# Principles of Economics

## DEDICATION

For Nuala MMcD

For Susan RT

# Principles of Economics

Moore McDowell
Rodney Thom
Robert Frank
and
Ben Bernanke

The McGraw-Hill Companies

London Boston Burr Ridge, IL Dubuque, IA Madison, WI New York San Francisco
St. Louis Bangkok Bogotá Caracas Kuala Lumpur Lisbon Madrid Mexico City
Milan Montreal New Delhi Santiago Seoul Singapore Sydney Taipei Toronto

*Principles of Economics*
Moore McDowell, Rodney Thom, Robert Frank and Ben Bernanke
ISBN-13 978 007 710831 1
ISBN-10 0-07-710831-0

Published by McGraw-Hill Education
Shoppenhangers Road
Maidenhead
Berkshire
SL6 2QL
Telephone: 44 (0) 1628 502 500
Fax: 44 (0) 1628 770 224
Website: www.mcgraw-hill.co.uk

Reprinted 2006

**British Library Cataloguing in Publication Data**
A catalogue record for this book is available from the British Library

**Library of Congress Cataloging in Publication Data**
The Library of Congress data for this book has been applied for from the Library of Congress

Acquisitions Editor: Mark Kavanagh
Development Editor: Hannah Cooper
Marketing Manager: Marca Wosoba
Senior Production Editor: Beverley Shields

Text design by Jonathan Coleclough
Cover design by Paul Fielding Design
Printed and bound in Spain by Mateu Cromo



ISBN-13 978 007 710831 1
ISBN-10 0-07-710831-0

# Brief Table of Contents


Preface *xvi*

**PART 1 Introduction**

1 Thinking Like an Economist *3*

2 Comparative Advantage: the Basis for Exchange *36*

3 Supply and Demand: an Introduction *58*

**PART 2 Competition and the 'Invisible Hand'**

4 Elasticity *93*

5 Demand: the Benefit Side of the Market *121*

6 Perfectly Competitive Supply: the Cost Side of the Market *153*

7 Efficiency and Exchange *182*

8 The Quest for Profit and the 'Invisible Hand' *208*

**PART 3 Market Imperfections**

9 Imperfect Competition and the Consequences of Market Power *241*

10 Thinking Strategically: Competition among the Few *273*

11 Externalities and Property Rights *312*

12 The Economics of Information *341*

**PART 4 Government in the Economy: Distribution, Regulation and the Provision of Public Goods**

13 Labour Markets, Income Distribution, Wealth and Poverty *365*

14 Government in the Market Economy: Regulation and Production of Public Goods and Other Services *397*

**PART 5 Trade and Integration**

15 International Trade and Trade Policy *429*

16 Trade, Factor Flows and Economic Integration: the Basic Economics of the European Union *455*

**PART 6 Macroeconomics: Issues and Data**

17 Macroeconomics: the Bird's-Eye View of the Economy *477*

18 Measuring Economic Activity: GDP and Unemployment *495*

19 Measuring the Price Level and Inflation *524*

**PART 7 The Economy in the Long Run**

20 Economic Growth, Productivity and Living Standards *555*

21 Workers, Wages and Unemployment in the Modern Economy *586*

22 Saving and Capital Formation *620*

23 Money, Prices and the European Central Bank *648*

24 Financial Markets and International Capital Flows *676*

**PART 8 The Economy in the Short Run**

25 Short-term Economic Fluctuations *703*

26 Stabilising the Economy: the Role of Fiscal Policy *738*

27 Stabilising the Economy: the Role of Monetary Policy *762*

28 Inflation and Aggregate Supply *792*

**PART 9 The International Economy**

29 Exchange Rates and the Open Economy *831*

30 Monetary Union: the Theory of Optimum Currency Areas *874*

Appendix: The IS-LM Model *895*

Glossary *912*

Index *925*

# Detailed Table of Contents


Preface *xvi*

Acknowledgements *xviii*

Guided Tour *xix*

Technology to Enhance Learning and Teaching *xxi*

**PART 1 Introduction**

**1 Thinking Like an Economist** *3*

Economics: studying choice in a world of scarcity *4*

Applying the Cost–Benefit Principle *5*

Economic surplus *6*

Opportunity cost *6*

The role of economic models *7*

RECAP Cost–benefit analysis *7*

Four important decision pitfalls *8*

Pitfall 1: measuring costs and benefits as proportions rather than absolute money amounts *8*

Pitfall 2: ignoring opportunity costs *9*

Pitfall 3: failure to ignore sunk costs *10*

Pitfall 4: failure to understand the average–marginal distinction *10*

RECAP Four important decision pitfalls *13*

Economics: micro and macro *14*

The approach of this text *14*

Economic naturalism *15*

Summary *18*

Review questions *18*

Problems *19*

Answers to in-chapter exercises *20*

Appendix A *21*

Answers to in-appendix exercises *27*

Appendix B *28*

Answers to in-appendix exercises *34*

References *35*

**2 Comparative Advantage: the Basis for Exchange** *36*

Exchange and opportunity cost *37*

The Principle of Comparative Advantage *38*

Sources of comparative advantage *41*

RECAP Exchange and opportunity cost *43*

Comparative advantage and production possibilities *43*

The production possibilities curve *43*

How individual productivity affects the slope and position of the PPC *45*

The gains from specialisation *46*

A PPC for a many-person economy *48*

RECAP Comparative advantage and production possibilities *49*

Factors that shift the economy's PPC *49*

Why have some countries been slow to specialise? *51*

Can we have too much specialisation? *52*

Comparative advantage and international trade *52*

RECAP Comparative advantage and international trade *53*

Summary *54*

Review questions *54*

Problems *55*

Answers to in-chapter exercises *56*

References *57*

**3 Supply and Demand: an Introduction** *58*

What, how and for whom? Central planning versus the market *60*

Buyers and sellers in markets *61*

The demand curve *62*

The supply curve *64*

RECAP Demand and supply curves *65*

Market equilibrium *65*

Rent controls reconsidered *69*

Pizza price controls? *72*

RECAP Market equilibrium *72*

Predicting and explaining changes in prices and quantities *73*

Shifts in demand *73*

Shifts in the supply curve *77*

Four simple rules *80*

RECAP Factors that shift supply and demand *81*

Markets and social welfare *83*

Cash on the table *83*

Smart for one, dumb for all *84*

RECAP Markets and social welfare *85*

Summary *86*

Review questions *87*

Problems *88*

Answers to in-chapter exercises *89*

## PART 2 Competition and the 'Invisible Hand'

### 4 Elasticity *93*

Price elasticity of demand *94*
- Price elasticity defined *94*
- Determinants of price elasticity of demand *95*
- RECAP Factors that influence price elasticity *96*
- Some representative elasticity estimates *96*
- Using price elasticity of demand *97*
- A graphical interpretation of price elasticity *99*
- Price elasticity changes along a straight-line demand curve *101*
- Two special cases *102*
- The midpoint formula *103*
- RECAP Calculating price elasticity of demand *104*
- Elasticity and total expenditure *104*
- Income elasticity and cross-price elasticity of demand *107*
- RECAP Cross-price and income elasticities *108*

The price elasticity of supply *108*
- Determinants of supply elasticity *111*
- Unique and essential inputs: the ultimate supply bottleneck *115*

Summary *116*
- Review questions *117*
- Problems *117*
- Answers to in-chapter exercises *119*
- References *120*

### 5 Demand: the Benefit Side of the Market *121*

The law of demand *122*
- The origins of demand *123*
- Needs versus wants *123*

Translating wants into demand *125*
- Measuring wants; the concept of utility *125*
- Allocating a fixed income between two goods *127*
- The rational spending rule *131*
- Income and substitution effects revisited *131*
- RECAP Translating wants into demand *133*

Applying the rational spending rule *133*
- Substitution at work *134*
- The importance of income differences *135*
- RECAP Applying the rational spending rule *136*

Indifference curve analysis and the demand curve *136*
- The model *138*
- RECAP Indifference curve analysis of rational choice *143*

Individual and market demand curves *143*
- Horizontal addition *144*
- Demand and consumer surplus *145*
- Calculating economic surplus *145*

Summary *148*
- Review questions *149*
- Problems *149*
- Answers to in-chapter exercises *151*

### 6 Perfectly Competitive Supply: the Cost Side of the Market *153*

Thinking about supply: the importance of opportunity cost *154*

Profit-maximising firms in perfectly competitive markets *157*
- Profit-maximisation *157*
- The demand curve facing a perfectly competitive firm *158*
- Production in the short run *159*
- Some important cost concepts *160*
- Choosing output to maximise profit *161*
- A note on the firm's shutdown condition *162*
- Average variable cost and average total cost *163*

A graphical approach to profit maximisation *163*
- Price = marginal cost: the maximum-profit condition *165*

The 'law' of supply *167*
- RECAP The competitive firm's supply curve *168*

Determinants of supply revisited *168*
- Technology *168*
- Input prices *168*
- The number of suppliers *168*
- Expectations *169*
- Changes in prices of other products *169*
- RECAP Determinants of supply *169*

Applying the theory of supply *169*
- When recycling is left to private market forces, why are many more aluminium beverage containers recycled than glass ones? *169*
- Supply and producer surplus *172*
- Calculating producer surplus *172*

Summary *173*
- Review questions *174*
- Problems *174*
- Answers to in-chapter exercises *177*

Appendix *179*

### 7 Efficiency and Exchange *182*

Market equilibrium and efficiency *183*

Efficiency is not the only goal *185*

Why efficiency should be the first goal *186*
- RECAP Equilibrium and efficiency *186*

The cost of preventing price adjustments *186*
- Price ceilings *186*
- Price subsidies *189*

First-come, first-served policies *191*
RECAP The cost of blocking price adjustments *195*
Marginal cost pricing of public services *195*
RECAP Marginal cost pricing of public services *196*
Taxes and efficiency *196*
Who pays a tax imposed on sellers of a good? *196*
How a tax collected from a seller affects economic surplus *198*
Taxes, elasticity and efficiency *200*
Taxes, external costs and efficiency *201*
RECAP Taxes and efficiency *202*
Summary *202*
Review questions *203*
Problems *203*
Answers to in-chapter exercises *206*

**8 The Quest for Profit and the 'Invisible Hand'** *208*
The central role of economic profit *209*
Three types of profit *209*
RECAP The central role of economic profit *212*
The 'invisible hand' theory *212*
Two functions of price *212*
Responses to profits and losses *213*
The importance of free entry and exit *219*
RECAP The 'invisible hand' theory *220*
Economic rent versus economic profit *220*
RECAP Economic rent versus economic profit *222*
The 'invisible hand' in action *222*
The 'invisible hand' at the supermarket and on the motorway *222*
The 'invisible hand' and cost-saving innovations *222*
The 'invisible hand' in regulated markets *224*
The 'invisible hand' in anti-poverty programmes *226*
The 'invisible hand' in the stock market *227*
The efficient markets hypothesis *229*
RECAP The 'invisible hand' in action *231*
The distinction between an equilibrium and a social optimum *232*
Smart for one, dumb for all *232*
RECAP Equilibrium versus social optimum *233*
Summary *234*
Review questions *235*
Problems *235*
Answers to in-chapter exercises *237*
References *238*

**PART 3 Market Imperfections**

**9 Imperfect Competition and the Consequences of Market Power** *241*
Imperfect competition *242*
Different forms of imperfect competition *242*
The essential difference between perfectly and imperfectly competitive firms *243*
RECAP Imperfect competition *243*
Five sources of market power *244*
Exclusive control over important inputs *244*
Patents and copyrights *244*
Government licences or franchises *244*
Economies of scale (natural monopolies) *245*
Network economies *245*
RECAP Five sources of market power *246*
Economies of scale and the importance of fixed costs *246*
RECAP Economies of scale and the importance of fixed costs *249*
Profit-maximisation for the monopolist *249*
Marginal revenue for the monopolist *250*
The monopolist's profit-maximising decision rule *251*
Being a monopolist does not guarantee an economic profit *253*
RECAP Profit-maximisation for the monopolist *254*
Why the 'invisible hand' breaks down under monopoly *254*
RECAP Why the monopolist produces 'too little' output *256*
The rigorous analysis of profit-maximisation *256*
Using discounts to expand the market: monopoly power at work for you? *257*
Price discrimination defined *258*
How price discrimination affects output *258*
The hurdle method of price discrimination *260*
Is price discrimination a bad thing? *261*
Examples of price discrimination *261*
RECAP Using discounts to expand the market *263*
Public policy toward natural monopoly *263*
State ownership and management *263*
State regulation of private monopolies *264*
Exclusive contracting for natural monopoly *265*
Vigorous enforcement of anti-trust laws *266*
RECAP Public policy toward natural monopoly *267*
Summary *268*
Review questions *269*
Problems *269*
Answers to in-chapter exercises *271*

**10 Thinking Strategically: Competition among the Few** *273*
The theory of games *274*
The three elements of a game *274*
Nash equilibrium *276*
RECAP The theory of games *277*
The prisoner's dilemma *278*
The original prisoner's dilemma *278*

Prisoners' dilemmas confronting imperfectly competitive firms *279*
Prisoners' dilemmas in everyday life *283*
Tit-for-tat and the repeated prisoner's dilemma *285*
RECAP The prisoner's dilemma *286*
Games in which timing matters *286*
The ultimatum bargaining game *286*
Credible threats and promises *288*
Commitment problems *291*
RECAP Games in which timing matters *292*
The strategic role of preferences *292*
Are people fundamentally selfish? *293*
Preferences as solutions to commitment problems *294*
RECAP The strategic role of preferences *295*
Games, timing, beliefs and behaviour: oligopolistic markets *295*
Two basic tools of analysis *296*
Repeated games *300*
Summary *304*
Review questions *305*
Problems *306*
Answers to in-chapter exercises *309*
References *311*

**11 Externalities and Property Rights** *312*
External costs and benefits *312*
How externalities affect resource allocation *313*
The graphical portrayal of externalities *314*
The Coase theorem *316*
Legal remedies for externalities *320*
The optimal amount of negative externalities is not zero *322*
RECAP External costs and benefits *323*
Property rights and the tragedy of the commons *323*
The problem of unpriced resources *324*
The effect of private ownership *326*
When private ownership is impractical *328*
RECAP Property rights and the tragedy of the commons *329*
Positional externalities *329*
Payoffs that depend on relative performance *330*
Positional arms races *331*
Positional arms control agreements *332*
Social norms as positional arms control agreements *333*
Summary *335*
Review questions *336*
Problems *336*
Answers to in-chapter exercises *339*
References *340*

**12 The Economics of Information** *341*
How the middleman adds value *342*
RECAP How the middleman adds value *343*
The optimal amount of information *344*
The cost–benefit test *344*
The free-rider problem *344*
Two guidelines for rational search *345*
The gamble inherent in search *346*
The commitment problem when search is costly *347*
RECAP The optimal amount of information *348*
Asymmetric information *348*
The 'lemons' model *349*
The credibility problem in trading *350*
The costly-to-fake principle *351*
Conspicuous consumption as a sign of ability *353*
Statistical discrimination *354*
Adverse selection *355*
Moral hazard *356*
RECAP Asymmetric information *356*
Disappearing political discourse *357*
Summary *359*
Review questions *360*
Problems *361*
Answers to in-chapter exercises *362*
References *362*

**PART 4 Government in the Economy: Distribution, Regulation and the Provision of Public Goods**

**13 Labour Markets, Income Distribution, Wealth and Poverty** *365*
The economic value of work *366*
RECAP The economic value of work *368*
The equilibrium wage and employment levels *369*
The demand for labour *369*
The supply curve of labour *369*
Market shifts *370*
RECAP Equilibrium in the labour market *370*
Explaining differences in earnings *371*
The human capital explanation *371*
Trade unions *372*
Compensating wage differentials *376*
Discrimination in the labour market *377*
Discrimination by employers *377*
Discrimination by others *378*
Parental discrimination *379*
Other sources of the wage gap *379*
Winner-take-all markets *380*

RECAP Explaining differences in earnings among people *381*
Trends in inequality *382*
Measuring the distribution of income or wealth *383*
Inequality: a moral problem? *384*
RECAP Why is income inequality: a moral problem? *385*
Methods of income redistribution *385*
Welfare payments and in-kind transfers *386*
Universality and means testing *387*
Income tax and redistribution *387*
Minimum wages *388*
The earned income tax credit *389*
Summary *391*
Review questions *392*
Problems *393*
Answers to in-chapter exercises *395*
References *395*

## 14 Government in the Market Economy: Regulation and Production of Public Goods and Other Services *397*

Government and regulation *397*
Regulatory blunders: the security of supply neurosis *398*
The regulatory framework *399*
Three case studies *400*
RECAP Using price incentives in environmental regulation *404*
RECAP Workplace safety regulation *409*
Public health and safety *409*
Government in the economy: producing public goods *411*
Public goods versus private goods *411*
Paying for public goods *413*
The demand curve for a public good *416*
Private provision of public goods *418*
Summary *421*
Review questions *422*
Problems *422*
Answers to in-chapter exercises *423*
References *425*

# PART 5 Trade and Integration

## 15 International Trade and Trade Policy *429*

Comparative advantage as a basis for trade *430*
Production and consumption possibilities and the benefits of trade *431*
The two-worker PPC *431*
The many-worker PPC *433*
RECAP PPCs *434*
Consumption possibilities with and without international trade *434*
RECAP Consumption possibilities and production possibilities *439*
A supply and demand perspective on trade *439*
Winners and losers from trade *441*
RECAP Trade winners and losers *442*
Protectionist policies: tariffs and quotas *443*
Tariffs *443*
Quotas *445*
The inefficiency of protectionism *449*
Summary *449*
Review questions *450*
Problems *451*
Answers to in-chapter exercises *453*
References *454*

## 16 Trade, Factor Flows and Economic Integration: the Basic Components of the European Union *455*

The birth and growth of the Union *456*
The economics of freeing trade *457*
The gains from trade *457*
The consequences of trade restrictions *461*
The economic implications of imposing and removing tariffs *462*
Import taxes, export taxes and subsidies *463*
RECAP The impact of trade and trade restrictions of economic welfare *464*
International integration: free-trade areas, customs unions, common markets, monetary unions and economic unions *465*
Why are FTAs formed? *466*
Why proceed to establish a customs union? *466*
Why might a common market be established once a customs union is in place? *466*
Why move from a common market to a monetary union? *467*
Why move to a full economic union? *468*
RECAP The process of integration *468*
Trade regimes and trade flows: trade creation and trade diversion in the European Union *468*
What is at stake: the economic gains from free trade *469*
The Single Market Programme *470*
The Single European Act and the Single Market *470*
The static gains from integrating factor markets *470*
The dynamic gains: the car industry as an example *471*
The impact of integration on the underlying trend in economic growth *472*
Summary *472*
Review questions *473*

Answers to in-chapter exercises 473
References 474

## PART 6 Macroeconomics: Issues and Data

### 17 Macroeconomics: the Bird's-Eye View of the Economy 477

The major macroeconomics issues 478
Economic growth and living standards 478
Productivity 480
Recessions and expansions 483
Unemployment 483
Inflation 484
Economic interdependence among nations 485
RECAP The major macroeconomics issues 486
Macroeconomic policy 487
Types of macroeconomic policy 487
Positive versus normative analyses of macroeconomic policy 488
RECAP Macroeconomic policy 488
Aggregation 489
RECAP Aggregation 490
Studying macroeconomics: a preview 491
Summary 492
Review questions 492
Problems 493
Answers to in-chapter exercises 493
References 494

### 18 Measuring Economic Activity: GDP and Unemployment 495

Gross domestic product: measuring the economy's output 496
Market value 496
Final goods and services 499
Produced within a country during a given period 501
RECAP Measuring GDP 502
The expenditure method for measuring GDP 502
RECAP Expenditure components of GDP 505
GDP and the incomes of capital and labour 505
Nominal GDP versus real GDP 506
RECAP Nominal GDP versus real GDP 509
Real GDP is not the same as economic well-being 509
Leisure time 509
Non-market economic activities 510
Environmental quality and resource depletion 510
Quality of life 511
Poverty and economic inequality 511
GDP is related to economic well-being 511
Availability of goods and services 512
Health and education 512
RECAP Real GDP and economic well-being 514
The unemployment rate 514
Measuring unemployment 514
The costs of unemployment 517
The duration of unemployment 517
The unemployment rate versus 'true' unemployment 518
Summary 519
Review questions 520
Problems 520
Answers to in-chapter exercises 521
References 523

### 19 Measuring the Price Level and Inflation 524

The consumer price index: measuring the price level 525
Inflation 527
Adjusting for inflation 529
Deflating a nominal quantity 530
Indexing to maintain buying power 532
RECAP Methods to adjust for inflation 533
Does the CPI measure 'true' inflation? 533
The costs of inflation: not always what you think 536
The true costs of inflation 537
'Shoe-leather' costs 538
'Noise' in the price system 539
Distortions of the tax system 540
Unexpected redistribution of wealth 541
Interference with long-run planning 542
RECAP The true costs of inflation 542
Hyperinflation 543
Inflation and interest rates 544
Inflation and the real interest rate 544
The Fisher effect 547
Summary 548
Review questions 549
Problems 549
Answers to in-chapter exercises 551
References 552

## PART 7 The Economy in the Long Run

### 20 Economic Growth, Productivity and Living Standards 555

The remarkable rise in living standards: the record 556
Why 'small' differences in growth matter 557
Why nations become rich: the crucial role of average labour productivity 559

RECAP Economic growth and productivity 561
Determinants of average labour productivity 561
Human capital 561
Physical capital 563
Land and other natural resources 565
Technology 566
Entrepreneurship and management 567
The political and legal environment 568
RECAP Determinants of average labour productivity 571
The worldwide productivity slowdown – and recovery? 571
The costs of economic growth 573
Promoting economic growth 573
Policies to increase human capital 573
Policies that promote saving and investment 574
Policies that support research and development 575
The legal and political framework 575
The poorest countries: a special case? 575
Are there limits to growth? 578
RECAP Economic growth: developments and issues 580
Summary 581
Review questions 582
Problems 582
Answers to in-chapter exercises 584
References 585

**21 Workers, Wages and Unemployment in the Modern Economy** 586
Five important labour market trends 586
Trends in real wages 587
Trends in employment and unemployment 588
RECAP Important labour market trends 588
Supply and demand in the labour market 588
Wages and the demand for labour 589
Shifts in the demand for labour 591
The supply of labour 594
Shifts in the supply of labour 595
RECAP Supply and demand in the labour market 595
Explaining the trends in real wages 596
Increasing wage inequality 598
Both sides gain from free trade 603
RECAP Explaining the trends in real wages 605
Labour force trends: unemployment 605
Types of unemployment and their costs 606
Impediments to full employment 608
RECAP Unemployment 613
Summary 613
Review questions 615
Problems 615
Answers to in-chapter exercises 618

**22 Saving and Capital Formation** 620
Saving and wealth 620
Stocks and flows 621
Capital gains and losses 622
RECAP Saving and wealth 623
Why do people save? 623
Saving and the real interest rate 626
Saving, self-control and demonstration effects 628
RECAP Why do people save? 629
National saving and its components 629
The measurement of national saving 629
Private and public components of national saving 630
Public saving and the government budget 632
RECAP National saving and its components 635
Investment and capital formation 635
RECAP Features that affect investment 639
Saving, investment and financial markets 639
Summary 642
Review questions 643
Problems 643
Answers to in-chapter exercises 646

**23 Money, Prices and the European Central Bank** 648
Money and its uses 649
Measuring money 651
RECAP Money and its uses 652
Commercial banks and the creation of money 652
The money supply with both currency and deposits 656
RECAP Commercial banks and the creation of money 657
The European Central Bank 657
Decision-making bodies of the ECB 658
Voting rights in the Governing Council 658
ECB independence 659
A mandate for price stability 660
RECAP The European Central Bank 661
Controlling the money supply: open-market operations 663
Main refinancing operations 664
Controlling the money supply: changing reserve requirements 665
Money and prices 667
Velocity 668
Money and inflation in the long run 669
RECAP Money and prices 671
Summary 671
Review questions 673
Problems 673
Answers to in-chapter exercises 675
References 675

**24 Financial Markets and International Capital Flows** *676*

The financial system and the allocation of saving to productive uses *677*

The banking system *677*

Bonds and shares *679*

RECAP Factors affecting share prices *683*

Bond markets, stock markets and the allocation of saving *683*

The informational role of bond and stock markets *683*

Risk-sharing and diversification *683*

International capital flows *685*

Capital flows and the balance of trade *686*

Determinants of international capital flows *689*

Saving, investment and capital inflows *690*

The saving rate and the trade deficit *692*

RECAP International capital flows and the balance of trade *694*

Summary *695*

Review questions *696*

Problems *696*

Answers to in-chapter exercises *698*

**PART 8 The Economy in the Short Run**

**25 Short-Term Economic Fluctuations** *703*

Recessions and expansions *703*

RECAP Recessions, booms and their characteristics *706*

Output gaps and cyclical unemployment *706*

Potential output and the output gap *707*

The natural rate of unemployment and cyclical unemployment *708*

RECAP Output gaps and cyclical unemployment *709*

Why do short-term fluctuations occur? A preview and a parable *710*

Spending and output in the short run *713*

John Maynard Keynes and the Keynesian revolution *713*

John Maynard Keynes *713*

The Keynesian revolution *714*

The Keynesian model's crucial assumption: firms meet demand at pre-set prices *715*

Planned aggregate expenditure *717*

Planned spending versus actual spending *717*

Consumer spending and the economy *718*

Planned aggregate expenditure and output *719*

RECAP Planned aggregate expenditure *722*

Short-run equilibrium output *722*

Planned spending and the output gap *726*

The multiplier *728*

RECAP Finding short-run equilibrium output *731*

Summary *731*

Review questions *733*

Problems *734*

Answers to in-chapter exercises *735*

Appendix The multiplier in the basic Keynesian model *737*

**26 Stabilising the Economy: the Role of Fiscal Policy** *738*

Discretionary fiscal policy: changes in government purchases *739*

Discretionary fiscal policy: changes in taxes and transfers *741*

RECAP Fiscal policy and planned spending *744*

Automatic stabilisers *745*

The problem of deficits *748*

Interest rates *749*

Exchange rates *749*

Debt sustainability *750*

The SGP and automatic stabilisers *752*

Problems with the SGP *754*

Fiscal policy as a stabilisation tool: two qualifications *757*

Fiscal policy and the supply side *757*

The relative inflexibility of fiscal policy *757*

Summary *758*

Review questions *759*

Problems *759*

Answers to in-chapter exercises *761*

**27 Stabilising the Economy: the Role of Monetary Policy** *762*

The ECB and interest rates *763*

The demand for money *763*

The Rossis, Kim and the ECB *766*

Macroeconomic factors that affect the demand for money *766*

The money demand curve *767*

RECAP Money demand *768*

The supply of money and money market equilibrium *769*

How the ECB controls the nominal interest rate *770*

Can the ECB control the real interest rate? *772*

RECAP The ECB and interest rates *773*

The effects of ECB actions on the economy *773*

Planned aggregate expenditure and the real interest rate *774*

The ECB fights a recession 776
The ECB fights inflation 778
The ECB's policy reaction function 781
RECAP Monetary policy and the economy 784
Monetary policy making: art or science? 784
Summary 785
Review questions 786
Problems 786
Answers to in-chapter exercises 788
Appendix Monetary policy in the basic Keynesian model 790
References 791

**28 Inflation and Aggregate Supply** 792
Inflation, spending and output: the aggregate demand curve 793
Inflation, the ECB and the *AD* curve 794
Other reasons for the downward slope of the *AD* curve 794
Shifts of the *AD* curve 795
Shifts of the *AD* curve versus movements along the *AD* curve 797
RECAP The aggregate demand (*AD*) curve 798
Inflation and aggregate supply 798
Inflation inertia 799
The output gap and inflation 801
The aggregate demand–aggregate supply diagram 802
The self-correcting economy 805
RECAP *AD–AS* and the self-correcting economy 806
Sources of inflation 806
Excessive aggregate spending 806
Inflation shocks 808
Shocks to potential output 810
RECAP Sources of inflation 813
Controlling inflation 814
RECAP Controlling inflation 817
Summary 818
Review questions 819
Problems 820
Answers to in-chapter exercises 822
Appendix The algebra of aggregate demand and aggregate supply 825
Answers to in-appendix exercises 827
References 827

**PART 9 The International Economy**

**29 Exchange Rates and the Open Economy** 831
Exchange rates 832
Nominal exchange rates 833
Flexible versus fixed exchange rates 835
The real exchange rate 836
RECAP Exchange rates 839
Determination of the exchange rate 839
A simple theory of exchange rates: purchasing power parity 839
Determination of the exchange rate: a supply and demand analysis 843
Monetary policy and the exchange rate 846
RECAP Determining the exchange rate 847
Fixed exchange rates 847
How to fix an exchange rate 848
Speculative attacks 851
Exchange rate systems 852
Monetary policy and the fixed exchange rate 859
RECAP Fixed exchange rates 866
Should exchange rates be fixed or flexible? 867
Summary 868
Review questions 870
Problems 870
Answers to in-chapter exercises 872

**30 Monetary Union: the Theory of Optimum Currency Areas** 874
Costs and benefits of a common currency 875
Costs: the loss of policy independence 875
Costs: the importance of flexible markets and inflation inertia 879
Costs: the importance of labour mobility 880
Benefits: eliminating transaction costs 881
Benefits: eliminating exchange rate uncertainty 882
RECAP Costs and benefits of a common currency 882
Comparing costs and benefits: the *CC* and *BB* schedules 883
Summary 892
Review questions 893
References 894

Appendix: The IS-LM Model 895
Glossary 912
Index 925

# Preface

When we agreed with McGraw-Hill to prepare a European Edition of Frank and Bernanke, it was with the experience of having used the original, US text for two years in University College Dublin. Both of us had found that the text was clear, easy to use, and, more important in some ways, a source of constant challenge to our students. This challenge reflected the emphasis on continually asking the reader to think about real-world phenomena and to analyse them using the relevant concepts drawn from economics. The point was to make clear to students that economics offers a powerful intellectual tool set that helps us understand a much wider set of behaviours and institutions than would initially be thought of as being matter for economic analysis. The end result being sought was an ability to look at the world in a new way, and to understand its workings by applying an analytical approach that is coherent and highly predictive.

We are, however, aware that there are significant risks in adding to, subtracting from and modifying a book that has been very well received on the basis of its innovative approach to introductory economics. Hence in preparing a European Edition we have attempted to maintain the text's analytical approach to economic principles but to place them in a context which is relevant to the European reader. Apart from changes in language and spelling from 'American' to 'English English', there are several major content changes from the original text. The most obvious revision was the need to recast the chapters dealing with central banking, macroeconomic policy and exchange rates to reflect the European experience. While the basic theory of macroeconomics remains the same, the practical aspects of fiscal and monetary policy inside and outside the eurozone required a rewrite of key chapters in the macroeconomic sections. We have also included two new chapters. Chapter 16 builds on the existing trade chapter and contains both relevant theory and an historical account of the process of economic integration in Europe, while Chapter 30 discusses the economic rationale for monetary integration and asks if the introduction of the euro can be justified on purely economic grounds.

A second change is a slightly more rigorous treatment of theory in both the microeconomic and macroeconomic sections. This reflects our view that if a text is to prepare European students to continue with economics it should introduce some additional analytical tools that are required for this purpose and should seek to familiarise students with the use of simple algebraic approaches to theory. In the macroeconomics sections greater use is made of algebra to develop the basic model of income determination as a complement to graphical analysis. In the microeconomics sections the indifference curve approach to demand theory is embodied in the main text, although it can be skipped. Calculus is used (sparingly) to derive the familiar conditions for consumer and producer equilibrium and the treatment of competition among the few has been extended to cover reaction functions at an elementary level.

## FEATURES

### Economic naturalism

We have enthusiastically continued the Frank and Bernanke approach to instruction based on what they describe as 'economic naturalism' – developing concepts in relation to a real-world setting. This has involved in some cases dropping US-based material and replacing it by European material. In other cases, where the US material was simply incapable of improvement from a European perspective, we have left it unchanged. Some representative examples of additional European-orientated economic naturalists are:

- Emissions Trading in the EU: what can trading deliver?
- Why did the EU persist in using quotas to ensure that sugar was obtained expensively from domestic production rather than import sugar at much lower cost from the West Indies?
- Why, for many years, were Britain's most popular chocolate bars sold in wrappers that did not mention the word 'chocolate'?
- Why does Europe need a Stability and Growth Pact (SGP)?
- What are the advantages of an independent Central Bank?
- What are Chancellor Gordon Brown's economic tests for joining the euro?

## An active learning approach

In addition to the economic naturalist feature, exercises, review questions and problems are included within chapters, so that knowledge can be applied and assessed across each topic.

## Advanced technical analysis

Elements of working with equations, supply and the Keynesian model are demonstrated in appendixes throughout the book, for those students who require more rigorous analysis.

Although not included in every principles of economics course, we have also included an appendix on the IS-LM model, as we feel it is an important component of macroeconomics.

# Acknowledgements

We have been greatly helped in producing this edition by the comments from our colleagues in the School of Economics at University College Dublin and from reviewers of early drafts who offered critiques on an anonymous referee basis. Our sincere thanks are due to them for their painstaking efforts to help us improve what we were producing. We must also express our thanks to many people at McGraw-Hill, who have supported and prodded us where necessary, in particular Mark Kavanagh, Caroline Prodger, Hannah Cooper, Marca Wosoba and Beverley Shields, and to Barbara Docherty for her copy-editing skills.

The Publishers would like to thank the following reviewers for their comments at various stages in the text's development:

Martin Kenneally – University College Cork
Andreas Johnson – Jönköping International Business School
Helen Julia Paul – St Andrews University
Dinky Daruvala – Karlstad University
Joerg Oechssler – Heidelberg University
Gianni de Fraaja – Leicester University
Andrew Henley – University of Wales, Aberystwyth
Alex Tackie – Kingston University
Giovanni Caggiano – Glasgow University

Every effort has been made to trace and acknowledge copyright and to obtain permissions to reproduce material in the text. The Publishers would be pleased to make arrangements to clear permission with any copyright holders it has not been possible to contact.

# Guided Tour

## Key terms

These are highlighted throughout the chapter, with page number references at the end of each chapter so that they can be found quickly and easily.

## Examples

Examples throughout the text apply the theory discussed to practical contexts.

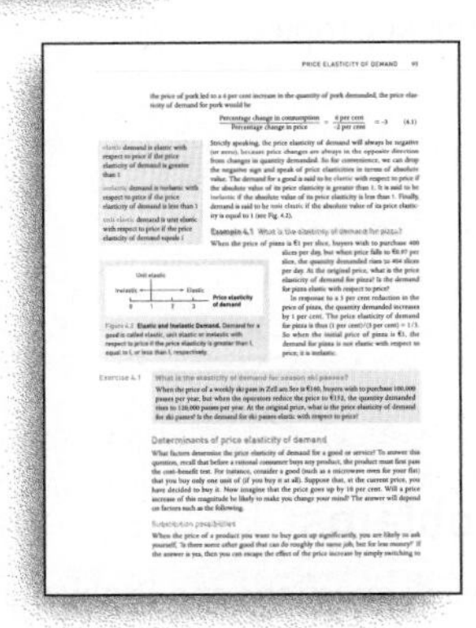

## Exercises

Exercises feature throughout the chapters, to enable you to practise the techniques you have been taught and apply the methodology to real-world situations.

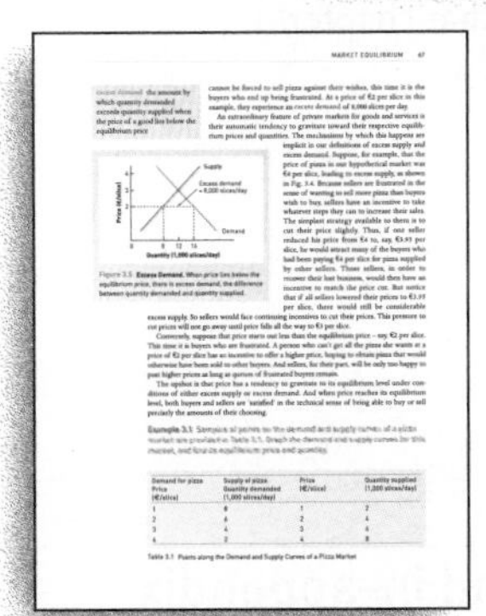

## Figures and tables

Each chapter provides a number of figures and tables to help you to visualise the various economic models, and to illustrate and summarise important concepts.

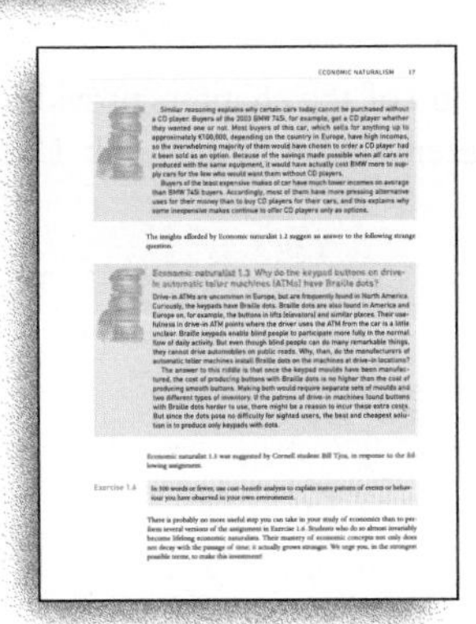

## Economic naturalist boxes

This feature applies economic perspectives to real-world situations, encouraging you to 'think like an economist'.

## Recaps

This feature highlights key themes throughout the text, linking what you have learned in previous sections of the chapter to new material.

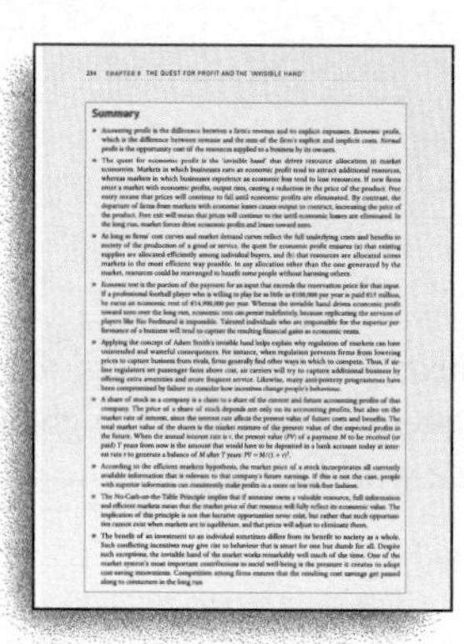

## Summary

This briefly reviews and reinforces the main topics you will have covered in each chapter to ensure you have acquired a solid understanding of the key topics.

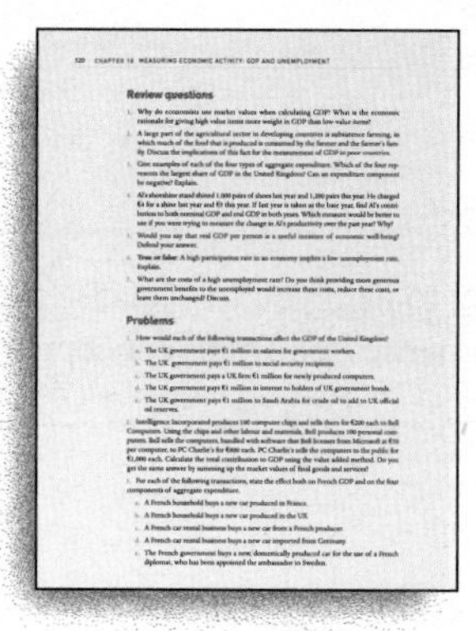

## Review questions and problems

Each chapter ends with a set of Review questions and Problems ranging in difficulty to consolidate learning of the material in that chapter.

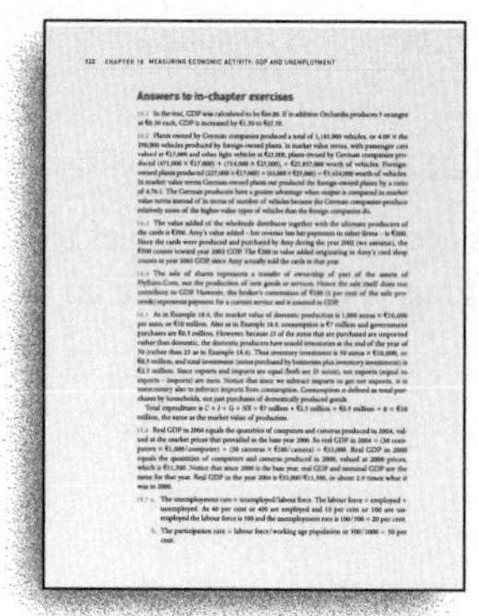

## Answers to in-chapter and in-appendix exercises

This feature at the end of the chapters provides the answers to the questions and exercises set in the book. Use it to check your workings.

# Technology to Enhance Learning and Teaching

## Online Learning Centre (OLC)

After completing each chapter, log on to the supporting Online Learning Centre website. Take advantage of the study tools offered to reinforce the material you have read in the text, and to develop your knowledge of economics in a fun and effective way.

Resources for students include:

- Learning objectives
- Self-test questions
- Crosswords
- Glossary by chapter
- Lecture / chapter outlines
- Solutions to questions in the book
- Colour PowerPoint slides
- Economic naturalist exercises from the text
- Test bank

## For lecturers: Primis Content Centre

If you need to supplement your course with additional cases or content, create a personalised e-Book for your students.

Visit www.primiscontentcenter.com or e-mail primis_euro@mcgraw-hill.com for more information.

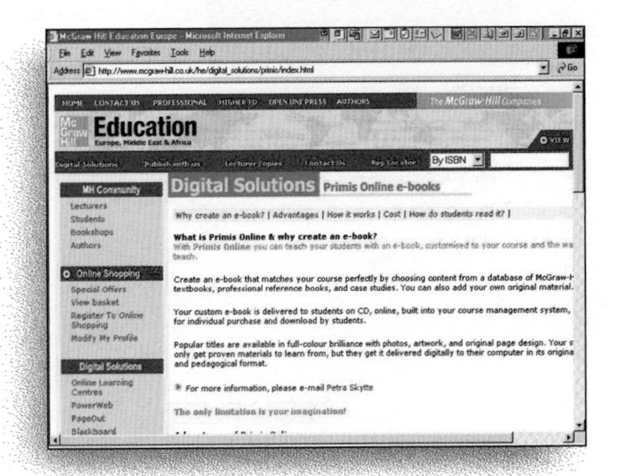

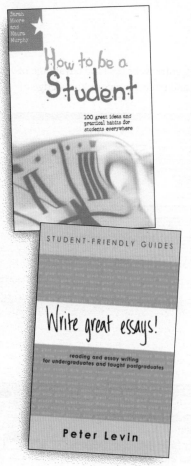

# Part 1
# Introduction

For many students reading this text it will be their first economics text. Others, of course, will have had some exposure to economics before. In either case it is important to understand that economics is not a collection of settled facts, to be copied down and memorised. Mark Twain said that nothing is older than yesterday's newspaper, and the same can be said of yesterday's economic statistics. Indeed, the only prediction about the economy that can be made with confidence is that there will continue to be large, and largely unpredictable, changes.

If economics is not a set of durable facts, then what is it? Fundamentally, it is a way of *thinking about the world*. Over many years economists have developed some simple but widely applicable principles that can help us to understand almost any economic situation (and a multitude of situations that at first sight might not appear to be concerned with economics), from the relatively simple ones such as economic decisions that individuals make every day, to the workings of highly complex markets, such as international financial markets. The principal objective of this book is to help you learn these principles and how to apply them to a variety of economic questions and issues.

The three chapters of Part 1 lay out the basic economic principles that will be used throughout the book. Chapter 1 introduces the notion of *scarcity* – the unavoidable fact that, although our needs and wants are boundless, the resources available to satisfy them are limited. The chapter goes on to show that deciding whether to take an action by comparing the cost and benefit of it is a useful approach for dealing with the inevitable trade-offs that scarcity creates. Chapter 1 then discusses several important decision pitfalls and concludes by introducing the concept of *economic naturalism*. Chapter 2 goes beyond individual decision making to consider trade, among both individuals and countries. An important reason for trade is that it permits people (or countries) to *specialise* in the production of particular goods and services, which in turn enhances productivity and raises standards of living. Finally, Chapter 3 presents an overview of the concepts of *supply* and *demand*, perhaps the most basic and familiar tools used by economists.

# 1 Thinking Like an Economist

How many students are there in your introductory economics class? Class sizes differ greatly between universities, and between countries. Some classes have just 20 or so; others average 35, 100, or 200 students. Indeed introductory classes of 400 are far from rare. Which size is best?

If cost were no object, the best size for an introductory economics course – or any other course, for that matter – might be a single student. Everything could be customised or tailored to that student's background and ability. The material could be covered at just the right pace. This tutorial format would also promote close communication and personal trust between student and professor. The grade for the course would depend more heavily on what had actually been learned than on any element of luck when taking multiple-choice exams. Studies by educational psychologists strongly suggest that students learn best in the tutorial format.

Why, then, do so many universities continue to schedule introductory classes with hundreds of students? The simple reason is that costs *do* matter. They matter not just to the university administrators who must build classrooms and pay faculty salaries, but also to *you*. The direct cost of providing you with your own personal introductory economics course – most notably, the lecturer's salary and the expense of providing a classroom in which to meet – might easily top £13,000 or €20,000 per semester. *Someone* has to pay these costs. In North American private universities, a large share of the cost would be recovered directly from higher fees; in state universities, or universities with substantial state support, more typical of Europe, the burden would be split between higher fees and higher tax payments. But in either case, the course would be unaffordable for many, if not most, students. Or it would bankrupt the tax-payers if there were no tuition fees.

With a larger class size, of course, the cost per student goes down. For example, in a class of 300 students, the cost of an introductory economics course might come to as little as €100 per student. But a class that large would surely compromise the quality of the learning environment. Compared with the customised tutorial format, however, it would be dramatically more affordable.

In choosing what size introductory economics course to offer, then, university administrators confront a classic economic *trade-off*. In making the class larger, they lower the quality of instruction – a bad thing – but at the same time, they reduce costs, and hence the tuition students must pay – a good thing.

## Economics: studying choice in a world of scarcity

By historical standards and in comparison with less fortunate countries in the Third World, societies such as those of the US and Western Europe at the beginning of the twenty-first century are rich. Even in rich societies, however, *scarcity* is a fundamental fact of life. There is never enough time, money or energy to do everything we want to do or have everything we would like to have. **Economics** is the study of how people make choices under conditions of scarcity, and of the results of those choices for society.

**economics** the study of how people make choices under conditions of scarcity and of the results of those choices for society

In the class-size example just discussed, a motivated economics student might definitely prefer to be in a class of 20 rather than a class of 100, everything else being equal. But other things, of course, are not equal. Students can enjoy the benefits of having smaller classes, but only at the price of having less money for other activities. The student's choice inevitably will come down to the relative importance of competing activities.

That such trade-offs are widespread and important is one of the core principles of economics. We call it the **Scarcity Principle**, because the simple fact of scarcity makes trade-offs necessary. Another name for the scarcity principle is the **No-Free-Lunch Principle** (which comes from the observation that even lunches that are given to you are never really free – somebody, somehow, always has to pay for them).

The Scarcity Principle (also called the No-Free-Lunch Principle): Although we have boundless needs and wants, the resources available to us are limited. So having more of one good thing usually means having less of another. Hence the cliché, 'There ain't no such thing as a free lunch', sometimes reduced to the acronym TANSTAAFL.

Inherent in the idea of a trade-off is the fact that choice involves compromise between competing interests. Economists resolve such trade-offs by using *cost–benefit analysis*, which is based on the disarmingly simple principle that an action should be taken if, and only if, its benefits exceed its costs. We call this statement the **Cost–Benefit Principle**, and it, too, is one of the core principles of economics:

The Cost–Benefit Principle: An individual (or a firm, or a society) should take an action if, and only if, the extra benefits from taking the action are at least as great as the extra costs.

With the Cost–Benefit Principle in mind, let us think about our class-size question again. Imagine that classrooms come in only two sizes – 100-seat lecture halls and 20-seat classrooms – and that your university currently offers introductory economics courses to classes of 100 students.

**Question:** Should administrators reduce the class size to 20 students?

**Answer:** Reduce if, and only if, the value of the improvement in instruction outweighs its additional cost.

This rule sounds simple, but to apply it we need some way to *measure* the relevant costs and benefits – a task that is often difficult in practice. If we make a few simplifying assumptions, however, we can see how the analysis might work. On the cost side, the primary expense of reducing class size from 100 to 20 is that we will now need five professors instead of just one. We'll also need five smaller classrooms rather than a single big one, and this too may add slightly to the expense of the move. For the sake of discussion, suppose that the cost with a class size of 20 turns out to be €1,000 per student more than the cost per student when the class size is 100. Should administrators switch to the smaller class size? If they apply the cost–benefit principle, they will realize that the reduction in class size makes sense only if the *value of attending the smaller class is at least €1,000 per student greater than the value of attending the larger class.*

With the Cost–Benefit Principle in mind, let us think about our class-size question again. Imagine that classrooms come in only two sizes – 100-seat lecture halls and 20-seat classrooms – and that your university currently offers introductory economics courses to classes of 100 students.

**Question:** Should administrators reduce the class size to 20 students?

**Answer:** Reduce if, and only if, the value of the improvement in instruction outweighs its additional cost.

Would you (or your family) be willing to pay an extra €1,000 for a smaller economics class? If not, and if other students feel the same way, then sticking with the larger class size makes sense. But if you and others would be willing to pay the extra tuition, then reducing the class size to 20 makes good economic sense.

*Notice that the 'best' class size, from an economics point of view, will generally not be the same as the 'best' size from the point of view of an educational psychologist.* The difference arises because the economics definition of 'best' takes into account both the benefits *and* the costs of different class sizes. The psychologist ignores costs and looks only at the learning benefits of different class sizes.

In practice, of course, different people will feel differently about the value of smaller classes. People with high incomes, for example, tend to be willing to pay more for the advantage, which helps to explain why average class size is smaller, and tuition higher, at private schools whose students come predominantly from high-income families.

Scarcity and the trade-offs that result also apply to resources other than money. Bill Gates is one of the richest men on earth. His wealth was once estimated at over €100 billion – more than the combined wealth of the poorest 40 per cent of Americans. Gates has enough money to buy more houses, cars, holidays and other consumer goods than he could possibly use. Yet Gates, like the rest of us, has only 24 hours each day and a limited amount of energy. So even he confronts trade-offs, in that any activity he pursues – whether it be building his business empire or redecorating his mansion – uses up time and energy that he could otherwise spend on other things. Indeed, someone once calculated that the value of Gates' time is so great that pausing to pick up a €100 bill from the road simply wouldn't be worth his while.

## Applying the Cost–Benefit Principle

In studying choice under scarcity, we shall usually begin with the premise that people are **rational**, which means they have well-defined goals and try to fulfil them as best they can. The Cost–Benefit Principle illustrated in our class-size example is a fundamental tool for the study of how rational people make choices.

**rational person** someone with well-defined goals who tries to fulfil those goals as best she can

As in the class-size example, often the only real difficulty in applying the cost–benefit rule is to come up with reasonable measures of the relevant benefits and costs. Only in rare instances will exact money measures be conveniently available. But the cost–benefit framework can lend structure to your thinking even when no relevant market data are available.

To illustrate how we proceed in such cases, the following example asks you to decide whether to perform an action whose cost is described only in vague, qualitative terms.

### Example 1.1 Should you walk to the centre of town to save €10 on a €25 computer game?

Imagine you are about to buy a €25 computer game at the nearby college book shop when a friend tells you that the same game is on sale at a city centre store for only €15. If the store in question is a 30-minute walk away, where should you buy the game?

The Cost–Benefit Principle tells us that you should buy it from the store in the city centre if the benefit of doing so exceeds the cost. The benefit of taking any action is the money value of everything you gain by taking it. Here, the benefit of buying elsewhere is exactly €10, since that is the amount you will save on the purchase price of the game. The cost of taking any action is the money value of everything you give up by taking it. Here, the cost of buying in the city centre is the money value you assign to the time and trouble it takes to make the trip. But how do we estimate that money value?

One way is to perform the following hypothetical auction. Imagine that a stranger has offered to pay you to do an errand that involves the same walk to the centre of town (perhaps to drop off a letter for her at the post office). If she offered you a payment of, say, €1,000, would you accept? If so, we know that your cost of walking to the centre of town and back must be less than €1,000. Now imagine her offer being reduced in small increments until you finally refuse the last offer. For example, if you would agree to walk there and back for €9.00 but not for €8.99, then your cost of making the trip is €9.00. In this case, you should buy the game in the town centre, because the €10 you'll save (your benefit) is greater than your €9.00 cost of making the trip.

But suppose, alternatively, that your cost of making the trip had been greater than €10. In that case, your best bet would have been to buy the game from the nearby college book shop. Confronted with this choice, different people may choose differently, depending on how costly they think it is to make the trip into town. But although there is no uniquely correct choice, most people who are asked what they would do in this situation say they would buy the game from the city centre store.

## Economic surplus

Suppose again that in Example 1.1 your 'cost' of making the trip to the city centre was €9. Compared with the alternative of buying the game at the college store, buying it elsewhere resulted in an **economic surplus** of €1, the difference between the benefit of making the trip and its cost. In general, your goal as an economic decision maker is to choose those actions that generate the largest possible economic surplus. This means taking all actions that yield a positive total economic surplus, which is just another way of restating the Cost–Benefit Principle.

**economic surplus** the economic surplus from taking any action is the benefit of taking that action minus its cost

Note that the fact that your best choice was to buy the game in the city doesn't imply that you *enjoy* making the trip, any more than choosing a large class means that you prefer large classes to small ones. It simply means that the trip is less unpleasant than the prospect of paying €10 extra for the game. Once again, you've faced a trade-off – in this case, the choice between a cheaper game and the free time gained by avoiding the trip.

## Opportunity cost

Of course, your mental 'auction' could have produced a different outcome. Suppose, for example, that the time required for the trip is the only time you have left to study for a difficult test the next day. Or suppose you are watching one of your favourite movies on cable, or that you are tired and would love a short nap. In such cases, we say that the **opportunity cost** of making the trip – that is, the value of what you must sacrifice to walk to the city and back – is high, and you are more likely to decide against making the trip.

**opportunity cost** the opportunity cost of an activity is the value of the next-best alternative that must be forgone in order to undertake the activity

In this example, if watching the last hour of the cable TV movie is the most valuable opportunity that conflicts with the trip to the city centre, the opportunity cost of making the trip is the money value you place on pursuing that opportunity – that is, the largest amount you'd be willing to pay to avoid missing the end of the movie. Note that the opportunity cost of making the trip is not the combined value of *all* possible activities you could have pursued, but only the value of your *best* alternative – the one you would have chosen had you not made the trip.

Throughout the text we will pose exercises like Exercise 1.1. You will find that pausing to answer them will help you to master key concepts in economics. Because doing these exercises isn't very costly (indeed, many students report that they are actually fun), the Cost–Benefit Principle indicates that it's well worth your while to do them.

**Exercise 1.1** You would again save €10 by buying the game in the city rather than at the college store, but your cost of making the trip is now €12, not €9. How much economic surplus would you get from buying the game in the city? Where should you buy it?

## The role of economic models

Economists use the Cost–Benefit Principle as an abstract model of how an idealised rational individual would choose among competing alternatives. (By 'abstract model' we mean a simplified description that captures the essential elements of a situation and allows us to analyse them in a logical way.) A computer model of a complex phenomenon such as climate change, which must ignore many details and include only the major forces at work, is an example of an abstract model.

Non-economists are sometimes harshly critical of the economist's cost–benefit model on the grounds that people in the real world never conduct hypothetical mental 'auctions' before deciding whether to make trips to town. But this criticism betrays a fundamental misunderstanding of how abstract models can help to explain and predict human behaviour. Economists know perfectly well that people don't conduct hypothetical mental 'auctions' when they make simple decisions. All the Cost–Benefit Principle really says is that a rational decision is one that is explicitly or implicitly based on a *weighing of costs and benefits*.

Most of us make sensible decisions most of the time, without being consciously aware that we are weighing costs and benefits, just as most people ride a bike without being consciously aware of what keeps them from falling off. Through trial and error, we gradually learn what kinds of choices tend to work best in different contexts, just as bicycle riders internalise the relevant laws of physics, usually without being conscious of them.

Even so, learning the explicit principles of cost–benefit analysis can help us make better decisions, just as knowing a little physics can help in learning how to ride a bicycle or drive a car.

A model is to an economist in many ways what a laboratory experiment is to a physical scientist. If you climbed the Leaning Tower of Pisa to test Newton's theory of gravity by dropping a feather and a kilogram of lead, you might conclude that gravity affects metals to a greater degree than it does organic material. The lead fell faster and hit the ground first. A physicist would demonstrate that this is not the case by creating a vacuum and repeating the experiment. We live in a real world where air pressure and resistance affect how objects fall. We create a simplified world to test the gravity hypothesis by removing the pressure and resistance effects. Would you agree with someone who said that there is little value in talking about the impact of gravity because in the real world we don't live in a vacuum?

### RECAP Cost–benefit analysis

Scarcity is a basic fact of economic life. Because of it, having more of one good thing almost always means having less of another (the Scarcity Principle). The Cost–Benefit Principle holds that an individual (or a firm, or a society) should take an action if, and only if, the extra benefit from taking the action is at least as great as the extra cost. The benefit of taking any action minus the cost of taking the action is called the *economic surplus* from that action. Hence the Cost–Benefit Principle suggests that we take only those actions that create additional economic surplus.

## Four important decision pitfalls[1]

Rational people will apply the Cost–Benefit Principle most of the time, although probably in an intuitive and approximate way rather than through explicit and precise calculation. Knowing that rational people tend to compare costs and benefits enables economists to predict their likely behaviour. As noted earlier, for example, we can predict that students from wealthy families are more likely than others to attend colleges that offer small classes. (Again, while the cost of small classes is the same for all families, the benefit of small classes, as measured by what people are willing to pay for them, tends to be higher for wealthier families.)

### Pitfall 1: measuring costs and benefits as proportions rather than absolute money amounts

As Example 1.2 makes clear, the Cost–Benefit Principle proves helpful in another way. Example 1.2 demonstrates that people are not born with an infallible instinct for weighing the relevant costs and benefits of many daily decisions. Indeed, one of the rewards of studying economics is that it can improve the quality of your decisions.

#### **Example 1.2** Should you walk 3 km to save €10 on a €2,000 laptop computer?

You are about to buy a €2,000 laptop computer at the nearby college store when a friend tells you that the same computer is on sale at a city centre store for only €1,990. If the latter is half an hour's walk away, where should you buy the computer?

Assuming that the laptop is light enough to carry without effort, the structure of this example is exactly the same as that of Example 1.1 – the only difference being that the price of the laptop is dramatically higher than the price of the computer game. As before, the benefit of buying in town is the money you'll save, namely, €10. And since it's exactly the same trip, its cost must also be the same as before. So if you are perfectly rational, you should make the same decision in both cases. Yet when real people are asked what they would do in these situations, the overwhelming majority say they would walk to town to buy the game but would buy the laptop at the college store. When asked to explain, most of them say something like: 'The trip was worth it for the game because you save 40 per cent, but not worth it for the laptop because you save only €10 out of €2,000.'

This is faulty reasoning. The benefit of the trip to town is not the *proportion* you save on the original price. Rather, it is the *absolute money amount* you save. Since the benefit of walking to the city to buy the laptop is €10 – exactly the same as for the computer game – and since the cost of the trip must also be the same in both cases, the economic surplus from making both trips must be exactly the same. And that means that a rational decision maker would make the same decision in both cases. Yet, as noted, most people choose differently.

**Exercise 1.2** Which is more valuable, saving £100 on a £2,000 plane ticket from London to Tokyo or saving £90 on a £200 plane ticket from London to Paris?

The pattern of faulty reasoning in the decision just discussed is one of several decision pitfalls to which people are prone. In the discussion that follows, we will identify three additional decision pitfalls. In some cases, people ignore costs or benefits that they ought to take into account, while on other occasions they are influenced by costs or benefits that are irrelevant.

[1] The examples in this section reflect the work of Daniel Kahneman and the late Amos Tversky. Kahneman was awarded the 2003 Nobel Prize in economics for his efforts to integrate insights from psychology into economics.

## Pitfall 2: ignoring opportunity costs

Sherlock Holmes, Arthur Conan Doyle's legendary detective, was successful because he saw details that most others overlooked. In *Silver Blaze*, Holmes is called on to investigate the theft of an expensive racehorse from its stable. A Scotland Yard inspector assigned to the case asks Holmes whether some particular aspect of the crime requires further study. 'Yes,' Holmes replies, and describes 'the curious incident of the dog in the night-time.' 'The dog did nothing in the night-time,' responds the puzzled inspector. But as Holmes realised, that was precisely the problem. The watchdog's failure to bark when Silver Blaze was stolen meant that the watchdog knew the thief. This clue ultimately proved the key to unravelling the mystery.

Just as we often don't notice when a dog fails to bark, many of us tend to overlook the implicit value of activities that fail to happen. As discussed earlier, however, intelligent decisions require taking the value of *forgone opportunities* properly into account.

The opportunity cost of an activity, once again, is the value of the next-best alternative that must be forgone in order to engage in that activity. If buying a computer game in the town means not watching the last hour of a movie, then the value to you of watching the end of that movie is an opportunity cost of the trip. Many people make bad decisions because they tend to ignore the value of such forgone opportunities. To avoid overlooking opportunity costs, economists often translate questions like 'Should I walk to the pub?' into ones like 'Should I walk to the pub or watch the end of the movie on TV?'

### **Example 1.3** How should you use your father's frequent-flyer points?

It is May. You are interested in going to the United States for the summer, where you hope to work and make next year's pocket money. You expect to make €600 after all costs in the United States. The round-trip airfare to New York is €800. Your father tells you that he has accumulated sufficient frequent-flyer points to buy you the return ticket. However, you now hear that your sister is to be married in Nairobi in September. Your attendance is non-negotiable. The cost of a package return ticket to Nairobi and accommodation is €700. You could use the points instead to cover the cost of the Nairobi trip. Which should you use the points for? The Cost–Benefit Principle tells us that you should go to New York if the benefits of the trip exceed its costs. If it were not for the complication of the frequent-flyer points, solving this problem would be a straightforward matter of comparing your benefit from the summer in the United States with all the relevant costs. And since your airfare exceeds the net amount you expect to earn you would not go to New York.

But what about the possibility of using your frequent-flyer coupon to make the trip? Using it for that purpose might make the flight to New York seem free, suggesting you would reap an economic surplus of €600 by making the trip. But doing so would also mean you would have to pay €700 for your airfare and accommodation costs for Nairobi. So the opportunity cost of using your coupon to go to New York is really €700. If you use the points to go to New York, the trip still ends up being a loser, because the cost, €700, exceeds the benefit by €100. In cases like these, you are much more likely to decide sensibly if you ask yourself: 'Should I use the frequent-flyer points for this trip or save it for an upcoming trip?'

We cannot emphasise strongly enough that the key to using the concept of opportunity cost correctly lies in recognising precisely what taking a given action *prevents us from doing*. Exercise 1.3 illustrates this point by modifying the details of Example 1.3 slightly.

**Exercise 1.3**

The same as Example 1.3, except that now your frequent-flyer coupon expires before September, so your only chance to use it will be for the New York trip. Should you use your coupon?

## Pitfall 3: failure to ignore sunk costs

The opportunity cost pitfall is one in which people ignore costs they ought to take into account. In another common pitfall, the reverse is true: people are influenced by costs they ought to ignore. The only costs that should influence a decision about whether to take an action are those that we can *avoid by not taking the action*. As a practical matter, however, many decision makers appear to be influenced by **sunk costs** – costs that are beyond recovery at the moment a decision is made. For example, money spent on a non-transferable, non-refundable airline ticket is a sunk cost.

**sunk cost** a cost that is beyond recovery at the moment a decision must be made

Because sunk costs must be borne *whether or not an action is taken*, they are irrelevant to the decision of whether to take the action. The sunk-cost pitfall (the mistake of being influenced by sunk costs) is illustrated clearly in Example 1.4.

### **Example 1.4** How much should you eat at an all-you-can-eat restaurant?

The Rajput, an Indian restaurant in Berlin, offers an all-you-can-eat lunch buffet for €15. Customers pay €15 at the door, and no matter how many times they refill their plates, there is no additional charge. One day, as a goodwill gesture, the owner of the restaurant tells 20 randomly selected guests that their lunch is on the house. The remaining guests pay the usual price. If all diners are rational, will there be any difference in the average quantity of food consumed by people in these two groups?

Having eaten their first helping, diners in each group confront the following question: 'Should I go back for another helping?' For rational diners, if the benefit of doing so exceeds the cost, the answer is yes; otherwise it is no. Note that at the moment of decision about a second helping, the €15 charge for the lunch is a sunk cost. Those who paid it have no way to recover it. Thus, for both groups, the (extra) cost of another helping is exactly zero. And since the people who received the free lunch were chosen at random, there is no reason to suppose that their appetites or incomes are different from those of other diners. The benefit of another helping thus should be the same, on average, for people in both groups. And since their respective costs and benefits of an additional helping are the same, the two groups should eat the same number of helpings, on average.

Psychologists and economists have experimental evidence, however, that people in such groups do not eat similar amounts.[2] In particular, those for whom the luncheon charge is not waived tend to eat substantially more than those for whom the charge is waived. People in the former group seem somehow determined to 'get their money's worth'. Their implicit goal is apparently to minimise the average cost per bite of the food they eat. Yet minimising average cost is not a particularly sensible objective. It brings to mind the man who drove his car on the highway at night, even though he had nowhere to go, because he wanted to boost his average fuel economy. The irony is that diners who are determined to get their money's worth usually end up eating too much, as evidenced later by their regrets about having gone back for their last helpings.

The fact that the cost–benefit criterion failed the test of prediction in this example does nothing to invalidate its advice about what people *should* do. If you are letting sunk costs influence your decisions, you can do better by changing your behaviour.

## Pitfall 4: failure to understand the average–marginal distinction

Often we are confronted with the choice of whether or not to engage in an activity (for example, whether or not to shop in the city). But in many situations, the issue is not whether to pursue the activity at all, but rather the *extent* to which it should be pursued. We can apply the Cost–Benefit

[2] See, for example, Thaler (1980).

marginal cost the increase in total cost that results from carrying out one additional unit of an activity

marginal benefit the increase in total benefit that results from carrying out one additional unit of an activity

Principle in such situations by repeatedly asking the question: 'Should I increase the level at which I am currently pursuing the activity?'

In attempting to answer this question, the focus should always be on the benefit and cost of an *additional* unit of activity. To emphasise this focus, economists refer to the cost of an additional unit of activity as the **marginal cost** of the activity. Similarly, the benefit of an additional unit of the activity is the **marginal benefit** of the activity.

When the problem is to discover the proper level at which to pursue an activity, the cost–benefit rule is to keep increasing the level as long as the marginal benefit of the activity exceeds its marginal cost. As Example 1.5 illustrates, however, people often fail to apply this rule correctly.

### **Example 1.5** Should the European Space Agency (ESA) expand the Ariane programme from four launches per year to five?

Suppose it has been estimated by the economists working for the ESA that the gains from the programme are currently €12 billion per year (an average of €3 billion per launch) and that its costs are currently €10 billion per year (an average of €2.5 billion per launch). On the basis of these estimates, the ESA sends its chief economist to Brussels to persuade the Commission to provide increased EU funding to expand the launch vehicle programme. Should the Commission agree?

To discover whether expanding the programme makes economic sense, we must compare the marginal cost of a launch with its marginal benefit. The economists' estimates, however, tell us only the **average cost** and **average benefit** of the programme – which are, respectively, the total cost of the programme divided by the number of launches and the total benefit divided by the number of launches. Knowing the average benefit and average cost per launch for all satellites launched thus far is simply not useful for deciding whether to expand the programme. Of course, the average cost of the launches undertaken so far *might* be the same as the cost of adding another launch. But it might also be either higher or lower than the marginal cost of a launch. The same statement holds true regarding average and marginal benefits.

average cost the total cost of undertaking *n* units of an activity divided by *n*

average benefit the total benefit of undertaking *n* units of an activity divided by *n*

Suppose, for the sake of discussion, that the benefit of an additional launch is in fact the same as the average benefit per launch thus far, €3 billion. Should the ESA add another launch? Not if the cost of adding the fifth launch would be more than €3 billion. And the fact that the average cost per launch is only €2.5 billion simply does not tell us anything about the marginal cost of the fifth launch.

Suppose, for example, that the relationship between the number of satellites launched and the total cost of the programme is as described in Table 1.1. The average cost per launch (column (3)) when there are four launches would then be €10 billion/4 = €2.5 billion per

| Number of launches (1) | Total cost (€ billion) (2) | Average cost (€ billion) (3) |
|---|---|---|
| 0 | 0 | 0 |
| 1 | 2.00 | 2.00 |
| 2 | 4.25 | 2.125 |
| 3 | 6.75 | 2.25 |
| 4 | 10.0 | 2.50 |
| 5 | 15.0 | 5.0 |

**Table 1.1** Total Cost and Satellite Launches

launch. But note that in column (2) of Table 1.1 that adding a fifth launch would raise costs from €10 billion to €15 billion, making the marginal cost of the fifth launch €5 billion. So if the benefit of an additional launch is €3 billion, increasing the number of launches from four to five would make absolutely no economic sense.

Example 1.6 illustrates how to apply the Cost–Benefit Principle correctly in this case.

### Example 1.6 How many space vehicles should the ESA launch?

The ESA must decide how many vehicles to launch. The benefit of each launch is estimated to be €3 billion, and the total cost of the programme again depends on the number of launches, in the manner shown in Table 1.1. How many vehicles should be launched ?

The ESA should continue to launch satellites as long as the marginal benefit of the programme exceeds its marginal cost. In Example 1.6, the marginal benefit is constant at €3 billion per launch, regardless of the number of launches. The ESA should thus keep launching as long as the marginal cost per launch is less than or equal to €3 billion (Table 1.2).

| Number of launches (1) | Total cost (€ billion) (2) | Average cost (€ billion) (3) | Marginal cost (€ billion) (4) |
|---|---|---|---|
| 0 | 0 | 0 | |
| | | | 2.0 |
| 1 | 2.0 | 2.0 | |
| | | | 2.25 |
| 2 | 4.25 | 2.125 | |
| | | | 2.5 |
| 3 | 6.75 | 2.25 | |
| | | | 3.25 |
| 4 | 10.0 | 2.5 | |
| | | | 5.0 |
| 5 | 15.0 | 5.0 | |

**Table 1.2** Marginal Cost and Satellite Launches

Applying the definition of marginal cost to the total cost entries in column (2) of Table 1.1 yields the marginal cost values in column (3) of Table 1.2. (Because marginal cost is the change in total cost that results when we change the number of launches by one, we place each marginal cost entry midway between the rows showing the corresponding total cost entries.) Thus, for example, the marginal cost of increasing the number of launches from one to two is €2.25 billion, the difference between the €4.25 billion total cost of two launches and the €2 billion total cost of one launch.

As we see from a comparison of the €6 billion marginal benefit per launch with the marginal cost entries in column (3) of Table 1.2, the first three launches satisfy the cost–benefit test, but the fourth and fifth launches do not. The ESA should thus launch three space satellites. The Commission should actually reduce its funding.

**Exercise 1.4** If the marginal benefit of each launch had been not €3 billion but €4.5 billion, how many satellites should the ESA have launched?

The cost–benefit framework emphasises that the only relevant costs and benefits in deciding whether to pursue an activity further are *marginal* costs and benefits – measures that correspond to the *increment* of activity under consideration. In many contexts, however, people seem more inclined to compare the *average* cost and benefit of the activity. As Example 1.5 has made clear, increasing the level of an activity may not be justified, even though its average benefit at the current level is significantly greater than its average cost.

Exercise 1.5 further illustrates the importance of the average–marginal distinction.

**Exercise 1.5**

Liverpool, fresh from their 2005 triumph over AC Milan, and assuming they will make the cut in 2006, decide to beef up team management in preparation and hire a new assistant manager. He notices that one player, Steven Gerrard, scores on average a higher percentage of his penalty shots than any other player on the squad. Based on this information, the assistant suggests to the manager that the star player should take *all* the shots. That way, he reasons, the team will score more points and win more games. On hearing this suggestion, the manager fires his assistant for incompetence. What was wrong with the assistant's idea?

Examples 1.2–1.5 make the point that people *sometimes* choose irrationally. We must stress that our purpose in discussing these examples was not to suggest that people *generally* make irrational choices. On the contrary, most people appear to choose sensibly most of the time, especially when their decisions are important or familiar ones. The economist's focus on rational choice thus offers not only useful advice about making better decisions, but also a basis for predicting and explaining human behaviour. We used the cost–benefit approach in this way when discussing how rising faculty salaries have led to larger class sizes. And as we shall see, similar reasoning helps to explain human behaviour in virtually every other domain.

## RECAP Four important decision pitfalls

- **The pitfall of measuring costs or benefits proportionally** Many decision makers treat a change in cost or benefit as insignificant if it constitutes only a small proportion of the original amount. *Absolute money amounts*, not proportions, should be employed to measure costs and benefits.
- **The pitfall of ignoring opportunity costs** When performing a cost–benefit analysis of an action, it is important to account for all relevant *opportunity costs*, defined as the values of the most highly valued alternatives that must be forgone in order to carry out the action. A resource (such as a frequent-flyer coupon) may have a high opportunity cost, even if you originally got it 'for free', if its best alternative use has high value. The identical resource may have a low opportunity cost, however, if it has no good alternative uses.
- **The pitfall of not ignoring sunk costs** When deciding whether to perform an action, it is important to ignore *sunk costs* – those costs that cannot be avoided even if the action is not taken. Even though a ticket to a concert may have cost you €100, if you have already bought it and cannot sell it to anyone else, the €100 is a sunk cost and should not influence your decision about whether to go to the concert.
- **The pitfall of using average instead of marginal costs and benefits** Decision makers often have ready information about the total cost and benefit of an activity, and from these it is simple to compute the activity's average cost and benefit. A common mistake is to conclude that an activity should be increased if its average benefit exceeds its average cost. The Cost–Benefit Principle tells us that the level of an activity should be increased if, and only if, its *marginal* benefit exceeds its *marginal* cost.

Some costs and benefits, especially marginal costs and benefits and opportunity costs, are important for decision making, while others, such as sunk costs and average costs and benefits, are essentially irrelevant. This conclusion is implicit in our original statement of the Cost–Benefit Principle (an action should be taken if, and only if, the extra benefits of taking it exceed the extra costs). Yet so important are the pitfalls of using proportions instead of absolute money amounts, of ignoring opportunity costs, of taking sunk costs into account, and of confusing average and marginal costs and benefits that we enumerate these pitfalls separately as one of the core ideas for repeated emphasis.

The Not-All-Costs-and-Benefits-Matter-Equally Principle: Some costs and benefits (for example, opportunity costs and marginal costs and benefits) matter in making decisions, whereas others (for example, sunk costs and average costs and benefits) don't.

## Economics: micro and macro

By convention, we use the term **microeconomics** to describe the study of individual choices and of group behaviour in individual markets. **Macroeconomics**, by contrast, is the study of the performance of national economies and of the policies that governments use to try to improve that performance. Macroeconomics tries to understand the determinants of such things as the national unemployment rate, the overall price level and the total value of national output.

**microeconomics** the study of individual choice under scarcity and its implications for the behaviour of prices and quantities in individual markets

**macroeconomics** the study of the performance of national economies and the policies that governments use to try to improve that performance

Our focus in this chapter is on issues that face the individual decision maker, whether that individual confronts a personal decision, a family decision, a business decision, a government policy decision, or indeed any other type of decision. Further on, we shall consider economic models of groups of individuals, such as all buyers or all sellers in a specific market. Later still, we shall turn to broader economic issues and measures.

No matter which of these levels is our focus, however, our thinking will be shaped by the fact that although economic needs and wants are effectively unlimited, the material and human resources that can be used to satisfy them are finite. Clear thinking about economic problems must therefore always take into account the idea of *trade-offs* – the idea that having more of one good thing usually means having less of another. Our economy and our society are shaped to a substantial degree by the choices people have made when faced with such trade-offs.

## The approach of this text

Choosing the number of students to register in each class is just one of many important decisions in planning an introductory economics course. Another decision, to which the scarcity principle applies just as strongly, concerns which of many different topics to include on the course syllabus. There is a virtually inexhaustible set of topics and issues that might be covered in an introductory course, but only limited time in which to cover them. There is no free lunch: covering some topics inevitably means omitting others.

All textbook authors are necessarily forced to pick and choose. A textbook that covered all the issues ever written about in economics would take up more than a whole floor of your university library. It is our firm view that most introductory textbooks try to cover far too much. A relatively short list of the discipline's core ideas can explain a great deal of the behaviour and events we see in the world around us. So rather than cover a large number of ideas at a superficial level, our strategy is to focus on this short list of core ideas, returning to each entry again and again, in many different contexts. This strategy will enable you to internalise these ideas remarkably well in the brief span of a single course. And the benefit of learning a small number of important ideas well will far outweigh the cost of having to ignore a host of other, less important ideas.[3]

---

[3] The famous Australian economist, W. Max Corden, a charming and brilliant teacher as well as a prolific and innovative researcher, was fond of saying to graduate students at a seminar series attended by one of us at Nuffield College, Oxford, that if you couldn't explain something by using the basic tools and concepts of supply and demand it probably wasn't worth explaining in the first place.

So far, we've already encountered three core ideas: the Scarcity Principle, the Cost–Benefit Principle and the principle that not all costs and benefits matter equally. As these core ideas re-emerge in the course of our discussions, we shall call your attention to them. And shortly after a *new* core idea appears, we shall highlight it by formally restating it.

A second important element in the philosophy of this text is our belief in the importance of active learning. In the same way that you can learn Spanish only by speaking and writing it, or tennis only by playing the game, you can learn economics only by *doing* economics. And because we want you to learn how to do economics, rather than just to read or listen passively as the authors or your instructor does economics, we shall make every effort to encourage you to stay actively involved.

For example, instead of just telling you about an idea, we shall usually first motivate the idea by showing you how it works in the context of a specific example. Often, these examples will be followed by exercises for you to try, as well as applications that show the relevance of the idea to real life. Try working the exercises *before* looking up the answers (which are at the back of the relevant chapter).

Think critically about the applications: Do you see how they illustrate the point being made? Do they give you new insight into the issue? Work the problems at the end of the chapters, and take extra care with those relating to points that you do not fully understand. Apply economic principles to the world around you. (We shall say more about this when we discuss economic naturalism below.) Finally, when you come across an idea or example that you find interesting, tell a friend about it. You'll be surprised to discover how much the mere act of explaining it helps you understand and remember the underlying principle. The more actively you can become engaged in the learning process, the more effective your learning will be.

## Economic naturalism

With the rudiments of the cost–benefit framework under your belt, you are now in a position to become an 'economic naturalist', someone who uses insights from economics to help make sense of observations from everyday life. People who have studied biology are able to observe and marvel at many details of nature that would otherwise have escaped their notice. For example, on a walk in the woods in early April the novice may see only trees whereas the biology student notices many different species of trees and understands why some are already in leaf while others still lie dormant. Likewise, the novice may notice that in some animal species males are much larger than females, but the biology student knows that such a pattern occurs only in species in which males take several mates. Natural selection favours larger males in those species because their greater size helps them prevail in the often bloody contests among males for access to females. By contrast, males tend to be roughly the same size as females in monogamous species, in which there is much less fighting for mates.

In similar fashion, learning a few simple economic principles enables us to see the mundane details of ordinary human existence in a new light. Whereas the uninitiated often fail even to notice these details, the economic naturalist not only sees them, but becomes actively engaged in the attempt to understand them. Let us consider a few examples of questions that economic naturalists might pose for themselves.

Economic naturalist 1.1 illustrates a case in which the *benefit* of a product depends on the number of other people who own that product. As the next example demonstrates, the *cost* of a product may also depend on the number of others who own it.

### Economic naturalist 1.1 Why do many hardware manufacturers include more than €1,000 worth of 'free' software with a computer selling for only slightly more than that?

The software industry is different from many others in the sense that its customers care a great deal about product compatibility. When you and your classmates are working on a project together, for example, your task will be much simpler if you all use the same word-processing program. Likewise, an executive's life will be easier at tax return time if her financial software is the same as her accountant's.

The implication is that the benefit of owning and using any given software program increases with the number of other people who use that same product. This unusual relationship gives the producers of the most popular programs an enormous advantage and often makes it hard for new programs to break into the market.

Recognising this pattern, the Intuit Corporation offered computer makers free copies of *Quicken*, its personal financial management software. Computer makers, for their part, were only too happy to include the program, since it made their new computers more attractive to buyers. *Quicken* soon became the standard for personal financial management programs. By giving away free copies of the program, Intuit 'primed the pump', creating an enormous demand for upgrades of *Quicken* and for more advanced versions of related software. Thus *TurboTax* and *Macintax*, Intuit's personal income tax software, have become the standards for tax-preparation programs.

Inspired by this success story, other software developers have jumped on to the bandwagon. Most hardware now comes bundled with a host of free software programs. Some software developers are even rumoured to *pay* computer makers to include their programs!

### Economic naturalist 1.2 Why don't car manufacturers make cars without heaters?

Virtually every new car sold in the Europe today has a heater. But not every car has a CD player yet, although this is changing. The car's heating system costs more than the cost of a CD player. Why the difference?

One might be tempted to answer that although everyone *needs* a heater, people can get along without CD players. Yet heaters are of little use in hot climates, and car rental companies that keep their cars for six months or less, and buy a lot of cars, could well rent cars without heaters (they rent cars without air conditioning!). What is more, cars produced as recently as the 1960s did *not* all have heaters.

Although heaters cost extra money to manufacture and may not be of much use to all purchasers, they do not cost *much* money and are useful on at least a few days each year in most parts of the continent. As time passed and people's incomes grew, manufacturers found that people were ordering fewer and fewer cars without heaters. At some point it actually became cheaper to put heaters in all cars, rather than bear the administrative expense of making some cars with heaters and others without. No doubt a few buyers would still order a car without a heater if they could save some money in the process. But catering for these customers is just no longer worth it.

Similar reasoning explains why certain cars today cannot be purchased without a CD player. Buyers of the 2003 BMW 745i, for example, got a CD player whether they wanted one or not. Most buyers of this car, which sells for anything up to approximately €100,000, depending on the country in Europe, have high incomes, so the overwhelming majority of them would have chosen to order a CD player had it been sold as an option. Because of the savings made possible when *all* cars are produced with the same equipment, it would have actually cost BMW more to supply cars for the few who would want them without CD players.

Buyers of the least expensive makes of car have much lower incomes on average than BMW 745i buyers. Accordingly, most of them have more pressing alternative uses for their money than to buy CD players for their cars, and this explains why some inexpensive makes continue to offer CD players only as options.

The insights afforded by Economic naturalist 1.2 suggest an answer to the following strange question.

## Economic naturalist 1.3 Why do the keypad buttons on drive-in automatic teller machines (ATMs) have Braille dots?

Drive-in ATMs are uncommon in Europe, but are frequently found in North America. Curiously, the keypads have Braille dots. Braille dots are also found in America and Europe on, for example, the buttons in lifts (elevators) and similar places. Their usefulness in drive-in ATM points where the driver uses the ATM from the car is a little unclear. Braille keypads enable blind people to participate more fully in the normal flow of daily activity. But even though blind people can do many remarkable things, they cannot drive automobiles on public roads. Why, then, do the manufacturers of automatic teller machines install Braille dots on the machines at drive-in locations?

The answer to this riddle is that once the keypad moulds have been manufactured, the cost of producing buttons with Braille dots is no higher than the cost of producing smooth buttons. Making both would require separate sets of moulds and two different types of inventory. If the patrons of drive-in machines found buttons with Braille dots harder to use, there might be a reason to incur these extra costs. But since the dots pose no difficulty for sighted users, the best and cheapest solution is to produce only keypads with dots.

Economic naturalist 1.3 was suggested by Cornell student Bill Tjoa, in response to the following assignment.

**Exercise 1.6** In 500 words or fewer, use cost–benefit analysis to explain some pattern of events or behaviour you have observed in your own environment.

There is probably no more useful step you can take in your study of economics than to perform several versions of the assignment in Exercise 1.6. Students who do so almost invariably become lifelong economic naturalists. Their mastery of economic concepts not only does not decay with the passage of time; it actually grows stronger. We urge you, in the strongest possible terms, to make this investment!

## SUMMARY

- Economics is the study of how people make choices under conditions of scarcity and of the results of those choices for society. Economic analysis of human behaviour begins with the assumption that people are *rational* – that they have well-defined goals and try to achieve them as best they can. In trying to achieve their goals, people normally face trade-offs: because material and human resources are limited, having more of one good thing means making do with less of some other good thing.
- Our focus in this chapter has been on how rational people make choices among alternative courses of action. Our basic tool for analysing these decisions is *cost–benefit analysis*. The Cost–Benefit Principle says that a person should take an action if, and only if, the benefit of that action is at least as great as its cost. The benefit of an action is defined as the largest money amount the person would be willing to pay in order to take the action. The cost of an action is defined as the money value of everything the person must give up in order to take the action.
- Often the question is not whether to pursue an activity but rather how many units of it to pursue. In these cases, the rational person pursues additional units as long as the marginal benefit of the activity (the benefit from pursuing an additional unit of it) exceeds its marginal cost (the cost of pursuing an additional unit of it).
- In using the cost–benefit framework, we need not presume that people *choose rationally* all the time. Indeed, we identified four common pitfalls that plague decision makers in all walks of life: a tendency to treat small proportional changes as insignificant, a tendency to ignore opportunity costs, a tendency not to ignore sunk costs, and a tendency to confuse average and marginal costs and benefits.
- *Microeconomics* is the study of individual choices and of group behaviour in individual markets, while *macroeconomics* is the study of the performance of national economies and of the policies that governments use to try to improve economic performance.

## Key terms

**average benefit** (11)
**average cost** (11)
**economic surplus** (6)
**economics** (4)
**macroeconomics** (14)
**marginal benefit** (11)
**marginal cost** (11)
**microeconomics** (14)
**opportunity cost** (6)
**rational person** (5)
**sunk cost** (10)

## Review questions

1. A friend of yours on the tennis team says: 'Private tennis lessons are definitely better than group lessons.' Explain what you think he means by this statement. Then use the Cost–Benefit Principle to explain why private lessons are not necessarily the best choice for everyone.
2. True or false: Your willingness to drive to town to save €30 on a new appliance should depend on what fraction of the total selling price €30 is. Explain.
3. Why might someone who is trying to decide whether to see a movie be more likely to focus on the €9 ticket price than on the €20 she would fail to earn by not babysitting?
4. Many people think of their air travel as being free when they use frequent-flyer coupons. Explain why these people are likely to make wasteful travel decisions.

5. Is the non-refundable tuition payment you made to your university this year a sunk cost? How would your answer differ if your university were to offer a full tuition refund to any student who dropped out of school during the first two months of the semester?

## Problems

Problems marked with an asterisk (*) are more difficult.

1. The most you would be willing to pay for having a freshly washed car before going out on a date is €6. The smallest amount for which you would be willing to wash someone else's car is €3.50. You are going out this evening, and your car is dirty. How much economic surplus would you receive from washing it?

2. To earn extra money in the summer, you grow tomatoes and sell them at the farmers' market for 30 cents per kg. By adding compost to your garden, you can increase your yield as shown in the table below. If compost costs 50 cents per kg and your goal is to make as much money as possible, how many kilograms of compost should you add?

| Kg of compost | Kg of tomatoes |
|---|---|
| 0 | 100 |
| 1 | 120 |
| 2 | 125 |
| 3 | 128 |
| 4 | 130 |
| 5 | 131 |
| 6 | 131.5 |

3. Residents of your city are charged a fixed weekly fee of €6 for garbage collection. They are allowed to put out as many bins as they wish. The average household disposes of three bins of garbage per week under this plan. Now suppose that your city changes to a 'tag' system. Each bin to be collected must have a tag affixed to it. The tags cost €2 each and are not reusable. What effect do you think the introduction of the tag system will have on the total quantity of garbage collected in your city? Explain briefly.

4. Once a week, Smith purchases a six-pack of cola and puts it in his refrigerator for his two children. He invariably discovers that all six cans are gone on the first day. Jones also purchases a six-pack of cola once a week for his two children but, unlike Smith, he tells them that each may drink no more than three cans. If the children use cost–benefit analysis each time they decide whether to drink a can of cola, explain why the cola lasts much longer at Jones' house than at Smith's.

5. Tom is a mushroom farmer. He invests all his spare cash in additional mushrooms, which grow on otherwise useless land behind his barn. The mushrooms double in weight during their first year, after which time they are harvested and sold at a constant price per kilogram. Tom's friend Dick asks Tom for a loan of €200, which he promises to repay after one year. How much interest will Dick have to pay Tom in order for Tom to recover his opportunity cost of making the loan? Explain briefly.

6. Suppose that in the last few seconds you devoted to Question 1 on your physics exam you earned 4 extra points, while in the last few seconds you devoted to Question 2 you earned 10 extra points. You earned a total of 48 and 12 points, respectively, on the two questions, and the total time you spent on each was the same. If you could take the exam again, how – if at all – should you reallocate your time between these questions?

7. Martha and Sarah have the same preferences and incomes. Just as Martha arrived at the theatre to see a play, she discovered that she had lost the €10 ticket she had purchased earlier. Sarah had also just arrived at the theatre planning to buy a ticket to see the same play when she discovered that she had lost a €10 note from her purse. If both Martha and Sarah are rational and both still have enough money to pay for a ticket, is one of them more likely than the other to go ahead and see the play anyway?

8.* You and your friend Joe have identical tastes. At 2 p.m., you go to the local Ticketmaster outlet and buy a €30 ticket to a football match to be played that night 50 km away. Joe plans to attend the same game, but because he cannot get to the Ticketmaster outlet, he plans to buy his ticket at the game. Tickets sold at the game cost only €25, because they carry no Ticketmaster surcharge. (Many people nonetheless pay the higher price at Ticketmaster, to be sure of getting good seats.) At 4 p.m., an unexpected snowstorm begins, making the prospect of the 50 km drive much less attractive than before (but assuring the availability of good seats). If both you and Joe are rational, is one of you more likely to attend the game than the other?

9.* For each long-distance call anywhere in the continental United States, a new phone service will charge users 30 cents per minute for the first 2 minutes and 2 cents per minute for additional minutes in each call. Tom's current phone service charges 10 cents per minute for all calls, and his calls are never shorter than 7 minutes. If Tom's dorm switches to the new phone service, what will happen to the average length of his calls?

10.* The meal plan at university A lets students eat as much as they like for a fixed fee of €500 per semester. The average student there eats 250 kg of food per semester. University B charges €500 for a book of meal tickets that entitles the student to eat 250 kg of food per semester. If the student eats more than 250 kg, he or she pays €2 for each additional kilogram; if the student eats less, he or she gets a €2 per kg refund. If students are rational, at which university will average food consumption be higher? Explain briefly.

## Answers to in-chapter exercises

1.1 The benefit of buying the game in the city is again €10 but the cost is now €12, so your economic surplus from buying it in town would be €10 – €12 = –€2. Since your economic surplus from making the trip would be negative, you should buy at the college store.

1.2 Saving €100 is €10 more valuable than saving €90, even though the percentage savings is much greater in the case of the Paris ticket.

1.3 Since you now have no alternative use for your coupon, the opportunity cost of using it to pay for the earlier flight is zero. Your economic surplus from using it on the earlier trip is positive, so you should use it for that trip.

1.4 The marginal benefit of the fourth launch is €4.5 billion, which exceeds its marginal cost of €3.5 billion, so the fourth launch should be added. But the fifth launch should not, since its marginal cost (€5 billion) exceeds its marginal benefit (€4.5 billion).

1.5 If the star player takes one more shot, some other player must take one less. The fact that the star player's *average* success rate is higher than the other player's does not mean that the probability of scoring with his *next* shot (the marginal benefit of having him shoot once more) is higher than the probability of another player scoring with his next shot. Indeed, if the best player took all his team's shots, the other team would focus its defensive effort entirely on him, in which case letting others shoot would definitely pay.

# Appendix A

## Working with equations, graphs and tables

Although many of the examples and most of the end-of-chapter problems in this book are quantitative, none requires mathematical skills beyond rudimentary high school algebra and geometry. In this brief appendix we shall review some of the skills you will need for dealing with these examples and problems.

One important skill is to be able to read simple verbal descriptions and translate the information they provide into the relevant equations or graphs. You will also need to be able to translate information given in tabular form into an equation or graph, and sometimes you will need to translate graphical information into a table or equation. The following examples illustrate all the tools you will need.

## Using a verbal description to construct an equation

We begin with an example that shows how to construct a long-distance telephone billing equation from a verbal description of the billing plan.

**Example 1A.1** Your long-distance telephone plan charges you €5 per month plus 10 cents per minute for long-distance calls. Write an equation that describes your monthly telephone bill.

An **equation** is a simple mathematical expression that describes the relationship between two or more **variables**, or quantities that are free to assume different values in some range. The most common type of equation we shall work with contains two types of variable: **dependent variable** and **independent variable**. In this example, the dependent variable is the money amount of your monthly telephone bill, and the independent variable is the variable on which your bill depends – namely, the volume of long-distance calls you make during the month. Your bill also depends on the €5 monthly fee and the 10 cents per minute charge. But in this example, those amounts are **constants**, not variables. A constant, also called a **parameter**, is a quantity in an equation that is fixed in value, not free to vary. As the terms suggest, the dependent variable describes an outcome that depends on the value taken by the independent variable.

**equation** a mathematical expression that describes the relationship between two or more variables

**variable** a quantity that is free to take a range of different values

**dependent variable** a variable in an equation whose value is determined by the value taken by another variable in the equation

**independent variable** a variable in an equation whose value determines the value taken by another variable in the equation

**constant (or parameter)** a quantity that is fixed in value

Once you have identified the dependent variable and the independent variable, choose simple symbols to represent them. In algebra courses, $X$ is typically used to represent the independent variable and $Y$ the dependent variable. Many people find it easier to remember what the variables stand for, however, if they choose symbols that are linked in some straightforward way to the quantities that the variables represent. Thus, in this example, we might use $B$ to represent your monthly *bill* in money terms and $T$ to represent the total *time* in minutes you spent during the month on long-distance calls.

Having identified the relevant variables and chosen symbols to represent them, you are now in a position to write the equation that links them:

$$B = 5 + 0.10T \tag{1A.1}$$

where $B$ is your monthly long-distance bill in money terms and $T$ is your monthly total long-distance calling time in minutes. The fixed monthly fee (5) and the charge per minute (0.10) are parameters in this equation. Note the importance of being clear about the units of measure. Because $B$ represents the monthly bill, we must also express the fixed monthly fee and the per-minute monetary charge, which is why the latter number appears in Eq.(1A.1) as 0.10 rather than 10. Equation (1A.1) follows the normal convention in which the dependent variable appears by itself on the left-hand side while the independent variable or variables and constants appear on the right-hand side.

Once we have the equation for the monthly bill, we can use it to calculate how much you will owe as a function of your monthly volume of long-distance calls. For example, if you make 32 minutes of calls, you can calculate your monthly bill by simply substituting 32 minutes for $T$ in Eq. (1A.1):

$$B = 5 + 0.10(32) = 8.20 \qquad (1A.2)$$

Your monthly bill when you make 32 minutes of calls is thus equal to €8.20.

**Exercise 1A.1** Under the monthly billing plan described in Example 1A.1, how much would you owe for a month during which you made 45 minutes of long-distance calls?

## Graphing the equation of a straight line

Example 1A.2 shows how to portray the billing plan described in Example 1A.1 as a graph.

**Example 1A.2** Construct a graph that portrays the monthly long-distance telephone billing plan described in Example 1A.1, putting your telephone charges, in money per month, on the vertical axis, and your total volume of calls, in minutes per month, on the horizontal axis.

The first step in responding to this instruction is the one we just took, namely, to translate the verbal description of the billing plan into an equation. When graphing an equation, the normal convention is to use the vertical axis to represent the dependent variable and the horizontal axis to represent the independent variable. In Fig. 1A.1, we therefore put $B$ on the vertical axis and $T$ on the horizontal axis. One way to construct the graph shown in Fig. 1A.1 is to begin by plotting the monthly bill values that correspond to several different total amounts of long-distance calls. For example, someone who makes 10 minutes of calls during the month would have a bill of $B = 5 + 0.10(10) =$ €6. Thus, in Fig. 1A.1 the value of 10 minutes per month on the horizontal axis corresponds to a bill of €6 per month on the vertical axis (point $A$). Someone who makes 30 minutes of long-distance calls during the month will have a monthly bill of $B = 5 + 0.10(30) =$ €8, so the value of 30 minutes per month on the horizontal axis corresponds to €8 per month on the vertical axis (point $C$). Similarly, someone who makes 70 minutes of long-distance calls during the month will have a monthly bill of $B = 5 + 0.10(70)$ = €12, so the value of 70 minutes on the horizontal axis corresponds to €12 on the vertical axis (point $D$). The line joining these points is the graph of the monthly billing in Eq. (1A.1).

**vertical intercept** in a straight line, the value taken by the dependent variable when the independent variable equals zero

**slope** in a straight line, the ratio of the vertical distance the straight line travels between any two points (**rise**) to the corresponding horizontal distance (**run**)

As shown in Fig. 1A.1, the graph of the equation $B = 5 + 0.10T$ is a straight line. The parameter 5 is the **vertical intercept** of the line – the value of $B$ when $T = 0$, or the point at which the line intersects the vertical axis. The parameter 0.10 is the **slope** of the line, which is the ratio of the **rise** of the line to the corresponding **run**. The ratio rise/run is simply the vertical distance between any two points on the line divided by the horizontal distance between those points. For example, if we choose points $A$ and $C$ in Fig. 1A.1, the rise is $8 - 6 = 2$ and the corresponding run is $30 - 10 = 20$, so rise/run $= 2/20 = 0.10$. More generally, for the graph of any equation $Y = a + bX$, the parameter $a$ is the vertical intercept and the parameter $b$ is the slope.

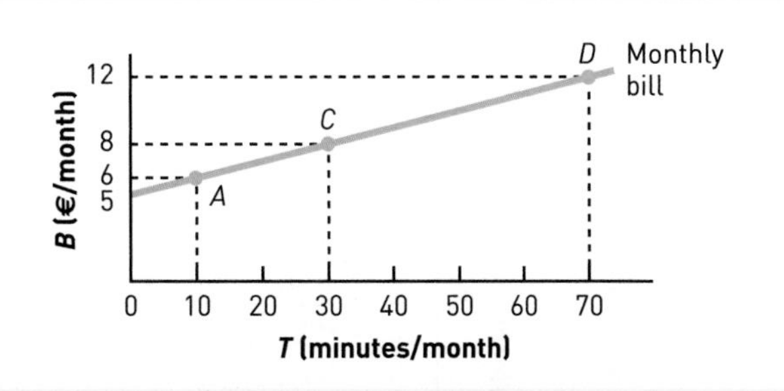


**Figure 1A.1 The Monthly Telephone Bill in Example 1A.1.** The graph of the equation $B = 5 + 0.10T$ is the straight line shown. Its vertical intercept is 5, and its slope is 0.10.

## Deriving the equation of a straight line from its graph

Example 1A.3 shows how to derive the equation for a straight line from a graph of the line.

**Example 1A.3** Figure 1A.2 shows the graph of the monthly billing plan for a new long-distance plan. What is the equation for this graph? How much is the fixed monthly fee under this plan? How much is the charge per minute?

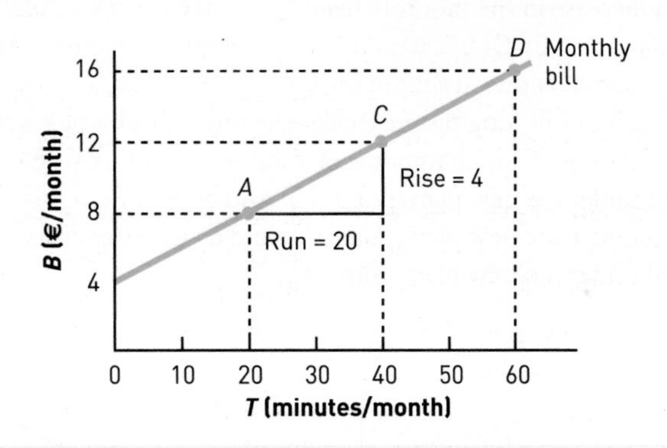


**Figure 1A.2 Another Monthly Long-Distance Plan.** The vertical distance between points $A$ and $C$ is $12 - 8 = 4$ units, and the horizontal distance between points $A$ and $C$ is $40 - 20 = 20$, so the slope of the line is $4/20 = 1/5 = 0.20$. The vertical intercept (the value of $B$ when $T = 0$) is 4. So the equation for the billing plan shown is $B = 4 + 0.20T$.

The slope of the line shown in Fig. 1A.2 is the rise between any two points divided by the corresponding run. For points $A$ and $C$, rise $= 12 - 8 = 4$, and run $= 40 - 20 = 20$, so the slope equals rise/run $= 4/20 = 1/5 = 0.20$. And since the horizontal intercept of the line is 4, its equation must be given by

$$B = 4 + 0.20T \tag{1A.3}$$

Under this plan, the fixed monthly fee is the value of the bill when $T = 0$, which is €4. The charge per minute is the slope of the billing line, 0.20, or 20 cents per minute.

**Exercise 1A.2** Write the equation for the billing plan shown in the graph below. How much is its fixed monthly fee? Its charge per minute?

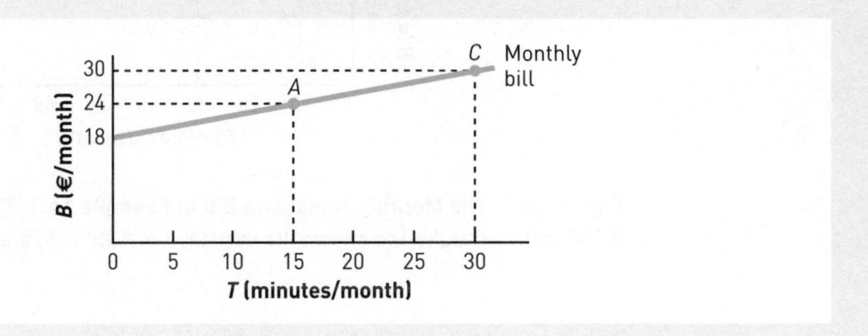


## Changes in the vertical intercept and slope

Examples 1A.4 and 1A.5 and Exercises 1A.3 and 1A.4 provide practice in seeing how a line shifts with a change in its vertical intercept or slope.

**Example 1A.4** Show how the billing plan whose graph is in Fig. 1A.2 would change if the monthly fixed fee were increased from €4 to €8.

An increase in the monthly fixed fee from €4 to €8 would increase the vertical intercept of the billing plan by €4 but would leave its slope unchanged. An increase in the fixed fee thus leads to a parallel upward shift in the billing plan by €4, as shown in Fig. 1A.3. For any given number of minutes of long-distance calls, the monthly charge on the new bill will be €4 higher than on the old bill. Thus 20 minutes of calls per month costs €8 under the original plan (point *A*) but €12 under the new plan (point *A'*). And 40 minutes costs €12 under the original plan (point *C*), €16 under the new plan (point *C'*); and 60 minutes costs €16 under the original plan (point *D*), €20 under the new plan (point *D'*).

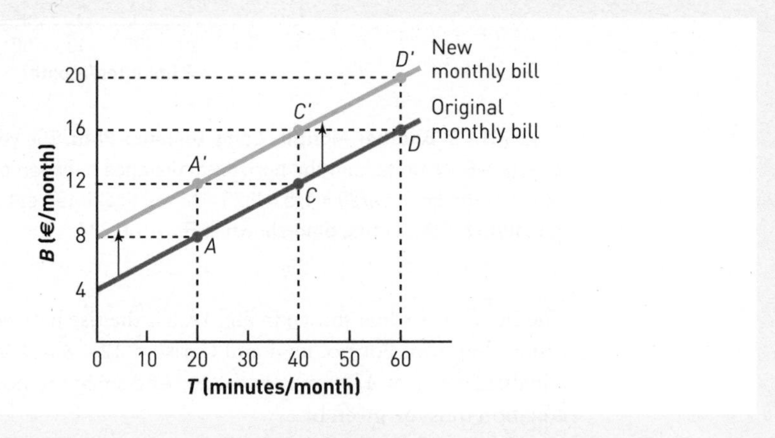


**Figure 1A.3 The Effect of an Increase in the Vertical Intercept.** An increase in the vertical intercept of a straight line produces an upward parallel shift in the line.

**Exercise 1A.3** Show how the billing plan whose graph is in Fig. 1A.2 would change if the monthly fixed fee were reduced from €4 to €2.

**Example 1A.5** Show how the billing plan whose graph is in Fig. 1A.2 would change if the charge per minute were increased from 20 cents to 40 cents.

Because the monthly fixed fee is unchanged, the vertical intercept of the new billing plan continues to be 4. But the slope of the new plan, shown in Fig. 1A.4, is 0.40, or twice the slope of the original plan. More generally, in the equation $Y = a + bX$, an increase in $b$ makes the slope of the graph of the equation steeper.

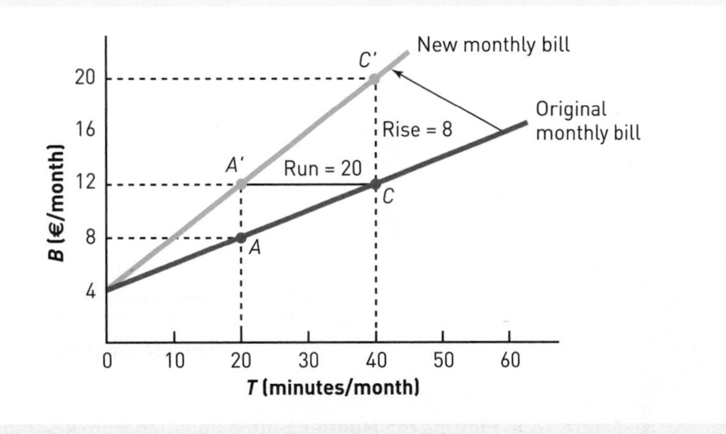


**Figure 1A.4 The Effect of an Increase in the Charge per Minute.** Because the fixed monthly fee continues to be €4, the vertical intercept of the new plan is the same as that of the original plan. With the new charge per minute of 40 cents, the slope of the billing plan rises from 0.20 to 0.40.

**Exercise 1A.4** Show how the billing plan whose graph is in Fig. 1A.2 would change if the charge per minute were reduced from 20 cents to 10 cents.

Exercise 1A.4 illustrates the general rule that in an equation $Y = a + bX$, a reduction in $b$ makes the slope of the graph of the equation less steep.

## Constructing equations and graphs from tables

Example 1A.6 and Exercise 1A.5 show how to transform tabular information into an equation or graph.

**Example 1A.6** Table 1A.1 shows four points from a monthly long-distance telephone billing equation. If all points on this billing equation lie on a straight line, find the vertical intercept of the equation and graph it. What is the monthly fixed fee? What is the charge per minute? Calculate the total bill for a month with 1 hour of long-distance calls.

**Table 1A.1** Points on a Long-Distance Billing Plan

| Long-distance bill (€/month) | Total long-distance calls (minutes/month) |
|---|---|
| 10.50 | 10 |
| 11.00 | 20 |
| 11.50 | 30 |
| 12.00 | 40 |

One approach to this problem is simply to plot any two points from Table 1A.1 on a graph. Since we are told that the billing equation is a straight line, that line must be the one that passes through any two of its points. Thus, in Fig. 1A.5 we use $A$ to denote the point from Table 1A.1 for which a monthly bill of €11 corresponds to 20 minutes per month of calls (row 2) and $C$ to denote the point for which a monthly bill of €12 corresponds to 40 minutes per month of calls (row 4). The straight line passing through these points is the graph of the billing equation.

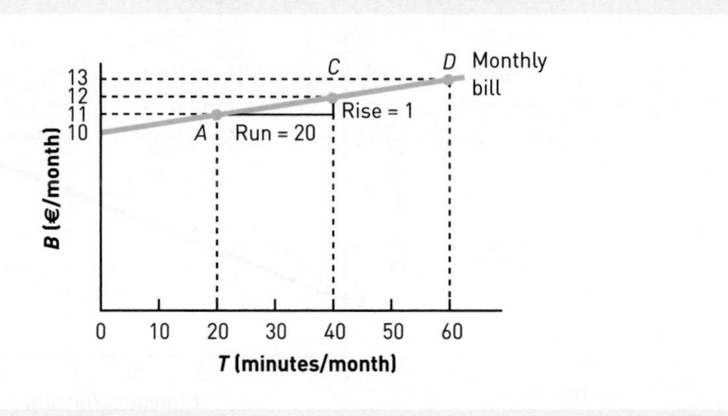


**Figure 1A.5 Plotting the Monthly Billing Equation from a Sample of Points.** Point $A$ is taken from row 2, Table 1A.1, and point $C$ from row 4. The monthly billing plan is the straight line that passes through these points.

Unless you have a steady hand, however, or use extremely large graph paper, the method of extending a line between two points on the billing plan is unlikely to be very accurate. An alternative approach is to calculate the equation for the billing plan directly. Since the equation is a straight line, we know that it takes the general form $B = f + sT$, where $f$ is the fixed monthly fee and $s$ is the slope. Our goal is to calculate the vertical intercept $f$ and the slope $s$. From the same two points we plotted earlier, $A$ and $C$, we can calculate the slope of the billing plan as $s = \text{rise}/\text{run} = 1/20 = 0.05$.

So all that remains is to calculate $f$, the fixed monthly fee. At point $C$ on the billing plan, the total monthly bill is €12 for 40 minutes, so we can substitute $B = 12$, $s = 0.05$ and $T = 40$ into the general equation $B = f + sT$ to obtain

$$12 = f + 0.05(40) \qquad (1A.4)$$

or

$$12 = f + 2 \qquad (1A.5)$$

which solves for $f = 10$. So the monthly billing equation must be

$$B = 10 + 0.05T \qquad (1A.6)$$

For this billing equation, the fixed fee is €10 per month, the calling charge is 5 cents per minute (€0.05/minute), and the total bill for a month with 1 hour of long-distance calls is $B = 10 + 0.05(60) = €13$, just as shown in Fig. 1A.5.

**Exercise 1A.5** The table below shows four points from a monthly long-distance telephone billing plan.

| Long-distance bill (€/month) | Total long-distance calls (minutes/month) |
|---|---|
| 20.00 | 10 |
| 30.00 | 20 |
| 40.00 | 30 |
| 50.00 | 40 |

If all points on this billing plan lie on a straight line, find the vertical intercept of the corresponding equation without graphing it. What is the monthly fixed fee? What is the charge per minute? How much would the charges be for 1 hour of long-distance calls per month?

## Key terms

constant (or parameter) (21)
dependent variable (21)
equation (21)
independent variable (21)
rise (22)
run (22)
slope (22)
variable (21)
vertical intercept (22)

## Answers to in-appendix exercises

1A.1 To calculate your monthly bill for 45 minutes of calls, substitute 45 minutes for $T$ in Eq. (1A.1) to get $B = 5 + 0.10(45) =$ €9.50.

1A.2 Calculating the slope using points $A$ and $C$, we have rise $= 30 - 24 = 6$ and run $= 30 - 15 = 15$, so rise/run $= 6/15 = 2/5 = 0.40$. And since the horizontal intercept of the line is 18, its equation is $B = 18 + 0.40T$. Under this plan, the fixed monthly fee is €18, and the charge per minute is the slope of the billing line, 0.40, or 40 cents per minute.

1A.3 A €2 reduction in the monthly fixed fee would produce a downward parallel shift in the billing plan by €2.

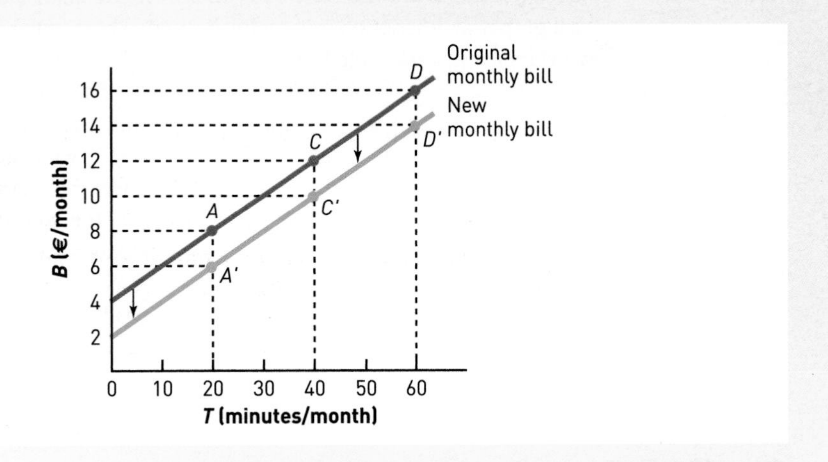

1A.4 With an unchanged monthly fixed fee, the vertical intercept of the new billing plan continues to be 4. The slope of the new plan is 0.10, half the slope of the original plan.

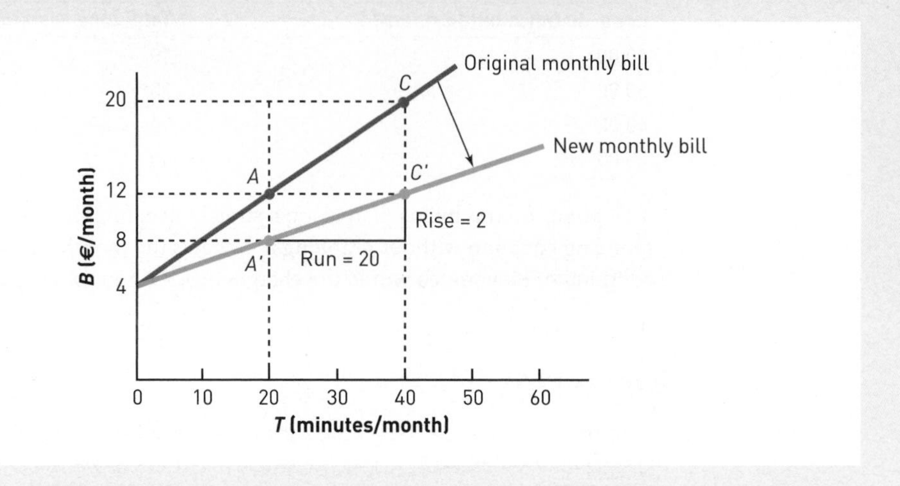


1A.5 Let the billing equation be $B = f + sT$, where $f$ is the fixed monthly fee and $s$ is the slope. From the first two points in the table, calculate the slope $s$ = rise/run = 10/10 = 1.0. To calculate $f$, we can use the information in row 1 of the table to write the billing equation as $20 = f + 1.0(10)$ and solve for $f = 10$. So the monthly billing equation must be $B = 10 + 1.0T$. For this billing equation, the fixed fee is €10 per month, the calling charge is €1 per minute, and the total bill for a month with 1 hour of long-distance calls is $B = 10 + 1.0(60) =$ €70.

# Appendix B

## Elements of calculus for use in economics

### *Why use calculus?*

Graphs may be considered as a pictorial description of the relationship between the variables on the axes. As such, they are limited in their ability to treat the relationship in an exact and unambiguous fashion, since they depend on the accuracy with which the graphical account of the relationship is drawn. They also suffer from the unavoidable restriction that even the most exact graphical description is in reality limited to portraying properly the relationship between two variables in a tractable fashion.

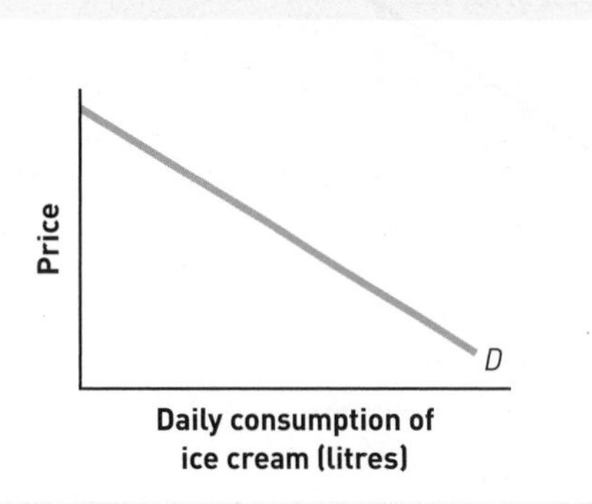


**Figure 1B.1 The Demand Curve for Ice Cream.** The effect of unit price on consumption.

This means that a normal graph can show only the relationship between two variables, $X$ and $Y$, while holding all other factors that might affect the relationship constant. Take, for example, the well-established relationships between temperature, price and consumption of ice cream. Any competent marketing study would easily show that in any location the quantity of ice cream sold on a given day will be inversely related to the unit price at which it is sold. Or, as an economist would put it, the demand curve for ice cream has a negative slope (Fig. 1B.1). Here, following the convention in economics, and in defiance of the mathematical tradition,

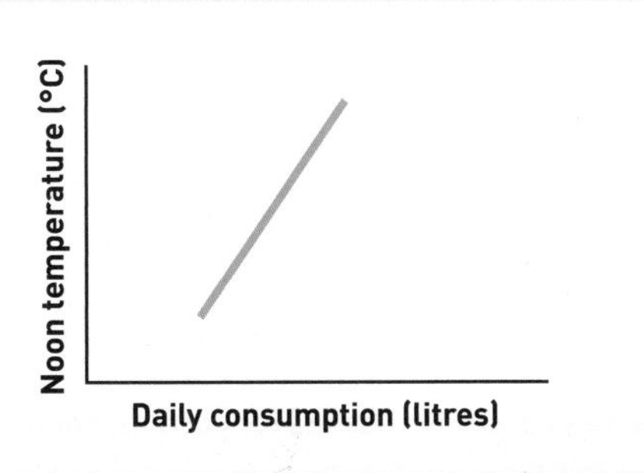


**Figure 1B.2 Temperature Effect on Daily Ice Cream Consumption.**

the consumption of ice cream, the dependent or endogenous variable, is shown on the horizontal axis, while the unit price, the independent, causative or exogenous variable, is shown on the vertical axis.

The marketing analyst would also produce data indicating that at any give unit price, the quantity sold would rise with the ambient temperature. Less is sold in winter than in summer, when it is raining than when the sun is splitting the pavement. That relationship is shown by using temperature (in degrees) on the vertical axis and consumption on the horizontal (Fig. 1B.2).

**Exercise 1B.1** If you were given the information that produced Fig. 1B.2, and wanted to show how the temperature–consumption relationship is affected by a price change, what would you do?

Neither Fig. 1B.1 nor Fig. 1B.2 can deal satisfactorily with the problem that both price and temperature may vary as between days, something that makes it difficult to separate the price and temperature effects. As an expedient, when using graphic analysis we assume we know each of the effects from prior information, and adjust one for any change in the other. Thus, if we know the price–consumption relationship (the demand curve), we can shift it to make allowance for a change in temperature (Fig. 1B.3).

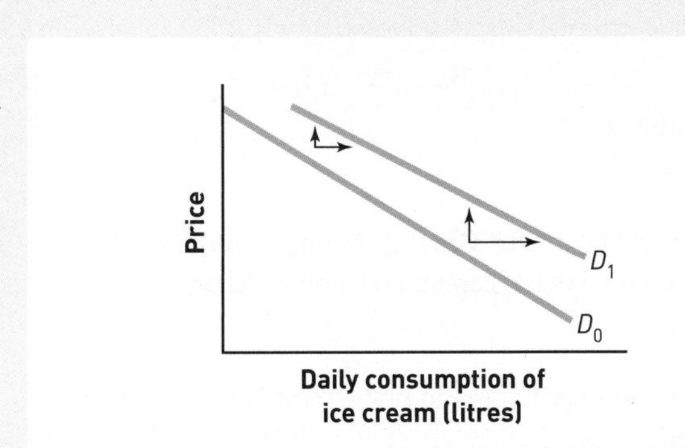


**Figure 1B.3 The Demand Curve for Ice Cream.** A rise in temperature increases consumption at any price.

In this case, we show a hypothetical demand curve for choc ices at a holiday resort (a) when the noon temperature is 18°C, and (b) when it is 27°C. Suppose, however, we wanted to establish what a small change in price and temperature would do to sales. In practice this approach would not be very helpful, since we would need to be very exact in moving the demand curve to take the temperature effect into account. We could, of course, try to draw a three-dimensional graph, using some form of perspective, as shown in Fig. 1B.4, but measuring the impact of changes using this approach is extremely difficult other than in an inexact fashion.

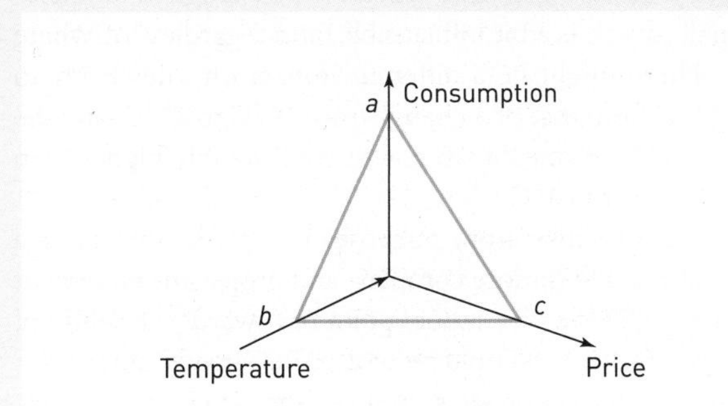


**Figure 1B.4 The Surface *abc* shows the Price and Temperature Effects on Consumption, Holding Other Things Constant.**

Even if we did adopt this approach this we could not deal with the following problem. Sales will also be affected by the number of visitors to the holiday resort. Our demand curve shift approach and our three-dimensional graph approach will both be incapable of allowing for a change in the final factor, the number of potential consumers.

### *Dealing with the problem*

If we use simple mathematical notation the basis of the problem and its solution becomes clear. Use $Q$ to represent the volume of sales (in litres – or, if we prefer, in number of choc ices). Let $P$ represent the unit price (e.g. €0.75 per choc ice). Let $T$ be the temperature at noon, and let $N$ be the number of potential customers.

We are saying that $Q$ is a *function* of $P$, $T$ and $N$, which we can write as:

$$Q = Q(P,T,N)$$

Furthermore, let us suppose that market analysis has established for each independent variable its impact on $Q$. To make this tractable we will suppose that we know that these are as follows:

$$Q = a - bP$$

This, if graphed, would give us a demand curve such as in Fig. 1B.1. The 'coefficient' $b$ tells us by how much $Q$ changes (sales rise or fall) as $P$ changes. It is the slope of the straight line demand curve.[4]

We will also suppose that the temperature and population effects are known and are equally simple:

$$Q = cT$$

meaning that, controlling for price, consumption will rise with temperature in a predictable fashion and

$$Q = dN$$

meaning that, controlling for the other factors, more people means more sales. Putting these together, we can write the whole relationship as

$$Q = a - bP + cT + dN$$

Any change in $Q$ from one day to the next will be due to a change in one or more of the independent variables. Use the Greek letter $\Delta$ (capital delta, capital D) to mean 'change in':

$$\Delta Q = - b\Delta P + c\Delta T + f\Delta N$$

Now, assuming all this, and assuming we know the changes in price, temperature and population, we can determine the change in sales.

All very simple? Alas, no.

We have made it all very easy by assuming straight-line relationships. That is, the slopes in each case are constant, so that the absolute impact of a large or small change in $P$, $T$ and $N$ is given; the ratios $\Delta Q/\Delta P$, $\Delta Q/\Delta T$ and $\Delta Q/\Delta N$ are the same whether the change in temperature, price or population is large or small, which is a bit implausible, and regardless of where we measure it from a starting point. There might be a different impact on sales from an increase in temperature from 11°C to 14°C from that of a change from 19°C to 22°C, and the impact of a change from 19°C to 22°C (3°C) in one day might be considerably higher than three times the impact of a change from 19°C to 20°C.

Using straight-line relationships is fine for explanatory purposes in a classroom, or as a rough approximation to likely effects, but real life is more complex, and proper measurement of such effects cannot depend on this method. However, it does point us towards the solution.

Return to the simple demand curve of Fig. 1B.1. It could be written, as already noted, $Q = a - bP$. The value of $b$ tells us the change (in litres) of sales for a change (in cents) of price. Suppose it was in fact $Q = 2{,}000 - 10\,P$. In this case $\Delta Q/\Delta P = -10$, which is true whether $P$ is 5 cents or 15 cents, and whether the starting price is 75 cents or 65 cents.

---

[4] Actually, in geometric terms it is the *inverse* of the slope, because slope measures vertical ($P$) change over horizontal ($Q$) change, but this need not concern us here.

| Price (cents per choc ice) | Volume sold (litres) |
|---|---|
| 0 | 2,000 |
| 10 | 1,900 |
| 50 | 1,500 |
| 75 | 1,250 |
| 100 | 1,000 |
| 150 | 500 |
| 200 | 0 |

**Table 1B.1** Sales at Various Prices

In this case, holding the other factors constant we could set down in a table the level of sales at various prices (Table 1B.1), and the relationship, if graphed, would give us our straight-line demand curve. At a price of zero and for a given number in the resort, and for a given temperature (ice cream is free) people would consume 2,000 litres a day. At a price of €2 a bar, no ice cream would be sold.

Now, suppose the demand curve was not a straight line, which is more than possible. Suppose it was curved, as in Fig. 1B.5.

Then, remembering what the slope of the curve means (the rate at which sales change as price changes), we see that (a) it changes as we move down the curve, and (b) the impact of a change in price depends on where we start from. To add to our woes, there is no reason to believe that the temperature effect or the population effect is linear (a straight line) either.

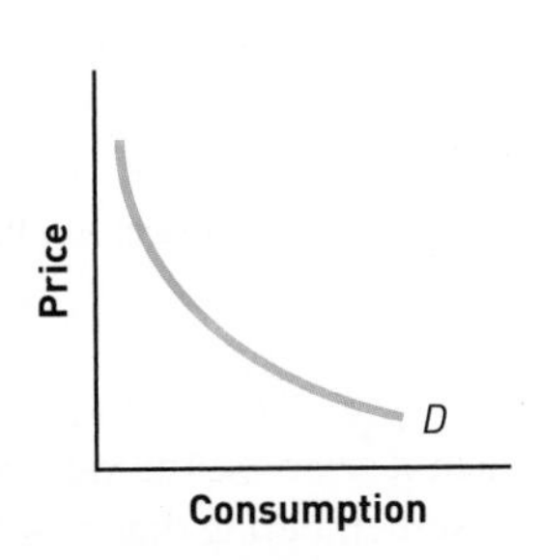


**Figure 1B.5 A 'Curved' Demand Curve.**

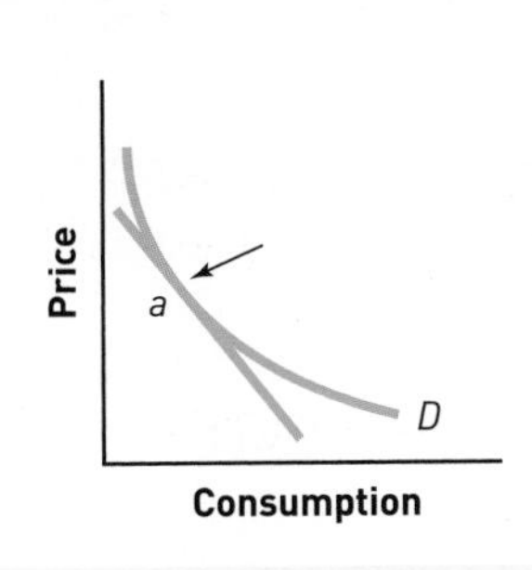


**Figure 1B.6 A 'Curved' Demand Curve.** The slope at *a* is found by drawing the tangent to the curve at *a* and getting the slope of the tangent.

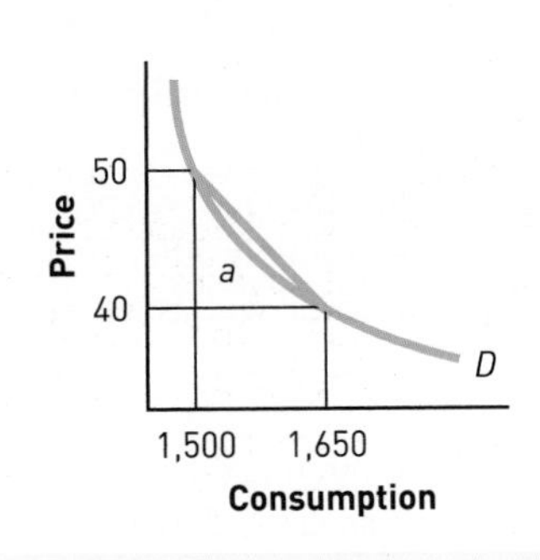


**Figure 1B.7 Differentiating.**

## *How do we deal with this?*

At its simplest, and using a graph, we would measure the slope by getting the slope of a tangent to the curve at the relevant point (Fig. 1B.6). This is unsatisfactory, since we would need to provide the value of the tangent slope at every point on the curve ... and there is an infinite number of such points; so, operationally, we would have to calculate a large number of tangent slopes in order to make good predictions of price change effects on consumption (or weather or population effects).

## *The solution: use calculus — differentiating*

Go back to the definition of a slope: it is the rate of change of sales (in this example) with respect to the change in price (ignoring the other effects). It is $\Delta Q/\Delta P$. In Fig. 1B.7, starting from a price of 50, if we lower price to 40 we see that sales will rise to 1,650. $\Delta Q/\Delta P$ is 150/10, or 15:1. That is an approximation to, but only an approximation to, the sales increase from any reduction of between 1 cent and 10 cents starting from 50, and not very different from that of a reduction from, say, 48 cents to 47 cents. But it is only an approximation, and will not accurately predict the impact of reducing price by 1 cent at any point in this interval. For that, it would appear we need either tangent values or something else.

We start by noting that if at any point $A$ on the curve if $\Delta P$ is very small, $\Delta Q/\Delta P$ will be close to the value of the slope at that point.

If we keep making $\Delta P$ smaller and smaller around $A$, the slope of the straight line approaches that of the tangent at $A$, and eventually coincides with it. The slope of the tangent is the slope of the curve between two points that are infinitely close to each other (coincide). Or the slope of the tangent is given by $\Delta Q/\Delta P$ when $\Delta P$ and $\Delta Q$ are extremely small ($\Delta P \rightarrow 0$).

For any expression $y = y(x)$ the value of $\Delta y/\Delta x$ as $\Delta x \rightarrow 0$ is written $\mathrm{d}y/\mathrm{d}x$, and is described as the 'first derivative' of $y$ with respect to $x$. Obtaining it is done by 'differentiating' $y$ with respect to $x$.

**differentiation** finding the slope or rate of change of a function using algebra rather than geometry

The *differential calculus* is the procedure that enables us to obtain the value of $\mathrm{d}y/\mathrm{d}x$ from the original expression $y = y(x)$ , or to **differentiate** $y$ with respect to $x$.

For simple algebraic functions this turns out to be easy to learn (although we will not prove it here: this is not a rigorous text in mathematics).

Take an expression

$$Y = a + bX + cX^2 + dX^3$$

$\mathrm{d}Y/\mathrm{d}X$ is found by multiplying the coefficient of each $X$ term on the right-hand side by the power of $X$ concerned and reducing that power by 1. Remembering that $X^0 = 1$, and $X^1 = X$ the expression can be rewritten:

$$Y = aX^0 + bX^1 + cX^2 + dX^3$$

$$\mathrm{d}Y/\mathrm{d}X = 0aX^{-1} + 1bX^0 + 2cX^1 + 3dX^2$$

or

$$\mathrm{d}Y/\mathrm{d}X = b + 2cX + 3dX^2$$

So, if we had a non-linear demand curve:

$$Q = 2{,}000 - 350\,P + 5\,P^2$$

we can find the slope, $\mathrm{d}Q/\mathrm{d}P$, at any point by differentiating $Q$ with respect to $P$ and solving:

$$\mathrm{d}Q/\mathrm{d}P = -350 + 10\,P$$

**Exercise 1B.2** Obtain this result by the procedure just outlined.

For $P = 1$, $\mathrm{d}Q/\mathrm{d}P = -340$; for $P = 5$, $\mathrm{d}Q/\mathrm{d}P = -300$; for $P = 15$, $\mathrm{d}Q/\mathrm{d}P = -200$

$$\Delta Q = (\mathrm{d}Q/\mathrm{d}P)\,\Delta P$$

That is, for a small change in $P$ (e.g. raise price by 1) sales would fall by 350/1 or 350 if the existing price is 1, by 300 if the existing price is 5, and so on.

Now, let us go back to our ice cream example. If all that changed was price, and we wanted to estimate the impact of a price change on sales we would simply differentiate the expression for $Q$ with respect to price and estimate the impact in the same way as we have just done.

But suppose that price, temperature and numbers in town are all changing. How do we estimate the impact of all these on sales?

We start with a small change in notation. In these circumstances, where sales, $Q$, are dependent on (in this case) three variables, $P$, $T$ and $N$, we shall use $\mathrm{d}Q$ to mean change in sales, $\mathrm{d}P$ change in price, $\mathrm{d}T$ change in temperature and $\mathrm{d}N$ change in potential number of customers. We shall use the small Greek letter delta $\delta$ (d), to indicate the rate of change obtained by differentiating where $Q$ is being differentiated with respect to just one of the variables that determine it (or 'partially differentiated').

Since (if we have properly specified the demand relationship) we know that changes in $Q$ are due to the impact of the three independent variables, we can state this formally:

$$dQ = (\delta Q/\delta P)dp + (\delta Q/\delta T)dT + (\delta Q/\delta N)dN$$

Exactly the same procedure as before is used to obtain the rates of change values: but if you want to isolate the effect of $T$, for example, you differentiate with respect to $T$, and any term in the expression not including $T$ is ignored (or treated as being multiplied by $T^0$, which is the same thing).

**Exercise 1B.3**

$$Q = 3{,}000 - 15\,P + 3\,P^2 + 2.5\,T - 6\,T^{\frac{1}{2}} + 15N - 2{,}000\,N^{\frac{1}{2}}$$

(i) Write down the expression for $dQ/dP$.
(ii) What is $dQ/dP$ if $P = 50$? What is $dQ/dT$ if $T = 16$?
(iii) By how much will sales rise if the numbers in town rise from 10,000 to 10,500? (Remember that raising a number to the power of $\frac{1}{2}$ means its square root, and a negative power means the reciprocal of the positive value, i.e. $X^{-1} = 1/X$.)

There are three other useful differentiation rules for economists.

1. Suppose we know that $Y$ is a product of two variables, each of which is a function of $X$:

   $Y = UV$, where $U = U(X)$ and $V = V(X)$

   and we want to find the impact of a change in $X$ on $Y$.
   How do we differentiate $Y$ with respect to $X$?
   The rule is a simple one:

   $$dY/dX = UdV/dX + V\,dU/dX$$

   This is called the *product chain rule*.

   **Example**

   $Y = UV$
   $U = 10 - 2X$ and $V = -5 + 8X$
   $dU/dX = -2$ and $dV/dX = 8$
   $dY/dX = (100 - 2X)(8) + (-5 + 8X)(-2) = 90$

2. Suppose that $Y = U/V$, where $U$ and $V$ are both functions of $X$.
   The rule is:

   $$dY/dX = [(VdU/dX) - (UdV/dX)]/V^2$$

   This is the *divisor chain rule*.

   **Example**

   $Y = U/V$
   $U = 10 + 2.X$ and $V = 5 + 8.X$
   $dY/dX = [(5 + 8.X)(2) - (10 + 2.X)(8)]/(-5 + 8.X)^2$
   $= 70/(25 - 80X + 64X^2)$

3. Finally, suppose that the relation between $Y$ and $X$ is of the form

   $$Y = (a + bX)^n = (f(X))^n$$

The rule for deriving $dY/dX$ is:

$$dY/dX = [n(fX)^{n-1}][d(f(X)d(X)]$$

This is the *function chain rule*.

**Example**

$Y = (10 + 5X)^2$

$dY/dX = 2(10 + 5X)5 = 100 + 50X$

**Exercise 1B.4** (i) Show that the function chain rule is correct in this case by extending the bracket term in the function rule example and differentiating $Y$ with respect to $X$.
(ii) Show that the divisor chain rule is correct by turning the terms in the example into a product:

$$Y = (10 + 2X)(5 + 8X)^{-1}$$

## Key term

differentiation (32)

## Answers to in-appendix exercises

1B.1 Since a fall in price, other things being equal, raises consumption, and a rise in price reduces it, at any given temperature a fall in price will shift the temperature–consumption relationship, increasing consumption. The line in Fig. 1B.2 will be shifted to the right. A rise in price will shift it to the left.

1B.2

$$Q = 2{,}000 - 350P + 5P^2$$
$$= 2{,}000P^0 - 350\,P^1 + 5P^2$$
$$dQ/dP = (0)(2{,}000)P^{-1} - (1)350P^0 + (2)5P^1$$
$$= -350 + 10P$$

1B.3 (i) $dQ/dP = -15 + 6P$

(ii) $dQ/dP = 285$

(iii) $dQ/dT = 2.5 - 3T^{-\frac{1}{2}} = 2.5 - 3/\sqrt{T}$; if $T = 16$, $dQ/dT = 1.75$

(iv) $\Delta Q = (dQ/dN)\,\Delta N$
$dQ/dN = 15 - 1{,}000/\sqrt{N}$
for $N = 10{,}000$ $dQ/dN = 15 - 1{,}000/100 = 5$
therefore $\Delta Q = (dQ/dN)\,\Delta N = 5(500) = 2{,}500$

1B.4 (i) Follow the procedure for expansion of the bracketed term:

$$Y = 100 + 100X + 25X^2$$

$$dY/dX = 100 + 50X$$

(ii) $Y = UV$ where $V = (5 + 8X)^{-1}$;
$dY/dX = U(dV/dX) + V(dU/dX)$;
$dV/dX = -1(5 + 8X)^{-2}8 = -8/(5 + 8X)^2$
hence $dY/dX = (10 + 2X)\,[-8/(5 + 8X)^2] + 2/(5+8X)$
$= [2(5 + 8X) - 8(10 + 2X)]/(5 + 8X)^2 = [V(dU/dX) - U(dV/dX)]/V^2$

## References

Thaler, R. (1980) 'Towards a Positive Theory of Consumer Choice', *Journal of Economic Behaviour and Organization*, 1(1).

# 2

# Comparative Advantage: the Basis for Exchange

If you visit or work in an underdeveloped country a common fact of life that you will observe is that people tend to be able to turn their hands to a very wide range of activities. A good cook may also work part time as a tinsmith and carpenter, and do a little repair work on mechanical devices, while also helping to build houses and cure leather. That is certainly a feature of many people in, for example, Nepal. Such a variety of skills in a single person is rare in advanced countries, where people specialise and hire others to do things for them. Why this difference in skills and employment?

One might be tempted to answer that the Nepalese are simply too poor to hire others to perform these services. Nepal is indeed a poor country, with an income per person less than one one-hundredth that of any of the richer countries in Europe. Few Nepalese have spare cash to spend on outside services. But as reasonable as this poverty explanation may seem, the reverse is actually the case. The Nepalese do not perform their own services because they are poor; rather, they are poor largely *because* they perform their own services.

The alternative to a system in which everyone is a jack-of-all-trades is one in which people *specialise* in particular goods and services, then satisfy their needs by trading among themselves. Economic systems based on specialisation and the exchange of goods and services are generally far more productive than those with less specialisation. Our task in this chapter is to investigate why this is so. In doing so we shall explore why people choose to exchange goods and services in the first place, rather than having each person produce his or her own food, cars, clothing, shelter and the like.

As this chapter will show, the reason that specialisation is so productive is the existence of what economists call *comparative advantage*. A person has a comparative advantage at producing a particular good or service, say, haircuts, if that person is *relatively* more efficient at producing haircuts than at producing other goods or services. We shall see that we can all have more of *every* good and service if each of us specialises in the activities at which we have a comparative advantage.

This chapter will also introduce the *production possibilities curve* (PPC), which is a graphical method of describing the combinations of goods and services that an economy can produce. The development of this tool will allow us to see much more precisely how specialisation enhances the productive capacity of even the simplest economy.

So, what does this tell us about Nepal or any other seriously underdeveloped and poor country? If it is the failure to specialise that is the root cause of poverty, what is to stop the Nepalese becoming richer simply by specialising? Unfortunately, it's not quite as simple as all that. Yes, if they specialised they would be richer ... but specialisation may require training or skills that are hard to acquire. It may require capital in the form of dedicated equipment, which is costly to acquire. For it to make sense it may be necessary that others specialise at the same time, so as to create a market for the potentially increased supply of goods and services that specialists produce. It will certainly be necessary that the extra output derived from specialisation can be got to market, and the infrastructure may not be sufficient. There is also an element of a 'chicken and egg' problem: specialisation increases the value of goods and services being produced (the size of the economy), but the incentive to specialise may depend on the existing size of the economy.

These problems are the concern of what is known as 'development economics' and, interesting as it is, development economics is outside the scope of an introductory text. However, what we are going to look at in this chapter is fundamental to understanding why countries – and people – become better off through specialisation and exchange. To do so, we look at the problem in a simplified and rather abstract fashion, so as to avoid the kind of difficulties just described.

## Exchange and opportunity cost

The *Scarcity Principle* (see Chapter 1) reminds us that the opportunity cost of spending more time on any one activity is having less time available to spend on others. As Example 2.1 makes clear, this principle helps explain why everyone can do better by concentrating on those activities at which he or she performs best *relative* to others.

### **Example 2.1** Should Mrs Blair write her own will?

In 2004, Cherie Booth, QC, wife of the UK's Prime Minister, Tony Blair (who uses her name before marriage when she is in court), was one of the top counsel in Britain, or so the press said. Mrs Blair has, no doubt, found herself from time to time, like most of us, in a position where legal services were needed. In general, of course, just as a doctor is advised not to diagnose and prescribe for himself, a lawyer is advised not to rely on giving herself legal advice on contentious matters. However, some legal matters are strictly routine, and just as a doctor with a headache will look for the aspirin on his own, a lawyer (or most of them, at any rate) can write a simple will. So let us assume that Mrs Blair wished to write a simple will. Should she do it herself?

Let us assume Mrs Blair can command fees of €3,000 a day, or €250 an hour, as an advocate, and is highly skilled at drawing up wills. People would be willing to pay her €150 an hour to draft a will. Suppose a competent solicitor can offer his services in drafting wills through his firm for €100 per hour, and will also be able to act as an advocate at that price. Even if she is just as good at drafting wills as the solicitor, and even if she could do it in half the time, it would be economically irrational for Mrs Blair to devote one or more hours to drawing up her own will. The opportunity cost of an hour of her time drafting a will (€250) exceeds the cost of hiring the solicitor, which is the opportunity cost of an hour of his time. She is better off by €100 for each hour spent in advocacy to pay for the solicitor to write her will.

**absolute advantage** one person has an absolute advantage over another if an hour spent in performing a task earns more than the other person can earn in an hour at the task

If Mrs Blair is better than the solicitor at the task, she has an **absolute advantage** in drawing up wills. If she is better at advocacy than the solicitor, she also has an absolute advantage as an advocate. But if her opportunity cost of drawing up a will is higher than that of the solicitor

Mrs Blair has a **comparative advantage** in advocacy, while the solicitor, who is at an *absolute disadvantage* in both functions, has a comparative advantage in drawing up a will.

The ratio of the income Mrs Blair could earn from an hour's will drafting to that earned from an hour's advocacy is the opportunity cost in time to her of an hour's advocacy. It is 150/250, or 0.6. That of will drafting is 250/150 = 1.67. For the solicitor, an hour earns him the same in both activities, so the ratio for both is 1.0. His opportunity cost of time spent drafting wills is less than hers; her opportunity cost of an hour's advocacy is less than his.

**comparative advantage** one person has a comparative advantage over another in a task if his or her opportunity cost of performing a task is lower than the other person's opportunity cost

The point of Example 2.1 is not that people whose time is valuable should never perform their own services. If that were the case most DIY stores would have many fewer customers. Example 2.1 made the implicit assumption that Mrs Blair would have been equally happy to spend an hour preparing a will or preparing for a trial. But suppose she was tired of trial preparation and felt it might be enjoyable to refresh her knowledge of probate law. Preparing a will might then have made perfect sense! But unless she expected to gain special satisfaction from performing that task, she would almost certainly do better to hire a probate lawyer. The probate lawyer would also benefit, or else he wouldn't have offered to prepare a will for the agreed price.

So the answer to our initial question is that if Mrs Blair has limited time and is paid more per hour for her own work than a probate lawyer, she should probably let the probate lawyer draft her will. The answer depends on whether she could earn more in the time it would take her to draft her will than it would cost her to have someone else do it.

## The Principle of Comparative Advantage

One of the most important insights of modern economics is that when two people (or two nations) have different opportunity costs of performing various tasks, they can always increase the total value of available goods and services by trading with one another. Example 2.2 captures the logic behind this insight.

### **Example 2.2** Should Paula update her own web page?

Consider a small community in which Paula is the only professional bicycle mechanic and Beth is the only professional HTML programmer. Paula also happens to be an even better HTML programmer than Beth. If the amount of time each of them takes to perform these tasks is as shown in Table 2.1, and if each regards the two tasks as equally pleasant (or unpleasant), does the fact that Paula can program faster than Beth imply that Paula should update her own web page?

| | Time to update a web page (minutes) | Time to complete a bicycle repair (minutes) |
|---|---|---|
| Paula | 20 | 10 |
| Beth | 30 | 30 |

**Table 2.1** Productivity Information for Paula and Beth

The entries in Table 2.1 show that Paula has an absolute advantage over Beth in both activities. While Paula, the mechanic, needs only 20 minutes to update a web page, Beth, the programmer, needs 30 minutes. Paula's advantage over Beth is even greater when the task is fixing bikes: she can complete a repair in only 10 minutes, compared with Beth's 30 minutes.

But the fact that Paula is a better programmer than Beth does *not* imply that Paula should update her own web page. As with the lawyer who litigates instead of preparing her own will, Beth has a comparative advantage over Paula at programming: she is *relatively* more productive at programming than Paula. Similarly, Paula has a comparative advantage in bicycle repair. (Remember that a person has a comparative advantage at a given task if his or her opportunity cost of performing that task is lower than another person's.)

What is Beth's opportunity cost of updating a web page? Since she takes 30 minutes to update each page – the same amount of time she takes to fix a bicycle – her opportunity cost of updating a web page is one bicycle repair. In other words, by taking the time to update a web page, Beth is effectively giving up the opportunity to do one bicycle repair. Paula, in contrast, can complete two bicycle repairs in the time she takes to update a single web page. For her, the opportunity cost of updating a web page is two bicycle repairs. Paula's opportunity cost of programming, measured in terms of bicycle repairs forgone, is twice as high as Beth's. Thus Beth has a comparative advantage at programming.

The interesting and important implication of the opportunity cost comparison summarised in Table 2.2 is that the total number of bicycle repairs and web updates accomplished if Paula and Beth both spend part of their time at each activity will always be smaller than the number accomplished if each specialises in the activity in which she has a comparative advantage. Suppose, for example, that people in their community demand a total of 16 web page updates per day. If Paula spent half her time updating web pages and the other half repairing bicycles, an eight-hour workday would yield 12 web page updates and 24 bicycle repairs. To complete the remaining four updates, Beth would have to spend two hours programming, which would leave her six hours to repair bicycles. And since she takes 30 minutes to do each repair, she would have time to complete 12 of them. So when the two women try to be jacks-of-all-trades, they end up completing a total of 16 web page updates and 36 bicycle repairs.

| | **Opportunity cost of updating a web page** | **Opportunity cost of a bicycle repair** |
|---|---|---|
| Paula | 2 bicycle repairs | 0.5 web page updates |
| Beth | 1 bicycle repair | 1 web page update |

**Table 2.2** Opportunity Costs for Paula and Beth

Consider what would have happened had each woman specialised in her activity of comparative advantage. Beth could have updated 16 web pages on her own, and Paula could have performed 48 bicycle repairs. Specialisation would have created an additional 12 bicycle repairs out of thin air.

When computing the opportunity cost of one good in terms of another, we must pay close attention to the form in which the productivity information is presented. In Example 2.2, we were told how many minutes each person needed to perform each task. Alternatively, we might be told how many units of each task each person can perform in an hour. Work through Exercise 2.1 to see how to proceed when information is presented in this alternative format.

**Exercise 2.1**

Consider a small community in which Barbara is the only professional bicycle mechanic and Pat is the only professional HTML programmer. If their productivity rates at the two tasks are as shown in the table, and if each regards the two tasks as equally pleasant (or unpleasant), does the fact that Barbara can program faster than Pat imply that Barbara should update her own web page?

| | Productivity in programming (per hour) | Productivity in bicycle repair (per hour) |
|---|---|---|
| Pat | 2 web page updates | 1 repair |
| Barbara | 3 web page updates | 3 repairs |

The principle illustrated by Examples 2.1 and 2.2 is so important that we state it formally as one of the core principles of the course:

The Principle of Comparative Advantage: Everyone does best when each person (or each country) concentrates on the activities for which his or her opportunity cost is lowest.

Indeed, the gains made possible from specialisation based on comparative advantage constitute the rationale for *market exchange*. They explain why each person does not devote 10 per cent of his or her time to producing cars, 5 per cent to growing food, 25 per cent to building housing, 0.0001 per cent to performing brain surgery, and so on. By concentrating on those tasks at which we are relatively more productive, we can together produce vastly more than if we all tried to be self-sufficient.

Specialisation and its effects provide ample grist for the economic naturalist. Here is an example from the world of sports.

## Economic naturalist 2.1 What has happened to football (soccer)? They just don't seem to be able to score goals like they used to![1]

In 1954 Roger Bannister broke the 4-minute mile barrier. By the end of the century sub-4-minute miles were frequent events at top athletics meeting. The standards of athletes and their performances have steadily improved right across the spectrum of sports as intensive and scientific training and the application of technology (permitted) and more questionable methods have been increasingly used to improve performance. Most observers would agree that professionalism has greatly improved the skills and performances of sports in general. In recent years this has been abundantly evident in the case of rugby football. But has it happened in soccer? Consider the following. Look at the scoring record in the World Cup since the 1930s. Between 1930 and 1954 the average number of goals scored in World Cup games rose on a trend from 3.88 to 5.36. From 1954 there was a fairly steady decline to 2.21 in 1990. There seems to have been a small recovery since 1990: 2.71 in 1994, 2.67 in 1998 and 2.52 in 2002.

One suggestion was that it was getting harder to score in recent decades because goalkeepers were getting bigger... but no one suggested that they were getting smaller between 1930 and 1954. However, something did happen in the mid-1950s. It became more and more common to put most of a team's effort (in the form of the formation in which players took the field) into defence. The old 3–2–5 formation (five attackers) gave way to 4–3–3 and 4–4–2. For some reason, teams began to shift the weight of specialisation from attack to defence, and this has been maintained to the present, with 4–5–1 not being unknown. On that basis the fall in the average score becomes easy to understand, and when account is taken of the

[1] We are indebted to a colleague in University College Dublin's Economics School, David Madden, for suggesting the material for Economic nauralist 2.1.

fall in the percentage of attackers, the goal score per attacker may even have risen, consistent with the professionalisation story. The lower score rates, then, reflect not a falling skill among attackers but increased specialisation in defence and a consequent increased ability of teams to defend. But what might have driven the move to emphasise and specialise in defence? A possible explanation may lie in the increased amounts of money going into football and the consequent potential cost to a club of losing matches and facing relegation. If teams are risk averse they would be expected to respond to this by putting more effort into specialising in defence and less into attack. What do you think?

## Sources of comparative advantage

At the individual level, comparative advantage often appears to be the result of inborn talent. For instance, some people seem to be naturally gifted at programming computers while others seem to have a special knack for fixing bikes. But comparative advantage is more often the result of education, training or experience. Thus we usually leave the design of kitchens to people with architectural training, the drafting of contracts to people who have studied law and the teaching of physics to people with advanced degrees in that field.

At the national level, comparative advantage may derive from differences in natural resources or from differences in society or culture. The United States, which has a disproportionate share of the world's leading research universities, has a comparative advantage in the design of electronic computing hardware and software. Canada, which has one of the world's highest per capita endowments of farm and forest land, has a comparative advantage in the production of agricultural products. Topography and climate explain why Colorado specialises in the skiing industry while Hawaii specialises as an ocean resort.

Seemingly non-economic factors can also give rise to comparative advantage. For instance, the emergence of English as the *de facto* world language gives English-speaking countries a comparative advantage over non-English-speaking nations in the production of books, movies and popular music. Even a country's institutions may affect the likelihood that it will achieve comparative advantage in a particular pursuit. For example, cultures that encourage entrepreneurship will tend to have a comparative advantage in the introduction of new products, whereas those that promote high standards of care and craftsmanship will tend to have a comparative advantage in the production of high-quality variants of established products.

### Economic naturalist 2.2 1 Televisions and videocassette recorders (VCRs) were developed and first produced in the United States, but today the country accounts for only a minuscule share of total world production of these products. Why did the United States fail to retain its lead in these markets?

That televisions and VCRs were developed in the United States is explained in part by the country's comparative advantage in technological research, which in turn was supported by an outstanding system of higher education. Other contributing factors were high expenditures on the development of electronic components for the military and a culture that actively encouraged entrepreneurship. As for the production of these products, America enjoyed an early advantage partly because the product designs were themselves evolving rapidly, which favoured production

facilities located in close proximity to the product designers. Early production techniques also relied intensively on skilled labour, which was abundant in the United States. In time, however, product designs stabilised and many of the more complex manufacturing operations were automated. Both of these changes gradually led to greater reliance on less skilled production workers. And at that point, factories located in high-wage countries like the United States could no longer compete with those located in low-wage areas overseas.

## 2 Whatever happened to the British shipbuilding industry?

In 1843 the world's first (and for a considerable time largest) iron-hulled, screw-propelled passenger ship, the SS *Great Britain*, designed by Isambard Kingdom Brunel, was launched in Bristol. This marked the beginning of a golden age for UK shipyards. In the nineteenth century and into the twentieth century the United Kingdom was the world's most important designer and producer of merchant shipping and warships. The world's largest passenger liners (e.g. the Cunard liners *Queen Elizabeth* and *Queen Mary*) and unluckiest (the White Star liner RMS *Titanic*) were launched from UK slipways. Britain effectively invented and led world production of iron- and later steel-hulled commercial shipping. The UK's comparative advantage in shipbuilding was based on the engineering skills developed in the Industrial Revolution, on suitable locations for building and launching ships, and on its iron and steel industry. This was not confined to commercial shipping: British shipyards built battleships for most of the world. Indeed, one of the things that tipped Turkey into siding with Germany and Austria-Hungary in 1914 was the fact that when war broke out the Admiralty seized two dreadnoughts (battleships) on the point of completion for Turkey in British yards, renamed them and took them into the Royal Navy facing the Imperial German Navy's High Seas Fleet in the North Sea. The Sultan of Turkey was not amused ... and the Germans took advantage of this. They happened to have a modern battlecruiser, SMS *Goeben*, in the Mediterranean. *Goeben*'s life expectancy was rather short, given the size and firepower of the Royal Navy's Mediterranean Fleet. The German Kaiser's government ordered it to steam to the Golden Horn on the Bosphorus where it was handed over to the Turks, who shortly afterwards declared war on Britain and her allies.

But all this has changed. By the end of the twentieth century, apart from some highly specialised activities and some strategic production for the Royal Navy, commercial shipbuilding in the United Kingdom had become virtually extinct. In 2003, it was announced that a French firm would be the lead firm in delivering the Royal Navy's next generation of aircraft carriers, and in the same year a French shipyard delivered the *Queen Mary 2* to the Cunard Line. *Comparative advantage changes*. In this case, we can identify a series of factors that led to the decline in the importance of the United Kingdom as a producer as comparative advantage changed. First, the process became more mechanised: welding replaced skilled and specialised labour-intensive riveting as a technique. Steel became available cheaply elsewhere. Labour costs (even though the technology was becoming more capital-intensive) rose in Britain relative to the Far East. Ship designing as a skill was available on at least as high a quality basis outside Britain. British firms could no longer compete because their costs were higher and there were no vital inputs that demanded that British yards be used.

**RECAP Exchange and opportunity cost**

Gains from exchange are possible if trading partners have comparative advantages in producing different goods and services. You have a comparative advantage in producing, say, web pages, if your opportunity cost of producing a web page – measured in terms of other production opportunities forgone – is smaller than the corresponding opportunity costs of your trading partners. Maximum production is achieved if each person specialises in producing the good or service in which he or she has the lowest opportunity cost (the principle of comparative advantage). Comparative advantage makes specialisation worthwhile even if one trading partner is more productive than others, in absolute terms, in every activity.

# Comparative advantage and production possibilities

Comparative advantage and specialisation allow an economy to produce more than if each person tries to produce a little of everything. In this section we gain further insight into the advantages of specialisation by introducing a graph that can be used to describe the various combinations of goods and services that an economy can produce.

## The production possibilities curve

We begin with a hypothetical economy in which only two goods are produced: coffee and pine nuts. It is a small island economy, and 'production' consists either of picking coffee beans that grow on small bushes on the island's central valley floor or of picking pine nuts that grow on trees on the steep hillsides overlooking the valley. The more time workers spend picking coffee, the less time they have available for picking nuts. So if people want to drink more coffee, they must make do with a smaller amount of nuts.

**production possibilities curve** a graph that describes the maximum amount of one good that can be produced for every possible level of production of the other good

If we know how productive workers are at each activity, we can summarise the various combinations of coffee and nuts they can pick each day. This menu of possibilities is known as the **production possibilities curve** (PPC).

To keep matters simple, we begin with an example in which the economy has only a single worker who can divide her time between the two activities.

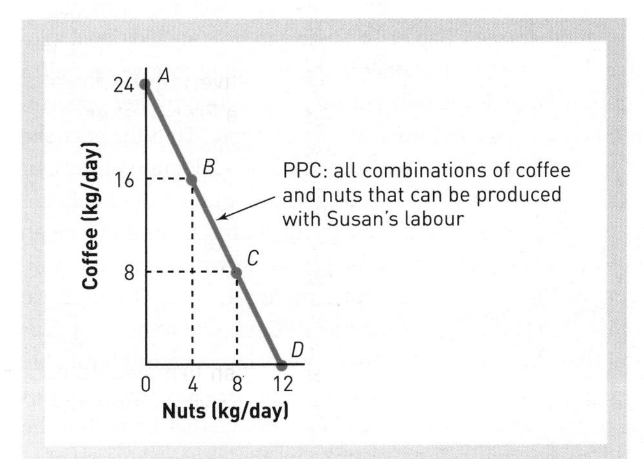


**Figure 2.1 Susan's Production Possibilities.** For the production relationships given, the PPC is a straight line.

**Example 2.3** What is the PPC for an economy in which Susan is the only worker?

Consider a society consisting only of Susan, who allocates her production time between coffee and nuts. She is short and has nimble fingers, two qualities that make her more productive at picking coffee than at picking nuts. She can pick 2 kg of nuts or 4 kg of coffee in an hour. If she works a total of 6 hours per day, describe her PPC – the graph that displays, for each level of nut production, the maximum amount of coffee that Susan can pick.

The vertical axis in Fig. 2.1 shows Susan's daily production of coffee, and the horizontal axis shows her daily production of nuts. Let us begin by looking at two extreme allocations of her time. First, suppose she employs her entire workday (6 hours) picking coffee. In that case, since she can pick 4 kg of coffee per hour, she would pick 24 kg per day of coffee and zero kg of nuts. That combination of coffee and nut production is represented by point *A* in Fig. 2.1. It is the vertical intercept of Susan's PPC.

Now suppose, instead, that Susan devotes all her time to picking nuts. Since she can pick 2 kg of nuts per hour, her total daily production would be 12 kg of nuts. That combination is represented by point *D* in Fig. 2.1, the horizontal intercept of Susan's PPC. Because Susan's production of each good is exactly proportional to the amount of time she devotes to that good, the remaining points along her production possibilities curve will lie on the straight line that joins *A* and *D*.

For example, suppose that Susan devotes 4 hours each day to picking coffee and 2 hours to picking nuts. She will then end up with (4 hours/day) × (4 kg/hour) = 16 kg of coffee per day and (2 hours/day) × (2 kg/hour) = 4 kg of nuts. This is the point labelled *B* in Fig. 2.1. Alternatively, if she devotes 2 hours to coffee and 4 to nuts, she will get (2 hours/day) × (4 kg/hour) = 8 kg of coffee per day and (4 hours/day) × (2 kg/hour) = 8 kg of nuts. This alternative combination is represented by point *C* in Fig. 2.1.

Since Susan's PPC is a straight line, its slope is constant. The absolute value of the slope of Susan's PPC is the ratio of its vertical intercept to its horizontal intercept: (24 kg of coffee/day)/(12 kg of nuts/day) = (2 kg of coffee)/(1 kg of nuts). (Be sure to keep track of the units of measure on each axis when computing this ratio.) This ratio means that Susan's *opportunity cost of an additional kilogram of nuts is 2 kg of coffee.*

Note that Susan's opportunity cost (*OC*) of nuts can also be expressed as the following simple formula:

$$OC_{nuts} = \frac{\text{Loss in coffee}}{\text{Gain in nuts}} \tag{2.1}$$

where 'loss in coffee' means the amount of coffee given up, and 'gain in nuts' means the corresponding increase in nuts. Likewise, Susan's opportunity cost of coffee can be expressed by this formula:

$$OC_{coffee} = \frac{\text{Loss in nuts}}{\text{Gain in coffee}} \tag{2.2}$$

To say that Susan's opportunity cost of an additional kilogram of nuts is 2 kg of coffee is thus equivalent to saying that her opportunity cost of a kilogram of coffee is $\frac{1}{2}$ kg of nuts.

The downward slope of the PPC shown in Fig. 2.1 illustrates the scarcity principle – the idea that because our resources are limited, having more of one good thing generally means having to settle for less of another (see Chapter 1). Susan can have an additional kilogram of coffee if she wishes, but only if she is willing to give up half a kilogram of nuts. If Susan is the only person in the economy, her opportunity cost of producing a good becomes, in effect, its *price*. Thus the price she has to pay for an additional kilogram of coffee is half a kilogram of nuts; or the price she has to pay for an additional kilogram of nuts is 2 kg of coffee.

**attainable point** any combination of goods that can be produced using currently available resources

**unattainable point** any combination of goods that cannot be produced using currently available resources

**inefficient point** any combination of goods for which currently available resources enable an increase in the production of one good without a reduction in the production of the other

Any point that lies either along the PPC or within it is said to be an **attainable point**, meaning that it can be produced with currently available resources. In Fig. 2.2, for example, points *A*, *B*, *C*, *D* and *E* are attainable points. Points that lie outside the PPC are said to be **unattainable**, meaning that they cannot be produced using currently available resources. In Fig. 2.2, *F* is an unattainable point because Susan cannot pick 16 kg of coffee per day *and* 8 kg of nuts. Points that lie within the curve are said to be **inefficient points**, in the sense that existing resources would allow for production of more of at least one good without sacrificing the production of any other good. At *E*, for example,

**efficient point** any combination of goods for which currently available resources do not allow an increase in the production of one good without a reduction in the production of the other

Susan is picking only 8 kg of coffee per day and 4 kg of nuts, which means that she could increase her coffee harvest by 8 kg per day without giving up any nuts (by moving from *E* to *B*). Alternatively, Susan could pick as many as 4 additional kilograms of nuts each day without giving up any coffee (by moving from *E* to *C*). An **efficient point** is one that lies along the PPC. At any such point, more of one good can be produced only by producing less of the other.

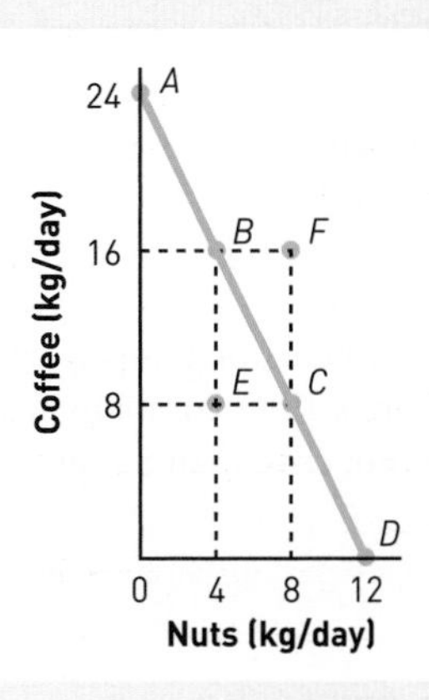


**Figure 2.2 Attainable and Efficient Points on Susan's PPC.** Points that lie either along the PPC (for example, *A*, *B*, *C* and *D*) or within it (for example, *E*) are said to be attainable. Points that lie outside the PPC (for example, *F*) are unattainable. Points that lie along the PPC are said to be efficient, while those that lie within the PPC are said to be inefficient.

**Exercise 2.2**

For the PPC shown in Fig. 2.2, state whether the following points are attainable and/or efficient:

a. 20 kg per day of coffee, 4 kg per day of nuts.
b. 12 kg per day of coffee, 6 kg per day of nuts.
c. 4 kg per day of coffee, 8 kg per day of nuts.

## How individual productivity affects the slope and position of the PPC

To see how the slope and position of the PPC depend on an individual's productivity, let us compare Susan's PPC to that of Tom, who is less productive at picking coffee but more productive at picking nuts.

**Example 2.4** How do changes in productivity affect the opportunity cost of nuts?

Tom is tall and an agile climber, qualities that make him especially well suited for picking nuts that grow on hillside trees. He can pick 4 kg of nuts or 2 kg of coffee per hour. If Tom were the only person in the economy, describe the economy's PPC.

We can construct Tom's PPC the same way we did Susan's. Note first that if Tom devotes an entire workday (6 hours) to coffee picking, he ends up with (6 hours/day) × (2 kg/hour) = 12 kg of coffee per day and 0 kg of nuts. So the vertical intercept of Tom's PPC is *A* in Fig. 2.3. If instead he devotes all his time to picking nuts, he gets (6 hours/day) × (4 kg/hour) = 24 kg of nuts per day and no coffee. That means that the horizontal intercept of his PPC is *D*

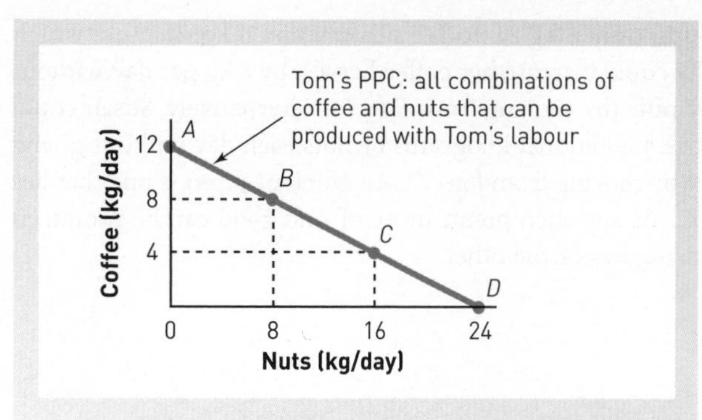


**Figure 2.3 Tom's PPC.** Tom's opportunity cost of producing 1 kg of nuts is only $\frac{1}{2}$ kg of coffee.

in Fig. 2.3. Because Tom's production of each good is proportional to the amount of time he devotes to it, the remaining points on his PPC will lie along the straight line that joins these two extreme points.

For example, if Tom devotes 4 hours each day to picking coffee and 2 hours to picking nuts, he will end up with (4 hours/day) × (2 kg/hour) = 8 kg of coffee per day and (2 hours/day) × (4 kg/hour) = 8 kg of nuts per day. This is the point labelled *B* in Fig. 2.3. Alternatively, if he devotes 2 hours to coffee and 4 to nuts, he will get (2 hours/day) × (2 kg/hour) = 4 kg of coffee per day and (4 hours/day) × (4 kg/hour) = 16 kg of nuts. This alternative combination is represented by point *C* in Fig. 2.3.

How does Tom's PPC compare with Susan's? Note in Fig. 2.4 that because Tom is absolutely less productive than Susan at picking coffee, the vertical intercept of his PPC lies closer to the origin than Susan's. By the same token, because Susan is absolutely less productive than Tom at picking nuts, the horizontal intercept of her PPC lies closer to the origin than Tom's. For Tom, the opportunity cost of an additional kilogram of nuts is $\frac{1}{2}$ kg of coffee, which is one-quarter Susan's opportunity cost of nuts. This difference in opportunity costs shows up as a difference in the slopes of their PPCs: the absolute value of the slope of Tom's PPC is $\frac{1}{2}$ whereas Susan's is 2.

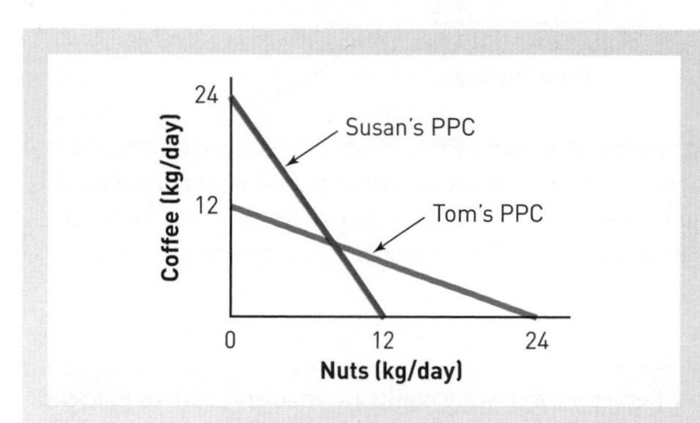


**Figure 2.4 Individual PPCs Compared.** Tom is less productive in coffee than Susan, but more productive in nuts.

In this example, Tom has both an absolute advantage and a comparative advantage over Susan in picking nuts. Susan, for her part, has both an absolute advantage and a comparative advantage over Tom in picking coffee.

We cannot emphasise too strongly that the Principle of Comparative Advantage is a *relative* concept – one that makes sense only when the productivities of two or more people (or countries) are being compared. To cement this idea, work through Exercise 2.3.

**Exercise 2.3**

Suppose Susan can pick 2 kg of coffee per hour or 4 kg of nuts per hour; Tom can pick 1 kg of coffee per hour and 1 kg of nuts per hour. What is Susan's opportunity cost of picking 1 kg of nuts? What is Tom's opportunity cost of picking 1 kg of nuts? Where does Susan's comparative advantage now lie?

## The gains from specialisation

Earlier we saw that a comparative advantage arising from disparities in individual opportunity costs creates gains for everyone (see Examples 2.1 and 2.2). Example 2.5 shows how the same point can be illustrated using PPCs.

### Example 2.5 How costly is failure to specialise?

Suppose that in Example 2.4 Susan and Tom had divided their time so that each person's output consisted of half nuts and half coffee. How much of each good would Tom and Susan have been able to consume? How much could they have consumed if each had specialised in the activity for which he or she enjoyed a comparative advantage?

Since Tom can pick twice as many kg of nuts in an hour as kg of coffee, to pick equal quantities of each he must spend 2 hours picking coffee for every hour he devotes to picking nuts. And since he works a 6-hour day, that means spending 2 hours picking nuts and 4 hours picking coffee. Dividing his time in this way, he will end up with 8 kg of coffee and 8 kg of nuts per day.

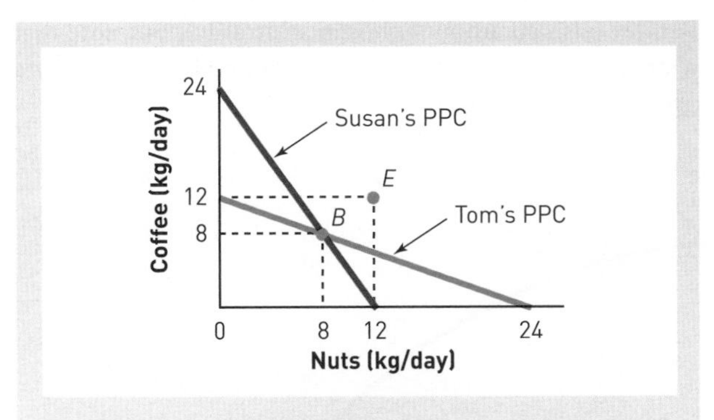


**Figure 2.5 Production without Specialisation.** When Tom and Susan divide their time so that each produces the same number of kilograms of coffee and nuts, they can consume a total of 16 kg of coffee and 16 kg of nuts each day.

Similarly, since Susan can pick twice as many kg of coffee in an hour as kg of nuts, to pick equal quantities of each she must spend 2 hours picking nuts for every hour she devotes to picking coffee. And since she too works a 6-hour day, that means spending 2 hours picking coffee and 4 hours picking nuts. So, like Tom, she will end up with 8 kg of coffee per day and 8 kg of nuts (see Fig. 2.5). Their combined daily production will thus be 16 kg of each good. By contrast, had they each specialised in their respective activities of comparative advantage, their combined daily production would have been 24 kg of each good.

If they exchange coffee and nuts with one another, each can consume a combination of the two goods that would have been unattainable if exchange had not been possible. For example, Susan can give Tom 12 kg of coffee in exchange for 12 kg of nuts, enabling each to consume 4 kg per day more of each good than when each produced and consumed alone. Note that point *E* in Fig. 2.5, which has 12 kg per day of each good, lies beyond both Tom's and Susan's PPC, yet is easily attainable with specialisation and exchange.

As Exercise 2.4 illustrates, the gains from specialisation grow larger as the difference in opportunity costs increases.

**Exercise 2.4** How do differences in opportunity cost affect the gains from specialisation?

Susan can pick 5 kg of coffee or 1 kg of nuts in an hour. Tom can pick 1 kg of coffee or 5 kg of nuts in an hour. Assuming they again work 6-hour days and want to consume coffee and nuts in equal quantities, by how much will specialisation increase their consumption compared with the alternative in which each produced only for his or her own consumption?

Although the gains from specialisation and exchange grow with increases in the differences in opportunity costs among trading partners, these differences alone still seem insufficient to account for the enormous differences in living standards between rich and poor countries. Average income in the 20 richest countries in 2000, for example, was over €27,000 per person, compared with only €211 per person in the 20 poorest countries. Although we will say more later about the role of specialisation in explaining these differences, we first discuss how to construct the PPC for an entire economy and examine how factors other than specialisation might cause it to shift outward over time.

## A PPC for a many-person economy

Although most actual economies consist of millions of workers, the process of constructing a PPC for an economy of that size is really no different from the process for a one-person economy. Consider again an economy in which the only two goods are coffee and nuts, with coffee again on the vertical axis and nuts on the horizontal axis. The vertical intercept of the economy's PPC is the total amount of coffee that could be picked if all available workers worked full-time picking coffee. Thus the maximum attainable amount of coffee production is shown for the hypothetical economy in Fig. 2.6 as 100,000 kg per day (an amount chosen arbitrarily, for illustrative purposes). The horizontal intercept of the PPC is the amount of nuts that could be picked if all available workers worked full-time picking nuts, shown for this same economy as 80,000 kg per day (also an amount chosen arbitrarily). But note that the PPC shown in Fig. 2.6 is not a straight line – as in the earlier examples involving only a single worker – but rather a curve that is bowed out from the origin.

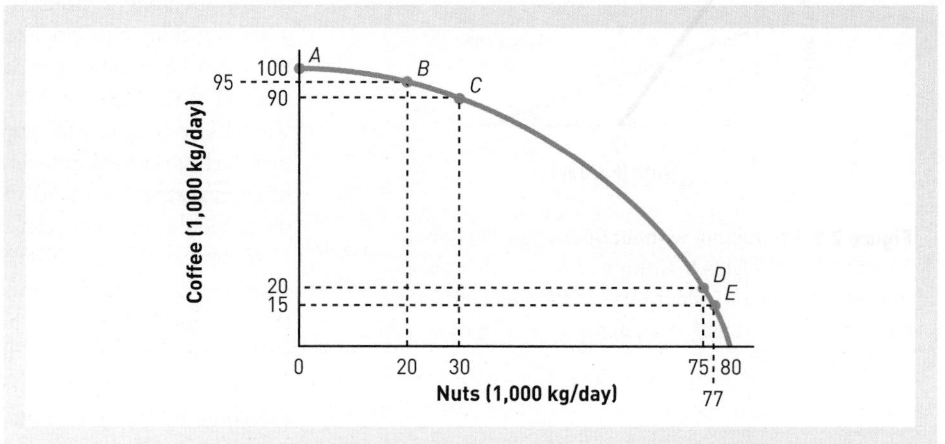


**Figure 2.6 PPC for a Large Economy.** For an economy with millions of workers, the PPC typically has a gentle outward bow shape.

We shall say more in a moment about the reasons for this 'bow' shape. But first note that a bow-shaped PPC means that the opportunity cost of producing nuts increases as the economy produces more of them. Notice, for example, that when the economy moves from *A*, where it is producing only coffee, to *B*, it gets 20,000 kg of nuts per day by giving up only 5,000 kg per day of coffee. When nut production is increased still further, however – for example, by moving from *B* to *C* – the economy again gives up 5,000 kg per day of coffee yet this time gets only 10,000 additional kg of nuts. This pattern of *increasing opportunity cost* persists over the entire length of the PPC. For example, note that in moving from *D* to *E*, the economy again gives up 5,000 kg per day of coffee but now gains only 2,000 kg a day of nuts. Note, finally, that the same pattern of increasing opportunity cost applies to coffee. Thus, as more coffee is produced, the opportunity cost of producing additional coffee – as measured by the amount of nuts that must be sacrificed – also rises.

Why is the PPC for the multi-person economy bow-shaped? The answer lies in the fact that some resources are relatively well suited for picking nuts while others are relatively well suited for picking coffee. If the economy is initially producing only coffee and wants to begin producing some nuts, which workers will it reassign? Recall Susan and Tom, the two workers discussed in Example 2.5, in which Tom's comparative advantage was picking nuts and Susan's comparative advantage was picking coffee. If both workers were currently picking coffee and you wanted to reassign one of them to pick nuts instead, whom would you send? Tom would be the clear choice, because his departure would cost the economy only half as much coffee as Susan's and would augment nut production by twice as much.

The principle is the same in any large multi-person economy, except that the range of opportunity cost differences across workers is even greater than in Example 2.5. As we keep reassigning workers from coffee production to nut production, sooner or later we must withdraw even coffee specialists like Susan from coffee production. Indeed, we must eventually reassign others whose opportunity cost of producing nuts is far higher than hers.

The shape of the PPC shown in Fig. 2.6 illustrates the general principle that when resources have different opportunity costs, we should always exploit the resource with the lowest opportunity cost first. We call this the *Low-Hanging-Fruit Principle,* in honour of the fruit picker's rule of picking the most accessible fruit first:

The Principle of Increasing Opportunity Cost (also called 'The Low-Hanging-Fruit Principle'): In expanding the production of any good, first employ those resources with the lowest opportunity cost, and only afterwards turn to resources with higher opportunity costs.

### A note on the logic of the fruit picker's rule

Why should a fruit picker harvest the low-hanging fruit first? This rule makes sense for several reasons. For one, the low-hanging fruit is easier (and hence cheaper) to pick, and if he or she planned on picking only a limited amount of fruit to begin with, they would clearly come out ahead by avoiding the less accessible fruit on the higher branches. But even if they planned on picking all the fruit on the tree, they would do better to start with the lower branches first, because this would enable them to enjoy the revenue from the sale of the fruit sooner.

The fruit picker's job can be likened to the task confronting a new chief executive officer (CEO) who has been hired to reform an inefficient, ailing company. The CEO has limited time and attention, so it makes sense to focus first on the problems that are relatively easy to correct and whose elimination will provide the biggest improvements in performance – the low-hanging fruit. Later on, the CEO can worry about the many smaller improvements needed to raise the company from very good to excellent.

Again, the important message of the Low-Hanging-Fruit Principle is to be sure to take advantage of your most favourable opportunities first.

### RECAP Comparative advantage and production possibilities

For an economy that produces two goods, the PPC describes the maximum amount of one good that can be produced for every possible level of production of the other good. Attainable points are those that lie on or within the curve, and efficient points are those that lie along the curve. The slope of the PPC tells us the opportunity cost of producing an additional unit of the good measured along the horizontal axis. The Principle of Increasing Opportunity Cost, or the Low-Hanging-Fruit Principle, tells us that the slope of the PPC becomes steeper as we move downward to the right. The greater the differences among individual opportunity costs, the more bow-shaped the PPC will be, and the more bow-shaped the PPC, the greater will be the potential gains from specialisation.

## Factors that shift the economy's PPC

As its name implies, the PPC provides a summary of the production options open to any society. At any given moment, the PPC confronts society with a *trade-off*: the only way people can produce and consume more nuts is to produce and consume less coffee. In the long run, however, it is often possible to increase production of all goods. This is what is meant when people speak of economic growth. As shown in Fig. 2.7, economic growth is an outward shift

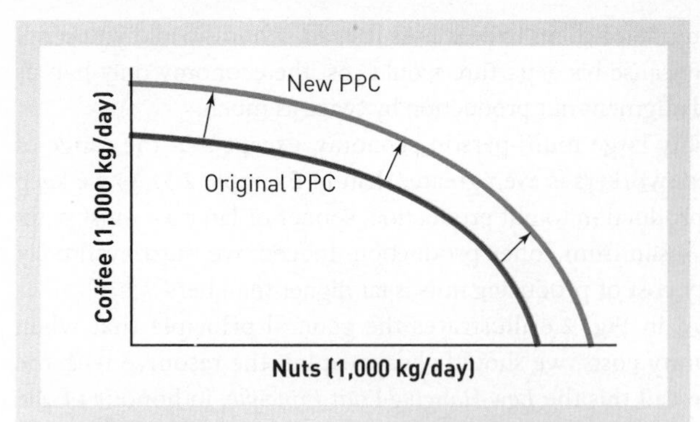


**Figure 2.7 Economic Growth: An Outward Shift in the Economy's PPC.** Increases in productive resources (such as labour and capital equipment) or improvements in knowledge and technology cause the PPC to shift outward. They are the main factors that drive economic growth.

in the economy's PPC. It can result from increases in the amount of productive resources available or from improvements in knowledge or technology that render existing resources more productive.

What causes the quantity of productive resources to grow in an economy? One factor is *investment* in new factories and equipment. When workers have more and better equipment to work with, their productivity increases, often dramatically. This is surely an important factor behind the differences in living standards between rich and poor countries. According to one study, for example, the value of capital investment per worker in the United States is about $30,000, while in Nepal the corresponding figure is less than $1,000.[2]

Such large differences in capital per worker do not occur all at once. They are a consequence of decades – even centuries – of differences in rates of savings and investment. Over time, even small differences in rates of investment can translate into extremely large differences in the amount of capital equipment available to each worker. Differences of this sort are often *self-reinforcing*: not only do higher rates of saving and investment cause incomes to grow, but the resulting higher income levels also make it easier devote additional resources to savings and investment. Over time, then, even small initial productivity advantages from specialisation can translate into very large income gaps.

Population growth also causes an economy's PPC curve to shift outward and thus is often listed as one of the sources of economic growth. But because population growth also generates more mouths to feed, it cannot by itself raise a country's standard of living. Indeed it may even cause a decline in the standard of living if existing population densities have already begun to put pressure on available land, water and other scarce resources.

Perhaps the most important source of economic growth is improvements in *knowledge and technology*. As economists have long recognised, such improvements often lead to higher output through increased specialisation. Improvements in technology often occur spontaneously, but more frequently they are directly or indirectly the result of increases in education.

In Exercise 2.4 we discussed a two-person example in which individual differences in opportunity cost led to a threefold gain from specialisation. Real-world gains from specialisation often are far more spectacular than those in the example. One reason is that specialisation not only capitalises on pre-existing differences in individual skills but also deepens those skills through practice and experience. Moreover, it eliminates many of the switching and start-up costs people incur when they move back and forth among numerous tasks. These gains apply not only to people but also to the tools and equipment they use. Breaking a task down into simple steps, each of which can be performed by a different machine, greatly multiplies the productivity of individual workers.

Even in simple settings, these factors can combine to increase productivity hundreds- or even thousands-fold. Adam Smith, the Scottish moral philosopher who is remembered today as the founder of modern economics, was the first to recognise the magnitude of the gains made possible by the division and specialisation of labour. Consider, for instance, his description of work in an eighteenth-century Scottish pin factory:

[2] Heston and Summers (1991).

> One man draws out the wire, another straightens it, a third cuts it, a fourth points it, a fifth grinds it at the top for receiving the head; to make the head requires two or three distinct operations ... I have seen a small manufactory of this kind where only ten men were employed ... [who] could, when they exerted themselves, make among them about twelve kgs of pins in a day. There are in a kg upwards of four thousand pins of middling size. Those ten persons, therefore, could make among them upwards of forty-eight thousand pins in a day. Each person, therefore, making a tenth part of forty-eight thousand pins, might be considered as making four thousand eight hundred pins in a day. But if they had all wrought separately and independently, and without any of them having been educated to this peculiar business, they certainly could not each of them have made twenty, perhaps not one pin in a day.[3]

The gains in productivity that result from specialisation are indeed often prodigious. They constitute the single most important explanation for why societies that don't rely heavily on specialisation and exchange are rapidly becoming relics.

## Why have some countries been slow to specialise?

You may be asking yourself, 'If specialisation is such a great thing, why don't people in poor countries like Nepal just specialise?' If so, you are in good company. Adam Smith spent many years attempting to answer precisely the same question. In the end, his explanation was that *population density* is an important precondition for specialisation. Smith, ever the economic naturalist, observed that work tended to be far more specialised in the large cities of England in the eighteenth century than in the rural highlands of Scotland:

> In the lone houses and very small villages which are scattered about in so desert a country as the Highlands of Scotland, every farmer must be butcher, baker and brewer for his own family ... A country carpenter ... is not only a carpenter, but a joiner, a cabinet maker, and even a carver in wood, as well as a wheelwright, a ploughwright, a cart and wagon maker.[4]

In contrast, each of these same tasks was performed by a different specialist in the large English and Scottish cities of Smith's day. Scottish highlanders would also have specialised had they been able to, but the markets in which they participated were simply too small and fragmented. Of course, high population density by itself provides no guarantee that specialisation will result in rapid economic growth. But especially before the arrival of modern shipping and electronic communications technology, low population density was a definite obstacle to gains from specialisation.

Nepal remains one of the most remote and isolated countries on the planet. In the mid-1960s, its average population density was less than 30 people per km$^2$ (Thailand, which has developed much more rapidly than Nepal, had a density of some 140 per km$^2$ in 1960). Specialisation was further limited by Nepal's rugged terrain. Exchanging goods and services with residents of other villages was difficult, because the nearest village in most cases could be reached only after trekking several hours, or even days, over treacherous Himalayan trails. More than any other factor, this extreme isolation accounts for Nepal's long-standing failure to benefit from widespread specialisation.

Population density is by no means the only important factor that influences the degree of specialisation. Specialisation may be severely impeded, for example, by *laws and customs* that limit people's freedom to transact freely with one another. The communist governments of North Korea and the former East Germany (GDR) restricted exchange severely, which helps

[3] This quotation is from Book 1 of Smith's *An Enquiry into the Nature and Causes of the Wealth of Nations*, usually referred to today as *The Wealth of Nations*, originally published in 1776 and frequently said to have launched the discipline of economics (Smith, 1776, book 1).

[4] Smith op.cit, book 1, ch. 3.

explain why those countries achieved far less specialisation than South Korea and the former West Germany (FRG), whose governments were far more supportive of exchange.

Finally, specialisation (in Smith's example taking the form of the division of labour whereby the process of producing a pin is broken down into separate operations performed by different people) is limited by the *size of the market*. It is worth doing only if a significant quantity of output is to be produced. Hence the 'chicken and egg' problem in a country like Nepal: large-scale production, high productivity and high income depend on division of labour, but division of labour is worthwhile only to the extent that the level of demand for the final products produced by labour warrants it. Because there is little specialisation, Nepal is poor ... but because it is poor there is little incentive to specialise.

### Can we have too much specialisation?

Of course, the mere fact that specialisation boosts productivity does not mean that more specialisation is always better than less, for specialisation also entails *costs*. For example, most people appear to enjoy variety in the work they do, yet variety tends to be one of the first casualties as workplace tasks become ever more narrowly specialised. Indeed, one of Karl Marx's central themes was that the fragmentation of workplace tasks often exacts a heavy psychological toll on workers:

> All means for the development of production ... mutilate the labourer into a fragment of a man, degrade him to the level of an appendage of a machine, destroy every remnant of charm in his work and turn it into hated toil.[5]

Do the extra goods made possible by specialisation simply come at too high a price? We must certainly acknowledge at least the *potential* for specialisation to proceed too far. Yet specialisation need not entail rigidly segmented, mind-numbingly repetitive work. And it is important to recognise that *failure* to specialise entails costs as well. Those who don't specialise must accept low wages or work extremely long hours.

When all is said and done, we can expect to meet life's financial obligations in the shortest time – thereby freeing up more time to do whatever else we wish – if we concentrate at least a significant proportion of our efforts on those tasks for which we have a comparative advantage.

## Comparative advantage and international trade

The same logic that leads the individuals in an economy to specialise and exchange goods with one another also leads nations to specialise and trade among themselves. As with individuals, each nation can benefit from exchange, even though one may be generally more productive than the other in absolute terms.

### Economic naturalist 2.3 If trade between nations is so beneficial, why are free-trade agreements so controversial?

One of the most heated issues in the 1996 US presidential campaign was President Clinton's support for the North American Free Trade Agreement (NAFTA), a treaty to sharply reduce trade barriers between the United States and its immediate neighbours, Canada and Mexico. The treaty attracted fierce opposition from third-party candidate Ross Perot, who insisted that it would mean unemployment for

[5] Marx (1867, pp. 708–9).

millions of American workers. It was also widely opposed by trade unions in the United States.

Right from its inception at the beginning of 1957, what is now the European Union (EU) has been legally and politically committed to free trade among its members, and to encouraging free trade on a global basis. However, when the record is examined in relation to trade with non-members, the position is quite different. In the late 1990s the level of protection of EU markets was effectively much higher than might have been suspected from the fact that the maximum official value for the EU's single tariff against imports from outside the Union was only 6 per cent. For foodstuffs, when other protective devices were computed for their tariff equivalent effect the effective rate of protection was over 32 per cent in 1996. For all goods the effect was 7.7 per cent.[6] (It has to be said that since then there has been a significant reduction in the level of EU protection.)

If free trade and exchange is so beneficial, why does anyone oppose it?

The answer is that while reducing barriers to international trade increases the total value of all goods and services produced in each nation, it does not guarantee that each individual citizen will do better. This will be explained more fully in Chapters 15 and 16. One specific American concern regarding NAFTA was that it would help Mexico to exploit a comparative advantage in the production of goods made by unskilled labour. Although US consumers would benefit from reduced prices for such goods, many Americans feared that unskilled workers in the United States would lose their jobs to workers in Mexico. In the end, NAFTA was enacted over the vociferous opposition of American labour unions. So far, however, studies have failed to detect significant job losses among US unskilled workers.

The European Union's principal protectionist programme has been aimed at shielding Union farmers from competition from food producers outside the Union. This was the reason for the highly expensive and inefficient Common Agricultural Policy (CAP) that pays EU farmers to produce food that people do not want to consume while excluding more efficient and lower-cost food producers from outside the Union, a policy that was a major barrier to raising Third World incomes. The costs and consequences of the policy have eventually led to its slowly being dismantled, a process that is far from being complete. It was in some measure the decline in the political importance of farming votes and the rise of organised consumer interests that made the old CAP unsustainable. The other factor was that some countries gained from it (France, Ireland and Italy, for example) while others (especially the United Kingdom) lost because they traditionally produced little of their own food requirements.

## RECAP Comparative advantage and international trade

Nations, like individuals, can benefit from exchange, even though one trading partner may be more productive than the other in absolute terms. The greater the difference between domestic opportunity costs and world opportunity costs, the more a nation benefits from exchange with other nations. But expansion in exchange does not guarantee that each individual citizen will do better. In particular, unskilled workers in high-wage countries may be hurt in the short run by the reduction of barriers to trade with low-wage nations.

[6] Jørgensen, Lüthje and Schröder (2001).

## Summary

- One person has an *absolute* advantage over another in the production of a good if she can produce more of that good than the other person. One person has a *comparative* advantage over another in the production of a good if she is relatively more efficient than the other person at producing that good, meaning that her opportunity cost of producing it is lower than her counterpart's. Specialisation based on comparative advantage is the basis for economic exchange. When each person specialises in the task at which he or she is relatively more efficient, the economic pie is maximised, making possible the largest slice for everyone.
- At the *individual* level, comparative advantage may spring from differences in talent or ability, or from differences in education, training and experience. At the *national* level, sources of comparative advantage include these innate and learned differences, as well as differences in language, culture, institutions, climate, natural resources and a host of other factors.
- The *production possibilities curve* (PPC) is a simple device for summarising the possible combinations of output that a society can produce if it employs its resources efficiently. In a simple economy that produces only coffee and nuts, a graph of the PPC shows the maximum quantity of coffee production (vertical axis) possible at each level of nut production (horizontal axis). The slope of the PPC at any point represents the opportunity cost of nuts at that point, expressed in kg of coffee.
- All PPCs slope downward because of the *Scarcity Principle*, which states that the only way a consumer can get more of one good is to settle for less of another. In economies whose workers have different opportunity costs of producing each good, the slope of the PPC becomes steeper as consumers move downward along the curve. This change in slope illustrates the Principle of Increasing Opportunity Cost (or the Low-Hanging-Fruit Principle), which states that in expanding the production of any good, a society should first employ those resources that are relatively efficient at producing that good, only afterwards turning to those that are less efficient.
- Factors that cause a country's PPC to shift outward over time include *investment* in new factories and equipment, *population growth* and improvements in *knowledge and technology*.
- The same logic that prompts individuals to specialise in their production and exchange goods with one another also leads nations to specialise and trade with one another. On both levels, each trading partner can benefit from an exchange, even though one may be more productive than the other, in absolute terms, for each good. For both individuals and nations, the benefits of exchange tend to be larger the larger are the differences between the trading partners' *opportunity costs*.

## Key terms

**absolute advantage** (37)
**attainable point** (44)
**comparative advantage** (38)
**efficient point** (45)
**inefficient point** (44)
**production possibilities curve** (43)
**unattainable point** (44)

## Review questions

1. Explain what 'having a comparative advantage' in producing a particular good or service means. What does 'having an absolute advantage' in producing a good or service mean?
2. How will a reduction in the number of hours worked each day affect an economy's PPC?

3. How will technological innovations that boost labour productivity affect an economy's PPC?

4. Why does saying that people are poor because they do not specialise make more sense than saying that people perform their own services because they are poor?

5. What factors have helped the United States to become the world's leading exporter of movies, books and popular music?

## Problems

Problems marked with an asterisk (*) are more difficult.

1. Ted can wax 4 cars per day or wash 12 cars. Tom can wax 3 cars per day or wash 6. What is each man's opportunity cost of washing a car? Who has a comparative advantage in washing cars?

2. Ted can wax a car in 20 minutes or wash a car in 60 minutes. Tom can wax a car in 15 minutes or wash a car in 30 minutes. What is each man's opportunity cost of washing a car? Who has a comparative advantage in washing cars?

3. Toby can produce 5 litres of apple cider or 2.5 kg of feta cheese per hour. Kyle can produce 3 litres of apple cider or 1.5 kg of feta cheese per hour. Can Toby and Kyle benefit from specialisation and trade? Explain.

4. Nancy and Bill are auto mechanics. Nancy takes 4 hours to replace a clutch and 2 hours to replace a set of brakes. Bill takes 6 hours to replace a clutch and 2 hours to replace a set of brakes. State whether anyone has an absolute advantage at either task and, for each task, identify who has a comparative advantage.

5. Consider a society consisting only of Helen, who allocates her time between sewing dresses and baking bread. Each hour she devotes to sewing dresses yields 4 dresses, and each hour she devotes to baking bread yields 8 loaves of bread. If Helen works a total of 8 hours per day, graph her PPC.

6. Refer to Problem 5. Which of the points listed below is efficient? Which is attainable?

   a. 28 dresses per day, 16 loaves per day.
   b. 16 dresses per day, 32 loaves per day.
   c. 18 dresses per day, 24 loaves per day.

7. Suppose that in Problem 5 a sewing machine is introduced that enables Helen to sew 8 dresses per hour rather than only 4. Show how this development shifts her PPC.

8. Refer to Problem 7 to explain what is meant by the following statement: 'An increase in productivity with respect to any one good increases our options for producing and consuming all other goods.'

9. Susan can pick 4 kg of coffee in an hour or 2 kg of nuts. Tom can pick 2 kg of coffee in an hour or 4 kg of nuts. Each works 6 hours per day.

   a. What is the maximum number of kg of coffee the two can pick in a day?
   b. What is the maximum number of kg of nuts the two can pick in a day?
   c. If Susan and Tom were picking the maximum number of kg of coffee when they decided that they would like to begin picking 4 kg of nuts per day, who would pick the nuts, and how many kg of coffee would they still be able to pick?
   d. Now suppose that Susan and Tom were picking the maximum number of kg of nuts when they decided that they would like to begin picking 8 kg of coffee per day. Who would pick the coffee, and how many kg of nuts would they still be able to pick?
   e. Would it be possible for Susan and Tom to pick a total of 26 kg of nuts and 20 kg of coffee each day? If so, how much of each good should each person pick?

10.* Refer to the two-person economy described in Problem 9.

a. Is the point (30 kg of coffee per day, 12 kg of nuts per day) an attainable point? Is it an efficient point? What about the point (24 kg of coffee per day, 24 kg of nuts per day)?
b. On a graph with kg of coffee per day on the vertical axis and kg of nuts per day on the horizontal axis, show all the points you identified in Problem 9, parts (a)–(e), and in Problem 10(a). Connect these points with straight lines. Is the result the PPC for an economy consisting of Susan and Tom?
c. Suppose that Susan and Tom could buy or sell coffee and nuts in the world market at a price of €2 per kg for coffee and €2 per kg for nuts. If each person specialised completely in the good for which he or she had a comparative advantage, how much could they earn by selling all their produce?
d. At the prices just described, what is the maximum amount of coffee Susan and Tom could buy in the world market? The maximum amount of nuts? Would it be possible for them to consume 40 kg of nuts and 8 kg of coffee each day?
e. In light of their ability to buy and sell in world markets at the stated prices, show on the same graph all combinations of the two goods it would be possible for them to consume.

## Answers to in-chapter exercises

2.1

| | Productivity in programming (per hour) | Productivity in bicycle repair (per hour) |
|---|---|---|
| Pat | 2 web page updates | 1 repair |
| Barbara | 3 web page updates | 3 repairs |

The entries in the table tell us that Barb has an absolute advantage over Pat in both activities. While Barbara (the mechanic) can update 3 web pages per hour, Pat (the programmer) can update only 2. Barbara's absolute advantage over Pat is even greater in the task of fixing bikes – 3 repairs per hour versus Pat's 1.

But as in Example 2.2, the fact that Barbara is a better programmer than Pat does not imply that Barb should update her own web page. Barbara's opportunity cost of updating a web page is 1 bicycle repair, whereas Pat must give up only half a repair to update a web page. Pat has a comparative advantage over Barb at programming, and Barbara has a comparative advantage over Pat at bicycle repair.

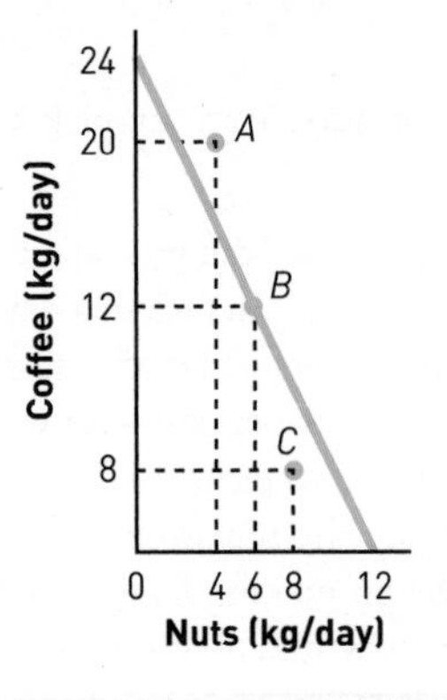


2.2 In the graph on the left, *A* (20 kg per day of coffee, 4 kg per day of nuts) is unattainable; *B* (12 kg per day of coffee, 6 kg per day of nuts) is both attainable and efficient; and *C* (4 kg per day of coffee, 8 kg per day of nuts) is both attainable and inefficient.

2.3 Susan's opportunity cost of picking 1 kg of nuts is now $\frac{1}{2}$ kg of coffee, and Tom's opportunity cost of picking 1 kg of nuts is now only 1 kg of coffee. So Tom has a comparative advantage at picking coffee, and Susan has a comparative advantage at picking nuts.

2.4 Since Tom can pick five times as many kilograms of nuts in an hour as kilograms of coffee, to pick equal quantities of each, he must spend 5 hours picking coffee for every hour he devotes to picking nuts. And since he works a 6-hour day, that means spending 5 hours picking coffee and 1 hour picking nuts. Dividing his time in this way, he will end up with 5 kg of each good. Similarly, if she is to pick equal quantities of each good, Susan must spend 5 hours picking nuts and 1 hour picking coffee. So she, too, picks 5 kg of each good if she divides her 6-hour day in this way. Their combined daily production will thus be 10 kg of each good. By working together and specialising, however, they can produce and consume a total of 30 kg per day of each good.

## References

Heston, A. and R. Summers (1991) 'The Penn World Table (Mark 5): An Expanded Set of International Comparisons, 1950–1988', *Quarterly Journal of Economics*, May, pp. 327–68.

Jørgensen, J. G., T. Lüthje and P. J. H. Schröder (2001) 'Trade: the Work-Horse of Integration', Chapter 6 in J. D. Hansen (ed.), *European Integration – An Economic Perspective* (Oxford: Oxford University Press).

Marx, K. (1867) *Das Kapital* (New York: Modern Library).

Smith, A. (1776) *An Enquiry into the Nature and Causes of the Wealth of Nations* (New York: Everyman's Library).

# 3

# Supply and Demand: an Introduction

In any European city, if we could aggregate the total stock of food held by supermarkets, grocery and other food stores, restaurants, wholesalers and households and other end users, we would probably find that the amount involved was sufficient to feed that city's population for at most a week or so. Little or no food is actually produced within the city. Nevertheless, most people in most cities have nutritionally adequate and varied diets on an ongoing basis. That requires that in the case of a large city – London, Manchester, Paris, Frankfurt – thousands of tonnes of food must be delivered to an enormous number of locations in the city every day.

If you live in one of these cities (and even if you do not) it is doubtful whether when you sit down to eat you give much thought to the quite extraordinary co-ordination of people and resources needed to feed the population of such a city on a day-to-day basis. If you do think about it, it should occur to you that it is truly remarkable that somehow it all seems to happen without being centrally controlled. If food were some simple and homogeneous commodity it would be an impressive feat to secure these deliveries to so many locations in varying quantities sufficient to provide what was needed. But when you think about the incredible variety of different products involved, the fact that what is wanted in any location is available as and when it is wanted might strike you as close to miraculous.

In fact, it is even more complex and astonishing when you think that it is not simply a question of delivering the various commodities as and when demanded, but that there is also the question of how the different quantities of the enormous number of products consumed get produced in the first place. In each case, and in respect of each delivery, and of each kilogram or litre being produced, some individual somewhere is making a decision that determines what is produced, and where it goes. And in the end it is individual decisions, made by those making the decisions without any detailed knowledge about who needs what, where and when, that somehow produces the end result whereby what end users want in terms of quantity and variety is available when and where they want it.

In the case of all these goods consumed someone has to decide where each particular type of food gets produced, and how, and by whom. Someone must decide how much of each type of food gets delivered to *each* of the thousands of restaurants, hospitals, supermarkets and grocery stores in a large city. Someone must determine whether the deliveries should be made in big trucks or small ones, arrange for the trucks to be in the right place at the right time, and ensure that fuel and qualified drivers are available.

Thousands of individuals must decide what role, if any, they will play in this collective effort. Some people – just the right number – must choose to drive food-delivery trucks rather than trucks that deliver concrete. Others must become the mechanics who fix these trucks rather than carpenters who build houses. Others must become farmers rather than architects or bricklayers. Still others must become chefs in up-market restaurants, or flip burgers at McDonald's, instead of becoming plumbers or electricians.

Yet despite the almost incomprehensible number and complexity of the tasks involved, somehow the supplying of the city manages to get done remarkably smoothly. Yes, from time to time a supermarket will run out of stuffed olives, or you may sometimes be told that someone else has just ordered the last serving of roast duck. But if episodes like these stick in your memory, it is only because they are so rare. For the most part the city's food delivery system functions so smoothly that it attracts virtually no notice.

But if we look at some other aspects of what we need to live, things are not always as smoothly organised. In most European and North American cities there are perennial problems affecting the rental housing market. New York is a particularly striking example of this problem, but to a greater or lesser degree the same thing can be seen in a very great number of larger cities and towns in Europe.

According to one recent estimate, New York needs between 20,000 and 40,000 new housing units each year merely to keep up with population growth and to replace existing housing that has deteriorated beyond repair. The actual rate of new construction in the city, however, is of the order of only 6,000 units per year. As a result, America's most densely populated city has been experiencing a protracted housing shortage. Yet, paradoxically, in the midst of this shortage, apartment houses are being demolished; and in the vacant plots left behind, people from the neighbourhoods are planting flower gardens! In common with other cities in Europe and America, New York is experiencing not only a growing shortage of rental housing, but also chronically strained relations between landlords and tenants. Why?

The market for health care services is one in which in several European countries (as well as in the United States) things do not appear to work as smoothly as in the case of food supplies in major conurbations. During the 1990s there were several attempts to reorganise the delivery of UK health services, because the tax-financed National Health Service (NHS) was not seen as delivering care as required when required and at reasonable cost. The reforms, in so far as they have been implemented, have achieved relatively little. In Ireland, where there is a state system parallel to a private market largely insurance-financed, waiting lists are endemic in the state system and, despite increasing the level of state funding to the state system from 5 per cent to 7 per cent of GNP between 1999 and 2003, the waiting lists (a sure sign of a market not working) are as long as ever.

It is an interesting problem. Housing services and food are both basic requirements of life, and both are needed in any large city. But in the case of the food industry, goods and services are available in wide variety, and people (at least those with adequate income) are generally satisfied with what they receive and the choices available to them. In contrast, in the rental housing industry, chronic shortages and chronic dissatisfaction are rife among both buyers and sellers. Why this difference?

Adequate availability of health care is seen as a basic requirement in modern societies, but despite the steady growth in spending per head on health care in countries in Western Europe and America, in some, but not all, countries this spending does not call forth the level and type of care that people regard as desirable, while in others it does. Complaints about the availability and quality of health care seem to be much less common in France or Germany than they are in Britain or Ireland. Why?

The case of housing in New York (as echoed in other cities in Europe and America) provides a clue as to what is going on. The brief answer is that New York relies on a complex system of administrative rent regulations to allocate housing units but leaves the allocation of food essentially in the hands of market forces – the forces of supply and demand. The allocation mechanism used in the case of housing in New York is (with some modifications) that used to allocate health care in systems like Britain's NHS. Although intuition might suggest otherwise, both theory and experience suggest that the seemingly chaotic and unplanned outcomes of market forces can in most cases do a better job of allocating economic resources than can (for example) a government agency, even if the agency has the best of intentions.

In this chapter we shall explore how markets allocate food, housing and other goods and services, usually with remarkable efficiency despite the complexity of the tasks. To be sure, markets are by no means perfect, and our stress on their virtues is to some extent an attempt to counteract what most economists view as an underappreciation by the general public of their remarkable strengths. But in the course of our discussion we shall see why markets function so smoothly most of the time, and why bureaucratic rules and regulations rarely work as well in solving complex economic problems.

To convey an understanding of how markets work is a major goal of this book, and in this chapter we provide only a brief introduction and overview. As the course proceeds we shall discuss the economic role of markets in considerably more detail, paying attention to some of the problems of markets as well as their strengths.

## What, how and for whom? Central planning versus the market

No city, state or society – regardless of how it is organised – can escape the need to answer certain basic economic questions. For example, how much of our limited time and other resources should we devote to building housing, how much to the production of food and how much to providing other goods and services? What techniques should we use to produce each good? Who should be assigned to each specific task? And how should the resulting goods and services be distributed among people?

In the thousands of different societies for which records are available, issues such as these have been decided in essentially one of two ways. One approach is for all economic decisions to be made *centrally*, by an individual or small number of individuals on behalf of a larger group. For example, in many agrarian societies throughout history, families or other small groups consumed only those goods and services that they produced for themselves, and a single clan or family leader made most important production and distribution decisions. On an immensely larger scale, the economic organisation of the former Soviet Union (and other communist countries) was also largely centralised. In so-called centrally planned communist nations, a central bureaucratic committee established production targets for the country's farms and factories, developed a master plan for how to achieve the targets (including detailed instructions concerning who was to produce what) and set up guidelines for the distribution and use of the goods and services produced.

Neither form of centralised economic organisation is much in evidence today. When implemented on a small scale, as in a self-sufficient family enterprise, centralised decision making is certainly feasible. For the reasons discussed in Chapter 2, however, the jack-of-all-trades approach was doomed once it became clear how dramatically people could improve their living standards by specialisation – that is, by having each individual focus his or her efforts on a relatively narrow range of tasks. After the collapse of the Soviet Union between 1989 and 1991 and the overthrow of the Soviet-backed regimes in the East European countries that had been Soviet satellites since the late 1940s, there remained in 2006 only three countries worldwide that formally operate or claim to operate communist economies with **central planning**: Cuba, North Korea and China. The first two of these appear to be on their last legs, economically speaking, and China has by now largely abandoned any attempt to control produc-

**central planning** the allocation of economic resources is determined by a political and administrative mechanism that gathers information as to technology, resource availability and end demands for goods and services

tion and distribution decisions from the centre. The major remaining examples of centralised allocation and control now reside in the bureaucratic agencies that administer programmes such as New York City's rent controls or Britain's NHS – programmes that are themselves becoming increasingly rare.

At the beginning of the twenty-first century we are therefore left, for the most part, with the second major form of economic system, one in which production and distribution decisions are left to individuals interacting in private markets. In the so-called **capitalist economies**, or **free-market economies**, people decide for themselves which careers to pursue and which products to produce or buy. In fact, there are no *pure* free-market economies today. Modern industrial countries are characterised by a mixture of structures that deliver goods and services to end users. Where markets do the job, they are commonly subject to various forms of regulation. In the case of some services, collective provision via state structures is common. Public transport is an obvious example. Hence, modern economies are more properly described as *mixed economies*, meaning that goods and services are allocated by a combination of free markets, regulation and other forms of collective control. Still, it makes sense to refer to such systems as free-market economies, or at least market economies, because people are for the most part free to start businesses, to shut them down or to sell them. And, within broad limits, the distribution of goods and services is determined by individual preferences backed by individual purchasing power, which in most cases comes from the income people earn in the labour market.

In country after country, markets have replaced centralised control, for the simple reason that they tend to assign production tasks and consumption benefits much more effectively. This has not been without controversy. For example, the UK experiment in privatising rail transport has been the subject of considerable criticism, and indeed has been effectively partially reversed. One result of the controversies over the manner in which privatisation occurred, and its consequences, has been to reinforce the reputation of the economics profession as chronically unable to agree on correct answers to problems. The popular press, conventional wisdom and politicians seeking to deflect criticism often assert that economists disagree about important issues, or, if they do agree, get it wrong. (As someone once quipped: 'If you laid all the economists in the world end to end, you still wouldn't get an agreed, correct and practicable answer to a question.') The fact is, however, that there is overwhelming agreement among economists about a broad range of issues, with the great majority accepting the efficacy of markets as means for allocating society's scarce resources. In most cases, the experience of privatisation and reliance on markets has been shown to be correct. For example, a survey found that more than 90 per cent of American professional economists believe that rent regulations like those implemented by New York do more harm than good. That the stated aim of these regulations – to make rental housing more affordable for middle- and low-income families – was clearly benign was not enough to prevent them from wreaking havoc on New York's housing market. And no one seriously disputes the proposition that the privatisation and deregulation of the air traffic sector across Europe, long called for by transport economists, has revolutionised the choices and costs facing people who want to fly. Ryanair is the standing proof of markets working where state provision and restricted competition have failed.

To see why this is the case, we must explore how goods and services are allocated in private markets, and why non-market means of allocating goods and services often do not produce the expected results.

## Buyers and sellers in markets

Beginning with some simple concepts and definitions, we shall explore how the interactions among buyers and sellers in markets determine the prices and quantities of the various goods

**market** the market for any good consists of all buyers or sellers of that good

and services traded in those markets. We begin by defining a **market**: the market for any good consists of all the buyers and sellers of that good. So, for example, the market for pizza on a given day in a given place is just the set of people (or other economic actors, such as firms) potentially able to buy or sell pizza at that time and location.

In the market for pizza, sellers comprise the individuals and companies that either do sell – or might, under the right circumstances, sell – pizza. Similarly, buyers in this market include all individuals who buy – or might buy – pizza. What would some one have to pay to buy a slice of pizza? Not very much, is the answer: depending on location and quality you would expect to be able to buy a slice for less than €3. Where does the market price of pizza come from? Looking beyond pizza to the vast array of other goods that are bought and sold every day, we may ask: 'Why are some goods cheap and others expensive?' Aristotle had no idea. Nor did Plato, nor Copernicus, nor Newton. On reflection, it is astonishing that, for almost the entire span of human history, not even the most intelligent and creative minds on earth had any real inkling of how to answer that seemingly simple question. Even Adam Smith suffered confusion on this issue.

Smith and other early economists (including Karl Marx) thought that the market price of a good was determined by its *cost of production*. But although costs do affect prices, they cannot explain why one of Pablo Picasso's paintings sells for so much more than one of Jackson Pollock's, or why a Juan Gris sells for more than a Francis Bacon.

Stanley Jevons and other nineteenth-century economists tried to explain price by focusing on the value people derived from consuming different goods and services. It certainly seems plausible that people will pay a lot for a good they value highly. Yet willingness to pay cannot be the whole story, either. Deprive a person in the desert of water, for example, and he will be dead in a matter of hours, and yet water sells for just a few cents per litre. By contrast, human beings can get along perfectly well without gold, and yet gold sells for more than €250 an ounce.

Cost of production? Value to the user? Which is it? The answer, which seems obvious to today's economists, is that both matter. Writing in the late nineteenth century, the British economist Alfred Marshall was among the first to show clearly how *costs* and *value* interact to determine both the prevailing market price for a good, and the amount of it that is bought and sold. Our task in the pages ahead will be to explore Marshall's insights and gain some practice in applying them. As a first step, we introduce the two main components of Marshall's path-breaking analysis: the **demand curve** and the supply curve.

**demand curve** a schedule or graph showing the quantity of a good that buyers wish to buy at each price

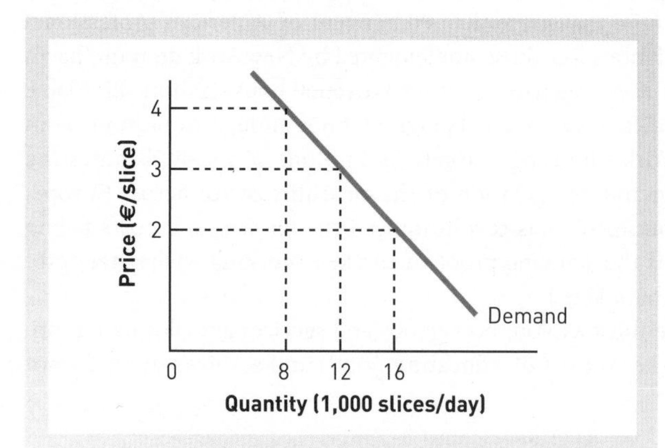


**Figure 3.1 The Daily Demand Curve for Pizza.** The demand curve for any good is a downward-sloping function of its price.

## The demand curve

In the market for pizza, the demand curve for pizza is a simple schedule or graph that tells us how many slices people would be willing to buy at different prices. By convention, economists usually put price on the vertical axis of the demand curve and quantity on the horizontal axis.

A fundamental property of the demand curve is that it is *downward-sloping* with respect to price. For example, the demand curve for pizza tells us that as the price of pizza falls, buyers will buy more slices. Thus the daily demand curve for pizza in Manchester or Milan on a given day might look like the curve seen in Fig. 3.1. (Although economists usually refer to demand and supply 'curves', we often draw them as straight lines in examples.)

The demand curve in Fig. 3.1 tells us that when the price of pizza is low – say, €2 per slice – buyers will want to buy 16,000 slices per day, whereas they will want to buy only 12,000 slices at a price of €3, and only 8,000 at a price of €4. The demand curve for pizza – as for any other good – slopes downward for many reasons. Some of these reasons have to do with the individual consumer's reactions to price changes. Thus, as pizza becomes more expensive, a consumer may switch to chicken sandwiches, hamburgers, or other foods that substitute for pizza. This is called the **substitution effect** of a price change. In addition, a price increase reduces the quantity demanded because it reduces purchasing power: a consumer simply can't afford to buy as many slices of pizza at higher prices as at lower prices. This is called the **income effect** of a price change.

**substitution effect** the change in the quantity demanded of a good that results because buyers switch to substitutes when the price of the good changes

**income effect** the change in the quantity demanded of a good that results because of a change in real income of purchasers arising from the price change

**buyer's reservation price** the largest euro amount the buyer would be willing to pay for a good

Another reason that the demand curve slopes downward is that consumers differ in terms of how much they are willing to pay for the good. The Cost–Benefit Principle (Chapter 1) tells us that a given person will buy the good if the benefit she expects to receive from it exceeds its cost. The benefit is the **buyer's reservation price**, the highest euro amount she would be willing to pay for the good. The cost of the good is the actual amount that the buyer actually must pay for it, which is the market price of the good. In most markets, different buyers have different reservation prices. Thus when the good sells for a high price, it will satisfy the cost–benefit test for fewer buyers than when it sells for a lower price.

To put this same point another way, the fact that the demand curve for a good is downward-sloping reflects the fact that the reservation price of the marginal buyer declines as the quantity of the good bought increases. Here the marginal buyer is the person who purchases the last unit of the good that is sold. If buyers are currently purchasing 12,000 slices of pizza a day in Fig. 3.1, for example, the reservation price for the buyer of the 12,000th slice must be €3. (If someone had been willing to pay more than that, the quantity demanded at a price of €3 would have been more than 12,000 to begin with.) By similar reasoning, when the quantity sold is 16,000 slices per day, the marginal buyer's reservation price must be only €2.

We defined the demand curve for any good as a schedule telling how much of it consumers wish to purchase at various prices. This is called the *horizontal interpretation* of the demand curve. Using the horizontal interpretation, we start with price on the vertical axis and read the corresponding quantity demanded on the horizontal axis. Thus, at a price of €4 per slice, the demand curve in Fig. 3.1 tells us that the quantity of pizza demanded will be 8,000 slices per day. *It tells us the quantity that will be demanded as a function of the price at which it is made available.*

The demand curve can also be interpreted in a second way, which is to start with quantity on the horizontal axis and then read the marginal buyer's reservation price on the vertical axis. Thus, when the quantity of pizza sold is 8,000 slices per day, the demand curve in Fig. 3.1 tells us that the marginal buyer's reservation price is €4 per slice. This second way of reading the demand curve is called the *vertical interpretation*. This means that the demand curve tells us what the market price will be if any given amount is made available (in this case, if 8,000 slices are offered for sale the price sellers will receive is €4). *It tells us the market price as a function of the available amount.*

**Exercise 3.1** In Fig. 3.1, what is the marginal buyer's reservation price when the quantity of pizza sold is 10,000 slices per day? For the same demand curve, what will be the quantity of pizza demanded at a price of €2.50 per slice?

## The supply curve

In the market for pizza, the **supply curve** is a simple schedule or graph that tells us, for each possible price, the total number of slices that all pizza vendors would be willing to sell at that price. What does the supply curve of pizza look like? The answer to this question is based on the logical assumption that suppliers should be willing to sell additional slices as long as the price they receive is sufficient to cover their opportunity costs of supplying them. Thus, if what someone could earn by selling a slice of pizza is insufficient to compensate her for what she could have earned if she had spent her time and invested her money in some other way, she will not sell that slice. Otherwise, she will.

**supply curve** a curve or schedule showing the quantity of a good that sellers wish to sell at each price

Just as buyers differ with respect to the amounts they are willing to pay for pizza, sellers also differ with respect to their opportunity costs of supplying pizza. For those with limited education and work experience, the opportunity cost of selling pizza is relatively low (because such individuals typically do not have a lot of high-paying alternatives). For others the opportunity cost of selling pizza is of moderate value, and for still others – like rock stars and professional athletes – it is prohibitively high. In part because of these differences in opportunity cost among people, the daily supply curve of pizza will be *upward-sloping* with respect to price. As an illustration see Fig. 3.2, which shows a hypothetical supply curve on a given day.

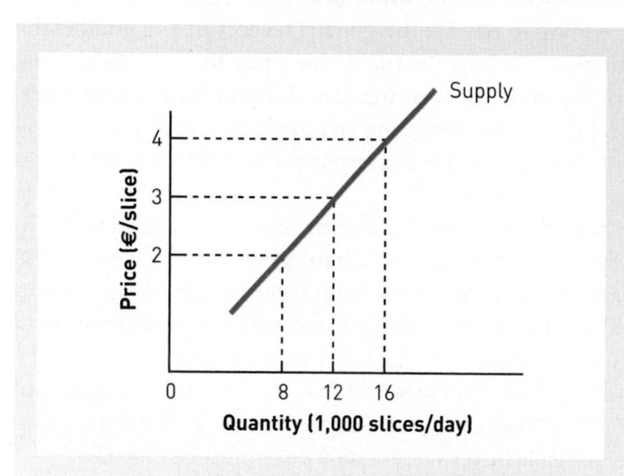


**Figure 3.2 The Daily Supply Curve of Pizza.** At higher prices, sellers generally offer more units for sale.

The fact that the supply curve slopes upward may be seen as a consequence of the *Low-Hanging-Fruit Principle*, discussed in Chapter 2. This principle tells us that as we expand the production of pizza, we turn first to those whose opportunity costs of producing pizza are lowest, and only then to others with higher opportunity costs. It also reflects the fact that if a producer faces increasing opportunity costs for producing a product, it will be necessary to pay more per unit to get more produced.

Like the demand curve, the supply curve can be interpreted either horizontally or vertically. Under the horizontal interpretation, we begin with a price, then go over to the supply curve to read the quantity that sellers wish to sell at that price on the horizontal axis. For instance, at a price of €2 per slice, sellers in Fig. 3.2 wish to sell 8,000 slices per day. *It tells us the quantity that producers will supply as a function of the price they expect to receive.*

Under the vertical interpretation, we begin with a quantity, then go up to the supply curve to read the corresponding marginal cost on the vertical axis. Thus, if sellers in Fig. 3.2 are currently supplying 12,000 slices per day, the opportunity cost of the marginal seller is €3 per slice. In other words, the supply curve tells us that the marginal cost of producing the 12,000th slice of pizza is €3. (If someone could produce a 12,001st slice for less than €3, she would have an incentive to supply it, so the quantity of pizza supplied at €3 per slice would not have been 12,000 slices per day to begin with.) By similar reasoning, when the quantity of pizza supplied is 16,000 slices per day, the marginal cost of producing another slice must be €4. The **seller's reservation price** for selling an additional unit of a good is her marginal cost of producing that good. It is the smallest euro amount for which she would not be financially worse off if she sold an additional

**seller's reservation price** the smallest money amount for which a seller would be willing to sell an additional unit, generally equal to marginal cost

unit. Under the vertical interpretation the supply curve tells us the sellers' reservation price for any given quantity. *It tells us the amount that will have to be paid to deliver any quantity as a function of quantity.*

**Exercise 3.2** In Fig. 3.2, what is the marginal cost of a slice of pizza when the quantity of pizza sold is 10,000 slices per day? For the same supply curve, what will be the quantity of pizza supplied at a price of €3.50 per slice?

### RECAP Demand and supply curves

The *market* for a good consists of the actual and potential buyers and sellers of that good. For any given price, the *demand curve* shows the quantity that demanders would be willing to buy, and the *supply curve* shows the quantity that suppliers of the good would be willing to sell. Suppliers are willing to sell more at higher prices (supply curves slope upward) and demanders are willing to buy less at higher prices (demand curves slope downward).

## Market equilibrium

The concept of **equilibrium** is employed in both the physical and social sciences, and it is of central importance in economic analysis. In general, a system is in equilibrium when all forces at work within the system are cancelled by others, resulting in a *stable*, *balanced*, or *unchanging* situation. In physics, for example, a ball hanging from a spring is said to be in equilibrium when the spring has stretched sufficiently that the upward force it exerts on the ball is exactly counterbalanced by the downward force of gravity. The ball does not move. *Its position does not change.* Equilibrium in this sense is a *static* concept. Now consider a falling object. It accelerates and then its speed becomes a constant. This happens when the force of gravity is just offset by the increase in the resistance as it falls though the air. It reaches its terminal velocity. *Its position in space changes at a constant rate.* This is a *dynamic equilibrium*. In economics, a market for a good or service is said to be in equilibrium when no participant in the market has any reason to alter his or her behaviour, so that there is no tendency for production or price in that market to change. This is a *static equilibrium*. If we think about *inflation* – the phenomenon of generally increasing prices for all goods and services – we will realise that the average rate at which prices rise over time is variable. Inflation measures the average rate of increase of prices. The causes of inflation are considered in macroeconomics. When these are such that inflation is constant (the average of prices is rising at a constant rate) we have a *dynamic equilibrium* in prices.

**equilibrium** a system is in equilibrium when there is no tendency for it to change

If we want to determine the final position of a ball hanging from a spring, we need to find the point at which the forces of gravity and spring tension are balanced and the system is in equilibrium. Similarly, if we want to find the price at which a good will sell (which we will call the **equilibrium price**) and the quantity of it that will be sold (the **equilibrium quantity**), we need to find the equilibrium in the market for that good. The basic tools for finding the equilibrium in a market for a good are the supply and demand curves for that good. For reasons that we shall explain, the equilibrium price and equilibrium quantity of a good are the price and quantity at which the supply and demand curves for the good intersect. For the hypothetical supply and demand curves shown earlier for the pizza market, the equilibrium price will therefore be €3 per slice and the equilibrium quantity of pizza sold will be 12,000 slices per day, as shown in Fig. 3.3.

**equilibrium price** and **equilibrium quantity** the values of price and quantity for which quantity supplied and quantity demanded are equal

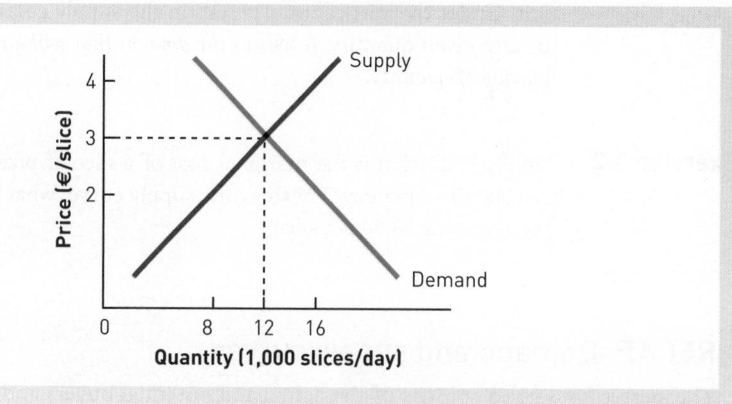


**Figure 3.3 The Equilibrium Price and Quantity of Pizza.** The equilibrium quantity and price of a product are the values that correspond to the intersection of the supply and demand curves for that product.

In Fig. 3.3, note that at the equilibrium price of €3 per slice, both sellers and buyers are 'satisfied' in the following sense: buyers are buying exactly the quantity of pizza they wish to buy at that price (12,000 slices per day) and sellers are selling exactly the quantity of pizza they wish to sell (also 12,000 slices per day). And since they are satisfied in this sense, *neither buyers nor sellers face any incentives to change their behaviour*.

**market equilibrium** occurs in a market when all buyers and sellers are satisfied with their respective quantities at the market price

**excess supply** the amount by which quantity supplied exceeds quantity demanded when the price of a good exceeds the equilibrium price

Note the limited sense of the term 'satisfied' in the definition of **market equilibrium**. It does not mean that sellers would not be pleased to receive a price higher than the equilibrium price. Rather, it means only that they are able to sell all they wish to sell at that price. Similarly, to say that buyers are 'satisfied' at the equilibrium price doesn't mean that they would not be happy to pay less than the equilibrium price. Rather, it means only that they are able to buy exactly as many units of the good as they wish to at the equilibrium price.

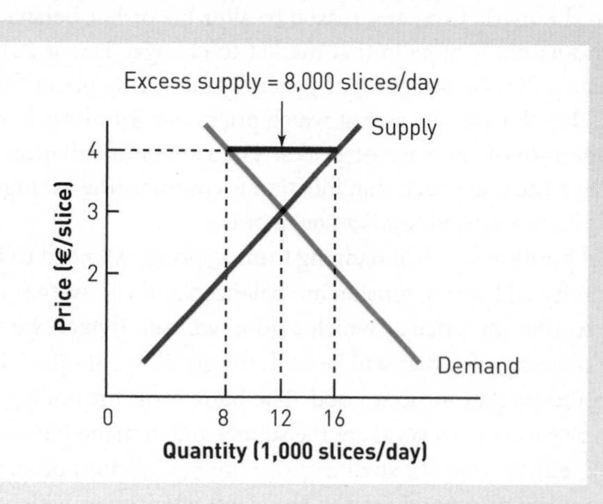


**Figure 3.4 Excess Supply.** When price exceeds the equilibrium price, there is excess supply, or surplus, the difference between quantity supplied and quantity demanded.

Note also that if the price of pizza in our market were anything other than €3 per slice, either buyers or sellers would frustrated. Suppose, for example, that the price of pizza were €4 per slice, as shown in Fig. 3.4. At that price, buyers wish to buy only 8,000 slices per day, but sellers wish to sell 16,000. And since no one can force someone to buy a slice of pizza against her wishes, this means that buyers will buy only the 8,000 slices they wish to buy. So when the price exceeds the equilibrium price, it is sellers who end up being frustrated. At a price of €4 in this example, they are left with an **excess supply** of 8,000 slices per day.

Conversely, suppose that the price of pizza were less than the equilibrium price – say, €2 per slice. As shown in Fig. 3.5, buyers want to buy 16,000 slices per day at that price, whereas sellers want to sell only 8,000. And since sellers

**excess demand** the amount by which quantity demanded exceeds quantity supplied when the price of a good lies below the equilibrium price

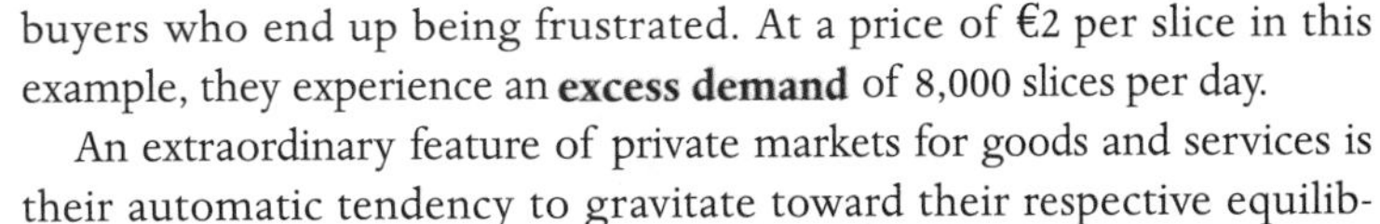

cannot be forced to sell pizza against their wishes, this time it is the buyers who end up being frustrated. At a price of €2 per slice in this example, they experience an **excess demand** of 8,000 slices per day.

An extraordinary feature of private markets for goods and services is their automatic tendency to gravitate toward their respective equilibrium prices and quantities. The mechanisms by which this happens are implicit in our definitions of excess supply and excess demand. Suppose, for example, that the price of pizza in our hypothetical market was €4 per slice, leading to excess supply, as shown in Fig. 3.4. Because sellers are frustrated in the sense of wanting to sell more pizza than buyers wish to buy, sellers have an incentive to take whatever steps they can to increase their sales. The simplest strategy available to them is to cut their price slightly. Thus, if one seller reduced his price from €4 to, say, €3.95 per slice, he would attract many of the buyers who had been paying €4 per slice for pizza supplied by other sellers. Those sellers, in order to recover their lost business, would then have an incentive to match the price cut. But notice that if all sellers lowered their prices to €3.95 per slice, there would still be considerable excess supply. So sellers would face continuing incentives to cut their prices. This pressure to cut prices will not go away until price falls all the way to €3 per slice.

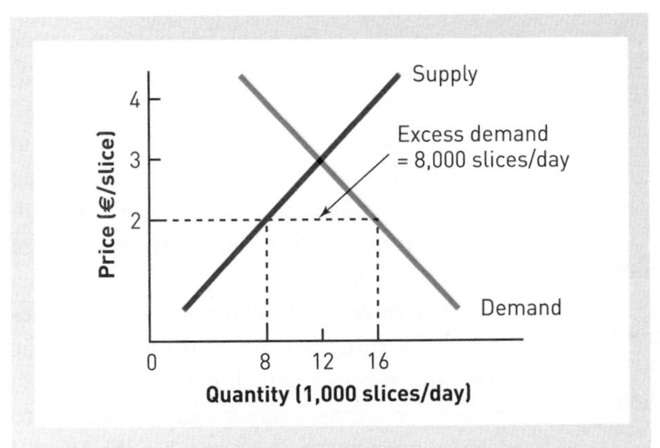


**Figure 3.5 Excess Demand.** When price lies below the equilibrium price, there is excess demand, the difference between quantity demanded and quantity supplied.

Conversely, suppose that price starts out less than the equilibrium price – say, €2 per slice. This time it is buyers who are frustrated. A person who can't get all the pizza she wants at a price of €2 per slice has an incentive to offer a higher price, hoping to obtain pizza that would otherwise have been sold to other buyers. And sellers, for their part, will be only too happy to post higher prices as long as queues of frustrated buyers remain.

The upshot is that price has a tendency to gravitate to its equilibrium level under conditions of either excess supply or excess demand. And when price reaches its equilibrium level, both buyers and sellers are 'satisfied' in the technical sense of being able to buy or sell precisely the amounts of their choosing.

**Example 3.1** **Samples of points on the demand and supply curves of a pizza market are provided in Table 3.1. Graph the demand and supply curves for this market, and find its equilibrium price and quantity.**

| Demand for pizza Price (€/slice) | Supply of pizza Quantity demanded (1,000 slices/day) | Price (€/slice) | Quantity supplied (1,000 slices/day) |
|---|---|---|---|
| 1 | 8 | 1 | 2 |
| 2 | 6 | 2 | 4 |
| 3 | 4 | 3 | 6 |
| 4 | 2 | 4 | 8 |

**Table 3.1** Points along the Demand and Supply Curves of a Pizza Market

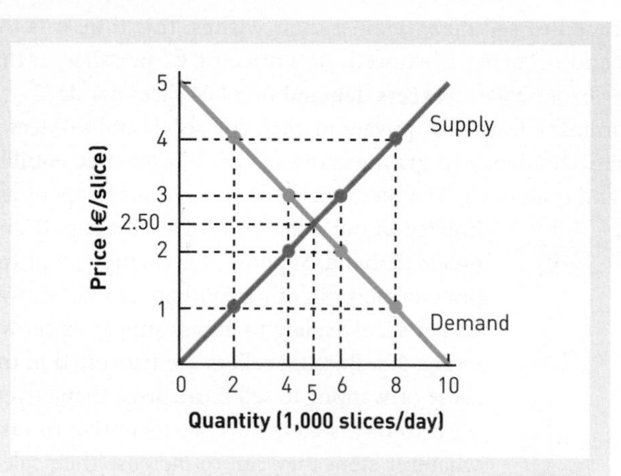


**Figure 3.6 Graphing Supply and Demand and Finding the Equilibrium Price and Quantity.** To graph the demand and supply curve, plot the relevant points given in Table 3.1 and then join them with a line. The equilibrium price and quantity occur at the intersection of these curves.

The points in Table 3.1 are plotted in Fig. 3.6. and then joined to indicate the supply and demand curves for this market. These curves intersect to yield an equilibrium price of €2.50 per slice and an equilibrium quantity of 5,000 slices per day.

We emphasise that market equilibrium does not necessarily produce an ideal outcome for all market participants. Thus, in Example 3.1, market participants are satisfied with the amount of pizza they buy and sell at a price of €2.50 per slice, but for a poor buyer this may signify little more than that he *can't* buy additional pizza without sacrificing other more highly valued purchases.

Indeed, buyers with extremely low incomes often have difficulty purchasing even basic goods and services, which has prompted governments in almost every society to attempt to ease the burdens of the poor. Yet the laws of supply and demand cannot simply be repealed by an act of the legislature. In the next section we will see that when legislators attempt to prevent markets from reaching their equilibrium prices and quantities, they often do more harm than good.

## Economic naturalist 3.1 Do prices actually adjust to offset excess demand or supply?

Two examples from the motor trade show that they do ... but sometimes do so in a covert fashion. The Morgan is a traditional sports car produced by a small UK specialist producer with very limited production capacity. It has traditionally been sold at a price that indicates excess demand: there is a long waiting list for a car. What happens in these circumstances? One thing that has been observed is people buying freshly produced Morgans at a premium from those who had queued to buy one new. Unusually, used car prices then exceed new prices. Those who hold on to their cars rather than sell them on, of course, are paying a significantly higher price than that handed over to the Morgan's producer. They pay in waiting time, and, perhaps, in the form of booking deposit paid up-front. And they forgo any premium that they might get by selling it on. So, even if the list price does not change, the real price does. A more interesting question is why the Morgan's producers do not simply raise the price in the first place and capture the extra price per unit sold. There are several factors that may be at play here. One is that selling at the *market-clearing price* might mean incurring marketing costs. A second is that excess demand means certainty of sales, which means lower inventory costs for the producer. Another factor is that perceived depreciation is lower, which supports demand.

The other example is what happens at the end of a car model's life cycle. The prospect of a newer model arriving in the showrooms, coupled to competition from new offerings by rival producers, drives demand down and makes it difficult to sustain sales, a particular problem if production volumes are not easily adjusted. Distributors and dealers have difficulty in moving the stock that they have bought from the producer. Frequently (but not always) producers do not announce lower prices to clear the market (eliminate excess supply). Instead, they offer specification improvements, easy credit terms, deferred payment, enhanced trade-in values and so on. In reality, of course, these are just disguised reductions in price. So why not just cut price? The best answer is a marketing one: people who bought the car six months earlier will not be amused to see advertisements implying that they had 'paid too much', and are unlikely to repeat the mistake by buying that producer's models in the future.

## Rent controls reconsidered

Consider again the market for rental housing units in New York, and suppose that the demand and supply curves for one-bedroom apartments are as shown in Fig. 3.7. This market, left alone, would reach an equilibrium monthly rent of $1,600, at which 2 million one-bedroom apartments would be rented. Both landlords and tenants would be 'satisfied', in the sense that they would not wish to rent either more or fewer units at that price.

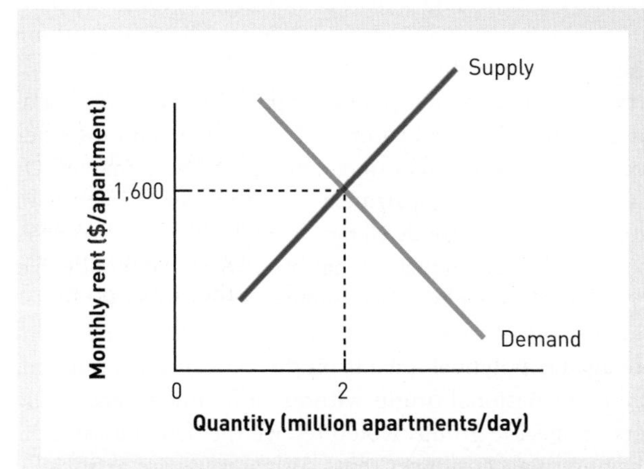


**Figure 3.7 An Unregulated Housing Market.** For the supply and demand curves shown, the equilibrium monthly rent is $1,600, and 2 million apartments will be rented at that price.

This would not necessarily mean, of course, that all is well and good. Many potential tenants, for example, might simply be unable to afford a rent of $1,600 per month and thus be forced to remain homeless (or to move out of the city to a cheaper location). Suppose that, acting purely out of benign motives, legislators made it unlawful for landlords to charge more than $800 per month for one-bedroom apartments. Their stated aim in enacting this law was that no person should have to remain homeless because decent housing was unaffordable.

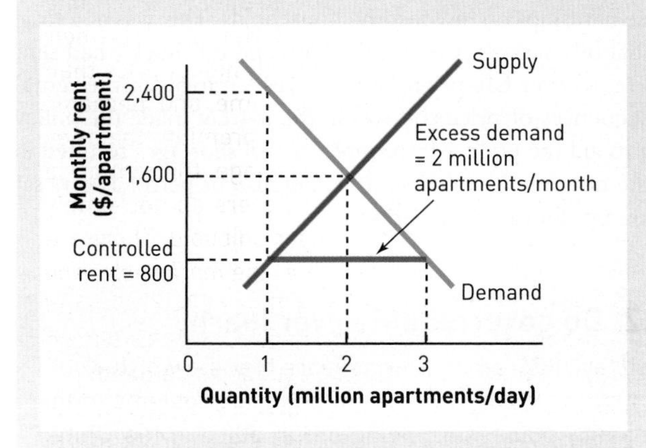


**Figure 3.8 Rent Controls.** When rents are prohibited from rising to the equilibrium level, the result is excess demand in the housing market.

But note in Fig. 3.8 that when rents for one-bedroom apartments are prevented from rising above $800 per month, landlords are willing to supply only 1 million apartments per month, 1 million fewer than at the equilibrium monthly rent of $1,600. Note also that at the controlled rent of $800 per month, tenants want to rent 3 million one-bedroom apartments per month. (For example, many people who would have decided to live across the Hudson River in New Jersey rather than pay $1,600 a month in New York will now choose to live in the city.) So when rents are prevented from rising above $800 per month, we see an excess demand for one-bedroom apartments of 2 million units each month. Put another way, the rent controls result in a housing shortage of 2 million units each month. What is more, the number of apartments actually available *declines* by 1 million units per month.

If the housing market were completely unregulated, the immediate response to such a high level of excess demand would be for rents to rise sharply. But here the law prevents them from rising above $800. Many other ways exist, however, in which the pressures of excess demand can make themselves felt. For instance, owners will quickly learn that they are free to spend less on maintaining the quality of their rental units. After all, if there are scores of renters knocking at the door of each vacant flat, a landlord has considerable room to manoeuvre. Leaking pipes, peeling paint, broken central heating and other problems are less likely to receive prompt attention – or, indeed, any attention at all – when rents are set well below market-clearing levels.

Nor are reduced availability of apartments and poorer maintenance of existing apartments the only difficulties. With an offering of only 1 million apartments per month, we see in Fig. 3.8 that there are renters who would be willing to pay as much as $2,400 per month for an apartment. This pressure almost always finds ways, legal or illegal, of expressing itself. In New York, for example, it is not uncommon to see 'finder's fees' or 'key deposits' as high as several thousand dollars. Owners who cannot charge a market-clearing rent for their apartments also have the option of putting the properties up for sale, thus realising something close to their open market rental value as a lump sum.

Even when rent-controlled apartment owners do not raise their prices in these ways, serious misallocations can result. For instance, ill-suited room-mates often remain together despite their constant bickering, because each is reluctant to re-enter the housing market. Or a widow might steadfastly remain in her seven-room apartment even after her children have left home, because it is much cheaper than alternative dwellings not covered by rent control. It would be much better for all concerned if she relinquished that space to a larger family that valued it more highly. But under rent controls, she has no economic incentive to do so.

There is also another more insidious cost of rent controls. In markets without rent controls, landlords cannot discriminate against potential tenants on the basis of race, religion, sexual orientation, physical disability, or national origin without suffering an economic penalty. Refusal to rent to members of specific groups would reduce the demand for their apartments, which would mean having to accept lower rents. When rents are artificially pegged below their equilibrium level, however, the resulting excess demand for flats enables landlords to engage in discrimination with no further economic penalty.

Rent controls are not the only instance in which governments have attempted to repeal the law of supply and demand in the interest of helping the poor. During the late 1970s, for example, several governments on both sides of the Atlantic tried to hold the prices of oil products (petrol, central heating oil, etc.) below their equilibrium levels out of concern that higher prices imposed unacceptable hardships on low-income households. This was at a time when supply interruptions in global oil markets (the so-called 'second oil shock') had sent prices up from about €15 per barrel to over €30 per barrel. As with controls in the rental housing market, unintended consequences of price controls in the market made the policy an extremely costly way of trying to aid the poor. For example, petrol shortages resulted in long queues at the pumps – a waste not only of valuable time, but also of petrol as cars sat idling or moving slowly up to the pumps for extended periods.

## Economic naturalist 3.2 Do governments ever learn?

Apparently they do not. In late May 2004, amid growing fears that the world would face oil supply problems yet again as a consequence of political problems in the Near and Middle East, contingency plans were being put in place in the United Kingdom to deal with such an eventuality. Remembering the shortages in 1979–80, if press reports are to be believed, the British government started to prepare for the introduction of rationing procedures to allocate scarce supplies, naturally giving priority to public service demand for fuel. Ration books, limited entitlements, restrictions on sales would all play their part in ensuring that the quantity available was just equal to the demand for it. Why not simply let prices do the job? The answer is that the government believed that this would be unfair, since some people with a lower willingness and ability to pay would obtain less petrol, while those who were prepared to pay more would get more. This was seen as posing political problems, so the government prepared to take steps to use rationing. Would it be unfair to suggest that another reason might influence the government: the government could pre-empt supplies for its own preferred purposes while paying less than the going price?

In their opposition to rent controls and similar measures, are economists revealing a total lack of concern for the poor? Although this claim is sometimes made by those who don't understand the issues, or who stand to benefit in some way from government regulations, there is little justification for it. Economists simply realise that there are *much more effective ways to help poor people than to try to give them apartments and other goods at artificially low prices.*

One straightforward approach would be to give the poor additional income and let them decide for themselves how to spend it. True, there are also practical difficulties involved in transferring additional purchasing power into the hands of the poor – most importantly, the difficulty of targeting cash to the genuinely needy without weakening others' incentives to fend for themselves. But there are practical ways to overcome this difficulty. For example, for far less than the waste caused by price controls, the government could afford generous subsidies to the wages of the working poor and could sponsor public service employment for those who are unable to find jobs in the private sector.

Regulations that peg prices below equilibrium levels have far-reaching effects on market outcomes. Exercise 3.3 asks you to consider what happens when a price control is established at a level above the equilibrium price.

**Exercise 3.3** In the rental housing market whose demand and supply curves are shown below, what will be the effect of a law that prevents rents from rising above €1,200 per month?

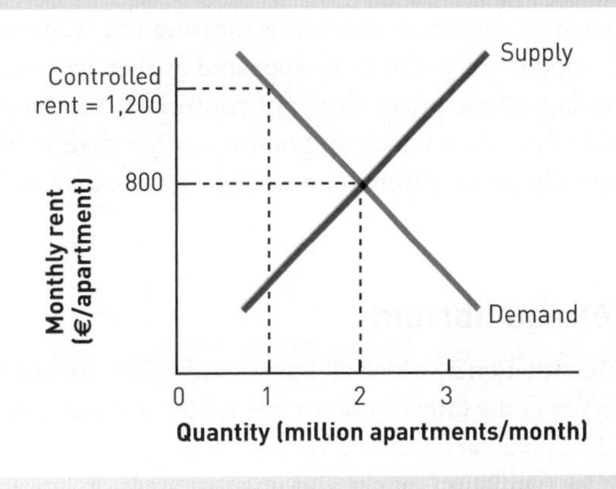

## Pizza price controls?

The sources of the contrast between the rent-controlled housing market and the largely unregulated food markets in New York can be seen more vividly by trying to imagine what would happen if concern for the poor led a city's leaders to implement price controls on pizza. Suppose, for example, that the supply and demand curves for pizza are as shown in Fig. 3.9, and that the city imposes a **price ceiling** of €2 per slice, making it unlawful to charge more than that amount. At €2 per slice, buyers want to buy 16,000 slices per day, but sellers want to sell only 8,000.

**price ceiling** a maximum allowable price, specified by law

At a price of €2 per slice, every pizza restaurant in the city will have long queues of buyers trying unsuccessfully to purchase pizza. Frustrated buyers will behave rudely to cooks, who will respond in kind. Friends of restaurant managers will begin to get preferential treatment. Devious pricing strategies will begin to emerge (such as the €2 slice of pizza sold in combination with a €5 cup of Coke). Pizza will be made from poorer-quality ingredients. Rumours will begin to circulate about sources of black-market pizza. And so on.

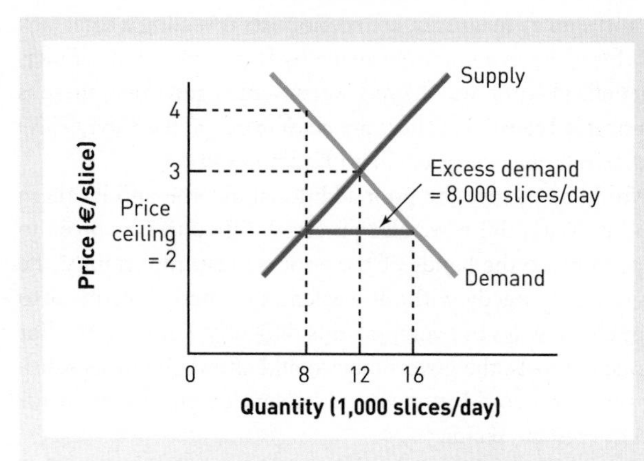


**Figure 3.9 Price Controls in the Pizza Market.** A price ceiling below the equilibrium price of pizza would result in excess demand for pizza.

The very idea of not being able to buy a pizza seems absurd, yet precisely such things happen routinely in markets in which prices are held below the equilibrium levels. For example, prior to the collapse of communist governments, it was considered normal in those countries for people to queue for hours to buy basic goods, while the politically connected had first choice of those goods that were available. Nor is this confined to the world of socialist planning. At one point during the 1970s a shortage of potatoes in Western Europe sent potato prices soaring. Potatoes had a high weighting in the procedure by which inflation was measured in Belgium. (This reflected the Belgian passion for *pommes frites*.) The Belgian government sought to hold down the consumer price index (CPI, the measure of inflation) by freezing the price of potatoes. The intervention was a great success, if 'success' is measured by what happened to the CPI. Unfortunately available supplies of potatoes disappeared as they were exported to the Netherlands, France and Germany where prices were not controlled. So, the price index didn't rise ... because people couldn't get their hands on potatoes (other than in black-market transactions). *Pommes frites* simply disappeared from menus. The controls were rapidly abandoned.

## RECAP Market equilibrium

*Market equilibrium*, the situation in which all buyers and sellers are satisfied with their respective quantities at the market price, occurs at the intersection of the supply and demand curves. The corresponding price and quantity are called the *equilibrium price* and the *equilibrium quantity*.

Unless prevented by regulation, prices and quantities are driven toward their equilibrium values by the actions of buyers and sellers. If the price is initially too high, so that there is excess supply, frustrated sellers will cut their price in order to sell more. If the price is initially too low, so that there is excess demand, competition among buyers drives the price upward. This process continues until equilibrium is reached.

## Predicting and explaining changes in prices and quantities

If we know how the factors that govern supply and demand curves are changing, we can make informed predictions about how prices and the corresponding quantities will change. But when describing changing circumstances in the marketplace, we must take care to recognise some important terminological distinctions. For example, we must distinguish between the meanings of the seemingly similar expressions **change in the quantity demanded** and **change in demand.**

**change in the quantity demanded** a movement along the demand curve that occurs in response to a change in price

**change in demand** a shift of the entire demand curve

When we speak of a 'change in the quantity demanded', this means the change in the quantity that people wish to buy that occurs in response to a change in price. For instance, Fig. 3.10(a) depicts an increase in the quantity demanded that occurs in response to a reduction in the price of tuna. When the price falls from €5 to €4 per can, the quantity demanded rises from 2,000 to 4,000 cans per day. By contrast, when we speak of a 'change in demand', this means a *shift in the entire demand curve*. For example, Fig. 3.10(b) depicts an increase in demand, meaning that at every price the quantity demanded is higher than before. In summary, a 'change in the quantity demanded' refers to a movement *along* the demand curve, and a 'change in demand' means a *shift* of the entire curve.

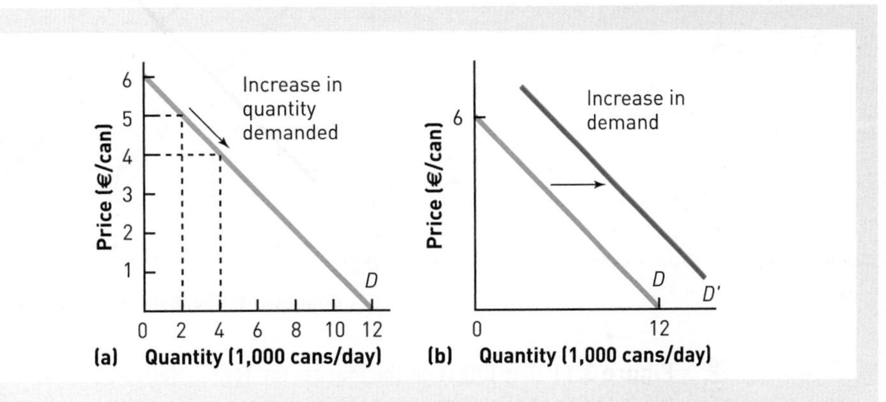


**Figure 3.10 An Increase in the Quantity Demanded versus an Increase in Demand.** (a) An increase in quantity demanded describes a downward movement along the demand curve as price falls. (b) An increase in demand describes an outward shift of the demand curve.

**change in supply** a shift of the entire supply curve

**change in the quantity supplied** a movement along the supply curve that occurs in response to a change in price

A similar terminological distinction applies on the supply side of the market. A **change in supply** means a shift in the entire supply curve, whereas a **change in the quantity supplied** refers to a movement along the supply curve.

Alfred Marshall's supply and demand model is one of the most useful tools of the economic naturalist. Once we understand the forces that govern the placements of supply and demand curves, we are suddenly in a position to make sense of a host of interesting observations in the world around us.

### Shifts in demand

To get a better feel for how the supply and demand model enables us to predict and explain price and quantity movements, it is helpful to begin with a few simple examples. Example 3.2 illustrates a shift in demand that results from events outside the particular market itself.

### Example 3.2 What will happen to the equilibrium price and quantity of tennis balls if court-rental fees decline?

Let the initial supply and demand curves for tennis balls be as shown by the curves *S* and *D* in Fig. 3.11, where the resulting equilibrium price and quantity are €1 per ball and 40 million balls per month, respectively. Tennis courts and tennis balls are what economists call **complements**, goods that are more valuable when used *in combination* than when used alone. Tennis balls, for example, would be of little value if there were no tennis courts on which to play. As tennis courts become cheaper to use, people will respond by playing more tennis, and this will increase their demand for tennis balls. A decline in court-rental fees will thus shift the demand curve for tennis balls rightward to *D*′. (A 'rightward shift' of a demand curve can also be described as an 'upward shift'. These distinctions correspond, respectively, to the horizontal and vertical interpretations of the demand curve.)

**complements** two goods are complements in consumption if an increase in the price of one causes a leftward shift in the demand curve for the other (or if a decrease causes a rightward shift)

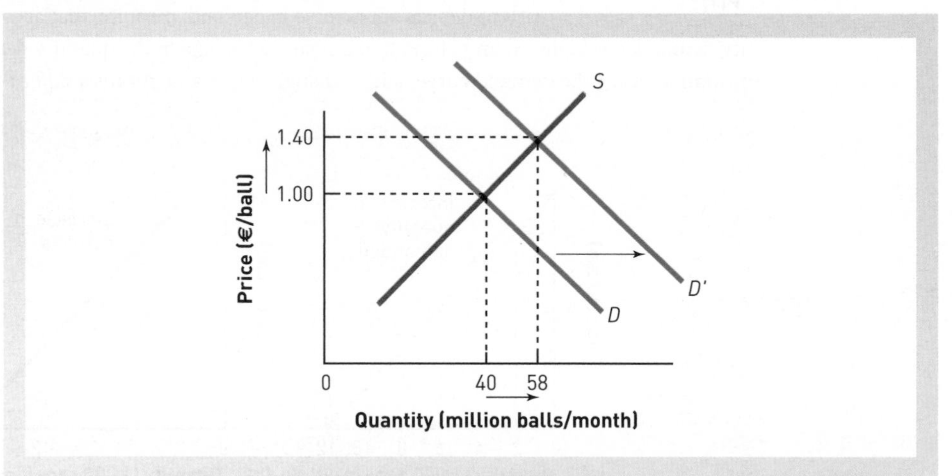


**Figure 3.11 The Effect on the Market for Tennis Balls of a Decline in Court-Rental Fees.** When the price of a complement falls, demand shifts right, causing equilibrium price and quantity to rise.

Note in Fig. 3.11 that for the illustrative demand shift shown, the new equilibrium price of tennis balls, €1.40, is higher than the original price, and the new equilibrium quantity, 58 million balls per month, is higher than the original quantity.

### Example 3.3 What will happen to the equilibrium price and quantity of overnight letter courier service as the price of Internet access falls?

Suppose the initial supply and demand curves for overnight letter deliveries are as shown by the curves *S* and *D* in Fig. 3.12, and that the resulting equilibrium price and quantity are denoted *P* and *Q*. Email messages and overnight letters are examples of what economists call **substitutes** – meaning that, in many applications at least, the two serve similar functions. When two goods or services are substitutes, a decrease in the price of one will cause a leftward shift in the demand curve for the other. (A 'leftward shift' in a demand curve can also be described as a 'downward shift'.) Diagrammatically, the demand curve for overnight delivery service shifts from *D* to *D*′ in Fig. 3.12.

**substitutes** two goods are substitutes in consumption if an increase in the price of one causes a rightward shift in the demand curve for the other (or if a decrease causes a leftward shift)

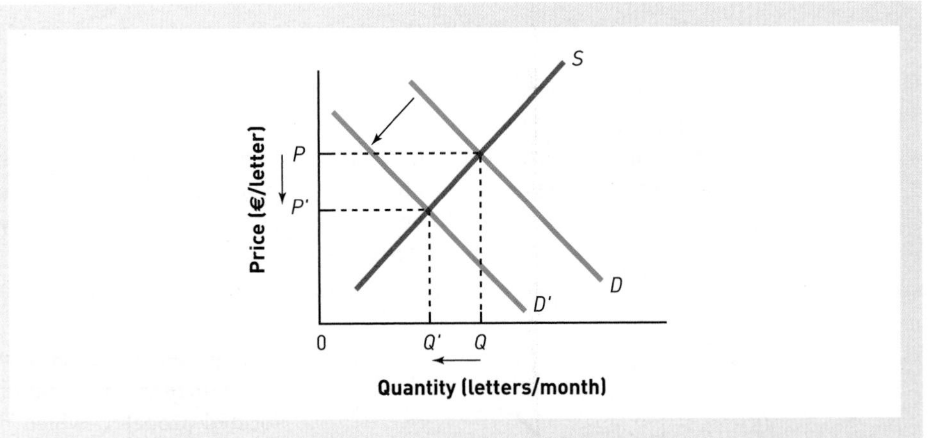


**Figure 3.12 The Effect on the Market for Overnight Letter Delivery of a Decline in the Price of Internet Access.** When the price of a substitute falls, demand shifts left, causing equilibrium price and quantity to fall.

As Fig. 3.12 shows, both the new equilibrium price, $P'$, and the new equilibrium quantity, $Q'$, are lower than the initial values, $P$ and $Q$. Cheaper Internet access probably won't put Federal Express and UPS out of business, but it will definitely cost them many customers.

To summarise, economists define goods as substitutes if an increase in the price of one causes a rightward shift in the demand curve for the other. By contrast, goods are complements if an increase in the price of one causes a leftward shift in the demand curve for the other.

The concepts of substitutes and complements enable you to answer questions such as that posed in Exercise 3.4.

**Exercise 3.4** How will a decline in air fares between Britain and France affect cross-Channel ferry fares and the price of hotel rooms in resort communities in France?

Demand curves are shifted not just by changes in the prices of substitutes and complements but also by other factors that change the amounts that people are willing to pay for a given good or service. One of the most important such factors is *income*.

## Economic naturalist 3.3 When a city's public transport authority opens or upgrades a rapid transit rail line, why do property prices and rental costs rise close to stations on the line relative to those in other locations in the city?

More efficient public transport reduces travel costs for people inversely in relation to their distance from the transport facility. That is equivalent to an increase in their real incomes even if their money incomes remain constant. Ownership of, or a lease on, property close to the rail line is what increases their real income. Hence, the market price of such property, whether for sale or rent, will rise since it confers this increase in real incomes on the occupants because the demand for such property increases relative to the demand for other property. Suppose the initial demand and supply curves for typical properties close to the rail line are as shown in Fig. 3.13. Following the investment in the improved transport structure, some people who live further away will be willing and able to use part of their extra income to bid for the more conveniently located properties, and those who already live in such apartments will be willing and able to pay more to keep them. The effect of transport structure investment is thus to shift the demand curve for conveniently located properties to the right, as indicated by the demand curve labelled *D'* in Fig. 3.13. As a result, both the equilibrium price and quantity of such properties, *P'* and *Q'*, will be higher than before.

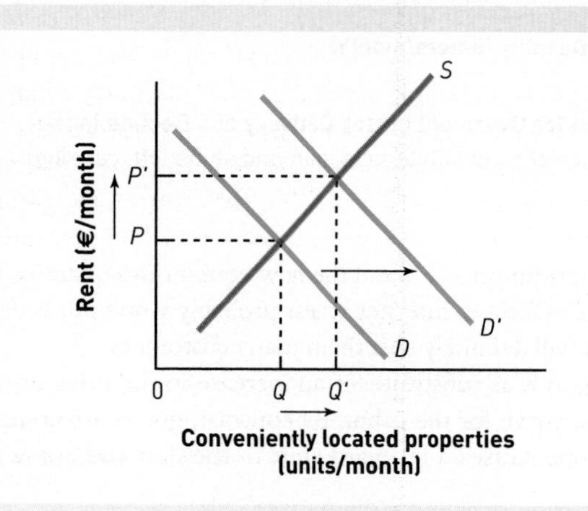


**Figure 3.13 The Effect of Improved Transport Structure on the Rent for Conveniently Located Properties.** An increase in transport structure shifts demand for a normal good to the right, causing equilibrium price and quantity to rise.

It might seem natural to ask how there could be an increase in the number of conveniently located property, which might appear to be fixed by the constraints of geography. But one must never underestimate the ingenuity of sellers when they confront an opportunity to make money by supplying more of something that people want. For example, if rents rose sufficiently, some landlords might respond by converting warehouse space to residential use. Or perhaps people with cars who do not place high value on living near a station might sell their properties, thereby making them available to people eager to rent them or buy them. (Note that these responses constitute movements *along* the supply curve of conveniently located property, as opposed to *shifts* in that supply curve.)

When incomes increase, the demand curves for most goods will behave like the demand curve for conveniently located property, and in recognition of that fact, economists have chosen to call such goods **normal goods**.

**normal good** one whose demand curve shifts rightward when the incomes of buyers increase and leftward when the incomes of buyers decrease

**inferior good** one whose demand curve shifts leftward when the incomes of buyers increase and rightward when the incomes of buyers decrease

Not all goods are normal goods, however. In fact, the demand curves for some goods actually shift leftward when income goes up, and such goods are called **inferior goods**.

When would having more money tend to make you want to buy less of something? In general, this will happen in the case of goods for which there exist attractive substitutes that sell for only slightly higher prices. Property in an unsafe, inconveniently located neighbourhood are an example. Most residents would choose to move out of such neighbourhoods as soon as they could afford to, which means that an increase in income would cause the demand for such property to shift leftward.

Ground or minced beef with high fat content is another example of an inferior good. For health reasons, most people prefer grades of meat with a low fat content, and when they do buy high-fat meats it is usually a sign of budgetary pressure. When people in this situation receive higher incomes, they usually switch quickly to leaner grades of meat.

Preferences, or tastes, are another important factor that determines whether a given good will meet the cost–benefit test. Steven Spielberg's film *Jurassic Park* appeared to kindle a powerful, if previously latent, preference among children for toy dinosaurs. When this film was

### Economic naturalist 3.4 If it is true that investments in public transport reduce transport costs and raise the real incomes of those able to use it, why did investment in commuter public transport decline in the 1950s to 1970s in so many European and American cities?

As long as road space was available, and especially as long as driving costs were relatively low, as people became richer they opted to consume less public transport and spend more on transport by car. This was more common in Britain, Ireland and America than in countries such as France or Italy, but even there commuting by car became more usual. The technical characteristics of using a car (flexibility, convenience, privacy, comfort, speed) dominated those of public transport. Consequently, as real incomes increased, people switched to private transport. Public transport was an 'inferior' good. The demand for investment in public transport since the 1980s is in part a consequence of environmental considerations, but also reflects the fact that the relative advantage of using a car has decreased as more people use it, with increased travel time and congestion costs associated with commuting by car being the main drivers of the demand for an alternative mode of transport.

first released, the demand for such toys shifted sharply to the right. And the same children who couldn't find enough dinosaur toys suddenly seemed to lose interest in toy designs involving horses and other modern animals, whose respective demand curves shifted sharply to the left.

Expectations about the future are another factor that may cause demand curves to shift. If Apple Macintosh users hear a credible rumour, for example, that a cheaper or significantly upgraded model will be introduced next month, the demand curve for the current model is likely to shift leftward.

## Shifts in the supply curve

The preceding examples involved changes that gave rise to shifts in demand curves. Next, we shall look at what happens when supply curves shift. Because the supply curve is based on costs of production, anything that changes production costs will shift the supply curve, and hence will result in a new equilibrium quantity and price.

### **Example 3.4** What will happen to the equilibrium price and quantity of skateboards if the price of fibreglass, a substance used for making skateboards, rises?

Suppose the initial supply and demand curves for skateboards are as shown by the curves *S* and *D* in Fig. 3.14, resulting in an equilibrium price and quantity of €60 per skateboard and 1,000 skateboards per month, respectively. Since fibreglass is one of the ingredients used to produce skateboards, the effect of an increase in the price of fibreglass will be to raise the marginal cost of producing skateboards. How will this affect the supply curve of skateboards? Recall that the supply curve is upward-sloping because when the price of skateboards is low, only those potential sellers whose marginal cost of making skateboards is low can sell boards profitably, whereas at higher prices those with higher marginal costs can also enter the market profitably (again, the Low-Hanging-Fruit Principle from Chapter 2). So if the cost of one of the ingredients used to produce skateboards rises, the number of potential sellers who can profitably sell skateboards at any given price will fall. And this, in turn, implies a leftward shift in the supply curve for skateboards. Note that a 'leftward shift' in a supply curve can also be viewed as an 'upward shift' in the same curve. The first corresponds to the *horizontal* interpretation of the supply curve, while the second corresponds to the *vertical* interpretation. We shall use these expressions to mean exactly the same thing. The new supply curve (after the price of fibreglass rises) is the curve labelled *S′* in Fig. 3.14.

Does an increase in the cost of fibreglass have any effect on the demand curve for skateboards? The demand curve tells us how many skateboards buyers wish to purchase at each price. Any given buyer is willing to purchase a skateboard if her reservation price for it exceeds its market price. And since each buyer's reservation price, which is based on the benefits of owning a skateboard, does not depend on the price of fibreglass, there should be no shift in the demand curve for skateboards.

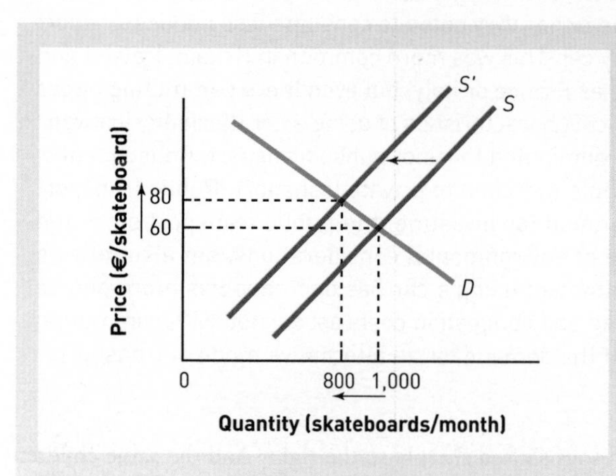


**Figure 3.14 The Effect on the Skateboard Market of an Increase in the Price of Fibregalss.** When input prices rise, supply shifts left, causing equilibrium price to rise and equilibrium quantity to fall.

In Fig. 3.14, we can now see what happens when the supply curve shifts leftward and the demand curve remains unchanged. For the illustrative supply curve shown, the new equilibrium price of skateboards, €80, is higher than the original price, and the new equilibrium quantity, 800 per month, is lower than the original quantity. (These new equilibrium values are merely illustrative. There is insufficient information provided in Example 3.4 to determine their exact values.) People who don't place a value of at least €80 on owning a skateboard will choose to spend their money on something else.

The effects on equilibrium price and quantity run in the opposite direction whenever marginal costs of production decline, as illustrated in Example 3.5.

**Example 3.5** What will happen to the equilibrium price and quantity of new houses if the wage rate of carpenters falls?

Suppose that the initial supply and demand curves for new houses are as shown by the curves *S* and *D* in Fig. 3.15, resulting in an equilibrium price of €120,000 per house and an equilibrium quantity of 40 houses per month. A decline in the wage rate of carpenters reduces the marginal cost of making new houses, and this means that, for any given price of houses, more builders can profitably serve the market than before. Diagrammatically, this means a rightward shift in the supply curve of houses, from *S* to *S′*in Fig. 3.15 (A 'rightward shift' in the supply curve can also be described as a 'downward shift'.)

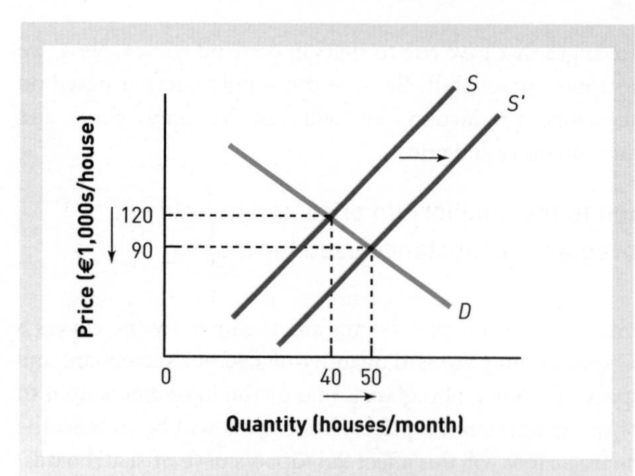


**Figure 3.15 The Effect on the Market for New Houses of a Decline in Carpenters' Wage Rates.** When input prices fall, supply shifts right, causing equilibrium price to fall and equilibrium quantity to rise.

Does a decrease in the wage rate of carpenters have any effect on the demand curve for houses? The demand curve tells us how many houses buyers wish to purchase at each price. Because carpenters are now earning less than before, the maximum amount that they are willing to pay for houses may fall, which would imply a leftward shift in the demand curve for houses. But because carpenters make up only a tiny fraction of all potential home buyers, we may assume that this shift is negligible. Thus a reduction in carpenters' wages produces a significant rightward shift in the supply curve of houses, but no appreciable shift in the demand curve.

We see from Fig. 3.15 that the new equilibrium price, €90,000 per house, is lower than the original price, and the new equilibrium quantity, 50 houses per month, is higher than the original quantity.

Examples 3.4 and 3.5 both involved changes in the cost of an *ingredient*, or *input*, in the production of the good in question – fibreglass in the production of skateboards and carpenters' labour in the production of houses. As Economic naturalist 3.5 illustrates, supply curves also shift when *technology* changes.

## Economic naturalist 3.5 Why do major undergraduate essays, assignments and projects go through so many more revisions today than in the 1970s?

In the days before word processors were in widespread use, students could not make even minor revisions in their essays or assignments without having to retype their entire manuscripts from scratch. The availability of word-processing technology has, of course, radically changed the picture. Instead of having to retype the entire draft, now only the changes need be entered.

In Fig. 3.16, the curves labelled *S* and *D* depict the supply and demand curves for revisions in the days before word processing, and the curve *S*´ depicts the supply curve for revisions today. As Fig. 3.16 shows, the result is not only a sharp decline in the price per revision, but also a corresponding increase in the equilibrium number of revisions.

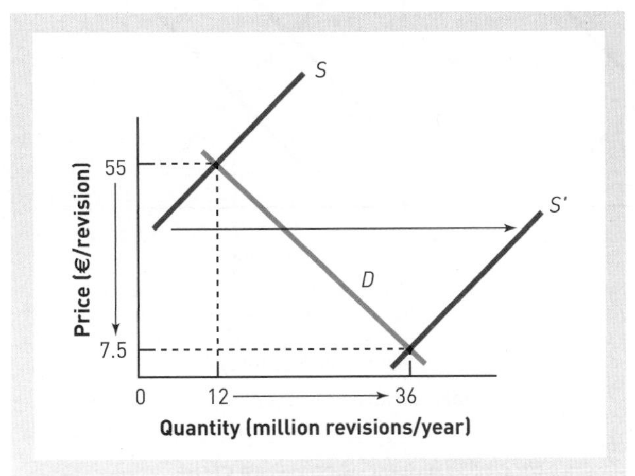


**Figure 3.16 The Effect of Technical Change on the Market for Essay Revisions.** When a new technology reduces the cost of production, supply shifts right, causing equilibrium quantity to rise.

Note that in the preceding discussion we implicitly assumed that students purchased typing services in a market. In fact, however, many students type their own essays or assignments. Does that make a difference? Even if no money actually changes hands, students pay a price when they revise their essays – namely, the opportunity cost of the time it takes to perform that task. Because technology has radically reduced that cost, we would expect to see a large increase in the number of essay revisions even if most students type their own work.

Changes in input prices and technology are two of the most important factors that give rise to shifts in supply curves. In the case of agricultural commodities, *weather* may be another important factor, with favourable conditions shifting the supply curves of such products to the right, and unfavourable conditions shifting them to the left. (Weather may also affect the supply curves of non-agricultural products through its effects on the national transportation system.) Expectations of future price changes may also shift current supply curves, as when the expectation of poor crops from a current drought causes suppliers to withhold supplies from existing stocks in the hope of selling at higher prices in the future. Changes in the number of *sellers* in the market can also cause supply curves to shift.

## Four simple rules

For supply and demand curves that have the conventional slopes (upward-sloping for supply curves, downward-sloping for demand curves), the preceding examples illustrate the four basic rules that govern how shifts in supply and demand affect equilibrium prices and quantities. These rules are summarised in Fig. 3.17 (a)–(d).

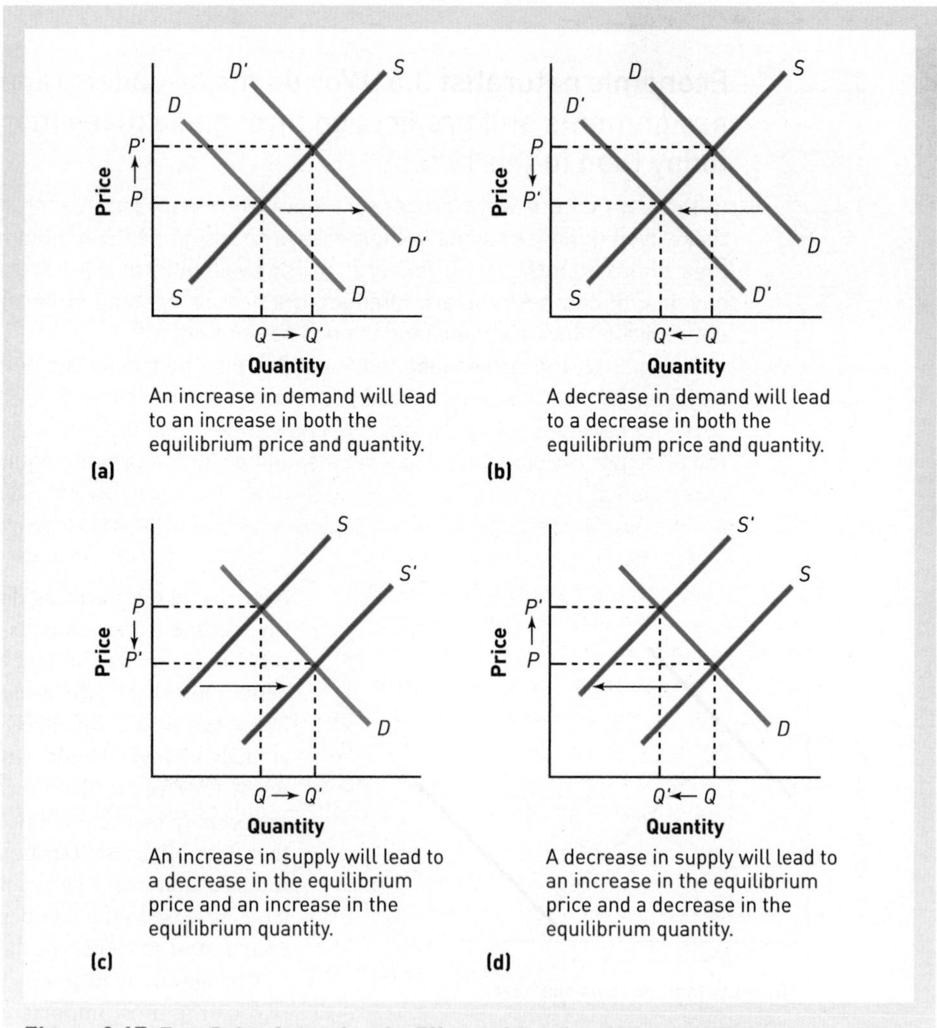

Price
Quantity
D'
S
D
P'
P
D'
S
D
Q → Q'
An increase in demand will lead to an increase in both the equilibrium price and quantity.
(a)
D
S
D'
P
P'
D
S
D'
Q' ← Q
A decrease in demand will lead to a decrease in both the equilibrium price and quantity.
(b)
S
S'
P
P'
D
Q → Q'
An increase in supply will lead to a decrease in the equilibrium price and an increase in the equilibrium quantity.
(c)
S'
S
P'
P
D
Q' ← Q
A decrease in supply will lead to an increase in the equilibrium price and a decrease in the equilibrium quantity.
(d)

**Figure 3.17** **Four Rules Governing the Effects of Supply and Demand Shifts.**

## RECAP Factors that shift supply and demand

- **Factors that cause an increase (rightward or upward shift) in demand:**

1. A decrease in the price of complements to the good or service.
2. An increase in the price of substitutes for the good or service.
3. An increase in income (for a normal good).
4. An increased preference by demanders for the good or service.
5. An increase in the population of potential buyers.
6. An expectation of higher prices in the future.

When these factors move in the opposite direction, demand will shift left.

- **Factors that cause an increase (rightward or downward shift) in supply:**

1. A decrease in the cost of materials, labour or other inputs used in the production of the good or service.
2. An improvement in technology that reduces the cost of producing the good or service.
3. A improvement in the weather (especially for agricultural products).
4. An increase in the number of suppliers.
5. An expectation of lower prices in the future.

When these factors move in the opposite direction, supply will shift left.

The qualitative rules summarised in Fig. 3.17 hold for supply or demand shifts of any magnitude, provided that the curves have their conventional slopes. But as the Example 3.6 demonstrates, when both supply and demand curves shift at the same time, the direction in which equilibrium price or quantity changes will depend on the *relative magnitudes* of the shifts.

### Example 3.6 How do shifts in *both* demand and supply affect equilibrium quantities and prices?

What will happen to the equilibrium price and quantity in the corn tortilla chip market if both of the following events occur: (1) researchers prove that the oils in which tortilla chips are fried are harmful to human health; and (2) the price of corn harvesting equipment falls?

The conclusion regarding the health effects of the oils will shift the demand for tortilla chips to the left, because many people who once bought chips in the belief that they were healthful will now switch to other foods. The decline in the price of harvesting equipment will shift the supply of chips to the right, because additional farmers will now find it profitable to enter the corn market. In Fig. 3.18(a) and 3.18(b), the original supply and demand curves are denoted by *S* and *D*, while the new curves are denoted by *S′* and *D′*. Note that in panels (a) and (b), the shifts lead to a decline in the equilibrium price of chips.

Note also, however, that the effect of the shifts on equilibrium quantity cannot be determined without knowing their relative magnitudes. Taken separately, the demand shift causes a decline in equilibrium quantity, whereas the supply shift causes an increase in equilibrium quantity. The net effect of the two shifts thus depends on which of the individual effects is larger. In Fig. 3.18(a), the demand shift dominates, so equilibrium quantity declines. In Fig. 3.18(b), the supply shift dominates, so equilibrium quantity goes up.

Exercise 3.5 asks you to consider a simple variation on the problem posed in Example 3.6.

**Exercise 3.5** What will happen to the equilibrium price and quantity in the corn tortilla chip market if both of the following events occur: (1) researchers discover that a vitamin found in corn helps protect against cancer and heart disease; and (2) a swarm of locusts destroys part of the corn crop?

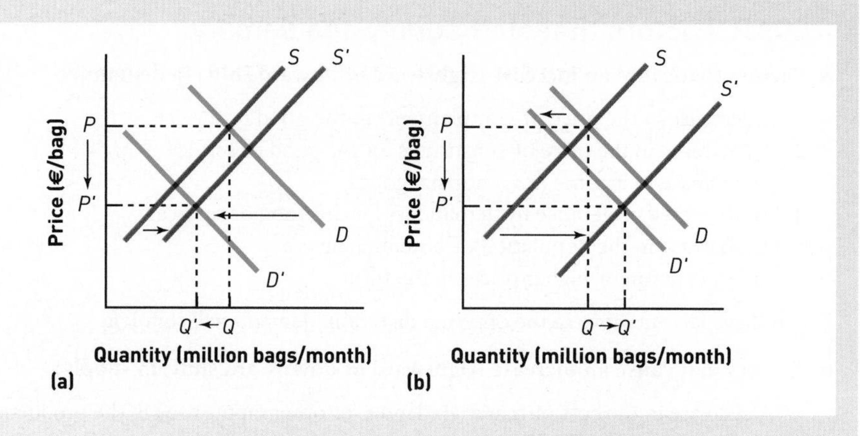


**Figure 3.18 The Effects of Simultaneous Shifts in Supply and Demand.** When demand shifts left and supply shifts right, equilibrium price falls, but equilibrium quantity may either rise (b) or fall (a).

## Economic naturalist 3.6 Why do the prices of some goods (such as airline tickets from Europe to the United States) go up during the months of heaviest consumption, while others (such as the price of strawberries) go down?

Seasonal price movements for airline tickets are primarily the result of *seasonal variations in demand*. Thus ticket prices on the North Atlantic routes are highest during the summer months because the demand for tickets is highest during those months, as shown in Fig. 3.19(a), where the *w* and *s* subscripts denote winter and summer values, respectively.

By contrast, seasonal price movements for strawberries are primarily the result of *seasonal variations in supply*. In the winter months strawberries offered for sale in Europe are for the most part produced under glass or are imported into Europe. The costs involved are higher than in the summer months, when seasonal factors permit production in the open across a large part of Europe. Costs are lower: the supply curve shifts to the right. The price of strawberries is lowest in the summer months because their supply is highest during those months, as seen in Fig. 3.19(b).

**Figure 3.19 Seasonal Variation in the Air Travel and Strawberry Markets.** (a) Prices are highest during the period of heaviest consumption when heavy consumption is the result of high demand. (b) Prices are lowest during the period of heaviest consumption when heavy consumption is the result of high supply.

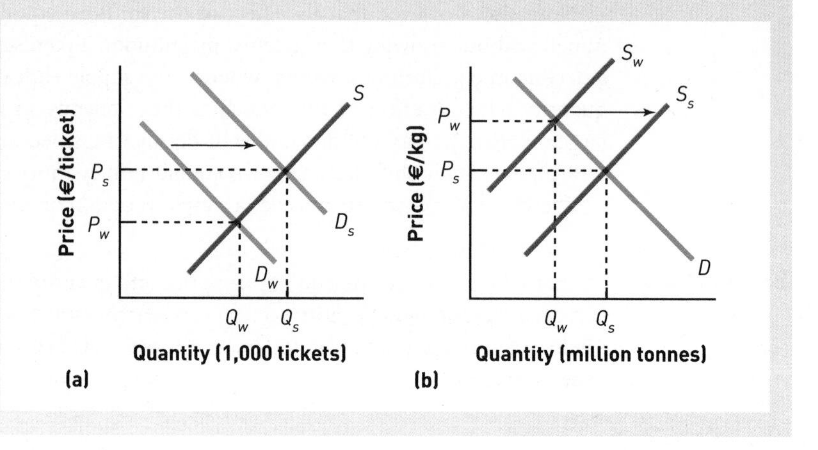

## Markets and social welfare

Markets represent a highly effective system of *allocating resources*. When a market for a good is in equilibrium, the equilibrium price conveys important information to potential suppliers about the value that potential demanders place on that good. At the same time, the equilibrium price informs potential demanders about the opportunity cost of supplying the good. This rapid, two-way transmission of information is the reason that markets can co-ordinate an activity as complex as supplying London or Paris with food and drink, even though no one person or organisation oversees the process.

But are the prices and quantities determined in market equilibrium socially optimal, in the sense of maximising total economic surplus? That is, does equilibrium in unregulated markets always maximise the difference between the total benefits and total costs experienced by market participants? As we shall see, the answer is 'it depends': a market that is out of equilibrium, such as the market for rented housing in cities with rent control laws, always creates opportunities for individuals to arrange transactions that will increase their individual economic surplus. As we shall see, however, a market for a good that is in equilibrium makes the largest possible contribution to total economic surplus only when its supply and demand curves fully reflect the costs and benefits associated with the production and consumption of that good.

### Cash on the table

**buyer's surplus** the difference between the buyer's reservation price and the price he or she actually pays

**seller's surplus** the difference between the price received by the seller and his or her reservation price

**total surplus** the difference between the buyer's reservation price and the seller's reservation price

In economics, we assume that all exchange is purely voluntary. This means that a transaction cannot take place unless the buyer's reservation price for the good exceeds the seller's reservation price. When that condition is met and a transaction takes place, both parties receive an economic surplus. The **buyer's surplus** from the transaction is the difference between her reservation price and the price she actually pays. The **seller's surplus** is the difference between the price she receives and her reservation price. The **total surplus** from the transaction is the sum of the buyer's surplus and the seller's surplus. It is also equal to the difference between the buyer's reservation price and the seller's reservation price.

Suppose that there is a potential buyer whose reservation price for an additional slice of pizza is €4 and a potential seller whose reservation price is only €2. If this buyer purchases a slice of pizza from this seller for €3, the total surplus generated by this exchange is €4 – €2 = €2, of which €4 – €3 = €1 is the buyer's surplus and €3 – €2 = €1 is the seller's surplus.

A regulation that prevents the price of a good from reaching its equilibrium level unnecessarily prevents exchanges of this sort from taking place, and in the process reduces total economic surplus. Consider again the effect of price controls imposed in the market for pizza. The demand curve in Fig. 3.20 tells us that if a price ceiling of €2 per slice were imposed, only 8,000 slices of pizza per day would be sold. At that quantity, the vertical interpretations of the supply and demand curves tell us that a buyer would be willing to pay as much as €4 for an additional slice and that a seller would be willing to sell one for as little €2. The difference – €2 per slice – is the additional economic sur-

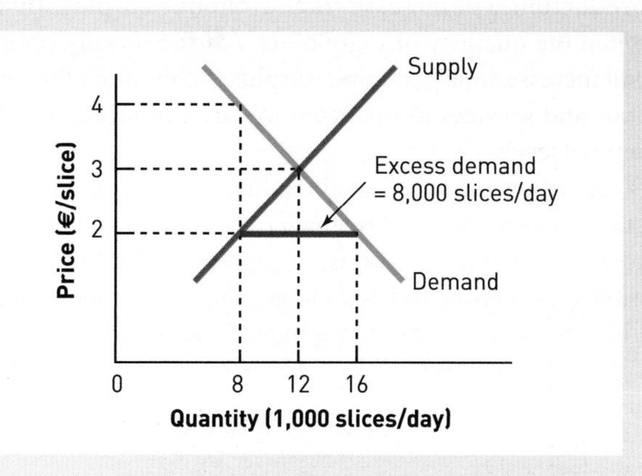


**Figure 3.20 Price Controls in the Pizza Market.** A price ceiling below the equilibrium price of pizza would result in excess demand for pizza.

plus that would result if an additional slice were produced and sold. As noted earlier, an extra slice sold at a price of €3 would result in an additional €1 of economic surplus for both buyer and seller.

When a market is out of equilibrium, it is always possible to identify *mutually beneficial exchanges* of this sort. When people have failed to take advantage of all mutually beneficial exchanges, we often say that there is **'cash on the table'** – the economist's metaphor for unexploited opportunities. When the price in a market is below the equilibrium price, there is cash on the table, because the reservation price of sellers (marginal cost) will always be lower than the reservation price of buyers. In the absence of a law preventing buyers paying more than €2 per slice, restaurant owners would quickly raise their prices and expand their production until the equilibrium price of €3 per slice were reached. At that price, buyers would be able to get precisely the 12,000 slices of pizza they want to buy each day. All mutually beneficial opportunities for exchange would have been exploited, leaving no more cash on the table.

**'cash on the table'** economic metaphor for unexploited gains from exchange

Buyers and sellers in the marketplace have an uncanny ability to detect the presence of cash on the table. It is almost as if unexploited opportunities gave off some exotic scent triggering neuro-chemical explosions in the olfactory centres of their brains. The desire to scrape cash off the table and into their pockets is what drives sellers in each of any large city's thousands of individual food outlets to work diligently to meet their customers' demands. That they succeed to a far higher degree than participants in the city's rent-controlled housing market is plainly evident. Whatever flaws it might have, the market system moves with considerably greater speed and agility than any centralised allocation mechanisms yet devised. But as we emphasise in the following section, this does not mean that markets *always* lead to the greatest good for all.

## Smart for one, dumb for all

The **socially optimal quantity** of any good is the quantity that maximises the total economic surplus that results from producing and consuming the good. From the Cost–Benefit Principle (Chapter 1), we know that we should keep expanding production of the good as long as its marginal benefit is at least as great as its marginal cost. This means that the socially optimal quantity is that level for which the marginal cost and marginal benefit of the good are the same.

**socially optimal quantity** the quantity of a good that results in the maximum possible economic surplus from producing and consuming the good

When the quantity of a good is less than the socially optimal quantity, boosting its production will increase total economic surplus. By the same token, when the quantity of a good exceeds the socially optimal quantity, reducing its production will increase total economic surplus. **Economic efficiency**, or **efficiency**, occurs when all goods and services in the economy are produced and consumed at their respective socially optimal levels.

*Efficiency* is an important social goal. Failure to achieve efficiency means that total economic surplus is smaller than it might have been. Movements toward efficiency make the total economic 'pie' larger, making it possible for everyone to have a larger slice. The importance of efficiency will be a recurring theme as we move forward, and we state it here as one of the core principles:

**economic efficiency** (also called **efficiency**) occurs when all goods and services are produced and consumed at their respective socially optimal levels

The Efficiency Principle: Efficiency is an important social goal, because when the economic 'pie' grows larger, everyone can have a larger slice.

Is the market equilibrium quantity of a good efficient? That is, does it maximise the total economic surplus received by participants in the market for that good? When the private market for a given good is in equilibrium, we can say that the cost *to the seller* of producing an additional unit of the good is the same as the benefit *to the buyer* of having an additional unit. If all costs of producing the good are borne directly by sellers, and if all benefits from the good accrue directly to buyers, it follows that the market equilibrium quantity of the good will equate the marginal cost and marginal benefit of the good. And this means that the equilibrium quantity also maximises total economic surplus.

Sometimes the production of a good entails costs that fall on people *other than those who sell the good*. This will be true, for instance, for goods whose production generates significant levels of environmental pollution (a topic we shall explore in much greater detail in Chapter 11). As extra units of these goods are produced, the extra pollution harms other people besides sellers. In the market equilibrium for such goods, the benefit *to buyers* of the last good produced is, as before, equal to the cost incurred by sellers to produce that good. But since producing that good also imposed pollution costs on others, we know that the *full* marginal cost of the last unit produced – the seller's private marginal cost plus the marginal pollution cost borne by others – must be higher than the benefit of the last unit produced. So in this case the market equilibrium quantity of the good will be larger than the socially optimal quantity. Total economic surplus would be higher if output of the good were lower. Yet neither sellers nor buyers have any incentive to alter their behaviour.

Another possibility is that people *other than those who buy* a good may receive significant benefits from it. For instance, when someone purchases a vaccination against measles from her doctor, she not only protects herself against measles, but she also makes it less likely that others will catch this disease. From the perspective of society as a whole, we should keep increasing the number of vaccinations until their marginal cost equals their marginal benefit. The marginal benefit of a vaccination is the value of the protection it provides for the person vaccinated *plus* the value of the protection it provides for all others. Private consumers, however, will choose to be vaccinated only if the marginal benefit *to them* exceeds the price of the vaccination. In this case, then, the market equilibrium quantity of vaccinations will be smaller than the quantity that maximises total economic surplus. Again, however, individuals would have no incentive to alter their behaviour.

Situations like those just discussed provide examples of behaviours that we may call 'smart for one, dumb for all'. In each case, the individual actors are behaving rationally. They are pursuing their goals as best they can, and yet there remain unexploited opportunities for gain from the point of view of the whole society. The difficulty is that these opportunities cannot be exploited by individuals acting alone. In subsequent chapters we shall see how people can often *organise collectively* to exploit such opportunities. For now, we simply summarise this discussion in the form of the following core principle:

The Equilibrium Principle (also called the 'No-Cash-On-The-Table' Principle): A market in equilibrium leaves no unexploited opportunities for individuals, but may not exploit all gains achievable through collective action.

## RECAP Markets and social welfare

When the supply and demand curves for a good reflect all significant costs and benefits associated with the production and consumption of that good, the *market equilibrium price* will guide people to produce and consume the quantity of the good that results in the largest possible economic surplus.

## Summary

- Eighteenth-century economists tried to explain differences in the prices of goods by focusing on differences in their *cost of production*. But this approach cannot explain why a conveniently located house sells for more than one that is less conveniently located. Early nineteenth-century economists tried to explain price differences by focusing on differences in what buyers were willing to pay. But this approach cannot explain why the price of a life-saving appendectomy is less than that of a surgical facelift.
- Alfred Marshall's model of supply and demand explains why neither cost of production nor value to the purchaser (as measured by willingness to pay) is, by itself, sufficient to explain why some goods are cheap and others are expensive. To explain variations in price, we must examine the *interaction of cost and willingness to pay*. As we have seen in this chapter, goods differ in price because of differences in their respective supply and demand curves.
- The demand curve is a downward-sloping line that tells what quantity buyers will demand at any given price. The supply curve is an upward-sloping line that tells what quantity sellers will offer at any given price. *Market equilibrium* occurs when the quantity buyers demand at the market price is exactly the same as the quantity that sellers offer. The equilibrium price–quantity pair is the one at which the demand and supply curves intersect. In equilibrium, market price measures both the value of the last unit sold to buyers and the cost of the resources required to produce it.
- When the price of a good lies above its equilibrium value, there is an *excess supply* of that good. Excess supply motivates sellers to cut their prices, and price continues to fall until the equilibrium price is reached. When price lies below its equilibrium value, there is *excess demand*. With excess demand, frustrated buyers are motivated to offer higher prices, and the upward pressure on prices persists until equilibrium is reached. A remarkable feature of the market system is that, relying only on the tendency of people to respond in self-interested ways to market price signals, it somehow manages to co-ordinate the actions of literally billions of buyers and sellers worldwide. When excess demand or excess supply occurs, it tends to be small and brief, except in markets where regulations prevent full adjustment of prices.
- The efficiency of markets in *allocating resources* does not eliminate social concerns about how goods and services are distributed among different people. For example, we often lament the fact that many buyers enter the market with too little income to buy even the most basic goods and services. Concern for the well-being of the poor has motivated many governments to intervene in a variety of ways to alter the outcomes of market forces. Sometimes these interventions take the form of laws that peg prices below their equilibrium levels. Such laws almost invariably generate harmful, if unintended, consequences. Programmes such as rent-control laws, for example, lead to severe housing shortages, black marketeering and a rapid deterioration of the relationship between landlords and tenants.
- If the difficulty is that the poor have too little money, the best solution is to discover ways of boosting their incomes directly. The law of supply and demand cannot be repealed by the legislature. But legislatures do have the capacity to *alter the underlying forces* that govern the shape and position of supply and demand schedules.
- The basic *supply and demand model* is a primary tool of the economic naturalist. Changes in the equilibrium price of a good, and in the amount of it traded in the marketplace, can be predicted on the basis of shifts in its supply or demand curves. The following four rules hold for any good with a downward-sloping demand curve and an upward-sloping supply curve:
  - An increase in demand will lead to an increase in equilibrium price and quantity.
  - A reduction in demand will lead to a reduction in equilibrium price and quantity.
  - An increase in supply will lead to a reduction in equilibrium price and an increase in equilibrium quantity.
  - A decrease in supply will lead to an increase in equilibrium price and a reduction in equilibrium quantity.

- Incomes, tastes, population, expectations and the prices of substitutes and complements are among the factors that shift *demand schedules*. *Supply schedules*, in turn, are primarily governed by such factors as technology, input prices, expectations, the number of sellers – and, especially for agricultural products – the weather.
- When the supply and demand curves for a good reflect all significant costs and benefits associated with the production and consumption of that good, the market equilibrium price will guide people to produce and consume the quantity of the good that results in the largest possible economic surplus. This conclusion, however, does not apply if others, beside buyers, benefit from the good (as when someone benefits from his neighbour's purchase of a vaccination against measles), or if others beside sellers bear costs because of the good (as when its production generates pollution). In such cases, market equilibrium *does not result in the greatest gain for all.*

## Key terms

**buyer's reservation price** (63)
**buyer's surplus** (83)
**'cash on the table'** (84)
**central planning** (60)
**change in demand** (73)
**change in the quantity demanded** (73)
**change in the quantity supplied** (73)
**change in supply** (73)
**complements** (74)
**demand curve** (62)
**economic efficiency** (84)
**equilibrium** (65)
**equilibrium price** (65)
**equilibrium quantity** (65)
**excess demand** (67)
**excess supply** (66)
**income effect** (63)
**inferior good** (76)
**market** (62)
**market equilibrium** (66)
**normal good** (76)
**price ceiling** (72)
**seller's reservation price** (64)
**seller's surplus** (83)
**socially optimal quantity** (84)
**substitutes** (74)
**substitution effect** (63)
**supply curve** (64)
**total surplus** (83)

## Review questions

1. Why is knowing the cost of producing a good not sufficient to predict its market price?
2. Distinguish between the meaning of the expressions 'change in demand' and 'change in the quantity demanded'.
3. Last year a government official proposed that motor fuel price controls be imposed to protect the poor from rising motor fuel prices. What evidence could you consult to discover whether this proposal was enacted?
4. Explain the distinction between the horizontal and vertical interpretations of the demand curve.
5. Give an example of behaviour you have observed that could be described as 'smart for one, dumb for all'.

## Problems

1. State whether the following pairs of goods are complements or substitutes. (If you think a pair is ambiguous in this respect, explain why.)
   a. Tennis courts and squash courts.
   b. Squash racquets and squash balls.
   c. Ice cream and chocolate.
   d. Cloth nappies and paper nappies.
2. How would each of the following affect the EU market supply curve for corn?
   a. A new and improved crop rotation technique is discovered.
   b. The price of fertiliser falls.
   c. The EU Commission offers new subsidies to farmers growing wheat.
   d. A tornado sweeps through northern France in July.
3. Indicate how you think each of the following would shift demand in the indicated market:
   a. Incomes of buyers in the market for Spanish sun holidays increase.
   b. Buyers in the market for pizza read a study linking hamburger consumption to heart disease.
   c. Buyers in the market for CDs learn of an increase in the price of audio cassettes (a substitute for CDs).
   d. Buyers in the market for CDs learn of an increase in the price of CDs.
4. A German student claims to have spotted a UFO over the countryside south of Munich How will his claim affect the *supply* (not the quantity supplied) of binoculars in Munich stores?
5. What will happen to the equilibrium price and quantity of olives in Italy if the wage paid to olive pickers rises?
6. How will an increase in the birth rate affect the equilibrium price of land?
7. What will happen to the equilibrium price and quantity of fish if fish oils are found to help prevent heart disease?
8. What will happen to the equilibrium price and quantity of beef if the price of chicken-feed increases?
9. Use supply and demand analysis to explain why hotel room rental rates near your college at the very beginning of the year and on a graduation weekend might differ from the rates charged during the rest of the year.
10. How will a new law mandating an increase in required levels of automobile insurance affect the equilibrium price and quantity in the market for new automobiles?
11. Suppose the current issue of the *Le Monde* reports an outbreak of mad cow disease in the Dordogne as well as the discovery of a new breed of chickens that gain more weight than existing breeds that consume the same amount of food. How will these developments affect the equilibrium price and quantity of chicken sold in the France?
12. What will happen to the equilibrium quantity and price of potatoes if the population increases and a new, higher-yielding variety of potato plant is developed?
13. What will happen to the equilibrium price and quantity of apples if apples are discovered to help prevent colds and a fungus kills 10 per cent of existing apple trees?

14. What will happen to the equilibrium quantity and price of corn on the cob (sweetcorn) if the price of butter (a complement) increases and the price of fertiliser decreases?

15. In the 1970s, tofu was available only from small businesses operating in predominantly Asian sections of large cities in North America. Today tofu has become popular as a high-protein health food and is widely available in supermarkets throughout the United States and Europe. At the same time, tofu production has evolved to become factory-based using modern food-processing technologies. Draw a diagram with demand and supply curves depicting the market for tofu in 1975 and the market for tofu today. Given the information above, what does the demand–supply model predict about changes in the volume of tofu sold in the United States and Europe between then and now? What does it predict about changes in the price of tofu?

## Answers to in-chapter exercises

3.1 At a quantity of 10,000 slices per day, the marginal buyer's reservation price is €3.50 per slice. At a price of €2.50 per slice, the quantity demanded will be 14,000 slices per day.

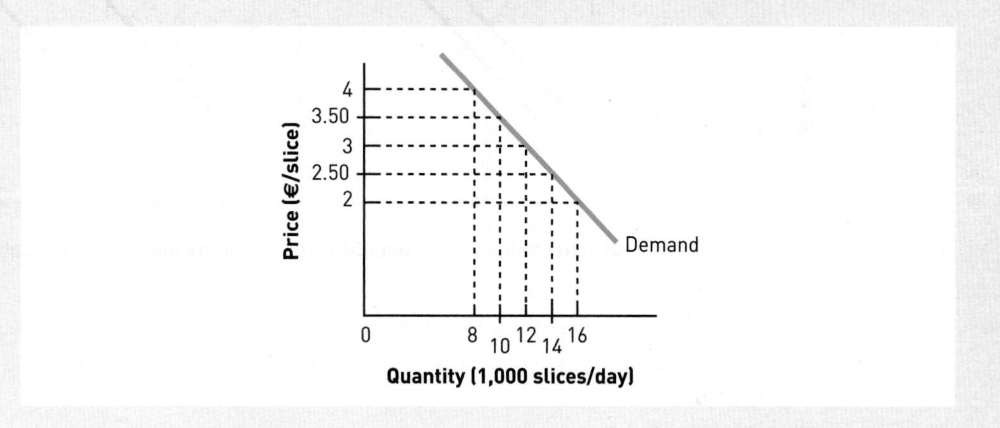


3.2 At a quantity of 10,000 slices per day, the marginal cost of pizza is €2.50 per slice. At a price of €3.50 per slice, the quantity supplied will be 14,000 slices per day.

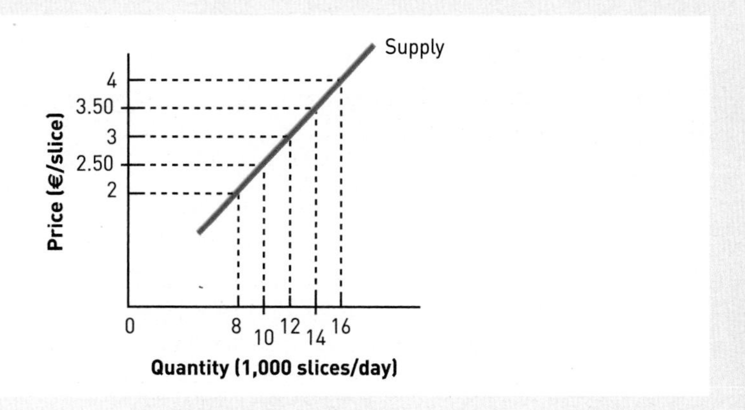

3.3 Since landlords are permitted to charge less than the maximum rent established by rent-control laws, a law that sets the maximum rent at €1,200 will have no effect on the rents actually charged in this market, which will settle at the equilibrium value of €800 per month.

3.4 Travel by air and travel by cross-Channel ferry are substitutes, so a decline in air fares will shift the demand for ferry travel to the left, resulting in lower ferry fares and fewer ferry trips taken. Travel by air and the use of resort hotels are complements, so a decline in air fares will shift the demand for resort hotel rooms to the right, resulting in higher hotel rates and an increase in the number of rooms rented.

3.5 The vitamin discovery shifts the demand for chips to the right, and the crop losses shift the supply of chips to the left. Both shifts result in an increase in the equilibrium price of chips. But depending on the relative magnitude of the shifts, the equilibrium quantity of chips may either rise (panel (a)) or fall (panel (b)).

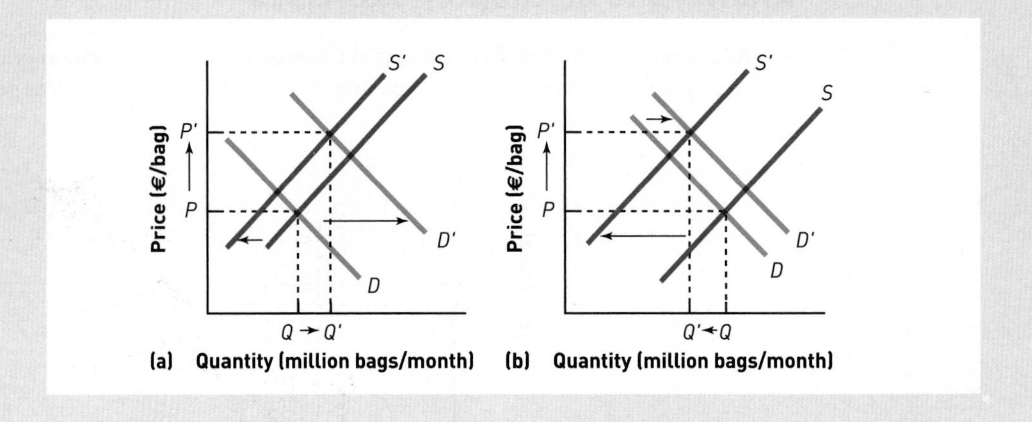

# Part 2

# Competition and the 'Invisible Hand'

Part 1 of the book laid down some basic core principles of economics. In Part 2 we aim to provide a sharper understanding of how consumers and firms behave. Our starting point is to analyse how things would work in an idealised, perfectly competitive economy in which consumers are perfectly informed and no firm has market power.

We begin in Chapter 4 by exploring the concept of *elasticity*, which describes the sensitivity of demand and supply to variations in prices, incomes and other economic factors. In our review of supply and demand in Part 1, we asked you simply to assume the law of demand, which says that demand curves are downward-sloping. In Chapter 5 we shall see that this law is a simple consequence of the fact that people spend their limited incomes in rational ways: that is, it follows from the concept of *consumer rationality*. In Chapter 6 our focus will shift to the seller's side of the market, where our task will be to see why upward-sloping supply curves are a consequence of production decisions taken by firms whose goal is to maximise profit: it reflects producer rationality.

In Chapter 7 we develop more carefully and fully the concept of economic surplus introduced in Part 1 and investigate the conditions under which unregulated markets generate the largest possible economic surplus. We shall also explore why attempts to interfere with market outcomes often lead to unintended and undesired consequences.

Finally, in Chapter 8 we shall investigate the economic forces by which the 'invisible hand' of the marketplace guides profit-seeking firms and satisfaction-seeking consumers in ways that, to a surprising degree, serve society's ends. These forces encourage aggressive cost cutting by firms, even though the resulting gains will eventually take the form of lower prices rather than higher profits. We shall also see why misunderstanding of competitive forces often results in costly errors, in both everyday decision making and in government policy.

# 4 Elasticity

Across Europe the laws on possession, supply and usage of 'controlled substances' (i.e. drugs) differ significantly by country. In recent years there have been changes in those laws in most Western European jurisdictions in the direction of penalising suppliers while reducing the penalties on users. In the case of some drugs (e.g. cannabis and 'hash') this has gone as far as *de facto* legalisation of consumption in the Netherlands (where Amsterdam's 'yellow cafés' are well known). In the case of the harder and more addictive drugs this process is much less advanced, with possession as well as supply being illegal in most circumstances in most countries. In part, this reflects a judgement that the drugs are by their nature so harmful that their consumption has to be strongly discouraged. In part, however, it is because there is a well-established connection between the consumption of illegal drugs such as heroin and the level of crime. In a sense, this is a tautology, since possession and use of the drugs concerned is in many countries a crime in itself. However, it is also the case that the level of crimes against property and the person seem to be connected to heroin addiction.

This is not surprising. Many illicit drug users commit crimes to finance their addiction. This connection between drugs and crime has led to calls for more vigorous efforts to stop the smuggling of illicit drugs. But can such efforts reduce the likelihood that your laptop computer will be stolen in the next month? If attempts to reduce the supply of illicit drugs are successful, their effect will be to increase the market price of drugs. (From our basic supply and demand analysis, we can see that this increase in price is caused by a leftward shift in the supply curve for drugs.) The law of demand tells us that drug users will respond by consuming a smaller quantity of drugs. But the amount of crime drug users commit depends not on the *quantity* of drugs they consume, but rather on their *total expenditure* on drugs. Depending on the specific characteristics of the demand curve for illicit drugs, a price increase might reduce total expenditure on drugs, but it could also raise total expenditure.

Suppose, for example, that increased activity by the police and the Customs and Excise services of an EU member state shift the supply curve in the market for illicit drugs in the country concerned to the left, as shown in Fig. 4.1. As a result, the equilibrium quantity of drugs would fall from 50,000 to 40,000 g per day, and the price of drugs would rise from €50 to €80 per g. The total amount spent on drugs, which was €2,500,000 per day (50,000 g/day × €50/g), would rise to €3,200,000 per day (40,000 g/day × €80/g). In this case, then, efforts to stem the supply of drugs would actually increase the likelihood of your laptop being stolen.

This effect was observed in several econometric studies of the incidence of crime in urban areas across the United States during the 1980s and early 1990s. Of course, it may be the case that the other benefits (reduced volume of consumption and consequent effects on the health and employment prospects for addicts) may be regarded as being sufficient to offset the increased incidence of crime, but for policy makers the possible impact on criminal behaviour is something that should be included in any cost–benefit analysis of drug law enforcement.

Our task in this chapter will be to introduce the concept of *elasticity*, a measure of the extent to which quantity demanded and quantity supplied respond to variations in price, income and other factors. In Chapter 3, we saw how shifts in supply and demand curves enabled us to predict the direction of change in the equilibrium values of price and quantity. An understanding of price elasticity will enable us to make even more precise statements about the effects of such changes. In the illicit drug example just considered, the decrease in supply led to an increase in total spending. In many other cases, a decrease in supply will lead to a reduction in total spending. Why this difference? The underlying phenomenon that explains this pattern, as we shall see, is the *price elasticity of demand*. We shall explore why some goods have higher price elasticity of demand than others, and the implications of that fact for how total spending responds to changes in price. We shall also discuss the *price elasticity of supply* and examine the factors that explain why it takes different values for different goods.

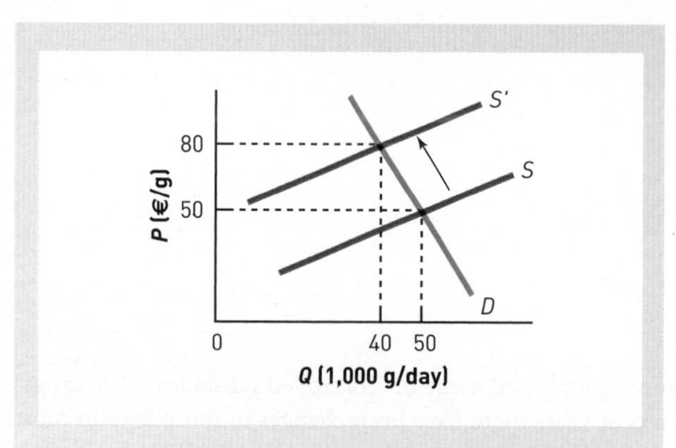


**Figure 4.1 The Effect of Extra Border Patrols on the Market for Illicit Drugs.** Extra patrols shift supply leftward and reduce the quantity demanded, but they may actually increase the total amount spent on drugs.

## Price elasticity of demand

When the price of a good or service rises, the quantity demanded falls. But to predict the effect of the price increase on total expenditure, we must also know how much quantity falls. The quantity demanded of some goods, such as salt, is not very sensitive to changes in price. Indeed, even if the price of salt were to double, or to fall by half, most people would hardly alter their consumption of it at all. For other goods, however, the quantity demanded is extremely responsive to changes in price. For example, when a luxury tax was imposed on yachts in the early 1990s, purchases of yachts plummeted.

### Price elasticity defined

The **price elasticity of demand** for a good is a measure of the responsiveness of the quantity demanded of that good to changes in its price. Formally, the price elasticity of demand for a good is defined as the percentage change in the quantity demanded that results from a 1 per cent change in its price. For example, if the price of beef falls by 1 per cent and the quantity demanded rises by 2 per cent, then the price elasticity of demand for beef has a value of –2.

**price elasticity of demand** percentage change in quantity demanded that results from a 1 per cent change in price

Although the definition just given refers to the response of quantity demanded to a 1 per cent change in price, it can also be adapted to other variations in price, provided that they are relatively small. In such cases, we calculate the price elasticity of demand as the percentage change in quantity demanded divided by the corresponding percentage change in price. Thus, if a 2 per cent reduction in the price of pork led to a 6 per cent increase in the quantity of pork demanded, the price elasticity of demand for pork would be

$$\frac{\text{Percentage change in consumption}}{\text{Percentage change in price}} = \frac{6 \text{ per cent}}{-2 \text{ per cent}} = -3 \qquad (4.1)$$

**elastic** demand is elastic with respect to price if the price elasticity of demand is greater than 1

**inelastic** demand is inelastic with respect to price if the price elasticity of demand is less than 1

**unit elastic** demand is unit elastic with respect to price if the price elasticity of demand equals 1

Strictly speaking, the price elasticity of demand will always be negative (or zero), because price changes are always in the opposite direction from changes in quantity demanded. So for convenience, we can drop the negative sign and speak of price elasticities in terms of absolute value. The demand for a good is said to be **elastic** with respect to price if the absolute value of its price elasticity is greater than 1. It is said to be **inelastic** if the absolute value of its price elasticity is less than 1. Finally, demand is said to be **unit elastic** if the absolute value of its price elasticity is equal to 1 (see Fig. 4.2).

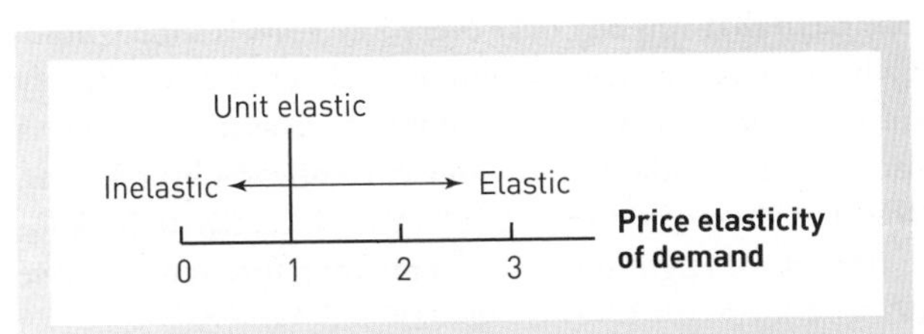


**Figure 4.2 Elastic and Inelastic Demand.** Demand for a good is called elastic, unit elastic or inelastic with respect to price if the price elasticity is greater than I, equal to I, or less than I, respectively.

### Example 4.1 What is the elasticity of demand for pizza?

When the price of pizza is €1 per slice, buyers wish to purchase 400 slices per day, but when price falls to €0.97 per slice, the quantity demanded rises to 404 slices per day. At the original price, what is the price elasticity of demand for pizza? Is the demand for pizza elastic with respect to price?

In response to a 3 per cent reduction in the price of pizza, the quantity demanded increases by 1 per cent. The price elasticity of demand for pizza is thus (1 per cent)/(3 per cent) = 1/3. So when the initial price of pizza is €1, the demand for pizza is not elastic with respect to price; it is inelastic.

**Exercise 4.1** **What is the elasticity of demand for season ski passes?**

When the price of a weekly ski pass in Zell am See is €160, buyers wish to purchase 100,000 passes per year, but when the operators reduce the price to €152, the quantity demanded rises to 120,000 passes per year. At the original price, what is the price elasticity of demand for ski passes? Is the demand for ski passes elastic with respect to price?

## Determinants of price elasticity of demand

What factors determine the price elasticity of demand for a good or service? To answer this question, recall that before a rational consumer buys any product, the product must first pass the cost–benefit test. For instance, consider a good (such as a microwave oven for your flat) that you buy only one unit of (if you buy it at all). Suppose that, at the current price, you have decided to buy it. Now imagine that the price goes up by 10 per cent. Will a price increase of this magnitude be likely to make you change your mind? The answer will depend on factors such as the following.

### Substitution possibilities

When the price of a product you want to buy goes up significantly, you are likely to ask yourself, 'Is there some other good that can do roughly the same job, but for less money?' If the answer is yes, then you can escape the effect of the price increase by simply switching to the substitute product. But if the answer is no, you are more likely to stick with your current purchase.

These observations suggest that the price elasticity of demand will tend to be higher for products for which *close substitutes* are readily available. Salt, for example, has no close substitutes, which is one reason that the demand for it is highly inelastic. Note, however, that while the quantity of salt people demand is highly insensitive to price, the same cannot be said of the demand for any *specific brand* of salt. After all, despite what salt manufacturers say about the special advantages of their own labels, consumers tend to regard one brand of salt as a virtually perfect substitute for another. Thus, if one producer were to raise the price of its salt significantly, many people would simply switch to some other brand.

The vaccine against rabies is another product for which there are essentially no attractive substitutes. A person who is bitten by a rabid animal and does not take the vaccine faces a certain and painful death. So most people in that position would pay any price they could afford rather than do without the vaccine.

### Budget share

Suppose the price of key rings suddenly were to double. How would that affect the number of key rings you buy? If you're like most people, it would have no effect at all. Think about it – a doubling of the price of a 25 cent item that you buy only every few years is simply nothing to worry about. By contrast, if the price of the new car you were about to buy suddenly doubled, you would definitely want to check out possible substitutes, such as a used car or a smaller new model. You might also consider holding on to your current car a little longer. *The larger the share of your budget an item accounts for*, the greater is your incentive to look for substitutes when the price of the item rises. High unit price items therefore tend to have higher price elasticities of demand.

### Time

Domestic appliances such as ovens or washing machines come in a variety of models, some more energy-efficient than others. As a general rule, the more efficient an appliance is, the higher its price. If you were about to buy a new dishwasher and the price per kWh of electricity suddenly rose sharply, it would be in your interest to buy a more efficient machine than you had originally planned. But suppose you had already bought the machine before you learned of the rate increase. In all likelihood, it would not pay you discard the machine right away and replace it with a more efficient model. Rather, you would wait until the machine wore out, or until you moved, before making the switch.

As this example illustrates, substitution of one product or service for another takes time. Some substitutions occur in the immediate aftermath of a price increase, but many others take place years or even decades later. For this reason, the price elasticity of demand for any good or service will be higher in the *long run* than in the *short run*.

### RECAP Factors that influence price elasticity

The price elasticity of demand for a good or service tends to be larger when *substitutes* for the good are more readily available, when the good's share in the consumer's budget is *larger* and when consumers have more time to *adjust* to a change in price.

## Some representative elasticity estimates

As the entries in Table 4.1 show, the price elasticities of demand for different products often differ substantially – in this sample, ranging from a high of 2.8 for green peas to a low of 0.18 for theatre and opera tickets. This variability is explained in part by the determinants of elasticity just discussed. Patrons of theatre and opera, for example, often tend to have high incomes, implying that the shares of their budgets devoted to these items are likely to be small. What is more, theatre and opera patrons are often highly knowledgeable and enthusiastic about these art forms; for many of them, there are simply no acceptable substitute forms of entertainment.

| Good or service | Price elasticity |
|---|---|
| Green peas | 2.80 |
| Restaurant meals | 1.63 |
| Automobiles | 1.35 |
| Electricity | 1.20 |
| Beer | 1.19 |
| Movies | 0.87 |
| Air travel (foreign) | 0.77 |
| Shoes | 0.70 |
| Coffee | 0.25 |
| Theatre, opera | 0.18 |

**Table 4.1** Price Elasticity Estimates for Selected Products
*Sources*: These short-run elasticity estimates are taken from Houthakker and Taylor (1970); Taylor (1975); Elzinga (1977); Fisher (1996).

Why is the price elasticity of demand almost 16 times larger for green peas than for theatre and opera performances? The answer cannot be that income effects loom any larger for green peas than for theatre tickets. Even though the average consumer of green peas earns much less than the average theatre or opera patron, the share of a typical family's budget devoted to green peas is surely very small. What differentiates green peas from theatre and opera performances is that there are so many more close substitutes for peas than for opera and theatre. The lowly green pea, which is mostly found in the canned goods or frozen foods sections of supermarkets, just does not seem to have inspired a loyal consumer following.

## Using price elasticity of demand

An understanding of the factors that govern price elasticity of demand is necessary not only to make sense of consumer behaviour, but also to design effective public policy. Consider, for example, the debate about how taxes affect smoking among teenagers.

### Economic naturalist 4.1 Will a higher tax on cigarettes curb teenage smoking?

Across the developed world public policy tries to discourage teenagers from starting to smoke. Smoking is so addictive that some experts feel it makes more sense to spend a given amount on resources to prevent people from starting to smoke than in encouraging smokers to give up the habit. In either case, one weapon in the armoury of governments is taxing cigarettes so as to increase their price. Higher taxes have been (not surprisingly) resisted by the tobacco industry. The tobacco industry has consistently maintained (and produced supportive consultancy reports) that peer pressure rather than affordability is what encourages teenagers to smoke. The main reason teenagers smoke is that their friends smoke, these consultants testified, and they concluded that higher taxes would have little effect.

The consultants are almost certainly right that peer influence is the most important determinant of teenage smoking. Other evidence suggests that the increase in smoking among young women is related to concerns about weight. Smoking reduces a person's appetite. But that does not imply that a higher tax on cigarettes would have little impact on adolescent smoking rates. Because most teenagers have little money to spend at their own discretion, cigarettes constitute a significant share of a typical teenage smoker's budget. The price elasticity of demand is thus likely to be far from negligible. For at least some teenage smokers, a higher tax would make smoking unaffordable. And even among those who could afford the higher prices, at least some would choose to spend their money on other things rather than pay the higher prices.

Given that the tax would affect at least *some* teenage smokers, the consultants' argument begins to unravel. If the tax deters even a small number of smokers directly through its effect on the price of cigarettes, it will also deter others indirectly, by reducing the number of peer role models who smoke. And those who refrain because of these indirect effects will in turn no longer influence others to smoke, and so on. So even if the direct effect of higher cigarette taxes on teenage smoking is small, the cumulative effects may be extremely large. The mere fact that peer pressure may be the primary determinant of teenage smoking therefore does not imply that higher cigarette taxes will have no significant impact on the number of teenagers who smoke.

Despite the rhetoric of the industry about prices being ineffective, evidence of the effects of restrictions on smoking actually undermine their case. Prohibiting smoking in some circumstances is analytically equivalent to a location- and/or time-specific extremely high price. To the extent that people do not fully (if at all) replace smoking not done where prohibited by an equivalent increase in smoking where permitted, this high pseudo-price has reduced smoking. The workplace smoking ban introduced in Ireland in 2004, which included pubs, does appear to have had the desired effect of reducing the total consumption of tobacco.

The real problem about tax on tobacco is twofold: (1) it is a regressive tax, hitting the poor more than the rich; and (2) it is easily evaded through smuggling unless all countries have the same high taxes.

## Economic naturalist 4.2 Why was the US Congress decision to impose a luxury tax on yachts such a disaster?

This is a well-known example of politicians getting it badly wrong in introducing a piece of populist tax law without investigating the likely consequences. The background to this was a need to increase taxes and cut spending to deal with a growing US federal budget deficit at the end of the Reagan presidency. To soften the blow on most taxpayers, the US Congress decided to introduce a tax that would hurt the better off significantly. Under the 1990 Omnibus Budget Reconciliation Act, Congress imposed a luxury tax on yachts costing more than $100,000, along with similar taxes on a handful of other luxury goods. Before these taxes were imposed, the Joint Committee on Taxation estimated that they would yield more than $31 million in revenue in 1991. But in fact their yield was little more than half that amount, $16.6 million. Several years later, the Joint Economic Committee estimated that the tax on yachts had led to a loss of 7,600 jobs in the US boating industry. Taking account of lost income taxes and increased unemployment benefits, the US government actually came out $7.6 million behind in the fiscal year 1991 as a result of its luxury taxes – almost $39 million worse than the initial projection. This meant either more taxes elsewhere, or less spending, or more borrowing. What went wrong?

Virtually all yachts and similar craft bought in the United States were produced by American suppliers. The tax was imposed on the sale of new yachts from US producers and boatyards. It did not apply to yachts built and purchased outside the United States. What Congress failed to consider was that such yachts are almost perfect substitutes for yachts built and purchased in the United States. And, no surprise, when prices on domestic yachts went up because of the tax, yacht buyers switched in droves to foreign models. A tax imposed on a good with high elasticity of demand stimulates large rearrangements of consumption but yields little revenue. Had Congress done its economic analysis properly, it would have predicted that this particular tax would be a big loser. Facing angry protests from unemployed New England shipbuilders, Congress repealed the luxury tax on yachts in 1993.

## A graphical interpretation of price elasticity

For small changes in price, the price elasticity of demand is the proportion by which quantity demanded changes divided by the corresponding proportion by which price changes. This formulation enables us to construct a simple expression for the price elasticity of demand for a good using only minimal information about its demand curve.

To illustrate, suppose we let $P$ represent the current price of the good and $Q$ the quantity demanded at that price. Similarly, let $\Delta P$ represent a small change in the current price and $\Delta Q$ the resulting change in quantity demanded (see Fig. 4.3). The expression $\Delta P/P$ will then stand for the proportion by which price changes when $P$ changes by $\Delta P$; and $\Delta Q/Q$ will stand for the corresponding proportion by which quantity changes. The formula for price elasticity may then be written as:

$$\text{Price elasticity} = \varepsilon = \frac{\Delta Q/Q}{\Delta P/P} \tag{4.2}$$

Suppose, for example, that 20 units were sold at the original price of 100, and that when the price rose to 105, quantity demanded fell to 15 units. Neglecting the negative sign of the

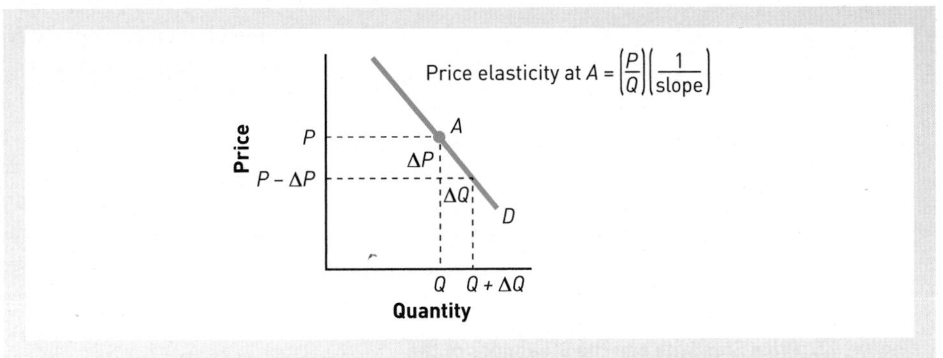


**Figure 4.3 A Graphical Interpretation of the Price Elasticity of Demand.** The price elasticity of demand at any point along a straight-line demand curve is the ratio of price to quantity at that point times the reciprocal of the slope of the demand curve.

quantity change, we would then have $\Delta Q/Q = 5/20$ and $\Delta P/P = 5/100$, which yields $\varepsilon = (5/20)/(5/100) = 5$.

One attractive feature of this formula is that it has a straightforward graphical interpretation. Thus, if we want to calculate the price elasticity of demand at point $A$ on the demand curve shown in Fig. 4.3, we can begin by rewriting the right-hand side of Eq. (4.2) as $(P/Q) \times (\Delta Q/\Delta P)$. And since the slope of the demand curve is equal to $\Delta P/\Delta Q$, $\Delta Q/\Delta P$ is the reciprocal of that slope: $\Delta Q/\Delta P = 1/\text{slope}$. So the price elasticity of demand at point $A$, denoted $\varepsilon_A$, has the following simple formula:

$$\varepsilon_A = \frac{P}{Q} \times \frac{1}{\text{Slope}} \tag{4.3}$$

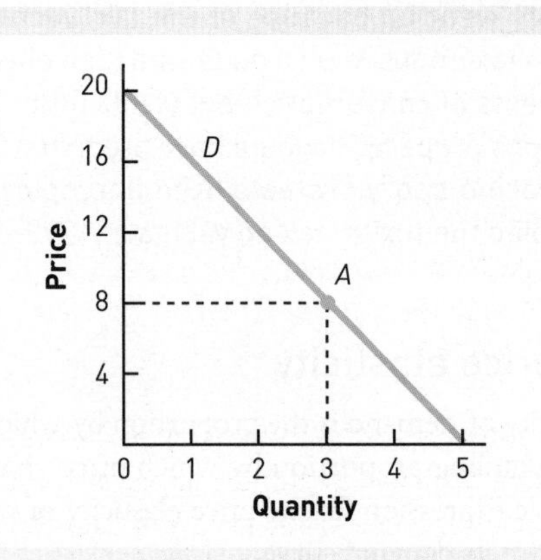


**Figure 4.4 Calculating the Price Elasticity of Demand.** The price elasticity of demand at $A$ is given by $(P/Q) \times (1/\text{slope}) = (8/3) \times (1/4) = 2/3$.

To demonstrate how convenient this graphical interpretation of elasticity can be, suppose we want to find the price elasticity of demand at point $A$ on the demand curve in Fig. 4.4. The slope of this demand curve is the ratio of its vertical intercept to its horizontal intercept: $20/5 = 4$. So $1/\text{slope} = 1/4$. (Actually, the slope is $-4$, but we again ignore the minus sign for convenience, since the price elasticity of demand always has the same sign.) The ratio $P/Q$ at point $A$ is $8/3$, so the price elasticity at point $A$ is equal to $(P/Q) \times (1/\text{slope}) = (8/3) \times (1/4) = 2/3$. This means that when the price of the good is 8, a 3 per cent reduction in price will lead to a 2 per cent increase in quantity demanded.

**Exercise 4.2** What is the price elasticity of demand when $P = 4$ on the demand curve in Fig. 4.4?

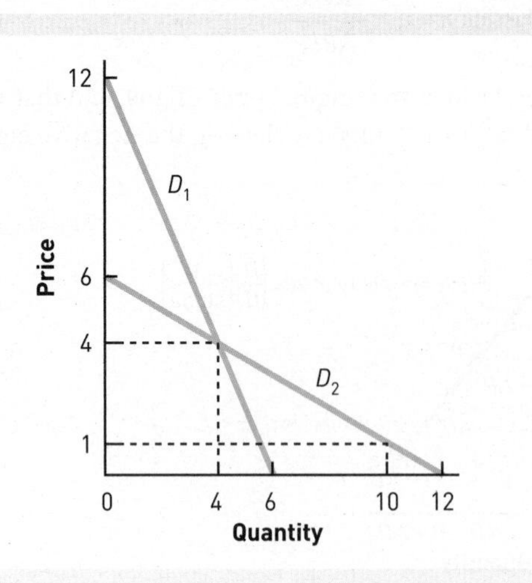


**Figure 4.5 Price Elasticity and the Steepness of the Demand Curve.** When price and quantity are the same, the price elasticity of demand is always greater for the less steep of two demand curves.

**Example 4.2** For the demand curves $D_1$ and $D_2$ shown in Fig. 4.5, calculate the price elasticity of demand when $P = 4$. What is the price elasticity of demand on $D_2$ when $P = 1$?

These elasticities can be calculated easily using the formula $\varepsilon = (P/Q) \times (1/\text{slope})$. The slope of $D_1$ is the ratio of its vertical intercept to its horizontal intercept: $12/6 = 2$. So $(1/\text{slope})$ is $1/2$ for $D_1$. Similarly, the slope of $D_2$ is the ratio of its vertical intercept to its horizontal intercept: $6/12 = 1/2$. So the reciprocal of the slope of $D_2$ is 2. For both demand curves, $Q = 4$ when $P = 4$, so $(P/Q) = 4/4 = 1$ for each. Thus the price elasticity of demand when $P = 4$ is $(1) \times (1/2) = 1/2$ for $D_1$ and $(1) \times (2) = 2$ for $D_2$. When $P = 1$, $Q = 10$ on $D_2$, so $(P/Q) = 1/10$. Thus price elasticity of demand $= (1/10) \times (2) \times 1/5$ when $P = 1$ on $D_2$.

Example 4.2 illustrates the general rule that if two demand curves have a point in common, the steeper curve must be the less elastic of the two with respect to price at that point. But note carefully that this does not mean that the steeper curve is less elastic at every point. Thus we saw that at $P = 1$, the price elasticity of demand on $D_2$ was only 1/5, or less than half the corresponding elasticity on the steeper $D_1$ at $P = 4$.

## Price elasticity changes along a straight-line demand curve

As a glance at our elasticity formula makes clear, price elasticity has a different value at every point along a straight-line demand curve. The slope of a straight-line demand curve is constant, which means that 1/slope is also constant. But the price–quantity ratio, $P/Q$, declines as we move down the demand curve. The elasticity of demand thus declines steadily as we move downward along a straight-line demand curve.

Since price elasticity is the percentage change in quantity demanded divided by the corresponding percentage change in price, this pattern makes sense. After all, a price movement of a given absolute size is small in percentage terms when it occurs near the top of the demand curve, where price is high, but large in percentage terms when it occurs near the bottom of the demand curve, where price is low. Likewise, a quantity movement of a given absolute value is large in percentage terms when it occurs near the top of the demand curve, where quantity is low, and small in percentage terms when it occurs near the bottom of the curve, where quantity is high.

The graphical interpretation of elasticity also makes it easy to see why the price elasticity of demand at the midpoint of any straight-line demand curve must always be 1.[1] Consider, for example, the price elasticity of demand at point $A$ on the demand curve $D$ shown in Fig. 4.6. At that point, the ratio $P/Q$ is equal to $6/3 = 2$. The slope of this demand curve is the ratio of its vertical intercept to its horizontal intercept, $12/6 = 2$. So $(1/\text{slope}) = 1/2$ (again, we neglect the

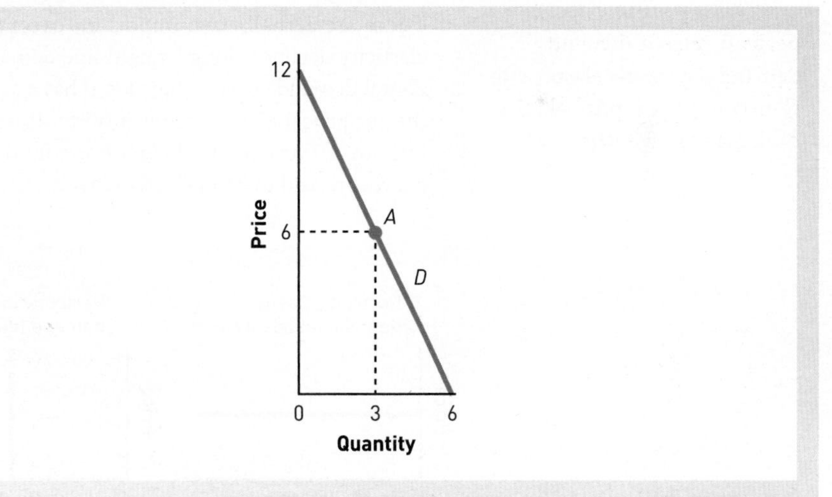


**Figure 4.6 Elasticity at the Midpoint of a Straight-Line Demand Curve.** The price elasticity of demand at the midpoint of any straight-line demand curve always takes the value 1.

[1] To see why, note that at the midpoint of any such curve, $P$, is exactly half the vertical intercept of the demand curve and $Q$ is exactly half the horizontal intercept. Since the ratio of the vertical intercept to the horizontal intercept is the slope of the demand curve, the ratio $(P/Q)$ must also be equal to the slope of the demand curve. And this means that $(1/\text{slope})$ will always be equal to $(Q/P)$. Thus the product $(P/Q) \times (1/\text{slope}) = (P/Q) \times (Q/P)$ will always be exactly 1 at the midpoint of any straight-line demand curve.

negative sign for simplicity). Inserting these values into the graphical elasticity formula yields $\varepsilon_A = (P/Q) \times (1/\text{slope}) = (2) \times (1/2) = 1$.

This result holds not just for the particular demand curve shown, but also for any other straight-line demand curve. A glance at the formula also tells us that since $P/Q$ declines as we move downward along a straight-line demand curve, price elasticity of demand must be less than 1 at any point below the midpoint. By the same token, price elasticity must be greater than 1 for any point above the midpoint. Figure 4.7 summarises these findings by denoting the elastic, inelastic and unit elastic portions of any straight-line demand curve.

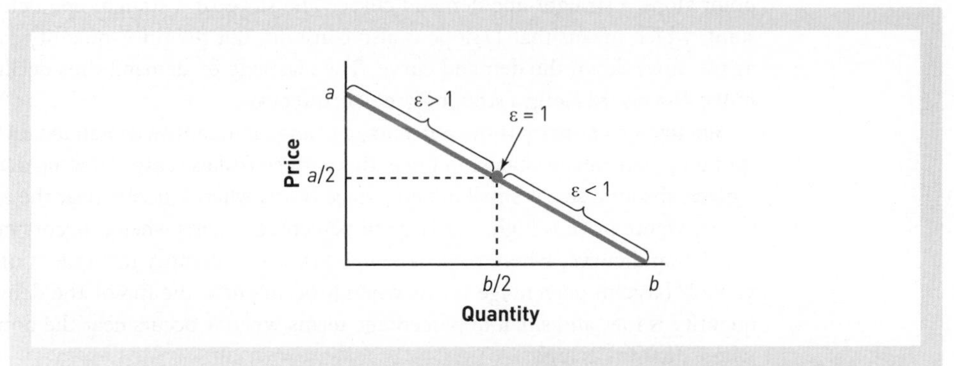


**Figure 4.7 Price Elasticity Regions along a Straight-Line Demand Curve.** Demand is elastic on the top half, unit elastic at the midpoint and inelastic on the bottom half of a straight-line demand curve.

## Two special cases

**perfectly elastic demand** demand is perfectly elastic with respect to price if price elasticity of demand is infinite

There are actually two important exceptions to the general rule that elasticity declines along straight-line demand curves. Note that the horizontal demand curve in Fig. 4.8(a) has a slope of zero, which means that the reciprocal of its slope is infinite. Price elasticity of demand is thus infinite at every point along a horizontal demand curve. Such demand curves are said to be **perfectly elastic**.

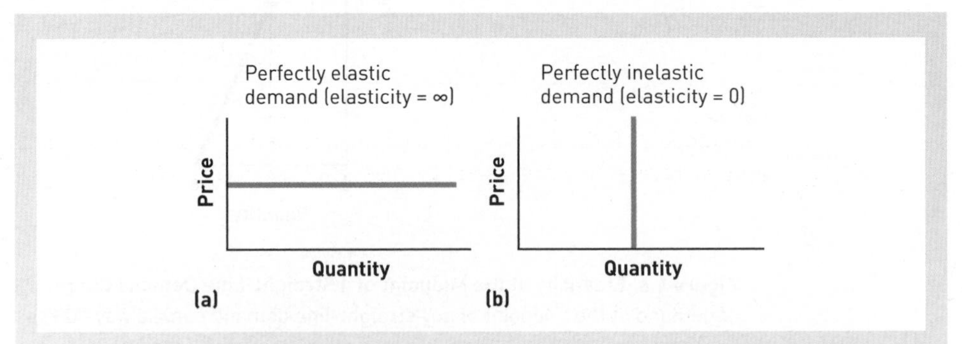


**Figure 4.8 Perfectly Elastic and Perfectly Inelastic Demand Curves.** The horizontal demand curve (a) is perfectly elastic, or infinitely elastic, at every point. Even the slightest increase in price leads consumers to desert the product in favour of substitutes. The vertical demand curve (b) is perfectly inelastic at every point. Consumers do not, or cannot, switch to substitutes even in the face of large increases in price.

**perfectly inelastic demand** demand is perfectly inelastic with respect to price if price elasticity of demand is zero

In contrast, the demand curve in Fig. 4.8(b) is vertical, which means that its slope is infinite. The reciprocal of its slope is thus equal to zero. Price elasticity of demand is thus exactly zero at every point along the curve. For this reason, vertical demand curves are said to be **perfectly inelastic**.

## The midpoint formula

Suppose that you encounter a question like the following in a standardised test in economics:

> At a price of 3, quantity demanded of a good is 6, while at a price of 4, quantity demanded is 4. What is the price elasticity of demand for this good?

Let us attempt to answer this question by using the formula $\varepsilon = (\Delta Q/Q)/(\Delta P/P)$. In Fig. 4.9 we first plot the two price–quantity pairs given in the question and then draw the straight-line demand curve that connects them. From the graph, it is clear that $\Delta P = 1$ and $\Delta Q = 2$. But what values do we use for $P$ and $Q$? If we use $P = 4$ and $Q = 4$ (point $A$), we get an elasticity of 2. But if we use $P = 3$ and $Q = 6$ (point $B$), we get an elasticity of 1. Thus, if we reckon price and quantity changes as proportions of their values at point $A$ we get one answer, but if we compute them as proportions of their values at point $B$ we get another. Neither of these answers is incorrect. The fact that they differ is merely a reflection of the fact that the elasticity of demand *differs at every point* along a straight-line demand curve.

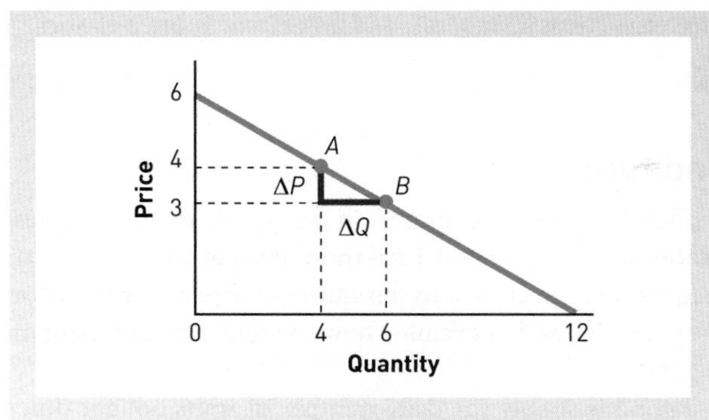


**Figure 4.9 Two Points on a Demand Curve.**

Strictly speaking, the original question ('What is the price elasticity of demand for this good?') was not well posed. To have elicited a uniquely correct answer, it should have been 'What is the price elasticity of demand at point $A$?' or 'What is the price elasticity of demand at point $B$?' Economists have nonetheless developed a convention, which we call the *midpoint formula*, for answering ambiguous questions like that originally posed. If the two points in question are $(Q_A, P_A)$ and $(Q_B, P_B)$, this formula is given by

$$\varepsilon = \frac{\Delta Q/[(Q_A + Q_B)/2]}{\Delta P/[(P_A + P_B)/2]} \tag{4.4}$$

The midpoint formula thus sidesteps the question of which price–quantity pair to use by using averages of the new and old values. The formula reduces to

$$\varepsilon = \frac{\Delta Q/(Q_A + Q_B)}{\Delta P/(P_A + P_B)} \tag{4.5}$$

For the two points shown in Fig. 4.9, the midpoint formula yields $\varepsilon = [2/(4 + 6)]/[1/(4 + 3)] = 1.4$, which lies between the values for price elasticity at $A$ and $B$.

We will not employ the midpoint formula again in this text. Hereafter, all questions concerning elasticity will employ the measure discussed earlier, which is called *point elasticity*.

### Technical note

Demand curves, of course, are not always (or even mostly) straight lines. Hence, the slope of the curve will vary along the curve. Hence, when we want to estimate the price elasticity of demand a formulation using the $(\Delta Q/Q)/(\Delta P/P)$ approach will of necessity be an approximation. This reflects the matters dealt with in Appendix B to Chapter 1: calculus. As a result, in estimating real-world elasticities economists will normally use the first derivative of the demand curve, $dP/dQ$, as the measure of slope, and define elasticity as

$$\varepsilon = (-)(dQ/dP)/(P/Q) \tag{4.6}$$

For the rest of the discussion in this chapter we shall stay with the $(\Delta Q/Q)/(\Delta P/P)$ approach.

## RECAP Calculating price elasticity of demand

The price elasticity of demand for a good is the percentage change in the quantity demanded that results from a 1 per cent change in its price. Mathematically, the elasticity of demand at a point along a demand curve is equal to $(P/Q) \times (1/\text{slope})$, where $P$ and $Q$ represent price and quantity and $(1/\text{slope})$ is the reciprocal of the slope of the demand curve at that point. Demand is elastic with respect to price if the absolute value of its price elasticity exceeds 1; inelastic if price elasticity is less than 1; and unit elastic if price elasticity is equal to 1.

## Elasticity and total expenditure

Sellers of goods and services will often have a strong interest in being able to answer questions like: 'Will consumers spend more on my product if I sell more units at a lower price or fewer units at a higher price?' As it turns out, the answer to this question depends critically on the price elasticity of demand. To see why, let us first examine how the total amount spent on a good varies with the price of the good.

The total daily expenditure on a good is simply the daily number of units bought times the price for which it sells. The market demand curve for a good tells us the quantity that will be sold at each price. We can thus use the information on the demand curve to show how the total amount spent on a good will vary with its price.

To illustrate, let us calculate how much moviegoers will spend on tickets each day if the demand curve is as shown in Fig. 4.10 and the price is €2 per ticket (Fig. 4.10(a)). The demand curve tells us that at a price of €2 per ticket, 500 tickets per day will be sold, so total expenditure at that price will be €1,000 per day. If tickets sell not for €2 but for €4 apiece, 400 tickets will be sold each day (Fig. 4.10(b)), so total expenditure at the higher price will be €1,600 per day.

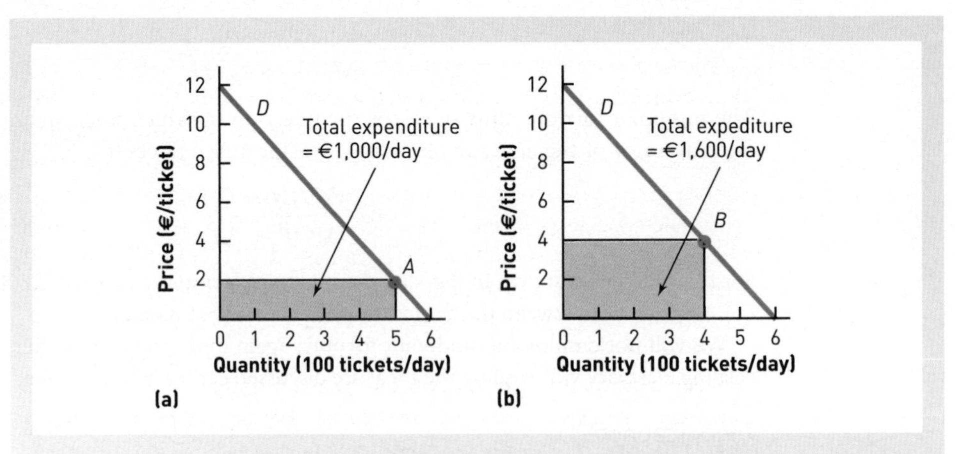


**Figure 4.10 The Demand Curve for Cinema Tickets: 1.** An increase in price from €2 to €4 per ticket increases total expenditure on tickets.

Note that the total amount consumers spend on a product each day must equal the total amount sellers of the product receive. That is to say, the terms *total expenditure* and *total revenue* are simply two sides of the same coin:

> **Total expenditure = Total revenue:** The euro amount that consumers spend on a product ($P \times Q$) is equal to the euro amount that sellers receive.

It might seem that an increase in the market price of a product should always result in an increase in the total revenue received by sellers. But although that happened in this case, it needn't always be so. The law of demand tells us that when the price of a good rises, people will buy less of it. The two factors that govern total revenue – price and quantity – will thus always move in opposite directions. When price goes up and quantity goes down, the product of the two may go either up or down.

Note, for example, that for the demand curve shown in Fig. 4.11 (which is the same as that in Fig. 4.10), a rise in price from €8 per ticket (Fig. 4.11(a)) to €10 per ticket (Fig. 4.11(b)) will cause total expenditure on tickets to go down. Thus people will spend €1,600 per day on tickets at a price of €8, but only €1,000 per day at a price of €10.

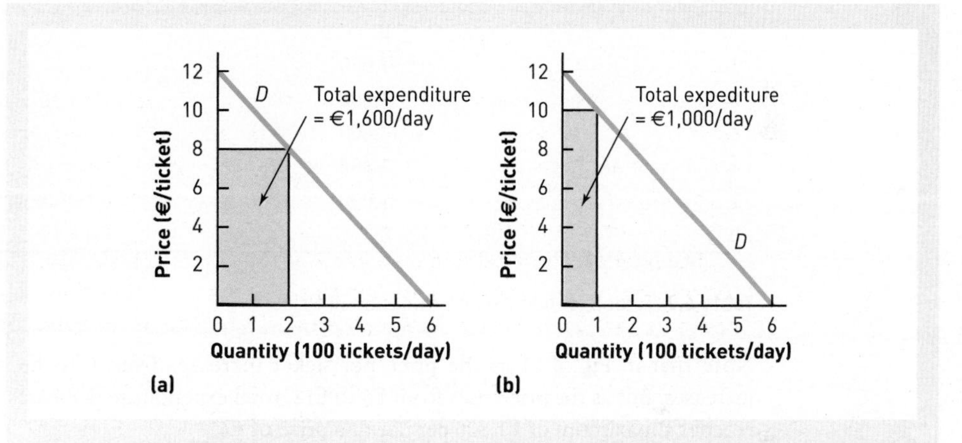


**Figure 4.11 The Demand Curve for Cinema Tickets: 2.** An increase in price from €8 to €10 per ticket results in a fall in total expenditure on tickets.

The general rule illustrated by Figs 4.10 and 4.11 is that a price increase will produce an increase in total revenue whenever it is greater, in percentage terms, than the corresponding percentage reduction in quantity demanded. Although the two price increases (from €2 to €4 and from €8 to €10) were of the same absolute value – €2 in each case – they are very different when expressed as a percentage of the original price. An increase from €2 to €4 represents a 100 per cent increase in price, whereas an increase from €8 to €10 represents only a 25 per cent increase in price. And although the quantity reductions caused by the two price increases are also equal in absolute terms, they, too, are very different when expressed as percentages of the quantities originally sold. Thus, although the decline in quantity demanded was 100 tickets per day in each case, it was just a 20 per cent reduction in the first case (from 500 units to 400 in Fig. 4.10) but a 50 per cent reduction in the second (from 200 units to 100 in Fig. 4.11). In the second case, the negative effect on total expenditure of the 50 per cent quantity reduction outweighed the positive effect of the 25 per cent price increase. The reverse happened in the first case: the 100 per cent increase in price (from €2 to €4) outweighed the 20 per cent reduction in quantity (from 5 units to 4 units).

Example 4.3 provides further insight into the relationship between total revenue and price.

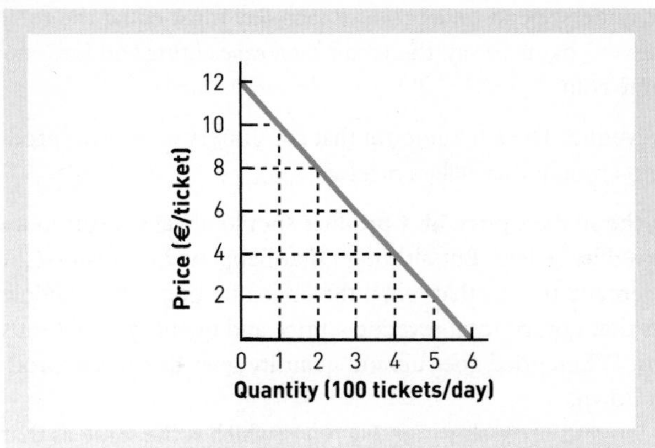


**Figure 4.12 The Demand Curve for Cinema Tickets: 3.**

**Example 4.3** For the demand curve shown in Fig. 4.12, draw a separate graph showing how total expenditure varies with the price of tickets.

The first step in constructing this graph is to calculate total expenditure for a sample of price points on the demand curve and record the results, as in Table 4.2. The next step is to plot total expenditure at each of the price points on a graph, as in Fig. 4.13. Finally, sketch the curve by joining these points. (If greater accuracy is required, you can use a larger sample of points than that shown in Table 4.2.)

| Price (€/ticket) | Total expenditure (€/day) |
|---|---|
| 12 | 0 |
| 10 | 1,000 |
| 8 | 1,600 |
| 6 | 1,800 |
| 4 | 1,600 |
| 2 | 1,000 |
| 0 | 0 |

**Table 4.2** Total Expenditure as a Function of Price

Note that in Fig. 4.13 as the price per ticket increases from 0 to €6, total expenditure increases. But as the price rises from €6 to €12, total expenditure decreases. Total expenditure reaches a maximum of €1,800 per day at a price of €6.

The pattern observed in Example 4.3 holds true in general. For a straight-line demand curve, total expenditure is highest at the price that lies *on the midpoint of the demand curve.*

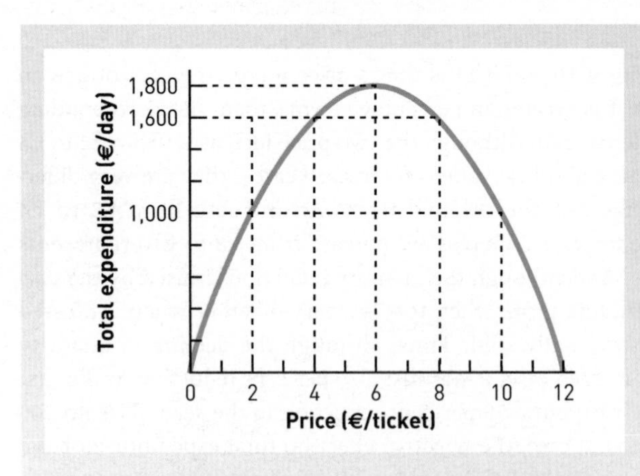


**Figure 4.13 Total Expenditure as a Function of Price.** For a good whose demand curve is a straight line, total expenditure reaches a maximum at the price corresponding to the midpoint of the demand curve.

Bearing in mind these observations about how expenditure varies with price, let us return to the question of how the effect of a price change on total expenditure depends on the price elasticity of demand. Suppose, for example, that the business manager of a rock band knows that he can sell 5,000 tickets to the band's weekly summer concerts if he sets the price at €20 per ticket. If the elasticity of demand for tickets is equal to 3, will total ticket revenue go up or down in response to a 10 per cent increase in the price of tickets?

Total revenue from tickets sold is currently (€20/ticket) × (5,000 tickets/week) = €100,000 per week. The fact that the price elasticity of demand for tickets is 3 implies that a 10 per cent increase in price will produce a 30 per cent reduction in the number of tickets sold, which means that quantity will fall to 3,500 tickets per week. Total expenditure on tickets will therefore fall to (3,500 tickets/week) × (€22/ticket) = €77,000 per week, which is significantly less than the current spending total.

What would have happened to total expenditure if the band manager had *reduced* ticket prices by 10 per cent, from €20 to €18? Again assuming a price elasticity of 3, the result would have been a 30 per cent increase in tickets sold – from 5,000 per week to 6,500 per week. The resulting total expenditure would have been (€18/ticket) × (6,500 tickets/week) = €117,000 per week, significantly more than the current total.

These examples illustrate the following important rule about how price changes affect total expenditure for an elastically demanded good:

> **When price elasticity is greater than 1**, changes in price and changes in total expenditure always move in opposite directions.

The intuition behind this rule is as follows. Total expenditure is the *product of price and quantity*. For an elastically demanded product, the percentage change in quantity will be larger than the corresponding percentage change in price. Thus the change in quantity will more than offset the change in revenue per unit sold.

Now let us see how total spending responds to a price increase when demand is *inelastic* with respect to price. Consider a case like that above, except that the elasticity of demand for tickets is not 3 but 0.5. How will total expenditure respond to a 10 per cent increase in ticket prices? This time the number of tickets sold will fall by only 5 per cent to 4,750 tickets per week, which means that total expenditure on tickets will rise to (4,750 tickets/week) × (€22/ticket) = €104,500 per week, or €4,500 per week more than the current expenditure level.

In contrast, a 10 per cent price reduction (from €20 to €18 per ticket) when price elasticity is 0.5 would cause the number to tickets sold to grow by only 5 per cent, from 5,000 per week to 5,250 per week, resulting in total expenditure of (€18/ticket) × (5,250 tickets/week) = €94,500 per week, significantly less than the current total.

As these examples illustrate, the effect of price changes on total expenditure when demand is inelastic is precisely the opposite of what it was when demand was elastic:

> **For a product whose price elasticity of demand is less than 1**, price changes and total expenditure changes always move in the same direction.

Again, the intuition behind the rule is straightforward. For a product whose demand is inelastic with respect to price, the percentage change in quantity demanded will be smaller than the corresponding percentage change in price. The change in revenue per unit sold (price) will thus more than offset the change in the number of units sold.

The relationship between elasticity and the effect of a price change on total revenue is summarised in Table 4.3, where the symbol $\varepsilon$ is used to denote elasticity.

Recall that in the example with which we began this chapter, an increase in the price of drugs led to an increase in the total amount spent on drugs. That will happen whenever the demand for drugs is inelastic with respect to price, as it was in that example. Had the demand for drugs instead been elastic with respect to price, the drug supply interruption would have led to a reduction in total expenditure on drugs.

## Income elasticity and cross-price elasticity of demand

> **cross-price elasticity of demand** the percentage by which the quantity demanded of the first good changes in response to a 1 per cent change in the price of the second

The elasticity of demand for a good can be defined not only with respect to its own price but also with respect to the prices of substitutes or complements, or even to income. For example, the elasticity of demand for peanuts with respect to the price of cashews – also known as the **cross-price elasticity of demand** for peanuts with respect to cashew prices – is the percentage by which the quantity of peanuts demanded changes in response to a 1 per cent change in the price of cashews. The

| If demand is... | A price increase will... | A price reduction will... |
|---|---|---|
| elastic ($\varepsilon > 1$) | reduce total expenditure<br>$P \times Q = PQ$ ↓ | increase total expenditure<br>$P \times Q = PQ$ ↑ |
| inelastic ($\varepsilon < 1$) | increase total expenditure<br>$P \times Q = PQ$ ↑ | reduce total expenditure<br>$P \times Q = PQ$ ↓ |

**Table 4.3** Elasticity and the Effect of a Price Change on Total Expenditure

**income elasticity of demand** for peanuts is the percentage by which the quantity demanded of peanuts changes in response to a 1 per cent change in income.

Unlike the elasticity of demand for a good with respect to its own price, these other elasticities may be either *positive* or *negative*, so it is important to note their algebraic signs carefully. The income elasticity of demand for inferior goods, for example, is negative, whereas the income elasticity of demand for normal goods is positive. When the cross-price elasticity of demand for two goods is positive – as in our peanuts/cashews example – the two goods are *substitutes*. When it is negative, the two goods are *complements*. The elasticity of demand for tennis racquets with respect to court-rental fees, for example, is less than zero.

**income elasticity of demand** the percentage by which quantity demanded changes in response to a 1 per cent change in income

**Exercise 4.3** If a 10 per cent increase in income causes the number of students who choose to attend private universities to go up by 5 per cent, what is the income elasticity of demand for private universities?

## RECAP Cross-price and income elasticities

When the elasticity of demand for one good with respect to the price of another good is positive, the two goods are *substitutes*; when this cross-price elasticity of demand is negative, the two goods are *complements*. A *normal* good has positive income elasticity of demand and an *inferior* good has negative income elasticity of demand.

## The price elasticity of supply

On the buyer's side of the market, we use price elasticity of demand to measure the responsiveness of quantity demanded to changes in price. On the seller's side of the market, the analogous measure is **price elasticity of supply**. It is defined as the percentage change in quantity supplied that occurs in response to a 1 per cent change in price. For example, if a 1 per cent increase in the price of peanuts leads to a 2 per cent increase in the quantity supplied, the price elasticity of supply of peanuts would be 2.

**price elasticity of supply** the percentage change in quantity supplied that occurs in response to a 1 per cent change in price

The mathematical formula for the price elasticity of supply at any point is the same as the corresponding expression for the price elasticity of demand:

$$\text{Price elasticity of supply} = \frac{\Delta Q/Q}{\Delta P/P} \tag{4.7}$$

where $P$ and $Q$ are the price and quantity at that point, $\Delta P$ is a small change in the initial price and $\Delta Q$ is the resulting change in quantity.

As with the corresponding expression for price elasticity of demand, Eq. (4.7) can be rewritten as $(P/Q) \times (\Delta Q/\Delta P)$. And since $(\Delta Q/\Delta P)$ is the reciprocal of the slope of the supply curve, the right-hand side of Eq. (4.7) is equal to $(P/Q) \times (1/\text{slope})$ – the same expression we saw for price elasticity of demand. Price and quantity are always positive, as is the slope of the typical supply curve, which implies that price elasticity of supply will be a positive number at every point.

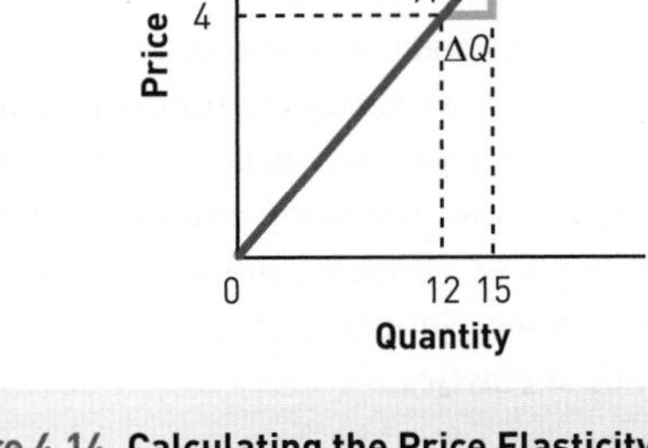


**Figure 4.14 Calculating the Price Elasticity of Supply Graphically.** Price elasticity of supply is $(P/Q) \times (1/\text{slope})$, which at $A$ is $(4/12) \times (12/4) = 1$, exactly the same as at $B$. The price elasticity of supply is equal to 1 at any point along a straight-line supply curve that passes through the origin.

Consider the supply curve shown in Fig. 4.14. The slope of this supply curve is $1/3$, so the reciprocal of this slope is 3. Using the formula, this means that the price elasticity of supply at $A$ is $(4/12) \times (3) = 1$. The corresponding expression at $B$, $(5/15) = (3)$, yields exactly the same value. Indeed, because the ratio $P/Q$ is the same at every point along the supply curve shown, price elasticity of supply will be exactly 1 at every point along this curve. Note the contrast between this result and our earlier finding that price elasticity of demand declines as we move downward along any straight-line demand curve.

Why price elasticity equals 1 at every point in Fig. 4.14 is explained by one special property: the supply curve was a straight line through the origin. For movements along any such line, both price and quantity always change in exactly the same proportion.

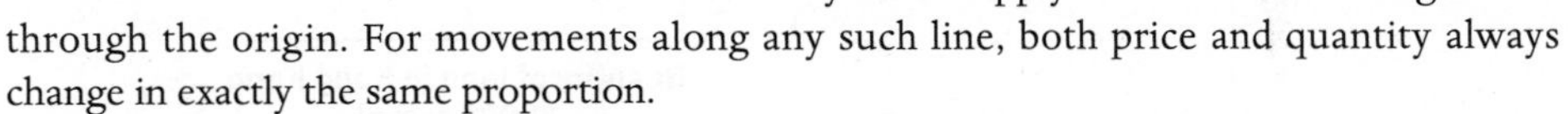

Elasticity is not constant, however, along straight-line supply curves like that in Fig. 4.15, which does not pass through the origin. Although the slope of this supply curve is equal to 1 at every point, the ratio $P/Q$ declines as we move to the right along the curve. Elasticity at $A$ is equal to $(4/2) \times (1) = 2$ and declines to $(5/3) \times (1) = 5/3$ at $B$.

### Technical note

As with the demand curve, strictly speaking the slope value is based on the first derivative, not on $\Delta Q/\Delta P$.

**Exercise 4.4** For the supply curve shown in Fig. 4.15, calculate the elasticity of supply when $P = 3$.

On the buyer's side of the market, two important polar cases were demand curves with infinite price elasticity and zero price elasticity. As Examples 4.4 and 4.5 illustrate, analogous polar cases exist on the seller's side of the market.

### Example 4.4 What is the elasticity of supply of land within the territory of Hong Kong?

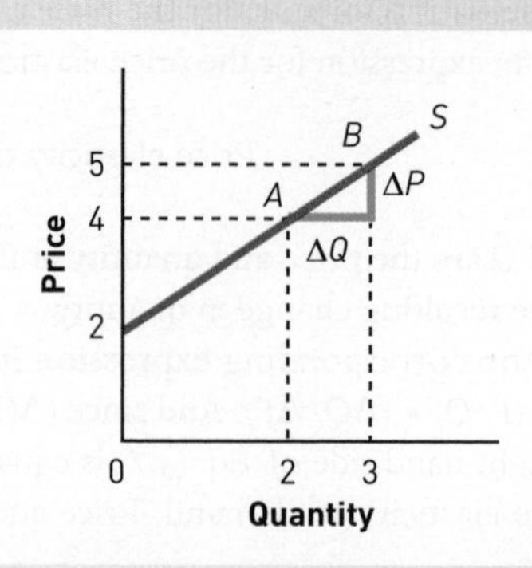


**Figure 4.15 A Supply Curve for which Price Elasticity Declines as Quantity Rises.** For the supply curve shown, (1/slope) is the same at every point, but the ratio $P/Q$ declines as $Q$ increases. So elasticity $= (P/Q) \times (1/\text{slope})$ declines as quantity increases.

Land in Hong Kong sells in the market for a price, just like steel or wheat or cars or any other product. And the demand for land in Hong Kong is a downward-sloping function of its price. For all practical purposes, however, its supply is completely fixed. No matter whether its price is high or low, the same amount of it is available in the market. The supply curve of such a good is *vertical*, and its price elasticity is zero at every price. Supply curves like that shown in Fig. 4.16 are said to be **perfectly inelastic.**

**perfectly inelastic supply** supply is perfectly inelastic with respect to price if elasticity is zero

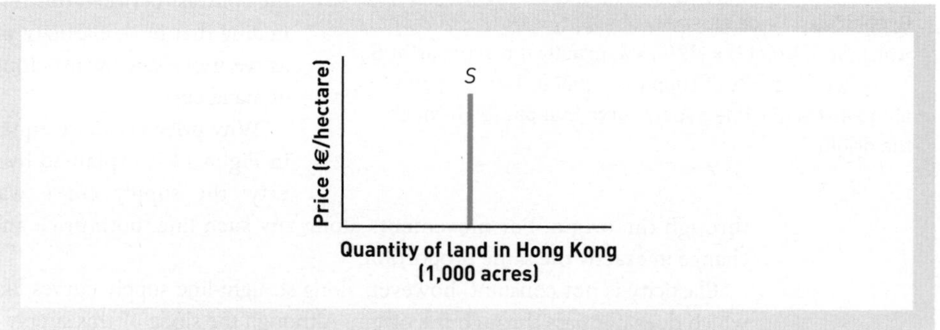


**Figure 4.16 A Perfectly Inelastic Supply Curve.** Price elasticity of supply is zero at every point along a vertical supply curve.

## Example 4.5 What is the elasticity of supply of lemonade?

Suppose that the ingredients required to bring a paper cup of lemonade to market and their respective costs are as follows:

| Ingredient | Cents |
|---|---|
| Paper cup | 2.0 |
| Lemon | 3.8 |
| Sugar | 2.0 |
| Water | 0.2 |
| Ice | 1.0 |
| Labour (30 seconds @ €6/hour) | 5.0 |

If these proportions remain the same, no matter how many of lemonade are made, and the inputs can be purchased in any quantities at the stated prices, draw the supply curve of lemonade and compute its price elasticity.

Since each cup of lemonade costs exactly 14 cents to make, no matter how many cups are made, the marginal cost of lemonade is constant at 14 cents per cup. And since each point on a supply curve is equal to marginal cost (see Chapter 3), this means that the supply curve of lemonade is not upward-sloping but is instead a horizontal line at 14 cents per cup (Fig. 4.17). The price elasticity of supply of lemonade is infinite.

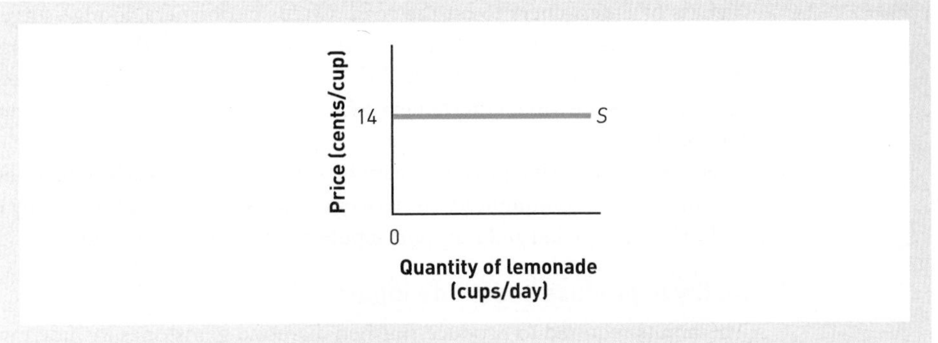


**Figure 4.17 A Perfectly Elastic Supply Curve.** The elasticity of supply is infinite at every point along a horizontal supply curve.

**perfectly elastic supply** supply is perfectly elastic with respect to price if elasticity of supply is infinite

Whenever additional units of a good can be produced by using the same combination of inputs, purchased at the same prices, as have been used so far, the supply curve of that good will be horizontal. Such supply curves are said to be **perfectly elastic**.

## Determinants of supply elasticity

Examples 4.4 and 4.5 suggest some of the factors that govern the elasticity of supply of a good or service. The lemonade case was one whose production process was essentially like a cooking recipe. For such cases, we can exactly double our output by doubling each ingredient. If the price of each ingredient remains fixed, the marginal cost of production for such goods will be constant – and hence their horizontal supply curves.

The Hong Kong land example is a contrast in the extreme. The inputs that were used to produce land in Hong Kong – even if we knew what they were – could not be duplicated at any price.

The key to predicting how elastic the supply of a good will be with respect to price is to know the terms on which *additional units* of the inputs involved in producing that good can be acquired. In general, the more easily additional units of these inputs can be acquired, the higher price elasticity of supply will be. The following factors (among others) govern the ease with which additional inputs can be acquired by a producer.

### Flexibility of inputs

To the extent that production of a good requires inputs that are also useful for the production of other goods, it is relatively easy to lure additional inputs away from their current uses, making supply of that good relatively elastic with respect to price. Thus the fact that lemonade production requires labour with only minimal skills means that a large pool of workers could shift from other activities to lemonade production if a profitable opportunity arose. Brain surgery, by contrast, requires highly trained and specialised labour, which means that even a large price increase would not increase available supplies, except in the very long run.

### Mobility of inputs

If inputs can be easily transported from one site to another, an increase in the price of a product in one market will enable a producer in that market to summon inputs from other markets. For example, the supply of agricultural products is made more elastic with respect to price by the fact that thousands of farm workers are willing to migrate northward during the growing season. The supply of entertainment is similarly made more elastic by the willingness of entertainers to hit the road. Circus performers, lounge singers, comedians and even exotic dancers often spend a substantial fraction of their time away from home. For instance, according to a 1996 *New York Times* article, the top exotic dancers 'basically follow the action, so the same entertainers who worked the Indianapolis 500 now head to Atlanta for the Olympics'.

For most goods, the price elasticity of supply increases each time a new highway is built, or when the telecommunications network improves, or indeed when any other development makes it easier to find and transport inputs from one place to another.

### Ability to produce substitute inputs

The inputs required to produce finished diamond gemstones include raw diamond crystal, skilled labour, and elaborate cutting and polishing machinery. In time, the number of people with the requisite skills can be increased, as can the amount of specialised machinery. The number of raw diamond crystals buried in the earth is probably fixed in the same way that Hong Kong land is fixed, but unlike Hong Kong land, rising prices will encourage miners to spend the effort required to find a larger proportion of those crystals. Still, the supply of natural gemstone diamonds tends to be relatively inelastic because of the difficulty of augmenting the number of diamond crystals.

The day is close at hand, however, when gemstone makers will be able to produce synthetic diamond crystals that are indistinguishable from real ones. Indeed, there are already synthetic crystals that fool even highly experienced jewellers. The introduction of a perfect synthetic substitute for natural diamond crystals would increase the price elasticity of supply of diamonds (or, at any rate, the price elasticity of supply of gemstones that look and feel just like diamonds).

### Time

Because it takes time for producers to switch from one activity another, and because it takes time to build new machines and factories and train additional skilled workers, the price elasticity of supply will be higher for most goods in the long run than in the short run. In the short run, a manufacturer's inability to augment existing stocks of equipment and skilled labour may make it impossible to expand output beyond a certain limit. But if a shortage of managers was the bottleneck, new MBAs can graduate in only two years. Or if a shortage of legal staff is the problem, new lawyers can be trained in three years. In the long run, firms can always buy new equipment, build new factories and hire additional skilled workers.

The conditions that gave rise to the perfectly elastic supply curve for lemonade in Example 4.5 are also satisfied for many other products in the long run. If a product can be copied (in the sense that any company can acquire the design and other technological information required to produce it), and if the inputs needed for its production are used in roughly fixed proportions and are available at fixed market prices, then the long-run supply curve for that product will be horizontal. But many products do not satisfy these conditions, and their supply curves remain steeply upward-sloping, even in the very long run.

## Economic naturalist 4.3 Why are fuel prices so much more volatile than car prices?

Car price changes usually occur just once a year, when manufacturers announce an increase of only a few percentage points. In contrast, petrol and diesel prices, at least in some European countries, often fluctuate noticeably on a week-to-week basis. The variability of the price of fuel in the United States is more pronounced than in Europe, reflecting the lower tax component in the final price to consumers. In early 2005, while petrol cost €0.95 - €1.20 per litre in Europe, it was only €0.27 - €0.35 in the United States (at the time, €1 ≅ $1.3). The difference is due to excise tax and VAT in Europe being much higher than excise plus sales tax in the United States. As shown in Fig. 4.18, for example, the highest daily fuel prices in California's two largest cities were three times higher than the lowest daily prices during 2001–02. Why this enormous difference in volatility?

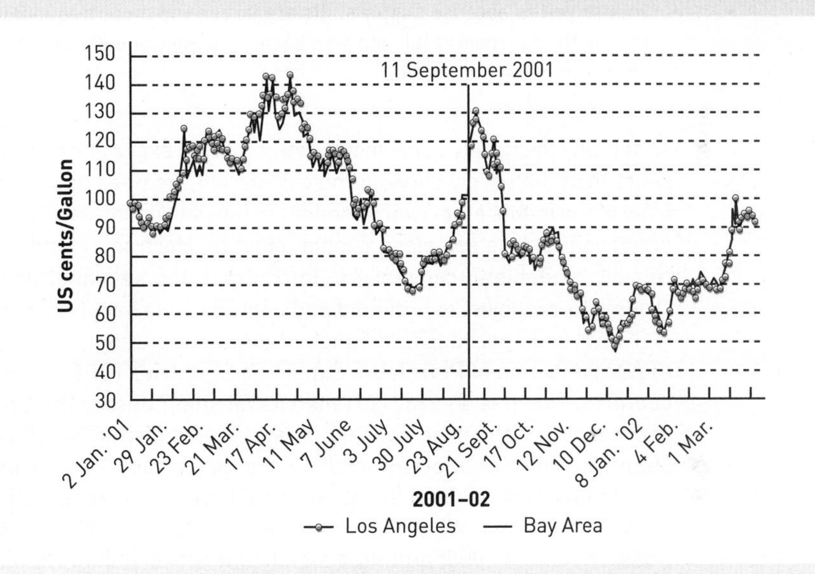


**Figure 4.18 Fuel Prices in Two California Cities.**
*Source*: Oil Price Information Service (http://www.opisnet.com).

With respect to price volatility, at least two important features distinguish the fuel market from the market for cars. One is that the short-run price elasticity of demand for fuel is much smaller than the corresponding elasticity for cars. The other is that supply shifts are much more pronounced and frequent in the fuel market than in the car market (see Fig. 4.19).

Why are the two markets different? Consider first the difference in price elasticities of demand. The quantity and type of fuel we demand depend largely on the kinds of cars we own and the amounts we drive them. In the short run, car ownership and commuting patterns are almost completely fixed, so even if the price of fuel were to change sharply, the quantity we demand will not change by much. In contrast, if there is a sudden dramatic change in the price of cars, we can always postpone or accelerate our next car purchase.

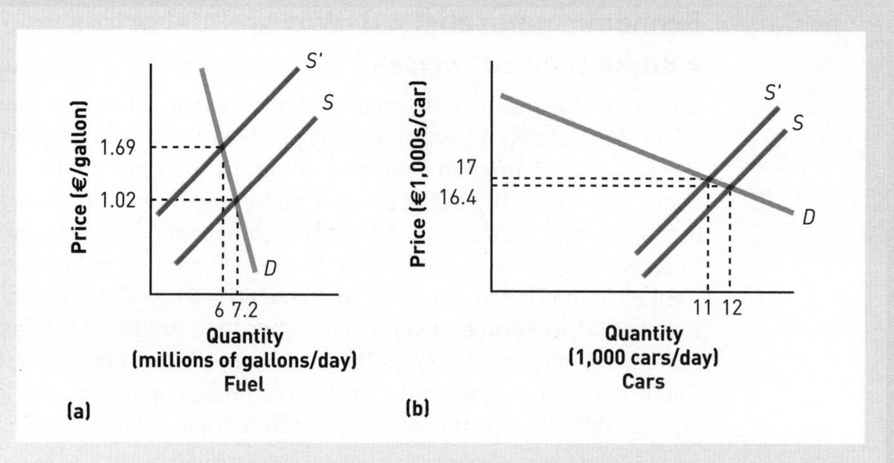


**Figure 4.19 Greater Volatility in Fuel Prices than in Car Prices.** Fuel prices are more volatile prices because supply shifts are larger and more frequent in the fuel market (a) than in the car market (b), and also because supply and demand are less elastic in the short run in the fuel market.

To see why the supply curve in the petrol market experiences larger and more frequent shifts than the supply curve in the car market, we need only examine the relative stability of the inputs employed by sellers in these two markets. Most of the inputs used in producing cars – steel, glass, rubber, plastics, electronic components, labour etc. – are reliably available to car makers. In contrast, the key input used in making petrol – crude oil – is subject to profound and unpredictable supply interruptions.

This is so in part because much of the world's supply of crude oil is controlled by the Organisation of Petroleum Exporting Countries (OPEC), a group of oil-exporting countries that has sharply curtailed its oil shipments to the United States on several occasions in the past. Even in the absence of formal OPEC action, however, large supply curtailments often occur in the oil market – for example, whenever producers fear that political instability might engulf the major oil-producing countries of the Middle East. When Hurricane Katrina devasted New Orleans and the US Gulf Coast in August 2005, putting a significant proportion of US oil production capacity out of use for several months, prices rose by several dollars a barrel.

Note the sharp spike in petrol prices in Fig. 4.18 that occurred just after the terrorist attacks on the World Trade Centre and Pentagon on 11 September 2001. Because many believed that the aim of these attacks was to provoke large-scale war between Muslim societies and the West, fears of an impending oil supply interruption were perfectly rational. And such fears alone can trigger a temporary supply interruption, even if war is avoided. The prospect of war creates the expectation of oil supply cutbacks that could cause higher prices in the future, which leads producers to withdraw some of their oil from current markets (in order to sell it at higher prices later). The consequence is oil being diverted from sale to end users into inventories. The same phenomenon led to a surge in oil prices from around $30 per barrel at the end of 2003 to over $40 per barrel by May 2004, as a consequence of fears of supply disruptions associated with unrest in the Middle East arising from the British- and US-led occupation of Iraq. But once the fear of war recedes, the supply curve of petrol reverts with equal speed to its earlier position. Given the low short-run price elasticity of demand for petrol, that's all it takes to generate the considerable price volatility we see in this market.

(The fallback in prices in 2004 turned out to be temporary, as a combination of supply restrictions and steadily increasing demand from China and India underpinned a much more durable upward movement in prices, which reached over $60 per barrel in 2005.)

Price volatility is also common in markets in which demand curves fluctuate sharply and supply curves are highly inelastic. One such market was California's unregulated market for wholesale electricity during the summer of 2000. The supply of electricity generating capacity was essentially fixed in the short run. And because air conditioning accounts for a large share of demand, several spells of unusually warm weather caused demand to shift sharply to the right. Price at one point reached more than four times its highest level from the summer of 1999.

## Unique and essential inputs: the ultimate supply bottleneck

Football (soccer) fans are an enthusiastic bunch. Directly through their purchases of tickets and indirectly through their support of television advertisers, they spend literally billions of pounds, kroner and euros every year on the sport. But this money is not distributed evenly across all teams. A disproportionate share of all revenues and product endorsement fees accrue to the people associated with consistently winning teams. In Europe at the top of the pile is the small number of top teams from the major football countries that play in the Champions' League.

Consider the task of trying to produce a new championship team (as opposed to being a Russian millionaire who can buy Chelsea). What are the inputs you would need? Talented players, a shrewd and dedicated manager and assistants, trainers, physicians, a stadium, practice facilities, means for transporting players to away games, a marketing staff and so on. And whereas some of these inputs can be acquired at reasonable prices in the marketplace, many others cannot. Indeed, the most important input of all – highly talented players – is in extremely limited supply. This is so because the very definition of talented player is inescapably relative – simply put, such a player is *one who is better than most others*.

Given the huge payoff that accrues to a championship team, it is no surprise that the bidding for the most talented players has become so intense. If there were a long list of superbly talented strikers, each of star quality, Real Madrid would not have had to pay €20 million plus to Manchester United for David Beckham, and then pay Beckham as much as €5 million a year. But, of course, the supply of such players is extremely limited.

Another source of supply bottlenecks arises from the existence of fixed numbers of places in a football league. It is conceivable that you could produce more and better players by spending more on them. But you can't produce more places at the top of the league. A place in the UK Premiership is an essential input to play against other Premiership clubs. There are many hungry football teams in Britain, France, Italy, Spain ... that would like nothing better than to play in the Champions' League. Every Championship team in England would like to get into the Premiership. But no matter how much each is willing to spend, only three or four can succeed. Similar restrictions apply in the Champions' League. The supply of places in the Premiership or the Champions' League is perfectly inelastic with respect to price even in the very long run.

Sports champions are by no means the only important product whose supply elasticity is constrained by the inability to reproduce unique and essential inputs. In the movie industry, for example, although the supply of movies starring Jim Carrey is not perfectly inelastic, there are only so many films he can make each year. Because his films consistently generate huge box office revenues, scores of film producers want to sign him for their projects. But because there isn't enough of him to go around, his salary per film is more than $20 million.

In the long run, *unique and essential inputs* are the only truly significant supply bottleneck. If it were not for the inability to duplicate the services of such inputs, most goods and services would have extremely high price elasticities of supply in the long run.

## Summary

- The price elasticity of demand is a measure of how strongly buyers respond to *changes in price*. It is the percentage change in quantity demanded that occurs in response to a 1 per cent change in price. The demand for a good is called elastic with respect to price if its price elasticity is more than 1; inelastic if its price elasticity is less than 1; and unit elastic if its price elasticity is equal to 1.
- Goods such as salt, which occupy only a small share of the typical consumer's budget and have few or no good substitutes, tend to have low price elasticity of demand. Goods such as new cars of a particular make and model, which occupy large budget shares and have many attractive substitutes, tend to have high price elasticity of demand. Price elasticity of demand is higher in the long run than in the short run because people often need time to *adjust to price changes*.
- The *price elasticity of demand* at a point along a demand curve can also be expressed as the formula $\varepsilon = (\Delta Q/Q)/(\Delta P/P)$. Here, $P$ and $Q$ represent price and quantity at that point and $\Delta Q$ and $\Delta P$ represent small changes in price and quantity. For straight-line demand curves, this formula can also be expressed as $\varepsilon = (P/Q) \times (1/\text{slope})$. These formulations tell us that price elasticity *declines in absolute terms* as we move down a straight-line demand curve.
- A cut in price will increase total spending on a good if demand is elastic but reduce it if demand is inelastic. An increase in price will increase total spending on a good if demand is inelastic but reduce it if demand is elastic. *Total expenditure* on a good reaches a maximum when price elasticity of demand is equal to 1.
- Analogous formulas are used to define the elasticity of demand for a good with respect to *income* and the *prices of other goods*. In each case, elasticity is the percentage change in quantity demanded divided by the corresponding percentage change in income or price.
- *The price elasticity of supply* is defined as the percentage change in quantity supplied that occurs in response to a 1 per cent change in price. The mathematical formula for the price elasticity of supply at any point is $(\Delta Q/Q)/(\Delta P/P)$, where $P$ and $Q$ are the price and quantity at that point, $\Delta P$ is a small change in the initial price and $\Delta Q$ is the resulting change in quantity. This formula can also be expressed as $(P/Q) \times (1/\text{slope})$, where $(1/\text{slope})$ is the reciprocal of the slope of the supply curve.
- The price elasticity of supply of a good depends on how difficult or costly it is to acquire *additional units* of the inputs involved in producing that good. In general, the more easily additional units of these inputs can be acquired, the higher the price elasticity of supply will be. It is easier to expand production of a product if the inputs used to produce that product are similar to the inputs used to produce other products, if inputs are relatively mobile, or if an acceptable substitute for existing inputs can be developed. And like the price elasticity of demand, the price elasticity of supply is greater in the long run than in the short run.

## Key terms

**cross-price elasticity of demand** (107)
**elastic** (95)
**income elasticity of demand** (108)
**inelastic** (95)
**perfectly elastic demand** (102)
**perfectly elastic supply** (111)
**perfectly inelastic demand** (103)
**perfectly inelastic supply** (110)
**price elasticity of demand** (94)
**price elasticity of supply** (108)
**unit elastic** (95)

## Review questions

1. Why does a consumer's price elasticity of demand for a good depend on the fraction of the consumer's income spent on that good?
2. Why does the elasticity of demand for a good with respect to its own price decline as we move down along a straight-line demand curve?
3. Under what conditions will an increase in the price of a product lead to a reduction in total spending for that product?
4. Why do economists pay little attention to the algebraic sign of the elasticity of demand for a good with respect to its own price, yet pay careful attention to the algebraic sign of the elasticity of demand for a good with respect to another good's price?
5. Why is supply elasticity higher in the long run than in the short run?

## Problems

Problems marked with an asterisk (*) are more difficult.

1. On the demand curve below, calculate the price elasticity of demand at points *A*, *B*, *C*, *D* and *E*.

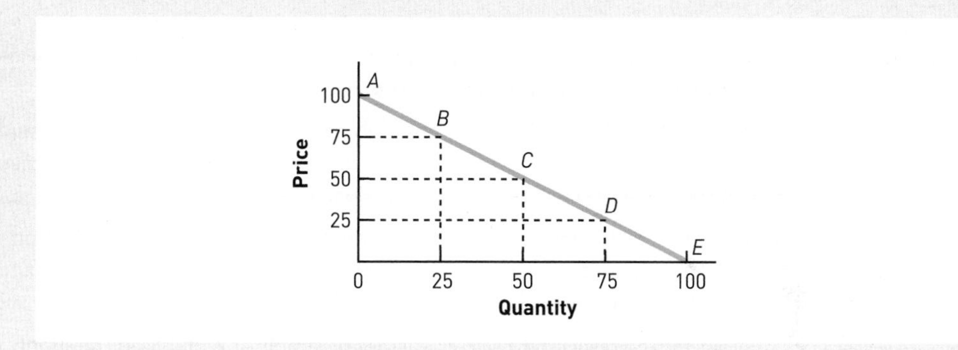


2. The schedule below shows the number of packs of bagels bought in Davis, California, each day at a variety of prices.

| Price of bagels (€/pack) | Number of packs purchased per day |
|---|---|
| 6 | 0 |
| 5 | 3,000 |
| 4 | 6,000 |
| 3 | 9,000 |
| 2 | 12,000 |
| 1 | 15,000 |
| 0 | 18,000 |

a. Graph the daily demand curve for packs of bagels in Davis.

b. Calculate the price elasticity of demand at the point on the demand curve at which the price of bagels is €3 per pack.

c. If all bagel shops increased the price of bagels from €3 per pack to €4 per pack, what would happen to total revenues?

**d.** Calculate the price elasticity of demand at a point on the demand curve where the price of bagels is €2 per pack.

**e.** If bagel shops increased the price of bagels from €2 per pack to €3 per pack, what would happen to total revenues?

**3.** Suppose, while rummaging through your uncle's attic, you found the original painting of *Dogs Playing Poker*, a valuable piece of art. You decided to set up a display in your uncle's garage. The demand curve to see this valuable piece of art is as shown in the graph below. What price should you charge if your goal is to maximise your revenues from tickets sold? On a graph, show the inelastic and elastic regions of the demand curve.

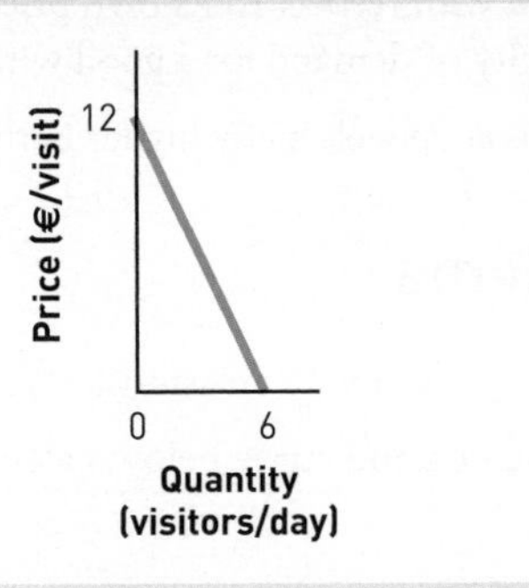


**4.** Is the demand for a particular brand of car, such as a Ford or a Volkswagen, likely to be more or less price elastic than the demand for all cars? Explain.

**5.** Among the following groups – senior executives, junior executives and students – which is likely to have the most and which is likely to have the least price elastic demand for membership in the Association of Business Professionals?

**6.** A 2 per cent increase in the price of milk causes a 4 per cent reduction in the quantity demanded of chocolate syrup. What is the cross-price elasticity of demand for milk with respect to the price of chocolate syrup? Are the two goods complements or substitutes?

**7.** What are the respective price elasticities of supply at *A* and *B* on the supply curve shown in the graph below?

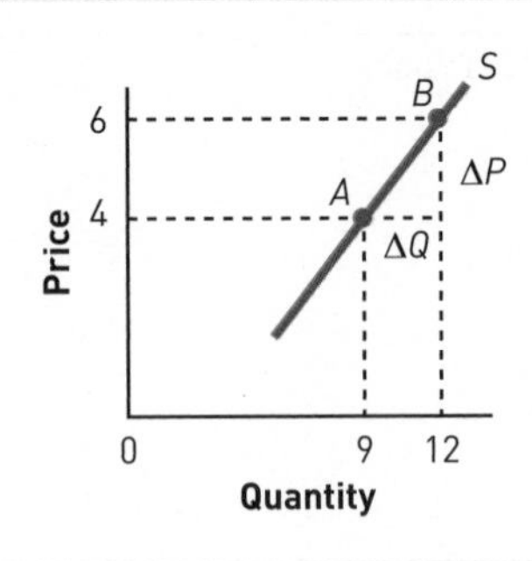

8. Suppose that the ingredients required to bring a slice of pizza to market and their respective costs are as listed in the table:

| Ingredient | Cents |
|---|---|
| Paper plate | 2 |
| Flour | 8 |
| Tomato sauce | 20 |
| Cheese | 30 |
| Labour (3 minutes @ €12/hour) | 60 |

If these proportions remain the same no matter how many slices are made, and the inputs can be purchased in any quantities at the stated prices, draw the supply curve of pizza slices and compute the price elasticity of a slice of pizza.

9.* At point *A* on the demand curve shown below, by what percentage will a 1 per cent increase in the price of the product affect total expenditure on the product?

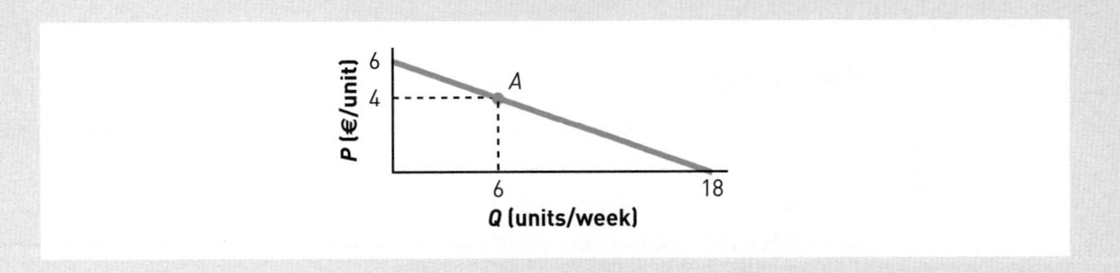


10.* In an attempt to induce citizens to conserve energy, the government enacted regulations requiring that all air conditioners be more efficient in their use of electricity. After this regulation was implemented, government officials were then surprised to discover that people used even more electricity than before. Using the concept of price elasticity, explain how this happened.

## Answers to in-chapter exercises

4.1 In response to a 5 per cent reduction in the price of ski passes, the quantity demanded increased by 20 per cent. The price elasticity of demand for ski passes is thus (20 per cent)/(5 per cent) = 4, and that means that at the initial price of €400, the demand for ski passes is elastic with respect to price.

4.2 At point *A* in the diagram below, $P/Q = 4/4 = 1$. The slope of this demand curve is $20/5 = 4$, so $\varepsilon = 1(1/\text{slope}) = 1/4$.

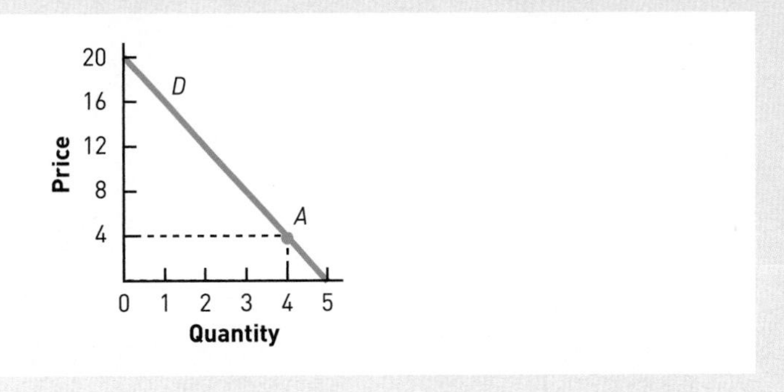

4.3 Income elasticity = percentage change in quantity demanded/percentage change in income = 5 per cent/10 per cent = 0.5.

4.4 For this supply curve, $Q = 1$ when $P = 3$, so elasticity of supply = $(P/Q) \times (1/\text{slope}) = (3) \times (1) = 3$.

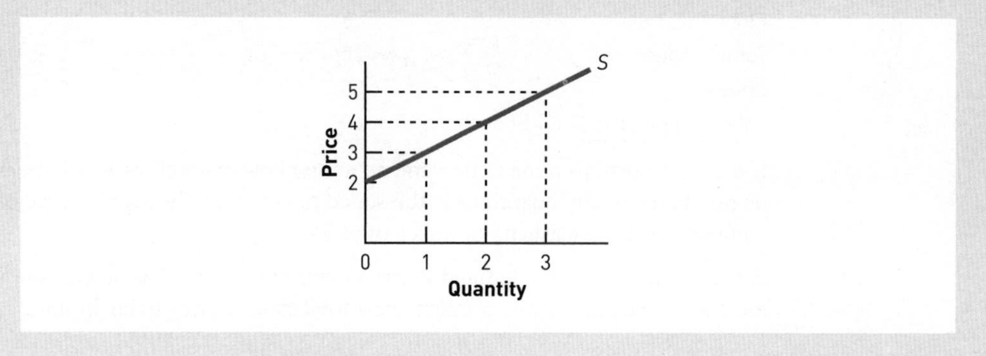


## References

Elzinga, K. (1971) 'The Beer Industry', in W. Adams (ed.), *The Structure of American Industry* (New York: Macmillan).

Fisher, R. (1996) *State and Local Public Finance* (Chicago: Irwin).

Houthakker, H.S. and L. Taylor (1970) *Consumer Demand in the United States: Analyses and Projections*, 2nd edn (Cambridge, MA: Harvard University Press).

Taylor, L. (1975) 'The Demand for Electricity: A Survey', *Bell Journal of Economics*, Spring.

# 5

# Demand: the Benefit Side of the Market

We start with an apocryphal story. X in Germany is famous for (among other things) its annual beer festival. In general, it seems, the city's beer cellars, pubs and other watering holes are full to capacity with locals and visitors for the duration of the festival. According to an urban myth, one year the municipal authorities decided that for the first day of the festival beer should be supplied free of charge in the beer cellars to get the festival off to a good start. The cost of this would be the cost of one day's consumption in the premises concerned, and this was reckoned to be a good investment for the city to attract extra visitors. Arrangements were made with the beer cellars that the city fathers would meet the cost of all the beer consumed in the premises concerned that day. This was done despite the advice of the police that the consequence would be a higher incidence of drunkenness and anti-social behaviour. After all, people, faced with the prospect of drinking for free will want to drink more, and the consequences are easy to predict. The city treasury said the plan would bankrupt the city, since at a zero price the amount that would be drunk would be enormous, and the cost to the city of the beer would reflect this. The owners of the other premises complained that they would do no business that day.

The story goes that at the end of the week the police had to admit that the threatened orgy of binge drinking on the first day did not materialise. Yes, consumption in the beer cellars was up somewhat, but the predictions of massive public drunkenness turned out to be wildly wrong. The accountants were delighted to report that the cost to the city was not much more than that of a normal beer festival bierkeller daily consumption. And the other premises had to admit that their sales hadn't been badly affected after all.

The police were at a loss to explain this outbreak of responsible drinking behaviour at a time when the city was *en fête*. The accountants could offer no plausible explanation. As it happens, however, the son of the Burgermeister (Mayor) of X was one of the best in the final-year economics class at the university that year, and his father had run the free-beer scheme past him before introducing the proposal. His son told him that there would be some increase in beer consumption, all right, but that the fears of the police were groundless. He explained that there was only so much capacity in the beer cellars, and that he expected that people would be forced to queue to get in to enjoy the free beer. Once in, they could indeed consume more ... but by and large each extra stein poured inside the cellar meant one stein less consumed by those outside waiting to get in. The queues outside would grow until the time cost of waiting acted as a deterrent to people joining the queue. Faced with this time price they would repair to the pubs that were not offering free beer. In effect, the cellars would supply not much more beer than would be normally the case, but it would be consumed by different individuals than if they sold it ... The end result would be that the available drink would be rationed not by a monetary price, but by a *time price* in the queue. The point was that the offer applied only to beer supplied in the beer cellars, and these had a fixed capacity to supply beer. Hence, it would not be possible for everyone in Munich that day to drink as much beer as they might like at a zero price, and those who drank beer 'free' would pay a time price to do so, while others would pay a money price but not have to queue.

When a good or service is scarce, it must somehow be *rationed* among competing users. In most markets, monetary prices perform that task. But in the case of free beer, waiting time becomes the effective rationing device. Having to stand in a queue is a cost, no less so than having to part with some money.

This story drives home the point that although the demand curve is usually described as a relationship between the quantity demanded of a good and its monetary price, the relationship is really a much more general one. At bottom, the demand curve is a relationship between the quantity demanded and all costs – monetary and non-monetary – associated with acquiring a good.

Our task in this chapter will be to explore the demand side of the market in greater depth than was possible in Chapter 3. There we merely asked you to accept as an intuitively plausible claim that the quantity demanded of a good or service declines as its price rises. This relationship is known as the law of demand, and we shall see how it emerges as a simple consequence of the assumption that people spend their limited incomes in rational ways. In the process, we shall see more clearly the dual roles of *income* and *substitution* as factors that account for the law of demand. We shall also see how to generate market demand curves by adding the demand curves for individual buyers horizontally. Finally, we shall see how to use the demand curve to generate a measure of the total benefit that buyers reap from their participation in a market.

The approach we take is to explain the basic concepts lying behind the idea of the demand curve, and then to use these to derive the proposition that demand curves in general will slope downward based on logic rather than on simple (and sometimes misleading) notions of common sense. In this chapter we offer first a relatively non-technical explanation based on an assumption concerning consumer behaviour that is referred to as *'diminishing marginal utility'*. This approach suffices for most purposes, but depends on restrictive assumptions concerning people's preferences. So, we then offer a more rigorous and more general analysis of preferences to demonstrate the logical basis for the slope of demand curves, and in doing so introduce a construct that is central to economics analysis after the introductory stage. This construct is the *'indifference curve'*. It is possible to skip this section without losing the thread of the argument in the chapter, but we recommend that you do not take this option if you intend going on to further study in economics.

## The law of demand

With our discussion of the 'free' beer offer in mind, let us restate the **law of demand**.

> **Law of demand:** People do less of what they want to do as the cost of doing it rises.

By stating the law of demand in this way, we can see it as a direct consequence of the *Cost–Benefit Principle* (Chapter 1), which says that an activity should be pursued if (and only if) its benefits are at least as great as its costs. Recall that we measure the benefit of an activity by the highest price we would be willing to pay to pursue it – namely, our *reservation price* for the activity. When the cost of an activity rises, it is more likely to exceed our reservation price, and we are therefore less likely to pursue that activity.

The law of demand applies to BMWs, cheap key rings and 'free' beer, not to mention compact discs, manicures, medical care and acid-free rain. It stresses that a 'cost' is the sum of *all* the sacrifices – monetary and non-monetary, implicit and explicit – we must make to engage in an activity.

## The origins of demand

How much are you willing to pay for the latest Alanis Morisette CD? The answer will clearly depend on how you feel about her music. To Morisette's diehard fans, buying the new release might seem absolutely essential; they'd pay a steep price indeed. But those who don't like Morisette's music may be unwilling to buy it at any price.

*Wants* (also called 'preferences' or 'tastes') are clearly an important determinant of a consumer's reservation price for a good. But that begs the question of where wants come from. Many tastes – such as the taste for water on a hot day or for a comfortable place to sleep at night – are largely biological in origin. But many others are heavily shaped by culture, and even basic cravings may be socially moulded. For example, people raised in southern India develop a taste for hot curry dishes, while those raised in England often prefer milder foods.

Tastes for some items may remain stable for many years, but tastes for others may be highly volatile. Although books about the *Titanic* disaster have been continuously available since the vessel sank in the spring of 1912, only with the appearance of James Cameron's blockbuster film did these books begin to sell in large quantities. In the spring of 1998, five of the 15 books on the *New York Times* paperback bestseller list were about the *Titanic* itself or one of the actors in the film. Yet none of these books, or any other book about the *Titanic*, made the bestseller list in 1999. Still, echoes of the film continued to reverberate in the marketplace. In the years since its release, for example, demand for ocean cruises has grown sharply, and several American television networks have introduced shows set on cruise ships.

*Peer influence* provides another example of how social forces often influence demand. Indeed, it is often the single most important determinant of demand. For instance, if our goal is to predict whether a young man will purchase an illegal recreational drug, our knowing how much income he has is not very helpful. Knowing the prices of whiskey and other legal substitutes for illicit drugs also tells us little. Although these factors do influence purchase decisions, by themselves they are weak predictors. But if we know that most of the young man's best friends are heavy drug users, there is a reasonably good chance that he will use drugs as well.

Another important way in which social forces shape demand is in the relatively common desire to consume goods and services that are recognised as the best of their kind. For instance, many people wanted to hear Luciano Pavorotti sing before he retired, not just because of the quality of his voice, but because he was widely regarded as the world's best – or at least the world's best-known – tenor.

Consider, too, the decision of how much to spend on an interview suit. As university employment advisers never tire of reminding students at the end of their time in college, when they are looking for a job, making a good first impression is extremely important when you go for an interview. At the very least, that means showing up in a suit that looks good. But 'looking good' is a relative concept. If everyone else shows up in a €200 suit, you'll look good if you show up in a €300 suit. But you won't look as good in that same €300 suit if everyone else shows up in suits costing €1,000. The amount you choose to spend on an interview suit, then, clearly depends on how much others in your circle are spending.

## Needs versus wants

In everyday language, we distinguish between goods and services people *need* and those they merely *want*. For example, we might say that someone wants a week's ski holiday in the

Austrian Tyrol, but what he really needs is a few days off from his daily routine; or that someone wants a house with a view, but what she really needs is shelter from the elements. Likewise, since people need protein to survive, we might say that a severely malnourished person needs more protein. But it would strike us as odd to say that anyone – even a malnourished person – needs more prime fillet of beef, since health can be restored by consuming far less expensive sources of protein.

Economists like to emphasise that once we have achieved bare subsistence levels of consumption – the amount of food, shelter and clothing required to maintain our health – we can abandon all reference to needs and speak only in terms of wants. This linguistic distinction helps us to think more clearly about the true nature of our choices.

Think about the perennial political problems arising in southern California over the availability of water (much of which is supplied from aquifers in the distant Sierra Nevada mountains). One typical viewpoint that is often expressed in the media is: 'Californians don't have nearly as much water as they need.' Anyone who says this (or agrees with it) will tend to think differently about water shortages than someone who says: 'Californians don't have nearly as much water as they want when the price of water is low.' The first person is likely to focus on regulations to prevent people from watering their lawns, or on projects to capture additional runoff from the Sierra Nevada mountains. The second person is more likely to focus on the low price of water in California. Whereas remedies of the first sort are often costly and extremely difficult to implement, raising the price of water is both simple and effective.

## Economic naturalist 5.1 Why does California experience chronic water shortages?

Some might respond that the state must serve the needs of a large population with a relatively low average annual rainfall. Yet other US states, such as New Mexico, have even less rainfall per person and do not experience water shortages as nearly as often as California. California's problem exists because local governments sell water at extremely low prices, which encourages Californians to use water in ways that make no sense for a state with low rainfall. For instance, rice, which is well suited for conditions in high-rainfall states like South Carolina, requires extensive irrigation in California. But because California farmers can obtain water so cheaply, they plant and flood hundreds of thousands of hectares of rice paddies each spring in the Central Valley. Two thousand tonnes of water are needed to produce one tonne of rice, but many other grains can be produced with only half that amount. If the price of California water were higher, farmers would simply switch to other grains.

Likewise, cheap water encourages home owners in Los Angeles and San Diego to plant water-intensive lawns and shrubs, like those common in the East and Midwest. By contrast, residents of cities such as Santa Fe, New Mexico, where water prices are high, choose rock gardens and native plantings that require little or no watering.

In the light of this you might like to consider why, although people complain about the level of water charges, from time to time it has been considered necessary to ban the use of garden hoses in suburban England. You might also ask whether the water shortages in France during the heatwave of the summer of 2005 could have been more appropriately dealt with than by a ban on car washes, pool filling and garden watering.

# Translating wants into demand

It is a simple fact of life that although our resources are finite, our appetites for good things are boundless. Even if we had unlimited bank accounts, we'd quickly run out of the time and energy needed to do all the things we wanted to do. Our challenge is to use our *limited resources* to fulfil our desires to the greatest possible degree. And that leaves us with this practical question: How should we allocate our incomes among the various goods and services that are available? To answer this question, it is helpful to begin by recognising that the goods and services we buy are not ends in themselves, but rather means for satisfying our desires.

## Measuring wants: the concept of utility

Economists use the concept of *utility* to represent the satisfaction people derive from their consumption activities. The assumption is that people try to allocate their incomes so as to maximise their satisfaction, a goal that is referred to as *utility maximisation*.

Early economists imagined that the utility associated with different activities might some day be subject to precise measurement. The nineteenth-century British economist Jeremy Bentham, for example, wrote of a 'utilometer', a device that could be used to measure the amount of utility provided by different consumption activities. Although no such device existed in Bentham's day, contemporary neuro-psychologists now have equipment that can generate at least crude measures of satisfaction.

For Bentham's intellectual enterprise, however, the absence of a real utilometer was of no practical significance. Even without such a machine, he could continue to envision the consumer as someone whose goal was to maximise the total utility he or she obtained from the goods consumed. Bentham's 'utility maximisation model', we shall see, affords important insights about how rational consumers ought to spend their incomes. To explore how the model works, we begin with an unusually simple problem, that facing a consumer who reaches the front of the queue at a free ice cream stand. How many cones of ice cream should this person, whom we'll call Sarah, ask for? Table 5.1 shows the relationship between the total number of ice cream cones Sarah eats per hour and the total utility, measured in utils per hour, she derives from them. Note that the measurements in the table are stated in terms of cones per hour and utils per hour. Why 'per hour'? Because without an explicit time dimension we would have no idea whether a given quantity was a lot or a little. Five ice cream cones in a lifetime isn't much, but five in an hour would be more than most of us would care to eat.

| Cone quantity (cones/hour) | Total utility (utils/hour) |
|---|---|
| 0 | 0 |
| 1 | 50 |
| 2 | 90 |
| 3 | 120 |
| 4 | 140 |
| 5 | 150 |
| 6 | 140 |

**Table 5.1** Sarah's Total Utility from Ice Cream Consumption

As the entries in Table 5.1 show, Sarah's total utility increases with each cone she eats, up to the fifth cone. Eating 5 cones per hour makes her happier than eating 4, which makes her happier than eating 3, and so on. But beyond 5 cones per hour, consuming more ice cream actually makes Sarah less happy. Thus the sixth cone reduces her total utility from 150 utils per hour to 140 utils per hour.

We can display the utility information in Table 5.1 graphically, as in Fig. 5.1. Note in the graph that the more cones per hour Sarah eats, the more utils she gets – but again only up to the fifth cone. Once she moves beyond 5, her total utility begins to decline. Sarah's happiness reaches a maximum of 150 utils when she eats 5 cones per hour. At that point she has no incentive to eat the sixth cone, even though it's absolutely free. Eating it would actually make her worse off.

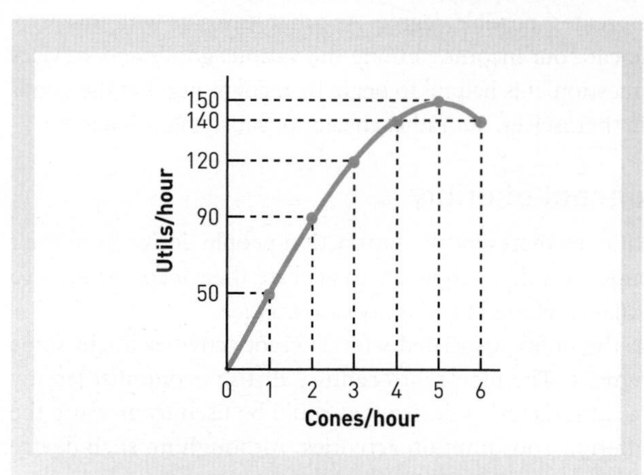


**Figure 5.1 Sarah's Total Utility from Ice Cream Consumption.** For most goods, utility rises at a diminishing rate with additional consumption.

Table 5.1 and Fig. 5.1 illustrate another important aspect of the relationship between utility and consumption – namely, that the additional utility from additional units of consumption declines as total consumption increases. Thus, whereas 1 cone per hour is a *lot* better – by 50 utils – than zero, 5 cones per hour is just a *little* better than 4 (just 10 utils' worth).

The term **marginal utility** denotes the amount by which total utility changes when consumption changes by one unit. In Table 5.2, column (3) shows the marginal utility values that correspond to changes in Sarah's level of ice cream consumption. For example, the second entry in column (3) represents the increase in total utility (measured in utils per cone) when Sarah's consumption rises from 1 cone per hour to 2. Note that the marginal utility entries in column (3) are placed midway between the rows of the preceding columns. We do this to indicate that marginal utility corresponds to the movement from one consumption quantity to the next. Thus we would say that the marginal utility of moving from 1 to 2 cones per hour is 40 utils per cone.

**marginal utility** the additional utility gained from consuming an additional unit of a good

| Cone quantity (cones/hour) (1) | Total utility (utils/hour) (2) | Marginal utility (utils/cone) (3) |
|---|---|---|
| 0 | 0 | – |
| 1 | 56 | |
| | | 40 |
| 2 | 90 | |
| | | 30 |
| 3 | 120 | |
| | | 20 |
| 4 | 140 | |
| | | 10 |
| 5 | 150 | |
| | | −10 |
| 6 | 140 | |

$$\text{Marginal utility} = \frac{\text{Change in utility}}{\text{Change in consumption}} = \frac{90 \text{ utils} - 50 \text{ utils}}{2 \text{ cones} - 1 \text{ cone}} = 40 \text{ utils/cone}$$

**Table 5.2** Sarah's Total and Marginal Utility from Ice Cream Consumption

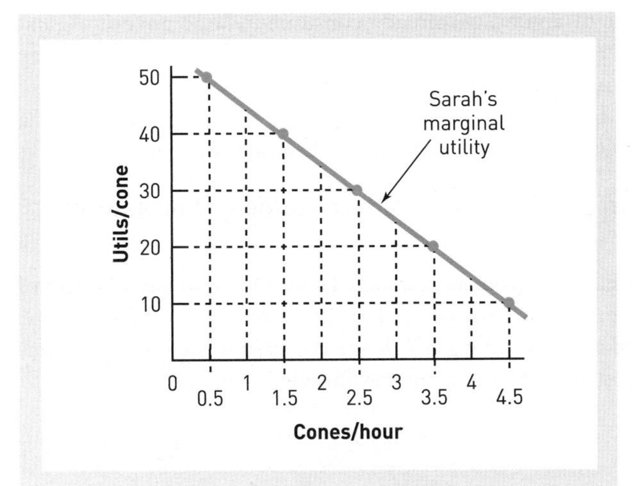


**Figure 5.2 Diminishing Marginal Utility.** The more cones Sarah consumes each hour, the smaller her marginal utility will be. For Sarah, consumption of ice cream cones satisfies the law of diminishing marginal utility.

Because marginal utility is the change in utility that occurs as we move from one quantity to another, when we graph marginal utility we normally adopt the convention of plotting each specific marginal utility value halfway between the two quantities to which it corresponds. Thus, in Fig. 5.2, we plot the marginal utility value of 40 utils per cone midway between 1 cone per hour and 2 cones per hour and so on. (In this example, the marginal utility graph is a downward-sloping straight line for the region shown, but this need not always be the case.)

**law of diminishing marginal utility** the tendency for the additional utility gained from consuming an additional unit of a good to diminish as consumption increases beyond some point

The tendency for marginal utility to decline as consumption increases beyond some point is called the **law of diminishing marginal utility**. It holds not just for Sarah's consumption of ice cream here, but also for most other goods for most consumers. If we have one cake or one Ferrari, we're happier than we are with none; if we have two, we'll be even happier – but not twice as happy – and so on. Though this pattern is called a *law*, there are exceptions. Indeed, some consumption activities even seem to exhibit *increasing* marginal utility. For example, an unfamiliar song may seem irritating the first time you hear it, then gradually become more tolerable the next few times you hear it. Before long, you may discover that you *like* the song, and you may even find yourself singing it in the shower. Notwithstanding such exceptions, the law of diminishing marginal utility is a plausible characterisation of the relationship between utility and consumption for many goods. Unless otherwise stated, we shall assume that it holds for the various goods we discuss.

What will Sarah do when she gets to the front of the queue? At that point, the opportunity cost of the time she spent waiting is a *sunk cost*, and is hence irrelevant to her decision about how many cones to order. And since there is no monetary charge for the cones, the cost of ordering an additional one is zero. According to the Cost–Benefit Principle, Sarah should therefore continue to order cones as long as the marginal benefit (here, the marginal utility she gets from an additional cone) is greater than or equal to zero. As we can see from the entries in Table 5.2, marginal utility is positive up to and including the fifth cone but becomes negative after 5 cones. Thus, as noted earlier, Sarah should order 5 cones.

In this highly simplified example, Sarah's *utility-maximisation* problem is just like the one she would confront if she were deciding how much water to drink from a public fountain. (**Solution**: Keep drinking until the marginal utility of water declines to zero.)

## Allocating a fixed income between two goods

Most of us confront considerably more complex purchase decisions than the one Sarah faced. For one thing, we generally must make decisions not just about a single good but about many. Another complication is that the cost of consuming additional units of each good will rarely be zero.

To see how to proceed in more complex cases, let us suppose that Sarah must decide how to spend a fixed sum of money on two different goods, each with a positive price. Should she spend all of it on one of the goods, or part of it on each? The law of diminishing marginal utility suggests that spending it all on a single good isn't a good strategy. Rather than devote more and more money to the purchase of a good we already consume in large quantities (and whose marginal utility is therefore relatively low), we generally do better to spend that money on other goods that we don't have much of, whose marginal utility will likely be higher.

The simplest way to illustrate how economists think about the spending decisions of a utility-maximising consumer is to work through a scenario like Example 5.1.

### Example 5.1 Is Sarah maximising her utility from consuming chocolate and vanilla ice cream: 1?

Chocolate ice cream sells sell for €2 per carton and vanilla sells for €1. Sarah has a budget of €400 per year to spend on ice cream, and her marginal utility from consuming each type varies with the amount consumed as shown in Fig. 5.3. If she is currently buying 200 cartons of vanilla and 100 cartons of chocolate each year, is she maximising her utility?

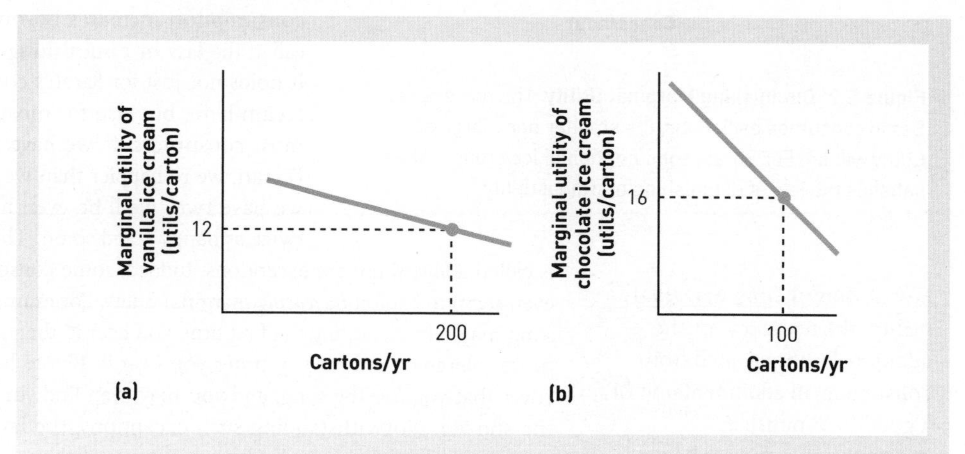


**Figure 5.3 Marginal Utility Curves for Two Flavours of Ice Cream: 1.** At Sarah's current consumption levels, her marginal utility of chocolate ice cream is 25 per cent higher than her marginal utility of vanilla. But chocolate is twice as expensive as vanilla.

Note first that with 200 cartons per year of vanilla and 100 cartons of chocolate, Sarah is spending €200 per year on each type of ice cream, for a total expenditure of €400 per year on ice cream, exactly the amount in her budget. By spending her money in this fashion, is she getting as much utility as possible? Note in Fig. 5.3(b) that her marginal utility from chocolate ice cream is 16 utils per carton. Since chocolate costs €2 per carton, her current spending on chocolate is yielding additional utility at the rate of (16 utils/carton)/(€2/carton) = 8 utils per euro. Similarly, note in Fig. 5.3(a) that Sarah's marginal utility for vanilla is 12 utils per carton. And since vanilla costs only €1 per carton, her current spending on vanilla is yielding (12 utils/carton)/(€1/carton) = 12 utils per euro. In other words, at her current rates of consumption of the two flavours, her spending yields higher marginal utility per euro for vanilla than for chocolate. And this means that Sarah cannot possibly be maximising her total utility.

To see why, note that if she spent €2 less on chocolate (that is, if she bought one carton less than before), she would lose about 16 utils;[1] but with the same €2, she could buy two additional cartons of vanilla, which would boost her utility by about 24 utils,[2] for a net gain of about 8 utils. Under Sarah's current budget allocation, she is thus spending too little on vanilla and too much on chocolate.

---

[1] The actual reduction would be slightly larger than 16 utils, because her marginal utility of chocolate rises slightly as she consumes less of it.

[2] The actual increase will be slightly smaller than 24 utils, because her marginal utility of vanilla falls slightly as she buys more of it.

In Example 5.2, we shall see what happens if Sarah spends €100 per year less on chocolate and €100 per year more on vanilla.

### Example 5.2 Is Sarah maximising her utility from consuming chocolate and vanilla ice cream: 2?

Sarah's total ice cream budget and the prices of the two flavours are the same as in Example 5.1. If her marginal utility from consuming each type varies with the amount consumed, as shown in Fig. 5.4, and if she is currently buying 300 cartons of vanilla and 50 cartons of chocolate each year, is she maximising her utility?

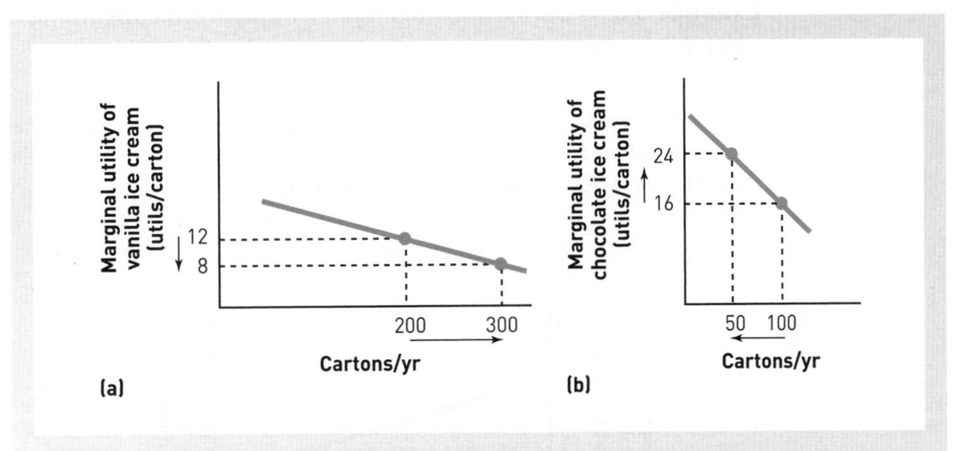


**Figure 5.4 Marginal Utility Curves for Two Flavours of Ice Cream: 2.** When Sarah increases her consumption of vanilla (a), her marginal utility of vanilla falls. Conversely, when she reduces her consumption of chocolate (b), her marginal utility of chocolate rises.

Note first that the direction of Sarah's rearrangement of her spending makes sense in light of Example 5.1, in which we saw that she was spending too much on chocolate and too little on vanilla. Spending €100 less on chocolate ice cream causes her marginal utility from that flavour to rise from 16 to 24 utils per carton (Fig. 5.4(b)). By the same token, spending €100 more on vanilla ice cream causes her marginal utility from that flavour to fall from 12 to 8 utils per carton (Fig. 5.4(a)). Both movements are a simple consequence of the law of diminishing marginal utility.

Since chocolate still costs €2 per carton, her spending on chocolate now yields additional utility at the rate of (24 utils/carton)/(€2/carton) = 12 utils per euro. Similarly, since vanilla still costs €1 per carton, her spending on vanilla now yields additional utility at the rate of only (8 utils/carton)/(€1/carton) = 8 utils per euro. So at her new rates of consumption of the two flavours, her spending yields higher marginal utility per euro for chocolate than for vanilla – precisely the opposite of the ordering we saw in Example 5.1.

Sarah has thus made too big an adjustment in her effort to remedy her original consumption imbalance. Starting from the new combination of flavours (300 cartons per year of vanilla and 50 cartons per year of chocolate), for example, if she then bought two fewer cartons of vanilla (which would reduce her utility by about 16 utils) and used the €2 she saved to buy an additional carton of chocolate (which would boost her utility by about 24 utils), she would experience a net gain of about 8 utils. So again, her current combination of the two flavours fails to maximise her total utility. This time, she is spending too little on chocolate and too much on vanilla.

**Exercise 5.1** Using the prices in Example 5.1, verify that the stated combination of flavours in Example 5.2 costs exactly the amount that Sarah has budgeted for ice cream.

**optimal combination of goods** the affordable combination that yields the highest total utility

What is Sarah's **optimal combination** of the two flavours? In other words, among all the combinations of vanilla and chocolate ice cream that Sarah can afford, which one provides the maximum possible total utility? Example 5.3 illustrates the condition that this optimal combination must satisfy.

### Example 5.3 Is Sarah maximising her utility from consuming chocolate and vanilla ice cream: 3?

Sarah's total ice cream budget and the prices of the two flavours are again as in Examples 5.1 and 5.2. If her marginal utility from consuming each type varies with the amounts consumed as shown in Fig. 5.5, and if she is currently buying 250 cartons of vanilla and 75 cartons of chocolate each year, is she maximising her utility?

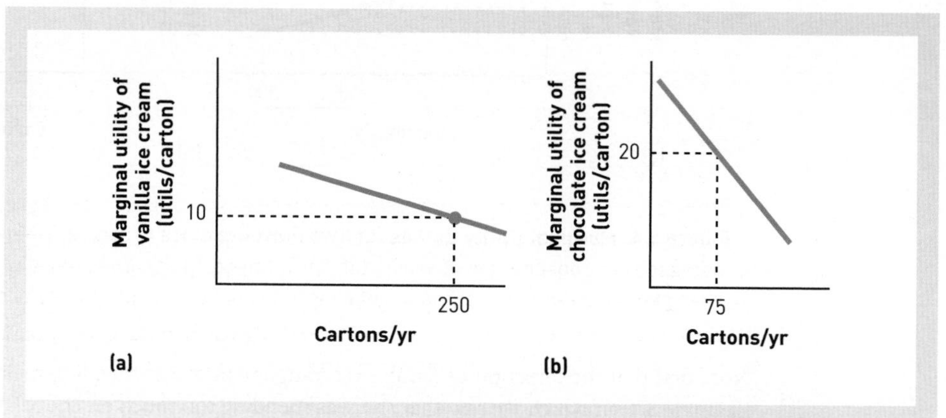


**Figure 5.5 Marginal Utility Curves for Two Flavours of Ice Cream: 3.** At her current consumption levels, marginal utility per euro is exactly the same for each flavour.

As you can easily verify, the combination of 250 cartons per year of vanilla and 75 cartons per year of chocolate again costs a total of €400, exactly the amount of Sarah's ice cream budget. Her marginal utility from chocolate is now 20 utils per carton (Fig. 5.5(b)), and since chocolate still costs €2 per carton, her spending on chocolate now yields additional utility at the rate of (20 utils/carton)/(€2/carton) = 10 utils per euro. Sarah's marginal utility for vanilla is now 10 utils per carton (Fig. 5.5(a)), and since vanilla still costs €1 per carton, her last euro spent on vanilla now also yields (10 utils/carton)/(€1/carton) = 10 utils per euro. So at her new rates of consumption of the two flavours, her spending yields precisely the same marginal utility per euro for each flavour. Thus, if she spent a little less on chocolate and a little more on vanilla (or vice versa), her total utility would not change at all. For example, if she bought two more cartons of vanilla (which would increase her utility by 20 utils) and one less carton of chocolate (which would reduce her utility by 20 utils), both her total expenditure on ice cream and her total utility would remain the same as before. When her marginal utility per euro is the same for each flavour, *it is impossible for Sarah to rearrange her spending to increase total utility*. So 250 cartons of vanilla and 75 cartons of chocolate per year is the optimal combination of the two flavours.

## The rational spending rule

Example 5.3 illustrates the **rational spending rule** for solving the problem of how to allocate a fixed budget across different goods. The optimal, or utility-maximising, combination must satisfy this rule.

> **Rational spending rule:** Spending should be allocated across goods so that the marginal utility per euro is the same for each good.

The rational spending rule can be expressed in the form of a simple formula. If we use $MU_C$ to denote marginal utility from chocolate ice cream consumption (again measured in utils per carton), and $P_C$ to denote the price of chocolate (measured in euros per carton), then the ratio $MU_C/P_C$ will represent the marginal utility per euro spent on chocolate, measured in utils per euro. Similarly, if we use $MU_V$ to denote the marginal utility from vanilla ice cream consumption and $P_V$ to denote the price of vanilla, then $MU_V/P_V$ will represent the marginal utility per euro spent on vanilla. The marginal utility per euro will be exactly the same for the two types – and hence total utility will be maximised – when the following simple equation for the rational spending rule for two goods is satisfied:

$$MU_C/P_C = MU_V/P_V$$

The rational spending rule is easily generalised to apply to spending decisions regarding large numbers of goods. In its most general form, it says that the ratio of marginal utility to price must be the same for each good the consumer buys. If the ratio were higher for one good than for another, the consumer could always increase her total utility by buying more of the first good and less of the second.

Strictly speaking, the rational spending rule applies to goods that are *perfectly divisible*, such as milk or petrol. Many other goods, such as bus rides and television sets, can be consumed only in whole-number amounts. In such cases, it may not be possible to satisfy the rational spending rule exactly. For example, when you buy one television set, your marginal utility per euro spent on televisions may be somewhat higher than the corresponding ratio for other goods, yet if you bought a second set the reverse might well be true. Your best alternative in such cases is to allocate each additional euro you spend to the good for which your marginal utility per euro is highest.[3]

Notice that we have not chosen to classify the rational spending rule as one of the core principles of economics. We omit it from this list not because the rule is unimportant, but because it follows directly from the cost–benefit principle. And as we noted earlier, there is considerable advantage in keeping the list of core principles as small as possible. (If we included 200 principles on this list, there's a good chance you wouldn't remember any of them a few years from now.)

## Income and substitution effects revisited

In Chapter 3, we saw that the quantity of a good that consumers wish to purchase depends on its own price, the prices of substitutes and complements and on consumer incomes. We also saw that when the price of a good changes, the quantity of it demanded changes for two reasons – the *substitution* effect and the *income* effect. The substitution effect refers to the fact that when the price of a good goes up, substitutes for that good become relatively more attractive, causing some consumers to abandon the good for its substitutes.

The income effect refers to the fact a price change makes the consumer either poorer or richer in real terms. Consider, for instance, the effect of a change in the price of one of the ice cream flavours in Example 5.3. At the original prices (€2 per carton for chocolate, €1 per

[3] See Problems 6 and 10 at the end of the chapter for examples.

carton for vanilla), Sarah's €400 annual ice cream budget would have enabled her to buy at most 200 cartons per year of chocolate or 400 cartons per year of vanilla. If the price of vanilla rose to €2 per carton, that would reduce not only the maximum amount of vanilla she could afford (from 400 to 200 cartons per year) but also the maximum amount of chocolate she could afford in combination with any given amount of vanilla. For example, at the original price of €1 per carton for vanilla, Sarah could afford to buy 150 cartons of chocolate while buying 100 cartons of vanilla; but when the price of vanilla rises to €2, she can buy only 100 cartons of chocolate while buying 100 cartons of vanilla. As noted in Chapter 3, a reduction in real income shifts the demand curves for normal goods to the left.

The rational spending rule helps us see more clearly why a change in the price of one good affects demands for other goods. The rule requires that the *ratio of marginal utility to price* be the same for all goods. This means that if the price of one good goes up, the ratio of its current marginal utility to its new price will be lower than for other goods. Consumers can then increase their total utility by devoting smaller proportions of their incomes to that good and larger proportions to others.

### **Example 5.4** How should Sarah respond to a reduction in the price of chocolate ice cream?

Sarah's total ice cream budget is again €400 per year and prices of the two flavours are again €2 per carton for chocolate and €1 per carton for vanilla. Her marginal utility from consuming each type varies with the amounts consumed as shown in Fig. 5.6. She is currently buying 250 cartons of vanilla and 75 cartons of chocolate each year, which is the optimal combination for her at these prices (see Example 5.3). How should she reallocate her spending among the two flavours if the price of chocolate ice cream falls to €1 per carton?

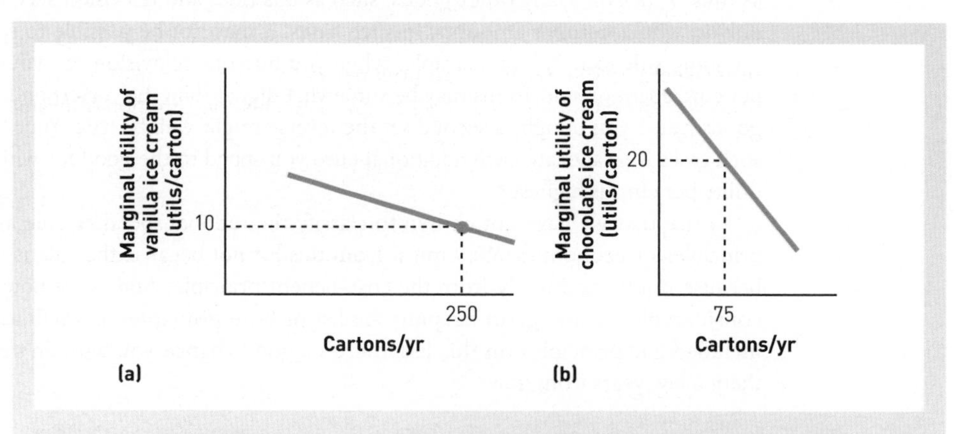


**Figure 5.6 Marginal Utility Curves for Two Flavours of Ice Cream: 4.** At the current combination of flavours, marginal utility per euro is the same for each flavour. When the price of chocolate falls, marginal utility per euro becomes higher for chocolate than for vanilla. To redress this imbalance, Sarah should buy more chocolate and less vanilla.

Because the quantities shown in Fig. 5.6 constitute the optimal combination of the two flavours for Sarah at the original prices, they must exactly satisfy the rational spending rule:

$$MU_C P_C = (20 \text{ utils/carton})/€2/\text{carton}) = 10 \text{ utils/euro}$$
$$= MU_V P_V = (10 \text{ utils/carton})/(€/\text{carton})$$

When the price of chocolate falls to €1 per carton, the original quantities will no longer satisfy the rational spending rule, because the marginal utility per euro for chocolate will suddenly be twice what it was before:

$$MU_C P_C = (20 \text{ utils/carton})/€1/\text{carton}) = 20 \text{ utils/euro}$$
$$> MU_V P_V = (10 \text{ utils/euro})$$

To redress this imbalance, Sarah must rearrange her spending on the two flavours in such a way as to increase the marginal utility per euro for vanilla relative to the marginal utility per euro for chocolate. And as we see in Fig. 5.6, that will happen if she buys a larger quantity than before of chocolate and a smaller quantity than before of vanilla.

**Exercise 5.2**

John spends all of his income on two goods, food and shelter. The price of food is €5 per kg and the price of shelter is €10 per $m^2$. At his current consumption levels, his marginal utilities for the two goods are 20 utils per kg and 30 utils per $m^2$, respectively. Is John maximising his utility? If not, how should he reallocate his spending?

In Chapter 1 we saw that people often make bad decisions because they fail to appreciate the distinction between average and marginal costs and benefits. As Example 5.5 illustrates, this pitfall also arises when people attempt to apply the economist's model of utility maximisation.

### Example 5.5 Should Eric consume more apples?

Eric gets a total of 1,000 utils per week from his consumption of apples and a total of 400 utils per week from his consumption of oranges. The price of apples is €2 each, the price of oranges is €1 each, and he consumes 50 apples and 50 oranges each week. **True or false:** Eric should consume more apples and fewer oranges.

Eric spends €100 per week on apples and €50 on oranges. He thus averages (1,000 utils/week)/(€100/week) = 10 utils per euro from his consumption of apples and (400 utils/week)/(€50/week) = 8 utils per euro from his consumption of oranges. Many might be tempted to respond that because Eric's average utility per euro for apples is higher than for oranges, he should consume more apples. But knowing only his average utility per euro for each good simply does not enable us to say whether his current combination is optimal. To make that determination, we need to compare Eric's marginal utility per euro for each good. The information given simply doesn't permit us to make that comparison.

### RECAP Translating wants into demand

The Scarcity Principle (Chapter 1) challenges us to allocate our incomes among the various goods that are available so as to fulfil our desires to the greatest possible degree. The optimal combination of goods is the *affordable combination that yields the highest total utility*. For goods that are perfectly divisible, the rational spending rule tells us that the optimal combination is one for which the marginal utility per euro is the same for each good. If this condition were not satisfied, the consumer could increase utility by spending less on goods for which the marginal utility per euro was lower and more on goods for which the marginal utility per euro was higher.

## Applying the rational spending rule

The real payoff from learning the law of demand and the rational spending rule lies not in working through hypothetical examples, but in using these abstract concepts to make sense of the world around you. To encourage you in your efforts to become an economic naturalist, we turn now to a sequence of examples in this vein.

## Substitution at work

In the first of these examples, we focus on the role of *substitution*. When the price of a good or service goes up, rational consumers generally turn to less expensive substitutes. Can't afford the monthly repayments for a new car? Then buy a used one, or rent a flat on a bus route or rail line. French cuisine restaurants are too expensive? Then go out for Chinese, or eat at home more often. Cup Final tickets cost too much? Watch the game on television, or read a book. Can't afford a book? Borrow one from your local library, or download some reading matter from the Internet. Once you begin to see substitution at work, you will be amazed by the number and richness of the examples that confront you every day.

### Economic naturalist 5.2 Why do the wealthy in Manhattan, London, Paris or Rome live in smaller houses than the wealthy in Seattle, the Dordogne, Taunton or Parma?

Microsoft co-founder Bill Gates lives in a 4,000 $m^2$ house in Seattle, Washington. The floor area is 0.4 hectares, large even by the standards of Seattle, many of whose wealthy residents live in houses with more than 1,000 $m^2$ of floor space. By contrast, persons of similar wealth in Manhattan rarely live in houses or apartments larger than 500 $m^2$. Michael Smurfit of the Jefferson Smurfit Corporation lives in a luxurious apartment in Monaco that is a fraction of the size of the mansion of Tony Ryan (one of the original founders of Ryanair) 30 km from the centre of Dublin. Why this difference?

For people trying to decide how large a house to buy, the most obvious difference between Manhattan and Seattle or London and Taunton is the huge difference in housing prices. The cost of land alone is several times higher in Manhattan or London than in Seattle or Taunton, and construction costs are also much higher. Although plenty of New Yorkers could *afford* to build a 4,000 $m^2$ mansion, Manhattan housing prices are so high that they simply choose to live in smaller houses and spend what they save in other ways – on lavish summer homes in eastern Long Island, for instance. Rich Londoners and New Yorkers also eat out and go to the theatre more often than their wealthy counterparts in other parts of Britain and the United States.

An especially vivid illustration of substitution occurred during the late 1970s, when fuel shortages brought on by interruptions in the supply of oil from the Middle East led to sharp increases in the price of petrol and other fuels. In a variety of ways – some straightforward, others remarkably ingenious – consumers changed their behaviour to economise on the use of energy. They formed car pools; switched to public transport; moved closer to work; took fewer trips; turned down their central heating thermostats; installed insulation, double glazing and solar heaters; and bought more efficient washing machines and similar appliances. In the United States, many people even moved south to the sunshine belt states, especially Florida, to escape high winter heating bills.

As Economic naturalist 5.3 points out, consumers not only abandon a good in favour of substitutes when it gets more expensive, but they also return to that good when prices return to their original levels.

### Economic naturalist 5.3 After the oil shocks of 1974 and 1979 Europeans did not change significantly the size of car they drove on average. Americans, however, with higher average incomes, switched dramatically from V8 5 litre engine cars to 2 litre four-cylinder cars. Why the difference? And why did they switch back in the 1990s, while there was a much smaller shift in consumption in Europe?

In 1973, the price of petrol was 38 cents per US gallon (approximately 3.5 litres; the Imperial gallon is approximately 4.5 litres). In 1974 the price shot up to 52 cents per gallon in the wake of a major disruption of oil supplies. A second disruption in 1979 drove the 1980 price to $1.19 per gallon. These sharp increases in the price of petrol led to big increases in the demand for cars with four-cylinder engines, which delivered much better fuel economy than the six- and eight-cylinder cars most people had owned. After 1980, however, fuel supplies stabilised, and prices rose only slowly, reaching $1.40 per gallon by 1999. Yet despite the continued rise in the price of petrol, the switch to smaller engines did not continue. By the late 1980s, the proportion of cars sold with six- and eight-cylinder engines began rising again. Why this reversal?

The first key to explaining these patterns is to focus on changes in the **real price** of petrol. When someone decides how big an automobile engine to choose, what matters is not the **nominal price** of petrol, but the price of petrol *relative* to all other goods. After all, for a consumer faced with a decision of whether to spend €1 on a litre of petrol, the important question is how much utility she could get from other things she could purchase with the same money. Even though the price of petrol has continued to rise slowly in nominal, or euro, terms since 1981, it has declined sharply relative to the price of other goods. Even in the aftermath of the Iraq war, petrol prices in Europe were lower in real terms than in 1985. Indeed, in terms of real purchasing power, in America the 1999 price was actually slightly lower than the 1973 price. (That is, in 1999 $1.40 bought slightly more goods and services than 38 cents bought in 1973.) It is this decline in the real price of petrol that accounts for the reversal of the trend toward smaller engines.

**real price** the euro price of a good relative to the average euro price of all other goods

**nominal price** the absolute price of a good in euro terms

What about Europe? The second key is to focus on the fact that the *relative increase* in petrol prices was much lower than in the United States. This reflects the fact that high taxes on petrol were and are universal in Europe. In the United States they were and are very low. Hence a doubling of the price of oil typically meant an increase of well under 50 per cent in the price to motorists in Europe, while the increase was close to 100 per cent in the United States. The incentive to shift consumption patterns based on relative price changes was much smaller in Europe. European motorists have, however, shown a willingness to react to higher fuel prices as predicted by economic theory in a way that has not been seen in the United States. They have shifted from smoother and more lively petrol engines to diesels.

## The importance of income differences

The most obvious difference between the rich and the poor is that the rich have higher incomes. To explain why the wealthy generally buy larger houses than the poor, we need not assume that the wealthy feel more strongly about housing than the poor. A much simpler explanation is that the total utility from housing, as with most other goods, increases with the amount that one consumes. As Economic naturalist 5.4 next example illustrates, income influences the demand not only for housing and other goods, but also for quality of service.

### Economic naturalist 5.4 Why should you not be surprised to find longer checkout queues at Aldi or Lidl than at Tesco in Britain or Conad in Italy?

Aldi, Lidl and other discount supermarkets offer a narrower range of goods at lower prices than the older supermarket chains in Britain. They originated in Germany, so it is not surprising that this pattern is repeated in other countries across Europe. People with lower incomes are disproportionately more likely to take advantage of these prices by going to the discount stores. One way that prices are reduced by the discounters is by reducing staffing levels, especially at the checkout. If we make the plausible assumption that people with higher incomes are more willing than others to pay to avoid standing in a queue, we should expect to see shorter queues in the conventional (but higher-priced) supermarkets. Keeping queues short at *any* grocery store means hiring more checkout staff, which means charging higher prices. High-income consumers are more likely than others to be willing to pay for shorter queues.

### RECAP Applying the rational spending rule

Application of the rational spending rule highlights the important roles of *income* and *substitution* in explaining differences in consumption patterns – among individuals, among communities and across time. The rule also highlights the fact that *real*, as opposed to nominal, prices and income are what matter. The demand for a good falls when the real price of a substitute falls or the real price of a complement rises.

## Indifference curve analysis and the demand curve

*This section of the chapter is more technically demanding than the rest of the chapter. It can be skipped as it is not necessary to read it or master its content in order to continue the analysis of demand, but it introduces concepts that are fundamental to further study of economics. It also offers a rigorous basis for the proposition that demand curves slope downward, and recasts rigorously the concept of consumer rationality.*

So far, the analysis used to explain why demand curves slope down and the concept of consumer rationality has explicitly assumed that goods are subject to **diminishing marginal utility** (DMU) for a representative consumer. As a working hypothesis this is fine. There is plenty of evidence in the real world to support the proposition that DMU is a pervasive aspect of individual behaviour. It is also intuitively plausible.

**DMU a 'law'?** It doesn't always hold true, so it is really an assumption.

Unfortunately, it doesn't take too much thought for someone to come up with counter-examples, cases where DMU does not, or certainly appears not to, apply. Consider, for example, activities in which as the saying goes, 'practice makes perfect'. If you have ever gone on a ski holiday you will immediately recognise the problem. The first day's skiing is (usually) much less enjoyable than the second, and the fifth (when you manage to get down a mountain without falling) beats the fourth. Where is DMU? The same applies to things such as stamp collecting, classical music and so on. Of course, even in these cases we expect DMU to set in at some stage, but it is clear that it is not in fact a universal aspect of consumer choice. That should raise some doubts as to whether we can establish that demand curves slope downward in general if we rely on a doubtfully general assumption as to how consumers value goods.

That is not the end of the matter. There is a second problem, which pertains to *measurement*. Earlier we made use of the assumption that we could measure satisfaction in objective units that we called utils. We did this as a pedagogic device, but in fact it is an assumption that is implicit in circumstances that are much more serious than demand theory in an introductory text.

For example, we implicitly appeal to the concept when we argue that society is better off if we transfer wealth from the rich to the poor, because we reckon that the increase in the welfare of the recipients of the transfer exceeds the reduction in the welfare of those who are asked to pay. Philosophically, and empirically, it could obviously be true that the reverse was true in the tax transfer example. Or we might say it is nonsensical to measure satisfaction in objective units anyway. For example, you might be able to answer the question 'Are you happier today than yesterday?' and be quite unable to answer the question 'By how much are you happier today than yesterday?' But DMU implies being able to make that kind of evaluation.

These two considerations lead to the conclusion that a 'proof' of the downward-sloping demand curve and the rational spending criterion that depends on DMU is at best a partial proof, and at worst may be no proof at all.

To deal with this, and also to introduce a tool of analysis that is widely used in economics, we drop any assumption of DMU, and start with a set of assumptions about rational choice.

First we posit that an individual has a *preference ordering*. By that we mean that we have some means whereby we can in principle define an individual's preferences as to various bundles of goods or services he might consume. We make this as general and unrestrictive as possible.

**Assumption 1:** The individual's preferences are **complete**. By this we mean that the individual can compare any two bundles of goods and services and say which is preferred or whether one is as good as the other. This is fundamental: the individual can *choose between bundles*.

**Assumption 2:** The individual's preference ordering over bundles is **ordinal**, rather than **cardinal**. By this we mean that we only require a ranking, but don't require the individual to be able to answer the type of question given above about 'how much happier'. To do that the ranking has to be cardinal. The cardinal numbers are 1, 2, 3 ... The ordinal numbers are 1st, 2nd, 3rd ... A cardinal ordering enables us to say 'I am 50 per cent happier'. The ordinal ranking is a much less restrictive assumption or requirement.

**Cardinal or ordinal?** DMU implies that utility is measured cardinally.

**Assumption 3:** The individual's preferences are **transitive**. By this we mean that if you say you prefer bundle *A* to bundle *B*, and bundle *B* to bundle *C*, you must prefer bundle *A* to bundle *C*.

**Assumption 4:** The individual's satisfaction level is **monotonically increasing** with respect to any good. This is a technical way of saying that 'more of a good is better', so that, other things being equal, the individual is better off with more of any one good as long as she has the same amount as before of all other goods.

**Assumption 5:** The individual's preferences are **continuous**. By this we mean that the individual can rank bundles that are very similar, for example containing a small amount more or less of any good or goods.

**Assumption 6:** We assume that the individual's preferences display a **diminishing marginal rate of substitution**. This will be explained in context later on.

Assumptions 1–5 inclusive enable us to say that the individual's preferences over bundles of goods can be written as a **utility function**. Assumption 6 is an assumption about the function. By a utility function we mean that we can write an individual's preferences in the form

$$U_i = U_i\,(X, Y, \ldots, Z)$$

where $U_i$ means the individual's utility, and the $X, Y, \ldots, Z$ are the bundles she is enjoying: her satisfaction is a function of the goods she consumes in the mathematical sense.

**Utility function assumption:** The preference ordering can be written as a utility function; this permits trade-offs.

The basic feature of all this is that it means that the individual can trade off bundles in terms of their composition while maintaining a given level of satisfaction. While that may seem blindingly obvious, in fact it is not. Frequently, ethical or political choices are made between states of the world in a manner that does not permit trade-offs. An obvious case of this is the question of whether or not, and in what circumstances, abortion should be permitted. Suppose that abortion is completely forbidden, and the government proposes that it should be introduced in circumstances where an estimated 100 special cases a year could avail themselves of it. Opponents of abortion are not likely to say 'we are against abortion being available, but if, say, everyone was given €1,000 a year more we would allow some abortion'. Instead they rank states of the world on the basis that there is no compensation they would accept that would leave them as happy as before if a little abortion was allowed.

## The model

The consumer has an income, $Y$, which is to be spent on two goods, $A$ and $B$. The unit price of $A$ is $P_a$ and the unit price of $B$ is $P_b$. Her income is exhausted on the two goods, and from this we derive her *budget constraint* (budget line):

$$Y = P_a A + P_b B$$

where $A$ is the number of units of $A$ consumed and $B$ is the number of units of $B$ consumed. In Fig. 5.7 we see a number of bundles of $A$ and $B$ that might be consumed. The line $Y/P_a$ to $Y/P_b$ is the budget constraint (budget line). Bundle 1 lies within the constraint, this bundle would not exhaust her income. Bundles 2 and 4 lie outside it: she hasn't enough income to buy either. Bundle 3 lies on the constraint. Only bundles on the constraint will exhaust her income. Given the assumptions above, she will never settle for a bundle lying within the constraint, because she can buy more of one or both and derive a higher level of utility.

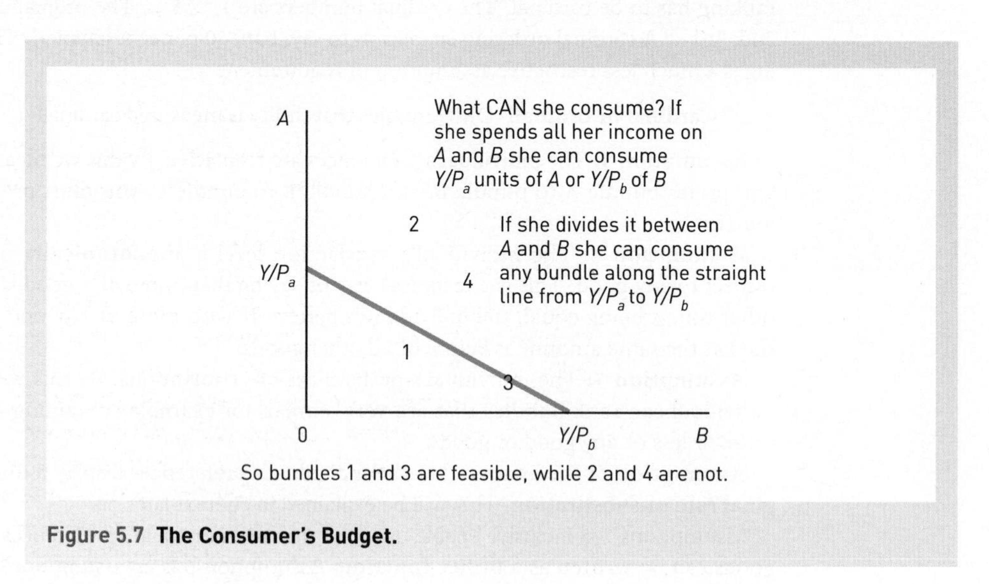


**Figure 5.7 The Consumer's Budget.**

If her income rises she can consume more, and bundle 4 becomes feasible (Fig. 5.8.)

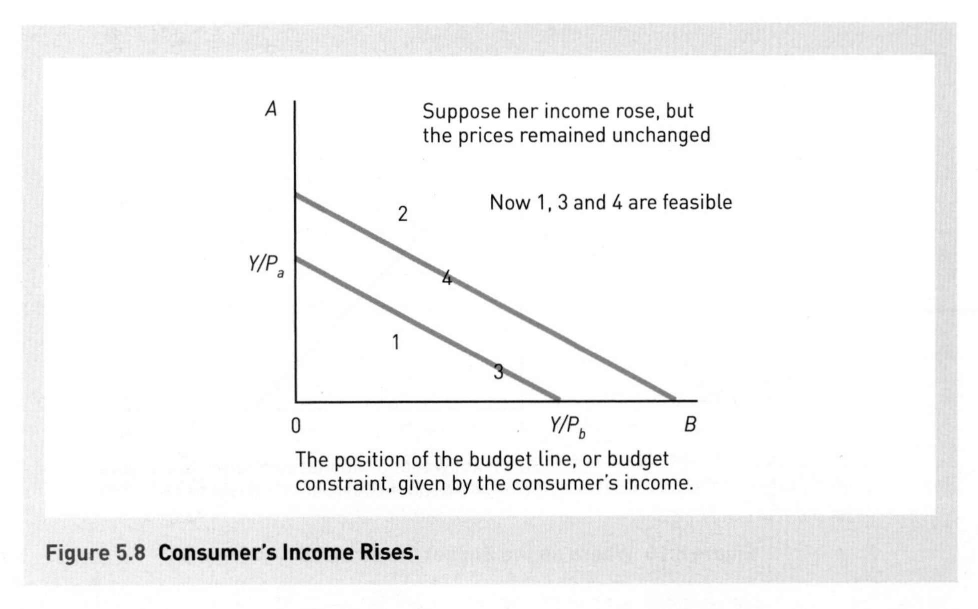


**Figure 5.8 Consumer's Income Rises.**

If the price of good *A* fell, her budget constraint would be shifted out on the *A* axis (Fig. 5.9).

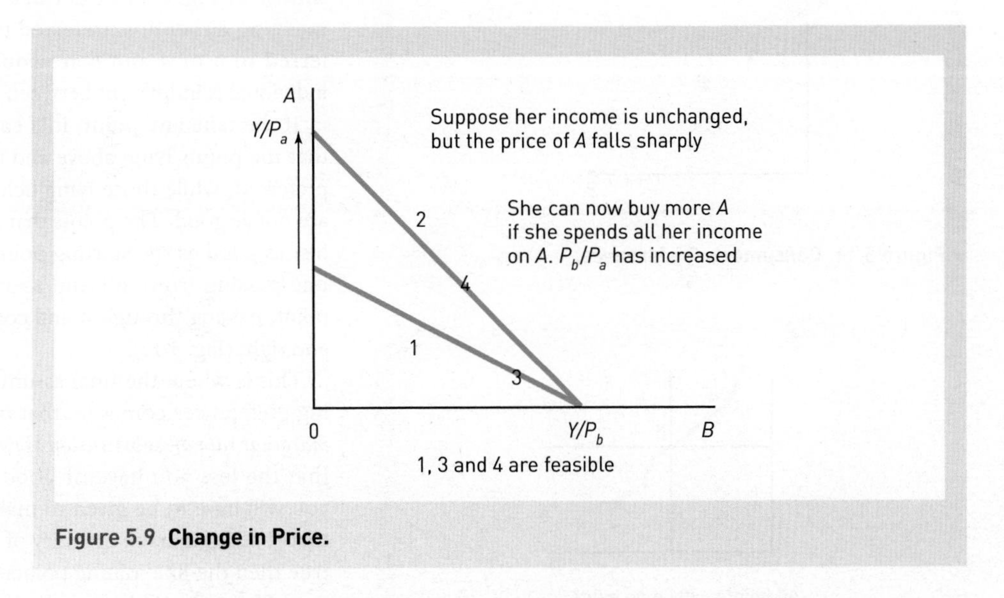


**Figure 5.9 Change in Price.**

The rational consumer will always be on her budget constraint … but where (Fig. 5.10)?

There is insufficient information so far to answer this question posed in Fig. 5.10. To do so, we have to go back to the *consumer's preferences*. In Fig. 5.11, for any points $\alpha$, $\beta$, $\gamma$ ... the preference assumptions tell us that on a pair-wise comparison the individual can say whether the bundle is preferred to (has higher utility) the other, is regarded as less desirable than the other (lower utility), or is the same as the other (she is indifferent between the bundles).

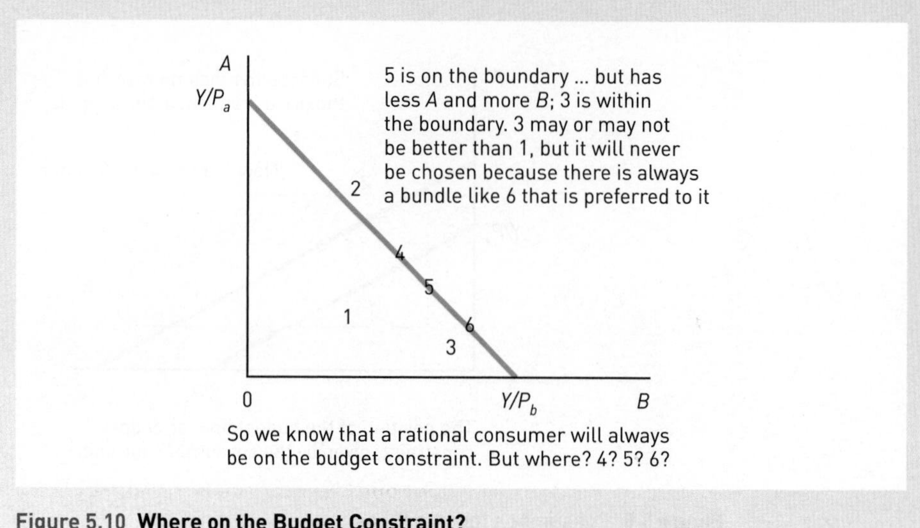


**Figure 5.10 Where on the Budget Constraint?**

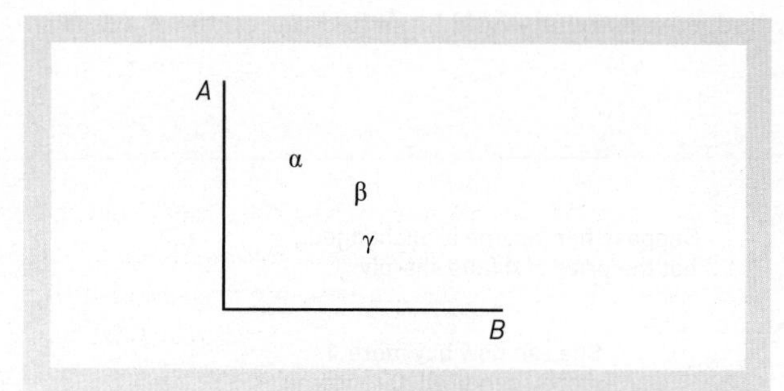


**Figure 5.11 Consumer's Preferences.**

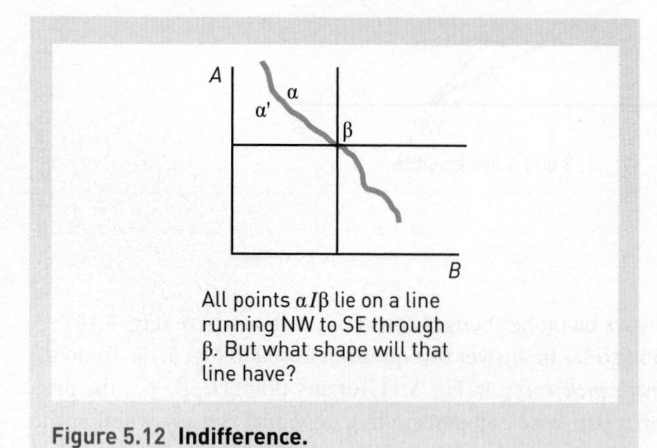

A
α
α'
β
B
All points α/β lie on a line running NW to SE through β. But what shape will that line have?


**Figure 5.12 Indifference.**

Formally, for any points *a* and *b* in the space shown in Fig. 5.11 either *aPb* or *bPa* or *aIb*, meaning either *a* is preferred to *b* or *b* is preferred to *a* or *a* and *b* are equally good (the individual is indifferent between them).

If we take any point, it is easy to establish that the points lying above and to the right are preferred, while those lying below and the left are not as good. The points that are regarded as just as good as the starting point must lie on a line passing from left and above the starting point, passing through it and continuing below and right (Fig. 5.12).

This is where the final assumption concerning preferences comes in, that of a *diminishing marginal rate of substitution* (DMRS). It means that the less you have of good *A* the more *B* you will have to be given to make up for a further reduction in the quantity of *A*. If this holds true then the line joining points of indifference as in Fig. 5.12 will have to look as in Fig. 5.13. As you move along the indifference curve you trade units of *A* for *B* or vice versa while your utility is unchanged (hence you are indifferent). The slope of the **indifference curve** shows the marginal rate of substitution. DMRS implies that it is smoothly convex.

**indifference curve** a smoothly convex curve; its slope is the consumer's marginal rate of substitution (MRS) between two goods

There is in principle an infinite number of indifference curves (Fig. 5.14), one for each level of satisfaction, and the further out the curve the higher the level of satisfaction to which it refers, since any point on it contains more of both goods than a point below and to the right. The more of both goods the consumer has, the higher is her satisfaction.

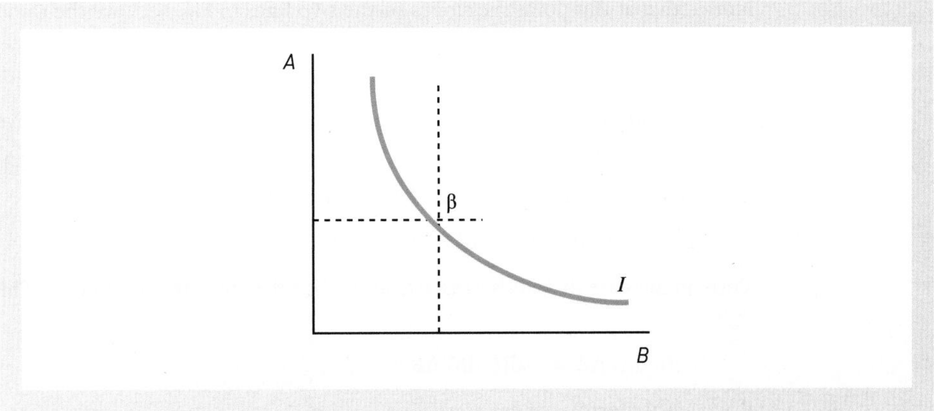


Figure 5.13 **The Convex Indifference Curve.**

Hence we can think of moving out from the origin on the graph as ascending a 'utility mountain', with the curves being contour lines on the map, just like contour lines on the physical map of a country. *Transitivity* implies that the curves cannot cross.

**Exercise 5.3** To demonstrate this, draw two curves crossing and show why this is a contradiction in terms.

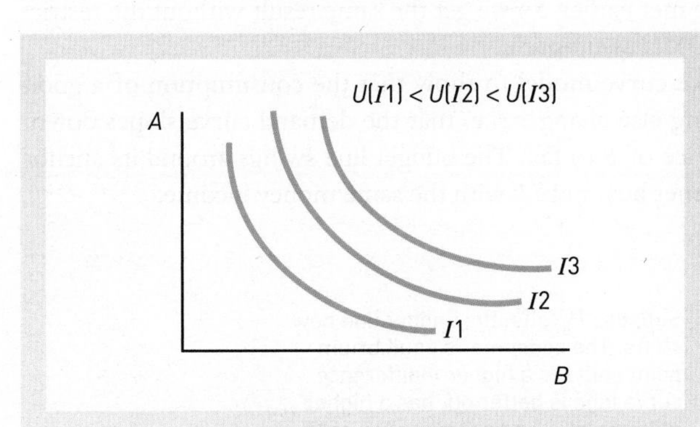


Figure 5.14 **Indifference Curves and Satisfaction Levels.**

At this stage we bring the pieces together, the budget constraint and the indifference map. The consumer wants to maximise her utility but has to remain on her budget constraint. This happens (Fig. 5.15) when she is at a point on the constraint where it is a tangent to an indifference curve. Some such point must exist because of the continuity assumption about preferences.

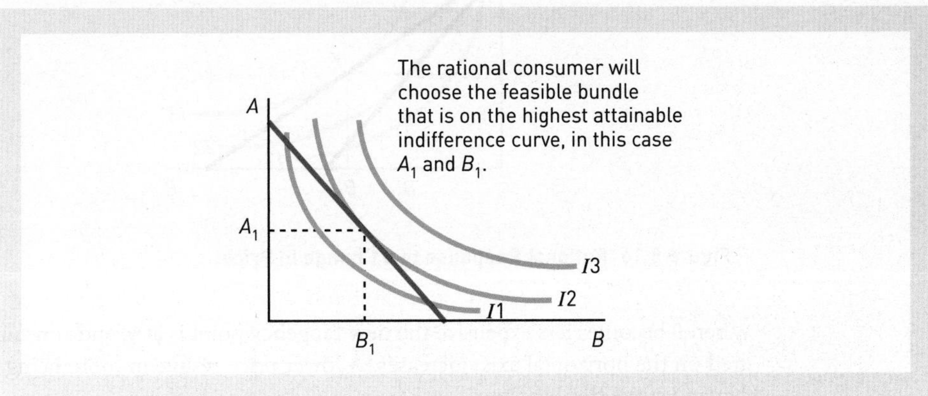


Figure 5.15 **Rational Choice.**

Notice that at this point the slopes of the two lines in Fig. 5.15 are the same. The slope of the indifference curve is the MRS; that of the budget line is $P_a/P_b$, relative prices. If the individual displays *consumer rationality*, she will allocate her spending so that MRS equals relative price.

**Consumer rationality:** Allocate spending so that MRS equals relative price.

Since the indifference curve traces out the points offering the same level of utility, a move along it leaves utility unchanged. This can be written

$$\Delta U = (dU/dA)\ \Delta A + (dU/dB)\ \Delta B = 0$$

since an increase in $A$ adds satisfaction that is offset by a reduction in $B$. This equation implies that

$$(dU/dA)\ \Delta A = -(dU/dB)\ \Delta B$$

If we gather terms, we get:

$$\Delta A/\Delta B = -(dU/dB)/(dU/dA)$$

The left-hand side is the slope of the indifference curve, the MRS; the right-hand side is the ratio of marginal utilities.

When the consumer is in equilibrium, maximising utility, the two curves are tangents, and the MRS equals the price ratio. That means that $P_a/P_b = (dU/dB)/(dU/dA)$ (we ignore the sign). That in turn implies that

$$(dU/dA)/P_a = (dU/dB)/P_b$$

which is the familiar $MU/P$ rule we met earlier. So we get the same result without the restrictive assumptions lying behind the DMU assumption.

We can now use the indifference curve model to show that the consumption of a good will rise if its price falls and nothing else changes (i.e. that the demand curve slopes downward). In Fig. 5.16 we allow the price of $B$ to fall. The budget line swings around its anchor point on the $A$ axis to let the consumer buy more $B$ with the same money income.

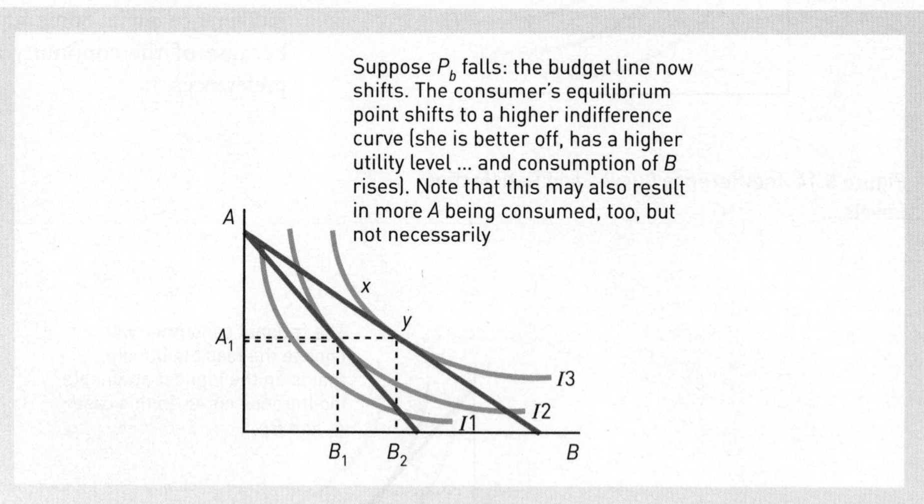

Suppose $P_b$ falls: the budget line now shifts. The consumer's equilibrium point shifts to a higher indifference curve (she is better off, has a higher utility level ... and consumption of *B* rises). Note that this may also result in more *A* being consumed, too, but not necessarily
A
x
y
$A_1$
I3
I2
I1
$B_1$
$B_2$
B


**Figure 5.16 Rational Response to a Change in Price.**

When $B$ becomes less expensive the new tangency point is at $y$, and consumption of $B$ (measured on the horizontal axis) increases. A lower price results in more being demanded, or the demand curve slopes down.

Indifference curve analysis has, therefore, enabled us to conclude that if the price of a good falls, other things being equal, a rational consumer will purchase more of it. That means that the consumer's demand curve slopes down from left to right, which was one of the things that we set out to prove without assuming either DMU or that utility could be measured cardinally.

This also demonstrates that the concept of consumer rationality that states that a consumer will allocate his or her budget between goods so that the ratio of marginal utility to price is the same across all goods is independent of any assumption that DMU applies.

The indifference curve approach has a further dividend. It makes clear the difference between the *income* and *substitution* effects of a price change. When the price of *B* fell the consumer's income permitted her to consume more of both goods that before. That fact alone means she is better off, and if she is, and if *B* is a normal good, she will consume more *B*. This is the *income* effect of the price change. But it also reduces the relative price of *B*, encouraging her to substitute some of the now cheaper good for some of what is now more expensive. This is the *substitution* effect of the price change.

To see both of these, imagine that instead of the price of *B* falling the consumer's money income was increased just enough to enable her to get on to *I3* in Fig. 5.16. This would be shown by moving her original budget line out without changing its slope until it was a tangent with *I3*. The tangency point would be on *I3* above and to the right of the tangency point *y* in Fig. 5.16. It would be at a point such as *x*. The distance between these two tangency points, *x* and *y*, is a measure of the impact of the relative price change, or the substitution effect. The move from *I2* to *I3* at *x* is a measure of the income effect. The movement on the horizontal axis, the increase in consumption of *B*, may be seen combining as a move from *I2* to *I3* (the income effect of the price change) at *x* and a movement along *I3* from *x* to *y* (the substitution effect of the price change).

**Exercise 5.4** Suppose good *B* is an inferior good. Draw an indifference curve diagram that has the effect that a rise in the consumer's money income leads to a fall in consumption of *B*.

### RECAP Indifference curve analysis of rational choice

Instead of assuming DMU, we suppose that a consumer's preferences are such that we can say that she has a *utility function*. This enables us to analyse the consumer's behaviour as deriving the maximum utility from the budget at her disposal. Analytically this means choosing the 'best' point on the budget line. That happens when the budget line is tangent to an *indifference curve*, a contour of the utility function. Indifference curves are assumed to be smoothly convex. A change in the price of a good, other things remaining unchanged, means a change in the amount of that good the consumer can buy, and a corresponding change in the slope of the budget line. This gives an unambiguous prediction: a fall (rise) in the price for a good leads to an increase (reduction) in the amount the rational consumer will purchase, which gives us the individual's downward-sloping demand curve. The change in the amount bought can be decomposed into an income and a substitution effect of the price change.

## Individual and market demand curves

If we know what each individual's demand curve for a good looks like, how can we use that information to construct the market demand curve for the good? We must *add the individual demand curves together*, a process that is straightforward but requires care.

## Horizontal addition

Suppose that there only two buyers – Smith and Jones – in the market for canned tuna, and that their demand curves are as shown in Fig. 5.17(a) and (b). To construct the market demand curve for canned tuna, we simply announce a sequence of prices and then add the quantity demanded by each buyer at each price. For example, at a price of €4 per can, Smith demands 6 cans per week (Fig. 5.17(a)) and Jones demands 2 cans per week (Fig. 5.17(b)), for a market demand of 8 cans per week (Fig. 5.17(c)).

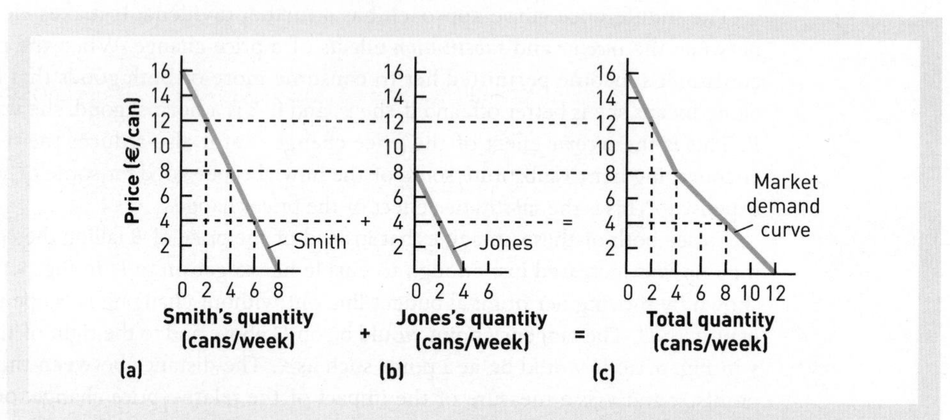


**Figure 5.17 Individual and Market Demand Curves for Canned Tuna.** The quantity demanded at any price on the market demand curve (c) is the sum of the individual quantities demanded at that price, (a) and (b).

The process of adding individual demand curves to get the market demand curve is known as *horizontal addition*, a term used to emphasise that we are adding *quantities*, which are measured on the horizontal axes of individual demand curves.

**Exercise 5.5**

The buyers' side of the market for cinema tickets consists of two consumers whose demands are as shown in the diagram below. Graph the market demand curve for this market.

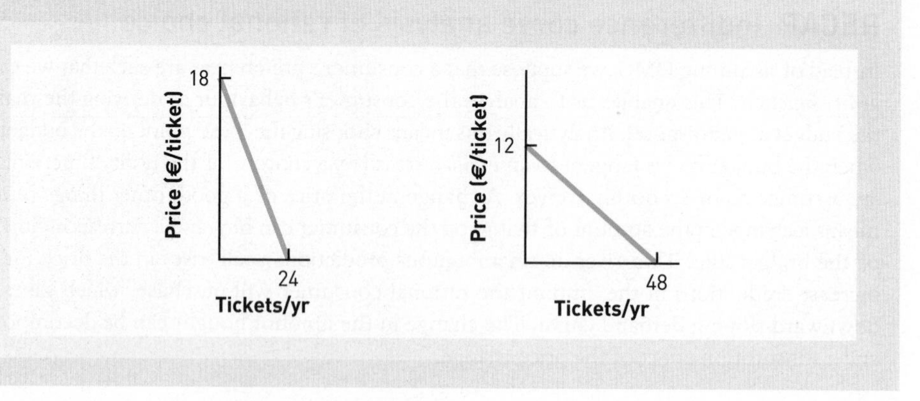


Figure 5.18 illustrates the special case in which each of 1,000 consumers in the market has the same demand curve (Fig. 5.18(a)). To get the market demand curve (Fig. 5.18(b)) in this case, we simply multiply each quantity on the representative individual demand curve by 1,000.

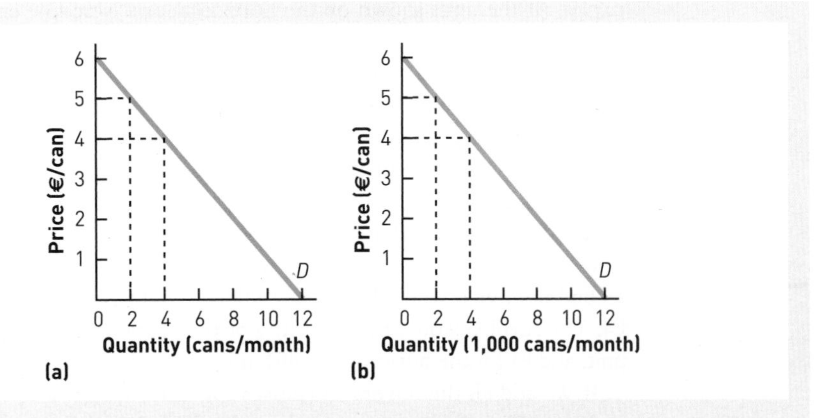


**Figure 5.18 The Individual and Market Demand Curves When All Buyers Have Identical Demand Curves.** When individual demand curves are identical, we get the market demand curve (b) by multiplying each quantity on the individual demand curve (a) by the number of consumers in the market.

## Demand and consumer surplus

In Chapter 1 we first encountered the concept of economic surplus, which in a buyer's case is the difference between the most she would have been willing to pay for a product and the amount she actually pays for it. The economic surplus received by buyers is often referred to a **consumer surplus**.

**consumer surplus** the difference between a buyer's reservation price for a product and the price actually paid

The term 'consumer surplus' sometimes refers to the surplus received by a single buyer in a transaction. On other occasions it is used to denote the total surplus received by all buyers in a market or collection of markets.

## Calculating economic surplus

For performing cost–benefit analysis it is often important to be able to measure the *total consumer surplus* received by all the buyers who participate in a given market. For example, a road linking a mountain village and a port city would create a new market for fresh fish in the mountain village; in deciding whether the road should be built, analysts would want to count as one of its benefits the gains that would be reaped by buyers in this new market.

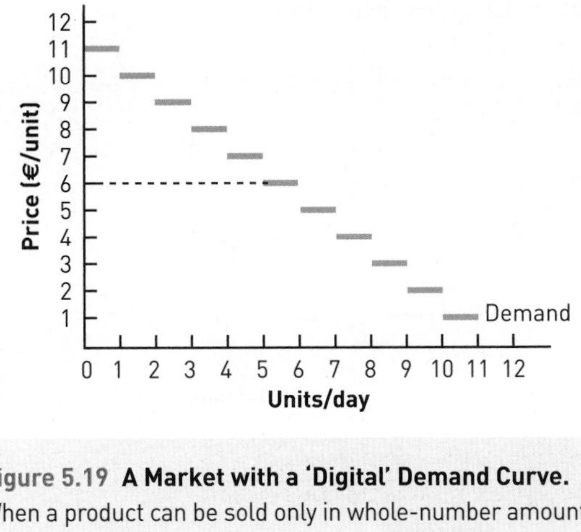

**Figure 5.19 A Market with a 'Digital' Demand Curve.** When a product can be sold only in whole-number amounts, its demand curve has the 'staircase' shape shown.

To illustrate how economists actually measure consumer surplus, we shall consider a hypothetical market for a good with 11 potential buyers, each of whom can buy a maximum of one unit of the good each day. The first potential buyer's reservation price for the product is €11; the second buyer's reservation price is €10; the third buyer's reservation price is €9; and so on. The demand curve for this market will have the 'staircase' shape shown in Fig. 5.19. We can think of this curve as the digital counterpart of traditional analogue demand curves. (If the units shown on the horizontal axis were fine enough, this digital curve would be visually indistinguishable from its analogue counterparts.)

Suppose the good whose demand curve is shown in Fig. 5.19 were available at a price of €6 per unit. How much total consumer surplus would buyers in this market reap? At a price of €6, six units per day would be sold in this market. The buyer of the sixth unit would receive no economic surplus, since her reservation price for that unit was exactly €6, the same as its selling price. But the first five buyers would reap a surplus for their purchases. The buyer of the first unit, for example, would have been willing to pay as much as €11 for it, but since she would pay only €6, she would receive a surplus of exactly €5. The buyer of the second unit, who would have been willing to pay as much as €10, would receive a surplus of €4. The surplus would be €3 for the buyer of the third unit, €2 for the buyer of the fourth unit, and €1 for the buyer of the fifth unit.

If we add all the buyers' surpluses together, we get a total of €15 of consumer surplus each day. That surplus corresponds to the shaded area shown in Fig. 5.20.

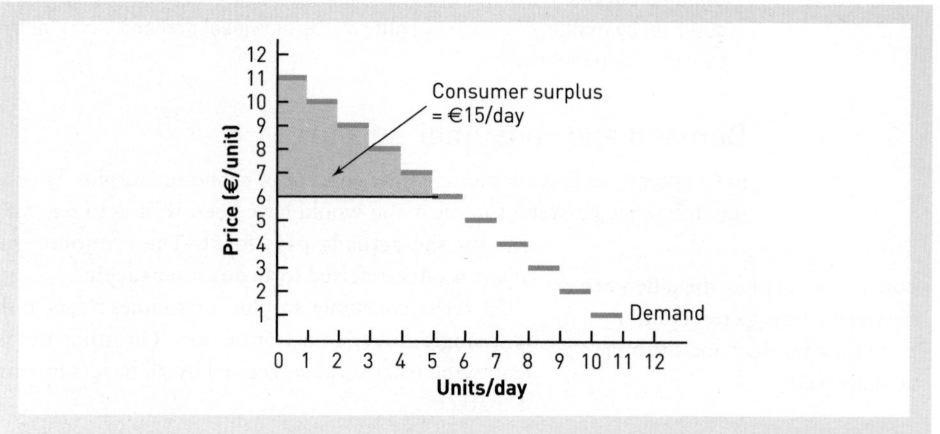


**Figure 5.20 Consumer Surplus.** Consumer surplus (shaded region) is the cumulative difference between the most that buyers are willing to pay for each unit and the price they actually pay.

**Exercise 5.6** Calculate consumer surplus for a demand curve like the one just described except that the buyers' reservation prices for each unit are €2 higher than before.

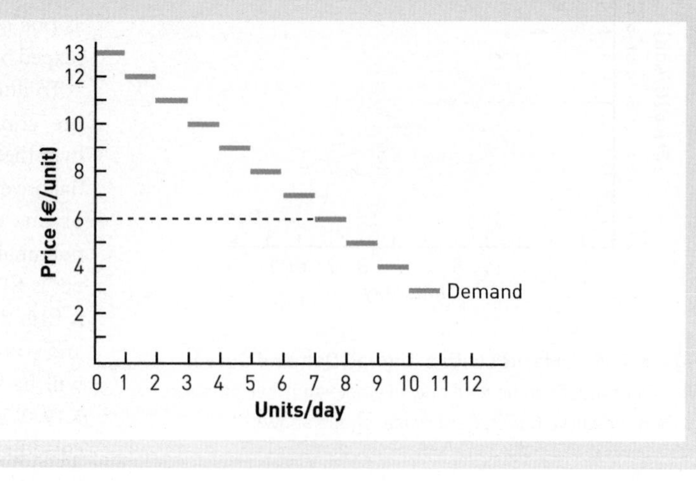

Now suppose we want to calculate consumer surplus in a market with a conventional straight-line demand curve. As Example 5.6 illustrates, this task is a simple extension of the method used for digital demand curves.

### **Example 5.6** How much do buyers benefit from their participation in the market for milk?

Consider the market for milk whose demand and supply curves are shown in Fig. 5.21, which has an equilibrium price of €2 per litre and an equilibrium quantity of 4,000 litres per day. How much consumer surplus do the buyers in this market reap?

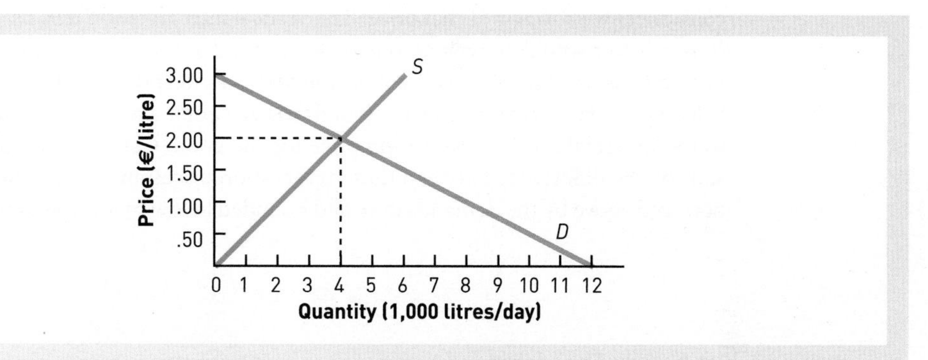


**Figure 5.21 Supply and Demand in the Market for Milk.** For the supply and demand curves shown, the equilibrium price of milk is €2 per litre and the equilibrium quantity is 4,000 litres per day.

In Fig. 5.21, note first that, as in Fig. 5.20, the last unit exchanged each day generates no consumer surplus at all. Note also that for all milk sold up to 4,000 litres per day, buyers receive consumer surplus, just as in Fig. 5.21. For these buyers, consumer surplus is the cumulative difference between the most they would be willing to pay for milk (as measured on the demand curve) and the price they actually pay.

Total consumer surplus received by buyers in the milk market is thus the shaded triangle between the demand curve and the market price in Fig. 5.22. Note that this area is a right triangle whose vertical arm is $h$ = €1/litre and whose horizontal arm is $b$ = 4,000 litres/day.

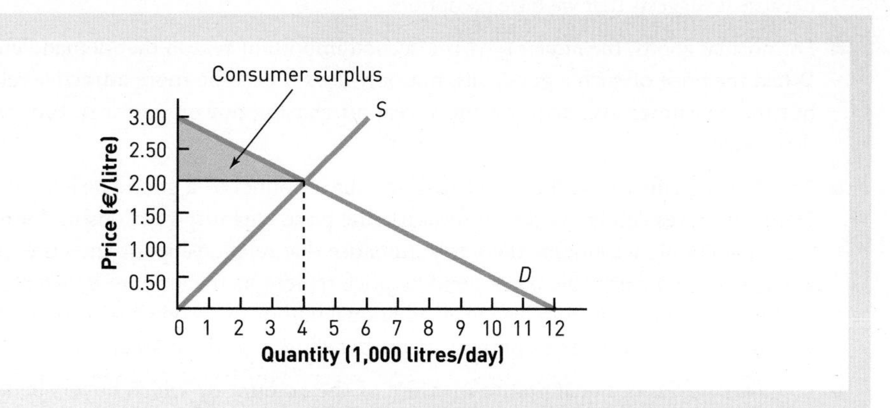


**Figure 5.22 Consumer Surplus in the Market for Milk.** Consumer surplus in the area of the shaded triangle (€2,000/day).

And since the area of any triangle is equal to (1/2)(base × height), consumer surplus in this market is equal to

$$(1/2)(4{,}000 \text{ litres/day})(€1/\text{litre}) = €2{,}000/\text{day}$$

A useful way of thinking about consumer surplus is to ask what is the highest price consumers would pay, in the aggregate, for the right to continue participating in this milk market. The answer is €2,000 per day, since that is the amount by which their *combined benefits exceed their combined costs*.

As discussed in Chapter 3, the demand curve for a good can be interpreted either horizontally or vertically. The horizontal interpretation tells us, for each price, the total quantity that consumers wish to buy at that price. The vertical interpretation tells us, for each quantity, the most a buyer would be willing to pay for the good at that quantity. For the purpose of computing consumer surplus, we rely on the vertical interpretation of the demand curve. The value on the vertical axis that corresponds to each point along the demand curve corresponds to the marginal buyer's reservation price for the good. Consumer surplus is the cumulative sum of the differences between these reservation prices and the market price. It is the area bounded above by the demand curve and bounded below by the market price.

## Summary

- If diminishing marginal utility is assumed the rational consumer allocates income among different goods so that the marginal utility gained from the last euro spent on each good is the same. This rational spending rule gives rise to the law of demand, which states that people do less of what they want to do as the cost of doing it rises. Here, 'cost' refers to the *sum of all monetary and non-monetary sacrifices* – explicit and implicit – that must be made in order to engage in the activity.
- *Indifference curve analysis* states that consumer rationality implies allocating expenditure between two goods so as to equate the marginal rate of substitution between any two goods to their relative price. This implies that demand curves will slope down from left to right, the basic law of demand.
- The ability to substitute one good for another is an important factor behind the law of demand. Because virtually every good or service has at least some substitutes, economists prefer to speak in terms of *wants* rather than needs. We face choices, and describing our demands as 'needs' is misleading because it suggests that we have no options.
- For normal goods, the *income effect* is a second important reason that demand curves slope downward. When the price of such a good falls, not only does it become more attractive relative to its substitutes, but the consumer also acquires more real purchasing power, and this, too, augments the quantity demanded.
- The demand curve is a schedule that shows the amounts of a good *people want to buy at various prices*. Demand curves can be used to summarise the price–quantity relationship for a single individual, but more commonly we employ them to summarise that relationship for an entire market. At any quantity along a demand curve, the corresponding price represents the amount by which the consumer (or consumers) would benefit from having an additional unit of the product. For this reason, the demand curve is sometimes described as a summary of the benefit side of the market.
- *Consumer surplus* is a quantitative measure of the amount by which buyers benefit as a result of their ability to purchase goods at the market price. It is the area between the demand curve and the market price.

## Key terms

consumer surplus (145)
indifference curve (140)
law of diminishing marginal utility (127)
marginal utility (126)
nominal price (135)
optimal combination of goods (130)
real price (135)

## Review questions

1. Why do economists prefer to speak of demands arising out of 'wants' rather than 'needs'?
2. Explain why economists consider the concept of utility useful, even if psychologists cannot measure it precisely.
3. Why does the law of diminishing marginal utility encourage people to spread their spending across many different types of goods?
4. Explain why a good or service that is offered at a monetary price of zero is unlikely to be a truly 'free' good from an economic perspective.
5. Give an example of a good that you have consumed for which your marginal utility increased with the amount of it you consumed.
6. Give examples of cardinal and ordinal measurements.
7. Show how the concept of consumer rationality is the same whether you use DMU or indifference curves to explain demand curves.
8. Show, using indifference curves, how a price rise for one good affects consumption of that good (a) by lowering the consumer's real income, and (b) by altering relative prices of the two goods.

## Problems

Problems marked with an asterisk (*) are more difficult.

1. In which type of restaurant do you expect the service to be more prompt and courteous: an expensive gourmet restaurant or an inexpensive diner? Explain.

2. You are having lunch at an all-you-can-eat buffet. If you are rational, what should be your marginal utility from the last morsel of food you swallow?

3. Martha's current marginal utility from consuming orange juice is 75 utils per centilitre and her marginal utility from consuming coffee is 50 utils per centilitre. If orange juice costs 25 cents per centilitre and coffee costs 20 cents per centilitre, is Martha maximising her total utility from the two beverages? If so, explain how you know. If not, how should she rearrange her spending?

4. Toby's current marginal utility from consuming peanuts is 100 utils per gram and his marginal utility from consuming cashews is 200 utils per gram. If peanuts cost 10 cents per gram and cashews cost 25 cents per gram, is Toby maximising his total utility from the two kinds of nuts? If so, explain how you know. If not, how should he rearrange his spending?

5. Sue gets a total of 20 utils per week from her consumption of pizza and a total of 40 utils per week from her consumption of yogurt. The price of pizza is €1 per slice, the price of yogurt is €1 per carton, and she consumes 10 slices of pizza and 20 cartons of yogurt each week. **True or false:** Sue is consuming the optimal combination of pizza and yogurt.

6. Anna Lucia lives in Cremona and commutes by train each day to her job in Milan (20 round trips per month). When the price of a round trip goes up from €10 to €20, she responds by

consuming exactly the same number of trips as before, while spending €200 per month less on restaurant meals.

a. Does the fact that her quantity of train travel is completely unresponsive to the price increase imply that Anna Lucia is not a rational consumer?

b. Explain why an increase in train travel might affect the amount she spends on restaurant meals.

7. For the demand curve shown below, find the total amount of consumer surplus that results in the petrol market if petrol sells for €2 per litre.

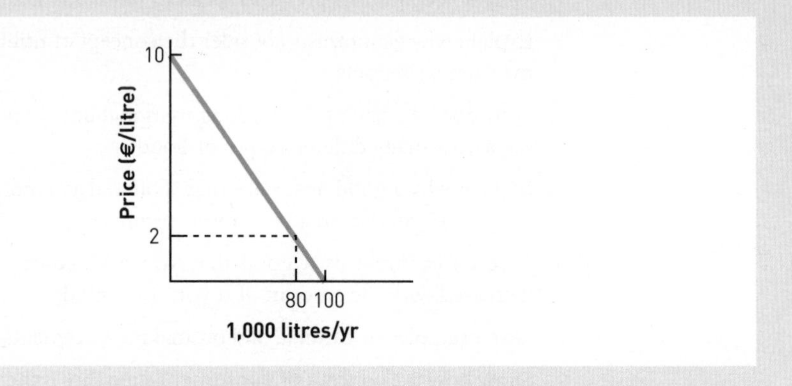


8. Tom has a weekly allowance of €24, all of which he spends on pizza and movie rentals, whose prices are €6 per slice and €3 per rental, respectively. If slices of pizza and movie rentals are available only in whole-number amounts, list all the possible combinations of the two goods that Tom can purchase each week with his allowance.

9.* Refer to Problem 8. Tom's total utility is the sum of the utility he derives from pizza and movie rentals. If these utilities vary with the amounts consumed as shown in the table below, and pizzas and movie rentals are again consumable only in whole-number amounts, how many pizzas and how many movie rentals should Tom consume each week?

| Pizzas/week | Utils/week from pizza | Movie rentals/ week | Utils/week from rentals |
|---|---|---|---|
| 0 | 0 | 0 | 0 |
| 1 | 20 | 1 | 40 |
| 2 | 38 | 2 | 46 |
| 3 | 54 | 3 | 50 |
| 4 | 68 | 4 | 54 |
| 5 | 80 | 5 | 56 |
| 6 | 90 | 6 | 57 |
| 7 | 98 | 7 | 57 |
| 8 | 104 | 8 | 57 |

10.* The buyers' side of the market for amusement park tickets consists of two consumers whose demands are as shown in the diagram below.

a. Graph the market demand curve for this market.

b. Calculate the total consumer surplus in the amusement park market if tickets sell for €12 each.

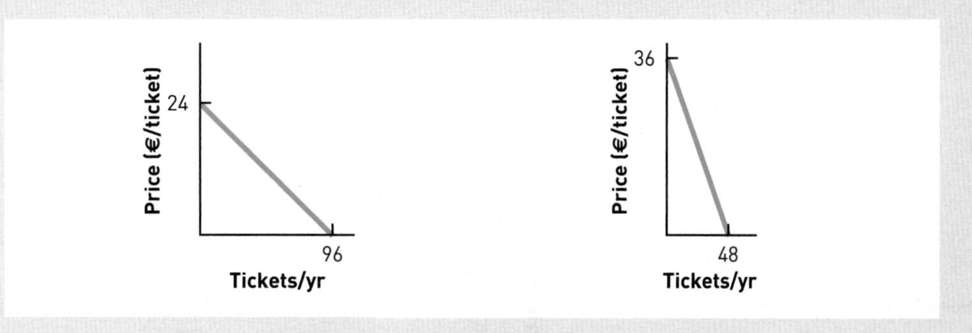


## Answers to in-chapter exercises

5.1 The combination of 300 cartons per year of vanilla (€300) and 50 cartons of chocolate (€100) costs a total of €400, which is exactly equal to Sarah's ice cream budget.

5.2 The rational spending rule requires $MU_F/P_F = MU_S/P_S$ where $MU_F$ and $MU_S$ are John's marginal utilities from food and shelter and $P_F$ and $P_S$ are the prices of food and shelter, respectively. At John's original combination, $MU_F/P_F = 4$ utils per euro and $MU_S/P_S = 3$ utils per euro. John should thus spend more of his income on food and less on shelter.

5.3 Draw two curves crossing. Mark a point *A* on one of the curves to the left of the intersection and a point *B* to the right. On the other curve mark a point *C* to the left and a point *D* to the right. *A* and *B* are on the same curve *AIB*. Similarly *CID*. But *C* is on a curve further out from *A*, so *CPA*, and, of course *BPD* for the same reason. But *CPA* and *AIB* implies *CPB*. *CPB* and *CID* implies *DPB*, which contradicts *BPD*. **QED**.

5.4 If *B* is an inferior good then as income rises (the budget line shifts out with no change in slope) the successive tangency points have to move closer to the *A* axis. This means that the indifference curves have to be 'bunched' in towards that axis. Only in this manner will a move out of the budget line lead to a series of tangency points involving a fall in the quantity of *B* chosen by the consumer.

5.5 Adding the two individual demand curves, (a) and (b), horizontally yields the market demand curve (c), as shown below.

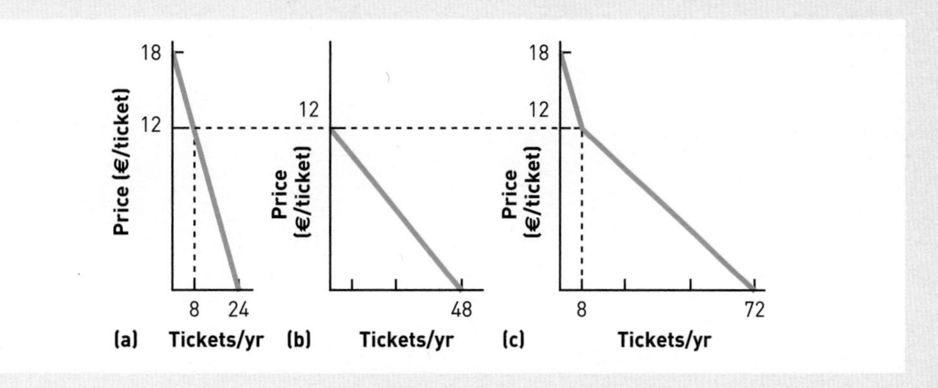

5.6 Consumer surplus is now the new shaded area, €28 per day, see below.

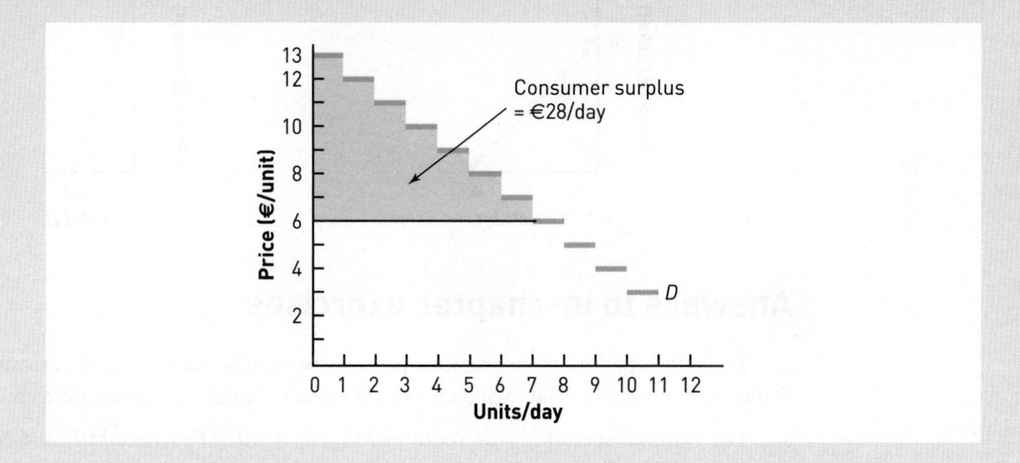

# 6

# Perfectly Competitive Supply: the Cost Side of the Market

Cars that took more than 50 hours to assemble in the 1970s are now built in less than 8 hours. Similar productivity growth has occurred in many other manufacturing industries. Yet in many service industries, productivity has grown only slowly, if at all. For example, the Vienna Philharmonic Orchestra performs Beethoven's Fifth Symphony with no fewer musicians today than it did in 1950. And it still takes a barber about half an hour to cut someone's hair, just as it always has.

Given the spectacular growth in manufacturing workers' productivity, it is no surprise that their real wages rose more than five-fold during the twentieth century. But why have real wages for service workers risen just as much? If barbers and musicians are no more productive than they were in the 1890s, why are they now paid five times as much?

An answer is suggested by the observation that the opportunity cost of pursuing any given occupation is the most one could have earned in some other occupation. Most people who become barbers or musicians could instead have chosen jobs in manufacturing. If workers in service industries were not paid roughly as much as they could have earned in other occupations, many of them would not have been willing to work in service industries in the first place.

The trajectories of wages in manufacturing and service industries illustrate the intimate link between the prices at which goods and services are offered for sale in the market and the opportunity cost of the resources required to produce them. Whereas our focus in Chapter 5 was on the buyers' side of the market, our focus here will be on sellers. Earlier, we saw that the demand curve is a schedule that tells how many units buyers wish to purchase at different prices. Our task here is to gain insight into the factors that shape the supply curve, the schedule that tells how many units suppliers wish to sell at different prices.

Although the demand side and the supply side of the market are different in several ways, many of these differences are superficial. Indeed, the behaviour of both buyers and sellers is in an important sense fundamentally the same. After all, the two groups confront essentially similar questions – in the buyer's case, 'Should I buy another unit?' and in the seller's, 'Should I sell another unit?' What is more, buyers and sellers use the same criterion for answering these questions. Thus a rational consumer will buy another unit if its benefit exceeds its cost; and a rational seller will sell another unit if the cost of making it is less than the extra revenue he can get from selling it (the familiar Cost–Benefit Principle again).

## Thinking about supply: the importance of opportunity cost

Many countries or local government areas have regulations that create incentives for people to return bottles and drinks cans directly or indirectly to the original seller for recycling. If you live or study where such a regime exists you will have probably noticed that while some people always return their own containers to receive the incentive (usually cash), others pass up this opportunity, leaving their used containers to be recycled by others, or simply get rid of them with other garbage. If you return your containers for recycling you are *supplying a service*, and its production obeys the same logic as applies to the production of other goods and services. As the following sequence of recycling examples makes clear, the supply curve for a good or service is rooted in the individual's choice of whether to produce it.

### **Example 6.1** How much time should Harry spend recycling soft drink containers?

Harry is trying to decide how to divide his time between his job as a dishwasher in the student cafeteria at his university, which pays €6 an hour for as many hours as he chooses to work, and gathering soft drink containers around the college to redeem for deposit, in which case his pay depends on both the deposit per container and the number of containers he finds. Earnings aside, Harry is indifferent between the two tasks, and the number of containers he will find depends, as shown in the table below, on the number of hours per day he searches.

| Search time (hours/day) (1) | Total number of containers found (2) | Additional number of containers found (3) |
|---|---|---|
| 0 | 0 | |
| | | 600 |
| 1 | 600 | |
| | | 400 |
| 2 | 1,000 | |
| | | 300 |
| 3 | 1,300 | |
| | | 200 |
| 4 | 1,500 | |
| | | 100 |
| 5 | 1,600 | |

If the containers may be redeemed for 2 cents each, how many hours should Harry spend searching for containers?

For each additional hour Harry spends searching for soft drink containers, he loses the €6 he could have earned as a dishwasher. This is his *hourly opportunity cost* of searching for soft drink containers. His benefit from each hour spent searching for containers is the number of additional containers he finds (shown in column (3) of the table) times the deposit he collects per container. Since he can redeem each container for 2 cents, his first hour spent collecting containers will yield earnings of 600(€0.02) = €12, or €6 more than he could have earned as a dishwasher.

By the Cost–Benefit Principle, then, Harry should spend his first hour of work each day searching for soft drink containers rather than washing dishes. A second hour searching for containers will yield 400 additional containers, for additional earnings of €8, so it, too, satisfies the cost–benefit test. A third hour spent searching yields 300 additional containers, for

300(€0.02) = €6 of additional earnings. Since this is exactly what Harry could have earned washing dishes, he is indifferent between spending his third hour of work each day on one task or the other. For the sake of discussion, however, we shall assume that when indifferent he opts to search for containers, in which case he will spend 3 hours each day searching for containers.

What is the lowest redemption price that would induce Harry to spend at least 1 hour per day recycling? Since he will find 600 containers in his first hour of search, a one cent deposit on each container would enable him to match his €6 per hour opportunity cost. More generally, if the redemption price is $p$, and the next hour spent searching yields $\Delta Q$ additional containers, then Harry's additional earnings from searching the additional hour will be $p(\Delta Q)$. This means that the smallest redemption price that will lead Harry to search another hour must satisfy the equation

$$p(\Delta Q) = €6 \tag{6.1}$$

How high would the redemption price of containers have to be to induce Harry to search for a second hour? Since he can find $\Delta Q = 400$ additional containers if he searches for a second hour, the smallest redemption price that will lead him to do so must satisfy $p(400) = €6$, which solves for $p = 1.5$ cents.

**Exercise 6.1** In Example 6.1, calculate the smallest container redemption prices that will lead Harry to search a third, fourth and fifth hour.

By searching for soft drink containers, Harry becomes, in effect, a supplier of container-recycling services. In Example 6.1, we saw that Harry's reservation prices for his third, fourth and fifth hours of container search are 2, 3 and 6 cents, respectively. Having calculated these reservation prices, we can now plot his supply curve of container-recycling services. This curve, which plots the redemption price per container on the vertical axis and the number of containers recycled each day on the horizontal axis, is shown in Fig. 6.1. Harry's individual supply curve of container-recycling services tells us the number of containers he is willing to recycle at various redemption prices.

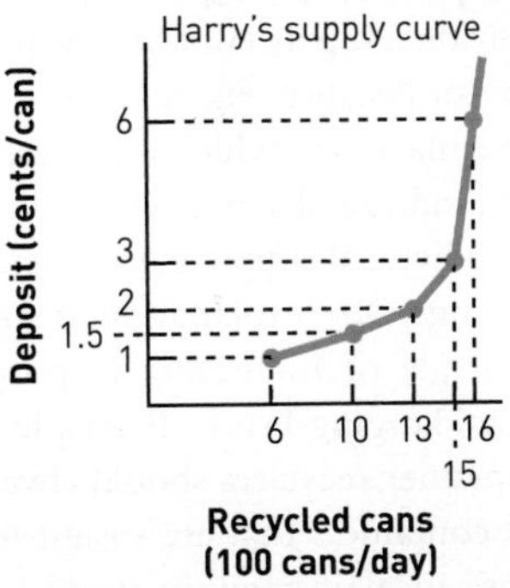

**Figure 6.1 An Individual Supply Curve for Recycling Services.** When the deposit price increases, it becomes attractive to abandon alternative pursuits to spend more time searching for soft drink containers.

Like those we saw in Chapter 3, the supply curve shown in Fig. 6.1 is upward-sloping. There are exceptions to this general rule, but sellers of most goods will offer higher quantities at higher prices than at lower prices.

The relationship between the individual and market supply curves for a product is analogous to the relationship between the individual and market demand curves. The quantity that corresponds to a given price on the market demand curve is the sum of the quantities demanded at that price by all individual buyers in the market. Likewise, the quantity that corresponds to any given price on the market supply curve is the sum of the quantities supplied at that price by all individual sellers in the market.

Suppose, for example, that the supply side of the recycling-services market consists only of Harry and his identical twin, Barry, whose individual supply curve is the same as Harry's. To generate the market supply curve, we first put the individual supply curves side by side, as shown in Fig. 6.2(a) and Fig. 6.2(b). We then announce a price, and for that price add the indi-

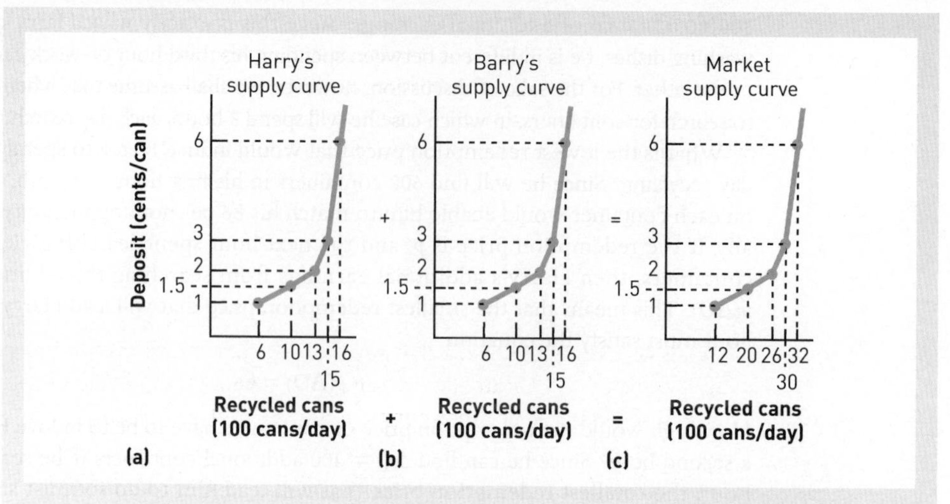


Figure 6.2 **The Market Supply Curve for Recycling Services.** To generate the market supply curve (c) from the individual supply curves (a) and (b), we add the individual supply curves horizontally.

vidual quantities supplied to obtain the total quantity supplied in the market. Thus, at a price of 3 cents per container, both Harry and Barry wish to recycle 1,500 cans per day, so the total market supply at that price is 3,000 cans per day. Proceeding in like manner for a sequence of prices, we generate the market supply curve for recycling services shown in Fig. 6.2(c). This is the same process of horizontal summation by which we generated market demand curves from individual demand curves in Chapter 5.

Alternatively, if there were many suppliers with individual supply curves identical to Harry's, we could generate the market supply curve by simply multiplying each quantity value on the individual supply curve by the number of suppliers. For instance, Fig. 6.3 shows the supply curve for a market in which there are 1,000 suppliers with individual supply curves like Harry's. Why do individual supply curves tend to be upward-sloping? One explanation is suggested by the Principle of Increasing Opportunity Cost, or Low-Hanging-Fruit Principle (Chapter 2). Container recyclers should always look first for the containers that are easiest to find – such as those in plain view in readily accessible locations. As the redemption price rises, it will pay to incur the additional cost of searching farther from the beaten path.

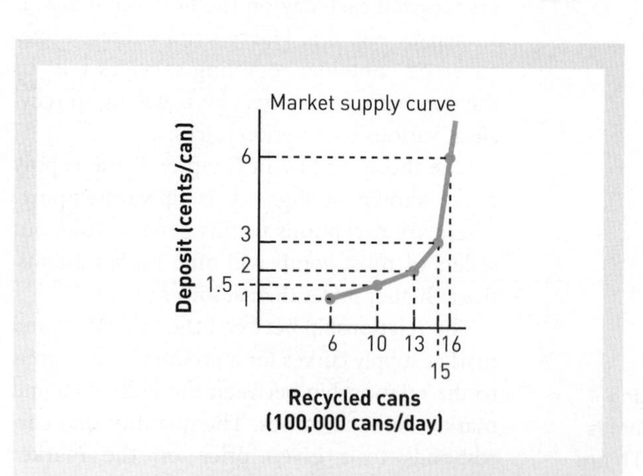


Figure 6.3 **The Market Supply Curve with 1,000 Identical Sellers.** To generate the market supply curve for a market with 1,000 identical sellers, we simply multiply each quantity value on the individual supply curve by 1,000.

If all individuals have identical upward-sloping supply curves, the market supply curve will be upward-sloping as well. But there is an important additional reason for the positive slope of market supply curves: individual suppliers generally differ with respect to their opportunity costs of supplying the product. (The Principle of Increasing Opportunity Cost applies not only to each individual searcher, but also *across* individuals.) Thus, whereas people facing unattractive employment opportunities in other occupations may be willing to recycle soft drink containers even when the redemption price is low, those with more attractive options will recycle only if the redemption price is relatively high.

In summary, then, the upward slope of the supply schedule reflects the fact that costs tend to rise when producers expand production, partly because each individual exploits her most attractive opportunities first, but also because different potential sellers face different opportunity costs.

## Profit-maximising firms in perfectly competitive markets

To explore the nature of the supply curve of a product more fully, we must say more about the goals of the organisations that supply the product and the kind of economic environment in which they operate. In virtually every economy, goods and services are produced by a variety of organisations that pursue a host of different motives. The Red Cross supplies blood because its organisers and donors want to help people in need; the local government fixes potholes because the mayor was elected on a promise to do so; karaoke singers perform because they like public attention; and car-wash employees are driven primarily by the hope of making enough money to pay their rent and other living expenses.

### Profit maximisation

Notwithstanding this rich variety of motives, *most* goods and services that are offered for sale in a market economy are sold by private firms whose main reason for existing is to earn **profit** for their owners. A firm's profit is the difference between the total revenue it receives from the sale of its product and all costs it incurs in producing it.

**profit** the total revenue a firm receives from the sale of its product minus all costs – explicit and implicit – incurred in producing it

**profit-maximising firm** a firm whose primary goal is to maximise the difference between its total revenues and total costs

**perfectly competitive market** a market in which no individual supplier has significant influence on the market price of the product

**price taker** a firm that has no influence over the price at which it sells its product

A **profit-maximising firm** is one whose primary goal is to maximise the amount of profit it earns. The supply curves that economists use in standard supply and demand theory are based on the assumption that the market can plausibly be treated as if the goods or services concerned are sold by profit-maximising firms in **perfectly competitive markets**, which are markets in which individual firms have no influence over the market prices of the products they sell. Because of their inability to influence market price, perfectly competitive firms are often described as **price takers**. Note that this does not mean that when economists use supply curves they are always strictly assuming that the markets concerned are perfectly competitive in this sense. For example, economists will frequently use supply and demand curves to analyse what is happening in the oil market, even though, strictly speaking, the major crude oil producers do not display all (or even many) of the characteristics of perfectly competitive producers. In such circumstances what is happening is that the analysis is based on an assumption that the outcome in the market is likely to be close to what would happen in a competitive market.

The following four conditions are often taken to be characteristic of markets that are perfectly competitive:

1. **All firms sell the same standardised product** Although this condition is almost never literally satisfied, it holds as a rough approximation for many markets. Thus the markets for concrete building blocks of a given size, or for apples of a given variety, may be described in this way. This condition implies that buyers are willing to switch from one seller to another if by so doing they can obtain a lower price.
2. **The market has many buyers and sellers, each of which buys or sells only a small fraction of the total quantity exchanged** This condition implies that individual buyers and

sellers will be price takers, regarding the market price of the product as a fixed number beyond their control. For example, a single farmer's decision to plant fewer hectares of wheat would have no appreciable impact on the market price of wheat, just as an individual consumer's decision to become a vegetarian would have no perceptible effect on the price of beef.

3. **Productive resources are mobile** This condition implies that if a potential seller identifies a profitable business opportunity in a market, he or she will be able to obtain the labour, capital and other productive resources necessary to enter that market. By the same token, sellers who are dissatisfied with the opportunities they confront in a given market are free to leave that market and employ their resources elsewhere.
4. **Buyers and sellers are well informed** This condition implies that buyers and sellers are aware of the relevant opportunities available to them. If that were not so, buyers would be unable to seek out sellers who charge the lowest prices, and sellers would have no means of deploying their resources in the markets in which they would earn the most.

The market for wheat closely approximates a perfectly competitive market. The market for operating systems for desktop computers, however, does not. More than 90 per cent of desktop operating systems are sold by Microsoft, giving the company enough influence in that market to have significant control over the price it charges. For example, if it were to raise the price of its latest edition of Windows by, say, 20 per cent, some consumers might switch to Macintosh or Linux, and others might postpone their next upgrade; but many – perhaps even most – would continue with their plans to buy.

By contrast, if an individual wheat farmer were to try to charge even just 10 cents more than the current market price for a tonne of wheat, he wouldn't be able to sell any of his wheat at all. And since he can sell as much wheat as he wishes at the market price, he has no motive to charge less.

## The demand curve facing a perfectly competitive firm

From the perspective of an individual firm in a perfectly competitive market, what does the demand curve for its product look like? Since it can sell as much or as little as it wishes at the prevailing market price, the demand curve for its product is perfectly elastic at the market price. Figure 6.4(a) shows the market demand and supply curves intersecting to determine a market price of $P_0$. Figure 6.4(b) shows the product demand curve, $D_i$, as seen by any individual firm in this market: a horizontal line at the price market price level $P_0$.

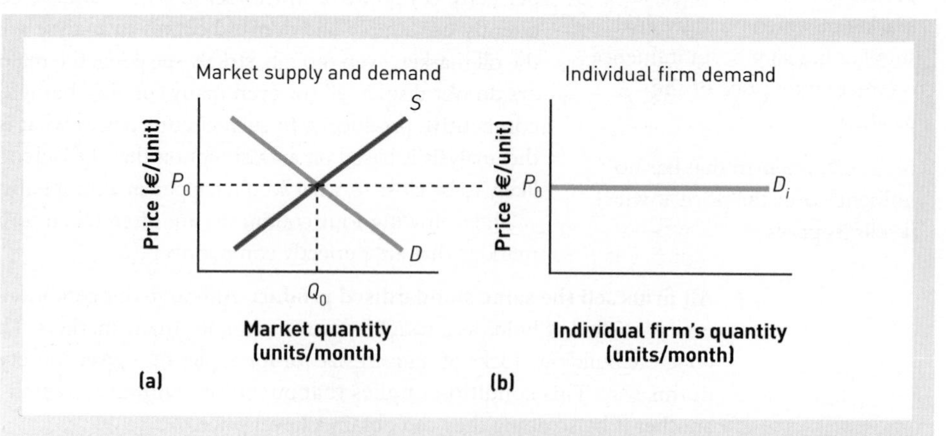


**Figure 6.4 The Demand Curve Facing a Perfectly Competitive Firm.** The market demand and supply curves intersect to determine the market price of the product (a). The individual firm's demand curve, $D_i$ (b), is a horizontal line at the market price.

Many of the conclusions of the standard supply and demand model also hold for **imperfectly competitive firms** – those firms, like Microsoft, that have at least some ability to vary their own prices. But certain other conclusions do not, as we shall see when we examine the behaviour of such firms more closely in Chapter 9.

**imperfectly competitive firm** a firm that has at least some control over the market price of its product

Since a perfectly competitive firm has no control over the market price of its product, it needn't worry about choosing the level at which to set that price. As we have seen, the equilibrium market price in a competitive market comes from the intersection of the industry supply and demand curves. The challenge confronting the perfectly competitive firm is to choose its *output level* so that it makes as much profit as it can at that price. As we investigate how the competitive firm responds to this challenge, we shall see once again the pivotal role of our core principle that some costs are more important than others.

## Production in the short run

To gain a deeper understanding of the origins of the supply curve, it is helpful to consider a perfectly competitive firm confronting the decision of how much to produce. The firm in question is a small company that makes glass bottles. To keep things simple, suppose that the silica required for making bottles is available free of charge from a nearby desert, and that the only costs incurred by the firm are the wages it pays its employees and the lease payment on its bottle making machine. The employees and the machine are the firm's only two **factors of production** – inputs used to produce goods and services. In more complex examples, factors of production might also include land, structures, entrepreneurship and possibly others, but for the moment we consider only labour and capital.

**factor of production** an input used in the production of a good or service

**short run** a period of time sufficiently short that at least some of the firm's factors of production are fixed

**long run** a period of time of sufficient length that all the firm's factors of production are variable

**law of diminishing returns** a property of the relationship between the amount of a good or service produced and the amount of a variable factor required to produce it; it says that when some factors of production are fixed, increased production of the good eventually requires ever-larger increases in the variable factor

**fixed factor of production** an input whose quantity cannot be altered in the short run

**variable factor of production** an input whose quantity can be altered in the short run

When we refer to the **short run**, we mean a period of time during which at least some of the firm's factors of production cannot be varied. For our bottle maker, we will assume that the number of employees can be varied at short notice but that the capacity of its bottle making machine can be altered only with significant delay. For this firm, then, the short run is simply that period of time during which the firm cannot alter the capacity of its bottle making machine. By contrast, when we speak of the **long run**, we refer to a time period of sufficient length that all the firm's factors of production are variable.

Table 6.1 shows how the company's bottle production depends on the number of hours its employees spend on the job each day. The output–employment relationship described in Table 6.1 exhibits a pattern that is common to many such relationships. Each time we add an additional unit of labour, output grows; but beyond some point the additional output that results from each additional unit of labour begins to diminish. Note in column (2), for example, that output gains begin to diminish with the third employee. Economists refer to this pattern as the **law of diminishing returns**, and it always refers to situations in which at least some factors of production are fixed. Here, the **fixed factor** is the bottle making machine, and the **variable factor** is labour. In the context of this example, the law of diminishing returns says simply that successive increases in the labour input eventually yield smaller and smaller increments in bottle output. (Strictly speaking, the law ought to be called the law of *eventually* diminishing returns, because output may initially grow at an increasing rate with additional units of the variable factor.)

| Total number of employees per day (1) | Total number of bottles per day (2) |
|---|---|
| 0 | 0 |
| 1 | 80 |
| 2 | 200 |
| 3 | 260 |
| 4 | 300 |
| 5 | 330 |
| 6 | 350 |
| 7 | 362 |

**Table 6.1** Employment and Output for a Glass Bottle Maker

Typically, returns from additional units of the variable input eventually diminish because of some form of *congestion*. For instance, in an office with three secretaries and only a single desktop computer, we would not expect to get three times as many letters typed per hour as in an office with only one secretary, because only one person can use a computer at a time.

## Some important cost concepts

For the bottle making firm described in Table 6.1, suppose that the lease payment for the company's bottle making machine is €40 per day, which must be paid whether the company makes any bottles or not. This payment is both a **fixed cost** (since it does not depend on the number of bottles per day the firm makes) and, for the duration of the lease, a sunk cost. Columns (1) and (2) of Table 6.2 reproduce the employment and output entries (columns (1) and (2)) from Table 6.1, and the firm's fixed cost appears in column (3).

**fixed cost** the sum of all payments made to the firm's fixed factors of production

| Employees per day (1) | Bottles per day (2) | Fixed cost (€/day) (3) | Variable cost (€/day) (4) | Total cost (€/day) (5) | Marginal cost (€/bottle) (6) |
|---|---|---|---|---|---|
| 0 | 0 | 40 | 0 | 40 | |
| | | | | | 0.15 |
| 1 | 80 | 40 | 12 | 52 | |
| | | | | | 0.10 |
| 2 | 200 | 40 | 24 | 64 | |
| | | | | | 0.20 |
| 3 | 260 | 40 | 36 | 76 | |
| | | | | | 0.33 |
| 4 | 300 | 40 | 48 | 88 | |
| | | | | | 0.40 |
| 5 | 330 | 40 | 60 | 100 | |
| | | | | | 0.60 |
| 6 | 350 | 40 | 72 | 112 | |
| | | | | | 1.00 |
| 7 | 362 | 40 | 84 | 124 | |

**Table 6.2** Fixed, Variable and Total Costs of Bottle Production

**variable cost** the sum of all payments made to the firm's variable factors of production

**total cost** the sum of all payments made to the firm's fixed and variable factors of production

**marginal cost** as output changes from one level to another, the change in total cost divided by the corresponding change in output

The company's payment to its employees is called **variable cost** because, unlike fixed cost, it varies with the *number of bottles* the company produces. The variable cost of producing 200 bottles per day, for example, is shown in column (4) of Table 6.2 as €24 per day. Column (5) shows the firm's **total cost**, which is the *sum of its fixed and variable costs*. Column (6), finally, shows the firm's **marginal cost**, a measure of how its *total cost changes when its output changes*. Specifically, marginal cost is defined as the change in total cost divided by the corresponding change in output. Note, for example, that when the firm expands production from 80 to 200 bottles per day, its total cost goes up by €12, which gives rise to the marginal cost entry of (€12/day)/(120 bottles/day) = €0.10 per bottle. To emphasise that marginal cost refers to the change in total cost when quantity changes, we place the marginal cost entries between the corresponding quantity rows of Table 6.2.

## Choosing output to maximise profit

In the following examples and exercises, we shall explore how the company's decision about how many bottles to produce depends on the price of bottles, the wage and the cost of capital.

**Example 6.2** If bottles sell for 35 cents each, how many bottles should the company described in Table 6.2 produce each day?

To answer this question, we need simply apply the Cost–Benefit Principle to the question: 'Should the firm expand its level of output?' If its goal is to maximise its profit, the answer to this question will be to expand as long as the *marginal benefit from expanding is at least as great as the marginal cost*. Since the perfectly competitive firm can sell as many bottles as it wishes at the market price of €0.35 per bottle, its marginal benefit from selling an additional bottle is €0.35. If we compare this marginal benefit with the marginal cost entries shown in column (6) of Table 6.2, we see that the firm should keep expanding until it reaches 300 bottles per day (4 employees per day). To expand beyond that level it would have to hire a fifth employee, and the resulting marginal cost (€0.40 per bottle) would exceed the marginal benefit.

To confirm that the Cost–Benefit Principle thus applied identifies the profit-maximising number of bottles to produce, we can calculate profit levels directly, as in Table 6.3. Column (3) of Table 6.3 reports the firm's revenue from the sale of bottles, which is calculated as the product of the number of bottles produced per day and the price of €0.35 per bottle. Note, for example, that in the third row of column (3), total revenue is (200 bottles/day)

| Employees per day (1) | Output (bottles/day) (2) | Total revenue (€/day) (3) | Total cost (€/day) (4) | Profit (€/day) (5) |
|---|---|---|---|---|
| 0 | 0 | 0 | 40 | -40 |
| 1 | 80 | 28 | 52 | -24 |
| 2 | 200 | 70 | 64 | 6 |
| 3 | 260 | 91 | 76 | 15 |
| 4 | 300 | 105 | 88 | 17 |
| 5 | 330 | 115.50 | 100 | 15.50 |
| 6 | 350 | 122.50 | 112 | 10.50 |
| 7 | 362 | 126.70 | 124 | 2.70 |

**Table 6.3** Output, Revenue, Costs and Profit

(€0.35/bottle) = €70 per day. Column (5) reports the firm's total daily profit, which is just the difference between its total revenue (column (3)) and its total cost (column (4)). Note that the largest profit entry in column (5), €17 per day, occurs at an output of 300 bottles per day, just as suggested by our earlier application of the Cost–Benefit Principle.

As Exercise 6.2 demonstrates, an increase in the price of the product gives rise to an increase in the profit-maximising level of output.

**Exercise 6.2** Same as Example 6.2, except now bottles sell for 62 cents each.

Exercise 6.3 illustrates that a fall in the wage rate leads to a decline in marginal cost, which also causes an increase in the profit-maximising level of output.

**Exercise 6.3** Same as Example 6.2, except now employees receive a wage of €6 per day.

Suppose that in Example 6.2 the firm's fixed cost had been not €40 per day but €45 per day. How, if at all, would that have affected the firm's profit-maximising level of output? The answer is 'not at all': each entry in the profit column of Table 6.3 would have been €5 per day smaller than before, but the maximum profit entry still would have been 300 bottles per day.

The observation that the profit-maximising quantity does not depend on fixed costs is not an idiosyncrasy of this example. That it holds true in general is an immediate consequence of the Cost–Benefit Principle, which says that a firm should increase its output if, and only if, the *marginal* benefit exceeds the *marginal* cost. Neither the marginal benefit of expanding (which is the market price of bottles) nor the marginal cost of expanding is affected by a change in the firm's fixed cost.

When the law of diminishing returns applies (that is, when some factors of production are fixed), marginal cost goes up as the firm expands production beyond some point. Under these circumstances, the firm's best option is to keep expanding output as long as *marginal cost is less than price*.

Note that in Example 6.2 if the company's fixed cost had been any more than €57 per day, it would have made a loss at *every* possible level of output. As long as it still had to pay its fixed cost, however, its best bet would have been to continue producing 300 bottles per day. It is better, after all, to experience a smaller loss than a larger one. If a firm in that situation expected conditions to remain the same, though, it would want to get out of the bottle business as soon as its equipment lease expired.

## A note on the firm's shutdown condition

It may seem that a firm that can sell as much output as it wishes at a constant market price would *always* do best in the short run by producing and selling the output level for which price equals marginal cost. But there are exceptions to this rule. Suppose, for example, that the market price of the firm's product falls so low that its revenue from sales is smaller than its variable cost at all possible levels of output. The firm should then cease production for the time being. By shutting down, it will suffer a loss equal to its fixed costs. But by remaining open, it will suffer an even larger loss.

More formally, if $P$ denotes the market price of the product and $Q$ denotes the number of units produced and sold, then $P \times Q$ is the firm's total revenue from sales, and if we use $VC$ to denote the firm's variable cost, the rule is that the firm should shut down in the short run if $P \times Q$ is less than $VC$ for every level of $Q$:

**Short-run shutdown condition:** $P \times Q < VC$ for all levels of $Q$

**Exercise 6.4** In Example 6.2, suppose that bottles sold not for €0.35 but only €0.10. Calculate the profit corresponding to each level of output, as in Table 6.3, and verify that the firm's best option is to cease operations in the short run.

### Average variable cost and average total cost

Suppose that the firm is unable to cover its variable cost at any level of output – that is, suppose that $P \times Q < VC$ for all levels of $Q$. It must then also be true that $P < VC/Q$ for all levels of $Q$, since we obtain the second inequality by simply dividing both sides of the first one by $Q$. $VC/Q$ is the firm's **average variable cost** – its variable cost divided by its output. The firm's short-run shutdown condition may thus be restated a second way: discontinue operations in the short run if the product price is less than the minimum value of its average variable cost (AVC). Thus:

**average variable cost (AVC)** variable cost divided by total output

**Short-run shutdown condition** (alternative version): $P <$ minimum value of $AVC$

As we shall see in the next section, this version of the shutdown condition often enables us to tell at a glance whether the firm should continue operations.

A related cost concept that facilitates assessment of the firm's profitability is **average total cost** (ATC), which is total cost ($TC$) divided by output ($Q$): $ATC = TC/Q$. The firm's profit, again, is the difference between its total revenue ($P \times Q$) and its total cost. And since total cost is equal to average total cost times quantity, the firm's profit is also equal to $(P \times Q) - (ATC \times Q)$. A firm is said to be **profitable** if its revenue ($P \times Q$) exceeds its total cost ($ATC \times Q$). A firm can thus be profitable only if the price of its product price ($P$) exceeds its $ATC$ for some level of output.

**average total cost (ATC)** total cost divided by total output

**profitable firm** a firm whose total revenue exceeds its total cost

Keeping track of all these cost concepts may seem tedious. In the next section, however, we will see that the payoff from doing so is that it enables us to recast the profit-maximisation decision in a simple graphical framework.

## A graphical approach to profit maximisation

For our bottle making firm, average variable cost and average total cost values are shown in columns (4) and (6) of Table 6.4. Using the entries in Table 6.4, we plot the firm's average total cost, average variable cost and marginal cost curves in Fig. 6.5. (Because marginal cost corresponds to the change in total cost as we move between two output levels, each marginal cost value in Table 6.4 is plotted at an output level midway between those in the adjacent rows.)

We call your attention to several features of the cost curves in Fig. 6.5. Note, for example, that the upward-sloping portion of the marginal cost curve ($MC$) corresponds to the region of diminishing returns discussed earlier. Thus, as the firm moves beyond two employees per day (200 bottles per day), the increments to total output become smaller with each additional employee, which means that the cost of producing additional bottles ($MC$) must be increasing in this region.

Note also that the definition of marginal cost implies that the marginal cost curve must intersect both the average variable cost curve ($AVC$) and the average total cost curve ($ATC$) at their respective minimum points. To see why, consider the logic that explains what happens to the average weight of children in an elementary school class when a new student joins the class. If the new (marginal) student is lighter than the previous average weight for the class, average weight will fall, but if the new student is heavier than the previous average, average

| Employees per day | Bottles per day | Variable cost (€/day) | Average variable cost (€/unit of output) | Total cost (€/day) | Average total cost (€/unit of output) | Marginal cost (€/bottle) |
|---|---|---|---|---|---|---|
| (1) | (2) | (3) | (4) | (5) | (6) | (7) |
| 0 | 0 | 0 | | 40 | | |
| | | | | | | *0.15* |
| 1 | 80 | 12 | 0.15 | 52 | 0.65 | |
| | | | | | | *0.10* |
| 2 | 200 | 24 | 0.12 | 64 | 0.32 | |
| | | | | | | *0.20* |
| 3 | 260 | 36 | 0.138 | 76 | 0.292 | |
| | | | | | | *0.33* |
| 4 | 300 | 48 | 0.16 | 88 | 0.293 | |
| | | | | | | *0.40* |
| 5 | 330 | 60 | 0.182 | 100 | 0.303 | |
| | | | | | | *0.60* |
| 6 | 350 | 72 | 0.206 | 112 | 0.32 | |
| | | | | | | *1.00* |
| 7 | 362 | 84 | 0.232 | 124 | 0.343 | |

**Table 6.4** Average Variable Cost and Average Total Cost of Bottle Production

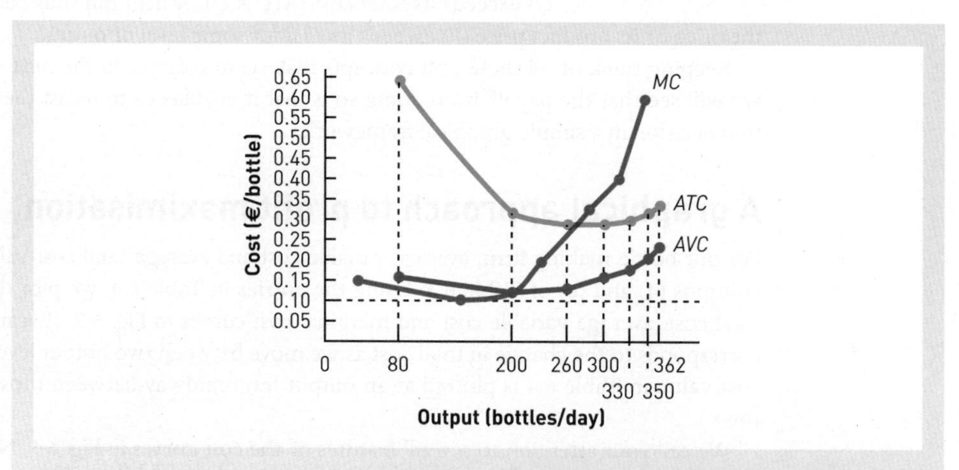


**Figure 6.5 The Marginal, Average Variable and Average Total Cost Curves for a Bottle Manufacturer.** The *MC* curve cuts both the *AVC* and *ATC* curves at their minimum points. The upward-sloping portion of the marginal cost curve corresponds to the region of diminishing returns.

weight will rise. By the same token, when marginal cost is below average total cost or average variable cost, the corresponding average cost must be falling and vice versa. And this ensures that the marginal cost curve must pass through the *minimum points* of both average cost curves.

Seeing the bottle maker's *AVC* curve displayed graphically makes the question posed in Exercise 6.4 much easier to answer. The question, you should recall, was whether the firm should shut down in the short run if the price of a bottle was only €0.10. A glance at Fig. 6.5

reveals that the firm should indeed shut down, because this price lies below the minimum value of its *AVC* curve, making it impossible for the firm to cover its variable costs at any output level.

## Price = marginal cost: the maximum-profit condition

In Example 6.2, we implicitly assumed that the bottle maker could employ workers only in whole-number amounts. Under these conditions, we saw that the profit-maximising output level was one for which marginal cost was somewhat less than price (because adding yet another employee would have pushed marginal cost higher than price). In Example 6.3, we shall see that when output and employment can be varied continuously, the maximum-profit condition is that price be equal to marginal cost.

Example 6.3 For the bottle maker whose cost curves are shown in Fig. 6.6, find the profit-maximising output level if bottles sell for €0.20 each. How much profit will this firm earn? What is the lowest price at which this firm would continue to operate in the short run?

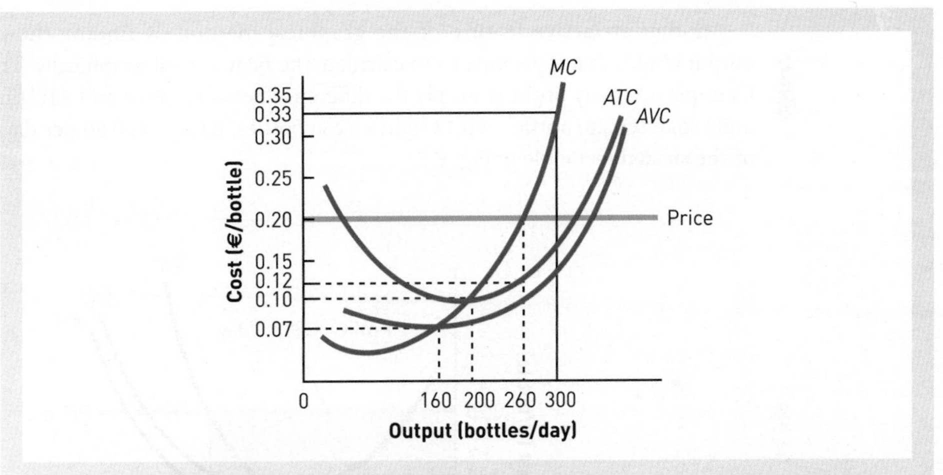


**Figure 6.6 Price = Marginal Cost: the Perfectly Competitive Firm's Proft-Maximising Supply Rule.** If price is greater than marginal cost, the firm can increase its profit by expanding production and sales. If price is less than marginal cost, the firm can increase its profit by producing and selling less output.

The Cost–Benefit Principle tells us that this firm should continue to expand as long as price is at least as great as marginal cost. In Fig. 6.6 we see that we see that if the firm follows this rule, it will produce 260 bottles per day, the quantity at which *price and marginal cost are equal*. To gain further confidence that 260 must be the profit-maximising quantity when the price is €0.20 per bottle, first suppose that the firm had sold some amount less than that – say, only 200 bottles per day. Its benefit from expanding output by one bottle would then be the bottle's market price, here 20 cents. The cost of expanding output by one bottle is equal (by definition) to the firm's marginal cost, which at 200 bottles per day is only 10 cents (see Fig. 6.6). So by selling the 201st bottle for 20 cents and producing it for an extra cost of only 10 cents, the firm will increase its profit by 20 – 10 = 10 cents per day. In a similar way, we can show that for *any* quantity less than the level at which price equals marginal cost, the seller can boost profit by expanding production.

Conversely, suppose that the firm was currently selling more than 260 bottles per day – say, 300 – at a price of 20 cents each. In Fig. 6.6 we see that marginal cost at an output of 300 is 33 cents per bottle. If the firm then contracted its output by one bottle per day, it would cut its costs by 33 cents while losing only 20 cents in revenue. As a result, its profit would grow by 13 cents per day. The same argument can be made regarding any quantity larger than 260, so if the firm is currently selling an output at which price is less than marginal cost, it can always do better by producing and selling fewer bottles.

We have thus established that if the firm sold fewer than 260 bottles per day, it could earn more profit by expanding; and if it sold more than 260, it could earn more by contracting. It follows that at a market price of 20 cents per bottle, the seller maximises its profit by selling 260 units per week, the quantity for which price and marginal cost are exactly the same.

At that quantity the firm will collect total revenue of $P \times Q$ = (€0.20/bottle) (260 bottles/day) = €52 per day. Note in Fig. 6.6 that at 260 bottles per day the firm's average total cost is *ATC* = €0.12 per bottle, which means that its total cost is $ATC \times Q$ = (€0.12/bottle)(260 bottles/day) = €31.20 per day. The firm's profit is the difference between its *total revenue and its total cost*, or €20.80 per day. Note, finally, that the minimum value of the firm's *AVC* curve is €0.07. So if the price of bottles fell below 7 cents each, the firm would shut down in the short run.

Another attractive feature of the graphical method of finding the profit-maximising output level is that it permits us to calculate the firm's profit graphically. Thus, for the firm in Example 6.3, daily profit is simply the difference between price and *ATC* times the number of units sold: (€0.20/bottle – €0.12/bottle)(260 bottles/day) = €20.80 per day, which is the area of the shaded rectangle in Fig. 6.7.

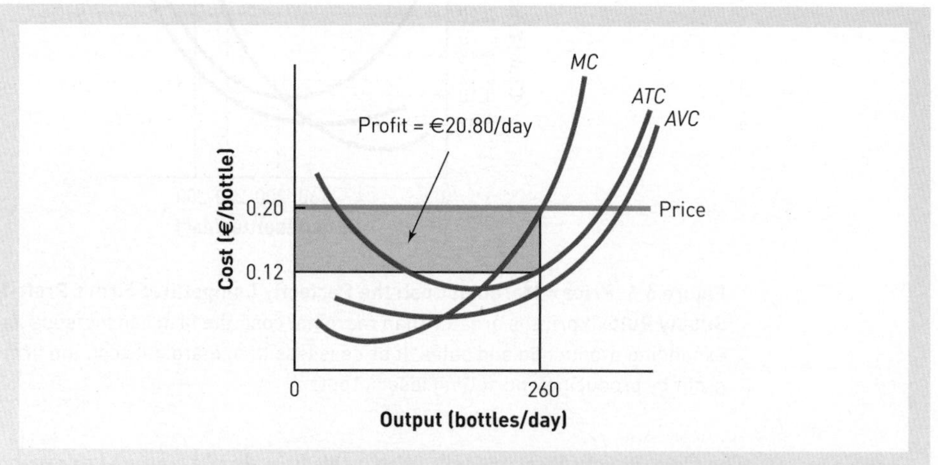


**Figure 6.7 Measuring Profit Graphically.** Profit is equal to $(P - ATC) \times Q$, which is equal to the area of the shaded rectangle.

Not all firms are as fortunate as the one shown in Fig. 6.7. Suppose, for example, that the price of bottles had been not 20 cents but only 8 cents. Since that price is greater than the minimum value of *AVC* (see Fig. 6.8), the firm should continue to operate in the short run by producing the level of output for which price equals marginal cost (180 bottles per day). But because price is less than *ATC* at that level of output, the firm will now experience a loss, or negative profit, on its operations. This profit is calculated as $(P - ATC) \times Q$ = (€0.08/bottle – €0.10/bottle) × (180 bottles/day) = –€3.60 per day, which is equal to the area of the shaded rectangle in Fig. 6.8.

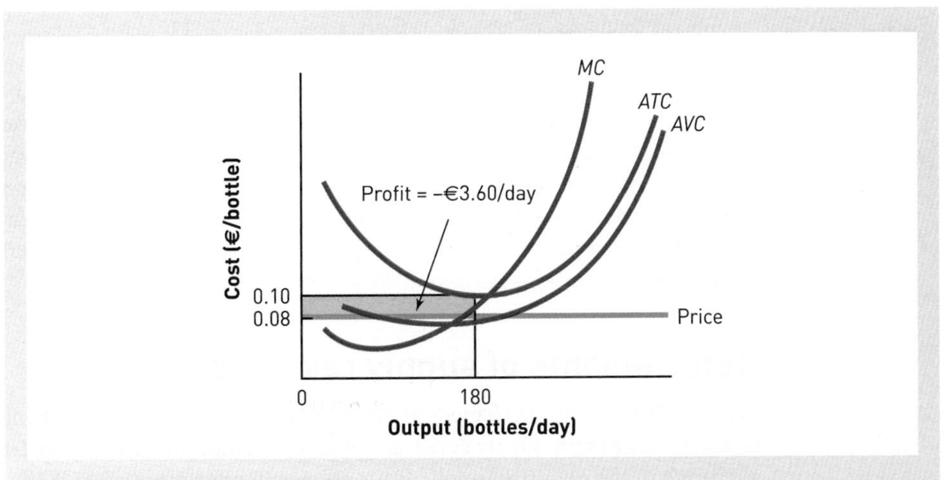


**Figure 6.8 A Negative Profit.** When price is less than *ATC* as the profit-maximising quantity, the firm experiences a loss, which is equal to the area of the shaded rectangle.

In Chapter 8, we shall see how firms move resources in response to the incentives implicit in profits and losses. But such movements occur in the long run, and our focus here is on production decisions in the short run.

## The 'law' of supply

The law of demand tells us that consumers buy less of a product when its price rises. If there were an analogous law of supply, it would say that producers offer more of a product for sale when its price rises. Is there such a law? We know that supply curves are essentially *marginal cost curves*, and that because of the law of diminishing returns, marginal cost curves are upward-sloping in the short run. And so there is indeed a law of supply that applies in the short run.

In the long run, however, the law of diminishing returns does not apply. (Recall that it holds only if at least *some* factors of production are fixed.) Because firms can vary the amounts of *all* factors of production they use in the long run, they can often double their production by simply doubling the amount of each input they use. In such cases costs would be exactly proportional to output, and the firm's marginal cost curve in the long run would be horizontal, not upward-sloping. So for now we shall say only that the 'law' of supply holds in the short run but not necessarily in the long run. For both the long run and the short run, however, the perfectly competitive firm's supply curve is its *marginal cost curve*.[1]

Every quantity of output along the market supply curve represents the summation of all the quantities individual sellers offer at the corresponding price. So the correspondence between price and marginal cost exists for the market supply curve as well as for the individual supply curves that lie behind it. That is, for every price–quantity pair along the market supply curve, *price will be equal to each seller's marginal cost of production.*

This is why we sometimes say that the supply curve represents the *cost side* of the market, whereas the demand curve represents the *benefit side* of the market. At every point along a market demand curve, price represents what buyers would be willing to pay for an additional unit of the product – and this, in turn, is how we measure the amount by which they would benefit by having an additional unit of the product. Likewise, at every point along a market supply curve, price measures what it would cost producers to expand production by one unit.

[1] Again, this rule holds subject to the provision that total revenue exceeds variable production costs at the output level or which price equals marginal cost.

## RECAP The competitive firm's supply curve

The perfectly competitive firm faces a *horizontal demand curve* for its product, meaning that it can sell any quantity it wishes at the market price. In the short run, the firm's goal is to choose the level of output that maximises its profits. It will accomplish this by choosing the output level for which its marginal cost is equal to the market price of its product, provided that price exceeds average variable cost. The perfectly competitive firm's supply curve is the portion of its marginal cost curve that lies above its average variable cost curve. At the profit-maximising quantity, the firm's profit is the product of that quantity and the difference between price and average total cost.

# Determinants of supply revisited

What factors give rise to changes in supply? (Again, remember that a 'change in supply' refers to a shift in the entire supply curve, as opposed to a movement along the curve, which we call a 'change in the quantity supplied'.) A seller will offer more units if the benefit of selling extra output goes up relative to the cost of producing it. And since the benefit of selling output in a perfectly competitive market is a fixed market price that is beyond the seller's control, our search for factors that influence supply naturally focuses on the cost side of the calculation. The preceding examples suggest why the following factors, among others, will affect the likelihood that a product will satisfy the cost–benefit test for a given supplier.

## Technology

Perhaps the most important determinant of production cost is *technology*. Improvements in technology make it possible to produce additional units of output at lower cost. This shifts each individual supply curve downward (or, equivalently, outward) and hence shifts the market supply curve downward as well. Over time, the introduction of more sophisticated machinery has resulted in dramatic increases in the number of goods produced per hour of effort expended. Every such development gives rise to an outward shift in the market supply curve.

But how do we know that technological change will reduce the cost of producing goods and services? Might not new equipment be so expensive that the producers who use it will have higher costs than those who rely on earlier designs? If so, then rational producers simply will not use the new equipment. The only technological changes that rational producers will adopt are those that will reduce their cost of production.

## Input prices

Whereas technological change generally (although not always) leads to gradual shifts in supply, changes in the prices of *important inputs* can give rise to large supply shifts literally overnight. As discussed in Chapter 4, for example, the price of crude oil, which is the most important input in the production of motor fuel, often fluctuates sharply, and the resulting shifts in supply cause fuel prices to exhibit corresponding fluctuations.

Similarly, when *wage rates* rise, the marginal cost of any business that employs labour also rises, shifting supply curves to the left (or, equivalently, upward). When interest rates fall, the opportunity cost of capital equipment also falls, causing supply to shift to the right.

## The number of suppliers

Just as demand curves shift to the right when population grows, supply curves also shift to the right as the number of *individual suppliers* grows. For example, if container recyclers die or retire at a higher rate than new recyclers enter the industry, the supply curve for recycling services will shift to the left. Conversely, if a rise in the unemployment rate leads more people to recycle soft drink containers (by reducing the opportunity cost of time spent recycling), the supply curve of recycling services will shift to the right.

### Expectations

Expectations about *future price movements* can affect how much sellers choose to offer in the current market. Suppose, for example, that recyclers expect the future price of aluminium to be much higher than the current price because of the growing use of aluminium components in cars. The rational recycler would then have an incentive to withhold aluminium from the market at today's lower price, in order to have more available to sell at the higher future price. Conversely, if recyclers expect next year's price of aluminium to be lower than this year's, their incentive would be to offer more aluminium for sale in today's market.

### Changes in prices of other products

Apart from technological change, perhaps the most important determinant of supply is variation in the prices of *other goods and services* that sellers might produce. Prospectors, for example, search for those precious metals for which the surplus of benefits over costs is greatest. When the price of silver rises, many stop looking for gold and start looking for silver. Conversely, when the price of platinum falls, many platinum prospectors shift their attention to gold.

**RECAP** Determinants of supply

Among the relevant factors *causing supply curves to shift* are new technologies, changes in input prices, changes in the number of sellers, expectations of future price changes and changes in the prices of other products that firms might produce.

## Applying the theory of supply

Whether the activity is producing new soft drink containers or recycling used ones – or, indeed, any other production activity at all – the same logic governs all supply decisions in perfectly competitive markets (and in any other setting in which sellers can sell as much as they wish to at a constant price): keep expanding output until marginal cost is equal to the price of the product. This logic helps us understand why recycling efforts are more intensive for some products than others (see also the Appendix to this chapter).

### When recycling is left to private market forces, why are many more aluminium beverage containers recycled than glass ones?

In both cases, recyclers gather containers until their marginal costs are equal to the containers' respective redemption prices. When recycling is left to market forces, the redemption price for a container is based on what companies can sell it (or the materials in it) for. Aluminium containers can be easily processed into scrap aluminium, which commands a high price, and this leads profit-seeking companies to offer a high redemption price for aluminium cans. By contrast, the glass from which glass containers are made has only limited resale value, primarily because the raw materials required to make new glass are so cheap. This difference leads profit-seeking companies to offer much lower redemption prices for glass containers than for aluminium ones.

The high redemption prices for aluminium cans induce many people to track them down, whereas the low redemption prices for glass containers leads most people to ignore them. If recycling is left completely to market forces, then, we would expect to see aluminium soft drink containers quickly recycled, whereas glass containers would increasingly litter the landscape. This is in fact the pattern we do see in countries without recycling laws. (More on how these laws work in a moment.) This pattern is a simple consequence of the fact that the supply curves of container-recycling services are upward-sloping.

The acquisition of valuable raw materials is only one of two important benefits from recycling. The second is that, by removing litter, recycling makes the environment more pleasant for everyone. As Example 6.4 suggests, this second benefit might easily justify the cost of recycling substantial numbers of glass containers.

### **Example 6.4** What is the socially optimal amount of recycling of glass containers?

Suppose that the 60,000 citizens of Chinon in the Loire Valley in France would collectively be willing to pay 6 centimes for each glass container removed from their local environment. If the local market supply curve of glass container–recycling services is as shown in Fig. 6.9, what is the socially optimal level of glass container recycling?

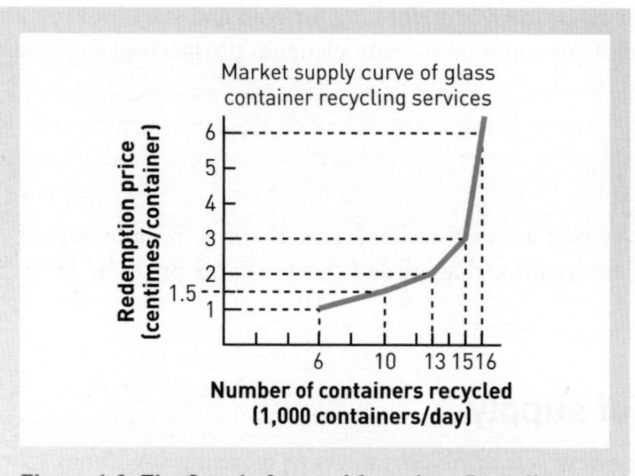


**Figure 6.9 The Supply Curve of Container Recycling Services for Chinon, France.**

Suppose the citizens of Chinon authorise their Commune to collect tax money to finance litter removal. If the benefit of each glass container removed, as measured by what residents are collectively willing to pay, is 6 centimes, the government should offer to pay 6 centimes for each glass container recycled. To maximise the total economic surplus from recycling, we should recycle that number of containers for which the marginal cost of recycling is equal to the 6 centimes marginal benefit. Given the market supply curve shown in Fig 6.9, the optimal quantity is 16,000 containers per day, and that is how many will be redeemed when the government offers 6 centimes per container.

Although 16,000 containers per day will be removed from the environment in Example 6.4, others will remain. After all, some are discarded in remote locations, and a redemption price of 6 centimes per container is simply not high enough to induce people to track them all down.

So why not offer an even higher price, and get rid of *all* glass container litter? For the case in Example 6.4, the reason is that the *marginal cost* of removing the 16,001st glass container each day is greater than the benefit of removing it. Total economic surplus is largest when we remove litter only up to the point that the marginal benefit of litter removal is equal to its marginal cost, which occurs when 16,000 containers per day are recycled. To proceed past that point is actually wasteful.

Many people become upset when they first hear economists say that the socially optimal amount of litter is greater than zero. In the minds of these people, the optimal amount of litter is *exactly* zero. But this position completely ignores the scarcity principle. Granted, there would be benefits from reducing litter further, but there would also be costs. Spending more on litter removal therefore means spending less on other useful things. No one would insist that the optimal amount of dirt in his own home is zero. (If someone does make this claim, ask her why she doesn't stay home all day vacuuming the dust that is accumulating in her absence.) If it doesn't pay to remove all the dust from your house, it doesn't pay to remove all the bottles from the environment. Precisely the same logic applies in each case.

If 16,000 containers per day is the optimal amount of litter removal, can we expect the individual spending decisions of private citizens to result in that amount of litter removal? Unfortunately we cannot. The problem is that anyone who paid for litter removal individually would bear the full cost of those services while reaping only a tiny fraction of the benefit. In Example 6.4, the 60,000 citizens of Chinon reaped a total benefit of 6 centimes per container removed, which means a benefit of only $(6/60{,}000) = 0.0001$ centime per person! Someone who paid 6 centimes for someone else to remove a container would thus be incurring a cost 60,000 times greater than his share of the resulting benefit.

Note that the *incentive problem* here is similar to that discussed in Chapter 3 for the person deciding whether to be vaccinated against an illness. The problem was that the incentive to be vaccinated was too weak, because even though the patient bears the full cost of the vaccination many of the resulting benefits accrue to others. Thus an important part of the extra benefit from any one person being vaccinated is that others also become less likely to contract the illness.

In the case of glass container litter, in short, we have an example in which private market forces do not produce the best attainable outcome for society as a whole. Even people who carelessly toss containers on the ground, rather than recycle them, are often offended by the unsightly landscape to which their own actions contribute. Indeed, this is why they often support laws mandating adequate redemption prices for glass containers.

Activities that generate litter are a good illustration of the equilibrium principle described in Chapter 3 (also called, for reasons this example makes clear, the *'smart for one, dumb for all'* principle). People who litter do so not because they don't care about the environment, but because their private incentives make littering misleadingly attractive. Recycling requires some effort, after all; yet no individual's recycling efforts have a noticeable effect on the quality of the environment. The soft drink container-deposit laws that have been enacted by numerous US states are a simple way to bring individual interests more closely into balance with the interests of society as a whole. The vast majority of container litter has disappeared almost literally overnight in the states that enacted these laws.

## Economic naturalist 6.1 Why have the plastic grocery bags that disfigured the Irish countryside almost entirely disappeared?

Ireland depends heavily on tourism, and 'sells' the image of a green and unspoilt countryside. This is hardly surprising since few people would come to Ireland (or Britain, for that matter) in search of sun, sand and cheap wine: the weather and penal taxes on alcohol rule that out. Unfortunately, during the 1980s and 1990s increased prosperity and other factors let to the prolific use of plastic bags in retailing. A large proportion of these ended up being blown into hedgerows and littering the streets. In 2002, in an attempt to clean up this massive eyesore, the Irish Minister for the Environment persuaded the Minister for Finance to impose a 15 cent per bag tax on plastic bags provided by retail establishments in the budget for 2003 (there were some small exceptions associated with fresh food). There were loud complaints from supermarkets and other grocery and convenience outlets. The government stood its ground. In 2003 the government derived virtually no revenue from the tax ... and plastic bags were about as common as hens' teeth. The impact on the environment was dramatic. Of course, purists among the economics profession were heard to argue that the outcome was sub-optimal since the optimal level of littering is not zero. Do you think anyone listened? If not, what does this tell us about the costs and benefits involved?

**Exercise 6.5** If the supply curve of glass container-recycling services is as shown in the diagram below, and each of the city's 60,000 citizens would be willing to pay 0.00005 cents for each glass container removed from the landscape, at what level should the city government set the redemption price for glass containers, and how many will be recycled each day?

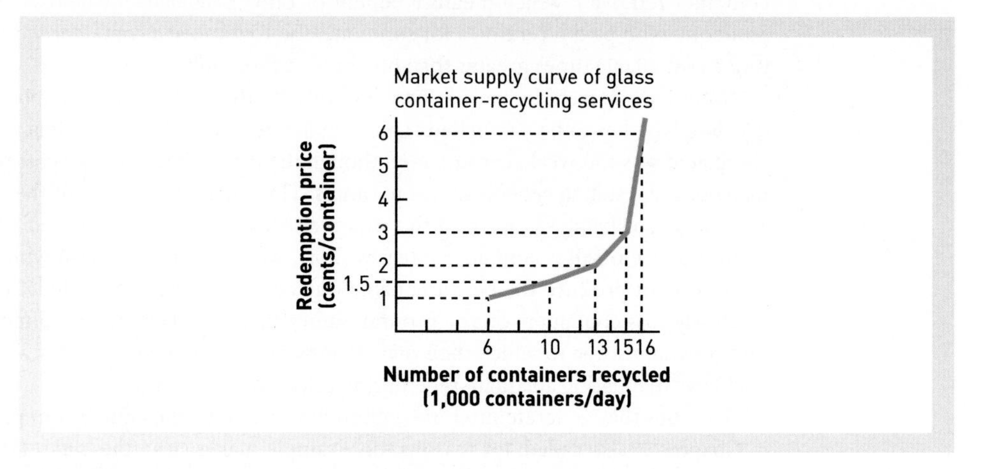


## Supply and producer surplus

**producer surplus** the amount by which price exceeds the seller's reservation price

The economic surplus received by a buyer is called *consumer surplus*. The analogous construct for a seller is **producer surplus**, the difference between the price a seller actually receives for the product and the lowest price for which she would have been willing to sell it (her reservation price, which in general will be her marginal cost).

As in the case of consumer surplus, the term 'producer surplus' sometimes refers to the surplus received by a single seller in a transaction, while on other occasions it describes the total surplus received by all sellers in a market or collection of markets.

## Calculating producer surplus

In Chapter 5 we saw that consumer surplus in a market is the area bounded above by the demand curve and bounded below by the market price. Producer surplus in a market is calculated in an analogous way. As Example 6.5 illustrates, it is the area bounded above by the market price and bounded below by the market supply curve.

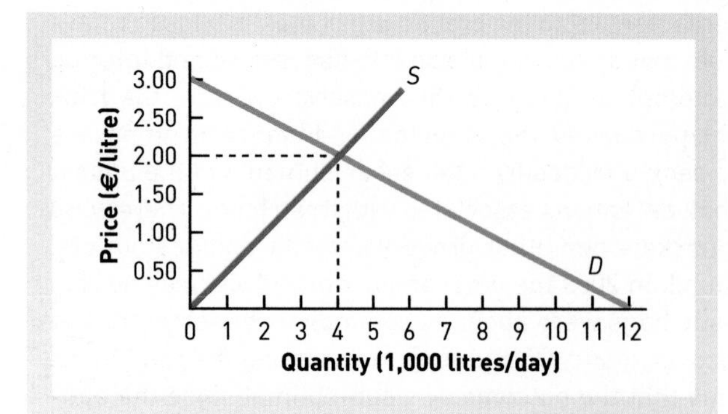


**Figure 6.10 Supply and Demand in the Market for Milk.** For the supply and demand curves shown, the equilibrium price of milk is €2 per litre and the equilibrium quantity is 4,000 litres per day.

### Example 6.5 How much do sellers benefit from their participation in the market for milk?

Consider the market for milk whose demand and supply curves are shown in Fig. 6.10, which has an equilibrium price of €2 per litre and an equilibrium quantity of 4,000 litres per day. How much producer surplus do the sellers in this market reap?

In Fig. 6.10, note first that for all milk sold up to 4,000 litres per day, sellers receive a surplus equal to the difference between the market price of €2 per litre and their reservation price as given by the supply curve. Total producer surplus received by buyers in the milk market is thus the shaded triangle between the supply

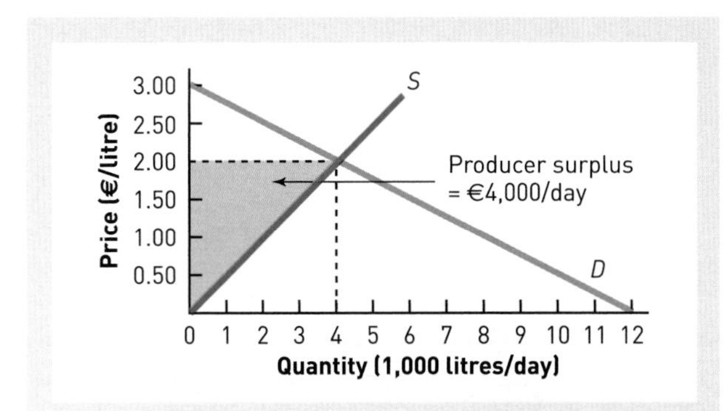


**Figure 6.11 Producer Surplus in the Market for Milk.** Producer surplus is the area of the shaded triangle (€4,000/day).

curve and the market price in Fig. 6.11. Note that this area is a right-angled triangle whose vertical arm is $h = €2/\text{litre}$ and whose horizontal arm is $b = 4{,}000$ litres/day. And since the area of any triangle is equal to $(1/2)bh$, producer surplus in this market is equal to

$$(1/2)(4{,}000 \text{ litres/day})(€2/\text{litre}) = €4{,}000/\text{day}$$

Producer surplus in this example may be thought of as the highest price sellers would pay, in the aggregate, for the right to continue participating in the milk market. It is €4,000 per day, since that is the amount by which their *combined benefits exceed their combined costs*.

As discussed in Chapter 3, the supply curve for a good can be interpreted either horizontally or vertically. The horizontal interpretation tells us, for each price, the total quantity that producers wish to sell at that price. The vertical interpretation tells us, for each quantity, the smallest amount a seller would be willing to accept for the good. For the purpose of computing producer surplus, we rely on the vertical interpretation of the supply curve. The value on the vertical axis that corresponds to each point along the supply curve corresponds to the marginal seller's reservation price for the good, which is the marginal cost of producing it. Producer surplus is the cumulative sum of the differences between the market price and these reservation prices. It is the area bounded above by market price and bounded below by the supply curve.

## Summary

- The supply curve for a good or service is a schedule that for any price tells us the *quantity that sellers wish to supply at that price*. The prices at which goods and services are offered for sale in the market depend, in turn, on the opportunity cost of the resources required to produce them.
- Supply curves tend to be upward-sloping, at least in the short run, in part because of the low-hanging-fruit principle. In general, rational producers will always take advantage of their best opportunities first, moving on to more difficult or costly opportunities only after their best ones have been exhausted. Reinforcing this tendency is the *law of diminishing returns*, which says that when some factors of production are held fixed, the amount of additional variable factors required to produce successive increments in output grows larger.
- For perfectly competitive markets – or, more generally, for markets in which individual sellers can sell whatever quantity they wish at constant price – the seller's best option is to sell that quantity of output for which *price equals marginal cost*, provided price exceeds the minimum value of average variable cost. The supply curve for the seller thus coincides with the portion of his marginal cost curve that exceeds average variable cost. This is why we sometimes say that the supply curve represents the cost side of the market (in contrast to the demand curve, which represents the benefit side of the market).
- An important terminological distinction from the demand side of the market also applies on the supply side of the market. A 'change in supply' means a shift in the entire supply curve, whereas a 'change in the quantity supplied' means a movement along the supply curve. The factors that cause *supply curves to shift* include technology, input prices, the number of sellers, expectations of future price changes and the prices of other products that firms might produce.
- *Producer surplus* is a measure of the economic surplus reaped by a seller or sellers in a market. It is the cumulative sum of the differences between the market price and their reservation prices, which is the area bounded above by market price and bounded below by the supply curve.

## Key terms

average total cost (*ATC*) (163)
average variable cost (*AVC*) (163)
factor of production (159)
fixed cost (160)
fixed factor of production (159)
imperfectly competitive firm (159)
law of diminishing returns (159)
long run (159)
marginal cost (161)
perfectly competitive market (157)
price taker (157)
producer surplus (172)
profit (157)
profitable firm (163)
profit-maximising firm (157)
short run (159)
total cost (161)
variable cost (161)
variable factor of production (159)

## Review questions

1. Explain why you would expect supply curves to slope upward on the basis of the principle of increasing opportunity cost.
2. Which do you think is more likely to be a fixed factor of production for an ice cream producer during the next two months: its factory building or its workers who operate the machines? Explain.
3. Economists often stress that congestion helps account for the law of diminishing returns. With this in mind, explain why it would be impossible to feed all the people on earth with food grown in a single flowerpot, even if unlimited water, labour, seed, fertiliser, sunlight and other inputs were available.
4. **True or false:** The perfectly competitive firm should always produce the output level for which price equals marginal cost.
5. Why do we use the vertical interpretation of the supply curve when we measure producer surplus?

## Problems

Problems marked with an asterisk (*) are more difficult.

1. Zoe is trying to decide how to divide her time between her job as a wedding photographer, which pays €27 per hour for as many hours as she chooses to work, and as a fossil collector, in which her pay depends both on the price of fossils and the number of them she finds. Earnings aside, Zoe is indifferent between the two tasks, and the number of fossils she can find depends on the number of hours a day she searches, as shown in the table below.

| Hours per day (1) | Total fossils per day (2) |
|---|---|
| 1 | 5 |
| 2 | 9 |
| 3 | 12 |
| 4 | 14 |
| 5 | 15 |

   a. Derive a table with price in euro increments from €0 to €30 in column (1) and the quantity of fossils Zoe is willing to supply per day at that price in column (2).

   b. Plot these points in a graph with price on the vertical axis and quantity per day on the horizontal. What is this curve called?

2. A price-taking firm makes air conditioners. The market price of one of their new air conditioners is €120. Its total cost information is given in the table below.

| Air conditioners per day | Total cost (€ per day) |
|---|---|
| 1 | 100 |
| 2 | 150 |
| 3 | 220 |
| 4 | 310 |
| 5 | 405 |
| 6 | 510 |
| 7 | 650 |
| 8 | 800 |

How many air conditioners should the firm produce per day if its goal is to maximise its profit?

3. The Paducah Slugger Company makes baseball bats out of lumber supplied to it by Acme Sporting Goods, which pays Paducah €10 for each finished bat. Paducah's only factors of production are lathe operators and a small building with a lathe. The number of bats per day it produces depends on the number of employee-hours per day, as shown in the table below.

| Number of bats per day | Number of employee-hours per day |
|---|---|
| 0 | 0 |
| 5 | 1 |
| 10 | 2 |
| 15 | 4 |
| 20 | 7 |
| 25 | 11 |
| 30 | 16 |
| 35 | 22 |

a. If the wage is €15 per hour and Paducah's daily fixed cost for the lathe and building is €60, what is the profit-maximising quantity of bats?

b. What would be the profit-maximising number of bats if the firm's fixed cost were not €60 per day but only €30?

4. In Question 3, how would Paducah's profit-maximising level of output be affected if the government imposed a tax of €10 per day on the company? (**Hint:** Think of this tax as equivalent to a €10 increase in fixed cost.) What would Paducah's profit-maximising level of output be if the government imposed a tax of €2 per bat? (**Hint:** Think of this tax as a €2 per bat increase in the firm's marginal cost.) Why do these two taxes have such different effects?

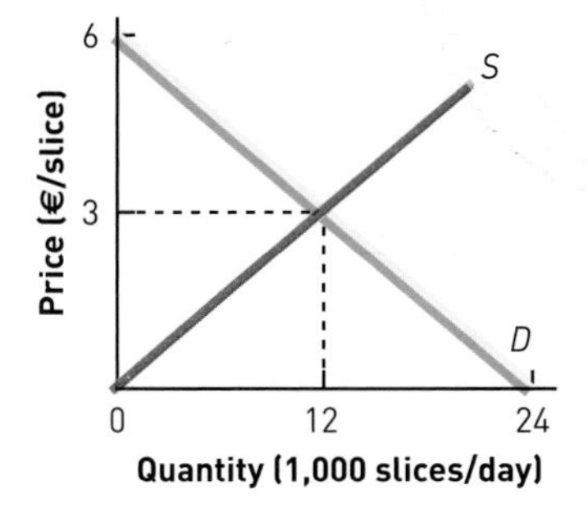


5. The supply curves for the only two firms in a competitive industry are given by $P = 2Q_1$ and $P = 2 + Q_2$, where $Q_1$ is the output of firm 1 and $Q_2$ is the output of firm 2. What is the market supply curve for this industry? (**Hint:** Graph the two curves side by side, then add their respective quantities at a sample of different prices.)

6. Calculate daily producer surplus for the market for pizza whose demand and supply curves are shown in the graph on the left.

7. For the pizza seller whose marginal, average variable and average total cost curves are shown in the diagram below, what is the profit-maximising level of output and how much profit will this producer earn if the price of pizza is €2.50 per slice?

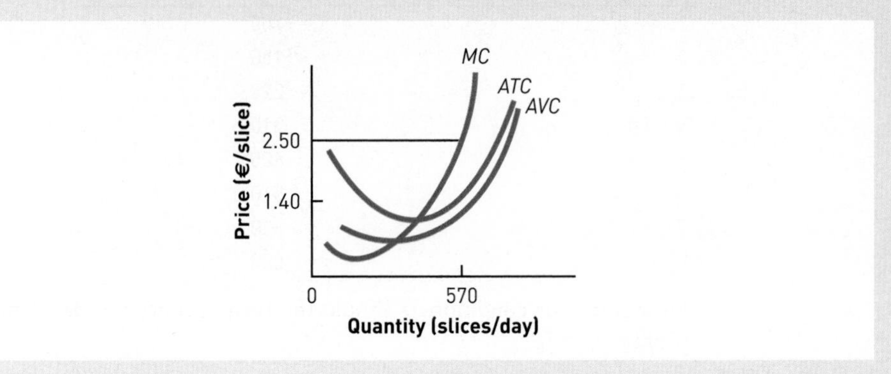


8. For the pizza seller whose marginal, average variable and average total cost curves are shown in the diagram below, what is the profit-maximising level of output and how much profit will this producer earn if the price of pizza is €0.80 per slice?

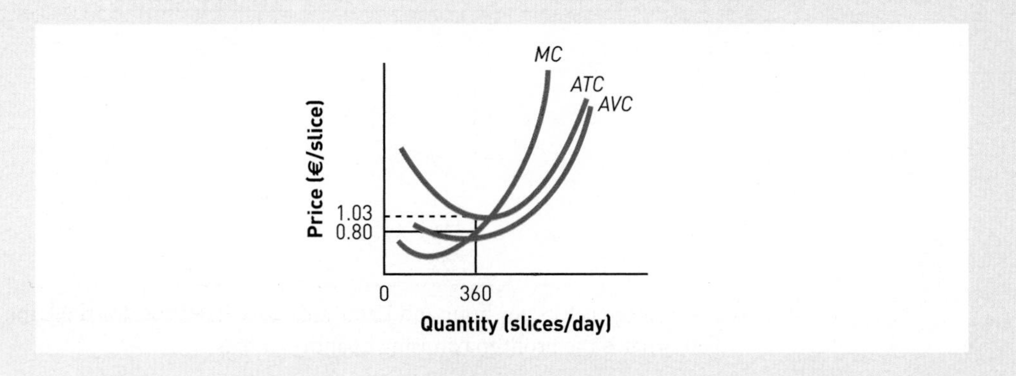


9.* For the pizza seller whose marginal, average variable and average total cost curves are shown in the diagram below, what is the profit-maximising level of output and how much profit will this producer earn if the price of pizza is €0.50 per slice?

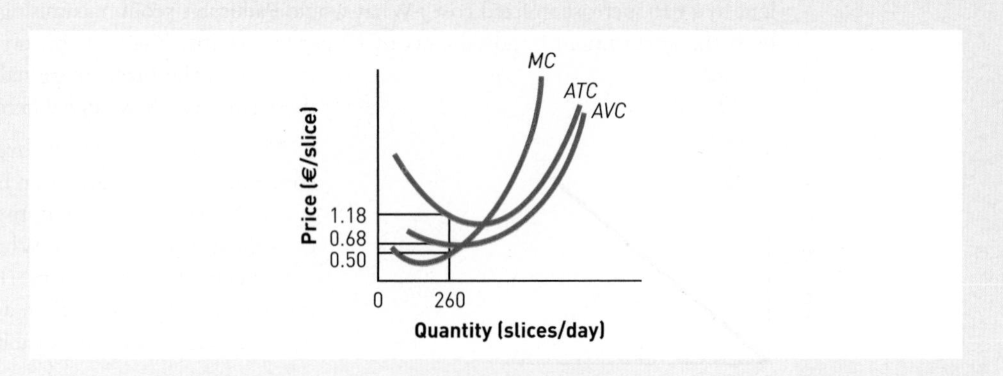

10.* For the pizza seller whose marginal, average variable and average total cost curves are shown in the diagram below (who is the same seller as in Problem 9), what is the profit-maximising level of output and how much profit will this producer earn if the price of pizza is €1.18 per slice?

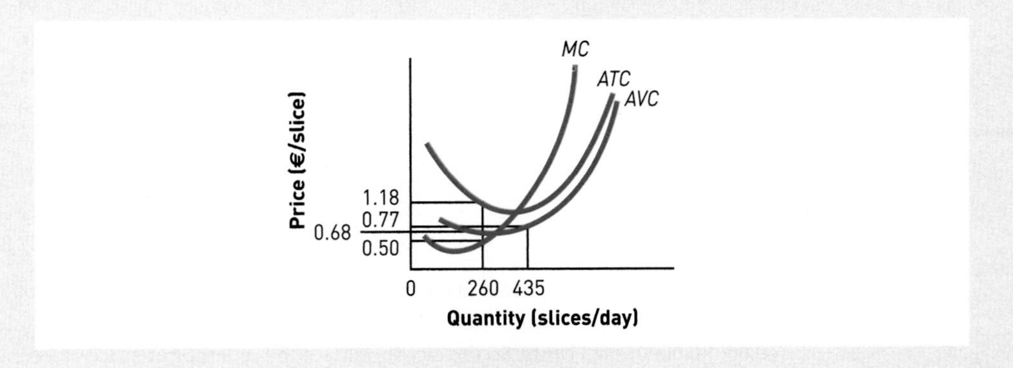


## Answers to in-chapter exercises

6.1 Since Harry will find 300 containers if he searches for a third hour, we find his reservation price for searching for a second hour by solving $p(300) = €6$ for $p = 2$ pence. His reservation prices for additional hours of search are calculated in an analogous way.

Fourth hour: $p(200) = €6$, so $p = 3$ cents.

Fifth hour: $p(100) = €6$, so $p = 6$ cents.

6.2 If bottles sell for 62 cents each, the firm should continue to expand up to and including the sixth employee (350 bottles per day).

6.3 The relevant costs are now as shown in the table below. With each variable and marginal cost entry half what it was in Example 6.2, the firm should now hire six employees and produce 350 bottles per day.

| Employees per day | Bottles per day | Fixed cost (€/day) | Variable cost (€/day) | Total cost (€/day) | Marginal cost (€/bottle) |
|---|---|---|---|---|---|
| 0 | 0 | 40 | 0 | 40 | |
| | | | | | 0.075 |
| 1 | 80 | 40 | 6 | 46 | |
| | | | | | 0.05 |
| 2 | 200 | 40 | 12 | 52 | |
| | | | | | 0.10 |
| 3 | 260 | 40 | 18 | 58 | |
| | | | | | 0.167 |
| 4 | 300 | 40 | 24 | 64 | |
| | | | | | 0.20 |
| 5 | 330 | 40 | 30 | 70 | |
| | | | | | 0.30 |
| 6 | 350 | 40 | 36 | 76 | |
| | | | | | 0.50 |
| 7 | 362 | 40 | 42 | 82 | |

6.4 Because the firm makes its smallest loss when it hires zero employees, it should shut down in the short run.

| Employees per day | Output (bottles/day) | Total revenue (€/day) | Total cost (€/day) | Profit (€/day) |
|---|---|---|---|---|
| 0 | 0 | 0 | 40 | -40 |
| 1 | 80 | 8 | 52 | -44 |
| 2 | 200 | 20 | 64 | -44 |
| 3 | 260 | 26 | 76 | -50 |
| 4 | 300 | 30 | 88 | -58 |
| 5 | 330 | 33 | 100 | -67 |
| 6 | 350 | 35 | 112 | -77 |
| 7 | 362 | 36.20 | 124 | -87.80 |

6.5 The fact that each of the city's 60,000 residents is willing to pay 0.00005 cents for each container removed means that the collective benefit of each container removed is (60,000)(0.00005) = 3 cents. So the city should set the redemption price at 3 cents, and from the supply curve we see that 15,000 containers per day will be recycled at that price.

# Appendix

In the main body of the chapter we have derived some key aspects of the theory of supply in an informal fashion. In this Appendix the propositions concerned are derived rigorously, but not in a manner that is technically difficult to follow. As with earlier analysis of demand, the point here is twofold. In the first place conclusions based on illustrative examples or on the shapes of graphs may lack persuasiveness, in that while they are plausible a reader could be concerned that they did not stand up to rigorous analysis. Hence, deriving them formally demonstrates their validity. The second objective is to accustom students to using formal and mathematical analysis in approaching economics as a discipline.

The first proposition that we demonstrate is that the *marginal cost curve must cut the average cost curve at its lowest point*. In the main body of the chapter this was supported by reference to an example of the average weight of an elementary school class. In this Appendix we make use of the chain rule contained in Appendix B to Chapter 1 on differentiation.

## Margins, averages and all that

The marginal cost curve must cut the average cost curve at its lowest point.

Average cost is total cost at any level of output produced divided by the number of units of output being produced. Write this as $AC = TC/q$. The value of average cost will depend on the level of production. Note that this can be rewritten as $TC = AC.q$, and that $AC$ is a function of $q$ (varies with $q$), so $TC = AC(q).q$

Marginal cost is the change in total cost from producing one more or one less unit of output. It is, therefore the rate of change of total cost as output changes at any level of output. Write this as $MC = \mathrm{d}TC/\mathrm{d}q$. The value of marginal cost will also depend on the level of production. Hence, $MC = \mathrm{d}TC/\mathrm{d}q = \mathrm{d}[AC(q).q]/\mathrm{d}q$.

From the chain rule,

$$\mathrm{d}TC/\mathrm{d}q = AC(q)[\mathrm{d}q/\mathrm{d}q] + q\,[\mathrm{d}AC(q)/\mathrm{d}q)] \qquad (6A.1)$$

$\mathrm{d}q/\mathrm{d}q = 1$, therefore

$$\mathrm{d}TC/\mathrm{d}Q = MC = AC(q) + q[\mathrm{d}C(q)/\mathrm{d}q] \qquad (6A.2)$$

Or,

$$MC = AC + q[\mathrm{d}AC/\mathrm{d}q] \qquad (6A.3)$$

If $AC$ is falling, the second term on the right-hand side is negative; if $AC$ is rising the term is positive. Hence, if $AC$ is falling, $MC < AC$; and if it is rising, $MC > AC$. From this it follows that if $AC$ is neither rising nor falling (i.e. is constant or is turning), $MC = AC$. Therefore $MC$ equals (cuts) $AC$ at its lowest point.

This is true of the relation between any marginal value and its corresponding average.

## The simple mathematics of profit maximisation under perfect competition

The simplest way to approach this is initially via a graph. For a perfectly competitive firm, price is outside its control: the firm is a *price taker*. The amount it sells has no effect on the price per unit sold it receives. Hence, total sales revenue is simply price (which is given) multiplied by the number of units sold. In Fig. 6A.1 it is a straight line from the origin, the slope of which is price.

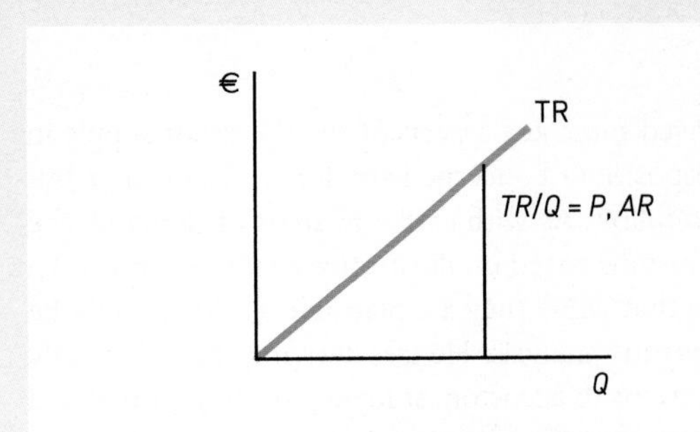


**Figure 6A.1 *TR, AR* and *MR* under Perfect Competition.**

Total cost is *fixed cost* (independent of whether or not production takes place) plus *variable cost*. The level of fixed cost on the vertical axis marks the point from which the total cost curve is drawn. Assuming diminishing returns, the total cost curve will slope upward at an accelerating rate.

The profits associated with any level of output are simply the *vertical distance* between the two curves. The profit-maximising output is that for which this distance is greatest. The distance will be greatest where the slopes of the two curves are the same. The slope of total cost is marginal cost; the slope of the total revenue curve in this case is price. Hence, profits are maximised at that output for which *marginal cost equals price*.

That said, let us derive the result formally.

Profits are the difference between Total Sales Revenue derived from sales of a production a period and Total Costs incurred in production of the product for sale in that period.

Let $B$ be profits; the level of profits depends on the level of sales and of costs, both of which depend on the level of production of the good or service sold. Hence, profits are a function of the level of production.

Formally,

$$B = B(q) \tag{6A.4}$$

where $q$ is the level of output. The problem is to find the level or value of $q$ that results in a maximum value for $B$.

To find the maximum value of a function we obtain the first derivative of the function and set it equal to zero. The slope of its graph is zero. At this value, it is either a maximum or a minimum. If the second derivative is negative, the value for $q$ is that which maximises the function

$$B = TR(q) - TC(q) \tag{6A.5}$$

$$B' = \mathrm{d}B/\mathrm{d}q = \mathrm{d}TR/\mathrm{d}q - \mathrm{d}TC/\mathrm{d}q \tag{6A.6}$$

For a maximum value of $B$ it is necessary that this be equal to zero. That means

$$\mathrm{d}TR/\mathrm{d}q = \mathrm{d}TC/\mathrm{d}q \tag{6A.7}$$

But $\mathrm{d}TR/\mathrm{d}q$ and $\mathrm{d}TC/\mathrm{d}q$ are (in the competitive case) simply price and marginal cost, respectively. Hence this necessary condition says that to maximise profits you produce the level of output that equates price to marginal cost.

Is this a maximum? To answer this requires that we know more about $TR$ and $TC$. $TR$ is easy. Under perfect competition

$$TR = p.q \tag{6A.8}$$

$TC$ is the sum of fixed plus variable costs. Fixed cost are a constant, $a$. Variable costs, because of diminishing returns, have the form

$$TVC = b.q + c.q^2 \tag{6A.9}$$

meaning that average variable cost increases with $q$.

Hence, the total cost function is

$$TC = a + b.q + c.q^2 \tag{6A.10}$$

Hence, the profits function may be written $B = p.q - a - b.q - c.q^2$ (6A.11)

The second derivative of this function with respect to $q$ is

$$d^2B/dq^2 = -2c < 0 \tag{6A.12}$$

hence this is a maximum.

## The monopoly (market power) case

For completeness at this stage we move beyond the competitive model to derive a result that is implicit in the competitive case but needs to be made explicit. This will be of use in Chapter 9, when we look at markets in which firms enjoy some degree of market power, the limiting case of which is when a firm is a monopolist.

Market power (in the limiting case, monopoly) implies that the firm knows that the price it obtains per unit sold will fall if it offers more to the market because the demand curve slopes downward. This means that the price per unit the firm receives for the amount it puts on the market is a function of the amount being sold:

$$p = p(q) \tag{6A.13}$$

in contrast with perfect competition, where the firm perceives price as given and independent of how much it chooses to sell.

The firm's profits function is, therefore, written:

$$B = p(q).q - a - b.q - c.q^2 \tag{6A.14}$$

The first derivative is now

$$B' = dB/dq = p + q(dp/dq) - b - 2c.q \tag{6A.15}$$

The first two terms on the right-hand side are the value of $dTR/dq$ (MR) when $TR = p(q)q$. However, the expression $q(dp/dq)$ is negative, since $dp/dq$ is the negative slope of the demand curve. Therefore

$$p + q(dp/dq) < p \tag{6A.16}$$

which means that $MR < P$.

Just as the slope of the total cost curve is marginal cost, the slope of the total revenue curve, $dTR/dQ$, is (by definition), marginal revenue. Hence, the condition for profit maximisation is setting $MR = MC$. The perfect competition case reflects the fact that under perfect competition, where firms have no market power, *price and marginal revenue are the same thing*. When a firm has market power it faces a downward-sloping demand curve. This means that it can raise its price without losing all its sales, and can increase its sales by lowering its price. $TR = pq$, $AR = TR/q$; therefore $p$ and $AR$ are the same thing. Since $p$ falls as $q$ increases along the demand curve, $AR$ is falling by definition. Since $AR$ is falling we know that $MR < AR$. Hence, $MR < p$.

Note the implication that in the presence of market power the chosen level of output is one for which $p > MC$, implying loss of surplus relative to the perfectly competitive case.

# 7 Efficiency and Exchange

The free-enterprise system of economic organisation has been frequently described in such glowing terms as 'the greatest engine of progress mankind has ever witnessed'. Its ability to deliver a high and rising standard of living to everyone (even if not equally to everyone) has been summed up in the saying: 'A rising tide lifts all boats.'

If you have heard these optimistic expressions extolling the free market but were struggling to make ends meet in one of the poorer areas of the Paris suburbs largely populated by immigrant workers from North Africa you might be somewhat sceptical. Urban violence, a drab and deteriorating environment, a long and expensive commute to a poorly paid job in the city centre and all the other unpleasant aspects of urban ghettoes would probably be your lot. If you were a 55-year-old unemployed ex-coal miner in County Durham in England in the late 1990s you may have wondered whether you were in a boat that had sprung a leak: there were simply no jobs available for you. If you were a white-collar worker who had lost a job in Seattle because Boeing was losing market share to Airbus, and were now working as a pallet pusher in a supermarket distribution centre and unable to afford adequate treatment for an asthmatic child because you no longer had company health cover, you might regard those expressions as descriptions of an entirely different economic universe from the one you lived in. In all these cases you would have found yourself enduring a poor and declining standard of living and an inability to better your position and an inability to find suitable work and to afford the basic necessities of a decent existence by society's standards.

For someone in any of these positions a degree of scepticism about the virtues of the system of free markets and private ownership of economic resources that we call 'free enterprise' would be entirely understandable.

Informed students of the market system understand that it could never be expected to avoid all these problems, and others like them, in the first place. *In certain domains* – indeed, in very broad domains – markets are every bit as remarkable as their strongest proponents assert. Yet there are many problems they simply cannot be expected to solve. For example, private markets cannot by themselves guarantee an income distribution that most people regard as fair. Nor can they ensure clean air, uncongested roads or safe neighbourhoods for all. And unemployment can persist even in a booming economy.

Yet markets do enable society to produce sufficient resources to meet all these goals, and more. But the types of problems just described point to an unavoidable conclusion. There are circumstances in which markets do not operate well and the outcome is less than acceptable. As a result, and even in the most successful free-market economies, markets are supplemented by active political co-ordination and collective provision of goods and services in at least some instances. We will almost always achieve our goals more effectively if we know what tasks private markets can do well, and then allow them to perform those tasks.

Unfortunately, the discovery that markets cannot solve *every* problem seems to have led some critics to conclude that markets cannot solve *any* problems. This misperception is a dangerous one, because it has prompted attempts to prevent markets from doing even those tasks for which they are ideally suited. Our task in this chapter will be to explore why many tasks are best left to the market. We shall explore the conditions under which unregulated markets generate the largest possible economic surplus. We shall also discuss why attempts to interfere with market outcomes often lead to unintended and undesired consequences. We shall see why public utilities can more efficiently serve their customers if they set prices in a way that closely mimics the market. And we shall also discuss why the economic burden of a tax does not always fall most heavily on the parties from whom it is directly collected.

## Market equilibrium and efficiency

As noted in Chapter 3, the mere fact that markets co-ordinate the production of a large and complex list of goods and services is reason enough to marvel at them. But economists make an even stronger claim – namely, that markets not only produce these goods, but also produce them as *efficiently* as possible.

The term **efficient**, as economists use it, has a narrow technical meaning. When we say that market equilibrium is efficient, we mean simply this: *If price and quantity take anything other than their equilibrium values, a transaction that will make at least some people better off without harming others can always be found.* This conception of efficiency is also known as Pareto efficiency, after Vilfredo Pareto, the nineteenth-century Italian economist who introduced it.

**efficient (or Pareto efficient)** a situation is efficient if no change is possible that will help some people without harming others

Why is market equilibrium 'efficient' in this sense? The answer is that when a market is not in equilibrium it is always possible to construct an exchange that helps some without harming others. In a sense, a 'free lunch' exists. Suppose, for example, that the supply and demand curves for milk are as shown in Fig. 7.1, and that the current price of milk is €1 per litre. At that price, sellers offer only 2,000 litres of milk a day. At that quantity, the marginal buyer values an extra litre of milk at €2. This is the price that corresponds to 2,000 litres a day on the demand curve, which represents what the marginal buyer is willing to pay for an additional litre (another application of the vertical interpretation of the demand curve). We also know that the cost of producing an extra litre of milk is only €1. This is the price that corresponds to 2,000 litres a day on the supply curve, which equals marginal cost (another application of the vertical interpretation of the supply curve).

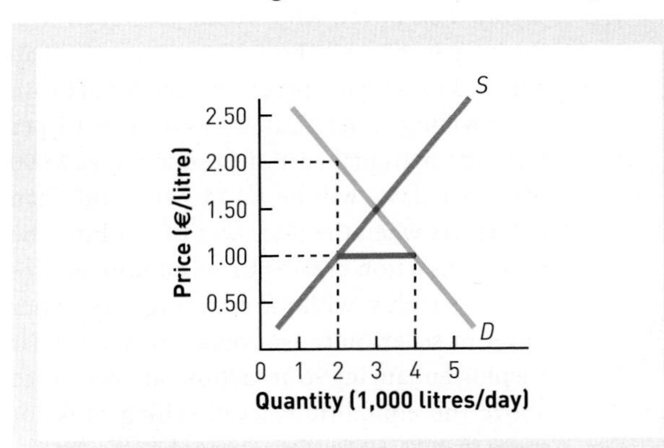


**Figure 7.1 A Market in which Price is Below the Equilibrium Level.** In this market, milk is currently selling for €1 per litre, €0.50 below the equilibrium price of €1.50 per litre.

Furthermore, a price of €1 per litre leads to excess demand of 2,000 litres per day, which means that many frustrated buyers cannot buy as much milk as they want at the going price.

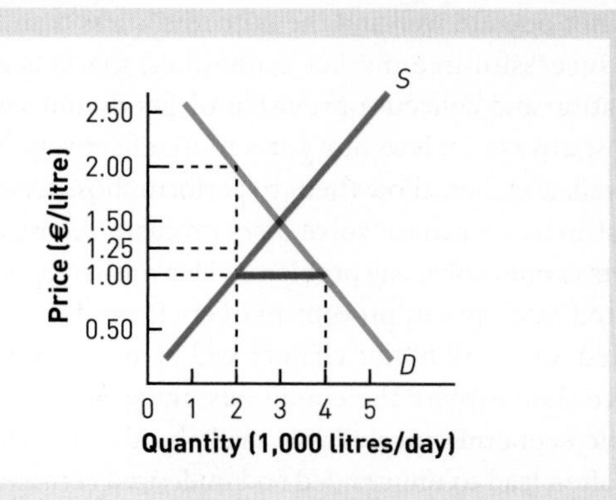


**Figure 7.2 How Excess Demand Creates an Opportunity for a Surplus-Enhancing Transaction.** At a market price of €1 per litre, the most intensely dissatisfied buyer is willing to pay €2 for an additional litre, which a seller can produce at a cost of only €1. If this buyer pays the seller €1.25 for the extra litre, the buyer gains an economic surplus of €0.75 and the seller gains an economic surplus of €0.25.

Now suppose a supplier sells an extra litre of milk to the most eager of these buyers for €1.25, as in Fig. 7.2. Since the extra litre cost only €1 to produce, the seller is €0.25 better off than before. And since the most eager buyer values the extra litre at €2, that buyer is €0.75 better off than before. In sum, the transaction creates an extra €1 of economic surplus out of thin air!

Note that none of the other buyers or sellers is harmed by this transaction. Thus milk selling for only €1 per litre cannot be efficient. As Exercise 7.1 illustrates, there was nothing special about the price of €1 per litre. Indeed, if milk sells for *any* price below €1.50 per litre (the market equilibrium price), we can design a similar transaction, which means that selling milk for any price less than €1.50 per litre cannot be efficient.

**Exercise 7.1** In Fig. 7.1, suppose that milk initially sells for 50 cents per litre. Describe a transaction that will create additional economic surplus for both buyer and seller without causing harm to anyone else.

What is more, it is always possible to describe a transaction that will create additional surplus for both buyer and seller whenever the price lies above the market equilibrium level. Suppose, for example, that the current price is €2 per litre in the milk market shown in Fig. 7.1. At that price, we have excess supply of 2,000 litres per day (see Fig. 7.3). Suppose the most dissatisfied producer sells a litre of milk for €1.75 to the buyer who values it most highly. This buyer, who would have been willing to pay €2, will be €0.25 better off than before. Likewise the producer, who would have been willing to sell milk for as little as €1 per litre (the marginal cost of production at 2,000 litres per day), will be €0.75 better off than before. As when the price was €1 per litre, the new transaction creates €1 of additional economic surplus without harming any other buyer or seller. Since we could design a similar surplus-enhancing transaction at any price above the equilibrium level, selling milk for more than €1.50 per litre cannot be efficient.

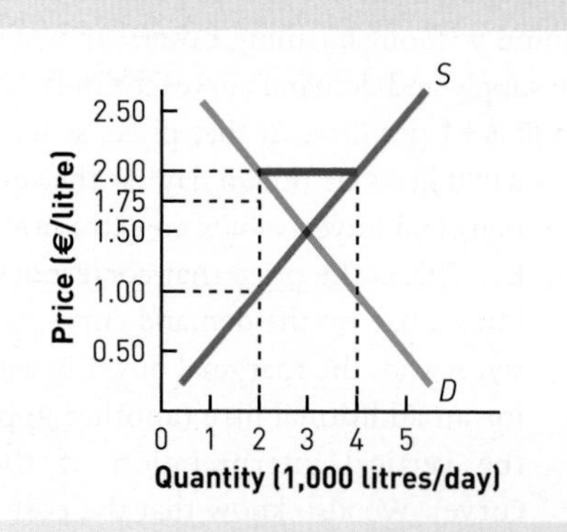


**Figure 7.3 How Excess Supply Creates an Opportunity for a Surplus-Enhancing Transaction.** At a market price of €2 per litre, dissatisfied sellers can produce an additional litre of milk at a cost of only €1, which is €1 less than a buyer would be willing to pay for it. If the buyer pays the seller €1.75 for an extra litre, the buyer gains an economic surplus of €0.25 and the seller gains an economic surplus of €0.75.

The vertical interpretations of the supply and demand curves thus make it clear why only the equilibrium price in a market can be efficient. *When the price realised is either higher or lower than the equilibrium price, the quantity exchanged in the market will always be lower than the equilibrium quantity.*

If the price is below equilibrium, the quantity sold will be the amount that *sellers offer*. If the price is above equilibrium, the quantity sold will be the amount that *buyers wish to buy*. In either case, the vertical value on the demand curve at the quantity exchanged, which is the value of an extra unit to buyers, must be larger than the vertical value on the supply curve, which is the marginal cost of producing that unit.

So the market equilibrium price is the only price at which buyers and sellers cannot design a surplus-enhancing transaction. The market equilibrium price leads, in other words, to the largest possible total economic surplus. In this specific, limited sense, free markets are said to produce and distribute goods and services efficiently.

Actually, to claim that the observed market equilibrium in terms of prices and quantities is always efficient even in this limited sense is an overstatement. The claim holds only if the following conditions are met:

1. *Buyers and sellers are well informed*. If people do not know the quality of a good or service they may find it difficult to evaluate the price they are prepared to pay for it.
2. *Markets are perfectly competitive*. A monopolist can use market power to drive a wedge between marginal cost and price, and hence between the cost of producing a good and what people are prepared to pay for it.
3. The *demand and supply curves satisfy certain other restrictions*. For example, market equilibrium will not be efficient if the individual marginal cost curves that add up to the market supply curve fail to include all relevant costs of producing the product. Thus, as we saw in Chapter 3, the true cost of expanding output will be higher than indicated by the market supply curve if production generates pollution that harms others. The equilibrium output will then be inefficiently large and the equilibrium price inefficiently low. Likewise, market equilibrium will not be efficient if the individual demand curves that make up the market demand curve do not capture all the relevant benefits of buying additional units of the product. For instance, if a home owner's willingness to pay for ornamental shrubs is based only on the enjoyment she herself gains from them, and not on any benefits that may accrue to her neighbours, the market demand curve for shrubs will understate their value to the neighbourhood. The equilibrium quantity of ornamental shrubs will be inefficiently small, and the market price for shrubs will be inefficiently low.
4. *Transaction costs are low*. For example, high tax costs on buying and selling houses can result in demand for existing housing space not being equal to supply; high travel costs can result in excess demand for labour in one part of a city and excess supply persisting in another.

We shall take up such market imperfections in greater detail in Chapters 9–12. For now, we shall confine our attention to perfectly competitive markets whose demand curves capture all relevant benefits and whose supply curves capture all relevant costs. For such goods, market equilibrium will always be 'efficient' in the limited sense described earlier.

## Efficiency is not the only goal

The fact that market equilibrium maximises economic surplus is an attractive feature of the market system. However, 'efficient' does not mean the same thing as 'good'. For example, the market for milk may be in equilibrium at a price of €1.50 per litre, yet many poor families may be unable to afford milk for their children at that price. Still others may not even have a place for their children to sleep.

Efficiency is a concept that is based on predetermined attributes of buyers and sellers – their incomes, tastes, abilities, knowledge and so on. Through the combined effects of individual cost–benefit decisions, these attributes give rise to the supply and demand curves for each good produced in an economy. If we are concerned about inequality in the distribution of attributes such as income, we should not be surprised to discover that markets do not always yield the outcomes we like.

Most of us could agree, for example, that the world would be a better one if all people had enough income to feed their families adequately. The claim that equilibrium in the market for milk is efficient means simply that, *taking people's incomes as given*, the resulting allocation of milk cannot be altered so as to help some people without at the same time harming others.

To this a critic of the market system might respond, 'So what?' As such critics rightly point out, imposing costs on others may be justified if doing so will help those with sufficiently important unmet demands. For example, most people would prefer to provide some funding out of taxes to provide housing for the homeless rather than let the homeless freeze to death. This kind of reasoning led to a decision in the United States in the 1970s to impose price controls on home heating oil when crude oil prices rose sharply after the second oil shock (see below). Many might agree that if the alternative had been to take no action at all, price controls might have been justified in the name of social justice.

But the economists' concept of market efficiency makes it clear that there *must* be a better alternative policy. Price controls on oil prevent the market from reaching equilibrium, and that means forgoing transactions that would benefit some people without harming others. It would have been more efficient to allow heating oil prices to rise, but to give those on low incomes money with which to buy it, rather than reduce prices for everyone and induce a shortage because demand exceeded supply.

## Why efficiency should be the first goal

Efficiency is important not because it is a desirable end in itself, but because it enables us to achieve all our other goals to the fullest possible extent. Whenever a market is out of equilibrium, it is always possible to generate additional economic surplus. To gain additional economic surplus is to gain more of the resources we need to do the things we want to do. Whenever any market is out of equilibrium, there is *waste*, and waste is always bad thing.

### RECAP Equilibrium and efficiency

When a market is not in equilibrium – because price is either above the equilibrium level or below it – the quantity exchanged is always *less than the equilibrium level.* At such a quantity, a transaction can always be made in which both buyer and seller benefit from the exchange of an additional unit of output. A market in equilibrium is said to be efficient, or Pareto efficient, meaning that no reallocation is possible that will benefit some people without harming others. Total economic surplus in a market is maximised when exchange occurs at the equilibrium price. But the fact that equilibrium is 'efficient' in this sense does not mean that it is 'good'. All markets can be in equilibrium, yet many people may lack sufficient income to buy even basic goods and services. Still, permitting markets to reach equilibrium is important, because when economic surplus is maximised, it is possible to pursue every goal more fully.

## The cost of preventing price adjustments

### Price ceilings

During 1979, after the second oil shock, the price of home heating oil across America rose by more than 100 per cent. (The percentage increase in Europe was much lower. Why?) Concern about the hardship this sudden price increase would impose on poor families in northern states led the US government to impose a price ceiling in the market for home heating oil. This price ceiling prohibited sellers from charging more than a specified amount for heating oil.

Example 7.1 illustrates why imposing a price ceiling on heating oil, though well intended, was a bad idea.

### Example 7.1 How much waste does a price ceiling on heating oil cause?

Suppose the demand and supply curves for home heating oil are as shown in Fig. 7.4, in which the equilibrium price is €1.40 per litre. And suppose that, at that price, many poor families cannot heat their homes adequately. Out of concern for the poor, legislators pass a law setting the maximum price at €1 per litre. How much lost economic surplus does this policy cost society?

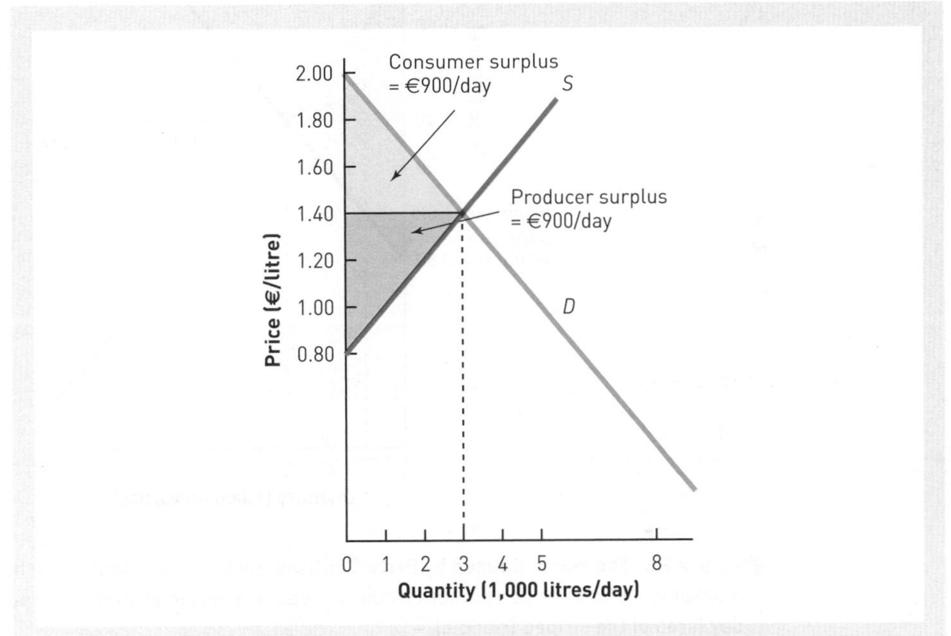


**Figure 7.4 Economic Surplus in an Unregulated Market for Home Heating Oil.** For the supply and demand curves shown, the equilibrium price of home heating oil is €1.40 per litre, and the equilibrium quantity is 3,000 litres per day. Consumer surplus is the area of the upper shaded triangle (€900 per day). Producer surplus is the area of the lower shaded triangle (also €900 per day).

First, we can calculate total economic surplus without price controls. If this market is not regulated, 3,000 litres per day will be sold at a price of €1.40 per litre. In Fig. 7.4, the economic surplus received by buyers is the area of the upper shaded triangle. Since the height of this triangle is €0.60 per litre, and its base is 3,000 litres per day, its area is equal to (1/2)(3,000 litres/day)(€0.60/litre) = €900 per day. The economic surplus received by producers is the area of the lower shaded triangle. Since this triangle also has an area of €900 per day, total economic surplus in this market will be €1,800 per day.

If the price of heating oil is prevented from rising above €1 per litre, only 1,000 litres per day will be sold, and the total economic surplus will be reduced by the area of the striped triangle shown in Fig. 7.5. Since the height of this triangle is €0.80 per litre, and its base is 2,000 litres per day, its area is (1/2)(2,000 litres/day)(€0.80/litre) = €800 per day. Producer surplus falls from €900 per day in the unregulated market to the area of the lower shaded triangle, or (1/2)(1,000 litres/day)(€0.20/litre) = €100 per day, which is a loss of €800 per day. Thus the loss in total economic surplus is equal to the loss in producer surplus, which means that the new consumer surplus must be the same as the original consumer surplus. To verify this, note that consumer surplus with the price ceiling is the area of the upper shaded area in Fig. 7.5, which is again €900 per day. (**Hint:** To compute this area in Fig. 7.5, first split it into a rectangle and a triangle.) By preventing the home heating oil market from reaching equilibrium, price controls waste €800 of producer surplus per day without creating any additional surplus for consumers!

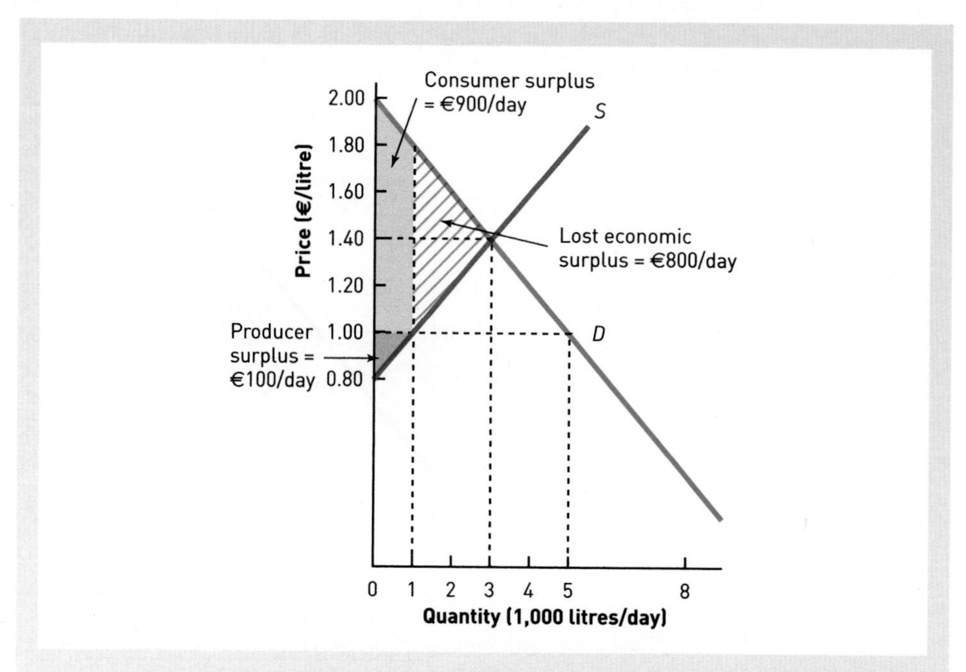


**Figure 7.5 The Waste Caused by Price Controls.** By limiting output in the home heating oil market to 1,000 litres per day, price controls cause a loss in economic surplus of €800 per day (area of the striped triangle).

**Exercise 7.2** In Example 7.1, by how much would total economic surplus have been reduced if the price ceiling had been set not at €1 but at €1.20 per litre?

For several reasons, the reduction in total economic surplus shown in Fig. 7.5 is a conservative estimate of the waste caused by attempts to hold price below its equilibrium level. For one thing, the analysis assumes that each of the 1,000 litres per day that are sold in this market will end up in the hands of the consumers who value them most – in Fig. 7.5, those whose reservation prices are above €1.80 per litre. But since any buyer whose reservation price is above €1 per litre will want to buy at the ceiling price, much of the oil actually sold is likely to go to buyers whose reservation prices are below €1.80. Suppose, for example, that a buyer whose reservation price was €1.50 per litre made it into the queue outside a heating oil supplier just ahead of a buyer whose reservation price was €1.90 per litre. If each buyer had a 20-litre tank to fill, and if the first buyer got the last of the day's available oil, then total surplus would be smaller by €8 that day than if the oil had gone to the second buyer.

A second reason that the reduction in surplus shown in Fig. 7.5 is likely to be an underestimate is that shortages typically prompt buyers to take costly actions to enhance their chances of being served. For example, if the heating oil distributor begins selling its available supplies at 6.00 a.m., many buyers may arrive several hours early to ensure a place near the front of the queue.

Notwithstanding the fact that price ceilings reduce total economic surplus, their defenders might argue that controls are justified because they enable at least some low-income families to buy heating oil at affordable prices. Yes, but the same objective could have been accomplished in a much less costly way – namely, by giving the poor more income with which to buy heating oil.

It may seem natural to wonder whether the poor, who have limited political power, can really hope to receive income transfers that would enable them to heat their homes. On reflection, the answer to this question would seem to be yes, if *the alternative is to impose price controls that would be even more costly than the income transfers*. After all, the price ceiling as implemented ends up costing heating oil sellers €800 per day in lost economic surplus. So they ought to be willing to pay some amount less than €800 a day in additional taxes in order to escape the burden of controls. The additional tax revenue could finance income transfers that would be far more beneficial to the poor than price controls.

This point is so important, and so often misunderstood by voters and policy makers, that we will emphasise it by putting it another way. Think of the economic surplus from a market as a pie to be divided among the various market participants. Figure 7.6(a) represents the €1,000 per day of total economic surplus available to participants in the home heating oil market when the government limits the price of oil to €1 per litre. We have divided this 'pie' into two slices, labelled *R* and *P*, to denote the surpluses received by rich and poor participants. Figure 7.6(b) represents the €1,800 per day of total economic surplus available when the price of home heating oil is free to reach its equilibrium level. This 'pie' is divided among rich and poor participants in the same proportion as the 'pie' in the panel (a).

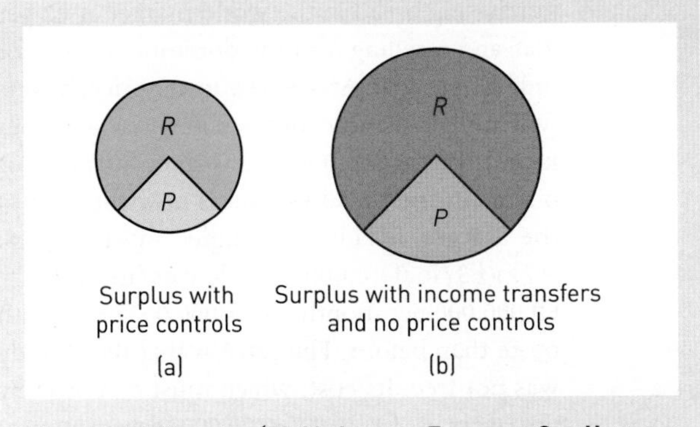


**Figure 7.6 When the 'Pie' is Larger, Everyone Can Have a Bigger Slice.** Any policy that reduces total economic surplus is a missed opportunity to make everyone better off.

The important point to notice is this: *Because the pie in panel (b) is larger, both rich and poor participants in the home heating oil market can get a bigger slice of the 'pie' than they would have had under price controls*. Rather than tinker with the market price of oil, it is in everyone's interest to simply transfer additional income to the poor.

Supporters of price controls may object that income transfers to the poor might weaken people's incentive to work, and thus might prove extremely costly in the long run. Difficult issues do indeed arise in the design of programmes for transferring income to the poor. But for now, suffice it to say that ways exist to transfer income without undermining work incentives significantly. Given such programmes, transferring income to the poor will always be more efficient than trying to boost their living standard through price controls.

## Price subsidies

Sometimes governments try to assist low-income consumers by subsidising the prices of 'essential' goods and services. France and Russia, for example, have taken this approach at various times by subsidising the price of bread. But as Example 7.2 illustrates, such subsidies are like price ceilings in that they reduce total economic surplus.

**Example 7.2** By how much do subsidies reduce total economic surplus in the market for bread?

A small island nation imports bread for its population at the world price of €2 per loaf. If the domestic demand curve for bread is as shown in Fig. 7.7, by how much will total economic surplus decline in this market if the government provides a €1 per loaf subsidy?

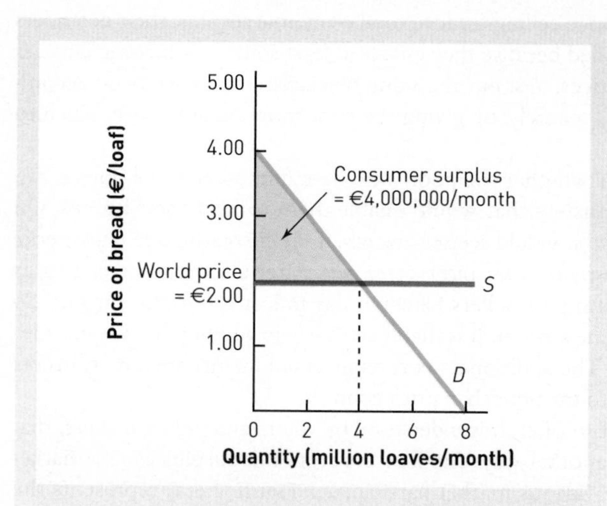


**Figure 7.7 Economic Surplus in a Bread Market without Subsidy.** For the demand curve shown, consumer surplus (area of the shaded triangle) is €4,000,000. This amount is equal to total economic surplus in the domestic bread market, since no bread is produced domestically.

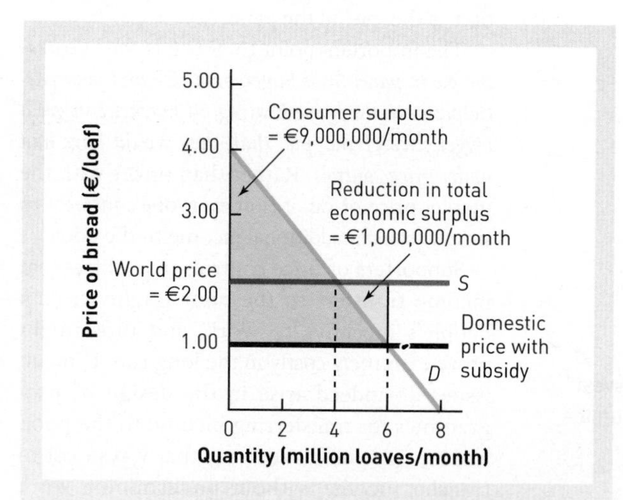


**Figure 7.8 The Reduction in Economic Surplus from a Subsidy.** Since the marginal cost of bread is €2 per loaf, total economic surplus is maximised at 4,000,000 loaves per month, the quantity for which the marginal buyer's reservation price is equal to marginal cost. The reduction in economic surplus from consuming an additional 2,000,000 loaves per month is €1,000,000 per month, the area of the smaller shaded triangle.

With no subsidy, the equilibrium price of bread in this market would be the world price of €2 per loaf, and the equilibrium quantity would be 4,000,000 loaves per month. The shaded triangle in Fig. 7.7 represents consumer economic surplus for buyers in the domestic bread market. The height of this triangle is €2 per loaf, and its base is 4,000,000 loaves per month, so its area is equal to (1/2)(4,000,000 loaves/month)(€2/loaf) = €4,000,000 per month. Because the country can import as much bread as it wishes at the world price of €2 per loaf, supply is *perfectly elastic* in this market. Because the marginal cost of each loaf of bread to sellers is exactly the same as the price buyers pay, producer surplus in this market is zero. So total economic surplus is exactly equal to consumer surplus, which, again, is €4,000,000 per month.

Now suppose that the government administers its €1 per loaf subsidy programme by purchasing bread in the world market at €2 per loaf and reselling it in the domestic market for only €1 per loaf. At the new lower price, buyers will now consume not 4,000,000 loaves per month but 6,000,000. Consumer surplus for buyers in the bread market is now the area of the larger shaded triangle in Fig. 7.8: (1/2)(€3/loaf)(6,000,000 loaves/month) = €9,000,000 per month, or €5,000,000 per month more than before. The catch is that the subsidy was not free. Its cost, which must be borne by taxpayers, is (€1/loaf)(6,000,000 loaves/month) = €6,000,000 per month. So even though consumer surplus in the bread market is larger than before, the net effect of the subsidy programme is actually to reduce total economic surplus by €1,000,000 per month.

Another way to see why the subsidy reduces total economic surplus by this amount is to note that total economic surplus is maximised at 4,000,000 loaves per month, the quantity for which the marginal buyer's reservation price is equal to marginal cost, and that the subsidy induces additional consumption of 2,000,000 loaves per month. Each additional loaf has a marginal cost of €2 but is worth less than that to the buyer (as indicated by the fact that the vertical co-ordinate of the demand curve lies below €2 for consumption beyond 4,000,000). As monthly consumption expands from 4,000,000 to 6,000,000 loaves per month, the cumulative difference between the marginal cost of bread and its value to buyers is the area of the smaller shaded triangle in Fig. 7.8, which is €1,000,000 per month.

This reduction in economic surplus constitutes pure waste – no different, from the perspective of participants in this market, from someone siphoning that much cash out of their bank account each month and throwing it into a bonfire.

**Exercise 7.3** How much total economic surplus would have been lost if the bread subsidy had been set at €0.50 per loaf instead of €1.00?

Compared with a bread subsidy, a much better policy would be to give low-income people some additional income and then let them bid for bread on the open market. Subsidy advocates who complain that tax-payers would be unwilling to give low-income people income transfers must be asked to explain why people would be willing to tolerate subsidies, which are so much more costly than income transfers. Logically, if voters are willing to support subsidies, they should be even more eager to support income transfers to low-income persons.

This is not to say that the poor reap no benefit at all from bread subsidies. Since they get to buy bread at lower prices and since the subsidy programme is financed by taxes collected primarily from middle- and upper-income families, poor families probably come out ahead on balance. *The point is that, for the same expense, we could do much more to help the poor.* Their problem is that they have too little income. The simplest and best solution is not to try to peg the prices of the goods they and others buy below equilibrium levels, but rather to give them some additional money.

## First-come, first-served policies

Governments are not the only institutions that attempt to promote social goals by preventing markets from reaching equilibrium. Some event promoters, for example, attempt to protect access by low-income purchasers to concerts and sporting events by selling a limited number of tickets below the market-clearing price on a first-come, first-served basis.[1]

The commercial airline industry was an early proponent of the use of the first-come, first-served allocation method, which it employed to ration seats on overbooked flights. Throughout the industry's history, most airlines have routinely accepted more reservations for their flights than there are seats on those flights. Most of the time, this practice causes no difficulty, because many reservation holders don't show up to claim their seats. Indeed, if airlines did not overbook their flights, most flights would take off with many more empty seats, forcing airlines to charge higher ticket prices to cover their costs.

The only real difficulty is that every so often, more people actually do show up for a flight than there are seats on the plane. Until the late 1970s (i.e. before deregulation increased competition), US airlines dealt with this problem by boarding passengers on a first-come, first-served basis. For example, if 120 people showed up for a flight with 110 seats, the last 10 to arrive were 'bumped', or forced to wait for the next available flight.

[1] That is certainly the stated reason. We shall see in Chapter 9, however, when dealing with pricing strategies of firms with market power, that this form of discounting may also be a discriminatory mechanism that may be expected to increase the sellers' revenues.

The 'bumped' passengers often complained bitterly, and no wonder, since many of them ended up missing important business meetings or family events. As Economic naturalist 7.1 illustrates, there was, fortunately, a simple solution to this problem.

## Economic naturalist 7.1 Why does no one complain any longer about being 'bumped' from an overbooked flight?

In 1978, as regulation of the business ended, airlines in the US abandoned their first-come, first-served policy in favour of a new procedure. Since then, their practice has been to solicit volunteers to give up their seats on oversold flights in return for a cash payment or free ticket. Now, the only people who give up their seats are those who volunteer to do so in return for compensation, hence the complete disappearance of complaints about being 'bumped' from overbooked flights. As the airline business has been moving towards deregulation in Europe, the same phenomenon has been observed. Airlines may routinely overbook flights, relying on 'no-shows' to balance capacity with demand. When this didn't happen, they in effect 'bought back' seats by offering cash or other compensation. For reasons that are far from clear, the EU Commission has now moved to imposing fixed compensation amounts. This is clearly inefficient. Can you explain why? (See Exercise 7.4 below.)

Which of the two policies – first-come, first-served or compensation for volunteers – is more efficient? The difficulty with the first-come, first-served policy is that it gives little weight to the interests of passengers with pressing reasons for arriving at their destination on time. Such passengers can sometimes avoid losing their seats by showing up early, but passengers coming in on connecting flights often cannot control when they arrive. And the cost of showing up early is likely to be highest for precisely those people who place the highest value on not missing a flight (such as business executives, whose opportunity cost of waiting in airports is high).

For the sake of illustration, suppose that 37 people show up for a flight with only 33 seats. One way or another, four people will have to wait for another flight. Suppose we ask each of them, 'What is the most you would be willing to pay to fly now rather than wait?' Typically, different passengers will have different reservation prices for avoiding the wait. Suppose that the person who is most willing to pay would pay up to €60 rather than miss the flight; that the person second-most willing to pay would pay up to €59; that the person third-most willing to pay would pay up to €58; and so on. In that case, the person with the smallest reservation price for avoiding the wait would have a reservation price of €24. For the entire group of 37 passengers, the average reservation price for avoiding the wait would be (€60 + €59 + €58 + ... + €24)/37 = €42.

Given the difficulty of controlling airport arrival times, the passengers who get 'bumped' under the first-come, first-served policy are not likely to differ systematically from others with respect to their reservation price for not missing the flight. On average, then, the total cost imposed on the four 'bumped' passengers would be four times the average reservation price of €42, or €168. As far as those four passengers are concerned, that total is a pure loss of consumer surplus.

How does this cost compare with the cost imposed on 'bumped' passengers when the airline compensates volunteers? Suppose that the airline solicits volunteers by conducting an informal auction, increasing its cash compensation offer by €1 increments until it has the desired number of volunteers. As the incentive to stay behind rises, more people will volunteer; those whose reservation prices are the lowest will volunteer first. In this example, offers below €24 would generate no volunteers. An offer of €24 would generate one volunteer; an offer of €25 would generate two volunteers; and so on. A compensation payment of €27 would generate the necessary four volunteers.

What is the net cost of the compensation policy? While the airline pays out (4)(€27) = €108 in compensation payments, not all that amount represents lost economic surplus. Thus the passenger whose reservation price for missing the flight is €24 receives a net gain in economic surplus of €3 – the difference between the €27 compensation payment and her €24 reservation price. Similarly, those whose reservation prices were €25 and €26 receive a net gain of €2 and €1, respectively. The cost of the cash compensation policy net of these gains is thus €108 – €6 = €102, or €66 less than under the first-come, first-served policy.

The compensation policy is more efficient than the first-come, first-served policy because it establishes a market for a scarce resource that would otherwise be allocated by non-market means. Figure 7.9 shows the supply and demand curves for seats under the compensation policy. In this market, the equilibrium price of not having to wait is €27. People who choose not to volunteer at that price incur an opportunity cost of €27 in order not to miss the flight. The four people who do volunteer accept €27 as ample compensation – indeed, more than ample for three of them.

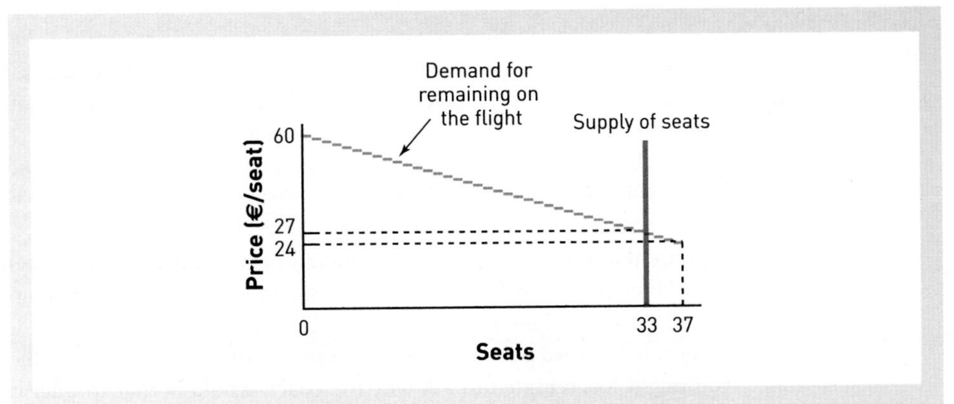


**Figure 7.9 Equilibrium in the Market for Seats on Oversold Flights.** The demand curve for remaining on the flight is generated by plotting the reservation prices in descending order. The equilibrium compensation payment for volunteers who give up their seats is €27 – the price at which four passengers volunteer to wait and the remaining 33 choose not to wait.

Given all this, it is hard to understand US consumer reaction when the compensation mechanism was introduced. There were strong protests from the Aviation Consumer Action Project (ACAP), a group that portrayed itself as a watchdog for the interests of airline passengers. ACAP's concern was that the shift to a system of compensation payments would mean that poor people would most often end up waiting for the next flight. The new policy, therefore, as far as ACAP was concerned, damaged poor people more than better-off people.

**Exercise 7.4** The ACAP objections to the change were inconsistent with what we know about markets. Can you indicate some reasons why ACAP was wrong?

**Exercise 7.5** In the light of this, what conclusion should we draw regarding the decision by the EU Commission to intervene in the airline passenger ticket market in Europe, announced in 2004? The Commission proposed that airlines should be obliged to pay any passenger who was 'bumped' a fixed amount, initially set at €250, plus meeting certain costs. This is to replace any 'buy-back' of seats (implicit in what happens in the United States).

### **Example 7.3** How should a professional tennis coach handle the overbooking problem?

Anticipating a high proportion of 'no-shows', a tennis coach routinely books five people for each of his group lesson slots, even though he is able to teach only three people at a time. One day, all five people show up for their lessons at 10 a.m., the first lesson slot of the morning. Their respective arrival times and the maximum amounts each would be willing to pay to avoid postponing his or her lesson are as given in the table below.

| Player | Arrival time (a.m.) | Reservation price (€) |
|---|---|---|
| Ann | 9.50 | 4 |
| Bill | 9.52 | 3 |
| Carrie | 9.55 | 6 |
| Dan | 9.56 | 10 |
| Earl | 9.59 | 3 |

If the coach accommodates the players on a first-come, first-served basis, by how much will total economic surplus be smaller than if he had offered cash compensation to induce two volunteers to reschedule? Which system is more efficient?

The result of using a first-come, first-served policy will be that Dan and Earl, the last two to arrive, will have to postpone their lessons. Since the cost of waiting is €10 for Dan and €3 for Earl, the total cost of the first-come, first-served policy is €13.

Suppose that the coach had instead offered cash compensation payments to elicit volunteers. If he offered a payment of €3, both Bill and Earl would be willing to wait. The total cost of the cash compensation policy would therefore be only €6, or €7 less than under the first-come, first-served policy. So the cash compensation policy is more efficient.

You might feel tempted to ask why the coach would bother to offer cash compensation when he has the option of saving the €6 by continuing with his current policy of first-come, first-served. Or you might wonder why an airline would bother to offer cash compensation to elicit volunteers to wait for the next flight. But we know that it is possible for *everyone* to do better under an efficient policy than under an inefficient one. (When the pie is bigger, everyone can have a larger slice.) Exercise 7.6 asks you to design such a transaction for the tennis-lesson example.

**Exercise 7.6** Describe a set of cash transfers in Example 7.3 that would make each of the five students and the coach better off than under the first-come, first-served policy. (**Hint:** Imagine that the coach tells his clients that he will stick with first-come, first-served unless they agree to contribute to the compensation pool as he requests.)

In practice, transactions like that called for in Example 7.6 would be cumbersome to administer. Typically, the seller is in a position to solve such problems more easily by offering cash payments to elicit volunteers, and then financing those cash payments by charging slightly higher prices. Buyers, for their part, are willing to pay the higher prices because they value the seller's promise not to cancel their reservations without compensation.

## RECAP The cost of blocking price adjustments

In an effort to increase the economic welfare of disadvantaged consumers, governments often implement policies that attempt to prevent markets from reaching equilibrium. Price ceilings and subsidies attempt to make housing and other basic goods more affordable for poor families. Private organisations also implement policies that prevent markets from reaching equilibrium, such as allocation on a first-come, first-served basis. Such policies always *reduce total economic surplus* relative to the alternative of letting prices seek their equilibrium levels. It is always possible to design alternative policies under which rich and poor alike fare better.

# Marginal cost pricing of public services

The largest possible total economic surplus is achieved in private markets when goods are exchanged at equilibrium prices, where the value of the last unit to the buyer is exactly equal to the seller's marginal cost of producing it. Suppose that the government has decided to become the provider of a good or service, such as water or electricity. If the government's goal is to maximise the resulting total economic surplus, how much should it charge its customers? The theory of *market exchange*, normally applied to perfectly competitive firms that can sell any quantity they choose at a constant market price, helps to answer this question. Consider Example 7.4, in which a local government supplies water to its residents.

### Example 7.4 What is the marginal cost of water in Sharm el Sheikh?

Sharm el Sheik, at the head of the Gulf of Aqaba on the Red Sea, is a thriving tourist resort. Locals and tourists use a great deal of water, which is supplied by the municipal authorities. The municipal water supply company has three potential sources of water: an underground spring, a nearby lake and the Red Sea. The spring can supply up to 10 million litres per day at a cost of 0.2 cents per litre. The lake can supply an additional 20 million litres per day at a cost of 0.8 cents per litre. Additional water must be distilled using a desalination plant from the sea at a cost of 4.0 cents per litre. Draw the marginal cost curve for water in Sharm el Sheikh.

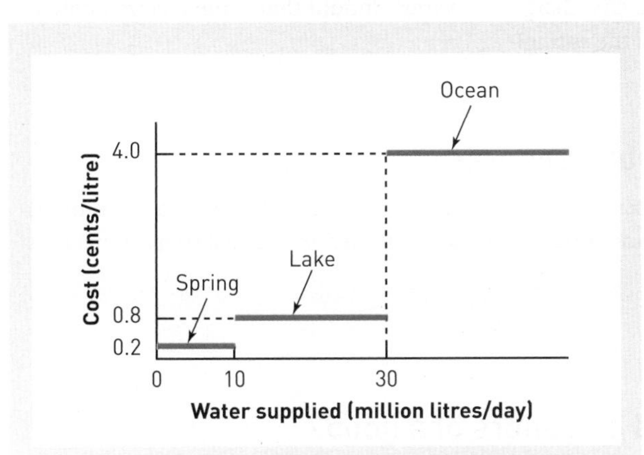


**Figure 7.10 The Marginal Cost Curve for Water.** The current marginal cost of water is the cost of producing an extra litre by means of the most expensive production source currently in use.

The *Low-Hanging-Fruit Principle* (Chapter 2) tells us that the city will use the cheapest source of water first (the spring). Only when the quantity demanded exceeds the spring's capacity will the city turn to the next least expensive source, the lake; and only when the lake's capacity is exhausted will the city supply water from the ocean. The marginal cost curve will thus be as shown in Fig. 7.10.

As Example 7.5 illustrates, total economic surplus is maximised when the government charges each customer *exactly the marginal cost* of the water he or she consumes.

### Example 7.5 How much should the municipal authority charge for water?

In Example 7.4, suppose that if the price of water were 4.0 cents per litre, citizens of and visitors to Sharm el Sheikh would consume 4 million litres per day. Given the marginal cost curve shown in Fig. 7.10, how much should the city charge a citizen whose water comes from the underground spring? How much should it charge someone whose water comes from the lake?

The citizens of Sharm el Sheikh will enjoy the largest possible economic surplus if the price they pay for water exactly equals the marginal cost of providing it. Since the total amount of water demanded at 4.0 cents per litre exceeds 3 million litres per day, the city will have to supply at least some households with water distilled from the Red Sea, at a cost of 4.0 cents per litre. At 4 million litres per day, the marginal cost of water is thus 4.0 cents per litre, and *this is true no matter where the water comes from*. As long as the city must get *some* of its water from the ocean, the marginal cost of water taken from the underground spring is also 4.0 cents per litre. Water taken from the lake has a marginal cost of 4.0 cents per litre as well.

This statement might seem to contradict the claim that water drawn from the spring costs only 0.2 cents per litre, water drawn from the lake only 0.8 cents per litre. But there is no contradiction. To see why, ask yourself how much the city would save if a family that currently gets its water from the spring were to reduce its consumption by 1 litre per day. The cutback would enable the city to divert that litre of spring water to some other household that currently gets its water from the ocean, which in turn would reduce consumption of ocean water by 1 litre. So if a family currently served by the spring were to reduce its daily consumption by 1 litre, the cost savings would be exactly 4.0 cents. And that, by definition, is the marginal cost of water.

To encourage the efficient use of water, the city should charge every household 4.0 cents per litre for all the water it consumes. Charging any household less than that would encourage households to use water whose marginal benefit is less than its marginal cost. For example, suppose the city charged households who get their water from the spring only 0.2 cents per litre. Those households would then expand their use of water until the benefit they received from the last litre used equalled 0.2 cents. Because that litre could have been used to serve someone who is currently using water distilled from the ocean, for whom the value of the marginal litre is 4 cents, its use would entail a loss in economic surplus of 3.8 cents.

**Exercise 7.7**

Suppose that at a price of 0.8 cents per litre of water, the citizens of Sharm el Sheikh would consume a total of only 2 million litres per day. If the marginal cost of water is as shown in Fig. 7.10, how much should the city charge for water? Should that same charge apply to people who get their water from the spring?

### RECAP Marginal cost pricing of public services

When a good is provided by a public utility from several sources, the marginal cost of serving a customer is the cost associated with the *least efficient source in use*. A public utility should set price equal to marginal cost if its goal is to maximise economic surplus.

## Taxes and efficiency

### Who pays a tax imposed on sellers of a good?

Politicians of all stripes seem loath to propose new taxes. But when additional public revenue must be raised, most seem to feel more comfortable proposing taxes paid by sellers than taxes paid by consumers. When pressed to explain why, many respond that businesses can more easily afford to pay extra taxes. Yet the burden of a tax collected from the sellers of a good need not fall exclusively on sellers. Suppose, for example, that a tax of €1 per kg is collected from potato farmers in the market whose demand and supply curves are shown as *D* and *S* in Fig. 7.11.

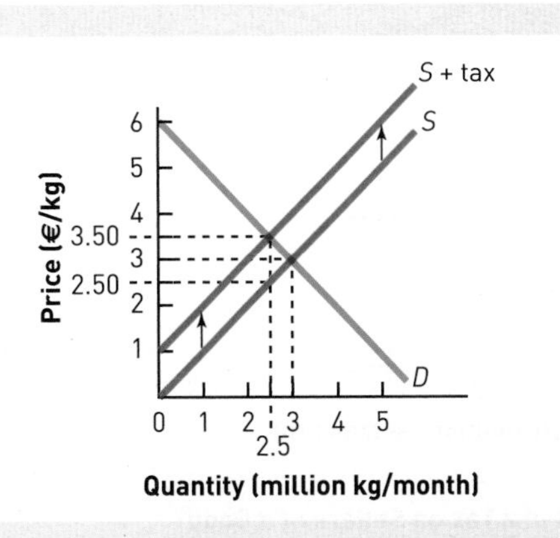


**Figure 7.11 The Effect of a Tax on the Equilibrium Quantity and Price of Potatoes.** With no tax, 3 million kg of potatoes are sold each month at a price of €3 per kg. With a tax of €1 per kg collected from sellers, consumers end up paying €3.50 per kg (including tax), while sellers receive only €2.50 per kg (net of tax). Equilibrium quantity falls from 3 million kg per month to 2.5 million.

In this market the initial equilibrium price and quantity are €3 per kg and 3 million kg per month, respectively. From the farmers' perspective, the imposition of a tax of €1 per kg is essentially the same as a €1 increase in the marginal cost of producing each kg of potatoes, and hence the tax results in an upward shift in the supply curve by €1 per kg.

As shown in Fig. 7.11, the new equilibrium price (including the tax) will be €3.50, and the new equilibrium quantity will be 2.5 million kg per month. The net price per kg received by producers is one euro less than the price paid by the consumer, or €2.50. Even though the tax was collected entirely from potato sellers, the burden of the tax fell on both buyers and sellers – on buyers, because they pay €0.50 per kg more than before the tax and on sellers, because they receive €0.50 per kg less than before the tax.

The burden of the tax need not fall equally on buyers and sellers, as in the illustration just discussed. Indeed, as Economic naturalist 7.2 illustrates, a tax levied on sellers may end up being paid entirely by buyers.

## Economic naturalist 7.2 How will a tax on cars affect their prices in the long run?

Suppose that, given sufficient time, all the inputs required to produce cars can be acquired in unlimited quantities at fixed market prices. If the inputs required to produce each car cost €20,000, how will the long-run equilibrium price of cars be affected if a tax of €100 per car is levied on manufacturers?

The fact that all the inputs needed to build cars can be acquired at constant prices suggests that the long-run marginal cost of making cars is constant – or, in other words, that the long-run supply curve of cars is horizontal at €20,000 per car. A tax of €100 per car effectively raises marginal cost by €100 per car, and thus shifts the supply curve upward by exactly €100. If the demand curve for cars is as shown by curve *D* in Fig. 7.12, the effect is to raise the equilibrium price of cars by exactly €100, to €20,100. The equilibrium quantity of cars falls from 2 million per month to 1.9 million.

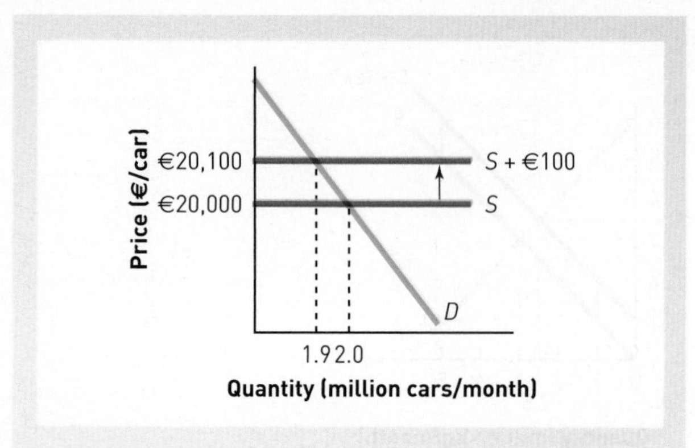


**Figure 7.12 The Effect of a Tax on Sellers of a Good with Infinite Price Elasticity of Supply.** When the supply curve for a good is perfectly elastic, the burden of a tax collected from sellers falls entirely on buyers.

Although the long-run supply curve shown in Fig. 7.12 is in one sense an extreme case (since its price elasticity is infinite), it is by no means an unrepresentative one. For, as we discussed in Chapter 4, the long-run supply curve will tend to be horizontal when it is possible to acquire more of all the necessary inputs at constant prices. As a first approximation, this can be accomplished for many – perhaps even most – goods and services in a typical economy.

For goods with perfectly elastic supply curves, the entire burden of any tax is borne by the buyer.[2] That is, the increase in the equilibrium price is exactly equal to the tax. For this empirically relevant case, then, there is special irony in the common political practice of justifying taxes on business by saying that businesses have greater ability to pay than consumers.

## How a tax collected from a seller affects economic surplus

We saw earlier that perfectly competitive markets distribute goods and services efficiently if demand curves reflect all relevant benefits and supply curves reflect all relevant costs. If a tax is imposed on sellers in such a market, will the new market equilibrium still be efficient? Consider again the potato market discussed in Fig. 7.11, whose supply and demand curves are reproduced in Fig. 7.13. In the absence of a tax, 3 million kg of potatoes a month would be sold in this market at a price of €3 per kg, and the resulting total economic surplus would be €9 million per month (the area of the shaded triangle).

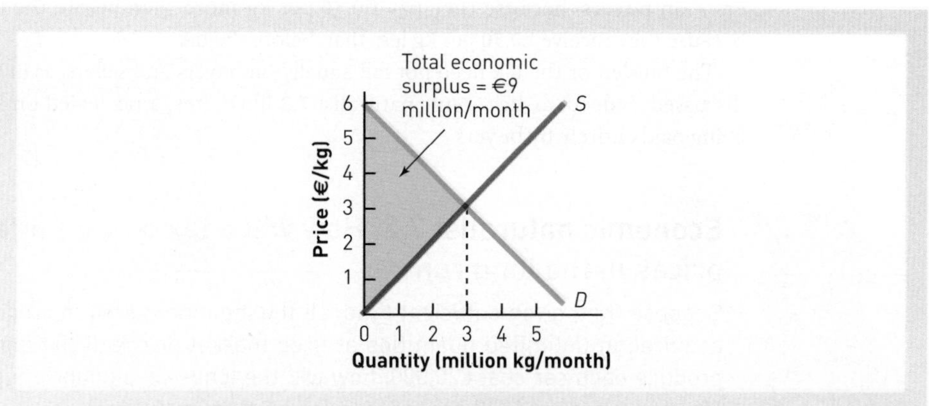


**Figure 7.13 The Market for Potatoes without Taxes.** Without taxes, total surplus in the potato market equals the area of the shaded triangle, €9 million per month.

With a tax of €1 per kg collected from potato sellers, the new equilibrium price of potatoes would be €3.50 per kg (of which sellers receive €2.50, net of tax), and only 2.5 million kg of potatoes would be sold each month (see Fig. 7.14). The total economic surplus reaped by buyers and sellers in the potato market would be the area of the shaded triangle shown in Fig. 7.14, which is €6.25 million per month – or €2.75 million less than before.

---

[2] In the example given, the tax was collected from sellers. The same conclusions will apply when a tax is collected from buyers. It raises the supply price by the same amount.

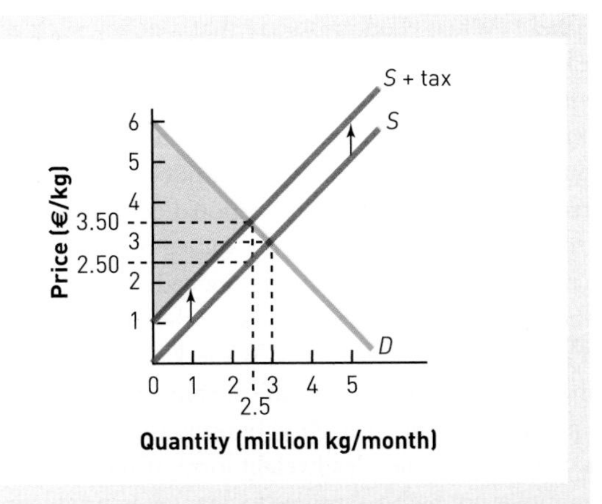


**Figure 7.14 The Effect of a €1 per kg Tax on Potatoes.** A €1 per kg tax on potatoes would cause an upward shift in the supply curve by €1. The sum of producer and consumer surplus would shrink to the area of the shaded triangle, €6.25 million per month.

This drop in surplus may sound like an enormous loss, but it is a misleading figure because it fails to take account of the value of the *additional tax revenue collected*, which is equal to €2.5 million per month (€1 per kg on 2.5 million kg of potatoes). If the government needs to collect no more than a given total amount of tax revenue in order to pay for the services it provides, then the potato tax revenue should enable it to reduce other taxes by €2.5 million per month. So although buyers and sellers lose €2.75 million per month in economic surplus from their participation in the potato market, they also enjoy a €2.5 million reduction in the other taxes they pay. On balance, then, the net reduction in total economic surplus is only €0.25 million.

Graphically, the loss in total economic surplus caused by the imposition of the tax can be shown as the small shaded triangle in Fig. 7.15. This loss in surplus is often described as the **deadweight loss** from the tax.

**deadweight loss** the reduction in total economic surplus that results from the adoption of a policy

Still, a loss in economic surplus, however small, is something that people would prefer to avoid, and taxes like that just described undoubtedly reduce economic surplus in the markets on which they are imposed. As the long-time US Federal Reserve Board (FRB, the equivalent in the United States of the European Central Bank or ECB in the European Union) chairman Alan Greenspan, who retired in 2006, once remarked: 'All taxes are a drag on economic growth. It's only a question of degree.'[3]

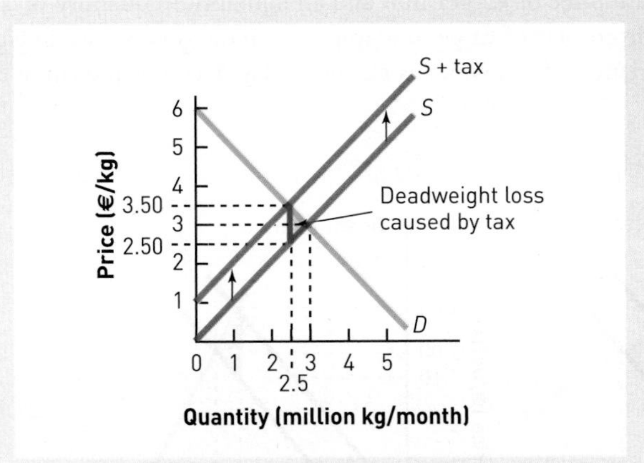


**Figure 7.15 The Deadweight Loss Caused by a Tax.** For the market shown, the loss in economic surplus caused by a tax of €1 per kg of potatoes equals the area of the small shaded triangle, or €250,000 per month.

A tax reduces economic surplus because it distorts the basic cost–benefit calculation that would ordinarily guide efficient decisions about production and consumption. In the example just considered, the Cost–Benefit Principle tells us that we should expand potato production up to the point at which the benefit of the last kilogram of potatoes consumed (as measured by what buyers are willing to pay for it) equals the cost of producing it (as measured by the producers' marginal cost). That condition was satisfied in the potato market before the tax, but it is not satisfied once the tax is imposed. In Fig. 7.15, for example, note that when potato consumption is 2.5 million kg per month, the value of an additional kilogram of potatoes to consumers is €3.50, whereas the cost to producers is only €2.50, not including the tax. (The cost to producers, including the tax, is €3.50 per kg, but again we note that this tax is not a cost to society as a whole because it offsets other taxes that would otherwise have to be collected.)

[3] *The Wall Street Journal*, 26 March 1997, p. A1.

Is a tax on potatoes necessarily 'bad'? (When economists say that a policy, such as a tax, is 'bad', they mean – or ought to mean – that it lowers total economic surplus.) To answer this question, we must first identify the *best alternative to taxing potatoes*. You may be tempted to say: 'Don't tax anything at all!' On a moment's reflection, however, you will realise that this is surely not the best option. After all, a country that taxed nothing could not pay for even minimal public services, such as road maintenance, fire protection and national defence. On balance, if taxing potatoes were the best way to avoid doing without highly valued public services, then a small deadweight loss in the potato market would be a small price indeed.

So the real question is whether there are other things we could tax that would be better than taxing potatoes. The problem with a tax on any activity is that if market incentives encourage people to pursue the 'right' amount of the activity (that is, the surplus-maximising amount), then a tax will encourage them to pursue too little of it. As economists have long recognised, this observation suggests that taxes will cause smaller deadweight losses if they are imposed on goods for which the equilibrium quantity is not highly sensitive to changes in production costs.

## Taxes, elasticity and efficiency

Suppose that the government put a tax of 50 cents per kg on table salt. How would this affect the amount of salt you and others use? In Chapter 4 we saw that the demand for salt is highly inelastic with respect to price, because salt has few substitutes and occupies only a minuscule share in most family budgets. Because the imposition of a tax on table salt would not result in a significant reduction in the amount of it consumed, the deadweight loss from this tax would be relatively small. More generally, the deadweight loss from a per-unit tax imposed on the seller of a good will be smaller the smaller is the price elasticity of demand for the good.

Figure 7.16 illustrates how the deadweight loss from a tax declines as the demand for a good becomes less elastic with respect to price. In both Figs 7.16 (a) and (b), the original supply and demand curves yield an equilibrium price of €2 per unit and an equilibrium quantity of 24 units per day. The deadweight loss from a tax of €1 per unit imposed on the good shown in Fig. 7.16(a) is the area of the shaded triangle in (a), which is €2.50 per day. The demand curve in

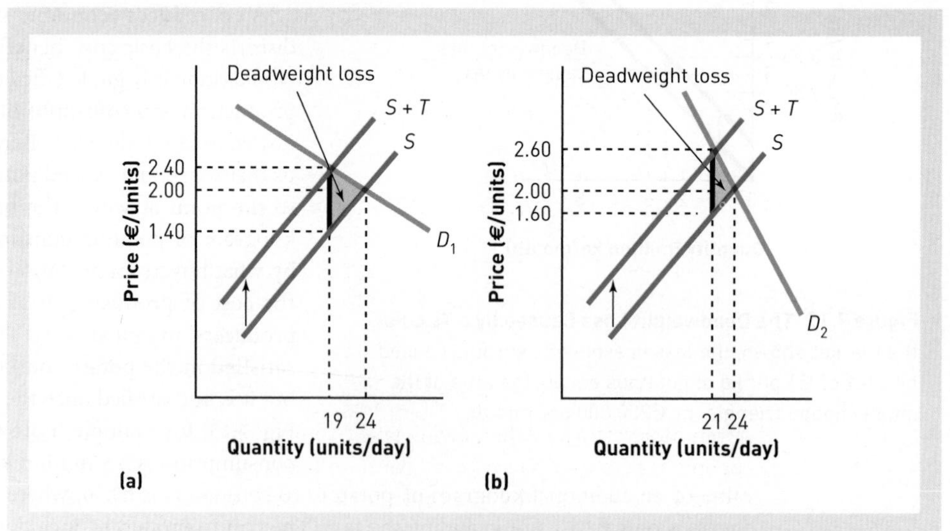


**Figure 7.16 Elasticity of Demand and the Deadweight Loss from a Tax.** At the equilibrium price and quantity, price elasticity of demand is smaller for the good shown in (b) than for the good shown in (a). The area of the deadweight loss triangle in (b), €1.50 per day, is smaller than the area of the deadweight loss triangle in (a), €2.50 per day.

Fig. 7.16(b), $D_2$, is less elastic at the equilibrium price of €2 than the demand curve in (a), $D_1$ (this follows from the fact that $P/Q$ is the same in both cases, whereas 1/slope is smaller in (b)). The deadweight loss from the same €1 per unit tax imposed on the good in Fig. 7.16(b) is the area of the shaded triangle in (b), which is only €1.50 per day.

The reduction in equilibrium quantity that results from a tax on a good will also be smaller the smaller is the elasticity of supply of the good. In Fig. 7.17, for example, the original supply and demand curves for the markets portrayed in (a) and (b) yield an equilibrium price of €2 per unit and an equilibrium quantity of 72 units per day. The deadweight loss from a tax of €1 per unit imposed on the good shown in Fig. 7.17(a) is the area of the shaded triangle in (a), which is €7.50 per day. The supply curve in Fig. 7.17(b), $S_2$, is less elastic at the equilibrium price than the supply curve in (a), $S_1$ (again because $P/Q$ is the same in both cases, whereas 1/slope is smaller in (b)). The deadweight loss from the same €1 per unit tax imposed on the good in Fig. 7.17(b) is the area of the shaded triangle in (b), which is only €4.50 per day.

The deadweight loss from a tax imposed on a good whose supply curve is perfectly inelastic will be zero. This explains why many economists continue to favour the tax advocated by Henry George in the nineteenth century. George proposed that all taxes on labour and goods be abolished and replaced by a *single tax on land*. Such a tax, he argued, would cause no significant loss in economic surplus because the supply of land is almost perfectly inelastic.

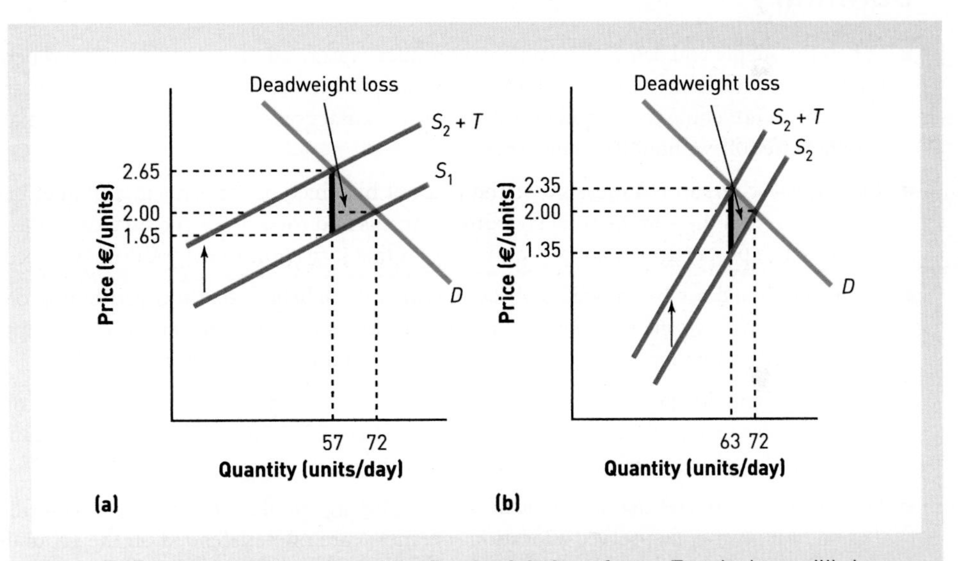


**Figure 7.17 Elasticity of Supply and the Deadweight Loss from a Tax.** At the equilibrium price and quantity, price elasticity of supply is smaller for the good shown in (b) than for the good shown in (a). The area of the deadweight loss triangle in (b), €4.50 per day, is smaller than the area of the deadweight loss triangle in (a), €7.50 per day.

## Taxes, external costs and efficiency

Even more attractive than taxing land, from an efficiency standpoint, is taxing activities that people tend to *pursue to excess*. We have mentioned activities that generate environmental pollution as one example; in Chapter 11 we shall discuss others. Whereas a tax on land does not reduce economic surplus, a tax on pollution can actually increase total economic surplus. Taxes on activities that cause harm to others kill two birds with one stone: they generate revenue to pay for useful public services and at the same time discourage people from pursuing the harmful activities. The notion that taxes always and everywhere constitute an obstacle to efficiency simply does not withstand careful scrutiny.

## RECAP Taxes and efficiency

A tax levied on the seller of a product has the same effect on equilibrium quantity and price as a rise in marginal cost equal to the amount of the tax. The burden of a tax imposed on sellers will generally be shared among both buyers and sellers. In the extreme case of a good whose elasticity of supply is infinite, the entire burden of the tax is borne by buyers.

A tax imposed on a product whose supply and demand curves embody all relevant costs and benefits associated with its production and use will result in a *deadweight loss* – a reduction in total economic surplus in the market for the taxed good. Such taxes may nonetheless be justified if the value of the public services financed by the tax outweighs this deadweight loss. In general, the deadweight loss from a tax on a good will be smaller the smaller are the good's price elasticities of supply and demand. Taxes on activities that generate harm to others may produce a net gain in economic surplus, even apart from the value of public services they finance.

## Summary

- When the supply and demand curves for a product capture all the relevant costs and benefits of producing that product, then market equilibrium for that product will be *efficient*. In such a market, if price and quantity do not equal their equilibrium values, a transaction can be found that will make at least some people better off without harming others.
- *Total economic surplus* is a measure of the amount by which participants in a market benefit by participating in it. It is the sum of total consumer surplus and total producer surplus in the market. One of the attractive properties of market equilibrium is that it maximises the value of total economic surplus.
- Efficiency should not be equated with *social justice*. If we believe that the distribution of income among people is unjust, we shall not like the results produced by the intersection of the supply and demand curves based on that income distribution, even though those results are efficient.
- Even so, we should always strive for efficiency because it enables us to achieve all our other goals to the fullest possible extent. Whenever a market is out of equilibrium, the economic 'pie' can be made larger. And with a larger pie, everyone can have a larger slice.
- Regulations or policies that *prevent markets from reaching equilibrium* – such as price ceilings, price subsidies and first-come, first-served allocation schemes – are often defended on the grounds that they help the poor. But such schemes reduce economic surplus, meaning that we can find alternatives under which both rich and poor would be better off. The main difficulty of the poor is that they have too little income. Rather than trying to control the prices of the goods they buy, we could do better by enacting policies that raise the incomes of the poor and then letting prices seek their equilibrium levels. Those who complain that the poor lack the political power to obtain such income transfers must explain why the poor have the power to impose regulations that are far more costly than income transfers.
- Even when a good is provided by a *public utility* rather than a private firm, the theory of competitive supply has important implications for how to provide the good most efficiently. The general rule is that a public utility maximises economic surplus by charging its customers the marginal cost of the goods it provides.
- Critics often complain that taxes make the economy less efficient. A tax will indeed reduce economic surplus if the supply and demand curves in the market for the taxed good reflect all the relevant costs and benefits of its production and consumption. But this decline in surplus may be more than offset by the increase in economic surplus made possible by public goods financed with the *proceeds of the tax*. The best taxes are imposed on activities that would otherwise be pursued to excess, such as activities that generate environmental pollution. Such taxes not only do not reduce economic surplus; they actually increase it.

## Key terms

**deadweight loss** (199)

**efficient (or Pareto efficient)** (183)

## Review questions

1. Why do economists emphasise efficiency as an important goal of public policy?
2. You are a politician considering how to vote on a policy that would increase the economic surplus of workers by €100 million per year but reduce the economic surplus of retirees by €1 million per year. What additional measure might you combine with the policy to ensure that the overall result is a better outcome for everyone?
3. Why does the loss in total economic surplus directly experienced by participants in the market for a good that is taxed overstate the overall loss in economic surplus that results from the tax?
4. Why is compensating volunteers to relinquish their seats on overbooked flights more efficient than a policy of first-come, first-served?
5. Why do price ceilings reduce economic surplus?

## Problems

Problems marked with an asterisk (*) are more difficult.

1. Suppose the weekly demand and supply curves for used DVDs in Brussels, are as shown in the graph below. Calculate:

   a. The weekly consumer surplus.
   b. The weekly producer surplus.
   c. The maximum weekly amount that producers and consumers in Brussels would be willing to pay to be able to buy and sell used DVDs in any given week.

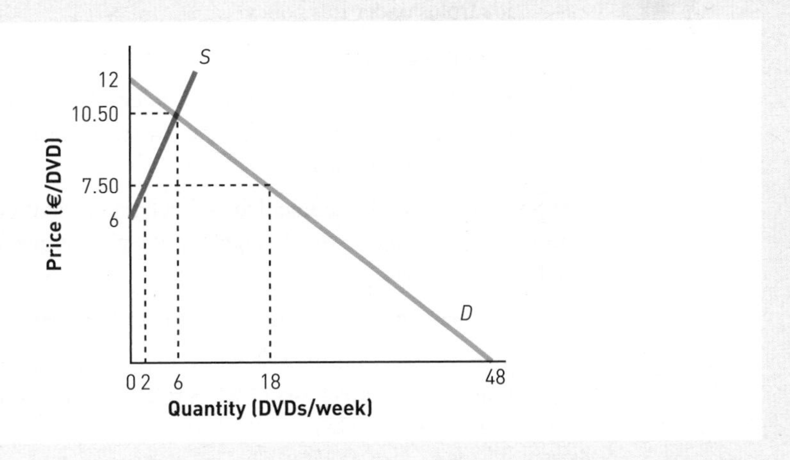

2. Refer to Problem 1. Suppose a coalition of students from a Brussels secondary school succeeds in persuading the local government to impose a price ceiling of €7.50 on used DVDs, on the grounds that local suppliers are taking advantage of teenagers by charging exorbitant prices.

a. Calculate the weekly shortage of used DVDs that will result from this policy.

b. Calculate the total economic surplus lost every week as a result of the price ceiling.

3. The Kubak crystal caves are renowned for their stalactites and stalagmites. The warden of the caves offers a tour each afternoon at 2 p.m. sharp. The caves can be shown to only four people per day without disturbing their fragile ecology. Occasionally, however, more than four people want to see the caves on the same day. The table below lists the people who wanted to see the caves on 24 September 2005, together with their respective times of arrival and reservation prices for taking the tour that day.

| | Arrival time | Reservation price (€) |
|---|---|---|
| Herman | 1.48 | 20 |
| Jon | 1.50 | 14 |
| Kate | 1.53 | 30 |
| Jack | 1.56 | 15 |
| Penny | 1.57 | 40 |
| Fran | 1.59 | 12 |
| Faith | 2.00 | 17 |

a. If the tour is 'free' and the warden operates it on a first-come, first-served basis, what will the total consumer surplus be for the four people who get to go on the tour on that day?

b. Suppose the warden solicits volunteers to postpone their tour by offering increasing amounts of cash compensation until only four people still wish to see the caves that day. If he gives each volunteer the same compensation payment, how much money will he have to offer to generate the required number of volunteers? What is the total economic surplus under this policy?

c. Why is the compensation policy more efficient than the first-come, first-served policy?

d. Describe a way of financing the warden's compensation payments that will make everyone, including the warden, either better off or no worse off than under the first-come, first-served approach.

4. Suppose the weekly demand for a certain good, in thousands of units, is given by the equation $P = 8 - Q$, and the weekly supply of the good is given by the equation $P = 2 + Q$, where $P$ is the price in euros.

a. Calculate the total weekly economic surplus generated at the market equilibrium.

b. Suppose a per-unit tax of €2, to be collected from sellers, is imposed in this market. Calculate the direct loss in economic surplus experienced by participants in this market as a result of the tax.

c. How much government revenue will this tax generate each week? If the revenue is used to offset other taxes paid by participants in this market, what will be their net reduction in total economic surplus?

5. Is a companys' producer surplus the same as its profit? (**Hint:** A company's total cost is equal to the sum of all marginal costs incurred in producing its output, plus any fixed costs.)

6. In Dubrovnik, Croatia, citizens can get their electric power from two sources: a hydroelectric generator and a coal-fired steam generator. The hydroelectric generator can supply up to 100 units of power per day at a constant marginal cost of 1 cent per unit. The steam generator can supply any additional power that is needed at a constant marginal cost of 10 cents per unit. When electricity costs 10 cents per unit, residents of Dubrovnik demand 200 units per day.

  a. Draw the marginal cost curve of electric power production in Dubrovnik.

  b. How much should the city charge for electric power? Explain. Should it charge the same price for a family whose power comes from the hydroelectric generator as it does for a family whose power comes from the steam generator?

7. The municipal water works of Cortland draws water from two sources: an underground spring and a nearby lake. Water from the spring costs 2 cents per 100 litres to deliver, and the spring has a capacity of 1 million litres per day. Water from the lake costs 4 cents per 100 litres to deliver and is available in unlimited quantities. The demand for water in the summer months in Cortland is $P = 20 - 0.001Q$, where $P$ is the price of water in cents per 100 litres, and $Q$ is quantity demanded in hundreds of litres per day. The demand curve for water in the winter months is $P = 10 - 0.001Q$. If the water works wants to encourage efficient water use, how much should it charge for water in the summer months? In the winter months?

8.* Phil's demand curve for visits to a private sector health clinic is given by $P = 48 - 8Q$, where $P$ is the price per visit in euros and $Q$ is the number of visits per season. The marginal cost of providing medical services at the clinic is €24 per visit. Phil has a choice between two health policies, *A* and *B*. Both policies cover all the costs of any serious illness from which Phil might suffer. Policy *A* also covers the cost of visits to the clinic, whereas policy *B* does not. Thus if Phil chooses policy *B*, he must pay €24 per visit to the clinic.

  a. If the premiums the insurance company charges for policies *A* and *B* must cover their respective costs, by how much will the two premiums differ, and what will be the difference in Phil's total expenditure for medical care under the two policies?

  b. Which policy will Phil choose?

  c. What is the most Phil would be willing to pay for the right to continue buying that policy?

9.* The government of Islandia, a small island nation, imports heating oil at a price of €2 per litre and makes it available to citizens at a price of €1 per litre. If Islandians' demand curve for heating oil is given by $P = 6 - Q$, where $P$ is the price per litre in euros and $Q$ is the quantity in millions of litres per year, how much economic surplus is lost as a result of the government's policy?

10.* Refer to Problem 9. Suppose each of the 1 million Islandian households has the same demand curve for heating oil.

  a. What is the household demand curve?

  b. How much consumer surplus would each household lose if it had to pay €2 per litre instead of €1 per litre for heating oil, assuming that there were no other changes in the household budget?

  c. With the money saved by not subsidising oil, by how much could the Islandian government afford to cut each family's annual taxes?

  d. If the government abandoned its oil subsidy and implemented the tax cut, by how much would each family be better off?

  e. How does the resulting total gain for the 1 million families compare with your calculation of the lost economic surplus in Problem 9?

## Answers to in-chapter exercises

7.1 At a price of 50 cents per litre, there is excess demand of 4,000 litres per day. Suppose a seller produces an extra litre of milk (marginal cost = 50 cents) and sells it to the buyer who values it most (reservation price = €2.50) for €1.50. Both buyer and seller will gain additional economic surplus of €1, and no other buyers or sellers will be hurt by the transaction.

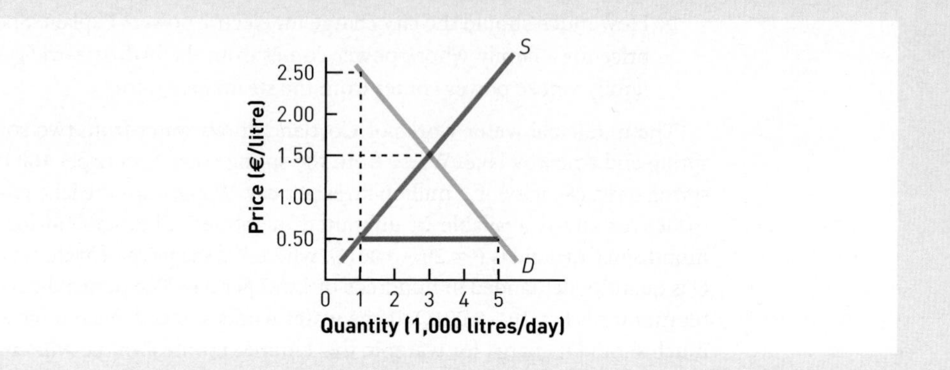


7.2 As shown in the graph below, the new loss in total economic surplus is €200 per day.

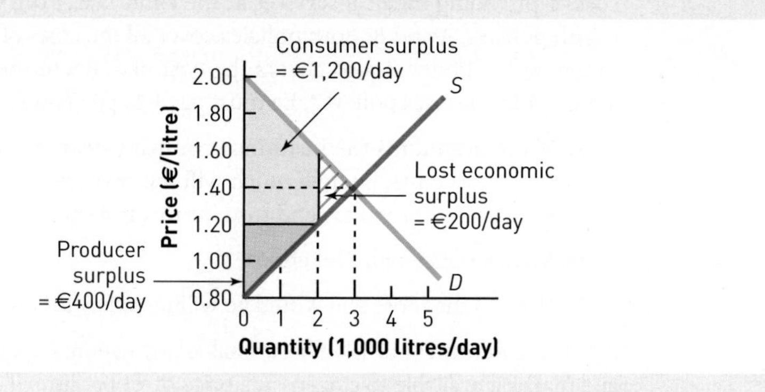


7.3 With a €0.50 per loaf subsidy, the new domestic price becomes €1.50 per loaf. The new lost surplus is the area of the small shaded triangle in the graph below: (1/2)(€0.50/loaf)(1,000,000 loaves/month) = €250,000 per month.

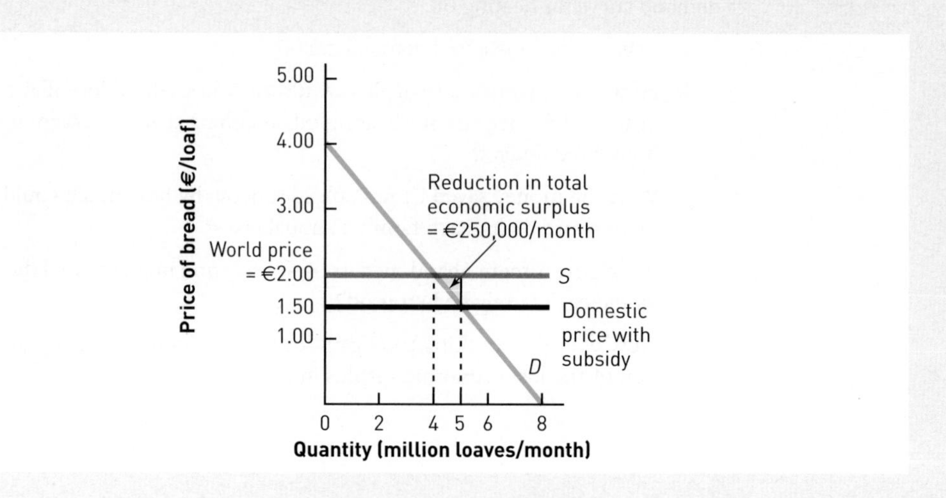

7.4 In the first place, and assuming that it is indeed predominantly poor people who volunteer to wait for the next flight, they are by definition better off by doing so since they reveal that the amount of compensation offered exceeds the value of getting on to the first flight. The policy, therefore, increases the net worth of poor people who volunteer to give up their places. Secondly, a poor person might place a higher value on getting on to the earlier flight than a richer person. In that case, it will be the richer person who volunteers to take the later flight in return for compensation. The compensation system, therefore, increases the net worth of that poor person by transferring the other person's ticket.

7.5 The EU Commission decision is economically inefficient. The airlines are being obliged to pay a fixed amount, regardless of whether it is necessary to pay that amount to secure the release of a seat. Some seats would have been made available at a lower price. The US auction system enables airlines to pre-sell a greater percentage of their seats and, therefore, to lower their fares. This will increase their costs and therefore the level of fares. In addition, in the case of passengers who hold seats but would be willing to sell them back for, say, €100, the airlines are paying more, which increases their costs. Secondly, some 'bumped' passengers would have been willing to pay more to get a seat than the €250 they are being offered. Under an auction system as operated in the United States, seats will be transferred from lower-value users (who have a seat) to higher-value users (who have been 'bumped'). The EU proposal makes this less likely. **Conclusion:** Once again, the bureaucrats' solution is sub-optimal.

7.6 Under first-come, first-served, Dan will have to postpone his lesson. Since Dan would be willing to pay up to €10 to avoid postponing it, he will be better off if the coach asks for a contribution of, say, €8, and then lets him take Bill's place at the scheduled time. The coach could then give €4 to Bill, which would make him €1 better off than if he had not postponed his lesson. The remaining €4 of Dan's payment could be distributed by giving €1 each to Ann, Carrie, Earl and the tennis coach.

| Player | Arrival time (a.m.) | Reservation price (€) |
|---|---|---|
| Ann | 9.50 | 4 |
| Bill | 9.52 | 3 |
| Carrie | 9.55 | 6 |
| Dan | 9.56 | 10 |
| Earl | 9.59 | 3 |

7.7 At a consumption level of 2 million litres per day, the marginal source of water is the lake, which has a marginal cost of 0.8 cents per litre. The city should charge everyone 0.8 cents per litre, including those who get their water from the spring.

# 8

# The Quest for Profit and the 'Invisible Hand'

In New York, in London, indeed in any major city in the 1970s, you would find a very large population of small secretarial firms offering typing, copying and printing services. Some survive today, but they are few in number compared with the position in the 1970s. In those years in most American cities several firms also offered telephone answering services. Today they have nearly all disappeared, or if they survive, it is not as answering services. On the other hand, Manhattan offers a large choice of dog-walking service suppliers today; London offers an extraordinary number of yoga and transcendental meditation (TM) instruction services, more or less unheard of in the 1970s.

There has been an explosion in the choice of restaurants available in any big city. On the other hand, the choice of bookshops has sharply contracted: they are now concentrated into fewer and larger outlets, and most offer the same services.

Try to have your watch repaired today and you will find that watch repair firms are few and far between. Similarly, it is hard in a modern European city to find a cobbler to mend shoes. In contrast, if you need immediate access to the Internet, cyber cafés abound.

The reasons for these changes are in some cases obvious. The PC has revolutionised document preparation, and electronic watches are cheap and disposable. Increased leisure and higher incomes have increased the demand for recreational services. Other changes, however, require deeper study to explain them.

However, what is of interest here is not the underlying cause of these changes, but what actually *happens to bring them about*. That is the process whereby firms are set up, or disappear, or firms change what they do.

Driving these changes is the business owner's quest for profit. Businesses migrate to industries and locations in which profit opportunities abound and desert those whose prospects appear bleak. In perhaps the most widely quoted passage from his landmark treatise, *The Wealth of Nations* (1776), Adam Smith wrote:

> It is not from the benevolence of the butcher, the brewer, or the baker that we expect our dinner, but from their regard of their own interest. We address ourselves not to their humanity, but to their self-love, and never talk to them of our necessities, but of their advantage.

Smith went on to argue that although the entrepreneur 'intends only his own gain', he is 'led by an invisible hand to promote an end which was no part of his intention'. As Smith saw it, even though self-interest is the prime mover of economic activity, the end result is an allocation of goods and services that serves society's collective interests remarkably well. If producers are offering 'too much' of one product and 'not enough' of another, profit opportunities immediately alert entrepreneurs to that fact and provide incentives for them to take remedial action. All the while, the system exerts relentless pressure on producers to hold the price of each good close to its cost of production – and, indeed, to reduce that cost in any ways possible.

The object of this chapter is to provide a deeper insight into the nature of the forces that guide the invisible hand. This involves confronting three questions.

1. What exactly does 'profit' mean, and how is it measured?
2. How does the pursuit of profit serve society's ends, as is asserted by economists who support the use of markets to allocate resources?
3. If competition holds price close to the cost of production, why do so many entrepreneurs become fabulously wealthy?

We shall also discuss cases in which a misunderstanding of Smith's theory can result in costly errors, in both everyday decision making and in the realm of government policy.

## The central role of economic profit

The economic theory of business behaviour is built on the assumption that the firm's goal is to *maximise its profit*. So we must be clear at the outset about what, exactly, 'profit' means.

### Three types of profit

The economist's understanding of profit is different from the accountant's, and the distinction between the two is important to understanding how the 'invisible hand' works. Accountants define the annual profit of a business as the difference between the revenue it takes in and its **explicit costs** for the year, which are the actual payments the firm makes to its factors of production and other suppliers. Profit thus defined is called **accounting profit**:

Accounting profit = Total revenue – Explicit costs

Accounting profit is the most familiar profit concept in everyday discourse. It is the one that companies use, for example, when they provide statements about their profits in press releases or annual reports. It is what the tax authorities use to compute corporation tax liabilities.

Economists, by contrast, define profit as the difference between the firm's total revenue and not just its explicit costs, but also its **implicit costs**, which are the opportunity costs of all the resources supplied by the firm's owners. Profit thus defined is called **economic profit, supernormal profit** or **excess profit**:

Economic profit = Total revenue – Explicit costs – Implicit costs

To illustrate the difference between accounting profit and economic profit, consider a firm with €400,000 in total annual revenue whose only explicit costs are workers' salaries of €250,000 per year. The owners of this firm have supplied machines and other capital equipment with a total resale value of €1 million. This firm's accounting profit, then, is the difference between its total revenue of €400,000 per year and its explicit costs of €250,000 per year, or €150,000 per year.

**explicit costs** the actual payments a firm makes to its factors of production and other suppliers

**accounting profit** the difference between a firm's total revenue and its explicit cost

**implicit costs** the opportunity costs of the resources supplied by the firm's owners

**economic profit (or supernormal profit or excess profit)** the difference between a firm's total revenue and the sum of its explicit and implicit costs

To calculate the firm's economic profit, we must first calculate the opportunity cost of the resources supplied by the firm's owners, *the equity capital of the firm*. Suppose that the current annual interest rate on savings accounts is 10 per cent. Had owners not invested in capital equipment, they could have earned an additional €100,000 per year interest by depositing their €1 million in a savings account. So the firm's economic profit is €400,000 per year – €250,000 per year – €100,000 per year = €50,000 per year.

Note that this economic profit is smaller than the accounting profit by exactly the amount of the firm's *implicit costs* – the €100,000 per year opportunity cost of the resources supplied by the firm's owners. This difference between a business's accounting profit and its economic profit is called its **normal profit**. Normal profit is simply the opportunity cost of the resources supplied to a business by its owners.

**normal profit** the opportunity cost of the resources supplied by a firm's owners, equal to accounting profit minus economic profit

Figure 8.1 illustrates the difference between accounting and economic profit. Figure 8.1(a) represents a firm's total revenues, while Figs. 8.1(b) and (c) show how these revenues are apportioned among the various cost and profit categories.

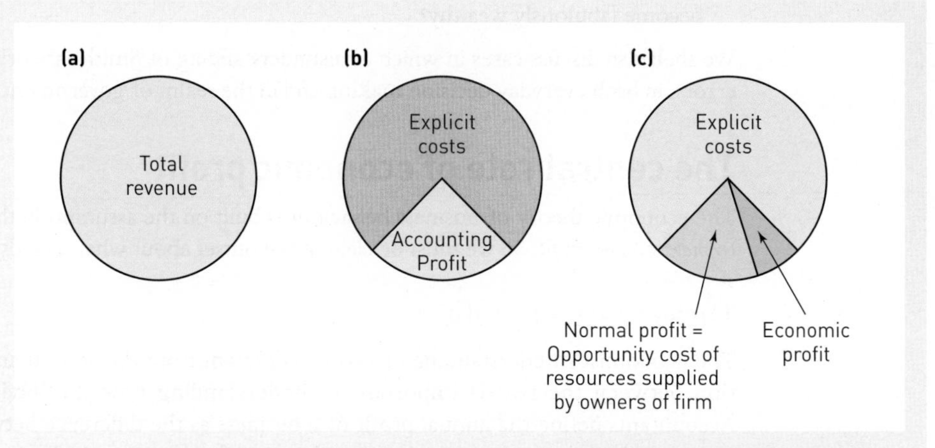


**Figure 8.1 The Difference between Accounting Profit and Economic Profit.** Accounting profit (b) is the difference between total revenue (a) and explicit costs. Normal profit (c) is the opportunity cost of all resources supplied by firm's owners. Economic profit (c) is the difference between total revenue and all costs, explicit and implicit (also equal to the difference between accounting profit and normal profit).

Examples 8.1 and 8.2 illustrate why the distinction between accounting and economic profit is so important.

### Example 8.1 With the changes taking place in the EU's Common Agricultural Policy should we expect the number of farmers to remain unchanged even if the farms appear to remain profitable?

Since the 1990s successive reforms of the price supports for farm produce available to help farmers in the European Union have been reduced. As a consequence, the prices farmers have been receiving for what they produce have fallen in real terms (i.e. allowing for inflation). As is well known, not only have farm interest groups been complaining vociferously about farm incomes, but it is clear from census data that the numbers in farming have been dropping steadily. At the same time it has often been pointed out that farming remains profitable, and farmers have been paying income taxes, something that would not happen if they were losing money. To understand (and reconcile) these positions, the following two sets of data in Tables 8.1 and 8.2 (p. 212) will be helpful.

| Total revenue (€/year) | Explicit costs (€/year) | Implicit costs (€/year) | Accounting profit (= total revenue - explicit costs) (€/year) | Economic profit (= total revenue - explicit costs - implicit costs) (€/year) | Normal profit (= implicit costs) (€/year) |
|---|---|---|---|---|---|
| 22,000 | 10,000 | 11,000 | 12,000 | 1,000 | 11,000 |

**Table 8.1** Revenue, Cost and Profit Summary for Example 8.1

Table 8.1 summarises the following scenario. A wheat farmer in northern France pays €6,000 rent (the going rate) to his elderly uncle for his land and also pays the cost of his various pieces of farm equipment and other inputs. The total for rent and other cost payments comes to €10,000 a year. He supplies only his own labour, and he considers farming just as attractive as his only other employment opportunity, managing a retail store in a nearby town at a salary of €11,000 per year. Apart from the matter of pay, he is indifferent between farming and being a manager. Wheat sells for a constant price per tonne effectively determined by EU price supports. The farmer's revenue from wheat sales is €22,000 per year.

- What is his accounting profit?
- His economic profit?
- His normal profit?
- Should he remain in farming?

As shown in Table 8.1, accounting profit is €12,000 per year, the difference between his €22,000 annual revenue and his €10,000 yearly payment for land, equipment and supplies. His economic profit is that amount less the opportunity cost of his labour. Since the latter is the €11,000 per year he could have earned as a store manager, he is making an economic profit of €1,000 per year. Finally, his normal profit is the €11,000 opportunity cost of the only resource he supplies – namely, his labour. Given that he is otherwise indifferent between the two types of work, he will be better off by €1,000 per year if he remains in farming. He earns an economic profit of €1,000 by remaining on the land.

**Exercise 8.1** Suppose the European Union lowers the effective support price, and the value of the annual wheat production on the farm falls to €20,000. What advice would you give the farmer?

**economic loss** an economic profit that is less than zero

If you work through Exercise 8.1, you will conclude that the farmer now has an economic profit of –€1,000 per year. A negative economic profit is an **economic loss**. If he expects to sustain an economic loss indefinitely, his best bet would be to abandon farming in favour of managing a retail store. Note that he is still earning an accounting profit.

### Example 8.2 Does owning the land rather than paying rent to the owner make a difference?

Now suppose that his uncle dies and leaves the land to the farmer. Clearly he is better off, because he doesn't have to pay the uncle €500 a month as rent. Should he now revise his opinion? Would you tell him that he should now stay on in farming because he doesn't have to pay the rent, and has an extra €6,000 at the end of the year?

The answer is that he should still take the other job, as is shown in Table 8.2. If he continues to farm his own land, his accounting profit will be €16,000 per year, or €6,000 more than before. But his economic profit will still be the same as before – that is, –€1,000 per year – because he should deduct the €6,000 per year opportunity cost of farming his own land, even though he no longer must make an explicit payment to his uncle for it. Why? Because he could rent it to someone else at the going rate. The normal profit from owning and operating his farm will be €17,000 per year – the opportunity cost of the land and labour he provides. But since he earns an accounting profit of only €16,000, he will again do better to abandon farming for the managerial job.

| Total revenue (€/year) | Explicit costs (€/year) | Implicit costs (€/year) | Accounting profit (= total revenue - explicit costs) (€/year) | Economic profit (= total revenue - explicit costs - implicit costs) (€/year) | Normal profit (= implicit costs) (€/year) |
|---|---|---|---|---|---|
| 20,000 | 4,000 | 17,000 | 16,000 | −1,000 | 17,000 |

**Table 8.2** Revenue, Cost and Profit Summary for Example 8.2

He would obviously be wealthier as an owner than he was as a renter. But the question of whether to remain a farmer is answered the same way whether he rents his farmland or owns it. He should stay in farming only if that is the option that yields the highest economic profit.

So, as a matter of probability we should expect the numbers on the land to fall, even if the farms remain profitable in an accounting sense, when the real price of what is produced on the land falls. This is because a fall in farm output prices will result in some farmers not making an economic profit from staying in the business.

### RECAP The central role of economic profit

A firm's *accounting profit* is the difference between its revenue and the sum of all explicit costs it incurs. *Economic profit* is the difference between the firm's revenue and all costs it incurs – both explicit and implicit. *Normal profit* is the opportunity cost of the resources supplied by the owners of the firm. When a firm's accounting profit is exactly equal to the opportunity cost of the inputs supplied by the firm's owners, the firm's economic profit is zero. For a firm to remain in business in the long run, it must earn an economic profit greater than or equal to zero.

## The 'invisible hand' theory

**rationing function of price** to distribute scarce goods to those consumers who value them most highly

**allocative function of price** to direct resources away from overcrowded markets and toward markets that are underserved

**'invisible hand' theory** Adam Smith's theory that the actions of independent, self-interested buyers and sellers will often result in the most efficient allocation of resources

### Two functions of price

In the free-enterprise system, market prices serve two important and distinct functions. The first, the **rationing function of price**, is to distribute scarce goods among potential claimants, ensuring that those who get them are the ones who value them most. Thus, if three people want the only antique clock for sale at an auction, the clock goes home with the person who bids the most for it.

The second function, the **allocative function of price**, is to direct productive resources to different sectors of the economy. Resources leave markets in which price cannot cover the cost of production and enter those in which price exceeds the cost of production.

Both the allocative and rationing functions of price underlie Adam Smith's celebrated theory of the '**invisible hand**' of the market. Smith believed and taught that the market system channels the selfish interests of individual buyers and sellers so as to promote the greatest good for society. The carrot of economic profit and the stick of economic loss, he argued, were the only forces necessary to ensure not only that existing supplies in any market would be allocated efficiently, but also that resources would be allocated across markets to produce the most efficient possible mix of goods and services.

## Responses to profits and losses

To understand how the invisible hand works, we begin by looking at how market forces respond to economic profits and losses. If a firm is to remain in business in the long run, it must cover all its costs, both explicit and implicit. A firm's normal profit should be treated as a cost of doing business. Thus the owner of a firm that earns no more than a normal profit has managed only to recover the opportunity cost of the resources invested in the firm. By contrast, the owner of a firm that makes a positive economic profit earns more than the opportunity cost of the invested resources, and earns more than a normal profit.

Naturally, everyone would be delighted to earn more than a normal profit, and no one wants to earn less. The result is that those markets in which firms are earning an economic profit tend to attract additional resources, whereas markets in which firms are experiencing economic losses tend to lose resources.

To see how this happens, we examine the workings of a hypothetical market for a product (in this case, wheat) whose short-run supply and demand curves are shown in Fig. 8.2(a). Figure 8.2(b) depicts the marginal and average total cost curves for a representative farm. The equilibrium price of €2 per tonne is determined by the supply–demand intersection in (a). The representative farm whose *MC* and *ATC* curves are shown in (b) then maximises its profit by producing the quantity for which price equals marginal cost, 130,000 tonnes of wheat per year.

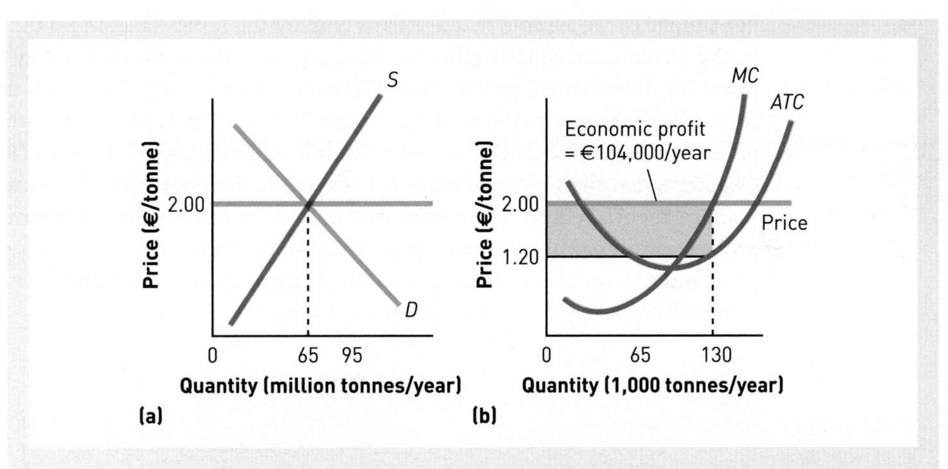


**Figure 8.2 Economic Profit in the Short Run in the Wheat Market.** At an equilibrium price of €2 per tonne (a), the typical farm earns an economic profit of €104,000 per year (b).

From Chapter 6 we know that average total cost (*ATC*) any output level is the sum of all costs divided by output. The difference between price and *ATC* is thus equal to the average amount of economic profit earned per unit sold. In Fig. 8.2(b), that difference is €0.80 per unit. With 130,000 tonnes per year sold, the representative farm thus earns an economic profit of €104,000 per year.

The existence of positive economic profit in the wheat market means that producers in that market are earning more than their opportunity cost of farming. For simplicity, we assume that the inputs required to enter the wheat market – land, labour, equipment and the like – are available at constant prices and that anyone is free to enter this market if he or she chooses. The key point is that since price exceeds the opportunity cost of the resources required to enter the market, others *will* want to enter. As they add their wheat production to the amount already on offer, supply shifts to the right, causing the market equilibrium price to fall, as shown in Fig. 8.3(a). At the new price of €1.50 per tonne, the representative farm now earns much less economic profit than before, only €50,400 per year (Fig. 8.3(b)).

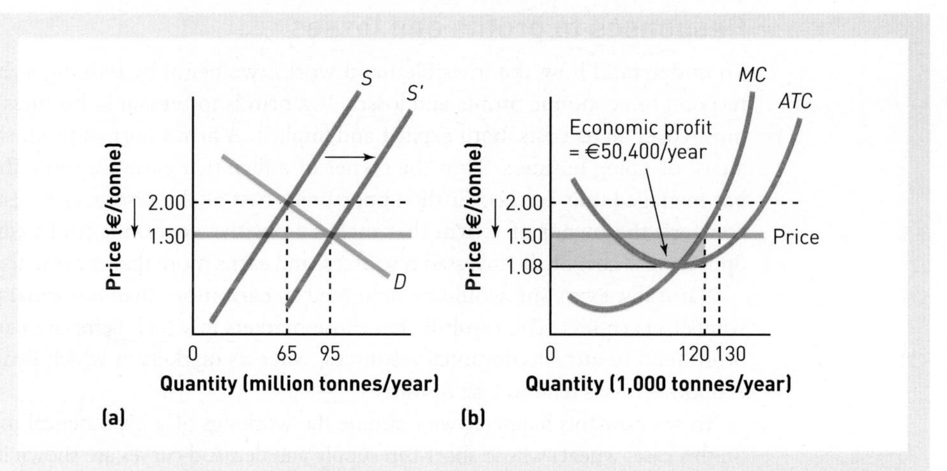


**Figure 8.3 The Effect of Entry on Price and Economic Profit.** At the original price of €2 per tonne, existing farmers earned economic profit, prompting new farmers to enter. With entry, supply shifts right (from *S* to *S'* in (a)) and equilibrium price falls, as does economic profit (b).

For simplicity, we assume that all farms employ the same standard production method (that is, the farmers are equally efficient, have access to the same technology and pay the same prices for their inputs), so that their *ATC* curves are identical. Entry will then continue until price falls all the way to the minimum value of *ATC*. (At any price higher than that, economic profit would still be positive, and entry would continue, driving price still lower.) Recall from Chapter 6 that the short-run marginal cost curve intersects the *ATC* curve at the minimum point of the *ATC* curve. This means that once price reaches the minimum value of *ATC*, the profit-maximising rule of setting price equal to marginal cost results in a quantity for which price and *ATC* are the same. And when that happens, economic profit for the representative farm will be exactly zero, as shown in Fig. 8.4(b).

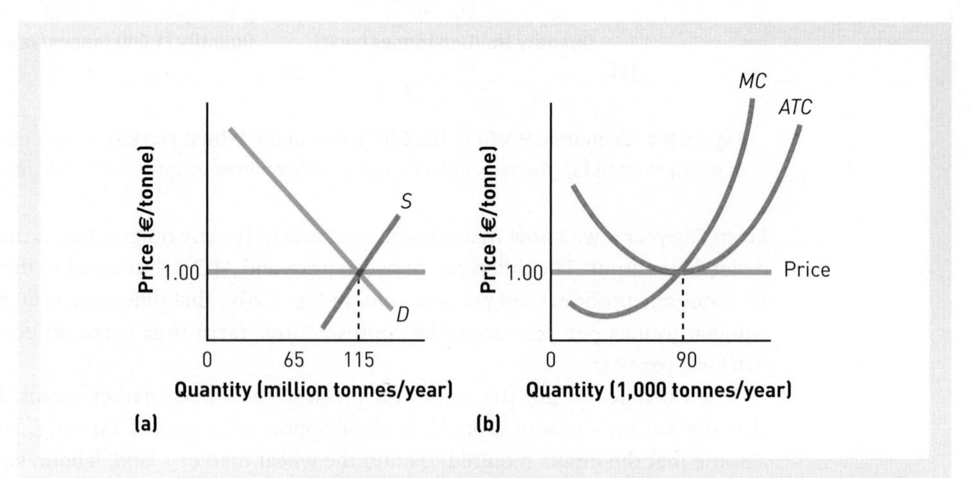


**Figure 8.4 Equilibrium when Entry Ceases.** Further entry ceases once price falls to the minimum value of *ATC*. At that point all farms earn a normal economic profit. Equivalently, each earns an economic profit of zero.

In the adjustment process just considered, the initial equilibrium price had been above the minimum value of *ATC*, giving rise to positive economic profits. Suppose instead that the market demand curve for wheat had intersected the short-run supply curve at a price below the minimum value of each farm's *ATC* curve, as shown in Fig. 8.5(b). As long as this price is above the minimum value of average variable cost, each farm will supply that quantity of wheat for which price equals marginal cost, shown as 70,000 tonnes per year in Fig. 8.5(b). Note, however, that at that quantity, the farm's average total cost is €1.05 per tonne, or €0.30 more than the price for which it sells each tonne. As shown in (b), the farm thus sustains an economic loss of €21,000 per year.

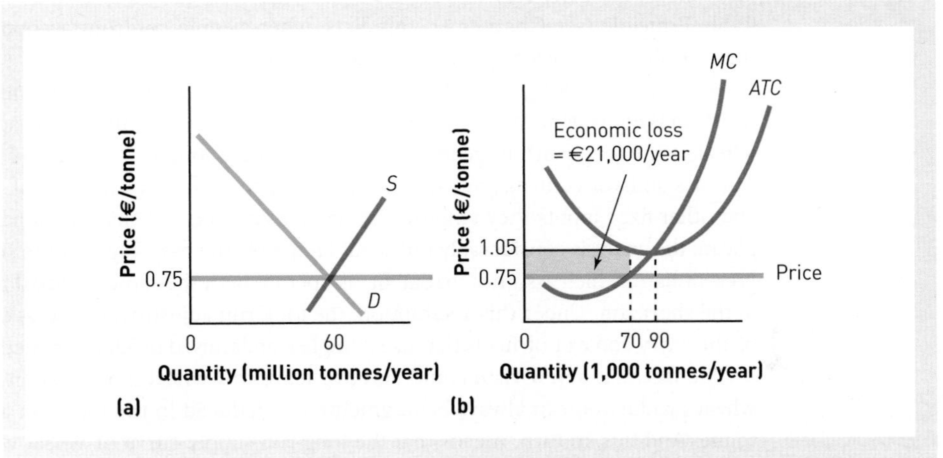


**Figure 8.5 A Short-Run Economic Loss in the Wheat Market.** When price is below the minimum value of *ATC* (a), each farm sustains an economic loss (b).

If the demand curve that led to the low price and resulting economic losses in Fig. 8.5 is expected to persist, farmers will begin to abandon farming for other activities that promise better returns. This means that the supply curve for wheat will shift to the left, resulting in higher prices and smaller losses. Exit from wheat farming will continue, in fact, until price has again risen to €1 per tonne, at which point there will be no incentive for further exit. Once again we see a stable equilibrium in which price is €1 per tonne, as shown in Fig. 8.6.

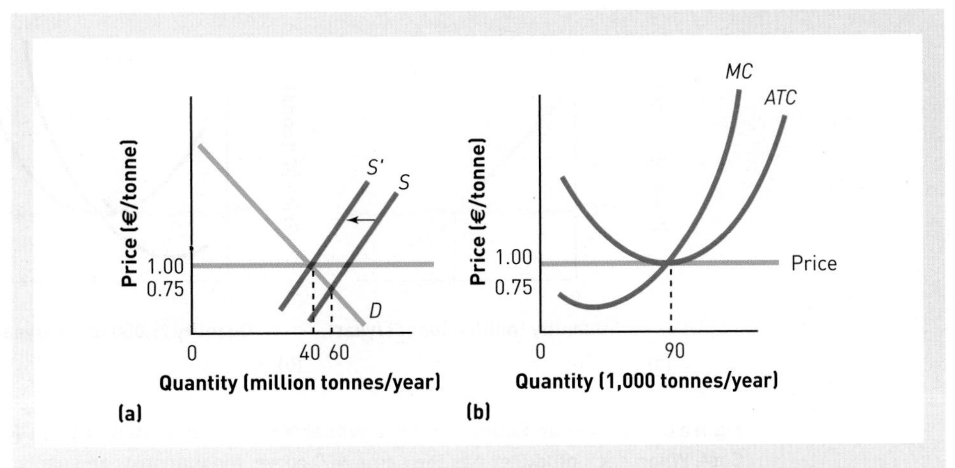


**Figure 8.6 Equilibrium when Exit Ceases.** Further exit ceases once price rises to the minimum value of *ATC*. At that point all farms earn a normal economic profit. Equivalently, each earns an economic profit of zero.

Given our simplifying assumptions that all wheat farms employ a standardised production method and that inputs can be purchased in any quantities at fixed prices, the price of wheat cannot remain above €1 per tonne (the minimum point on the *ATC* curve) in the long run. Any higher price would stimulate additional entry until price again fell to that level. Further, the price of wheat cannot remain below €1 per tonne in the long run, because any lower price would stimulate exit until the price of wheat again rose to €1 per tonne.

The fact that firms are free to enter or leave an industry at any time ensures that in the long run all firms in the industry will to tend earn zero economic profit. Their goal is not to earn zero profit. Rather, the zero-profit tendency is a consequence of the price movements associated with entry and exit. As the *Equilibrium Principle* – also called the No-Cash-on-the-Table Principle (see Chapter 3) – predicts, when people confront an opportunity for gain, they are almost always quick to exploit it.

What does the long-run supply curve look like in the wheat market just discussed? This question is equivalent to asking: 'What is the marginal cost of producing additional tonnes of wheat in the long run?' In general, adjustment in the long run may entail not just entry and exit of standardised firms, but also the ability of firms to alter the mix of capital equipment and other fixed inputs they employ. Explicit consideration of this additional step would complicate the analysis considerably but would not alter the basic logic of the simpler account we present here, which assumes that all firms operate with the same standard mix of fixed inputs in the short run. Under this assumption, the long-run adjustment process consists exclusively of the entry and exit of firms that use a single standardised production method.

The fact that a new firm could enter or leave this wheat market at any time means that wheat production can always be augmented or reduced in the long run at a cost of €1 per tonne. And this, in turn, means that the long-run supply curve of wheat will be a horizontal line at a price equal to the minimum value of the *ATC* curve, €1 per tonne. Since the long-run marginal cost (*LMC*) of producing wheat is constant, so is the long-run average cost (*LAC*) and it, too, is €1 per tonne, as shown in Fig. 8.7(a). Figure 8.7(b) shows the *MC* and *ATC* curves of a representative wheat farm. At a price of €1 per tonne, this wheat market is said to be in *long-run equilibrium*. The representative farm produces 90,000 tonnes of wheat each year, the quantity for which price equals its marginal cost. And since price is exactly equal to *ATC*, this farm also earns an economic profit of zero.

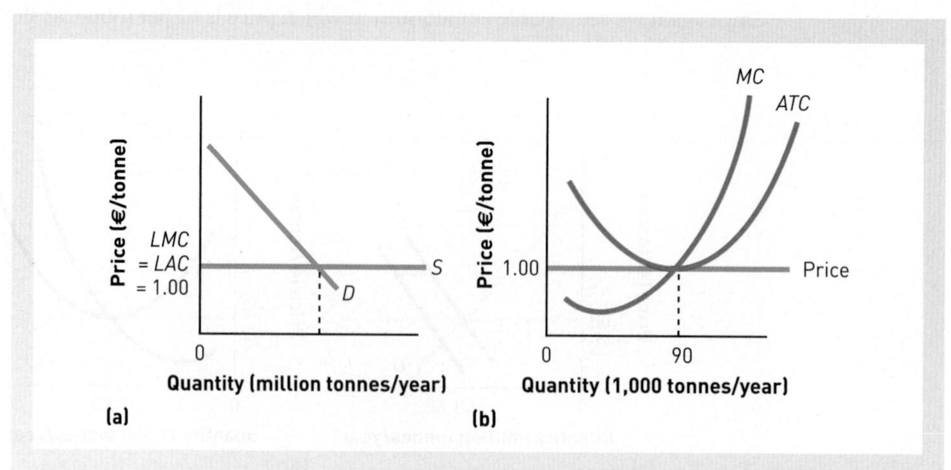


**Figure 8.7 Long-Run Equilibrium in a Wheat Market with Constant Long-Run Average Cost.** When each producer has the same *ATC* curve, the industry can supply as much or as little output as buyers wish to buy at a price equal to the minimum value of *ATC* (a). At that price, the representative producer (b) earns zero economic profit.

These observations call attention to two attractive features of the invisible hand concept:

1. The first is that the *market outcome is efficient in the long run*. Note, for example, that when the wheat market is in long-run equilibrium, the value to buyers of the last unit of wheat sold is €1 per tonne, which is exactly the same as the long-run marginal cost of producing it. Thus there is no possible rearrangement of resources that would make some participants in this market better off without causing harm to some others. If farmers were to expand production, for example, the added costs incurred would exceed the added benefits; and if they were to contract production, the cost savings would be less than the benefits forgone.
2. The second attractive feature of long-run competitive equilibrium is that the market outcome can be described as fair, in the sense that the price buyers must pay is no higher than the cost incurred by suppliers. That cost includes a normal profit, the opportunity cost of the resources supplied by owners of the firm.

We must emphasise that Smith's 'invisible hand' does not mean that market allocation of resources is optimal in every way. It simply means that markets are 'efficient' in the limited technical sense discussed in Chapter 7. Thus, if the current allocation differs from the market equilibrium allocation, the 'invisible hand' theory implies that we can reallocate resources in a way that makes some people better off without harming others.

Example 8.3 affords additional insight into how Smith's 'invisible hand' works in practice.

### Example 8.3 What happens in a city with 'too many' hair stylists and 'too few' aerobics instructors?

At the initial equilibrium quantities and prices in the markets for haircuts and aerobics classes shown in Fig. 8.8, all suppliers are currently earning zero economic profit. Now suppose that styles suddenly change in favour of longer hair and increased physical fitness. If the long-run marginal cost of altering current production levels is constant in both markets, describe how prices and quantities will change in each market, in both the short run and the long run. Are the new equilibrium quantities socially optimal?

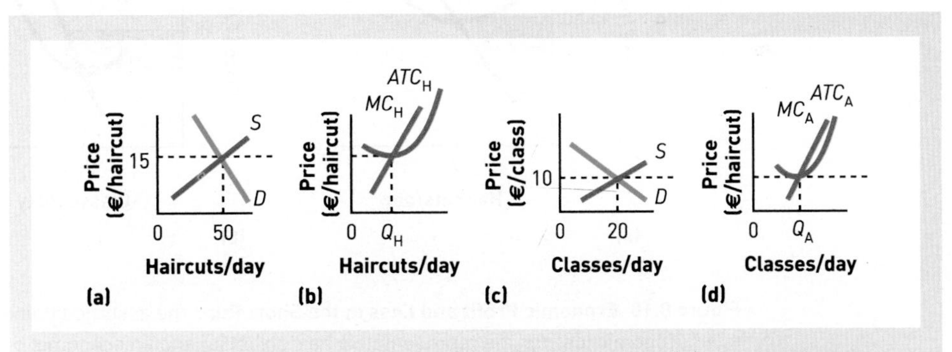


**Figure 8.8 Initial Equilibrium in the Markets for (a) Haircuts and (b) Aerobics Classes.** $MC_H$ and $ATC_H$ are the marginal cost and average total cost curves for a representative hair stylist, and $MC_A$ and $ATC_A$ are the marginal cost and average total cost curves for a representative aerobics instructor. Both markets are initially in long-run equilibrium, with sellers in each market earning zero economic profit.

The shift to longer hair styles means a leftward shift in the demand for haircuts, while the increased emphasis on physical fitness implies a rightward shift in the demand curve for aerobics classes, as seen in Fig. 8.9. As a result of these demand shifts, the new short-run equilibrium prices change. For the sake of illustration, these new prices are shown as €12 per haircut and €15 per aerobics class.

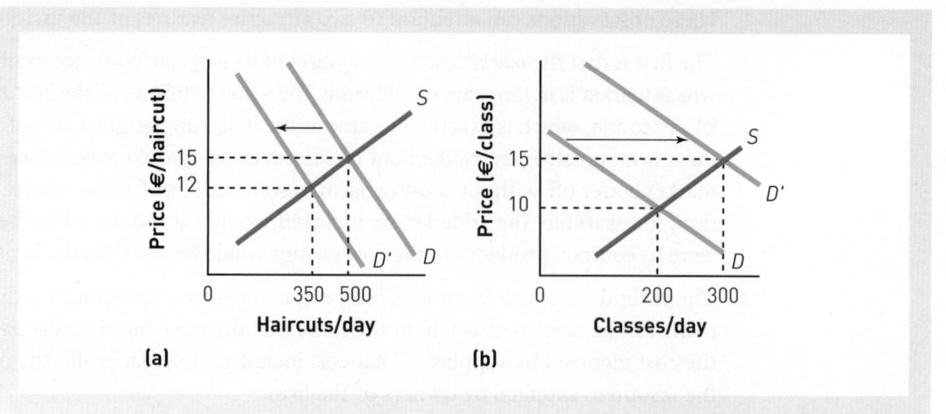


**Figure 8.9 The Short-Run Effect of Demand Shifts in Two Markets.** The decline in demand for haircuts causes the price of haircuts to fall from €15 to €12 in the short run (a), while the increase in demand for areobics classes cuases the price of classes to rise from €10 to €15 in the short run (b).

Because each producer was earning zero economic profit at the original equilibrium prices, hair stylists will experience economic losses and aerobics instructors will experience economic profits at the new prices, as seen in Fig. 8.10.

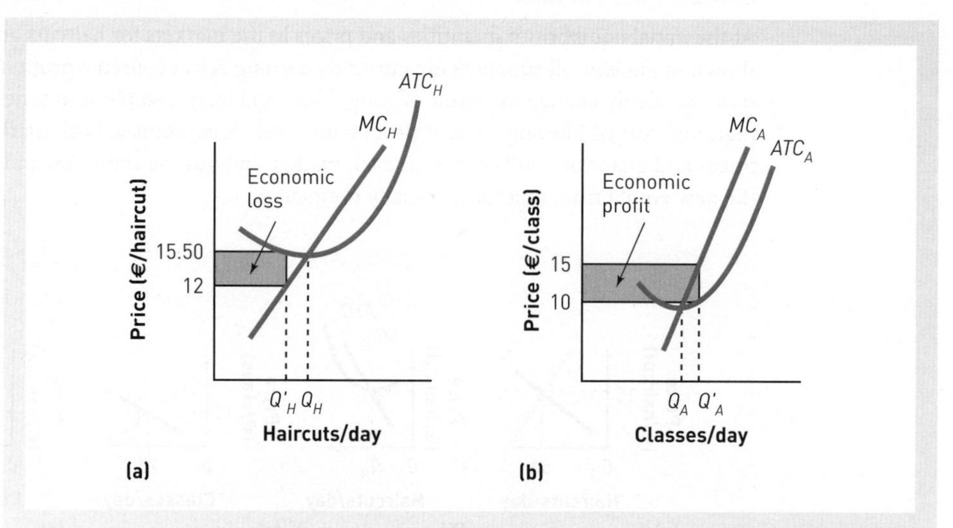


**Figure 8.10 Economic Profit and Loss in the Short Run.** The assumed demand shifts result in an economic loss for the representative hair stylist (a) and an economic profit for the representative aerobics instructor (b).

Because the short-run equilibrium price of haircuts results in economic losses for hair stylists, some hair stylists will begin to leave that market in search of more favourable opportunities elsewhere. As a result, the short-run supply curve of haircuts will shift leftward, resulting in a higher equilibrium price. Exit of hair stylists will continue until the price of haircuts rises sufficiently to cover the long-run opportunity cost of providing them, which by assumption is €15.

By the same token, because the short-run equilibrium price of aerobics classes results in economic profits for instructors, outsiders will begin to enter that market, causing the short-run supply curve of classes to shift rightward. New instructors will continue to enter until the price of classes falls to the long-run opportunity cost of providing them. By assumption, that cost is €10. Once all adjustments have taken place, there will be fewer hair stylists and more aerobics classes than before. But because marginal costs in both markets were assumed constant in the long run, the prices of the two goods will again be at their original levels.

It bears mention that those stylists who leave the hair-cutting market will not necessarily be the same people who enter the aerobics teaching market. Indeed, given the sheer number of occupations a former hair stylist might choose to pursue, the likelihood of such a switch is low. Movements of resources will typically involve several indirect steps. Thus a former hair stylist might become a secretary, and a former postal worker might become an aerobics instructor.

We also note that the invisible hand theory says nothing about *how long* these adjustments might take. In some markets, especially labour markets, the required movements might take months or even years. Think of what happened in the coal mining areas of Britain during the 1980s when coal mining was drastically reduced (and in many areas closed down completely). By way of contrast, consider the consequences of the collapse of MG Rover early in 2005. No one believes that the workers who lost their jobs would for the most part remain unemployed for long. But even in the worst case (as in coal mining) if the supply and demand curves remain stable, the labour markets will eventually reach equilibrium prices and quantities. And the new prices and quantities will be socially optimal in the same sense as before. Because the value to buyers of the last unit sold will be the same as the marginal cost of producing it, no additional transactions will be possible that benefit some without harming others.

## The importance of free entry and exit

The allocative function of price cannot operate unless firms can enter new markets and leave existing ones at will. If new firms could not enter a market in which existing firms were making a large economic profit, economic profit would not tend to fall to zero over time, and price would not tend to gravitate toward the marginal cost of production.

Forces that inhibit firms from entering new markets are sometimes called **barriers to entry**. In the book publishing market, for example, the publisher of a book enjoys copyright protection granted by the government. Copyright law forbids other publishers from producing and selling their own editions of protected works. This barrier allows the price of a popular book to remain significantly above its cost of production for an extended period, all the while generating an economic profit for its publisher. (A copyright provides no *guarantee* of a profit, and indeed most new books actually generate an economic loss for their publishers.)

**barrier to entry** any force that prevents firms from entering a new market

Barriers to entry may result from practical as well as legal constraints. Some economists, for example, have argued that the compelling advantages of *product compatibility* have created barriers to entry in the computer software market. Since more than 90 per cent of new desktop computers come with Microsoft's Windows operating system (OS) software already installed, rival companies have difficulty selling other operating systems that may make it difficult for users to exchange files with friends and colleagues. The bundling of MSWord with Windows, coupled to problems of importing documents prepared with other word-processing (WP) packages into MSWord, is just one factor that has undermined demand for other WP packages, especially WordPerfect, whose users will swear that it is a much superior product to MSWord. These compatibility problems, more than all other factors, are widely believed to explain Microsoft's spectacular profit history.

This last effect may be overstated. The emergence of the 'open architecture' freeware operating system, Linux, has seriously undermined Microsoft's position in the OS market, something that would have been expected by economists of the Chicago School, who have always argued that markets tend to erode positions of market power.

No less important than the freedom to enter a market is the freedom to leave. When the US domestic airline industry was regulated by the federal government, air carriers were often required to serve specific markets, even though they were losing money in them. Similar constraints continue to be imposed by national and EU regulation on a variety of utilities across Europe. They are termed 'universal service obligations' (USOs) in the literature on regulation, and they have the effect of increasing operating costs for suppliers subject to them. When firms discover that a market, once entered, is difficult or impossible to leave, they become reluctant to enter new markets. Barriers to exit thus become barriers to entry. Without reasonably free entry and exit, then, the implications of Adam Smith's 'invisible hand' theory cannot be expected to hold.

All things considered, however, producers enjoy a high degree of freedom of entry in most sectors of the market economies of the West. Recognition of the importance of ease of entry and exit has meant that even where, in countries or sectors, firms enjoy a lower degree of freedom, the consequences (arthritic economies) have led to pressure for change. Because free entry and exit is one of the defining characteristics of perfectly competitive markets, we shall, unless otherwise stated, assume its existence.

### RECAP The 'invisible hand' theory

In market economies, the *allocative* and *rationing* functions of prices guide resources to their most highly valued uses. Prices influence how much of each type of good gets produced (the allocative function). Firms enter industries in which prices are sufficiently high to sustain an economic profit and leave those in which low prices result in an economic loss. Prices also direct existing supplies of goods to the buyers who value them most (the rationing function). Industries in which firms earn a positive economic profit tend to attract new firms, shifting industry supply to the right. Firms tend to leave industries in which they sustain an economic loss, shifting supply curves to the left. In each case, the supply movements continue until economic profit reaches zero. In long-run equilibrium, the value of the last unit produced to buyers is equal to its marginal cost of production, leaving no possibility for additional mutually beneficial transactions.

## Economic rent versus economic profit

Microsoft chairman Bill Gates is said to be one of the wealthiest men in the world. This, it is widely believed, is largely because the problem of compatibility prevents rival suppliers from competing effectively in the many software markets dominated by his company. This has led to regulatory and judicial confrontations on both sides of the Atlantic as anti-trust policy has been invoked to curb Microsoft's alleged abuses of its market position. Yet numerous people have become fabulously rich even in markets with no conspicuous barriers to entry. If market forces push economic profit toward zero, how can that happen?

The answer to this question hinges on the distinction between economic profit and economic rent. When people use the term 'rent' in everyday circumstances they are referring to the payment they might make to a landlord for a flat, or to a car hire company for the use of a car. In economics, however, the term 'rent' has a different meaning, although it is connected to the everyday term in some cases. In economics *'economic rent'* (or simply, *rent*) is that portion of the payment for an input that is above the supplier's reservation price for that input, which is by definition the supply price of that input. Suppose, for example, that a landowner's reservation price for a hectare of land is €100 per year, reflecting its value to the landowner if he used it himself. That is, suppose he would be willing to lease it to a farmer as long as he received an annual payment of at least €100, but for less than that amount he would rather leave it fallow. If competition between would-be farmers resulted in one of them offering him an annual payment (in everyday usage, rents the land from the landowner) not of €100 but of €1,000, the landowner's *economic rent* from that

**economic rent** that part of the payment for a factor of production that exceeds the owner's reservation price

payment would be €900 per year. If the land had no other use as far as the landowner was concerned, and he would be willing to let it for a very small sum, virtually the entire payment received would be an economic rent.

If an economist working for a civil service department is paid €90,000 a year, and if the next best employment available to someone with that skill set and experience in economics was in a university department at a salary of €80,000, €10,000 of the civil servant's salary would be an economic rent.

In our landowner's example, if the supply price of land was €100 per hectare, and large quantities of land were on offer, we would expect rents (in the everyday sense) to be competed down to €100: there would be no *economic* rent earned by landowners. Similarly, in our economist's example, if it were easy for academic economists to leave universities and seek employment in the civil service, we would expect to see the economic rent element in civil service economists' earnings disappear, unless there existed non-pecuniary benefits for academic economists (which has been traditionally the case in much of the English-speaking world).

Economic profit is like economic rent in that it, too, may be seen as the difference between what someone is paid (the business owner's total revenue) and the reservation price for remaining in business (the sum of all costs, explicit and implicit). But whereas competition pushes economic profit toward zero (by increasing supply and driving down price), it has no such effect on the economic rent for inputs if they cannot be replicated easily. For example, although the lease payments for land may remain substantially above the land owner's reservation price, year in and year out, new land cannot come on to the market to reduce or eliminate the economic rent through competition. There is, after all, only so much land to be had.

As Example 8.4 illustrates, economic rent can accrue to people as well as land.

### **Example 8.4** How much economic rent will a talented chef get?

France prides itself on the quality of its restaurants. There are thousands of them. Most are ordinary and unassuming (even if they might appear to be much better than run-of-the-mill eating establishments in less fortunate countries). And there is a small number of really outstandingly good restaurants, epitomised, perhaps, by *La Tour d'Argent* in Paris. The key to a restaurant's standing is the skill of the chef. In ordinary restaurants a chef might expect to be paid between €25,000 and €50,000 a year depending on experience and some modest differences in skills. But in establishments like *La Tour d'Argent*, the master chef could expect a significant multiple of that level of earnings.

Why? Because France takes gastronomy very seriously. Indeed, in early 2003 Bernard Loiseau, the chef–owner of one of the country's most famous hostelries, *La Côte d'Or* in Saulieu in Burgundy, shook France to its core when he committed suicide after the restaurant was downgraded from 19 to 17 on a 20-point scale by a rating body.

Because French (and other) diners are prepared to pay through the nose to consume the creations of the most talented chefs in France, the restaurants that employ them can charge enormous prices. Consequently, restaurants compete fiercely for talented chefs, and their earnings reflect this competition for the small number of extraordinary *artistes de cuisine*. The bulk of chefs will be paid something like their supply price: what they could earn outside the industry. Their earnings contain little or no economic rent. Master chefs, on the other hand, earning sums of up to €200,000 and more, have the same supply price ... and most of their earnings are rent, being derived from the fact they are few in number and supply cannot expand to meet demand.

Since the talented chef's opportunities outside the restaurant industry are no better than an ordinary chef's, why is it necessary to pay the talented chef so much? Suppose the employer were to pay him only €80,000, which they both would consider a generous salary, since it is twice what ordinary chefs earn. The employer would then earn a significant economic profit since his annual revenue would be an order of magnitude higher than that of ordinary restaurants, but his costs would be only €30,000 to €40,000 more.

But this economic profit would create an opportunity for the owner of some other restaurant to bid the talented chef away. For example, if the owner of a competing restaurant were to hire the talented chef at a salary of €90,000, the chef would be €10,000 per year better off, and the rival owner would earn an economic profit. Furthermore, if the talented chef is the sole reason that a restaurant earns a positive economic profit, the bidding for that chef should continue as long as any economic profit remains. This bidding process assumes, of course, that the reason for the chef's superior performance is that he or she concerned possesses some personal culinary skills that cannot be replicated or copied. If instead it were the result of, say, training at a culinary institute in France, then his privileged position would be eroded over time, as other chefs sought similar training.

### RECAP Economic rent versus economic profit

Economic rent is the amount by which the payment to a factor of production exceeds the supplier's reservation price. Unlike economic profit, which is driven toward zero by competition, economic rent may persist for extended periods, especially in the case of factors with special talents that cannot easily be duplicated.

## The 'invisible hand' in action

To help develop your intuition about how the invisible hand works, we will examine how it can help us gain insight into the patterns we observe in a wide variety of different contexts. In each case, the key idea we want you to focus on is that opportunities for private gain seldom remain unexploited for very long. Perhaps more than any other, this idea encapsulates the essence of that distinctive mind-set known as 'thinking like an economist'.

### The 'invisible hand' at the supermarket and on the motorway

As Economic naturalist 8.1 illustrates, the No-Cash-on-the-Table Principle refers not just to opportunities to earn economic profits in cash, but also to any other opportunity to achieve a more desirable outcome.

### Economic naturalist 8.1 Why do supermarket checkout queues all tend to be roughly the same length?

Pay careful attention the next few times you go grocery shopping, and you will notice that the queues at all the checkout points tend to be roughly the same length. Suppose you saw one queue that was significantly shorter than the others as you wheeled your cart toward the checkout area. Which queue would you choose? The shorter one, of course; and because most shoppers would do the same, the short queue seldom remains shorter for long.

**Exercise 8.2** Use the No-Cash-on-the-Table Principle (Chapter 3) to explain why all lanes on a crowded, multi-lane motorway move at about the same speed.

### The 'invisible hand' and cost-saving innovations

When economists speak of perfectly competitive firms, they have in mind businesses whose contribution to total market output is too small to have a perceptible impact on market price. As explained in Chapter 6, such firms are often called *price takers*: they take the market price of their product as given and then produce that quantity of output for which marginal cost equals that price.

This characterisation of the competitive firm gives the impression that the firm is essentially a passive actor in the marketplace. Yet, for most firms, that is anything but the case. As Example 8.5 illustrates, even those firms that cannot hope to influence the market prices of their products have very powerful incentives to develop and introduce cost-saving innovations.

### **Example 8.5** How do cost-saving innovations affect economic profit in the short run? In the long run? And what have markets and incentives to do with this?

Consider the following scenario involving the dissemination of technology. Suppose 40 merchant marine companies operate supertankers that carry oil from the Middle East to Western Europe. The market is close to perfectly competitive. The cost per trip, including a normal profit, is €500,000. An engineer at one of these companies develops a more efficient propeller design that results in fuel savings of €20,000 per trip. How will this innovation affect the company's accounting and economic profits? Will these changes persist in the long run?

In the short run, the reduction in a single firm's costs will have no impact on the market price of transoceanic shipping services. The firm with the more efficient propeller will thus earn an economic profit of €20,000 per trip (since its total revenue will be the same as before, while its total cost will now be €20,000 per trip lower). As other firms learn about the new design, however, they will begin to adopt it, causing their individual supply curves to shift downward (since the marginal cost per trip at these firms will drop by €20,000). The shift in these individual supply curves will cause the market supply curve to shift, which in turn will result in a lower market price for shipping and a decline in economic profit at the firm where the innovation originated. When all firms have adopted the new, efficient design, the long-run supply curve for the industry will have shifted downward by €20,000 per trip, and each company will again be earning only a normal profit. At that point, any firm that did *not* adopt the new propeller design would suffer an economic loss of €20,000 per trip.

The importance of inter-firm competition and the profit motive is central to all this. In a paper in an academic economics journal[1] Maurizio Iacopetta of Georgia Institute of Technology in the United States has argued that the failure to disseminate technology in the former Soviet Union (USSR) was a major factor in explaining the failure of the Soviet economy in the long Cold War productivity competition with the West. Despite major achievements in the Soviet Union, in terms of advancing production technologies through research and development (R&D), the USSR's manufacturing capacity fell steadily behind that of the Organisation for Economic Co-operation and Development (OECD) in terms of productivity and product quality. The reason for this was argued to be the fact that in the planned economy of the Soviet Union, managers of firms did not face the same incentives as in the West, and responded less promptly to the possibilities of new technologies than their Western counterparts. Soviet managers were paid for meeting output targets, not for reducing costs or improving quality. This gave an incentive to managers to give changes in products or in production methods a low priority compared with meeting the targets that the planner imposed upon firms. They stuck with what they had.

The incentive to come up with cost-saving innovations in order to reap economic profit is one of the most powerful forces on the economic landscape. Its beauty, in terms of the invisible hand theory, is that competition among firms ensures that the resulting cost savings will be passed along to consumers in the long run.

---

[1] Iacopetta (2004).

## The 'invisible hand' in regulated markets

The carrot of economic profit and the stick of economic loss guide resource movements in regulated markets no less than in unregulated ones. Consider the taxi industry, which many cities regulate by licensing taxi-cabs, and restricting their numbers. These licences are often referred to as 'plates' or 'medallions', because they are issued in the form of a metal disc that must be fixed to the cab, where enforcement officials can easily see it. Cities that regulate cabs in this fashion typically issue fewer medallions than the equilibrium number of taxi-cabs in similar markets that are not regulated. Officials then allow the medallions to be bought and sold in the marketplace. As Economic naturalist 8.2 demonstrates, the issuance of taxi medallions alters the equilibrium quantity of taxi-cabs but does not change the fundamental rule that resources flow in response to profit and loss signals.

### Economic naturalist 8.2 A tale of two cities: regulation and taxi plates in New York and Dublin

Until the early 2000s, New York and Dublin had something more than a rash of Irish pubs in common. They both regulated the number of taxis that could operate on their streets. There was in Dublin, and still is in New York, plenty of evidence of excess demand in the form of people trying to get a taxi and not being able to find one. To add to the problem, in both cities prices (fares) were also regulated, and could not adjust to clear the market, or give an incentive to the taxis to respond by working longer hours. Despite this, we know that the restriction on the number of taxis resulted in higher incomes for taxi drivers. Why? Because the taxi plates/medallions were traded at substantial prices. Put another way, people were willing to pay significant amounts of money for permission to work as taxi drivers. In Dublin in 2001, taxi plates/medallions were worth about IRL£90,000 (€112,000). In New York they were traded for more than $200,000 (€200,000).

The fact that the plates/medallions commanded these prices meant that taxi drivers were earning more than their opportunity cost: the earnings they could make elsewhere. In fact the medallion price is the market capitalisation of the average excess of taxi drivers' annual earnings over their supply price, a form of monopoly profit, a *scarcity rent*. Buying a plate/medallion was an investment decision. If you had funds earning, say 8 per cent, or could borrow at 8 per cent, and a plate yielded €20,000 a year over and above what you could otherwise earn, it would be worth buying at anything up to €250,000 (the sum that would earn you €20,000 at 8 per cent) and, with competition to buy medallions, that is what they would trade for.

At these prices, new drivers do not earn supernormal profits. Why? Because they have had to hand over to previous drivers the capitalisation of those profits.

The plates/medallions represent an asset to the holder, with a market value as long as excess demand persists. And it is here that the two cities diverge. In 2002 the Irish government liberalised the taxi regime under pressure from huge public discontent. At that time there were about 2,000 taxis in Dublin. From then on, anyone who wanted to drive a taxi, had a suitable car and had passed certain personal characteristic tests (convictions for certain crimes against the person disqualified you for obvious reasons) could do so on paying an annual licence fee to the city. In 2004 Dublin had 10,000 taxis and, with the exception of some irreducible peak-time problems, taxis could be had on demand. In New York, no such change took place, and people still grumble. In Dublin, the only grumbling is from those who had (unwisely) bought plates/medallions in the run-up to 2001.The market value of a plate fell from

€115,000 to zero. And the drivers had to work longer hours (offer more capacity) to earn any target income. It will not come as a surprise to learn that the drivers' association is using its considerable party political influence with the Irish government to have the 2001 decision reversed, or at least seriously amended.

**Exercise 8.3** What would happen to the price of a taxi plate if the interest rate was 4 per cent in Economic naturalist 8.2, rather than 8 per cent?

Another regulated market in which the invisible hand was very much in evidence was the regulated commercial airline industry. In the Unites States, until late 1978, airlines were heavily regulated by the Civil Aeronautics Board (CAB), an agency of the federal government. In Europe it took strong pressure from the European Union from the early 1990s onwards to force national governments to liberalise the market, and the process is still not fully finished.

In the United States, carriers could not provide air service between two cities unless they were given explicit permission to do so. The CAB also prescribed the fares that carriers could charge. In Europe, national regulations not only determined who could fly on what route, and at what fares, but even how many flights they could put on a route. One of the declared objects of these regulatory regimes was to ensure an 'adequate' service on less popular routes. The standard practice was to set fares well above the cost of providing a service on most routes, and then require carriers to use some of the resulting economic profit to pay for service on sparsely travelled routes. But as Economic naturalist 8.3 illustrates, the regulators failed to reckon with the invisible hand if they thought that high prices on some routes would produce profits to subsidise passengers on other routes.

## Economic naturalist 8.3 Why did some US airlines install piano bars on the upper decks of Boeing 747s in the 1970s? Why has deregulation and increased competition resulted in customers paying for food and drink on many airline operators' routes in Europe, while food is not paid for on the Atlantic routes?

The answer to these questions lies in thinking about why food and drink were supplied free of charge under the less competitive regulated regime. The old regime enabled planes to fly profitably with many empty seats. But if they could fill those seats, it would be even better. They could not compete on price (fixed by regulators) and had only limited freedom to compete on frequency. So they sought to compete on 'quality'. In the United States, at one stage this led to the installation of piano bars on the upper decks of Boeing 747s. In Europe, with shorter haul flights predominant, quality meant hiring more (and more attractive) cabin crew and offering trimmings such as food and drink. These were on offer whether or not people wanted them, and were consumed in quantities reflecting a zero price at point of sale. Their costs ate into the profitability of the airlines and so were 'bundled' into the airlines' fare structures.

Competition under deregulation made paying for food and drink in Europe inevitable. Why? If an airline charged a price that covered expected costs of 'free' food and drink it would always be possible for a competitor to offer a lower fare structure that excluded food and drink while selling the latter separately to those who were willing to pay the cost of provision. By 'unbundling' the price of the seat from the price of the food the airlines could increase economic surplus.

So why is food still supplied free on competitive long-haul routes? The answer is that the airlines believe that virtually everyone would want to buy a meal on a six-hour or longer flight. Hence, a 'bundled' price does not oblige people to pay for something they don't want to consume to any significant extent. That limits the potential for competing by 'unbundling'. Add to that the cost of extracting payment and it is easy to see why 'bundling' is a cost-effective competitive strategy.

As it happened, American regulation did not apply to intra-state services in states such as California. Unregulated carriers in California provided a service on the San Francisco to San Diego route for about half the fare charged by regulated carriers on the Washington to Boston route of the same distance. Though the California carriers were free to offer more frequent service and more elaborate in-flight amenities, passengers voted with their dollars to sacrifice those amenities for lower airfares. California was the birthplace of the no-frills airline, which has spread to Europe with deregulation here.

Ryanair, easyJet and others took advantage of deregulation to offer low or no-frills services on a point-to-point basis (i.e. without interconnection and baggage check-through), and did so successfully. It is clear from the problems of the 'full-service' airlines in their operations within Europe that the regulated regime involved serious economic welfare losses (efficiency losses). The original idea behind regulation was to create profits to finance 'social' (i.e. low-density) routes. It is now clear that, for the most part, low fares make low-density routes viable where regulation failed to do so. Regulation in this case was a waste of time from the start ... as economists preached continuously while governments did not listen.

**Exercise 8.4** From what was discussed in Economic naturalist 8.3, can you offer an explanation for the fact that it is now almost universal practice that airlines on the North Atlantic charge standard-fare passengers for alcoholic drinks but not for soft drinks?

## The 'invisible hand' in anti-poverty programmes

As Example 8.6 shows, failure to understand the logic of the invisible hand can lead not only to inefficient government regulation, but also to anti-poverty programmes that are doomed to fail.

### Example 8.6 How will an irrigation project affect the incomes of poor farmers?

The World Bank and other development agencies are always under pressure to increase the flows of funds to projects that are designed to increase the incomes of low-productivity agricultural producers in some of the world's poorest countries. The funds flow, all right, but the outcome in terms of the incomes of those working the land frequently turns out to be disappointing. Accusations are then made that either the World Bank is not directing the money to the correct targets, or that the money is being siphoned of by corrupt officials in the recipient countries. No doubt either or both of these may be correct in some cases. However, as the following example is designed to illustrate, part (most?) of the answer may lie in a failure to understand the workings of the invisible hand.

Consider a small and unnamed country somewhere in southern Asia. It has a large population of tenant farmers growing rice, a staple of the local diet. Recently, Western investment has resulted in the establishment of a textile industry turning out t-shirts (factories that have replaced similar establishments in Ireland or France). Suppose unskilled workers must choose between working in a textile factory, earning €4,000 per year and growing rice on a rented parcel of farmland. One worker can farm 80 ha of rise paddy, which rents for €2,500 a year. Such holdings yield a crop that earns €8,000 per year in revenue, and the total non-labour costs of bringing the crop to market are €1,500 per year. The net incomes of rice farmers are thus €4,000 per year – the same as those of textile workers.

The landowners, few in number, receive the rental income from the land, which greatly exceeds the income per head of the peasant farmers who grow the rice. This inequitable distribution of income leads to calls for actions to support the incomes of the large numbers of poor farmers who are handing over a lot of money to the few and very rich landlords. As a result of pressure from Oxfam and other organisations, the World Bank announces that it will fund an irrigation project that would double the output of rice on farms operated by tenant farmers. Rice, of course, is an internationally traded good, so the level of output in this Third World country has no discernible effect on the world (and, therefore, domestic) price of rice. How will the project affect the absolute and relative incomes of tenant farmers in the long run?

Suppose that the irrigation project succeeds in doubling rice yields, which means that each farmer will sell €16,000 worth of rice per year rather than €8,000. If nothing else changed, farmers' incomes would rise from €4,000 per year to €12,000 per year. But the no-cash-on-the-table principle tells us that farmers cannot sustain this income level. Think about the impact on the new textile sector. The firms face a given price for the output of the factories. But to textile workers, there is cash on the table in farming. Seeing an opportunity to triple their incomes, many will want to switch to farming. But since the supply of land is fixed, farm rents will rise as textile workers begin bidding for them. They will continue to rise as long as farmers can earn more than textile workers. The long-run effect of the project, then, will be to raise the rent on rice farms, from €2,500 per year to €10,500 (since at the higher rent the incomes of rice farmers and textile workers will again be the same). Thus the irrigation project will increase the wealth of landowners but will have no long-run effect on the incomes of tenant farmers.

**Exercise 8.5**

Suppose the government imposes a rent freeze, so that existing farmers do not have to pay more to landlords, and cannot be evicted for not doing so. Can you explain why, after a few years, the World Bank is likely to find the rice still being grown by peasants earning a net €4,000 a year (assuming that nothing else has changed)?

## The 'invisible hand' in the stock market

The world's great stock markets (London, Frankfurt, New York and Tokyo are the most important), in which dealers trade in shares (stock) and bonds (fixed interest securities, debt of governments and firms) are among the most competitive markets in the world. Unfortunately, as we shall see, public understanding of how the invisible hand works in these markets is often no better than the state legislator's understanding of how the rice market works.

### Calculating the value of a share of stock

A share of stock in a company is a claim to a share of the current and future accounting profits of that company. Thus, if you own 1 per cent of the total number of shares of a company's stock, you effectively own 1 per cent of the company's annual accounting profit, both now and in the future. (We say 'effectively' because companies generally do not distribute their accounting profit to shareholders each year; many reinvest their earnings in the company's operations. Such reinvestment benefits the stockholder by enlarging the company and increasing its future accounting profit.) The price of a share of stock depends not only on a company's accounting profit, however, but also on the market rate of interest, as Example 8.7 illustrates.

### Example 8.7 How much will a share of stock sell for?

Suppose we know with certainty that a company's accounting profit will be €1 million this year and every year. If the company has issued a total of 200,000 shares of stock, and the annual interest rate is 5 per cent, at what price will each share sell?

Because there are 200,000 shares of stock, each share entitles its owner to1/200,000 of the company's annual accounting profit, or €5 per year. Owning this stock is like having a bank deposit that earns €5 per year in interest. To calculate the economic value of the stock, therefore, we need only ask how much an investor would need to deposit in the bank at 5 per cent interest to generate an annual interest payment of €5. The answer is €100, and that is the price that each share will command in the stock market.

### Calculating the present value of future costs and benefits

Someone who is trying to estimate how much a business is worth must take account of the fact that earnings received in the future are less valuable than earnings received today. Consider a company whose only accounting profit, €14,400, will occur exactly two years from now. At all other times its accounting profit will be exactly zero. How much is ownership of this company worth?

To answer this question, we need to employ the concept of the **time value of money** – the fact that money deposited in an interest-bearing account today will *grow in value over time.*

Our goal is to compute what economists call the **present value** (*PV*) of a €14,400 payment to be received in two years. We can think of this present value as the amount that would have to be deposited in an interest-bearing bank account today to generate a balance of €14,400 two years from today. Let *PV* denote present value and $r$ the market rate of interest, measured as a fraction. (For example, an annual interest rate of 10 per cent would correspond to $r = 0.10$.) If we put €100 in an account today at 10 per cent annual interest, we will have €100(1.10) = €110 in the account after one year. If we leave €100 in the same account for two years, we will have €100(1.10)(1.10) = €100$(1.10)^2$ = €121.

**time value of money** the fact that a given euro amount today is equivalent to a larger euro amount in the future, because the money can be invested in an interest-bearing account in the meantime. After *T* years: $PV – M/(1 – r)T$

**present value** for an annual interest rate $r$, the present value (*PV*) of a payment (*M*) to be received *T* years from now is the amount that would have to be deposited today at interest rate $r$ to generate a balance of *M*

More generally, if we put *PV* in the bank today at the interest rate $r$, we will have $PV(1 + r)$ one year from now and $PV(1 + r)^2$ two years from now. So to find the present value of a €14,400 payment to be received two years from now we simply solve the equation €14,400 = $PV(1 + r)^2$ and get $PV$ = €14,400/$(1 + r)^2$. If the interest rate is 20 per cent, then $PV$ = €14,400/$(1.2)^2$ = €10,000. To verify this answer, note that €10,000 deposited at 20 per cent interest today would grow to €10,000(1 + 0.2) = €12,000 by the end of one year, and that amount left on deposit for a second year would grow to €12,000(1 + 0.2) = €14,400.

More generally, when the interest rate is $r$, the present value of a payment $M$ to be received $T$ years from now is given by the equation

$$PV = M/(1 + r)^T$$

**Exercise 8.6** What is the present value of a payment of €1,728 to be received three years from now if the annual interest rate is 20 per cent?

## The efficient markets hypothesis

In practice, of course, no one knows with any certainty what a company's future profits will be. So the current price of a share will depend not on the actual amount of future profits, but on investors' estimates of them. These estimates incorporate information about current profits, prospects for the company's industry, the state of the economy, demographic trends and a host of other factors. As this information changes, investors' estimates of future profits change with it, along with the prices of a share of stock.

How fast does new information affect the price of a stock? With blazing speed, according to the **efficient markets hypothesis**. This hypothesis states that the current price of any company's shares incorporates all available information relevant to the company's earnings. The plausibility of this theory is evident if we think for a moment about what might happen if it were false. Suppose, for example, that at 9.00 a.m. on Monday, 14 October, some investors acquire new information to the effect that the company in Example 8.7 will realise accounting profits not of €1 million per year, but of €2 million. This information implies that the new equilibrium price for each share of its stock should be €200. Now suppose that the price were to remain at its current level (€100) for 24 hours before rising gradually to €200 over the next two weeks. If so, an investor privy to this information could double her wealth in two weeks without working hard, taking any risk, or even being lucky. All she would have to do is invest all her wealth in the stock at today's price of €100 per share.

**efficient markets hypothesis** the theory that the current price of stock in a company reflects all the relevant information about its current and future earnings prospects

We may safely assume that there is no shortage of investors who would be delighted to double their wealth without having to work hard or take risks. But in the case just described, they would have to buy shares of the stock within 24 hours of learning of the new profit projections. As eager investors rushed to buy the stock, its price would rise quickly, so that those who waited until the end of the day to buy would miss much of the opportunity for gain. To get the full advantage of the new information, they would have to make their purchases earlier in the day. As more and more investors rushed to buy shares, the window of opportunity would grow narrower and narrower. In the end, the duration of the opportunity to profit from the new information may be just a few minutes long.

In practice, of course, new information often takes time to interpret, and different investors may have different beliefs about exactly what it means. Early information may signal an impending change that is far from certain. As time passes, events may confirm or contradict the implications of the earlier information. The usual pattern is for information to emerge in bits and pieces, and for stock prices to adjust in small increments as each new bit of information emerges. But this does not mean that the price of a stock adjusts gradually to new information. Rather, it means that new information usually emerges gradually. And as each piece of new information emerges, the market reacts almost instantly.

For example, in the United States in July 1996 a Florida jury awarded a lung cancer patient $750,000 in damages. The price of tobacco stocks plummeted roughly 20 per cent *within minutes*. The award broke a long series of legal precedents in which tobacco companies had not been held liable for the illnesses suffered by smokers. When the verdict was announced, no one knew whether it would be reversed on appeal or whether it would influence future verdicts in such cases. Yet investors who had been monitoring the case carefully knew instantly that massive new financial liabilities had become much more likely.

Despite such persuasive evidence in favour of the efficient markets hypothesis, many investors seem to believe that information about the next sure investment bonanza is as close as their stockbroker's latest newsletter. In most financial centres a large population of salespeople make a living telephoning potential investors to offer the latest tips on how to invest their money. The weekend quality newspapers across Europe have pages devoted to share analysis and advice on whether to buy, hold or sell various shares. The difficulty is that, according to the efficient markets hypothesis, by the time information reaches investors in this way, days, weeks or even months will have gone by, and the information will have already been incorporated into any stock prices for which it might have been relevant. By the time you've read about a share worth buying in the newspaper the reason for buying it will be history.

The *Wall Street Journal* publishes a feature in which a group of leading investment advisers predict which stocks will increase most in price during the coming months. The *Journal* then compares the forecasts with the performance of a randomly selected set of stocks. The usual finding is that the randomly selected portfolios perform little differently from those chosen by the 'experts'. Some of the experts do better than average, others worse. This pattern is consistent with the economist's theory that the invisible hand moves with unusual speed to eliminate profit opportunities in financial markets.

## Economic naturalist 8.4 Why isn't a stock portfolio consisting of America's, or Britain's, or Germany's 'best-managed companies' a good investment?

Each year *Fortune* magazine asks executives at America's largest companies to list those US firms, excluding their own, that are managed most efficiently. Imagine that you see the results of this survey and immediately purchase 100 shares of stock in each of the top 10 companies on the list. How well might you expect those stocks to perform relative to a randomly selected portfolio?

A stock is said to 'perform well' if its price rises more rapidly than the prices of other stocks. Changes in the price of a company's stock depend not on investors' current beliefs about the company's accounting profit, but on *changes in those beliefs*. Suppose, for the sake of argument, that the 'best-managed' companies had higher accounting profits than other companies at the time of the *Fortune* survey. Because the prices you paid for their stocks would have reflected those higher earnings, there would be no reason to expect their prices to rise more rapidly than those of other stocks.

But won't the accounting profits of a well-managed company be likely to grow more rapidly than those of other companies? Perhaps; but even if so, beliefs to that effect would also be reflected in current stock prices. Indeed, the stocks of many software, biotechnology and Internet commerce companies sell at high prices years before they ever post their first euro of accounting profit.

An understanding of the invisible hand theory might even lead us to question whether a 'well-managed' company will have higher accounting profit than other companies. After all, if an unusually competent manager were known to be the reason a company consistently posted a positive economic profit, other companies could be expected to bid for her services, causing her salary to rise. And the market for her services will not reach equilibrium until her salary has captured all the gains for which her talent is responsible.

We must stress that our point in Economic naturalist 8.4 is *not* that good management does not matter. Good management is obviously better than bad management, for it increases total economic surplus. The point is that the reward for good performance tends to be captured by those who provide that performance. And that is a good thing, in so far as it provides powerful incentives for everyone to perform well.

## Economic naturalist 8.5 What happens when good management departs?

In late November 2004, the *Wall Street Journal* and the *Financial Times*, as well as a large number of European daily newspapers, carried the story that the three top executives in Aer Lingus, the Irish state-owned airline that had been tipped for privatisation, had tendered their resignations, to take effect in 2005. The apparent reason was an unwillingness on the part of the Irish government to proceed with the privatisation along the lines favoured by the management team. The team had turned the airline from a loss-making full-service airline into a highly profitable low-cost airline over three years, and the estimated stock market value of the company was about €600 million. By general consent, the effect of the departure of what was seen as one of Europe's most successful aviation management teams was to wipe €200 million (about one-third) off the sale value of the company. The irony is that the government's reluctance to proceed to privatise along the lines being suggested by the management was that it involved a management buy-out. For some reason, the government was not prepared to countenance the concept of a buy-out because it would have meant that the management would have bought the company and made money. For what other reason they would have contemplated buying it is not clear. The government's reluctance to see them making money cost the Irish tax-payer about €200 million. That is the capitalisation of the annual amount that the market reckoned that the team could have earned from managing the company ... and which they would have had to pay to buy it. If they had bought it, and then sold on shares to the public, the return on the investment by new shareholders would be expected to be the same as if the company was sold without the exiting management for €400 million.

By way of footnote, in March 2005, British Airways announced that it was appointing a new CEO to take up full duties later in the year. His name: Willie Walsh; his previous job: the outgoing CEO of Aer Lingus.

## RECAP The 'invisible hand' in action

Because individuals and firms are generally eager to improve their position, opportunities for gain seldom remain unexploited for long. Early adopters of *cost-saving innovations* enjoy temporary economic profits. But as additional firms adopt the innovations, the resulting downward supply shift causes price to fall. In the long run, economic profit returns to zero, and all cost savings are passed on to consumers.

The quest for advantage guides resources not only in perfectly competitive markets, but also in heavily regulated markets. Firms can almost always find ways to expand sales in markets in which the regulated price permits an economic profit or withdraw service from markets in which the regulated price results in an economic loss. An understanding of the invisible hand theory is also important for the design of anti-poverty programmes. An irrigation programme that makes land more productive, for example, will raise the incomes of tenant farmers only temporarily. In the long run, the gains from such projects tend to be captured as higher rents to landowners. The efficient markets hypothesis says that the price of a firm's stock at any moment reflects all available information that is relevant for predicting the firm's future earnings. This hypothesis identifies several common beliefs as false – among them that stocks in well-managed companies perform better than stocks in poorly managed ones and that ordinary investors can make large financial gains by trading stocks on the basis of information reported in the news media.

## The distinction between an equilibrium and a social optimum

The Equilibrium, or No-Cash-on-the-Table, Principle (Chapter 3) tells us that when a market reaches equilibrium, no further opportunities for gain are available to individuals. This principle implies that the market prices of resources that people own will eventually reflect their *economic value*. (As we shall see in later chapters, the same cannot be said of resources that are not owned by anyone, such as fish in international waters.)

The No-Cash-on-the-Table Principle is sometimes misunderstood to mean that there are *never* any valuable opportunities to exploit. For example, the story is told of two American economists on their way to lunch when they spot what appears to be a $100 bill lying on the pavement. When the younger economist stoops to pick up the bill, his older colleague restrains him, saying: 'That can't be a genuine $100 dollar bill.' 'Why not?' asks the younger colleague. 'If it were, someone would have picked it up by now,' the older economist replies.

The No-Cash-on-the-Table Principle means not that there *never* are any unexploited opportunities, but that there are none when the market is *in equilibrium*. Occasionally a $100 bill does lie on the pavement, and the person who first spots it and picks it up gains a windfall. Likewise, when a company's earnings prospects improve, *somebody* must be the first to recognise the opportunity, and that person can make a lot of money by purchasing the stock quickly.

Still, the No-Cash-on-the-Table Principle is important. It tells us, in effect, that there are only three ways to earn a big payoff: to work especially hard; to have some unusual skill, talent or training; or simply to be lucky. The person who finds a big banknote on the pavement is lucky, as are many of the investors whose stocks perform better than average. Other investors whose stocks do well achieve their gains through hard work or special talent. For example, the legendary investor Warren Buffett, whose portfolio has grown in value at almost three times the stock market average for the past 40 years, spends long hours studying annual financial reports and has a remarkably keen eye for the telling detail. Thousands of others work just as hard yet fail to beat the market averages.

It is important to stress, however, that a market being in equilibrium implies only that no additional opportunities are available *to individuals*. It does not imply that the resulting allocation is necessarily best from the point of view of society as a whole.

### Smart for one, dumb for all

Adam Smith's profound insight was that the individual pursuit of self-interest often promotes the broader interests of society. But unlike some of his modern disciples, Smith was under no illusion that this is *always* the case. Note, for example, Smith's elaboration on his description of the entrepreneur led by the invisible hand 'to promote an end which was no part of his intention':

> Nor is it *always* the worse for society that it was no part of it. By pursuing his own interest he *frequently* promotes that of society more effectively than when he really intends to promote it'. (Smith, 1776, book 4, ch. 2)

As Smith was well aware, the individual pursuit of self-interest often does not coincide with society's interest. In Chapter 3 we cited activities that generate environmental pollution as an example of conflicting economic interests, noting that behaviour in those circumstances may be described as 'smart for one, dumb for all'. As Economic naturalist 8.6 suggests, extremely high levels of investment in earnings forecasts can also be 'smart for one, dumb for all'.

## Economic naturalist 8.6 Are there 'too many' smart people working as corporate earnings forecasters?

Stock analysts use complex mathematical models to forecast corporate earnings. The more analysts invest in the development of these models, the more accurate the models become. Thus the analyst whose model produces a reliable forecast sooner than others can reap a windfall by buying stocks whose prices are about to rise. Given the speed with which stock prices respond to new information, however, the results of even the second-fastest forecasting model may come too late to be of much use. Individual stock analysts thus face a powerful incentive to invest more and more money in their models, in the hope of generating the fastest forecast. Does this incentive result in the socially optimal level of investment in forecast models?

Beyond some point, increased speed of forecasting is of little benefit to society as a whole, whose interests suffer little when the price of a stock moves to its proper level a few hours more slowly. If *all* stock analysts spent less money on their forecasting models, *someone's* model would still produce the winning forecast, and the resources that might otherwise be devoted to fine-tuning the models could be put to more valued uses. Yet if any one individual spends less, he can be sure the winning forecast will not be his.

The 'invisible hand' went awry in the situation just described because the benefit of an investment to the individual who made it was larger than the benefit of that investment to society as a whole. In later chapters we shall discuss a broad class of investments with this property. In general, the efficacy of the invisible hand depends on the extent to which the individual costs and benefits of actions taken in the marketplace coincide with the respective costs and benefits of those actions to society. These exceptions notwithstanding, some of the most powerful forces at work in competitive markets clearly promote society's interests.

## RECAP Equilibrium versus social optimum

A market in *equilibrium* is one in which no additional opportunities for gain remain available to individual buyers or sellers. The No-Cash-on-the Table Principle describes powerful forces that help push markets toward equilibrium. But even if all markets are in equilibrium, the resulting allocation of resources need not be socially optimal. Equilibrium will not be socially optimal when the costs or benefits to individual participants in the market differ from those experienced by society as a whole.

## Summary

- *Accounting* profit is the difference between a firm's revenue and its explicit expenses. *Economic* profit, which is the difference between revenue and the sum of the firm's explicit and implicit costs. *Normal* profit is the opportunity cost of the resources supplied to a business by its owners.
- The quest for economic profit is the 'invisible hand' that drives resource allocation in market economies. Markets in which businesses earn an economic profit tend to attract additional resources, whereas markets in which businesses experience an economic loss tend to lose resources. If new firms enter a market with economic profits, output rises, causing a reduction in the price of the product. Free entry means that prices will continue to fall until economic profits are eliminated. By contrast, the departure of firms from markets with economic losses causes output to contract, increasing the price of the product. Free exit will mean that prices will continue to rise until economic losses are eliminated. In the long run, market forces drive economic profits and losses toward zero.
- As long as firms' cost curves and market demand curves reflect the full underlying costs and benefits to society of the production of a good or service, the quest for economic profit ensures (a) that existing supplies are allocated efficiently among individual buyers, and (b) that resources are allocated across markets in the most efficient way possible. In any allocation other than the one generated by the market, resources could be rearranged to benefit some people without harming others.
- *Economic rent* is the portion of the payment for an input that exceeds the reservation price for that input. If a professional football player who is willing to play for as little as €100,000 per year is paid €15 million, he earns an economic rent of €14,900,000 per year. Whereas the invisible hand drives economic profit toward zero over the long run, economic rent can persist indefinitely, because replicating the services of players like Rio Ferdinand is impossible. Talented individuals who are responsible for the superior performance of a business will tend to capture the resulting financial gains as economic rents.
- Applying the concept of Adam Smith's invisible hand helps explain why regulation of markets can have unintended and wasteful consequences. For instance, when regulation prevents firms from lowering prices to capture business from rivals, firms generally find other ways in which to compete. Thus, if airline regulators set passenger fares above cost, air carriers will try to capture additional business by offering extra amenities and more frequent service. Likewise, many anti-poverty programmes have been compromised by failure to consider how incentives change people's behaviour.
- A share of stock in a company is a claim to a share of the current and future accounting profits of that company. The price of a share of stock depends not only on its accounting profits, but also on the market rate of interest, since the interest rate affects the present value of future costs and benefits. The total market value of the shares is the market estimate of the present value of the expected profits in the future. When the annual interest rate is $r$, the present value ($PV$) of a payment $M$ to be received (or paid) $T$ years from now is the amount that would have to be deposited in a bank account today at interest rate $r$ to generate a balance of $M$ after $T$ years: $PV = M/(1 + r)^T$.
- According to the efficient markets hypothesis, the market price of a stock incorporates all currently available information that is relevant to that company's future earnings. If this is not the case, people with superior information can consistently make profits in a more or less risk-free fashion.
- The No-Cash-on-the-Table Principle implies that if someone owns a valuable resource, full information and efficient markets mean that the market price of that resource will fully reflect its economic value. The implication of this principle is not that lucrative opportunities never exist, but rather that such opportunities cannot exist when markets are in equilibrium, and that prices will adjust to eliminate them.
- The benefit of an investment to an individual sometimes differs from its benefit to society as a whole. Such conflicting incentives may give rise to behaviour that is smart for one but dumb for all. Despite such exceptions, the invisible hand of the market works remarkably well much of the time. One of the market system's most important contributions to social well-being is the pressure it creates to adopt cost-saving innovations. Competition among firms ensures that the resulting cost savings get passed along to consumers in the long run.

## Key terms

**accounting profit** (209)
**allocative function of price** (212)
**barrier to entry** (219)
**economic loss** (211)
**economic profit** (209)
**economic rent** (220)
**efficient markets hypothesis** (229)
**explicit costs** (209)
**implicit costs** (209)
**'invisible hand' theory** (212)
**normal profit** (210)
**present value** (228)
**rationing function of price** (212)
**time value of money** (228)

## Review questions

1. Why do most cities now have more radios but fewer radio repair shops than they did in 1960?
2. How can a business owner who earns 10 million per year from his business credibly claim to earn zero economic profit?
3. Why do market forces drive economic profit but not economic rent toward zero?
4. Why did airlines that once were regulated by the government generally fail to earn an economic profit, even on routes with relatively high fares?
5. Why is a payment of 10,000 to be received one year from now more valuable than a payment of 10,000 to be received two years from now?

## Problems

1. Explain why the following statements are **true** or **false**:
   a. The economic maxim 'There's no cash on the table' means that there are never any unexploited economic opportunities.
   b. Firms in competitive environments make no accounting profit when the market is in long-run equilibrium.
   c. Firms that can introduce cost-saving innovations can make an economic profit in the short run.
2. Explain why new software firms that give away their software products at a short-run economic loss are nonetheless able to sell their stock at positive prices.
3. John Jones owns and manages a café whose annual revenue is €5,000. The annual expenses are as in the table below.

| Expense | € |
|---|---|
| Labour | 2,000 |
| Food and drink | 500 |
| Electricity | 100 |
| Vehicle lease | 150 |
| Rent | 500 |
| Interest on loan for equipment | 1,000 |

   a. Calculate John's annual accounting profit.
   b. John could earn €1,000 per year as a recycler of aluminium cans. However, he prefers to run the café. In fact, he would be willing to pay up to €275 per year to run the café rather than to recycle cans. Is the café making an economic profit? Should John stay in the business? Explain.

c. Suppose the café's revenues and expenses remain the same, but recyclers' earnings rise to €1,100 per year. Is the café still making an economic profit? Explain.

d. Suppose John had not had to get a €10,000 loan at an annual interest rate of 10 per cent to buy equipment, but instead had invested €10,000 of his own money in equipment. How would your answers to parts (a) and (b) change?

e. If John can earn €1,000 a year as a recycler, and he likes recycling just as well as running the café, how much additional revenue would the café have to collect each year to earn a normal profit?

4. A city has 200 advertising companies, 199 of which employ designers of normal ability at a salary of €100,000 a year. Paying this salary, each of the 199 firms makes a normal profit on €500,000 in revenue. However, the 200th company employs Janus Jacobs, an unusually talented designer. This company collects €1,000,000 in revenues because of Jacobs' talent.

a. How much will Jacobs earn? What proportion of his annual salary will be economic rent?

b. Why will the advertising company for which Jacobs works not be able to earn an economic profit?

5. Explain carefully why, in the absence of a patent, a technical innovation invented and pioneered in one tofu factory will cause the supply curve for the entire tofu industry to shift to the right. What will finally halt the rightward shift?

6. The government of the Republic of Self-Reliance has decided to limit imports of machine tools, to encourage development of locally made machine tools. To do so, the government offers to sell a small number of machine-tool import licences. To operate a machine-tool import business costs €30,000, excluding the cost of the import licence. An importer of machine tools can expect to earn €50,000 per year. If the annual interest rate is 10 per cent, for how much will the government be able to auction the import licences? Will the owner of a licence earn an economic profit?

7. Unskilled workers in a poor cotton-growing region must choose between working in a factory for €6,000 a year or being a tenant cotton farmer. One farmer can work a 120-hectare farm, which rents for €10,000 a year. Such farms yield €20,000 worth of cotton each year. The total non-labour cost of producing and marketing the cotton is €4,000 a year. A local politician whose motto is 'working people come first' has promised that, if he is elected, his administration will fund a fertiliser, irrigation and marketing scheme that will triple cotton yields on tenant farms at no charge to tenant farmers.

a. If the market price of cotton would be unaffected by this policy and no new jobs would be created in the cotton-growing industry, how would the project affect the incomes of tenant farmers in the short run? In the long run?

b. Who would reap the benefit of the scheme in the long run? How much would they gain each year?

8. You have a friend who is a potter. He holds a permanent patent on an indestructible teacup whose sale generates €30,000 a year more revenue than his production costs. If the annual interest rate is 20 per cent, what is the market value of his patent?

9. You have an opportunity to buy an apple orchard that produces €25,000 per year in total revenue. To run the orchard, you would have to give up your current job, which pays €10,000 per year. If you would find both jobs equally satisfying, and the annual interest rate is 10 per cent, what is the highest price you would be willing to pay for the orchard?

10. Louisa, a renowned chef, owns one of the 1,000 spaghetti restaurants in Sicily. Each restaurant serves 100 plates of spaghetti a night at €5 per plate. Louisa knows she can develop a new sauce at the same cost as the current sauce, which would be so tasty that all 100,000 spaghetti eaters would buy her spaghetti at €10 per plate. There are two problems: developing the new sauce would require some experimental cost; and the other spaghetti producers could figure out the recipe after one day.

a. What is the highest experimental cost Louisa would be willing to incur?

b. How would your answer change if Louisa could enforce a year-long patent on her new sauce? (Assume that the interest rate is zero.)

## Answers to in-chapter exercises

8.1 Accounting profit is now €10,000, the difference between €20,000 annual revenue and the €10,000 per year payment for land, equipment and supplies. His economic profit is that amount minus the opportunity cost of his labour – again, the €11,000 per year he could have earned as a store manager. The farmer is now earning a negative economic profit, – €1,000 per year. As before, his normal profit is the €11,000 per year opportunity cost of his labour. Although an accountant would say that the farmer is making an annual profit of €10,000, that amount is less than a normal profit for his activity. An economist would therefore say that he is making an economic loss of €1,000 per year. Since the farmer likes the two jobs equally well, he will be better off by €1,000 per year if he leaves farming to become a manager.

8.2 If each lane did not move at about the same pace, any driver in a slower lane could reduce his travel time by simply switching to a faster one. People will exploit these opportunities until each lane moves at about the same pace.

8.3 If the taxi plate/medallion were available for free, it would still command an economic profit of €20,000 per year. So its value is still the answer to the question: 'How much would you need to put in the bank to generate interest earnings of €20,000 per year?' When the interest rate is 4 per cent a year, the answer is €500,000, or twice what the medallion was worth at an interest rate of 8 per cent.

8.4 You might be tempted to say that it is something to do with encouraging lower alcohol consumption for a variety of reasons, and this may indeed have been part of the airlines' thinking. However, they could have achieved this just by rationing. So it is logical to assume something else is going on. In fact it can be explained in exactly the same way as the decision to charge for food on short-haul routes. A significant number of people do not want to drink alcohol while flying. To supply it to those who do want it (in whatever quantities) is costly. Hence, in a competitive market it makes sense to 'unbundle' alcohol consumption prices from ticket prices.

8.5 If the government imposed a rent freeze so that landlords could not extract the increased value of the land, one of two things would happen. In the first case, existing tenants would be able to sub-let their holdings to other workers for €4,000. Alternatively (and reminiscent of the taxi plate problem, they could sell the tenancy to others for the capitalisation of the difference between the return from working the land and the next-best earning (wages in the textile sector). Either way we would see those working the land making the same (net) as those in the textile sector.

8.6 $PV = €1{,}728/(1.2)^3 = €1{,}000$.

## References

Iacopetta, M. (2004) 'Dissemination of Technology in Planned and Market Economies', *Contributions to Macroeconomics*, 4(1).

Smith, A. (1776) *An Enquiry into the Nature and Causes of the Wealth of Nations.*

# Part 3
# Market Imperfections

We now move away from the world implicitly and to a lesser extent explicitly assumed by Adam Smith. In that world, exchange is frictionless, parties to exchanges are fully informed and no one has significant market power. This means investigating what happens when people and firms interact in markets plagued by a variety of imperfections. Not surprisingly, the invisible hand that served society so well in the perfectly competitive world often goes astray in this new environment.

Our focus in Chapter 9 will be on how markets served by only one or a small number of firms differ from those served by perfectly competitive firms. We shall see that although monopolies often escape the pressures that constrain the profits of their perfectly competitive counterparts, the two types of firm also have many important similarities.

In Chapter 10 we shall investigate how the allocation of resources is affected when activities generate costs or benefits that accrue to people not directly involved in those activities. We shall see that if parties cannot easily negotiate with one another, the self-serving actions of individuals usually will not lead to efficient outcomes.

In Chapters 1–10 economic decision makers confronted an environment that was essentially fixed. By that we mean that an individual could take the decisions and actions of others as given, and unaffected by his or her own decisions. In Chapter 11, however, we shall discuss cases in which people can expect their actions to alter the behaviour of others, as when a firm's decision to advertise or launch a new product induces a rival to follow suit. Interdependencies of this sort are the rule rather than the exception, and we shall explore how to take them into account using simple theories of games.

Although the invisible hand theory assumes that buyers and sellers are perfectly informed about all relevant options, this assumption is almost never satisfied in practice. In Chapter 12 we shall explore how basic economic principles can help imperfectly informed individuals and firms make the best use of the limited information they possess.

# 9
# Imperfect Competition and the Consequences of Market Power

Parents, faced with demands from their offspring that they be supplied with the latest fashion trainers, produced by Nike, New Balance, or whatever is in fashion, usually try (and fail) to persuade the youngsters that there is no real difference between the trainers they want and much less expensive brands that will perform much the same functions and just as well. The difference in price between the high-fashion brands and the more generic products can hardly be accounted for by differences in costs of production. Clearly, there can be differences in the quality and finish of trainers that involve additional expenses in production of higher-quality variants. However, no one really believes that this alone is what explains the differences in retail price. It is reasonable to assume that the higher-priced fashion brands yield higher profits to the producers than the other brands. This, of course, even if explained, cuts little ice with the average teenager.

As an economist, however, under these circumstances you might expect that producers of training shoes would flood the market with imitations of the high-fashion brands. There is, after all, 'cash on the table'. Indeed, anyone who has travelled in the Far East or North Africa will be happy to recount bargain purchases of trainers that are produced locally and are indistinguishable from the branded products sold in the West. But this doesn't happen, on a large scale at any rate, in Britain, France or other EU states.

The reason this producer reaction is uncommon in the West is because the producers of Nike and similar products have a *legally enforceable monopoly* on their brands – and, frequently, on the designs of their products. As a result, they can restrict output, safe from competition from replicas, and obtain a higher price for their products based on fashion (which is more or less the same as saying that people will pay more for something simply because it is in short supply and demonstrates the purchaser's ability to pay). Sociologists refer to such goods as 'positional' goods, meaning that they are bought in order to demonstrate *status* or *wealth*.

This particular legal ability to prevent imitations being produced is just one way in which producers of goods can *differentiate* their offerings from those of rivals. By doing so, they put themselves in a position to become **price setters** rather than price takers. They still have to compete for sales with producers of other variants of the good in question. These will offer their own particular brands, or may decide to compete on price by selling more or less generic products.

**price setter** a firm with at least some latitude to set its own price

When producers can, for whatever reason, differentiate their products from those of their rivals, with whom they compete, economists refer to the market concerned as being *imperfectly competitive*, and the firms as being **imperfectly competitive firms**. The key to this type of market is that the output of any producer is not perfectly substitutable for that of another producer. Hence, the purchaser of a unit of the product is not indifferent as to the identity of the producer. If this were not the case, the producer would be a price taker, since if he tried to increase his price, people would simply buy someone else's product.

**imperfectly competitive firms** firms that differentiate their products from those of their rivals, with whom they compete

Our focus in this chapter will be on the ways in which markets served by imperfectly competitive firms differ from those served by perfectly competitive firms. One salient difference is the imperfectly competitive firm's ability, under certain circumstances, to charge more than its cost of production. Nike can sell its latest trainers for €150 a pair (where production costs are perhaps €10). Nike may be the only permitted producer of Nike trainers but, given the intensity of competition from other brands and from the much-despised generic trainers, its pricing freedom is far from absolute. We shall also see how some imperfectly competitive firms manage to earn an economic profit, even in the long run, and even without government protections such as copyright. And we shall explore why Adam Smith's invisible hand is less in evidence in a world served by imperfectly competitive firms.

# Imperfect competition

The concept of a perfectly competitive market should be thought of as an extreme version of competition, in a sense, an ideal; the actual markets we encounter in everyday life differ from the ideal in varying degrees. In a classification scheme whose arbitrariness most economists would feel hard-pressed to defend, economics texts usually distinguish among three types of imperfectly competitive market structure.

## Different forms of imperfect competition

Furthest from the perfectly competitive ideal is the **pure monopoly**, a market in which a single firm is the lone seller of a unique product. A real-life example of a full-blown monopolist is not all that easy to find, unless the monopoly is created by law (e.g. a postal monopoly). In the 1980s, anyone in England or Wales who wanted to use electricity had to buy the power supplied by Britain's Central Electricity Generation Board (CEGB). In France there is still only one serious supplier of electricity, Electricité de France.

**pure monopoly** the only supplier of a unique product with no close substitutes

Somewhat closer to the perfectly competitive ideal is *oligopoly*, the market structure in which only a few firms (**oligopolists**) sell a given product. Examples include the market for mobile (cellular) phone services, in which firms like Vodafone, $O_2$ and others are the principal providers. Although there are thousands of retail outlets selling grocery products in most countries, in general the large supermarket chains, of which there are in any country only a handful, are accepted as being in a separate market from small convenience stores. As such, they form an oligopoly (and it was this factor that led the UK Competition Commission to intervene in the sale of the Safeway operation in 2003, by preventing its sale to any other large national chain ... it was eventually sold to Morrison). Closer still to perfect competition is the industry structure known as *monopolistic competition*, which typically consists of a relatively large number of firms that sell the same product with slight differentiations. Examples of **monopolistically competitive firms** include local petrol (gasoline) stations, which differ not so much in what they sell as in

**oligopolist** a firm that produces a product for which only a few rival firms produce close substitutes

**monopolistically competitive firm** one of a large number of firms that produce slightly differentiated products that are reasonably close substitutes for one another

their physical locations (in practice, the products actually sold in a petrol station carrying the logo of one brand will frequently actually be supplied by the producer of another brand).

As we shall see in the next section, the essential characteristic that differentiates imperfectly competitive firms from perfectly competitive firms is the same in each of the three cases. So for convenience, we shall use the term *monopolist* to refer to the price-setting ability of any of the three types of imperfectly competitive firms.

## The essential difference between perfectly and imperfectly competitive firms

In advanced economics courses, lecturers generally devote much attention to the analysis of subtle differences in the behaviour of different types of imperfectly competitive firms. Far more important for our purposes, however, will be to focus on the single, common feature that differentiates all imperfectly competitive firms from their perfectly competitive counterparts, namely, that whereas the perfectly competitive firm faces a perfectly elastic demand curve for its product, *the imperfectly competitive firm faces a downward-sloping demand curve.*

In the perfectly competitive industry, the supply and demand curves intersect to determine an equilibrium market price. At that price, the perfectly competitive firm can sell as many units as it wishes. It has no incentive to charge more than the market price, because it won't sell anything if it does so. Nor does it have any incentive to charge less than the market price, because it can sell as many units as it wants to at the market price. The perfectly competitive firm's demand curve is thus a horizontal line at the market price, as we saw in Chapter 6.

By contrast, if a local petrol retailer or convenience store – an imperfect competitor – charges a little more than its rivals for some or all of what it sells, some of its customers may desert it. But others will remain, perhaps because they are willing to pay a little extra to continue shopping at their most convenient location. An imperfectly competitive firm thus faces a negatively sloped demand curve. Figure 9.1 summarises this contrast between the demand curves facing perfectly competitive and imperfectly competitive firms.

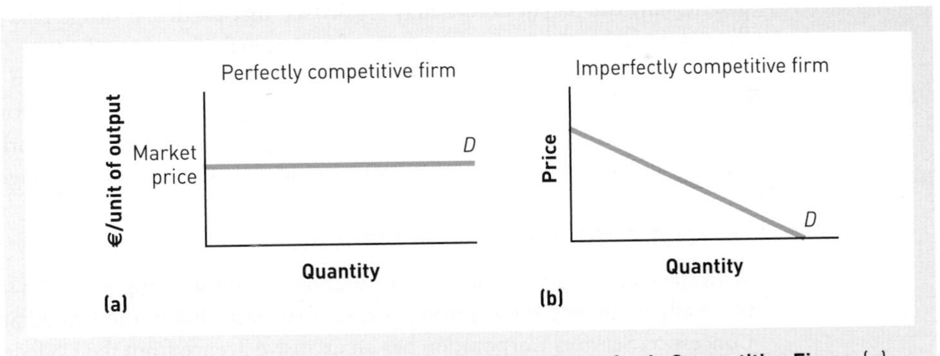


**Figure 9.1 The Demand Curves Facing Perfectly and Imperfectly Competitive Firms.** (a) The demand curve confronting a perfectly competitive firm is perfectly elastic at the market price. (b) The demand curve confronting an imperfectly competitive firm is downward-sloping.

## RECAP Imperfect competition

Perfect competition is an ideal case, at best only approximated in actual industries. Economists study three other types of market structure that differ in varying degrees from perfect competition: *monopoly*, an industry with only one seller of a unique product; *oligopoly*, an industry with only a few sellers; and *monopolistic competition*, an industry in which many firms sell products that are close, but imperfect, substitutes for one another. The demand curve confronting a perfectly competitive firm is perfectly elastic at the market price, while the demand curve confronting an imperfectly competitive firm is downward-sloping.

## Five sources of market power

Firms that confront downward-sloping demand curves are said to enjoy **market power**, a term that refers to their ability to *set the prices* of their products. A common misconception is that a firm with market power can sell any quantity at any price it wishes. It cannot: all it can do is pick a price–quantity combination along its demand curve. If the firm chooses to raise its price, it must settle for reduced sales.

**market power** a firm's ability to raise the price of a good without losing all its sales

Why do some firms have market power while others do not? Since market power often carries with it the ability to charge a price above the cost of production, such power tends to arise from factors that limit competition. In practice, the following five factors often confer such power: exclusive control over important inputs; patents and copyrights; government licences or franchises; economies of scale; and network economies.

### Exclusive control over important inputs

If a single firm controls an input *essential to the production* of a given product, that firm will have market power. For example, to the extent that some commercial tenants are willing to pay a premium for office space in the tallest building in the United States (as of 2003), the Sears Tower, the owner of that building has market power.

### Patents and copyrights

Patents give the inventors or developers of new products the exclusive right to sell those products for a specified period of time. By insulating sellers from competition for an interval, patents enable innovators to charge higher prices to recoup their product's *development costs*. Pharmaceutical companies, for example, spend millions of euros on research in the hope of discovering new drug therapies for serious illnesses. The drugs they discover are insulated from competition for an interval by the granting of government patents. For the life of the patent, only the patent holder may legally sell that particular drug. This protection enables the patent holder to set a price above the marginal cost of production. The profits on the sales of the drug are expected to be sufficient (at least) to recoup the cost of the research on the drug. In the same way, copyrights protect the authors of movies, software, music, books and other published works. And the property right in the Nike trade mark protects its trainers from imitations. (Or does it? Ask street vendors in Casablanca or Shanghai.)

### Government licences or franchises

With the increasing incidence of privatisation and outsourcing of public services, it may not be totally surprising for a European reader to learn that in the United States the Yosemite Concession Services Corporation has an exclusive licence from the US federal government to run the lodging and food and drink concession operations at Yosemite National Park in California. One of the government's goals in granting this monopoly was to preserve the wilderness character of the area to the greatest degree possible. And indeed, the inns and cabins offered by the Yosemite Concession Services Company blend nicely with the valley's scenery. No garish neon signs mar the national park as they do in places where rival firms compete for the tourists' purchases of their services.

A similar rationale applies to the granting of postal service monopoly franchises to (usually state-owned) operators. The goal in this case is the provision of a single-price universal postal delivery service. This, it is felt, would not be possible if the universal service operator faced competition in lucrative urban markets, the profits from which are said to be necessary to cross-subsidise loss-making operations in other parts of the country.

## Economies of scale (natural monopolies)

When a firm doubles all its factors of production, what happens to its output? If output exactly doubles, the firm's production process is said to exhibit **constant returns to scale**. If output more than doubles, the production process is said to exhibit **increasing returns to scale**, or **economies of scale**. When production is subject to economies of scale, the average cost of production declines as the number of units produced increases. For example, in the generation of electricity, the use of larger generators lowers the unit cost of production. The markets for such products tend to be served by a single seller, or perhaps only a few sellers, because having a large number of sellers would result in significantly higher costs. Hence, competition between them results in a smaller number of surviving firms. A monopoly that results from economies of scale is called a **natural monopoly**.

**constant returns to scale** a production process is said to have constant returns to scale if, when all inputs are changed by a given proportion, output changes by the same proportion

**increasing returns to scale** a production process is said to have increasing returns to scale if, when all inputs are changed by a given proportion, output changes by more than that proportion; also called **economies of scale**

**natural monopoly** a monopoly that results from economies of scale

A classic example of the impact of scale economies is the evolution of the structure of the passenger and military aircraft markets. In this case, the economies arise not just from the production process but from the enormous costs of designing and marketing new aircraft. In the United Kingdom, the main aircraft-producing country in Europe after the Second World War, there were in the early 1950s at least 10 major firms producing military and commercial fixed-wing aircraft: Hawker, English Electric, Vickers, Bristol, Avro, Handley-Page, Gloster, De Havilland, Blackburn and Airspeed. By the early 1970s the industry had just two firms, resulting from mergers and exits: BAC and Hawker Siddeley. By the beginning of the twenty-first century no UK independent producer of large aircraft survived, and virtually the entire British industry (one firm, BAe plc) had become part of a small number of larger multinational operations, being involved with EADS (the producer of Airbus) and Lockheed-Martin (the US producer of the next generation of STOVL strike fighters to replace the Harrier in service in the United States, United Kingdom and other countries). For large commercial passenger planes, airlines (outside the Soviet bloc) that could choose among the offerings of two European and three North American suppliers as recently as 1980 are now effectively limited to choosing between two, Airbus and Boeing, all the others having either merged or exited the industry.

## Network economies

Although most of us don't care what brand of dental floss others use, many products do become much more valuable to us as more people use them. In the case of home recorders, for instance, the VHS format's defeat of the competing Betamax format was explained not by its superior picture quality – indeed, on most important technical dimensions, Betamax was regarded by experts as superior to VHS. Rather, VHS won simply because it managed to gain a slight sales edge on the initial version of Betamax, which could not record programmes longer than one hour. Although Betamax later corrected this deficiency, the VHS lead proved insuperable. Once the fraction of consumers owning VHS passed a critical threshold, the reasons for choosing it became compelling – variety and availability of tape rental, access to repair facilities, the capability to exchange tapes with friends and so on. A similar contest is now starting in the market for the successor technology to the ubiquitous DVD, which in its time drove out the VHS system.

A similar network economy helped to account for the dominant position of Microsoft's Windows operating system, which is currently installed in more than 90 per cent of all personal computers. Because Microsoft's initial sales advantage (in turn due to supplying the original MS DOS operations system for the original IBM Personal Computer) gave software developers a strong incentive to write for the Windows format, the inventory of available software in the Windows format is now vastly larger than that for any competing operating system. And although general-purpose software such as word-processors and spreadsheets continues to be available for multiple operating systems, specialised professional software and games usually appear first – and often only – in the Windows format. This 'software gap' and the desire to achieve compatibility for file-sharing gave people a good reason for choosing Windows, even if, as in the case of many Apple Macintosh users, they believed a competing system was otherwise superior.

By far the most important and enduring of these sources of market power are economies of scale and network economies. Firms can often evade patent laws by making slight changes in the design of products. Patent protection is only temporary, in any case. Finally, governments grant very few franchises each year. But economies of scale are both widespread and enduring.

Firmly entrenched network economies can be as persistent a source of natural monopoly as economies of scale. Indeed, network economies are essentially similar to economies of scale. When network economies are of value to the consumer, a product's quality increases as the number of users increases, so we can say that any given quality level can be produced at a lower cost as sales volume increases. Thus network economies may be viewed as just another form of economies of scale in production, and that is how we'll treat them here.

## RECAP Five sources of market power

A firm's power to raise its price without losing its entire market stems from exclusive control of important inputs, patents and copyrights, government licences, economies of scale, or network economies. By far the most important and enduring of these are *economies of scale* and *network economies*.

## Economies of scale and the importance of fixed costs

As we saw in Chapter 6, variable costs are those that vary with the level of output produced, while fixed costs are independent of output. Strictly speaking, there are no fixed costs in the long run, because all inputs can be varied. But as a practical matter, start-up costs often loom large for the duration of a product's useful life. Most of the costs involved in the production of computer software, for example, are fixed costs of this sort, one-time costs incurred in writing and testing the software. Once those tasks are done, additional copies of the software can be produced at a very low marginal cost. A good such as software, whose production entails large fixed costs and low variable costs, will be subject to significant economies of scale. Because, by definition, fixed costs don't increase as output increases, the average total cost of production for such goods will decline sharply as output increases.

To illustrate, consider a production process for which total cost is given by the equation $TC = F + MQ$, where $F$ is fixed cost, $M$ is marginal cost (assumed constant in this illustration) and $Q$ is the level of output produced. For the production process with this simple total cost function, variable cost is simply $MQ$, the product of marginal cost and quantity. Average total cost, $TC/Q$, is equal to $(F/Q) + M$. As $Q$ increases, average cost declines steadily, because the fixed costs are spread out over more and more units of output.

Figure 9.2 shows the total production cost (panel (a)) and average total cost (panel (b)) for a firm with the total cost curve $TC = F + MQ$ and the corresponding average total cost curve $ATC = (F/Q) + M$. The average total cost curve (panel (b)) shows the decline in per-unit cost as output grows. Though average total cost is always higher than marginal cost for this firm, the difference between the two diminishes as output grows. At extremely high levels of

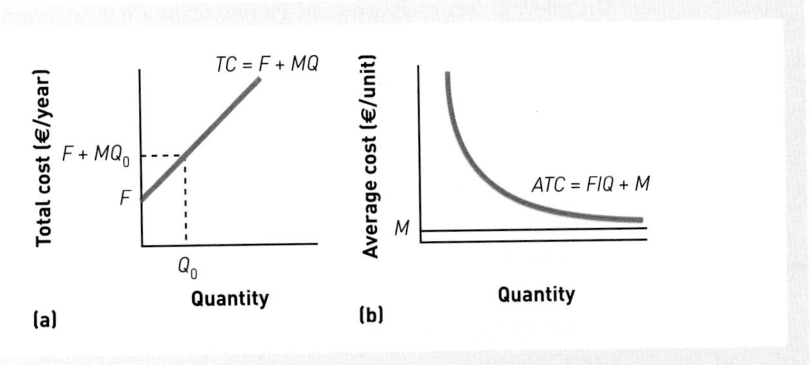


**Figure 9.2 Total and Average Total Costs for a Production Process with Economies of Scale.** For a firm whose total cost curve of producing $Q$ units of output per year is $TC = F + MQ$, total cost (a) rises at a constant rate as output grows, while average total cost (b) declines. Average total cost is always higher than marginal cost for this firm, but the difference becomes less significant at high output levels.

output, average total cost becomes very close to marginal cost ($M$). Because the firm is spreading out its fixed cost over an extremely large volume of output, the fixed cost per unit becomes almost insignificant.

As Examples 9.1 and 9.2 illustrate, the importance of economies of scale depends on how large *fixed cost* is in relation to *marginal cost*.

**Example 9.1** Two video game producers, Nintendo and Playstation, each have fixed costs of €200,000 and marginal costs of €0.80 per game. If Nintendo produces 1 million units per year and Playstation produces 1.2 million, how much lower will Playstation's average total production cost be?

Table 9.1 summarises the relevant cost categories for the two firms. Note in the bottom row that Playstation enjoys only a 3 cent average cost advantage over Nintendo. Even though Nintendo produces 20 per cent fewer copies of its video game than Playstation, it does not suffer a significant cost disadvantage because fixed cost is a relatively small part of total production cost.

| Cost | Nintendo | Playstation |
|---|---|---|
| Annual production | 1,000,000 | 1,200,000 |
| Fixed cost | €200,000 | €200,000 |
| Variable cost | €800,000 | €960,000 |
| Total cost | €1,000,000 | €1,160,000 |
| Average total cost per game | €1.00 | €0.97 |

**Table 9.1** Costs for Two Computer Game Producers: 1

But note how the picture changes when fixed cost looms large relative to marginal cost.

**Example 9.2** Two video game producers, Nintendo and Playstation, each have fixed costs of €10,000,000 and marginal costs of €0.20 per video game. If Nintendo produces 1 million units per year and Playstation produces 1.2 million, how much lower will Playstation's average total cost be?

The relevant cost categories for the two firms are now summarised in Table 9.2. The bottom row shows that Playstation enjoys a €1.67 average total cost advantage over Nintendo, substantially larger than in Example 9.1.

| Cost | Nintendo | Playstation |
|---|---|---|
| Annual production | 1,000,000 | 1,200,000 |
| Fixed cost | €100,000,000 | €10,000,000 |
| Variable cost | €200,000 | €240,000 |
| Total cost | €10,200,000 | €10,240,000 |
| Average total cost per game | €10.20 | €8.53 |

**Table 9.2** Costs for Two Computer Game Producers: 2

If the video games the two firms produce are essentially similar, the fact that Playstation can charge significantly lower prices and still cover its costs should enable it to attract customers away from Nintendo. As more and more of the market goes to Playstation, its cost advantage will become self-reinforcing. Table 9.3 shows how a shift of 500,000 units from Nintendo to Playstation would cause Nintendo's average total cost to rise to €20.20 per unit, while Playstation's average total cost would fall to €6.08 per unit. The fact that a firm could not long survive at such a severe disadvantage explains why the video game market is served now by only a small number of firms.

| Cost | Nintendo | Playstation |
|---|---|---|
| Annual production | 500,000 | 1,700,000 |
| Fixed cost | €10,000,000 | €10,000,000 |
| Variable cost | €100,000 | €340,000 |
| Total cost | €10,100,000 | €10,340,000 |
| Average total cost per game | €20.20 | €6.08 |

**Table 9.3** Costs for Two Computer Game Producers: 3

**Exercise 9.1** How big will Playstation's unit cost advantage be if it sells 2,000,000 units per year, while Nintendo sells only 300,000?

An important worldwide economic trend since the 1970s is that an increasing share of the value embodied in the goods and services we buy stems from *fixed investment in R&D*. For example, in 1984 some 80 per cent of the cost of a computer was in its hardware; the remaining 20 per cent was in its software. With the cost of memory and computing power roughly halving in real terms every couple of years, by 1999 these proportions were reversed. Hardware is cheap ... but software, which is to an even greater degree than hardware the result of fixed investment in R&D, now accounts for most of the cost of a computer. Fixed costs account for about 85 per cent of total costs in the computer software industry, whose products are included in a growing share of ordinary manufactured goods.

### Economic naturalist 9.1 Why does Intel sell the overwhelming majority of all microprocessors used in personal computers?

Producing memory and computer processing unit (CPU) chips is relatively cheap. Most of us are blissfully unaware of what is going on inside the computer, so we rationally shouldn't care who makes the bits as long as they work. Under these circumstances it might seem hard to understand why Intel sells about 80 per cent of the microprocessors in PCs. Part of the answer lies in branding and reputation, but that can't be the whole explanation. Knowledgeable purchasers might be expected to prefer, say, an equally powerful chip made by AMD if there is a price difference, while price-conscious, low-intensity home users would also be expected to look for the best value for money.

Intel may be thought of as an innovating chip producer: it is first to market with newer, better chips, the product of its heavy fixed cost investment in R&D. It sells these initially at high prices to high-value users, those with a particular need for more powerful chips. It also sells them at these prices to people who want the best anyway. Then, as (a) other players start to produce competing chips (possibly based on reverse engineering) and as (b) the high-value users have been serviced, it lowers its prices. This gives it a first-mover advantage, based on its R&D, that sustains its market share – which, of course, is also a reflection of its heavy investment (another fixed cost) in brand advertising. If industry sources are correct in forecasting that R&D investment in increasing computing power by improving chip performance is rapidly running into diminishing returns, we would expect to see Intel's share of the chip market start to decline to the extent that it is not based simply on branding.

### RECAP Economies of scale and the importance of fixed costs

Research, design, engineering and other fixed costs account for an increasingly large share of all costs required to bring products successfully to market. For products with large fixed costs, marginal cost is lower, often substantially, than average total cost, and average total cost declines, often sharply, as output grows. This cost pattern explains why many industries are dominated by either a *single firm* or a *small number of firms*.

## Profit-maximisation for the monopolist

Regardless of whether a firm is a price taker or a price setter, economists assume that its basic goal is to *maximise its profit*. They also assume that in either case the operational decision confronting each firm is to select the output level that results in the greatest possible difference between total revenue and total cost. But there are some important differences in how the two types of firm carry out this decision.

For both the perfectly competitive firm and the monopolist, the marginal benefit of expanding output is the additional revenue the firm will receive if it sells one additional unit of output. In both cases, this marginal benefit is called the firm's **marginal revenue**. For the perfectly competitive firm, marginal revenue is exactly equal to the market price of the product. The position for a price-setting firm is different. This is because the amount sold affects the price at which all units are sold.

**marginal revenue** the change in a firm's total revenue that results from a one-unit change in output

## Marginal revenue for the monopolist

The logic of profit-maximisation is precisely the same for the monopolist as for the perfectly competitive firm. In both cases, the firm keeps expanding output as long as the benefit of doing so exceeds the cost. The calculation of marginal cost is also precisely the same for the monopolist as for the perfectly competitive firm. The only significant difference between the two cases concerns the calculation of *marginal revenue.*

As we have seen, marginal revenue for a competitive firm is simply the market price. If that price is €6, then the marginal benefit of selling an extra unit is exactly €6. To a monopolist, in contrast, the marginal benefit of selling an additional unit is *strictly less than the market price*. As the following discussion will make clear, the reason is that while the perfectly competitive firm can sell as many units as it wishes at the market price, the monopolist can sell an additional unit only if it cuts the price – and it must do so not just for the additional unit but for the units it is *currently selling.*

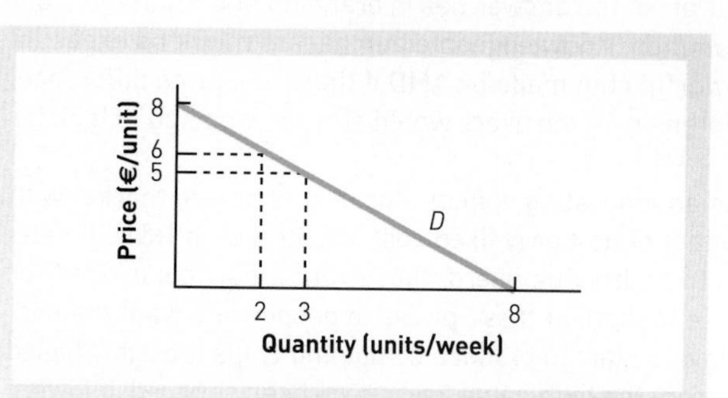


**Figure 9.3 The Monopolist's Benefit from Selling an Additional Unit.** The monopolist shown receives €12 per week in total revenue by selling 2 units per week at a price of €6 each. This monopolist could earn €15 per week by selling 3 units per week at a price of €5 each. In that case, the benefit from selling the third unit would be €15 - €12 = €3, less than its selling price of €5.

Suppose, for example, that a monopolist with the demand curve shown in Fig. 9.3 is currently selling 2 units of output at a price of €6 per unit. What would be its marginal revenue from selling an additional unit?s

This monopolist's total revenue from the sale of 2 units per week is (€6 per unit) (2 units per week) = €12 per week. Its total revenue from the sale of 3 units per week would be €15 per week. The difference – €3 per week – is the marginal revenue from the sale of the third unit each week. Note that this amount is not only smaller than the original price (€6) but smaller than the new price (€5) as well.

**Exercise 9.2** Calculate marginal revenue for the monopolist in Fig. 9.3 as it expands output from 3 to 4 units per week, and then from 4 to 5 units per week.

For the monopolist whose demand curve is shown in Fig. 9.3, a sequence of increases in output – from 2 to 3, from 3 to 4 and from 4 to 5 – will yield marginal revenue of €3, €2 and €1, respectively. We can display these results in tabular form, as in Table 9.4

| Quantity | Marginal revenue |
|---|---|
| 2 | |
| | 3 |
| 3 | |
| | 1 |
| 4 | |
| | -1 |
| 5 | |

**Table 9.4** Marginal Revenue for a Monopolist (€ per unit)

Note that in Table 9.4 the marginal revenue values are displayed between the two quantity figures to which they correspond. For example, when the firm expanded its output from 2 units per week to 3, its marginal revenue was €3 per unit. Strictly speaking, this marginal revenue corresponds to neither quantity but to the *movement between* those quantities, hence its placement in Table 9.4. Likewise, in moving from 3 to 4 units per week, the firm earned marginal revenue of €1 per unit so that figure is placed midway between the quantities of 3 and 4 in Table 9.3 and so on.

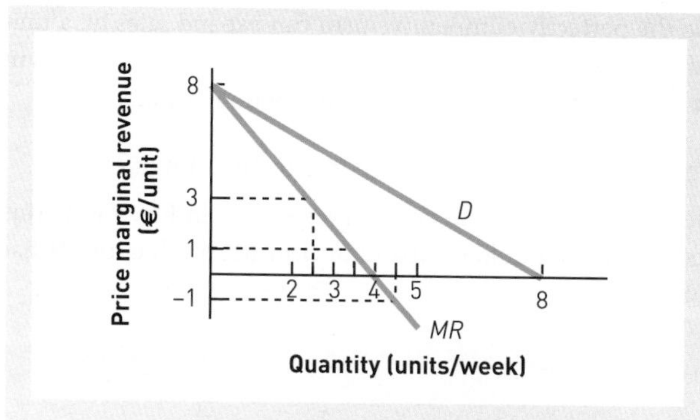


**Figure 9.4 Marginal Revenue in Graphical Form.** Because a monopolist must cut price to sell an extra unit, not only for the extra unit sold but also for all existing units, marginal revenue from the sale of the extra unit is less than its selling price.

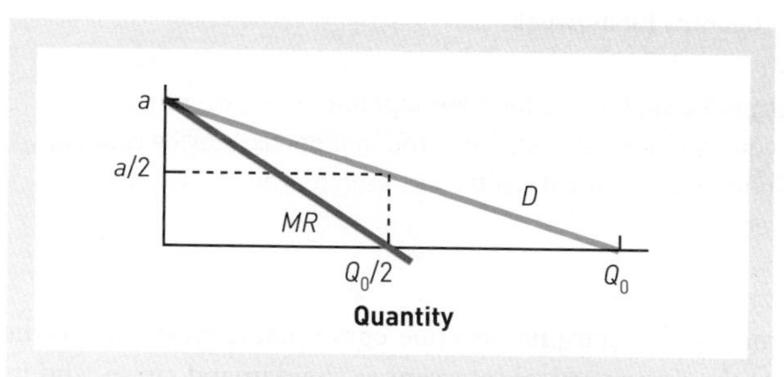


**Figure 9.5 The Marginal Revenue Curve for a Monopolist with a Straight-Line Demand Curve.** For a monopolist with the demand curve shown, the corresponding marginal revenue curve has the same vertical intercept as the demand curve, and a horizontal intercept only half as large as that of the demand curve.

To graph marginal revenue as a function of quantity, we would plot the marginal revenue for the movement from 2 to 3 units of output per week (€3) at a quantity value of 2.5, because 2.5 lies midway between 2 and 3. Similarly, we would plot the marginal revenue for the movement from 3 to 4 units per week (€1) at a quantity of 3.5 units per week, and the marginal revenue for the movement from 4 to 5 units per week (€1) at a quantity of 4.5. The resulting marginal revenue curve *MR*, is shown in Fig. 9.4.

More generally, consider a monopolist with a straight-line demand curve whose vertical intercept is $a$ and whose horizontal intercept is $Q_0$, as shown in Fig. 9.5. This monopolist's marginal revenue curve will also have a vertical intercept of $a$, and it will be twice as steep as the demand curve. Thus its horizontal intercept will be not $Q_0$, but $Q_0/2$, as shown in Fig. 9.5.

Marginal revenue curves can also be expressed algebraically. If the formula for the monopolist's demand curve is $P = a - bQ$, then the formula for its marginal revenue curve will be $MR = a - 2bQ$. This will be demonstrated in the section on the rigorous derivation of the rule for profit-maximisation below. If you have done calculus, this relationship is easy to derive,[1] but even without calculus you can verify it by working through a few numerical examples. First translate the formula for the demand curve into a diagram, and then construct the corresponding marginal revenue curve graphically. Reading from the graph, write the formula for that marginal revenue curve.

## The monopolist's profit-maximising decision rule

Having derived the monopolist's marginal revenue curve, we are now in a position to describe how the monopolist chooses the output level that maximises profit. As in the case of the perfectly competitive firm, the Cost–Benefit Principle says that the monopolist should continue to expand output as long as the gain from doing so exceeds the cost. At the current level of output, the benefit from expanding output is the marginal revenue value that corresponds to that output level. The cost of expanding output is the marginal cost at that level of output. Whenever marginal revenue exceeds marginal cost, the firm should expand.

[1] Total revenue is average revenue (demand) multiplied by $Q$. $TR = aQ - bQ^2$; marginal revenue is $dTR/dQ$ or $MR = a - 2bQ$.

Conversely, whenever marginal revenue falls short of marginal cost, the firm should reduce its output. Profit is maximised at the level of output for which *marginal revenue precisely equals marginal cost.*

When the monopolist's profit-maximising rule is stated in this way, we can see that the perfectly competitive firm's rule is actually a special case of the monopolist's rule. When the perfectly competitive firm expands output by one unit, its marginal revenue exactly equals the product's market price (because the perfectly competitive firm can expand sales by a unit without having to cut the price of existing units). So when the perfectly competitive firm equates price with marginal cost, it is also equating marginal revenue with marginal cost.

### Example 9.3 What is the monopolist's profit-maximising output level?

Consider a monopolist with the demand and marginal cost curves shown in Fig. 9.6. If this firm is currently producing 12 units per week, should it expand or contract production? What is the profit-maximising level of output?

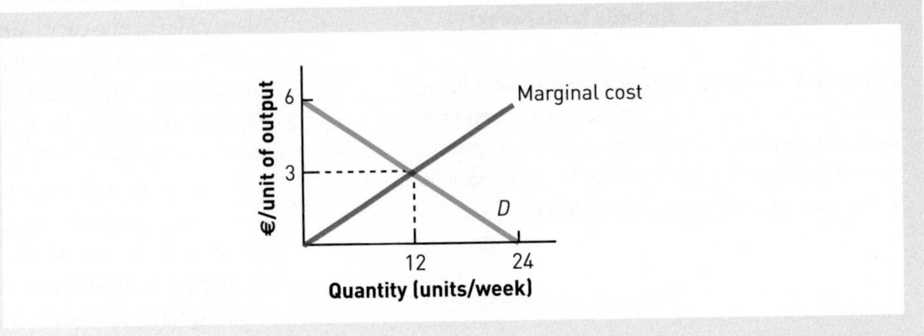


**Figure 9.6 The Demand and Marginal Cost Curves for a Monopolist.** At the current output level of 12 units per week, price equals marginal cost. Since the monopolist's price is always greater than marginal revenue, marginal revenue must be less than marginal cost, which means this monopolist should produce less.

In Figure 9.7, we begin by constructing the marginal revenue curve that corresponds to the monopolist's demand curve. It has the same vertical intercept as the demand curve, and its horizontal intercept is half as large. Note that the monopolist's marginal revenue at 12 units per week is zero, which is clearly less than its marginal cost of €3 per unit. This monopolist

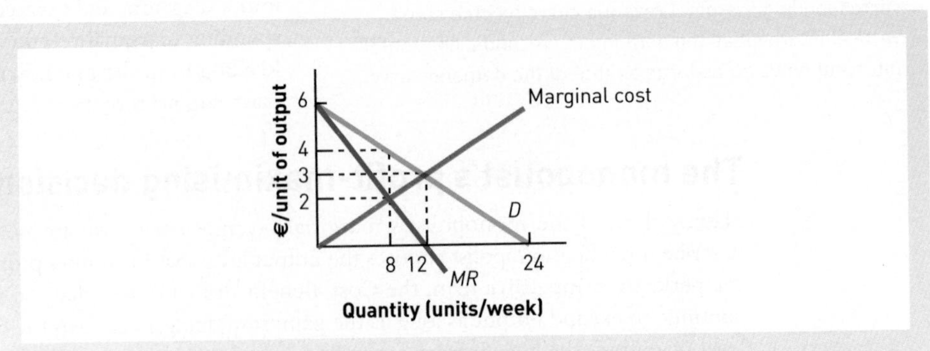


**Figure 9.7 The Monopolist's Profit-Maximising Output Level.** This monopolist maximises profit by selling 8 units per week, the output level at which marginal revenue equals marginal cost. The profit-maximising price is €4 per unit, the price that corresponds to the profit-maximising quantity on the demand curve.

will therefore earn a higher profit by contracting production until marginal revenue equals marginal cost, which occurs at an output level of 8 units per week. At this profit-maximising output level the firm will charge €4 per unit, the price that corresponds to 8 units per week on the demand curve.

**Exercise 9.3**

Find the profit-maximising price and level of output for a monopolist with the demand curve $P = 12 - Q$ and the marginal cost curve $MC = 2Q$, where $P$ is the price of the product in euros per unit and $Q$ is output in units per week.

## Being a monopolist does not guarantee an economic profit

The fact that the profit-maximising price for a monopolist will always be greater than marginal cost provides no assurance that the monopolist will earn an economic profit. Consider, for example, the long-distance telephone service provider whose demand, marginal revenue, marginal cost and average total cost curves are shown in Fig. 9.8(a). This monopolist maximises its daily profit by selling 20 million minutes per day of calls at a price of €0.10 per minute. At that quantity, $MR = MC$, yet price is €0.02 per minute less than the company's average total cost of €0.12 per minute. As a result, the company sustains an economic loss of €0.02 per minute on all calls provided, or a total loss of (€0.02 per minute)(20,000,000 minutes per day) = €400,000 per day.

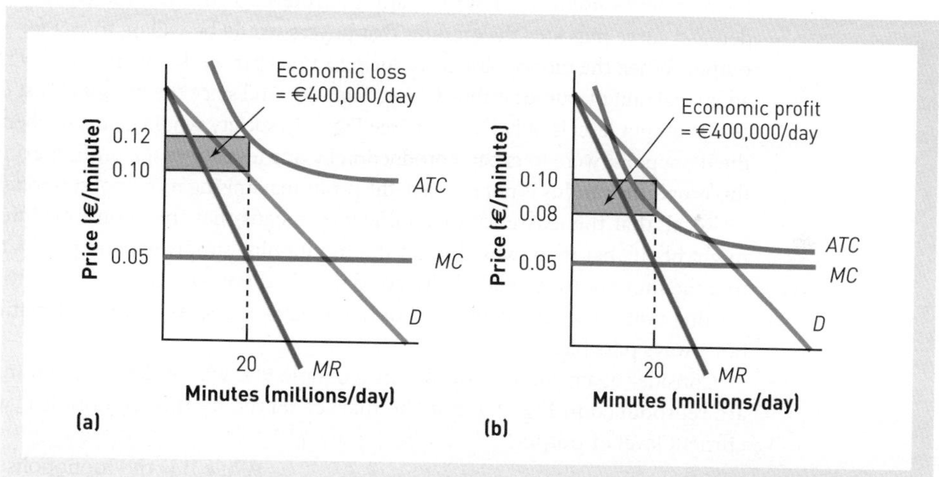


**Figure 9.8 Even a Monopolist May Suffer an Economic Loss.** The monopolist in (a) maximises its profit by selling 20 million minutes per day of calls but suffers an economic loss of €400,000 per day in the process. Because the profit-maximising price of the monopolist in (b) exceeds *ATC*, this monopolist earns an economic profit.

The monopolist in Fig. 9.8(a) suffered a loss because its profit-maximising price was lower than its *ATC*. If the monopolist's profit-maximising price exceeds its average total cost, however, the company will of course earn an economic profit. Consider, for example, the long-distance provider shown in Fig. 9.8(b). This firm has the same demand, marginal revenue and marginal cost curves as the firm shown in Fig. 9.8(a). But because the firm in panel (b) has lower fixed costs, its *ATC* curve is lower at every level of output than the *ATC* curve in (a). At the profit-maximising price of €0.10 per minute, the firm in Fig. 9.8(b) earns an economic profit of €0.02 per minute, for a total economic profit of €400,000 per day.

## RECAP Profit-maximisation for the monopolist

Both the perfectly competitive firm and the monopolist maximise profit by choosing the output level at which marginal revenue equals marginal cost. But whereas marginal revenue equals market price for the perfectly competitive firm, it is always less than market price for the monopolist. A monopolist will earn an economic profit only if price exceeds average total cost at the *profit-maximising level of output*.

## Why the 'invisible hand' breaks down under monopoly

In our discussion of equilibrium in perfectly competitive markets in Chapters 7 and 8, we saw conditions under which the self-serving pursuits of consumers and firms were consistent with the broader interests of society as a whole. This was what was described as the workings of Adam Smith's 'invisible hand'.

The obvious analytical question that arises from the discussion so far in this chapter is to what extent Smith's conclusions regarding the invisible hand are robust in the sense of what happens if we change assumptions about the market. Smith, after all, was implicitly assuming that markets were 'efficient' in the sense that perfectly competitive markets are (of course, he didn't use the term, which had not been invented, but it is clear what he had in mind). To answer this question, we start with the case of monopoly.

Consider the monopolist in Example 9.3. Is this firm's profit-maximising output level efficient from society's point of view? For any given level of output, the corresponding price on the demand curve indicates the amount that buyers would be willing to pay for an additional unit of output. When the monopolist is producing 8 units per week, the marginal benefit to society of an additional unit of output is thus €4 (see Fig. 9.7). And since the marginal cost of an additional unit at that output level is only €2 (again, see Fig. 9.7), society would gain a net benefit of €2 per unit if the monopolist were to expand production by one unit above the profit-maximising level. Because this economic surplus is not realised, the profit-maximising monopolist is *socially inefficient*.

Recall that the existence of inefficiency means that the economic 'pie' is smaller than it might be. If that is so, why doesn't the monopolist simply expand production? The answer is that the monopolist would gladly do so if only there were some way to maintain the price of existing units and cut the price of only the extra units. As a practical matter, however, that is not always possible.

Consider again the monopolist in Example 9.3, whose demand and marginal cost curves are reproduced in Fig. 9.9. For the market served by this monopolist, what is the socially efficient level of output?

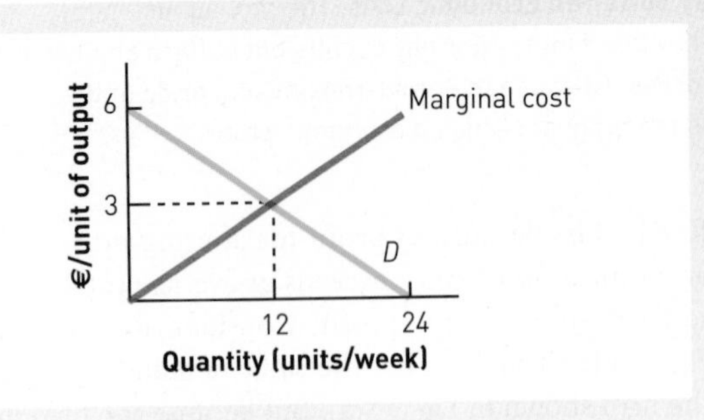


**Figure 9.9 The Demand and Marginal Curves for a Monopolist.** The socially optimal output level is 12 units per week, the quantity for which the marginal benefit *to the public* is exactly the same as marginal cost.

While it is the monopolist who pays the cost of using resources, it will in general be the case that the price he has to pay represents the opportunity cost of the *resources* he uses. It follows that at any output level, the cost to society of an additional unit of output is the same as the cost to the monopolist, namely, the amount shown on the monopolist's marginal cost curve. However, the marginal benefit to society from another unit being produced is not the same as the marginal benefit to the monopolist. The marginal benefit to *society* (not to the monopolist) of an extra unit of output is simply the amount people are willing to pay for it, which is the amount shown on the monopolist's demand curve. To achieve social efficiency, the monopolist should expand production until the marginal benefit to society equals the marginal cost, which in this case occurs at a level of 12 units per week. Social efficiency is thus achieved at the output level at which the market demand curve intersects the monopolist's marginal cost curve.

Unfortunately, the marginal benefit to the monopolist is not what people would be willing to pay for another unit, but the change in his total sales revenues from selling one more unit, or marginal revenue. It is this inequality between the value to society of an extra unit of output (its current price) and the value to the monopolist (its marginal revenue) that is the key factor. His calculus of benefit will lead him to equate marginal cost not with price but with marginal revenue. Since the monopolist's demand curve slopes downward, to sell more he has to lower unit price (and remember, price is average revenue). We already know that if any average (in this case price or average revenue) is declining, the marginal curve must lie below it. The marginal revenue curve for a monopolist will always lie below the demand curve if he has to lower price for all units sold to increase sales.

The fact that marginal revenue is less than price for the monopolist results in a *deadweight loss*. For the monopolist just discussed, the size of this deadweight loss is equal to the area of the shaded triangle in Fig. 9.10, which is (1/2)(€2 per unit)(4 units per week) = €4 per week. That is the amount by which total economic surplus is reduced because the monopolist produces too little.

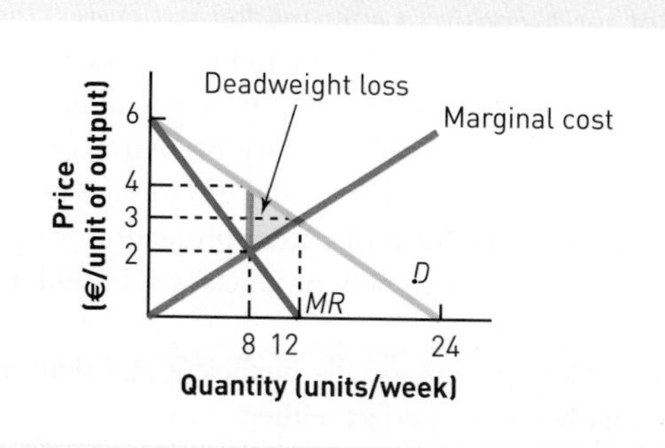


**Figure 9.10 The Deadweight Loss from Monopoly.** A loss in economic surplus results because the profit-maximising level of output (8 units per week) is less than the socially optimal level of output (12 units per week). This deadweight loss is the area of the shaded triangle, €4 per week.

For a monopolist, profit-maximisation occurs when marginal cost equals marginal revenue. Since the monopolist's marginal revenue is always less than price, the monopolist's profit-maximising output level is always below the socially efficient level. Under perfect competition, by contrast, profit-maximisation occurs when marginal cost equals the market price – the same criterion that must be satisfied for social efficiency. This difference explains why the invisible hand of the market is less evident in monopoly markets than in perfectly competitive markets.

Given that monopoly is socially inefficient, why not legislate it out of existence? A cynical response might well be that it would be ironic if parliaments that create monopolies (usually in the public sector) should decide that they are a bad thing in the first place. But it's not as simple as that. Monopolies can (if infrequently) evolve simply through the pressure of competition (which is accepted as a socially beneficial process). In this case, market forces produce concentration of production into a single firm, a natural monopoly, a firm that can produce the output at a lower average resource cost to society than if it were divided between two equally sized firms. Secondly (and this is a view that is firmly held among economists of the Chicago School, a view they have inherited from the influential economists of the mid-twentieth-century Austrian School such as Schumpeter, Hayek and Von Mises), many economists believe that monopoly power is transient, and contains within itself the seeds of its own destruction, as its profitability incites competition and innovation to break it down.

Although legal regimes do provide for breaking up monopolies (this is particularly true of the United States), for the most part they provide for its regulation. In part this probably reflects the acceptance that monopolies may derive their existence from scale economies, so that breaking them up would increase total costs of production. It also probably reflects a view that while a monopoly may be a problem, deciding what exactly should replace it may not be a tractable problem for bureaucrats and legislators. Two firms? Three firms? Four firms? ...

The UK experience of experiments in devising structures for industry through political intervention in the 1960s and 1970s does not inspire confidence in such interventions. Shipbuilding, steel, aviation, car production and road passenger transport were all the beneficiaries of state intervention to improve industrial efficiency by restructuring via state ownership. In every case the intervention had to be reversed when it was seen to have been a costly failure. (By the same token, state intervention to create what were hoped to be viable and competitive private sector structures from state monopolies has not been a great success in Britain, either. The controversial history of rail privatisation and the establishment of the privately owned Railtrack corporation is fresh in most people's memories.)

It has to be said that the US experience has not been as bad. There, it is the courts, for the most part, or threats of court actions, that have driven restructuring of monopolies. Early in the twentieth century the US courts broke up the Rockefeller oil monopoly (Standard Oil). More recently, and more controversially in terms of results, the US Department of Justice used threats of legal action to secure a restructuring of the US telephone sector (in the late 1970s, before mobile phones, by breaking up AT&T).

Apart from the poor track records of intervention to alter market structures, there are other reasons for reluctance to use the coercive power of the state to break monopoly power. Suppose, for example, that a monopoly results from a patent that prevents all but one firm from manufacturing some highly valued product. Would society be better off without patents? Probably not, because eliminating such protection would discourage innovation. Virtually all successful industrial nations grant some form of patent protection, which gives firms a chance to recover the R&D costs without which new products would seldom reach the market.

In short, we live in an imperfect world. Monopoly is socially inefficient and that, needless to say, is bad. But the alternatives to monopoly are not perfect, either.

### RECAP Why the monopolist produces 'too little' output

The monopolist maximises profit at the output level for which marginal revenue equals marginal cost. Because its profit-maximising price exceeds marginal revenue, and hence also marginal cost, the benefit to society of the last unit produced (the market price) must be greater than the cost of the last unit produced (the marginal cost). So the output level for an industry served by a profit-maximising monopolist is *smaller* than the socially optimal level of output.

## The rigorous analysis of profit-maximisation

At this point, we shall recast the analysis of monopoly in terms of the rigorous analysis of profit-maximisation included as an Appendix to Chapter 6. You can skip this section without losing the plot. However, we think it will repay the effort in the longer term if you want to take further courses in economics.

The starting point is the fact that the firm's demand curve slopes downward (the firm is a price setter rather than a price taker and quantity setter). The firm knows that the price it obtains per unit sold will fall if it offers more to the market because the demand curve slopes downward. This means that the price at which it sells its output is a function of the amount being sold:

$$p = p(q)$$

in contrast with perfect competition where the firm perceives price as given and independent of how much it chooses to sell. Using the same notation as in Chapter 6, we assume the firm has a cost function, written as

$$TC = a + bq + cq^2$$

Total revenue, $TR$, is $pq$, or $p(q)q$. Profit, $B$, is $TR - TC$.

The firm's profit function is, therefore, written

$$B = p(q)q - a - bq - cq^2$$

The value of $q$ that maximises this expression is the profit-maximising level of output, and the price that produces that level of sales is the profit-maximising price. To find this value for $q$, differentiate the profit function with respect to $q$, and set the result, the first derivative, equal to zero, and solve for $q$.

We then get the first derivative as

$$B' = \mathrm{d}B/\mathrm{d}q = p + q(\mathrm{d}p/\mathrm{d}q) - b - 2cq$$

If this is equal to zero, then

$$p + q(\mathrm{d}p/\mathrm{d}q) = b + 2cq$$

The left-hand side is the value of $\mathrm{d}TR/\mathrm{d}q$ when $TR = p(q)q$. $\mathrm{d}TR/\mathrm{d}q$ is $MR$. The right-hand side is $\mathrm{d}TC/\mathrm{d}q$, or $MC$. So, for profits to be maximised, you have to choose the value of $q$ at which $MR = MC$. This, of course, is the result we obtained graphically above.

**Example 9.4** To show how this result can be used, take the following example. There is a type of doughnut sold in Germany known as a Berliner. (This is not a joke: it explains why there were a few chuckles when President John F. Kennedy in 1963 expressed his solidarity with the inhabitants of that city, after the Berlin Wall had divided it, in the lapidary phrase: 'Ich bin ein Berliner.')

Suppose we know that the demand curve for Berliners in Berlin (and we suppose there is only one Berliner producer in Berlin) is known to be:

$$€p = 20{,}000 - 6q$$

where $q$ is thousands of doughnuts for sale in a week. Suppose the weekly fixed cost is $€TC = 2{,}000q$. Then

$$TR = 20{,}000q - 6q^2;\ TC = 2{,}000q$$

$$MR = 20{,}000 - 12q;\ MC = 2{,}000;\ MR = MC \rightarrow 18{,}000 = 12q, \text{ or } q = 1{,}500$$

If $q = 1{,}500$, $p = 11{,}000$, and each doughnut sells for €1.10.

**Exercise 9.4** What are the firm's profits? What is the deadweight loss?

## Using discounts to expand the market: monopoly power at work for you?

The source of inefficiency in monopoly markets is the fact that the benefit to the monopolist of expanding output is less than the corresponding benefit to society. From the monopolist's point of view, the price reduction the firm must grant existing buyers to expand output is a loss. But from the point of view of those buyers, each euro or dollar of price reduction is a gain – one dollar or euro more in their pockets.

Note the tension in this situation, which is similar to the tension that exists in all other situations in which the economic 'pie' is smaller than it might otherwise be. As the efficiency principle reminds us, when the economic 'pie' grows larger, everyone can have a larger slice. To say that monopoly is inefficient means that steps could be taken to make some people better off without harming others. If people have a healthy regard for their own self-interest, why doesn't someone take those steps? Why, for example, doesn't the monopolist from the earlier examples sell 8 units of output at a price of €4, and then once those buyers are out the door, cut the price for more price-sensitive buyers? The answer is that frequently that is exactly what he does. Think back to the story in Economic naturalist 9.1, and the strategy of Intel.

## Price discrimination defined

Charging different buyers different prices for the same good or service is a practice known as **price discrimination**. Examples of price discrimination include senior citizens' and children's discounts on cinema tickets. DIY superstores in many European countries offer old age pensioners special deals on certain days. In France and Italy a standard practice is to offer access to art galleries and museums to the over-60s at a reduced rate. Something that is starting to be used in Europe but is widespread in the United States is the use of cut-out newspaper coupons entitling users to get discounts at supermarkets or other retail outlets. This is a subtle form of price discrimination: the goods are sold at a lower price to those with the time and money constraints that result in their spending time cutting out coupons. Other consumers, more pressed for time or with more money, pay more.

**price discrimination** the practice of charging different buyers different prices for essentially the same good or service

Attempts at price discrimination seem to work effectively in some markets but not in others. Buyers are not stupid, after all; if the monopolist periodically offered a 50 per cent discount on the list price, those who were paying the list price might anticipate the next price cut and postpone their purchases to take advantage of it. In some markets, however, buyers may not know, or simply may not take the trouble to find out, how the price they pay compares with the prices paid by other buyers. Alternatively, the monopolist may be in a position to prevent some groups from buying at the discount prices made available to others. In such cases, the monopolist can price discriminate effectively.

### Economic naturalist 9.2 Why do many cinemas offer discount tickets to students?

Whenever a firm offers a discount, it aims that discount at buyers who would not purchase the product without it. People with low incomes generally have lower reservation prices for movie tickets than people with high incomes. Because students generally have lower disposable incomes than working adults, cinema owners can expand their audiences by charging lower prices to students than to adults. Student discounts are one practical way of doing so. Believe us: it's not because they feel sorry for penniless students (who does?). It's because they can make higher profits by selling more tickets via a *discriminatory price structure*.

## How price discrimination affects output

Curiously, as we shall now see, this use of price discrimination to extract more profits can have the counter-intuitive consequence of making society as a whole better off. The unexpected result of this reasoning arises from the fact that we (reasonably) assume that higher prices that produce higher profits involve less being offered for sale. But this is not necessarily the case.

Suppose in a small village with a single doctor there are 10 households. The doctor is a monopolist, and can set a single price at which he will maximise his profits. Figure 9.10 (p. 255) describes this position. Assume that whatever he says at village meetings about the ethic of public service, he is concerned to maximise his profits. Let us also assume that medical regulations require that he has to post his prices for a month in advance, and sell his services to all and sundry at the posted price. The price is his charge for a visit to his surgery.

Armed with sufficient knowledge as to the villagers' demand for health care, he will set the price that maximises his profits (or, equivalently choose the weekly number of hours he will make available) by setting $MC = MR$, and selecting the relevant price and quantity.

Suppose the 10 families (reflecting their incomes, number of children and health status) have differing reservation prices for a weekly visit to the doctor. Rank them from the highest to the lowest as in Table 9.5.

| Family | Reservation price (€ per visit) |
|---|---|
| 1 | 80 |
| 2 | 75 |
| 3 | 70 |
| 4 | 65 |
| 5 | 60 |
| 6 | 55 |
| 7 | 50 |
| 8 | 45 |
| 9 | 40 |
| 10 | 35 |

**Table 9.5** Family Reservation Prices

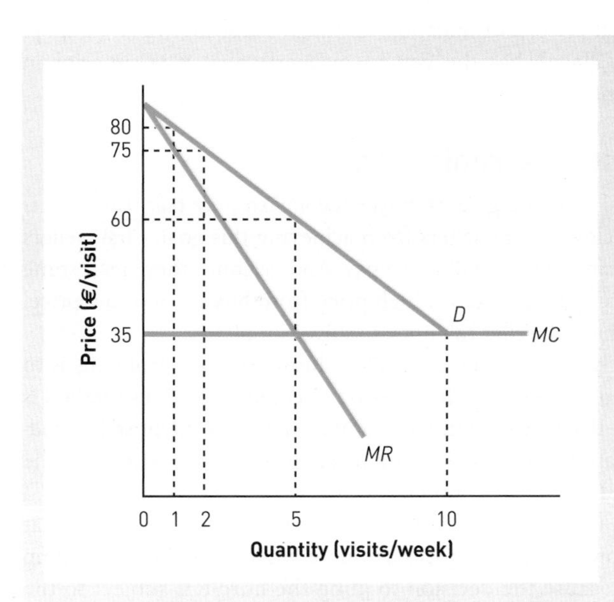


**Figure 9.11 Demand Curve for a Weekly Doctor's Visit.**

To make life easy, suppose that the doctor has a constant marginal cost of seeing a patient (this makes the story simpler, but changes nothing). Suppose his $MC$ is 35. We could use this data to derive a village demand curve for a weekly visit (Fig. 9.11).

Under price regulations the profit-maximising doctor will charge a price of €60, and see five families in the week. At this price, village welfare is not maximised. Maximisation of economic surplus would require seeing 10 families (where $MC = P$).

The doctor's profits are €(5 × 25) = €125. Families 1–5 have a joint consumer surplus of €(20 + 15 +10 + 5 + 0) = €50. Total surplus is, therefore, €175.

Now suppose that the regulation determining the doctor's pricing policy is removed, and he is allowed to charge each family its reservation price. He sells the visit to family 1 at €80, to family 2 at €75 and so on (Fig. 9.11). As long as a family is prepared to cover his marginal cost he has an incentive to see the family. He will see all the families, since the reservation price of family 10 is just equal to his *MC*. Each family pays its reservation price and so keeps no consumer surplus. The doctor has a profit of €(45 +40 + 35 + 30 + 25 + 20 + 15 + 10 + 5 + 0) = €225. This is the total surplus.

Total surplus is higher; more output is produced; the level of output is the efficient level ($P = MC$). Of course, from the point of view of families 1–5 this is a rough deal, but families 6–10 are better off (because they have chosen to purchase) even though they have no consumer surplus. The entire surplus has been appropriated by the doctor, who at the next village meeting is hailed as a latter-day Robin Hood because he appears to be charging more to the rich to finance supplying the poor.

The doctor in this case is described as a **perfectly discriminating monopolist**. This is a monopolist who can sell each unit he produces at its reservation price. He is engaging in 'first-degree' price discrimination. A firm with market power that can discriminate between groups of purchasers in a market is said to be engaging in 'second-degree' price discrimination. An airline that sells tickets at different prices to different groups reflecting willingness to pay (business and tourist, off-peak and peak-time travel) is an example of a firm practising second-degree price discrimination. A firm that can segment whole markets is a third-degree price discriminator. An example is Levi-Strauss. It has used trade restrictions that have been sanctioned by the European Court of Justice (ECJ) to sell jeans at much lower prices in countries such as India than the prices it charges in the European Union.

**perfectly discriminating monopolist** a firm that charges each buyer exactly his or her reservation price

In practice, of course, perfect price discrimination can never occur, because no seller knows each and every buyer's precise reservation price. But even if some sellers did know, practical difficulties would stand in the way of their charging a separate price to each buyer. For example, in many markets the seller could not prevent buyers who bought at low prices from reselling to other buyers at higher prices, capturing some of the seller's business in the process. Despite these difficulties, price discrimination is widespread, but it is generally *imperfect price discrimination* – that is, price discrimination in which at least some buyers are charged less than their reservation prices.

However, it remains the case that price discrimination, although redistributive and unpopular and in some circumstances illegal, has the general property that it is superior in efficiency terms to single price monopoly.

## The hurdle method of price discrimination

The profit-maximising seller's goal is to charge each buyer the *highest price that that buyer is willing to pay*. Two primary obstacles prevent sellers from achieving this goal. First, sellers don't know exactly how much each buyer is willing to pay. And, second, they need some means of excluding those who are willing to pay a high price from buying at a low price. These are formidable problems, which no seller can hope to solve completely.

One common method by which sellers achieve a crude solution to both problems is to require buyers to overcome some obstacle to be eligible for a discount price. This method is called the **hurdle method of price discrimination**. For example, the seller might sell a product at a standard list price and offer a rebate to any buyer who takes the trouble to mail in a rebate coupon.

**hurdle method of price discrimination** the practice by which a seller offers a discount to all buyers who overcome some obstacle

The hurdle method solves both the seller's problems, provided that buyers with low reservation prices are more willing than others to jump the hurdle. Because the decision to jump the hurdle is subject to the cost–benefit test, such a link seems to exist. As noted earlier, buyers with low incomes are more likely than others to have low reservation prices (at least in the case of normal goods). Because of the low opportunity cost of their time, they are more likely than others to take the trouble to send in rebate coupons. Rebate coupons thus target a discount toward those buyers whose reservation prices are low and who therefore might not buy the product otherwise.

A **perfect hurdle** is one that separates buyers precisely according to their reservation prices, and in the process imposes no cost on those who jump the hurdle. With a perfect hurdle, the highest reservation price among buyers who jump the hurdle will be lower than the lowest reservation price among buyers who choose not to jump the hurdle. In practice, perfect hurdles do not exist. Some buyers will always jump the hurdle even though their reservation prices are high. And hurdles will always exclude at least some buyers with low reservation prices. Even so, many commonly used hurdles do a remarkably good job of targeting discounts to buyers with low reservation prices

**perfect hurdle** a threshold that completely segregates buyers whose reservation prices lie above it from others whose reservation prices lie below it, imposing no cost on those who jump the hurdle

## Is price discrimination a bad thing?

We are so conditioned to think of discrimination as 'bad' that we may be tempted to conclude that price discrimination must run counter to the public interest. Consider, however, the price coupon example. It is two weeks before Christmas. A supermarket advertises in a local paper, and states that anyone who cuts out and presents to the supermarket manager the coupon in the advertisement will receive a discount of 5 per cent on any oven-ready turkey in the week before Christmas.

On average, the supermarket believes that only those with low opportunity costs of time and a high marginal utility of money income (i.e. the less well off) will take the trouble to jump the hurdle. Inevitably, some inveterate high-income bargain hunters will do so as well, but an astute supermarket chain will set the hurdle so as to ensure that most of those who jump it have a lower reservation price than those who don't.

By definition, the real income of those who jump the hurdle is improved by doing so: the cost is more than offset by the benefit from paying less for the turkey. Faced with the option of paying more and/or buying a smaller turkey, but not expending effort to jump the hurdle, or jumping, they jump. Their total surplus has increased. That of those who did not jump has not been reduced. The surplus of the supermarket operator must have increased as well … otherwise he would not have made the offer. The acid test is to ask whether a prohibition on coupons would have increased or reduced the total of consumer and producer surplus.

## Examples of price discrimination

Once you grasp the principle behind the hurdle method of price discrimination, you will begin to see examples of it all around you. Next time you visit a grocery, hardware store, or electrical goods retail outlet, for instance, notice how many different product promotions include cash rebates. Temporary sales are another illustration of the hurdle method. Most of the time, stores sell most of their merchandise at the 'regular' price, but periodically they offer special sales at a significant discount. The hurdle in this instance is taking the trouble to find out when and where the sales will occur and then the cost of waiting before going to the store during that period. This technique works because buyers who care most about price (mainly those with low reservation prices) are more likely to monitor advertisements carefully and buy only during sale periods.

To give another example, book publishers typically launch a new book in hardcover form at a price from €20 to €30, and a year later they bring out a paperback edition priced between €5 and €15. In this instance, the hurdle involves having to wait the extra year and accepting a slight reduction in the quality of the finished product. People who are strongly concerned about price end up waiting for the paperback edition, while those with high reservation prices usually go for the hardback.

Consider the way in which major movies are released. The general rule is that they are released to cinemas first, then to terrestrial and satellite TV for pay-per-view, then to DVD or VCR for rental, and finally to free-to-air TV. Only movies that are not believed to have initial high reservation prices from a significant number of potential viewers appear in rental outlets first. Basically, this is the same story as in the hardback and paperback book case. The hurdle is willingness to wait to see the movie.

Commercial airlines have perfected the hurdle method to an extent matched by almost no other seller. Their supersaver fares are often less than half their regular economy class fares. To be eligible for these discounts, travellers must purchase their tickets 7–21 days in advance, and their journey must include a Saturday night stayover. Vacation travellers can more easily satisfy these restrictions than business travellers, whose schedules often change at the last moment and whose trips seldom involve Saturday stayovers. And – no surprise – the business traveller's reservation price tends to be much higher than the vacation traveller's. Using the technology of online sales they can vary prices continuously over time, and even as between purchases at any point in time (if you ask for four tickets from London to Paris you may be quoted a different price from that which would be charged for two tickets).

Or take the example of car manufacturers, who typically offer several different models of what is basically the same car with different external appearances, some technical differences and differences in trim and accessories. In Europe the classic example of this is the VW group. It sells its cars under four brands: VW, Audi, Skoda and Seat. In many cases the different marques are produced in the same factory and, for example, the Seat Ibiza shares most of its mechanical and under-the-skin components with the VW Polo. Production costs differ marginally, but by much less than the price to a purchaser. This reflects a strategy of designing and pricing models to appeal to buyer groups with different reservation prices. In the United States, Ford operates the same strategy in differentiating between Ford and Mercury offerings. In Italy, Fiat does exactly the same thing by using the Fiat, Alfa Romeo and Lancia brands (although in the case of Alfa Romeo, there are performance-enhancing modifications as well as external appearance differences). General Motors in the United States has used this strategy for over 70 years.

Recall that the efficiency loss from single-price monopoly occurs because to the monopolist the benefit of expanding output is smaller than the benefit to society as a whole. The hurdle method of price discrimination reduces this loss by giving the monopolist a practical means of cutting prices for price-sensitive buyers only. In general, the more finely the monopolist can partition a market using the hurdle method, the smaller the efficiency loss. Hurdles are not perfect, however, and some degree of efficiency will inevitably be lost.

## Economic naturalist 9.3 Why might a US appliance retailer instruct its sales staff to hammer dents into the sides of its stoves and refrigerators?

The US department store chain, Sears Roebuck, operates an occasional 'Scratch 'n' Dent Sale'. Many Sears stores hold an annual sale in which they display appliances with minor scratches and blemishes in the parking lot at heavy discounts. This is another example of how retailers use quality differentials to segregate buyers according to their reservation prices. People who don't care much about price are unlikely to turn out for these events, but those with very low reservation prices often get up early to be first in line. Indeed, these sales have proved so popular that it might even be in a retailer's interest deliberately to put dents in some of its sale items.

### RECAP Using discounts to expand the market

A price-discriminating monopolist is one who charges different prices to different buyers for essentially the same good or service. A common method of price discrimination is the hurdle method, which involves granting a discount to buyers who jump over a hurdle, such as mailing a rebate coupon. An *effective hurdle* is one that is more easily cleared by buyers with low reservation prices than by buyers with high reservation prices. Such a hurdle enables the monopolist to expand output and thereby reduce the deadweight loss from monopoly pricing.

## Public policy toward natural monopoly

Monopoly is problematic not only because of the loss in efficiency associated with restricted output but also because the monopolist as a seller earns an economic profit at the buyer's expense. Many people are understandably uncomfortable about having to purchase from the sole provider of any good or service. For this reason, voters in many societies have empowered government to adopt policies aimed at controlling natural monopolists.

There are several ways to achieve this aim. A government may assume ownership and control of a natural monopoly, or it may merely attempt to regulate the prices it charges. In some cases government solicits competitive bids from private firms to produce natural monopoly services. In still other cases, governments attempt to dissolve natural monopolies into smaller entities that compete with one another. But many of these policies create economic problems of their own. In each case, the practical challenge is to come up with the solution that yields the greatest surplus of benefits over costs. Natural monopoly may be inefficient and unfair but, as noted earlier, the alternatives to natural monopoly are far from perfect.

The need to achieve social control of natural monopolies was the generally accepted rationale that led to virtually all the network industries in Europe coming into state ownership: railways, postal services, telephone systems, airlines. In many cases the question of whether or not the cost structure of the sector concerned actually had the technical character of a natural monopoly was never rigorously examined. Indeed, there was a sort of circularity of argument in many cases: the state set up state-owned firms or nationalised private firms and amalgamated them, gave them monopoly rights and justified continuing public ownership on natural monopoly grounds.

### State ownership and management

Natural monopoly is inefficient because the monopolist's profit-maximising price is greater than its marginal cost. But even if the natural monopolist *wanted* to set price equal to marginal cost, it could not do so and hope to remain in business. After all, the defining feature of a natural monopoly is *economies of scale in production*, which means that marginal cost will always be less than average total cost. Setting price equal to marginal cost would fail to cover average total cost, which implies an economic loss.

Consider the case of a local cable television company. Once an area has been wired for cable television, the marginal cost of adding an additional subscriber is very low. For the sake of efficiency, all subscribers should pay a price equal to that marginal cost. Yet a cable company that priced in this manner would never be able to recover the fixed cost of setting up the network. This same problem applies not just to cable television companies but to all other natural monopolies. Even if such firms wanted to set price equal to marginal cost (which, of course, they do not, since they will earn more by setting marginal revenue equal to marginal cost), they cannot do so without suffering an economic loss.

One way to attack the efficiency and fairness problems is for the government to take over the industry, set price equal to marginal cost and then absorb the resulting losses out of general tax revenues. This approach has been followed with good results in the state-owned electric utility industry in France, Electricité de France, whose efficient pricing methods have set the standard for electricity pricing worldwide.

But state ownership and efficient management do not always go hand in hand. Granted, the state-owned natural monopoly is free to charge marginal cost, while the private natural monopoly is not. Yet private natural monopolies often face a much stronger incentive to cut costs than their government-owned counterparts. When the private monopolist figures out a way to cut €1 from the cost of production, its profit goes up by €1. But when the government manager of a state-owned monopoly cuts €1 from the cost of production, the government typically cuts the monopoly's budget by €1 or demands a dividend.

To the extent that this is a serious issue, we have an example of what economists call **X-inefficiency**, whereby monopoly power results in higher costs being incurred as a means of absorbing the inherent profitability of the monopoly enterprise. It happens to a degree in firms in the private sector with market power, but is a much more serious problem in the public sector because, in the private sector, shareholders can (and do) fire inefficient managers so as to realise profits, while, in the public sector, governments have weak incentives to act decisively to curb waste in public sector firms, and poor information on which to act. Whether the efficiency that is gained by being able to set price equal to marginal cost outweighs the inefficiency that results from a weakened incentive to cut costs is an empirical question.

**X-inefficiency** where market power results in inefficient production rather than higher profits

## State regulation of private monopolies

Dissatisfaction with public ownership (costly, slow to innovate, poor responses to changes in demand ...) has led to widespread divestment of state enterprise across Europe. However, the consequences have frequently been the creation of privately owned suppliers with substantial market power, bordering on monopoly. As a result, privatisation has been accompanied by increased emphasis on regulation: legal and administrative structures that are entitled to lay down operational requirements and controls (pricing, availability, quality ...) for the firms concerned. While this is relatively new in Europe (dating for the most part from the 1980s), it has been the standard US procedure for dealing with natural monopolies and similar circumstances for a very long time. The most common US method of curbing monopoly profits is for government merely to regulate the natural monopoly rather than own it. Most US states, for example, take this approach with electricity utilities, natural gas providers, local telephone companies and cable television companies. The standard procedure in these cases is called **cost-plus regulation**: government regulators gather data on the monopolist's explicit costs of production and then permit the monopolist to set prices that cover those costs, plus a mark-up to assure a normal return on the firm's investment.

While it may sound reasonable, cost-plus regulation has several pitfalls. First, it generates costly administrative proceedings in which regulators and firms quarrel over which of the firm's expenditures can properly be included in the costs it is allowed to recover. This question is difficult to answer even in theory. Consider a firm such as Pacific Telesis, originally the Californian telecommunications operator, but now a communications conglomerate. Its local telephone service is subject to cost-plus regulation but other products and services are unregulated. Many Pacific Telesis employees, from the president down, are involved in both regulated and unregulated activities. How should their salaries be allocated between the two? The company has a strong incentive to argue for greater allocation to the regulated activities, which allows it to capture more revenue from captive customers in the local telephone market.

**cost-plus regulation** a method of regulation under which the regulated firm is permitted to charge a price equal to its explicit costs of production plus a mark-up to cover the opportunity cost of resources provided by the firm's owners

A second problem with cost-plus regulation is that it blunts the firm's incentive to adopt cost-saving innovations, for, when it does, regulators require the firm to cut its rates. The firm gets to keep its cost savings in the current period, which is a stronger incentive to cut costs than that facing a government-owned monopoly. But the incentive to cut costs would be stronger still if the firm could retain its cost savings indefinitely. Furthermore, in cases in which regulators set rates by allowing the monopolist to add a fixed mark-up to costs incurred, the regulated monopolist may actually have an incentive to *increase* costs rather than reduce them. Outrageous though the thought may be, the monopolist may earn a higher profit by installing gold-plated water taps in the company rest rooms.

Finally, cost-plus regulation does not solve the natural monopolist's basic problem, the inability to set price equal to marginal cost without losing money. Although these are all serious problems, governments seemed to be in no hurry to abandon cost-plus regulation.

Another mechanism frequently used is *rate of return* regulation. This lays down the maximum profits a supplier may earn by reference to the capital employed. For example, it could be obliged to set prices on the basis that they permit a 15 per cent return to capital employed. If profits exceed this amount they are either taken away from the firm or it is obliged to reduce prices. *X-inefficiency* is a problem here, too, since a firm can allow other costs to increase since it will lose the profits anyway. More seriously, it can lead to firms investing in capital assets not on the basis of their contribution to net output but simply to permit retention of profits.

For these reasons, recent developments in European regulation have emphasised using *price rules* to sweat productivity out of regulated industries. A classic example of this is the RPI-X approach of the UK regulator in the electricity sector, Ofelec. RPI means the retail price index, for a long time the main UK measure for inflation. The RPI-X approach sets a rule: your price may rise only at *X* per cent less than the inflation rate. *X* is set at a level designed to oblige the firm to implement cost-saving technology as it becomes available, and to rely on productivity gains rather than higher price–cost margins to generate profits.

Such a rule also has its problems, because it can lead to cost cutting at the expense of consumer safety (alleged in the United Kingdom in the case of Railtrack, the entity which was vested with the ownership of the railway infrastructure), and requires the regulator to have accurate knowledge of the potential for cost savings from new technology and productivity improvements that may in fact be difficult to know at all, or knowledge that is in effect confined to the firms being regulated.

## Exclusive contracting for natural monopoly

One of the most promising methods for dealing with natural monopoly is for the government to invite private firms to bid for the natural monopolist's market. The government specifies in detail the service it wants – cable television, fire protection, refuse collection – and firms submit bids describing how much they will charge for the service. The lowest bidder wins the contract.

The incentive to cut costs under such an arrangement is every bit as powerful as that facing ordinary competitive firms. Competition among bidders should also eliminate any concerns about the fairness of monopoly profits. And if the government is willing to provide a cash subsidy to the winning bidder, exclusive contracting even allows the monopolist to set price equal to marginal cost.

Contracting has been employed with good results in municipal fire protection and refuse collection. US communities that employ private companies to provide these services often spend only half as much as adjacent communities served by municipal fire and sanitation departments.

Despite these attractive features, however, exclusive contracting is not without problems, especially when the service to be provided is complex or requires a large fixed investment in capital equipment. In such cases, contract specifications may be so detailed and complicated that they become tantamount to regulating the firm directly. And in cases involving a large fixed investment – electricity generation and distribution, for example – officials face the question of how to transfer the assets if a new firm wins the contract. The winning firm naturally wants to acquire the assets as cheaply as possible, but the retiring firm is entitled to a fair price for them. What, in such cases, is a 'fair price'? Fire protection and refuse collection are simple enough, so the costs of contracting out these functions is not prohibitive. But in other cases such costs might easily outweigh any savings made possible by exclusive contracting.

This approach is becoming very common. In Europe. The highest bridge in Europe, in Tarn in France, was built by a private sector firm that won the contract to build and toll the bridge. It was opened in December 2004. Motorway construction in Ireland is increasingly being undertaken on the basis of competitive contracting to build and operate (i.e. toll) the roads. A significant proportion of London bus transport is by franchised private operators. In New Zealand, although it remains in state ownership, the postal service is operated by New Zealand Post under a franchise contract with the government.

## Vigorous enforcement of anti-trust laws

The nineteenth century witnessed the accumulation of massive private fortunes, the likes of which had never been seen in the industrialised world. This was particularly true in the protected industrial sector of the booming US economy. Public sentiment ran high against the so-called 'robber barons' of the period – the Carnegies, Mellons, Rockefellers and others. In 1890, the US Congress passed the Sherman Act, which declared illegal any conspiracy 'to monopolise, or attempt to monopolise ... any part of the trade or commerce among the several States'. In 1914, Congress passed the Clayton Act, whose aim was to prevent corporations from acquiring shares in a competitor if the transaction would 'substantially lessen competition or create a monopoly'.

Since the Second World War, but mostly since the requirements of EU membership began to take effect, European countries and the Union have followed the US example by legislation and regulation affecting market structure (mergers and acquisitions (M&A) controls) and the behaviour of firms with substantial market power (in EU language, prohibitions on the 'abuse of a dominant position'). These are built into the grounding treaty provisions of the Union in Articles 81 and 82 of the Treaty of Amsterdam (Articles 85 and 86 of the Rome Treaty it updates).

The generic term most widely used to cover this activity is 'anti-trust laws', recognising their origin in the United States. Anti-trust laws have helped to prevent the formation of *cartels*, or coalitions of firms that collude to raise prices above competitive levels. An early European example of this was the action of the EEC (as it was then) Commission to punish United Brands, the largest banana supplier in Europe, for third-degree price discrimination by segmenting the EEC markets of six states in the 1960s. More recently, the French authorities and the Union imposed heavy fines on the cement producers of Europe who were found to be operating a cartel. The motor trade in Europe has been radically changed in the early 2000s by EU anti-trust actions designed to outlaw vertical distribution agreements operated by manufacturers and retailers that reduce intra-brand and inter-brand competition in the sector.

But such activities have also caused some harm. For example, US federal anti-trust officials spent more than a decade trying to break up the IBM Corporation in the belief that it had achieved an unhealthy dominance in the computer industry. That view was proved comically wrong by IBM's subsequent failure to foresee and profit from the rise of the personal computer. By breaking up large companies and discouraging mergers between companies in the same industry, anti-trust laws may help to promote competition, but they may also prevent companies from achieving *economies of scale*. Similarly, the US and EU cases against Microsoft have been criticised in some quarters as a waste of time, as they assumed that Microsoft's position, undoubtedly bolstered by some dubious practices in 'bundling' and in generating artificial incompatibilities, needed legal action to remedy the situation. And then along comes Linux ...

A final possibility is simply to ignore the problem of natural monopoly: to let the monopolist choose the quantity to produce and sell it at whatever price the market will bear. The obvious objections to this policy are the two we began with – namely, that a natural monopoly is not only inefficient but also unfair. But just as the hurdle method of price discrimination mitigates efficiency losses, it also lessens the concern about taking unfair advantage of buyers.

Consider first the source of the natural monopolist's economic profit. This firm, recall, is one with economies of scale, which means that its average production cost declines as output increases. Efficiency requires that price be set at marginal cost, but because the natural monopolist's marginal cost is lower than its average cost, it cannot charge all buyers the marginal cost without suffering an economic loss.

The depth and prevalence of discount pricing suggests that whatever economic profit a natural monopolist earns will generally not come out of the discount buyer's pocket. Although discount prices are higher than the monopolist's marginal cost of production, in most cases they are lower than the average cost. Thus the monopolist's economic profit, if any, must come from buyers who pay the list price. And since those buyers have the option, in most cases, of jumping a hurdle and paying a discount price, their contribution, if not completely voluntary, is at least not strongly coerced.

So much for the source of the monopolist's economic profit. What about its disposition? Who gets it? A large chunk goes to government via a corporation tax. The remainder is paid out to shareholders, some of whom are wealthy and some of whom are not. However, when we realise that over 80 per cent of shares are held by 'institutions', mostly pension funds, the redistributive consequences of monopoly power become much less clear.

Both the source of the monopolist's economic profit (the list-price buyer) and the disposition of that profit (largely, to fund public services) cast doubt on the claim that monopoly profit constitutes a social injustice on any grand scale. Nevertheless, the hurdle method of differential pricing cannot completely eliminate the fairness and efficiency problems that result from monopoly pricing. In the end, then, we are left with a choice among imperfect alternatives. As the Cost–Benefit Principle emphasises, the best choice is the one for which the balance of benefits over costs is largest. But which choice that is will depend on the circumstances at hand.

## RECAP Public policy toward natural monopoly

The natural monopolist sets price above marginal cost, resulting in too little output from society's point of view (the *efficiency* problem). The natural monopolist may also earn an economic profit at buyer's expense (the *fairness* problem). Policies for dealing with the efficiency and fairness problems include state ownership and management, state regulation, exclusive contracting and vigorous enforcement of anti-trust laws. Each of these remedies entails problems of its own.

## Summary

- Our concern in this chapter was the conduct and performance of the *imperfectly competitive firm*, a firm that has at least some latitude to set its own price. Economists often distinguish among three different types of imperfectly competitive firms: the pure monopolist, the lone seller of a product in a given market; the oligopolist, one of only a few sellers of a given product; and the monopolistic competitor, one of a relatively large number of firms that sell similar though slightly differentiated products.
- Although advanced courses in economics devote much attention to differences in behaviour among these three types of firm, our focus was on the common feature that differentiates them from perfectly competitive firms. Whereas the perfectly competitive firm faces an infinitely elastic demand curve for its product, the imperfectly competitive firm faces a *downward-sloping demand curve*. For convenience, we use the term *monopolist* to refer to any of the three types of imperfectly competitive firms.
- Monopolists are sometimes said to enjoy *market power*, a term that refers to their power to set the price of their product. Market power stems from exclusive control over important inputs, from economies of scale, from patents and government licences or franchises and from network economies. The most important and enduring of these five sources of market power are economies of scale and network economies.
- Unlike the perfectly competitive firm, for which marginal revenue exactly equals market price, the monopolist realises a *marginal revenue that is always less than its price*. This shortfall reflects the fact that to sell more output, the monopolist must cut the price not only to additional buyers but to existing buyers as well. For the monopolist with a straight-line demand curve, the marginal revenue curve has the same vertical intercept and a horizontal intercept that is half as large as the intercept for the demand curve.
- Whereas the perfectly competitive firm maximises profit by producing at the level at which marginal cost equals the market price, the monopolist maximises profit by equating marginal cost with marginal revenue, which is significantly lower than the market price. The result is an output level that is best for the monopolist but smaller than the level that would be best for society as a whole. At the *profit-maximising* level of output, the benefit of an extra unit of output (the market price) is greater than its cost (the marginal cost). At the *socially efficient* level of output, where the monopolist's marginal cost curve intersects the demand curve, the benefit and cost of an extra unit are the same.
- Both the monopolist and its potential customers can do better if the monopolist can grant discounts to price-sensitive buyers. The extreme example is the *perfectly discriminating monopolist*, who charges each buyer exactly his or her reservation price. Such producers are socially efficient, because they sell to every buyer whose reservation price is at least as high as the marginal cost.
- One common method of targeting discounts toward price-sensitive buyers is the *hurdle method* of price discrimination, in which the buyer becomes eligible for a discount only after overcoming some obstacle, such as mailing in a rebate coupon. This technique works well because those buyers who care most about price are more likely than others to jump the hurdle. While the hurdle method reduces the efficiency loss associated with single-price monopoly, it does not completely eliminate it.
- The various policies that governments employ to mitigate concerns about fairness and efficiency losses arising from natural monopoly include state ownership and management of natural monopolies, state regulation, private contracting and vigorous enforcement of anti-trust laws. Each of these remedies entails costs as well as benefits. In some cases, a *combination* of policies will produce a better outcome than simply allowing natural monopolists to do as they please. But in other cases, a *hands-off* policy may be the best available option.

## Key terms

constant returns to scale (245)
cost-plus regulation (264)
hurdle method of price discrimination (260)
imperfectly competitive firm (242)
increasing returns to scale (245)
marginal revenue (249)
market power (244)
monopolistically competitive firm (242)
natural monopoly (245)
oligopolist (242)
perfect hurdle (261)
perfectly discriminating monopolist (260)
price discrimination (258)
price setter (241)
pure monopoly (242)
X-inefficiency (264)

## Review questions

1. What important characteristic do all three types of imperfectly competitive firm share?
2. **True or false:** A firm with market power can sell whatever quantity it wishes at whatever price it chooses.
3. Why do most successful industrial societies offer patents and copyright protection, even though these protections enable sellers to charge higher prices?
4. Why is marginal revenue always less than price for a monopolist but equal to price for a perfectly competitive firm?
5. **True or false:** Because a natural monopolist charges a price greater than marginal cost, it necessarily earns a positive economic profit.

## Problems

1. Two car manufacturers, Saab and Volvo, have fixed costs of €1 billion and marginal costs of €10,000 per car. If Saab produces 50,000 cars per year and Volvo produces 200,000, calculate the average production cost for each company. On the basis of these costs, which company's market share do you think will grow in relative terms?

In Problems 2–4 state whether the statements are **true or false**, and explain why.

2. a. In a perfectly competitive industry the industry demand curve is horizontal, whereas for a monopoly it is downward-sloping.
   b. Perfectly competitive firms have no control over the price they charge for their product.
   c. For a natural monopoly, average cost declines as the number of units produced increases over the relevant output range.
3. A single-price profit-maximising monopolist:
   a. Causes excess demand, or shortages, by selling too few units of a good or service.
   b. Chooses the output level at which marginal revenue begins to increase.
   c. Always charges a price above the marginal cost of production.
   d. Also maximises marginal revenue.
   e. None of the above statements is true.
4. If a monopolist could perfectly price discriminate:
   a. The marginal revenue curve and the demand curve would coincide.
   b. The marginal revenue curve and the marginal cost curve would coincide.

c. Every consumer would pay a different price.

d. Marginal revenue would become negative at some output level.

e. The resulting pattern of exchange would still be socially inefficient.

5. Explain why price discrimination and the existence of slightly different variants of the same product tend to go hand in hand. Give an example from your own experience.

6. What is the socially desirable price for a natural monopoly to charge? Why will a natural monopoly that attempts to charge the socially desirable price invariably suffer an economic loss?

7. TotsPoses, a profit-maximising business, is the only photography business in town that specialises in portraits of small children. George, who owns and runs TotsPoses, expects to encounter an average of eight customers per day, each with a reservation price shown in the table below.

| Customer | Reservation price (€ per photo) |
|---|---|
| *A* | 50 |
| *B* | 46 |
| *C* | 42 |
| *D* | 38 |
| *E* | 34 |
| *F* | 30 |
| *G* | 26 |
| *H* | 22 |

a. If the total cost of each photo portrait is €12, how much should George charge if he must charge a single price to all customers? At this price, how many portraits will George produce each day? What will be his economic profit?

b. How much consumer surplus is generated each day at this price?

c. What is the socially efficient number of portraits?

d. George is very experienced in the business and knows the reservation price of each of his customers. If he is allowed to charge any price he likes to any consumer, how many portraits will he produce each day, and what will his economic profit be?

e. In this case, how much consumer surplus is generated each day?

f. Suppose that George is permitted to charge two prices. He knows that customers with a reservation price above $30 never bother with coupons, whereas those with a reservation price of €30 or less always use them. At what level should George set the list price of a portrait? At what level should he set the discount price? How many photo portraits will he sell at each price?

g. In this case, what is George's economic profit, and how much consumer surplus is generated each day?

7. Suppose that a university student cinema is a local monopoly whose demand curve for adult tickets on Saturday night is $P = 12 - 2Q$, where $P$ is the price of a ticket in euros and $Q$ is the number of tickets sold in hundreds. The demand for children's tickets on Sunday afternoon is $P = 8 - 3Q$, and for adult tickets on Sunday afternoon, $P = 10 - 4Q$. On both Saturday night and Sunday afternoon, the marginal cost of an additional patron, child or adult, is €2.

a. What is the marginal revenue curve in each of the three sub-markets?

b. What price should the cinema charge in each of the three sub-markets if its goal is to maximise profit?

8. Suppose you are a monopolist in the market for a specific video game. Your demand curve is given by $P = 80 - Q/2$, and your marginal cost curve is $MC = Q$. Your fixed costs equal €400.

a. Graph the demand and marginal cost curve.

b. Derive and graph the marginal revenue curve.

c. Calculate and indicate on the graph the equilibrium price and quantity.

d. What is your profit?

e. What is the level of consumer surplus?

9. Beth is an 8-year-old who old sells home-made lemonade on a street corner in a suburban neighbourhood. Each paper cup of lemonade costs Beth 20 cents to produce; she has no fixed costs. The reservation prices for the 10 people who walk by Beth's lemonade stand each day are listed in the table below.

| Person | A | B | C | D | E | F | G | H | I | J |
|---|---|---|---|---|---|---|---|---|---|---|
| Reservation price (€) | 1.00 | 0.90 | 0.80 | 0.70 | 0.60 | 0.50 | 0.40 | 0.30 | 0.20 | 0.10 |

Beth knows the distribution of reservation prices (that is, she knows that one person is willing to pay €1, another €0.90, and so on), but she does not know any specific individual's reservation price.

a. Calculate the marginal revenue of selling an additional cup of lemonade. (Start by figuring out the price Beth would charge if she produced only one cup of lemonade, and calculate the total revenue; then find the price Beth would charge if she sold two cups of lemonade; and so on.)

b. What is Beth's profit-maximising price?

c. At that price, what are Beth's economic profit and total consumer surplus?

d. What price should Beth charge if she wants to maximise total economic surplus?

Now suppose that Beth can tell the reservation price of each person. What price would she charge each person if she wanted to maximise profit? Compare her profit to the total surplus calculated in part (c).

## Answers to in-chapter exercises

9.1 The relevant cost figures are as shown in the table below, which shows that Playstation's unit-cost advantage is now €50.20 – €5.20 = €45.00.

| | Nintendo | Playstation |
|---|---|---|
| Annual production | 200,000 | 2,000,000 |
| Fixed cost | €10,000,000 | €10,000,000 |
| Variable cost | €40,000 | €400,000 |
| Total cost | €10,040,000 | €10,400,000 |
| Average total cost per game | €50.20 | €5.20 |

9.2 When the monopolist expands from 3 to 4 units per week, total revenue rises from €15 to €16 per week, which means that the marginal revenue from the sale of the fourth unit is only $1 per week. When the monopolist expands from 4 to 5 units per week, total revenue drops from €16 to €15 per week, which means that the marginal revenue from the sale of the fifth unit is actually negative, or –€1 per week.

**9.3** For the demand curve $P = 12 - Q$, the corresponding marginal revenue curve is $MR = 12 - 2Q$. Equating $MR$ and $MC$, we solve the equation $12 - 2Q = 2Q$ for $Q = 3$. Substituting $Q = 3$ into the demand equation, we solve for the profit-maximising price, $P = 12 - 3 = 9$.

**9.4** Substitute the value of 1,500 into the expression for $TR$ and $TC$; subtract $TC$ from $TR$, and profit is what is left. Excess burden is given by the expression $(1/2)(P - MC)(q_{pc} - q)$, where $q$ is the value already found (1,500) and $q_{pc}$ is the competitive output, where price equals $MC$. Set $MC = p$ and solve for $q$. Profit is €15 million and deadweight loss is €6.75 million.

# 10

# Thinking Strategically: Competition among the Few

A US newspaper at the end of the 1990s[1] carried a story originating in that centre of wheeling, dealing and couch casting, Hollywood. At a Christmas Eve dinner party in 1997, actor Robert De Niro asked singer Tony Bennett if he would be willing to sing 'Got the World on a String' in the final scene of a film that De Niro would be acting in and which was to be produced by Warner Brothers. He was referring to the project that became the 1999 hit comedy *Analyze This*, in which the troubled head of a crime family, played by De Niro, seeks the counsel of a psychotherapist, played by Billy Crystal. In the script, both the mob boss and his therapist are big fans of Bennett's music. Bennett said he would be interested, and that was that ... for a year.

Then his son and agent, Danny Bennett, received a phone call from Warner Brothers to discuss terms. They had in mind a fee of $15,000 for Bennett Sr for singing the song in the final scene. That's not bad pay for an hour's work, so it was a very reasonable offer, and one any singer (or his agent) would be expected to accept in a semi-quaver. Unfortunately, the Warner negotiator let slip that the film was already in the can except for the final scene and the song, and the script clearly led up to this particular song and singer at the ending. Bennett Jr managed to get Warner Brothers up to $200,000. They were over the proverbial barrel. Had they put the offer to Bennett a year earlier, before shooting began, they would have been €185,000 better off. As they say: in life, timing is everything!

The payoff to many actions depends not only on the actions themselves but also on when they are taken and how they relate to actions taken by others. In Chapters 6–9, economic decision makers confronted an environment that was essentially fixed. This chapter will focus on cases in which people must consider the effect of their behavior on others. For example, an imperfectly competitive firm will in many circumstances want to weigh the likely responses of rivals when deciding whether to cut prices or to increase the advertising budget. *Interdependences* of this sort are the rule rather than the exception in economic and social life. To make sense of the world we live in, then, we must take these interdependences into account.

An analytical method for handling this type of problem is what is known as game theory. Its origins may be found in a book published in 1944 written by John von Neumann and

[1] *The New York Times*, 2 May 1999.

Oskar Morgenstern, *The Theory of Games and Economic Behavior*.[2] This book started from the premise that much economic behaviour can be analysed as a choice of a strategy in situations where people's interests do not coincide, so that *conflict between decision makers* is inevitable. Von Neumann and Morgenstern developed a mathematical methodology for analysing this type of situation. Then, in the early 1950s, John Nash,[3] a mathematician at Princeton, produced a couple of path-breaking papers dealing with the concept of an *equilibrium in a game* – meaning, loosely, an outcome that is stable and predictable given the motives of, and constraints facing, the players. Modern game theory has been built on these foundations, and Nash was subsequently awarded the Nobel Prize in Economics.

## The theory of games

In chess, tennis, or any other game, the payoff to a given move depends on *what your opponent does in response*. In choosing your move, therefore, you must anticipate your opponent's responses, how you might respond and what further moves your own response might elicit.

Consider the following problem that shows how this idea applies in economics. You have decided to open a small supermarket in your home town neighbourhood, where there is already an established store belonging to a major national chain. The reason is that you have good information that there is 'cash on the table' in the form of profits to be appropriated if you can attract a sufficient number of customers from the incumbent. You do so because you estimate that you can offer a better value-for-money service. You could do this by undercutting the prices of the incumbent. You could do this simply by offering a different choice of goods. You could do this by offering a service that that will attract a sufficient number of higher-income shoppers to you who are not satisfied with the one-size-fits-all offerings of the established chain. The market share you hope to achieve makes the proposal profitable. But will you achieve it? That depends on how the incumbent firm reacts.

It could decide that the loss of market share is such that it must respond by lowering prices (increasing value for money). It could decide that there is room in the market for both of you, and it might be happy (if you go up-market) to leave the upper end of the market (with all the problems of dealing with better-off and more demanding purchasers) to you. It could decide that if you succeed in this venture it is probable that others will imitate you in other local markets, threatening the financial viability of its operations as a whole, and so launch a price war designed to force you out, on the basis that the sight of a corpse hanging from a gibbet deters imitation. Whether or not you enter the market, and the strategy you adopt in the market, will reflect your opinion as to what the other side will do in response to your decision. It's not at all clear that it makes sense to enter just because you see a profitable opportunity in the form of 'cash on the table'. In order to analyse and to predict outcomes in such situations, in which the payoffs to different actors depend on the actions their opponents undertake, economists and other behavioural scientists have devised the mathematical theory of games.

**basic elements of a game** the players, the strategies available to each player and the payoffs each player receives for each possible combination of strategies

### The three elements of a game

Any game has three **basic elements:** the *players*, the list of possible actions (or *strategies*) each player can choose from and the *payoffs* the players receive for each combination of strategies. How these elements combine to form the basis of a theory of behaviour will become clear in the context of Examples 10.1–10.3.

[2] Von Neumann and Morgenstern (1944).

[3] Nash's sad life (he was diagnosed paranoid schizophrenic) was the subject of the movie *A Beautiful Mind*. For an economist, unfortunately, the movie is marred by its failure to make clear the significance, simple elegance and enormous analytical implications of his exposition of what is now known as the concept of a Nash equilibrium (see p. 276).

### Example 10.1 Should Lufthansa spend more money on advertising?

Suppose that Lufthansa and Alitalia are the only air carriers that serve the Frankfurt–Milan route. Each currently earns an economic profit of €6,000 per flight on this route. If Lufthansa increases its advertising spending in this market by €1,000 per flight and Alitalia spends no more on advertising than it does now, Lufthansa's profit will rise to €8,000 per flight and Alitalia's will fall to €2,000. If both spend €1,000 more on advertising, each will earn an economic profit of €5,500 per flight. These payoffs are symmetric, so if Lufthansa stands still while Alitalia increases its spending by €1,000, Lufthansa's economic profit will fall to €2,000 per flight and Alitalia's will rise to €8,000. If each must decide independently whether to increase spending on advertising, what should Lufthansa do?

Think of this situation as a game. What are its three elements? The players are the two airlines, each of which must choose one of two strategies: to raise spending by €1,000 or to leave it the same. The payoffs are the economic profits that correspond to the four possible scenarios resulting from their choices. One way to summarise the relevant information about this game is to display the players, strategies, and payoffs in the form of a simple table called a **payoff matrix** (see Table 10.1).

**payoff matrix** a table that describes the payoffs in a game for each possible combination of strategies

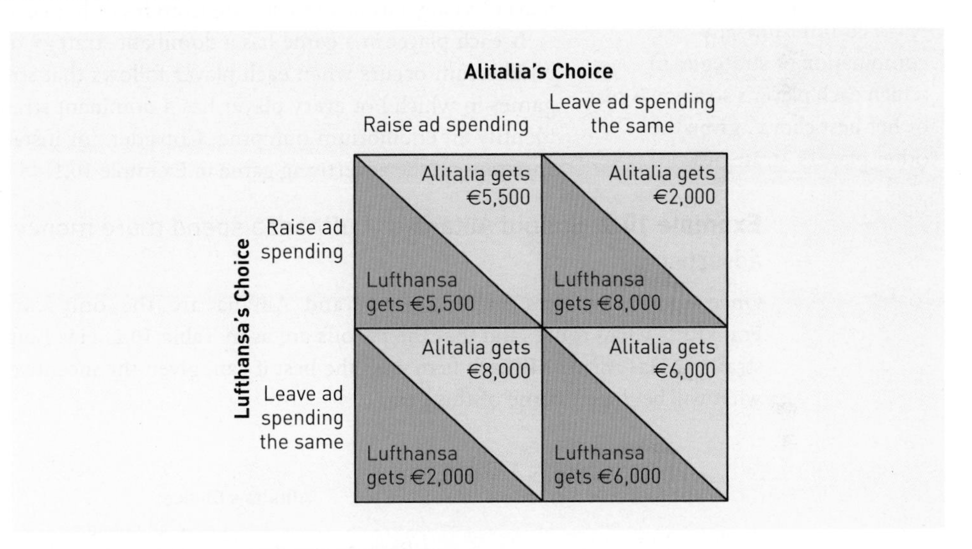

| Lufthansa's Choice | Alitalia's Choice: Raise ad spending | Alitalia's Choice: Leave ad spending the same |
|---|---|---|
| Raise ad spending | Alitalia gets €5,500<br>Lufthansa gets €5,500 | Alitalia gets €2,000<br>Lufthansa gets €8,000 |
| Leave ad spending the same | Alitalia gets €8,000<br>Lufthansa gets €2,000 | Alitalia gets €6,000<br>Lufthansa gets €6,000 |

**Table 10.1** The Payoff Matrix for an Advertising Game

Confronted with the payoff matrix in Table 10.1, what should Lufthansa do? The essence of strategic thinking is to begin by looking at the situation from the other party's point of view. Suppose Alitalia assumes that Lufthansa will raise its spending on advertising (the top row in Table 10.1). In that case, Alitalia's best bet would be to follow suit (the left column in Table 10.1). Why is the left column Alitalia's best response when Lufthansa chooses the top row? Alitalia's economic profits, given in the upper left cell of Table 10.1, will be €5,500 as compared with only €2,000 if it keeps spending level (see the upper right cell).

Alternatively, suppose Alitalia assumes that Lufthansa will keep its ad spending level (that is, Lufthansa will choose the bottom row in Table 10.1). In that case, Alitalia would still do better to increase spending, because it would earn €8,000 (the lower left cell) as compared with only €6,000 if it keeps spending level (the lower right cell). In this particular game, no matter which strategy Lufthansa chooses, Alitalia will earn a higher economic profit by increasing its spending on advertising. And since this game is perfectly symmetric, a similar conclusion holds for Lufthansa: no matter which strategy Alitalia chooses, Lufthansa will do better by increasing its spending on ads.

When one player has a strategy that yields a higher payoff no matter which choice the other player makes, that player is said to have a **dominant strategy**. Not all games involve dominant strategies, but both players in this game have one, and that is to increase spending on ads. For both players, to leave ad spending the same is a **dominated strategy** – one that leads to a lower payoff than an alternative choice, regardless of the other player's choice.

**dominant strategy** one that yields a higher payoff no matter what the other players in a game choose

**dominated strategy** any other strategy available to a player who has a dominant strategy

Notice, however, that when each player chooses the dominant strategy, the resulting payoffs are smaller than if each had left spending unchanged. When Lufthansa and Alitalia increase their spending on ads, each earns only €5,500 in economic profits as compared with the €6,000 each would have earned without the increase. (We'll say more below about this apparent paradox.)

## Nash equilibrium

A game is said to be in equilibrium if each player's strategy is the best he or she can choose, given the other players' chosen strategies. This definition of equilibrium is sometimes called a **Nash equilibrium**, after the Nobel Laureate John Nash. When a game is in equilibrium, no player has any incentive to deviate from his or her current strategy.

**Nash equilibrium** any combination of strategies in which each player's strategy is his or her best choice, given the other players' strategies

If each player in a game has a dominant strategy, as in Example 10.1, equilibrium occurs when each player follows that strategy. But even in games in which not every player has a dominant strategy, we can often identify an equilibrium outcome. Consider, for instance, the following variation on the advertising game in Example 10.1.

### **Example 10.2** Should Alitalia or Lufthansa spend more money on advertising?

Once again, suppose that Lufthansa and Alitalia are the only carriers serving the Frankfurt–Milan route, and that the payoffs are as in Table 10.2. Has Lufthansa a dominant strategy? Has Alitalia? If each firm does the best it can, given the incentives facing the other, what will be the outcome of this game?

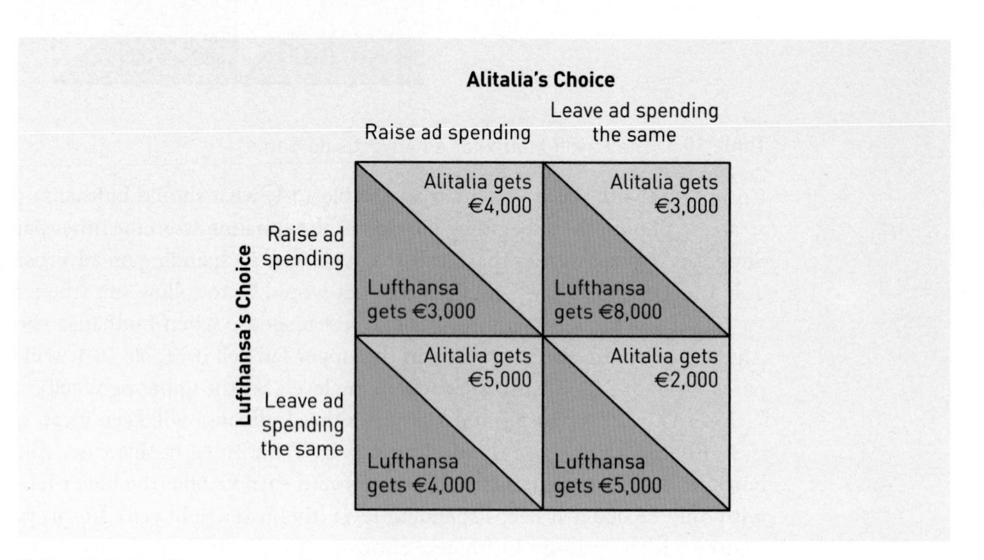

| Lufthansa's Choice \ Alitalia's Choice | Raise ad spending | Leave ad spending the same |
|---|---|---|
| Raise ad spending | Alitalia gets €4,000; Lufthansa gets €3,000 | Alitalia gets €3,000; Lufthansa gets €8,000 |
| Leave ad spending the same | Alitalia gets €5,000; Lufthansa gets €4,000 | Alitalia gets €2,000; Lufthansa gets €5,000 |

**Table 10.2** Equilibrium when One Player Lacks a Dominant Strategy

In this particular game, no matter what Lufthansa does, Alitalia will do better to raise its ad spending, so raising the advertising budget is a dominant strategy for Alitalia. Lufthansa, however, does not have a dominant strategy. If Alitalia raises its spending, Lufthansa will do better to stand still; if Alitalia stands still, however, Lufthansa will do better to spend more. But even though Lufthansa hasn't a dominant strategy, we can still predict what is likely to happen in this game. After all, Lufthansa's managers know what the payoff matrix is, so they can predict that Alitalia will spend more on ads (since that is Alitalia's dominant strategy). Thus the best strategy for Lufthansa, given the prediction that Alitalia will spend more on ads, is to keep its own spending level. If both players do the best they can, taking account of the incentives each faces, this game will end in the lower left cell of the payoff matrix in Table 10.2: Alitalia will raise its spending on ads and Lufthansa will not. (Note that when both players are positioned in the lower left cell, neither has any incentive to change its strategy.)

Note that the choices corresponding to the lower left cell in Table 10.2 satisfy the definition of a Nash equilibrium. If Lufthansa found itself in that cell, its alternative would be to raise its ad spending, a move that would reduce its payoff from €4,000 to €3,000. So Lufthansa has no incentive to abandon the lower left cell. Similarly, if Alitalia found itself in the lower left cell of Table 10.2, its alternative would be to leave ad spending the same, a move that would reduce its payoff from €5,000 to €2,000. So Alitalia also has no incentive to abandon the lower left cell. And that means that the lower left cell of Table 10.2 is a Nash equilibrium – a combination of strategies for which each player's choice is the best available option, given the choice made by the other player.

**Exercise 10.1** What should Lufthansa and Alitalia do if their payoff matrix is modified as follows?

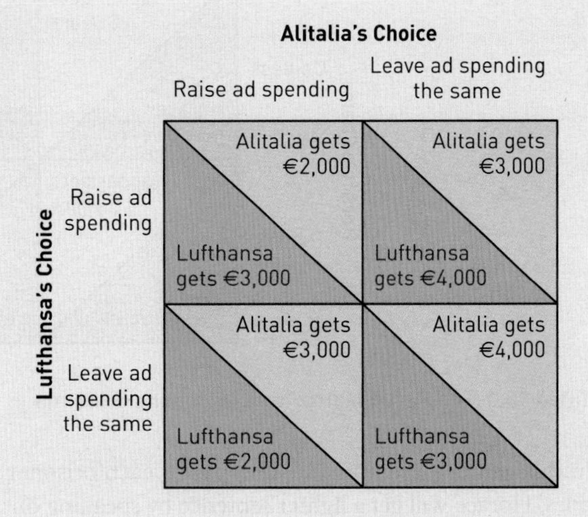


## RECAP The theory of games

The three elements of any game are the players, the list of strategies from which they can choose and the payoffs to each combination of strategies. Players in some games have a *dominant strategy*, one that yields a higher payoff regardless of the strategies.

*Equilibrium* in a game occurs when each player's strategy choice yields the highest payoff available, given the strategies by other players. Such a combination of strategies is called a *Nash equilibrium*.

## The prisoner's dilemma

**prisoner's dilemma** a game in which each player has a dominant strategy, and when each plays it, the resulting payoffs are smaller than if each had played a dominated strategy

The game in Example 10.1 belongs to an important class of games called the **prisoner's dilemma**. In the prisoner's dilemma, when each player chooses his dominant strategy, the result is unattractive to the group of players as a whole.

### The original prisoner's dilemma

Example 10.3 recounts the original scenario from which the prisoner's dilemma drew its name.

**Example 10.3** Should the prisoners confess?

Two prisoners, Horace and Jasper, are being held in separate cells for a serious crime that they did in fact commit. The prosecutor, however, has only enough hard evidence to convict them of a minor offence, for which the penalty is 1 year in jail. Each prisoner is told that if one confesses while the other remains silent, the confessor will be released without prosecution, and the other will spend 20 years in prison. If both confess, they will get an intermediate sentence of 5 years. (These payoffs are summarised in Table 10.3.) The two prisoners are not allowed to communicate with one another. Do they have a dominant strategy? If so, what is it?

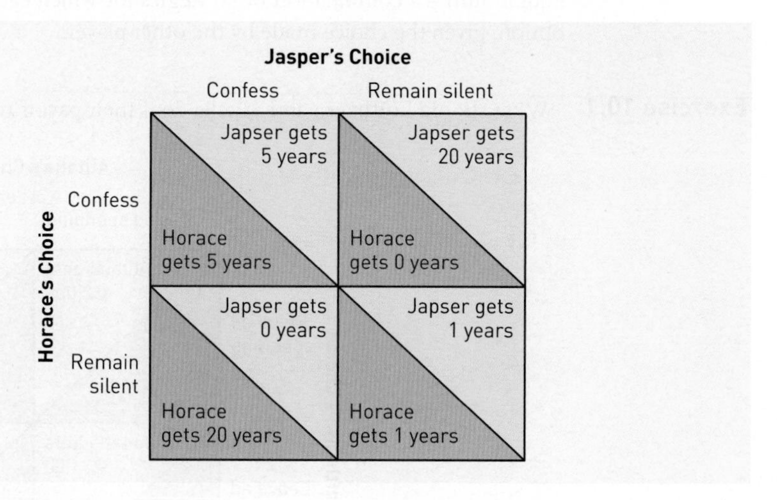


**Table 10.3** The Payoff Matrix for a Prisoner's Dilemma

In this game, the dominant strategy for each prisoner is to confess. No matter what Jasper does, Horace will get a lighter sentence by speaking out. If Jasper confesses, Horace will get 5 years (upper left cell in Table 10.3) instead of 20 (lower left cell). If Jasper remains silent, Horace will go free (upper right cell) instead of spending a year in jail (lower right cell). Because the payoffs are perfectly symmetrical: Jasper will also do better to confess, no matter what Horace does. The difficulty is that when each follows his dominant strategy and confesses, both will do worse than if each had said nothing. When both confess, they each get 5 years (upper left cell) instead of the 1 year they would have received by remaining silent (lower right cell). Hence the name of this game, the prisoner's dilemma (or, indeed, prisoners' dilemma).

**Exercise 10.2** GM and Chrysler must both decide whether to invest in a new process. Games 1 and 2 show how their profits depend on the decisions they might make. Which of these games is a prisoner's dilemma?

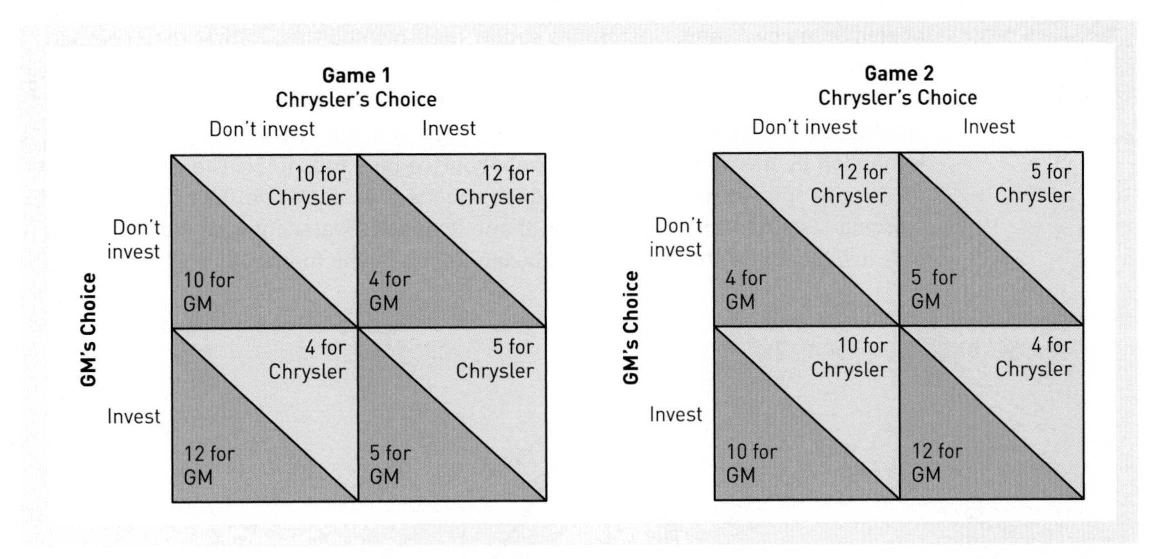


The prisoner's dilemma is one of the most powerful metaphors in all of human behavioural science. Countless social and economic interactions have payoff structures analogous to the one confronted by the two prisoners. Some of those interactions occur between only two players, as in the examples just discussed; many others involve larger groups. But regardless of the number of players involved, the common thread is one of conflict between the narrow self-interest of individuals and the broader interests of larger communities.

## Prisoners' dilemmas confronting imperfectly competitive firms

A **cartel** is any coalition of firms or producers that conspires to restrict production for the purpose of earning an economic profit by increasing price and widening the gap between price and cost. The world's best-known (and for some reason widely tolerated) cartel is OPEC, the Organisation of Petroleum Exporting Countries, formed in 1960 to control oil production. Its members account for a very large share of the world's oil production. After the surge in oil prices in 2004 from $20 to $55 per barrel, due for the most to precautionary stockpiling because of the situation in Iraq, as oil prices fell back toward $40, and looked as if they would continue to decline, OPEC announced that it intended to cut production in order to maintain prices at or around $40. This was not treated very seriously by most industry observers because over the previous 30 years it had been shown that after initial increases in prices sparked by OPEC production cuts, prices always fell back as OPEC members broke ranks and non-members took advantage of OPEC cuts to raise production. OPEC is not only the best-known cartel, but the best-known example of the problem besetting all cartels: how to get them to work. History shows that cartels are notoriously unstable. As we shall see in Economic naturalist 10.1, the problem confronting oligopolists who are trying to form a cartel is a classic illustration of the prisoner's dilemma.

**cartel** a coalition of firms that agrees to restrict output for the purpose of earning an economic profit

## Economic naturalist 10.1 Why are cartel agreements notoriously unstable?

Consider a market for bottled water served by only two firms, Aquapure and Mountain Spring. Each firm can draw water free of charge from a mineral spring located on its own land. Customers supply their own bottles. Rather than compete with one another, the two firms decide to collude by selling water at the price a profit-maximising pure monopolist would charge. Under their agreement (which constitutes a cartel), each firm would produce and sell half the quantity of water demanded by the market at the monopoly price (see Fig. 10.1). The agreement is not legally enforceable, however, which means that each firm has the option of charging less than the agreed price. If one firm sells water for less than the other firm, it will capture the entire quantity demanded by the market at the lower price.

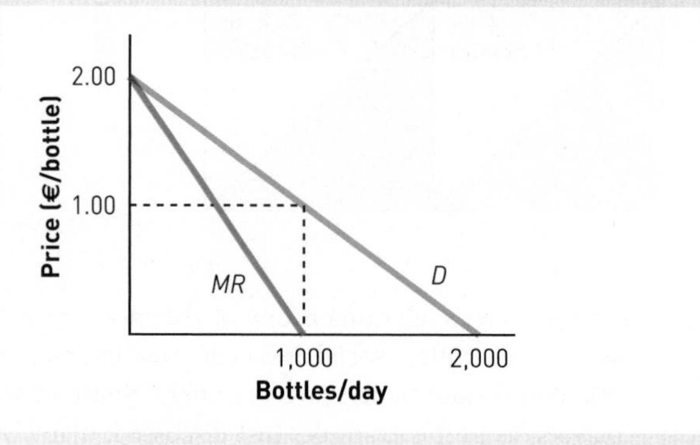


**Figure 10.1 The Market Demand for Mineral Water.** Faced with the demand curve shown, a monopolist with zero marginal cost would produce 1,000 bottles per day (the quantity at which marginal revenue equals zero) and sell them at a price of €1.00 per bottle.

Why is this agreement likely to collapse?

Since the marginal cost of mineral water is zero, the profit-maximising quantity for a monopolist with the demand curve shown in Fig. 10.1 is 1,000 bottles per day, the quantity for which marginal revenue equals marginal cost. At that quantity, the monopoly price is €1 per bottle. If the firms abide by their agreement, each will sell half the market total, or 500 bottles per day at a price of €1 per bottle, for an economic profit of €500 per day.

But suppose Aquapure reduced its price to €0.90 per bottle. By underselling Mineral Spring, it would capture the entire quantity demanded by the market which, as shown in Fig. 10.2 is 1,100 bottles per day. Aquapure's economic profit would rise from €500 per day to (€0.90 per bottle) (1,100 bottles per day) = €990 per day, almost twice as much as before. In the process, Mountain Spring's economic profit would fall from €500 per day to zero. Rather than see its economic profit disappear, Mountain Spring would match Aquapure's price cut, recapturing its original 50 per cent share of the market. But when each firm charges €0.90 per bottle and sells 550 bottles per day, each earns an economic profit of (€0.90 per bottle) (550 bottles per day) = €495 per day, or €5 per day less than before.

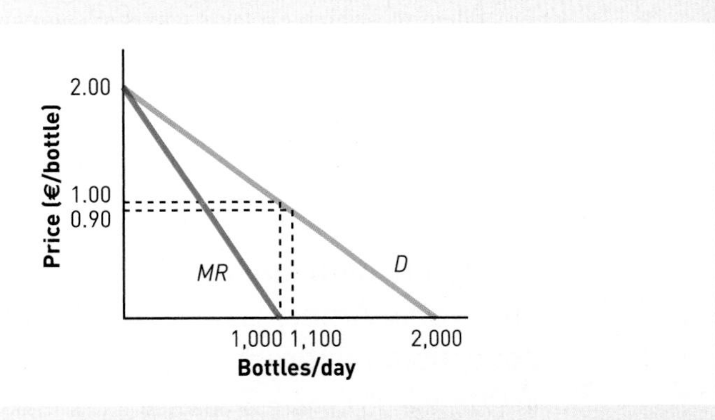


**Figure 10.2 The Temptation to Violate a Cartel Agreement.** By cutting its price from €1 per bottle to €0.90 per bottle, Aquapure can sell the entire market quantity demanded at that price, 1,100 bottle per day, rather than half the monopoly quantity of 1,000 bottles per day.

Suppose we view the cartel agreement as an economic game in which the two available strategies are to sell for €1 per bottle or to sell for €0.90 per bottle. The payoffs are the economic profits that result from these strategies. Table 10.4 shows the payoff matrix for this game. Each firm's dominant strategy is to sell at the lower price, yet in following that strategy each earns a lower profit than if each had sold at the higher price.

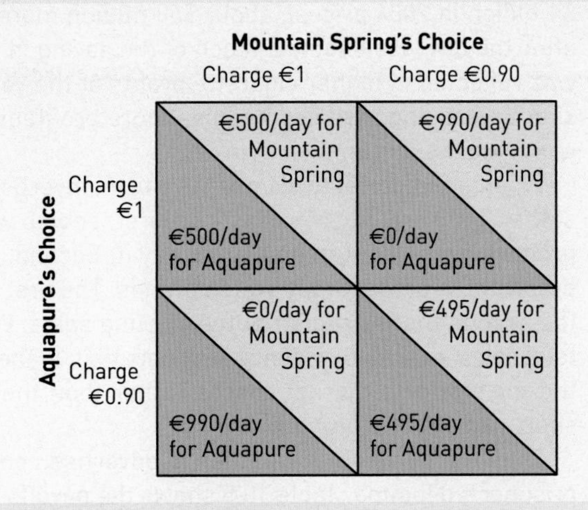

| Aquapure's Choice | Mountain Spring's Choice: Charge €1 | Mountain Spring's Choice: Charge €0.90 |
|---|---|---|
| Charge €1 | €500/day for Mountain Spring; €500/day for Aquapure | €990/day for Mountain Spring; €0/day for Aquapure |
| Charge €0.90 | €0/day for Mountain Spring; €990/day for Aquapure | €495/day for Mountain Spring; €495/day for Aquapure |

**Table 10.4** The Payoff Matrix for a Cartel Agreement

The game does not end with both firms charging €0.90 per bottle. Each firm knows that if it cuts the price a little further, it can recapture the entire market, and in the process earn a substantially higher economic profit. At every step the rival firm will match any price cut, until the price falls all the way to the marginal cost – in this example, zero.

Cartel agreements confront participants with the economic incentives inherent in the prisoner's dilemma, which explains why such agreements have historically been so unstable. Usually a cartel involves not just two firms, but several, an arrangement that can make retaliation against price-cutters extremely difficult. In many cases, discovering which parties have broken the agreement is difficult. For example, OPEC, has no practical way to prevent member countries from secretly pumping oil offshore in the dead of night.

## Economic naturalist 10.2 How did governments in Europe and North America unwittingly solve the television advertising dilemma confronting cigarette producers?

In 1970, the US Congress enacted a law making cigarette advertising on television illegal after 1 January 1971. Since the 1960s a similar restriction has been progressively introduced by all Western European countries and is now part of the Union's '*acquis communautaire*' (the body of rules and practices that have evolved and are accepted as binding on existing and new members). In the United States, given the evidence of the steadily declining proportion of Americans who smoke, this law seems to have achieved its stated purpose of protecting citizens against a proven health hazard. In Europe, this has been to some extent offset by an increase in the number of women who smoke, but is widely credited as having contributed to the decline in the total number of smokers and the total amount of smoking. But these laws also had an unintended effect, which was to increase the economic profit of cigarette makers, at least in the short run. In the year before the law's passage, US tobacco manufacturers spent more than $300 million on advertising (well over $1 billion in 2004 prices), about $60 million more than they spent during the year after the law was enacted. Much of the saving in advertising expenditures in 1971 was reflected in higher cigarette profits at the year-end. But if eliminating television advertising made companies more profitable, why didn't the manufacturers eliminate the ads on their own?

When an imperfectly competitive firm advertises its product, its demand curve shifts rightward, for two reasons. First, people who have never used that type of product learn about it, and some buy it. Second, people who consume a different brand of the product may switch brands. The first effect boosts sales industrywide; the second merely redistributes existing sales. Whatever the long-run effects on total sales, available evidence suggests that, in the short run, tobacco advertising in the main affects market shares rather than the size of the market. Its primary short-run effect is *brand switching*.

Thus the decision of whether to advertise confronts the individual firm with a prisoner's dilemma. Table 10.5 shows the payoffs facing a pair of US cigarette producers trying to decide whether to advertise. If both firms advertise on TV (the upper left cell), each earns a profit of only $10 million per year as compared with a profit of $20 million per year for each if neither advertises (the lower right cell). Clearly, both will benefit if neither advertises.

Yet note the powerful incentive that confronts each firm. RJR sees that if Philip Morris doesn't advertise, RJR can earn higher profits by advertising ($35 million per year) than by not advertising ($20 million per year). RJR also sees that if Philip Morris does advertise, RJR will again earn more by advertising ($10 million per year) than by not advertising ($5 million per year). Thus RJR's dominant strategy is to advertise. And because the payoffs are symmetric, Philip Morris' dominant strat-

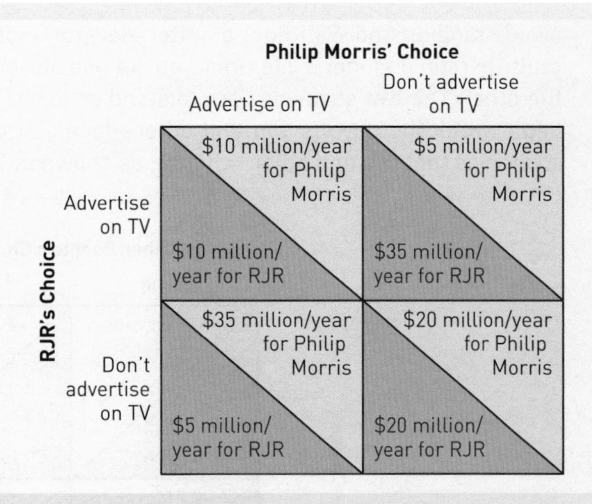

| RJR's Choice | Philip Morris' Choice: Advertise on TV | Philip Morris' Choice: Don't advertise on TV |
|---|---|---|
| Advertise on TV | $10 million/year for Philip Morris; $10 million/year for RJR | $5 million/year for Philip Morris; $35 million/year for RJR |
| Don't advertise on TV | $35 million/year for Philip Morris; $5 million/year for RJR | $20 million/year for Philip Morris; $20 million/year for RJR |

**Table 10.5** Cigarette Advertising as a Prisoner's Dilemma

egy is also to advertise. So when each firm behaves rationally from its own point of view, the two together do worse than if they had both shown restraint. The congressional ad ban forced cigarette manufacturers to do what they could not have accomplished on their own.

## Prisoners' dilemmas in everyday life

As Economic naturalists 10.3 and 10.4 make clear, the prisoner's dilemma helps us to make sense of human behaviour not only in the world of business but in other domains of life as well.

### Economic naturalist 10.3 Why do people often stand at rock concerts, even though they can see just as well when everyone sits?

A few years ago, an economic naturalist went with friends to hear Diana Ross sing. They bought good seats, some 20 rows from the stage. But before Ross had finished her first song, several people in front of them rose to their feet, presumably to get a better view. In doing so, they blocked the line of sight for others behind them, forcing those people to stand to see better. Before long, the entire crowd was standing. Then a few people in the front rows climbed on top of their seats, blocking the views of those behind them and forcing them to stand on their seats too. The seats had fold-up bottoms, so from time to time someone who stood too close to the pivot point would tumble as the seat popped into its vertical position. All things considered, the outcome was far less satisfactory than if everyone had remained seated. Why this pattern of self-defeating behaviour?

To understand what happened at the concert, note that standing is self-defeating only when viewed from the group's perspective. From the individual's perspective, however, standing passes the cost–benefit test. No matter what others do, an individual gets a better view by standing than by sitting. Suppose for the sake of discussion that you and other members of the audience would be willing to pay €2 to avoid standing and €3 to get a better view (or avoid having a worse one). In this multi-person prisoner's dilemma, you are one player and the rest of the audience is the other. The two strategies are to stand or to sit. Suppose everyone is seated to begin with. The payoffs you and others face will depend on the combination of strategies that you and others choose, as shown in Table 10.6.

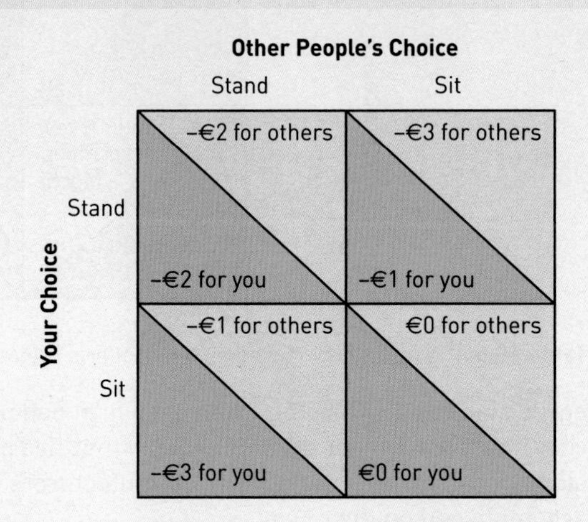

Other People's Choice
Stand
Sit
Your Choice
Stand
Sit
-€2 for others
-€2 for you
-€3 for others
-€1 for you
-€1 for others
-€3 for you
€0 for others
€0 for you


**Table 10.6** Standing versus Sitting at a Concert as a Prisoner's Dilemma

The payoff of €0 in the lower right cell of the payoff matrix in Table 10.6 reflects the fact that when everyone remains seated, everyone is just as well off as before. Your payoff of -€3 in the lower left cell reflects the fact that if you sit while others stand, you will have a worse view. Your payoff of -€2 in the upper left cell reflects the fact that when you and others stand, you must endure the €2 cost of standing, even though you don't get a better view. Finally, your €1 payoff in the upper right cell represents the difference between your €3 benefit and your €2 cost of standing when you stand while others sit.

These payoffs mean that your dominant strategy is to stand. If others stand, you will get -€2 by standing, which is better than the -€3 you will get by sitting. If others sit, you will get €1 by standing, which is better than the €0 you will get by sitting. Since this game is symmetric, the dominant strategy for others is also to stand. Yet when everyone stands, everyone gets a payoff of -€2, which is €2 worse than if everyone had remained seated. As in all prisoner's dilemmas, the choice that is more attractive from the perspective of the individual turns out to be less attractive from the perspective of the group.

And here is something else to think about: Why does the problem of standing at critical moments not occur at the opera? After all, there is no reason to believe that most opera lovers have read much economics.

## Economic naturalist 10.4 Why do people shout at parties?

Whenever large numbers of people gather for conversation in a closed space, the ambient noise level rises sharply. After attending such gatherings, people often complain of sore throats and hoarse voices. If everyone spoke at a normal volume at parties, the overall noise level would be lower, and people would hear just as well. So why do people shout?

Again, the problem involves the difference between individual incentives and group incentives. Suppose everyone starts by speaking at a normal level. But because of the crowded conditions, conversation partners have difficulty hearing one another, even when no one is shouting. The natural solution, from the point of view of the individual, is to simply raise one's voice a bit. But that is also the natural solution for everyone else. When everyone speaks more loudly, the ambient noise level rises, so no one hears any better than before.

No matter what others do, the individual will do better by speaking more loudly. Doing so is a dominant strategy for everyone, in fact. Yet when everyone follows the dominant strategy, the result is worse (no one can hear well) than if everyone had continued to speak normally. While shouting is wasteful, individuals acting alone have no better option. If anyone were to speak softly while others shout, that person wouldn't be heard. No one wants to go home with raw vocal cords, but people apparently prefer that cost to the alternative of not being heard at all.

Here's another version of the last problem: Do people shout at summer garden parties at Buckingham Palace?

**Exercise 10.3** It was reported at the end of 2004 that (as many have suspected) the use of mobile phones on planes does not pose a safety hazard. Consequently legal restrictions on their use would in all probability be lifted. How likely is it that all airlines will completely lift the restriction even if it is no longer legally binding on them to impose it?

## Tit-for-tat and the repeated prisoner's dilemma

When all players co-operate in a prisoner's dilemma, each gets a higher payoff than when all defect. So people who confront a prisoner's dilemma will be on the lookout for ways to create incentives for mutual co-operation. What they need is some way to *penalise* players who defect. When players interact with one another only once, this turns out to be difficult to achieve. But when they expect to interact repeatedly, new possibilities emerge.

**repeated prisoner's dilemma** a standard prisoner's dilemma that confronts the same players repeatedly

**tit-for-tat** a strategy for the repeated prisoner's dilemma in which players co-operate on the first move, then mimic their partner's last move on each successive move

A **repeated prisoner's dilemma** is a standard prisoner's dilemma that confronts the same players not just once but many times. Experimental research on repeated prisoner's dilemmas in the 1960s identified a simple strategy that proves remarkably effective at limiting defection. The strategy is called **tit-for-tat**, and here is how it works. The first time you interact with someone, you co-operate. In each subsequent interaction you simply do what that person did in the previous interaction. Thus, if your partner defected on your first interaction, you would then defect on your next interaction with her. If she then co-operates, your move next time will be to co-operate as well.

On the basis of elaborate computer simulations, University of Michigan political scientist Robert Axelrod showed that tit-for-tat was a remarkably effective strategy, even when pitted against a host of ingenious counter-strategies that had been designed for the explicit purpose of trying to exploit it. The success of tit-for-tat requires a reasonably stable set of players, each of whom can remember what other players have done in previous interactions. It also requires that players have a significant stake in what happens in the future, for it is the fear of *retaliation* that deters people from defecting.

Since rival firms in the same industry interact with one another repeatedly, it might seem that the tit-for-tat strategy would ensure widespread collusion to raise prices. And yet, as noted earlier, cartel agreements are notoriously unsuccessful. One difficulty is that tit-for-tat's effectiveness depends on there being only two players in the game. In competitive and monopolistically competitive industries there are generally many firms, and even in oligopolies there are often several. When there are more than two firms, and one defects now, how do the co-operators selectively punish the defector later? By cutting price? That will penalise everyone, not just the defector. Even if there are only two firms in an industry, these firms realise that other firms may enter their industry. So the would-be cartel members have to worry not only about each other, but also about the entire list of firms that might decide to compete with them. Each firm may see this as an impossible task and decide to defect now, hoping to reap at least some economic profit in the short run. What seems clear, in any event, is that the practical problems involved in implementing tit-for-tat have made it difficult to hold cartel agreements together for long.

### RECAP The prisoner's dilemma

The *prisoner's dilemma* is a game in which each player has a dominant strategy, and in which the payoff to each player when each chooses that strategy is smaller than if each had chosen a dominated strategy. Incentives analogous to those found in the prisoner's dilemmas help to explain a broad range of behaviour in business and everyday life – among them, excessive spending on advertising, cartel instability, standing at concerts and shouting at parties. Co-operation in repeated prisoner's dilemmas can often be sustained by the *tit-for-tat* strategy, in which players co-operate on the first move and mimic their partner's previous move thereafter.

## Games in which timing matters

In the games discussed so far, players were assumed to choose their strategies simultaneously, and which player moved first didn't particularly matter. For example, in the prisoner's dilemma, players would follow their dominant strategies even if they knew in advance what strategies their opponents had chosen. But in other situations, such as the negotiations between Warner Brothers and Tony Bennett described at the beginning of this chapter, timing is of the essence.

### The ultimatum bargaining game

The following example illustrates another game in which timing plays a crucial role.

#### Example 10.4 Should Michael accept Tom's offer?

Tom and Michael are subjects in an experiment. The experimenter begins by giving €100 to Tom, who must then propose how to divide the money between himself and Michael. Tom can propose any division he chooses, provided the proposed amounts are whole euros and he offers Michael at least €1. Suppose Tom proposes €$X$ for himself and €$(100 - X)$ for Michael, where $X$ is a whole number no larger than 99. Michael must then say whether he accepts the proposal. If he does, each will get the proposed amount. But if Michael rejects the proposal, each player will get zero, and the €100 will revert to the experimenter. If Tom and Michael know they will play this game only once, and each wants to make as much money for himself as possible, what should Tom propose?

A payoff matrix is not a useful way to summarise the information in this game, because it says nothing about the timing of each player's move. For games in which timing matters, a **decision tree**, or **game tree**, is more useful. This type of diagram describes the possible moves in the sequence in which they may occur and lists the final payoffs for each possible combination of moves.

**decision tree (or game tree)** a diagram that describes the possible moves in a game in sequence and lists the payoffs that correspond to each possible combination of moves

The decision tree for the game in Example 10.4 is shown in Fig. 10.3. At *A*, Tom begins the game by making his proposal. At *B*, Michael responds to Tom's proposal. If he accepts (the top branch of the tree), Tom will get €*X* and Michael will get €(100 – *X*). If he refuses (the bottom branch of the tree), both will get nothing.

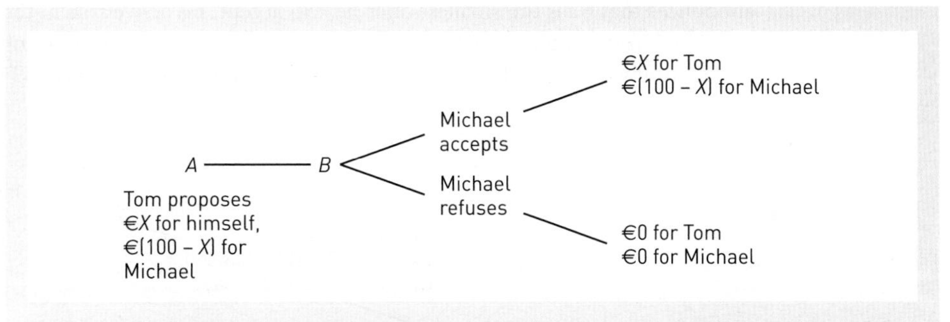


**Figure 10.3 Decision Tree for Example 10.4.** This decision tree shows the possible moves and payoffs for the game in Example 10.4 in the sequence in which they may occur.

In thinking strategically about this game, the key for Tom is to put himself in Michael's shoes and imagine how he might react to various proposals. Because he knows that Michael's goal is to make as much money as possible, he knows that Michael will accept his offer no matter how small, because the alternative is to reject it and get nothing. For instance, suppose that Tom proposes €99 for himself and only €1 for Michael (see Fig. 10.4). At *B*, Michael's best option is to accept the offer. This is a Nash equilibrium, because neither player has any incentive to deviate from the strategy he chose.

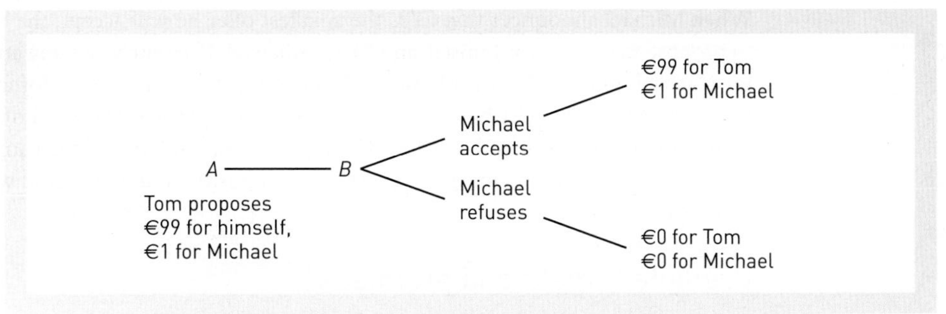


**Figure 10.4 Tom's Best Strategy in an Ultimatum Bargaining Game.** Because Tom can predict that Michael will accept any positive offer, Tom's income-maximising strategy at *A* is to offer Michael the smallest positive amount possible, €1.

**ultimatum bargaining game** one in which the first player has the power to confront the second player with a take-it-or-leave-it offer

This type of game has been called the **ultimatum bargaining game**, because of the power of the first player to confront the second player with a take-it-or-leave-it offer. Michael could refuse a one-sided offer from Tom, but doing so would make him worse off than if he accepted it.

Example 10.5 illustrates the importance of the *timing of moves* in determining the outcome of the ultimatum bargaining game.

### Example 10.5 What should Michael's acceptance threshold be?

Suppose we change the rules of the ultimatum bargaining game slightly so that Michael has the right to specify *in advance* the smallest offer he will accept. Once Michael announces this number, he is bound by it. If Tom's task is again to propose a division of the €100, what amount should Michael specify?

This seemingly minor change in the rules completely alters the game. Once Michael announces that €$Y$ is the smallest offer he will accept, his active role in the game is over. If $Y$ is €60 and Tom proposes €$X$ for himself and €$(100 - X)$ for Michael, his offer will be rejected automatically if $X$ exceeds 40. The decision tree for this game is shown in Fig. 10.5.

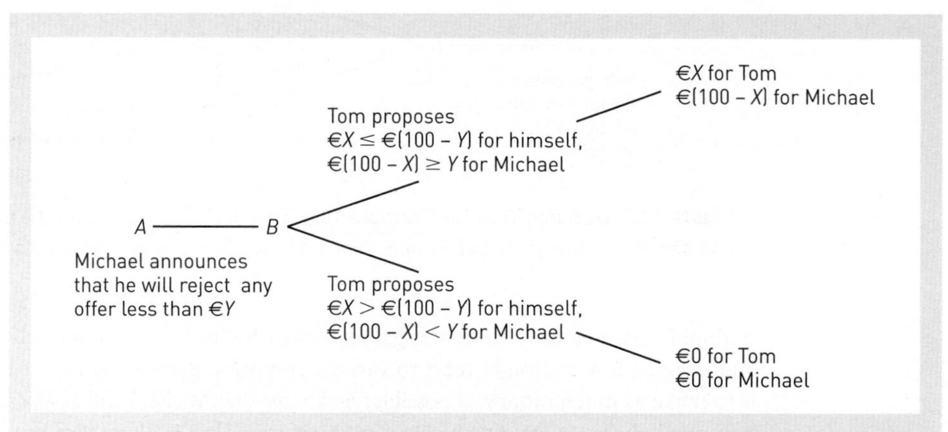


**Figure 10.5 The Ultimatum Bargaining Game with an Acceptance Threshold.** If Michael can commit himself to a minimum acceptable offer threshold at $A$, he will fare dramaticallly better than in the standard ultimatum bargaining game.

When Michael announces that €$Y$ is the smallest offer he will accept, the best Tom can do is to propose €$(100 - Y)$ for himself and €$Y$ for Michael. If he proposes any amount less than €$Y$ for Michael, both will get nothing at all. Since this reasoning holds for any value of $Y$ less than 100, Michael's best bet is to announce an acceptance threshold of €99 – the largest whole number that is less than €100. The equilibrium outcome of the game will then be €99 for Michael and only €1 for Tom, exactly the opposite of the outcome when Tom had the first move.

## Credible threats and promises

**credible threat** a threat to take an action that is in the threatener's interest to carry out

Why couldn't Michael have threatened to refuse a one-sided offer in the original version of the game? While nothing prevented him from doing so, such a threat would not have been credible. In the language of game theory, a **credible threat** is one that is in the threatener's interest to carry out when the time comes to act. The problem in the original version of the game is that Michael would have no reason to carry out his threat to reject a one-sided offer in the event that he actually received one. Once Tom announced such an offer, refusing it would not pass the cost–benefit test.

The concept of a credible threat figured prominently in the negotiations between Warner Brothers managers and Tony Bennett over the matter of Bennett's fee for performing in *Analyze This*. Once most of the film had been shot, managers knew they couldn't threaten credibly to refuse Bennett's salary demand, because at that point adapting the film to another singer would have been prohibitively costly. In contrast, a similar threat made before production of the movie had begun would have been credible.

Example 10.6 is another case in which one person suffers as a result of the inability to make a credible threat.

### **Example 10.6** Is it safe to steal Veronica's briefcase?

When Veronica travels out of town on business, she usually brings along an expensive briefcase. A stranger takes a liking to her briefcase and assumes that because Veronica is an economist, she must be a self-interested, rational person.[4] If the cost to Veronica of pressing charges in the event that her briefcase is stolen exceeds the value of the briefcase, can the stranger safely steal it?

Provided that the thief's assumptions about Veronica are correct, he can get away with his crime. To press charges once her briefcase has been stolen, Veronica must call the police and will probably miss her flight home. Months later, she will have to return to testify at the thief's trial, and she may have to endure hostile cross-examination by the thief's lawyer. Since these costs clearly exceed the value of the briefcase, a rational, self-interested person would simply write it off. But if Veronica could somehow have made a credible threat to press charges in the event that her briefcase was stolen, she could have deterred the thief. The problem is that the thief knows the cost of retaliation will exceed the benefit, so the threat is not credible.

**credible promise** a promise that is in the interests of the promissor to keep when the time comes to act.

Just as in some games credible threats are impossible to make, in others **credible promises** are impossible.

### **Example 10.7** Should the business owner open a remote office?

The owner of a thriving business wants to start up an office in a distant city. If she hires someone to manage the new office, she can afford to pay a weekly salary of €1,000 – a premium of €500 over what the manager would otherwise be able to earn – and still earn a weekly economic profit of €1,000 for herself. The owner's concern is that she will not be able to monitor the manager's behaviour. The owner knows that by managing the remote office dishonestly, the manager can boost his take-home pay to €1,500 while causing the owner an economic loss of €500 per week. If the owner believes that all managers are selfish income maximisers, will she open the new office?

The decision tree for the remote office game is shown in Fig. 10.6. At *A*, the managerial candidate promises to manage honestly, which brings the owner to *B*, where she must decide whether to open the new office. If she opens it, they reach *C*, where the manager must decide whether to manage honestly. If the manager's only goal is to make as much money as he can, he will manage dishonestly (bottom branch at *C*), since that way he will earn €500 more than by managing honestly (top branch at *C*).

[4] Experiments with the ultimatum game have uncovered something that may not surprise you. When classroom experiments are played using sociology students, literature students and similar groups as test populations, the offers that are made are usually much closer to a 50/50 split than when they are carried out using economics students. There, the general trend is toward a 90/10 to 70/30 split. Figure that out! Does economics make you 'rational', or do more 'rational' people take economics?

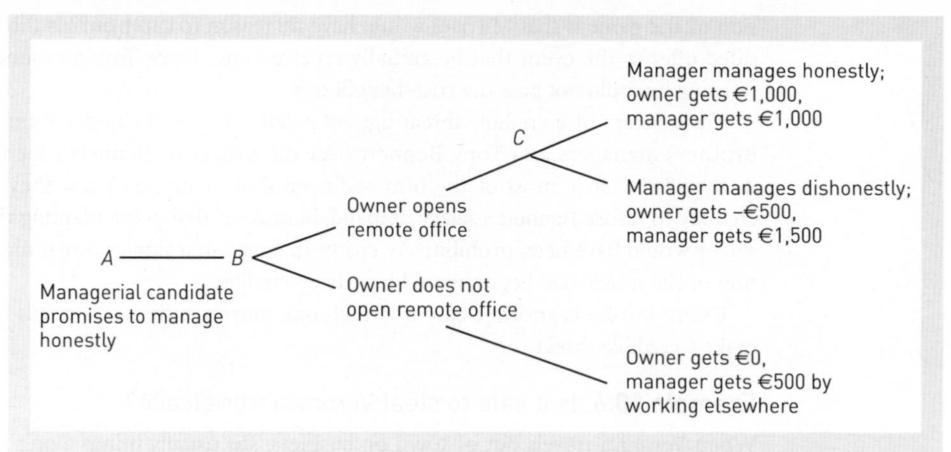


**Figure 10.6 Decision Tree for the Remote Office Game.** The best outcome is for the manager to open the office at *B* and for the manager to manage the office honestly at *C*. But if the manager is purely self-interested and the owner knows it, this path will not be an equilibrium outcome.

So if the owner opens the new office, she will end up with an economic loss of €500. If she had not opened the office (bottom branch at *B*), she would have realised an economic profit of zero. Since zero is better than –€500, the owner will choose not to open the remote office. In the end, the opportunity cost of the manager's inability to make a credible promise is €1,500: the manager's forgone €500 salary premium and the owner's forgone €1,000 return.

**Exercise 10.4** Smith and Jones are playing a game in which Smith has the first move at *A* in the following decision tree. Once Smith has chosen either the top or bottom branch at *A* Jones, who can see what Smith has chosen, must choose the top or bottom branch at *B* or *C*. If the payoffs at the end of each branch are as shown, what is the equilibrium outcome of this game? If, before Smith chose, Jones could make a credible commitment to choose either the top or bottom branch when his turn came, what would he do?

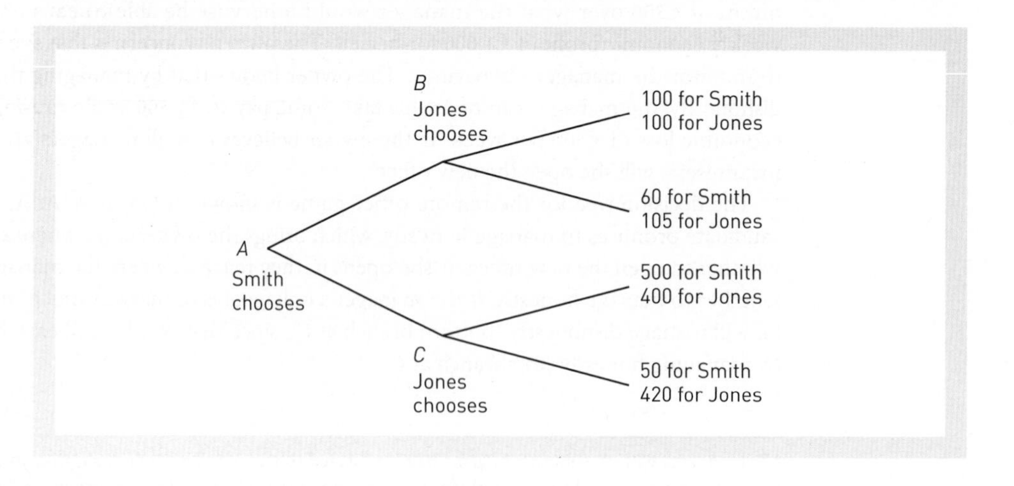

## Commitment problems

Games like that in Exercise 10.3, as well as the prisoner's dilemma, the cartel game, the ultimatum bargaining game and the remote office game, confront players with a **commitment problem**, a situation in which they have difficulty achieving the desired outcome because they cannot make credible threats or promises. If both players in the prisoner's dilemma (Example 10.3) could make a binding promise to remain silent, both would be assured of a shorter sentence. Hence the logic of the underworld code of *omertà*, under which the family of anyone who provides evidence against a fellow mob member is killed. A similar logic explains the adoption of military arms control agreements, in which opponents sign an enforceable pledge to curtail weapons spending.

**commitment problem** a situation in which people cannot achieve their goals because of an inability to make credible threats or promises

The commitment problem in a game can be solved if the potential beneficiary can find some way of committing himself to a course of action in the future. For example, suppose firm *A* wants to discourage firm *B* from price cutting, and knows that to do so involves acting in a way that makes *B* confident that *A* will not overtly or tacitly engage in price cutting itself. It could sell firm *B* a 'put' option, whereby firm *B* could oblige firm *A* to buy specified quantities of its output at some critical price below today's price. A tacit promise not to cut prices would be made credible by this **commitment device**.

**commitment device** a way of changing incentives so as to make otherwise empty threats or promises credible

Business owners seem well aware of commitment problems in the workplace and have adopted a variety of commitment devices to solve them. Consider, for example, the problem confronting the owner of a restaurant. She wants her table staff to provide good service so that customers will enjoy their meals and come back in the future. And since good service is valuable to her, she would be willing to pay waiters extra for it. For their part, waiters would be willing to provide good service in return for the extra pay. The problem is that the owner cannot always monitor whether the waiters do provide good service. Her concern is that, having been paid extra for it, the waiters may slack off when she isn't looking. Unless the owner can find some way to solve this problem, she will not pay extra, the waiters will not provide good service, and she, they and the diners will suffer. A better outcome for all concerned would be for the waiters to find some way to commit themselves to good service.

Restaurateurs in many countries have tried to solve this commitment problem by encouraging diners to leave tips at the end of their meals. The attraction of this solution is that the diner is *always* in a good position to monitor service quality. The diner should be happy to reward good service with a generous tip, since doing so will help to ensure good service in the future. And the waiter has a strong incentive to provide good service, because he knows that the size of his tip may depend on it.

The various commitment devices just discussed – the underworld code of *omertà*, military arms control agreements, the tip for the waiter – all work because they change the material incentives facing the decision makers. But as Example 10.8 illustrates, sometimes this simple calculus of incentives is not a complete explanation.

### Example 10.8 Will Federico leave a tip when dining on the road?

Federico has just finished a €30 dinner at Ristorante Stendhal,[5] just off the Milan–Ancona autostrada near Parma, some 300 km from home. The meal was superb, and the waiter provided good service. If Federico cares only about himself, will he leave a tip?

[5] It exists, in a little village on the banks of the Po. One of us has been there a couple of times. It's well worth the detour ... and you can have a great meal and have change out of €30 each (2004 prices). Watch out for the advertising sign beside the autostrada near Parma, or look it up on the web. And, yes, a tip was left!

Once the waiter has provided good service, there is no way for him to take it back if the diner fails to leave a tip. In restaurants patronised by local diners, failure to tip is not a problem, because the waiter can simply provide poor service the next time a non-tipper comes in. And no one wants to appear mean in front of people who might care. But the waiter lacks that leverage with out-of-town diners eating alone. Having already received good service, Federico must choose between paying €30 or €35 for his meal. If he is an essentially selfish person, the former choice may be a compelling one. But if you know that the waiter depends for much of his living on tips you are likely to tip anyway, even if not overgenerously, for the same reason as most people do not engage in shoplifting even when they know they would get away with it: our moral sense overrides our instinct for self-advancement.

## RECAP Games in which timing matters

The outcomes in many games depend on the *timing* of each player's move. For such games, the payoffs are best summarised by a *decision tree* rather than a payoff matrix.

The inability to make credible threats and promises often prevents people from achieving desired outcomes in many games. Games with this property are said to confront players with *commitment problems*. Such problems can sometimes be solved by employing *commitment devices* – ways of changing incentives to facilitate making credible threats or promises.

# The strategic role of preferences

In all the games we have discussed so far, players were assumed to care only about obtaining the best possible outcome for themselves. Thus each player's goal was to get the highest monetary payoff, the shortest jail sentence, the best chance of survival and so on. The irony, in most of these games, is that players do not attain the best outcomes. Better outcomes can sometimes be achieved by altering the material incentives selfish players face, but not always.

If altering the relevant material incentives is not possible, commitment problems can sometimes be solved by altering people's psychological incentives. As Example 10.9 illustrates, in a society in which people are strongly conditioned to develop moral sentiments – feelings of guilt when they harm others, feelings of sympathy for their trading partners, feelings of outrage when they are treated unjustly – commitment problems arise less often than in more narrowly self-interested societies.

### **Example 10.9** In a moral society, will the business owner open a remote office?

Consider again the owner of the thriving business who is trying to decide whether to open an office in a distant city (Example 10.7). Suppose the society in which she lives is one in which all citizens have been strongly conditioned to behave honestly. Will she open the remote office?

Suppose, for instance, that the managerial candidate would suffer guilt pangs if he embezzled money from the owner. Most people would be reluctant to assign a monetary value to guilty feelings. But for the sake of discussion, let us suppose that those feelings are so unpleasant that the manager would be willing to pay at least €10,000 to avoid them. On this assumption, the manager's payoff if he manages dishonestly will not be €1,500 but €1,500 – €10,000 = –€8,500. The new decision tree is shown in Fig. 10.7.

In this case, the best choice for the owner at *B* will be to open the remote office, because she knows that at *C* the manager's best choice will be to manage honestly. The irony, of course, is that the honest manager in this example ends up richer than the selfish manager in Example 10.7, who earned only a normal salary.

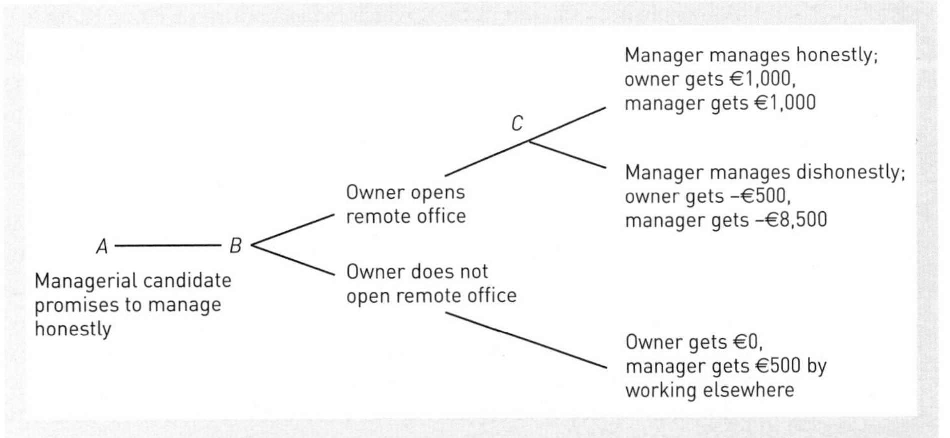


**Figure 10.7 The Remote Office Game with an Honest Manager.** If the owner can identify a managerial candidate who would choose to manage honestly at *C*, she will hire that candidate at *B* and open the remote office.

## Are people fundamentally selfish?

As Examples 10.7 and 10.8 suggest, the assumption that people are 'self-interested' in the narrow sense of the term does not always capture the full range of motives that govern choice in strategic settings. Federico's case is well documented as quite normal. Researchers have found that tipping rates in restaurants patronised mostly by out-of-town diners are essentially the same as in restaurants patronised mostly by local diners.

Reflect also on how you would behave in some of the other games we have discussed. In the ultimatum bargaining game, what would you do if your partner proposed €99 for himself and only €1 for you? Would you reject the offer? If so, you are not alone. Two findings of extensive laboratory studies of the ultimatum bargaining game challenge the assumption that most players are narrowly self-interested. First, the most common proposal by the first player in this game is not a 99/1 split, but a 50/50 split. And second, on the few occasions when the first player does propose a highly one-sided split, the second player almost always rejects it. Subjects who reject the offer often mention the satisfaction they experienced at having penalised the first player for an 'unfair' offer.

Indeed, there are many exceptions to the outcomes predicted on the basis of the assumption that people are self-interested in the most narrow sense of the term. People who have been treated unjustly often seek 'revenge' even at ruinous cost to themselves. Every day people walk away from profitable transactions whose terms they believe to be 'unfair'.

American decision makers, immersed in the doctrine of strategic deterrence and mutually assured destruction (MAD), found it hard to understand the British decision to spend vast sums, lose lives and risk the core of the Royal Navy's surface fleet to recover the desolate Falkland Islands in 1982, even though they had little empire left against which to deter future aggression. Presumably the Argentine *junta* was of a similar mind. After all, as the Argentine writer Jorge Luis Borges observed, the Falkland War made about as much sense to North and South Americans as two bald men fighting over a comb.[6] It looked like a case of other values taking precedence over narrow self-interest. Possibly true: Mrs Thatcher was no ordinary Prime Minister, but rejoiced in the nickname of the 'Iron Lady'. At the time, Spain was putting pressure on Britain over Gibraltar, and Britain was facing difficult negotiations with China over the future administration of Hong Kong after the 99-year lease of most of the

[6] Quoted in Barnstone (1993).

colony's territory ran out in 1997, which made a return of Hong Kong to China unavoidable. And the UK government was facing internal opposition from the unionised coal miners who were threatening general strikes if the industry was rationalised. In these circumstances, does it seem so economically irrational to demonstrate that you will not be trampled on?

## Preferences as solutions to commitment problems

Economists tend to view preferences as ends in themselves. Taking them as given, they calculate what actions will best serve those preferences. This approach to the study of behaviour is widely used by other social scientists and by game theorists, military strategists, philosophers and others. In its standard form, it assumes purely self-interested preferences for present and future consumption goods of various sorts, leisure pursuits and so on. Concerns about fairness, guilt, honour, sympathy and the like typically play no role.

Preferences clearly affect the choices people make in strategic interactions. Sympathy for one's trading partner can make a businessperson trustworthy even when material incentives favour cheating. A sense of justice can prompt a person to incur the costs of retaliation, even when incurring those costs will not undo the original injury. It can also induce people to reject one-sided offers, even when their wealth would be increased by accepting them.

Note, however, that although preferences can clearly shape behaviour in these ways, that alone does not solve commitment problems. The solution to such problems requires not only that a person *have* certain preferences, but also that others have some way of *discerning* them. Unless the business owner can identify the trustworthy employee, that employee cannot land a job whose pay is predicated on trust. Unless the predator can identify a potential victim whose character will motivate retaliation, that person is likely to become a victim. And unless a person's potential trading partners can identify him as someone predisposed to reject one-sided offers, he will not be able to deter such offers.

From among those with whom we might engage in ventures requiring trust, can we identify reliable partners? If people could make *perfectly* accurate character judgements, they could always steer clear of dishonest persons. That people continue to be victimised, at least occasionally, by dishonest persons suggests that perfectly reliable character judgements are either impossible to make or prohibitively expensive.

Vigilance in the choice of trading partners is an essential element in solving (or avoiding) commitment problems, for if there is an advantage in being honest and being perceived as such, there is an even greater advantage in only *appearing* to be honest. After all, a liar who appears trustworthy will have better opportunities than one who glances about furtively, sweats profusely and has difficulty making eye contact. Indeed, the liar will have the same opportunities as an honest person but will get higher payoffs because the liar will exploit them to the full.

In the end, the question of whether people can make reasonably accurate character judgements is an empirical one. Experimental studies have shown that even on the basis of brief encounters involving strangers, subjects are adept at predicting who will co-operate and who will defect in prisoners' dilemma games. For example, in one experiment in which only 26 per cent of subjects defected, the accuracy rate of predicted defections was more than 56 per cent. One might expect that predictions regarding those we know well would be even more accurate.

Do you know someone who would return an envelope containing €1,000 in cash to you if you lost it at a crowded concert? If so, then you accept the claim that personal character can help people to solve commitment problems. As long as honest individuals can identify at least some others who are honest and can interact selectively with them, honest individuals can prosper in a competitive environment.

## RECAP The strategic role of preferences

Most applications of the theory of games assume that players are 'self-interested' in the narrow sense of the term. In practice, however, many choices, such as leaving tips in out-of-town restaurants, appear inconsistent with this assumption.

The fact that people seem driven by a more complex range of motives makes behaviour more difficult to predict but also creates new ways of solving commitment problems. *Psychological incentives* can often serve as commitment devices when changing players' material incentives is impractical. For example, people who are able to identify honest trading partners and interact selectively with them are able to solve commitment problems that arise from lack of trust.

# Games, timing, beliefs and behaviour: oligopolistic markets

*This section of the chapter contains some advanced analysis that can be skipped if you wish. It expands what has already been covered and introduces you to how economics approaches the analysis of firm behaviour in small-number markets, an analysis that underlies contemporary competition policy.*

The concepts developed up to this point in this chapter are helpful in explaining, and even predicting, the behaviour of firms in markets where a small number of large firms determine product characteristics, prices and output levels. The menu of possible outcomes in such markets is long and varied, reflecting permutations and combinations of firm strategies, firm beliefs, modes of competition, and numbers and sizes of firms. In this section, we shall look at some basic models that are of use in indicating how differences in structure of markets, firms' beliefs as to other firms' responses and the manner in which firms compete can affect prices and outputs in those markets.

- **Structure** By 'market structure' we mean the degree of *similarity or difference between* firms (players, in game theory terms) and the *number of firms*. For example, in most parts of Britain or France the everyday grocery trade is shared by a small number of similar-sized large firms (small convenience stores abound, especially in Britain, but they largely sell into another market). On the other hand, retail sales of clothing is divided between a small number of large chain stores (Marks and Spencer, C&A, Debenhams, Galeries Lafayette ...) and a very large number of much smaller outlets.
- **Beliefs** In the prisoner's dilemma, the outcome reflected the *knowledge and beliefs of each of the players about the other*. The outcome depends on the idea that each expects the other to behave independently in a one-off situation to maximise his own utility subject to no external influence or concern about the future. This may (or may not) be plausible in terms of suspects in police custody, but a wider set of beliefs, etc. is plausible in the case of firms interacting in markets.
- **Competition** Firms also differ as to how they *compete*, usually reflecting the products they are engaged in producing. For example, car producers can plausibly be modelled as deciding on a volume of output of a particular type of car, for which they tool up (commit themselves to produce, hoping to be able to sell them). Quantity is the decision competition variable: the firm lets market demand determine how much it realises for a given volume of production, or average revenue, meaning unit price. If firms compete by setting quantities, competition between firms is called 'Cournot competition' (see p. 298 below). A life assurance producer is best thought of as developing a financial product range, pricing it and waiting to see how many units of the product it can sell. Price is the decision variable, with market demand determining the amount sold. If firms compete by setting prices, competition is called 'Bertrand competition' (again, see p. 298)

## Two basic tools of analysis

### The residual demand curve

To understand this concept, consider the following problem. A large firm faces a number of smaller firms serving a market. The large firm has the advantage of lower costs of production, but has to settle on a profit-maximising price and output level in the knowledge that the price adopted will determine how much the smaller firms offer for sale.

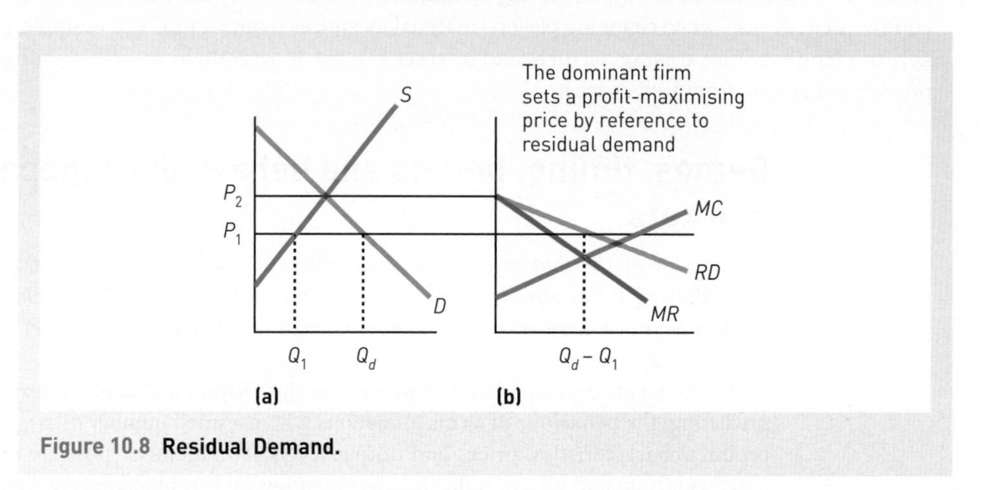


**Figure 10.8 Residual Demand.**

In panel (a) of Fig. 10.8, we show the supply curve for the combined output of the small firms, and the market demand curve. From this, we can see how much of total demand at any price will be met by the output of the small firms. Thus at $P_1$ they will produce only $Q_1$, leaving the balance of demand at that price to be supplied (if it wants to do so) by the large firm. At $P_2$, the small firms would produce sufficient output to satisfy market demand, and at that price there would be no room for the large firm to produce any output, given what the small firms would produce.

In panel (b) of Fig. 10.8, we draw the demand curve facing the large firm based on panel (a). It shows market demand at any price after the output of the smaller firms is subtracted. Thus, at $P_2$ there is no demand for output from the large firm, and at $P_1$ the demand for its output is the difference between total demand in panel (a) minus the output of the smaller firms at that price. Based on this **'residual' demand curve** we draw a marginal revenue curve; the profit-maximising output and price for the large ('dominant') firm are given by the intersection of its *MC* curve with this *MR* curve.

**residual demand curve** shows the price and output combinations available to a firm given other firms' decisions

The concept of the residual demand curve can be derived in any market. Thus, in a two-firm market (a 'duopoly') we can derive for each firm the residual demand curve reflecting the market space left to it for different prices facing the other firm. This would describe part of the strategic problem facing, for example, Boeing and Airbus in the markets for very large commercial passenger and freight planes, for which they are the only producers. At the smaller end of the market (B737, Airbus 318–321) they both face competition from other suppliers (e.g. Embraer in Brazil, De Havilland Canada, SAAB in Sweden and a few other regional jet producers, as well as emerging producers in some Asian countries).

**Exercise 10.5** Use residual demand curve analysis to illustrate Boeing's decision not to compete head-to-head with Airbus when the latter had committed itself to producing the A380, a super-jumbo with a capacity 50–70 per cent greater than Boeing's B747 jumbo.

## The reaction function

In the simple game theory examples used earlier we considered whether a dominant strategy existed for either or both players. In those cases, there were two possible actions by each player, and payoffs derived from these produced a single-equilibrium outcome. It described the best choice of action contingent on what the other player might do. However, where pricing or output decisions are concerned there is a theoretical infinity of choices a firm can make, with related payoffs. Hence we have a range of *best values* for one firm depending on the choices of the other. This leads us to develop the concept of a 'reaction function' or a 'reaction curve'. This will show the preferred action of a given firm as a function of the action of the other firm(s).

**reaction function** shows the preferred response of a firm in terms of a decision variable as a response to a value of that variable chosen by the other firm(s)

A widely used variant of this concept describes how output levels are determined in markets in which firms choose profit-maximising outputs. We develop it here for a duopoly in which firms compete by setting quantities which they offer to the market.

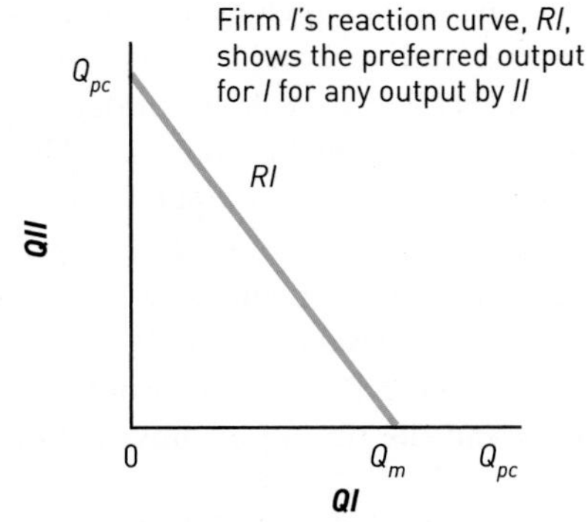

Firm *I*'s reaction curve, *RI*, shows the preferred output for *I* for any output by *II*

$Q_{pc}$ *RI* *QII* 0 $Q_m$ $Q_{pc}$ *QI*

**Figure 10.9 Firm *I*'s Reaction Curve, *RI*.**

Using a residual demand curve for Firm *I* (Fig. 10.9) we can determine its profit-maximising output for any output by Firm *II*. This is indicated on the horizontal axis in Fig. 10.9. Firm *II*'s output is indicated on the vertical axis. Thus, if Firm *II* produced the perfectly competitive output ($Q_{pc}$), with price equal to average cost, and no profits, it would not pay Firm *I* to produce any output. If Firm *II* chose to produce nothing, leaving the entire market to Firm *I* the best output for Firm *I* is the monopoly output. With some not too restrictive assumptions about demand curves and cost curves, the reaction curve for Firm *I* will be a straight line as drawn in Fig. 10.9. It runs from the monopoly output on Firm *I*'s axis to the competitive output on Firm *II*'s axis. It shows the profit-maximising output for Firm *I* for any output by Firm *II*. The further out a firm is on its reaction curve the lower are its profits. For either firm, the closer its output is to the monopoly output on its own axis the higher are its profits.

If both players choose their outputs independently, and face the same demand and cost conditions the result will be the Nash equilibrium output shown by the intersection of the reaction curves at *X*.
If Firm *I* can move first and Firm *II* must follow the outcome will be at a point like *Y*, with lower profits overall, but higher profits for Firm *I* than at *X*. The lines joining $Q_m$ $Q_m$ and $Q_{pc}$ $Q_{pc}$ represent the monopoly and competitive outputs shared between the firms

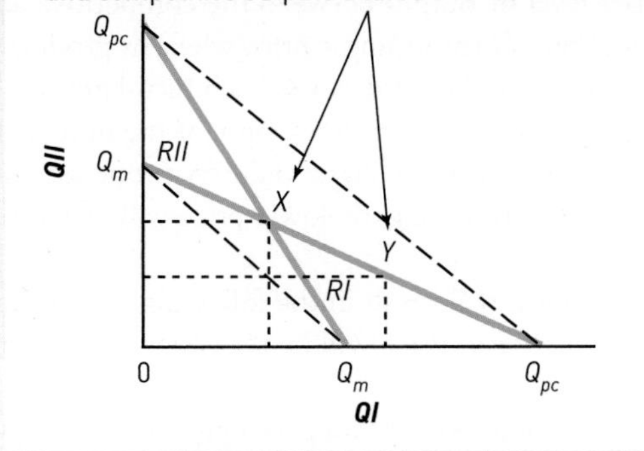


**Figure 10.10 If Both Players Choose Their Outputs Independently.**

In Fig. 10.10 we show the reaction curves for both firms. For ease of analysis we assume that the firms have identical costs and the products are highly substitutable (so that they face similar demand conditions). Notice also the broken lines joining $Q_{pc}$ on each axis and $Q_m$ on each axis. These represent the competitive output and monopoly output divided between the two firms in proportion to the shares indicated by any point on the line. They also, therefore, represent the competitive level of profits (zero) and the monopoly level similarly divided between them. The firm outputs given by the intersection of the two reaction curves involves a level of profits below the monopoly level and above the competitive level shared equally,

What will be the outcome? That depends on firms' beliefs and how the firms can choose how and when to move.

Figure 10.10 illustrates the choices we looked at in the prisoner's dilemma game (Example 10.3). If they can co-operate (collude rather than compete) they can share the monopoly profits. If they have to choose independently what to do, and each believes that the other faces the same problem and the same payoffs, and they can be thought of as deciding what to do simultaneously (as in the prisoner's dilemma), neither can do better than select the output indicated by the intersection of the two reaction curves. This is a dominant strategy for both, and the outcome is a Nash equilibrium outcome.

Suppose, however, that Firm *I* moves first, and believes (correctly) that Firm *II* will follow its move, rather than move independently (a leader and follower game). Firm *I* knows that Firm *II* will choose an output on the basis of its reaction curve. That curve becomes the set of outputs for the two firms among which Firm *I* has to choose. The Nash equilibrium is a feasible choice for Firm *I*, but an output level and share that is preferable for Firm *I* exists. It is at a point like *Y* in Fig. 10.10. Total output is higher, and price and industry profits are lower than at the Nash equilibrium. This is shown by the fact that a line drawn through *Y* parallel to the line joining the competitive output on both axes (the total output shared between the two firms as indicated by point *X*) lies nearer to the competitive output line than the Nash equilibrium output line, meaning an output level that is higher and industry profits that are lower than at the Nash equilibrium output. There exists some point like *X* such that Firm *I*'s output share is sufficiently large to give Firm *I* a higher level of profit despite lower prices than at the Nash equilibrium, meaning of course that Firm *II* does much worse.

**This illustrates the fact that firms' beliefs and the timing of moves affect the end result.**

Competition as in this case when firms choose *output levels* is described as **Cournot competition**, after the French nineteenth-century economist, A. A. Cournot, who considered the problem of duopoly decision making on output levels as long ago as 1838, and arrived at the conclusion that the solution to the problem was what would today be described as the Nash equilibrium solution.

**Cournot competition** firms choose an output and accept the market price

**Bertrand competition** firms choose a price and accept that quantity sold depends on demand at that price

Suppose, however, that firms compete on *price*. This possibility was analysed by another French mathematician and economist, Joseph Bertrand, who argued that the Cournot solution did not generally hold and derived an alternative result where firms decided on prices rather than output levels – this is **Bertrand competition.**

We saw that under prisoner's dilemma circumstances in the Cournot game the outcome was a level of output between the competitive and the monopoly levels. Now suppose we think about a firm setting a price when its product is identical to that of the other firm, and they each have the same costs. Each firm knows that for any price it chooses which is higher than marginal cost the best response of the other firm is to set a price that is a little lower. If it sets the same price it shares industry profits equally, since it will sell the same amount as the competitor. But a slightly lower price will give it the whole market and all the profits.

You can try this as a problem, but a little thought will result in the following conclusion. Each firm will choose a price at which profits are zero. Price will be set equal to marginal cost, and with constant costs this means zero profits.

This leads to what has been called the 'Bertrand Paradox'. As long as there are at least two similar firms in the market the dominant strategy is for each to set price equal to cost. Increasing the number beyond two, or reducing the number as long as there are at least two results in a zero price cost margin. Industry structure has no apparent effect on price.

**This result points to different conclusions depending on whether firms can best be treated as competing on quantity or price**.

But if we look around, we can see that there are cases where firms can plausibly be treated as competing in terms of setting *prices* (Bertrand as opposed to Cournot competitors), and profits are not zero. We can also see examples of higher prices and profit margins in Bertrand markets when there are fewer competitors. Petrol retailing in local markets is an obvious example of both these market characteristics.

How do we square this with the Bertrand model just described?

There are two bases on which to suggest that the Bertrand Paradox outcome is not an equilibrium one. The first is that the products of the firms may not be *perfectly substitutable*. If that is so the products will not have to be sold at the same price (different brands of toothpaste are sold on the same supermarket shelves at different prices). When this is the case, it is possible to look at a firm's pricing decision in the same way as we looked at the output decision in the basic Cournot model. We construct a reaction curve for each firm, showing its preferred price given any price set by the competitor (Fig. 10.11).

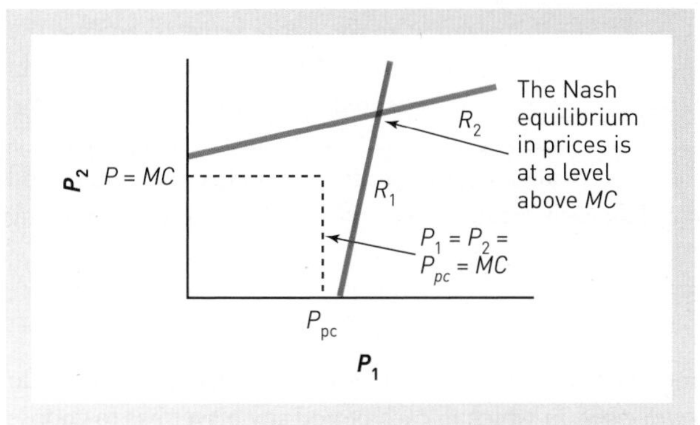


Figure 10.11 The Nash Equilibrium in Prices.

In this case, $R_1$ shows Firm *I*'s preferred price for its own product given (as a function of) Firm *II*'s price. $R_2$ is Firm *II*'s reaction curve. Neither will set a price below marginal cost, and each will set a price equal to marginal cost only if the other prices below marginal cost. Assuming constant unit cost and price elasticity of demand symmetry the reaction curves will (conveniently) be straight lines, and a Nash equilibrium in prices is where they intersect. Once again, this price (and the joint profits of the firms) will be lower than if they colluded to set the monopoly price and shared the market. However, the point is that the Nash equilibrium does not mean that prices are set equal to marginal cost. Positive profits can be earned in equilibrium without collusion. Furthermore, if there are more firms/products on offer, meaning that each firm/product faces closer substitutes, a firm's reaction curve becomes steeper, and the Nash equilibrium approaches the perfectly competitive price ($P = MC$). In the absence of co-operative behaviour, the more petrol stations there are in a town the lower we would expect prices to be.

There is a second, and even more important, reason for not expecting prices to fall to marginal cost under Bertrand competition, even if the products of each firm are very similar to those of others. That is the fact that the analysis so far treats the pricing decision as if it were taken just once, and never changed. In fact, of course, firms have to make decisions on price frequently through time. As supply costs move, and/or as demand conditions change, the 'correct' price for a firm to set changes too. We must assume that firms have memories. We must also assume that firms know how to signal how they will respond to price cutting, and how to indicate by their pricing behaviour whether or not they intend competing aggressively or adopting a 'live and let live' approach. Put another way, pricing decisions involve choosing not just a set of prices for your products, but deciding on a *pricing strategy*, or adopting a rule on setting prices as circumstances change.

The consequences of this approach to pricing include a high degree of 'price stickiness' in small-number markets where players can observe accurately what their competitors are doing as far as prices are concerned. This is sometimes illustrated in terms of what is called the 'kinked oligopoly demand curve' (Fig. 10.12). Given the price being charged, a firm will be reluctant to change it because it fears that an increase in price will leave it exposed to a col-

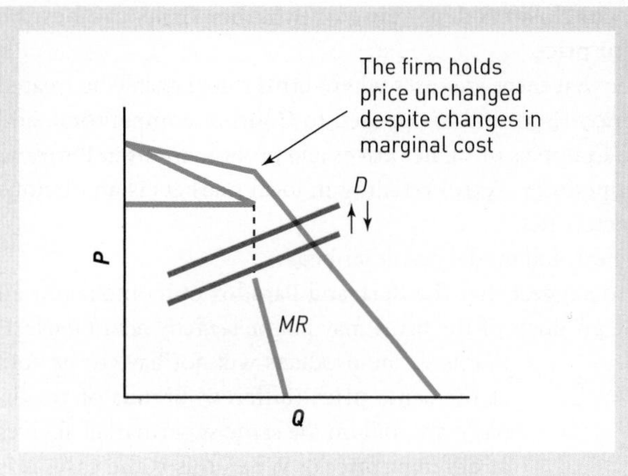


Figure 10.12 **Kinked Demand Curve.**

lapse in market share, while if it lowers its price the others will follow. Hence, if costs rise or fall, the firm holds its price.

There are several limitations of this approach. It does not explain how the observed price emerged. Nor does it suggest that firms will respond to market conditions by changing prices, something that we observe as a widespread phenomenon even in markets with a small number of similar-sized firms (i.e. there is no dominant firm price leader as in Fig. 10.8).

Instead, it makes more sense to analyse the pricing behaviour of firms in these markets in terms of repeated games, pricing rules, signalling and tacit collusion. This approach is also useful because it helps us understand when and why this *tacitly co-ordinated behaviour* breaks down, and we see price wars breaking out.

## Repeated games

Think of a cartel, and ask why a member of it might decide to break ranks. One way to do this is to analyse the cartel as a *repeated game*, in which in each period any player has to choose whether or not to stick by the cartel rules, restrict output and sell at a price at which the firm's marginal revenue exceeds its marginal cost. The single-period dominant strategy (and the consequent Nash equilibrium) suggests breaking the rules, because by breaking them while everyone else obeys the rules you stand to clean up. However, if all the players know the game is going to be repeated indefinitely into the future, the calculation changes. Even if you clean up this week, by undermining the cartel you know that profits in future weeks will be lower. As a result, it is reasonable to believe that you might compare the present value of two profit streams into the future: profits if you undercut the other players this week, but everyone sells at a much lower price into the future, and profits if you – and, you hope, the others – stick by the rules.

Of course, you might reason that since you are a small player, and provided you don't lower prices by too much, the others will prefer to ignore your behaviour – or, better still, may not even be aware of it. Suppose, however, that either by experience, or by some explicit and credible threat, it was clear to you that cheating would not be tolerated, and selective price cuts by large and close competitors were the expected response to any deviation from the rule. How would that affect your choice of strategy? Suppose trade magazines published frequent, reliable and detailed information on who was charging what prices for which goods. Would that encourage you to shave your price?

On the other hand, if it was difficult to observe the quality-adjusted price because the product as sold differs among customers, does that help price fixing? If you had very poor information as to what the market was going to look like in the future, so that future profits are highly uncertain, what effect would that have? Or suppose you were in debt to a financial institution that was charging a high rate of interest on your loan, but the loan could be paid off by a quick killing in the market. High interest rates act as a disincentive to stick by cartel rules.

In practice, of course, we are not usually dealing with an actual cartel. Under competition law in Europe, the United States and other OECD countries, such arrangements are illegal. Participation not only results in being liable to substantial financial penalties, but in some circumstances can result in a prison sentence for those responsible. However, and especially in

**tacit collusion** firms behaving in a manner that resembles what might emerge from a collusive agreement because they recognise their interdependence

small-number situations, firms can decide to operate a pricing policy that is based on a recognition that how they behave affects others' behaviour and vice versa. Recognition of *interdependence of decisions* leads to a situation in which the observed behaviour resembles what might flow from an explicit agreement not to compete aggressively on price. For this reason this behaviour is frequently described as **tacit collusion**.

## Economic naturalist 10.5 Tacit collusion or a cartel? The great cement scandal

There had long been rumours that all was not well with competition among cement producers in Europe when these were confirmed by the findings of the EU Commission's Competition Directorate in 1994.[7] Dismissing arguments about parallel pricing and tacit collusion, it found that Europe's largest cement producers had been operating a cartel for several years – fixing prices, sharing the EU market and administering production quotas. The industry was one in which all the conditions for tacit collusion were present. The product was homogeneous across producers, technology and costs were similar among producers, pricing was transparent, in any country producers were large and few in number and faced similar costs, and entry was difficult. However, from whistle-blower and dawn raid evidence, the Commission was satisfied that parallel pricing and output decisions were not simply the result of tacit collusion but the consequence of a fully orchestrated cartel covering most of the major producers. The Commission identified a starting date of January 1983, when, at a meeting, senior representatives of the European cement industry agreed on a rule of 'non-transhipment to home markets'. This was designed to prohibit any export of cement within Europe which might 'destabilise' neighbouring markets. A fine of about €250 million was imposed on the firms involved.

Tacit collusion in oligopolistic and imperfectly competitive industries is frequently supported by *pricing* and *signalling* strategies designed to discourage competition and reinforce co-operative behaviour. One common device, which to an uninformed observer looks like aggressive competition on price, is a commitment to match or beat any price by guaranteeing to be the lowest-price seller. This is very widespread as a promotional device but, on closer examination may in fact operate to support existing prices rather than ensure that buyers face the lowest possible prices. When a large white goods retailer makes such a promise he is signalling credibly to competitors small and large that if they lower prices, he will lower his.

## Economic naturalist 10.6 Why was Statoil forced to abandon a rebate scheme that would have helped petrol retailers cut their prices?

In 2002 the Competition Authority in Dublin threatened legal action against Statoil as a result of an arrangement it had entered into with its retailers in a country town in Ireland.[8] Statoil's scheme involved (a) fixing a maximum price at which petrol

[7] The text of the decision and the facts and reasoning behind it are published as 94/815/EC, 30/11/1994, available on the EU website or in the EU *Official Journal*, OJ L33/1 1995.

[8] The Competition Authority has described the confrontation and its outcome in Decision E/03/002, which is available on its website: www.TCA. ie.

could be sold, and (b) offering a rebate to its dealers to enable them to cut their prices if other petrol outlets cut their prices below a marker price. While the first might have been part of a campaign to persuade people that Statoil petrol was a good buy (people notoriously appear not to pay much attention to actual prices per litre), the second element meant that other dealers knew that there was no point reducing price below the marker price since Statoil dealers could costlessly follow them down. This would clearly dampen price competition. Statoil withdrew the scheme.

Conditions facilitating tacit collusion do not always exist, even where there are few firms and they recognise the fact that their behaviour affects that of the others. First of all, firms may face different cost structures. This can result in significant differences between them in terms of what pricing structure and behaviour maximise profits when demand conditions change. For example, the lower a firm's variable costs relative to its fixed costs, the more likely it is to prefer to cut price rather than to cut output if demand weakens.

Pricing may not be transparent, with each unit being sold at a price negotiated with the purchaser on a confidential basis. Tacit collusion on pricing becomes meaningless. This factor on its own is probably the main reason why we see cut-throat competition between Boeing and Airbus.

Differences in product characteristics may mean that firms face different price elasticities of demand. This means they differ in terms of how they view the consequences of a change in prices.

As a result, we do not observe high prices supported by tacit collusion as inevitably following an observation of a small number of large producers in a market. And even when it does occur, it is frequently undermined by repeated episodes of price wars.

When do price wars break out, and how do they end?

In mid-2004 the Chinese Ministry of Information announced that it was stepping up its regulatory supervision of pricing in the telecoms sector in China in order to avoid price wars. Until earlier in the year mobile telephony charges had been set by the Ministry, which was also the regulator. In order to encourage the development of the sector, these price controls were relaxed. As elsewhere in the world, mobile telephony in China was dominated by a small number of players, all large. As soon as price controls were relaxed, a price war broke out, as firms slashed prices to increase market share in what was seen as an expanding market. The government, however, wanted the companies to maintain high profit margins and use them to finance qualitative upgrading of the mobile network. When the government intervened to restrict price cutting, of course, the industry greeted this warmly.[9] Regulation produced higher profits.

One possibility here is that under a tight regulatory regime firms had not been able to learn how others would react to price changes, nor been able to estimate demand elasticities correctly. This would interpret the price war as flowing from poor information as to demand conditions and the degree of interdependence of pricing. Another possibility is that, even with good information, tacit collusion and weak price competition was unlikely under deregulation because of the extraordinary degree of non-transparency of pricing: mobile phone pricing packages are numerous, complex and difficult to compare.

The impact of poor information is a useful starting point. Suppose a firm sees its sales falling, and has poor information as to market conditions. Three possible reasons will arise. The first is that market demand has weakened, and it is sharing the pain with other firms.

[9] The story can be found in the English-language *China Daily*, at its website www2.chinadaily.cn/English/doc/2004-07/03/content_345216.htm.

The second is that for some reason it has lost competitiveness. The third is that supply has increased as a competitor has increased production. Unfortunately, the firm is not able with any degree of certainty to establish what exactly is going on.

If it had been content not to compete aggressively on price up to this point, it now faces a problem. Suppose its best guess is that there has been a fall in demand. It must choose between (a) tacit collusion on the basis that this is a temporary blip in demand, everyone is in the same boat and price cutting will achieve nothing as it will be imitated; (b) price cutting anyway because the demand reduction may be permanent so that even if everyone is similarly affected there are fewer seats in the boat than potential passengers, and the last to cut prices exits the market. Suppose, however, it suspects that it has lost competitiveness. The options are not to do anything and accept a lower volume of sales (and possibly further falls) or reduce price to make its products more attractive. Finally, it might suspect that the problem is not its own offerings, or demand in the market, but a competitor increasing production. If it does nothing, it accepts a lower market share. If it wishes to protect its market share and signal its intention to do so to anyone who wants to raise theirs, it will respond by reducing price.

What will happen? In all three scenarios, cutting price looks a better bet, even if a case can be made for not cutting price. Betting against a price cut under uncertainty as to what is going on looks unwise. Hence, it is easy to understand why price wars can be triggered by falling demand or by an overestimate of market demand.

Notice, too, that the scenarios point to a further reason for price wars: market disciplining and market 'restructuring'. Responding to price cuts by one supermarket operator by a 'race to the bottom' may not seem to make much sense until you reflect that the expectation that this will happen in future will be reinforced by an aggressive response. It can also be a mechanism to secure a shake-up in an industry leading to a consolidation among players.

### Economic naturalist 10.7 How the structure of the US tobacco industry was changed by a price war in the 1990s

Philip Morris cut the price of the world's best-selling cigarette, Marlboro, in the spring of 1993 by almost 20 per cent. Price competition from generic and mid-range brands over a period of years had reduced significantly the share of the premium cigarette producers, who at first accommodated the expansion of the cheaper producers and even increased prices in what was a declining market overall. The price cut by Philip Morris hit the mid-range producers worst, and the main firm producing in this range, American Tobacco, exited the market and sold its business to British American Tobacco. The generic producers appear to have taken the hint, and by 1995 Philip Morris had regained its lost market share and both premium and generic cigarette prices were rising together, if slowly.[10] In effect the Marlboro price managed simultaneously to exacerbate and end an ongoing price war, while restoring Philip Morris' position as market leader and consolidating the market.

And finally, of course, an episode of price cutting can arise as a consequence of changes on the supply side. New entrants to a market can disturb a collusive equilibrium. Even with tacit collusion, a fall in input costs can result in the collusive equilibrium level of prices falling. Alternatively, a significant fall in one firm's costs that is not enjoyed by other firms can lead to the lower-cost firm seeking to increase share on the back of lower costs.

[10] A full account of the episode, on which Economic naturalist 10.6 is based, is available in an article by John Kay, *Financial Times*, 5 July 1996.

Do oligopolistic firms always behave in a fashion that looks rational from a game theory perspective? Example 10.10 suggests otherwise.

### Example 10.10 The Inverness bus war of 1988–91

After bus deregulation in 1986, many municipal bus companies in Britain found themselves facing competition from private sector bus companies. In May 1988, an entrant, ITL, started to compete with the incumbent public sector operator, HSO, in Inverness in the Scottish Highlands, by running minibuses on the routes operated by HSO. HSO responded by increasing its frequency (the volume of service) and, eventually, by replacing some of its conventional buses by minibuses. ITL in August increased its frequencies, and HSO responded in kind. Both firms made substantial losses, and by mid-1989 ITL was effectively bankrupt and had to sell out to a national bus operator. The latter continued to operate in Inverness, and in 1991 HSO withdrew from the town. Britain's Monopolies and Mergers Commission (MMC) investigated the matter and concluded that HSO had engaged in predatory pricing to drive out the entrant. Predatory pricing is selling at below cost to eliminate competition so as to be able to raise prices later and maintain monopoly profits.

In 1993, an academic paper appeared that undermined the MMC's conclusions, and indicated that the unfortunate experience of ITL and HSO was due to a series of miscalculations.[11] The economist authors estimated the Cournot reaction curves for the two firms in the market, and showed that (a) if ITL had entered at a lower level of frequency it could have done so profitably, and (b) that the level at which it entered made it impossible for the incumbent or the entrant to cover costs. Worse, when the losses mounted, and HSO had cut its costs by introducing minibuses, both sides decided to try to establish a leadership position and force the other to cut back capacity. In effect, in terms of Fig. 10.10, both tried to get to a point like $Y$ on the other's reaction curve. If you add the two firm's production at points like $Y$ you will see that total output exceeds the competitive output so that both must make losses. ITL buckled first, but faced with the might of a major national concern operating ITL's services, HSO had to exit the market a couple of years later.

## Summary

- Economists use the mathematical theory of games to analyse situations in which the payoffs of one's actions depend on the actions *taken by others*. Games have three basic elements: the *players*; the list of *possible actions*, or *strategies*, from which each player can choose; and the *payoffs* the players receive for those strategies. The *payoff matrix* is the most useful way to summarise this information in games in which the timing of the players' moves is not decisive. In games in which the timing of moves does matter, a *decision tree* summarises the information in a much more useful format.
- A *dominant strategy* is one that yields a higher payoff regardless of the strategy chosen by the other player. In some games, such as the prisoner's dilemma, each player has a dominant strategy. The equilibrium occurs in such games when each player chooses his or her dominant strategy. In other games, not all players have a dominant strategy.
- Although the equilibrium outcome of any game is any combination of choices in which each player does the best he can, given the choices made by others, the result is often unattractive from the perspective of players as group. The prisoner's dilemma has this feature. The *incentive structure* of this game

[11] Dodgson, Katsoulakos and Newton (1993).

helps explain such disparate social dilemmas as excessive advertising, military arms races and failure to reap the potential benefits of interactions requiring trust.

- Individuals can often resolve these dilemmas if they can make *binding commitments* to behave in certain ways. Some commitments, such as those involved in military arms control agreements, are achieved by altering the material incentives confronting the players. Other commitments can be achieved by relying on psychological incentives to counteract material payoffs. Moral sentiments such as guilt, sympathy and a sense of justice often foster better outcomes than can be achieved by narrowly self-interested players. For this type of commitment to work, the relevant moral sentiments must be discernible by one's potential trading partners.
- Building on the idea of payoffs and games enables economists to construct models that indicate the importance of such things as beliefs and modes of competition in understanding how *small-number markets operate*.
- These models yield interesting and plausible conclusions that explain some features of *market behaviour* that are not explained by the simple models of perfect competition or monopolistic competition.

## Key terms

**basic elements of a game** (274)
**Bertrand competition** (298)
**cartel** (279)
**Cournot competition** (298)
**commitment device** (291)
**commitment problem** (291)
**credible promise** (289)
**credible threat** (288)
**decision tree (or game tree)** (287)
**dominant strategy** (276)
**dominated strategy** (276)
**Nash equilibrium** (276)
**payoff matrix** (275)
**prisoner's dilemma** (278)
**reaction function** (297)
**repeated prisoner's dilemma** (285)
**residual demand curve** (296)
**tacit collusion** (301)
**tit-for-tat** (285)
**ultimatum bargaining game** (288)

## Review questions

1. Explain why a military arms race is an example of a prisoner's dilemma.
2. Why did Warner Brothers make a mistake by waiting until the filming of *Analyze This* was almost finished before negotiating with Tony Bennett to perform in the final scene?
3. Suppose General Motors is trying to hire a small firm to manufacture the door handles for Opel saloon cars. The task requires an investment in expensive capital equipment that cannot be used for any other purpose. Why might the president of the small firm refuse to undertake this venture without a long-term contract fixing the price of the door handles?
4. Would you be irrational to refuse a one-sided offer in an ultimatum bargaining game if you knew that you would be playing that game many times with the same partner?
5. Can you show where (approximately) prices would settle if firm 1 were a leader and firm 2 a follower in the price-setting game (the equivalent to point *Y* in Fig. 10.10)?
6. Describe the commitment problem that narrowly self-interested diners and waiters confront at restaurants located on interstate highways. Given that in such restaurants tipping does seem to assure reasonably good service, do you think people are always selfish in the narrowest sense?

## Problems

Problems marked with an asterisk (*) are more difficult.

1. In studying for his economics final, Sam is concerned about only two things: his grade and the amount of time he spends studying. A good grade will give him a benefit of 20; an average grade, a benefit of 5; and a poor grade, a benefit of 0. By studying a lot, Sam will incur a cost of 10; by studying a little, a cost of 6. Moreover, if Sam studies a lot and all other students study a little, he will get a good grade and they will get poor ones. But if they study a lot and he studies a little, they will get good grades and he will get a poor one. Finally, if he and all other students study the same amount of time, everyone will get average grades. Other students share Sam's preferences regarding grades and study time.
    a. Model this situation as a two-person prisoner's dilemma in which the strategies are to study a little and to study a lot, and the players are Sam and all other students. Include the payoffs in the matrix.
    b. What is the equilibrium outcome in this game? From the students' perspective, is it the best outcome?

2. Consider the following 'dating game', which has two players, *A* and *B*, and two strategies, to buy a cinema ticket or a football ticket. The payoffs, given in points, are as shown in the matrix below. Note that the highest payoffs occur when both *A* and *B* attend the same event.

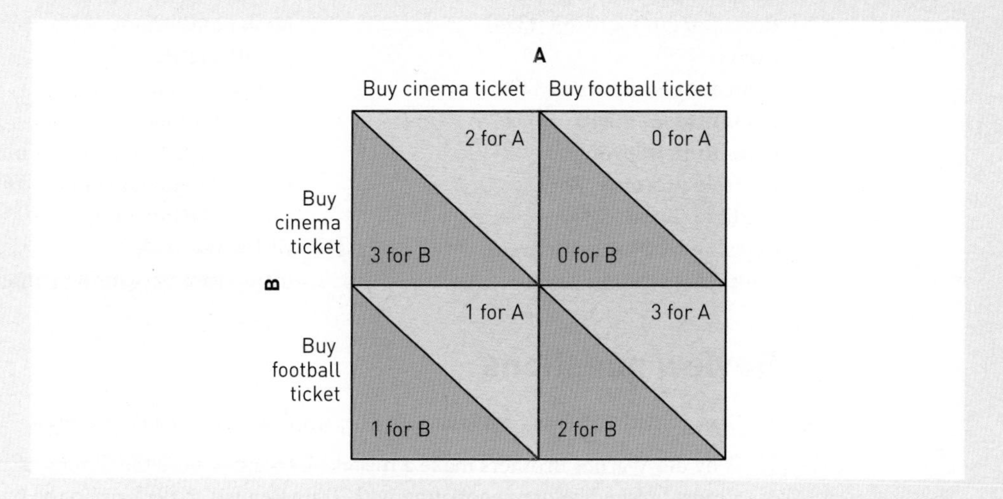


Assume that players *A* and *B* buy their tickets separately and simultaneously. Each must decide what to do knowing the available choices and payoffs but not what the other has actually chosen. Each player believes the other to be rational and self-interested.

   a. Does either player have a dominant strategy?
   b. How many potential equilibria are there? (**Hint:** To see whether a given combination of strategies is an equilibrium, ask whether either player could get a higher payoff by changing his or her strategy.)
   c. Is this game a prisoner's dilemma? Explain.
   d. Suppose player *A* gets to buy her ticket first. Player *B* does not observe *A*'s choice but knows that *A* chose first. Player *A* knows that player *B* knows she chose first. What is the equilibrium outcome?
   e. Suppose the situation is similar to part (d), except that player *B* chooses first. What is the equilibrium outcome?

3. Blackadder and Baldrick are rational, self-interested criminals imprisoned in separate cells in a dark medieval dungeon. They face the prisoner's dilemma displayed in the matrix below.

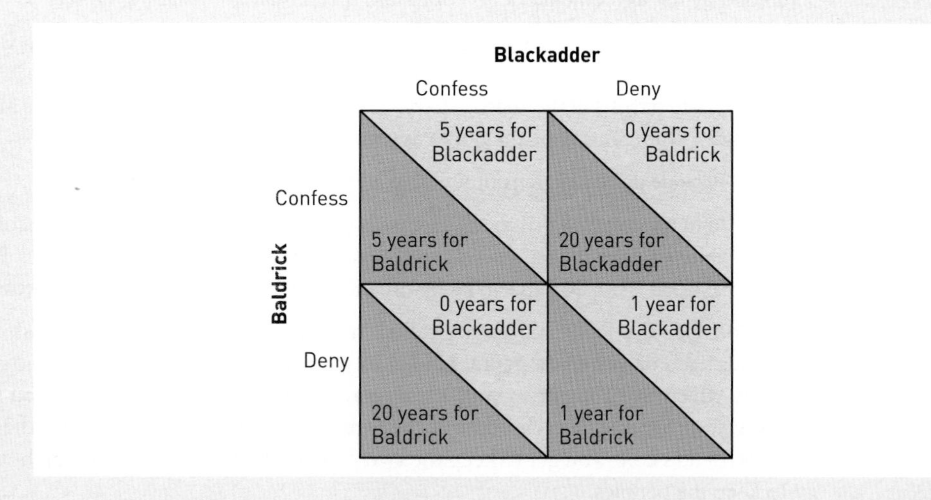


Assume that Blackadder is willing to pay 1,000 ducats for each year by which he can reduce his sentence below 20 years. A corrupt jailer tells Blackadder that before he decides whether to confess or deny the crime, he can tell him Baldrick's decision. How much is this information worth to Blackadder?

4. The owner of a thriving business wants to open a new office in a distant city. If he can hire someone who will manage the new office honestly, he can afford to pay that person a weekly salary of €2,000 (€1,000 more than the manager would be able to earn elsewhere) and still earn an economic profit of €800. The owner's concern is that he will not be able to monitor the manager's behaviour and that the manager will therefore be in a position to embezzle money from the business. The owner knows that if the remote office is managed dishonestly, the manager can earn €3,100 while causing the owner an economic loss of €600 per week.

a. If the owner believes that all managers are narrowly self-interested income-maximisers, will he open the new office?

b. Suppose the owner knows that a managerial candidate is a devoutly religious person who condemns dishonest behaviour and who would be willing to pay up to €15,000 to avoid the guilt she would feel if she were dishonest. Will the owner open the remote office?

5. Imagine yourself sitting in your car in a university car park that is currently full, waiting for someone to pull out so that you can park your car. Somebody pulls out, but at the same moment a driver who has just arrived overtakes you in an obvious attempt to park in the vacated spot before you can. Suppose this driver would be willing to pay up to €10 to park in that spot and up to €30 to avoid getting into an argument with you. (That is, the benefit of parking is €10, and the cost of an argument is €30.) At the same time the other driver guesses, accurately, that you too would be willing to pay up to €30 to avoid a confrontation and up to €10 to park in the vacant spot.

a. Model this situation as a two-stage decision tree in which the other driver's bid to take the space is the opening move and your strategies are (1) to protest and (2) not to protest. If you protest (initiate an argument), the rules of the game specify that the other driver has to let you take the space. Show the payoffs at the end of each branch of the tree.

b. What is the equilibrium outcome?

c. What would be the advantage of being able to communicate credibly to the other driver that your failure to protest would be a significant psychological cost to you?

6. Newfoundland's fishing industry has declined sharply due to overfishing, even though fishing companies were supposedly bound by a quota agreement. If all fishing companies had abided by the agreement, yields could have been maintained at high levels.

   a. Model this situation as a prisoner's dilemma in which the players are Company *A* and Company *B* and the strategies are to keep the quota and break the quota. Include appropriate payoffs in the matrix. Explain why overfishing is inevitable in the absence of effective enforcement of the quota agreement.

   b. Provide another environmental example of a prisoner's dilemma.

   c. In many potential prisoners' dilemmas, a way out for a would-be co-operator is to make reliable character judgements about the trustworthiness of potential partners. Explain why this solution is not available in many situations involving degradation of the environment.

7. Consider the following game, called 'matching pennies', which you are playing with a friend. Each of you has a penny hidden in your hand, facing either heads up or tails up (you know which way the one in your hand is facing). On the count of 'three' you simultaneously show your pennies to each other. If the face-up side of your coin matches the face-up side of your friend's coin, you get to keep the two pennies. If the faces do not match, your friend gets to keep the pennies.

   a. Who are the players in this game? What are each player's strategies? Construct a payoff matrix for the game.

   b. Is there a dominant strategy? If so, what?

   c. Is there an equilibrium? If so, what?

8. Consider the following game. Harry has four 20 pence pieces. He can offer Sally from one to four of them. If she accepts his offer, she keeps the coins Harry offered her and Harry keeps the others. If Sally declines Harry's offer, they both get nothing. They play the game only once, and each cares only about the amount of money he or she ends up with.

   a. Who are the players? What are each player's strategies? Construct a decision tree for this ultimatum bargaining game.

   b. Given their goal, what is the optimal choice for each player?

9. Two aeroplane manufacturers are considering the production of a new product, a 550-passenger jet. Both are deciding whether to enter the market and produce the new plane. The payoff matrix is as shown (payoff values are in million euros).

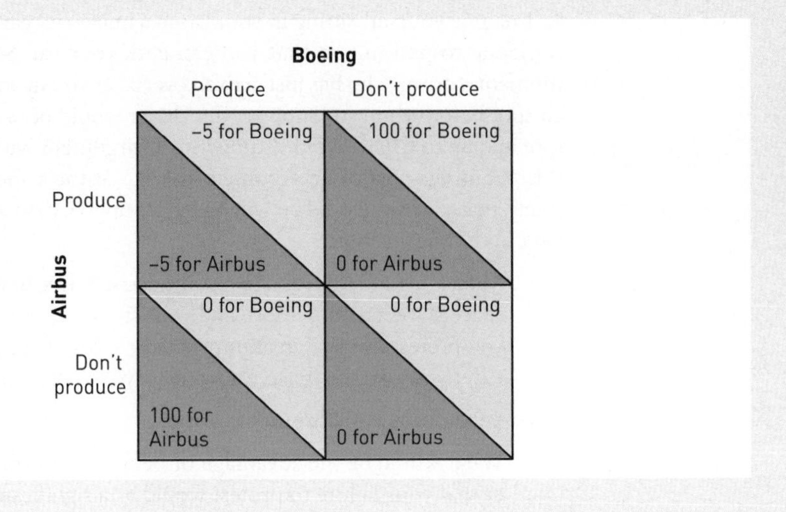

The implication of these payoffs is that the market demand is large enough to support only one manufacturer. If both firms enter, both will sustain a loss.

a. Identify two possible equilibrium outcomes in this game.

b. Consider the effect of a subsidy. Suppose the European Union decides to subsidise the European producer, Airbus, with a subsidy of €25 million if it enters the market. Revise the payoff matrix to account for this subsidy. What is the new equilibrium outcome?

c. Compare the two outcomes (pre- and post-subsidy). What qualitative effect does the subsidy have?

**10.*** Jill and Jack both have two pails that can be used to carry water down from a hill. Each makes only one trip down the hill, and each pail of water can be sold for €5. Carrying the pails of water down requires considerable effort. Both the children would be willing to pay €2 each to avoid carrying one bucket down the hill and an additional €3 to avoid carrying a second bucket down the hill.

a. Given market prices, how many pails of water will each child fetch from the top of the hill?

b. Jill and Jack's parents are worried that the two children don't co-operate enough with one another. Suppose they make Jill and Jack share their revenues from selling the water equally. Given that both are self-interested, construct the payoff matrix for the decisions Jill and Jack face regarding the number of pails of water each should carry. What is the equilibrium outcome?

## Answers to in-chapter exercises

**10.1** No matter what Alitalia does, Lufthansa will do better to raise ad spending. No matter what Lufthansa does, Alitalia will do better to leave ad spending the same. So each player will play its dominant strategy: Lufthansa will raise its ad spending, and Alitalia will leave its ad spending the same, as in the table below.

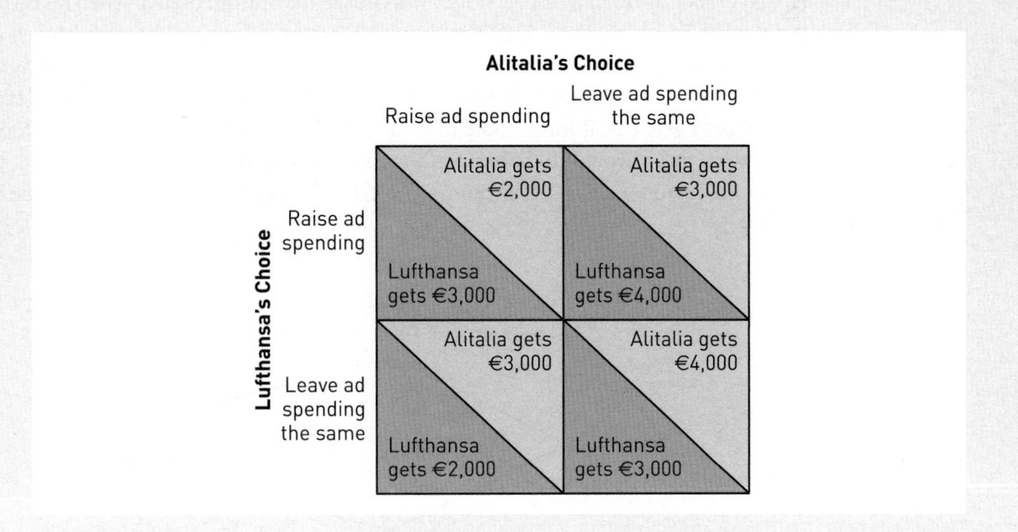


**10.2** In game 1, no matter what Chrysler does, General Motors (GM) will do better to invest, and no matter what GM does, Chrysler will do better to invest (see the table below). Each has a dominant strategy, but in following it, each does worse than if it had not invested. So game 1

is a prisoner's dilemma. In game 2, no matter what Chrysler does, GM again will do better to invest; but no matter what GM does, Chrysler will do better *not* to invest. Each has a dominant strategy, and in following it, each gets a payoff of 10 – that is, 5 more than if each had played its dominated strategy. So game 2 is not a prisoner's dilemma.

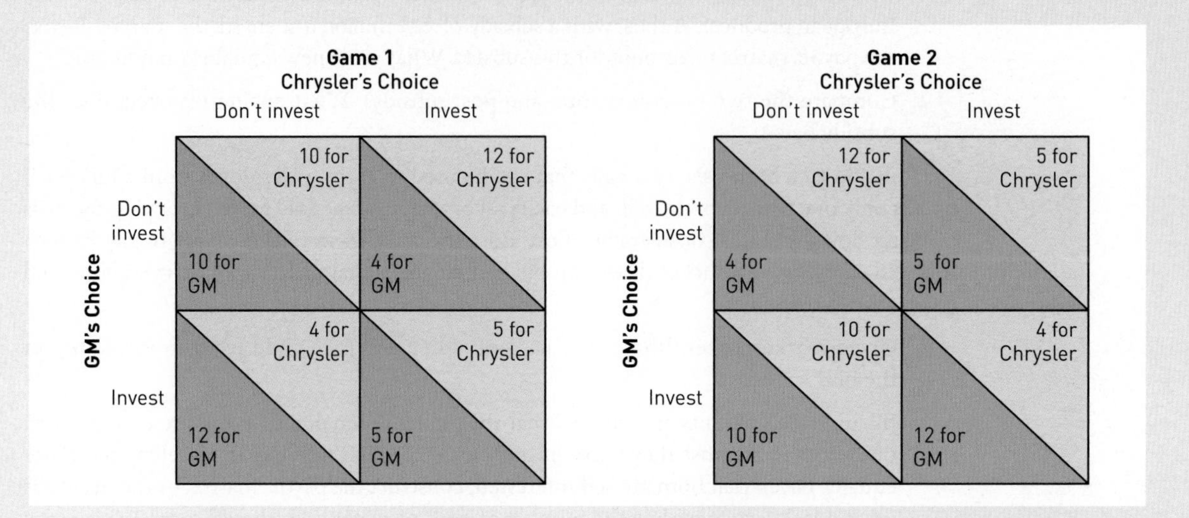


**10.3** People may well collectively prefer the absence of mobile phones while personally wishing to be able to use them. This another prisoner's dilemma problem: everyone would be better off if no one used a phone, but each person's dominant strategy is to use it. In these circumstances an airline could well conclude that its services would have a competitive advantage if it prohibited mobile phone usage. It could even seek to introduce a 'hurdle' to price discriminate on the basis of permission to use mobile phones in a separate cabin. It would be surprising if the absence of a legal prohibition resulted in a free for all. We shall see.

**10.4** Smith assumes that Jones will choose the branch that maximises his payoff, which is the bottom branch at either *B* or *C*. So Jones will choose the bottom branch when his turn comes, no matter what Smith chooses. Since Smith will do better (60) on the bottom branch at *B* than on the bottom branch at *C* (50), Smith will choose the top branch at *A*. So the equilibrium in this game is for Smith to choose the top branch at *A* and Jones to choose the bottom branch at *B*. Smith gets 60, and Jones gets 105. If Jones could make a credible commitment to choose the top branch no matter what, both would do better. Smith would choose the bottom branch at *A* and Jones would choose the top branch at *C*, giving Smith 500 and Jones 400 (see the decision tree below).

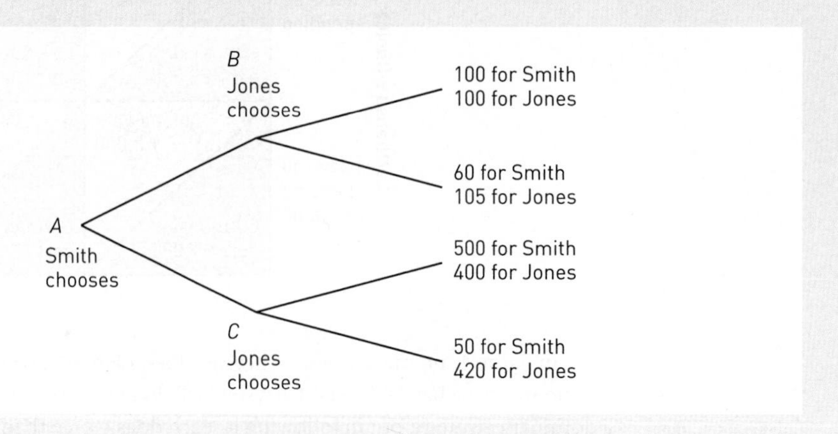

**10.5** Given its expected demand for super-jumbos over the life of the production run, Airbus thinks that it makes a profit by producing and selling 400 A380s and reckons that the maximum possible volume of profitable sales is 500 units. It would maximise its profits if it could sell 450. Suppose it now commits itself to sell 450, and expects to get €300 million per plane. The position facing Boeing is that it can sell planes only if it accepts a maximum price (for one plane) of €300 million, and to sell more (given that Airbus is committed to producing 450) can do so only if it is prepared to accept prices indicated by the residual demand curve in the diagram below. However, the residual demand curve lies below the long-run average cost curve, so it can never be profitable for Boeing to commit itself (incur sunk costs) to producing its planes once Airbus has done so provided it does not believe that Airbus has underestimated demand (in fact, Boeing believed that Airbus was being wildly optimistic).

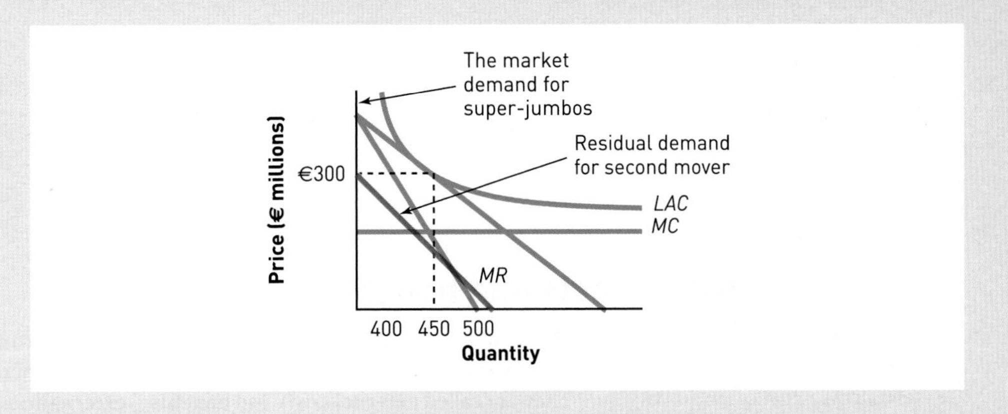


## References

Barnstone, W. (1993) *With Borges on an Ordinary Evening in Buenos Aires* (Champaign, IL: University of Illinois Press).

Dodgson, J. S., Y. Katsoulakos and C. R. Newton (1993) 'An Application of the Economic Modeling Approach to the Investigation of Population', *Journal of Transport Economics and Policy*, pp. 153–70.

Von Neumann, J. and O. Morgenstern (1944) *The Theory of Games and Economic Behavior* (Princeton, NJ: Princeton University Press).

# 11 Externalities and Property Rights

## External costs and benefits

**external cost (or negative externality)** a cost of an activity that falls on people other than those who pursue the activity

**external benefit (or positive externality)** a benefit of an activity received by people other than those who pursue the activity

**externality** an external cost or benefit of an activity

Many activities generate costs or benefits that accrue to people not directly involved in those activities. These effects are generally unintended. They are called **external costs** and **benefits** – **externalities**, for short.

When parents decide to inoculate a newborn child against a variety of infectious diseases they do so because they are concerned for the child's welfare. One of these diseases is rubella (so-called 'German measles'). Rubella is in most cases a not very disabling condition; however, if contracted by a pregnant woman it can cause physical and/or mental defects in her unborn child. No inoculation is without some risk, but well-intentioned parents calculate the benefits expected for the child and compare them with the possible risks. In having the child inoculated, however, they confer benefits on other, unidentified parents and children. This is because, in addition to protecting their own child from rubella, they also reduce the probability of some one else being infected, as they eliminate part of the transmission vector for the infection. It is reasonable to assume that the parents' decision reflects the costs (risk) and benefits (protection) to their own child. They do not calculate the benefits to others flowing from their decision. If the inoculation was financially costly, it is equally reasonable to assume that fewer children would be inoculated, with the consequence that the incidence of rubella among pregnant women would increase.

In this example, the decision to incur the cost reflects the private calculus of costs and benefits. These are 'internalised' into the decision-making process. What are not internalised are the costs and benefits *to others* of their decision. These are described as 'external effects' (spillover effects) of the actions they take. These effects are described in economics as 'externalities'.

In this case, inoculation involves a positive externality: it confers benefits on others at no cost to the decision maker, benefits that do not increase the welfare of the decision maker. Other actions involve negative externalities. They impose costs on others at no cost to the person undertaking the action. An example is a decision to use a car in an urban area during the rush-hour. The driver computes into his decision the costs and benefits to him of using the car to make a journey at that time. What does not enter into the calculation is that on the journey the driver may delay a large number of motorists, each by a small amount, because the road being used is already congested.

In general, where there are positive externalities private decision making tends to result in a less than socially optimal (marginal cost = marginal benefit) level of the activity concerned. This is because the resource allocation reflects *marginal private costs* and *marginal private benefits*. The problem is that marginal private benefits are not the same as marginal social benefits. Put another way, the decision maker does not capture all the benefits of his decision. For the same reason, negative externalities imply that 'too much' of the activity occurs, because the decision maker does not face personally all the costs that arise from his actions.

This chapter focuses on how externalities affect the allocation of resources. Adam Smith's theory of the 'invisible hand' (Chapter 8) applies to an ideal marketplace in which externalities do not exist. In such situations, Smith argued, the self-interested actions of individuals would lead to socially efficient outcomes. We shall see that when the parties affected by externalities can easily negotiate with one another, the 'invisible hand' will still produce an efficient outcome.

But in many cases, such as in the cases of rush-hour traffic and inoculation, negotiation is impractical. In those cases, the self-serving actions of individuals simply will not lead to efficient outcomes. Because externalities are widespread, the attempt to forge solutions to the problems they cause is one of the most important rationales not only for the existence of government but for a variety of other forms of collective action as well.

## How externalities affect resource allocation

The way in which externalities distort the allocation of resources can be seen clearly in Examples 11.1 and 11.2 and Economic naturalist 11.1.

### **Example 11.1** Does the honeybee keeper face the right incentives:I?

Phoebe earns her living as a keeper of honeybees. Her neighbours on all sides grow apples. Because bees pollinate apple trees as they forage for nectar, the more hives Phoebe keeps, the larger the harvests will be in the surrounding orchards. If Phoebe takes only her own costs and benefits into account in deciding how many hives to keep, will she keep the socially optimal number of hives?

For the orchard owners, Phoebe's hives constitute an external benefit, or a *positive* externality. If she takes only her own personal costs and benefits into account, she will add hives only until the added revenue she gets from the last hive just equals the cost of adding it. But since the orchard owners also benefit from additional hives, the total benefit of adding another hive at that point will be greater than its cost. Phoebe, then, will keep too few hives.

As we shall discuss later in the chapter, problems like that just discussed have several possible solutions. One is for orchard owners to pay beekeepers to keep additional hives. But such solutions often require complex negotiations between the affected parties. For the moment, we assume that such negotiations are not practical.

### **Example 11.2** Does the honeybee keeper face the right incentives: 2?

As in Example 11.1, Phoebe earns her living as a keeper of honeybees. But now her neighbours are not apple growers but an elementary school and a nursing home. The more hives Phoebe keeps, the more students and nursing home residents will be stung by bees. If Phoebe takes only her own costs and benefits into account in deciding how many hives to keep, will she keep the socially optimal number of hives?

For the students and nursing home residents, Phoebe's hives constitute an external cost, or a *negative* externality. If she considers only her own costs and benefits in deciding how many hives to keep, she will continue to add hives until the added revenue from the last hive is just enough to cover its cost. But since Phoebe's neighbours also incur costs when she adds a hive, the benefit of the last hive at that point will be smaller than its cost. Phoebe, in other words, will keep too many hives.

## Economic naturalist 11.1 It pays to know the facts!

The example of bees and orchards reflects an example of why markets 'fail' given by the Cambridge (UK) economist, A. C. Pigou, in a well-known textbook written in the 1930s. The point in the example is that neither side 'internalises' all the benefit of his or her investment decision. All that is considered is the *private benefit* in each case. As a result, there is underinvestment in both orchard and beekeeping. This is because the orchard owner cannot be made to pay for the activities of the bees, and the beekeeper cannot be made to pay for the nectar and pollen derived from the orchard. If payments could be exacted from the beneficiaries, there would be no problem. In fact, as anyone who knew anything about the economics of intensive fruit-growing could have told the Cambridge don, a well-developed market in the services of bees to orchards and vice versa actually does exist, as can be seen even today in the fruit-growing areas of the Central Valley of California. This is because the services of each to the other are valuable, and as a result beekeepers habitually move large numbers of hives around to serve orchard owners at blossom time, with one or other side paying depending on supply and demand. Clearly it was unwise to extrapolate from observations derived from the dreary fenland around Cambridge. Pigou could be said to have refused to let the facts get in the way of a good story!

Every activity involves *costs* and *benefits*. When all the relevant *costs* and *benefits* of an activity accrue directly to the person who carries it out – that is, when the activity generates no externalities – the level of the activity that is best for the individual will be best for society as a whole. But when an activity generates externalities, be they positive or negative, individual self-interest does not produce the best allocation of resources. Individuals who consider only their own costs and benefits will tend to engage too much in activities that generate negative externalities and too little in activities that generate positive externalities. When an activity generates both positive and negative externalities, private and social interests will coincide only in the unlikely event that the opposing effects offset one another exactly.

## The graphical portrayal of externalities

The effects of externalities on resource allocation can be portrayed graphically. Consider first the case of negative externalities. Figure 11.1(a) depicts the supply (Private *MC*) and demand curves for a product whose production involves no external costs or benefits. We may imagine, for example, that the energy that powers the factories in this market comes from non-polluting hydroelectric generators. The resulting equilibrium price and quantity in the market for this product will then be socially optimal, for the reasons discussed in Chapters 3 and 7: the value to buyers of the last unit of the product consumed will be exactly equal to the marginal cost of producing it (€1,300 per tonne in each case), leaving no further possible gains from exchange.

But now suppose that a protracted drought has eliminated hydroelectric power generation, forcing factories to rely instead on electric power produced by coal-burning generators. Now each tonne of output produced is accompanied by an external pollution cost of $XC$ = €1,000, as shown in Fig. 11.1(b). Since the external pollution cost falls not on firm owners but on others who live downwind from their factories, Private *MC* is again the supply curve for this product, and its demand curve is again as before, so that the equilibrium price and quantity will be exactly the same as in Fig. 11.1(a), as determined by the intersection of the demand curve (*D*) and the supply curve (Private *MC*). But this time the private market equilibrium is not socially optimal. To see why, note that at $Q_{pvt}$ = 12,000 tonnes per year, the value to consumers of the last unit of output produced was only €1,300 per tonne, while the

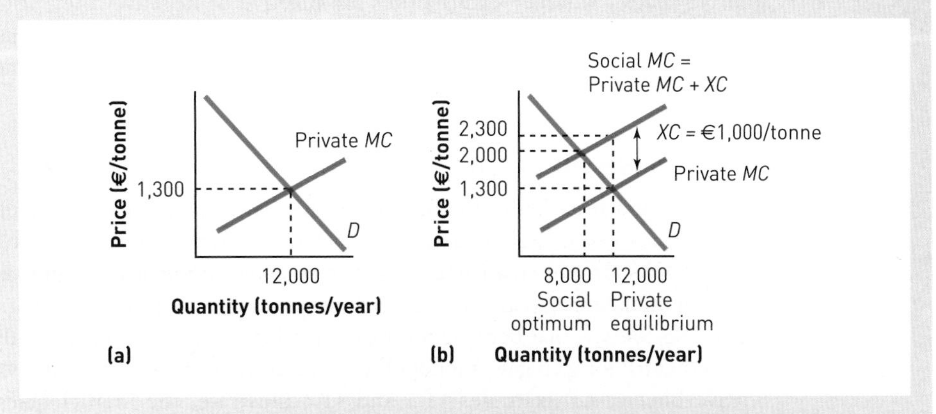


**Figure 11.1 How External Costs Affect Resource Allocation.** When a market has no external costs or benefits (a), the resulting equilibrium quantity and price are socially optimal. By contrast, when production of a good is accompanied by an external cost (b), the market equilibrium price (€1,300 per tonne) is too low, and the market equilibrium quantity (12,000 tonnes per year) is too high.

cost of producing that last unit (including the external cost) was €2,300 per tonne. This means that society could gain additional economic surplus by producing fewer units of the product. Indeed, the same conclusion will continue to hold whenever the current output exceeds 8,000 tonnes per year, the output level at which the demand curve intersects Social *MC*. Social *MC*, the socially optimal supply curve of the product, is the result of adding the external cost, *XC*, to every value along Private *MC*. The socially optimal level of output of the good shown in Fig. 11.1(b) is 8,000 tonnes per year, the level that exhausts all possibilities from exchange. For a good whose production generates external costs, the market equilibrium quantity will be higher than the socially optimal quantity.

What about a good whose production generates external benefits? In Fig. 11.2, Private demand is the demand curve for a product whose production generates an external benefit of *XB* per unit. The market equilibrium quantity of this good $Q_{pvt}$, is the output level at which Private demand intersects the supply curve of the product (*MC*). This time, market equilibrium quantity is smaller than the socially optimal level, denoted $Q_{soc}$. $Q_{soc}$ is the output level at which *MC* intersects the socially optimal demand curve (Social demand), which is obtained by adding the external benefit, *XB*, to every value along Private demand. Note that in Fig. 11.2 in the case of positive externalities the private market equilibrium again fails to exhaust all possible gains from exchange. Thus at $Q_{pvt}$ the marginal cost of producing an additional unit of output is only $MB_{pvt}$, which is smaller than the marginal benefit of an additional unit by the amount *XB*. For a good whose production generates external benefits, the market equilibrium quantity will be smaller than the socially optimal quantity.

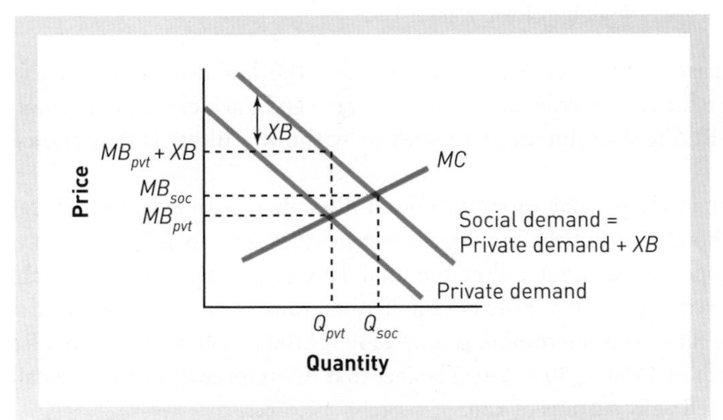


**Figure 11.2 A Good Whose Production Generates a Positive Externality for Consumers.** The market equilibrium quantity, $Q_{pvt}$ is smaller than the socially optimal quantity, $Q_{soc}$, because individual buyers are willing to pay only for the benefits they reap from directly consuming the product.

No matter whether externalities are positive or negative, they *distort the allocation of resources* in otherwise efficient markets. When externalities are present, the individual pursuit of self-interest will not result in the largest possible economic surplus. And when it does not, the outcome is by definition inefficient.

## The Coase theorem

To say that a situation is 'inefficient' means that it can be rearranged in a way that would make at least some people better off without harming others. Such situations, as we have seen, are a source of creative tension. The existence of inefficiency, after all, means that there is 'cash on the table' (Chapter 3), which usually triggers a race to see who can capture it. For example, we saw that because monopoly pricing results in an inefficiently low output level, the potential for gain gave monopolists an incentive to make discounts available to price-sensitive buyers. As Examples 11.3 and 11.4 illustrate, the inefficiencies that result from externalities create similar incentives for remedial action.

### **Example 11.3** Will Abercrombie dump toxins in the river: 1?

In nineteenth-century Lancashire an industrialist named Abercrombie has built a textile factory beside a river. The water supplies power, but is also used in the production process. The process produces a toxic waste by-product from the dyes used. If Abercrombie releases the water untreated back into the river the toxins cause damage to Fitch, a commercial fisherman located downstream. The toxins are short-lived and cause no damage to anyone other than Fitch. At a cost, Abercrombie can filter out the toxins, in which case Fitch will suffer no damage at all. The relevant gains and losses for the two individuals are listed in Table 11.1.

| | With filter | Without filter |
|---|---|---|
| Gains to Abercrombie | £100/day | £130/day |
| Gains to Fitch | £100/day | £50/day |

**Table 11.1** Costs and Benefits of Eliminating Toxic Waste: 1

If, as was generally the case in most countries at the time, the law does not penalise Abercrombie for dumping toxins in the river, and if Abercrombie and Fitch cannot communicate with one another, will Abercrombie operate with or without a filter? Is that choice socially efficient?

Since Abercrombie earns £330 per day more without a filter than with one, his natural incentive is to operate without one. But the outcome when he does so is socially inefficient. Thus, when Abercrombie operates without a filter, the total daily gain to both parties is only £130 + £50 = £180, compared with £100 + £100 = £200 if Abercrombie had operated with a filter. The daily cost of the filter to Abercrombie is only £130 – £100 = £30, which is smaller than its daily benefit to Fitch of £100 – £50 = £50. The fact that Abercrombie does not install the filter implies a squandered daily surplus of £20.

### **Example 11.4** Will Abercrombie dump toxins in the river: 2?

Suppose the costs and benefits of using the filter are as in Example 11.3 except that Abercrombie and Fitch can now communicate with one another at no cost. Even though the law does not require him to do so, will Abercrombie use a filter?

This time, Abercrombie will use a filter. Recall from Chapter 7 the observation that when the economic 'pie' grows larger, everyone can have a larger slice (the efficiency principle). Because use of a filter would result in the largest possible economic surplus, it would enable both Abercrombie and Fitch to have a larger net gain than before. Fitch thus has an incentive to *pay* Abercrombie to use a filter. For example, suppose Fitch offers Abercrombie £40 per day to compensate him for operating with a filter. Both Abercrombie and Fitch will then be exactly £10 per day better off than before, for a total daily net gain of £20.

**Exercise 11.1** In Example 11.4, what is the largest amount to the nearest pound by which Fitch could compensate Abercrombie for operating with a filter and still be better off than before?

Ronald Coase, a professor at the University of Chicago Law School, who was born in England and worked there as a professional economist before the Second World War, was the first to see clearly that if people can negotiate with one another at no cost over the right to perform activities that cause externalities, they will always arrive at an efficient solution. This insight, which is often called the **Coase theorem**, is a profoundly important idea, for which Coase was awarded the 1991 Nobel Prize in Economics.[1]

**Coase theorem** if at no cost people can negotiate the purchase and sale of the right to perform activities that cause externalities, they can always arrive at efficient solutions to the problems caused by externalities

Why, you might ask, should Fitch pay Abercrombie to filter out toxins that would not be there in the first place if it were not for Abercrombie's factory? The rhetorical force of this question is undeniable. Yet Coase points out that externalities are *reciprocal* in nature. The toxins do harm Fitch, to be sure, but preventing Abercrombie from emitting them would penalise Abercrombie, by exactly £30 per day. Why should Fitch necessarily have the right to harm Abercrombie? Indeed, as Example 11.5 illustrates, even if Fitch had that right, he would exercise it only if filtering the toxins proved the most efficient outcome.

### Example 11.5 Will Abercrombie dump toxins in the river: 3?

Suppose the law says that Abercrombie may *not* dump toxins in the river unless he has Fitch's permission. If the relevant costs and benefits of filtering the toxins are as shown in Table 11.2, and if Abercrombie and Fitch can negotiate with one another at no cost, will Abercrombie filter the toxins?

| | With filter | Without filter |
|---|---|---|
| Gains to Abercrombie | £100/day | £150/day |
| Gains to Fitch | £100/day | £70/day |

**Table 11.2** Costs and Benefits of Eliminating Toxic Waste: 3

Note that this time the most efficient outcome is for Abercrombie to operate without a filter, for the total daily surplus in that case will be £220 compared with only £200 with a filter. Under the law, however, Fitch has the right to insist that Abercrombie use a filter. We might expect him to exercise that right, since his own gain would rise from £70 to £100 per

[1] Coase's highly readable paper (and one of the most influential of the twentieth century) that enunciated what is now referred to as the Coase theorem appeared in 1960 (Coase 1960).

day if he did so. But because this outcome would be socially inefficient, we know that each party can do better.

Suppose, for example, that Abercrombie gives Fitch £40 per day in return for Fitch's permission to operate without a filter. Each would then have a net daily gain of £110, which is £10 better for each of them than if Fitch had insisted that Abercrombie use a filter. Abercrombie's pollution harms Fitch, sure enough, but failure to allow the pollution would have caused even greater harm to Abercrombie.

The Coase theorem tells us that regardless of whether the law holds polluters liable for damages, the affected parties will achieve efficient solutions to externalities if they can negotiate costlessly with one another. But note carefully that this does not imply that affected parties will be indifferent about whether the law holds polluters responsible for damages. If polluters are liable, they will end up with lower incomes and those who are injured by pollutants will end up with higher incomes than if the law does not hold polluters liable – even though the same efficient production methods are adopted in each case. When polluters are held liable, they must remove the pollution at their own expense. When they are not held liable, those who are injured by pollution must pay polluters to cut back.

Externalities are hardly rare and isolated occurrences. On the contrary, finding examples of actions that are altogether free of them is difficult. And because externalities can distort the allocation of resources, it is important to recognise them and deal intelligently with them. Consider Example 11.6, an externality that arises because of shared living arrangements.

### **Example 11.6** Will Ann and Betty share an apartment?

Ann and Betty can live together in a two-bedroom apartment in a small university town in Britain for £600 per month, or separately in two one-bedroom apartments, for £400 per month each. If the rent paid were the same for both alternatives, the two women would be indifferent between living together or separately, except for one problem: Ann talks constantly on the telephone. Ann would pay up to £250 per month for this privilege. Betty, for her part, would pay up to £150 per month to have better access to the phone. If the two cannot install a second phone line, should they live together or separately?

Ann and Betty should live together only if the benefit of doing so exceeds the cost. The benefit of living together is the reduction in their rent. Their benefit from living together is £200 per month. Their cost of living together is the least costly arrangement they can make to deal with Ann's objectionable telephone habits. Since Ann would be willing to pay up to £250 per month to avoid changing her behaviour, the £200 rent saving is too small to persuade her to change. But Betty is willing to put up with Ann's behaviour for a compensation payment of only £150 per month. Since that amount is smaller than the total saving in rent, the least costly solution to the problem is for Betty to live with Ann and simply put up with her behaviour.

Table 11.3 summarises the relevant costs and benefits of this shared living arrangement. The Cost–Benefit Principle tells us that Ann and Betty should live together if and only if the benefit of living together exceeds the cost. The cost of the shared living arrangement is not the sum of all possible costs but the least costly accommodation to the problem (or problems) of shared living. Since the £200 per month saving in rent exceeds the least costly accommodation to the phone problem, Ann and Betty can reap a total gain in economic surplus of £50 per month by sharing their living quarters.

An initial reaction to this problem might be that Ann and Betty should not live together, because if the two share the rent equally, Betty will end up paying £300 per month – which when added to the £150 cost of putting up with Ann's phone behaviour comes to £50 more than the cost of living alone. As persuasive as that argument may sound, however, it is mistaken. The source of the error, as Example 11.7 makes clear, is the assumption that the two must share the rent equally.

| Benefits of shared living | | | |
|---|---|---|---|
| **Total cost of separate apartments** | **Total cost of shared apartment** | | **Rent savings from sharing** |
| (2)(£400/month) = £800/month | £600/month | | £200/month |
| **Costs of shared living** | | | |
| **Problem** | **Ann's cost of solving problem** | **Betty's cost of solving problem** | **Least costly solution to the problem** |
| Ann's phone usage | Curtailed phone usage: £250/month | Tolerate phone usage: £150/month | Better tolerates Ann's phone usage: £150 /month |
| **Gain in surplus from shared living** | | | |
| Rent savings (£200/month) – | Least costly accommodation to shared living problems (£150/month) = | | Gain in surplus: £50/month |

**Table 11.3** The Gain in Surplus from Shared Living Arrangements

### **Example 11.7** What is the highest rent Betty would be willing to pay for the two-bedroom apartment?

In Example 11.6, what is the highest rent Betty would be willing to pay to share an apartment with Ann? Betty's alternative is to live alone, which would mean paying £400 per month, her reservation price for a living arrangement with no phone problem. Since the most she would be willing to pay to avoid the phone problem is £150 per month, the highest monthly rent she would be willing to pay for the shared apartment is £400 – £150 = £250. If she pays that amount, Ann will have to pay the difference, namely, £350 per month, which is clearly a better alternative for Ann than paying £400 to live alone.

### **Example 11.8** How much should Ann and Betty pay if they agree to split their economic surplus equally?

If Ann and Betty agree to live together and split the resulting gain in economic surplus equally, how much rent will each of them pay?

As we saw in Table 11.3, the total rent saving from the shared apartment is £200, and since the least costly solution to the phone problem is £150, the monthly gain in economic surplus is £50. We know that Ann's reservation price for living together is £400 per month and Betty's is £250 (see Example 11.7). So if the two women want to split the £50 monthly surplus equally, each should pay £25 less than her reservation price. Ann's monthly rent will thus be £375 and Betty's £225. The result is that each is £25 per month better off than if she had lived alone.

**Exercise 11.2** As in Example 11.6, Ann and Betty can live together in a two-bedroom apartment for £600 per month or separately in two one-bedroom apartments, each for £400 per month. Ann would pay up to £250 per month rather than moderate her telephone habits, and Betty would pay up to £150 per month to achieve reasonable access to the telephone. But Betty would also be willing to pay up to £60 per month to avoid the loss of privacy that comes with shared living space. Should the two women live together?

## Legal remedies for externalities

We have seen that efficient solutions to externalities can be found whenever the affected parties can negotiate with one another at no cost. But negotiation is not always practical. A motorist with a noisy exhaust silencer, for example, imposes costs on others, yet they cannot flag him down and offer him a compensation payment to fix it. In recognition of this difficulty, most governments simply require that cars have working silencers. Indeed, the explicit or implicit purpose of a large share – perhaps the lion's share – of laws is to solve problems caused by externalities. The goal of such laws is to help people achieve the solutions they might have reached had they been able to negotiate with one another.

When negotiation is costless, the task of adjustment generally falls on the party who can accomplish it at the lowest cost. For instance, in Example 11.6, Betty put up with Ann's annoying phone habits because doing so was less costly than asking Ann to change her habits. Many municipal noise abatement orders also place the burden of adjustment on those who can accomplish it at lowest cost. Consider, for example, the restrictions on loud party music, which often take effect at a later hour on weekends than on weekdays. This pattern reflects both the fact that the gains from loud music tend to be larger on weekends and the fact that such music is more likely to disturb people on weekdays. By setting the noise curfew at different hours on different days of the week, the law places the burden on partygoers during the week and on sleepers during the weekend. Similar logic explains why noise abatement orders allow motorists to honk their horns in most neighbourhoods but not in the immediate vicinity of a hospital.

**Exercise 11.3**

The exposition of the Coase theorem in Coase's 1960 paper referred to a case heard in the Chancery Division of the High Court in London in 1879.[2] The facts were as follows. A confectioner (Bridgeman) had for years operated a business from his premises on a London street that involved using mortars and pestles to grind and mix ingredients. A doctor, Sturges, who had a practice in an adjoining premises, built a consultation room up against the wall of Bridgeman's premises. The vibrations from the confectionery business interfered with the doctor's ability to listen to people's chests. He sued the confectioner for 'nuisance' (a tort under common law: a tort is an injury to a person or property). What would you have decided in this case (a) if you had never heard of the Coase theorem, and (b) if you were fully aware of the Coase theorem?

As Economic naturalists 11.2–11.6 demonstrate, economic naturalists can hone their craft by focusing on laws whose purpose is to solve the problems caused by externalities.

### Economic naturalist 11.2 What is the purpose of speed limits and other traffic laws?

The official line here (and there is much truth in it) is that the only reason for limits is an externality one. A motorist driving a car at high speed endangers not just her own life and property but also the lives and property of others. Speed limits, no-passing zones, right-of-way rules and a host of other traffic laws may be seen as reasoned attempts to limit the harm one party inflicts on another. Many countries even have laws requiring that motorists fit snow tyres on their cars by 1 November. In the Alps in France, Austria and Switzerland, such requirements are common. These laws pro-

[2] *Sturges v. Bridgeman*, 11 Chancery Division 852, 1879.

mote not just safety but also the smooth flow of traffic: a single motorist who can't get up a snow-covered hill delays not only herself but also the motorists behind her. People accept this rationale. The experience in Britain with speed cameras is illustrative. Once people began to feel that the enforcement of speed restrictions had another motive, pressure built up to have the system reviewed. The laws couldn't possibly have anything to do with raising revenues, could they?

## Economic naturalist 11.3 Why do most communities have zoning laws?

Most communities restrict the kinds of activities that take place in various parts of the city. Because many residents place a high value on living in an uncongested neighbourhood, some cities have enacted zoning laws specifying maximum housing densities. In places such as Manhattan, where a shortage of land encourages developers to build very large and tall buildings, zoning laws limit both a building's height and the proportion of a neighbourhood it may occupy. Such restrictions recognise that the taller a building is, and the greater the proportion of ground that it occupies, the more it blocks sunlight from reaching surrounding properties. The desire to control external costs also helps to explain why many cities establish separate zones for business and residential activity. Even within business districts, many cities limit certain kinds of commercial activity. For example, in an effort to revitalise the Times Square neighbourhood, New York City enacted a zoning law banning adult bookstores and pornographic movie theatres from the area. Soho in London was similarly 'cleaned up' in the 1970s.

## Economic naturalist 11.4 Why do many governments enact laws that limit the discharge of environmental pollutants?

Limitations on the discharge of pollutants into the environment are perhaps the clearest examples of laws aimed at solving problems caused by externalities. The details of these laws reflect the Cost–Benefit Principle. The discharge of toxic wastes into rivers, for example, tends to be most strictly regulated on those waterways whose commercial fishing or recreational uses are most highly valued. On other waterways, the burden of adjustment is likely to fall more heavily on fishermen, recreational sailors and swimmers. Similarly, air quality regulations tend to be strictest in the most heavily populated regions of the country, where the marginal benefit of pollution reduction is the greatest.

## Economic naturalist 11.5 What is the purpose of free speech laws?

At the end of 2004 a bill was introduced in the UK House of Commons that would have created a new offence. Under UK law it was already an offence to incite racial hatred. This bill would have made it an offence to make fun of a person's religious convictions. The reason for its introduction was heightened concern over possible conflicts between Britain's significant Muslim population, some born in Britain, some immigrants, and the rest of British society in the context of the events of September 2001 in the United States and the second Gulf War. The First Amendment to the original US Constitution provided protection for freedom of speech and the right freely to express opinions. Protection of free speech and the pattern of exceptions to that protection are another illustration of how legal remedies can be used to solve the problems caused by externalities. The First Amendment acknowledges the decisive value of open communication, as well as the practical difficulty of identifying and regulating acts of speech that cause more harm than good. Yet it does allow some important exceptions. For instance, it does not allow someone to yell 'fire' in a crowded theatre if there is no fire, nor does it allow someone to advocate the violent overthrow of the government. In those instances, the external benefits of free speech are far too small to justify the external costs. It would appear that in British circumstances of 2004 the right to freedom of expression would have to give way to the needs of civic peace. Jokes could have the same kind of effect as raising a false alarm in a crowded cinema. You may or may not agree, but it raises interesting issues from an economics perspective.

## Economic naturalist 11.6 Why does government subsidise the planting of trees on hillsides and subsidise economists to generate models of computable general equilibrium?

The laws discussed in Economic naturalists 11.2–11.5 are meant to regulate activities that generate negative externalities. But government also uses the law to encourage activities that generate positive externalities. We are encouraged to plant trees because they have a favourable impact on the environment – and, perhaps on the threat of global warming. The planting of trees on hillsides benefits not just the landowner but also his neighbours by limiting the danger of flooding. If the climate scenario experts are right, planting more trees may avert or delay the costly consequences of global warming a century or more from now, when no one involved in the planting decision will be here to see the results. Firms are prepared to invest in R&D; the EU Commission, the US Congress and all the governments of the OECD countries are prepared to raise and spend tax revenues to finance and encourage research, often of a non-commercial nature, in a range of disciplines (including economics), the immediate dividend from which is not obvious.

## The optimal amount of negative externalities is not zero

Curbing pollution and other negative externalities entails both costs and benefits. The Cost–Benefit Principle developed in Chapter 6 applies to public policy in relation to externalities. The best policy is to curtail pollution until the cost of further abatement (marginal cost) just equals the marginal benefit. In general, the marginal cost of abatement rises with the amount of pollution eliminated. (Following the Low-Hanging-Fruit Principle (Chapter 2), polluters use the cheapest clean-up methods first and then turn to more expensive ones.) And if diminishing marginal utility applies to environmental action, it suggests that, beyond some point, the marginal benefit of pollution reduction tends to fall as more pollution is removed. As a result, the marginal cost and marginal benefit curves almost always intersect at less than the maximum amount of pollution reduction.

The intersection of the two curves marks instead the *socially optimal level of pollution reduction*. If pollution is curtailed by any less than that amount, society will gain more than it will lose by pushing the clean-up effort a little further. But if regulators push beyond the point at which the marginal cost and benefit curves intersect, society will incur costs that exceed the benefits. The existence of a *socially optimal level of pollution* reduction implies the existence of a socially optimal level of pollution, and that level will almost always be greater than zero.

This point, a central tenet of the economic approach to policy making, is one that the public at large are not comfortable with. The concept implies that there is an acceptable level of something that people regard as intrinsically unacceptable, and leads to clashes between economists and other commentators on public policy issues. How often have you heard the statement that since human life is priceless there is no acceptable level of death on the roads? Actually, it is easy to show that we do put a price on life, even our own. And we do not in reality behave individually as if no road death is tolerable, even our own. However, because, as we saw in Chapter 6, people have been conditioned to think of pollution as bad, many cringe when they hear the phrase 'socially optimal level of pollution'. How can any positive level of pollution be socially optimal? But to speak of a socially optimal level of pollution is not the same as saying that *pollution is good*. It is merely to recognise that society has an interest in cleaning up the environment, but only up to a certain point. The underlying idea is no different from the idea of an optimal level of dirt in a flat. After all, even if you spent the whole day, every day, vacuuming your flat, there would be *some* dirt left in it. And because you have better things to do than vacuum all day, you probably tolerate substantially more than the minimal amount of dirt. A dirty apartment is not good, nor is pollution in the air you breathe. But in both cases, the clean-up effort should be expanded only until the marginal benefit equals the marginal cost.

### RECAP External costs and benefits

*Externalities* occur when the costs or benefits of an activity accrue to people other than those directly involved in the activity. The *Coase theorem* says that when affected parties can negotiate with one another without cost, activities will be pursued at efficient levels, even in the presence of positive or negative externalities. But when negotiation is prohibitively costly, inefficient behaviour generally results. Activities that generate negative externalities are pursued to excess, while those that generate positive externalities are pursued too little. Laws and regulations are often adopted in an effort to alter inefficient behaviour that results from externalities.

## Property rights and the tragedy of the commons

People who grow up in the industrialised nations tend to take the institution of private property for granted. Our intuitive sense is that people have the right to own any property they acquire by lawful means and to do with that property much as they see fit. In reality, however, property laws are considerably more complex in terms of the rights they confer and the obligations they impose. Moreover, the set of property rights created and enforced at law has significant implications in terms of the efficiency with which resources are used.

In 1968 an article was published in *Science* that gave the debate on economics and its impact on real life a memorable phrase that is now a commonplace term in the analysis of property rights and their implications.[3] The term used was the '**tragedy of the commons**'. The 'tragedy' is that when valuable assets are held in common so that their fruits may be shared the end result is usually that the assets are overexploited and wasted. Common ownership has the same consequences as *no ownership at all*.

**tragedy of the commons** the tendency for a resource that has no price to be used until its marginal benefit falls to zero

[3] Hardin (1968).

In 1975 two American economists from the University of Delaware published a paper demonstrating this point and its consequences.[4] They provided persuasive evidence of the effects of common ownership as opposed to private ownership of oyster fisheries on the US eastern seaboard. Common ownership resulted in lower output per head because the oyster beds were overexploited. Another way of putting it was that under common ownership there was insufficient investment in maintaining the productive potential of the beds. Anyone who refrained from harvesting a kilogram of oysters was investing the income forgone in maintaining production potential. But in doing so not only could he not benefit from the increased production in the future resulting from his actions, but he was conferring a 'free lunch' on all the others who were entitled to harvest the oysters. The inevitable consequence was over-exploitation of the biomass.

The collapse of fish stocks in north-west European waters in the 1990s led the EU Commission to propose drastic reductions in fishing quotas in 2004. This, too, was a reflection of the consequences of the exacerbation of a tragedy of the commons by the EU's Common Fisheries Policy (CFP). Under the European treaties the deep-sea fishery waters of all EU states must be open to fishing boats from any member state. It was bad enough when member state governments had to face the problem of overfishing of national waters by crews based in the various states. The richest fishing waters of western Euriope are those in what is, formally, the Irish economic zone. Even before full liberalisation of access, Irish drift net fishing in Irish coastal waters reduced the Atlantic salmon stocks in Irish rivers to close to extinction, and the government could or would do little about the problem. When boats from other states, frequently with exhausted waters at home, overfish Irish waters the Irish ability to police the problem is inadequate and the other states' governments are not unduly concerned. The result has been a fish stock crash. The EU is now acting, belatedly and crudely, to offset this tragedy of the commons problem.

## The problem of unpriced resources

The tragedy of the commons is part of a more general problem that arises when scarce resources are not priced to users, or are underpriced (a zero price is not even a limiting case: in some instances governments have permitted exploitation at a negative price – i.e. have subsidised people to undertake the exploitation; US federal policy in the nineteenth century on encouraging settlement of the west had this characteristic in some respects). To understand the laws that govern the use of property, we must begin by asking why societies created the institution of private property in the first place. Examples 11.9 and 11.10, which show what happens to property that nobody owns, suggest an answer.

### Example 11.9 How many cattle will villagers graze on the commons?

A village has five households, each of whom has accumulated savings of €100. The village has a commonly owned tract of grazing land. Each villager can use the money to buy a government bond that pays 13 per cent interest per year or to buy a year-old bullock, send it on to the commons to graze, and sell it after one year. The price the villager will get for the two-year-old animal depends on the amount of weight it gains while grazing on the commons, which in turn depends on the number of steers sent on to the commons, as shown in Table 11.4.

The price of a two-year-old steer declines with the number of cattle grazing on the commons, because the more cattle, the less grass available to each. The villagers make their investment decisions one at a time, and the results are public. If each villager decides how to invest individually, how many cattle will be sent on to the commons, and what will be the village's total income?

[4] Agnello and Donnelley (1975).

| Number of steers on the commons | Price per two-year-old steer (€) | Income per steer (€/year) |
|---|---|---|
| 1 | 126 | 26 |
| 2 | 119 | 19 |
| 3 | 116 | 16 |
| 4 | 113 | 13 |
| 5 | 111 | 11 |

**Table 11.4** The Relationship between Herd Size and Steer Price

If a villager buys a €100 government bond, he will earn €13 interest income at the end of one year. Thus he should buy and graze a bullock on the commons if and only if the animal will command a price of at least €113 as a two-year-old. When each villager chooses in this self-interested way, we can expect four households to send a steer on to the commons. (Actually, the fourth villager would be indifferent between investing in a steer or buying a bond, since he would earn €13 either way. For the sake of discussion, we shall assume that in the case of a tie, people choose to be cattle grazers.) The fifth household, seeing that he would earn only €11 by sending a fifth steer on to the commons, will choose instead to buy a government bond. As a result of these decisions, the total village income will be €65 per year – €13 for the one bondholder and 4 × (€13) = €52 for the four cattle grazers.

Has Adam Smith's invisible hand produced the most efficient allocation of these villagers' resources? We can tell at a glance that it has not, since their total village income is only €65 – precisely the same as it would have been had the possibility of cattle raising not existed. The source of the difficulty will become evident in Example 11.10.

### Example 11.10 What is the socially optimal number of cattle to graze on the commons?

Suppose the five households in Example 11.9 confront the same investment opportunities as before, except that this time they are free to make their decisions as a group rather than individually. How many bullocks will they send on to the commons, and what will be their total village income?

This time, the villagers' goal is to maximise the income received by the group as a whole. When decisions are made from this perspective, the criterion is to send a steer on to the commons only if its marginal contribution to village income is at least €13, the amount that could be earned from a government bond. As the entries in column (5) of Table 11.5 indicate, the first bullock clearly meets this criterion, since it contributes €26 to total village income. But the second does not. Sending it on to the commons raises the village's income from cattle

| Number of steers on the commons (1) | Price per two-year-old steer (€) (2) | Income per steer (€/year) (3) | Total cattle income (€/year) (4) | Marginal income (€/year) (5) |
|---|---|---|---|---|
| 1 | 126 | 26 | 26 | 26 |
| 2 | 119 | 19 | 38 | 12 |
| 3 | 116 | 16 | 48 | 10 |
| 4 | 113 | 13 | 52 | 4 |
| 5 | 111 | 11 | 55 | 3 |

**Table 11.5** Marginal Income and the Socially Optimal Herd Size

raising from €26 to €38, a gain of just €12. The €100 required to buy the second bullock would thus have been better invested in a government bond. Worse, the collective return from grazing a third animal is only €10; from a fourth, only €4; and from a fifth, only €3.

In sum, when investment decisions are made with the goal of *maximising total village income*, the best choice is to buy four government bonds and send only a single bullock on to the commons. The resulting village income will be €78: €26 from grazing the single animal and €52 from the four government bonds. That amount is €3 more than the total income that resulted when villagers made their investment decisions individually. Once again, the reward from moving from an inefficient allocation to an efficient one is that the economic 'pie' grows larger. And when the 'pie' grows larger, everyone can get a larger slice. For instance, if the villagers agree to pool their income and share it equally, each will get €15.60, or €2.60 more than before.

**Exercise 11.4** How would your answers to Examples 11.9 and 11.10 differ if the interest rate were not 13 per cent but 11 per cent per year?

Why do the villagers in Examples 11.9 and 11.10 do better when they make their investment decisions collectively? The answer is that when individuals decide alone, they ignore the fact that sending another steer on to the commons will cause existing steers to gain less weight. Their failure to consider this effect makes the return from sending another steer seem misleadingly high to them.

The grazing land on the commons is a valuable *economic resource*. When no one owns it, no one has any incentive to take the opportunity cost of using it into account. And when that happens, people will tend to use it until its marginal benefit is zero. This problem, and others similar to it, are examples of the tragedy of the commons. The essential cause of the tragedy of the commons is the fact that one person's use of commonly held property imposes an *external cost* on others by making the property less valuable. The tragedy of the commons also provides a vivid illustration of the Equilibrium Principle (see Chapter 3). Each individual villager behaves rationally by sending an additional steer on to the commons, yet the overall outcome falls far short of the attainable ideal.

## The effect of private ownership

As Example 11.11 illustrates, one solution to the tragedy of the commons is to place the village grazing land under private ownership.

### **Example 11.11** How much will the right to control the village commons sell for?

Suppose the five households face the same investment opportunities as before, except that this time they decide to auction off the right to use the commons to the highest bidder. Assuming that the villagers can borrow as well as lend at an annual interest rate of 13 per cent, what price will the right to use the commons fetch? How will the owner of that property right use it, and what will be the resulting village income?

To answer these questions, simply ask yourself what you would do if you had complete control over how the grazing land were used. As we saw in Example 11.10, the most profitable way to use this land is to send only a single steer to graze on it. If you do so, you will earn a total of €26 per year. Since the opportunity cost of the €100 you spent on the single yearling steer is the €13 in interest you could have earned from a bond, your economic profit from sending a single steer on to the commons will be €13 per year, provided you can use the land for free. But you cannot; to finance your purchase of the property right, you must borrow money (since you used your €100 savings to buy a year-old bullock).

What is the most you would be willing to pay for the right to use the commons? Since its use generates an income of €26 per year, or €13 more than the opportunity cost of your investment in the bullock, the most you would pay is €100 (because that amount used to purchase a bond that pays 13 per cent interest would also generate income of €13 per year). If the land were sold at auction, €100 is precisely the amount you would have to pay. Your annual earnings from the land would be exactly enough to pay the €13 interest on your loan and cover the opportunity cost of not having put your savings into a bond.

Note that when the right to use the land is auctioned to the highest bidder, the village achieves a more efficient allocation of its resources, because the owner has a strong incentive to take the opportunity cost of more intensive grazing fully into account. Total village income in this case will again be €78. If the annual interest on the €100 proceeds from selling the land rights is shared equally among the five villagers, each will again have an annual investment income of €15.60.

The logic of *economic surplus maximisation* helps to explain why the most economically successful nations have all been ones with well-developed private property laws. Property that belongs to everyone belongs, in effect, to no one. Not only is its potential economic value never fully realised, it usually ends up being of no value at all.

Bear in mind, however, that in most countries the owners of private property are not free to do *precisely* as they wish with it. For example, local planning regulations or zoning laws may give the owner of a plot of residential building land the right to build a three-storey house but not a six-storey house. Here, too, the logic of economic surplus maximisation applies, for a fully informed and rational legislature would define property rights so as to create the largest possible total economic surplus. In practice, of course, such ideal legislatures never really exist. Yet one view of the essence of politics is the creation of arrangements that make people better off. If a legislator could propose a change in the planning regime affecting his constituency that would enlarge the total economic surplus for the people in that constituency, he could also propose a scheme that would give each constituent a larger income by sharing out the gain, thus enhancing his chances for re-election.

## Economic naturalist 11.7 The phenomenon of 'bungalow blitz'

In the late 1990s environmentalists in Ireland began to put pressure on the government to halt the rash of one-off single-storey dwellings being built in rural districts in the country's more scenic areas. Local planning laws, which favoured concentrating construction in existing towns, villages and settlements were routinely set aside by the local councils. The demand for new housing reflected (a) rising population in the areas concerned, and (b) city dwellers building holiday homes. It was made possible precisely because local legislators (councillors) behaved exactly as outlined at the end of Example 11.11. In these areas, it increased economic surplus to permit development. The legislators didn't have to worry about sharing land out because the rest of the local population gained through higher land prices and/or by selling more services to the new households.

However, in doing this the councillors were maximising local surplus but only at the expense of exporting costs to the rest of the country. The costs were environmental degradation (ruined scenery) and development costs that had to be paid by the central government (i.e. tax-payers as a whole) rather than by the local tax-payers. The landscape was being supplied free to local people, and the costs of services (utilities) being extended to remote, single houses was not being fully met from the pockets of those building or occupying them.

Maximising total surplus would require collective action from central government. But central government relied on maintaining majority support in parliament, and a large number of parliamentary deputies represented rural constituencies . . .

As an economic naturalist, challenge yourself to use this framework when thinking about the various restrictions you encounter in private property laws: zoning laws that constrain what you can build and what types of activities you can conduct on your land; traffic laws that constrain what you can do with your car; employment and environmental laws that constrain how you can operate your business. Your understanding of these and countless other laws will be enhanced by the insight that everyone can gain when the private property laws are defined so as to create the largest total economic surplus.

## When private ownership is impractical

Do not be misled into thinking that the law provides an *ideal* resolution of all problems associated with externalities and the tragedy of the commons. Defining and enforcing efficient property rights entails costs, after all, and sometimes, as in Economic naturalists 11.7 and 11.8, the costs outweigh the gains.

### Economic naturalist 11.8 Why do blackberries in public parks get picked too soon?

Wild blackberries grow profusely at the edge of a wooded area in a crowded city park. The blackberries will taste best if left to ripen fully, but they still taste reasonably good if picked and eaten a few days early. Will the blackberries be left to ripen fully?

Obviously, the costs of defining and enforcing the property rights to blackberries growing in a public park are larger than the potential gains, so the blackberries will remain common property. That means that whoever picks them first gets them. Even though everyone would benefit if people waited until the berries were fully ripe, everyone knows that those who wait are likely to end up with no berries at all. And that means that the berries will be picked too soon.

### Economic naturalist 11.9 Why are shared milkshakes consumed too quickly?

Sara and Susan are identical twins who love chocolate milkshakes. Their mother buys them each a 25 cl carton each Saturday at the shopping centre. The girls take 10 minutes to finish their milkshakes. Their mother gets 10 minutes' peace. One weekend the mother buys them a 50 cl carton, and two straws (the 50 cl shake costs less than two 25 cl shakes). The carton is empty in 3 minutes. Bad decision on the mother's part. Why? If each has a straw and each knows that the other is self-interested, will the twins consume the milkshake at an optimal rate? Because drinking a milkshake too quickly chills the taste buds, the twins will enjoy their shake more if they drink it slowly. Yet each knows that the other will drink any part of the milkshake she doesn't finish herself. The result is that each will consume the shake at a faster rate than she would if she had half a shake all to herself.

Here are some further examples of the type of tragedy of the commons that is not easily solved by defining private ownership rights.

### Harvesting timber on remote public land

On remote public lands, enforcing restrictions against cutting down trees may be impractical. Each tree cutter knows that a tree that is not harvested this year will be bigger, and hence more valuable, next year. But he also knows that if he doesn't cut the tree down this year, someone else will. In contrast, private companies that grow trees on their own land have no incentive to harvest timber prematurely and a strong incentive to prevent outsiders from doing so.

### Harvesting whales in international waters

Each individual whaler knows that harvesting an extra whale reduces the breeding population, and hence the size of the future whale population. But the whaler also knows that any whale that is not harvested today will be taken by some other whaler. The solution would be to define and enforce property rights to whales. But the oceans are vast, and the behaviour of whalers is hard to monitor. And even if their behaviour could be monitored, the concept of national sovereignty would make the international enforcement of property rights problematic.

More generally, the animal species that are most severely threatened with extinction tend to be those that are economically valuable to humans but that are not privately owned by anyone. This is the situation confronting whales. Contrast it with the situation confronting chickens, which are also economically valuable to humans but which, unlike whales, are governed by traditional laws of private property. This difference explains why no one worries that Colonel Sanders might threaten the extinction of chickens. It also explains why allowing people to harvest ivory legally from herds that they own may be the best way to protect elephants from poachers in sub-Saharan Africa, and ecotourism is the best hope for the survival of the South East Asian tiger population.

### Controlling multinational environmental pollution

Each individual polluter may know that if he and all others pollute, the damage to the environment will be greater than the cost of not polluting. But if the environment is common property into which all are free to dump, each has a powerful incentive to pollute. If all polluters live under the jurisdiction of a single government, enforcing laws and regulations that limit the discharge of pollution may be practical. But if polluters come from many different countries, solutions are much more difficult to implement. Thus the Mediterranean Sea has long suffered serious pollution, because none of the many nations that border it has an economic incentive to consider the effects of its discharges on other countries. The smaller number of countries involved (and the fact that almost all were members of the then EEC) permitted agreements to be reached to control and reduce the pollution of the River Rhine which suffered on a similar basis to that of the Mediterranean.

As the world's population continues to grow, the absence of an effective system of international property rights will become an economic problem of increasing significance.

### RECAP Property rights and the tragedy of the commons

When a valuable resource has a price of zero, people will continue to exploit it as long as its marginal benefit remains positive.The tragedy of the commons describes situations in which valuable resources are squandered because users are not charged for them. In many cases, an efficient remedy for such waste is to define and enforce rights to the use of valuable property. But this solution is difficult to implement for resources such as the oceans and the atmosphere, because no single government has the authority to *enforce property rights* for these resources.

## Positional externalities

Steffi Graf received more than €1.6 million in tournament winnings in 1992; her endorsement and exhibition earnings totalled several times that amount. By any reasonable measure, the quality of her play was outstanding, yet she consistently lost to arch-rival Monica Seles.

But in April 1993, Seles was stabbed in the back by a deranged fan and forced to withdraw from the tour. In the ensuing months, Graf's tournament winnings accumulated at almost double her 1992 pace, despite little change in the quality of her play.

## Payoffs that depend on relative performance

In professional tennis and a host of other competitive situations, the rewards people receive typically depend not only on how they perform in absolute terms but also on how they perform relative to their closest rivals. David Beckham in soccer, Brian O'Driscoll in rugby, are similar to Monica Seles in tennis. In these situations, competitors have an incentive to take actions that will increase their odds of winning. For example, tennis players can increase their chances of winning by hiring personal fitness trainers and sports psychologists to travel with them on the tour. That is why the Olympics are plagued by the performance enhancing drugs problem. Yet the simple mathematics of competition tells us that the sum of all individual payoffs from such investments will be larger than the collective payoff. In any tennis match, for example, each contestant will get a sizeable payoff from money spent on fitness trainers and sports psychologists, yet each match will have exactly one winner and one loser, no matter how much players spend. The overall gain to tennis spectators is likely to be small, and the overall gain to players as a group must be zero. To the extent that each contestant's payoff depends on his or her relative performance, then, the incentive to undertake such investments will be excessive, from a collective point of view. Consider Economic naturalist 11.10

### Economic naturalist 11.10 Why do American football players take anabolic steroids?

The sheer size of professional football players in America is astounding to those who follow other codes. Not even rugby, which is certainly a serious contact sport, has average heights and weights that are comparable with those in the US National Foootball League teams (there are, of course, a couple of exceptions: Jonah Lomu would not have been out of place in the ranks of the 49ers). The offensive linemen of many National Football League (NFL) teams currently average more than 150 kg. In the 1970s, by contrast, offensive linemen in the league averaged barely 127 kg, and the all-decade linemen of the 1940s averaged only 104 kg. One reason that today's players are so much heavier is that players' salaries have escalated sharply since the 1980s, which has intensified competition for the positions. Size and strength are the two cardinal virtues of an offensive lineman and, other things being equal, the job will go to the larger and stronger of two rivals.

Size and strength, in turn, can be enhanced by the consumption of anabolic steroids. But if all players consume these substances, the rank ordering of players by size and strength – and hence the question of who lands the jobs – will be largely unaffected. And since the consumption of anabolic steroids entails potentially serious long-term health consequences, as a group football players are clearly worse off if they consume these drugs. So why do football players take steroids?

The problem here is that contestants for starting berths on the offensive line confront a prisoner's dilemma, like those analysed in Chapter 10. Consider two closely matched rivals – Smith and Jones – who are competing for a single position. If neither takes steroids, each has a 50 per cent chance of winning the job and a starting salary of €1 million per year. If both take steroids, each again has a 50 per cent chance of winning the job. But if one takes steroids and the other doesn't, the first is sure to win the job. The loser ends up working in a call centre for €25,000 per year.

Neither likes the fact that the drugs may have adverse health consequences, but each would be willing to take that risk in return for a shot at the big salary. Given these choices, the two competitors face a payoff matrix like that shown in Table 11.6.

| | | Jones: Don't take steroids | Jones: Take steroids |
|---|---|---|---|
| Smith | Don't take steroids | Second best for each | Best for Jones Worst for Smith |
| | Take steroids | Best for Smith Worst for Jones | Third best for each |

**Table 11.6** Payoff Matrix for Steroid Consumption

Clearly, the dominant strategy for both Smith and Jones is to take steroids. Yet when they do, each gets only the third-best outcome, whereas they could have got the second-best outcome by not taking the drugs. Hence the attraction of rules forbidding consumption of anabolic steroids.

## Positional arms races

**positional externality** occurs when an increase in one person's performance reduces the expected reward of another in situations in which reward depends on relative performance

The steroid problem is an example of a **positional externality**. Whenever the payoffs to one contestant depend at least in part on how he or she performs relative to a rival, any step that improves one side's relative position must necessarily worsen the other's. The standing-at-concerts example discussed in Economic naturalist 10.3 is another instance of a positional externality. Just as the invisible hand of the market is weakened by the presence of standard externalities, it is also weakened by positional externalities.

### Economic naturalist 11.11 Why do many US grocery stores stay open all night, even in small towns?

Most European countries have legal or zoning restrictions of some form on hours of opening of retail outlets. Germany is the best-known example. Economists have argued that this is clearly anti-competitive. In general in big-city America, and even in small towns, it is possible to find a good number of grocery stores open 24 hours a day. Ithaca, New York, has seven large supermarkets, five of which are open 24 hours a day. The convenience of all-night shopping could be maintained at lower cost if all but one of the stores were to close during late-night hours. Why do many remain open?

Most people do the bulk of their shopping at one supermarket. If other relevant factors – price, location, merchandise quality and so on – are essentially the same, people will choose the store with the most convenient hours. Suppose the two leading stores, Tops and Wegmans, currently close at midnight and are considering whether to stay open until 1 a.m. If one does so and the other doesn't, the store that is open longer will obviously capture all the business from midnight to 1 a.m. Less obviously, it will capture some of the business of the other store that would have gone to that store before midnight since they were obliged to shop before midnight, and in these circumstances chose the other store, but now have the choice of shopping after midnight. We're back to our old friend, the prisoner's dilemma. The optimum strategy is for the second store to stay open too. The extra cost of staying open may well exceed the willingness of people to pay at that time (as they can always choose to shop earlier). Each store will then face a payoff matrix like that shown in Table 11.7. In that case, costs rise relative to total sales revenues, and if the market is really competitive the end result will be higher prices through the day.

| | | **Wegmans** | |
|---|---|---|---|
| | | Close at midnight | Close at 1.00 a.m |
| **Tops** | Close at midnight | Second best for each | Best for Wegmans Worst for Tops |
| | Close at 1.00 a.m. | Best for Tops Worst for Wegmans | Third best for each |

**Table 11.7** Payoff Matrix for Extended Shopping Hours

In this situation, the dominant strategy for each store is to remain open an extra hour, even though each would be better off if both closed at midnight. And of course, the rivalry does not stop there, for if both stay open until 1 a.m., each will see an opportunity to better its rival by staying open until 2. As long as the cost of staying open another hour is small relative to the gains received, all stores will stay open 24 hours a day. But though consumers do gain when stores remain open longer, beyond some point the benefit to consumers is small relative to the costs borne by merchants. The problem is that for any individual merchant who fails to match a rival's hours, the costs may be even larger.

In such situations, the public might be well served by an amendment to the anti-trust laws that permits stores to co-operate to limit their hours, perhaps through an agreement calling for each store to serve in rotation as the only all-night grocery. Local statutes that limit business hours might serve the same purpose.

**Exercise 11.5** Before accepting this as a case for universal restrictions on opening hours, consider what would be the consequence of restricting stores to, say, 8 hours a day and no Sunday opening.

**positional arms race** a series of mutually offsetting investments in performance enhancement that is stimulated by a positional externality

**positional arms control agreement** an agreement in which contestants attempt to limit mutually offsetting investments in performance enhancement

We have seen that positional externalities often lead contestants to engage in an escalating series of mutually offsetting investments in performance enhancement. We call such spending patterns **positional arms races.**

## Positional arms control agreements

Because positional arms races produce inefficient outcomes, people have an incentive to curtail them. Steps taken to reduce positional arms races, such as rules against anabolic steroids, may therefore be thought of as **positional arms control agreements.**

Once you become aware of positional arms races, you will begin to see examples of them almost everywhere. You can hone your skills as an economic naturalist by asking these questions about every competitive situation you observe: What form do the investments in performance enhancement take? What steps have contestants taken to limit these investments? Sometimes positional arms control agreements are achieved by the imposition of formal rules or by the signing of legal contracts. We shall now consider examples of this type of agreement.

### Campaign spending limits

In the United States, presidential candidates routinely spend more than $100 million on advertising. Yet if both candidates double their spending on ads, each one's odds of winning will remain essentially the same. Recognition of this pattern led Congress to adopt strict spending limits for presidential candidates. (That those regulations have proved difficult to enforce does not call into question the logic behind the legislation.) Similar restrictions apply to parliamentary elections in many West European countries.

### Arbitration agreements

In the business world, contracting parties often sign a binding agreement that commits them to arbitration in the event of a dispute. By doing so, they sacrifice the option of pursuing their interests as fully as they might wish to later, but they also insulate themselves from costly legal battles. In the United Kingdom and Ireland what is called 'case management' is required by judges in many High Court civil cases. This means obliging the parties to exchange reports and have expert witnesses remove from consideration by the court matters on which there is no dispute, thus avoiding costly court time hearing testimony on which there is agreement between the parties.

### Mandatory starting dates for school

A child who is a year or so older than most of her elementary (primary) classmates is likely to perform better, in relative terms, than if she had entered school with children her own age. And since most parents are aware that admission to universities and eligibility for top jobs upon graduation depend largely on *relative* academic performance, many are tempted to keep their children out of kindergarten a year longer than necessary. Yet there is no social advantage in holding *all* children back an extra year, since their relative performance will essentially be unaffected. In many jurisdictions, therefore, the law requires children who reach a determined age by a given date in a year to start school in that year. However, this needs qualification. The use of the feminine pronoun in this case is deliberate, not simply politically correct. Most developmental psychologists will agree that, on average, between the ages of 12 and 18 boys develop mentally more slowly than girls (which is part of the reason teenage girls give boys in their classes such a hard time socially). It follows that if boys and girls take terminal exams and leave school at the same age, girls will do better than boys ... and better than if they were ranked at the same mental age. Requiring boys to start schooling at the same age as girls, then, is equivalent to giving girls as a group a slight edge in competitive exams at 18. Unfortunately, in today's political climate it looks rather unlikely that any government will pick up that hot potato.

## Social norms as positional arms control agreements

In some cases, *social norms* may take the place of formal agreements to curtail positional arms races. Here are some familiar examples.

### Nerd norms

Some students care more – in the short run, at least – about the grades they get than how much they actually learn. When such students are graded on the curve – that is, on the basis of their performance relative to other students – a positional arms race ensues, because if all students were to double the amount of time they studied, the distribution of grades would remain essentially the same. Students who find themselves in this situation are often quick to embrace 'nerd norms', which brand as social misfits those who 'study too hard'.

### Fashion norms

Social norms regarding dress and fashion often change quickly because of positional competitions. Consider, for instance, the person who wishes to be at the cutting edge of fashion. In some social circles during the 1950s, that goal could be accomplished by having pierced ears. But as more and more people adopted the practice, it ceased to communicate *avant-garde* status. At the same time, those who wanted to make a conservative fashion statement gradually became more able to have their ears pierced. For a period during the 1960s and 1970s, one could be on fashion's cutting edge by wearing two earrings in one earlobe. But by the 1990s multiple ear piercings had lost much of their social significance, the threshold of cutting-edge status having been raised to upward of a dozen piercings of each ear, or a smaller number of piercings of the nose, eyebrows or other body parts. A similar escalation has taken place in the number, size and placement of tattoos.

The increase in the required number of tattoos or body piercings has not changed the value of *avant-garde* fashion status to those who desire it. Being on the outer limits of fashion has much the same meaning now as it ever did. So to the extent that there are costs associated with body piercings, tattoos and other steps required to achieve *avant-garde* status, the current fashions are wasteful compared with earlier ones. In this sense, the erosion of the social norms against tattoos and body piercings has produced a social loss. Of course, the costs associated with this loss are small in most cases. Yet since each body piercing entails a small risk of infection, the costs will continue to rise with the number of piercings. And once those costs reach a certain threshold, support may mobilise on behalf of social norms that discourage body mutilation.

### Norms of taste

Similar cycles occur with respect to behaviours considered to be in bad taste. In the 1950s, for example, prevailing norms prevented major national magazines from accepting ads that featured nude photographs. Naturally, advertisers had a powerful incentive to chip away at such norms in an effort to capture the reader's limited attention. And indeed, taboos against nude photographs have eroded in the same way as taboos against body mutilation.

Consider, for instance, the evolution of nudity and sexual messages in advertising, especially in perfume ads. First came the nude silhouette; then, increasingly well-lit and detailed nude photographs; and, more recently, photographs of what appear to be group sex acts. Each innovation achieved just the desired effect: capturing the reader's instant and rapt attention. Inevitably, however, other advertisers followed suit, causing a shift in our sense of what is considered attention-grabbing. Photographs that once would have shocked readers now often draw little more than a bored glance.

Opinions differ, of course, about whether this change is an improvement. Many believe that the earlier, stricter norms were ill-advised, the legacy of a more prudish and repressive era. Yet even people who take that view are likely to believe that *some* kinds of photographic material ought not to be used in magazine advertisements. Obviously, what is acceptable will differ from person to person, and each person's threshold of discomfort will depend in part on current standards. But as advertisers continue to break new ground in their struggle to capture attention, the point may come when people begin to mobilise in favour of stricter standards of 'public decency'. Such a campaign would provide yet another example of a positional arms control agreement.

### Norms against vanity

Cosmetic and reconstructive surgery has produced dramatic benefits for many people, enabling badly disfigured accident victims to recover a more normal appearance. It has also eliminated the extreme self-consciousness felt by people born with strikingly unusual features. Such surgery, however, is by no means confined to the conspicuously disfigured. Increasingly, 'normal' people are seeking surgical improvements to their appearance. Demand has continued to grow steadily. Once a carefully guarded secret, these procedures are now sometimes offered as prizes in charity raffles. In America, undertakers have begun to complain that the non-combustible silicon implants used in breast and buttocks augmentation are clogging their crematoria (if he were writing *The Loved One* today, Evelyn Waugh might have titled it *Vile Bodies 2*).

In individual cases, cosmetic surgery may be just as beneficial as reconstructive surgery is for accident victims. Buoyed by the confidence of having a straight nose or a wrinkle-free complexion, patients sometimes go on to achieve much more than they ever thought possible. But the growing use of cosmetic surgery has also had an unintended side effect: it has altered the standards of normal appearance. A nose that once would have seemed only slightly larger than average may now seem jarringly big. The same person who once would have looked like an average 55-year-old may now look nearly 70. And someone who once would have tolerated slightly thinning hair or an average amount of cellulite may now feel compelled to undergo hair transplantation or liposuction. Because such procedures shift people's frame of reference, their payoffs to individuals are misleadingly large. From a social perspective, therefore, reliance on them is likely to be excessive.

Legal sanctions against cosmetic surgery are difficult to imagine. But some communities have embraced powerful social norms against cosmetic surgery, heaping scorn and ridicule on the consumers of facelifts and tummy tucks. In individual cases, such norms may seem cruel. Yet without them, many more people might feel compelled to bear the risk and expense of cosmetic surgery.

## Summary

- *Externalities* are the costs and benefits of activities that accrue to people who are not directly involved in those activities. When all parties affected by externalities can negotiate with one another at no cost, the invisible hand of the market will produce an efficient allocation of resources. According to the *Coase theorem*, the allocation of resources is efficient in such cases because the parties affected by externalities can compensate others for taking remedial action.
- Negotiation over externalities is often impractical, however. In these cases, the self-serving actions of individuals typically will not lead to an efficient outcome. The attempt to forge solutions to the problems caused by externalities is one of the most important rationales for *collective action*. Sometimes collective action takes the form of laws and government regulations that alter the incentives facing those who generate, or are affected by, externalities. Such remedies work best when they place the burden of accommodation on the parties who can accomplish it at the lowest cost. Traffic laws, zoning laws, environmental protection laws and free speech laws are examples
- Curbing pollution and other negative externalities entails *costs* as well as *benefits*. The optimal amount of pollution reduction is the amount for which the marginal benefit of further reduction just equals the marginal cost. In general, this formula implies that the socially optimal level of pollution, or of any other negative externality, is greater than zero.

- When grazing land and other valuable resources are owned in common, no one has an incentive to take into account the opportunity cost of using those resources. This problem is known as the *tragedy of the commons*. Defining and enforcing private rights governing the use of valuable resources is often an effective solution. Not surprisingly, most economically successful nations have well-developed institutions of private property. Property that belongs to everyone belongs, in effect, to no one. Not only is its potential economic value never fully realised, it usually ends up having no value at all.
- The difficulty of *enforcing* property rights in certain situations explains a variety of inefficient outcomes, such as the excessive harvest of whales in international waters and the premature harvest of timber on remote public lands. The excessive pollution of seas that are bordered by many countries also results from a lack of enforceable property rights.
- Situations in which people's rewards depend on how well they perform in relation to their rivals give rise to *positional externalities*. In these situations, any step that improves one side's relative position necessarily worsens the other's. Positional externalities tend to spawn positional arms races – escalating patterns of mutually offsetting investments in performance enhancement. Collective measures to curb positional arms races are known as *positional arms control agreements*. These collective actions may take the form of formal regulations or rules, such as rules against anabolic steroids in sports, campaign spending limits, and binding arbitration agreements. Informal social norms can also curtail positional arms races.

## Key terms

**Coase theorem** (317)
**external benefit (or positive externality)** (312)
**external cost (or negative externality)** (312)
**externality** (312)
**positional arms control agreement** (332)
**positional arms race** (332)
**positional externality** (331)
**tragedy of the commons** (323)

## Review questions

1. Shoes may be viewed as the result of a positional externality. What incentive problem explains why the freeways in cities such as Los Angeles suffer from excessive congestion?
2. How would you explain to a friend why the optimal amount of freeway congestion is not zero?
3. If a country's government could declare any activity that imposes external costs on others illegal, would such legislation be advisable?
4. Why does the Great Salt Lake, which is located wholly within the state of Utah, suffer lower levels of pollution than Lake Erie, which is bordered by several states and Canada?

## Problems

Problems marked with an asterisk (*) are more difficult.

1. Determine whether the following statements are **true or false**, and briefly explain why.
   a. A given total emission reduction in a polluting industry will be achieved at the lowest possible total cost when the cost of the last unit of pollution curbed is equal for each firm in the industry.
   b. In an attempt to lower their costs of production, firms sometimes succeed merely in shifting costs to outsiders.

2. Phoebe keeps a bee farm next door to an apple orchard. She chooses her optimal number of beehives by selecting the honey output level at which her private marginal benefit from beekeeping equals her private marginal cost.

a. Assume that Phoebe's private marginal benefit and marginal cost curves from beekeeping are normally shaped. Draw a diagram of them.

b. Phoebe's bees help to pollinate the blossoms in the apple orchard, increasing the fruit yield. Show the social marginal benefit from Phoebe's beekeeping in your diagram.

c. Phoebe's bees are Africanised killer bees that aggressively sting anyone who steps into their flight path. Phoebe, fortunately, is naturally immune to the bees' venom. Show the social marginal cost curve from Phoebe's beekeeping in your diagram.

d. Indicate the socially optimal quantity of beehives on your diagram. Is it higher or lower than the privately optimal quantity? Explain.

3. Suppose the supply curve of boom box rentals at a holiday resort in the Mediterranean is given by $P = 5 + 0.1Q$, where $P$ is the daily rent per unit in euros and $Q$ is the volume of units rented in hundreds per day. The demand curve for boom boxes is $20 - 0.2Q$. If each boom box imposes €3 per day in noise costs on others, by how much will the equilibrium number of boom boxes rented exceed the socially optimal number?

4. Refer to Problem 3. How would the imposition of a tax of €3 per unit on each daily boom box rental affect efficiency in this market?

5. Suppose the law says that Jones may *not* emit smoke from his factory unless he gets permission from Smith, who lives downwind. If the relevant costs and benefits of filtering the smoke from Jones' production process are as shown in the table below, and if Jones and Smith can negotiate with one another at no cost, will Jones emit smoke?

| | **Jones emits smoke (€)** | **Jones does not emit smoke (€)** |
|---|---|---|
| Surplus for Jones | 200 | 160 |
| Surplus for Smith | 400 | 420 |

6. John and Karl can live together in a two-bedroom flat for €500 per month, or each can rent a single-bedroom flat for €350 per month. Aside from the rent, the two would be indifferent between living together and living separately, except for one problem: John leaves dirty dishes in the sink every night. Karl would be willing to pay up to €175 per month to avoid John's dirty dishes. John, for his part, would be willing to pay up to €225 to be able to continue his sloppiness. Should John and Karl live together? If they do, will there be dirty dishes in the sink? Explain.

7. How, if at all, would your answer to Problem 6 differ if John would be willing to pay up to €30 per month to avoid giving up his privacy by sharing quarters with Karl?

8. Barton and Statler are neighbours in an apartment complex in London's Canary Wharf. Barton is a concert pianist, and Statler is a poet working on an epic poem. Barton rehearses his concert pieces on the baby grand piano in his front room, which is directly above Statler's study. The matrix below shows the monthly payoffs to Barton and Statler when Barton's front room is and is not soundproofed. The soundproofing will be effective only if it is installed in Barton's apartment.

a. If Barton has the legal right to make any amount of noise he wants and he and Statler can negotiate with one another at no cost, will Barton install and maintain soundproofing? Explain. Is his choice socially efficient?

b. If Statler has the legal right to peace and quiet and can negotiate with Barton at no cost, will Barton install and maintain soundproofing? Explain. Is his choice socially efficient?

c. Does the attainment of an efficient outcome depend on whether Barton has the legal right to make noise, or Statler the legal right to peace and quiet?

| | Soundproofed | Not soundproofed |
|---|---|---|
| Gains to Barton | £100/month | £150/month |
| Gains to Statler | £120/month | £80/month |

9. Refer to Problem 8. Barton decides to buy a full-sized grand piano. The new payoff matrix is as follows:

| | Soundproofed | Not soundproofed |
|---|---|---|
| Gains to Barton | £100/month | £150/month |
| Gains to Statler | £120/month | £60/month |

a. If Statler has the legal right to peace and quiet and Barton and Statler can negotiate at no cost, will Barton install and maintain soundproofing? Explain. Is this outcome socially efficient?

b. Suppose that Barton has the legal right to make as much noise as he likes and that negotiating an agreement with Barton costs £15 per month. Will Barton install and maintain soundproofing? Explain. Is this outcome socially efficient?

c. Suppose Statler has the legal right to peace and quiet, and it costs £15 per month for Statler and Barton to negotiate any agreement. (Compensation for noise damage can be paid without incurring negotiation cost.) Will Barton install and maintain soundproofing? Is this outcome socially efficient?

d. Why does the attainment of a socially efficient outcome now depend on whether Barton has the legal right to make noise?

10.* A village has six residents, each of whom has accumulated savings of €100. Each villager can use this money either to buy a government bond that pays 15 per cent interest per year or to buy a year-old llama, send it on to the commons to graze, and sell it after one year. The price the villager gets for the two-year-old llama depends on the quality of the fleece it grows while grazing on the commons. That in turn depends on the animal's access to grazing, which depends on the number of llamas sent to the commons, as shown in the table below.

The villagers make their investment decisions one after another, and their decisions are public.

a. If each villager decides individually how to invest, how many llamas will be sent on to the commons, and what will be the resulting net village income?

b. What is the socially optimal number of llamas for this village? Why is that different from the actual number? What would net village income be if the socially optimal number of llamas were sent on to the commons?

c. The village committee votes to auction the right to graze llamas on the commons to the highest bidder. Assuming villagers can both borrow and lend at 15 per cent annual interest, how much will the right sell for at auction? How will the new owner use the right, and what will be the resulting village income?

| Number of llamas on the commons | Price per two-year-old llama (€) |
|---|---|
| 1 | 122 |
| 2 | 118 |
| 3 | 116 |
| 4 | 114 |
| 5 | 112 |
| 6 | 109 |

## Answers to in-chapter exercises

**11.1** Since Fitch gains £50 per day when Abercrombie operates with a filter, he could pay Abercrombie as much as £49 per day and still come out ahead.

**11.2** If the two were to live together, the most efficient way to resolve the telephone problem would be as before: for Betty to give up reasonable access to the phone. But on top of that cost, which is £150, Betty would also bear a £60 cost from the loss of her privacy. The total cost of their living together would thus be £210 per month. Since that amount is greater than the £200 saving in rent, the two should live separately.

**11.3** The court found for the doctor. This was despite a common law restriction on the right to sue when the plaintiff 'came to the nuisance' as the doctor did. It has to be a matter of opinion, but independently of Coase considerations this decision was peculiar, to say the least. If the court had been interested in the economic consequences of the decision it might have sought to establish the relative costs involved (it didn't) in whatever verdict it delivered rather than deciding on the basis that the external effect ran from the confectioner's business. If the court had understood the issues as expounded by Coase it might well have sent them home to bargain and reach a settlement.

**11.4** The income figures from the different levels of investment in cattle would remain as before, as shown in the table below. What is different is the opportunity cost of investing in each steer, which is now €11 per year instead of €13. Column (5) of the table shows that the socially optimal number of steers is now 2 instead of 1. And if individuals still favour holding cattle, all other things being equal, they will now send 5 steers on to the land, as shown in column (3).

| Number of steers on the commons (1) | Price per two-year-old steer(€) (2) | Income per steer (€/year) (3) | Total cattle income (€/year) (4) | Marginal income (€/year) (5) |
|---|---|---|---|---|
| | | | | 26 |
| 1 | 126 | 26 | 26 | |
| | | | | 12 |
| 2 | 119 | 19 | 38 | |
| | | | | 10 |
| 3 | 116 | 16 | 48 | |
| | | | | 4 |
| 4 | 113 | 13 | 52 | |
| | | | | 3 |
| 5 | 111 | 11 | 55 | |

**11.5** Unit sales costs to the supermarkets may fall (not certain, since the stories may have to hire more checkout staff and install more checkouts if the total volume of sales is compacted into 48 hours a week). Unless, however, the numbers of those who would prefer to shop later in any day or on Sunday is small, and the cost to them of doing their shopping in the restricted time (the marginal utility of extra hours' availability) is small, the likelihood is that total surplus will fall. People will face a restriction on when to purchase and (probably) longer waiting time when purchasing. The indicator will be the extent to which more expensive convenience stores, if not covered by the restriction, pick up more business.

## References

Agnello, R. J. and L. Donnelly (1975) 'Property Rights and Efficiency in the Oyster Industry', *Journal of Law and Economics*, 18.

Coase, R. (1960) 'The Problem of Social Cost', *Journal of Law and Economics*, 4.

Hardin, G. (1968) 'The Tragedy of the Commons', *Science*, 162.

# 12

# The Economics of Information

Consider the following problem. You are on your first visit to Istanbul. You visit the famous bazaar, and are tempted to make a purchase. In the bazaar it is expected that purchaser and seller will bargain before any deal is done. No one in his right mind (except perhaps a naive tourist) would agree to pay the seller's initial asking price. This is by custom a considerable amount greater than the seller's reservation price. So what will you offer for the brass ornament, or silk scarf, or whatever has caught your eye? It is easy to say that you will not offer more than your own reservation price. But if you can obtain the object at less than your reservation price (that is, at a price greater or equal to the seller's reservation price, but less than yours), while both sides gain you will have done better than if you had paid your reservation price. Typically therefore, you will offer a price below your reservation price. After prolonged haggling a deal is either done or is not done. We know that it will not be done if your reservation price is below the seller's. But can we be sure it will be done if your reservation price exceeds his?

Before saying that it will of course be done, reflect for a moment. What in fact drives your reservation price in this one-on-one bargaining situation? If we think of it simply as the money value you place on the object then the deal will be done. But suppose you believe that another seller in the bazaar might be prepared to accept less than your reservation price, would you agree to hand that amount over to the first seller?

In this second case, your willingness to pay reflects other people's valuations. There is nothing unusual about this. If you walk into an antique shop and see an eighteenth-century Hogarth print that you would like at the price, but a friend whispers to you that an identical print was sold at auction three weeks ago for 50 per cent of the dealer's price, would you pay the asking price?

Before saying that you would not, reflect again. If you are well versed in eighteenth-century prints you might well say that the auction price was an aberration, reflecting the tastes of the people in the room that day, and that in general a higher price would be expected. Then you would probably reject the friend's advice and make the purchase. But if you did not have this information it is more probable that you would leave without buying the print.

Your willingness to pay will, therefore, in some circumstances reflect your own *relevant knowledge*, and may reflect your beliefs about other people's willingness to pay. Both factors may be summed up as 'information'. You may be well or poorly informed when contemplating a decision to buy or sell. This has significant implications for how markets work.

Adam Smith's invisible hand theory presumes that buyers are fully informed about the myriad ways in which they might spend their money: what goods and services are available, what prices they sell for, how long they last, how frequently they break down and so on. But of course no one is ever really *fully* informed about anything. And sometimes people are completely ignorant of even the most basic information. Still, life goes on, and most people muddle through somehow.

Consumers employ a variety of strategies for gathering information, some of which are better than others. They read *Which?* magazine, talk to family and friends, visit stores, kick the tyres on used cars and so on. But one of the most important aspects of choosing intelligently without having complete information is having at least some idea of the *extent of one's ignorance*. Someone once said that there are two kinds of consumers in the world: those who don't know what they're doing and those who don't know that they don't know what they're doing. The people in the second category are the ones who are most likely to choose foolishly. Auctioneers just love them. They walk away with the prize, but are victims of the 'winner's curse': they won the prize only because they were prepared to pay, and did pay, more than anyone else would pay ... meaning that they would not get their money back if they changed their minds.

Basic economic principles can help you in identifying those situations in which additional information is most likely to prove helpful. In this chapter, we shall explore what those principles tell us about how much information to acquire, and how to make the best use of limited information.

## How the middleman adds value

One of the most common problems consumers confront is the need to choose among different versions of a product whose many complex features they do not fully understand. As Example 12.1 illustrates, in such cases consumers can sometimes rely on the knowledge of others.

**Example 12.1** How should a consumer decide which pair of skis to buy?

On a ski holiday in Zell am See you decide to buy a new pair of skis, but because the technology has changed considerably since you bought your last pair (or, possibly, because all you know is which end is the front), you don't know which of the current brands and models would be best for you. The big ski goods shop beside the main gondola lift has the largest selection, so you go there and ask for advice. The salesperson appears to be well informed; after asking about your experience level and how aggressively you ski, he recommends the Salomon X-Scream 9. You buy a pair for €600, then head back to your chalet near Kaprun and show them to your room-mate, who helpfully tells you that you could have bought them on the Internet for only €400. How do you feel about your purchase? Are the different prices charged by the two suppliers related to the services they offer? Were the extra services you got by shopping in Zell am See worth the extra €200?

Internet retailers can sell for less because their costs are so much lower than those of full-service retail stores. Those stores, after all, must hire knowledgeable salespeople, put their merchandise on display, rent expensive retailing space and so on. Internet retailers and mail-order houses, by contrast, typically employ unskilled telephone clerks and they store their merchandise in cheap warehouses. But if you are a consumer who doesn't know which is the right product for you, the extra expense of shopping at a speciality retailer is likely to be a good investment. Spending €600 on the right skis is smarter than spending €400 on the wrong ones.

Many people believe that wholesalers, retailers and other agents who assist manufacturers in the sale of their products play a fundamentally different economic role from the one played by those who actually make the products. In this view, the production worker is the ultimate source of *economic value added*. Sales agents are often disparaged as mere middlemen, parasites on the efforts of others who do the real work.

On a superficial level, this view might seem to be supported by the fact that many people go to great lengths to avoid paying for the services of sales agents. Many manufacturers cater to them by offering consumers a chance to 'buy direct' and sidestep the middleman's commission. But on closer examination, we can see that the economic role of sales agents is essentially the same as that of production workers. Consider Example 12.2.

### Example 12.2 How does better information affect economic surplus?

You have inherited a pair of nineteenth-century silver candlesticks. Needing some money (and perhaps being unable to afford to insure them), you decide to sell them. How do you go about it? In the small town where you live there is no (trustworthy) antique dealer. Your reservation price is €300. You realise that as an alternative to putting an advertisement in the local newspaper, offering them to the highest bidder, you could decide to auction them off on eBay. The cost of the advertisement would be €20; the commission payable to eBay is 5 per cent of the amount paid by the winning bidder. In each case, this represents the costs of providing the service.

Advertising means (you hope) being offered the highest reservation price from the local population. Using eBay means that a much larger number of potential bidders will be aware of what is for sale. Now suppose that the local highest reservation price is €400, while in the much larger population of potential bidders on eBay there are two people with reservation prices of €800 and €900, respectively. In the eBay auction the object is sold to the highest bidder, but at the second-highest bidder's highest offer. This is called a second-price auction, rather than an English auction, where the highest bidder's highest offer is paid. One reason for using this system is that it avoids the winner's curse problem,[1] and so encourages people to bid their true reservation price.

Consider now the implications of using eBay rather than the local newspaper in terms of economic surplus. You will receive (net) €760, €460 more than your reservation price. The purchaser will receive surplus of €100 (why?). The total surplus is €560. If you use the newspaper the total surplus will be (€400 – 300 – 20) or €80. If you sell at €400 the surplus is yours; at a price below €400 it is divided between you and the local bidder. But the total, no matter at what price you sell, is €80.

eBay in this example is providing a service by making information available (nineteenth-century candlesticks for sale) to people who can make good use of it. A real increase in economic surplus results when an item ends up in the hands of someone who values it more highly than the person who otherwise would have bought it. That increase is just as valuable as the increase in surplus that results from manufacturing cars, growing corn, or any other productive activity.

### RECAP How the middleman adds value

In a world of incomplete information, sales agents and other middlemen add genuine *economic value* by increasing the extent to which goods and services find their way to the consumers who value them most. When a sales agent causes a good to be purchased by a person who values it by €20,000 more than the person who would have bought it in the absence of a sales agent, that agent augments total economic surplus by €20,000, an achievement on a par with the production of a €20,000 car.

[1] This is the problem that the only reason you have bought the item is because no one else was prepared to pay that much for it, suggesting that you may have paid too much for it. It can have the effect of dampening your willingness to indicate in your bidding your reservation price for the object.

## The optimal amount of information

Without a doubt, having more information is better than having less. But information is generally costly to acquire. In most situations, the value of additional information will decline beyond some point. And because of the Low-Hanging-Fruit Principle (Chapter 2), people tend to gather information from the cheapest sources first before turning to more costly ones. Typically, then, the marginal benefit of information will decline, and its marginal cost will rise, as the amount of information gathered increases.

### The cost–benefit test

Information-gathering is an activity like any other. The Cost–Benefit Principle (Chapter 1) tells us that a rational consumer will continue to gather information as long as its marginal benefit exceeds its marginal cost. Suppose, for the sake of discussion, that analysts have devised a scale that permits us to measure units of information, as on the horizontal axis of Fig. 12.1. If the relevant marginal cost and marginal benefit curves are as shown in Fig. 12.1, a rational consumer will acquire $I^*$ units of information, the amount for which the marginal benefit of information equals its marginal cost.

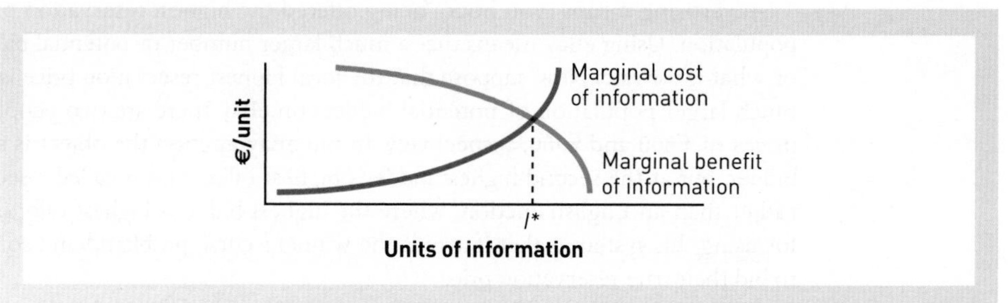


**Figure 12.1 The Optimal Amount of Information.** For the marginal cost and benefit curves shown, the optimal amount of information is $I^*$. Beyond that point, information costs more to acquire than it is worth.

Another way to think about Fig. 12.1 is that it shows the *optimal level of ignorance*. When the cost of acquiring information exceeds its benefits, acquiring additional information simply does not pay. If information could be acquired free, decision makers would, of course, be glad to have it. But when the cost of acquiring the information exceeds the gain in value from the decision it will facilitate, people are better off remaining ignorant.

### The free-rider problem

Does the invisible hand assure that the optimal amount of advice will be made available to consumers in the marketplace? Economic naturalist 12.1 suggests one reason that it might not.

**Exercise 12.1** Apart from its possible contribution to free-rider problems, how is increased access to the Internet likely to affect total economic surplus?

### Economic naturalist 12.1 Why is finding knowledgeable sales assistants to help you often difficult?

People can choose for themselves whether to bear the extra cost of retail shopping. Those who value advice and convenience can pay slightly higher prices, while those who know what they want can buy for less over the web or by mail order. **True or false:** it follows that private incentives lead to the optimal amount of retail service.

The market would provide the optimal level of retail service except for one practical problem – namely, that consumers can make use of the services offered by retail outlets without paying for them. After benefiting from the advice of informed salespersons and after inspecting the merchandise, the consumer can return home and buy the same item from an Internet retailer or mail-order house. Not all consumers do so, of course. But the fact that customers can benefit from the information provided by retail stores without paying for it is an example of the **free-rider problem**, an incentive problem that results in too little of a good or service being produced. Because retail outlets have difficulty recovering the cost of providing information, private incentives are likely to yield less than the socially optimal level of retail service. So the statement above is **false**.

**free-rider problem** an incentive problem in which too little of a good or service is produced because non-payers cannot be excluded from using it

## Two guidelines for rational search

In practice, of course, the exact value of additional information is difficult to know, so the amount of time and effort one should invest in acquiring it is not always obvious. But as Examples 12.3 and 12.4 suggest, the Cost–Benefit Principle provides a strong conceptual framework for thinking about this problem.

### **Example 12.3** Should a person living in Paris, Texas, spend more or less time searching for a flat than someone living in Paris, France?

Suppose that rents for one-bedroom flats in Paris, Texas, vary between €300 and €500 per month, with an average rent of €400 per month. Rents for similar one-bedroom flats in Paris, France, vary between €1,500 and €2,500 per month, with an average rent of €2,000. In which city should a rational person expect to spend a longer time searching for a flat?

In both cities, visiting additional flats entails a cost, largely the opportunity cost of one's time. In both cities, the more flats someone visits, the more likely it is that he or she will find one near the lower end of the rent distribution. But because rents are higher and are spread over a broader range in Paris, France, the expected saving from further time spent searching will be greater there than in Paris, Texas. And so a rational person will expect to spend more time searching for a flat in France.

Example 12.3 illustrates the principle that spending additional search time is more likely to be worthwhile for expensive items than for cheap ones. For example, one should spend more time searching for a good price on a diamond engagement ring than for a good price on a stone made of cubic zirconia; more time searching for a low fare from London to Sydney than for a low fare from Paris to Frankfurt; and more time searching for a car than for a bicycle. By extension, hiring an agent – someone who can assist with a search – is more likely to be a good investment in searching for something expensive than for something cheap. For example, people typically engage estate agents to help them find a house, but they seldom hire agents to help them have their car serviced.

### Example 12.4 Who should expect to search longer for a good price on a used piano?

Both Tom and Tim are shopping for a used upright piano. To examine a piano listed in the classified ads, they must travel to the home of the piano's current owner. If Tom has a car and Tim does not and both are rational, which one should expect to examine fewer pianos before making his purchase?

The benefits of examining an additional piano are the same in both cases – namely, a better chance of finding a good instrument for a low price. But because it is more costly for Tim to examine pianos, he should expect to examine fewer of them than Tom.

Example 12.4 makes the point that when searching becomes more costly, we should expect to do less of it. And as a result, the prices we expect to pay will be higher when the cost of a search is higher.

## The gamble inherent in search

Suppose you are in the market for a one-bedroom flat and have found one that rents for €400 per month. Should you rent it or should you search further in the hope of finding a cheaper flat? Even in a large market with many vacant flats, there is no guarantee that searching further will turn up a cheaper or better one. Searching further entails a cost, which might outweigh the gain. In general, someone who engages in further search must accept certain costs in return for unknown benefits. Thus further search invariably carries an element of risk.

**expected value of a gamble** the sum of the possible outcomes of the gamble multiplied by their respective probabilities

**fair gamble** a gamble whose expected value is zero

**better-than-fair gamble** a gamble whose expected value is positive

**risk neutral person** someone who would accept any gamble that is fair or better

**risk averse person** someone who would refuse any fair gamble

In thinking about whether to take any gamble, a helpful first step is to compute its **expected value** – the average amount you would win (or lose) if you played that gamble an infinite number of times. To calculate the expected value of a gamble with more than one outcome, we first multiply each outcome by its corresponding probability of occurring, and then add. For example, suppose you win €1 if a coin flip comes up heads and lose €1 if it comes up tails. Since 1/2 is the probability of heads (and also the probability of tails), the expected value of this gamble is $(1/2)(€1) + (1/2)(-€1) = 0$. A gamble with an expected value of zero is called a **fair gamble**. If you played this gamble a large number of times, you wouldn't expect to make money, but you also wouldn't expect to lose money.

A **better-than-fair gamble** is one with a *positive* expected value. (For example, a coin flip in which you win €2 for heads and lose €1 for tails is a better-than-fair gamble.) A **risk neutral** person is someone who would accept any gamble that is fair or better. A **risk averse** person is someone who would refuse to take any fair gamble.

**Exercise 12.2** Consider a gamble in which you win €4 if you flip a coin and it comes up heads and lose €2 if it comes up tails. What is the expected value of this gamble? Would a risk neutral person accept it?

In Example 12.5 we apply these concepts to the decision whether to search further for a flat.

### Example 12.5 Should you search further for a flat?

You have arrived in San Francisco for a one-month summer visit and are searching for a one-bedroom sublet for the month. There are only two kinds of one-bedroom flats in the neighbourhood in which you wish to live, identical in every respect except that one rents for €400 and the other for €360. Of the vacant flats in this neighbourhood, 80 per cent are of the first type and 20 per cent are of the second type. The only way you can discover the rent for a vacant flat is to visit it in person. The first flat you visit is one that rents for €400. If you are risk neutral and your opportunity cost of visiting an additional flat is €6, should you visit another flat or rent the one you've found?

If you visit one more flat, you have a 20 per cent chance of it being one that rents for €360 and an 80 per cent chance of it being one that rents for €400. If the former, you'll save €40 in rent, but if the latter, you'll face the same rent as before. Since the cost of a visit is €6, visiting another flat is a gamble with a 20 per cent chance to win €40 – €6 = €34 and an 80 per cent chance of losing €6 (which means 'winning' –€6). The expected value of this gamble is thus (0.20)(€34) + (0.80)(–€6) = €2. Visiting another flat is a better-than-fair gamble, and since you are risk neutral, you should take it.

**Exercise 12.3** Refer to Example 12.5. Suppose you visit another flat and discover it, too, is one that rents for €400. If you are risk neutral, should you visit a third flat?

## The commitment problem when search is costly

When most people search for a flat, they want a place to live not for just a month but for a year or more. Most landlords, for their part, are also looking for long-term tenants. Similarly, few people accept a full-time job in their chosen field unless they expect to hold the job for several years. Firms, too, generally prefer employees who will stay for an extended period. Finally, when most people search for mates, they are looking for someone with whom to settle down.

Because in all these cases search is costly, examining every possible option will never make sense. Flat hunters don't visit every vacant flat, nor do landlords interview every possible tenant. Job seekers don't visit every employer, nor do employers interview every job seeker. And not even the most determined searcher can manage to date every eligible mate. In these and other cases, people are rational to end their searches, even though they know a more attractive option surely exists out there somewhere.

But herein lies a difficulty. What happens when, by chance, a more attractive option comes along after the search has ceased? Few people would rent a flat if they thought the landlord would kick them out the moment another tenant came along who was willing to pay higher rent. Few landlords would be willing to rent to a tenant if they expected her to move out the moment she discovers a cheaper flat. Employers, job seekers and people who are looking for mates would have similar reservations about entering relationships that could be terminated if a better option happened to come along.

This potential difficulty in maintaining stable matches between partners in ongoing relationships would not arise in a world of perfect information. In such a world, everyone would end up in the best possible relationship, so no one would be tempted to renege. But when information is costly and the search must be limited, there will always be the potential for existing relationships to dissolve.

In most contexts, people solve this problem not by conducting an exhaustive search (which is usually impossible, in any event) but by committing themselves to remain in a relationship once a mutual agreement has been reached to terminate the search. Thus landlords and tenants sign a lease that binds them to one another for a specified period, usually six months or a year. Employees and firms enter into employment contracts, either formal or informal, under which each promises to honour the obligations to the other, except under extreme circumstances. And in most countries a marriage contract penalises those who abandon their spouses. Entering into such commitments limits the freedom to pursue one's own interests. Yet most people freely accept such restrictions, because they know that the alternative is failure to solve the search problem.

## RECAP The optimal amount of information

Additional information creates value, but it is also *costly to acquire*. A rational consumer will continue to acquire information until its marginal benefit equals its marginal cost. Beyond that point, it is rational to remain uninformed.

Markets for information do not always function perfectly. *Free-rider* problems often hinder retailers' efforts to provide information to consumers.

Search inevitably entails an element of *risk*, because costs must be incurred without any assurance that search will prove fruitful. A rational consumer can minimise this risk by concentrating search efforts on goods for which the variation in price or quality is relatively high and on those for which the cost of search is relatively low.

## Asymmetric information

One of the most common information problems occurs when the participants in a potential exchange are not equally well informed about the product or service that is offered for sale.

**asymmetric information** where buyers and sellers are not equally informed about the characteristics of products or services

For instance, the owner of a used car may know that the car is in excellent mechanical condition, but potential buyers cannot know that merely by inspecting it or taking it for a test drive. Economists use the term **asymmetric information** to describe situations in which buyers and sellers are not equally well informed about the characteristics of products or services. In these situations, sellers are typically much better informed than buyers, but sometimes the reverse will be true.

As Example 12.6 illustrates, the problem of asymmetric information can easily prevent exchanges that would benefit both parties.

### Example 12.6 Selling your car privately

You own a Ford Fiesta, four years old, with 100,000 km on the clock. You have always driven it carefully, and have had it regularly serviced in line with the manufacturer's instructions. It has never been damaged in an accident. In short, you know the car to be in excellent condition. Now, for whatever reason, you have decided to sell it privately. The going price for four-year-old Fiestas is €6,000

Someone who sees the advertisement in the local paper wants to buy a good four-year-old Fiesta, for which he would pay €8,000 if it is in excellent condition (like yours), but only €6,000 if it is in average condition for that age and all he has to go on is your description and a bunch of receipts. (He could hire a mechanic to examine the car, but doing so is expensive, and many problems cannot be detected even by a mechanic.) Will he buy your car? Is this outcome efficient?

Because your car looks the same as other four-year-old Fiestas, he is unlikely to be willing to pay €8,000 for it. After all, for only €6,000, he can buy some other car that is in just as good condition, as far as he can tell. The probability is that he will buy another Fiesta. He therefore will buy someone else's car, and yours will go unsold. This outcome is not efficient.

## The 'lemons' model

Example 12.6 serves as a useful introduction to what is called the problem of the 'market for lemons' or George Akerlof's **lemons model**. In colloquial American usage in the late 1960s and early 1970s a 'lemon' was a car that was, or might be, in poor condition in a way that would be unknowable to a buyer. In Britain at the time (the era of Peter Sellers playing Jack Kite in *I'm All Right, Jack*) the equivalent was known as a 'Monday' car: one assembled by a hung-over workforce at British Leyland on a Monday morning: it might look all right, but was almost guaranteed to break down about 10 minutes after leaving the showroom.

**'lemons' model** George Akerlof's explanation of how asymmetric information tends to reduce the average quality of goods offered for sale

The problem lies in the *economic incentives* created by asymmetric information. These suggest that the selection of used cars of any given age being offered for sale will be of lower quality than the average in the total population of used cars of that age. One reason is that people who mistreat their cars, or whose cars were never very good to begin with, are more likely than others to want to sell them. Buyers know from experience that cars for sale on the used car market are more likely to be 'lemons' than cars that are not for sale. This realisation causes them to lower their reservation prices for a used car.

But that's not the end of the story. Once used car market prices have fallen, the owners of cars that are in good condition have an even stronger incentive to hold on to them. That causes the average quality of the cars offered for sale on the used car market to decline still further. It helps explain why new cars depreciate so much once they have been bought. University of California at Berkeley economist George Akerlof, a Nobel Laureate, was the first to explain the logic behind this downward spiral.[2] Economists use the term 'lemons model' to describe Akerlof's explanation of how asymmetric information affects the average quality of the used goods offered for sale.

As Example 12.7 suggests, the lemons model has important practical implications for consumer choice.

### Economic naturalist 12.2 Should you buy your aunt's car?

One of the almost universal pieces of folk wisdom is that you should never buy a car from a close friend or a member of your family. The reasoning is that if things go wrong with the car the impact on relationships can be serious. Actually, a good economic naturalist would probably ignore it. You want to buy a used Honda Accord. Your Aunt Germaine buys a new car every four years, and she has a four-year-old Accord that she is about to trade in. You believe her report that the car is in good condition, and she is willing to sell it to you for €10,000, which is the current 'blue book' value for four-year-old Accords. (The 'blue book' value of a car is the average price for which cars of that age and model sell in the used car market.) Should you buy your aunt's Honda?

Akerlof's lemons model tells us that cars for sale in the used car market will be of lower average quality than cars of the same vintage that are not for sale. If you believe your aunt's claim that her car is in good condition, then being able to buy it for its 'blue book' value is definitely a good deal for you, since the 'blue book' price is the equilibrium price for a car that is of lower quality than your aunt's.

[2] Akerlof (1970).

Examples 12.7 and 12.8 illustrate the conditions under which asymmetric information about product quality results in a market in which *only* lemons are offered for sale.

### Example 12.7 How much will a naive buyer pay for a used car?

Consider a world with only two kinds of cars: good ones and lemons. An owner knows with certainty which type of car she has, but potential buyers cannot distinguish between the two types; 10 per cent of all new cars produced are lemons. Good used cars are worth €10,000 to their owners, but lemons are worth only €6,000. Consider a naive consumer who believes that the used cars currently for sale have the same quality distribution as new cars (i.e. 90 per cent good, 10 per cent lemons). If this consumer is risk neutral, how much would she be willing to pay for a used car?

Buying a car of unknown quality is a gamble, but a risk neutral buyer would be willing to take the gamble provided it is fair. If the buyer can't tell the difference between a good car and a lemon, the probability that she will end up with a lemon is simply the proportion of lemons among the cars from which she chooses. The buyer believes she has a 90 per cent chance of getting a good car and a 10 per cent chance of getting a lemon. Given the prices she is willing to pay for the two types of car, her expected value of the car she buys will thus be 0.90(€10,000) + 0.10(€6,000) = €9,600. And since she is risk neutral, that is her reservation price for a used car.

**Exercise 12.4** How would your answer to the question posed in Example 12.7 differ if the proportion of new cars that are lemons had been not 10 per cent but 20 per cent?

### Example 12.8 Who will sell a used car for what the naive buyer is willing to pay?

Refer to Example 12.7. If you were the owner of a good used car, what would it be worth to you? Would you sell it to a naive buyer? What if you owned a lemon?

Since you know that your car is good, it is worth €10,000 to you, by assumption. But since a naive buyer would be willing to pay only €9,600, neither you nor any other owner of a good car would be willing to sell to that buyer. If you had a lemon, of course, you would be happy to sell it to a naive buyer, since the €9,600 the buyer is willing to pay is €3,600 more than the lemon would be worth to you. So the only used cars for sale will be lemons. In time, buyers will revise their naively optimistic beliefs about the quality of the cars for sale on the used car market. In the end, all used cars will sell for a price of €6,000, and all will be lemons.

In practice, of course, the mere fact that a car is for sale does not guarantee that it is a lemon, because the owner of a good car will sometimes be forced to sell it, even at a price that does not reflect its condition. The logic of the lemons model explains this owner's frustration. The first thing sellers in this situation want a prospective buyer to know is the reason they are selling their cars. For example, classified ads often announce, 'Just had a baby, must sell my 2002 Lotus' or 'Transferred to Germany, must sell my 2003 Rover 75'. Any time you pay the 'blue book' price for a used car that is for sale for some reason unrelated to its condition, you are beating the market.

## The credibility problem in trading

Why can't someone with a high-quality used car simply *tell* the buyer about the car's condition? The difficulty is that buyers' and sellers' interests tend to conflict. Sellers of used cars, for example, have an economic incentive to overstate the quality of their products. Buyers, for their part, have an incentive to understate the amount they are willing to pay for used cars and other products (in the hope of bargaining for a lower price). Potential employees may be tempted to overstate their qualifications for a job. And people searching for mates have been known to engage in deception.

That is not to say that most people *consciously* misrepresent the truth in communicating with their potential trading partners. But people do tend to interpret ambiguous information in ways that promote their own interests. Thus, 92 per cent of factory employees surveyed in one study rated themselves as more productive than the average factory worker.[3]

Notwithstanding the natural tendency to exaggerate, the parties to a potential exchange can often gain if they can find some means to communicate their knowledge truthfully. In general, however, mere statements of relevant information will not suffice. People have long since learned to discount the used car salesman's inflated claims about the cars he is trying to unload. But as Example 12.9 illustrates, though communication between potential adversaries may be difficult, it is not impossible.

### Example 12.9 How can a used car seller signal high quality credibly?

You knew your Fiesta to be in excellent condition, and the potential purchaser would have been willing to pay your reservation price if he could be confident of getting such a car. What kind of signal about the car's quality would the purchaser find credible?

Again, the potential conflict between the buyer's and seller's interests suggests that mere statements about the car's quality may not be persuasive. But suppose you offer a warranty, under which you agree to remedy any defects the car develops over the next six months. You can afford to extend such an offer because you know that the car is unlikely to need expensive repairs. In contrast, a person who knows his car has a cracked engine block would never extend such an offer. The warranty is a credible signal that the car is in good condition. It enables the purchaser to buy the car with confidence, to both his and the seller's benefit.

## The costly-to-fake principle

Examples 12.7–12.9 illustrate the **costly-to-fake principle**, which holds that if parties whose interests potentially conflict are to communicate credibly with one another, the signals they send must be costly or difficult to fake. If the seller of a defective car could offer an extensive warranty just as easily as the seller of a good car, a warranty offer would communicate nothing about the car's quality. But warranties entail costs that are significantly higher for defective cars than for good cars – hence their credibility as a signal of product quality.

**costly-to-fake principle** to communicate information credibly to a potential rival, a signal must be costly or difficult to fake

To the extent that sellers have an incentive to portray a product in the most flattering light possible, their interests conflict with those of buyers, who want the most accurate assessment of product quality possible. Note that in Economic naturalist 12.3, the costly-to-fake principle applies to a producer's statement about the quality of a product.

### Economic naturalist 12.3 Why do firms insert the phrase 'As advertised on TV' when they advertise their products in magazines and newspapers?

Company *A* sponsors an expensive national TV advertising campaign on behalf of its compact disc player, claiming it has the clearest sound and the best repair record of any CD player in the market. Company *B* makes similar claims in a sales brochure but does not advertise its product on TV. If you had no additional information to go on, which company's claim would you find more credible? Why do you

[3] Some psychologists call this phenomenon the 'Lake Wobegon effect', after Garrison Keillor's mythical Minnesota town, where 'all the children are above average'.

suppose Company *A* mentions its TV ads when it advertises its CD player in the print media?

Accustomed as we are to discounting advertisers' inflated claims, the information given might seem to provide no real basis for a choice between the two products. On closer examination, however, we see that a company's decision to advertise its product on national TV constitutes a credible signal about the product's quality. The cost of a national TV campaign can run well into the millions of euros, a sum a company would be foolish to spend on an inferior product.

For example, in 2002 Pepsi paid Britney Spears $8 $million to appear in its two 30-second US Super Bowl ads and it paid more than $3.5 million to Fox TV for broadcasting those ads. National TV ads can attract the potential buyers' attention and persuade a small fraction of them to try a product. But these huge investments pay off only if the resulting initial sales generate other new business – either repeat sales to people who tried the product and liked it or sales to others who heard about the product from a friend.

Because ads cannot persuade buyers that a bad product is a good one, a company that spends millions of euros advertising a bad product is wasting its money. An expensive national advertising campaign is therefore a credible signal that the producer *thinks* that its product is a good one. Of course, the ads don't guarantee that a product *is* a winner, but in an uncertain world, they provide one more piece of information. Note, however, that the relevant information lies in the *expenditure on the advertising campaign*, not in what the ads themselves say.

These observations may explain why some companies mention their TV ads in their print ads. Advertisers understand the costly-to-fake principle and hope that consumers will understand it as well.

As Economic naturalist 12.4 illustrates, the costly-to-fake principle is also well known to many employers.

## Economic naturalist 12.4 Why do many companies care so much about elite educational credentials?

Microsoft is looking for a hard-working, smart person for an entry-level managerial position in a new technical products division in north-west France. Two candidates, Iain and Jean-Pierre, both economists, seem alike in every respect but one: Iain graduated with first-class honours from New College, Oxford, while Jean-Pierre graduated with a C1 average from Nanterre. Whom should Microsoft hire?

If you want to persuade prospective employers that you are both hard working and intelligent, there is perhaps no more credible signal than to have graduated with distinction from a highly selective educational institution. Most people would like potential employers to think of them as hard working and intelligent. But unless you actually have both those qualities, graduating with the highest honours from a university like Oxford will be extremely difficult. The fact that Jean-Pierre graduated from a much less selective institution and earned only a C1 average is not proof positive that he is not diligent and talented, but companies are forced to play the percentages. In this case, the odds strongly favour Iain.

This may help explain why the better UK universities are so concerned about being required to be less selective in their admissions policies in order to improve the chances of youngsters from socially disadvantaged parts of the UK gaining access.

## Conspicuous consumption as a signal of ability

Some individuals of high ability are not highly paid. (Remember the best schoolteacher you ever had.) And some people, such as the multi-billionaire investor Warren Buffett, earn a lot, yet spend very little. Virgin CEO Richard Branson dresses in jeans and open-neck shirts. So does Michael O'Leary of Ryanair. But such cases run counter to general tendencies. In competitive markets, the people with the most ability tend to receive the highest salaries. And as suggested by the Cost–Benefit Principle (Chapter 1), the more someone earns, the more she is likely to spend on high-quality goods and services. As Economic naturalist 12.5 suggests, these tendencies often lead us to infer a person's ability from the amount and quality of the goodss he consumes.

### Economic naturalist 12.5 Why do management consultants wear Armani suits when visiting clients while a top barrister may turn up at a consultation in a baggy sports jacket?

Your company is threatened by bankruptcy arising from a failure to exercise proper credit control and keep its product line up to date. You want the best advice available from management consultants. Your choice is between two corporate gurus who appear identical in all respects except for the things they buy. One of them wears a cheap polyester suit and arrives at the presentation at your office in a 10-year-old rust-eaten Toyota. The other wears an impeccably hand-tailored suit and drives a new Jaguar S-type. If this were the *only* information available to you at the time you chose, which guru would you hire?

We assume that there is a strong correlation between earnings and the abilities buyers value most in management consultancy. A consultant whose clients usually benefit from his advice will be much more in demand than one whose clients generally go out of business, and their fees will reflect the difference. The fact that one of the consultants spends much more than the other does not *prove* that he is better, but if that is the only information you have, you can ill afford to ignore it.

And the barrister? He is retained by a knowledgeable solicitor who has other (and objective) means to evaluate suitability for the case in hand. He does not have to try to convey information as to his ability by his clothes or his car. If, of course, legal reforms led to direct hiring of barristers by the public, then, as in the United States, we might see more conspicuous consumption by barristers.

If the less able guru loses business because of the suits he wears and the car he drives, why doesn't he simply buy better suits and a more expensive car? His choice is between saving for retirement or spending more on his car and clothing. In one sense, he cannot afford to buy a more expensive car, but in another sense, he cannot afford *not* to. If his current car is discouraging potential clients from hiring him, buying a better one may simply be a prudent investment. But because *all* consultants have an incentive to make such investments, their effects tend to be mutually offsetting.

When all is said and done, the things people consume will continue to convey relevant information about their respective ability levels. The costly-to-fake principle tells us that the Jaguar S-type is an effective signal precisely because the consultant of low ability cannot afford one, no matter how little he saves for his retirement. Yet from a social perspective, the resulting spending pattern is inefficient, for the same reason that other *positional arms races* are inefficient (see Chapter 11). Society would be better off if everyone spent less and saved more for retirement.

The problem of conspicuous consumption as an ability signal does not arise with equal force in every environment. In smaller towns, where people tend to know one another well, an accountant who tries to impress people by spending beyond her means is likely to succeed only in demonstrating how foolish she is. Thus the wardrobe a professional person 'needs' in towns like Inverness or Perugia costs less than the wardrobe the same person would need in Edinburgh or Rome.

## Statistical discrimination

In a competitive market with perfect information, the buyer of a service would pay the seller's cost of providing the service. In many markets, however – the market for fire insurance is one example – the seller does not know the exact cost of serving each individual buyer.

In such cases, the missing information has an *economic value*. If the seller can come up with even a rough estimate of the missing information, she can improve her position. As Economic naturalist 12.6 illustrates, firms often impute characteristics to individuals on the basis of the groups to which they belong.

### Economic naturalist 12.6 Why do Irish males under 25 years of age pay more than Irish females of the same age, and both more than their British equivalents, for car insurance?

The accident death rate on Irish roads is significantly higher than on British roads, which are among the safest in Europe. There are fewer motorways in Ireland, and on some of those that exist, to save money for the Exchequer (politicians and bureaucrats tend to limit considerations of costs to whatever the Exchequer has to pay), the government chose not to put crash barriers in the central reservation when building them. In addition, the cost per accident is higher for a variety of reasons, including a greater resort to judicial decisions involving expensive outings to the High Court. That explains a higher level of motor insurance costs in Ireland. What it does not explain is why Irish (and other) males pay more than females, and why this is even more the case in Ireland than in many other EU countries. One is tempted to say, discrimination: a charge that would certainly be laid were rates for women drivers higher. But it has nothing to do with discrimination on gender grounds. It reflects *expected costs*.

The expected cost to an insurance company of insuring any given driver depends on the probability that the driver will be involved in an accident. No one knows what that probability is for any given driver, but insurance companies can estimate rather precisely the proportion of drivers in specific groups who will be involved in an accident in any given year. Irish males under 25 are much more likely than older males and females of any age to become involved in road accidents. (Testosterone seems to have something to do with it. So does alcohol. The combination can be lethal.) Irish young males drink more than their elders, or other EU equivalents, drive more (the population density is lower than in the United Kingdom or most of continental Europe, and public transport is less universal) and crash more often. Because of high Irish taxes on cars, they also drive smaller and lighter cars than the average in most other countries. The consequences are obvious.

To remain in business, an insurance company must collect enough money from premiums to cover the cost of the claims it pays out, plus whatever administrative expenses it incurs. Consider an insurance company that charges lower rates for young males with clean driving records than for females with blemished ones.

Given that the former group is more likely to have accidents than the latter, the company cannot break even unless it charges females more, and males less, than the respective costs of insuring them. But if it does so, rival insurance companies will see cash-on-the-table (Chapter 3): they can offer females slightly lower rates and lure them away from the first company. The first company will end up with only young male policyholders and thus will suffer an economic loss at the low rates it charges. That is why, in equilibrium, young males with clean driving records pay higher insurance rates than young females with blemished records.

The insurance industry's policy of charging high rates to young male drivers is an example of **statistical discrimination**. Other examples include the common practice of paying higher salaries to people with college degrees than to people without them. Statistical discrimination occurs whenever people or products are judged on the basis of the *groups to which they belong*.

**statistical discrimination** the practice of making judgements about the quality of people, goods or services based on the characteristics of the groups to which they belong

Even though everyone *knows* that the characteristics of specific individuals can differ markedly from those of the group to which they belong, competition promotes statistical discrimination. For example, insurance companies know perfectly well that *some* young males are careful and competent drivers. But unless they can identify *which* males are the better drivers, competitive pressure forces them to act on their knowledge that, as a group, young males are more likely than others to generate insurance claims.

Similarly, employers know that many people with only a secondary education are more productive than the average university graduate. But because employers usually cannot tell in advance who those people are, competitive pressure leads them to offer higher wages to graduates, who are more productive, on average, than those with only a secondary education.

Statistical discrimination is the *result* of observable differences in group characteristics, not the cause of those differences. Young males, for example, do not generate more insurance claims because of statistical discrimination. Rather, statistical discrimination occurs because insurance companies know that young males generate more claims. Nor does statistical discrimination cause young males to pay insurance rates that are high in relation to the claims they generate. Among any group of young male drivers, some are careful and competent, and others are not. Statistical discrimination means the more able males will pay high rates relative to the volume of claims they generate, but it also means the less able male drivers will pay low rates relative to the claims they generate. On average, the group's rates will be appropriate to the claims its members generate.

Still, these observations do little to ease the frustration of the young male who knows himself to be a careful and competent driver, or the school leaver who knows herself to be a highly productive employee. Competitive forces give firms an incentive to identify such individuals and treat them more favourably whenever practical. Insurance companies in Ireland and elsewhere are now introducing programmes to help identify 'careful' drivers from among the young male population. These include voluntary limitations on time of driving (most fatalities occur between 11.00 p.m. and 5.00 a.m.), drinking and speed, as well as taking advanced driving courses.

## Adverse selection

Although insurance companies routinely practise statistical discrimination, each individual within a group pays the same rate, even though individuals within the group often differ sharply in terms of their likelihood of filing claims. Within each group, buying insurance is thus most attractive to those individuals with the highest likelihood of filing claims. As a result, high-risk individuals are more likely to buy insurance than low-risk individuals, a pattern known as **adverse selection**. Adverse selection forces insurance companies to raise their premiums, which makes buying insurance even less attractive to low-risk individuals, which raises still further the average risk level of those who remain insured. In some cases, only those individuals faced with extreme risks may continue to find insurance an attractive purchase.

**adverse selection** the pattern in which insurance tends to be purchased disproportionately by those who are most costly for companies to insure

## Moral hazard

**Moral hazard** is another problem that makes buying insurance less attractive for the average person. This problem refers to the fact that some people take fewer precautions when they know they are insured. Someone whose car is insured, for example, may take less care to prevent it from being damaged or stolen. Driving cautiously and searching for safe parking spaces require effort, after all, and if the losses from failing to engage in these precautions are covered by insurance, some people will become less vigilant.

**moral hazard** the tendency of people to expend less effort protecting those goods that are insured against theft or damage

By offering policies with deductible provisions (excesses), insurance companies help many of their potential clients soften the consequences of problems such as moral hazard and adverse selection. Under the terms of an automobile collision insurance policy with, say, a €1,000 excess provision, the insurance company covers only those collision repair costs in excess of €1,000. For example, if you have an accident in which €3,000 in damage occurs to your car, the insurance company covers only €2,000, and you pay the remaining €1,000.

An excess means that the insured is sharing part of the risk with the insurer. For this reason this is sometimes referred to as an example of 'co-insurance'. Carrying more of the risk makes the insured party take more precautions. A system of no-claims bonuses operates in the same way: if you make a claim your costs will increase when the time comes to renew the policy. That reduces the incentive to make a claim rather than carry the full cost of an accident yourself.

How does the availability of such policies mitigate the negative effects of adverse selection and moral hazard? Since the policies are cheaper for insurance companies to provide, they sell for lower prices. The lower prices represent a much better bargain, however, for those drivers who are least likely to file insurance claims, since those drivers are least likely to incur any uncovered repair costs. Policies with deductible provisions also confront careless drivers with more of the extra costs for which they are responsible, giving them additional incentives to take precautions.

These policies benefit insurance buyers in another way. Because the holder of a policy with an excess provision will not file a claim at all if the damage to his car in an accident is less than the deductible threshold, insurance companies require fewer resources to process and investigate claims, savings that get passed along in the form of lower premiums.

## RECAP Asymmetric information

Asymmetric information describes situations in which not all parties to a potential exchange are *equally well informed*. In the typical case, the seller of a product will know more about its quality than the potential buyers. Such asymmetries often stand in the way of mutually beneficial exchange in the markets for high-quality goods, because buyers' inability to identify high quality makes them unwilling to pay a commensurate price.

Information asymmetries and other communication problems between potential exchange partners can often be solved through the use of signals that are costly or difficult to fake. *Product warranties* are such a signal, because the seller of a low-quality product would find them too costly to offer.

Buyers and sellers also respond to asymmetric information by attempting to judge the qualities of products and people on the basis of the *groups to which they belong*. A young male may know he is a good driver, but auto insurance companies must nonetheless charge him high rates because they know only that he is a member of a group that is frequently involved in accidents.

## Disappearing political discourse

An intriguing illustration of statistical discrimination arises when a politician decides what to say about controversial public issues. Politicians have an interest in supporting the positions they genuinely believe in, but they also have an interest in winning re-election. As Example 12.10 and Economic naturalist 12.7 illustrate, the two motives often conflict, especially when a politician's statements about one subject convey information about her beliefs on other subjects.

### **Example 12.10** Why do opponents of the death penalty in the United States often remain silent?

The United States is now the only Western democracy in which the death penalty is imposed. It is a matter on which from time to time fierce debate takes place. The issues are both ethical and practical: quite apart from the question of whether execution of convicted criminals is morally legitimate, there are important practical arguments against capital punishment. For one thing, it is extremely expensive relative to the alternative of life without parole, because of judicial safeguards against the execution of innocent persons. In each capital case prosecuted in the United States, these safeguards consume thousands of person-hours from attorneys and other officers of the court, at a cost that runs well into the millions of dollars.[4] Such efforts notwithstanding, the record is replete with examples of executed persons who are later shown to have been innocent. Another argument against capital punishment is that many statistical studies find that it does not deter people from committing capital crimes. Though many political leaders in both parties find these and other arguments against capital punishment compelling, few politicians voice their opposition to capital punishment publicly. Why not?

A possible answer to this puzzle is suggested by the theory of statistical discrimination. Voters supporting both Republicans and Democrats are concerned about crime and want to elect politicians who take the problem seriously. Suppose there are two kinds of politicians: some who in their heart of hearts take the crime issue seriously and others who merely pay lip service to it. Suppose also that voters classify politicians in a second way: those who publicly favour the death penalty or remain silent, and those who publicly oppose it. Some politicians will oppose the death penalty for the reasons just discussed, but others will oppose it because they are simply reluctant to punish criminals – perhaps because they believe that crime is ultimately more society's fault than the criminal's. (Politicians in the latter category are the ones voters think of as being 'not serious about crime'; they are the ones most voters want to get rid of.) These two possible motives for opposing the death penalty suggest that the proportion of death penalty opponents who take the crime issue seriously, in the public's view, will be somewhat smaller than the corresponding proportion among proponents of the death penalty. For the sake of discussion, imagine that 95 per cent of politicians who favour the death penalty and only 80 per cent of politicians who oppose the death penalty are 'serious about crime.'

[4] See Cook and Slawson (1993).

If you are a voter who cares about crime, how will your views about a politician be affected by hearing that he opposes the death penalty? If you knew nothing about that politician to begin with, your best guess on hearing his opposition to the death penalty would be that there is an 80 per cent chance that he is serious about crime. Had he instead voiced support for the death penalty, your best guess would be that there is a 95 per cent chance that he is serious about crime. And since voters are looking for politicians who are serious about crime, the mere act of speaking out against the death penalty will entail a small loss of political support even for those politicians who are extremely serious about crime.

Knowing this tendency on the part of voters, some politicians who are only marginally opposed to the death penalty may prefer to keep their views to themselves. As a result, the composition of the group that speaks out publicly against the death penalty will change slightly so that it is more heavily weighted with people reluctant to punish criminals in any way. Suppose, for example, that the proportion of death penalty opponents who are serious about crime falls from 80 to 60 per cent. Now the political cost of speaking out against the death penalty rises, leading still more opponents to remain silent. Once the dust settles, very few opponents of capital punishment will risk stating their views publicly. In their desire to convince voters that they are tough on crime, some may even become outspoken proponents of the death penalty. In the end, public discourse will strongly favour capital punishment. But that is no reason to conclude that most leaders – or even most voters – genuinely favour it.

**disappearing political discourse** the theory that people who support a position may remain silent, because speaking out would create a risk of being misunderstood

The economist Glen Loury was the first to call attention to the phenomenon described in Example 12.10. We call it the problem of **disappearing political discourse**. Once you understand it, you will begin to notice examples not just in the political sphere but in everyday discourse as well.

## Economic naturalist 12.7 Why do proponents of legalising drugs remain silent?

That addictive drugs like heroin, cocaine and methamphetamines cause enormous harm is not a matter of dispute. The clear intent of laws that ban commerce in these drugs is to prevent that harm. But the laws also entail costs. By making the drugs illegal, they substantially increase their price, leading many addicts to commit crimes to pay for drugs. The high incomes of illicit drug dealers also divert many people from legitimate careers and result in 'turf battles' that often have devastating consequences for both participants and bystanders. If these drugs were legal, drug-related crime would vanish completely. Drug use would also rise, how significantly we do not know. In short, it is at least *conceivable* that legalising addictive drugs might be sound public policy. Why, then, do so few politicians in Western Europe publicly support such a policy?

Many politicians may simply believe that legalising drugs is a bad idea. Theoretically, legalisation could lead to such a steep rise in drug consumption that the cost of the policy might far outweigh its benefits. This concern, however, is not supported by experience in countries such as Britain and the Netherlands, which have tried limited forms of legalisation. A second explanation is that politicians who favour legalisation are reluctant to speak out for fear that others will misinterpret them. Suppose that some people favour legalisation based on careful analysis of the costs and benefits, while other proponents are merely crazy. If the proportion of crazies is higher among supporters than among opponents of legalisation, someone who speaks out in favour of legalisation may cause those who do not know her to increase their estimate of the likelihood she is crazy. This possibility deters some proponents from speaking out, which raises the proportion of crazies among the remaining public supporters of legalisation – and so on in a downward spiral, until most of the remaining public supporters really are crazy.

The disappearing political discourse problem helps to explain why the United States had difficulty re-establishing normal diplomatic relations with China, which were severed in the wake of the Communist Revolution. One could oppose communist expansionism and yet still favour normalised relations with China on the grounds that war is less likely when antagonists communicate openly. In the Cold War environment, however, American politicians were under enormous pressure to demonstrate their steadfast opposition to communism at every opportunity. Fearing that support for the normalisation of relations with China would be misinterpreted as a sign of 'softness' toward communism, many supporters of the policy remained silent. Not until Richard Nixon – whose anti-communist credentials no one could question – was elected president were diplomatic relations with China finally reopened.

It may also help explain why voting in EU referenda on amendments to the treaties in the 1990s showed quite a gap between what mainstream politicians were prepared to say and what their voters actually voted for. Opposition to the Nice and earlier treaties in opinion polls and votes was much greater than opposition from politicians, most of whom clustered in the camp of support for the proposals. But to oppose the changes would have meant being linked to neo-Nazis in Germany, the British National Party (BNP) in Britain, Jean-Marie Le Pen's National Front affiliates in France and Sinn Fein in Ireland. No mainstream politician looking for re-election would feel comfortable sharing a platform with any of these groups.

## Summary

- Virtually every market exchange takes place on the basis of *less than complete information*. More information is beneficial both to buyers and to sellers, but information is costly to acquire. The rational individual therefore acquires information only up to the point at which its marginal benefit equals its marginal cost. Beyond that point one is rational to remain ignorant.
- Retailers and other sales agents are important sources of information. To the extent that they enable consumers to find the right products and services, they add economic value. In that sense they are no less productive than the workers who manufacture goods or perform services directly. Unfortunately, the *free-rider problem* often prevents firms from offering useful product information.
- Several principles govern the *rational search for information*. Searching more intensively makes sense when the cost of a search is low, when quality is highly variable, or when prices vary widely. Further search is always a gamble. A risk neutral person will search whenever the expected gains outweigh the expected costs. A rational search will always terminate before all possible options have been investigated. Thus in a search for a partner in an ongoing bilateral relationship, there is always the possibility that a better partner will turn up after the search is over. In most contexts, people deal with this problem by entering into contracts that commit them to their partners once they have mutually agreed to terminate the search.
- Many potentially beneficial transactions are prevented from taking place by *asymmetric information* – the fact that one party lacks information that the other has. For example, the owner of a used car knows

whether it is in good condition, but potential buyers do not. Even though a buyer may be willing to pay more for a good car than the owner of such a car would require, the fact that the buyer cannot be sure that she is getting a good car often discourages the sale. More generally, asymmetric information often prevents sellers from supplying the same quality level that consumers would be willing to pay for.

- Both buyers and sellers can often gain by finding ways of communicating what they know to one another. But because of the potential conflict between the interests of buyers and sellers, mere statements about the relevant information may not be credible. For a signal between potential trading partners to be credible, it must be *costly to fake*. For instance, the owner of a high-quality used car can credibly signal the car's quality by offering a warranty – an offer that the seller of a low-quality car could not afford to make.
- Firms and consumers often try to estimate missing information by making use of what they know about the *groups to which people or things belong*. For example, insurance firms estimate the risk of insuring individual young male drivers on the basis of the accident rates for young males as a group. This practice is known as *statistical discrimination*. Other examples include paying college graduates more than school leavers and charging higher life insurance rates to 60-year-olds than to 20-year-olds. Statistical discrimination helps to explain the phenomenon of disappearing political discourse, which occurs when opponents of a practice such as the death penalty remain silent when the issue is discussed publicly.

## Key terms

**adverse selection** (356)
**asymmetric information** (348)
**better-than-fair gamble** (346)
**costly-to-fake principle** (351)
**disappearing political discourse** (358)
**expected value of a gamble** (346)
**fair gamble** (346)
**free-rider problem** (345)
**'lemons' model** (349)
**moral hazard** (356)
**risk averse person** (346)
**risk neutral person** (346)
**statistical discrimination** (355)

## Review questions

1. Can it be rational for a consumer to buy a Toyota without having first taken test drives in competing models built by Ford, VW, Renault, Honda and others?
2. Explain why a gallery owner who sells a painting might actually create more economic surplus than the artist who painted it.
3. Explain why used cars offered for sale are different, on average, from used cars not offered for sale.
4. Explain why the used-car market would be likely to function more efficiently in a community in which moral norms of honesty are strong than in a community in which such norms are weak.
5. Why might leasing a new Porsche be a good investment for an aspiring Hollywood film producer, even though he can't easily afford the monthly payments?

## Problems

1. State whether the following are **true or false**, and briefly explain why.

   a. Companies spend billions of euros advertising their products on network TV primarily because the texts of their advertisements persuade consumers that the advertised products are of high quality.

   b. Because of the free-rider problem you may not get the optimal level of advice from a retail shop when you go in to buy a lamp for your bike.

   c. If you need a lawyer, and all your legal expenses are covered by insurance, you should *always* choose the best-dressed lawyer with the most expensive car and the most ostentatiously furnished office.

   d. The benefit of searching for a spouse is affected by the size of the community you live in.

2. Consumers know that some fraction $x$ of all new cars produced and sold in the market are defective. The defective ones cannot be identified except by those who own them. Cars do not depreciate with use. Consumers are risk neutral and value non-defective cars at €10,000 each. New cars sell for €5,000 and used ones for €2,500. What is the fraction $x$?

3. Carlos is risk neutral and has an ancient farmhouse with great character for sale in Granada in Spain. His reservation price for the house is €130,000. The only possible local buyer is Whitney, whose reservation price for the house is €150,000. The only other houses on the market are modern houses that sell for €125,000, which is exactly equal to each potential buyer's reservation price for such a house. Suppose that if Carlos does not hire an estate agent, Whitney will learn from her neighbour that Carlos' house is for sale and will buy it for €140,000. However, if Carlos hires an estate agent, he knows that the agent will put him in touch with an enthusiast for old farmhouses who is willing to pay up to €300,000 for the house. Carlos also knows that if he and this person negotiate, they will agree on a price of €250,000. If agents charge a commission of 5 per cent of the selling price and all agents have opportunity costs of €2,000 for negotiating a sale, will Carlos hire an agent? If so, how will total economic surplus be affected?

4. Ann and Barbara are computer programmers in Nashville in Tennessee who are planning to move to Portland in Oregon. Each owns a house that has just been valued at $100,000. But whereas Ann's house is one of hundreds of highly similar houses in a large, well-known suburban development, Barbara's is the only one that was built from her architect's design. Who will benefit more by hiring an estate agent to assist in selling her house, Ann or Barbara?

5. For each pair of occupations listed, identify the one for which the kind of car a person drives is more likely to be a good indication of how good she is at her job.

   a. Primary school teacher; estate agent.

   b. Dentist; municipal government administrator.

   c. Engineer in the private sector; engineer in the military.

6. Brokers who sell stocks over the Internet can serve many more customers than those who transact business by mail or over the phone. How will the expansion of Internet access affect the average incomes of stockbrokers who continue to do business in the traditional way?

7. Whose income do you predict will be more affected by the expansion of Internet access:

   a. Stockbrokers or lawyers?

   b. Doctors or pharmacists?

   c. Bookshop owners or the owners of galleries that sell original oil paintings?

8. How will growing Internet access affect the number of film actors and musicians who have active fan clubs?

9. Fred, a retired accountant, and Jim, a senior civil servant, are 63-year-old identical twins who collect antique pottery. Each has an annual income of €100,000 (Fred's from a pension, Jim's from salary). One buys most of his pottery at local auctions, and the other buys most of his from a local dealer. Which brother is more likely to buy at an auction, and does he pay more or less than his brother who buys from the local dealer?

10. Female heads of state (e.g. Israel's Golda Meir, India's Indira Gandhi, Britain's Margaret Thatcher) have often been described as more bellicose in foreign policy matters than the average male head of state. Using Loury's theory of disappearing political discourse, suggest an explanation for this pattern.

## Answers to in-chapter exercises

12.1 Internet search is a cheap way to acquire information about many goods and services, so the effect of increased Internet access will be a downward shift in the supply curve of information. In equilibrium, people will acquire more information, and the goods and services they buy will more closely resemble those they would have chosen in an ideal world with perfect information. These effects will cause total economic surplus to grow. Some of these gains, however, might be offset if the Internet makes the free-rider problem more serious.

12.2 The probability of getting heads is 0.5, the same as the probability of getting tails. Thus the expected value of this gamble is (0.5)(€4) + (0.5)(–€2) = €1. Since the gamble is better than fair, a risk neutral person would accept it.

12.3 Since you still have a 20 per cent chance of finding a cheaper flat if you make another visit, the expected outcome of the gamble is again €2, and you should search again. The bad outcome of any previous search is a *sunk cost* and should not influence your decision about whether to search again.

12.4 The expected value of a new car will now be 0.8(€10,000) + 0.2(€6,000) = €9,200. Any risk neutral consumer who believed that the quality distribution of used cars for sale was the same as the quality distribution of new cars off the assembly line would be willing to pay €9,200 for a used car.

## References

Akerlof, G. (1970) 'The Market for Lemons', *Quarterly Journal of Economics*, 84.

Cook, P. J. and D. B. Slawson (1993) *The Costs of Processing Murder Cases in North Carolina* (Durham, NC: Sandford Institute of Public Policy, Duke University).

# Part 4

# Government in the Economy: Distribution, Regulation and the Provision of Public Goods

Why do some people earn so much more money than others? No other single question in economics has stimulated nearly as much interest and discussion. Our aim in Chapter 13 will be to apply simple economic principles in an attempt to answer this question. We shall discuss the human capital model, which emphasises the importance of differences in personal characteristics. But our focus will be on why people with similar personal characteristics often earn sharply different incomes. Among the factors we shall consider are labour unions, winner-take-all markets, discrimination and the effect of non-wage conditions of employment. In this chapter we shall also explore whether income inequality is something society should be concerned about and, if so, whether practical remedies exist for it. We shall see that government programmes to redistribute income have costs as well as benefits.

In Chapter 14 we shall explore two further aspects of government action in a market economy. The first of these is the function of government as 'regulator': taking legal and administrative steps to change the way in which firms or households behave from what they would do in an unrestricted environment. The second is the role of the government as producer of goods and services. In most Western economies, governments produce goods and services that could easily be (and in many cases are) produced by firms through markets. Why? There are, however, some activities of government as producer that cannot easily be replicated through markets. Why?

# 13

# Labour Markets, Income Distribution, Wealth and Poverty

Differences in incomes are sometimes hard to rationalise in terms of differences in the abilities of the people concerned. The returns to winning (and retaining!) an Olympic gold medal in, say, swimming, may be quite substantial in terms of advertising, appearance money, endorsements and so on. The winner may be (and usually is) only very marginally superior as an athlete to the silver and bronze medallists. But, typically, the latter tend to sink from public consciousness, and their lifetime earnings are small fractions of those of gold medallists who do not significantly outrank them in terms of inherent performance ability.

And when we look at the incomes of people with similar abilities in different countries or in different sectors of the same country we can frequently observe substantial differences in what they earn, controlling for the amount of work they undertake. In recent years, for example, Western health sector employers have taken advantage of very large differences in the earnings of trained nurses in countries such as the Philippines and Western Europe to recruit nursing staff from those countries to meet staff shortages in Europe. High-quality economists working in government departments typically earn lower salaries than equally competent analysts working in the financial sector or in consultancy firms.

Why do some people earn so much more than others? No other single question in economics has stimulated as much interest and discussion. In case you think it is simply a matter of whether you live in a rich country or a poor country, the fact is that, say, although the United States is an extremely rich country American citizenship is neither necessary nor sufficient for receiving a high income. Many of the wealthiest people in the world come from extremely poor countries, and many Americans are homeless and malnourished.

Our aim in this chapter will be to employ simple economic principles in an attempt to explain why different people earn different incomes. We shall discuss the human capital model, which emphasises the importance of differences in personal characteristics. But our focus will be on why people with similar personal characteristics often earn sharply different incomes. Among the factors we shall consider are trade unions, discrimination, the effect of non-wage conditions of employment and winner-take-all markets. We shall explore whether *income inequality* is something society should be concerned about and, if so, whether practical remedies for it exist. As we shall see, government programmes to redistribute income have costs as well as benefits: as always, policy makers must compare an imperfect status quo with the practical consequences of imperfect government remedies.

Our approach is based on the tried and tested technique of applying the analysis of markets to the problem, on the basis that a person's earnings from labour can be thought of as reflecting the price received for an hour of work and the number of hours worked (i.e. sold by the worker and bought by the employer). The same applies to incomes earned from the ownership of productive assets.

## The economic value of work

In some respects, the sale of human labour is profoundly different from the sale of other goods and services. For example, although someone may legally relinquish all future rights to the use of her TV set by selling it, in societies with legal systems based on the Western model the law no longer permits people formally to sell themselves into slavery or to trade in people in the sense of selling and buying an absolute right of disposal of a person's services. The law does, however, permit employers to 'rent' our services. And in many ways the rental market for labour services functions much like the market for most other goods and services. Each specific category of labour has a *demand curve* and a *supply curve*. These curves intersect to determine both the *equilibrium wage* and the *equilibrium quantity of employment* for each category of labour.

What is more, shifts in the relevant demand and supply curves produce changes analogous to those produced by shifts in the demand and supply curves for other goods and services. For instance, an increase in the demand for a specific category of labour will generally increase both the equilibrium wage and the equilibrium quantity of employment in that category. By the same token, an increase in the supply of labour to a given occupation will tend to increase the level of employment and lower the wage rate in that occupation.

As in our discussions of other markets, our strategy for investigating how the labour market works will be to go through a series of examples that shed light on different parts of the picture. In Economic naturalist 13.1, we focus on how the equilibrium principle can help us to understand how wages will differ among workers with different levels of productive ability.

### Economic naturalist 13.1 If there is no such thing as slavery, how did the media report that Manchester United sold David Beckham to Real Madrid for several millions of pounds sterling?

The answer is that they didn't sell Beckham. Real Madrid had to pay Beckham to come to play for them and pay Manchester United a sum to allow Beckham to terminate his existing contract obligations to United. Labour contracts frequently have a *time dimension* to them and these impose restrictions on one or both sides in terms of freedom to end the relationship. These are the consequences of explicit contract negotiations between the parties and/or legal requirements imposed by labour law. Beckham entered into a contract with Real Madrid to play for them for a period of time in return for a package that included a lump sum and a scale of salary and bonus payments. United, which might well have initiated the process, accepted payment for relinquishing their existing contractual right to retain Beckham as a player, rights that were contained in a previous contract entered into by Beckham. Beckham simply changed employer. No one bought him. But some one did buy out his *contractual obligations*. Football commentators may understand the game . . . but if their use of language reflects their understanding of the economics behind it, they need to take a refresher course.

### Example 13.1 How much will the potters earn?

Go into any garden centre or DIY outlet in Europe and you are likely to find glazed earthenware pots for sale. These are mostly made in China and nearby countries in the Far East. In many cases, the pots are made unglazed and then sold to firms that apply the glazing. It is at this stage that the pots become distinctive. As originally produced, the output of one pottery producer is more or less the same as that of any other producer. It is something close to what we would describe as a perfectly competitive industry. Suppose that Peking Pottery Works (PPW) is one of numerous identical companies in China that hire potters who mould clay into standard pots. These companies sell the pots for 1.20 yuan each to a finishing company that glazes and fires them and then sells them in the retail marketplace. Clay and water, both available free of charge in unlimited quantities, are the only inputs used by the potters. The equipment is owned by the proprietor of PPW, who rents it to the potters for 0.10 yuan per pot to cover his costs and allow him some income for his efforts. Currently only two potters work for PPW, whose only cost other than potters' salaries is a 0.10 yuan handling cost for each pot it delivers to the finisher. Potter Han delivers 100 pots per week and potter Lee delivers 120. If the labour market for potters is perfectly competitive, how much will each be paid?

We begin with the assumption that Han and Lee have decided to work full time as potters, so our focus is not on how much they will work but on how much they will be paid. After taking handling costs and the equipment charge into account, the value of the pots that Han delivers is 100 yuan per week, and that is the amount PPW will pay him. To pay him less would risk having him bid away by a competitor. For example, if PPW paid Han only 90 yuan per week, the company would then enjoy an economic profit of 10 yuan per week as a result of hiring him. Seeing this cash on the table (Chapter 3), a rival firm could then offer Han 91 yuan, thus earning an additional economic profit of 9 yuan per week by bidding him away from PPW. So under the bidding pressure from rival employers, PPW will have difficulty keeping Han if it pays him less than 100 yuan per week. And the company would suffer an economic loss if it pays him more than 100 yuan per week. Similarly, the value of the pots delivered each week by Lee is 120 yuan, and this will be her competitive equilibrium wage.

In Example 13.1, the number of pots each potter delivered each week was that potter's **marginal physical product** (or **marginal product, MP, of labour** for short). More generally, a worker's marginal product is the extra output the firm gets as a result of hiring that worker. When we multiply a worker's marginal product by the net price for which each unit of the product sells, we get that worker's **value of marginal product**, or **VMP of labour**. (In Example 13.1, the 'net price' of each pot was 1.00 yuan – the difference between the 1.20 sale price and the 0.20 handling and equipment charge.) The general rule in competitive labour markets is that a worker's pay in long-run equilibrium will be *equal to her VMP, which is the net contribution she makes to the employer's revenue*. Employers would be delighted to pay workers less than their respective VMPs, but if labour markets are truly competitive they cannot get away with doing so for long.

**marginal product of labour (MP)** the additional output a firm gets by employing one additional unit of labour

**value of marginal product of labour (VMP)** the money value of the additional output a firm gets by employing one additional unit of labour

In Example 13.1, each worker's VMP was independent of the number of other workers employed by the firm. In such cases, we cannot predict how many workers a firm will hire. PPW could break even with two potters, with 10, or even with 1,000 or more. In many other situations, however, we can predict exactly how many workers a firm will hire. Consider Example 13.2.

### Example 13.2 How many workers should the WTK AG hire?

Wilhelm Tell Kunstfabrik AG (WTK), located in Zurich, hires workers in a competitive labour market at a wage of Sfr350 per week to make cuckoo clock cases from scrap wood that is available free of charge. If the cases sell for Sfr20 each and the company's weekly output varies with the number of workers hired, as shown in Table 13.1, how many workers should WTK hire?

| Number of workers (1) | Total number of clock cases/week (2) | MP (extra clock cases/week) (3) | VMP (Sfr/week) (4) |
|---|---|---|---|
| 0 | 0 | | |
| | | 30 | 600 |
| 1 | 30 | | |
| | | 25 | 500 |
| 2 | 55 | | |
| | | 21 | 420 |
| 3 | 76 | | |
| | | 18 | 360 |
| 4 | 94 | | |
| | | 14 | 280 |
| 5 | 108 | | |

**Table 13.1** Employment and Productivity in WTK (when clock cases sell for Sfr20 each)

In Example 13.1 our focus was on wage differences for employees whose productive abilities differed. In contrast, we assume here that all workers are equally productive and the firm faces a fixed market wage for each. The fact that the marginal product of labour declines with the number of workers hired is a consequence of the *law of diminishing returns*. (As discussed in Chapter 6, this law says that when a firm's capital or other productive inputs are held fixed in the short run, adding workers beyond some point results in ever-smaller increases in output.) Column (3) of Table 13.1 reports the marginal product for each additional worker, and column (4) reports the value of each successive worker's marginal product – the number of clock cases he or she adds times the selling price of Sfr20. WTK should keep hiring as long as the next worker's VMP is at least Sfr350 per week (the market wage). The first four workers have VMPs larger than Sfr350, so WTK should hire them. But since hiring the fifth worker would add only Sfr280 to weekly revenue, WTK should not hire that worker.

Note the similarity between the perfectly competitive firm's decision about how many workers to hire and the perfectly competitive firm's output decision we considered in Chapter 6. When labour is the only variable factor of production, the two decisions are essentially the same. Because of the unique correspondence between the firm's total output and the total number of workers it hires, deciding how many workers to hire is the same as deciding *how much output to supply*.

The worker's attractiveness to the employer depends not only on how many clock cases she produces, but also on the price of clock cases and on the wage rate. For example, because VMP rises when product price rises, an increase in product price will lead employers to hire more workers. Employers will also increase hiring when the wage rate falls.

**Exercise 13.1** In Example 13.2, how many workers should WTK hire if the price of clock cases rises to Sfr26?

**Exercise 13.2** How many workers should WTK hire if the wage rate falls to Sfr275 per week?

## RECAP The economic value of work

In competitive labour markets, employers face pressure to pay each worker the value of his or her marginal product. When a firm can hire as many workers as it wishes at a given market wage, it should expand employment as long as the value of *marginal product of labour exceeds the market wage*.

## The equilibrium wage and employment levels

As we saw in Chapter 3, the equilibrium price and quantity in any competitive market occur at the intersection of the relevant supply and demand curves. The same is true in competitive markets for labour.

### The demand for labour

An employer's reservation price for a worker is the most the employer could pay without suffering a decline in profit. As already discussed, this reservation price for the employer in a perfectly competitive labour market is simply VMP, the value of the worker's marginal product. Because of the law of diminishing returns, we know that the marginal product of labour, and hence VMP, declines in the short run as the quantity of labour rises. The individual employer's demand curve for labour in any particular occupation – say, computer programmers – may thus be shown, as in Fig. 13.1(a), as a downward-sloping function of the wage rate. Suppose firm 1 (panel (a)) and firm 2 (panel (b)) are the only two firms that employ programmers in a given community. The demand for programmers in that community will then be the horizontal sum of the individual firm demands (panel (c)).

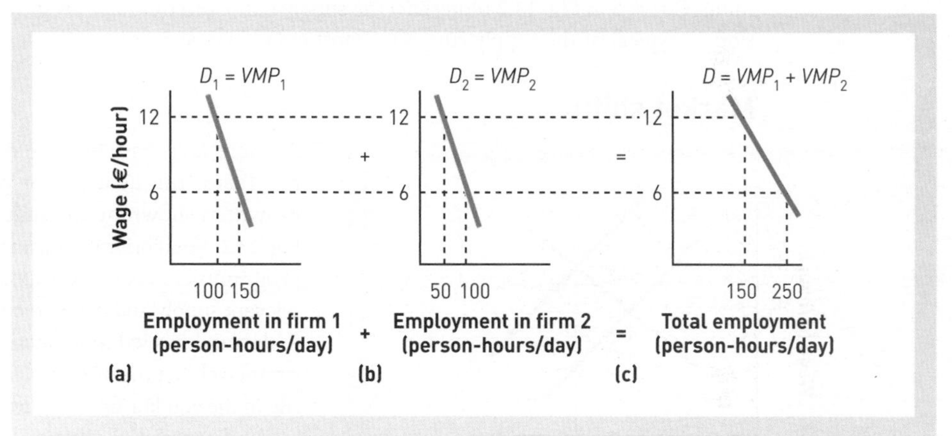


**Figure 13.1 The Occupational Demand for Labour.** If firm 1 and firm 2 are the only firms that employ labour in a given occupation, we generate the demand curve for labour in that occupation by adding the individual demand curves horizontally.

### The supply curve of labour

What does the supply curve of labour for a specific occupation look like? Will more labour be offered at high wage rates than at low wage rates? An equivalent way to pose the same question is to ask whether consumers will wish to consume *less leisure* at high wage rates than at low wage rates. By themselves, the principles of economic theory do not provide an answer to this question, because a change in the wage rate exerts two opposing effects on the quantity of leisure demanded. One is the *substitution* effect, which says that, at a higher wage, leisure is more expensive, leading consumers to consume less of it. The second is the *income* effect, which says that, at a higher wage, consumers have more purchasing power, leading them to consume more leisure. Which of these two opposing effects dominates is an empirical question.

For the economy as a whole during the past several centuries, the working week has been declining and real wages have been rising. This pattern might seem to suggest that the supply curve of labour is downward-sloping, and for the economy as a whole it may be. There is also evidence that individual workers may sometimes work fewer hours when wage rates are high than when they are low. A study of taxicab drivers in New York City, for example, found that drivers quit earlier on rainy days (when the effective wage is high because of high demand for cab rides) than on sunny days (when the effective wage is lower).[1]

The same effect was observed in Dublin after the taxi market was liberalised in 2001. The consequence of liberalisation was that the expected number of fares per hour (and, therefore, the expected hourly income of a representative taxi driver) fell as a result of liberalisation. Previously, with chronic excess demand, taxi drivers could expect their cars to be full any time they chose to take them on to the streets. Now with a big increase in the number of taxis, drivers had to go looking for fares. The reaction of the taxi drivers was to demand restrictions on entry because they were now 'obliged' (i.e. chose) to work more hours as a consequence of the fall in the expected hourly income.

Whether any individual's labour supply curve is upward-sloping depends on income and substitution effects. When we move to groups of workers this can still be the case, provided that they are shielded from competition from new entrants. These observations notwithstanding, with easy entry to an occupation the supply of labour *to any particular occupation* is almost surely upward-sloping, because wage differences among occupations influence occupational choice. It is no accident, for example, that many more people are choosing jobs as computer programmers now than in 1970. Wages of programmers have risen sharply since the 1970s, which has led many people to forsake other career paths in favour of programming. Curve *S* in Fig. 13.2 represents the supply curve of computer programmers. Its positive slope is typical of the supply curves for most individual occupations.

## Market shifts

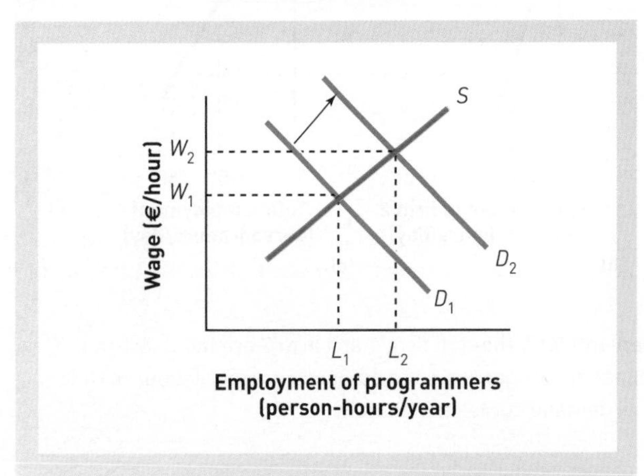


**Figure 13.2 The Effect of an Increase in the Demand for Computer Programmers.** An increase in the demand for programmers from $D_1$ to $D_2$ results in an increase in the equilibrium level of employment (from $L_1$ to $L_2$) and an increase in the equilibrium wage (from $W_1$ to $W_2$).

As more tasks have become computerised since the 1980s, the demand for programmers has grown, as shown by the shift from $D_1$ to $D_2$ in Fig. 13.2. Equilibrium in the market for computer programmers occurs at the intersection of the relevant supply and demand curves. The increase in demand has led to an increase in the equilibrium level of programmers from $L_1$ to $L_2$ and a rise in the equilibrium wage from $W_1$ to $W_2$.

As discussed in Chapter 8, the market for stocks and other financial assets reaches equilibrium very quickly in the wake of shifts in the underlying supply and demand curves. Labour markets, by contrast, are often much slower to adjust. When the demand for workers in a given profession increases, shortages may remain for months, or even years, depending on how long it takes people to acquire the skills and training needed to enter the profession.

## RECAP Equilibrium in the labour market

The demand for labour in a perfectly competitive labour market is the horizontal sum of each employer's VMP curve. The supply curve of labour for an individual labour market is upward-sloping, even though the supply curve of labour for the economy as a whole may be vertical or even downward-sloping. In each labour market, the demand and supply curves intersect to determine the *equilibrium wage and level of employment.*

[1] Babcock, Camerer, Loewenstein and Thaler (1997).

## Explaining differences in earnings

The theory of competitive labour markets tells us that differences in pay reflect differences in the corresponding VMPs. Thus, in Example 13.1, Lee earned 20 per cent more than Han because she made 20 per cent more pots each week than he did. That begs the obvious question: why was Lee able to (and/or chose to) produce more pots than Han? Note that if it simply represented a decision by Han to work less hard there is nothing that really needs explaining: he took more tea breaks, and took some of his real income that way. However, if this is not the case we need to explain why Lee was more productive than Han in order to explain the difference in their incomes. It could simply be talent: Lee is naturally more dexterous than Han. Or it could be that Lee has been working at the job longer than Han and has improved skill levels arising from this experience. Or it could be that Lee took a course in pot throwing at the local technological institute, and Han did not.

We often see (or think we see) large salary differences even among people who appear equally talented and hard-working. Why, for example, do some lawyers earn so much more than those plumbers who are just as smart as they are and work just as hard? And why do surgeons usually earn so much more than general practitioners? These wage differences might seem to violate the no-cash-on-the-table principle, which says that only differences in talent, luck or hard work can account for long-run differences in earnings. For example, if plumbers could earn more by becoming lawyers, why don't they just switch occupations? Similarly, if general practitioners could boost their incomes by becoming surgeons, why didn't they become surgeons in the first place?

### The human capital explanation

Answers to these questions are suggested by **human capital theory**, which holds that an individual's VMP is proportional to his or her stock of **human capital** – an amalgam of factors such as education, experience, training, intelligence, energy, work habits, trustworthiness and initiative. According to this theory, some occupations pay better than others because they require larger stocks of human capital. For example, a general practitioner could become a surgeon, but only by undertaking formal training for several more years. An even larger investment in additional education is required for a plumber to become a lawyer.

**human capital theory** a theory of pay detemination that says a worker's wage will be proportional to his or her stock of human capital

**human capital** an amalgam of factors such as education, training, experience, intelligence, energy, work habits, trustworthiness and initiative that affect the value of a worker's marginal product

There are two angles to this account of differences in earnings. On the one hand, other things being equal, the more human capital you possess the higher will be your earnings, because human capital increases your VMP. On the other hand, because human capital is in most cases costly to acquire (money costs of training, time and opportunity costs of earnings forgone) it is relatively scarce and commands a high price. Put another way, the payment received by owners of human capital is the *supply price* of that capital, the social benefit of which is increased labour productivity – and, therefore, income per head – in society as a whole.

Differences in demand can result in some kinds of human capital being more valuable than others. Consider two occupations: tax accountants and computer programmers. Both occupations require demanding technical training. Since the 1970s there has been a steady increase in the demand for skilled programmers in virtually all advanced Western economies. During that period, the demand for the services of US tax accountants has fallen as more and more American tax-payers have used tax-preparation software in lieu of hiring accountants to help them with their taxes. This is less evident in Europe, where online tax returns are a fairly recent development, and where the combination of complex tax codes and high marginal tax rates have supported the use of tax accountants and equivalent professionals in dealing with the tax authorities. In the United States, incomes of computer programmers have risen relative to the incomes of people employed as tax accountants because the training of programmers (the human capital of programmers) now yields a higher return in the labour market.

## Trade unions

Two workers with the same amount of human capital may earn different wages if one of them belongs to a **labour union** and the other does not. A labour (or trade) union is an organisation through which workers attempt to bargain collectively with employers for better wages and working conditions.

**labour union** a group of workers who bargain collectively with employers for better wages and working conditions

The impact of trades unions in labour markets is something about which there is considerable controversy in economics, a controversy which is reflected in a wider political and social debate about the role of unions and the protection they receive in law from the legal redress sought by those hurt by their actions. At one end of the spectrum there are many, including economists, who believe that unions can have the effect of ensuring levels of real income and working conditions to employees as a whole in excess of those that would be provided in a labour market without unions. Obviously, this view is widely held by members of trades unions and their professional advisers. At the other end are economists who believe that whatever value unions may have had in the early twentieth century in protecting disorganised workers from exploitation by capitalists enjoying market power in the labour market has largely disappeared. Instead, they regard unions as affecting labour markets in much the same way that cartels affect product markets. To illustrate, consider a simple economy with two labour markets, neither of which is unionised initially. Suppose the total supply of labour to the two markets is fixed at $S_0 = 200$ workers per day, and that the demand curves are as shown by $VMP_1$ and $VMP_2$ in Fig. 13.3(a) and (b). The sum of the two demand curves, $VMP_1 + VMP_2$ (panel (c)), intersects the supply curve to determine an equilibrium wage of €9 per hour. At that wage, firms in market 1 hire 125 workers per day (panel (a)), and firms in market 2 hire 75 (panel (b)).

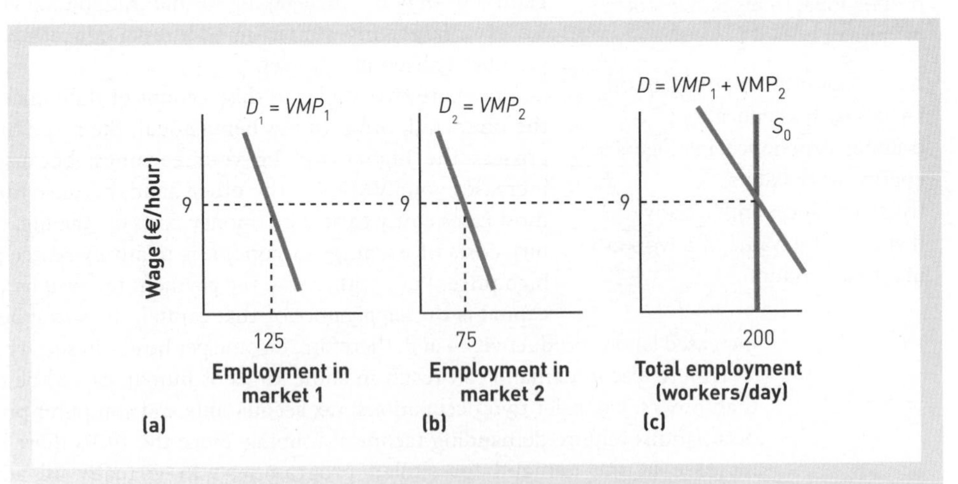


**Figure 13.3 An Economy with Two Non-unionised Labour Markets.** Supply and demand intersect to determine a market wage of €9 per hour (c). At that wage, employers in market 1 hire 125 workers per day and employers in market 2 hire 75 workers per day. The VMP is €9 in each market.

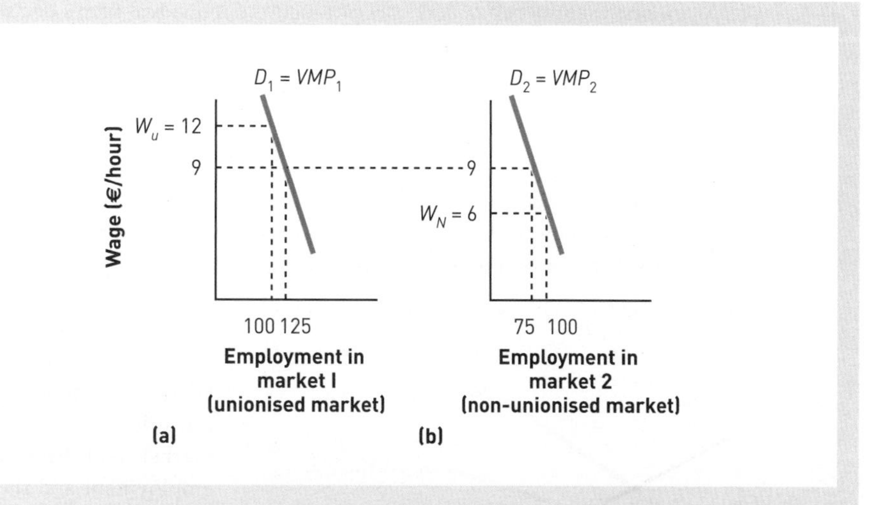


**Figure 13.4 The Effect of a Union Wage Above the Equilibrium Wage.** When the unionised wage is pegged at $W_u$ = €12/hour (a), 25 workers are discharged. When these workers seek employment in the non-unionised market, the wage in that market falls to $W_N$ = €6/hour (b).

Now suppose that workers in market 1 form a union and refuse to work for less than €12 per hour. Because demand curves for labour are downward-sloping, employers of unionised workers reduce employment from 125 workers per day to 100 (Fig. 13.4(a)). The 25 displaced workers in the unionised market would of course be delighted to find other jobs in that market at €12 per hour. But they cannot, and so they are forced to seek employment in the non-unionised market. The result is an excess supply of 25 workers in the non-union market at the original wage of €9 per hour. In time, wages in that market decline to $W_N$ = €6 per hour, the level at which 100 workers can find jobs in the non-unionised market (Fig. 13.4(b)).

It might seem that the gains of the unionised workers are exactly offset by the losses of non-unionised workers. On closer inspection, however, we see that pegging the union wage above the equilibrium level actually *reduces* the value of total output. If labour were allocated efficiently between the two markets, its value of marginal product would have to be the same in each. Otherwise, the total value of output could be increased by moving workers from the low-VMP market to the high-VMP market. With the wage set initially at €9 per hour in both markets, the condition for efficient allocation was met, because labour's VMP was €9 per hour in both markets. But because the collective bargaining process drives wages (and hence VMPs) in the two markets apart, the value of total output is no longer maximised. To verify this claim, note that if a worker is taken out of the non-unionised market, the reduction in the value of output there will be only €6 per hour, which is less than the €12 per hour gain in the value of output when that same worker is added to the unionised market.

**Exercise 13.3** In Fig. 13.4, how much would the total value of output be increased if the wage rate were €9 per hour in each market?

However, the above analysis implicitly assumes that competitive conditions apply in labour markets in the absence of unions. If this assumption is dropped, and it is assumed instead that potential employers are few in number, then the position changes. In a competitive market employers are *price takers*: any one firm's employment decision has no appreciable impact on wage rates. If they are few in number, employers have market power analogous to a small number of sellers of a product: the individual firm's decisions affects prices. 'Market power' here does not mean harsh, Dickensian employers using their position to grind workers into poverty (although that may indeed be the case). It simply means not being price takers. This results in lower wages, lower employment and lower production than if the labour market were competitive. If this is indeed the case, the argument that unions distort resource allocation and worsen the incomes of those outside the unions has to be reassessed.

To illustrate this, consider Fig. 13.5 (panels (a) and (b)). This looks at the position of a single employer of labour in a relevant labour market. The employer is a local 'monopsonist', or sole buyer of a product (labour) being offered by a large number of competing workers.

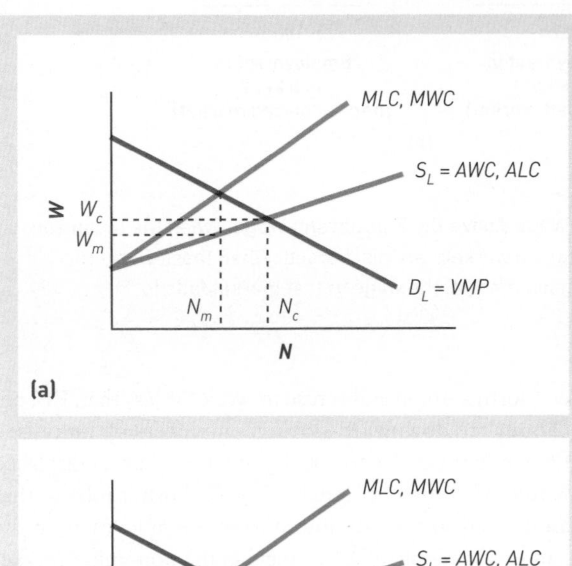


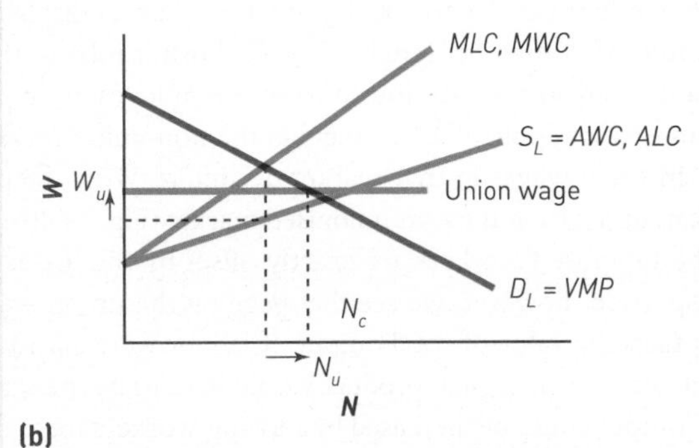


**Figure 13.5 How a Union Can Increase Employment when the Employer has Market Power.**

The employer's demand curve for labour (the *VMP* curve) is, as usual, downward-sloping. He faces an upward-sloping supply curve of labour. The more labour he demands the higher the price (wages) he will have to pay. If the market had been competitive the level of employment and the level of wages would be determined by the intersection of the supply curve and the demand curve ($W_c$ and $N_c$) (panel (a)). But, if the market is monopsonistic, and the employer wishes to maximise profits this will not happen. Why?

The supply curve of labour represents the *average cost of labour to the employer* (because total labour cost is simply the rectangle formed by the level of employment and the corresponding point on the labour supply curve). For this reason, it is also labelled *ALC*. Note that this is increasing as the employer purchases more labour (because he is not a price taker in the labour market). To maximise profits the employer will hire that quantity of labour for which the *marginal* cost of labour, not the average cost of labour, equals the value marginal product. Since *AWC* is upward-sloping, the marginal cost of labour must lie above it: the *MLC* line. That intersects the *VMP* curve to the left of the hypothetical competitive level of employment. The monopsonistic employer will purchase less labour than in the case of a competitive market, $N_m$. Nor is that the end of the matter: if he seeks only that amount of labour, the market-clearing wage rate is $W_m$, from the labour supply curve (*ALC*). He not only purchases less labour, but will pay a lower wage than if the market were competitive.

Now suppose a union appears and organises the workers. It then confronts the employer with a demand for $W_u > W_m$, and enters into a contract with the employer (formal or informal) to the effect that provided he pays $W_u$ he may hire as much or as little labour as he likes. If this is conceded (and the alternative is a strike), the employer now faces a fixed *ALC* curve (and when an average is constant, the marginal equals the average). Hence his *MLC* is now a horizontal line from $W_u$, and, to maximise profits he will purchase the quantity of labour for which *MLC* = *VMP*. The consequence of the arrival of the union is higher wages and higher employment. Total surplus in the economy is increased because, other things being equal, more labour hired means more goods being produced and lower product prices.

There is, therefore, a respectable case for arguing for exactly the opposite conclusions as to the consequences of unionisation. Is this just another example of two-handed economics resulting in no conclusions? On balance, we think not. Although the second approach is useful in explaining some aspects of the labour market (for example, the role of unions in the public sector in mixed economies, where the employer is protected from competition and is the only employer), the assumption of weak competition among employers (market power) is less plausible than it seems once a longer-term view of labour markets in modern circumstances is adopted. In these circumstances, an assumption that markets are more rather than less competitive is in most circumstances more plausible. This reflects the observation that (especially given sufficient time) markets for final goods and markets for labour are subject to relatively free entry and exit.

Ease of entry into the final goods market reduces the market power of incumbent firms as purchasers of labour: they are likely to find themselves competing for labour more intensively and having to pay 'the going rate'. The monopsonistic market model has an implicit assumption that the employer is the only person to whom the workers can in effect sell their labour. But if workers are mobile as between jobs and as between locations, this is hard to sustain: mobility forces employers to compete. And if they have to compete then they cannot exploit market power to pay wages that are below competitive levels, which, of course, reduces the incentive to join a union in the first place. In fact, the evidence of declining union membership across the developed world is the strongest argument for the competitive model's basic plausibility in the context of a modern capitalist economy.

Wages paid to workers in a unionised firm are sometimes 50 per cent or more above the wages paid to their non-unionised counterparts. To the alert Economic naturalist, this difference prompts a question.

## Economic naturalist 13.2 If unionised firms have to pay more, how do they manage to survive in the face of competition from their non-unionised counterparts?

In fact, non-unionised firms sometimes do drive unionised firms out of business. To a considerable degree, the problems of the national flag carrier airlines in Europe reflect the erosion of their markets by the 'no-frills' low-cost airlines epitomised by Ryanair. The latter are in general non-unionised, while the flag carriers are heavily unionised. The flight of the British newspapers from Fleet Street in central London to out-of-town sites such as Wapping in the 1980s was in large measure a flight from unionised to non-unionised production processes in order to survive. Even so, unionised and non-unionised firms often manage to compete head-to-head for extended periods. If their costs are significantly higher, how do the unionised firms manage to survive?

The observed pay differential actually overstates the difference between the labour costs of the two types of firm. Because the higher union wage attracts an excess supply of workers, unionised employers can adopt more stringent hiring requirements than their non-unionised counterparts. As a result, unionised workers tend to be more experienced and skilled than non-unionised workers. Studies estimate that the union wage premium for US workers with the same amount of human capital is only about 10 per cent.

Another factor is that unions may actually boost the productivity of workers with any given amount of human capital, perhaps by improving communication between management and workers. Similarly, the implementation of formal grievance procedures, in combination with higher pay, may boost morale among unionised workers, leading to higher productivity. Labour turnover is also significantly lower in unionised firms, which reduces hiring and training costs. Studies suggest that union productivity may be sufficiently high to compensate for the premium in union wages. So even though wages are higher in unionised firms, these firms may not have significantly higher labour costs per unit of output than their non-unionised counterparts.

Unionisation is a more plausible explanation of wage differentials in Europe than in the United States. In the United States, unionisation now involves about 14 per cent of the workforce (down from 20 per cent in the early 1980s and 35 per cent in 1954). Furthermore, while the average is around 14 per cent, when public sector employment is ignored, the average falls to 10 per cent (about 40 per cent of US public sector employees are in a union). Because the union wage premium is small and applies to only a small fraction of the labour force, US union membership is probably not an important explanation for why workers with similar qualifications often earn sharply different incomes.

In Western Europe the average is higher although, in most countries, falling. In the EU15 in 2001, unionisation was about 30 per cent (measured as 'union density', the percentage of the workforce belonging to a union). Within this average there was enormous variation: at one end, Sweden's union density was close to 90 per cent, while Spain's was 15 per cent. Germany, France, Italy, the United Kingdom and the Netherlands were all within about 5 per cent of the average (not surprising, since they account for most of the EU15's employment). The pattern in Europe resembles that in the United States to this extent: in general, union density is much higher in the public sector ... and, of course, the public sector is a larger element in the economies of Western Europe than in those of North America. In the United Kingdom, 60 per cent of public sector employees are in unions, and over 70 per cent of public sector 'professionals' (educators, scientists, accountants and so on) are in a union. Only 20 per cent of private sector employees are in a union, and this percentage is falling steadily.

The wage and work condition differentials that unionisation helps to explain in some European countries are those between public sector employees and those in the private sector. Not only is employment in the public sector less volatile, but pension entitlements are notoriously much greater, and in many sectors the relative wages of public sector workers have risen as a consequence of the exercise of union power in parts of the economy that are sheltered from competition. However, under EU liberalisation programmes, this is likely to be a diminishing influence on relative wages as between public and private sector employees.

The impact of unions on wage developments is also likely to be reduced by increased globalisation, especially reflecting the growing importance of foreign direct investment (FDI) in Europe. One reason for the decline in unionisation is the increasing resistance of new employers to union recognition. The Irish experience points this out dramatically. Ireland has received a proportionately much greater share of non-EU FDI into the Union since the 1980s than any other EU15 country. The largest component of this *inward investment* came from US companies. But, while 80 per cent of FDI set-ups from other EU countries in Ireland between 1987 and 1997 involved union recognition (and 20 per cent did not), in the case of US-sourced FDI in Ireland the percentages were 90 per cent non-recognition and 10 per cent recognition.[2]

## Compensating wage differentials

If people are paid the value of what they produce, why do panel beaters in a car repair shop earn more than lifeguards on a crowded summer beach? Repairing cars is obviously important, but is it more valuable than saving the life of a drowning child? If your central heating unit

[2] Gunnigle and O'Sullivan (2003).

breaks down and you call out a repair service, the hourly rate at which the repair technician is paid is likely to be higher than the hourly rate for an intensive care unit staff nurse. Is cleaning a burner more important than monitoring a critically ill post-operative accident victim? In each case, you will almost certainly answer no. However, the amount paid to someone is not simply a matter of the value of what that person does, but, as Example 13.3 illustrates, the wage for a particular job depends not only on the value of what workers produce in that job, but also on how attractive they find the *working conditions* associated with the job.

### Example 13.3 Why do some public relations (PR) personnel earn more than others?

You are about to graduate and plan to pursue a career in PR and have two job offers. One is in a firm that specialises in dealing with the problems of organisations such as Oxfam and Médecins Sans Frontières. The other represents the interests of Imperial Tobacco, British American Tobacco and a couple of the oil majors. Except for the subject matter, working conditions are identical in the two jobs. If each job paid €30,000 per year and offered the same prospects for advancement, which would you choose? When a similar question was recently posed to a sample of final-year undergraduate students at the US Cornell University, almost 90 per cent of them chose the first type of job. When asked how much more they would have to be paid to induce them to switch to the second type of job, their median response was a premium of €15,000 per year. (The offer was in dollars, since they were American students.) At any given salary, most preferred the first type of job, and would take an implicit wage cut to retain it. As Example 13.3 suggests, employers who offer jobs with less attractive working conditions cannot hope to fill them unless they also offer higher salaries.

Other things being equal, jobs with attractive working conditions will pay less than jobs with less attractive conditions. Wage differences associated with differences in working conditions are known as **compensating wage differentials**. Economists have identified compensating differentials for a host of different specific working conditions. Studies have found, for example, that safe jobs tend to pay less than otherwise similar jobs that entail greater risks to health and safety. Studies have also found that wages vary in accord with the attractiveness of the work schedule. For instance, working night shifts commands a wage premium, and teachers must accept lower wages in part because many of those with children value having hours that coincide with the school calendar.

**compensating wage differential** a difference in the wage rate – negative or positive – that reflects the attractiveness of a job's working conditions

## Discrimination in the labour market

Women and minorities continue to receive lower wage rates, on average, than white males with similar measures of human capital. This pattern poses a profound challenge to standard theories of competitive labour markets, which hold that competitive pressures will eliminate wage differentials not based on differences in productivity. Defenders of standard theories attribute the wage gap to unmeasured differences in human capital, and/or to preferences on the parts of different categories of workers, and/or to differences in non-wage costs of employment across different groups of workers. Many critics of these theories reject the idea that labour markets are effectively competitive, and instead attribute the gap to various forms of *discrimination*.

## Discrimination by employers

**employer discrimination** an arbitrary preference by an employer for one group of workers over another

**Employer discrimination** is the term used to describe wage differentials that arise from an arbitrary preference by an employer for one group of workers over another. An example occurs if two labour force groups, such as males and females, are equally productive, on average, yet some employers (discriminators) prefer hiring males and are willing to pay higher wages to do so. While much of the controversy and analysis has focused on earnings, similar considerations apply to career prospects and promotions, summed up in the case of gender differentials in the concept of the 'glass ceiling', the invisible barrier that is claimed to affect the ability of women to secure career advancement on the same basis as men.

Most consumers are not willing to pay more for a product produced by males than for an identical one produced by females (if indeed they even *know* which type of worker produced the product). If product price is unaffected by the composition of the workforce that produces the product, and if men are paid more than women for comparable work, a firm's profit will be smaller the more males it employs, because males cost more yet are no more productive (on the assumption that discrimination is the cause of the wage gap). Thus the most profitable firms will be ones that employ only females.

Arbitrary wage gaps are an apparent violation of the No-Cash-on-the-Table Principle (Chapter 3). The initial wage differential provides an opportunity for employers who hire mostly females to grow at the expense of their rivals. Because such firms make an economic profit on the sale of each unit of output, their incentive is to expand as rapidly as they possibly can. And to do that, they would naturally want to continue hiring only the cheaper females. But as profit-seeking firms continue to pursue this strategy, the supply of females at the lower wage rate will run out. The short-run solution is to offer females a slightly higher wage. But this strategy works only if other firms do not pursue it. Once they, too, start offering a higher wage, females will again be in short supply. The only stable outcome occurs when the wage of females reaches parity with the wage of males. The wage for both males and females will thus settle at the common value of their VMP.

Another way of looking at this is to consider the circumstances under which discrimination is feasible, even if not profit-maximising. Suppose a firm discriminates by paying, say, fair-haired workers more than dark-haired workers (or, equivalently, hiring less productive fair-haired rather than more productive dark-haired at a common wage). In doing so the employer must, by definition, increase his unit costs. If he faces competition in the market into which he is selling the product of the firm he will be undercut by firms that do not discriminate on hair-colour grounds. Eventually he must cease discrimination or go out of business. Discrimination increases his costs; he forgoes profits in order to discriminate. This is feasible only as long as there are potential profits to be absorbed by the costs of discrimination. Competition from other firms eliminates that source of funds to finance discrimination.

Any employer who wants to voice a preference for hiring males must now do so by paying males a wage in excess of the VMP. Employers can discriminate against females if they wish, but only if they are willing to pay premium wages to males out of their own profits. Not even the harshest critics of the competitive model seem willing to impute such behaviour to the owners of capitalist enterprises ... unless, of course, the owners are protected from the consequences of their actions either by government or by the absence of competitive pressure.

## Discrimination by others

**customer discrimination** the willingness of consumers to pay more for a product produced by members of a favoured group, even if the quality of the product is unaffected

If employer discrimination is not the primary explanation of the wage gap in competitive markets, what is? In some instances, **customer discrimination** may provide a plausible explanation. For example, if people believe that juries and clients are less likely to take female or minority ethnic group lawyers seriously, members of these groups will face a reduced incentive to attend law school, and law firms will face a reduced incentive to hire those who do. Fanciful? Consider Economic naturalist 13.3.

### Economic naturalist 13.3 Why are Irish barristers permitted to continue to wear wigs, and English barristers permitted to achieve the status of Queen's Counsel?

In the ceaseless pursuit of modernisation, the Irish government proposed in 1996 to prohibit by legislation the wearing of wigs by barristers in court (an inheritance of the British courts tradition in which barristers appearing in court wear gowns, white collar tabs – a token, according to some, of mourning for Queen Anne, who died in 1714 – dark clothes and horsehair wigs based on those worn by males in the late eighteenth century – think of Kavanagh QC!). A few months later, the government retreated to making the wearing of wigs a matter of choice (up to then it had been a requirement under court rules), and wigs continue to be worn by most barristers. In 2003, the Lord Chancellor of England, who is a member of the cabinet (and who, incidentally, also in pursuit of modernisation, was at the same time proposing the abolition of his own 1,400-year-old office) announced that he intended to abolish the status of Queen's (King's) Counsel (QC or KC), a mark of achievement and expertise among advocacy lawyers dating from the sixteenth century. A year later the Lord Chancellor dropped the proposal (and subsequently announced that he was also dropping the proposal for his own abolition).

Traditionalists and economists who argued that (a) tradition was important, and (b) in neither case could the traditional practice convincingly be shown to damage end user interests (by raising costs or reducing quality of service by lawyers) made little headway against the modernisers. Then, in the Irish case, women barristers let it be known that they favoured wigs because it put them on a level playing field with their male colleagues. Without wigs, clients would not take them as seriously as they would male lawyers. In England, lawyers from minority racial groups made the same case for QC status. Acquiring QC status was a means of advancing the position of minority advocates and showing that they could deliver a superior service to clients. In both countries, the government immediately changed its mind.

## Parental discrimination

Another possible source of persistent wage gaps is discrimination and socialisation within the family. For example, families may provide less education for their female children, or they may socialise them to believe that lofty career ambitions are not appropriate.

## Other sources of the wage gap

Part of the wage gap may be explained by compensating wage differentials that spring from differences in preferences for other non-wage elements of the compensation package. Jobs that involve exposure to physical risk, for example, command higher wages, and if men are relatively more willing to accept such risks they will earn more than females with otherwise identical stocks of human capital. (The same difference would result if employers felt constrained by social norms not to assign female employees to risky jobs.)

Elements of human capital that are difficult to measure may also help to explain earnings differentials. For example, productivity is influenced not only by the quantity of education an individual has, which is easy to measure, but also by its *quality*, which is much harder to measure. Part of the observed aggregate black–white differential in US wages may thus be due to the fact that schools in black neighbourhoods have not been as good, on average, as those in white neighbourhoods.

Differences in the courses people take at university or other tertiary-level institutions appear to have similar implications for differences in productivity. For instance, students in maths, engineering or business – both male and female – tend to earn significantly higher salaries than those who study the humanities and do not acquire other professional training after graduating. The fact that males are disproportionately represented in the former group gives rise to a male wage premium that is unrelated to employer discrimination.

As economists have grown more sophisticated in their efforts to measure human capital and other factors that influence individual wage rates, unexplained wage differentials by sex and race have grown steadily smaller, and have even disappeared altogether in some studies.[3] Some work, however, continues to find significant unexplained differentials by race and sex. Debate about discrimination in the workplace will continue until the causes of these differentials are more fully understood.

## Winner-take-all markets

Differences in human capital do much to explain observed differences in earnings. Yet earnings differentials have also grown sharply in many occupations within which the distribution of human capital among workers seems essentially unchanged. Consider Economic naturalist 13.4.

### Economic naturalist 13.4 Why do Renée Fleming and Angela Gheorghiu earn millions more than sopranos of only slightly lesser ability?

Although the best sopranos have always earned more than others with slightly lesser talents, the earnings gap is sharply larger now than it was in the nineteenth century. Today, top singers such as Fleming and Gheorghiu earn millions of euros per year – hundreds or even thousands of times what sopranos only marginally less talented earn. Given that listeners in 'blind hearings' often have difficulty identifying the most highly paid singers, why is this earnings differential so large?

The answer lies in a fundamental change in the way in which we consume most of our music. That change is the consequence of the technology of recording. As late as the early 1950s, recordings were more or less confined to 78 rpm graphite discs. Then came vinyl LPs, and in the mid-1980s digital recording on CD. These developments made it possible to hear music at least as well as at a live performance and more cheaply and on demand. But before recording, in the nineteenth century, to hear a professional singer it was necessary to attend a live performance, usually in a concert hall. In any one day, therefore a singer could perform for at most a thousand people. Today a singer can perform instantaneously and simultaneously for hundreds of millions.

Nineteenth-century audiences would have been delighted to listen to the world's best soprano, but no one singer could hope to perform in more than a tiny fraction of the world's concert halls, of which there were a great number (remember the story of the building of an opera house in Manaus in the middle of the Matto Grosso!). As a result, given the demand for good singing, it could be met only by a large number of good singers. Given the total willingness to pay for singing, it would be divided over a large number of singers. Given that the differences

[3] Polackek and Kim (1994).

between the best and the next-best was not large, we would expect the differences in earnings of singers to be limited to what could be extracted from a limited number of live performances. Being better would yield a higher income, but the spread of incomes would be limited. People would still pay to listen to other singers.

Today, in contrast, most of the music we hear comes in recorded form, which enables the best soprano to be literally everywhere at once. As soon as the master recording has been made, Renée Fleming's performance can be burned on to compact discs at the same low cost as for a slightly less talented singer's. Tens of millions of buyers worldwide are willing to pay a few cents extra to hear the most talented performers. This means that the demand for the singing of less talented performers is sharply reduced. Recording companies would be delighted to hire the best singers at modest salaries, for by so doing they would earn an enormous economic profit. But that would unleash bidding by rival recording companies for the best singers. Such bidding ensures that the top singers will earn multimillion-euro annual salaries (most of which constitute economic rents, as discussed in Chapter 8). Slightly less talented singers earn much less, because the recording industry simply does not need them.

The market for sopranos is an example of a **winner-take-all labour market**, one in which small differences in ability or other dimensions of human capital translate into large differences in pay. Such markets have long been familiar in entertainment and professional sports. But as technology has enabled the most talented individuals to serve broader markets, the winner-take-all reward structure has become an increasingly important feature of modern economic life, permeating such diverse fields as law, journalism, consulting, medicine, investment banking, corporate management, publishing, design, fashion and even the hallowed halls of academe.

**winner-take-all labour market** one in which small differences in human capital translate into large differences in pay

Contrary to what the name seems to imply, a winner-take-all market does not mean a market with literally only one winner. Indeed, hundreds of professional musicians earn multimillion-euro annual salaries. Yet tens of thousands of others, many of them nearly as good, struggle to pay their bills.

The fact that small differences in human capital often give rise to extremely large differences in pay might seem to contradict human capital theory. Note, however, that the winner-take-all reward pattern is completely consistent with the competitive labour market theory's claim that individuals are paid in accordance with the contributions they make to the *employer's net revenue*. The leverage of technology often amplifies small performance differentials into very large ones.

## RECAP Explaining differences in earnings among people

Earnings differ among people in part because of differences in their *human capital*, an amalgam of personal characteristics that affects productivity. But pay often differs substantially between two people with the same amount of human capital. This can happen for many reasons: one person may belong to a labour union while the other does not; one may work in a job with less pleasant conditions; one may be the victim of discrimination; or one may work in an arena in which technology or other factors provide greater leverage to human capital.

## Trends in inequality

It is widely believed that since the mid-1970s *inequality of outcome* (in terms of the incomes households enjoy) has increased in most advanced world economies. In most market economies most citizens receive most of their income from the sale of their own labour. An attractive feature of the free-market system is that it rewards initiative, effort and risk taking: the harder, longer and more effectively a person works, the more he or she will be paid.

Yet relying on the marketplace to distribute income also entails an important drawback: those who do well often end up with vastly more money than they can spend, while those who fail often cannot afford even basic goods and services. Hundreds of thousands of American families are homeless, and still larger numbers go to bed hungry each night. Many distinguished philosophers have argued that such poverty in the midst of plenty is impossible to justify on moral grounds. It is thus troubling that income inequality has been growing rapidly since the 1970s. The data in Table 13.2 offer an indication of the extent of this problem in the US context.

| Quintile (per cent) | 1980 | 1990 | 2000 |
|---|---|---|---|
| Bottom 20 | 12,756 | 12,625 | 14,232 |
| Second 20 | 27,769 | 29,448 | 32,268 |
| Middle 20 | 41,950 | 45,352 | 50,925 |
| Fourth 20 | 58,200 | 65,222 | 74,918 |
| Top 20 | 97,991 | 121,212 | 155,527 |
| Top 5 | 139,302 | 190,187 | 272,349 |

**Table 13.2** Mean Income Received by Families in Each Income Quintile and by the Top 5 Per Cent of Families, 1980–2000 (2000 dollars)

The period from the end of the Second World War until the early 1970s was one of balanced income growth in the United States. During that period, incomes grew at almost 3 per cent a year for rich, middle-class and poor Americans alike. In the ensuing years, however, the pattern of income growth has been dramatically different.

In the first row of Table 13.2, for example, notice that families in the bottom 20 per cent of the income distribution saw their real incomes grow by less than 12 per cent from 1980 to 2000 (a growth rate of less than one-half of 1 per cent per year).

The third row of Table 13.2 indicates that the real incomes of families in the middle quintile grew by less than 22 per cent during the same 20-year period (a growth rate of less than 1 per cent per year). In contrast, real incomes jumped more than 58 per cent for families in the top quintile

Between 1980 and 2000, incomes for families in the top 5 per cent jumped by more than 95 per cent. Even for these families, however, income growth rates were low relative to those of the immediate post-Second World War decades.

The only people whose incomes have grown substantially faster than in that earlier period are those at the very pinnacle of the income ladder. Real earnings of the top 1 per cent of US earners, for example, have more than doubled since 1980, and those even higher up have taken home paycheques that might have seemed unimaginable in 1980.

It is important to emphasise that being near the bottom of the income distribution in one year does not necessarily mean being stranded there for ever. Many chief executive officers (CEOs) now earning multimillion-dollar paycheques, for example, were struggling young graduate students in 1980, and were classified in the bottom 20 per cent of the income distribution for that year. We must bear in mind, too, that not all economic mobility is *upward*. Many US blue-collar workers, for instance, had higher real incomes in 1980 than they do today.

## Measuring the distribution of income or wealth

Is the US situation different from, and if so by how much, than in other countries – Sweden or the United Kindom, for example? By how much has this position changed over, say, a twenty-year period? Has income distribution in, say, Britain, changed in the same way as that in the United States? How have any measures adopted to alter the distribution affected their target? To be in a position to answer questions like these we must have an *agreed and objective measure of income distribution*. It must also be *cardinal* rather than simply ordinal. There are in fact several such measures available, but the one that is most widely used and easiest to both understand and compute is what is known as the **Gini coefficient**. It does not, note, 'explain' the level or change in any distribution; it does not evaluate distributions (that in country *X* is worse or better than that in country *Y*); it merely provides a basis for *comparing distributions* on an objective numerical basis.

**Gini coefficient** a measure of equality of distribution that compares the actual distribution with a benchmark of absolute equality

The measure was developed by the great Italian statistician, Corrado Gini (1884–1965), in a monograph published in 1912.[4] It measures the degree to which an observed distribution differs from a hypothetical perfectly equal distribution. It is demonstrated in graph form in Fig. 13.6.

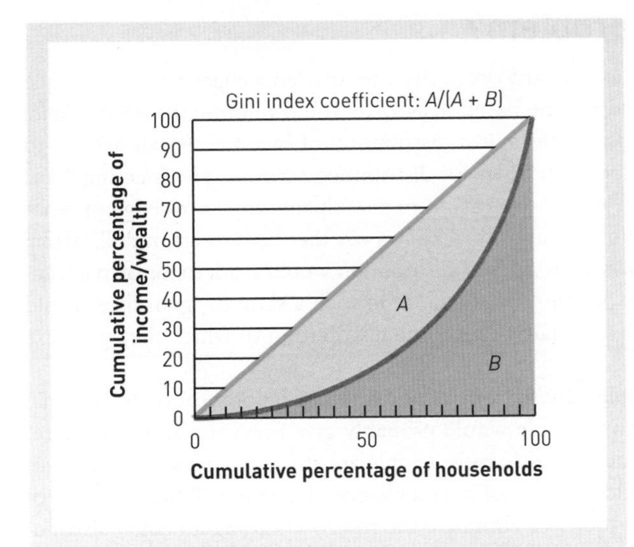


**Figure 13.6 Gini Index: a Measure of Distribution.**

On the vertical axis is given the percentiles of the magnitude being measured, in this case, income, from 0 to 100 per cent. On the horizontal axis is given percentiles of the population over which the distribution is being measured. If the income of the population was perfectly equally distributed, then any 1 per cent of the population would earn 1 per cent of total population income, and any 10 per cent or 20 per cent would earn 10 per cent or 20 per cent of the total. Starting, then, with an arbitrary 1 per cent of the population, then 2 per cent, then 3 per cent and so on, and graphing the percentage of the total income they account for, we would get the 45° straight line in Fig. 13.6. Then, taking the actual distribution, we start with the poorest 1 per cent or 5 per cent on the horizontal axis and plot their share of total income, then that of the bottom 2 per cent (or 5 per cent, depending on the statistics available) and continue until we have accounted for the entire population. The graph we get is called the **Lorenz curve**.[5]

**Lorenz curve** the graph of the cumulative distribution of income or wealth by percentages of households or individuals from poorest to richest

The Gini coefficient is the ratio of the area between the Lorenz curve (*A*) to the total area under the 45° line (*A* + *B*). It has a value somewhere between 0 (everyone has the same income, perfect equality) and 1 (one person has all the income, perfect inequality). The higher the value, the less equal is the distribution.

Table 13.3 contains data on Gini coefficients for a number of OECD countries in 2004. The results are not all that surprising: the Scandinavian economies, with highly developed 'cradle-to-grave' welfare systems financed out of high taxation have more equal distributions

[4] Gini (1912).

[5] Max Otto Lorenz (1880–1962) was an American economist. He developed the concept to describe income inequalities in a paper published in 1905 (Lorenz 1905).

| | |
|---|---|
| Japan | 0.249 |
| Sweden | 0.250 |
| Germany | 0.283 |
| France | 0.327 |
| Australia | 0.352 |
| Ireland | 0.359 |
| United Kingdom | 0.360 |
| United States | 0.408 |
| Russia | 0.456 |
| Nigeria | 0.506 |
| Argentina | 0.522 |

**Table 13.3** Gini Coefficients by Country, 2004
*Source*: UN, *Human Development Report* (2004).

than countries with more market-orientated economies. The United States has a less equal distribution than the United Kingdom – but not enormously less equal.

Table 13.4 shows what has happened to income distributions in the United States and the United Kingdom over the years 1980–2001/2.

| Country | 1980 | 1985 | 1990 | 1995 | 2000 | 2001/2 |
|---|---|---|---|---|---|---|
| UK | 0.28 | 0.29 | 0.36 | 0.33 | 0.35 | 0.33 |
| US | 0.40 | 0.42 | 0.43 | 0.45 | 0.46 | 0.47 |

**Table 13.4** UK and US Gini Coefficients, 1980–2001/2
*Source*: US Bureau of the Census; UK National Statistics (2005).
UK data refer to household disposable income pre-tax (2002); US data refer to household income, pre-tax (2001).

## Inequality: a moral problem?

John Rawls, a moral philosopher at Harvard University, constructed a cogent ethical critique of the marginal productivity system, one based heavily on the economic theory of *choice* itself.[6] In thinking about what constitutes a 'just distribution of income', Rawls asks us to imagine ourselves meeting to choose the rules for distributing income. The meeting takes place behind a 'veil of ignorance', which conceals from participants any knowledge of what talents and abilities each has. Because no individual knows whether he is smart or dull, strong or weak, fast or slow, no one knows what rules of distribution would work to his own advantage. Rawls argues that the rules people would choose in such a state of ignorance would necessarily be fair; and if the rules are fair, the income distribution to which they give rise will also be fair.

What sort of rules would people choose from behind a veil of ignorance? If the national income were a fixed amount, most people would probably give everyone an equal share. That scenario is likely, Rawls argues, because most people are strongly risk averse. Since an unequal income distribution would involve not only a chance of doing well but a chance of doing poorly, most people would prefer to eliminate the risk by choosing an equal distribution. If diminishing marginal utility applies to wealth, a given chance of a given gain over the average income is less valuable than avoiding the same chance of the same loss relative to the average. An individual for whom this is the case is said to be *risk averse*.

Imagine, for example, that you and two friends have been told that an anonymous benefactor donated €300,000 to divide among you. How would you split it? If you are like most people, you would propose an equal division, or €100,000 for each of you. Most of us, most of the time, behave in a risk averse fashion. The logical extreme of the Rawlsian thought experiment is that people would choose a fully egalitarian outcome if they could not choose (or influence) their position in society. Given this, an egalitarian distribution is ethically superior to an unequal one.

Rawls' logic is appealing ... but is not necessarily convincing, at least in its extreme version. It depends first of all on an assumption that a person's economic welfare depends on his income alone, and that no benefits are derived by anyone from the activities of those who are better off: no pop-stars; no patrons of the arts. It also expressly assumes that the size of the cake is independent of the way it is sliced. This is fine for real cakes, but not for the 'cake' of gross national product (GNP). While there are several dissenting voices, most economists

[6] Rawls (1971).

would support the proposition that a successful market economy cannot function properly (i.e. maximise the size of the 'cake') without incentives that imply some *inequality of outcome*. If either or both of these factors is built into Rawls' thought experiment it is not at all obvious that a risk averse individual would choose a highly equal distribution from behind a veil of ignorance.

Whatever the choice made from behind that veil, the attraction of a commitment to a high degree of equality is far from absolute when we consider its impact in a the real world. For many, the goal of absolute equality is quickly trumped by other concerns when we set about making the rules for distributing wealth in modern market economies. Wealth, after all, generally doesn't grow on trees; we must produce it. In a large economy, if each person were guaranteed an equal amount of income, few would invest in education or the development of special talents; and the incentive to work would be sharply reduced. In a country without rewards for hard work and risk taking, national income would be dramatically smaller than in a country with such rewards. Of course, material rewards for effort and risk taking necessarily lead to inequality.

Rawls accepts, to be fair, that people would be willing to accept a certain degree of inequality as long as these rewards produced a sufficiently large increase in the total amount of output available for distribution. But how much inequality would people accept? Much less than the amount produced by purely competitive markets, Rawls argues. The idea is that, behind the veil of ignorance, each person would fear ending up in a disadvantaged position, so each would choose rules that would produce a more equal distribution of income than exists under the marginal productivity system. And since such choices *define* the just distribution of income, Rawls argues, fairness requires at least some attempt to reduce the inequality produced by the market system. Most people would agree with this weaker Rawls proposition. After all, most people voluntarily redistribute income through gifts and donations to the poor or disaster relief: look at the global, non-governmental response to the tsunami catastrophe of Christmas 2004 in South East Asia.

### RECAP Why is income inequality a moral problem?

John Rawls argues that the degree of inequality typical of unregulated market systems is unfair because people would favour substantially less inequality if they chose distributional rules from *behind a veil of ignorance*.

## Methods of income redistribution

A political consensus that the existing distribution of income is less than optimal leads to policies by government designed to improve the distribution. These take two basic forms. The first is to do something to change the *underlying factors* that produce the observed distribution. The second is to compensate for the *outcome observed*. An example of the first would be to improve the ability of children from poor families to obtain tertiary-level education. An example of the second would be direct payments to households with incomes below some threshold value.

Although we, as a society, have an interest in limiting income inequality, programmes for reducing it are often fraught with practical difficulties. The challenge is to find ways to raise the incomes of those who cannot fend for themselves, without at the same time undermining their incentive to work, and without using scarce resources to subsidise those who are not poor. The manner in which the funds are raised will also be subject to a similar test: To what extent does the raising of the funds reduce the *global income* from which the funds are raised? Of course, some people simply cannot work, or cannot find work that pays enough to live on. In a world of perfect information, the government could make generous cash payments to those people, and withhold support from those who can fend for themselves. In practice, however, the two groups are often hard to distinguish. So we must choose among imperfect alternative measures.

*Redistribution* takes place through one or both of two channels. In the first place, the design of the *tax structure*, which produces the revenues to finance government spending, can be skewed in such a way that those with greater resources pay more for the services provided to all, or to some. If this is the case the incidence of taxation is 'progressive' (as opposed to 'regressive', when the incidence is heavier on those with fewer resources). In the second place the *composition of public spending* can be biased toward providing income or services to those with fewer resources. The net redistributive impact of the government reflects the balance of the effects of policies on taxation and spending. In this respect it can be misleading to treat a particular tax or spending item without looking at the overall impact of all taxes and spending structures in order to judge the effectiveness of the government in terms of income redistribution.

## Welfare payments and in-kind transfers

In all advanced countries the government tries to alter the distribution of income and wealth by creating entitlements to money payments and the provision of goods and services free of charge or at a price that is below the cost of provision. Economists have long argued the merits of these two approaches. The balance of conclusions is that *money payments* are preferable to provision of what are really benefits in kind.

**In-kind transfers** are direct transfers of goods or services to low-income individuals or families. This includes both free-of-charge provision and provision at below cost. Examples are subsidised public housing, subsidised school meals, education without fees and 'free' medical care. In many European jurisdictions they also include some more dubious features such as benefits to defined groups of people: for example, the elderly benefit from such things as free public transport, exemption from refuse collection charges, reductions in the price of electricity – and even free TV licences. Economists criticise these on two grounds. The first is that (unless you do not trust those on low incomes to spend wisely) it is axiomatically true that it is welfare enhancing for the poor to give them money to spend as they wish rather than to constrain them to consume a predetermined bundle of goods of equal cost. The second is that in-kind transfers tend not to be accurately related to the means of those receiving them. At its most obvious, why should we think that all those over 65 (the elderly) are poor? The same, of course, applies to some monetary payments: most West European countries offer payments to families (in some cases to mothers) on the basis of the number of children they have. This benefits the rich equally with the poor. The motivation is to help poor families with a large number of children. The effect is to transfer real resources to families with children, regardless of their means.

> **in-kind transfer** a payment made not in the form of cash, but in the form of a good or service

*Monetary transfers* consist in cash (or equivalent) payments to recipients who are designated by some standard as entitled to the payment. Non-contributory old age pensions are an example of this kind of payment in many European countries. Children's allowances are another. The single most important element in this structure is *unemployment relief*: people who are unable to find work are entitled to a replacement of their earnings by a sum paid by the state. In the United States, such payments are severely limited in terms of the duration of any period of receipt of payments. European countries are mostly much more liberal. Obviously, unemployment is the most important proximate cause of poverty, so entitling the unemployed to cash income support tackles poverty head-on. Unfortunately, it can have perverse incentive effects, since it can discourage people from accepting employment. This is why there is growing pressure in Europe to follow the US model and make it limited in duration – and, where it is already limited, to reduce the period further.

## Universality and means testing

In the United States, there is a strong bias toward a system of cash or in-kind benefits based on objective means testing. To qualify for Medicaid, households have to demonstrate a level of income that is sufficiently low to qualify for the health cost benefit. The Aid to Families with Dependent Children (AFDC) programme is **means-tested** on a sliding scale. In Europe, there is a stronger emphasis on universalist provision. The UK's universal National Health Service (NHS) is a classic example. Child support payments, a common feature of European social support structures in one form or another, are a further example.

**means-tested** a benefit programme whose benefit level declines as the recipient earns additional income

On the face of it, it must appear wasteful and illogical to raise taxes in order to make payments to the very people from whom the tax is raised rather than raise less taxation and deliver the funds to those who are less well off. There are, however, two strong counter-arguments supporting a universalist approach. The first is an administrative one, and one that also has an element of social sensitivity in it. That is the argument that (a) it is significantly more costly to devise, administer and modify a social spending programme that is based on establishing recipients' entitlement to receive the transfers involved, and (b) it is kinder and more effective to grant support to people in need of support without requiring them to devote time and resources to proving that they meet the legal requirements of an entitlement. The second argument concerns what is known as the *poverty trap*. If a family that as of now is entitled to, say, a rent subsidy manages to increase its income but in so doing ceases to be eligible for the subsidy, the loss of the subsidy is in effect a tax on the extra income the family has earned. If a social support programme offers resources to people who are unemployed, then it implies a tax on taking up a job offer. Programmes of support to single mothers frequently mean that if the father co-habits with the mother and helps support the family, the support is withdrawn. That does not exactly encourage two-parent families. This kind of thing can lead to a position in which poorer families face an extremely high *effective marginal tax rate* if they take steps that will reduce their poverty and, as a result, have a very weak incentive to take those steps, thus creating for them the 'poverty trap'.

## Income tax and redistribution

One obvious way of dealing with the issues just discussed is to apply income tax to any universal social support programme receipts. That has the effect of (a) ensuring that the benefits flow preponderantly to those on lower incomes, and (b) the level of payment can be increased without increasing taxes generally. The potential to use the tax system as the engine for redistribution that this raises has been the subject of debate among both economists and social workers. It has been suggested that it might be possible to replace the whole panoply of income support programmes by a reform of the tax code. The central element in this proposal is what is called **negative income tax** (NIT).

**negative income tax (NIT)** a system under which the government would grant every citizen a cash payment each year, financed by an additional tax on earned income

There are several variants of this concept, but they have in common the idea that income tax takes away a proportion of the payer's income over some threshold, and that the threshold could be used as a basis for paying money to people whose incomes are below that threshold. For example, suppose there is a 25 per cent income tax on family incomes above, say, €10,000 per annum. This would be replaced by a tax of 25 per cent of (income – €10,000). A household with an income of €8,000 would face a tax bill of €0.25(8000 – 10000) = –€500. A negative tax bill is, of course, a receipt. The family would receive a cheque for €500, an NIT payment. In this case everyone, regardless of income faces the same effective tax rate. If a family with €15,000 earns an extra €1,000, it retains €750 (75 per cent) and pays €250 (25 per cent) in tax. A family with €8,000 that earns an extra €1,000 keeps the whole €1,000, but receives €250 rather than €500. The extra €1,000 leaves it with a net increase of €750 (75 per cent) as it loses the €250 (25 per cent) NIT payment.

The big problem with this type of proposal is the incentive difficulty. Note that in the last example a household with no income at all would receive €2,500. Suppose (rather unrealistically) that this constituted what the government considered to be the **poverty threshold**, the level of income below which a family is 'poor' – i.e. has insufficient income to sustain an acceptable lifestyle. At a marginal effective tax rate of 25 per cent, no one would pay any tax to the Exchequer until they had an income four times the poverty level. A widely used and far from generous poverty threshold is 40 per cent of the average industrial wage. On that basis no one earning less than 160 per cent of the average industrial wage would pay any income tax. In most Western economies that would mean about 60 per cent of households paying no income tax. It doesn't take a genius to work out that you couldn't finance current government spending programmes if only 40 per cent of people paid any income taxes, and then only at 25 per cent for some time after hitting the threshold, unless taxes on the rest were confiscatory, something that would have very serious incentive effects on work effort and risk taking.

**poverty threshold** the level of income below which a family is 'poor'

**Exercise 13.4** Using the data above, what would the tax rate have to be if everyone below and those just above the tax threshold (€10,000) were to face the same effective tax rate while the poverty threshold is set at half the tax threshold?

Finally, the higher the basic payment (the poverty threshold) relative to the income tax threshold the lower is the incentive to work at all, since work does, you will remember, have an *opportunity cost*: what you can do with the time you spend working if you don't work.

## Minimum wages

Nearly all industrialised countries have sought to increase the standard of living of low-wage workers by enacting minimum wage legislation – laws that prohibit employers from paying workers less than a specified hourly wage. This rate varies from country to country. The federal minimum wage in the United States is currently (2005) set at $5.15 per hour, and several states have set minimum wage levels significantly higher. In Europe, minimum wage structures vary by country. Germany, where consideration is (late 2004) being given to a mandatory legal minimum wage, has sectoral minimum wages determined by collective agreements and legally enforceable. The United Kingdom has a general minimum wage for adult (over 22) workers of £4.85 (end 2004) or €6.90. Ireland has a similarly based minimum wage of €7.00 (end 2004). Spain has a monthly minimum wage of €512.90 (2005).

At one point, economists were almost unanimous in their opposition to minimum wage laws, arguing that those laws reduce total economic surplus, as do other regulations that prevent markets from reaching equilibrium. Even today, economists as a whole tend to be critical of minimum wage legislation on the grounds that elementary theory (see the discussion of the impact of unions on p. 372) suggests that such interventions in labour markets damage employment prospects and hurt those not covered by the minimum wage. Some economists have now questioned this blanket opposition to minimum wage laws, citing studies that have failed to show significant reductions in employment following increases in minimum wage levels. These studies may well imply that, as a group, low-income workers are better off with minimum wage laws than without them. But as we saw in Chapter 7, any

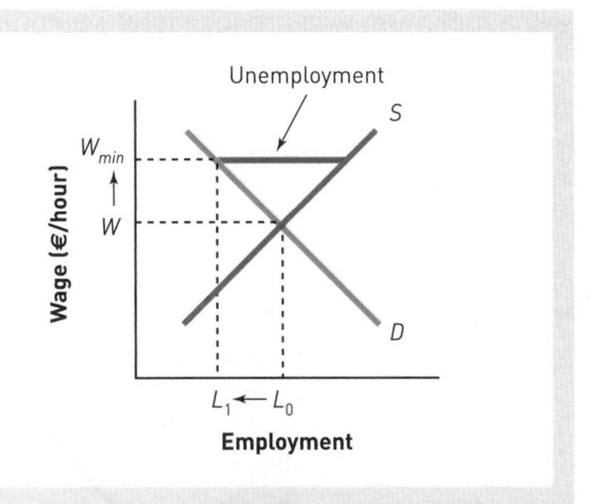


**Figure 13.7 The Effect of Minimum Wage Legislation on Employment.** If mimimum wage legislation requires employers to pay more than the equilibrium wage, the result will be a decline in employment for low-wage workers.

policy that prevents a market from reaching equilibrium causes a reduction in *total economic surplus* – which means society ought in principle to be able to find a more effective policy for helping low-wage workers.

How does a minimum wage affect the market for low-wage labour? In Fig. 13.7, note that when the law prevents employers from paying less than $W_{min}$, employers hire fewer workers (a decline from $L_0$ to $L_1$). Unemployment results. The $L_1$ workers who keep their jobs earn more than before, but the $L_0$–$L_1$ workers who lose their jobs earn nothing. Whether workers together earn more or less than before thus depends on the *elasticity of demand for labour.* If elasticity of demand is less than 1, workers as a group will earn more than before. If it is more than 1, workers as a group will earn less.

## The earned income tax credit

A US fiscal innovation in 1975 is an example of how it is possible to achieve the goals of minimum wage legislation without incurring its costs. First proposed by President Richard Nixon, the earned income tax credit (EITC) was enacted into law in 1975, and has drawn praise from both left and right on the political spectrum. The programme is essentially a *wage subsidy* in the form of a credit against the amount a family owes in federal income taxes. For example, a family of four with total earned income of $13,000 in 2001 would have received an annual tax credit of about $4,000. That is, the programme would have reduced the annual federal income tax payment of this family by roughly that amount. Families who earned less would have received a larger tax credit, and those who earned more would have received a smaller one. Families whose tax credit exceeds the amount of tax owed actually receive a check from the government for the difference. The EITC is thus essentially the same as a *negative income tax* (NIT), except that eligibility for the programme is confined to people who work. Like both the NIT and the minimum wage, the EITC puts extra income into the hands of workers who are employed at low wage levels. But unlike the minimum wage, the EITC creates no incentive for employers to lay off low-wage workers.

Contrast that intervention in the labour market with the decision of the Irish government in 2000 to introduce a minimum wage at a level of IRL£4.40 (€5.60). At the time this was the highest minimum wage in the OECD. We can think of the minimum wage as an *off-budget tax* on employers of low-wage workers, the proceeds of which are transferred to the employee rather than to the government. That's why it is expected to reduce demand for low-skill labour. However, at the time anyone on an hourly income of IRL£4.40 faced a marginal tax rate of 20 per cent plus social insurance contributions, giving an effective tax on the employee's marginal pound of about 26 per cent. By introducing the minimum wage on this basis the Irish government was taxing the employment of low-skill labour by employers (reducing the demand for such labour) and then taxing the tax in the hands of the recipient. This bizarre state of affairs, in which the incentives were strongly biased against increasing employment and real income for low-paid workers, continued until the end of 2004 when the government removed all those earning minimum wages from liability to income tax.

### Example 13.4 By how much will a minimum wage reduce total economic surplus?

Suppose the demand and supply curves for unskilled labour in the Birmingham labour market are as shown in Fig. 13.8. By how much will the imposition of a minimum wage at £7 per hour reduce total economic surplus? By how much do worker surplus and employer surplus change as a result of adopting the minimum wage?

**Figure 13.8 Worker and Employer Surplus in an Unregulated Labour Market.** For the demand and supply curves shown, worker surplus is the area of the lower shaded triangle, £12,5000 per day, the same as employer surplus (upper shaded triangle).

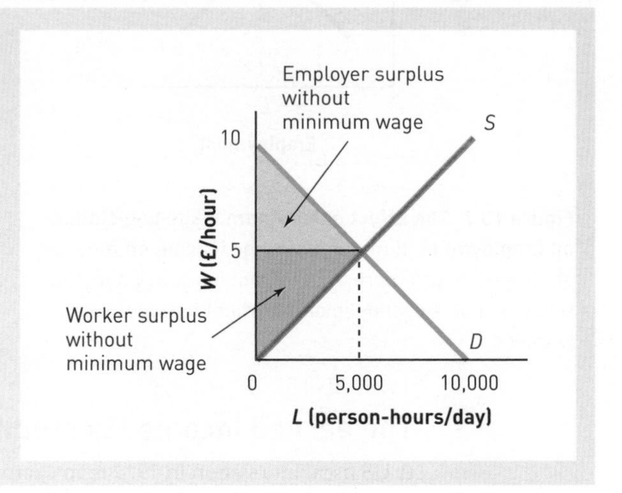


In the absence of a minimum wage, the equilibrium unskilled wage for Birmingham would be £5 per hour, and employment would be 5,000 person-hours per day. Both employers and workers would enjoy economic surplus equal to the area of the shaded triangles in Fig. 13.8, £12,500 per day.

With a minimum wage set at £7 per hour, employer surplus is the area of the upper shaded triangle in Fig. 13.9, £4,500 per day, and worker surplus is the area of the lower-left shaded area, £16,500 per day. The minimum wage thus reduces employer surplus by £8,000 per day and increases worker surplus by £4,000 per day. The net reduction in surplus is the area of the right-hand shaded triangle shown in Fig. 13.9, £4,000 per day.

**Figure 13.9 The Effect of a Minimum Wage on Economic Surplus.** A minimum wage of £7 per hour reduces employment in this market by 2,000 person-hours per day, for a reduction in total economic surplus of £4,000 per day (area of the right-hand shaded triangle). Employer surplus falls to £4,500 per day (area of upper shaded triangle), while worker surplus rises to £16,500 per day (lower-left shaded area).

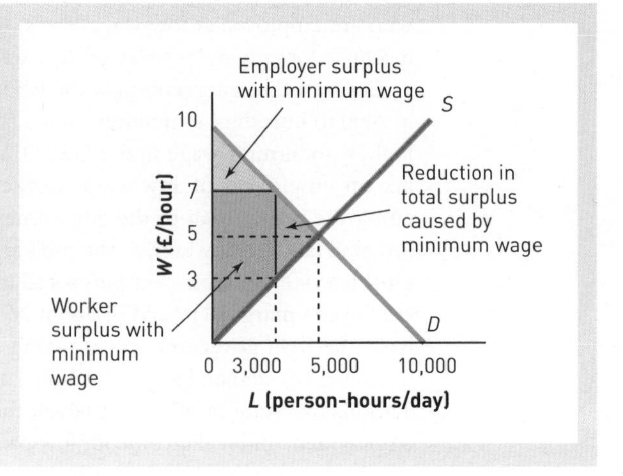

**Exercise 13.5** In Example 13.4, by how much would total economic surplus have been reduced by the £7 minimum wage if labour demand in Birmingham had been perfectly inelastic at 5,000 person-hours per day?

Example 13.5 illustrates the central message of the efficiency principle, which is that if the economic 'pie' can be made larger, everyone can have a larger slice.

**Example 13.5** Refer to Example 13.4. How much would it cost the government each day to provide EITC under which workers as a group receive the same economic surplus as they do under the £7 per hour minimum wage? (Assume for simplicity that the EITC has no effect on labour supply.)

With an EITC in lieu of a minimum wage, employment will be 5,000 person-hours per day at £5 per hour, just as in the unregulated market. Since worker surplus in the unregulated market was £4,000 per day less than under the minimum wage, the government would have to offer a tax credit worth £0.80 per hour for each of the 5,000 person-hours of employment to restore worker surplus to the level obtained under the £7 minimum wage. With an EITC of that amount in effect, worker surplus would be the same as under the £7 minimum wage.

If the EITC were financed by a £4,000 tax on employers, employer surplus would be £4,000 greater than under the £7 minimum wage.

We stress that our point is not that the minimum wage produces no gains for low-income workers, but rather that it is possible to provide even larger gains for these workers if we avoid policies that try to prevent labour markets from reaching equilibrium.

## Summary

- A worker's long-run equilibrium pay in a competitive labour market will be equal to the value of her marginal product (VMP) – the market value of whatever goods and services she produces for her employer. The law of diminishing returns says that when a firm's capital and other productive inputs are held fixed in the short run, adding workers beyond some point results in ever-smaller increases in output. Firms that purchase labour in competitive labour markets face a constant wage, and they will hire labour up to the point at which VMP equals the *market wage*.
- *Human capital theory* says that an individual's VMP is proportional to his stock of human capital – an amalgam of education, experience, training, intelligence and other factors that influence productivity. According to this theory, some occupations pay better than others simply because they require larger stocks of human capital.
- Wages often differ between individuals whose stocks of human capital appear nearly the same, as when one belongs to a labour union and the other does not. Compensating *wage differentials* – wage differences associated with differences in working conditions – are another important explanation for why individuals with similar human capital might earn different salaries. They help to explain why refuse collectors earn more than lifeguards and, more generally, why individuals with a given stock of human capital tend to earn more in jobs that have less attractive working conditions.
- Many firms pay members of certain groups – notably minority groups and women – less than they pay other people who seem to have similar employment characteristics. If such *wage gaps* are the result of employer discrimination, their existence implies profit opportunities for firms that do not discriminate.

Several other factors, including discrimination by customers and institutions other than firms, may explain at least part of the observed wage gaps.

- Technologies that allow the most productive individuals to serve broader markets can translate even small differences in human capital into enormous differences in pay. Such technologies give rise to *winner-take-all* markets, which have long been common in sports and entertainment, and which are now becoming common in other professions.
- Although incomes grew at almost 3 per cent a year for all income classes from the 1950s to the 1980s, the lion's share of income growth in the years since has been concentrated among the *top earners*.
- Philosophers have argued that at least some *income redistribution* is justified in the name of fairness, because if people chose society's distributional rules without knowing their own personal circumstances, most would favour less inequality than would be produced by market outcomes.
- Policies and programmes for *reducing poverty* include minimum-wage laws, the EITC, food and housing vouchers, subsidised school lunches, free health care, public housing and income supplements. Of these, all but the EITC fail to maximise total economic surplus, either by interfering with work incentives or by preventing markets from reaching equilibrium.
- The NIT works much like the EITC, except that it includes those who are not employed.

## Key terms

**compensating wage differential** (377)
**customer discrimination** (378)
**employer discrimination** (377)
**Gini coefficient** (383)
**human capital** (371)
**human capital theory** (371)
**in-kind transfer** (386)
**labour union** (372)
**Lorenz curve** (383)
**marginal product of labour** (MP) (367)
**means-tested** (387)
**negative income tax** (NIT) (387)
**poverty threshold** (388)
**value of marginal product of labour** (VMP) (367)
**winner-take-all labour market** (381)

## Review questions

1. Why is the supply curve of labour for any specific occupation likely to be upward-sloping, even if, for the economy as a whole, people work fewer hours when wage rates increase?
2. **True or false**: If the human capital possessed by two workers is nearly the same, their wage rates will be nearly the same. Explain.
3. How might recent changes in income inequality be related to the proliferation of technologies that enable the most productive individuals to serve broader markets?
4. Mention two self-interested reasons that a top earner might favour policies to redistribute income.
5. Why is exclusive reliance on the negative income tax unlikely to constitute a long-term solution to the poverty problem?

## Problems

Problems marked with an asterisk (*) are more difficult.

1. H2Oclean Ltd supplies domestic kitchen water filters to the retail market in Essex and hires workers to assemble the components. An air filter sells for €26, and H2Oclean can buy the components for each filter for €1. Kevin and Sharon are two workers for H2Oclean Ltd. Sharon can assemble 60 air filters per month, and Kevin can assemble 70. If the labour market is perfectly competitive, how much will each be paid?

2. Stone, Inc. owns a clothing factory, hiring workers in a competitive market to cut denim to make jeans. The fabric costs €5 per pair. The company's weekly output varies with labour usage, as shown in the table below.

| Number of workers | Jeans (pairs/week) |
|---|---|
| 0 | 0 |
| 1 | 25 |
| 2 | 45 |
| 3 | 60 |
| 4 | 72 |
| 5 | 80 |
| 6 | 85 |

a. If the jeans sell for €35 a pair, and the competitive market wage is €250 per week, how many workers should Stone hire? How many pairs of jeans will the company produce each week?

b. Suppose the Clothing Workers Union now sets a weekly minimum acceptable wage of €230 per week. All the workers Stone hires belong to the union. How does the minimum wage affect Stone's decision about how many workers to hire?

c. If the minimum wage set by the union had been €400 per week, how would the minimum wage affect Stone's decision about how many workers to hire?

d. If Stone again faces a market wage of €250 per week but the price of jeans rises to €45, how many workers will the company now hire?

3. Reacteurs de France, SA (RdF), supplier of engines for France's space exploration programme, hires workers to assemble the components. An engine sells for €30,000, and RdF can buy the components for each engine for €25,000. Belmondo and Halliday are two workers for RdF. Belmondo can assemble 1/5 of an engine per month, and Halliday can assemble 1/10. If the labour market is perfectly competitive and components are RdF's only other cost, how much will each be paid?

4. Carolyn owns a soda factory and hires workers in a competitive labour market to bottle the soda. Her company's weekly output of bottled soda varies with the number of workers hired, as shown in the table below.

| Number of workers | Cases/week |
|---|---|
| 0 | 0 |
| 1 | 200 |
| 2 | 360 |
| 3 | 480 |
| 4 | 560 |
| 5 | 600 |

a. If each case sells for €10 more than the cost of the materials used in producing it and the competitive market wage is €1,000 per week, how many workers should Carolyn hire? How many cases will be produced per week?

b. Suppose the Soda Bottlers Union now sets a weekly minimum acceptable wage of €1,500 per week. All the workers Carolyn hires belong to the union. How does the minimum wage affect Carolyn's decision about how many workers to hire?

c. If the wage is again €1,000 per week but the price of soda rises to €15 per case, how many workers will Carolyn now hire?

5. Suppose the equilibrium wage for unskilled workers in New Jersey is $7 per hour. How will the wages and employment of unskilled workers in New Jersey change if the state legislature raises the minimum wage from $5.15 per hour to $6 per hour?

6. Jones, who is currently unemployed, is a participant in three means-tested welfare programmes: food vouchers, rent vouchers and day care vouchers. Each programme grants him €150 per month in vouchers, which can be used like cash to purchase the good or service they cover.

a. If benefits in each programme are reduced by 40 cents for each additional dollar Jones earns in the labour market, how will Jones' economic position change if he accepts a job paying €120 per week?

b. In the light of your answer to part (a), explain why means testing for welfare recipients has undesirable effects on work incentives.

7. Sue is offered a job re-shelving books in the University of Limerick library from noon until 1 p.m. each Friday. Her reservation wage for this task is €10 per hour.

a. If the library director offers Sue €100 per hour, how much economic surplus will she enjoy as a result of accepting the job?

b. Now suppose the library director announces that the earnings from the job will be divided equally among the 400 students who live in Sue's residence. Will Sue still accept?

c. Explain how your answers to parts (a) and (b) illustrate one of the incentive problems inherent in income redistribution programmes.

8.* Suppose the demand and supply curves for unskilled labour in the Bremen labour market are as shown in the graph below. By how much will the imposition of a minimum wage of €12 per hour reduce total economic surplus? Calculate the amounts by which employer surplus and worker surplus change as a result of the minimum wage.

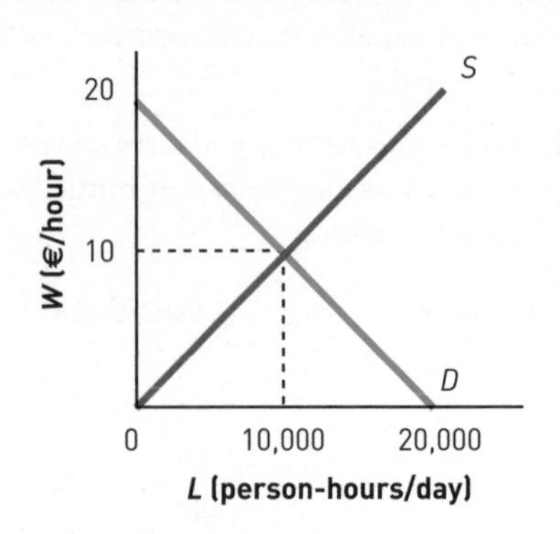

9.* Refer to Problem 8. How much would it cost the government each day to provide an EITC under which workers as a group receive the same economic surplus as they do under the €12 per hour minimum wage? (Assume for simplicity that the EITC has no effect on labour supply.)

## Answers to in-chapter exercises

13.1 At a price of Sfr26 per clock case, the fifth worker has a VMP of Sfr364 per week, so WTK should hire five workers.

13.2 Since the VMP of each worker exceeds Sfr275,WTK should hire five workers.

13.3 When the wage rate is €9 per hour in each market, 25 fewer workers will be employed in the non-unionised market and 25 more in the unionised market. The loss in output from removing 25 workers from the non-unionised market is the sum of the VMPs of those workers, which is the shaded area in panel (b) of the graph. This area is €187.50 per hour. (**Hint**: To calculate this area, first break the graph into a rectangle and a triangle.) The gain in output from adding 25 workers to the unionised market is the shaded area in panel (a), which is €262.50 per hour. The net increase in output is thus €262.50 – €187.50 = €75 per hour.

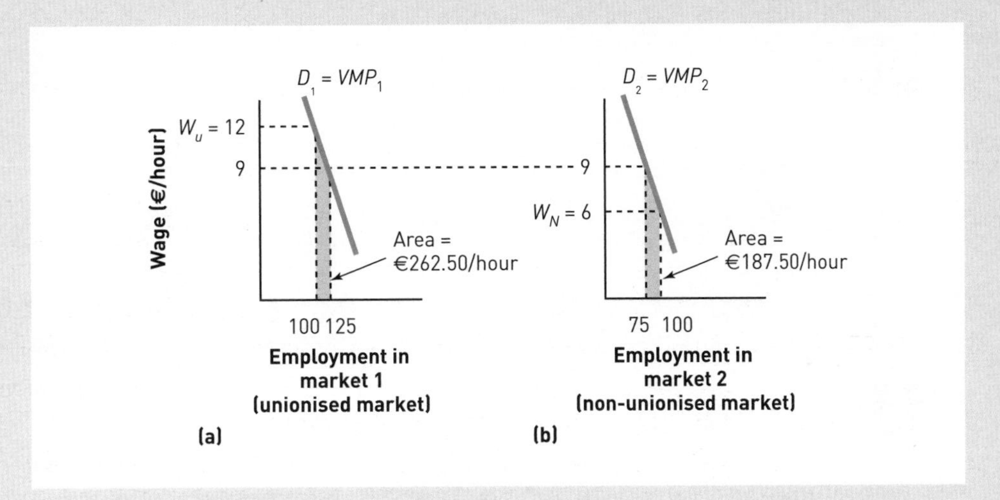


13.4 The tax rate would have to be 50 per cent.

13.5 With perfectly inelastic demand, employment would remain at 5,000 person-hours per day, so the minimum wage would cause no reduction in economic surplus.

## References

Babcock, L., C. Camerer, G. Loewenstein and R. Thaler (1997) 'Labor Supply of New York City Cab Drivers: One Day at a Time', *Quarterly Journal of Economics*, 111.

Gini, C. (1912) *Variabilità e mutabilità: contributo allo studio delle distribuzioni e delle relazioni statistiche* (Bologna: Tipografia di Paolo Cuppin).

Gunnigle, P. and M. O'Sullivan (2003) 'Organized Labour in the Celtic Tiger: Trends in Trade Union Penetration in the Republic of Ireland', paper delivered to the 13th Congress of the International Industrial Relations Association, Berlin.

Lorenz, M. O. (1905) 'Methods of Measuring the Concentration of Wealth', *Publications of the American Statistical Association*, 9, pp. 209–19.

Polackek, S. and M. Kim (1994) 'Panel Estimates of the Male–Female Earnings Functions', *Journal of Human Resources*, 29(2), pp. 406–28.

Rawls, J. (1971) *A Theory of Justice* (Cambridge, MA: Harvard University Press).

# 14

# Government in the Market Economy: Regulation and Production of Public Goods and Other Services

In the course of Chapter 9 we looked at the performance of firms that enjoy substantial market power. The limiting case of this is the model of monopoly. Several things emerged from that material. In the first place we saw that market power results in a reduction in economic efficiency in that we cannot generally expect firms to choose outputs and prices that equate price to marginal cost. We also saw that firms will exploit market power to extract profits derived from restricting output, something that transfers real income from consumers to producers.

To respond to this type of problem we saw that we rely on governmental (or, indeed, supranational) intervention in the form of **regulation**. This takes the form of restrictions on how firms operate, and on the structures of markets. It is the basis for regulation in the form of competition policy and mergers and acquisitions (M&A) policy.

**regulation** legal intervention in markets to alter the way in which firms or consumers behave

In this chapter we shall be looking at the role of government in the market economy under two headings. The first of these is its role as regulator in a broader context than simply that of competition and mergers policy. The second is the function of government as an agent in the economy in its own right, acting as a producer of goods and services. In this respect we shall in the main be considering the role of government in the provision of what are known as *public goods*.

## Government and regulation

What is common to the general problem of market failure and the narrow question of market power as an instance of market failure is that regulation is seen by economists as a means of correcting that failure. Our starting point is that if governments need to regulate economic activity they need to understand the economics foundations of regulatory intervention. When they don't they (and their critics) can end up pursuing irrational policies. Instead of market failure we have *regulatory failure*. Consider the following responses over concerns about 'security of supply'.

## Regulatory blunders: the security of supply neurosis

Whether due to misunderstanding, or whether reflecting underhand actions to protect certain interest groups, governments frequently take regulatory action to protect or improve 'security of supply'. The market, it is said, does not adequately provide security. It is necessary for the state to regulate how markets work in order to improve the situation. Since suppliers make profits by selling things to consumers, and since supply interruptions will undermine those profits, it might be thought that suppliers would be acutely aware of any potential threat, and take steps to provide security. Governments think otherwise, and frequently think somewhat hazily about regulation, taxation and market failure, as three examples, two concerning energy and one concerning food, make clear.

Consider first the arguments used to raise taxes on oil consumption or, equivalently, to subsidise or mandate use of renewables and/or domestic fuel supplies in order to reduce dependence on Middle Eastern oil. The justification is essentially one of correcting market failure. Oil consumers are not factoring into their decisions on oil consumption the implicit cost to the economy as a whole of its vulnerability to supply interruption. Whether or not, or to what extent, this is really the case is a moot point. After all, any large-scale seller or buyer of oil would be perfectly well aware of the consequences to his business of supply interruption, and could be assumed to have factored that into his plans for organising his business, including insuring against interruption. Presumably the same applies to the purchase of energy by households for domestic purposes.

Clearly unconvinced by these considerations, the Irish government has, since the 1980s, obliged consumers of oil products in Ireland to pay a small price premium to permit the oil companies to take some of their supplies from a small and elderly refinery near Cork in the south of the country and distant from the main energy markets. This is done on the basis that national security requires that there should exist a crude oil refining capacity in Ireland. Precisely how the country could find itself unable to lay its hands on refined oil while being able to get supplies of crude oil has never been explained.

The basis for the European Union's Common Agriculture Policy (CAP) was originally to ensure security of food supplies in Europe. Since the 1960s, Europeans have been paying higher than necessary prices and producing food they couldn't eat, while excluding imports from outside the Union, in order to ensure a secure supply.

Security of supply is not a neurosis peculiar to Europe. In 1979, in the wake of the second major oil supply interruption in a decade, the US government actively considered a proposal to reduce American dependence on imported oil by imposing a federal motor fuel tax of 50 cents per US gallon (approximately 15 cents per litre). Fierce opposition to the proposal resulted in its being dropped. It would be pleasant to think that this reflected a clearer understanding of the problem by the electorate than by the government. Unfortunately, the real reason it was dropped was because of economic illiteracy in Congress.

Anticipating objections that the tax would impose an unacceptable hardship on the poor, policy makers proposed to return the revenues from the tax to the people by reducing the payroll tax – the tax on wages that supports the social security system. Most economists, whatever they felt about the need for the tax, could see considerable merit in reducing a tax on labour. Proponents of the tax also argued that it would reduce air pollution and ease highway congestion. But critics, mostly in Congress, ridiculed the proposal, stating that if the revenues from the tax were returned to the people, the quantity of motor fuel demanded would remain essentially the same. Their argument tipped the debate, and officials never managed to implement the proposal. The argument was, however, nonsensical.

True, the proposed tax rebate meant that people *could* have bought just as much motor fuel as before the tax. Yet the tax would have given them a powerful incentive not to do so. As we saw in Chapter 5, consumers can change their behaviour to escape the effects of a steep rise in the after-tax price of motor fuel – by switching to cars with smaller, more fuel-efficient engines, forming car pools, and so on. Such changes free up money to spend on other goods and services, which become relatively more attractive because they are not taxed. Relative prices, not just disposable incomes, determine spending patterns.

## The regulatory framework

First, let us look at how regulation is implemented. At its basis is some form of legislative intervention that has the effect of modifying individuals' or firms' behaviour in the context of the legal framework of property rights and contract law that underpins the workings of markets. Without an adequate legal framework markets cannot function efficiently. Change that framework and you will change how firms and individuals will behave in terms of market transactions.

That is not to say there are no markets without the legal institutions provided by a state as we know it. A really good example of markets functioning in an almost lawless environment on a wide scale is what has happened in Somalia since the 1980s.[1] There are burgeoning markets in most goods and many relatively technologically complex services in a territory that has no functioning government making and enforcing laws. Instead, local warlords provide a set of enforced property rights, and enforce contracts where necessary … and take a cut of the action (a sort of informal tax system).

Within states with the full panoply of legal property rights and legal enforcement, markets can function outside the law. Prohibition in the United States gave the world the spectacle of a well-developed market in alcoholic drink entirely outside the law. And, while by definition the law does not provide the basis for exchange in illegal goods and services (such as heroin or prostitution), there are markets for those goods and services, with buyers and sellers. But transactions in these markets are very costly compared with transactions in markets that rely on the legal establishment and enforcement of property rights and contractual relations.

The legal framework lays down the ground rules for *market exchange*. Changes in that framework are the first form of regulation to be considered. For example, governments all over the world lay down by law certain workers' rights that supersede simple contracts between employers and employees (statutory notice periods, statutory holiday entitlements, entitlements to redundancy payments, working time restrictions and so on). Trade unions are usually exempt from parts of the law on contracts that firms must respect (ever since the 1906 Trades Disputes Act, unions in Britain have enjoyed a degree of protection from actions for breach of contract in relation to their members' activities in pursuing grievances). Germany was notorious for legal restrictions on opening hours for retail establishments that made German cities and towns commercial dead zones at weekends. In Italy, shops must close for a weekly rest period. In France only a very small number of outlets (known as '*tabacs*') may sell tobacco. In virtually all countries you cannot practise medicine unless you possess a set of qualifications laid down by law. In many countries there are legal restrictions on price cutting. For example, in some EU countries it is prohibited to sell a range of goods at less than the price on the invoice covering their purchase by a retailer.

In these cases we have examples of *direct legislative regulation*. The law defines the permissible range of activities, and the normal procedures for law enforcement are used to make sure the restrictions are respected.

While economists have always been interested in such basic forms of regulation and their consequences, most attention has been paid to the operations of *delegated regulation*. This refers to the system whereby the legislature sets up a body to regulate an industry or market along certain lines proscribed by legislation, and makes the agency so created the legal regulatory body. It in turn issues legally binding regulations and decisions affecting the structure and/or performance of the entities covered in its remit.

[1] If you are interested, read Cockburn (2002) which has provided the basis for this account of a market without laws.

Some agencies exist to moderate particular aspects of behaviour across all sectors of the economy. For example, there are two US agencies, the Department of Justice and the Federal Trade Commission, that act to regulate market behaviour by firms to counter abuse of market power. Under EU law all member states must have a 'competition authority' (although not necessarily using exactly that title: in the United Kingdom it has been the Competition Commission since 2000; in France it is the *Conseil de Concurrence*, or Competition Council). Subject to the guidelines set down under national and EU law, it is responsible for the implementation of competition policy within the member states. It polices markets in general to deal with problems such as collusive fixing of prices, and can stop or modify M&As that are larger than a defined threshold size. National competition authorities operate in collaboration with the Competition Directorate of the EU Commission that concerns itself with competition matters having a wider dimension than the member state, and whose findings have binding effects on the decisions of the national authorities.

There are also sector-specific regulatory agencies. These supervise the performance of specific industries. These regulators can, for example, typically determine what prices the firm or firms in a sector may charge. The idea is that these are industries where technical considerations suggest that there will be only one (a natural monopoly) supplier or at best a small number of suppliers (reflecting substantial economies of scale). In the United Kingdom, acronyms like Ofcom are used (in this case, the office that regulates telecommunications).

In this chapter we shall look at regulatory intervention in markets in three areas in order to demonstrate the problems facing regulators and the benefits and costs of well-designed and poorly designed regulation. These are (i) regulation to deal with externality problems in the form of environmental degradation; (ii) health and safety regulation affecting household and labour market behaviour; and (iii) regulation of public utilities (in this case, electricity production and sale). The importance of the issues discussed is twofold.

First, there is the question of *regulatory design and practice*. Regulation is supposed to correct market failure. The benefits of regulation can be thought of as the reduction (or elimination) of the costs associated with market failure. Poor performance by the regulator (if an agency) or design of legal regulation (if it is direct regulation) will result in a smaller reduction in the costs of market failure – or, worse, an exacerbation of those costs.

Secondly, some questions are raised by *poor regulation*. Why does it happen? How can it be reduced as a problem?

## Three case studies

### 1. Regulation to protect the environment from industrial pollution: using price incentives in environmental regulation

As we saw in Chapter 11, goods whose production generates negative externalities, such as atmospheric pollution, tend to be overproduced whenever negotiation among private parties is costly. Suppose we decide, as a society, that the best attainable outcome would be to have half as much pollution as would occur under completely unregulated conditions. In that case, how should the clean-up effort be distributed among those firms that currently discharge pollutants into the environment?

The most efficient – and hence best – distribution of effort is the one for which *each polluter's marginal cost of abatement is exactly the same*. To see why, imagine that under current arrangements the cost to one firm of removing a tonne of pollutant from the air is larger than the cost to another firm. Society could then achieve the same total reduction in pollution at lower cost by having the first firm discharge 1 tonne more into the air and the second firm 1 tonne less.

Unfortunately, government regulators seldom have detailed information on how the cost of reducing pollution varies from one firm to another. Traditionally, many pollution control regimes therefore require all polluters simply to cut back their emissions by the same proportion or to meet the same absolute emissions standards. If different polluters have different marginal costs of pollution abatement, however, these approaches will not be efficient. That is now changing, thanks to increased interest in using market devices to improve regulatory control of emissions.

### *Taxing pollution*

Alternative policies can distribute the clean-up more efficiently, even if the government lacks detailed information about how much it costs different firms to curtail pollution. One method is to tax pollution and allow firms to decide for themselves how much pollutant to emit. Example 14.1 illustrates the logic of this approach.

### **Example 14.1** What is the least costly way to cut pollution by half?

Each of two firms, Sludge Oil and Northwest Lumber, has access to five production processes, each of which has a different cost and creates a different amount of pollution. The daily costs of the processes and the number of tonnes of smoke emitted are shown in Table 14.1. Pollution is currently unregulated, and negotiation between the firms and those who are harmed by pollution is impossible, which means that each firm uses process A, the least costly. Each firm emits 4 tonnes of pollutant per day, for a total of 8 tonnes of pollutant per day.

| **Process (smoke)** | **A (4 tonnes/day)** | **B (3 tonnes/day)** | **C (2 tonnes/day)** | **D (1 tonne/day)** | **E (0 tonnes/day)** |
|---|---|---|---|---|---|
| Cost to Sludge Oil (€/day) | 100 | 200 | 600 | 1,300 | 2,300 |
| Cost to Northwest Lumber (€/day) | 300 | 320 | 380 | 480 | 700 |

**Table 14.1** Costs and Emissions for Different Production Processes

The government is considering two options for reducing total emissions by half. One is to require each firm to curtail its emissions by half. The other is to set a tax of €*T* per tonne of smoke emitted each day. How large must *T* be to curtail emissions by half? What would be the total cost to society under each alternative?

If each firm is required to cut pollution by half, each must switch from process A to process C. The result will be 2 tonnes per day of pollution for each firm. The cost of the switch for Sludge Oil will be €600 per day – €100 per day = €500 per day. The cost to Northwest Lumber will be €380 per day – €300 per day = €80 per day, for a total cost of €580 per day.

Consider now how each firm would react to a tax of €*T* per tonne of pollutant. If a firm can cut pollution by 1 tonne per day, it will save €*T* per day in tax payments. Whenever the cost of cutting a tonne of pollutant is less than €*T*, then, each firm has an incentive to switch to a cleaner process. For example, if the tax were set at €40 per tonne, Sludge Oil would stick with process A, because switching to process B would cost €100 per day extra but would save only €40 per day in taxes. Northwest Lumber, however, would switch to process B, because the €40 saving in taxes would be more than enough to cover the €20 cost of switching.

The problem is that a €40 per day tax on each tonne of pollutant results in a reduction of only 1 tonne per day, 3 short of the 4 tonne target. Suppose instead that the government imposed a tax of €101 per tonne. Sludge Oil would then adopt process B, because the €100 extra daily cost of doing so would be less than the €101 saved in taxes. Northwest Lumber would adopt process D, because for every process up to and including C, the cost of switching to the next process would be less than the resulting tax saving.

Overall, then, a tax of €101 per tonne would result in the desired pollutant reduction of 4 tonnes per day. The total cost of the reduction would be only €280 per day (€100 per day for Sludge Oil and €180 per day for Northwest Lumber), or €300 per day less than when each firm was required to cut its pollution by half. (The taxes paid by the firms do not constitute a cost of pollution reduction, because the money can be used to reduce whatever taxes would otherwise need to be levied on citizens.)

**Exercise 14.1** In Example 14.1, if the tax were €61 per tonne of pollutant emitted each day, which production processes would the two firms adopt?

The advantage of the tax approach is that it concentrates pollution reduction in the hands of the firms that can accomplish it *at least cost*. Requiring each firm to cut emissions by the same proportion ignores the fact that some firms can reduce pollution much more cheaply than others. Note that under the tax approach, the cost of the last tonne of smoke removed is the same for each firm, so the efficiency condition is satisfied.

One problem with the tax approach is that unless the government has detailed knowledge about each firm's cost of reducing pollution, it cannot know how high to set the pollution tax. A tax that is too low will result in too much pollution, while a tax that is too high will result in too little. Of course, the government could start by setting a low tax rate and gradually increasing the rate until pollution is reduced to the target level. But because firms often incur substantial *sunk costs* when they switch from one process to another, that approach might be even more wasteful than requiring all firms to cut their emissions by the same proportion.

### *Auctioning pollution permits*

Another alternative is to establish a target level for pollution and then auction off permits to emit that level. The virtues of this approach are illustrated in Example 14.2.

### **Example 14.2** How much will pollution permits sell for?

Two firms, Sludge Oil and Northwest Lumber, again have access to the production processes described earlier (which are reproduced in Table 14.2). The government's goal is to cut the current level of pollution, 8 tonnes per day, by half. To do so, the government auctions off four permits, each of which entitles the bearer to emit 1 tonne of smoke per day. No smoke may be emitted without a permit. What price will the pollution permits fetch at auction, how many permits will each firm buy and what will be the total cost of the resulting pollution reduction?

| Process (smoke) | A (4 tonnes/day) | B (3 tonnes/day) | C (2 tonnes/day) | D (1 tonne/day) | E (0 tonnes/day) |
|---|---|---|---|---|---|
| Cost to Sludge Oil (€/day) | 100 | 200 | 600 | 1,300 | 2,300 |
| Cost to Northwest Lumber (€/day) | 300 | 320 | 380 | 480 | 700 |

**Table 14.2** Costs and Emissions for Different Production Processes

If Sludge Oil has no permits, it must use process *E*, which costs €2,300 per day to operate. If it had one permit, it could use process *D*, which would save it €1,000 per day. Thus the most Sludge Oil would be willing to pay for a single 1 tonne pollution permit is €1,000 per day. With a second permit, Sludge Oil could switch to process C and save another €700 per day; with a third permit, it could switch to process B and save another €400; and with a fourth permit, it could switch to process A and save another €100. Using similar reasoning, we can see that Northwest Lumber would pay up to €220 for one permit, up to €100 for a second, up to €60 for a third and up to €20 for a fourth.

Suppose the government starts the auction at a price of €90. Sludge Oil will then demand four permits and Northwest Lumber will demand two, for a total demand of six permits. Since the government wishes to sell only four permits, it will keep raising the price until the two firms together demand a total of only four permits. Once the price reaches €101, Sludge Oil will demand three permits and Northwest Lumber will demand only one, for a total quantity demanded of four permits. Compared to the unregulated alternative, in which each firm used process A, the daily cost of the auction solution is €280: Sludge Oil spends €100 switching from process A to process B, and Northwest Lumber spends €180 switching from A to D. This total is €300 less than the cost of requiring each firm to reduce its emissions by half. (Again, the permit fees paid by the firms do not constitute a cost of clean-up, because the money can be used to reduce taxes that would otherwise have to be collected.)

The auction method has the same virtue as the tax method: it concentrates pollution reduction in the hands of those firms that can accomplish it *at the lowest cost*. But the auction method has other attractive features that the tax approach does not have. First, it does not induce firms to commit themselves to costly investments that they will have to abandon if the clean-up falls short of the target level. And, second, it allows private citizens a direct voice in determining where the emission level will be set. For example, any group that believes the pollution target is too lenient could raise money to buy permits at auction. By keeping those permits locked away in a safe, the group could ensure that they will not be used to emit pollution.

Several decades ago, when economists first proposed the auctioning of pollution permits, or **emissions trading**, outraged reactions were widely reported in the press, and in recent years the proposal has fallen foul of 'green' environmentalists. Most of those reactions amounted to the charge that the proposal would 'permit rich firms to pollute to their heart's content'. Such an assertion betrays a total misunderstanding of the forces that generate pollution. Firms pollute not because they *want* to pollute, but because dirty production processes are cheaper than clean ones. Society's only real interest is in keeping the *total amount of pollution* from becoming excessive, not in who actually does the polluting. And in any event, the firms that do most of the polluting under an auction system will not be rich firms, but those for whom pollution reduction is most costly.

**emissions trading** a system whereby firms can trade emission reductions, with the result that any given level of emissions reduction is undertaken by those with the lowest costs of achieving reductions

Economists have argued patiently against these misinformed objections to the auction system, and their efforts have finally borne fruit. The sale of pollution permits is now common in several parts of the United States, and there is growing interest in other countries in such an approach.

## Economic naturalist 14.1 Emissions trading in the EU: what can trading deliver?

As an instrument to achieve emissions reductions in line with the targets set at Kyoto the EU Commission published a Green Paper in 2000[2] outlining proposals for the establishment of a price-based mechanism to reduce emissions. This was the creation of an emissions trading regime. It envisaged the establishment of *national quotas* for emissions of carbon dioxide ($CO_2$), which the national governments would allocate and then permit firms to trade, buying or selling reflecting the costs of reducing emissions and the penalties for not doing so. The proposal provided the basis for a Council Directive in 2003[3] establishing an emissions trading regime and

[2] COM/2000/87, available on the Commission website, europa.eu.int/comm/index_en.htm.

[3] Council Directive 2003/87/EC.

which set down national allocations. The emissions trading regime began to function in January 2005.

Ignoring differences of detail, the essence of the scheme is that which was described in Example 14.2. Faced with legally binding national requirements to reduce emissions (and fines for non-compliance), firms could either reduce emissions or purchase the right not to do so. Given a fixed allocation for each country, and, therefore, for the Union as a whole, this created a market in the right to emit greenhouse gases, with the allocation being subject to reduction to comply with Kyoto targets. By reducing emissions a firm created a *saleable asset* (the reduction) that it could retain or sell. The implication, as in the examples above, is that a trading system would allocate the reduction in emissions as between firms (and, therefore, as between EU regions) in such a way as to ensure that the costs of reduction would be minimised.

A preliminary and somewhat aggregated estimate undertaken in 2000 suggested that if the EU15 was treated as six zones, and abatement costs in those zones were taken to represent the costs of reducing emissions, the cost of complying with Kyoto could be reduced by 25 per cent by permitting EU-wide emissions trading.[4] The annual cost with EU15-wide trading was estimated at 0.15 per cent of GDP for the EU15 as a whole. If the zones had to meet their targets without trading between zones, but using the most efficient means to reduce emissions within zones, the cost would amount to 0.20 per cent of GDP per annum. Using the most efficient methods within zones is equivalent to using emissions trading within zones.

Further work undertaken at the same time to establish the general cost implications of different approaches to managing emissions through regulation gives an idea of the degree to which different approaches affect the overall economic costs of reaching environmental targets. If we assumed that the target for emissions reduction agreed from achieving lower total liquid fuel usage is accepted and *then* imposed a national average target percentage emissions reduction on all sectors in each country across the EU15, the cost of reducing emissions by sector (as opposed to simply reducing liquid fuel usage) to reach Kyoto targets for $CO_2$ would be of the order of €20 billion per annum. If, however, we obtained the same total reduction based on permitting emissions trading within countries (i.e. the national target is met, but via trading within each country) the cost would be of the order of €9 billion per annum. This would be reduced further by €3 billion, or one-third, by permitting full EU15-wide trading.[5]

## RECAP Using price incentives in environmental regulation

An efficient programme for reducing pollution is one for which the *marginal cost of abatement* is the same for all polluters. Taxing pollution has this desirable property, as does the auction of pollution permits. The auction method also has the advantage that regulators can achieve a desired abatement target without having detailed knowledge of the abatement technologies available to polluters.

[4] Institute for Prospective Technological Studies (IPTS) (2000). The IPTS is a Directorate-General Research Centre.

[5] Capros and Mantzos (2000).

## 2: Using regulation to counteract the exploitation of market power: market failure and regulatory failure – the Californian power crisis

Regulation to control the pricing of electricity has become a familiar part of the EU political and economic landscape since 1990. The proximate cause has been the decisions taken since the early 1990s to liberalise energy markets as part of the programme to create the Single Market envisaged in the Maastricht Treaty. Prior to this, and in the United Kingdom prior to the ideological revolution associated with the premiership of Margaret Thatcher, the norm in Europe was for state-owned monopoly supply systems to operate in each country or region. Generation, transmission and distribution of electricity was in general vertically integrated, with a single state-controlled entity being responsible for the three functions: producing power, transmitting current to the user and selling the power to the user. By retaining the firms in public ownership, it was believed that any tendency to use a monopoly position to raise prices would be eliminated, since the supplier's management was appointed by the government and was subject to political control. Monopoly was believed to be unavoidable because it was generally accepted that electricity was a local (at least) natural monopoly.

In the United States, in contrast, the norm was for privately owned firms to produce and sell electricity. These firms were regional monopolies and, as in Europe, were in general vertically integrated. However, because they were privately owned it was felt necessary to subject them to regulatory control, in order to ensure that they could not abuse their monopoly position by generating huge profits by means of monopoly restrictions on output leading to higher prices to end users. So, regulation has been a feature of the US energy sector for much longer that in Europe.

From the late 1980s onwards there was growing pressure in California to 'deregulate' the electricity sector. Much of this came from the big power companies and from large commercial purchasers. The latter, under California's existing regulatory regime, had been paying higher prices for power in order to keep down prices to consumers and some politically sensitive commercial and other uses. In other words, these large commercial users were being obliged to *cross-subsidise* consumption of power by other users. In fact, 'deregulation' really meant 're-regulation' to permit increased competition in generation and distribution. Inevitably, this meant what has been referred to as 'rebalancing' of prices to reduce or eliminate cross-subsidisation between types of user, and to make power charges reflect the marginal cost of supplying power. That is what competitive markets do. Deregulation in 1996 was supposed to solve the industry's problems. As far as many in California were concerned, it did nothing, but rather resulted in the power crises of 2001 and 2002. These were put down by critics of deregulation to the short-term-maximising behaviour of the power companies.

However, one problem with the regulatory process is that it, too, is subject to failure. In the Californian case the regulatory regime discouraged power suppliers from investing in new capacity while simultaneously sheltering large numbers of consumers from paying the true cost of the power they were consuming (encouraging consumption of power in circumstances where the marginal willingness to pay was less than the marginal cost of production). This reflected the fact that the regulatory function had been 'captured' by powerful lobby groups. They ensured that prices to large numbers of end users were prevented from rising to reflect scarcity of capacity.

Rising demand (and supply problems arising from falling availability of low-cost power imports from hydroelectric sources in neighbouring states) led to shortages as domestic Californian generating capacity failed to expand to meet demand because price controls discouraged investment in new capacity while encouraging demand growth. The consequences in 2001–02 were a series of shortages leading to rationing and blackouts on a rolling basis.

Regulatory capture is seen by economists as a serious problem because it has the effect of perverting a process designed to reduce market failure so as to introduce further problems akin to those it was supposed to solve. In the Californian case, the regulatory process was captured by populist pressure groups. More often, however, the regulator may be captured by the entity being regulated. When this happens, regulation is used to protect producer interests at the expense of general economic efficiency. Classic cases of regulation protecting producer interest are where legislation permits self-regulation by a trade or profession. In recent years this has led to reforms in regulation procedures in areas such as legal services, accountancy services and some parts of the health services sector. Less obvious, but potentially equally damaging to economic efficiency, are cases where an 'independent' regulator is 'turned' over time by the industry being regulated. This can happen when the regulator depends on the industry being regulated for the information required to perform its functions.

## 3 Regulation and health and safety: remedying defective incentives

### *Workplace safety regulations*

Most industrialised countries have laws that attempt to limit the extent to which workers are exposed to health and safety risks on the job. These laws often are described as necessary to protect workers against exploitation by employers with market power. Given the working conditions we saw in the early stages of the Industrial Revolution, the idea that such exploitation pervades unregulated private markets has intuitive appeal.

The miserable conditions of factory workers, juxtaposed with the often opulent lifestyle enjoyed by factory owners, seemed to affirm the idea that owners were exploiting workers. But if conditions in the factories were in fact too dangerous, how much safer should they have been?

Consider the question of whether to install a specific safety device – say, a guard rail on a lathe. Many people are reluctant to employ the cost–benefit principle to answer such a question. To them, safety is an absolute priority, so the guard rail should be installed regardless of its cost. Yet most of us do not make personal decisions about our own health and safety that way. No one you know, for example, gets the brakes on his car checked every day, even though doing so would reduce the likelihood of being killed in an accident. The reason, obviously, is that daily brake inspections would be very costly and would not reduce the probability of an accident significantly compared with annual or semi-annual inspections.

The same logic can be applied to installing a guard rail on a lathe. If the amount one is willing to pay to reduce the likelihood of an accident exceeds the cost of the guard rail, it should be installed; otherwise, it should not be. And no matter how highly we value reducing the odds of an accident, we will almost surely settle for less than perfect safety. After all, to reduce the risk of an accident to nearly zero, one would have to enclose the lathe in a thick Plexiglas case and operate it with remote-controlled mechanical arms. Faced with the prohibitive cost of such an alternative, most of us would decide that the best approach is to add safety equipment whose benefit exceeds its cost and then use caution while operating the machine.

But will unregulated employers offer the level of workplace safety suggested by the Cost–Benefit Principle? Most nations appear to have decided that they will not. As noted, virtually every industrial country now has comprehensive legislation mandating minimum safety standards in the workplace – laws usually described as safeguards against the exploitation of workers.

Yet explaining safety regulation as an antidote for exploitation raises troubling questions. One difficulty stems from the economist's argument that competition for workers prods firms to provide the socially optimal level of amenities. For example, if an amenity – say, a guard rail on a lathe – costs €50 per month to install and maintain, and workers value it at €100 per month, then the firm must install the device or risk losing workers to a competitor that does. After all, if a competing firm were to pay workers €60 per month less than they currently earn, it could cover the cost of the device with €10 to spare, while providing a compensation package that is €40 per month more attractive than the first employer's.

Critics respond to this argument that in practice there is very little competition in the labour market. They argue that incomplete information, worker immobility and other frictions create situations in which workers have little choice but to accept whatever conditions employers offer. Alternatively, they argue that workers are poorly informed and unable to make 'rational' decisions in relation to health and safety. Finally, there is an argument to the effect that people will take more risks if someone else pays the costs. If society is committed to paying for medical treatment or to replacing earnings in the case of workplace injuries, this introduces 'moral hazard' and a higher level of injury than if workers and employers had to meet these costs.

The first of these arguments has the following weakness: even if a firm were the only employer in the market, it would still have an incentive to install a €50 safety device that is worth €100 to the worker. Failure to do so would be to leave cash on the table.

The defective information argument, too, is troubling, because competing firms would have a strong incentive to call the devices to the workers' attention. If the problem is that workers cannot move to the competing firm's location, then the firm can set up a branch near the exploited workers. Collusive agreements to restrain such competition should prove difficult to maintain, because each firm can increase its profit by cheating on the agreement.

In fact, worker mobility between firms is high, as is entry by new firms into existing markets; and, as noted in Chapter 10, cartel agreements have always been notoriously unstable. Information may not be perfect, but if a new employer in town is offering a better deal, sooner or later word gets around.

Finally, if, despite these checks, some firms still manage to exploit their workers, we should expect those firms to earn a relatively high profit. But in fact we observe just the opposite. Year in and year out, firms that pay the *highest* wages are the most profitable. And so we are left with a puzzle. The fear of exploitation by employers with market power has led governments to adopt sweeping and costly safety regulations; yet the evidence suggests that exploitation cannot be a major problem. As Example 14.3 suggests, however, safety regulation might prove useful even in a perfectly competitive environment with complete information.

The strongest argument is the third one: regulation is designed to shelter tax-payers from the costs of accidents. There is, however, another interesting argument in favour of regulation derived from the tools of game theory we developed in Chapter 10.

### **Example 14.3** Will Don and Michael choose the optimal amount of safety?

Suppose Don and Michael are the only two members of a hypothetical community. They get satisfaction from three things – their income, safety on the job and their position on the economic ladder. Suppose Don and Michael must both choose between two jobs, a safe job that pays €50 per week and a risky job that pays €80 per week. The value of safety to each is €40 per week. Having more income than one's neighbour is worth €40 per week to each; having less income than one's neighbour means a €40 per week reduction in satisfaction. (Having the same income as one's neighbour means no change in satisfaction.) Will Don and Michael make the best job choices possible in this situation?

Viewed in isolation, each person's decision should be to take the safe job. Granted, it pays €30 per week less than the risky job, but the extra safety it offers is worth €40 per week. So aside from the issue of relative income, the value of the safe job is €90 per week (its €50 salary plus €40 worth of safety), or €10 per week more than the risky job.

Once we incorporate concerns about relative income, however, the logic of the decision changes in a fundamental way. Now the attractiveness of each job depends on the job chosen by the other. The four possible combinations of choices and their corresponding levels of satisfaction are shown in Table 14.3. If each man chooses a safe job, he will get €50 of income, €40 worth of satisfaction from safety and – because each will have the same income – zero satisfaction from relative income. So if each man chooses the safe job, each will get a total of

€90 worth of satisfaction. If, instead, each man chooses the risky job, each will get €80 of income, zero satisfaction from safety, and because each has the same income as the other, zero satisfaction from relative income. If we compare the upper-left cell of Table 14.3 with the lower-right cell, then, we can say unequivocally that Don and Michael would be happier if each took a safe job at lower income than if each chose a risky job with more income.

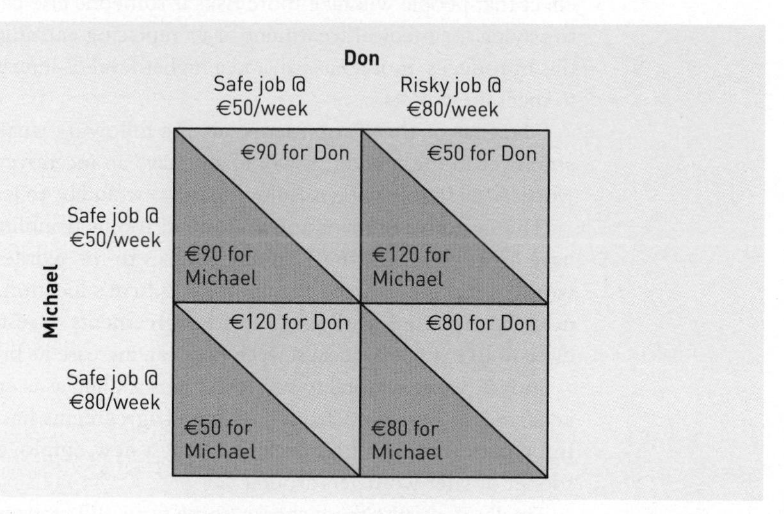

| Michael \ Don | Safe job @ €50/week | Risky job @ €80/week |
|---|---|---|
| Safe job @ €50/week | €90 for Don<br>€90 for Michael | €50 for Don<br>€120 for Michael |
| Safe job @ €80/week | €120 for Don<br>€50 for Michael | €80 for Don<br>€80 for Michael |

**Table 14.3** The Effect of Concern about Relative Income on Worker Choices Regarding Safety

But consider how the choice plays out once the two men recognise their *interdependence*. Suppose, for example, that Michael chooses the safe job. If Don then chooses the unsafe job, he ends up with a total of €120 of satisfaction – €80 in salary plus €40 from having more income than Michael. Michael, for his part, ends up with only €50 worth of satisfaction – €50 in salary plus €40 from safety, minus €40 from a having lower income than Don. Alternatively, suppose Michael chooses the risky job. Then Don will again do better to accept the risky job, for by doing so he gets €80 worth of satisfaction rather than €50.

In short, no matter which job Michael chooses, Don will get more satisfaction by choosing the risky job. Likewise, no matter which job Don chooses, Michael will do better by choosing the risky job. Yet when each follows his dominant strategy, they end up in the lower-right cell of the table, which provides only €80 per week of satisfaction to each – €10 less than if each had chosen the safe job. Thus their job–safety choice confronts them with a prisoner's dilemma (see Chapter 10). As in all such situations, when the players choose independently, they fail to make the most of their opportunities.

**Exercise 14.2** How would your answer to the question posed in Example 14.3 have differed if the value of safety had been not €40 per week, but €20?

Example 14.3 suggests an alternative explanation for safety regulation, one that is not based on the need to protect workers from exploitation. If Don and Michael could choose collectively, they would pick the safe job and maximise their combined satisfaction. Thus each might support legislation that establishes safety standards in the workplace.

Regulation, however, does not always improve matters. The labour market may not be perfect, but government regulators aren't perfect either.

The issue is not that there is no role for regulation, but that it is not clear that the regulations imposed are not more onerous than are necessary to correct the market failure, whatever it is. For this reason many economists favour programmes that increase employers' financial incentives to reduce workplace injuries. The worker's compensation insurance system provides a mechanism through which such a change might be achieved. If insurance premiums reflect the experience and safety record of the firm, poor risk employers will face higher premiums, and have an incentive to increase workplace safety.

Economists argue that revising insurance premiums to reflect the full social cost of the injuries sustained by each employer's workers would provide the optimal incentive to curtail injuries in the workplace. In effect, premiums set at this level would be an optimal tax on injuries, and this would be efficient for the same reason that a properly chosen tax on pollution is efficient. An injury tax set at the *marginal cost of injury* would encourage employers to adopt all safety measures whose benefits exceed their costs.

As in other domains, we are far more likely to achieve optimal safety levels in the workplace if we choose among policies on practical cost–benefit grounds rather than on the basis of slogans about the merits or flaws of the free market.

As Economic naturalist 14.2 illustrates, costs and benefits play a pivotal role in decisions about whether the government chooses to constrain individual choice in the safety domain, and if so, how.

### Economic naturalist 14. 2 Why does the government require safety seats for infants who travel in cars, but not for infants who travel in aeroplanes?

A mother cannot legally drive her six-month-old son to a nearby grocery store without first strapping him into a government-approved safety seat. Yet she can fly with him from London to Rome with no restraining device at all. Why this difference?

In case of an accident – whether in a car or an aeroplane – an infant who is strapped into a safety seat is more likely to escape injury or death than one who is unrestrained. But the probability of being involved in a serious accident is hundreds of times higher when travelling by car than when travelling by air, so the benefit of having safety seats is greater for trips made by car. Using safety seats is also far more costly on plane trips than on car trips. Whereas most cars have plenty of extra room for a safety seat, parents might need to purchase an extra ticket to use one on an aeroplane. Most parents appear unwilling to pay €600 more per trip for a small increment in safety, for either themselves or their children.

### RECAP Workplace safety regulation

Most countries regulate safety in the workplace, a practice often defended as needed to protect workers from being exploited by employers with market power. Yet safety regulation might be attractive even in perfectly competitive labour markets, because the *social payoff* from investment in safety often exceeds the private payoff. An injury tax set at the *marginal cost of injury* would encourage optimal investment in workplace safety.

## Public health and safety

Because public health and law enforcement officials are charged with protecting our health and safety, political leaders are often reluctant to discuss expenditures on public health and law enforcement in cost–benefit terms. But because we live in a world of scarcity, we cannot escape the fact that spending more in these areas means spending less on other things of value.

Illnesses, like accidents, are costly to prevent. The socially optimal expenditure on a health measure that reduces a specific illness is that amount for which the marginal benefit to society of the measure exactly equals its marginal cost. For example, in deciding how much to spend on vaccinating against measles, a rational public health policy would expand the proportion of the population vaccinated until the marginal cost of an additional vaccination was exactly equal to the marginal value of the illnesses thus prevented.

As Economic naturalist 14.3 illustrates, however, the decision whether to be vaccinated looks very different from each individual's perspective.

## Economic naturalist 14.3 Why do most governments encourage (and some actually require) vaccination against childhood illnesses?

Recent evidence on the epidemiology of vaccination has finally laid to rest the hypothesis that the combined inoculation of young children by one injection against measles, mumps and rubella (MMR) is linked to autism. While this fear was prevalent there was strong resistance to the MMR vaccination especially in the United Kingdom but also in other countries in Europe. The government line was consistent: even before the link was shown almost certainly not to exist, the benefits from the MMR injection greatly outweighed the costs, and it continued to encourage people to use the procedure.

This raises an interesting question. Why should the government encourage and subsidise vaccination? Free or highly subsidised vaccination against a variety of illnesses is a common feature of most advanced countries' health and social welfare systems. In some cases, vaccination is effectively compulsory in that access to state-financed education is conditional on a child's having been vaccinated. In the United States, proof of immunisation against diphtheria, measles, poliomyelitis and rubella is now universally required for entry into state schools. Most states also require immunisation against tetanus (49 states), pertussis (whooping cough) (44 states), mumps (43 states) and hepatitis B (26 states). Why these requirements?

Being vaccinated against a childhood illness entails a small but potentially serious risk. The vaccine against pertussis, for example, is believed to cause some form of permanent brain damage in 1 out of every 110,000 children vaccinated. Contracting the disease itself also poses serious health risks, and in an environment in which infections were sufficiently likely to occur, individuals would have a compelling reason to bear the risk of being vaccinated in order to reduce the even larger risk from infection. The problem is that in an environment in which most children were vaccinated, infection rates would be low, making the risk of vaccination loom understandably large in the eyes of individual families. The ideal situation from the perspective of any individual family would be to remain unvaccinated in an environment in which all other families were vaccinated. But as more and more families decided to forgo vaccination, infection rates would mount. Eventually the vaccination rate would stabilise at the point at which the additional risk to the individual family of becoming vaccinated would be exactly equal to the risk from remaining unvaccinated. But this calculation ignores the fact that a decision to remain unvaccinated poses risk not just to the individual decision maker, but also to others who have decided to become vaccinated (since no vaccine affords 100 per cent protection against infection).

Relegating the vaccination decision to individuals results in a sub-optimally low vaccination rate, because individual decision makers fail to take adequate account of the cost that their becoming infected will impose on others. It is for this reason that most states require vaccinations against specific childhood illnesses.

## Government in the economy: producing public goods

The second area of government activity that we want to consider is that of the government acting as a producer of goods and services that are either consumed or are inputs into further production. Economists usually consider such outputs under two headings: **merit goods** and **public goods**.

**merit goods** goods produced under non-market conditions by the state for political reasons

**public good** a good or service that, to at least some degree, is both non-rival and non-excludable

Merit goods are goods that could be, and frequently are, produced in markets, but for political reasons are produced under non-market conditions by the state. Obvious examples are health services (e.g. the UK NHS), education and housing. All these can be, and are, produced in markets in nearly all countries ... but are also produced by (or for) the state to allocate on a basis other than conventional demand expressed in terms of willingness to pay.

The term 'public goods' is used to describe certain outputs that for technical reasons simply cannot be produced efficiently if production is left to the interaction of the supply and demand sides of a market. By 'efficiently' is meant production resulting in the quantity being produced being that for which marginal benefits equal marginal costs.

The involvement of the state in provision of merit goods is pervasive, but in the end reflects political rather than economic pressures. Public goods provision, on the other hand, is the consequence of purely economic factors affecting the potential for market provision of certain types of outputs. As we shall see, the provision of public goods requires collective decisions on whether to produce them, how much to produce and finding the money to pay for provision.

### Public goods versus private goods

Government spending in OECD countries is equivalent to 30–50 per cent of GNP, varying as between countries. Much of this is, of course, *redistribution*. But typically half or more represents the cost of government direct provision of goods and services (the justice system, for example, or defence forces' salaries. Another tranche represents purchases of the output of private sector firms (for example, when roads, hospitals or ground attack fighters are produced.

In many cases these are 'merit' goods: goods whose production could efficiently be left to markets but, for political reasons, usually distributive, are determined by political choices. In the other cases, and in the case of some goods that might be treated as merit goods, the spending is on what are described as 'public' goods. In this treatment of the government as an *economic agent* we will be considering the issue of public goods provision.

**non-rival good** a good whose consumption by one person does not diminish its availability for others

**non-excludable good** a good that is difficult, or costly, to exclude non-payers from consuming

Public goods are those goods or services that are, in varying degrees, **non-rival** and **non-excludable**. A non-rival good is one whose consumption by one person does not diminish its availability for others. For example, if the armed forces prevent a hostile nation from invading your city, your enjoyment of that protection does not diminish its value to your neighbours. A good is non-excludable if it is difficult to exclude non-payers from consuming it. For instance, even if your neighbours don't pay their share of the cost of maintaining an army, they will still enjoy its protection.

Another example of a non-rival and non-excludable good is a terrestrial (i.e. not via cable or satellite) TV broadcast of *ER*, *Coronation Street* or *Match of the Day*. The fact that you tune in one evening does not make the programme any less available to others, and once the broadcast has been beamed out over the airwaves it is difficult to prevent anyone from tuning in. Similarly, when the millennium celebrations in many European cities involved magnificent fireworks displays, the municipal authorities concerned couldn't charge people for watching given the fact that the display was (and had to be) visible over a wide area. Curiously, private individuals could charge viewers if they owned or provided a limited amount of superior viewing facilities.

In contrast, the typical private good is diminished one-for-one by any individual's consumption of it. For instance, when you eat a sandwich, it is no longer available for anyone else. Moreover, people can be easily prevented from consuming sandwiches if they don't pay.

**Exercise 14.3** Which of the following, if any, is non-rival?

(A) The website of the EU Commission at 3 a.m.

(B) The World Cup soccer championship game watched in person.

(C) The World Cup soccer championship game watched on TV.

**pure public good** a good or service that, to a high degree, is both non-rival and non-excludable

Goods that are both highly non-excludable and non-rival are often called **pure public goods**. Two reasons favour government provision of such goods. First, for-profit private companies would have obvious difficulty recovering their cost of production. Many people might be willing to pay enough to cover the cost of producing the good, but if it is non-excludable, the company cannot easily charge for it (an example of the free-rider problem discussed in Chapter 12). And second, if the marginal cost of serving additional users is zero once the good has been produced, then charging for the good would be inefficient, even if there were some practical way to do so.

**collective good** a good or service that, to at least some degree, is non-rival but excludable

This inefficiency often characterises the provision of **collective goods** – non-rival goods for which it is possible to exclude non-payers. Pay-per-view cable television is an example. People who don't pay to get Sky TV may be unable to view some programmes as soon as subscribers. Remember the controversy over whether or not certain football games could be restricted to pay-TV channels? Since the marginal cost to society of those excluded from viewing is literally zero, excluding these viewers is wasteful.

**pure private good** one for which non-payers can easily be excluded and for which each unit consumed by one person means one less unit available for others

**pure commons good** one for which non-payers cannot easily be excluded and for which each unit consumed by one person means one less unit available for others

A **pure private good** is one from which non-payers can easily be excluded and for which one person's consumption creates a one-for-one reduction in the good's availability for others. The theory of perfectly competitive supply developed in Chapter 6 applies to pure private goods, of which basic agricultural products are perhaps the best examples.

A **pure commons good** is a rival good that is also non-excludable, so-called because goods with this combination of properties almost always result in a tragedy of the commons (see Chapter 11). Fish in ocean waters are an example.

The classification scheme defined by the non-rival and non-excludable properties is summarised in Table 14.4. The columns of the table indicate the extent to which one person's consumption of a good fails to diminish its availability for others. Goods in the right column are non-rival, and those in the left column are not. The rows of Table 14.4 indicate the difficulty of excluding non-payers from consuming the good. Goods in the top row are non-excludable, those in the bottom row, excludable. Private goods (lower-left cell) are rival and excludable.

Public goods (upper-right cell) are non-rival and non-excludable. The two hybrid categories are commons goods (upper-left cell), which are rival but non-excludable, and collective goods (lower-right cell), which are excludable but non-rival.

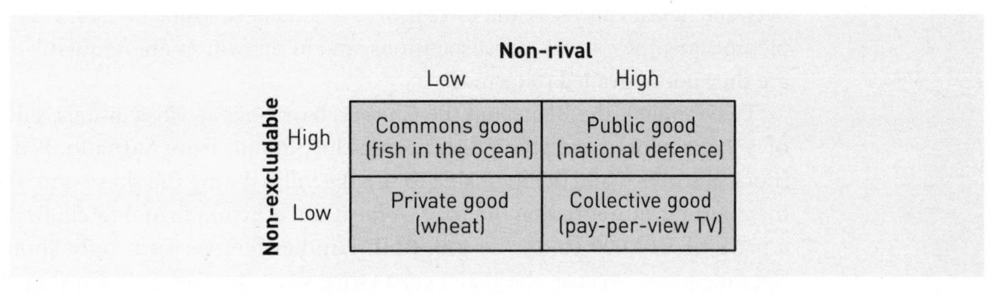

| Non-excludable | Non-rival: Low | Non-rival: High |
|---|---|---|
| High | Commons good (fish in the ocean) | Public good (national defence) |
| Low | Private good (wheat) | Collective good (pay-per-view TV) |

**Table 14.4** Private, Public and Hybrid Goods

Collective goods are provided sometimes by government, sometimes by private companies. Most pure public goods are provided by government, but even private companies can sometimes find profitable ways of producing goods that are both non-rival *and* non-excludable. An example is broadcast radio and TV, which covers its costs by selling airtime to advertisers.

The mere fact that a good is a pure public good does not necessarily mean that government ought to provide it. On the contrary, the only public goods the government should even *consider* providing are those whose benefits exceed their costs. The cost of a public good is simply the sum of all the explicit and implicit costs incurred to provide it. The benefit of a public good is measured by asking how much people would be willing to pay for it. Although that sounds similar to the way we measure the benefit of a private good, an important distinction exists. The benefit of an additional unit of a private good, such as a cheeseburger, is the highest sum that any individual buyer would be willing to pay for it. In contrast, the benefit of an additional unit of a public good, such as an additional broadcast episode of *Sesame Street*, is the sum of the reservation prices of all people who will watch that episode.

Even if the amount that all beneficiaries of a public good would be willing to pay exceeds its cost, government provision of that good makes sense only if there is no other less costly way of providing it. For example, whereas city governments often pay for fireworks displays, they almost invariably hire private companies to put on these events. Finally, if the benefit of a public good does not exceed its cost, we are better off without it.

## Paying for public goods

Not everyone benefits equally from the provision of a given public good. For example, some people find fireworks displays highly entertaining, but others simply don't care about them and still others actively dislike them. Ideally, it might seem that the most equitable method of financing a given public good would be to tax people in proportion to their willingness to pay for the good. To illustrate this approach, suppose Jones values a public good at €100, Smith values the same good at €200 and the cost of the good is €240. Jones would then be taxed €80, and Smith would be taxed €160. The good would be provided, and each tax-payer in this example would reap a surplus equal to 25 per cent of his tax payment: €20 for Jones, €40 for Smith.

In practice, however, government officials usually lack the information they would need to tax people in proportion to their willingness to pay for specific public goods. (Think about it: if a tax official asked you how much you would be willing to pay to have a new motorway and you knew you would be taxed in proportion to the amount you responded, what would you say?) Examples 14.4–14.6 illustrate some of the problems that arise in financing public goods, and suggest possible solutions to these problems.

### **Example 14. 4** Will rural roads in Tuscany be upgraded?

One of the picturesque features of the rolling and mountainous countryside in Tuscany, Umbria and Le Marche in Italy is the number of 'white' (i.e. unpaved) roads that wander between fields, vineyards and olive groves to small groups of houses. Unfortunately, although picturesque, they wreck car suspensions, and in the winter are frequently impassable. So why are they not upgraded to tarmac?

Two families, the Blairs and the Chiracs, have holiday villas in Italy, side by side at the end of a 2 km white road some distance up the Sibillini from Sarnano. Fed up with replacing shock absorbers, and being unable to use the villas during the ski season, they are considering the question of upgrading the road. A local construction firm, Fratelli Berlusconi, has quoted a price of €10,000 to do the job. Both families feel very strongly about having the road upgraded, but because the Blairs earn twice what the Chiracs earn they differ as to willingness to pay. For the Blairs, richer, and having more visitors, it is worth €8,000. To the Chiracs, with less money and being less sociable, it is worth only €4,000. Would either family be willing to foot the bill individually? Is it efficient for them to share the cost?

Neither will pay the full cost individually because each has a reservation price that is *below its cost*. But because the two together value the upgrading of the road at €12,000, sharing the cost would be socially efficient. If they were to do so, total economic surplus would be increased by €2,000. Since sharing the cost is the efficient outcome, we might expect that the Blairs and the Chiracs would quickly reach agreement to finance the project. Unfortunately, however, the joint purchase and sharing of facilities is often easier proposed than accomplished. One hurdle is that people must incur costs merely to get together to discuss joint purchases. With only two people involved, those costs might not be significant. But if hundreds or thousands of people were involved, communication costs could be prohibitive.

With large numbers of people, the free-rider problem also emerges (see Chapter 12). After all, everyone knows that the project will either succeed or fail independently of any one person's contribution to it. Everyone thus has an incentive to withhold contributions – or get a free ride – in the hope that others will contribute.

Finally, even when only a few people are involved, reaching agreement on a fair sharing of the total expense may be difficult. For example, the Blairs and the Chiracs might be reluctant to disclose their true reservation prices to one another because of what it revealed as to their relative incomes.

A solution could be to ask the Fratelli Berlusconi to use their local knowledge to get the Comune of Sarnano to do the job. Unfortunately, the Comune is likely to argue that if the road is upgraded at the tax-payers' expense the Blairs and the Chiracs will capture all the benefits while exporting the cost almost entirely to the other tax-payers. In any case, it is not clear to the Comune that the benefits actually exceed the costs. If they do, why do the two families not pay to get the job done? Now, if the Blairs and Chiracs were to consider allowing the Comune to tax them to pay for the work, the matter might be looked at again.

These practical concerns may lead us to empower government to buy public goods on our behalf. But, as Example 14.5 makes clear, this approach does not eliminate the need to reach political agreement on how public purchases are to be financed.

### **Example 14.5** Will the Comune get consent to upgrade the road if it is financed by an 'equal tax' rule?

Suppose the Blairs and the Chiracs could ask the Comune to help broker the road upgrading. And suppose that the regional government's tax policy must follow a 'non-discrimination' rule that prohibits charging any citizen more for a public good than it charges his or her neighbour. Another rule is that public goods can be provided only if a majority of citizens approve of them. What will happen?

**poll tax** a tax that collects the same amount from every tax-payer

**regressive tax** a tax under which the proportion of income paid in taxes declines as income rises

A tax that collects the same amount from every citizen is called a **poll tax**. A poll tax is an example of a **regressive tax**, one for which the proportion of a tax-payer's income that is paid in taxes declines as the tax-payer's income rises. If the government must rely on a poll tax, it must raise €5,000 from the Blairs and €5,000 from the Chiracs. But since the upgrading is worth only €4,000 to the Chiracs, they will vote against the project, thus denying it a majority.

This is a general problem with poll tax finance, leaving aside considerations of fairness. The point is not confined to the specific public good considered. It applies whenever tax-payers place significantly different valuations on public goods, as will almost always happen whenever people earn significantly different incomes. An equal-tax rule under these circumstances will almost invariably rule out the provision of many worthwhile public goods.

As Example 14.6 suggests, one solution to this problem is to allow taxes to vary by income.

### Example 14.6 Will the road be upgraded if the Comune can levy a proportional tax on income?

Suppose that the Chiracs propose that the revenue be raised by imposing a proportional tax on income. Will the Blairs agree?

**proportional income tax** one under which all tax-payers pay the same proportion of their incomes in taxes

A **proportional income tax** is one under which all tax-payers pay the same percentage of their incomes in taxes. Under such a tax, the Blairs would support the Chiracs' proposal because, otherwise, each family would fail to enjoy a public good whose benefit exceeds its share of its cost. Under the proportional tax on income, the Chiracs would contribute €3,333 toward the €10,000 cost of the road and the Blairs would contribute €6,667. The road would be upgraded, resulting in additional surpluses of €667 for the Chiracs and €1,333 for the Blairs.

Economic naturalist 14.4 makes the point that just as equal contributions are often a poor way to pay for public goods, they are also often a poor way to share expenses within the household.

### Economic naturalist 14.4 Why might a pre-nuptial agreement to share costs equally lead to a divorce?

Suppose David earns €20,000,000 per year while Victoria earns only €1,000,000. Given his income, David as an individual would probably want to spend much more than Victoria would on housing, travel, entertainment, education for their children, and the many other items they consume jointly. What will happen if the couple adopts a rule that each must contribute an equal amount toward the purchase of such items?

This rule would constrain the couple to live in a small (well, smaller) house, take only inexpensive vacations and skimp on entertainment, dining out and their children's education. It is therefore easy to see why David might argue for a change in the agreement. If Victoria's unwillingness to see spending rise could not be overcome, a divorce might be the only way out.

Public goods and jointly consumed private goods are different from individually consumed private goods in the following important way: different individuals are free to consume whatever quantity and quality of most private goods they choose to buy, but *jointly consumed goods must be provided in the same quantity and quality for all persons.*

As in the case of private goods, people's willingness to pay for public goods is generally an increasing function of income. Wealthy individuals tend to assign greater value to public goods than low-income people do, not because the wealthy have different tastes but because they have more money. A poll tax (head tax) would result in high-income persons getting smaller amounts of public goods than they want. By increasing the total economic surplus available for all to share, a tax system that assigns a larger share of the tax burden to people with higher incomes makes possible a better outcome for both rich and poor alike. Indeed, virtually all industrialised nations have at least mildly **progressive tax** systems, which means that the proportion of income paid in taxes actually rises with a family's income.

**progressive tax** one in which the proportion of income paid in taxes rises as income rises

Progressive taxation and even proportional taxation have often been criticised as being unfair to the wealthy, who are forced to pay more than others for public goods that all consume in common. The irony in this charge, however, is that exclusive reliance on poll taxes, or even proportional taxes, would curtail the provision of public goods and services that are of greatest value to high-income families. Studies have shown, for example, that the income elasticity of demand for public goods such as parks and recreation facilities, clean air and water, public safety, uncongested roads and aesthetically pleasing public spaces is substantially greater than 1. Failure to rely on progressive taxation would result in gross underprovision of such public goods and services.

In the examples considered thus far, the question was whether to provide a particular public good and, if so, how to pay for it. In practice, we often confront additional questions about what *level* and *quality* of a public good to provide.

## The demand curve for a public good

To calculate the socially optimal quantity of a public good, we must first construct the *demand curve* for that public good. The process for doing so differs in an important way from the one we use to generate the market demand curve for a private good.

For a private good, all buyers face the same price and each chooses the quantity she wishes to purchase at that price. Recall that to construct the demand curve for a private good from the demand curves for individual consumers, we place the individual demand curves side by side and add them horizontally. That is, for each of a series of fixed prices, we add the resulting quantities demanded on the individual demand curves. In Fig. 14.1, for example, we add the individual demand curves for a private good, $D_1$ and $D_2$ (panels (a) and (b)), horizontally to obtain the market demand curve for the good $D$ (panel (c)).

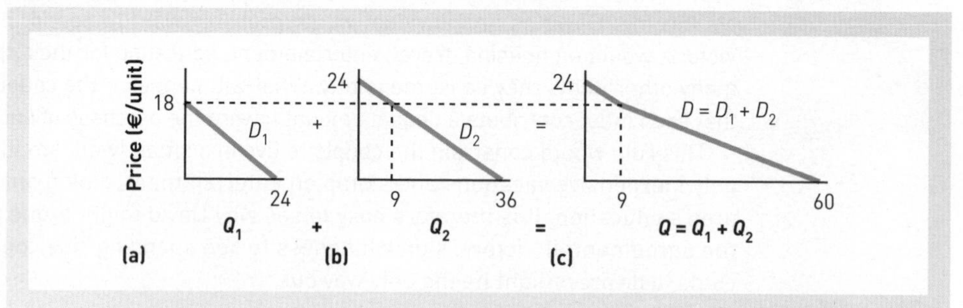


**Figure 14.1 Generating the Market Demand Curve for a Private Good.** To construct the market demand curve for a private good (c), we add the individual demand curves (a) and (b) horizontally.

For a public good, all buyers necessarily consume the same quantity, although each may differ in terms of willingness to pay for additional units of the good. Constructing the demand curve for a public good thus entails not horizontal summation of the individual demand curves but *vertical* summation. That is, for each of a series of quantity values, we must add the prices that individuals are willing to pay for an additional unit of the good. The curves $D_1$ and $D_2$ in Fig. 14.2(c) and (b) show individual demand curves for a public good by two different people. At each quantity, these curves tell how much the individual would be willing to pay for an additional unit of the public good. If we add $D_1$ and $D_2$ vertically, we obtain the total demand curve $D$ for the public good (panel (a)).

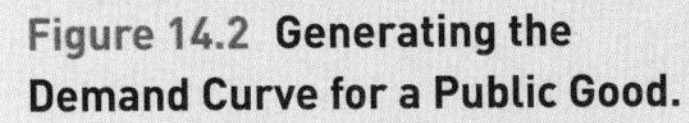

**Figure 14.2 Generating the Demand Curve for a Public Good.** To construct the demand curve for a public good (a), we add the individual demand curves (c) and (b) vertically.

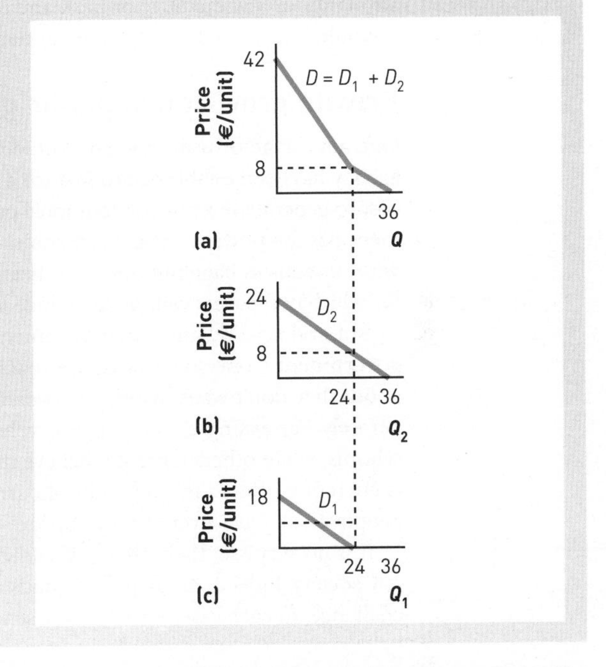


**Exercise 14.4** Bill and Tom are the only demanders of a public good. If Bill's demand curve is $P_B = 6 - 0.5Q$ and Tom's is $P_T = 1 - 2Q$, construct the demand curve for this public good.

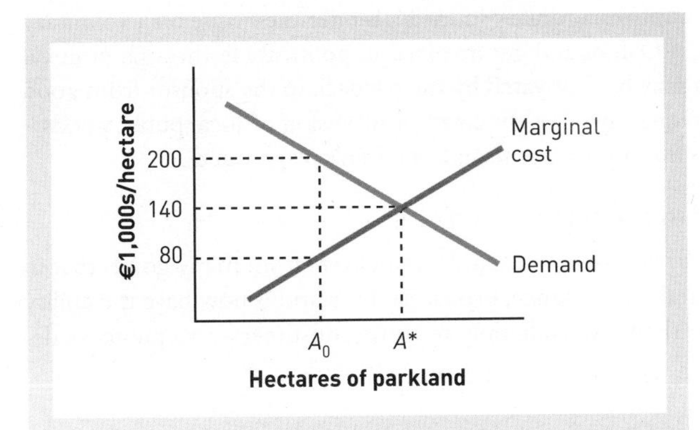


**Figure 14.3 The Optimal Quantity of Parkland.** The optimal number of hectares of urban parkland is $A^*$, the quantity at which the public's willingness to pay for additional parkland is equal to the marginal cost of parkland.

In Example 14.7, we see how the demand curve for a public good might be used in conjunction with information about costs to determine the optimal level of public park provision in a city.

### Example 14.7 What is the optimal quantity of urban park space?

The city government of a new, planned community must decide how much parkland to provide. The marginal cost curve and the public demand curve for urban parkland are as shown in Figure 14.3. Why is the marginal cost curve upward-sloping and the demand curve downward-sloping? Given these curves, what is the optimal quantity of parkland?

The marginal cost schedule for urban parkland is upward-sloping because of the Low-Hanging-Fruit Principle (Chapter 2): the city acquires the cheapest parcels of land first, and only then turns to more expensive parcels. Likewise, the marginal willingness-to-pay (WTP) curve is downward-sloping because of the law of diminishing marginal utility. Just as people are generally willing to pay less for their fifth hot dog than for their first, they are also willing to pay less for the 101st ha of parkland than for the 100th ha. Given these curves, $A^*$ is the optimal quantity of parkland. For any quantity less than $A^*$, the benefit of additional parkland exceeds its cost, which means that total economic surplus can be made larger by expanding the amount of parkland. For example, at $A_0$, the community would be willing to pay €200,000 for an additional hectare of urban parkland, but its cost is only €80,000. Similarly, for any quantity of parkland in excess of $A^*$, the community would gain more than it would lose by selling off some parkland.

## Private provision of public goods

One advantage of using the government to provide public goods is that once a tax collection agency has been established to finance a single public good, it can be expanded at relatively low cost to generate revenue for additional public goods. Another advantage is that because government has the power to tax, it can summarily assign responsibility for the cost of a public good without endless haggling over who bears what share of the burden. And in the case of goods for which non-payers cannot be excluded, the government may be the only feasible provider.

But exclusive reliance on government also entails disadvantages. Most fundamentally, the government's one-size-fits-all approach invariably requires many people to pay for public goods they don't want, while others end up having to do without public goods they want desperately. For example, many people vehemently oppose the provision of *any* sex education in schools, while others fervently believe that far more such instruction should be provided than is currently offered in most school curricula. In addition, mandatory taxation strikes many people as coercive, even if they approve of the particular public goods being provided.

It is no surprise, then, that governments are not the exclusive providers of public goods in any society. Indeed, many public goods are routinely provided through private channels. The challenge, in each case, is to devise a scheme for raising the required revenues.

### Funding by donation

Two well-known mechanisms that result in private provision of public goods are philanthropy and volunteer work effort; a third is commercial sponsorship. In the United States, and to a lesser extent in Europe, there is a strong tradition of endowment of research and the arts by wealthy individuals. In most countries, ordinary individuals offer their time on a voluntary basis to help such organisations as Oxfam and get involved in political life through political parties. Commercial sponsorship may be motivated by the payback to the sponsor from good publicity, but such sponsorship frequently takes the form of provision of local public goods – as, for example, when a firm pays for improvements in a children's playground.

### Development of new means to exclude non-payers

New electronic technology makes it possible to exclude non-payers from many goods that in the past could not be thus restricted. For instance, broadcast TV stations now have the ability to scramble their signals, making them available only to those consumers who purchase de-scrambling devices.

### Private contracting

More than 8 million Americans now live in gated private communities – private housing associations that wall off contiguous properties and provide various services to residents. They are increasingly the rule in middle-class areas in South Africa, and are starting to become common in parts of Europe. Many of these associations provide security services, schools and fire protection and in other ways function much like ordinary local governments. Recognising that individual incentives may not be strong enough to assure socially optimal levels of maintenance and landscaping, these associations often bill home owners for those services directly. Many of the rules imposed by these associations are even more restrictive than those imposed by local governments, a distinction that is defended on the grounds that people are always free to choose some other neighbourhood if they don't like the rule. Many people would be reluctant to tolerate a municipal ordinance that prevents people from painting their houses purple, yet such restrictions are common in the bylaws of housing associations.

### Sale of by-products

Many public goods are financed by the sale of rights or services that are generated as by-products of the public goods. For instance, as noted earlier, radio and TV programming is a public good that is paid for in many cases by the sale of advertising messages. Internet services are also underwritten in part by commercial messages that pop up or appear in the headers or margins of web pages. Franchising sales of souvenirs can be a means of financing the costs of maintaining heritage sites.

Given the quintessentially voluntary nature of privately provided public goods, it might seem that reliance on private provision might be preferred whenever it proved feasible. But as Economic naturalist 14.5 makes clear, private provision often entails problems of its own.

## Economic naturalist 14.5 Why do commercial TV channels favour programmes like *I'm a Celebrity* over Verdi operas?

In a given time slot, a television channel faces the alternative of broadcasting either *I'm a Celebrity – Get Me Out of Here* or Verdi's *Rigoletto*. Suppose that if it chooses *Celebrity*, it will win 20 per cent of the viewing audience, but only 18 per cent if it chooses *Rigoletto*. Suppose those who would choose *Celebrity* would collectively be willing to pay €20 million for the right to see that programme, while those who choose *Rigoletto* would be willing to pay €30 million. And suppose, finally, that the time slot is to be sponsored by a detergent company, that has acquired all the advertising airtime. Which programme will the network choose? Which programme would be socially optimal?The detergent maker cares primarily about the number of people who will see its advertisements and their spending habits and will thus choose the programme that will attract the largest audience, other things being equal – here, the *Celebrity* show. The fact that those who prefer *Rigoletto* would be willing to pay a lot more to see it is of little concern to the sponsor. But to identify the optimal result from society's point of view, we must take this difference into account. Because the people who prefer opera could pay the other viewers more than enough to compensate them for relinquishing the time slot, *Rigoletto* is the efficient outcome. But unless its supporters happen to buy more soap in total than the *Celebrity* viewers, the latter will prevail.

In short, reliance on advertising and other indirect mechanisms for financing public goods provides no assurance that the goods chosen will maximise economic surplus. This does not mean that it cannot be efficient. Even on the WTP figures already given it could be the case that it is still socially optimal. Suppose the detergent company is prepared to pay €15 million to sponsor the programme because it is a scarce resource that is of value to it, while the highest potential bidder for the slot if *Rigoletto* is played is a wine importer who would pay €3 million. The airtime is allocated to sponsor and audience with a joint willingness to pay of €35 million if *Celebrity* is broadcast, as opposed to €33 million in the case of *Rigoletto*. These methods allow viewers to register not just which programmes they prefer but also the strength of their preferences, as measured by how much they are willing to pay. But although pay-per-view TV is more likely to select the programmes the public most values, it is also less efficient than broadcast TV in one important respect. As noted earlier, charging each household a fee for viewing discourages some households from tuning in. And since the marginal social cost of serving an additional household is exactly zero, limiting the audience in this way is inefficient. Which of the two inefficiencies is more important – free TV's inefficiency in choosing among programmes or pay-TV's inefficiency in excluding potential beneficiaries – is an empirical question. In any event, the mix between private and public provision of public goods and services differs substantially from society to society and from arena to arena within any given society. These differences depend on the nature of available *technologies* for delivering and paying for public goods, and also on people's *preferences*.

One way to avoid the inefficiency that arises when advertisers choose programming is to employ pay-per-view methods of paying for television programming.

### Example 14.8 By how much is economic surplus reduced by a pay-per-view charge?

If a recently released movie is available on a pay-per-view channel on Thursdays at 10 p.m., the demand curve for each episode is given by $P = 20 - Q$, where $P$ is the price per household in euros and $Q$ is the number of households who choose to watch the programme (in millions). If the regulated pay-per-view charge is €10 per household, by how much would economic surplus rise if the same episode were shown instead on 'free' network TV?

With a fee of €10 per episode, 10 million households will watch (see Fig. 14.4). But if the same episode were shown on network TV, 20 million households would watch. The additional economic surplus reaped by the extra 10 million households is the area of the shaded triangle, €50 million. The marginal cost of permitting these additional households to watch is zero, so the total gain in surplus is €50 million. In general, charging a positive price for a good whose marginal cost is zero will result in a loss in surplus. As we saw in Chapter 7, the size of the loss that results when price is set above marginal cost depends on the *price elasticity of demand*. When demand is more elastic, the loss in surplus is greater. Exercise 14.5 provides an opportunity to see that principle at work.

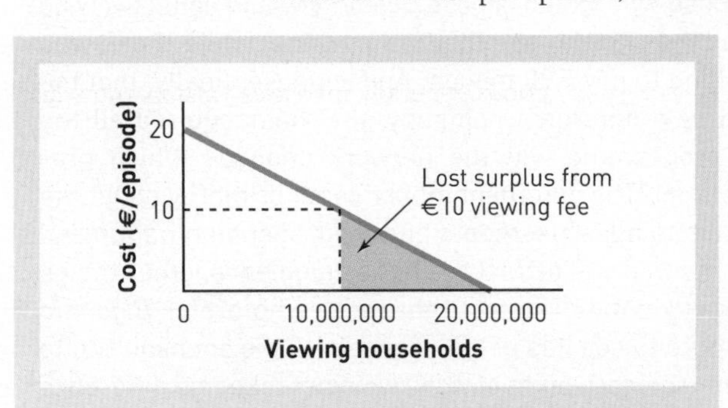


**Figure 14.4 The Loss in Surplus from a Pay-per-View Fee.** Twice as many households would watch the programme if its price were zero instead of €10. The additional economic surplus is the area of the shaded triangle, or €50 million.

**Exercise 14.5** How would your answer to Example 14.8 have been different if the demand curve had been given instead by $P = 15 - 2Q$?

## Summary

- Governments intervene in the market economy in two ways (other than to redistribute income and wealth): they seek to correct *market failure*, and they produce a range of *goods and services*.
- Just as markets are prone to market failure, policy makers need to recognise the possibility of *regulatory failure*. This arises when regulation is badly designed, or when the regulatory process is captured by those it seeks to regulate.
- Regulatory design is exemplified by the issues involved in environmental regulation. An understanding of the forces that give rise to environmental pollution can help to identify those policy measures that will achieve a desired reduction in pollution at the lowest possible cost. Both the taxing of pollution and the sale of transferable pollution rights promote this goal. Each distributes the cost of the environmental clean-up effort so that the *marginal cost of pollution abatement* is the same for all polluters.
- A perennially controversial topic is the application of the cost–benefit principle to policies involving public health, safety and security. Many critics feel that the use of cost–benefit analysis in this domain is not morally legitimate, because it involves putting a monetary price on human life. Yet the fundamental principle of scarcity applies to human health and safety, just as it does to other issues. Spending more on public health and safety necessarily means spending less on other things of value. Failure to weigh the relevant costs and benefits, then, means that society will be *less likely to achieve its stated goals*.
- One of government's principal tasks is to provide *public goods*, such as national defence and the criminal justice system. Such goods are, in varying degrees, *non-rival* and *non-excludable*. The first property describes goods for which one person's consumption does not diminish the amount available for others, while the second refers to the difficulty of preventing non-payers from consuming certain goods.
- Goods that are both highly non-excludable and non-rival are often called *pure public goods*. A collective good – such as pay-per-view cable television – is non-rival but excludable. Commons goods are goods that are rival but non-excludable.
- Because not everyone benefits equally from the provision of any given public good, charging all taxpayers equal amounts for the provision of public goods will generally not be either feasible or desirable. As in the case of private goods, people's WTP for public goods generally increases with income, and most governments therefore levy *higher taxes on the rich* than on the poor.
- The criterion for providing the optimal quantity or quality of a public good is to keep increasing quantity or quality as long as the marginal benefit of doing so exceeds the marginal cost. One advantage of using the government to provide public goods is that once a tax collection agency has been established to finance a single public good, it can be expanded at relatively low cost to generate revenue to finance additional public goods. A second advantage is that because government has the power to tax, it can easily assign responsibility for the cost of a public good. And in the case of goods for which non-payers simply cannot be excluded, the *government may be the only feasible provider*.
- One disadvantage to exclusive reliance on government for public goods provision is the element of coercion inherent in the tax system, which makes some people pay for public goods they don't want, while others do without public goods they do want. Many public goods are provided through private channels, with the necessary funding provided by donations, sale of by-products, by development of new means to exclude non-payers and in many cases by private contract. A *loss in surplus* results, however, whenever monetary charges are levied for the consumption of a non-rival good.

## Key terms

**collective good** (412)
**emissions trading** (403)
**merit goods** (411)
**non-excludable good** (411)
**non-rival good** (411)
**poll tax** (415)
**progressive tax** (416)
**proportional income tax** (415)
**public good** (411)
**pure commons good** (412)
**pure private good** (412)
**pure public good** (412)
**regressive tax** (415)
**regulation** (397)

## Review questions

1. Why is vaccination against many childhood illnesses a legal requirement for entry into state-funded schools in the United States?
2. Why do economists believe that pollution taxes and effluent permits are a more efficient way to curb pollution than laws mandating across-the-board cutbacks?
3. Does it make sense to require more sophisticated and expensive safety equipment in large commercial passenger jets than in small private planes?
4. a. Which of the following goods are non-rival?
   Apples
   Stephen King novels
   Street lighting in college grounds
   Public service radio broadcasts

   b. Which of the goods in part (a) are non-excludable?
5. Give examples of goods that are, for the most part:
   a. Rival but non-excludable
   b. Non-rival but excludable
   c. Both non-rival and non-excludable.
6. Why might even a wealthy person prefer a proportional income tax to a poll tax?
7. **True or false:** A tax on an activity that generates negative externalities will improve resource allocation in the private sector and also generate revenue that could be used to pay for useful public goods. Explain.

## Problems

1. Two firms, Sludge Oil and Northwest Lumber, have access to five production processes, each one of which has a different cost and creates a different amount of pollution. The daily costs of the processes and the corresponding number of tonnes of smoke emitted are as shown in the table below.

| Process (smoke) | A (4 tonnes/day) | B (3 tonnes/day) | C (2 tonnes/day) | D (1 tonne/day) | E (0 tonnes/day) |
|---|---|---|---|---|---|
| Cost to Sludge Oil (€/day) | 50 | 70 | 120 | 200 | 500 |
| Cost to Northwest Lumber (€/day) | 100 | 180 | 500 | 1,000 | 2,000 |

   a. If pollution is unregulated, which process will each firm use, and what will be the daily smoke emission?

b. The city council wants to curb smoke emissions by 50 per cent. To accomplish this, it requires each firm to curb its emissions by 50 per cent. What will be the total cost to society of this policy?

2. The city council in Problem 1 again wants to curb emissions by half. This time, it sets a tax of €*T* per day on each tonne of smoke emitted. How large will *T* have to be to effect the desired reduction? What is the total cost to society of this policy?

3. Refer to Problem 2. Instead of taxing pollution, the city council decides to auction off four permits, each of which entitles the bearer to emit 1 tonne of smoke per day. No smoke may be emitted without a permit. Suppose that the government conducts the auction by starting at €1 and asking how many permits each firm wants to buy at that price. If the total is more than four, it then raises the price by €1, and asks again, and so on, until the total quantity of demanded permits falls to four. How much will each permit sell for in this auction? How many permits will each firm buy? What will be the total cost to society of this reduction in pollution?

4. The table below shows all the marginal benefits for each voter in a small town whose town council is considering a new swimming pool with capacity for at least three citizens. The cost of the pool would be €18 per week and would not depend on the number of people who actually used it.

| Voter | Marginal benefit (€/week) |
|---|---|
| *A* | 12 |
| *B* | 5 |
| *C* | 2 |

a. If the pool must be financed by a weekly poll tax levied on all voters, will the pool be approved by majority vote? Is this outcome socially efficient? Explain.

b. The town council instead decides to auction a franchise off to a private monopoly to build and maintain the pool. If it cannot find such a firm willing to operate the pool, then the pool project will be scrapped. If all such monopolies are constrained by law to charge a single price to users, will the franchise be sold – and, if so, how much will it sell for? Is this outcome socially efficient? Explain.

5. Two consumers, Smith and Jones, have the following demand curves for broadcasts of recorded opera on Saturdays:

Smith: $P_S = 12 - Q$
Jones: $P_J = 12 - 2Q$

where $P_S$ and $P_J$ represent marginal willingness to pay values for Smith and Jones, respectively, and $Q$ represents the number of hours of opera broadcast each Saturday.

a. If Smith and Jones are the only broadcast listeners, construct the demand curve for opera broadcasts.

b. If the marginal cost of opera broadcasts is €15 per hour, what is the socially optimal number of hours of broadcast opera?

## Answers to in-chapter exercises

14.1 With a tax of €61 per tonne each day, Sludge Oil would adopt process A and Northwest Lumber would adopt process *C*.

| Process (smoke) | A (4 tonnes/day) | B (3 tonnes/day) | C (2 tonnes/day) | D (1 tonne/day) | E (0 tonnes/day) |
|---|---|---|---|---|---|
| Cost to Sludge Oil (€/day) | 100 | 200 | 600 | 1,300 | 2,300 |
| Cost to Northwest Lumber (€/day) | 300 | 320 | 380 | 480 | 700 |

**14.2** The payoff matrix would now be as shown below, and the best choice, both individually and collectively, would be the risky job.

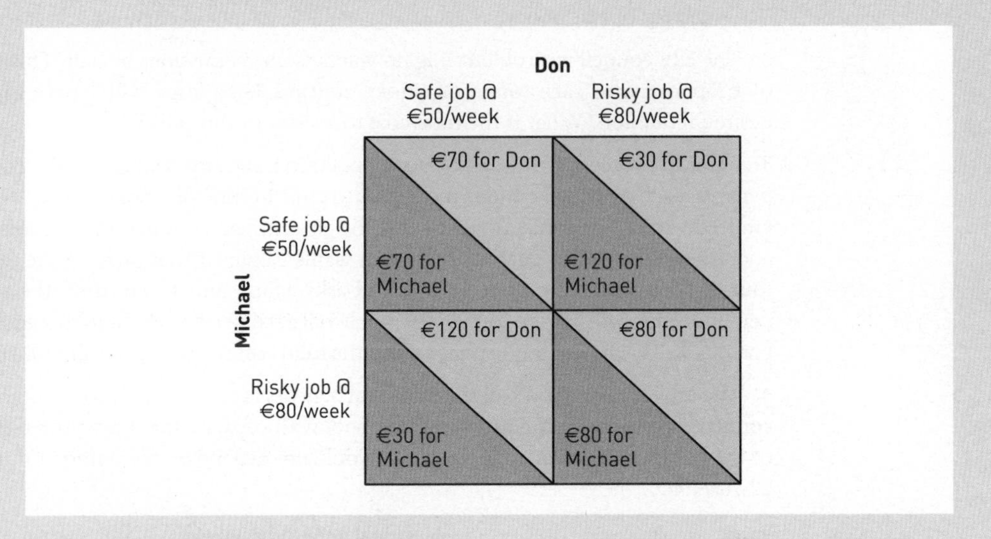


**14.3** a. The website at 3 a.m. in the morning has the capacity to serve far more users than it attracts, so an additional user calling up the site does not prevent some other user from doing so. Other websites, however do not show the non-rival property, at least during certain hours, because they attract more users than their servers can accommodate.

b. The stadium at the championship game is always full, so anyone who watches the game in person prevents someone else from doing so.

c. Additional people can watch the game on TV without diminishing the availability of the broadcast for others.

**14.4** To construct the demand curve (a), we first graph Bill's demand curve (c) and Tom's demand curve (b) and then add the two individual demand curves vertically. The equation for the demand curve is $P = 18 - 1.5Q$.

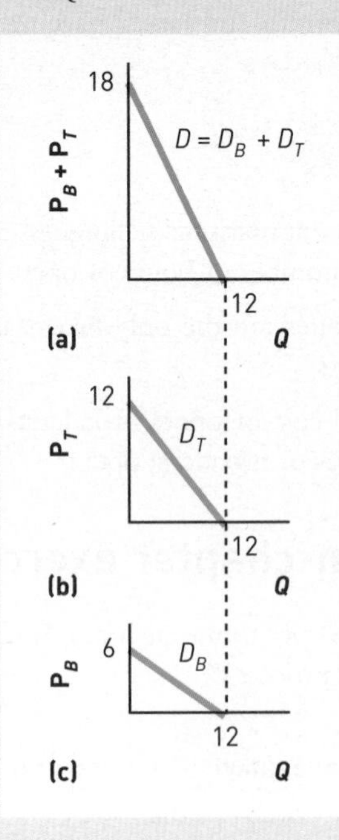

14.5 Whereas elasticity of demand was 1 at a price of €10 on the original demand curve, it is 1.5 on the new demand curve (see the graph below). As a result, the €10 fee now excludes 20 million viewers, and the resulting loss in surplus (again the area of the shaded triangle) is €100 million.

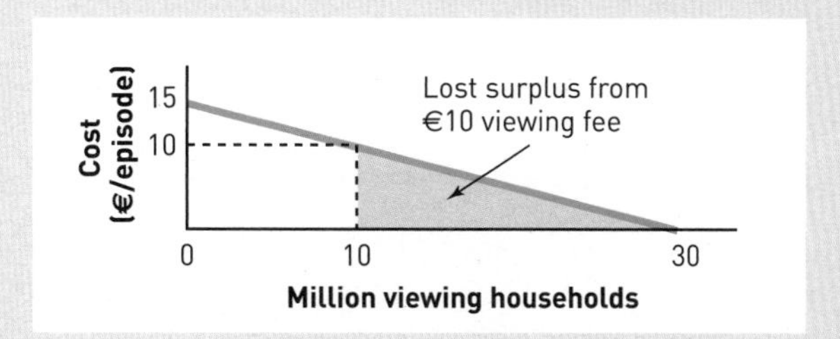


# References

Capros, P. and L. Mantzos (2000) *The Economic Effects of EU-Wide Industry-Level Emission Trading to Reduce Greenhouse Gases: Results from the PRIMES Energy Systems Model*, Brussels, May.

Cockburn, A. (2002) 'Somalia: A Failed State?', *National Geographic Magazine*, July, www.findarticles.com/p/articles/mi_hb3343/is_200207/ai–n8059104.

Institute for Prospective Technological Studies (IPTS) (2000) *Preliminary Analysis of the Implementation of an EU-wide Permit Trading Scheme on $CO_2$ Emissions Abatement Costs: Results from the POLES Model*, Brussels, April.

# Part 5
# Trade and Integration

In Chapter 15 we shall address international trade and its effects on the broader economy, showing that if trade is unrestricted, market forces will ensure that countries specialise in producing those goods in which they have a comparative advantage. We shall also show that although opening the economy to trade increases economic welfare overall, some groups – such as workers in industries that face competition from foreign producers – may be made worse off, which explains why proposals to expand trade often face political opposition.

Chapter 16 expands on the material in Chapter 15, and includes some factual material as well, in order to provide an introduction to the economics of integration, with special reference to the evolution of the European Union. It also provides the foundations for the discussion in the macroeconomics section of the book of the issues surrounding monetary integration and the euro.

# 15

# International Trade and Trade Policy

Governments appear to have contradictory attitudes towards trade and its effects on economic welfare. Consider the following. In April 1861, Southern troops fired on Fort Sumter in Charleston harbour, initiating the American Civil War. Less than a week later President Lincoln proclaimed a naval blockade of the South. The object of the blockade was to prevent the Confederacy from shipping cotton to Europe, where it could be traded for military equipment, clothing, foodstuffs and other supplies.

Historians are divided on the effectiveness of the Union blockade in choking off Confederate trade. By cutting off supplies of American cotton to Britain's textile industry the Union government increased the pressure on the British government to enter the war on the Confederate side. Nevertheless, and despite the efforts of Southern blockade runners (such as the fictitious Rhett Butler of *Gone With The Wind*), by 1864 the Southern war effort was seriously hampered by a lack of military equipment and supplies, at least in part as a result of the blockade.

Twice in the twentieth century Germany tried to defeat the coalition of powers facing her and her allies by cutting off Britain from trade with the United States and her Commonwealth sources of supply. Her efforts at enforcing this blockade resulted in the US entry into the First World War in 1917. Germany's defeat in the U-Boat campaign (submarine warfare against shipping) known as the Battle of the Atlantic between 1941 and 1943 determined the outcome of the Second World War in Europe. Germany's final defeat in the First World War was in large measure due to the economic collapse of that country as a result of the successful blockade of German ports by the UK Royal Navy, which strangled German trade with the world outside Europe.

The use of a naval blockade as a weapon of war highlights a paradox in contemporary attitudes toward trade between nations. In the middle 1860s, the United States threatened Japan with war if it did not permit free trade. An attempt by a foreign power to blockade US ports would today be considered a hostile act that would elicit a strong response from the government. Restricting an enemy's ability to trade freely with other countries is clearly, and correctly, seen as damaging to that country's economy. Consequently, restrictions on trade by others is seen as a device by which a country or countries can project power in pursuit of political goals to which the others are opposed. For nearly two decades Western governments with widespread public support, applied trade sanctions against South Africa in order to undermine the white supremacist regime (the Apartheid system). From 1991 (after the end of the first Gulf War) UN trade sanctions were in place against the regime of Saddam Hussein in Iraq until the Anglo-American led invasion of Iraq in 2003.

While behaving as if they believe that restricting a country's ability to trade is damaging to that country, governments also act from time to time as if they believe the exact opposite. In the debate over the proposed North American Free Trade Agreement (NAFTA), American politicians on all sides opposed efforts in the 1990s to open the United States to increased trade, in effect arguing that increased trade with other nations was harmful and should be restricted. This could be interpreted as a call for the United States to blockade its own ports on the grounds that it might cost American jobs. The European Union has for years engaged in a series of interventions designed to restrict imports or encourage exports ... to distort and restrict trade.

This hostility to free and undistorted trade is not confined to politicians. Since 2001, the 'anti-globalisation' movement has staged demonstrations in Washington, DC, and other world cities, disrupting meetings of the World Trade Organisation (WTO), an international body set up to promote trade and enforce trade agreements. It has picketed and attempted violently to disrupt intergovernmental meetings in order to protest against what it claims is the damage done to poor countries by efforts to free trade.

So, is freedom to trade a good thing or not? And if it is, why does it sometimes face determined and even violent opposition? Why do governments seek to use restrictions on trade to damage their adversaries ... and then introduce restrictions on and distortions of trade affecting their own citizens?

This chapter addresses international trade and its effects on the broader economy. We shall begin by reviewing the idea of *comparative advantage*, which was introduced in Chapter 2. We shall show that everyone can enjoy more goods and services if nations specialise in those products in which they have a comparative advantage, and then trade freely among themselves. Furthermore, if trade is unrestricted, market forces will ensure that countries produce those goods in which they have a comparative advantage.

Having shown the potential benefits of trade, we shall turn next to the reasons for opposition to trade. Although opening the economy to trade increases economic welfare overall, some groups – such as workers in industries that face competition from foreign producers – may be made worse off. The fact that open trade may hurt some groups creates political pressure to enact measures restricting trade, such as taxes on imported goods (called *tariffs*) and limits on imports (called *quotas*) (both defined later). We shall analyse the effects of these trade restrictions, along with other ways of responding to concerns about the affected industries and workers. From an economic point of view, providing direct assistance to those who are hurt by increased trade is preferable to blocking or restricting trade.

## Comparative advantage as a basis for trade

In Chapter 2 we saw that despite having the ability to perform a variety of functions well, the failure of individuals or countries to specialise to some degree is a cause of poverty. The paradox is that the ability to do many things well, when it results in doing all those things, results in an inability of an individual or country to become as productive in each separate activity as someone or some country that specialises entirely in that activity. The alternative to a nation of individuals where each person performs a wide variety of functions is one in which he specialises in the activity at which he is relatively more efficient, or has a *comparative advantage*.

This specialisation, combined with trade between producers of different goods and services, allows a society to achieve a higher level of productivity and standard of living than one in which each person is essentially self-sufficient.

This insight, that specialisation and trade among individuals can yield impressive gains in productivity, applies equally well to nations. Factors such as climate, natural resources, technology, workers' skills and education and culture provide countries with comparative advantages in the production of different goods and services. For example,the large number of leading research universities in the United States gives that nation a comparative advantage in the design of technologically sophisticated computer hardware and software. Likewise, the wide international use of the English language endows the United States with a comparative advantage in producing popular films and TV shows. Similarly, France's climate and topography, together with the accumulated knowledge of generations of vintners, provides that country a comparative advantage in producing fine wines, while Australia's huge expanses of arable land give that country a comparative advantage in producing grain.

The *Principle of Comparative Advantage* tells us that we can all enjoy more goods and services when each country produces according to its comparative advantage, and then trades with other countries. In the next section we explore this fundamental idea in greater detail.

## Production and consumption possibilities and the benefits of trade

In this section we shall consider how international trade benefits an individual country. To do so, we will contrast the production and consumption opportunities in a **closed economy** – one that does not trade with the rest of the world – with the opportunities in an **open economy** – one that does trade with other economies. Because we will make use of the production possibilities curve (PPC) – which was introduced in Chapter 2, we shall begin by briefly reviewing that concept. We shall look first at the PPC for a two-person economy and then at the PPC for a many-person economy. After reviewing the PPC, we shall see how a country's production possibilities are related to its citizens' ability to consume in a closed economy versus an open economy.

**closed economy** an economy that does not trade with the rest of the world

**open economy** an economy that trades with other countries

### The two-worker PPC

Recall that, for a two-good economy, the PPC is a graph that shows the maximum amount of each good that can be produced, at every possible level of production of the other good. To see how the PPC is constructed, let us consider in Example 15.1 a hypothetical economy, which we shall call Brazil, which has only two workers, Carlos and Maria. Each of these two workers can produce two goods, coffee and computers. The PPC for a two-worker economy is shown in Fig. 15.1.

#### Example 15.1 The PPC for a two-person economy

Two Brazilian workers, Carlos and Maria, can each produce coffee and computers. Carlos can produce either 100 kg of coffee or 1 computer per week. Maria can produce either 100 kg of coffee or 2 computers per week. Both Carlos and Maria work 50 weeks per year. Find the PPC for Brazil. To construct the PPC for this two-person economy, we ask first how much coffee Brazil could produce if both Carlos and Maria worked full time producing coffee. Between them they can produce 200 kg of coffee per week, so in 50 weeks they could produce 10,000 kg of coffee. Thus if we plot coffee production on the vertical axis of the graph of Brazil's PPC, the vertical intercept of the PPC will be 10,000 kg of coffee per year (point *A* in Fig. 15.1). Likewise, if Carlos and Maria produced only computers, between them they could produce 3 computers per week, or 150 computers per year. So the horizontal intercept of Brazil's PPC is 150 computers per year (point *B* in Fig. 15.1).

We have found where the Brazilian two-worker PPC intersects the two axes of the graph. To find the rest of the PPC, imagine that Carlos and Maria are producing only coffee (point *A* in Fig. 15.1), when they decide that they would like to have some computers as well. In this situ-

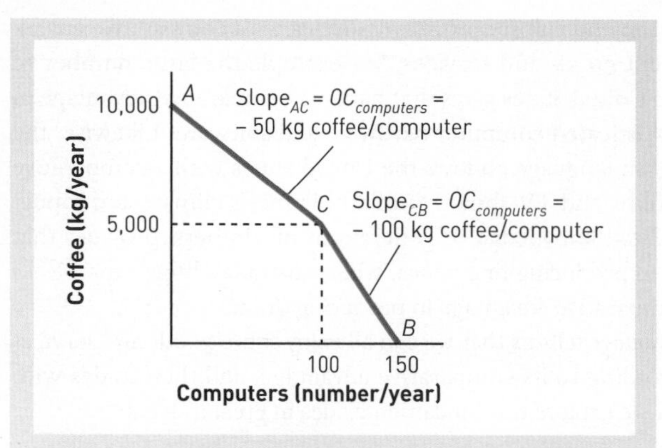


**Figure 15.1 PPC for a Two-Worker Economy.** In the portion of the PPC between points *A* and *C*, only Maria is producing computers, so the slope of the PPC in that range reflects Maria's opportunity cost of computers in terms of coffee production forgone. At point *C*, Maria spends all her time on computers and Carlos spends all his time on coffee. Between points *C* and *B*, any additional computers must be produced by Carlos. Thus between points *C* and *B* the slope of the PPC reflects Carlos' opportunity cost of producing computers, in terms of coffee production forgone.

ation, which worker should switch from producing coffee to producing computers?

To answer this question, we need to find the one with a *comparative advantage* in producing computers. To do this, we must calculate *opportunity costs*. Carlos can produce either 100 kg of coffee or 1 computer per week. Because producing a computer leaves him one week less to devote to coffee production, which reduces his coffee output by 100 kg, Carlos' opportunity cost of producing 1 computer is 100 kg of coffee. Maria can produce either 100 kg of coffee or 2 computers per week, so her opportunity cost of producing a computer is 100/2, or 50 kg of coffee. Because Maria's opportunity cost of producing a computer is lower than Carlos', she has a comparative advantage in producing computers. By the principle of comparative advantage, Maria should be the one to specialise in computer production. For his part, Carlos has a comparative advantage in producing coffee (see Exercise 15.1, below) so he should specialise in coffee.

Starting from point *A* in Fig. 15.1, where only coffee is produced, we can imagine that Maria begins to produce increasing numbers of computers. The slope of the line emanating from point *A* equals Maria's opportunity cost of producing a computer, $OC_{computers}$, where cost is measured as a negative quantity:

$$\begin{aligned}\text{Slope} &= \text{Maria's } OC_{computers} \\ &= (\text{loss in coffee})/(\text{gain in computers}) \\ &= (-100 \text{ kg coffee/week})/(2 \text{ computers/week}) = -50 \text{ kg coffee per computer}\end{aligned}$$

As Maria increases the share of her time devoted to computer production, we move down along the straight line from point *A* in Fig. 15.1. The slope of the PPC is constant in this region at 250 kg of coffee per computer, Maria's opportunity cost of computers.

Maria's time is limited to 50 weeks per year, however, so if she keeps increasing her computer production, she will eventually reach a point at which she produces only computers and no coffee. At that point annual production by the two workers taken together will be 100 computers (produced by Maria) and 5,000 kg of coffee (produced by Carlos, who spends all his time producing coffee). This combination of production is shown at point *C* on the PPC.

Once Maria's time is fully devoted to making computers, Brazil can increase its computer production only if Carlos begins to build some computers, too. However, Carlos' opportunity cost, measured as kg of coffee forgone per computer produced, is greater than Maria's. Hence at point *C* the slope of the PPC changes, creating a kink in the graph. The slope of the PPC to the right of point *C* is given by

$$\begin{aligned}\text{Slope} &= \text{Carlos' } OC_{computers} = (\text{loss in coffee})/(\text{gain in computers}) \\ &= (-100 \text{ kg coffee/week})/(1 \text{ computer/week}) \\ &= -100 \text{ kg coffee per computer}\end{aligned}$$

Note that the slope of the PPC to the right of point *C* is more negative than the slope to the left of point *C*, so that the PPC declines more sharply to the right of that point. The fact that the opportunity cost of a computer increases as more computers are produced (the *Principle of Increasing Opportunity Cost*) implies the outwardly bowed shape that is characteristic of a PPC, as shown in Fig. 15.1.

**Exercise 15.1**

Example 15.1 showed that Maria has a comparative advantage in producing computers. Show by comparison of opportunity costs that Carlos has a comparative advantage in producing coffee.

## The many-worker PPC

Although the economy considered in Example 15.1 included only two workers, the main ideas apply to economies with more workers. Suppose, for example, that we added a third Brazilian worker, Pedro, whose opportunity cost of producing computers is higher than Maria's but lower than Carlos'. The PPC curve for this three-person economy would look something like Fig. 15.2. Between points *A* and *C* on the PPC shown in Fig. 15.2, all computers are produced by Maria, who has the greatest comparative advantage in computer production. Thus the slope of the PPC between points *A* and *C* is determined by Maria's opportunity cost, measured as the amount of coffee production forgone for each additional computer produced.

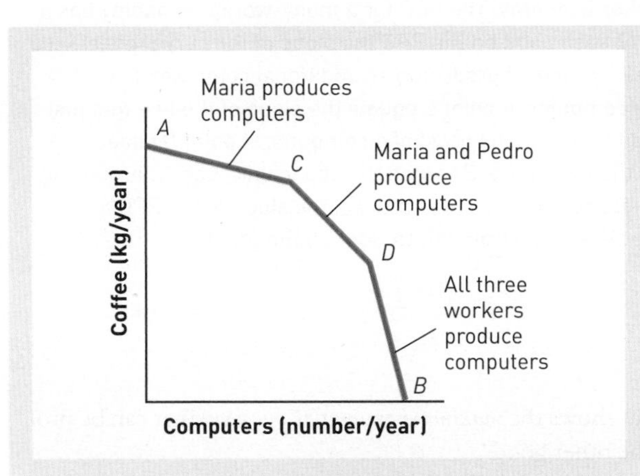


**Figure 15.2 PPC for a Three-Worker Economy.** The PPC for a three-person economy has two kinks, at points *C* and *D*. Between points *A* and *C* only Maria produces computers, and the slope of the PPC represents her opportunity cost of producing computers. At point *C* Maria is spending all her time making computers, so any additional computers will be produced by Pedro, whose comparative advantage is the next greatest. Between points *C* and *D* the slope of the PPC is determined by Pedro's opportunity cost. At point *D* Pedro is also fully occupied producing computers, so that Carlos must begin producing them if computer production is to increase further. Between points *D* and *B* the slope of the PPC reflects Carlos' opportunity cost.

At point *C* Maria is dedicating all her time to computer production, so someone else must produce any additional computers. Pedro has the next lowest opportunity cost of producing computers, so (following the Principle of Increasing Opportunity Cost) he begins to produce computers at point *C*. The slope of the PPC between points *C* and *D* is determined by Pedro's opportunity cost, which is greater (more negative) than Maria's opportunity cost. At point *D* in Fig. 15.2, Pedro is producing all the computers he can, so finally Carlos begins to produce computers as well. Thus the slope of the PPC between points *D* and *B* reflects Carlos' opportunity cost. Because opportunity cost increases as we move from left to right in Fig. 15.2, the slope of the PPC becomes more and more negative, leading once again to the outwardly bowed shape.

By a similar logic, we can construct a case in which there are many workers, perhaps millions. With many workers, the part of the nation's PPC that is associated with each individual worker becomes very small. As a result, the PPC for an economy with many workers has a smoothly bowed shape, as shown in Fig. 15.3. With a smoothly curved PPC, the slope at each point still reflects the opportunity cost of producing an additional computer, as illustrated in Fig. 15.3. For example, at point *C* in Fig. 15.3, the opportunity cost of producing an extra computer is given by the slope of the line that just touches the PPC at that point. Because computers will be produced first by workers with the greatest comparative advantage (the lowest opportunity cost), the slope of the PPC becomes more and more sharply negative as we read from left to right in Fig. 15.3.

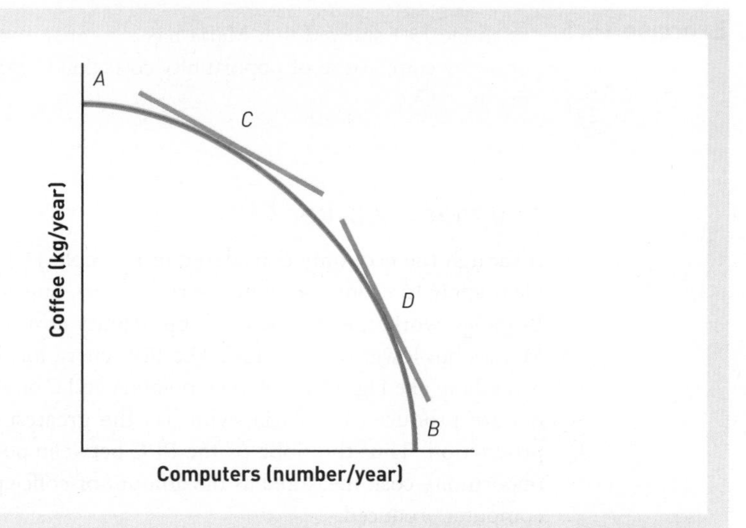


**Figure 15.3 PPC for a Many-Worker Economy.** The PPC for a many-worker economy has a smooth, outwardly bowed shape. At each point on the PPC the slope of the curve reflects the opportunity cost, in terms of coffee forgone, of producing an additional computer. For example, the opportunity cost of a computer at point *C* equals the slope of the line that just touches the PPC at that point, and the opportunity cost of a computer at point *D* equals the slope of the line that just touches the PPC there. Because the opportunity cost of producing another computer increases as more computers are produced, the slope of the PPC becomes more and more negative as we read from left to right on the graph.

## RECAP PPCs

- The PPC for a two-good economy is a graph that shows the *maximum amount of one good* that can be produced at every possible level of production of the other good.
- The slope of a PPC at any point indicates the *opportunity cost*, in terms of forgone production of the good on the vertical axis, of increasing production of the good on the horizontal axis by one unit.
- The more of a good that is already being produced, the greater the opportunity cost of increasing production still further. Thus the slope of the PPC becomes more and more *negative* as we read from left to right, imparting the characteristic outwardly bowed shape of the curve.

## Consumption possibilities with and without international trade

**consumption possibilities** the combinations of goods and services that a country's citizens might feasibly consume

A country's PPC shows the quantities of different goods that its economy can produce. However, economic welfare depends most directly not on what a country can *produce*, but on what its citizens can *consume*. The combinations of goods and services that a country's citizens might feasibly consume are called the country's **consumption possibilities**.

The relationship between a country's *consumption possibilities* and its *production possibilities* depends on whether the country is open to international trade. In a closed economy with no trade, people can consume only the goods and services produced within their own country. In a closed economy, then, *a society's consumption possibilities are identical to its production possibilities*. A situation in which a country is economically self-sufficient, producing everything its citizens consume, is called **autarky**.[1]

**autarky** a situation in which a country is economically self-sufficient

The case of an open economy, which trades with the rest of the world, is quite different. In an open economy, people are not restricted to consuming what is produced in their own country, because part of what they produce can be sent abroad in exchange for other goods and services. Indeed, we shall see in this section that opening an economy to trade may allow citizens to consume more of everything. Thus in an open economy, *a society's consumption possibilities are typically greater than (and will never be less than) its production possibilities*. We shall illustrate this critical point with reference to the two-worker economy studied earlier in the chapter, then briefly consider the more general case of a many-worker economy.

### Example 15.2 Brazil's consumption possibilities with trade

Two Brazilian workers, Carlos and Maria, can produce coffee and computers as described in Example 15.1. Initially the country is closed to trade, and Maria produces only computers, while Carlos produces only coffee. Then the country opens up to trade. World prices are such that 80 kg of coffee can be traded for 1 computer on the international market and vice versa. How does the opening of Brazil to trade affect Maria's and Carlos' opportunity to consume coffee and computers?

If Maria is producing only computers and Carlos is producing only coffee, then Brazil is at point *C* on the PPC shown in Fig. 15.4 (which is the same as the PPC shown in Fig. 15.1). At that point Maria is spending all her time producing 100 computers a year, and Carlos is spending all his time producing 5,000 kg of coffee a year. If Brazil were closed to trade, Maria and Carlos could obtain more coffee only by producing fewer computers. Specifically, starting at point *C* on the PPC, they could obtain 50 additional kg of coffee by giving up 1 computer – by having Maria work 1/2 week less on computers and 1/2 week more producing coffee.

If Brazil opens up to trade, however, then Maria and Carlos can get 80 kg of coffee in exchange for 1 computer simply by trading computers for coffee on the international market. In other words, they can get an extra 80 kg of coffee for each computer they give up. To illustrate the degree to which the opportunity to trade benefits Brazil, recall from Example 15.1 that, with no trade, Maria's and Carlos' maximum coffee consumption is 10,000 kg per year (the vertical intercept of the Brazilian PPC). With the opportunity to trade, however, Maria can trade the 100 computers produced at point *C* for 8,000 kg of coffee (80 kg of coffee per computer × 100 computers). Together with the 5,000 kg of coffee Carlos produces, the coffee obtained through trade raises Brazil's maximum annual coffee consumption from 10,000 to 13,000 kg per year, as indicated by point *F* in Fig. 15.4. Because trade creates the possibility for Brazil to consume as much as 13,000 kg of coffee per year, point *F* is included in Brazil's consumption possibilities, though it would have been unattainable to the Brazilians before the opening up of trade.

Furthermore, with the opportunity to trade, Maria and Carlos can consume any combination of coffee and computers represented on the straight line between points *F* and *C* in Fig. 15.4. This straight line has a slope of 280 kg of coffee per 1 computer, which is the rate at which the two goods can be exchanged on the international market. So, simply by trading

[1] The term is from a Greek verb, *autarkein*, meaning to be self-sufficient. It should not be confused with the term autarchy, meaning rule by one person, again from the Greek *autos*, meaning one or self, and *archein*, meaning to rule.

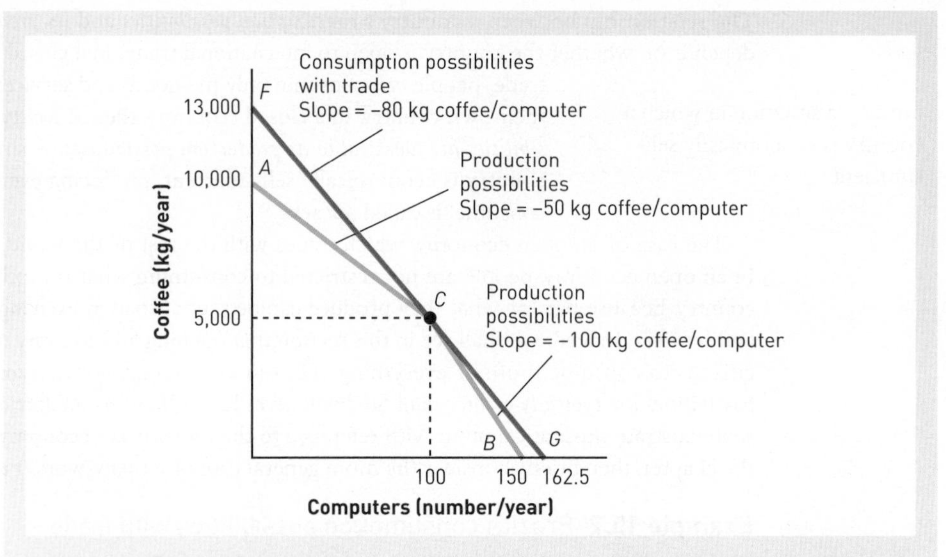


**Figure 15.4 Brazil's Consumption Possibilities with Trade.** Without the opportunity to trade. Brazil's consumption possibilities are the same as the Brazilian PPC, represented by line *ACB*. With the opportunity to trade, however, Brazilians can consume at any point along line *FG*.

computers for coffee, Maria and Carlos can improve their consumption possibilities at any point except *C*, where their production and consumption possibilities are the same.

Suppose instead that, starting from point *C* on Brazil's PPC, Maria and Carlos decide they want to consume more computers rather than more coffee. With no ability to trade, the opportunity cost of obtaining 1 more computer at point *C* would be 100 kg of coffee – that is, the amount of coffee that would be lost by having Carlos work 1 more week at producing an extra computer, and hence 1 week fewer at producing coffee. With trade, however, Brazilians can obtain an extra computer at the cost of only 80 kg of coffee (the price of computers on the international market). In the extreme, if they wanted to consume only computers, the Brazilians could trade the 5,000 kg of coffee Carlos produces at point *C* for 5,000/80 = 62.5 computers, for a total consumption (with the 100 computers Maria produces) of 162.5 computers. This maximum consumption amount is indicated by point *G* in Fig. 15.4. Comparing point *G* with point *B*, we can see that the opportunity to trade has increased Brazil's maximum consumption of computers from 150 to 162.5. (Consuming 162.5 computers a year means consuming 325 computers every two years.)

Furthermore, by trading various amounts of coffee for computers, Brazilians can consume any combination of computers and coffee on the straight line between points *C* and *G* in Fig. 15.4. Like the segment *FC*, segment *CG* has a slope equal to 280 kg of coffee per 1 computer, reflecting the rate at which coffee can be traded for computers on the international market. Note that since segments *FC* and *CG* have the same slopes, the line *FG* is a straight line. The line *FG* represents Brazil's consumption possibilities – the combinations of coffee and computers that Carlos and Maria might feasibly consume – when the Brazilian economy is open to trade. By comparing Brazil's consumption possibilities without trade (line *ACB*) and with trade (line *FG*), we can see that Maria and Carlos have a wider range of consumption opportunities when their economy is open.

**Exercise 15.2** Prior to the opening of trade, suppose that Brazilian residents consumed 80 computers per year. How much coffee were they able to consume each year? Suppose that the Brazilians open up to trade, but they choose to continue to consume 80 computers per year. Now how much coffee can they consume? In answering, use the PPC and consumption possibilities we found in Example 15.2. Does opening to trade make the Brazilians better off?

The same points just made in Example 15.2, which illustrates a two-worker economy, apply in the case of a many-worker economy. Figure 15.5 shows this more general case. With many workers, the PPC (curve *ACB* in Fig. 15.5) is smoothly bowed. Point *A*, where the PPC intercepts the vertical axis, indicates the maximum amount of coffee the economy can produce, and point *B*, the horizontal intercept of the PPC, shows the maximum number of computers the economy can produce. The intermediate points on the PPC represent alternative combinations of coffee and computers that can be produced. As in the two-worker economy, the slope at each point on the PPC indicates the opportunity cost of producing 1 additional computer. The more computers that are already being produced, the greater the opportunity cost of increasing computer production still further. Hence the slope of the PPC becomes increasingly negative as we read from left to right.

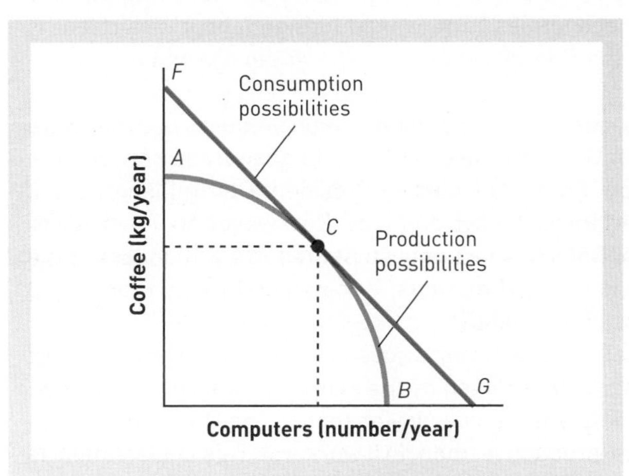


**Figure 15.5 Consumption Possibilities in a Many-Worker Economy.** The PPC for a many-worker economy is the smooth, outwardly bowed line *ACB*. If the country is open to trade, its consumption possibilities lie on the line *FG*, which just touches the PPC at point *C*. The slope of this line equals the rate at which coffee can be traded for computers at world prices. The country maximises its consumption possibilities by producing at point *C* and then trading so as to reach its most desired point on line *FG*.

Line *FG* in Fig. 15.5 shows the consumption possibilities for this economy if it is open to trade. This line has two key features. First, it is drawn so that it just touches the PPC, at point *C* in Fig. 15.5. Second, the slope of line *FG* is determined by the relative prices of coffee and computers on the world market. Specifically, as in the two-worker case (Fig. 15.4), the slope of line *FG* tells us how much coffee must be exchanged on world markets to obtain an additional computer.

With access to international trade, Brazil can consume the greatest amount of both coffee and computers by producing at point *C* on the PPC and trading on the international market to obtain the desired combination of coffee and computers on line *FG*. (The exact combination of coffee and computers Brazilians will choose depends on the needs and wants of the population.)

Why should the Brazilians produce at point *C*? At point *C*, and only at that point, the slope of the PPC equals the slope of the consumption possibilities line, *FG*. Hence only at point *C* is the opportunity cost of increasing domestic computer production equal to the opportunity cost of purchasing an extra computer on the world market. If the opportunity cost of producing a computer domestically exceeded the opportunity cost of purchasing a computer on the world market, Brazil would gain by reducing its computer production and importing more computers. Likewise, if the opportunity cost of producing a computer domestically were less than the opportunity cost of purchasing a computer abroad, Brazil would gain by increasing computer production and reducing computer imports. Brazil's best production combination, therefore, is at point *C*, where the domestic and international opportunity costs of acquiring an extra computer, measured in terms of coffee forgone, are equal.

We have already stated the general conclusion that can be drawn from this analysis. Once again, by opening itself up to trade, a country can consume more of *every* good than if it relied solely on its own production (a situation of *autarky*). Graphically, the consumption possibilities line in Fig. 15.5 lies above the PPC, showing that, through trade, Brazil can consume combinations of computers and coffee that would not be attainable if its economy were closed to trade.

## Economic naturalist 15.1 Does 'cheap' foreign labour pose a danger to high-wage economies?

Some people argue that high-wage industrialised countries lose by trading with low-wage developing nations. The concern is that the lower average wage that prevails in developing nations will allow those countries to produce most or all goods and services at lower cost. Unable to compete, the industrialised countries will suffer declining wages and rising unemployment. In the context of liberalising trade access to European markets for such things as textiles and call services, and of access to EU markets from East European applicant states, these arguments gained considerable currency in the years after 1999. Does 'cheap' foreign labour pose a danger to high-wage economies? The 'cheap foreign labour' argument is fallacious because it ignores the *Principle of Comparative Advantage* and the advantages of specialisation.

To illustrate the key issues, suppose the European Union produces both software and beef. Trade negotiators in Brussels have proposed to open trade between the union and a developing nation, Fredonia (ruled by President Otis T. Fisher, a.k.a. Groucho Marx) which produces the same two products. Real wages are much lower in Fredonia than in the Union. Does this fact imply that Fredonia will undersell the Union in both the software and the beef markets, threatening British, French and German workers with the loss of their jobs?

To answer this question, let's first ask *why* wages are lower in Fredonia. As we saw in Chapter 8, real wages are determined by the *marginal productivity of labour*. Hence, if real wages in Fredonia are radically lower than in the Union, Fredonian workers must be much less productive than EU workers. This observation is enough to show why Fredonian producers will not be able to undersell European producers in both industries. Even though Fredonian firms pay lower wages, because of differences in factors such as technology, physical capital and human capital a Fredonian worker produces much less output per hour than a European worker. Thus lower Fredonian wages do not necessarily translate into lower production costs.

Indeed, Fredonia's production costs will tend to be lower than EU production costs only in those industries in which Fredonia is *relatively* more productive. Recall the *Principle of Comparative Advantage*. Suppose that Fredonia is half as productive as the Union in producing beef, but only one-tenth as productive in producing software. In that case, the Union has an absolute advantage in producing both goods, but Fredonia has a comparative advantage in producing beef and the Union has a comparative advantage in producing software. As we have already seen in the examples in this chapter, the EU can gain by producing more software and trading the extra software to Fredonians for beef. Fredonia can gain, too, by trading its beef for software. Far from being hurt by trading with Fredonia, European consumers can have more of both goods through trade.

While the EU economy as a whole gains from trade with Fredonia, the European software sector will expand, while the beef sector will contract, as the Union moves along its PPF. EU software will be exported to Fredonia, but some EU-produced beef will be replaced by imported Fredonian beef. Hence, although opportunities for workers in the software sector will increase as a result of trade, employment and wages in the beef sector will fall. We shall discuss the sectoral impacts of trade in the next section.

## RECAP Consumption possibilities and production possibilities

- A country's consumption possibilities are the combinations of goods and services that its citizens *might feasibly consume*.
- In an economy that is closed to trade, residents can consume only what is produced *domestically* (a situation of *autarky*). Hence, in a closed economy, consumption possibilities equal production possibilities.
- The residents of an open economy can trade part of what they produce on international markets. According to the principle of comparative advantage, trade allows everyone to do better than they could otherwise. Thus, in an open economy, consumption possibilities are typically greater than, and will never be less than, *production possibilities*.
- Graphically, consumption possibilities in an open economy are described by a downward-sloping line that just touches the PPC. The slope of this line equals the amount of the good on the vertical axis that must be traded on the international market to obtain one unit of the good on the horizontal axis. A country maximises its consumption possibilities by producing at the point where the consumption possibilities line just touches the PPC, and then trading so as to reach its *most preferred point* on the consumption possibilities line.

# A supply and demand perspective on trade

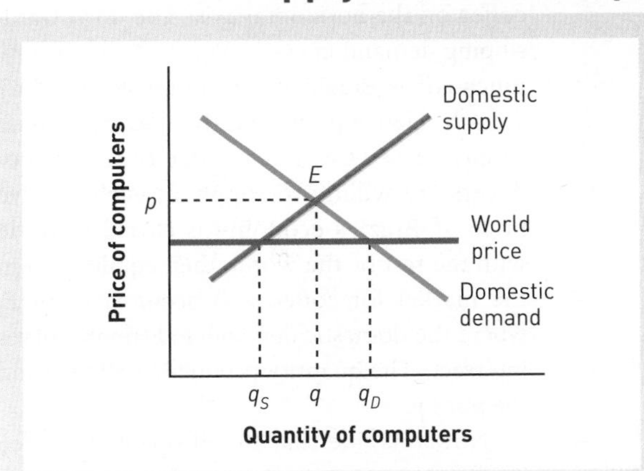


**Figure 15.6 The Market for Computers in Brazil.** If Brazil is closed to international trade, the equilibrium price and quantity of computers are determined by the intersection of the domestic supply and demand curves at point *E*. But if Brazil is open to trade, the domestic price of computers must equal the world price. At that price, Brazilians will demand $q_D$ computers, but domestic producers will supply only $q_S$ computers. Thus $q_D - q_S$ computers must be imported from abroad.

To this point we have shown that a country can improve its overall consumption possibilities by trading with other countries. In this section we shall look more carefully at how international trade affects supply and demand in the markets for specific goods. We shall see that when it is costly for workers and firms to change industries, opening up trade with other countries may create groups of winners and losers among producers, even as it helps consumers.

Let us see how trade affects the markets for computers and coffee in Brazil. Figure 15.6 shows the supply and demand for computers in that country. As usual, the price is shown on the vertical axis and the quantity on the horizontal axis. For now, think of the price of computers as being measured in terms of coffee rather than in terms of euros (in other words, we measure the price of computers *relative* to the price of the other good in the economy). As usual, the upward-sloping curve in Fig. 15.6 is the supply curve of computers, in this case for computers produced in Brazil; and the downward-sloping curve is the demand curve for computers by Brazilian residents. The supply curve for computers in Brazil reflects the opportunity cost of supplying computers (see Chapter 3). Specifically, at any level of computer production, the relative price at which Brazilian firms are willing to supply an additional computer equals their opportunity cost of doing so. The demand curve, which tells us the number of computers Brazilians will purchase at each relative price, reflects the preferences and buying power of Brazilian consumers.

If Brazil opens its market to trade, however, the relevant price for computers becomes the **world price** of computers, the price at which computers are traded internationally. The world price for computers is determined by the worldwide supply and demand for computers. If we assume that Brazil's computer market is too small to affect the world price for computers very much, the world price can be treated as fixed, and represented by a horizontal line in Fig. 15.6. Figure 15.6 shows the world price for computers as being lower than Brazil's closed-economy price.

**world price** the price at which a commodity is traded internationally

If Brazilians are free to buy and sell computers on the international market, then the price of computers in Brazil must be the same as the world price. (No one in Brazil will buy a computer at a price above the world price, and no one will sell one at a price below the world price.) Figure 15.6 shows that, at the world price, Brazilian consumers and firms demand $q_D$ computers, but Brazilian computer producers will supply only $q_S$ computers. The difference between the two quantities, $q_D - q_S$, is the number of computers that Brazil must import from abroad. Figure 15.6 illustrates a general conclusion: if the price of a good or service in a closed economy is greater than the world price, and that economy opens itself to trade, *the economy will tend to become a net importer of that good or service.*

A different outcome occurs in Brazil's coffee market, shown in Fig. 15.7. The price of coffee (measured relative to the price of computers) is shown on the vertical axis, and the quantity of coffee on the horizontal axis. The downward-sloping demand curve in Fig. 15.7 shows how much coffee Brazilian consumers want to buy at each relative price, and the upward-sloping supply curve how much coffee Brazilian producers are willing to supply at each relative price. If Brazil's economy is closed to trade with the rest of the world, then equilibrium in the market for coffee will occur at point $E$, where the domestic demand and supply curves intersect. The quantity produced will be $q$ and the price $p$.

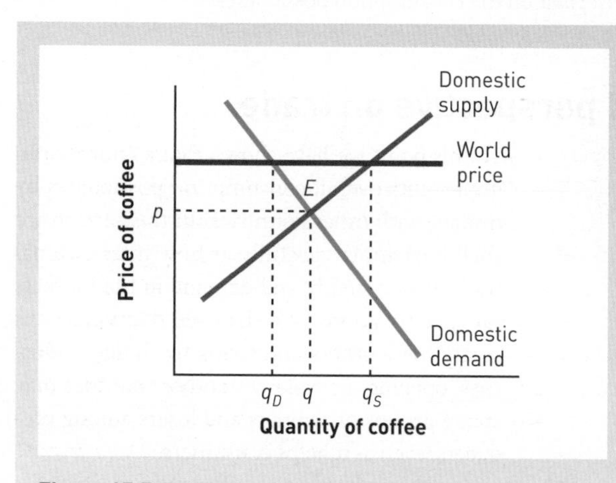


**Figure 15.7 The Market for Coffee in Brazil.** With no international trade, the equilibrium price and quantity of coffee in Brazil are determined by the intersection of the domestic supply and demand curves (point $E$). But if the country opens to trade, the domestic price of coffee must equal the world price. At the higher world price, Brazilians will demand the quantity of coffee $q_D$, less than the amount supplied by Brazilian producers, $q_S$. The excess coffee supplied by Brazilian producers, $q_S - q_D$, is exported.

Now imagine that Brazil opens its coffee market to international trade. As in the case of computers, if free trade in coffee is permitted, then the prevailing price for coffee in Brazil must be the same as the world price. Unlike the case of computers, however, the world price of coffee as shown in Fig. 15.7 is *higher* than the domestic equilibrium price. How do we know that the world price of coffee will be higher than the domestic price? Recall that the price of coffee is measured relative to the price of computers, and vice versa. If the price of computers relative to the price of coffee is higher in Brazil than in the world market, then the price of coffee relative to the price of computers must be lower, as each price is the reciprocal of the other. More generally, as we saw in Chapter 2, when two people or two countries trade with each other, neither can have a comparative advantage in *every* good and service. Thus, in an example with only two goods, if non-Brazilian producers have a comparative advantage in computers, reflected in the lower cost of computers relative to coffee in the world market, then Brazilian producers must have a comparative advantage in coffee. By definition, this comparative advantage implies that the opportunity cost of coffee in terms of computers must be lower in Brazil than in the rest of the world.

Figure 15.7 shows that at the world price for coffee, Brazilian producers are willing to supply $q_S$ coffee, while Brazilian consumers want to purchase a smaller amount, $q_D$. The difference between domestic production and domestic consumption, $q_S - q_D$, is exported to the world market. The general conclusion of Fig. 15.7 is this: if the price of a good or service in a closed economy is lower than the world price, and that economy opens itself to trade, *the economy will tend to become a net exporter of that good or service.*

These examples illustrate how the market translates comparative advantage into mutually beneficial gains from trade. If trade is unrestricted, then countries with a comparative advantage in a particular good will profit by supplying that good to the world market and using the revenue earned to import goods in which they do not have a comparative advantage. Thus the workings of the free market automatically ensure that goods will be produced where the opportunity cost is lowest, leading to the *highest possible consumption possibilities* for the world as a whole.

## Winners and losers from trade

If trade is so wonderful, why do politicians so often resist free trade and 'globalisation'? One reason is that although free trade benefits the economy as a whole, *specific groups* may not benefit. If groups who are hurt by trade have sufficient political influence, they may be able to persuade politicians to enact policies that restrict the free flow of goods and services across borders.

The supply and demand analyses shown in Figs 15.6 and 15.7 are useful in clarifying who gains and who loses when an economy opens up to trade. Look first at Fig. 15.6, which shows the market for computers in Brazil. When Brazil opens its computer market to international competition, Brazilian consumers enjoy a larger quantity of computers at a lower price. Clearly, Brazilian computer users benefit from the free trade in computers. In general, *domestic consumers of imported goods benefit from free trade.* However, Brazilian computer producers will not be so happy about opening their market to international competition. The fall in computer prices to the international level implies that less efficient domestic producers will go out of business, and that those who remain will earn lower profits. Unemployment in the Brazilian computer industry will rise and may persist over time, particularly if displaced computer workers cannot easily move to a new industry.[2] We see that, in general, *domestic producers of imported goods are hurt by free trade.*

Consumers are helped, and producers hurt, when imports increase. The opposite conclusions apply for an increase in exports (see Fig. 15.7). In the example of Brazil, an opening of the coffee market raises the domestic price of coffee to the world price and creates the opportunity for Brazil to export coffee. Domestic producers of coffee benefit from the increased market (they can now sell coffee abroad as well as at home) and from the higher price of their product. In short, *domestic producers of exported goods benefit from free trade.* Brazilian coffee drinkers will be less enthusiastic, however, since they must now pay the higher world price of coffee, and can therefore consume less. Thus *domestic consumers of exported goods are hurt by free trade.*

[2] If labour markets are competitive, the wage rate paid to Brazilian computer workers will also fall, reflecting the lower relative price of computers.

Free trade is *efficient* in the sense that it increases the size of the 'pie' available to the economy. Indeed, the efficiency of free trade is an application of the *Equilibrium Principle*: markets in equilibrium leave no unexploited opportunities for individuals. Despite the efficiency of free trade, however, some groups may lose from trade, which generates political pressures to block or restrict trade. In the next section we shall discuss the major types of policy used to restrict trade.

There is, formally at least, a second reason that is frequently cited for restricting trade. This is the argument that, for strategic reasons to do with security, an ability to dispense with imports is important. This used to be given as a rationalisation for UK policies to support British agriculture by means of subsidies known as deficiency payments. This was supposedly a reflection of Britain's experience in the First and Second World Wars. Self-sufficiency for similar reasons was also said to be the reason for the introduction of the EU's CAP.

A variant of this argument is sometimes used in decision making on defence procurement. It is argued that if, for example, the next generation of advanced air superiority fighters is not produced in Europe, but is bought off the shelf from America, the European aerospace sector will lose irretrievably the capacity to design and build such machines, and the countries of Europe will become dependent on US political goodwill for their security.

Note, however, that in both cases the arguments have the effect of increasing the incomes of those who work in the protected sectors, and do so by reducing the real incomes of people in the rest of the economy.

A third reason, and one that is rarely cited by politicians, is that it is possible to use tariffs to drive down the price a country pays for its imports relative to what it gets for its exports. Indeed, it is also possible by restricting trade to increase what a country gets for its exports. That is precisely what OPEC does when the cartel agrees to reduce oil production to get a higher price for oil. When a country can use trade restrictions to increase the relative price of its exports it is said to be shifting the 'terms of trade' in its favour. When this happens the country makes itself better off. It does so by implementing a deterioration in the terms of trade for the country or countries from whom it imports, making them worse off.

For this to work, the importing country has to represent a sufficiently large proportion of total demand for the commodity concerned that the price for the commodity will fall significantly as a consequence of a drop in demand in the importing country.

The political and ethical implications of all this help explain why politicians do not emphasise this aspect of trade restrictions. For years the European Union operated what was known as the Multi-Fibre Agreement (MFA), an arrangement that had the net effect of imposing quantitative restrictions on imports into Europe of textile products from a variety of countries. This was to protect European textile production. A side effect of this protection afforded to workers' incomes in the textile sector in Europe was to depress the incomes of textile workers in poorer countries affected by the restrictions.

## RECAP Trade winners and losers

**Winners**

- Consumers of imported goods
- Producers of exported goods

**Losers**

- Consumers of exported goods
- Producers of imported goods

## Protectionist policies: tariffs and quotas

**protectionism** the view that free trade is injurious and should be restricted

**tariff** a tax imposed on an imported good

**quota** a legal limit on the quantity of a good that may be imported

The view that free trade is injurious and should be restricted is known as **protectionism**. Supporters of this view believe the government should attempt to 'protect' domestic markets by raising legal barriers to imports. (Interestingly, protectionists rarely attempt to restrict exports, even though they hurt consumers of the exported good. Exceptions include OPEC, and also some coffee producers at times in the past.) Two of the most common types of such barriers are **tariffs** and **quotas**. A tariff is a tax imposed on an imported good. A quota is a legal limit on the quantity of a good that may be imported.

### Tariffs

The effects of tariffs and quotas can be explained using supply and demand diagrams. Suppose that Brazilian computer makers, dismayed by the penetration of 'their' market by imported computers, persuade their government to impose a tariff – that is, a tax – on every computer imported into the country. Computers produced in Brazil will be exempt from the tax. Figure 15.8 shows the likely effects of this tariff on the domestic Brazilian computer market. The lower of the two horizontal lines in Fig. 15.8 indicates the world price of computers, not including the tariff. The higher of the two lines indicates the price Brazilian consumers will actually pay for imported computers, including the tariff. We refer to the price of computers including the tariff as $p_T$. The vertical distance between the two lines equals the amount of the tariff that is imposed on each imported computer.

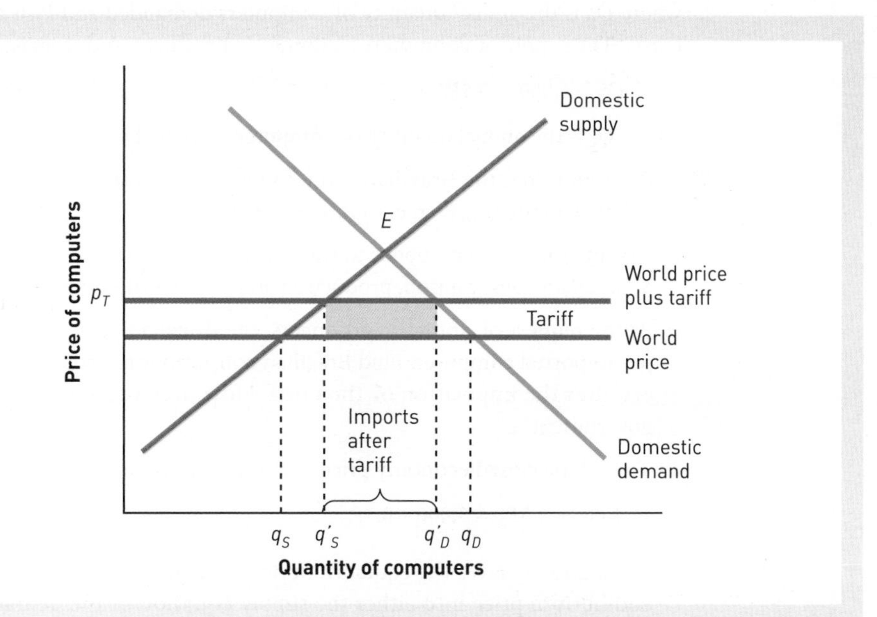


**Figure 15.8 The Market for Computers after the Imposition of an Import Tariff.** The imposition of a tariff on imported computers raises the price of computers in Brazil to the world price plus tariff, $p_T$, represented by the upper horizontal line. Domestic production of computers rises from $q_S$ to $q'_S$, domestic purchases of computers fall from $q_D$ to $q'_D$, and computer imports fall from $q_D - q_S$ to $q'_D - q'_S$. Brazilian consumers are worse off and Brazilian computer producers are better off. The Brazilian government collects revenue from the tariff equal to the area of the shaded rectangle.

From the point of view of domestic Brazilian producers and consumers, the imposition of the tariff has the same effects as an equivalent increase in the world price of computers. Because the price (including the tariff) of imported computers has risen, Brazilian computer producers will be able to raise the price they charge for their computers to the world price plus tariff, $p_T$. Thus the price Brazilian consumers must pay – whether their computers are imported or not – equals $p_T$, represented by the upper horizontal line in Fig. 15.8.

The rise in the price of computers created by the tariff affects the quantities of computers supplied and the quantities demanded by Brazilians. Domestic computer producers, facing a higher price for computers, increase their production from $q_S$ to $q'_S$ (see Fig. 15.8). Brazilian consumers, also reacting to the higher price, reduce their computer purchases from $q_D$ to $q'_D$. As a result, the number of imported computers – the difference between domestic purchases and domestic production – falls from $q_D - q_S$ to $q'_D - q'_S$.

Who, then, are the winners and the losers from the tariff? Relative to an environment with free trade and no tariff, the winners are the domestic computer producers, who sell more computers and receive a higher price for them. The clearest losers are Brazilian consumers, who must now pay more for their computers. Another winner is the government, which collects revenue from the tariff. The shaded area in Fig. 15.8 shows the amount of revenue the government collects, equal to the quantity of computer imports after the imposition of the tariff, $q'_D - q'_S$, times the amount of the tariff.

### Example 15.3 A tariff on imported computers

Suppose the demand for computers by Brazilian consumers is given by

$$Q_D = 3{,}000 - 0.5P_C$$

where $Q_D$ is the annual quantity of computers demanded and $P_C$ is the price per computer in euros. The supply of computers by domestic Brazilian producers is

$$Q_S = 1{,}000 + 0.5P_C$$

where $Q_S$ is the annual quantity of computers supplied.

a. Assuming that the Brazilian economy is closed to trade, find the equilibrium price and quantity in the Brazilian computer market.

b. Assume the economy opens to trade. If the world price of computers is €1,500, find annual Brazilian consumption, production and imports of computers.

c. At the request of domestic producers, the Brazilian government imposes a tariff of €300 per imported computer. Find Brazilian consumption, production and imports of computers after the imposition of the tariff. How much revenue does the tariff raise for the government?

a. To find the closed-economy price and quantity, we set supply equal to demand:

$$1{,}000 + 0.5P_C = 3{,}000 - 0.5P_C$$

Solving for $P_C$ gives the equilibrium price, equal to €2,000 per computer. Substituting this equilibrium price into either the supply equation or the demand equation, we find the equilibrium quantity of computers in the Brazilian market, equal to 2,000 computers per year. This equilibrium price and quantity correspond to a point like point $E$ in Fig. 15.8.

b. If the economy opens to trade, the domestic price of computers must equal the world price, which is €1,500. At this price, the domestic quantity demanded for computers is $3{,}000 - 0.5(1{,}500) = 2{,}250$ computers per year; the domestic quantity supplied is $1{,}000 + 0.5(1{,}500) = 1{,}750$ computers per year. These quantities correspond to $q_D$ and $q_S$, respectively, in Fig. 15.8. Imports equal the difference between domestic quantities demanded and supplied, or $2{,}250 - 1{,}750 = 500$ computers per year.

c. The imposition of a tariff of €300 per computer raises the price from €1,500 (the world price without the tariff) to €1,800. To find Brazilian consumption and production at this price, we set the price equal to €1,800 in the demand and supply equations. Thus the domestic quantity demanded is 3,000 – 0.5(1,800) = 2,100 computers per year; the domestic quantity supplied is 1,000 + 0.5(1,800) = 1,900 computers per year. Imports, the difference between the quantity demanded by Brazilians and the quantity supplied by domestic firms, is 2,100 – 1,900 = 200 computers per year. Thus the tariff has raised the price of computers by €300 and reduced imports by 300 computers per year. The tariff revenue collected by the government is €300/imported computer on 200 computers/year = €60,000 per year.

**Exercise 15.3** Repeat parts (b) and (c) of Example 15.3 under the assumption that the world price of computers is €1,200. What happens if the world price is €1,800?

## Quotas

An alternative to a tariff is a quota, or legal limit, on the number or value of foreign goods that can be imported. One means of enforcing a quota is to require importers to obtain a licence or permit for each good they bring into the country. The government then distributes exactly the same number of permits as the number of goods that may be imported under the quota.

How does the imposition of a quota on, say, computers affect the domestic market for computers? Figure 15.9, which is similar to Fig. 15.8, illustrates the effect of a quota on imported computers. As before, assume that at first there are no restrictions on trade.

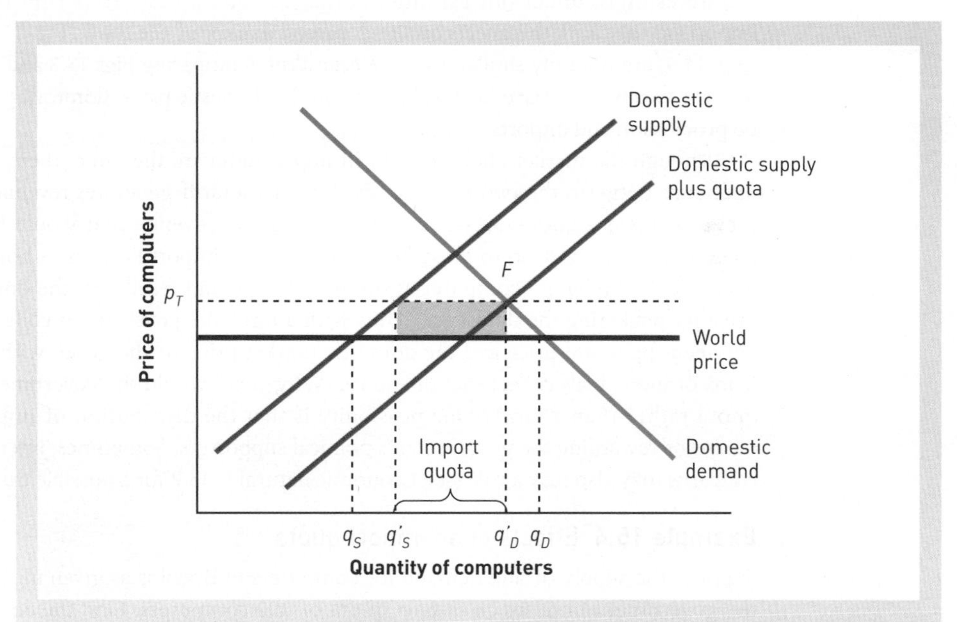


**Figure 15.9 The Market for Computers after the Imposition of an Import Quota.** The figure shows the effects of the imposition of a quota that permits only $q'_D - q'_S$ computers to be imported. The total supply of computers to the domestic economy equals the domestic supply curve shifted to the right by $q'_D - q'_S$ units (the fixed amount of imports). Market equilibrium occurs at point *F*. The effects of the quota on the domestic market are identical to those of the tariff analysed in Fig. 15.8. The domestic price rises to $p_T$, domestic production of computers rises from $q_S$ to $q'_S$, domestic purchases of computers fall from $q_D$ to $q'_D$ and computer imports fall from $q_D - q_S$ to $q'_D - q'_S$. The quota differs from the tariff in that under a quota system the government collects no revenue.

Consumers pay the world price for computers, and $q_D - q_S$ computers are imported. Now suppose once more that domestic computer producers complain to the government about competition from foreign computer makers, and the government agrees to act. However, this time, instead of a tariff, the government imposes a quota on the number of computers that can be imported. For comparability with the tariff analysed in Fig. 15.8, let's assume that the quota permits the same level of imports as entered the country under the tariff: specifically, $q'_D - q'_S$ computers.

What effect does this ruling have on the domestic market for computers?

After the imposition of the quota, the quantity of computers supplied to the Brazilian market is the production of domestic firms plus the $q'_D - q'_S$ imported computers allowed under the quota. Figure 15.9 shows the quantity of computers supplied inclusive of the quota. The total supply curve, labelled 'Domestic supply plus quota', is the same as the domestic supply curve shifted $q'_D - q'_S$ to the right.

The domestic demand curve is the same as in Fig. 15.8. Equilibrium in the domestic market for computers occurs at point *F* in Fig. 15.9, at the intersection of the supply curve including the quota and the domestic demand curve. Figure 15.9 shows that, relative to the initial situation with free trade, the quota (i) raises the domestic price of computers above the world price, to the level marked $p_T$ in Fig. 15.9; (ii) reduces domestic purchases of computers from $q_D$ to $q'_D$; (iii) increases domestic production of computers from $q_S$ to $q'_S$; and (iv) reduces imports to $q'_D - q'_S$, consistent with a quota. Like a tariff, the quota helps domestic producers by increasing their sales and the price they receive for their output, while hurting domestic consumers by forcing them to pay a higher price.

Interestingly, under our assumption that the quota is set to permit the same level of imports as the tariff, the effects on the domestic market of the tariff (Fig. 15.8) and the quota (Fig. 15.9) are not only similar, they are *equivalent*. Comparing Figs 15.8 and 15.9, you can see that the two policies have identical effects on the domestic price, domestic purchases, domestic production and imports.

Although the market effects of a tariff and a quota are the same, there is one important difference between the two policies, which is that a tariff generates revenue for the government, whereas a quota does not. With a quota, the revenue that would have gone to the government goes instead to those firms that hold the import licences. A holder of an import licence can purchase a computer at the world price and resell it in the domestic market at price $p_T$, pocketing the difference. Thus with a tariff the government collects the difference between the world price and the domestic market price of the good; with a quota, private firms or individuals collect that difference. Why, then, would the government ever impose a quota rather than a tariff? One possibility is that the distribution of import licences is a means of rewarding the government's political supporters. Sometimes, international political concerns may also play a role (see Economic naturalist 15.2 for a possible example).

### **Example 15.4** Effects of an import quota

Suppose the supply of and demand for computers in Brazil is as given in Example 15.3, and the government imposes an import quota of 200 computers. Find the equilibrium price in the domestic computer market, as well as the quantities produced by domestic firms and purchased by domestic consumers.

The quantity of computers supplied by domestic Brazilian producers was stated in Example 15.3 to be $1{,}000 + 0.5P_C$. The quota allows 200 computers per year to be imported. Thus the total quantity of computers supplied, including both domestic production and imports, is $1{,}000 + 0.5P_C + 200$, or $1{,}200 + 0.5P_C$. Setting the quantity supplied equal to the quantity demanded, we get

$$1{,}200 + 0.5P_C = 3{,}000 - 0.5P_C$$

Solving for $P_C$, we find that the price of computers in the domestic Brazilian market is €1,800. Domestic production of computers is 1,000 + 0.5(1,800) = 1,900 computers per year, while quantity demanded domestically is 3,000 – 0.5(1,800) = 2,100 computers per year. The difference between domestic quantity demanded and domestic production, 200 computers per year, is made up by imports.

Note that the domestic price, domestic production and domestic demand are the same in Examples 15.3 and 15.4. Thus the tariff and the quota have the same effects on the domestic market for computers. The only difference between the two policies is that, with a quota, the government does not get the tariff revenue it got in Example 15.3. That revenue goes instead to the holders of import licences, who can buy computers on the world market at €1,500 and sell them in the domestic market at €1,800.

## Economic naturalist 15.2 Who benefited from and who was hurt by voluntary export restraints on Japanese automobiles in the 1980s?

After the oil price increases of the 1970s, American consumers began to buy small, fuel-efficient Japanese automobiles in large numbers. Reeling from the new foreign competition, US automobile producers petitioned the US government for assistance. In response, in May 1981 the US government negotiated a system of so-called *voluntary export restraints*, or VERs, with Japan. Under the VER system, each Japanese auto producer would 'voluntarily' restrict exports to the United States to an agreed level. VER quotas were changed several times before the system was formally abandoned in 1994. Who benefited from, and who was hurt by, VERs on Japanese automobiles?

Several groups benefited from the VER system. As might be expected, US auto producers saw increased sales and profits when their Japanese competition was reduced. But Japanese automobile producers also profited from the policy, despite the reduction in their US sales. The restrictions on the supply of their automobiles to the US market allowed them to raise their prices in that market significantly – by several thousand dollars per car by the late 1980s, according to some estimates. From an economic point of view, the VERs functioned like a tariff on Japanese cars, except that the Japanese automobile producers, rather than the US government, got to keep the tariff revenue. A third group that benefited from the VERs was European automobile producers, who saw US demand for their cars rise when Japanese imports declined.

The biggest losers from the VER system were clearly American car buyers, who faced higher prices (particularly for Japanese imports) and reduced selection. During this period dealer discounts on new Japanese cars largely disappeared, and customers often found themselves paying a premium over the list price. Because the economic losses faced by American car buyers exceeded the extra profits received by US automobile producers, the VERs produced a net loss for the US economy that at its greatest was estimated at more than $3 billion per year.

The US government's choice of a VER system, rather than a tariff or a quota, was somewhat puzzling. If a tariff on Japanese cars had been imposed instead of a VER system, the US government would have collected much of the revenue that went instead to Japanese auto producers. Alternatively, a quota system with import licences given to US car dealers would have captured some revenue for domestic car dealers rather than Japanese firms. The best explanation for why the US government chose VERs is probably political. US policy makers may have been concerned that the Japanese government would retaliate against US trade restrictions by imposing its own restrictions on US exports. By instituting a system that did minimal financial harm to – or even helped – Japanese auto producers, they may have hoped to avoid retaliation from the Japanese.[3]

Note that while the owners of Japanese car producing firms made higher profits per car sold (and higher total profits, if we assume they agreed with the policy), fewer cars were produced by the firms concerned. This would have lowered the incomes of those working in the firms and supplying parts to them.

## Economic naturalist 15.3 Do VERs always work as desired?

Possibly not. The United States was not the only country to use VERs to protect car producers. In the late 1970s the remnants of Britain's native car industry, concentrated with government encouragement into the entity known as British Leyland Motor Corporation (BLMC), subsequently taken into state ownership, was experiencing severe competition from Japanese imports. Recent research[4] suggests that the UK government introduced quantitative restrictions (QRs) based on VERs to help BLMC, but in doing so may have helped to seal its fate. Initially Japanese producers agreed in the late 1970s to limit exports to Britain to about 10 per cent of new car sales for five years. Later, the EEC Commission got in on the act, and from the early 1980s extended this arrangement on a co-ordinated basis to the nine-member EEC, as it then was.

In addition to limiting the number of cars imported from Japan into Britain, the VERs also had the effect of encouraging Japanese producers to consider establishing manufacturing facilities in Britain, and these are today a major component of the EU motor industry.

However, what damaged BLMC was the reaction of Japanese producers to the QRs. Limited as to the number of cars they could sell, they reacted by moving away from the small, cheap and cheerful cars with which they had obtained their foothold in the market. They moved up-market, concentrating on selling larger, more profitable and 'loaded' cars (with optimal extras as standard). In doing so, they moved into the market segments where BLMC was most strongly represented, and its market share declined as a result, until eventually it had to be broken up and sold off.

Tariffs and quotas are not the only barriers to trade that governments erect. Importers may be subject to unnecessarily complex bureaucratic rules (so-called 'red tape barriers'), and regulations of goods that are nominally intended to promote health and safety sometimes have the side effect, whether intentionally or unintentionally, of restricting trade. One example is European restrictions on imports of genetically modified (GM) foods. Although these regula-

[3] The former US president, Ronald Reagan, states in his autobiography that other restrictions would have risked provoking a retaliatory response hitting American exports to Japan. See Reagan (1990, p. 274).

[4] 'The Japanese upgrading response was to expand sales in segments with higher profit magins. The most dramatic example of this was Toyota's development of the Lexus, but the more common result was for manufacturers to concentrate on selling medium rather then small family and mini cars. Since it was precisely the medium segment where British Leyland (BL) had a strong sales position, the effect of enhanced competition within that part of the market led to a fall in BL's sales and a contraction in profits' (Walker 2004).

tions were motivated in part by concerns about the safety of such foods, they also help to protect Europe's politically powerful farmers from foreign competition.

## The inefficiency of protectionism

Free trade is efficient because it allows countries to specialise in the production of goods and services in which they have the greatest comparative advantage. Conversely, protectionist policies that limit trade are inefficient – they reduce the total economic 'pie'. (Recall Chapter 3's *Efficiency Principle*, that efficiency is an important social goal.) Why, then, do governments adopt such policies? The reason is similar to why some city governments impose rent controls (see Chapter 3). Although rent controls reduce economic welfare overall, some people benefit from them – namely, the tenants whose rents are held artificially below the market level. Similarly, as we have seen in this section, tariffs and quotas benefit certain groups. Because those who benefit from these restrictions (such as firms facing import competition) are often better organised politically than those who lose from trade barriers (such as consumers in general), law makers are sometimes persuaded to enact the restrictions.

The fact that free trade is efficient suggests an alternative to trade restrictions, however. Because eliminating restrictions on trade increases the overall economic 'pie', in general the winners from free trade will be able to compensate the losers in such a way that everyone becomes better off. Government programmes that assist and retrain workers displaced by import competition are an example of such compensation. Spreading the benefits of free trade – or at least reducing its adverse effects on certain groups – reduces the incentives of those groups to inhibit free trade.

Although we have focused on the winners and losers from trade, not all opposition to free trade is motivated by economic interest. For example, many of the anti-trade protesters in Washington, DC in 2001 cited environmental concerns. Protecting the environment is an important and laudable goal, but once again the efficiency principle suggests that restricting trade is not the most effective means of achieving that goal. Restricting trade lowers world income, reducing the resources available to deal with environmental problems. (High levels of economic development are in fact associated with lower, not higher, amounts of pollution.) Furthermore, much of the income loss arising from barriers to trade is absorbed by poor nations trying to develop their economies. For this reason, the leaders of developing countries are among the strongest advocates of free trade.

## Summary

- According to the principle of comparative advantage, the best economic outcomes occur when each nation specialises in the goods and services at which it is *relatively more productive* and then trades with other nations to obtain the goods and services its citizens desire.
- The production possibilities curve (PPC) of a country is a graph that describes the maximum amount of one good that can be produced at every possible level of production of the other good. At any point the slope of a PPC indicates the *opportunity cost*, in terms of forgone production of the good on the vertical axis, of increasing production of the good on the horizontal axis by 1 unit. The more of a good that is already being produced, the greater the opportunity cost of increasing production still further. Thus the slope of a PPC becomes more and more negative as we read from left to right. When an economy has many workers, the PPC has a smooth, outwardly bowed shape.

- A country's *consumption possibilities* are the combinations of goods and services that might feasibly be consumed by its citizens. In a *closed economy* – one that does not trade with other countries – the citizens' consumption possibilities are identical to their production possibilities. But in an *open economy* – one that does trade with other countries – consumption possibilities are typically greater than, and never less than, the economy's production possibilities. Graphically, an *open economy's* consumption possibilities are described by a downward-sloping line that just touches the PPC, whose slope equals the amount of the good on the vertical axis that must be traded to obtain 1 unit of the good on the horizontal axis. A country achieves its highest consumption possibilities by producing at the point where the consumption possibilities line touches the PPC and then trading to obtain the most preferred point on the consumption possibilities line.
- In a closed economy, the relative price of a good or service is determined at the intersection of the supply curve of domestic producers and the demand curve of domestic consumers. In an open economy, the relative price of a good or service equals the *world price* – the price determined by supply and demand in the world economy. If the price of a good or service in a closed economy is greater than the world price and the country opens its market to trade, it will become a net importer of that good or service. But if the closed-economy price is below the world price and the country opens itself to trade, it will become a net exporter of that good or service.
- Although free trade is beneficial to the economy as a whole, some groups – such as the domestic producers of imported goods – are hurt by free trade. Groups that are hurt by trade may be able to induce the government to impose *protectionist* measures, such as tariffs or quotas. A *tariff* is a tax on an imported good that has the effect of raising the domestic price of the good. A higher domestic price increases domestic supply, reduces domestic demand and reduces imports of the good. A *quota*, which is a legal limit on the amount of a good that may be imported, has the same effects as a tariff, except that the government collects no tax revenue. (The equivalent amount of revenue goes instead to those firms with the legal authority to import goods.) Because free trade is efficient, the winners from free trade should be able to compensate the losers so that everyone becomes better off. Thus policies to assist those who are harmed by trade, such as assistance and retraining for workers made redundant by imports, are usually preferable to trade restrictions.

## Key terms

**autarky** (435)
**closed economy** (431)
**consumption possibilities** (434)
**open economy** (431)
**protectionism** (443)
**quota** (443)
**tariff** (443)
**world price** (440)

## Review questions

1. Sketch a PPC for a four-worker economy that produces two goods: hot dogs and hamburgers. Give an economic interpretation of the vertical intercept, the horizontal intercept and the slope of the graph.
2. What is meant by the 'consumption possibilities' of a country? How are consumption possibilities related to production possibilities in a closed economy? In an open economy?
3. A small, open economy is equally productive in producing coffee and tea. What will this economy produce if the world price of coffee is twice that of tea? Half that of tea? What will the country produce if the world price of coffee happens to equal the world price of tea?

4. **True or false:** If a country is more productive in every sector than a neighbouring country, then there is no benefit in trading with the neighbouring country. Explain.

5. Show graphically the effects of a tariff on imported automobiles on the domestic market for automobiles. Who is hurt by the tariff, and why? Who benefits, and why?

6. Show graphically the effects of a quota on imported cars on the domestic market for cars. Whom does the quota hurt, and who benefits? Explain.

## Problems

1. An economy has two workers, Anne and Bill. Per day of work, Anne can produce 100 apples or 25 bananas, and Bill can produce 50 apples or 50 bananas. Anne and Bill each work 200 days per year.

   a. Which worker has an absolute advantage in apples? Which has a comparative advantage? Calculate each worker's opportunity cost of producing an additional apple.

   b. Find the maximum number of each type of fruit that can be produced annually in this economy, assuming that none of the other type of fruit is produced. What is the most of each type that can be produced if each worker fully specialises according to his or her comparative advantage?

   c. Draw the PPC for annual production in this economy. Show numerical values for the vertical intercept, the horizontal intercept and the slopes of each segment of the PPC.

2. A developing economy requires 1,000 hours of work to produce a TV set and 10 hours of work to produce a tonne of corn. This economy has available a total of 1,000,000 hours of work per day.

   a. Draw the PPC for daily output of the developing economy. Give numerical values for the PPC's vertical intercept, horizontal intercept and slope. Relate the slope to the developing country's opportunity cost of producing each good. If this economy does not trade, what are its consumption possibilities?

   b. The developing economy is considering opening trade with a much larger, industrialised economy. The industrialised economy requires 10 hours of work to produce a TV and 1 hour of work to produce a tonne of corn. Show graphically how trading with the industrialised economy affects the developing economy's consumption possibilities. Is opening trade desirable for the developing economy? (**Hint:** When it opens to trade, the developing economy will be fully specialised in one product.)

3. Modifying Example 1.1, suppose that Brazilian worker Carlos can produce either 100 kg of coffee or 1 computer per week, and a second worker, Maria, can produce either 150 kg of coffee or 1 computer per week. Both Carlos and Maria work 50 weeks per year.

   a. Find the PPC for Brazil. Give numerical values for the graph's intercepts and slopes. How much of each good is produced if each worker fully specialises according to comparative advantage?

   b. World prices are such that 1 computer trades for 125 kg of coffee on international markets. If Brazil is open to trade, show Brazil's consumption possibilities graphically. What is the most of each good that Brazilians can consume when the economy is open? Compare this with the situation when the economy is closed.

   c. Repeat part (b) under the assumption that 1 computer trades for 80 kg of coffee on world markets.

4. Suppose that Carlos and Maria can produce coffee and computers as described in Problem 3. A third worker, Pedro, joins the Brazilian economy. Pedro can produce either 140 kg of coffee or 1 computer per week. Like the other two workers, Pedro works 50 weeks per year.

   a. Find the PPC for Brazil. Give numerical values of the PPC's intercepts and slopes.

   b. Find Brazil's consumption possibilities if the country is open and 1 computer trades for 125 kg of coffee on world markets. What is the most of each good that Brazilians can consume when the economy is open? Compare this with the situation when the economy is closed.

   c. Repeat part (b) assuming that 1 computer trades for 200 kg of coffee on world markets.

5. Suppose that a US worker can produce 1,000 pairs of shoes or 10 industrial robots per year. For simplicity, assume there are no costs other than labour costs and firms earn zero profits. Initially, the US economy is closed. The domestic price of shoes is $30 a pair, so that a US worker can earn $30,000 annually by working in the shoe industry. The domestic price of a robot is $3,000, so that a US worker can also earn $30,000 annually working in the robot industry.

   Now suppose that the United States opens trade with the rest of the world. Foreign workers can produce 500 pairs of shoes or 1 robot per year. The world price of shoes after the United States opens its markets is $10 a pair, and the world price of robots is $5,000.

   a. What do foreign workers earn annually, in dollars?

   b. When it opens to trade, which good will the United States import and which will it export?

   c. Find the real income of US workers after the opening to trade, measured in (i) the number of pairs of shoes annual worker income will buy and (ii) the number of robots annual worker income will buy. Compare this with the situation before the opening of trade. Does trading in goods produced by 'cheap foreign labour' hurt US workers?

   d. How might your conclusion in part (c) be modified in the short term if it is costly for workers to change industries? What policy response might help with this problem?

6. The demand for automobiles in a certain country is given by

   $D = 12{,}000 - 200P$

   where $P$ is the price of a car. Supply by domestic automobile producers is

   $S = 57{,}000 + 50P$

   a. Assuming that the economy is closed, find the equilibrium price and production of automobiles.

   b. The economy opens to trade. The world price of automobiles is 18. Find the domestic quantities demanded and supplied and the quantity of imports or exports. Who will favour the opening of the automobile market to trade, and who will oppose it?

   c. The government imposes a tariff of 1 unit per car. Find the effects on domestic quantities demanded and supplied and on the quantity of imports or exports. Also find the revenue raised by the tariff. Who will favour the imposition of the tariff, and who will oppose it?

   d. Can the government obtain the same results as you found in part (c) by imposing a quota on automobile imports? Explain.

7. Suppose the domestic demand and supply for automobiles is as given by Problem 6. The world price of automobiles is 16. Foreign car firms have a production cost of 15 per automobile, so they earn a profit of 1 per car.

a. How many cars will be imported, assuming this country trades freely?

b. Now suppose foreign car producers are asked 'voluntarily' to limit their exports to the home country to half of free-trade levels. What will be the equilibrium price of cars in the domestic market if foreign producers comply? Find the domestic quantities of cars supplied and demanded.

c. How will the 'voluntary' export restriction affect the profits of foreign car producers?

## Answers to in-chapter exercises

15.1 The opportunity cost of producing coffee equals the number of computers given up for each extra kg of coffee produced. Carlos can produce either 100 kg of coffee or 1 computer per week, so his opportunity cost is given by

$$\frac{\text{Loss in computers}}{\text{Gain in coffee}} = \frac{\text{21 computer/week}}{\text{100 kg of coffee/week}}$$

$$= \text{21/100 computer/kg of coffee}$$

Maria can produce either 100 kg of coffee or 2 computers per week, so her opportunity cost is

$$\frac{\text{Loss in computers}}{\text{Gain in coffee}} = \frac{\text{22 computers/week}}{\text{100 kg of coffee/week}}$$

$$= \text{21/50 computer/kg of coffee}$$

Since each kg of coffee Carlos produces requires the sacrifice of 1/100 of a computer, while each kg of coffee produced by Maria sacrifices 1/50 of a computer, Carlos has the smaller opportunity cost of producing coffee. Thus he has a comparative advantage in producing coffee.

15.2 When the economy is closed, the Brazilians can obtain 80 computers by having Maria work 40 weeks making computers. If Maria works the remaining 10 weeks producing coffee and Carlos works 50 weeks producing coffee, the Brazilians will be able to consume (10 + 50) × 100 = 6,000 kg of coffee per year.

The world price of computers is 80 kg of coffee, which is greater than Maria's opportunity cost of producing computers but less than Carlos' opportunity cost. Thus if the economy opens to trade, Maria will specialise in computers and Carlos will specialise in coffee. If Maria produces 100 computers, 80 of which are consumed domestically, 20 computers are available for export. Because a computer is worth 80 kg of coffee on the world market, the 20 exported computers can be traded for 1,600 kg of coffee. Carlos still produces 5,000 kg of coffee. Total coffee consumption in Brazil is thus 1,600 + 5,000 = 6,600 kg. Opening to trade has allowed the Brazilians to consume 10 per cent more coffee at no sacrifice in computers.

15.3 If the world price of computers is €1,200, domestic demand for computers is 3,000 – 0.5(1,200) = 2,400 computers. Domestic supply is 1,000 + 0.5(1,200) = 1,600 computers. The difference between the quantity demanded and the quantity supplied, 800 computers, is imported.

A tariff of €300 raises the domestic price of computers to €1,500. Now domestic demand is 3,000 – 0.5(1,500) = 2,250, and domestic supply is 1,000 + 0.5(1,500) = 1,750. The difference, 500 computers, equals imports. Revenue for the government is (300/computer) (500 imported computers) = €150,000.

If the world price of computers is €1,800 and there is no tariff, domestic demand is 3,000 – 0.5(1,800) = 2,100; domestic supply is 1,000 + 0.5(1,800) = 1,900; and imports are 200. A tariff of €300 raises the world price to €2,100, which is greater than the domestic price when there is no trade (€2,000). No computers are imported in this case and no tariff revenue is raised.

## References

Reagan, R. (1990) *An American Life* (New York: Simon & Schuster).

Walker, J. (2004) 'Voluntary "Export" Restraints between Britain and Japan: The Case of the Car Market (1971–1998)', paper presented at the Economic History Society Annual Conference.

# 16

# Trade, Factor Flows and Economic Integration: the Basic Economics of the European Union

The purpose of this chapter is to build on the material on trade that has been discussed in Chapter 15 in order to provide an understanding of the origins of the European Union, its evolution and the policy problems it faces. While most of its activities are unquestionably in the sphere of economics, narrowly defined, the reality is that the European Union (and its previous forms of existence as the European Economic Community, and subsequently the European Community (EC), often referred to as the 'Common Market') has always been fundamentally seen as having a deep political dimension, both in what it does and in terms of why it was established. Indeed, much of the frequently highly divisive debate between and within member states about the development of the Union is in reality a debate about the politics as much as the economics of integration.

In the economic analysis in this chapter we shall first look at what the economics of free trade and protection can tell us about why the Union was set up from an economics perspective, and how these factors have affected its evolution.

Secondly, we shall look at the connection between the formation of the economic union and its full flowering as a single market in terms of both the implications for economic policy in the member states and the secular trend towards enlargement of the Union. This enlargement has seen it evolve from the original six member states in 1958 to the present (2005) 25 states, and possibly 30 states by 2020, with a membership that includes Turkey, most of which is in fact in western Asia.

Thirdly, the chapter aims at providing a basis for understanding some of the issues behind the creation of the single European currency, the euro, and the continuing debate as to whether those countries that are members of the Union at present but not in the eurozone (Denmark, Sweden and the United Kingdom) should take that final step. The macroeconomic aspects of these problems are dealt with in the macroeconomics section of the text, but they in turn reflect some microeconomic aspects of the integration process. In addition to helping us understand the current position in terms of the single European currency, these considerations will obviously have implications for the economies of the new (mostly Eastern European) members and the applicant countries.

But before doing any of this it is necessary to give an overview of the political and economic forces that brought the Union into existence and shaped its developments. In what follows we shall normally use the current term 'European Union', or 'EU' rather than the older forms used in order to make the narrative simpler.

## The birth and growth of the Union

After the Second World War there was a widely shared view in the western part of the continent of Europe (the rest having been swallowed into the *de facto* empire of the Soviet Union (USSR), to which the various countries were fully subordinated in economics and politics) that it was desirable to take measures to ensure that a third conflict between Germany and France (and such allies as they had dragged in) could not happen. At the same time, the growing threat of the USSR to the independence and democratic institutions of Europe made it important to strengthen and unite (with the assistance of the United States).

The first steps in this direction were the Marshall Aid programme, by which the United States helped finance the reconstruction of the economies of Western Europe,[1] and the formation of the European Coal and Steel Community (the ECSC). The ECSC was an agreement to integrate and rationalise the coal and steel industries of the major producers in continental Europe. It covered Belgium, Luxembourg and the Netherlands (the Low Countries), France, Italy and West Germany.[2] The twin goals were to increase efficiency by rationalising production on a co-operative basis across the member countries and, as a consequence, to ensure that no country was self-sufficient in coal and steel, seen at the time as the necessary industries for a nation state to wage war.

The success of the arrangements under the ECSC treaty led to moves to deepen economic integration. This culminated in a major international conference at Messina in Sicily, in 1955. At this conference it was proposed that a full customs union and common market (these terms will be explained later) should be set up covering most of Western Europe. The United Kingdom and some other states declined to join, for a variety of reasons. In the UK case, the main reasons were geopolitical and trade-related. The United Kingdom still saw itself as a global rather than a European power, and was not willing to pool sovereignty to the modest degree envisaged. The alliance with the United States took priority over what were seen as potential entanglements in Europe. In addition, existing UK trade relations, in particular with the independent states of the Commonwealth, were seen as both vitally important and potentially at risk in any such European venture.

The six ECSC states moved to draw up a treaty, signed at Rome on 25 March 1957 and thereafter known as the Rome Treaty, setting up the European Economic Community (EEC), which came into existence on 1 January 1958. It was this arrangement that subsequently became the European Union. Britain responded by forming a looser free trade area, the European Free Trade Area (EFTA), with seven other European states: Austria, Denmark, Finland, Norway, Portugal, Sweden and Switzerland .

The changing world political balance, coupled with the clear evidence that the EEC was developing rapidly (while EFTA was rather moribund), led the United Kingdom to change its mind, and in 1961 it opened negotiations to join. France vetoed this in 1963. After the replacement of Charles de Gaulle as president of France in 1969, the United Kingdom re-opened negotiations. In 1973 the United Kingdom, Denmark, Norway and Ireland were offered membership. Norway subsequently decided in a referendum not to join. The EEC6 became the EEC9.

After the democratic reforms in Greece, Spain and Portugal these countries, too, applied to join. In the context of today's controversies about enlargement, it should be noted that the

[1] Actually, the Marshall Plan originally envisaged supporting reconstruction in Europe as a whole, including its eastern territories that were under Soviet control. Unfortunately, the Soviet Union refused to participate on behalf of its European satrapies.

[2] West Germany, the German Federal Republic (FRG), was established in the part of Germany occupied by America, Britain and France after 1945. After the collapse of communism in Eastern Europe, it absorbed the former German Democratic Republic (GDR) set up by the USSR in its zone of occupied Germany, usually referred to as East Germany.

decision to allow these countries to join was expressly taken in the light of the democratic reforms they had undertaken, and with a view to underpinning them, as well as with an eye to economic issues. Greece joined in 1983 and the other two in 1986. The EEC9 became the EEC12.

In the late 1980s the term 'European Community' (EC) came into vogue, and was associated with the increased tempo of economic and political integration under the Single Market Programme (SMP). This was designed to move the EC from being a customs union to becoming a *single integrated economic market* for goods, services, and labour and capital movements.

The collapse of the Soviet Union and its empire between 1989 and 1991 radically changed the European political landscape. This, coupled to the growing importance of the European Union as a trading partner, led Sweden and Austria (militarily neutral) and Finland (previously very much dependent on the goodwill of the Soviet Union, a dominant military neighbour and also its largest trading partner, to maintain its political independence) to apply for membership. When this was agreed in 1996 the EC12 became the EC15.

As a result of the Maastricht and Amsterdam treaties, which provided for increased economic integration and political co-operation respectively, the European Community became known as the European Union. In the aftermath of the collapse of the Soviet empire in Eastern Europe and the disintegration of Yugoslavia in the mid-to-late 1990s, most of the successor states sought the shelter of European Union membership. In 2004, eight of these – the Czech Republic, Estonia, Hungary, Latvia, Lithuania, Poland, Slovakia and Slovenia – plus Greek Cypriot Republic and Malta, were admitted. This brought the membership of the Union to 25. Ongoing negotiations could see this being expanded to 30 by 2020.

## The economics of freeing trade

The economic analysis of trade and tariffs in Chapter 15 is our starting point. Recall that, in Fig. 15.7, using supply and demand curves, we saw that imports occur when a country can purchase goods at a lower price than the market-clearing price that would obtain if it met domestic demand entirely from domestic output. Similarly (Chapter 15), exports occur if a country can obtain higher prices from purchasers in other countries than would obtain if its producers could sell only to domestic purchasers.

We also saw how the welfare gains and losses within a country from trade may be calculated. In the analysis in Chapter 15 this was done by examining who the winners and losers were when tariffs and quotas are used in order to restrict trade. Clearly, to see who wins and loses from freeing trade (reducing restrictions), all that is needed is to reverse the analysis used to explain the consequences of restricting trade.

However, while in Chapter 15 we saw in terms of PPCs how a country may gain from trade (by being able to exploit consumption possibilities that exceed its production possibilities, see Fig. 15.5), it is necessary at this stage to extend the supply and demand analysis somewhat to demonstrate gains and losses for both parties (indeed all parties) from free trade.

### The gains from trade

We do this by looking at how trade increases economic welfare, and barriers to trade reduce it, using a simplified model of the trading process. In Chapter 15, the analysis looked at the impact of trade on economic welfare, winners and losers, by considering what happens in the case of tariffs and trade related to just one good in one country. In this model, we examine trade between two countries that produce two goods. Even then, we deal explicitly with just one of the goods, on the basis that in the end in such circumstances trade must balance out. If people in one country import goods from other countries these goods have to be paid for, and this requires the importing country to export goods to the same value as its imports.

This means ignoring borrowing and lending between countries, and international flows of capital (foreign direct investment, FDI). In real life, these are very major influences on the impact of international trading relations on economic welfare, but the fundamental aspect that we shall look at is trade in goods and services and barriers to that trade. We shall also suppose that the countries have a common currency (such as the euro). A century ago this would have reflected the fact that all currencies were based on gold, so that gold was in effect a single currency. This enables us to avoid complications arising from changes in exchange rates.

In keeping with the analysis in Chapter 15 we shall assume that trade reflects *comparative advantage*. Countries, like individuals, will produce and sell, at home and abroad, those goods and services in which they have a competitive edge based on comparative advantage. However, how much will be traded will reflect supply and demand conditions in domestic and foreign markets, and the costs of trading, which include the costs of overcoming barriers to trade.

Start with a simple supply and demand curve in a country for some product, $Q$ (Fig. 16.1). If this country cannot trade with any other country for this product the quantity produced and the price to consumers is given by the intersection of the supply and demand curves. Output and price will be given by the intersection of supply and demand. Price will be $P_1$.

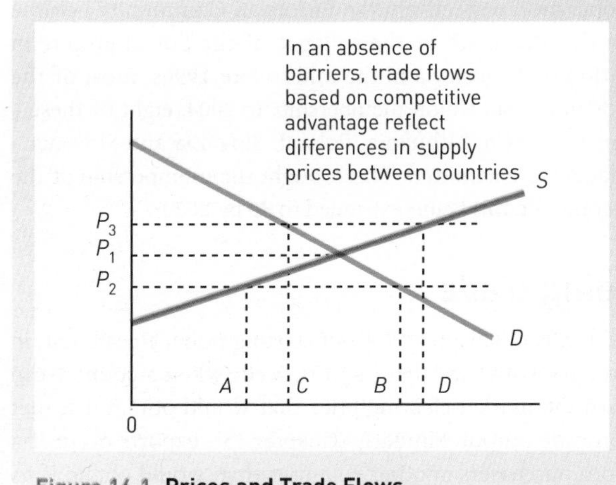


**Figure 16.1 Prices and Trade Flows.**

Suppose, however, the product is available from other countries at $P_2$. At that price, demand would be for the quantity $OB$, but at that price domestic producers would supply only $OA$. The difference, $AB$, would be supplied by producers in other countries. $AB$ is the level of imports at price $P_2$. Suppose, instead, that domestic producers could obtain $P_3$ for the product on world markets. They would produce $OD$ at that price. At that price, consumers in this country would consume only $OC$. The difference, $CD$, would be exported.

What this says is that, in the absence of barriers to trade, trade in commodities, reflecting competitive advantage, will reflect the difference between prices outside the country and what prices would be within the country if no trade were possible. If comparative advantage shifts, altering prices elsewhere relative to this benchmark price, trade will increase or decrease, and a commodity that at one time was imported can become an export and vice versa.

**Relative prices determine trade flows:** Whether goods are imported or exported depends on relative prices which can change.

We can take the analysis a step further by introducing a new concept: the trade curve (Fig. 16.2). This is derived from Fig. 16.1.

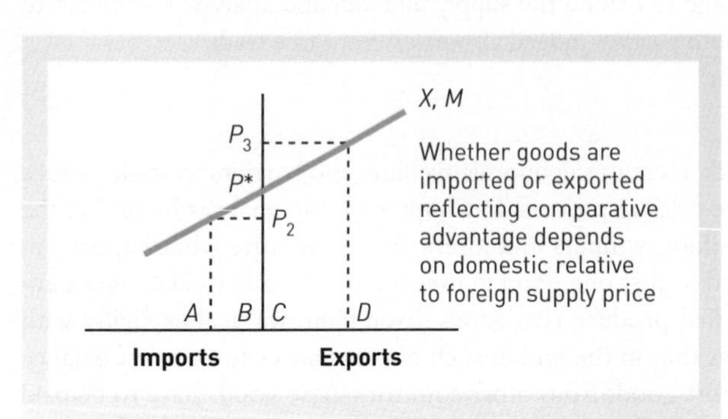


**Figure 16.2 Relative Prices and Trade.**

At $P^*$ in Fig. 16.2, there is no trade: *domestic production satisfies domestic demand*. As price is increased above $P^*$ the product is exported. The level of exports is the difference between domestic production at a price higher than $P^*$ in Fig. 16.1 and domestic consumption at that price. At prices below $P^*$ the good will be imported, the level of imports being the difference between domestic consumption at that price and domestic production in Fig. 16.1.

The line through the vertical axis at $P^*$ shows the level and direction of trade at prices relative to $P^*$. To the left of the vertical axis, we have imports of the good ($M$); to the right we have exports ($X$).

To proceed with the analysis, we now construct a model of trade in a world with two countries, $H$ (home) and $F$ (foreign). We also assume there are two goods, both of which would be produced in each country were there no trade, although prices would differ for the goods in the two countries in the absence of trade, with the prices reflecting comparative advantage. One country's export good is the other's import good.

Trade starts, and goods are exchanged between the countries. We look at the position for one of the goods, that in which $F$ has a comparative advantage. Call this good $MH$ or $XF$ (import into $H$ and export from $F$.) We construct a supply curve of exports of $MH$ from $F$ to $H$, and a demand curve in $H$ for imports from $F$ (Fig. 16.3).

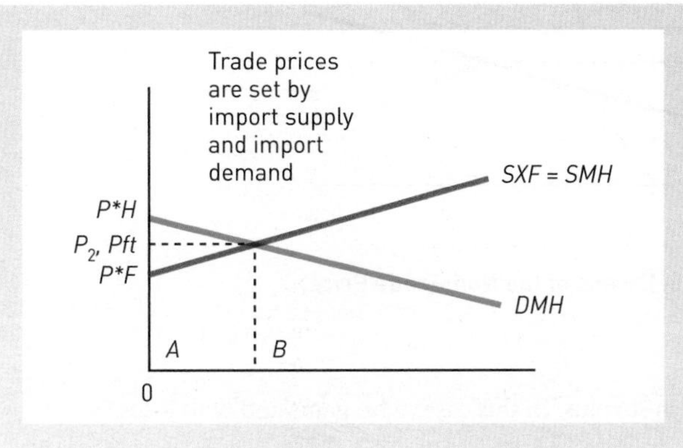


**Figure 16.3 Trade Prices.**

At a price of $P^*H$, import demand would be zero. At lower prices, import demand would increase from zero. In country $F$, at a price such as $P^*$ in Fig. 16.2 the product would be neither exported nor imported. This is shown as $P^*F$ in Fig. 16.3. An export from $F$ is an import into $H$. So we can now set down the import supply curve in $H$ (the supply of exports from $F$) as a function of prices in $H$. Similarly, we have the import demand curve in $H$ (the demand for exports from $F$).

In the background, of course, the trade volume and direction and the price of the other good are similarly determined, and trade has to be balanced by assumption. The price for this good in both countries is *simultaneously* determined by the demand curves in both countries and the supply curves in both countries, and these reflect *all the tariffs*, not just one of them.

**trade symmetry** freeing trade has symmetrical effects as between sectors and countries

This is important. It means that when we look at the impact of trade in one good in one country we must realise that there are symmetrical effects – **trade symmetry** – in the case of the other good and the other country. You can't simply derive the gains from trade by removing a tariff: you have to remove tariffs in general.

We are now able to restate the impact of trade on economic welfare, and the consequences for economic welfare for barriers to free trade.

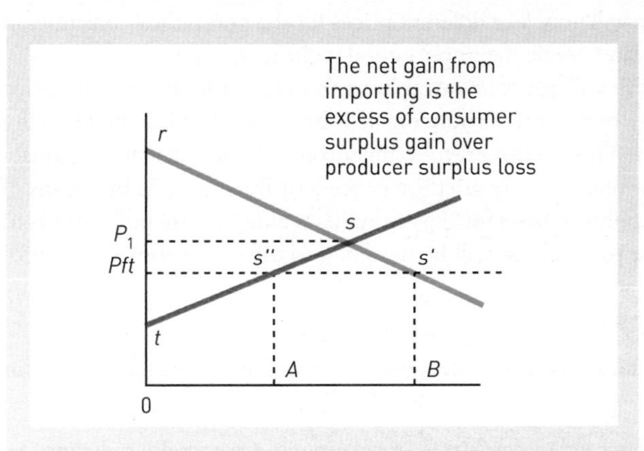


**Figure 16.4 The Net Welfare Gain from Trade.**

Again, we will take country $H$ as the case in point. From Fig. 16.3 we have the price of the good imported into $H$ in both countries (we assume no trading costs) if there is free trade. In Fig. 16.4 we show what happens in $H$ when trade results in the level of imports indicated by the equilibrium price in Fig. 16.3, *Pft*.

Before (or in the absence of) trade, total economic surplus is given by the triangle *rst*. This is the sum of consumer surplus ($rsP_1$) and producer surplus ($tsP_1$). When trade is opened and the free trade price of good $M$ is *Pft*, consumer surplus increases to *rs'Pft*. Producer surplus falls to *ts'Pft*. Subtract that from the gain in consumer surplus ($P_1ss'Pft$) and there remains the triangle *ss's"*. It is the *net gain in economic welfare* arising from being able to consume the good more cheaply because of trade. That is, the excess of the gains to gainers over losses to losers from freeing trade. The resources displaced by imports are absorbed (because trade is balanced) in *H*'s export sector, producing good *X*. This expands as a result of trade: after all, exports from *H* are imports into *F*, and just as the *M* sector contracts in *H* (and the *M* sector expands in *F*) the *X* sector has to contract in *F*. The two countries are moving along their PPCs, although in the opposite directions.

To take the impact on the expanding as well as the contracting sectors in either country into account is easy. Again, as in Fig. 16.5, we introduce a free-trade price in excess of the no-trade price, so that the good is exported, and the output of the good rises.

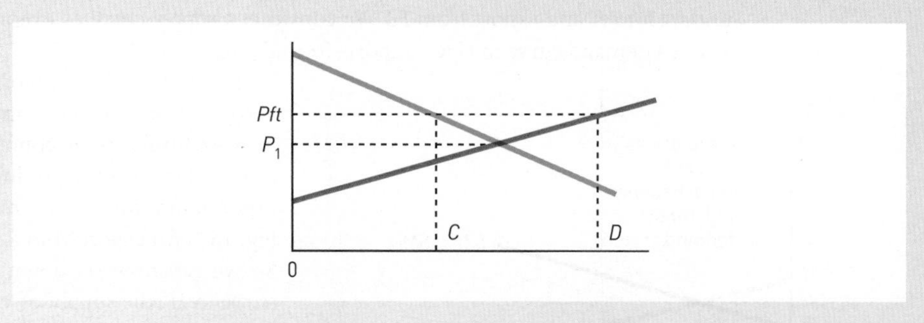


**Figure 16.5 A Free-Trade Price in Excess of the Non-Trade Price.**

**Exercise 16.1** In Fig. 16.5, identify the net gain in surplus. In this case, who gains and who loses?

In freeing trade, then, we enable producers as a whole and consumers in both countries to gain. The gain takes the form of *enhanced economic surplus.* This arises in the first place from replacing expensive domestic production with lower cost sources of supply in other countries. At the same time it enables countries to increase the value they receive for what they produce by selling it at a higher price abroad than they would obtain if they were restricted to selling those goods in their home market. But notice that while surplus is increased for both countries, because their combined resources are being used more efficiently to produce both goods, prices for both goods are equalised across both countries. That has implications for economic welfare in both countries. Both are better off in the aggregate, but freeing trade means expanding production of each country's export sector and contracting its import sector. This causes a shift in relative incomes as between the owners of resources tied to each sector. In each country, consumers gain overall, although they will now face different prices for the goods they consume. In each country the export good is dearer, while the import good is cheaper.

We can predict that consumers will react favourably to freeing trade despite the price changes because they are clearly better off. Producers will be divided, with those facing falling prices bearing all the pain. This asymmetry – concentrated losses, dispersed gains – gives the losers strong motives for seeking to restrict the process of freeing trade by means of political action. It also provides a political basis for governments seeking to use policy tools to aid the sectors that are feeling the pain. These will be designed to offset the consequences of freeing trade, either by finding some means of protecting the sectors concerned, or by enabling them to sell more via subsidies.

> **Gainers and losers:** The losers have strong motivation to mobilise political support for restrictions on trade.

However, to the extent that they succeed in doing this, governments are actually reducing the gains from trade overall. Their enthusiasm for freeing trade in the short term reflects the prospects for their export sectors rather than for their import sectors. However, for their export sectors to expand it is necessary that the import sectors in the other countries contract. Short-term considerations, however, give them strong motives to cheat: they will seek access for their exports to other markets on the basis of tariff reductions, but then seek to hinder access to their domestic markets by other countries' exporters.

This leads to a prisoner's dilemma problem. The outcome is likely to be restricted trade rather than free trade even though it is in everyone's long-term interests to have free trade. To resolve this requires that freeing trade be made the subject of binding rules. Organisations such as the WTO provide such arrangements on a worldwide basis. A free-trade area (FTA) or customs union agreement provides such rules on a regional basis. In the absence of such a framework the benefits of freeing trade are not likely to be achieved, and the impetus will be to restrict trade.

> **Prisoner's dilemma:** Obtaining the benefits from freeing trade requires entering into binding agreements.

It is this insight that provides the economic rationale (as opposed to political) for the creation of the EEC in 1958.

## The consequences of trade restrictions

Economists and policy makers recognise three types of intervention, all originating in policy decisions by governments, that are used to restrict trade. These are tariffs, QRs (quotas) and regulatory restrictions. Tariffs and quotas were dealt with in Chapter 15.

Regulatory restrictions arise from the impact of intervention by governments to affect *product characteristics* or *conditions of sale*. Governments can impose legal restrictions on the features of goods to be sold, or on the manner in which goods must be produced if they are to be legally offered for sale. When foreign suppliers pose a threat to domestic producers a government may impose restrictions that place foreign suppliers at a disadvantage. A well-known example was the German law affecting beer sales, now rescinded. For many years the *Reinheitsgebot*, or purity law, laid down strict restrictions on what could legally be sold as beer in Germany. Allegedly to protect consumers, its real purpose was to prevent foreign beers, which used different inputs from German beers, from being sold as 'beer' in Germany.

### Economic naturalist 16.1 Why for many years were Britain's most popular chocolate bars sold in wrappers that did not mention the word 'chocolate'?

The European Union introduced product standards for chocolate confectionery under pressure from producers on the mainland of Europe. These laid down the minimum requirement for cocoa content before confectionery could be sold as 'chocolate'. Chocolate produced in Britain and Ireland, reflecting tastes in those countries, contained less cocoa than was usual in France, the Low Countries and Germany. By adopting a product standard that approximated to continental norms the union outlawed using the description 'chocolate' to describe most UK and Irish products. The most famous casualty was Cadbury's Milk Chocolate, which for many years until 2003 could not be sold, even in Britain, as chocolate, and had to be branded and packaged accordingly.

Regulatory restrictions are pervasive, complex and difficult to quantify in terms of their effects. Their reduction and elimination is hard to achieve because, frequently, they have the appearance at least (and this may be genuine) of being grounded in public concern for product standards, or safety, or similar considerations.

In general, it can be shown that any quota has a tariff equivalent in many circumstances, As a result it is generally not very useful to analyse them separately, although this will be qualified later on. As a result, in this context we confine ourselves to considering how tariffs affect trade, since for most purposes the same conclusions can be drawn concerning quotas and regulatory restrictions.

## The economic implications of imposing and removing tariffs

At its simplest, this means just reversing the analysis used to show the effects of allowing trade in the first place. However, in order to be able to use the analysis later on in the context of European integration it will be helpful to treat the imposition of a tariff starting from a free-trade position.

We start with a very basic approach. In this model, we look at a country and economy that is small relative to the rest of the world. By this we mean that it can import as much as it wants of any good without this having any effect on the prices at which goods are sold to it. Bermuda or an island state in what used to be the British or French West Indies would be such an economy. Like the competitive firm, such a country is a *price taker*.

In Fig. 16.6 we illustrate the imposition of a tariff on an imported good by the government of Bermuda. This is similar to Fig. 16.5, but without any consideration of the supply-side consequences of a tariff.

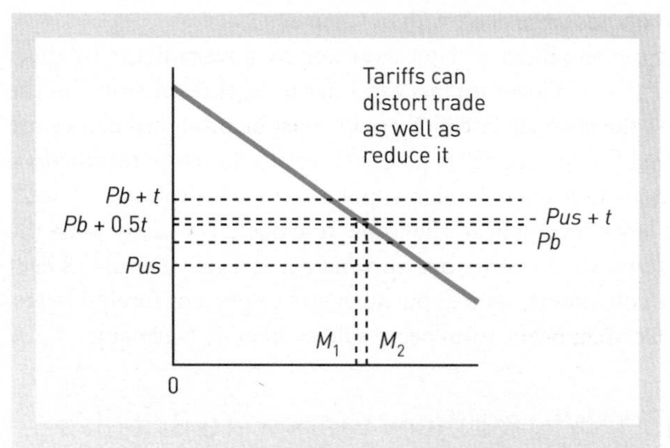


**Figure 16.6 Trade Distortion Effects of a Tariff.**

When the tariff is imposed the price to the islanders is increased by the amount of the tariff. We suppose that the tariff is in the form of an excise charge of $t$ cents per unit. The tariff raises the supply curve to the islanders from $P$ to $P + t$. Consumption of the good will fall and, if it is produced on the island, domestic production will rise. The implications for surplus are easy to establish – just check Figs 16.4 and 16.5. Remove the tariff again, and we can easily trace the economic welfare consequences.

Now let us introduce a little complication. We shall start (Fig. 16.6) with a tariff in place, and suppose that the good can be imported from Britain at a landed price *Pb*, or from the United States at a landed price *Pus*. The same tariff applies to imports from either country. Since US suppliers can supply at less than British suppliers, and the goods are perfect substitutes, all the imports will come from the United States, because $Pus + t < Pb + t$.

To cement good relations with Britain, the government of Bermuda decides to halve the tariff on British goods. British goods will now be available in Bermuda for $Pb + 0.5t$. Since $Pb + 0.5t$ in this example is less than $Pus + t$, Bermudans switch to buying from Britain, and the volume of imports rises. Look at Fig. 16.6. Are Bermudans better off?

Obviously, consumer surplus has risen. But look at what the cost to the Bermudan economy has become. The cost to the economy is the amount paid to the foreign supplier, because Bermuda has to produce exports to cover this. Notice that even if the quantity of imports hadn't changed, the cost would have risen, because it costs more per unit to buy from Britain excluding the tariff (which goes from Bermuda's consumers to the government who, we may assume, spends it on goodies to deliver to Bermudans). Of course this is a lower-bound estimate of the cost, since Bermuda actually imports more of the good, and at a higher price net of the tariff. Beforehand imports were $OM_1$; now they are $OM_2$. Bermuda has unambiguously lost an amount equal to $OM_1$ multiplied by the difference between *Pus* and *Pb*. It is also paying more than it has to for the extra imports, $M_1M_2$. Most of the gain in consumer surplus has come from lost revenue to the government, meaning fewer goodies being distributed to Bermudan households (unless taxes are raised elsewhere). This is **trade diversion**.

**trade diversion** replacing lower-cost imports by higher-cost imports

Suddenly, reducing the tariff doesn't look so smart after all. Where does that leave the conclusions drawn earlier in this chapter, and those derived in Chapter 15?

The difference between the earlier analysis of what happens when a tariff is reduced or eliminated and this scenario is that, in the former case, lowering tariffs meant *replacing expensive domestic production with lower-cost imports*. Here we are *replacing lower-cost imports with higher-cost imports*. The importance of this in the EU context will become apparent later.

Before going any further, two things should be noted. First, trade by definition involves expansion in a country's export-producing sector(s), and a contraction in its import competing sector(s). That means some income *redistribution* within a country. The second is the consequence for prices in countries *H* and *F* of introducing a tariff in *H* on imports from *F*. These are in effect being taxed, and part of the tax is borne by the suppliers in *F* who see demand for what they export fall. That means that by using the tariff *H* reduces its imports (bad for both) but gets what it does import at a lower price (good for *H*). It is possible that the price reduction more than compensates for the reduced trade volume as far as *H* is concerned.

## Economic naturalist 16.2 Why did the Union persist for years in using quotas to ensure that sugar was obtained expensively – mostly in France, Britain and Ireland, but also in many other temperate-climate EU states – from sugar beet, rather than import cane sugar at much lower cost from the West Indies?

Production of sugar from beet grown, harvested and milled in northern Europe is a much less efficient and much more resource-intensive business that letting the sub-tropical sun do the job by producing sugar cane. Traditionally, Britain imported sugar from her extensive possessions in the West Indies. France, on the other hand, having lost most of her possessions in the West Indies, relied on domestic production from beet. Concern for self-sufficiency in foodstuffs was a major factor in European policy on agriculture from the foundation of the EEC. Consequently, strict quotas were applied to imports of, among other things, sugar. Britain had to buy into this state of affairs, with some modifications, on joining the EEC in 1973. As we have noted, quotas and tariffs have comparable effects. These restrictions increased demand for European sugar (and farmers' incomes). They also drove down the price paid by Europeans for such sugar as was imported from cane sugar producers.

## Import taxes, export taxes and subsidies

Return for a moment to Chapter 15. Figure 15.5 (p. 437) shows a PPC for a two-good economy. It demonstrates how trade permits an economy to consume 'bundles' of goods that it cannot produce, thus increasing the country's economic welfare. Offered a set of prices, it produced the output indicated by point *C*. In Fig. 16.7 we have a similar graph, but we look at an economy producing two goods, *X* and *M*.

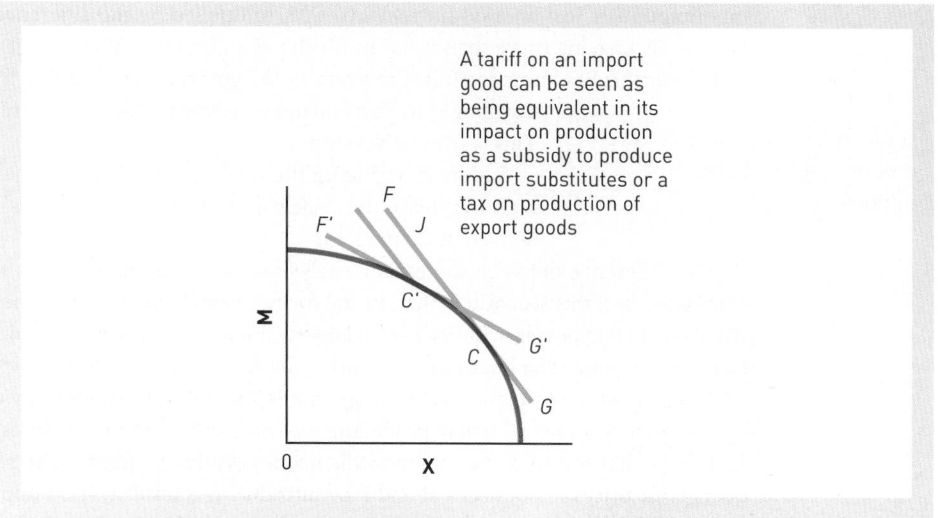


**Figure 16.7 Tariff and Subsidy Equivalence.**

The country faces world prices indicated by the line *FG* in Fig. 16.7. It has a comparative advantage in producing *X*, produces 'bundle' *C* and consumes a bundle *J*. Suppose that it imposes a tariff on *M*. In the country's markets the prices obtainable by domestic producers for *M* rise. Those received for *X* are unchanged As far as producers are concerned, the *FG* line has become *F'G'*, and *M* production increases ... while *X* production falls. The 'bundle' it consumes when it trades at world prices will be smaller than *J*. The protection afforded by the tariff on imports causes the other sector to contract. The tariff has the same effect as a subsidy to *M* production or a tax on production of *X*.

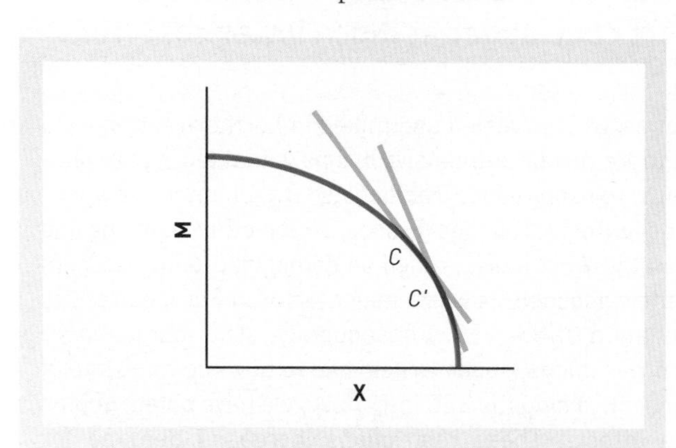


**Figure 16.8 Trade Effects of Taxes.**

Suppose that the government, instead of imposing a tariff on imports of *M*, imposed a tax on *M* whether produced at home or imported. The result is shown in Fig. 16.8. Starting from the initial equilibrium point, *C*, production of *M* will fall, and production of *X* will rise. So a tax on *all* sales of *M* has the same effect as a subsidy to production of *X*. More importantly, a subsidy to production of X is equivalent to a tariff on imports of *M* and a domestic tax on domestic production of *M*.

The importance of all this points will, we hope, become clear when we start to examine the economics of the integration process.

## RECAP The impact of trade and trade restrictions on economic welfare

By permitting trade (or an increase in trade) through reducing or eliminating trade restrictions it is possible to increase economic surplus in the countries concerned. In the aggregate, *both countries* are *better off*. Trade restrictions, on this logic, reduce economic welfare in both countries. Despite this, we observe trade restrictions across the world. This suggests that there is 'cash on the table' that is not being exploited. However, when we look at decisions on trade relations in a political – and, perhaps, adversarial – fashion, the income redistribution and import price consequences of trade restrictions provide some basis for rationalising the reluctance to the liberalise trade. Finally, regulation, domestic taxes and spending decisions can be used to restrict trade when tariffs or quotas may not be available.

## International integration: free-trade areas, customs unions, common markets, monetary unions and economic unions

First, some definitions. The different degrees of commitment to economic integration are now described. There is a widely held view that what is involved is a form of natural progression, at least up to a point. The idea is that if you set up a free-trade area (FTA), pressures that are inevitable will lead to step-by-step progress up (or down, depending on your viewpoint) the road to full integration.

**free-trade area** group of countries that has agreed to permit goods produced in one of them to be imported into any other member country free of tariff or quota restrictions

**customs union** 'the members, in addition to permitting free trade between them, agree to a single and common set of trade restrictions (or 'commercial policy') with respect to non-members

**common market** the member states agree to free up trade in services and to permit liberalised (in the limiting case, free) movement of labour and capital

- **Free-trade area (FTA)** This describes a group of countries that has agreed to permit goods produced in one of their number to be imported into *any other member country* free of any tariff or quota restrictions. The EFTA, set up in response to the establishment of the EEC, was an example.
- **Customs union** This goes a significant step further than an FTA. The members, in addition to permitting free trade between them, agree to a *single and common set of trade restrictions* (or 'commercial policy') with respect to non-members. Goods from non-members are imported under the same conditions into all member states. From its origins, the EEC aimed at being a customs union (and, indeed, going further).
- **Common market** A further stage in economic integration: the member states agree to free up *trade in services* and to permit liberalised (in the limiting case, free) *movement of labour and capital*. In addition, a common market implies removing the regulatory devices that impede trade in goods and services. For example, it restricts the ability of member states to operate separate health and safety regulations, or consumer protection regulations, in so far as those regulations discriminate between goods or services in different member states. Firms in one member state are permitted to establish operations in any member state. Establishment regulation is harmonised across member states. Restrictions are imposed on the freedom of member state governments to introduce or maintain aids to industry and similar subsidies.

**monetary union** the member states have a single currency

- **Monetary union** Building on a common market, a monetary union means introducing a *single currency* in the member states. This may be formal and complete, as with the euro, or informal and incomplete, where the member states' currencies have a rigidly fixed exchange rate. This was the position between 1999 and 2001 in the case of the countries now in the eurozone.

**economic union** there is centralised effective decision making on economic policies affecting the countries of the union

- **Economic union** A full economic union means that there is *centralised effective decision making* on economic policies affecting the countries of the union as a whole. It implies regulatory harmonization, the implementation of a single budgetary policy for most purposes, with union-wide tax and spending programmes. It is inseparable from a substantial degree of unified *political decision making*.

## Why are FTAs formed?

This may seem a trivial question, given that freeing trade is beneficial to all countries. But remember the prisoner's dilemma. What is best for both parties may not be what happens when each acts independently. Bargaining may be necessary to reach a superior outcome.

Suppose there are two countries, *A* and *B*, each protecting its import sector (the other's export sector). *A* unilaterally drops its tariffs. This increases the demand for *B*'s exports. *B*, however, increases its tariffs, reducing demand for *A's* exports. Overall, the demand for the goods produced in *B* rises, while the demand for the goods produced in *A* falls. The citizens of *B*, whose income reflects the demand for what they produce, gain at the expense of the citizens of *A*.

Knowing this, neither will be prepared to lower tariffs unilaterally, while if both get rid of their tariffs both gain. So they enter into an agreement to move jointly to lower tariffs. They establish an FTA (or, at least, a less restricted trade area).

## Why proceed to establish a customs union?

Introduce a third country, *C*. Both *A* and *B* trade freely, but *B* protects one of its industries from competition from producers in *C* by a tariff. *A* has no such tariff. Producers in *C* set up a finishing plant in *A*, import free of tariff the semi-finished good from their base plants in *C*, package it and send to consumers in *B* as imports (free of tariffs) from *A*. By doing this they avoid *B*'s tariffs 'by coming in through the backdoor'. This leads to enormous problems of defining where goods are produced ... or an agreement between *A* and *B* to have a single and mutually applied set of tariffs on *C*'s goods. The establishment of a *single external tariff* (SET) marks the creation of a customs union, and in the case of the EEC this was envisaged from the beginning.

## Why might a common market be established once a customs union is in place?

Deprived of the power to use tariffs and quotas, governments are still under pressure to shelter sectors, groups or single firms from competition from other member states. The potential for using regulatory intervention has already been discussed above, and also in Chapter 14. We have also seen that it is possible to achieve the same effects as those flowing from tariffs and quotas by judicious use of domestic taxes and government spending programmes. Hence, to ensure that governments do not take advantage of this possibility to distort trade for short- or long-term gains for their own populations it is necessary to extend the agreement structure to cover the policy areas concerned ... or create a 'common market'. This includes such matters as establishment rights and undistorted movements of capital and labour.

### Economic naturalist 16.3 Why is blackcurrant cordial a key element in the history of the integration of the economies of the European Union?

Cassis is an alcoholic cordial produced in France from blackcurrants. It is frequently used as a mixer with white wine to make *kir* (and with champagne to make *kir royale*). It has an alcohol content of 15–20 per cent. Cassis made in Dijon is said to be the *Crème de Cassis*. A German company sought in the late 1960s to import it for sale in Germany. Unfortunately, German law required that fruit liqueurs should have a minimum alcohol content of 25 per cent (normal for German products of this type). It could not, therefore, be sold as a fruit liqueur. It was not a wine or fortified wine, products that could be sold with the strength of Cassis, and so could not be sold as a wine. It was not distilled, so it could not be sold as a spirit. And it was far too strong to be sold as a beer. Existing regulations prohibited its sale in Germany because it did not meet German product classification standards. The importer took a case to the European Court of Justice (ECJ). In a landmark decision, the ECJ in 1979 declared that if a product *met product standards in the country of origin* it could be sold anywhere in the EEC unless a member state could demonstrate to a court that the product standard concerned posed a threat to the public interest in the country of importation, something that would rarely be possible. The *Cassis de Dijon* case was a critical element in eliminating the power of member states to use regulation to restrict trade.

## Why move from a common market to a monetary union?

Here we shall present a highly partial case. As will be seen in Part 6, this presentation is open to serious challenge. Monetary unions can exist without common markets, and common markets can exist without monetary unions.

A monetary union existed between Britain and Ireland between 1826 and 1979. This covered a period in which there were free-trade and free-factor flows between the islands (1826–1922), limited trade restrictions but free-factor flows (1922–32), severe trade and capital movement restrictions but free labour flows (1932–57), free-factor flows but restricted trade (1957–66), and free-trade and free-factor flows again (1966–79). It also covered periods in which there was a single effective government (1826–1922) and two sovereign governments (1922–79) in the islands, each with its own set of regulatory powers.

On the other hand, there is the example of the three former territories of British East Africa (Kenya, Uganda and Tanganyika). Under British rule there was a monetary union covering the three, the currency being the East African shilling. When they became independent in the early 1960s and each started to operate its own fiscal, commercial and regulatory policy regimes (and pursue separate goals in terms of political arrangements), the currency union collapsed rapidly.

Today, the United Kingdom, Denmark and Sweden are full members of the European Union, but not members of its monetary union. There is a full common market in virtually all respects in existence between the United Kingdom (which includes part of the island of Ireland) and the Irish Republic, which is in the eurozone.

These case studies show that it is not demonstrated by history that monetary union and common market arrangements can be seen to be inseparable. However, a strong case can be made for the economic desirability of a monetary union being implemented where a common market exits. That case rests on two premises. The first is that the full benefits of integration cannot be enjoyed without proceeding to a monetary union. The second is that the absence of monetary unification can pose a threat to the success of a common market.

The first of these will be examined in detail in Chapter 3. For the moment, it suffices to say that it argues that monetary union promotes trade and eases factor flows by removing an *implicit tax* on movement of goods and services between monetary regimes and across foreign exchange frontiers relative to movement of goods and services within a monetary regime. Currency conversion is costly, and this is a 'tax' on trade. Further, if it is possible for exchange rates to change, holding a foreign currency (or assets and liabilities denominated in a foreign currency) is inherently risky. To reduce or eliminate this risk, which is unavoidable when trading or investing across a foreign exchange frontier, is costly.

The second argument is closer to the subject matter of this chapter. We have seen how regulation can be used to distort competition and create barriers to imports. We know that governments can use subsidies to do the same thing by reducing costs to export industries. This means that the *misuse of policy instruments* can be undertaken by governments to undermine common market arrangements for domestic political reasons.

If a country has its own currency, the rate at which it can be exchanged for other currencies reflects the *supply* and *demand* for that currency on foreign exchange markets. A major potential source of supply of, and demand for, a countrys' currency is its own central bank, which can be controlled by the government. This means that a government has the power to manage the exchange rate within limits. This can be entirely desirable ... but it can be abused. By selling (supplying) its own currency and buying foreign exchange, the central bank can drive down the exchange rate, making imports more expensive to its own citizens and making its exports more competitive in other countries' markets, at least for a time. This is equivalent in effect to imposing tariffs on imports and subsidising exports, interventions that are prohibited in a common market. It is argued that to eliminate any such possibility of trade distortion through manipulating exchange rates within a common market a single currency is necessary.

### Why move to a full economic union?

The principal arguments here are for the most part macroeconomic, and will be dealt with in Chapter 30, where the budgetary implications of monetary unification are considered. However, there are microeconomic reasons that can be advanced as well. These are mainly related to the impact of taxation on investment and location decisions. It is a matter of dispute as to whether it is a good or bad thing, but unquestionably tax regimes affect firms' investment location decisions. This means that countries can compete for a tax base by choosing their tax rates. This opens the possibility that the allocation function of resource markets (labour and capital markets) can be distorted by manipulation of tax regimes. To deal with this it is argued that a monetary union needs to proceed to create a collective policy on such matters, leading to tax and social welfare financing harmonization.

### RECAP The process of integration

There are several distinct stages in the process of *economic integration*, starting with a simple FTA and ending with a full economic union, something that really implies a *political union*. It can be argued that establishing an agreement at any stage leads to decisions to move to the next stage. This is certainly plausible, but does not seem fully convincing when moving to a monetary union is under consideration.

## Trade regimes and trade flows: trade creation and trade diversion in the European Union

In Fig. 16.6 (p. 462) we saw that when trade is liberalised between countries on a partial basis the consequences can be less than optimal. In so far as free trade replaces more costly domestic production or imports with less costly goods, trade is welfare enhancing. This is referred to as the **trade creation** effect of reducing restrictions on trade. Reducing restrictions on trade between a subset of trading countries can have the effect already illustrated: replacing less expensive imports by more expensive imports. This happens because trade is driven by prices to end users. This does not necessarily reflect the costs to society as a whole. When this occurs the reduction in trade barriers is said to give rise to *trade diversion*.

**trade creation** replacing more costly domestic production by less costly imported goods

Trade diversion can occur as result of forming a trading bloc when internal trading conditions (in the case of the Union, free trade) are more favourable to trade than trade with non-member countries. The former EEC from the beginning operated a common trade policy with respect to non-members. This is what made it a *customs union*. The most visible element of this was a single set of tariffs on imports from outside the bloc. This external tariff structure, the common commercial tariff (CCT), was, however, only part of the story. In addition to tariffs, the EEC operated quota restrictions and preferential allocations of imports to favoured countries. These were most evident in relation to foodstuffs.

Within limits, the relative importance of these two effects can be gauged by looking at how trade patterns develop after the establishment of a customs union. If trade growth between members (*intra-union trade*) is greater than trade between the union and third countries (*extra-union trade*) this points to possible trade diversion effects, although it does not prove their existence. In the early years of the EEC up to the first expansion in 1973 intra-Union trade grew substantially more rapidly than extra-Union trade. This was exacerbated by UK adherence to the customs union in the years after 1973 as Britain switched its food imports away from its traditional overseas sources to domestic and other EEC sources, which was a major instance of trade diversion. Since the mid-1980s the overall pattern of EU trade suggests that EU expansion has not resulted in significant trade diversion, while trade creation has been substantial. In particular, the Single Market Programme (SMP) of the 1990s (see below) has been associated with considerable trade creation.[3]

## What is at stake: the economic gains from free trade

In the 1970s and into the 1980s empirical estimates of the potential for increased trade to lead to higher real incomes were mostly attempts to measure the *deadweight loss* arising from trade restrictions. They ignored the impact of increased competition on the efficiency with which resources were used. They also ignored the potential for economic gains arising from scale and scope economies as larger potential markets led to structural changes involving mergers and acquisitions.

The results were somewhat disappointing. First principles suggested that trade restrictions should have a significant impact on resource allocation and their removal should, therefore, produce significant gains in income per head. Casual observation of what had happened in Germany in the nineteenth century when internal trade barriers between the German states were dismantled under the *Zollverein* (the customs union for the German states established by Prussia), and of the rapid growth in income per head in the United States after the Civil War, supported the view that the potential gains from extending free trade were large.

A well-known study by Bela Balassa in 1975[4] estimated that the net impact of trade liberalisation within the original EEC had been to increase GNP per head by a mere 0.5 per cent – something that would hardly have warranted the efforts of the founding fathers of European unification. This small value is not really surprising when you consider that it reflects *marginal changes* in spending and production patterns as a result of price changes affecting a narrow range of goods (those affected by trade restrictions) while assuming that competitive pressures and scale factors are not operative.

Part of the reason for pushing ahead with increased economic integration, moving from a customs union to a common market, was a conviction that the gains from integration were in fact much greater than this purely static analysis of deadweight losses suggested. The result was the ambitious SMP.

---

[3] An easily understood and statistically rich discussion of the development of EU trade patterns can be found in Jørgensen, Lüthje and Schröder (2001).

[4] Balassa (1975).

# The Single Market Programme

## The Single European Act and the Single Market

In 1986 the member states of the then EC signed up to the implementation through national legislatures of what was described as the 'Single European Act' (SEA). This provided for the implementation of a genuine common market by creating the 'Single European Market' (SEM). It went further than providing for free trade in goods and services by establishing an *economic space without any internal frontiers*, a space that would permit fully free movement of persons and capital as well as full freedom to sell goods and services. The core idea was to allow competitive markets rather than political decisions to play a dominant role in resource allocation across the Community.

This required 'level playing fields' to be established across many aspects of economic life. As a result, it led to the liberalising of competition in sectors of national economies that up to then had been sheltered from competitive pressure, especially in the state-dominated network industries sector (transport, communications, energy). The ability of governments to grant aid to favoured sectors or firms was severely curtailed. This, in turn, resulted in increased private sector rather than state ownership of key areas of the member states' economies.

## The static gains from integrating factor markets

The static gains arising from integrating factor markets are those that result from allocating a scarce resource to higher-value uses. The impact of free movement of capital or labour on incomes per head in a common market is easy to demonstrate analytically.

In Fig. 16.9 we examine the consequences of permitting capital to flow between two regions where initially the returns to capital differ as between regions. On the horizontal axis is the sum total of capital available in the two regions. On the left-hand axis we measure the VMP of capital in region 2, and on the right-hand axis the VMP of capital in region 1. The VMP of capital in either region is found by dividing the total between the regions (as, for example, at *B*) and reading off the VMP by reference to each region's VMP curve.

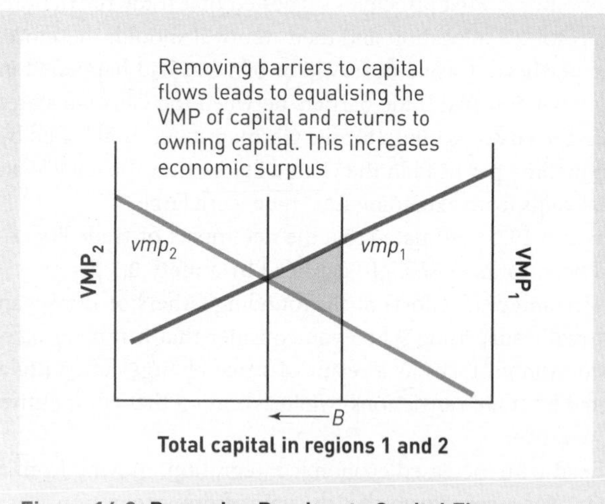


**Figure 16.9 Removing Barriers to Capital Flows.**

In this case at *B* the VMP in region 1 is higher than in region 2. This means that there is 'cash on the table' (Chapter 3). By moving capital from region 2 to region 1, VMP in region 2 will rise and VMP in region 1 will fall, until at *C* the return to capital (its VMP) is the same in both regions. The net gain is the shaded triangle: the increased output from employing more capital in region 1 less the reduced output from employing less capital in region 2. The triangle may be regarded as the *deadweight loss* of whatever restriction originally prevented resources from flowing freely between the regions.

That region 1 has gained is obvious: output there has increased. Has region 2 lost because capital has migrated to region 1? Actually, no. This is not a zero-sum game, it is *positive sum game*. Both regions win. How? Because although capital has flowed from region 2 to region 1 to earn a higher return, that return accrues to the owners of that capital in region 2. The capital may be employed in region 1, but it is owned in region 2, and the higher income accrues to its owners in region 2.

This provides us with the first reason for regarding the Balassa-type analysis of the returns to integration as an underestimate. We can think of factor flows as a partial substitute for trade in the goods produced by those factors. Country *A* might export goods to country *B* … or set up a factory in *B* to supply the *B* market. If there are restrictions on trade in goods, or high transport costs, allowing factors to move is an alternative. If we measure only the change in goods flows, we miss the gains from factor flows.

## Economic naturalist 16.4 Why are some Nissan cars made in Britain and some BMWs made in the United States?

Everyone knows that Nissan is a Japanese car producer (actually, Renault of France is a major shareholder), and BMW is a German car producer. Indeed, their market success reflects consumer attitudes to buying Japanese and German cars. Partly to 'jump' trade barriers, and partly to avoid transport costs, in each case instead of building the cars in Japan and Germany, the company has elected to set up production in the export market for at least a proportion of what it sells. This is an example of foreign direct investment (FDI) acting as a substitute for exports of goods. By definition, the investment means more value added and less costly supplies to consumers in the host country and a higher return on the capital of the firm undertaking the investment than if it had produced at home and exported – this is a win–win situation.

## The dynamic gains: the car industry as an example

In the 1960s German consumers bought mostly cars built in Germany, Italians bought cars built in Italy, Britons drove cars built in Britain and so on. In 1960, and ignoring minor luxury marques, there were approximately twenty car manufacturers in Western Europe. But trade restrictions and other factors meant that, for practical purposes, Italian and French purchasers could choose between three producers' offerings, Germans between seven, Britons between six; in each case those of domestic producers. Imports in each country accounted for a tiny proportion of sales. Check out any film made in the 1950s or early 1960s to confirm this.

Today there is one major producer in Italy, two in France and there are two US majors (Ford and GM) producing cars across Europe. There are two Japanese producers in Britain. There are three German producers, one of which has subsidiaries in Spain and the Czech Republic. And, of course, imports from outside Europe account for a large and growing proportion of sales. Leaving aside badge engineering (i.e. producing variants of what is essentially the same car, but superficially differentiated by minor details) and product differentiation, what has happened to competition?

The answer is that although there are fewer competing producers, most European customers can choose between more producers' offerings than in the early days of the EEC. A smaller number of much larger European producers are selling in much more competitive markets. That number is likely to fall in the face of increased penetration of EU markets by firms based outside the Union.

Economic integration is a major part of the explanation of the *consolidation of EU car production*. Scale economies can be exploited in the enlarged market by reducing the number of producers and increasing the size of production runs. Scope economies (spin-offs from producing several variants) can be exploited by concentrating marques as between producers (e.g. VW, producing the VW, Audi, Seat and Skoda variants). The impact of economic integration on the size of the market has led to massive *restructuring of production* in terms of plant size, location and marketing in order to hold down costs while offering higher-quality products.

At the same time, and separately from these supply-side effects, the increase in the number of effective competitors has increased the degree to which firms compete aggressively rather than rely on everyone accepting that a quiet life is better than active competition. When a small number of firms (two or three) share aggressive market competition on price, innovation or product quality is less likely (or tacit collusion is more likely) than when several firms (six or seven or more) do so.

## The impact of integration on the underlying trend in economic growth

When the SMP was launched, most commentators expected that in addition to the static and dynamic effects on total factor productivity (TFP), integration would raise the rate of growth of the EU economies as a whole. Growth means an increase in output per head of the employed population.

You can increase output per head by increasing the amount of capital per head. Hence, if integration led to increased investment it should have led to higher output per head, or measured economic growth. By encouraging more efficient resource allocation it might be expected that integration would increase the prospective return to investment – and, hence, stimulate growth.

Unfortunately, increasing physical capital per head runs into *diminishing returns*, so the growth effect of integration through encouraging investment will be temporary, if welcome. However, consider investment in knowledge and skills. There is no reason to believe that this form of capital must be subject to the same long-term diminishing returns. If that is the case, then in so far as the integrated market improves the return to investment in knowledge (R&D, human capital) we might expect some growth-rate dividend on a long-term basis.[5]

## Summary

- The present European Union is a *monetary union* and *common market*, although not yet a full economic union. It has evolved from the original EEC set-up with six members as a customs union with the object of promoting economic integration in Europe. It has grown through successive waves of expansion from six to 25 member states, in the process absorbing most of the members of EFTA as well as other West and East European countries.
- The case for economic integration is based in the first place on the *gains from freeing trade* between countries. The fundamentals of the analysis of the gains from trade were developed in Chapter 15. In this chapter, we note that when trade is freed between two countries, while overall both parties are expected to gain, the liberalised trade regime affects the *terms of trade* between the countries (the relative prices of imports and exports) and also has effects on relative incomes within the countries. Finally, *customs unions* treat member states differently from non-member states in terms of trade liberalisation, and this can distort trade patterns as well as increase trade.

[5] If you want to pursue this line of thought further, try looking at Chapter 7 in Baldwin and Wyplosz (2004).

- Forms of economic integration start with simple FTAs and exist on a spectrum of arrangements from FTA to full economic union. In some respects it is possible to argue that there is a sort of *natural progression* from FTA to full union, although this is far from being a fully deterministic process.
- Most observers agree that the European Union has had much less of a distortionary effect on trading patterns than a trade expansionary effect. The distortions, however, are significant, and are particularly important in terms of effects on poorer countries outside the Union. The actual static gains from trade are not all that large, and are swamped by the other *efficiency and competitiveness effects* of creating a large single market (SEM).
- The dynamic gains from full integration of the EU markets are the basis for the Single Market Programme (SMP) that is currently coming to fruition.

## Key terms

**common market** (465)
**customs union** (465)
**economic union** (465)
**free-trade area** (465)
**monetary union** (465)
**trade creation** (468)
**trade diversion** (463)
**trade symmetry** (459)

## Review questions

1. What was the motivation behind the original decision to establish the EEC?
2. How may a customs union distort trade rather than create trade?
3. Why is it important to harmonise regulations designed to protect consumers in order to integrate the EU economies?
4. Where have most of the economic gains from economic integration in Europe come from?
5. How can countries affect their terms of trade by tariff policy?
6. How does EU trade policy affect incomes in less developed countries?

## Answers to in-chapter exercises

16.1 See the figure below.

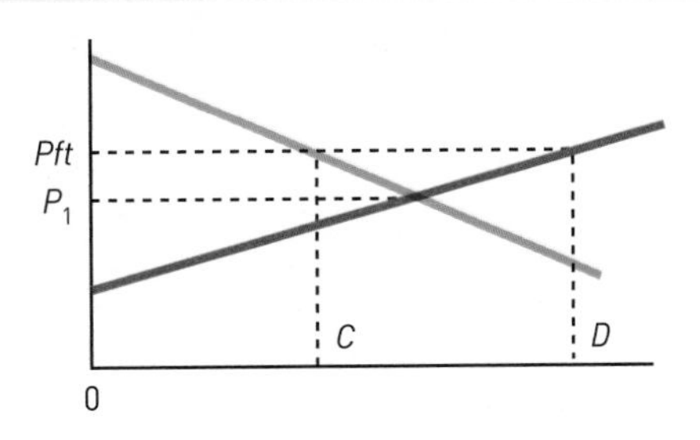


Producer surplus is increased, but part of this is offset by a decline in consumer surplus. The net increase is the inverted triangle above *CD*.

## References

Balassa, B. (1975) 'Trade Creation and Trade Diversion in the European Common Market', in B. Balassa (ed.), *European Economic Integration* (Amsterdam: North-Holland).

Baldwin, R. and C. Wyplosz (2004) *The Economics of European Integration* (Maidenhead: McGraw-Hill).

Jørgensen, J. G., T. Lüthje and P. J. H. Schröder (2001) 'Trade: the Work-Horse of Integration', Chapter 6 in J. D. Hansen (ed.), *European Integration – An Economic Perspective* (Oxford: Oxford University Press).

# Part 6

# Macroeconomics: Issues and Data

Physical scientists study the world on many different scales, ranging from the inner workings of the atom to the vast dimensions of the cosmos. Although the laws of physics are thought to apply at all scales, scientists find that some phenomena are best understood 'in the small' and some 'in the large'. Although the range of scales they must deal with is much more modest than in physics, economists also find it useful to analyse economic behaviour at both the small-scale, or 'micro' level, and the large-scale, or 'macro' level. This section introduces you to *macroeconomics*, the study of the performance of national economies. Unlike *microeconomics*, which focuses on the behaviour of individual households, firms and markets, macroeconomics takes a bird's-eye view of the economy. So, while a microeconomist might study the determinants of consumer spending on personal computers, macroeconomists analyse the factors that determine aggregate, or total, consumer spending. Experience has shown that, for many issues, the macroeconomic perspective is the more useful.

Chapter 17 begins our discussion of macroeconomics by introducing you to some of the key macroeconomic issues and questions. These include the search for the factors that cause economies to grow, productivity to improve and living standards to rise over long periods of time. Macroeconomists also study shorter-term fluctuations in the economy (called *recessions* and *expansions*), unemployment, inflation, and the economic interdependence among nations, among other topics. Macroeconomic policies – government actions to improve the performance of the economy – are of particular concern to macroeconomists, as the quality of macroeconomic policy making is a major determinant of a nation's economic health.

To study phenomena such as economic growth scientifically, economists must have accurate measurements. Chapters 18 and 19 continue the introduction to macroeconomics by discussing how some key macroeconomic concepts are measured and interpreted. Chapter 18 discusses two important measures of the level of economic activity, the *gross domestic product* (GDP) and the *unemployment rate*. Besides describing how these variables are constructed in practice, this chapter also discusses the issue of how these measures are related to the economic well-being of the typical person. Chapter 19 concerns the measurement of the price level and inflation and includes a discussion of the costs that inflation imposes on the economy. When you have completed Part 6, you will be familiar not only with the major questions that macroeconomists ask but also with some of the most important tools that they use to try to find the answers.

# 17

# Macroeconomics: the Bird's-Eye View of the Economy

In 1929 the economies of large industrial countries such as the United Kingdom, France, Germany and the United States slowed dramatically. Faced with declining sales, factories, shipyards, mines, railway companies and other producers of goods and services cut their output levels which in turn led to mass layoffs: Between 1928 and 1932, the British unemployment rate increased from 10 to 22 per cent of the labour force. In some other countries, conditions were even worse. In Germany, which had never fully recovered from its defeat in the First World War, the economy's output declined by 16 per cent and nearly a third of all workers were without jobs. Indeed, the desperate economic situation was a major reason for Adolf Hitler's election as chancellor of Germany in 1933. Introducing extensive government control over the economy, Hitler rearmed the country and ultimately launched the Second World War.

Historians now refer to the years following 1929 as the Great Depression. How could such an economic catastrophe have happened? One often-heard hypothesis is that the Great Depression was caused by wild financial speculation especially in the United States, which provoked the stock market crash of 1929. But though stock prices may have been unrealistically high in 1929, there is little evidence to suggest that the fall in stock prices was a major cause of the Depression. A similar crash in October 1987, when stock prices fell a record 23 per cent in one day – an event comparable in severity to the crash of October 1929 – did not slow the economy significantly. Another reason to doubt that the 1929 stock market crash caused the Great Depression is that, far from being confined to the United States, the Depression was a worldwide event, affecting countries that did not have well-developed stock markets at the time. The more reasonable conclusion is that the onset of the Depression probably caused the stock market crash, rather than the other way round.

Another explanation for the Depression, suggested by some economists in the 1930s, was that free-market economies such as those of the United States, Britain and Germany are 'naturally' unstable, prone to long periods of low production and high unemployment. But this idea, too, has fallen out of favour, since the period after the Second World War has generally been one of prosperity and economic growth throughout the industrialised world.

What *did* cause the Great Depression? Today most economists who have studied the period blame *poor economic policy making* in both Europe and the United States. Of course, policy makers did not set out to create an economic catastrophe. Rather, they fell prey to the misconceptions of the time about how the economy worked. In other words, the Great Depression, far from being inevitable, might have been avoided – if only the state of economic knowledge had been better. From today's perspective, the Great Depression was to economic policy making what the voyage of the *Titanic* was to ocean navigation.

One of the few benefits of the Great Depression was that it forced economists and policy makers of the 1930s to recognise that there were major gaps in their understanding of how the economy worked. This recognition led to the development of a new sub-field within economics, called *macroeconomics*. Recall from Chapter 1 that macroeconomics is the study of the performance of national economies and the policies governments use to try to improve that performance.

This chapter will introduce the subject matter and some of the tools of macroeconomics. Although understanding episodes such as the Great Depression remains an important concern of macroeconomists, the field has expanded to include the analysis of many other aspects of national economies. Among the issues that macroeconomists study are the sources of long-run economic growth and development, the causes of high unemployment and the factors that determine the rate of inflation. Appropriately enough in a world in which economic 'globalisation' preoccupies businesspeople and policy makers, macroeconomists also study how *national economies interact*. Since the performance of the national economy has an important bearing on the availability of jobs, the wages workers earn, the prices they pay and the rates of return they receive on their saving, it is clear that macroeconomics addresses bread-and-butter issues that affect virtually everyone.

In light of the Great Depression, macroeconomists are particularly concerned with understanding how macroeconomic policies work and how they should be applied. **Macroeconomic policies** are government actions designed to affect the performance of the economy as a whole (as opposed to policies intended to affect the performance of the market for a particular good or service, such as sugar or haircuts). The hope is that by understanding more fully how government policies affect the economy, economists can help policy makers do a better job – and avoid serious mistakes, such as those that were made during the Great Depression.

**macroeconomic policies** government actions designed to affect the performance of the economy as a whole

## The major macroeconomic issues

We defined macroeconomics as the study of the performance of the national economy as well as the policies used to improve that performance. Let us now take a closer look at some of the major economic issues that macroeconomists study.

### Economic growth and living standards

Although the wealthy industrialised countries (such as the United States, Canada, Japan and the countries of Western Europe) are certainly not free from poverty, hunger and homelessness, the typical person in those countries enjoys a standard of living better than at any previous time or place in history. By standard of living we mean the degree to which people have access to goods and services that make their lives easier, healthier, safer and more enjoyable. People with a high living standard enjoy more and better consumer goods: sports utility vehicles, camcorders, mobile phones and the like. But they also benefit from a longer life expectancy and better general health (the result of high-quality medical care, good nutrition and good sanitation), from higher literacy rates (the result of greater access to education), from more time and opportunity for cultural enrichment and recreation from more interesting and fulfilling career options and from better working conditions. Of course, the Scarcity Principle (Chapter 1) will always apply – even for the citizens of rich countries – having more of one good thing means having less of another. But higher incomes make these choices much less painful than they would be otherwise. Choosing between a larger flat and a nicer car is much easier than choosing between feeding your children adequately and sending them to school, the kind of hard choice people in the poorest nations face all the time.

Americans and Europeans sometimes take their standard of living for granted, or even as a 'right'. But we should realise that the way we live today is radically different from the way people have lived throughout most of history. The current standard of living in the Europe is the result of many years of *economic growth*, a process of steady increase in the quantity and quality of the goods and services the economy can produce. The basic equation is simple: the more we can *produce*, the more we can *consume*. Also, consumption does not only include cars, DVDs and foreign holidays, etc. It also includes access to the better health and education services which sustained economic growth makes possible. Though not everyone in a society shares equally in the fruits of economic growth, in most cases growth brings an improvement in the average person's standard of living.

To get a sense of the extent of economic growth over time, look at Fig. 17.1, which shows how the output of the European and American economies has increased since 1900. (We discuss the measure of output used here, real gross domestic product (GDP), in Chapter 18.) European output is measured as the aggregate or total output of the twelve largest economies in Western Europe. Although output fluctuates at times, the overall trend has been unmistakably upward. Indeed, in 2001 the output of the European economy was more than 11 times what it was in 1900 while the United States economy was 25 times larger:

- What caused this remarkable economic growth?
- Can it continue?
- Should it continue?

These are some of the questions macroeconomists try to answer.

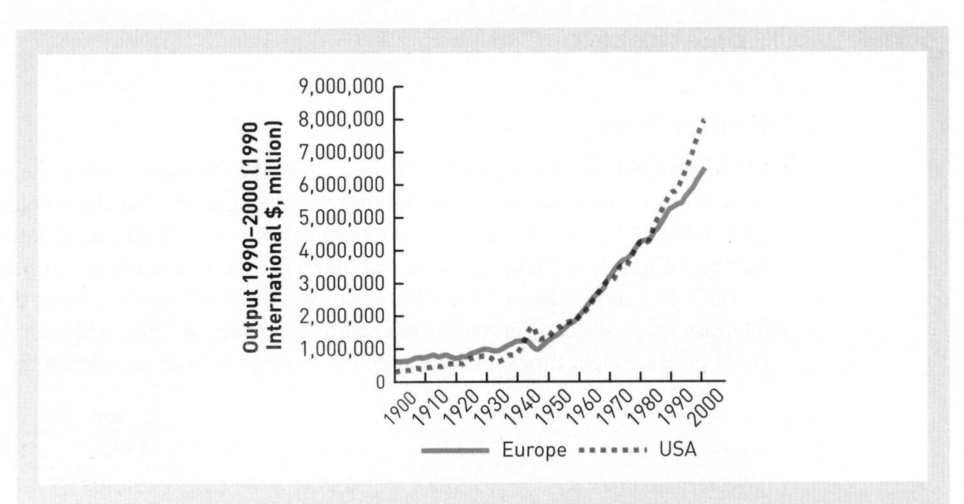


**Figure 17.1 Output: Europe and the United States, 1900–2000.** Output of the European (solid line) and American (dashed line) economies since 1900. The output of the European economy has inceased 11-fold since 1990 and the United States 25-fold.
*Source*: OECD (2003).

Population growth and an increasing number of workers available for production are important reasons underlying rapid output growth. Between 1900 and 2001 the population of the twelve largest European economies almost doubled while the US population increased fourfold over the same period. However, because of population growth, increases in *total* output cannot be equated with improvements in the general standard of living. Although increased output means that more goods and services are available, increased population implies that more people are sharing those goods and services. Because the population changes over time, output *per person* is a better indicator of the average living standard than total output. Figure 17.2 shows output per person in Europe (solid line) and the United States (dashed line) since 1900. Relative to 1900, output per person has increased about seven times in each economy.

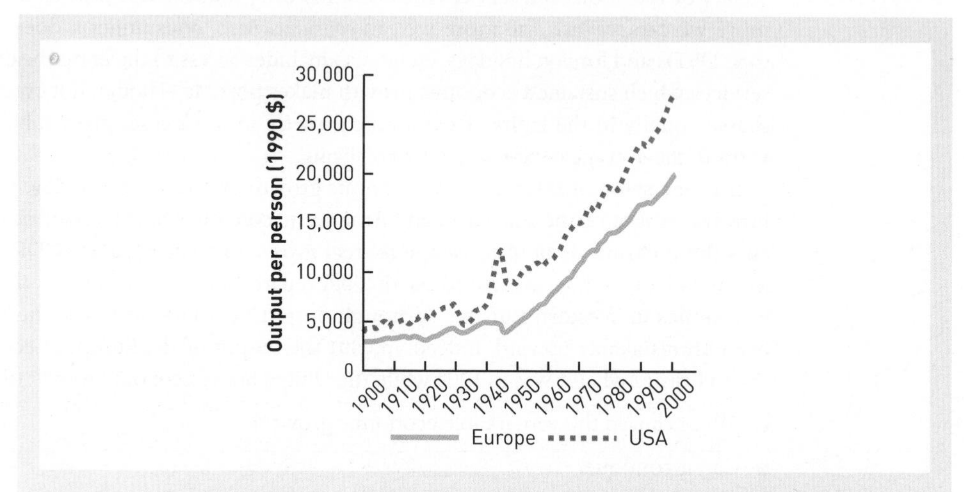


**Figure 17.2 Output per Person in Europe and the United States, 1900–2000.** Output *per person* in the European (solid line) and the American (dashed line) economies since 1900. Both have risen substantially since 1900. In both cases output per person in 2000 is nearly seven times more than in 1900.
*Source*: OECD (2003).

## Productivity

While growth in output per person is closely linked to changes in what the typical person can *consume*, macroeconomists are also interested in changes in what the average worker can *produce*. Table 17.1 shows how output per employed worker (that is, total output divided by the number of people working) has changed over a period of more than 120 years.

Table 17.1 shows that in 1998 a European worker could produce more than nine times the quantity of goods and services produced by a worker in 1870, while an American worker could produce eight times more, despite the fact that in both economies the working week is

| | 1870 | 1913 | 1950 | 1973 | 1990 | 1998 |
|---|---|---|---|---|---|---|
| Western Europe | 4,702 | 8,072 | 11,551 | 28,108 | 37,476 | 43,108 |
| France | 4,051 | 7,458 | 11,214 | 31,910 | 45,356 | 50,680 |
| Germany | 4,414 | 7,824 | 9,231 | 26,623 | 34,352 | 40,452 |
| Italy | 3,037 | 5,412 | 8,739 | 25,661 | 36,124 | 42,015 |
| United Kingdom | 7,614 | 11,296 | 15,529 | 26,956 | 35,061 | 40,875 |
| United States | 6,683 | 13,327 | 23,615 | 40,727 | 47,976 | 55,618 |
| Ratio: US/Europe | 1.42 | 1.65 | 2.04 | 1.44 | 1.28 | 1.29 |

**Table 17.1** Output per Person Employed, 1870–1998 (1990 International $)
*Source*: OECD (2003).

now much shorter than it was in 1870. Economists refer to output per employed worker as **average labour productivity**.

**average labour productivity**
output per person employed

The final row of Table 17.1 shows the ratio of US to European labour productivity. In 1950, US workers were twice as productive as their European counterparts but the ratio declined over the next fifty years and especially between 1950 and 1973 which is sometimes referred to as a *catch-up period*. Economic naturalist 17.1 looks at Europe's catch-up in greater detail.

**Exercise 17.1** The last row in Table 17.1 shows that between 1950 and 1973 average labour productivity in Western Europe increased at a faster rate than in the United States. Calculate the same ratio for each of the countries in Table 17.1. Was the rate of catch-up the same in all countries?

*Average labour productivity* and *output per person* are closely related. This relationship makes sense – as we noted earlier, the more we can produce, the more we can consume. Because of this close link to the average living standard, average labour productivity and the factors that cause it to increase over time are of major concern to macroeconomists.

Although the long-term improvement in output per worker is impressive, the *rate* of improvement has slowed somewhat since the 1970s. Between 1950 and 1973 output of the average European employed worker increased by about 6 per cent per year. But from 1973 to 1995 the average rate of increase in output per worker was 2.1 per cent per year. Slowing productivity growth leads to less rapid improvement in living standards, since the supply of goods and services cannot grow as quickly as it does during periods of rapid growth in productivity. Identifying the causes of productivity slowdowns and speed-ups is thus an important challenge for macroeconomists.

The current standard of living in Europe is not only much higher than in the past but also much higher than in many other nations today. Why have many of the world's countries, including the developing nations of Asia, Africa and Latin America as well as some former communist countries of Eastern Europe, not enjoyed the same rates of economic growth as the industrialised countries? How can the rate of economic growth be improved in these countries? Once again, these are questions of keen interest to macroeconomists.

## Economic naturalist 17.1 Explaining Europe's catch-up, 1950–73

Table 17.1 shows that in the seventy years preceding the Second World War American labour productivity not only exceeded European productivity, but that the gap between them widened. However in the decades following 1945 the reverse occurred and Europe closed the gap on the United States. Not only did the difference between American and European labour productivity decline between 1950 and 1973 but European output per person increased from 52 to 73 per cent of American output per person. Why did this catch-up occur after 1950? One obvious answer is that catch-up was the result of reconstructing Europe's war-ravaged economies, paid for in part by the US-financed Marshall Plan. Reconstruction certainly played a role but it is not the only reason for Europe's catch-up period between 1950 and 1973. The American Economist Robert J. Gordon discusses this issue and presents a number of reasons why Europe did so badly before the Second World War and so well afterwards.[1] One of Gordon's hypotheses is that we can understand Europe's catch-up only if we first understand why the United States surged ahead during the nineteenth century and the first half of the twentieth century. In answering this question, Gordon highlights the fact that America was a full

[1] Gordon (2004).

political, monetary and economic union long before Europe and that the creation of an internal or single market enabled the United States to exploit the advantages of mass production and key inventions such as electricity and the internal combustion engine. In contrast, Europe was fragmented by nation states, trade barriers and war. As Gordon puts it:

> Looking back at the long history of Europe falling behind the US and then catching up, it is hard to avoid the conclusion that this topic has more to do with politics and history rather than with economics. The sources of US advantage prior to 1913 centre on its internal common market, an achievement of the Founding Fathers, Abraham Lincoln and the Union Army, rather than any particular genius at business or technology, and free internal trade led in turn to exploitation of raw materials and leadership in materials-intensive manufacturing. Postwar Europe gradually rid itself of internal trade barriers and largely caught up to the American productivity frontier as a result.

Gordon's hypothesis raises several interesting questions. First, as the European Single Market, the common currency and the proposed constitution intensify the pace of economic and political integration, will Europe become 'more like America' and further close the gap on the United States? Second, and somewhat more trivial, Gordon's argument is an obvious boost to the 'what if' theorists. What if the Union Army had been defeated at Gettysburg in July 1863 and the Confederacy emerged victorious in the Civil War of 1861–65? Would America have fragmented into nation states and become 'more like Europe' with internal strife, trade barriers and impediments to the free movement of labour? If so, would the economic and political histories of Europe and America have been dramatically different?

### **Example 17.1** Productivity and living standards in China and Europe

In 2001 the value of the output in the People's Republic of China (PRC) was $1,160 billion (US). In the same year, the estimated value of output in Western Europe was $6,510 billion (we use dollars to facilitate the comparison). The populations of the China and Western Europe in 2001 were about 1,262 million and 325 million, respectively, while the number of employed workers in the two economies was approximately 710 million and 141 million

Find output per person and average labour productivity for the China and Western Europe in 2001. What do the results suggest about comparative living standards?

Output per person is simply total output divided by the number of people in an economy, and average labour productivity is output divided by the number of employed workers. Doing the arithmetic we get the following results for 2001:

| Standard | Europe ($) | China ($) |
|---|---|---|
| Output per person | 20,030 | 919 |
| Average labour productivity | 46,170 | 1,634 |

Note that although the total output of the Chinese economy is approximately 18 per cent that of European output, output per person and average labour productivity in China are each only about 4.5 and 3.5 per cent, respectively, of what they are in Europe. Thus, though the Chinese economy may some day rival the European economy in total output, for the time being there remains a large gap in *productivity*. This gap translates into striking differences in the living standard between the two economies – in access to consumer goods, health care, transportation, education and other benefits of affluence.

## Recessions and expansions

Economies do not always grow steadily; sometimes they go through periods of unusual strength or weakness. A look back at Fig. 17.1 shows that although output generally grows over time, it does not always grow smoothly. Particularly striking is the decline in output during the Great Depression of the 1930s, and in the case of the United States the sharp increase in output during the Second World War (1939–45). In contrast the war-torn economies of Western Europe experience a sharp fall in output between 1939 and 1945. But Fig. 17.1 shows many more moderate fluctuations in output as well.

Slowdowns in economic growth are called *recessions*; particularly severe economic slowdowns, like the one that began in 1929, are called *depressions*. In Europe and the United States, major recessions occurred in 1974–75 and 1981–82. More modest downturns occurred in 1990–91 and 2001. During recessions *economic opportunities* decline: jobs are harder to find, people with jobs are less likely to get wage increases, profits are lower and more companies go out of business. Recessions are particularly hard on economically disadvantaged people, who are most likely to be made redundant and have the hardest time finding new jobs.

Sometimes the economy grows unusually quickly. These periods of rapid economic growth are called *expansions*, and particularly strong expansions are called *booms*. In some European countries, and more especially in the United States, the recession of 1990–91 was followed by a period of relatively high economic growth which ended with the recession of 2001. During an expansion, jobs are easier to find, more people get rises and promotions, and most businesses thrive.

The alternating cycle of recessions and expansions raises some questions that are central to macroeconomics:

- What causes these short-term fluctuations in the rate of economic growth?
- Can government policy makers do anything about them?
- Should they try?

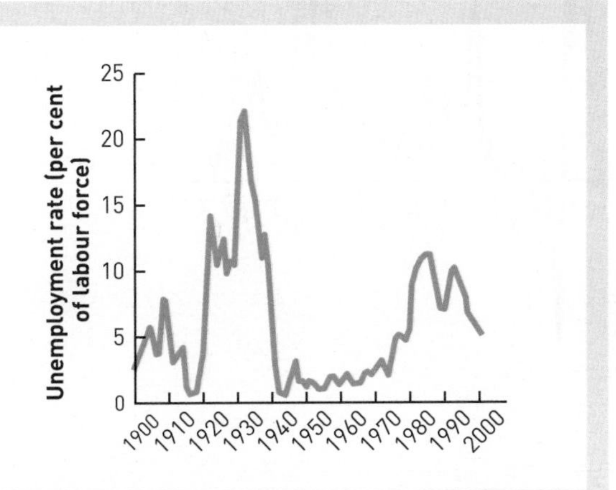


**Figure 17.3 The UK Unemployment Rate, 1900–2001.** The unemployment rate is the percentage of the labour force that is out of work. The unemployment rate spikes upward during recessions but is always positive, even during expansions.

*Sources: British Labour Historical Abstract (1900–68); The European Economy (1969–2001)*, Commission of the European Communities, www.europa_eu.int/comm-finance/publications.

## Unemployment

The *unemployment rate*, the percentage of the workforce who would like to be employed but can't find work, is a key indicator of the state of the labour market. When the unemployment rate is high, work is hard to find and people who do have jobs typically find it harder to get promotions or wage increases.

Figure 17.3 shows the unemployment rate in the United Kingdom since 1900. Unemployment rises during recessions – note the dramatic spike in unemployment during the Great Depression, as well as the increases in unemployment during the 1974–75 and 1981–82 recessions. But even in the so-called 'good times', such as the 1960s and the 1990s, some people are unemployed. Why does unemployment rise so sharply during periods of recession? And why are there always unemployed people, even when the economy is booming?

**Exercise 17.2** Find the most recent unemployment rates for France, Germany and the United Kingdom, and compare them with the most recent unemployment rate for the United States. Useful sources are the home pages of Eurostat (http://epp.eurostat.cec.eu.int), the statistical agency of the European Union and the Organisation for Economic Co-operation and Development (OECD), an organisation of industrialised countries (http://www.oecd.org/). Is unemployment still higher in the Western Europe than in the United States?

## Inflation

Another important economic statistic is the rate of *inflation*, which is the rate at which prices in general are increasing over time. As we discuss in Chapter 19, inflation imposes a variety of costs on the economy. And when the inflation rate is high, people on fixed incomes – such as pensioners who receive a fixed money payment each month – can't keep up with the rising cost of living.

In recent years, inflation has been relatively low in Western Europe, but that has not always been the case (see Fig. 17.4 for data on UK inflation since 1900). During the 1970s, inflation was a major problem in countries such as France and the United Kingdom where it peaked at 25 per cent in 1975. Why was inflation high in the 1970s, and why is it relatively low today? What difference does it make to the average person?

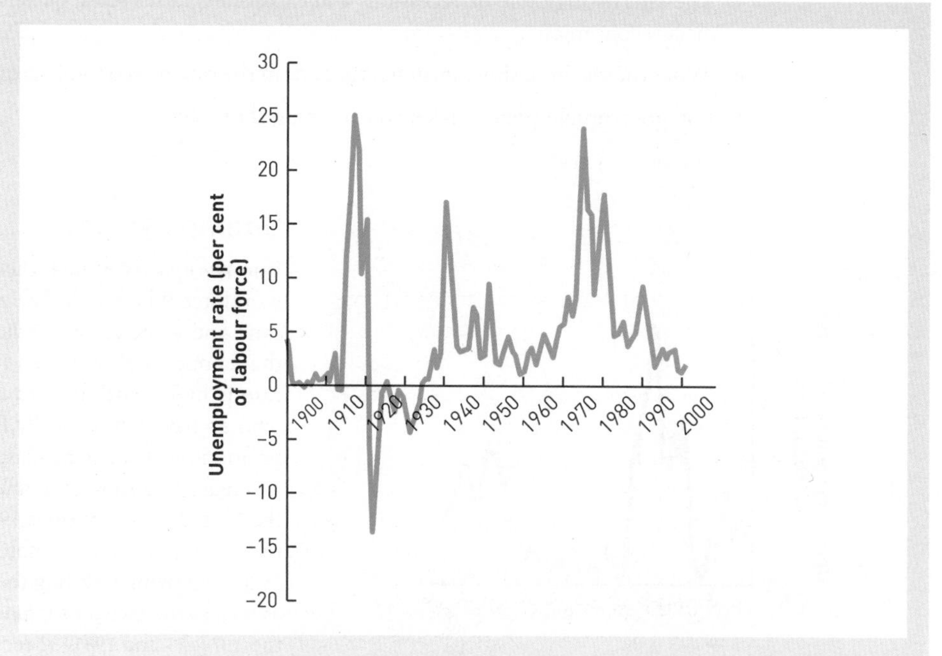


**Figure 17.4 The UK Inflation Rate, 1900–2001.** The inflation rate fluctuates over time. It was negative during the Great Depression and exceeded 20 per cent during the oil crises in the 1970s.

*Source*: *Inflation and the Value of the Pound*, House of Commons Research Paper, 99/20.

As with unemployment, inflation can differ markedly from country to country. For example, in 2001 the inflation rate was less than 3 per cent in most Western economies, but the Ukraine averaged over 400 per cent annual inflation for the whole decade of the 1990s. What accounts for such large differences in inflation rates between countries?

Inflation and unemployment are often linked in policy discussions. One reason for this linkage is the oft-heard argument that unemployment can be reduced only at the cost of higher inflation and that inflation can be reduced only at the cost of higher unemployment. Must the government accept a higher rate of inflation to bring down unemployment, and vice versa?

## Economic interdependence among nations

National economies do not exist in isolation but are increasingly *interdependent*. This is especially true for Europe where the introduction of the Single Market and the common currency (the euro) has dramatically increased the degree of integration and interdependences between EU member states. International trade is a key indicator of interdependences between countries. In 2003, total exports accounted for 34 per cent of aggregate EU output while imports accounted for 32 per cent. By comparison, the United States exported about 9 per cent of all the goods and services it produced and imported 14 per cent of the goods and services that Americans used. However, in the case of EU countries it is important to distinguish between *intra-EU* and *extra-EU* trade. Intra-EU trade is exports and imports *between* member states while extra-EU trade is trade with countries *outside* the Union. British exports to France are intra-EU trade, while imports from Norway are extra-EU trade. In 2003, intra-EU trade accounted for approximately 50 per cent of the total exports and imports.

Sometimes, international flows of goods and services become a matter of political and economic concern. For example, those who opposed the expansion of the European Union to include countries in Central and Eastern Europe (CEE) complained that low-priced imports of these countries threatened jobs in Western countries. Similar concerns were expressed following the creation of the North American Free Trade Agreement (or NAFTA) between the United States, Canada and Mexico. Are free-trade agreements, in which countries agree not to tax or otherwise block the international flow of goods and services, a good or a bad thing?

A related issue is the phenomenon of *trade imbalances*, which occur when the quantity of goods and services that a country sells abroad (its *exports*) differs significantly from the quantity of goods and services its citizens buy from abroad (its *imports*). The difference between exports and imports is often referred to as *net exports*.

Figure 17.5 shows French and British net exports of goods and services since 1960, measured as a percentage of each economy's total output. Prior to the 1990s France generally imported more than it exported, a situation called a *trade deficit*. Since the early 1990s, however, French exports have outstripped imports, creating a situation called a *trade surplus*. The United Kingdom, on the other hand, saw its surplus in the late 1970s and 1980s turned to a deficit in the 1990s. What causes trade deficits and surpluses? Are they harmful or helpful?

**Exercise 17.3**

Using the most recent data on exports and imports for the European Union find the EU's current trade deficit or surplus. Compare your results with the most recent trade data for the United States. Useful sources are the home pages of Eurostat (http://epp.eurostat.cec.eu.int), the EU statistical agency, and the OECD (http://www.oecd.org/).

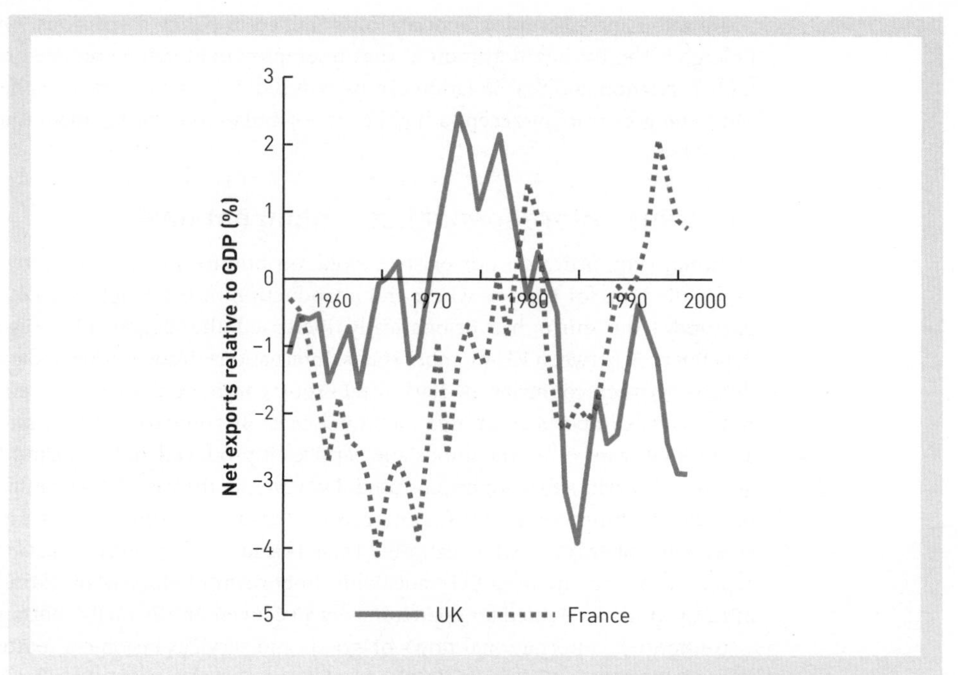


**Figure 17.5 Net Exports as a Share of Output, France and the United Kingdom, 1960–2000.** The figure shows next exports of goods and services (exports minus imports) for France (dashed line) and the United Kingdom (solid line) since 1960. On recent trends France has a surplus and the United Kingdom a deficit.

## RECAP The major macroeconomic issues

- *Economic growth and living standards* Since 1900 the industrialised nations have experienced remarkable economic growth and improvements in living standards. Macroeconomists study the reasons for this extraordinary growth and try to understand why growth rates vary markedly among nations.
- *Productivity* Average labour productivity, or output per employed worker, is a crucial determinant of living standards. Macroeconomists study the causes of variations in the rate of productivity growth.
- *Recessions and expansions* Economies experience periods of slower growth (recessions) and more rapid growth (expansions). Macroeconomists examine the sources of these fluctuations and the government policies that attempt to moderate them.
- *Unemployment* The unemployment rate is the fraction of the labour force who would like to be employed but can't find work. Unemployment rises during recessions, but there are always unemployed people even during good times. Macroeconomists study the causes of unemployment, including the reasons why it sometimes differs markedly across countries.
- *Inflation* The inflation rate is the rate at which prices in general are increasing over time. Questions macroeconomists ask about inflation include: Why does inflation vary over time and across countries? Must a reduction in inflation be accompanied by an increase in unemployment (or vice versa)?
- *Economic interdependence among nations* Modern economies are highly interdependent. Related issues studied by macroeconomists include the gains from closer economic integration, the desirability of free trade agreements and the causes and effects of trade imbalances.

## Macroeconomic policy

We have seen that macroeconomists are interested in why different countries' economies perform differently and why a particular economy may perform well in some periods and poorly in others. Although many factors contribute to economic performance, government policy is surely among the most important. Understanding the effects of various policies and helping government officials develop better policies are important objectives of macroeconomists.

### Types of macroeconomic policy

We defined macroeconomic policies as government policies that affect the performance of the economy as a whole, as opposed to the market for a particular good or service. There are three major types of macroeconomic policy: *monetary policy*, *fiscal policy* and *structural policy*.

The term **monetary policy** refers to the determination of the economy's money supply. (Cash and coin are the basic forms of money, although as we will see, modern economies have other forms of money as well.) For reasons that we will discuss in later chapters, most economists agree that changes in the money supply affect important macroeconomic variables, including aggregate output, employment, interest rates, inflation and exchange rates, and the value of one currency in terms of another. In virtually all countries, monetary policy is controlled by a government or publicly owned institution called the *central bank*. In January 1999, twelve European countries replaced their currencies with a common currency called the *euro* and transferred responsibility for monetary policy from national central banks to the newly created European Central Bank (ECB) located in Frankfurt. In the United States the central bank is known as the Federal Reserve System, often called the Fed for short, while the Bank of England is the central bank of the United Kingdom.

**monetary policy** determination of the nation's money supply

**Fiscal policy** refers to decisions that determine the government's budget, including the amount and composition of government expenditures and government revenues. The balance between government spending and taxes is a particularly important aspect of fiscal policy. When governments spend more than they collect in taxes, they run a *deficit*, and when they spend less, the government's budget is in *surplus*. As with monetary policy, economists generally agree that fiscal policy can have important effects on the overall performance of the economy. For example, many economists believe that large government deficits lead to instability and are harmful to growth and employment. Indeed, it is for this reason that European countries have attempted, with limited success, to restrict the size of government deficits by an agreement known as the Stability and Growth Pact (SGP).

**fiscal policy** decisions that determine the government's budget, including the amount and composition of government expenditures and government revenues

Finally, the term **structural policy** includes government policies aimed at changing the underlying structure, or institutions, of the economy. Structural policies come in many forms, from minor tinkering to ambitious overhauls of the entire economic system. The move away from government control of the economy and toward a more market-orientated approach in many formerly communist countries, such as Poland, the Czech Republic and Hungary, is a large-scale example of structural policy. Many developing countries have tried similar structural reforms. Supporters of structural policy hope that, by changing the basic characteristics of the economy or by remaking its institutions, they can stimulate economic growth and improve living standards.

**structural policy** government policies aimed at changing the underlying structure, or institutions, of the nation's economy

## Positive versus normative analyses of macroeconomic policy

Macroeconomists are frequently called upon to analyse the effects of a proposed policy. For example, if government is debating the merits of higher taxes on fossil fuels, economists may be asked to prepare an analysis of the likely effects on the overall economy, as well as on specific industries, regions or income groups. An objective analysis aimed at determining only the economic consequences of a particular policy – not whether those consequences are desirable – is called a **positive analysis**. In contrast, a **normative analysis** includes recommendations on whether a particular policy *should* be implemented. While a positive analysis is supposed to be objective and scientific, a normative analysis involves the *values* of the person or organisation doing the analysis – conservative, socialist or middle-of-the-road.

**positive analysis** addresses the economic consequences of a particular event or policy, not whether those consequences are desirable

**normative analysis** addresses the question of whether a policy *should* be used; normative analysis inevitably involves the values of the person doing the analysis

While pundits often joke that economists cannot agree among themselves, the tendency for economists to disagree is exaggerated. When economists do disagree, the controversy often centres on normative judgements (which relate to economists' personal values) rather than on positive analysis (which reflects an objective knowledge of the economy). For example, socialist and conservative economists might agree that a particular tax cut would increase the incomes of the relatively wealthy (positive analysis). But they might vehemently disagree on whether the policy *should* be enacted, reflecting their personal views about whether wealthy people deserve a tax break (normative analysis).

The next time you hear or read about a debate over economic issues, try to determine whether the differences between the two positions are primarily positive or normative. If the debate focuses on the actual effects of the event or policy under discussion, then the disagreement is over positive issues. But if the main question has to do with conflicting personal opinions about the *desirability* of those effects, the debate is normative. The distinction between positive and normative analyses is important, because objective economic research can help to resolve differences over positive issues. When people differ for normative reasons, however, economic analysis is of less use.

**Exercise 17.4**

Which of the following statements are positive and which are normative? How can you tell?

a. Banning smoking in public places will lead to lower employment in bars and restaurants.
b. Irrespective of its effect on employment, government should ban smoking in public places in order to protect public health.
c. A tax increase would be acceptable if most of the burden fell on those with incomes over €100,000.
d. Government should offer grants to first-time house buyers in order to promote home ownership.
e. Grants to first-time house buyers will lead to higher house prices.

## RECAP Macroeconomic policy

*Macroeconomic policies* affect the performance of the economy as a whole. The three types of macroeconomic policy are monetary policy, fiscal policy and structural policy. *Monetary policy*, which in the twelve countries using the euro as their currency is under the control of the ECB, refers to the determination of the nation's money supply. *Fiscal policy* involves decisions about the government budget, including its expenditures and tax collections. *Structural policy* refers to government actions to change the underlying structure or institutions of the economy. Structural policy can range from minor tinkering to a major overhaul of the economic system, as with the formerly communist countries that are attempting to convert to market-orientated systems.

The analysis of a proposed policy can be positive or normative. A positive analysis addresses the policy's likely economic consequences, but not whether those consequences are desirable. A normative analysis addresses the question of whether a proposed policy *should* be used. Debates about normative conclusions inevitably involve personal values and thus generally cannot be resolved by objective economic analysis alone.

## Aggregation

In Chapter 1, we discussed the difference between macroeconomics – the study of national economies – and microeconomics – the study of individual economic entities, such as households and firms, and the markets for specific goods and services. The main difference between the fields is one of perspective: macroeconomists take a 'bird's-eye view' of the economy, ignoring the fine details to understand how the system works as a whole. Microeconomists work instead at the 'ground level', studying the economic behaviour of individual households, firms and markets. Both perspectives are useful – indeed, essential – to understand what makes an economy work.

Although macroeconomics and microeconomics take different perspectives on the economy, the basic tools of analysis are much the same. In the chapters to come you will see that macroeconomists apply the same core principles as microeconomists in their efforts to understand and predict economic behaviour. Even though a national economy is a much bigger entity than a household, or even a large firm, the choices and actions of individual decision makers ultimately determine the performance of the economy as a whole. So, for example, to understand saving behaviour at the national level, the macroeconomist must first consider what motivates an individual family or household to save. The core principles introduced in Part 1 prove very useful for attacking such questions.

**Exercise 17.5**

Which of the following questions would be studied primarily by macroeconomists, and which by microeconomists? Explain.

a. Does increased government spending lower the unemployment rate?
b. Does Microsoft Corporation's dominance of the software industry harm consumers?
c. Would charging tuition fees to university students improve the quality of education?
d. Should the ECB aim to reduce inflation still further?
e. Why is the average rate of household saving higher in France than in the United States?
f. Does the increase in the number of consumer products being sold over the Internet threaten the profits of conventional retailers?

While macroeconomists use the core principles of economics to understand and predict individual economic decisions, they need a way to relate millions of individual decisions to the behaviour of the economy as a whole. One important tool they use to link individual behaviour to national economic performance is **aggregation**, the adding up of individual economic variables to obtain economywide totals.

**aggregation** the adding up of individual economic variables to obtain economywide totals

For example, macroeconomists don't care whether consumers drink red or white wine, go to the cinema or rent DVDs, live in rented or owner-occupied housing. These individual economic decisions are the province of microeconomics. Instead, macroeconomists add up consumer expenditures on all goods and services during a given period to obtain *aggregate*, or total, consumer expenditure.

Similarly, a macroeconomist would not focus on plumbers' wages versus electricians' but would concentrate instead on the average wage of all workers. By focusing on aggregate variables, such as total consumer expenditures or the average wage, macroeconomists suppress the mind-boggling details of a complex modern economy to see the broad economic trends.

### **Example 17.2** Aggregation: 1 – a national crime index

To illustrate not only why aggregation is needed but also some of the problems associated with it, consider an issue that is only partly economic: crime. Suppose policy makers want to know whether *in general* the problem of crime in a country such as the United Kingdom is getting better or worse. How could an analyst obtain a statistical answer to that question?

Police keep detailed records of the crimes reported in their jurisdictions, so in principle a researcher could determine precisely how many bag snatchings occurred last year on the London Underground. But data on the number of crimes of each type in each city and region would produce stacks of computer output. Is there a way to add up, or aggregate, all the crime data to get some sense of the national trend?

Government departments such as the UK Home Office use aggregation to obtain national *crime rates*, which are typically expressed as the total number of crimes reported to the police per 1,000 of the population (www.homeoffice.gov.uk). Although aggregation of crime statistics reveals the 'big picture', it may obscure important details. An aggregate index lumps together relatively minor crimes such as petty theft with more serious crimes involving violence. Most people would agree that violent crimes do far more damage than petty theft, so adding together these two very different types of crimes might give a false picture of UK crime. For example, according to Home Office aggregate data for 2003–04 the number of crimes reported by the police was down by 1 per cent on the previous year. Violent crime, however, increased by 12 per cent over the same period which is probably more significant than the fall in the overall or aggregate crime rate. This loss of detail is a cost of aggregation, the price analysts pay for the ability to look at broad economic or social trends.

### **Example 17.3** Aggregation: 2 – French exports

France exports a wide variety of products and services to many different countries. French manufacturing firms such as Airbus and Renault sell planes and cars to airlines and households in Europe, Africa, North America and Asia, and French vineyards sell wine all over the world. Suppose macroeconomists want to compare the total quantities of French-made goods sold to various regions of the world. How could such a comparison be made?

Economists can't add jumbo jets, cars and bottles of wine – the units aren't comparable. But they can add the *money values* of each – the revenue Airbus and car manufacturers earn from foreign sales and the euro value of French wine sold abroad. By comparing the euro values of French exports to other countries in a particular year, economists are able to determine which regions are the biggest customers for French-made goods.

### **RECAP** Aggregation

*Macroeconomics*, the study of national economies, differs from *microeconomics*, the study of individual economic entities (such as households and firms) and the markets for specific goods and services. Macroeconomists take a 'bird's-eye view' of the economy. To study the economy as a whole, macroeconomists make frequent use of *aggregation*, the adding up of individual economic variables to obtain economy-wide totals. For example, a macroeconomist is more interested in the determinants of total French exports, as measured by their total euro value, than in the factors that determine the exports of specific goods such as wine or aircraft. A cost of aggregation is that the fine details of the economic situation are often obscured.

## Studying macroeconomics: a preview

This chapter introduced many of the key issues of macroeconomics. In the chapters to come we shall look at each of these issues in more detail. Chapters 18 and 19 cover the *measurement* of economic performance, including key variables such as the level of economic activity, the extent of unemployment and the rate of inflation. Obtaining quantitative measurements of the economy, against which theories can be tested, is the crucial first step in answering basic macroeconomic questions like those raised in this chapter.

In Part 7 we shall study economic behaviour over relatively long periods of time. Chapter 20 examines economic growth and productivity improvement, the fundamental determinants of the average standard of living in the long run. Chapter 21 discusses the long-run determination of employment, unemployment and wages. In Chapter 22 we study saving and its link to the creation of new capital goods, such as factories and machines. The role played in the economy by money, and its relation to the rate of inflation, is covered in Chapter 23, which also introduces the ECB and discusses some of its policy tools. Chapter 24 looks at both domestic and international financial markets and their role in allocating saving to productive uses, in particular their role in promoting international capital flows.

John Maynard Keynes, a celebrated British economist, once wrote that 'In the long run, we are all dead'. Keynes' statement was intended as an ironic comment on the tendency of economists to downplay short-run economic problems on the grounds that 'in the long run', the operation of the free market will always restore economic stability. Keynes, who was particularly active and influential during the Great Depression, correctly viewed the problem of massive unemployment, whether 'short run' or not, as the most pressing economic issue of the time.

So why start our study of macroeconomics with the long run? Keynes' comment notwithstanding, long-run economic performance is extremely important, accounting for most of the substantial differences in living standards and economic well-being the world over. Furthermore, studying long-run economic behaviour provides an important background for understanding short-term fluctuations in the economy.

We turn to those short-term fluctuations in Part 8. Chapter 25 provides background on what happens during recessions and expansions and discusses one important source of short-term economic fluctuations: variations in aggregate spending. Chapter 26 discusses the role of fiscal policy in moderating economic fluctuations while the second major policy tool for stabilising the economy, monetary policy, is the subject of Chapter 27. Chapter 28 brings inflation into the analysis and discusses the circumstances under which macroeconomic policy makers may face a short-term trade-off between inflation and unemployment.

The international dimension of macroeconomics is the focus of Part 9. (Chapter 16 focused on the issue of international trade and the costs and benefits of unrestricted trade.) Chapter 29 introduces exchange rates between national currencies. We will discuss how exchange rates are determined and how they affect the workings of the economy and macroeconomic policy. Chapter 30 discusses the economic rationale for monetary union in Europe.

## Summary

- Macroeconomics is the study of the performance of national economies and of the policies governments use to try to improve that performance. The five broad issues macroeconomists study are:
  - Sources of economic growth and improved living standards
  - Trends in *average labour productivity*, or output per employed worker
  - Short-term fluctuations in the pace of economic growth (recessions and expansions)
  - Causes and cures of unemployment and inflation
  - Economic interdependence among nations.
- To help explain differences in economic performance among countries, or in economic performance in the same country at different times, macroeconomists study the implementation and effects of macroeconomic policies. *Macroeconomic policies* are government actions designed to affect the performance of the economy as a whole. Macroeconomic policies include *monetary policy* (the determination of the nation's money supply), *fiscal policy* (relating to decisions about the government's budget) and *structural policy* (aimed at affecting the basic structure and institutions of the economy).
- In studying economic policies, economists apply both *positive analysis* (an objective attempt to determine the consequences of a proposed policy) and *normative analysis* (which addresses whether a particular policy *should* be adopted). Normative analysis involves the values of the person doing the analysis.
- Macroeconomics is distinct from microeconomics, which focuses on the behaviour of individual economic entities and specific markets. Macroeconomists make heavy use of *aggregation*, which is the adding up of individual economic variables into economywide totals. Aggregation allows macroeconomists to study the 'big picture' of the economy, while ignoring fine details about individual households, firms and markets.

## Key terms

**aggregation** (489)
**average labour productivity** (481)
**fiscal policy** (487)
**macroeconomic policies** (478)
**monetary policy** (487)
**normative analysis** (488)
**positive analysis** (488)
**structural policy** (487)

## Review questions

1. How did the experience of the Great Depression motivate the development of the field of macroeconomics?
2. In general, how does the standard of living in Europe today compare with the standard of living in other countries? To the standard of living in the Europe a century ago?
3. Why is average labour productivity a particularly important economic variable?
4. **True or false**: Economic growth within a particular country generally proceeds at a constant rate. Explain.
5. **True or false**: Differences of opinion about economic policy recommendations can always be resolved by objective analysis of the issues. Explain.
6. What type of macroeconomic policy (monetary, fiscal, structural) might include each of the following actions?
   a. A broad government initiative to reduce the country's reliance on agriculture and promote high-technology industries

b. A reduction in income tax rates

c. Provision of additional cash to the banking system

d. An attempt to reduce the government budget deficit by reducing spending

e. A decision by a developing country to reduce government control of the economy and to become more market-orientated

## Problems

1. In the years to 2050 the Japanese population is expected to decline, while the fraction of the population that is retired is expected to increase sharply. What are the implications of these population changes for total output and average living standards in Japan, assuming that average labour productivity continues to grow? What if average labour productivity stagnates?

2. Is it possible for average living standards to rise during a period in which average labour productivity is falling? Discuss, using a numerical example for illustration.

3. Eurostat is the European agency that collects a wide variety of statistics about the European economy. From the Eurostat home page (http://epp.eurostat.cec.eu.int) find data for the most recent year available on EU exports and imports of goods and services. Is the Union running a trade surplus or deficit?

4. Which of the following statements are positive and which are normative?

   a. If the ECB raises interest rates, demand for housing is likely to fall.

   b. The ECB should be primarily concerned with keeping inflation low irrespective of the rate of unemployment.

   c. Share prices are likely to fall over the next year as the economy slows.

   d. A reduction in the capital gains tax (the tax on profits made in the stock market) would lead to a 10–20 per cent increase in stock prices.

   e. Government should not reduce capital gains taxes without also providing tax breaks for lower-income people.

5. Which of the following would be studied by a macroeconomist? By a microeconomist?

   a. The effect of higher oil prices on employment

   b. The effect of government subsidies on sugar prices

   c. Factors affecting average wages in the UK economy

   d. Inflation in developing countries

   e. The effects of tax cuts on consumer spending.

## Answers to in-chapter exercises

17.1 The table shows below the ratio of average labour productivity in the United States to that in each European country:

| Country | 1950 | 1973 |
|---|---|---|
| France | 2.11 | 1.26 |
| Germany | 2.56 | 1.53 |
| Italy | 2.70 | 1.59 |
| United Kingdom | 1.52 | 1.51 |

Average labour productivity in France, Germany and Italy follows the European trend by increasing relative to the United States. For example, in 1950 US productivity was 2.7 times that in Italy but by 1973 it was only 1.59 times greater. The United Kingdom is a clear outlier. Relative to the United States, British labour productivity in 1973 was much the same as in 1950.

17.2 Your answer will depend upon the current unemployment rate available at the Eurostat and OECD websites.

17.3 Your answer will depend upon the current export and import data available at the Eurostat and OECD websites.

17.4 a. **Positive**. This is a prediction of the effect of a policy, not a value judgement on whether the policy should be used.

b. **Normative**. Words like *should* express value judgements about the policy.

c. **Normative**. The statement is about the desirability of certain types of policies, not their likely effects.

d. **Normative**. The statement is about desirability of a policy.

e. **Positive**. The statement is a prediction of the likely effects of a policy, not a recommendation on whether the policy should be used.

17.5 a. **Macroeconomists**. Government spending and the unemployment rate are aggregate concepts pertaining to the national economy.

b. **Microeconomists**. Microsoft, though large, is an individual firm.

c. **Microeconomists**. The issue relates to the supply and demand for a specific service, education.

d. **Macroeconomists**. Inflation is an aggregate, economywide concept.

e. **Macroeconomists**. Average saving is an aggregate concept.

f. **Microeconomists**. The focus is on a relatively narrow set of markets and products rather than on the economy as a whole.

## References

Gordon, R. J. (2004) 'Two Centuries of Economic Growth: Europe Chasing the American Frontier', NBER Working Paper, 10662.

OECD (2003) *The World Economy: Historical Statistics* (Paris: OECD Development Centre)

# 18

# Measuring Economic Activity: GDP and Unemployment

> Economic growth slowed to 1 per cent last quarter ...
>
> Inflation appears subdued as the consumer price index registered an increase of only 0.2 per cent last month. ...
>
> The unemployment rate last month reached its highest level since 1999. ...

News reports like these fill the airwaves – some TV and radio stations carry nothing else. In fact, all kinds of people are interested in economic data. The average person hopes to learn something that will be useful in a business decision, a financial investment or a career move. The professional economist depends on economic data in much the same way that a doctor depends on a patient's vital signs – pulse, blood pressure and temperature – to make an accurate diagnosis. To understand economic developments and to be able to give useful advice to policy makers, businesspeople and financial investors, an economist must have up-to-date, accurate data. Political leaders and policy makers also need economic data to help them in their decisions and planning.

Interest in *measuring the economy*, and attempts to do so, date back as far as the mid-seventeenth century, when Sir William Petty (1623–87) conducted a detailed survey of the land and wealth of Ireland. The British government's purpose in commissioning the survey was to determine the capacity of the Irish people to pay taxes to the Crown. But Petty used the opportunity to measure a variety of social and economic variables and went on to conduct pioneering studies of wealth, production and population in several other countries. A firm believer in the idea that scientific progress depends first and foremost on accurate measurement, he once interrupted a meeting of the British Royal Society (a distinguished association of scientists, of which Petty was a founding member) to correct a speaker who had used the phrase 'considerably bigger'. A rule should be passed barring such vague terms, Petty proposed, so that 'no word might be used but what marks either number, weight, or measure'.[1]

Not until the twentieth century did economic measurement come into its own. The Second World War was an important catalyst for the development of accurate economic statistics, since its very outcome was thought to depend on the mobilization of economic resources. Two economists, Simon Kuznets in the United States and Richard Stone in the

[1] This story reported by Charles H. Hull (Hull 1900).

United Kingdom, developed comprehensive systems for measuring a nation's *output of goods and services*, which were of great help to Allied leaders in their wartime planning. Kuznets and Stone each received a Nobel Prize in Economics for their work, which became the basis for the economic accounts used today by almost all the world's countries.

In this chapter and Chapter 19 we shall discuss how economists measure three basic macroeconomic variables that arise frequently in analyses of the state of the economy: the **gross domestic product** (or **GDP**), the *rate of unemployment* and the *rate of inflation*. The focus of this chapter is on the first two of these statistics, GDP and the unemployment rate, which both measure the overall level of economic activity in a country.

**gross domestic product (GDP)** the market value of the final goods and services produced in a country during a given period

Measuring economic activity might sound like a straightforward and uncontroversial task, but that is not the case. Indeed, the basic measure of a nation's output of goods and services, GDP, has been criticised on many grounds. Some critics have complained that GDP does not adequately reflect factors such as the distribution of income and the effect of economic growth on the environment. Because of problems like these, they charge, policies based on GDP statistics are likely to be flawed. Unemployment statistics have also been the subject of some controversy. By the end of this chapter you will understand how official measures of output and unemployment are constructed and used, and will have gained some insight into these debates over their accuracy. Understanding the *strengths and limitations of economic data* is the first critical step toward becoming an intelligent user of economic statistics, as well as a necessary background for the economic analysis in the chapters to come.

## Gross domestic product: measuring the economy's output

Chapter 17 emphasised the link between an economy's output of goods and services and its living standard. We noted that high levels of output per person, and per worker, are typically associated with a high standard of living. But what, exactly, does 'output' mean? To study economic growth and productivity scientifically, we need to be more precise about how economists define and measure an economy's output.

The most frequently used measure of an economy's output is called *GDP*. GDP is intended to measure how much an economy produces in a given period, such as a quarter (three months) or a year. More precisely, GDP is the market value of the *final goods and services* produced in a country during a given period. To understand this definition, let us take it apart and examine each of its parts separately. The first key phrase in the definition is 'market value'.

### Market value

A modern economy produces many different goods and services, from toothpaste (a good) to acupuncture (a service). Macroeconomists are not interested in this kind of detail, however; rather, their goal is to understand the behaviour of the economy as a whole. For example, a macroeconomist might ask: Has the overall capacity of the economy to produce goods and services increased over time? If so, by how much?

To be able to talk about concepts such as the 'total output' or 'total production' – as opposed to the production of specific items such as toothpaste – economists need to *aggregate* the quantities of the many different goods and services into a single number. They do so by adding up the *market values* of the different goods and services the economy produces. A simple example will illustrate the process. In the imaginary economy of Orchardia, total production is 4 apples and 6 bananas. To find the total output of Orchardia, we could add the number of apples to the number of bananas and conclude that total output is 10 pieces of fruit. But what if this economy also produced 3 pairs of shoes? There really is no sensible way to add apples and bananas to shoes.

Suppose, though, that we know that apples sell for €0.25 each, bananas for €0.50 each and shoes for €20.00 a pair. Then the market value of this economy's production, or its GDP, is equal to

(4 apples × €0.25/apple) + (6 bananas × €0.50/banana) + (3 pairs of shoes × €20/pair) = €64.00

Notice that when we calculate total output this way, the more expensive items (the shoes) receive a higher weighting than the cheaper items (the apples and bananas). In general, the amount that people are willing to pay for an item is an indication of the *economic benefit* they expect to receive from it (see Chapter 3). For this reason, higher-priced items should count for more in a measure of aggregate output.

### Example 18.1 Orchardia's GDP

Suppose Orchardia were to produce 3 apples, 3 bananas and 4 pairs of shoes at the same prices as above. What is its GDP now? Now the Orchardian GDP is equal to

(3 apples × €0.25/apple) + (3 bananas × €0.50/banana) + (4 pairs of shoes × €20/pair) = €82.25

Notice that the market value of Orchardian GDP is higher in Example 18.1 than earlier, even though two of the three goods (apples and bananas) are being produced in smaller quantities than before. The reason is that the good whose production has increased (shoes) is much more valuable than the goods whose production has decreased (apples and bananas).

**Exercise 18.1**

Suppose Orchardia produces the same quantities of the three goods as originally at the same prices (see the discussion preceding Example 18.1). In addition, it produces 5 oranges at €0.30 each. What is the GDP of Orchardia now?

**Exercise 18.2**

The following are assumed monthly data on German production of passenger cars and other light vehicles (a category that includes minivans, light trucks and sports utility vehicles). The data are broken down into two categories: German car producers (Volkswagen, BMW, etc.) and foreign-owned plants (such as General Motors). The average selling price is €17,000 for passenger cars and €25,000 for other light vehicles.

| Producer | Passenger cars | Other light vehicles |
|---|---|---|
| German producers | 471,000 | 714,000 |
| Foreign-owned plants | 227,000 | 63,000 |

Compare the output of German producers to that of foreign-owned plants in terms of both the total number of vehicles produced and their market values (contribution to GDP). Explain why the two measures give different impressions of the relative importance of production by German-owned and foreign-owned plants.

*Market values* provide a convenient way to add together, or aggregate, the many different goods and services produced in a modern economy. A drawback of using market values, however, is that not all economically valuable goods and services are bought and sold in markets. For example, the unpaid work of a home maker, although it is of economic value, is not sold in markets and so is not counted in GDP. But paid housekeeping and child care services, which are sold in markets, do count. This distinction can create some pitfalls, as Example 18.2 shows.

**Example 18.2** Women's labour force participation and GDP measurement

The percentage of adult women working outside the home has increased dramatically since the 1960s. In the United Kingdom the percentage of females of working age who are classified as either working or actively seeking work has increased from less than 50 per cent in 1960 to about 70 per cent today. Similar trends have been observed in other European and North American countries This trend has led to a substantial increase in the demand for paid day care and housekeeping services, as working wives and mothers require more help at home. How have these changes affected measured GDP? The entry of many women into the labour market has raised measured GDP in two ways. First, the goods and services that women produce in their new jobs have contributed directly to increasing GDP. Second, the fact that paid workers took over previously unpaid housework and child care duties has increased measured GDP by the amount paid to those workers. The first of these two changes represents a genuine increase in economic activity, but the second reflects a transfer of existing economic activities from the unpaid sector to the market sector. Overall, then, the increase in measured GDP associated with increased participation in the labour force by women probably overstates the actual increase in economic activity.

## Economic naturalist 18.1 Why has female participation in the labour market increased by so much?

In a world governed only by economic principles – without social conventions, customs or traditions – home-making tasks such as cleaning, cooking and child rearing would be jobs like any other. As such, they would be subject to the principle of *comparative advantage*: those people (either men or women) whose comparative advantage lay in performing home-making tasks would specialise in them, freeing people whose comparative advantage lay elsewhere to work outside the home. In other words, home-making tasks would be done by those with the lowest opportunity cost in those tasks. In such a world, to see a woman with a medical degree doing housework would be very unusual – her opportunity cost of doing housework would be too high.

But of course we don't live in a world driven only by economic considerations. Traditionally, *social custom* has severely limited the economic opportunities of women (and in some societies it still does). However, social restrictions on women have weakened considerably since 1900, particularly in the industrialised countries, as a result of the increased educational attainment of women, the rise of the feminist movement and other factors. As traditional social restraints on women have loosened, domestic arrangements have moved in the direction dictated by comparative advantage – to an increasing degree, home-making tasks are now performed by paid specialists, while the majority of women (and men) work outside the home.

Although home-making activities are excluded from measured GDP, in a few cases goods and services that are not sold in markets are included in GDP. By far the most important are the goods and services provided by national and local governments. The protection provided by the army and navy, the transportation convenience of highway systems and the education provided by the state-funded school system are examples of publicly provided goods and services that are not sold in markets. As market prices for publicly provided goods and services do not exist, economic statisticians add to the GDP the *costs* of providing those goods and services as rough measures of their economic value. For example, to include public education in the GDP, the statisticians add to GDP the salaries of teachers and administrators, the costs of textbooks and supplies and the like. Similarly, the economic value of the national defence establishment is approximated, for the purposes of measuring GDP, by the *costs* of defence: the pay earned by soldiers and sailors, the costs of acquiring and maintaining weapons and so on.

With a few exceptions, like publicly provided goods and services, GDP is calculated by adding up market values. However, not all goods and services that have a market value are counted in GDP. As we shall see next, GDP includes only those goods and services that are the end products of the production process, called *final goods and services*. Goods and services that are used up in the production process are not counted in GDP.

## Final goods and services

Many goods are used in the production process. Before a baker can produce a loaf of bread, grain must be grown and harvested, the grain must then be ground into flour and, together with other ingredients, baked into bread. Of the three major goods that are produced during this process – the grain, the flour and the bread – only the bread is used by consumers. Because producing the bread is the ultimate purpose of the process, the bread is called a *final good*. In general, a **final good or service** is the end product of a process, the product or service that consumers actually use. The goods or services produced on the way toward making the final product – here, the grain and the flour – are called **intermediate goods or services**.

**final goods or services** goods or services consumed by the ultimate user; because they are the end products of the production process, they are counted as part of GDP

**intermediate goods or services** goods or services used up in the production of final goods and services and therefore not counted as part of GDP

Since we are interested in measuring only those items that are of direct economic value, only final goods and services are included in GDP. Intermediate goods and services are *not* included. To illustrate, suppose that the grain from the previous example has a market value of €0.50 (the price the milling company paid for the grain). The grain is then ground into flour, which has a market value of €1.20 (the price the baker paid for the flour). Finally, the flour is made into a loaf of fine French bread, worth €2.00 at the local supermarket. In calculating the contribution of these activities to GDP, would we want to add together the values of the grain, the flour and the bread? No, because the grain and flour are intermediate goods, valuable only because they can be used to make bread. So in this example, the total contribution to GDP is €2.00, the value of the loaf of bread, the *final product*.

Example 18.3 illustrates the same distinction, but this time with a focus on services.

### Example 18.3 The barber and his assistant

Your barber charges €20 for a haircut. In turn, the barber pays his assistant €5 per haircut in return for sharpening the scissors, sweeping the floor and other chores. For each haircut given, what is the total contribution of the barber and his assistant, taken together, to GDP?

The answer to this problem is €20, the price, or market value, of the haircut. The haircut is counted in GDP because it is the *final service*, the one that actually has value to the final user. The services provided by the assistant have value only because they contribute to the production of the haircut; thus they are not counted in GDP.

Example 18.4 illustrates that the same good can be either intermediate or final, depending on how it is used.

### Example 18.4 A good that can be either intermediate or final

Farmer Brown produces €100 worth of milk. He sells €40 worth of milk to his neighbours and uses the rest to feed his pigs, which he sells at his local market for €120. What is Farmer Brown's contribution to GDP?

The final goods in this example are the €40 worth of milk and the €120 worth of pigs sold at market. Adding €40 and €120, we get €160, which is Farmer Brown's contribution to GDP. Note that part of the milk Farmer Brown produced serves as an intermediate good and part as a final good. The €60 worth of milk that is fed to the pigs is an intermediate good, and so it is not counted in GDP. The €40 worth of milk sold to the neighbours is a final good, and so it is counted.

A special type of good that is difficult to classify as intermediate or final is a **capital good**. A capital good is a long-lived good, which is itself produced and used to produce other goods and services. Factories and machines are examples of capital goods. Capital goods do not fit the definition of final goods, since their purpose is to *produce other goods*. On the other hand, they are not used up during the production process, except over a very long period, so they are not exactly intermediate goods either. For purposes of measuring GDP, economists have agreed to classify newly produced capital goods as final goods. Otherwise, a country that invested in its future by building modern factories and buying new machines would be counted as having a lower GDP than a country that devoted all its resources to producing consumer goods.

**capital good** a long-lived good, which is itself produced and used to produce other goods and services

We have established the rule that only final goods and services (including newly produced capital goods) are counted in GDP. Intermediate goods and services, which are used up in the production of final goods and services, are not counted. In practice, however, this rule is not easy to apply, because the production process often stretches over several periods. To illustrate, recall the earlier example of the grain that was milled into flour, which in turn was baked into a loaf of French bread. The contribution of the whole process to GDP is €2, the value of the bread (the final product). Suppose, though, that the grain and the flour were produced near the end of the year 2002 and the bread was baked early the next year in 2003. In this case, should we attribute the €2 value of the bread to GDP for 2002 or to GDP for 2003?

Neither choice seems quite right, since part of the bread's production process occurred in each year. Part of the value of the bread should probably be counted in the year 2002 GDP and part in the year 2003 GDP. But how should we make the split? To deal with this problem, economists determine the market value of final goods and services indirectly, by adding up the **value added** by each firm in the production process. The value added by any firm equals the market value of its product or service minus the cost of inputs purchased from other firms. As we shall see, *summing the value added by all firms* (including producers of both intermediate and final goods and services) gives the same answer as simply adding together the value of final goods and services. But the value added method eliminates the problem of dividing the value of a final good or service between two periods.

**value added** for any firm, the market value of its product or service minus the cost of inputs purchased from other firms

To illustrate this method, let us revisit the example of French bread, which is the result of multiple stages of production. We have already determined that the total contribution of this production process to GDP is €2, the value of the bread. Let us show now that we can get the same answer by summing value added. Suppose that the bread is the ultimate product of three corporations: ABC Grain Company, Inc., produces grain; General Flour produces flour; and Hot'n'Fresh Baking produces the bread. If we make the same assumptions as before about the market value of the grain, the flour and the bread, what is the value added by each of these three companies?

ABC Grain Company produces €0.50 worth of grain, with no inputs from other companies, so ABC's value added is €0.50. General Flour uses €0.50 worth of grain from ABC to produce €1.20 worth of flour. The value added by General Flour is thus the value of its product (€1.20) less the cost of purchased inputs (€0.50), or €0.70. Finally, Hot'n'Fresh Baking buys €1.20 worth of flour from General Flour and uses it to produce €2.00 worth of bread. So the value added by Hot'n'Fresh is €0.80. These calculations are summarised in Table 18.1.

| Company | Revenues (€) | – Cost of purchased inputs (€) | = Value added (€) |
|---|---|---|---|
| ABC Grain | 0.50 | 0.00 | 0.50 |
| General Flour | 1.20 | 0.50 | 0.70 |
| Hot'n'Fresh | 2.00 | 1.20 | 0.80 |
| Total | | | 2.00 |

**Table 18.1** Value Added in Bread Production

You can see that summing the value added by each company gives the same contribution to GDP, €2.00, as the method based on counting final goods and services only. Basically, the value added by each firm represents the portion of the value of the final good or service that the firm creates in its stage of production. Summing the value added by all firms in the economy yields the total value of final goods and services, or GDP.

You can also see now how the value added method solves the problem of production processes that bridge two or more periods. Suppose that the grain and flour are produced during 2002 but the bread is not baked until 2003. Using the value added method, the contribution of this production process to 2002 GDP is the value added by the grain company plus the value added by the flour company, or €1.20. The contribution of the production process to 2003 GDP is the value added by the baker, which is €0.80. Thus part of the value of the final product, the bread, is counted in the GDP for each year, reflecting the fact that part of the production of the bread took place in each year.

**Exercise 18.3**

Amy's card shop receives a shipment of Valentine's Day cards in December 2002. Amy pays the wholesale distributor of the cards a total of €500. In February 2003 she sells the cards for a total of €700. What are the contributions of these transactions to GDP in 2002 and 2003?

We have now established that GDP is equal to the market value of final goods and services. Let us look at the last part of the definition, 'produced within a country during a given period'.

## Produced within a country during a given period

The word 'domestic' in the term 'gross domestic product' tells us that GDP is a measure of *economic activity* within a given country. Thus, only production that takes place within the country's borders is counted. For example, German GDP includes the market value of *all* cars produced within German borders, even if they are made in foreign-owned plants (recall Exercise 18.2). However, cars produced in the Czech Republic by a German-owned company such as Volkswagen are *not* counted. The market value of these cars are part of *Czech GDP*.

We have seen that GDP is intended to measure the amount of production that occurs during a given period, such as the calendar year. For this reason, only goods and services that are *actually produced* during a particular year are included in GDP for that year. Example 18.5 and Exercise 18.4 illustrate this.

### **Example 18.5** The sale of a house and GDP

A 20-year-old house in Manchester is sold to a young family for £200,000. The family uses an estate agent to find the house and pays a 5 per cent commission (or £10,000). The family also has to pay a solicitor a 3 per cent commission (or £6,000) to take care of the legal work. What is the contribution of this transaction to GDP?

Because the house was not produced during the current year, its value is *not* counted in this year's GDP. (The value of the house was included in the GDP 20 years earlier, the year the house was built.) In general, purchases and sales of existing assets, such as old houses or used cars, do not contribute to the current year's GDP. However, the £10,000 fee paid to the estate agent and the £6,000 paid to the solicitor represent the market value of the services the family purchased when buying the house. Since those services were provided during the current year, they are counted in current-year GDP. Hence the transaction contributes £16,000 to current-year GDP.

**Exercise 18.4** Joan Smith sells 100 shares in a low-fares airline called FlyEuro.Com for €50 per share. She pays her broker a 2 per cent commission for executing the sale. How does Joan's transaction affect the current-year GDP?

## RECAP Measuring GDP

**Gross domestic product (GDP) equals**

- **the market value**
  GDP is an *aggregate* of the market values of the many goods and services produced in the economy. Goods and services that are *not sold in markets*, such as unpaid housework, are not counted in GDP. An important exception is goods and services provided by the government, which are included in GDP at the government's cost of providing them.

- **of final goods and services**
  *Final goods and services* (which include capital goods, such as factories and machines) are counted in GDP. *Intermediate goods and services*, which are used up in the production of final goods and services, are not counted. In practice, the value of final goods and services is determined by the *value added method*. The value added by any firm equals the firm's revenue from selling its product minus the cost of inputs purchased from other firms. Summing the value added by all firms in the production process yields the value of the final good or service.

- **produced in a country during a given period**
  Only goods and services produced *within a nation's borders* are included in GDP.
  Only goods and services produced during the *current year* (or the portion of the value produced during the current year) are counted as part of the current-year GDP.

# The expenditure method for measuring GDP

GDP is a measure of the quantity of final goods and services *produced* by an economy. But any good or service that is produced will also be *purchased* and used by some economic agent – a consumer buying Christmas gifts or a firm investing in new machinery, for example. For many purposes, knowing not only how much is produced, but who *uses it* and *how*, is important.

Economic statisticians divide the users of the final goods and services that make up the GDP for any given year into four categories: *households, firms, governments* and the *foreign sector* (that is, foreign purchasers of domestic products). They assume that all the final goods and services that are produced in a country in a given year will be purchased and used by members of one or more of these four groups. Furthermore, the amounts that purchasers spend on various goods and services should be equal to the market values of those goods and services. As a result, GDP can be measured with equal accuracy by either of two methods: (1) adding up the market values of all the final goods and services that are produced domestically, or (2) adding up the total amount spent by each of the four groups on final goods and services and subtracting spending on imported goods and services. The values obtained by the two methods will be the same.

Corresponding to the four groups of final users are four components of expenditure: consumption, investment, government purchases and net exports. That is, households consume, firms invest, governments make government purchases and the foreign sector buys the nation's exports. Table 18.2 gives the values for each of these components for the British economy in 2003. Detailed definitions of the components of expenditure, and their principal sub-components, follow.

| | | |
|---|---|---|
| Consumption | | 721,083 |
| Investment | | 181,420 |
| Fixed investment[1] | 178,916 | |
| Inventory investment | + 2,504 | |
| Government purchases | | 229,892 |
| Net exports | | - 32,673 |
| Exports | 277,539 | |
| Imports | 310,212 | |
| | | 1,099,722 |

**Table 18.2** Expenditure Components of UK GDP, 2003 (£ million)

Note: 1. Fixed investment includes business and residential investment.

*Source*: *Economic Trends* (2004).

**consumption expenditure** (or **consumption**) spending by households on goods and services, such as food, clothing and entertainment

**Consumption expenditure** (or simply **consumption**) is spending by households on goods and services such as food, clothing and entertainment. Consumption expenditure is sub-divided into three sub-categories:

- *Consumer durables* are long-lived consumer goods such as cars and furniture. Note that new houses are not treated as consumer durables but as part of investment.
- *Consumer non-durables* are shorter-lived goods such as food and clothing.
- *Services*, a large component of consumer spending, include everything from haircuts and taxi rides to legal, financial and educational services.

**investment** spending by firms on final goods and services, primarily capital goods and housing

**Investment** is spending by firms on final goods and services, primarily capital goods and housing. Investment is divided into three sub-categories:

- *Business fixed investment* is the purchase by firms of *new capital goods* such as machinery, factories and office buildings. (Remember that for the purposes of calculating GDP, long-lived capital goods are treated as final goods rather than as intermediate goods.) Firms buy capital goods to increase their capacity to produce.
- *Residential investment* is construction of *new homes and flats*. For GDP accounting purposes, residential investment is treated as an investment by the business sector, which then sells the homes to households.
- *Inventory investment* is the addition of *unsold goods* to company inventories. In other words, the goods that a firm produces but doesn't sell during the current period are treated, for accounting purposes, as if the firm had bought those goods from itself. (This convention guarantees that production equals expenditure.) Inventory investment can take a negative value if the value of inventories on hand falls over the course of the year.

People often refer to purchases of financial assets, such as shares as 'investments'. That use of the term is different from the definition we give here. A person who buys a share issued by British Airways acquires partial ownership of the *existing* physical and financial assets controlled by the company. A share purchase does not usually correspond to the creation of *new* physical capital, however, and so is not 'investment' in the sense we are using the term in this chapter. We shall generally refer to purchases of financial assets, such as stocks and bonds, as 'financial investments', to distinguish them from a firm's investment in new capital goods, such as factories and machines. Indeed, as we shall see in Chapter 24, purchases of financial assets are a means by which households accumulate wealth and are really a form of saving rather than investment.

**Government purchases** are expenditures by central and local governments on final goods and services, such as computers, fighter planes, consultancy services and salaries paid to police, civil servants and schoolteachers. Government purchases do *not* include *transfer payments*, which are payments made by the government in return for which no current goods or services are received. Examples of transfer payments (which, again, are *not* included in government purchases) are unemployment benefits, pensions paid to government workers and welfare payments. Interest paid on the government debt is also excluded from government purchases.

**government purchases** purchases by central and local governments of final goods and services; government purchases do *not* include *transfer payments*, which are payments made by the government in return for which no current goods or services are received, nor do they include interest paid on the government debt

**net exports** exports minus imports

**Net exports** equal exports minus imports:

- *Exports* are domestically produced final goods and services that are sold abroad.
- *Imports* are purchases by domestic buyers of goods and services that were produced abroad. Imports are subtracted from exports to find the net amount of spending on domestically produced goods and services.

A country's net exports reflect the *net* demand by the rest of the world for its goods and services. Net exports can be negative, since imports can exceed exports in any given year.

The relationship between GDP and expenditures on goods and services can be summarised by an equation. Let

$Y$ = GDP, or output

$C$ = consumption expenditure

$I$ = investment

$G$ = government purchases

$NX$ = net exports

Using these symbols, we can write that GDP equals the sum of the four types of expenditure algebraically as

$$Y = C + I + G + NX$$

### Example 18.6 Measuring GDP by production and by expenditure

To illustrate the equivalence between the production and expenditure methods of measuring GDP, assume that the economy produces one good, automobiles. In a given year 1,000 automobiles are produced valued at €10,000 each.

Of these, 700 are sold to consumers, 200 are sold to businesses, 50 are sold to the government and 25 are exported abroad. No automobiles are imported. The automobiles left unsold at the end of the year are held in inventory by the auto producers. Find GDP in terms of (a) the market value of production and (b) the components of expenditure. You should get the same answer both ways.

The market value of the production of final goods and services in this economy is 1,000 autos × €10,000 per auto, or €10 million.

To measure GDP in terms of expenditure, we must add spending on consumption, investment, government purchases and net exports. Consumption is 700 autos × €10,000, or €7 million. Government purchases are 50 autos × €10,000, or €0.5 million. Net exports are equal to exports (25 autos at €10,000, or €0.25 million) – imports (0), so net exports are €0.25 million.

But what about investment? Here we must be careful. The 200 autos that are sold to businesses, worth €2 million, count as investment. But notice, too, that the auto companies produced 1,000 automobiles but sold only 975 (700 + 200 + 50 + 25). Hence 25 autos were unsold at the end of the year and were added to the automobile producers' inventories. This addition to producer inventories (25 autos @ €10,000, or €0.25 million) counts as inventory investment, which is part of total investment. Thus total investment spending equals the €2 million worth of autos sold to businesses plus the €0.25 million in inventory investment, or €2.25 million.

Total expenditure is $C + I + G + NX$ = €7 million + €2.25 million + €0.5 million + €0.25 = €10 million, the same as the market value of production.

**Exercise 18.5** Extending Example 18.6, suppose that 25 of the automobiles purchased by households are imported rather than domestically produced. Domestic production remains at 1,000 autos valued at €10,000 each. Once again, find GDP in terms of (a) the market value of production and (b) the components of expenditure.

## RECAP Expenditure components of GDP

GDP can be expressed as the sum of expenditures on domestically produced final goods and services. The four types of expenditure that are counted in the GDP, and the economic groups that make each type of expenditure, are as follows:

| Who makes the expenditure? | Type of expenditure | Examples |
|---|---|---|
| Households | Consumption | Food, clothes, haircuts, new cars |
| Business firms | Investment | New factories and equipment, new houses, increases in inventory stocks |
| Governments | Government purchases | New school buildings, new military hardware, salaries of soldiers, teachers and government officials |
| Foreign sector | Net exports, or exports minus imports | Exported manufactured goods, legal or financial services provided by domestic residents to foreigners |

## GDP and the incomes of capital and labour

GDP can be thought of equally well as a measure of *total production* or as a measure of *total expenditure* – either method of calculating GDP gives the same final answer. There is yet a third way to think of GDP, which is as the *incomes of capital and labour*.

Whenever a good or service is produced or sold, the revenue from the sale is distributed to the workers and the owners of the capital involved in the production of the good or service. Thus, except for some technical adjustments that we will ignore, GDP also equals labour income plus capital income. *Labour income* comprises wages, salaries and the incomes of the self-employed. *Capital income* is made up of payments to owners of physical capital (such as factories, machines and office buildings) and intangible capital (such as copyrights and patents). The components of capital income include items such as profits earned by business owners, the rents paid to owners of land or buildings, interest received by bondholders and the royalties received by the holders of copyrights or patents. Both labour income and capital income are to be understood as measured prior to payment of taxes; ultimately, of course, a portion of both types of income is captured by the government in the form of tax collections.

Figure 18.1 may help you visualise the three equivalent ways of thinking about GDP: the market value of production, the total value of expenditure and the sum of labour income and capital income. Figure 18.1 also roughly captures the relative importance of the expenditure and income components. For many Western economies, about 65 per cent of expenditure is consumption spending, about 20 per cent is government purchases and the rest is investment spending and net exports. Labour income is about 75 per cent of total income, with capital income making up the rest.

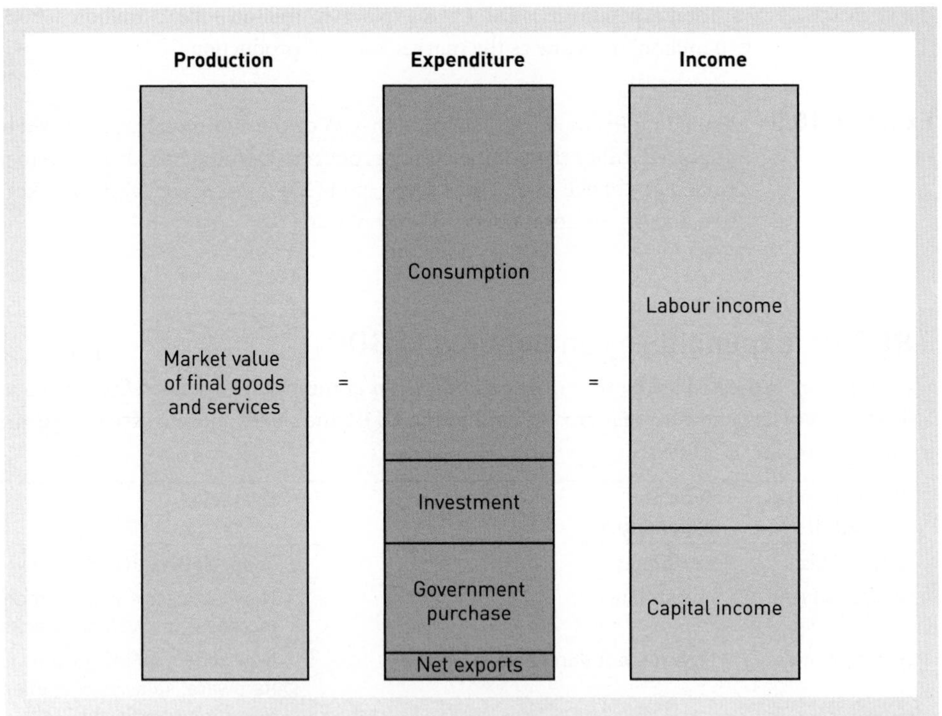


**Figure 18.1 The Three Faces of GDP.** GDP can be expressed equally well as (1) the market value of production, (2) total expenditure (consumption, investment, government purchases, net exports), or (3) total income (labour income and capital income).

## Nominal GDP versus real GDP

As a measure of the total production of an economy over a given period, such as a particular year, GDP is useful in comparisons of economic activity in different countries. For example, GDP data for 2004, broken down country by country, could be used to compare aggregate production in France and Germany during that year. However, economists are interested in comparing levels of economic activity not only in different *countries* but *over time* as well. For example, a government running for re-election on the basis of successful economic policies might want to know by how much GDP had increased during its term.

As the following example shows, using GDP to compare economic activity at two different points in time may give misleading answers. Suppose for the sake of illustration that the economy produces only computers and cameras. The prices and quantities of the two goods in 2000 and 2004, the beginning and end of the government's term, are shown in Table 18.3. If we calculate GDP in each year as the market value of production, we find that the GDP for 2000 is (10 computers × €1,000/computer) + (15 cameras × €100/camera) = €11,500. The GDP for 2004 is (20 computers × €1,200/computer) + (30 cameras × €110/camera) = €27,300. Comparing the GDP for 2004 to the GDP for 2000, we might conclude that it is 2.4 times greater (€27,300/€11,500).

| Year | Quantity of computers | Price of computers (€) | Quantity of cameras | Price of cameras (€) |
|---|---|---|---|---|
| 2000 | 10 | 1,000 | 15 | 100 |
| 2004 | 20 | 1,200 | 30 | 110 |

**Table 18.3** Prices and Quantities, 2000 and 2004

But look more closely at the data given in Table 18.3. Can you see what is wrong with this conclusion? The quantities of both computers and cameras produced in 2004 are exactly twice the quantities produced in 2000. If economic activity, as measured by actual production of both goods, exactly doubled over the four years, why do the calculated values of GDP show a greater increase?

The answer, as you also can see from Table 18.3, is that *prices* as well as *quantities* rose between 2000 and 2004. Because of the increase in prices, the *market value* of production grew more over those four years than the *physical volume* of production. So in this case, GDP is a misleading gauge of economic growth during the government's term, since the physical quantities of the goods and services produced in any given year, not the money values, are what determine people's economic well-being. Indeed, if the quantities produced had remained constant but the prices of computers and cameras had risen 2.4 times between 2000 and 2004, GDP would have risen 2.4 times as well, with no increase in physical production! In that case, the claim that the economy's (physical) output had more than doubled would obviously be wrong.

**real GDP** a measure of GDP in which the quantities produced are valued at the prices in a base year rather than at current prices; real GDP measures the actual *physical volume* of production

**nominal GDP** a measure of GDP in which the quantities produced are valued at current-year prices; nominal GDP measures the *current money value* of production

As this example shows, if we want to use GDP to compare economic activity at different points in time, we need some method of excluding the effects of price changes. In other words, we need to *adjust for inflation*. To do so, economists use a common set of prices to value quantities produced in different years. The standard approach is to pick a particular year, called the *base year*, and use the prices from that year to calculate the market value of output. When GDP is calculated using the prices from a base year, rather than the current year's prices, it is called **real GDP**, to indicate that it is a measure of *real physical production*. Real GDP is GDP adjusted for inflation. To distinguish real GDP, in which quantities produced are valued at base-year prices, from GDP valued at current-year prices, economists refer to the latter measure as **nominal GDP**.

### Example 18.7 Calculating the change in real GDP

Using data from Table 18.3 and assuming that 2000 is the base year, find real GDP for 2004 and 2000. By how much did real output grow between 2000 and 2004?

To find real GDP for the year 2004, we must value the quantities produced that year using the prices in the base year, 2000. Using the data in Table 18.3:

> Year 2004 real GDP = (year 2004 quantity of computers × year 2000 price of computers) + (year 2004 quantity of cameras × year 2000 price of cameras) = (20 × €1,000) + (30 × €100) = €23,000

The real GDP of this economy in 2004 is €23,000. What is the real GDP for 2000?

By definition, the real GDP for 2000 = 2000 quantities valued at base-year prices. The base year in this example happens to be 2000, so real GDP for 2000 equals 2000 quantities valued at 2000 prices, which is the same as nominal GDP for 2000. Hence real GDP for the base year 2000 is:

> Year 2000 real GDP = (year 2000 quantity of computers × year 2000 price of computers) + (year 2000 quantity of cameras × year 2000 price of cameras) = (10 × €1,000) + (15 × €100) = €11,500

In general, in the base year, real GDP and nominal GDP are the same. We can now determine how much real production has actually grown over the four-year period. Since real GDP was €11,500 in 2000 and €23,000 in 2004, the physical volume of production doubled between 2000 and 2004. This conclusion makes good sense, since Table 18.3 shows that the production of both computers and cameras exactly doubled over the period. By using real GDP, we have eliminated the effects of price changes and obtained a reasonable measure of the actual change in physical production over the four-year span.

In Example 18.7 the first year, 2000, was used as the base year. However, we get the same result if the last year, 2004, is used as the base year. Using 2004, as the base year, real GDP for 2000 is:

> Year 2000 real GDP = (year 2000 quantity of computers × year 2004 price of computers) + (year 2000 quantity of cameras × year 2004 price of cameras) = (10 × €1,200) + (15 × €110) = €13,650

As the base year real and nominal GDP are the same, using 2004 as the base year means that real GDP for 2004 is €27,300 which is exactly double real GDP for 2000. Hence we get the same result as using 2000 as the base year.

Of course, the production of all goods will not necessarily grow in equal proportion, as in Example 18.7. Exercise 18.6 asks you to find real GDP when computer and camera production grow at different rates.

**Exercise 18.6**

Suppose production and prices of computer and cameras in 2000 and 2004 are as follows:

| Year | Quantity of computers | Price of computers (€) | Quantity of cameras | Price of cameras (€) |
|---|---|---|---|---|
| 2000 | 10 | 1,000 | 15 | 100 |
| 2004 | 30 | 1,200 | 30 | 110 |

These data are the same as those in Table 18.3, except that computer production has tripled rather than doubled between 2000 and 2004. Find real GDP in 2004 and 2000, and calculate the growth in real output over the four-year period. (Continue to assume that 2000 is the base year.)

If you complete Exercise 18.6, you will find that the growth in real GDP between 2000 and 2004 reflects a sort of average of the growth in physical production of computers and cameras. Real GDP therefore remains a useful measure of overall physical production, even when the production of different goods and services grows at different rates.

**RECAP** Nominal GDP versus real GDP

Real GDP is calculated using the prices of goods and services that prevailed in a base year rather than in the current year. Nominal GDP is calculated using current-year prices. Real GDP is GDP adjusted for inflation; it may be thought of as measuring the physical volume of production. Comparisons of economic activity at different times should always be done using real GDP, not nominal GDP.

## Real GDP is not the same as economic well-being

Government policy makers pay close attention to real GDP, often behaving as if the greater the GDP, the better. However, real GDP is *not* the same as economic well-being. At best, it is an imperfect measure of economic well-being because, for the most part, it captures only those goods and services that are *priced and sold in markets*. Many factors that contribute to people's economic well-being are not priced and sold in markets and thus are largely or even entirely omitted from GDP. Maximising real GDP is not, therefore, always the right goal for government policy makers. Whether or not policies that increase GDP will also make people better off has to be determined on a case-by-case basis.

To understand why an increase in real GDP does not always promote economic well-being, let us look at some factors that are not included in GDP but do affect whether people are better off.

### Leisure time

Most Europeans (and most people in other industrialised countries as well) work many fewer hours than their great-grandparents did 100 years ago. Early in the twentieth century some industrial workers – steelworkers and coal miners, for example – worked as many as 12 hours a day, 7 days a week. Today, the 40-hour or shorter working week is typical. Today, most people also tend to start working later in life (after university or college) and, in many cases, they are able to retire earlier. The increased leisure time available to workers in industrialised countries – which allows them to pursue many worthwhile activities, including being with family and friends, participating in sports and hobbies, and pursuing cultural and educational activities – is a major benefit of living in a wealthy society. These extra hours of leisure are not priced in markets, however, and therefore are not reflected in GDP.

### Economic naturalist 18.2 Why do people work fewer hours today than their great-grandparents did?

Most Europeans start work later in life, retire earlier and in many cases work fewer hours per week than people of 50 or 100 years ago.

The *opportunity cost* of working less – retiring earlier, for example, or working fewer hours per week – is the earnings you forgo by not working. If you can make €400 per week at a summer job, for example, then leaving the job two weeks early to take a trip with some friends has an opportunity cost of €800. The fact that people are working fewer hours today suggests that their opportunity cost of forgone earnings is lower than their grandparents' and great-grandparents' opportunity cost. Why this difference?

Over the past century, rapid economic growth in industrialised countries has greatly increased the *purchasing power* of the average worker's wages (see Chapter 21). In other words, the typical worker today can buy more goods and services with his or her hourly earnings than ever before. This fact would seem to suggest that the opportunity cost of forgone earnings (measured in terms of what those earnings can buy) is greater, not smaller, today than in earlier times. But because the buying power of wages is so much higher today than in the past, Europeans can achieve a reasonable standard of living by working fewer hours than they did in the past. Thus, while your grandparents may have had to work long hours to pay the rent or put food on the table, today the extra income from working long hours is more likely to buy relative luxuries, like nicer clothes or a fancier car. Because such *discretionary purchases* are easier to give up than basic food and shelter, the true opportunity cost of forgone earnings is lower today than it was 50 years ago. As the opportunity cost of leisure has fallen, Europeans have chosen to enjoy more of it.

## Non-market economic activities

Not all economically important activities are bought and sold in markets; with a few exceptions, such as government services, non-market economic activities are omitted from GDP. We mentioned earlier the example of unpaid housekeeping services. Another example is volunteer services, such as the unpaid work for charity and aid agencies. The fact that these unpaid services are left out of GDP does *not* mean that they are unimportant. The problem is that, because there are no market prices and quantities for unpaid services, estimating their market values is very difficult.

How far do economists go wrong by leaving non-market economic activities out of GDP? The answer depends on the type of economy being studied. Although non-market economic activities exist in all economies, they are particularly important in poor economies. For example, in rural villages of developing countries, people commonly trade services with each other or co-operate on various tasks without exchanging any money. Families in these communities also tend to be relatively self-sufficient, growing their own food and providing many of their own basic services. Because such non-market economic activities are not counted in official statistics, GDP data may substantially understate the true amount of economic activity in the poorest countries. In 1999, according to the United Nations, the official GDP per person in Nepal was about €218, an amount that seems impossibly low. Part of the explanation for this figure is that, because the Nepalese seldom use formal markets, many economic activities that would ordinarily be included in GDP are excluded from it in Nepal.

Closely related to non-market activities is what is called the *underground economy*, which includes transactions that are never reported to government officials and data collectors. The underground economy encompasses both legal and illegal activities – from informal babysitting jobs to organised crime. For instance, some people pay temporary or part-time workers such as housecleaners and painters in cash, which allows these workers to avoid paying taxes on their income. Economists who have tried to estimate the value of such services by studying how much cash the public holds have concluded that these sorts of transactions are quite important, even in advanced industrial economies.

## Environmental quality and resource depletion

China has recently experienced tremendous growth in real GDP. But in expanding its manufacturing base, it has also suffered a severe decline in air and water quality. Increased pollution certainly detracts from the quality of life, but because air and water quality are not bought and sold in markets, the Chinese GDP does not reflect this downside of their economic growth.

The exploitation of finite natural resources also tends to be overlooked in GDP. When an oil company pumps and sells a barrel of oil, GDP increases by the value of the oil. But the fact that there is one fewer barrel of oil in the ground, waiting to be pumped sometime in the future, is not reflected in GDP.

A number of efforts have been made to incorporate factors such as air quality and resource depletion into a comprehensive measure of GDP. Doing so is difficult, since it often involves placing a euro value on *intangibles*, such as having a clean river to swim in instead of a dirty one. But the fact that the benefits of environmental quality and resource conservation are hard to measure in euros does not mean that they are unimportant.

### Quality of life

What makes a particular town or city an attractive place in which to live? Some desirable features you might think of are reflected in GDP: spacious, well-constructed homes, good restaurants and stores, a variety of entertainment and high-quality schools. However, other indicators of the good life are not sold in markets and so may be omitted from GDP. Examples include a low crime rate, minimal traffic congestion, active civic organisations and open space. Thus citizens of a rural area may be justified in opposing the construction of a new shopping centre because of its presumed negative effect on the quality of life – even though the new centre may increase GDP.

### Poverty and economic inequality

GDP measures the *total* quantity of goods and services produced and sold in an economy, but it conveys no information about who gets to enjoy those goods and services. Two countries may have identical GDPs but differ radically in the distribution of economic welfare across the population. Suppose, for example, that in one country – call it Equalia – most people have a comfortable middle-class existence; both extreme poverty and extreme wealth are rare. But in another country, Inequalia – which has the same real GDP as Equalia – a few wealthy families control the economy, and the majority of the population lives in poverty. While most people would say that Equalia has a better economic situation overall, that judgement would not be reflected in the GDPs of the two countries, which are the same.

In countries such as the United Kingdom and the United States, absolute poverty has been declining. Today, many families whose income is below today's official 'poverty line' own a television, a car and in some cases their own home. Some economists have argued that people who are considered 'poor' today live as well as many middle-class people did in the 1950s.

But, though absolute poverty seems to be decreasing, *inequality of income* has generally been rising. The chief executive officer of a large corporation may earn hundreds of times what the typical worker in the same firm receives. Psychologists tell us that people's economic satisfaction depends not only on their absolute economic position – the quantity and quality of food, clothing and shelter they have – but on what they have compared with what others have. If you own an old, dilapidated car but are the only person in your neighbourhood to have a car, you may feel privileged. But if everyone else in the neighbourhood owns a luxury car, you are likely to be less satisfied. To the extent that such comparisons affect people's well-being, *inequality* matters as well as absolute poverty. Again, because GDP focuses on total production rather than on the distribution of output, it does not capture the effects of inequality.

## GDP is related to economic well-being

You might conclude from the list of important factors omitted from the official figures that GDP is useless as a measure of economic welfare. Indeed, numerous critics have made that claim. Clearly, in evaluating the effects of a proposed economic policy, considering only the likely effects on GDP is not sufficient. Planners must also ask whether the policy will affect aspects of economic well-being that are not captured in GDP. Environmental regulations may reduce production of steel, for example, which reduces GDP. But that fact is not a sufficient basis on which to decide whether such regulations are good or bad. The right way to decide such questions is to apply the *Cost–Benefit Principle* (see Chapter 1). Are the benefits of cleaner air worth more to people than the costs the regulations impose in terms of lost output and lost jobs? If so, then the regulations should be adopted; otherwise, they should not.

Although looking at the effects of a proposed policy on real GDP is not a good enough basis on which to evaluate a policy, real GDP per person *does* tend to be positively associated with many things people value, including a high material standard of living, better health and life expectancies and better education. We discuss next some of the ways in which a higher real GDP implies greater economic well-being.

## Availability of goods and services

Obviously, citizens of a country with a high GDP are likely to possess more and better goods and services (after all, that is what GDP measures). On average, people in high-GDP countries enjoy larger, better-constructed and more comfortable homes, higher-quality food and clothing, a greater variety of entertainment and cultural opportunities, better access to transportation and travel, better communications and sanitation and other advantages. While social commentators may question the value of material consumption – and we agree that riches do not necessarily bring happiness or peace of mind – the majority of people in the world place great importance on achieving material prosperity.

## Health and education

Beyond an abundance of consumer goods, a high GDP brings other more basic advantages. Table 18.4 shows the differences between rich and poor countries with regard to some important indicators of well-being, including life expectancy, infant and child mortality rates, number of doctors, measures of nutrition and educational opportunity. Three groups of countries are compared: (1) developing countries as a group (total population, 4.6 billion); (2) the least developed countries (25 countries with a total population of about 600 million); and (3) the industrialised countries (25 countries, including the United States, Canada, the Western European countries and Japan, with a total population of 850 million). As the first row of Table 18.4 shows, these three groups of countries have radically different levels of GDP per person. Most notably, GDP per person in the industrialised countries is more than 20 times that of the least developed countries.[2]

How do these large differences in GDP relate to other measures of well-being? Table 18.4 shows that on some of the most basic measures of human welfare, the developing countries fare much worse than the industrial countries. A child born in one of the least developed countries has a 10 per cent (100/1,000) chance of dying before its first birthday and about a 16 per cent (159/1,000) chance of dying before its fifth birthday. The corresponding figures for the industrialised countries are 0.6 per cent (6/1,000) and 0.6 per cent (6/1,000), respectively. A child born in an industrialised country has a life expectancy of about 78 years, compared with about 52 years for a child born in one of the least developed countries. Superior nutrition, sanitation and medical services in the richer countries account for these large discrepancies in basic welfare. For treatment of the sick, industrialised countries have about 252 doctors per 100,000 people, compared to 30 doctors per 100,000 people in the least-developed countries. Doctors in

[2] The GDP data in Table 18.4 use US prices to value goods and services in developing nations. Since basic goods and services tend to be cheaper in poor countries, this adjustment significantly increases measured GDP in those countries.

| Indicator | All developing countries | Least developed countries | Industrialised countries |
|---|---|---|---|
| GDP per person ($) | 3,530 | 1,170 | 25,860 |
| Life expectancy at birth (years) | 64.5 | 51.7 | 78.0 |
| Infant mortality rate (per 1,000 live births) | 61 | 100 | 6 |
| Under-5 mortality rate (per 1,000 live births) | 89 | 159 | 6 |
| Doctors (per 100,000 people) | 78 | 30 | 252 |
| Incidence of HIV/AIDS (% in 15–49 age group) | 1.3 | 4.3 | 0.3 |
| Undernourished people (%) | 18 | 38 | Negligible |
| Primary school enrolment rate (as % of age group) | 85.7 | 60.4 | 99.9 |
| Secondary school enrolment rate (as % of age group) | 60.4 | 31.2 | 96.2 |
| Adult literacy rate (%) | 72.9 | 51.7 | 98.6 |

**Table 18.4** GDP and Basic Indicators of Well-Being

*Source*: United Nations, *Human Development Report* (2000–2001), available at http://hdr.undp.org/. All data are for 1999, except doctors per 100,000 people (1992–95), undernourished people (1996–98) and enrolment rates (1997). GDP data are adjusted to account for local differences in prices of basic commodities and services (adjusted for purchasing power parity, PPP).

the poorest countries, despite their fewer numbers, must contend with much higher rates of illness. For example, the incidence of HIV/AIDS in the least developed countries is 4.3 per cent of the population aged 15–49, about 14 times the rate in industrialised countries.

On another important dimension of human well-being, literacy and education rates, high-GDP countries also have the advantage. As Table 18.4 shows, in the industrialised countries the percentage of adults who can read and write exceeds 98 per cent, almost twice the percentage (52 per cent) in the poorest developing countries. The percentage of children of primary-school age who are enrolled in school is virtually 100 per cent in industrialised countries, compared with about 60 per cent in the least-developed countries. At the secondary (high-school) level the difference is even greater, with about 96 per cent of children enrolled in industrialised countries and 31 per cent enrolled in the poorest countries. Furthermore, enrolment rates do not capture important differences in the quality of education available in rich and poor countries, as measured by indicators such as the educational backgrounds of teachers and student–teacher ratios. Once again, the average person in an industrialised country seems to be better off than the average person in a poor developing country.

## Economic naturalist 18.3 Why do far fewer children complete high school in poor countries than in rich countries?

One possible explanation is that people in poor countries place a lower priority on getting an education than people in rich countries. But immigrants from poor countries often put a heavy emphasis on education – though it may be that people who emigrate from poor countries are unrepresentative of the population as a whole.

In economic naturalist's explanation for the lower schooling rates in poor countries would rely not on cultural differences but on differences in *opportunity cost*. In poor societies, most of which are heavily agricultural, children are an important source of labour. Beyond a certain age, sending children to school imposes a high opportunity cost on the family. Children who are in school are not available to help with planting, harvesting and other tasks that must be done if the family is to survive. In addition, the cost of books and school supplies imposes a major hardship on poor families. In rich, non-agricultural countries, school-age children have few work opportunities, and their potential earnings are small relative to other sources of family income. The low opportunity cost of sending children to school in rich countries is an important reason for the higher enrolment rates in those countries.

In Chapter 20 we shall discuss the costs and benefits of economic growth – which in practice means growth in real GDP per person – in greater depth. In that context, we shall return to the question of whether a growing real GDP must necessarily be equated with greater economic well-being.

### RECAP Real GDP and economic well-being

Real GDP is at best an imperfect measure of economic well-being. Among the factors affecting well-being *omitted from real GDP* are the availability of leisure time, non-market services such as unpaid home making and volunteer services, environmental quality and resource conservation and quality-of-life indicators such as a low crime rate. The GDP also does not reflect the degree of *economic inequality* in a country. Because real GDP is not the same as economic well-being, proposed policies should not be evaluated strictly in terms of whether or not they increase the GDP.

Although GDP is not the same as economic well-being, it is positively associated with many things that people value, including a higher material standard of living, better health, longer life expectancies and higher rates of literacy and educational attainment. This relationship between real GDP and economic well-being has led many people to emigrate from poor nations in search of a better life and has motivated policy makers in developing countries to try to increase their nations' rates of economic growth.

## The unemployment rate

In assessing the level of economic activity in a country, economists look at a variety of statistics. Besides real GDP, one statistic that receives much attention, from both economists and the general public, is the *rate of unemployment*. The **unemployment rate** is a sensitive indicator of conditions in the labour market. When the unemployment rate is low, jobs are secure and relatively easy to find. Low unemployment is often also associated with improving wages and working conditions, as employers compete to attract and retain workers.

**unemployment rate** the number of unemployed people divided by the labour force

We shall discuss labour markets and unemployment in detail in Chapter 21. This chapter will explain how the unemployment rate and some related statistics are defined and measured. It will close with a discussion of the costs of unemployment, to both the unemployed and to the economy as a whole.

### Measuring unemployment

In most countries a government agency publishes regular estimates of the numbers unemployed computed from the results of surveying randomly selected households. Although the precise methods may vary from country to country, most classify the population of working-age (normally over 15 or 16 years) into one of three categories:

1. *Employed* A person is employed if she worked *full-time or part-time* during the survey period or is on vacation or sick leave from a regular job.
2. *Unemployed* A person is unemployed if she is not employed but is *actively seeking employment.*
3. *Out of the labour force* A person is considered to be out of the labour force if she is *not employed or actively seeking employment*. In other words, people who are neither employed nor unemployed (in the sense of looking for work but not being able to find it) are 'out of the labour force'. Full-time students, unpaid home makers, retirees and people unable to work because of disabilities are examples of people who are out of the labour force.

Note the important distinction between unemployed who are *actively seeking employment* and those who are not working and are out of the labour force. The former are people who are not employed but will take a suitable job if offered. The latter are also people who are not employed but are not seeking employment. To find the unemployment rate, we must first calculate the size of the **labour force**. The labour force is defined as the total number of employed and unemployed people in the economy (the first two categories listed above). The unemployment rate is then defined as the number of unemployed people divided by the labour force. Notice that people who are out of the labour force (because they are in school, have retired or are disabled, for example) are not counted as unemployed and thus do not affect the unemployment rate. In general, a high rate of unemployment indicates that the economy is performing poorly.

**labour force** the total number of employed and unemployed people in the economy

**participation rate** the percentage of the working-age population in the labour force (that is, the percentage that is either employed or looking for work)

Another useful statistic is the **participation rate**, or the percentage of the working-age population in the labour force (that is, the percentage that is either employed or looking for work). The participation rate is calculated by dividing the labour force by the working-age (16+) population.

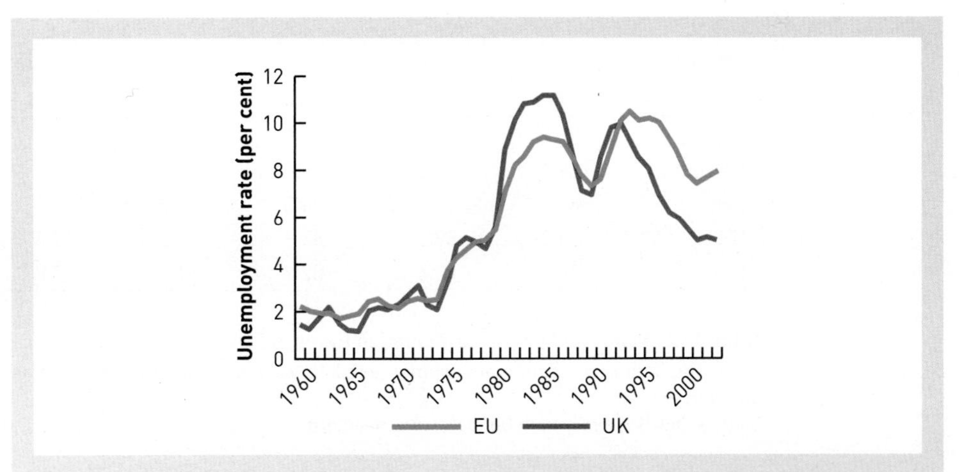


**Figure 18.2 Unemployment Rates for the United Kingdom and EU15, 1960–2003.** The unemployment rate or the percentage of the labour force that is unemployed was around 2 per cent in the 1960s and early 1970s. Throughout the 1960s and early years of the1970s European unemployment rates were exceptionally low but increased following the recessions at the start of each decade.

*Source*: *The European Economy*, Commission of the European Communities, www.europa_eu.int/comm_finance/publications.

Figure 18.2 shows unemployment rates for the United Kingdom and the EU15 since 1960. Throughout the 1960s and early 1970s European unemployment rates were exceptionally low but increased significantly from 1974–75 onwards. The rise in unemployment since the mid-1970s can be explained by a series of recessions which affected most Western countries in 1974, 1980, 1990 and 2001. Note that following the recession of 1990–91 British unemployment declined much more rapidly than the European average. Chapter 25 will look at these periods in greater detail.

Table 18.5 illustrates the calculation of key UK labour market statistics, using data published by the Office for National Statistics (ONS) (www.statistics.gov.uk) for the first quarter of 2004 (January, February, March). In that quarter, unemployment was 4.7 per cent of the labour force. The participation rate was 72.3 per cent – that is, more than two out of every three adults had a job or were looking for work.

| | |
|---|---|
| Employed | 28.346 |
| Plus: | |
| Unemployed | 1.413 |
| Equals: Labour force | 29.759 |
| Plus: | |
| Not in labour force | 17.378 |
| Equals: | |
| Working-age (16+) population | 47.137 |

**Table 18.5** UK Employment Data, First Quarter 2004 (millions)

*Notes*: 2004 Unemployment rate = unemployed/labour force = 1.413/29.759 = 4.7 per cent.
Participation rate = labour force/working-age population = 29.759/41.134 = 72.3 per cent.

Table 18.6 shows male and female participation rates for five EU countries in 1973, 1990 and 2003. For all countries, male participation rates have declined while female participation has increased. These trends are consistent with the discussion in Economic naturalist 18.1.

| Country | Male | | | Female | | |
|---|---|---|---|---|---|---|
| | 1973 | 1990 | 2003 | 1973 | 1990 | 2003 |
| France | 85.2 | 75.0 | 73.8 | 50.1 | 52.7 | 62.5 |
| Germany | 89.1 | 79.0 | 78.0 | 49.6 | 55.5 | 64.5 |
| Italy | 85.1 | 75.1 | 74.8 | 33.7 | 44.0 | 48.3 |
| UK | 93.0 | 88.3 | 83.9 | 53.2 | 67.3 | 69.2 |
| USA | 86.2 | 85.6 | 82.2 | 51.1 | 67.8 | 69.7 |

**Table 18.6** Male and Female Participation Rates in Five EU Countries

*Note*: The data refer to men and women aged 15–64 years who are classified as either employed or unemployed.
*Source*: OECD, *Employment Outlook*, www.oecd.org.

**Exercise 18.7**

Suppose that in a total population of working age of 1,000, 40 per cent are working and 10 per cent are unemployed but actively seeking employment.

a. Calculate the unemployment rate for this economy.
b. Calculate the labour force participation rate for this economy.

Suppose a new government scheme leads to 60 people who were neither working nor seeking work to start looking for employment. If the numbers unemployed falls by 16 find:

c. The change in the unemployment rate.
d. The change in the labour force participation rate.

## The costs of unemployment

Unemployment imposes *economic*, *psychological* and *social* costs on a nation. From an *economic* perspective, the main cost of unemployment is the output that is lost because the workforce is not fully utilised. Much of the burden of the reduced output is borne by the unemployed themselves, whose incomes fall when they are not working and whose skills may deteriorate from lack of use. However, society at large also bears part of the economic cost of unemployment. For example, workers who become unemployed are liable to stop paying taxes and start receiving government support payments, such as unemployment benefits. This net drain on the government's budget is a cost to all tax-payers.

The *psychological* costs of unemployment are felt primarily by unemployed workers and their families. Studies show that lengthy periods of unemployment can lead to a loss of self-esteem, feelings of loss of control over one's life, depression and even suicidal behaviour.[3] The unemployed worker's family is likely to feel increased psychological stress, compounded by the economic difficulties created by the loss of income.

The *social* costs of unemployment are a result of the economic and psychological effects. People who have been unemployed for a while tend not only to face severe financial difficulties but also to feel anger, frustration and despair. Not surprisingly, increases in unemployment tend to be associated with increases in crime, domestic violence, alcoholism, drug abuse and other social problems. The costs created by these problems are borne not only by the unemployed but by *society in general*, as more public resources must be spent to counteract these problems – for example, by hiring more police to control crime.

## The duration of unemployment

In assessing the impact of unemployment on jobless people, economists must know how long individual workers have been without work. Generally, the longer a person has been out of work, the more severe are the economic and psychological costs that person will face. People who are unemployed for only a few weeks, for example, are not likely to suffer a serious reduction in their standard of living, since for a short period they can draw upon their savings and perhaps on government benefits. Nor would we expect someone who is unemployed for only a short time to experience psychological problems such as depression or loss of self-esteem, at least not to the same extent as someone who has been out of work for months or years.

A period during which an individual is continuously unemployed is called an **unemployment spell**; it begins when the worker becomes unemployed and ends when the worker either finds a job or leaves the labour force. (Remember, people outside the labour force are not counted as unemployed.) The length of an unemployment spell is called its **duration**. The duration of unemployment rises during recessions, reflecting the greater difficulty of finding work during those periods.

**unemployment spell** a period during which an individual is continuously unemployed

**duration** the length of an unemployment spell

At any given time, a substantial fraction of unemployed workers will have been unemployed for six months or more; we shall refer to this group as the *long-term unemployed*. In 2002, 59 per cent of those unemployed in the European Union had been out of work for six months or more and 41 per cent for at least one year. Comparable figures for the United States were 18 and 8.5 per cent,

[3] For a survey of the literature on the psychological effects of unemployment, see Darity and Goldsmith (1996).

respectively. Chapter 21 discusses these differences between European and American unemployment in more detail. Long-term unemployment creates the highest economic, psychological and social costs, both for the unemployed themselves and for society as a whole. Workers who have been unemployed for shorter periods are often referred to as the *short-term unemployed*. Short-term unemployment can, however, be deceptive because short unemployment spells can arise from two very different patterns of labour market experience. Some people have short unemployment spells that end in their finding a stable long-term job. For the most part, these workers, whom we shall refer to as the short-term unemployed, do not bear a high cost of unemployment. But other workers have short unemployment spells that typically end either in their withdrawal from the labour force or in a short-term or temporary job that soon leaves the worker unemployed again. Workers whose unemployment spells are broken up by brief periods of employment or withdrawal from the labour force are referred to as the *chronically unemployed*. In terms of the costs of unemployment, the experience of these workers is similar to that of the long-term unemployed.

## The unemployment rate versus 'true' unemployment

Like GDP measurement, unemployment measurement has its critics. Most of them argue that the official unemployment rate understates the true extent of unemployment. They point in particular to two groups of people who are not counted among the unemployed: so-called *discouraged workers* and *involuntary part-time workers*.

**Discouraged workers** are people who say they would like to have a job but have not made an effort to find one in the recent past. Often, discouraged workers tell the survey takers that they have not searched for work because they have tried without success in the past, or because they are convinced that labour market conditions are such that they will not be able to find a job. Because they have not sought work, discouraged workers are counted as being out of the labour force rather than unemployed. Some observers have suggested that treating discouraged workers as unemployed would provide a more accurate picture of the labour market.

**discouraged workers** people who say they would like to have a job but have not made an effort to find one in the recent past

**involuntary part-time workers** people who say they would like to work full-time but are able to find only part-time work

**Involuntary part-time workers** are people who say they would like to work full-time but are able to find only part-time work. Because they do have jobs, involuntary part-time workers are counted as employed rather than unemployed. Some economists have suggested that these workers should be counted as partially unemployed.

Whether in an adjusted version, an unemployment rate that includes discouraged and involuntary part-time workers is a good overall indicator of labour-market conditions is a matter of conjecture. While it may give a more accurate picture, a high unemployment rate tends to be bad news even for those people who are employed, since pay raises and promotions are hard to come by in a 'slack' labour market. We shall discuss the causes and cures of unemployment at some length in Chapter 21 and subsequent chapters.

## Summary

- The basic measure of an economy's output is *gross domestic product (GDP)*, the market value of the final goods and services produced in a country during a given period. Expressing output in terms of market values allows economists to aggregate the millions of goods and services produced in a modern economy.
- Only *final goods and services* (which include *capital goods*) are counted in GDP, since they are the only goods and services that directly benefit final users. *Intermediate goods and services*, which are used up in the production of final goods and services, are not counted in GDP, nor are sales of existing assets, such as a 20-year-old house. Summing the value added by each firm in the production process is a useful method of determining the value of final goods and services.
- GDP can also be expressed as the sum of four types of expenditure: *consumption, investment, government purchases* and *net exports*. These four types of expenditure correspond to the spending of households, firms, the government and the foreign sector, respectively.
- To compare levels of GDP over time, economists must eliminate the effects of inflation. They do so by measuring the market value of goods and services in terms of the prices in a base year. GDP measured in this way is called *real GDP*, while GDP measured in terms of current-year prices is called *nominal GDP*. Real GDP should always be used in making comparisons of economic activity over time.
- Real GDP per person is an imperfect measure of economic well-being. With a few exceptions, notably government purchases of goods and services (which are included in GDP at their cost of production), GDP includes only those *goods and services* sold in markets. It excludes important factors that affect people's well-being, such as the amount of leisure time available to them, the value of unpaid or volunteer services, the quality of the environment, quality of life indicators such as the crime rate and the degree of economic inequality.
- Real GDP is still a useful indicator of *economic well-being*, however. Countries with a high real GDP per person not only enjoy high average standards of living; they also tend to have higher life expectancies, low rates of infant and child mortality and high rates of school enrolment and literacy.
- In most countries the *unemployment rate*, perhaps the best-known indicator of the state of the labour market, is based on survey data conducted by government agencies. These surveys classify all respondents of working age as employed, unemployed, or not in the labour force. The *labour force* is the sum of employed and unemployed workers – that is, people who have a job or are looking for one. The *unemployment rate* is calculated as the number of unemployed workers divided by the labour force. The *participation rate* is the percentage of the working-age population that is in the labour force.
- The *costs of unemployment* include the economic cost of lost output, the psychological costs borne by unemployed workers and their families and the social costs associated with problems such as increased crime and violence. The greatest costs are imposed by long *unemployment spells* (periods of unemployment). Critics of official unemployment rates argue that it understates 'true' unemployment by excluding *discouraged workers* and involuntary part-time workers.

## Key terms

**capital good** (500)
**consumption expenditure** (503)
**discouraged workers** (518)
**duration (of unemployment spell)** (517)
**final goods or services** (499)
**government purchases** (504)
**gross domestic product (GDP)** (496)
**intermediate goods or services** (499)
**investment** (503)
**involuntary-part-time workers** (518)
**labour force** (515)
**net exports** (504)
**nominal GDP** (507)
**participation rate** (515)
**real GDP** (507)
**unemployment rate** (514)
**unemployment spell** (517)
**value added** (500)

## Review questions

1. Why do economists use market values when calculating GDP? What is the economic rationale for giving high value items more weight in GDP than low-value items?
2. A large part of the agricultural sector in developing countries is subsistence farming, in which much of the food that is produced is consumed by the farmer and the farmer's family. Discuss the implications of this fact for the measurement of GDP in poor countries.
3. Give examples of each of the four types of aggregate expenditure. Which of the four represents the largest share of GDP in the United Kingdom? Can an expenditure component be negative? Explain.
4. Al's shoeshine stand shined 1,000 pairs of shoes last year and 1,200 pairs this year. He charged €4 for a shine last year and €5 this year. If last year is taken as the base year, find Al's contribution to both nominal GDP and real GDP in both years. Which measure would be better to use if you were trying to measure the change in Al's productivity over the past year? Why?
5. Would you say that real GDP per person is a useful measure of economic well-being? Defend your answer.
6. **True or false**: A high participation rate in an economy implies a low unemployment rate. Explain.
7. What are the costs of a high unemployment rate? Do you think providing more generous government benefits to the unemployed would increase these costs, reduce these costs, or leave them unchanged? Discuss.

## Problems

1. How would each of the following transactions affect the GDP of the United Kingdom?
   a. The UK government pays €1 million in salaries for government workers.
   b. The UK. government pays €1 million to social security recipients.
   c. The UK government pays a UK firm €1 million for newly produced computers.
   d. The UK government pays €1 million in interest to holders of UK government bonds.
   e. The UK government pays €1 million to Saudi Arabia for crude oil to add to UK official oil reserves.
2. Intelligence Incorporated produces 100 computer chips and sells them for €200 each to Bell Computers. Using the chips and other labour and materials, Bell produces 100 personal computers. Bell sells the computers, bundled with software that Bell licenses from Microsoft at €50 per computer, to PC Charlie's for €800 each. PC Charlie's sells the computers to the public for €1,000 each. Calculate the total contribution to GDP using the value added method. Do you get the same answer by summing up the market values of final goods and services?
3. For each of the following transactions, state the effect both on French GDP and on the four components of aggregate expenditure.
   a. A French household buys a new car produced in France.
   b. A French household buys a new car produced in the UK.
   c. A French car rental business buys a new car from a French producer.
   d. A French car rental business buys a new car imported from Germany.
   e. The French government buys a new, domestically produced car for the use of a French diplomat, who has been appointed the ambassador to Sweden.

4. Here are some data for an economy. Find its GDP. Explain your calculation.

| | |
|---|---|
| Consumption expenditures | €600 |
| Exports | 75 |
| Government purchases of goods and services | 200 |
| Construction of new homes and apartments | 100 |
| Sales of existing homes and apartments | 200 |
| Imports | 50 |
| Beginning-of-year inventory stocks | 100 |
| End-of-year inventory stocks | 125 |
| Business fixed investment | 100 |
| Government payments to retirees | 100 |
| Household purchases of durable goods | 150 |

5. The nation of Small-Land produces soccer balls, cases of beer and pain killers. Here are data on prices and quantities of the three goods in 2000 and 2005.

| | Balls | | Beer | | Pain Killers | |
|---|---|---|---|---|---|---|
| **Year** | **Quantity** | **Price (€)** | **Quantity** | **Price (€)** | **Quantity** | **Price (€)** |
| 2000 | 100 | 5 | 300 | 20 | 100 | 20 |
| 2005 | 125 | 7 | 250 | 20 | 110 | 25 |

Assume that 2000 is the base year. Find nominal GDP and real GDP for both years.

6. The government is considering a policy to reduce air pollution by restricting the use of 'dirty' fuels by factories. In deciding whether to implement the policy how, if at all, should the likely effects of the policy on real GDP be taken into account? Discuss.

7. Here is a report from a not-very-efficient labour force survey taker: 'There were 65 people in the houses I visited, 10 of them had children under 16 and 10 retired; 25 people had full-time jobs, and 5 had part-time jobs. There were 5 full-time home makers, 5 full-time students over age 16 and 2 people who were disabled and cannot work. The remaining people did not have jobs but all said they would like one. One of these people had not looked actively for work for more than a year, however.' Find the labour force, the unemployment rate and the participation rate implied by the report.

8. The towns of Littlehampton and Bighampton each have a labour force of 1,200 people. In Littlehampton, 100 people were unemployed for the entire year, while the rest of the labour force was employed continuously. In Bighampton every member of the labour force was unemployed for 1 month and employed for 11 months.

a. What is the average unemployment rate over the year in each of the two towns?

b. What is the average duration of unemployment spells in each of the two towns?

c. In which town do you think the costs of unemployment are higher? Explain.

## Answers to in-chapter exercises

18.1 In the text, GDP was calculated to be €64.00. If in addition Orchardia produces 5 oranges at €0.30 each, GDP is increased by €1.50 to €65.50.

18.2 Plants owned by German companies produced a total of 1,185,000 vehicles, or 4.09 × the 290,000 vehicles produced by foreign-owned plants. In market value terms, with passenger cars valued at €17,000 and other light vehicles at €25,000, plants owned by German companies produced (471,000 × €17,000) + (714,000 × €25,000) = €25,857,000 worth of vehicles. Foreign-owned plants produced (227,000 × €17,000) + (63,000 × €25,000) = €5,434,000 worth of vehicles. In market value terms, German-owned plants outproduced the foreign-owned plants by a ratio of 4.76:1. The German producers have a greater advantage when output is compared in market value terms instead of in terms of number of vehicles because the German companies produce relatively more of the higher-value types of vehicles than the foreign companies do.

18.3 The value added of the wholesale distributor together with the ultimate producers of the cards is €500. Amy's value added – her revenue less her payments to other firms – is €200. Since the cards were produced and purchased by Amy during the year 2002 (we assume), the €500 counts toward year 2002 GDP. The €200 in value added originating in Amy's card shop counts in year 2003 GDP, since Amy actually sold the cards in that year.

18.4 The sale of shares represents a transfer of ownership of part of the assets of FlyEuro.Com, not the production of new goods or services. Hence the sale itself does not contribute to GDP. However, the broker's commission of €100 (2 per cent of the sale proceeds) represents payment for a current service and is counted in GDP.

18.5 As in Example 18.6, the market value of domestic production is 1,000 autos × €10,000 per auto, or €10 million. Also as in Example 18.6, consumption is €7 million and government purchases are €0.5 million. However, because 25 of the autos that are purchased are imported rather than domestic, the domestic producers have unsold inventories at the end of the year of 50 (rather than 25 as in Example 18.6). Thus inventory investment is 50 autos × €10,000, or €0.5 million, and total investment (autos purchased by businesses plus inventory investment) is €2.5 million. Since exports and imports are equal (both are 25 autos), net exports (equal to exports – imports) are zero. Notice that since we subtract imports to get net exports, it is unnecessary also to subtract imports from consumption. Consumption is defined as total purchases by households, not just purchases of domestically produced goods.

Total expenditure is $C + I + G + NX$ = €7 million + €2.5 million + €0.5 million + 0 = €10 million, the same as the market value of production.

18.6 Real GDP in 2004 equals the quantities of computers and cameras produced in 2004, valued at the market prices that prevailed in the base year 2000. So real GDP in 2004 = (30 computers × €1,000/computer) + (30 cameras × €100/camera) = €33,000. Real GDP in 2000 equals the quantities of computers and cameras produced in 2000, valued at 2000 prices, which is €11,500. Notice that since 2000 is the base year, real GDP and nominal GDP are the same for that year. Real GDP in the year 2004 is €33,000/€11,500, or about 2.9 times what it was in 2000.

18.7 a. The unemployment rate = unemployed/labour force. The labour force = employed + unemployed. As 40 per cent or 400 are employed and 10 per cent or 100 are unemployed the labour force is 500 and the unemployment rate is 100/500 = 20 per cent.

b. The participation rate = labour force/working-age population or 500/1,000 = 50 per cent.

c. An additional 60 people start looking for employment, increasing the labour force to 560 and unemployment falls by 16 from 100 to 84. Hence the unemployment rate is 84/560 = 15 per cent, a fall of 5 per cent.

d. As the labour force has increased to 560 the participation rate is 560/1,000 = 56 per cent, a rise of 6 per cent.

## References

Darity, W., Jr and A. H. Goldsmith (1996) 'Social Psychology, Unemployment and Macroeconomics', *Journal of Economic Perspectives*, 10, pp. 121–40.

Hull, C.H. (1900) 'Petty's Place in the History of Economic Theory', *Quarterly Journal of Economics*, 14 May, pp. 307–40.

# 19

# Measuring the Price Level and Inflation

There is a story about an economics graduate, call her Roberta, who got a job with a Frankfurt-based bank. Five years on Roberta has been promoted several times and is a high earner with a salary of €100,000 per year. Roberta has a comfortable life and lives in a luxury apartment which costs €20,000 per year in rent. Despite her good fortune Roberta decides that she wants to see the world and asks her employer for two years' unpaid leave. Over the next two years Roberta travels extensively and uses her savings. On returning to Frankfurt she resumes her job at the bank at her old salary of €100,000 per year. However while Roberta was away Frankfurt has boomed as a financial centre and when she tries to rent her old apartment she finds that the monthly rent has doubled to €40,000. She also finds that prices for the other goods and services she likes to buy – haircuts, restaurant meals, theatre tickets, etc. – have also increased substantially. The problem that Roberta faces is that because of inflation the *real purchasing power* of her money income has been reduced. Roberta may have had a great time on her travels but at the price of a decline in her real standard of living as measured by the quantities of goods and services her income permits her to buy.

This story illustrates a simple but very important point, which is that the value of money depends entirely on the prices of goods and services one wants to buy. High and sustained inflation – a rapid and ongoing increase in the prices of most goods and services – can radically reduce the buying power of a given amount of money. €100,000 may be a substantial salary at the prices prevailing today but it becomes less attractive if these prices double or treble over a few years.

Inflation can also make a comparison of economic conditions at different points in time quite difficult. When the authors of this book were undergraduates 'essential' items like pints of beer and cinema tickets might have cost less than one euro (actually in those far-off days prices in the United Kingdom and Ireland were measured in non-decimal pounds, shillings and pence). Today the same items might cost five or six times as much. You might conclude from this that students were much better off in 'the good old days', but were they really? Without more information, we can't tell, for though the prices of beer and cinema tickets have gone up, so has the amount of spending money students have to buy these and other items such as books. The real question is whether young people's spending money has increased as much as or more than the prices of the things they want to buy. If so, then they are no worse off today than we were when we were young and a beer cost 1 shilling.

Inflation also creates uncertainty when we try to look into the future, to ask questions such as: 'How much should I plan to save for retirement?' The answer to this question depends on how much inflation is likely to occur before one retires (and thus how much heating, food and clothing will cost). Inflation can pose similar problems for policy makers. For example, to plan long-term government spending programmes they must estimate how much the government's purchases will cost several years in the future. How many times have you read newspaper reports on projects such has a new road or hospital which has run over its budget because inflation was higher than expected at the time the project was planned?

An important benefit of studying macroeconomics is learning how to avoid the confusion inflation interjects into comparisons of economic conditions over time or projections for the future. In this chapter, a continuation of our study of the construction and interpretation of economic data, we shall see how both prices and inflation are measured and how the money value of goods and services can be 'adjusted' to eliminate the effects of inflation. Quantities that are measured in euros (or other currency units) and then adjusted for inflation are called real quantities (recall, for example, the concept of real GDP in Chapter 18).

More important than the complications inflation creates for economic measurement are the costs that it imposes on the economy. In this chapter we shall see why high inflation can significantly impair an economy's performance, to the extent that economic policy makers claim a low and stable rate of inflation as one of their chief objectives. We shall conclude the chapter by showing how inflation is linked to another key economic variable, the rate of interest on financial assets.

## The consumer price index: measuring the price level

Suppose you are asked the following question: By how much did the 'cost of living' in France, Germany and the United Kingdom increase between 2000 and 2004? The *cost of living* is usually taken to mean the cost of an average or standard basket of goods and services (housing, food, clothing, transport, entertainment, etc.) purchased by a typical household. The basic tool economists use to answer this type of question is the **consumer price index** (or **CPI** for short). The CPI is a measure of the cost of living during a particular period. Specifically, the consumer price index (CPI) for any period measures the cost in that period of a standard set, or basket, of goods and services *relative* to the cost of the same basket of goods and services in a fixed year, called the base year.

**consumer price index (CPI)** for any period, measures the cost in that period of a standard basket of goods and services relative to the cost of the same basket of goods and services in a fixed year, called the *base year*

Although there may be differences in computational methods and the definition of an average basket of goods and services, the principles underlying the CPI are similar in most countries. To illustrate how a typical CPI is constructed, suppose that the government has designated 2000 as the base year. Assume for the sake of simplicity that in 2000 a typical household's monthly budget consisted of spending on just three items: rent, hamburgers and train tickets. In reality, of course, families purchase hundreds of different items each month, but the basic principles of constructing the CPI are the same no matter how many items are included. Suppose too that the family's average monthly expenditures in 2000, the base year, were as shown in Table 19.1.

| Item | Cost in 2000 (€) |
|---|---|
| Rent | 500 |
| Hamburgers (60 @ €2.00 each) | 120 |
| Train tickets (10 @ €6.00 each) | 60 |
| Total expenditure | 680 |

**Table 19.1** Monthly Household Budget of the Typical Family, 2000 (Base Year)

Now let's fast-forward to the year 2004. Over that period, the prices of various goods and services are likely to have changed; some will have risen and some fallen. Let's suppose that by 2004 the household's rent has risen to €630. Hamburgers now cost €2.50 each, and the price of train tickets has risen to €7.00 each. So, in general, prices have been rising.

By how much did the family's cost of living increase between 2000 and 2004? Table 19.2 shows that if the typical family wanted to consume the *same basket of goods and services* in the year 2004 as they did in the year 2000, they would have to spend €850 per month, or €170 more than the €680 per month they spent in 2000. In other words, to live the same way in the year 2004 as they did in the year 2000, the family would have to spend 25 per cent more (€170/€680) each month. So, in this example, the cost of living for the typical family rose 25 per cent between 2000 and 2004.

| Item | Cost in 2004 (€) | Cost in 2000 (€) |
|---|---|---|
| Rent | 630 | 500 |
| Hamburgers (60 @ €2.50 each) | 150 | 120 |
| Train tickets (10 @ €7.00 each) | 70 | 60 |
| Total expenditure | 850 | 680 |

**Table 19.2** Cost of Reproducing the 2000 (Base-Year) Basket of Goods and Services in 2004

In most countries, the government agency or department responsible for producing the CPI calculates the official CPI using essentially the same method. The first step in deriving the CPI is to pick a *base year* and determine the basket of goods and services that were consumed by the typical family during that year. In practice, the government learns how consumers allocate their spending through a detailed survey, called the Consumer or Household Expenditure Survey, in which randomly selected families record every purchase they make and the price they pay over a given month. Let's call the basket of goods and services that results the *base-year basket*. Then, each month, government employees visit thousands of stores and conduct numerous interviews to determine the current prices of the goods and services in the base-year basket. The CPI in any given year is computed using this formula:

$$\text{CPI} = \frac{\text{Cost of the base-year basket of goods and services in the current year}}{\text{Cost of the base-year basket of goods and services in the base year}}$$

Returning to the example of the typical family that consumes three goods, we can calculate the CPI in 2004 as

$$\text{CPI in 2004} = \frac{€850}{€680} = 1.25$$

In other words, in this example the cost of living in the year 2004 is 25 per cent higher than it was in 2000, the base year. Notice that the base-year CPI is always equal to 1.00, since in that year the numerator and the denominator of the CPI formula are the same. The CPI for a given period (such as a month or year) measures the cost of living in that period *relative* to what it was in the base year.

Often news reporters multiply the CPI by 100 to get rid of the decimal point. If we were to do that here, the year 2004 CPI would be expressed as 125 rather than 1.25, and the base-year CPI would be expressed as 100 rather than 1.00.

### Example 19.1 Measuring the typical family's cost of living

Suppose that in addition to the three goods and services the typical family consumed in 2000 they also bought four sweaters at €30 each. In 2004 the same sweaters cost €50 each. The prices of the other goods and services in 2000 and 2004 were the same as in Table 19.2. Find the change in the family's cost of living between 2000 and 2004.

In our CPI example in the text, the cost of the base-year (2000) basket was €680. Adding four sweaters at €30 each raises the cost of the base-year basket to €800. What does this same basket (including the four sweaters) cost in 2004? Rent, the price of hamburgers and the train tickets is €850, as before. Adding the cost of the four sweaters at €50 each raises the total cost of the basket to €1,050. The CPI equals the cost of the basket in 2004 divided by the cost of the basket in 2000 (the base year), or €1,050/€800 = 1.31. We conclude that the family's cost of living rose 31 per cent between 2000 and 2004.

**Exercise 19.1** Returning to the three-good example in Tables 19.1 and 19.2, find the 2004 CPI if the household's rent falls from €500 in 2000 to €400 in 2004. The prices for hamburgers and train tickets in the two years remain the same as in Tables 19.1 and 19.2.

A CPI is not itself the price of a specific good or service; it is a **price index**. A price index measures the average price of a class of goods or services relative to the price of those same goods or services in a base year. The CPI is an especially well-known price index, one of many that economists use to assess economic trends. For example, because manufacturers tend to pass on increases in the prices of raw materials to their customers, economists use indexes of raw materials' prices to try to forecast changes in the prices of manufactured goods. Other indexes are used to study the rate of price change in energy, food, health care and other major sectors.

**price index** a measure of the average price of a given class of goods or services relative to the price of the same goods and services in a base year

**Exercise 19.2** The CPI captures the cost of living for the 'typical' or average family. Suppose you were to construct a personal price index (PPI) to measure changes in your own cost of living over time. In general, how would you go about constructing such an index? Why might changes in your PPI differ from changes in the CPI?

## Inflation

The CPI provides a measure of the average *level* of prices relative to prices in the base year. *Inflation*, in contrast, is a measure of how fast the average price level is *changing* over time. The **rate of inflation** is defined as the annual percentage rate of change in the price level – as measured, for example, by the CPI. Suppose, for example, that the CPI has a value of 1.25 in 2004 and a value of 1.30 in 2005. The rate of inflation between 2004 and 2005 is the percentage increase in the price level, or the increase in the price level (0.05) divided by the initial price level (1.25), which is equal to 4 per cent.

**rate of inflation** the annual percentage rate of change in the price level, as measured, for example, by the CPI

### Example 19.2 Calculating inflation rates 1972–76

The table below gives CPI values for the United Kingdom in the years 1972–76 using 1974 as the base year (over this period the UK index was called the Retail Price Index or RPI). Find the rates of inflation between 1972 and 1973, 1973 and 1974, 1974 and 1975, and 1975 and 1976.

| Year | CPI |
|---|---:|
| 1972 | 78.7 |
| 1973 | 85.4 |
| 1974 | 100.0 |
| 1975 | 124.2 |
| 1976 | 144.8 |

The inflation rate between 1972 and 1973 is the percentage increase in the price level between those years, or (85.4 – 78.7)/78.7 = 6.7/78.7 = 0.085 = 8.5 per cent. Do the calculations on your own to confirm that inflation during each of the next three years was 17.2, 24.2 and 16.5 per cent, respectively. During the 1970s, inflation rates were much higher than the 2–3 per cent inflation rates that have prevailed in recent years.

**Exercise 19.3** Using the data in Example 19.2 recalculate the CPI and annual inflation rates using 1972 as the base year. Are the annual inflation rates the same?

### Example 19.3

The table below gives Japanese CPI values for the years 2000–04 (base year 1996 = 100). Find the rates of inflation in each year starting with 2001.

| Year | CPI |
|---|---|
| 2000 | 101.2 |
| 2001 | 101.1 |
| 2002 | 100.5 |
| 2003 | 100.3 |
| 2004 | 100.3 |

**deflation** a situation in which the prices of most goods and services are falling over time so that inflation is negative

The Japanese inflation rate between 2000 and 2001 was (101.1 – 102.2)/ 101.1 = –0.1 per cent. Likewise the inflation rates for 2002, 2003 and 2004 were –0.6, –0.2 and 0 per cent, respectively. Hence Japan experienced *negative* inflation over these years. A situation in which the prices of most goods and services are falling over time so that inflation is negative is called **deflation**.

## Economic naturalist 19.1 The EU's Harmonised Index of Consumer Prices

*National price indices* can vary widely in their coverage of goods and services and their methods of construction. For example, some countries include mortgage interest and credit charges while others treat these costs as financing costs rather than consumer expenditure and exclude them from their national CPIs. Likewise, some national CPIs are based exclusively on expenditure by domestic residents inside the country while others include expenditures in other countries. These differences in national price indices make it difficult to derive accurate international comparisons of living costs and national inflation rates. In particular, because the Maastricht Treaty charges the ECB with the responsibility of maintaining price stability, or low inflation, the Bank requires comparable price indices which can be used to compute the average inflation rate in the eurozone (those countries using the euro as their currency). In response to this Eurostat (the EU statistical office) has developed a *Harmonised Index of Consumer Prices* (or HICP), which can be used as a comparable measure of inflation in member states. Each member state of the European Union now produces a national HICP using a common methodology.

Using country weights which reflect differences in GDP these national HICPs can be aggregated to an EU harmonised price index. Hence changes in the aggregated HICP measure the average rate of inflation in the European Union. In addition to national and EU-wide HICPs, Eurostat also produces HICPs for other groupings. The most important of these is the *Monetary Union Index of Consumer Prices* (MUICP) which is a weighted average of national HICPs in the Eurosystem. The ECB uses the MUICP to monitor price stability which it now defines as a year-on-year increase of below 2 per cent in the MUICP.

Note that since 2003 the British HICP has been known as the CPI which should not be confused with the UK national price index known as the Retail Price Index (or RPI). Details on the construction and use of the HICP can be found at the Eurostat website, http://epp.eurostat.cec.eu.int.

### **Example 19.4** Making comparisons: Europe's most expensive city

Living costs differ from country to country and from city to city. Suppose you are asked to find the European capital city with the highest cost of living. You might compare national- or city-based CPIs, but as these may differ in terms of construction and the range of prices used, your results may be misleading. For example, rents for flats may be higher in London than in Paris but if British and French statisticians treat housing costs in different ways their cost of living indices may not be comparable. To address this type of problem Eurostat now produces a series of harmonised price indices for EU capital cities. Using Brussels as the 'base city' (setting the cost of living in Brussels at 100), the table below gives the July 2004 harmonised index of living costs in a range of capital cities.

| Madrid | Berlin | Rome | Paris | Dublin | London |
|---|---|---|---|---|---|
| 101 | 101 | 110 | 120 | 122 | 143 |

*Source*: http://epp.eurostat.cec.eu.int.

Hence in July 2004 the cost of living in Rome was 10 per cent greater than in Brussels. Madrid and Berlin were the lowest-cost cities and London the most expensive. Living costs for the average Londoner were 41 per cent (143 – 101)/143, higher than for the citizens of Madrid and Berlin.

## Adjusting for inflation

The CPI or HICP is an extremely useful tool. Not only does it allow us to measure changes in the cost of living; it can also be used to adjust economic data to *eliminate the effects of inflation*. In this section we shall see how the CPI can be used to convert quantities measured at current euro values into real terms, a process called **deflating**. By current euro values we mean measuring the value of a given *quantity* of goods and services in today's prices. We will also see that the CPI can be used to convert real quantities into current euro terms, a procedure called *indexing*. Both procedures are useful not only to economists but to anyone who needs to adjust payments, accounting measures or other economic quantities for the effects of inflation.

**deflating (a nominal quantity)** the process of dividing a nominal quantity by a price index (such as the CPI) to express the quantity in real terms

## Deflating a nominal quantity

**nominal quantity** a quantity that is measured in terms of its current euro value

An important use of the CPI is to adjust **nominal quantities** – quantities measured at their current euro values – for the effects of inflation. To illustrate, suppose we know that the typical family in a certain metropolitan area had a total income of €20,000 in 2000 and €22,000 in 2004. Was this family economically better off in 2004 than in 2000?

Without any more information than this we might be tempted to say yes. After all, its income rose by 10 per cent over the four-year period. But prices might also have been rising as fast as or faster than the family's income. Suppose the prices of the goods and services the family consumes rose 25 per cent over the same period. Since the family's income rose only 10 per cent, we would have to conclude that the family is worse off, in terms of the goods and services they can afford to buy, despite the increase in their *nominal*, or current euro, income.

We can make a more precise comparison of the family's purchasing power in 2000 and 2004 by calculating its income in those years in *real* terms. In general, a **real quantity** is one that is measured in *physical terms* – for example, in terms of quantities of goods and services.

**real quantity** a quantity that is measured in physical terms – for example, in terms of quantities of goods and services

To convert a nominal quantity into a real quantity, we must divide the nominal quantity by a price index for the period, as shown in Table 19.3. The calculations in Table 19.3 show that in *real* or purchasing power terms, the family's income actually *decreased* by €2,400, or 12 per cent of its initial real income of €20,000, between 2000 and 2004.

| Year | Nominal family income (€) | CPI | Real family income = Nominal family income/CPI (€) |
|---|---|---|---|
| 2000 | 20,000 | 1.00 | 20,000/1.00 = 20,000 |
| 2004 | 22,000 | 1.25 | 22,000/1.25 = 17,600 |

**Table 19.3** Comparing the Real Values of a Family's Income, 2000 and 2004

The problem for this family is that although its income has been rising in nominal (euro) terms, it has not kept up with inflation. Dividing a nominal quantity by a price index to express the quantity in real terms is called deflating the nominal quantity. (Be careful not to confuse the idea of deflating a nominal quantity with deflation, or negative inflation. *The two concepts are different.*)

Dividing a nominal quantity by the current value of a price index to measure it in *real or purchasing power terms* is a very useful tool. It can be used to eliminate the effects of inflation from comparisons of any nominal quantity – workers' wages, health care expenditures, college tuition fees, government expenditure on education – over time. Why does this method work? In general, if you know both how many euros you have spent on a given item and the item's price, you can figure out how much of the item you bought (by dividing your expenditures by the price). For example, if you spent €100 on hamburgers last month and hamburgers cost €2.50 each, you can determine that you purchased 40 hamburgers. Similarly, if you divide a family's nominal income or expenditures by a price index, which is a measure of the average price of the goods and services the family buys, you will obtain a measure of the real quantity of goods and services the family purchased. Such real quantities are sometimes referred to as *inflation-adjusted* quantities.

## Example 19.5 Winning Wimbledon: how much is it *really* worth?

In 1978 Martina Navratilova won the first of her nine Wimbledon singles titles. Her prize money was £17,100, or approximately $32,500 at the July 1978 exchange rate between the dollar and the pound. Navratilova won her last title in 1990 when the prize money was £171,000 or $273,600. Which prize was worth more to Navratilova?

As Martina Navratilova is a US resident it is more appropriate to use the dollar values and the US CPI to answer the question. Using the average of 1982–84 as the base year the American CPI was 0.66 in 1978 and 1.32 in 1990. Dividing the 1978 prize by 0.66, we obtain approximately €49,242, which is the value of the prize money 'in 1982–84 dollars'. Dividing the 1990 prize by that year's CPI, 1.32, gives $207,272 in 1982–84 dollars. We can now compare the two prizes. In money or current dollar terms the 1990 prize is about 8.4 times the 1978 prize (273,600/32,500). However in real or constant dollar (1982–84) terms the difference is much narrower, with the 1990 prize approximately 4.2 times the 1978 prize (207,272/49,242). Hence, although adjusting for inflation brings the two figures closer together (since part of increase in the prize money compensates for the increase in prices between 1978 and 1990), in real terms Navratilova's final championship still earned more than four times her first victory.

**real wage** the wage paid to workers measured in terms of real purchasing power; the real wage for any given period is calculated by dividing the nominal (euro) wage by the CPI for that period

Clearly, in comparing wages or earnings at two different points in time, we must adjust for changes in the price level. Doing so yields the **real wage** – the wage measured in terms of real purchasing power. The real wage for any given period is calculated by dividing the nominal (euro) wage by the CPI for that period.

**Exercise 19.4** In 2004 Maria Sharapova, also a US resident, won the Wimbledon title. Sharapova's prize money was £560,500 or approximately $1 million. In 2004 the CPI was 1.89. How did Sharapova's real earnings compare with Navratilova's 1990 winnings?

## Example 19.6 Real wages of British workers

Few very of us are lucky or talented enough to play at Wimbledon, let alone win a singles title. For most individuals and households, weekly or monthly wages and salaries constitute their major earnings. According to the British Office for National Statistics the average UK worker earned £6.34 per hour in 1990 and £12.03 per hour in 2003, an increase of almost 90 per cent. Compare the real wages of British workers in these years.

To find the real wage in 1990 and 2003, we need to know that the British RPI was 1.261 in 1990 and 1.813 in 2003 (using the 1987 as the base year). Dividing £6.43 by 1.261, we find that the real wage in 1990 was €5.10. Dividing £12.03 by 1.813, we find that the real wage in 2003 was £6.63, an increase of 30 per cent. Hence the increase in real wages was only one-third of the corresponding increase in nominal wages.

Figure 19.1 shows nominal wages and real weekly earnings for British production workers for the period 1960–2003. Notice the dramatic difference between the two trends.

Looking only at nominal wages, one might conclude that manufacturing workers were much better paid in 2003 than in 1960. But once wages are adjusted for inflation, we see that in terms of buying power workers' earnings have increased at a much lower rate than nominal earnings since the early 1970s. Example 19.6 illustrates the crucial importance of adjusting for inflation when comparing money values over time.

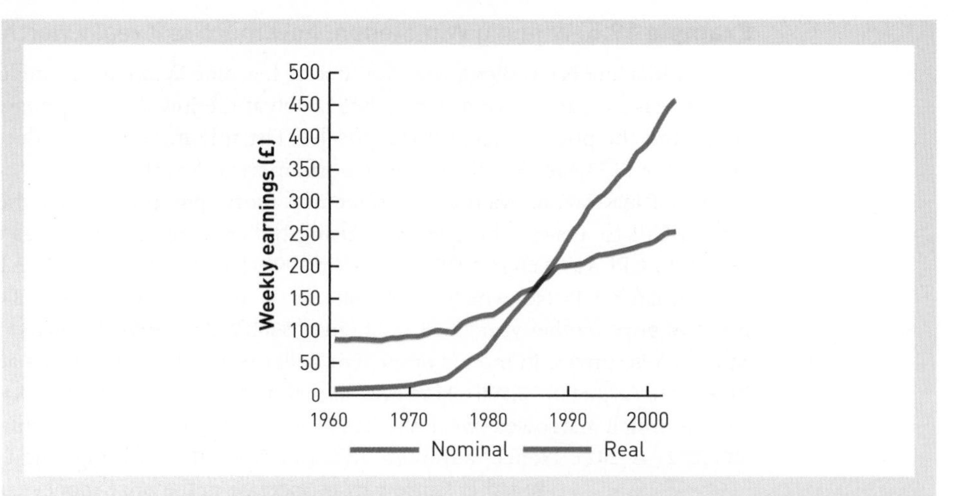


**Figure 19.1 Nominal and Real Wages in UK Manufacturing Industries, 1960–2003.** Though nominal wages have risen dramatically since the 1960s, real wages have increased at a much slower rate.

**Exercise 19.5** The average weekly wage for women working in UK manufacturing industries was £170.3 in 1990 and £356 in 2003, an increase of 109 per cent. The corresponding money wages for men are £282.20 in 1990 and £486.8, an increase of 73 per cent. Using the price data in Example 19.6, how does the real wage in 2003 compare with that in 1990?

## Indexing to maintain buying power

The CPI can also be used to convert real quantities to nominal quantities. Suppose, for example, that in 2000 the government paid full-time university students €500 per month in living grants. Let's assume that the government would like the buying power of these grants to remain constant over time so that the students' standard of living is unaffected by inflation. To achieve that goal, at what level should government set the monthly student grant in 2005?

The nominal, or euro, benefit government should pay in the year 2005 to maintain student purchasing power depends on how much inflation has taken place between 2000 and 2005. Suppose that the CPI has risen 20 per cent between 2000 and 2005. That is, on average the prices of the goods and services consumers buy have risen 20 per cent over that period. For students to 'keep up' with inflation, their benefit in the year 2005 must be €600 per month, or 20 per cent more than it was in 2000. In general, to keep purchasing power constant, the euro benefit must be increased each year by the percentage increase in the CPI.

**indexing** the practice of increasing a nominal quantity each period by an amount equal to the percentage increase in a specified price index; indexing prevents the purchasing power of the nominal quantity from being eroded by inflation

The practice of increasing a nominal quantity according to changes in a price index to prevent inflation from eroding purchasing power is called **indexing**. In some countries, government pensions are automatically indexed to inflation. Each year, without any action by government, benefits increase by an amount equal to the percentage increase in the CPI. Some labour contracts are indexed as well so that wages are adjusted fully or partially for changes in inflation.

### Example 19.7 An indexed labour contract

A labour contract provides for a first-year wage of €12.00 per hour and specifies that the real wage will rise by 2 per cent in the second year of the contract and by another 2 per cent in the third year. The CPI is 1.00 in the first year, 1.05 in the second year and 1.10 in the third year. Find the money wage that must be paid in the second and third years.

Because the CPI is 1.00 in the first year, both the nominal wage and the real wage are €12.00. Let $W_2$ stand for the nominal wage in the second year. Deflating by the CPI in the second year, we can express the real wage in the second year as $W_2/1.05$. The contract says that the second-year real wage must be 2 per cent higher than the real wage in the first year, so $W_2/1.05 = €12.00 \times 1.02 = €12.24$. Multiplying through by 1.05 to solve for $W_2$, we get $W_2 = €12.85$, the nominal wage required by the contract in the second year. In the third year, the nominal wage $W_3$ must satisfy the equation $W_3/1.10 = €12.24 \times 1.02 = €12.48$. (Why?) Solving this equation for $W_3$ yields €13.73 as the nominal wage that must be paid in the third year.

**Exercise 19.6** An accountant retires with an inflation-indexed pension of €2,000 per month. In the three years following his retirement inflation is 2, 3 and 4 per cent. What is the nominal value of the accountant's pension after three years?

### RECAP Methods to adjust for inflation

- *Deflating* To correct a nominal quantity, such as a family's euro income, for changes in the price level, divide it by a price index such as the CPI. This process, called *deflating* the nominal quantity, expresses the nominal quantity in terms of real purchasing power. If nominal quantities from two different years are deflated by a price index with the same base year, the purchasing power of the two deflated quantities can be compared.
- *Indexing* To ensure that a nominal payment, such as a wage or pension, represents a constant level of real purchasing power, increase the nominal quantity each year by a percentage equal to the rate of inflation for that year (a procedure known as *indexing*).

## Does the CPI measure 'true' inflation?

You may have concluded that measuring inflation is straightforward, but as with GDP and the unemployment rate, the issue is not free from controversy. Indeed, the question of whether inflation is properly measured has been the subject of serious debate. Because the CPI is one of the most important economic statistics, the issue is far from academic. Policy makers such as the Bank of England and the ECB pay close attention to the latest inflation numbers when deciding what actions to take. Furthermore, when inflation starts to increase, labour unions become more aggressive in seeking higher nominal wage increases to safeguard their members' real wages.

When a 1996 report for the American government concluded that changes in the CPI were a poor measure of 'true' inflation, a major controversy ensued. The report, prepared by a commission headed by Michael Boskin, formerly the chief economic adviser to President George H. W. Bush, concluded that the official CPI inflation rate *overstated* the true inflation rate by as much as one–two percentage points a year. In other words, if the official inflation rate is reported to be 3 per cent, the 'true' inflation rate might be 2 per cent, or even 1 per cent.

If this assessment is correct, then indexing pensions and other payments to the official inflation rate could be costing millions of euros more than necessary every year. In addition, an overstated rate of inflation would lead to an underestimation of the true improvement in living standards over time. If the typical family's nominal income increases by 3 per cent per year, and inflation is reported to be 2 per cent per year, economists would conclude that families are experiencing a 1 per cent increase in their real incomes. But if the 'true' inflation rate is really 1 per cent per year, then the family's real income is actually rising by 2 per cent per year (the 3 per cent increase in nominal income minus 1 per cent inflation).

The Boskin Commission gave a number of reasons why the official inflation rate might overestimate the true rate of inflation. Two are particularly important. First, in practice statisticians cannot always adjust adequately for changes in the *quality* of goods and services. Suppose a new personal computer (PC) has 20 per cent more memory, computational speed and data storage capacity than last year's model. Suppose, too, for the sake of illustration that its price is 20 per cent higher. Has there been inflation in computer prices? Economists would say no; although consumers are paying 20 per cent more for a computer, they are getting 20 per cent more computer power. The situation is really no different from paying 20 per cent more for a pizza that is 20 per cent bigger. However, because quality change is difficult to measure precisely and because they have many thousands of goods and services to consider, statisticians often miss or understate changes in quality. In general, whenever statisticians fail to adjust adequately for improvements in the quality of goods or services, they will tend to overstate inflation. This type of overstatement is called *quality-adjustment bias*.

An extreme example of quality-adjustment bias can occur whenever a totally new good becomes available. For example, the introduction of the first effective AIDS drugs significantly increased the quality of medical care received by AIDS patients. In practice, however, quality improvements that arise from totally new products are likely to be poorly captured by the CPI, if at all. The problem is that since the new good was not produced in the base year, there is no base-year price with which to compare the current price of the good. Statisticians use various approaches to correct for this problem, such as comparing the cost of the new drug to the cost of the next-best therapies. But such methods are necessarily imprecise and open to criticism.

The second problem emphasised by the Boskin Commission arises from the fact that the CPI is calculated for a *fixed basket of goods and services*. This procedure does not allow for the possibility that consumers can switch from products whose prices are rising to those whose prices are stable or falling. Ignoring the fact that consumers can switch from more expensive to less expensive goods leads statisticians to overestimate the true increase in the cost of living.

Suppose, for instance, that people like coffee and tea equally well and in the base year consumed equal amounts of each. But then a frost hits a major coffee-producing nation, causing the price of coffee to double. The increase in coffee prices encourages consumers to forgo coffee and drink tea instead – a switch that doesn't make them much worse off, since they like coffee and tea equally well. However, the CPI, which measures the cost of buying the base-year basket of goods and services, will rise significantly when the price of coffee doubles. This rise in the CPI, which ignores the fact that people can *substitute* tea for coffee without being made significantly worse off, exaggerates the true increase in the cost of living. This type of overstatement of inflation is called *substitution bias*.

### **Example 19.8** Substitution bias

Suppose the CPI basket for 2000, the base year, is as follows.

| Item | Expenditure (€) |
|---|---|
| Coffee (50 cups @ €1/cup) | 50.00 |
| Tea (50 cups @ €1/cup) | 50.00 |
| Scones (100 @ €1 each) | 100.00 |
| Total | 200.00 |

Assume that consumers are equally happy to drink coffee or tea with their scones. In 2000, coffee and tea cost the same, and the average person drinks equal amounts of coffee and tea.

In the year 2005, coffee has doubled in price to €2 per cup. Tea remains at €1 per cup, and scones are €1.50 each. What has happened to the cost of living as measured by the CPI? How does this result compare with the true cost of living?

To calculate the value of the CPI for the year 2005, we must first find the cost of consuming the 2000 basket of goods in that year. At year 2005 prices, 50 cups each of coffee and tea and 100 scones cost (50 × €2) + (50 × €1) + (100 × €1.50) = €300. Since consuming the same basket of goods cost €200 in 2000, the base year, the CPI in 2005 is €300/€200, or 1.50. This calculation leads us to conclude that the cost of living has increased 50 per cent between 2000 and 2005.

However, we have overlooked the possibility that consumers can substitute a cheaper good (tea) for the more expensive one (coffee). Indeed, since consumers like coffee and tea equally well, when the price of coffee doubles they will shift entirely to tea. Their new consumption basket – 100 cups of tea and 100 scones – is just as enjoyable to them as their original basket. If we allow for the substitution of less expensive goods, how much has the cost of living really increased? The cost of 100 cups of tea and 100 scones in 2005 is only €250, not €300. From the consumer's point of view, the true cost of living has risen by only €50, or 25 per cent. The 50 per cent increase in the CPI therefore overstates the increase in the cost of living as the result of substitution bias.

The Boskin Commission's findings have been controversial. While quality-adjustment bias and substitution bias undoubtedly distort the measurement of inflation, estimating precisely how much of an overstatement they create is difficult. (If economists knew exactly how big these biases were, they could simply correct the data.)

## Economic naturalist 19.2 Why is inflation in the health care sector apparently high?

Government statisticians report inflation rates for different categories of goods and services, as well as for the overall consumer basket. According to the official measures, since the 1980s the prices of medical services have tended to rise much more rapidly than the prices of other goods and services. Why is inflation in the health care sector apparently high?

Although inflation rates in the health care sector are high, some economists have argued that reported rates greatly overstate the true rate of inflation in that sector. The reason, claim critics, is the quality-adjustment bias. Health care is a dynamic sector of the economy, in which ongoing technological change has significantly improved the quality of care. To the extent that official data fail to account for improvements in the quality of medical care, inflation in the health care sector will be overstated.

Economists Matthew Shapiro and James Wilcox illustrated the problem with the example of changes in the treatment of cataracts, cloudiness in the lens of the eye that impairs vision.[1] The lens must still be removed surgically, but there have been important improvements in the procedure since the 1970s. First, surgeons can now replace the defective lens with an artificial one, which improves the patient's vision considerably without contact lenses or thick glasses. Second, the techniques for making and closing the surgical incision have been substantially improved. Besides

[1] Shapiro and Wilcox (1996).

reducing complications and therefore follow-up visits, the new techniques can be performed in the physician's surgery, with no hospital stay (older techniques frequently required three nights in hospital). Thus the new technologies have both improved patient outcomes and reduced the number of hours doctors and nurses spend on the procedure.

Shapiro and Wilcox point out that official measures of health care inflation are based primarily on data such as the doctor's hourly rate or the cost of a night in the hospital. They do not take into account either the reduction in a doctor's time or the shorter hospital stay now needed for procedures such as cataract surgery. Furthermore, Shapiro and Wilcox argue, official measures do not take adequate account of improvements in patient outcomes, such as the improved vision that cataract patients now enjoy. Because of the failure to adjust for improvements in the quality of procedures, including increased productivity of medical personnel, official measures may significantly overstate inflation in the health care sector.

## The costs of inflation: not always what you think

In the 1970s, when inflation in Europe and North America was considerably higher than it is now, opinion polls often suggested that the public viewed it as 'public enemy number one'. Although European and American inflation rates have not been very high in recent years, workers, employers, financial experts and government are still concerned about inflation, or the *threat of inflation*. Indeed, as we shall see in Chapter 23, the ECB has a primary mandate to maintain price stability, or low inflation, across those countries using the euro as their currency. Why do people worry so much about inflation? Detailed opinion surveys often find that many people are confused about the meaning of inflation and its economic effects. Before describing the true economic costs of inflation, which are real and serious, let us examine this confusion.

**price level** a measure of the overall level of prices at a particular point in time as measured by a price index such as the CPI

**relative price** the price of a specific good or service in comparison to the prices of other goods and services

We need first to distinguish between the **price level** and the **relative price** of a good or service. The price level is a measure of the overall level of prices at a particular point in time as measured by a price index such as the CPI. Recall that the inflation rate is the percentage change in the price level from year to year. In contrast, a relative price is the price of a specific good or service *in comparison to* the prices of other goods and services. For example, if the price of oil were to rise by 10 per cent while the prices of other goods and services were rising on average by 3 per cent, the relative price of oil would increase. But if oil prices rise by 3 per cent while other prices rise by 10 per cent, the relative price of oil would decrease. That is, oil would become cheaper *relative to other goods and services*, even though it has not become cheaper in absolute terms.

Public opinion surveys suggest that many people are confused about the distinction between inflation, or an increase in the overall *price level*, and an increase in a specific *relative price*. Suppose that hostilities in the Middle East were to double the prices of petrol and heating oil, leaving other prices unaffected. Appalled by the increase in petrol and oil prices, people might demand that the government do something about 'this inflation'. But while the increase in petrol and heating oil prices hurts consumers, is it an example of inflation? Petrol and heating oil are only two items in a consumer's budget, two of the thousands of goods and services that people buy every day. Thus the increase in the prices of petrol and oil might affect the overall price level, and hence the inflation rate, only slightly. In this example, inflation is not the real problem. What upsets consumers is the change in the *relative prices* of petrol and oil, particularly compared with the price of labour (wages). By increasing the cost of using a car and heating a home, the increase in the relative price of oil reduces the income that people have left over to spend on other things.

Again, changes in relative prices do *not* necessarily imply a significant amount of inflation. For example, increases in the prices of some goods could well be counter-balanced by decreases in the prices of other goods, in which case the price level and the inflation rate would be largely unaffected. Conversely, inflation can be high without affecting relative prices. Imagine, for example, that all prices in the economy, including wages and salaries, go up exactly 10 per cent each year. The inflation rate is 10 per cent, but relative prices are not changing. Indeed, because wages (the price of labour) are increasing by 10 per cent per year, people's ability to buy goods and services is unaffected by the inflation.

These examples show that changes in the average price level (inflation) and changes in the relative prices of specific goods are two quite different issues. The public's tendency to confuse the two is important, because the remedies for the two problems are different. To counteract changes in relative prices, the government would need to implement policies that affect the supply and demand for specific goods. In the case of an increase in oil prices, for example, the government could try to restore supplies by mediating the peace process in the Middle East. To counteract inflation, however, the government must resort (as we will see) to changes in macroeconomic policies, such as monetary or fiscal policies. If, in confusion, the public forces the government to adopt anti-inflationary policies when the real problem is a relative price change, the economy could actually be hurt by the effort. Example 19.9 shows why economic literacy is important, to both policy makers and the general public.

#### **Example 19.9** The price level, relative prices and inflation

Suppose the value of the CPI is 1.20 in 2000, 1.32 in 2001 and 1.40 in 2002. Assume also that the price of oil increases 8 per cent between 2000 and 2001 and another 8 per cent between 2001 and 2002. What is happening to the price level, the inflation rate and the relative price of oil?

The price level can be measured by the CPI. Since the CPI is higher in 2001 than in 2000 and higher still in 2002 than in 2001, the price level is rising throughout the period. The inflation rate is the *percentage increase* in the CPI. Since the CPI increases by 10 per cent between 2000 and 2001, the inflation rate between those years is 10 per cent ($1.32/1.20 = 1.10$). However, the CPI increases only about 6 per cent between 2001 and 2002 ($1.40/1.32 \approx 1.06$), so the inflation rate decreases to about 6 per cent between those years. The decline in the inflation rate implies that although the price level is still rising, it is doing so at a slower pace than the year before.

The price of oil rises 8 per cent between 2000 and 2001. But because the general inflation over that period is 10 per cent, the relative price of oil – that is, its price *relative to all other goods and services* – falls by about 2 per cent (8 per cent – 10 per cent = –2 per cent). Between 2001 and 2002 the price of oil rises by another 8 per cent, while the general inflation rate is about 6 per cent. Hence the relative price of oil rises between 2001 and 2002 by about 2 per cent (8 per cent – 6 per cent).

## The true costs of inflation

Having dispelled the common confusion between inflation and relative price changes, we are now free to address the *true economic costs of inflation*. There are a variety of such costs, each of which tends to reduce the efficiency of the economy. Five of the most important are discussed here.

## 'Shoe-leather' costs

As all shoppers know, *cash is convenient*. Unlike cheques, which are not accepted everywhere, and credit cards, for which a minimum purchase is often required, cash can be used in almost any routine transaction. Businesses, too, find cash convenient to hold. Having plenty of cash on hand facilitates transactions with customers and reduces the need for frequent deposits and withdrawals from the bank.

Inflation raises the cost of holding cash to consumers and businesses. Suppose you are given a present of €1,000 in cash and decide to keep it 'under the mattress' rather than spend it immediately or lodge it in a bank deposit. What happens to the buying power of the €1,000 over time? If inflation is zero so that on average the prices of goods and services are not changing, the buying power of the €1,000 does not change over time. At the end of a year your purchasing power is the same as it was at the beginning of the year. But suppose the inflation rate is 10 per cent. In that case, the purchasing power of the €1,000 will fall by 10 per cent each year. After a year, you will still have €1,000 in cash, but its purchasing power – or the amount of goods and services it can buy – will be reduced to only €900. In general, the higher the rate of inflation, the less people will want to hold cash because of the loss of *purchasing power* that they will suffer.

Technically, currency is a debt owed by the government or Central Bank to the currency holder. So when currency loses value, the losses to holders of cash are offset by gains to the government or Central Bank, which now owes less in real terms to currency holders. Thus, from the point of view of society as a whole, the loss of purchasing power is not in itself a cost of inflation, because it does not involve wasted resources. (Indeed, no real goods or services were used up when your €1,000 lost part of its value.) However, when faced with inflation, people are not likely to accept a loss in purchasing power but instead will take actions to try to 'economise' on their cash holdings. For example, instead of drawing out enough cash for a month the next time they visit the bank, they will draw out enough to last only a week. The inconvenience of visiting the bank or automated teller machine (ATM) more often to minimise one's cash holdings is a real cost of inflation. Similarly, businesses will reduce their cash holdings by sending employees to the bank more frequently, or by installing computerised systems to monitor cash usage. To deal with the increase in bank transactions required by consumers and businesses trying to use less cash, banks will need to hire more employees and expand their operations.

The costs of more frequent trips to the bank, new cash management systems and expanded employment in banks are real costs. They use up resources, including time and effort, that could be used for other purposes. Traditionally, the costs of economising on cash have been called *shoe-leather costs* – the idea being that shoe leather is worn out during extra trips to the bank. Shoe-leather costs probably are not a significant problem in Europe today, where inflation is only 2–3 per cent per year. But in economies with high rates of inflation, they can become quite significant.

### **Example 19.10** Shoe-leather costs at Manuel's Hardware

Manuel's Hardware needs €5,000 cash per day for customer transactions. Manuel has a choice between going to the bank first thing on Monday morning to withdraw €25,000 – enough cash for the whole week – or going to the bank first thing every morning for €5,000 each time. Manuel puts the cost of going to the bank, in terms of inconvenience and lost time, at €4 per trip. Assume that funds left in the bank earn precisely enough interest to keep their purchasing power unaffected by inflation.

How often will Manuel go to the bank to withdraw cash? Given the shoe-leather costs of €4 per trip the frequency of Manuel's visits to the bank will depend on the rate of inflation. If inflation is zero, there is no cost to holding cash. Manuel will go to the bank only once a week, incurring a shoe-leather cost of €4 per week. Assuming Manuel's store is open 50 weeks a year, going to the bank once per week at €4 per trip means 50 trips per year, at a total cost of €200. But if inflation is 10 per cent, Manuel may need to change his banking habits. If he continues to go to the bank only on Monday mornings, withdrawing €25,000 for the week, what will be Manuel's average cash holding over the week? At the beginning of each day, his cash holding will be as follows:

| Day | € |
|---|---|
| Monday | 25,000 |
| Tuesday | 20,000 |
| Wednesday | 15,000 |
| Thursday | 10,000 |
| Friday | 5,000 |

Averaging the holdings on those five days, we can calculate that Manuel's average cash holding at the beginning of each day is €75,000/5 = €15,000. If inflation is 10 per cent a year, over the course of a year the cost to Manuel, in terms of lost purchasing power, of holding an average of €15,000 in cash equals 10 per cent of €15,000, or €1,500. Also, going to the bank once per week at €4 per trip means 50 trips per year, at a total cost of €200. Hence with inflation at 10 per cent the total cost of making one €25,000 withdrawal per week is €1,700 as compared with €200 at zero inflation.

Suppose that with inflation at 10 per cent, Manuel goes to the bank every day rather than once per week. His average cash holding at the beginning of the day will be only €5,000. In that case, his losses from inflation will be €500 (10 per cent of €5,000) a year, a saving of €1,000 compared with one withdrawal per week. However, daily cash withdrawals mean 250 trips to the bank at a cost of €1,000 (€4 per trip) giving a total cost of €1,500 per year. As daily withdrawals reduce the total cost of holding cash (€1,500 as compared with €1,700), Manuel will begin going to the bank more often.

Manuel's *benefit* from reducing his daily cash holdings is €1,000 per year at the *cost* of an additional €800 in shoe-leather costs. These shoe-leather costs of a high inflation rate are the extra costs incurred to avoid holding cash. In this example they are the additional €800 per year associated with Manuel's daily trips to the bank.

## 'Noise' in the price system

In Chapter 3, we described the remarkable economic co-ordination that is necessary to provide the right amount and the right kinds of food to residents of large cities every day. This feat is not orchestrated by some food distribution ministry staffed by bureaucrats. It is done much better than a ministry ever could by the workings of free markets, operating without central guidance.

How do free markets transmit the enormous amounts of information necessary to accomplish complex tasks like the provisioning of a large metropolitan city such as London? The answer, as we saw in Chapter 3, is through the *price system*. When the owners of up-market fish restaurants in London cannot find sufficient quantities of John Dory, a relatively rare species, they bid up its market price. Fish suppliers notice the higher price for John Dory and realise that they can make a profit by supplying more John Dory to the market. At the same time, price-conscious diners will shift to cheaper, more available types of fish. The market for John Dory will reach equilibrium only when there are no more unexploited opportunities for profit, and both suppliers and demanders are satisfied at the market price (the

*Equilibrium Principle*, Chapter 3). Multiply this example a million times, and you will gain a sense of how the price system achieves a truly remarkable degree of economic co-ordination.

When inflation is high, however, the subtle signals that are transmitted through the price system become more difficult to interpret, much in the way that static, or 'noise', makes a radio message harder to interpret. In an economy with little or no inflation, the supplier of foodstuffs will immediately recognise the increase in John Dory prices as a signal to bring more to market. If inflation is high, however, the supplier must ask whether a price increase represents a true increase in the demand for John Dory or is just a result of the general inflation, which causes all food prices to rise. If the price rise reflects only inflation, the price of John Dory *relative to other goods and services* has not really changed. The supplier therefore should not change the quantity of fish he brings to market.

In an inflationary environment, to discern whether the increase in John Dory prices is a true signal of increased demand, the supplier needs to know not only the price of John Dory but also what is happening to the prices of other goods and services. Since this information takes time and effort to collect, the supplier's response to the change in John Dory prices is likely to be slower and more tentative.

In summary, price changes are the market's way of communicating information to suppliers and consumers. An increase in the price of a good or service, for example, tells consumers to economise on their use of the good or service and suppliers to bring more of it to market. But in the presence of inflation, prices are affected not only by changes in the supply and demand for a product but also by changes in the general price level. Inflation creates static, or 'noise', in the price system, obscuring the information transmitted by prices and reducing the efficiency of the market system. This reduction in efficiency imposes real economic costs.

## Distortions of the tax system

Most countries operate a progressive income tax system which levies higher rates of tax on higher levels of income. For example, the first €5,000 of income may be taxed at a zero rate, the next €20,000 at 20 per cent and the remainder at 40 per cent. Hence a household earning €50,000 per year would pay zero tax on the first €5,000, 20 per cent (or €4,000) on the next €20,000 and 40 per cent (or €10,000) on the remaining €25,000, giving a total tax bill of €14,000 which equals 28 per cent of pre-tax income (€50,000) – the system is *progressive* because a household earning €25,000 would pay €4,000 or 16 per cent of its income in tax. The divisions in the household's income, 0 – €5,000, €5,000 – €25,000 and greater than €25,000, are known as *tax brackets*. Now suppose that the household's income rises in line with inflation. If inflation is 10 per cent per year the household's annual income would increase by €5,000 to €55,000 and its annual tax bill would rise to €16,000 or 29 per cent of pre-tax income (€55,000). Hence the household is paying a higher proportion of its income in tax even though its real income has remained constant, a phenomenon known as *bracket creep*. This effect is called a *distortion* because the household is worse off in real terms even though the rates of income tax have remained unchanged. The household's after-tax income rises by 8.3 per cent, €36,000 to €39,000, but with inflation at 10 per cent the household's real purchasing power has declined. This distortion can be avoided by indexing the income tax brackets to inflation. For example suppose that the upper ends of the zero and 20 per cent brackets were increased by 20 per cent to €5,500 and €27,500, respectively. The household would now pay zero on the first €5,500, 20 per cent on the next €22,000 and 40 per cent on the remaining €27,5000, giving a total tax bill of €15,400 or 28 per cent of pre-tax income (€55,000). The household's after-tax income rises by 10 per cent, €36,000 to €39,600, keeping its real purchasing power constant.

Although indexing can solve the problem of bracket creep, many provisions of the various tax codes have not been indexed, either because of lack of political support or because of the complexity of the task. As a result, inflation can produce unintended changes in the taxes people pay, which in turn may cause them to change their behaviour in economically undesirable ways.

### Example 19.11 Accelerated depreciation

An important provision in the many tax codes for which inflation poses problems is a *depreciation allowance*. Suppose a firm buys a machine with a 10-year productive life for €1,000. With a depreciation allowance the firm can take a percentage of the purchase price as a deduction from its taxable profits in each of the 10 years. If the allowance is 10 per cent then the firm can reduce its taxable profits by €100 in each year of the machine's productive life. For example, if the tax rate on profits is 40 per cent then the firm can reduce its tax bill by €40 per year.

The idea behind this type of provision is that the wearing out of the machine is a *cost of doing business* that should be deducted from the firm's profit. Also, giving firms a tax break for investing in new machinery encourages them to invest and modernise their plants. What happens if capital depreciation allowances are not indexed to inflation? Suppose that, at a time when the inflation rate is high, a firm is considering purchasing a €1,000 machine. The managers know that the purchase will allow them to deduct €100 per year from taxable profits for the next 10 years. But that €100 is a fixed amount that is not indexed to inflation. Looking forward, managers will recognise that 5, 6, or 10 years into the future, the real value of the annual €100 tax deduction will be much lower than at present because of inflation. They will have less incentive to buy the machine and may decide not to make the investment at all. Indeed, many studies have found that a high rate of inflation can significantly reduce the rate at which firms invest in new factories and equipment.

One way round this distortion is to permit *accelerated* depreciation allowances. For example, suppose the firm is permitted to deduct the full purchase price in year 1. With a 40 per cent tax on profits the firm would be able to reduce the year 1 tax bill by €400 as compared with €40 per year over 10 years. Accelerated allowances therefore protect the firm from the effects of higher inflation in the future.

In many countries, tax codes are highly complex containing hundreds of provisions and tax rates. This lack of indexation means that inflation can seriously distort the incentives provided by the tax system for people to work, save and invest. The resulting adverse effects on economic efficiency and economic growth represent a real cost of inflation.

## Unexpected redistribution of wealth

Yet another concern about inflation is that it may arbitrarily *redistribute wealth* from one group to another. Consider a group of workers who signed a contract setting their wages for the next three years. If those wages are not indexed to inflation, then the workers will be vulnerable to upsurges in the price level. Suppose, for example, that inflation is much higher than expected over the three years of the contract. In that case the buying power of the workers' wages – their real wages – will be less than anticipated when they signed the contract.

From society's point of view, is the buying power that workers lose to inflation really 'lost'? The answer is no; the loss in their buying power is exactly matched by an unanticipated gain in the employer's buying power, because the real cost of paying the workers is less than anticipated. In other words, the effect of the inflation is not to *destroy* purchasing power but to *redistribute* it – in this case, from the workers to the employer. If inflation had been *lower* than expected, the workers would have enjoyed greater purchasing power than they anticipated and the employer would have been the loser.

Another example of the redistribution caused by inflation takes place between borrowers (debtors) and lenders (creditors). Suppose one of the authors of this book wants to buy a house and borrows €150,000 from the bank to pay for it. Shortly after signing the mortgage agreement, he learns that inflation is likely to be much higher than expected. How should he react to the news? Perhaps as a public-spirited macroeconomist he should be saddened to hear that inflation is rising, but as a borrower he should be pleased. In real terms, euros with which he will repay his loan in the future will be worth much less than expected. The lender should be distraught, because the interest and loan repayments the bank will receive will be worth less, in purchasing power terms, than expected at contract signing. Once again, no real wealth is 'lost' to the inflation; rather, the borrower's gain is just offset by the lender's loss. In general, unexpectedly high inflation rates *help borrowers at the expense of lenders*, because borrowers are able to repay their loans in less valuable euros. Unexpectedly low inflation rates, in contrast, help lenders and hurt borrowers by forcing borrowers to repay in euros that are worth more than expected when the loan was made.

Although redistributions caused by inflation do not directly destroy wealth, but only transfer it from one group to another, they are still bad for the economy. Our economic system is based on *incentives*. For it to work well, people must know that if they work hard, save some of their income and make wise financial investments, they will be rewarded in the long run with greater real wealth and a better standard of living. Some observers have compared a high-inflation economy to a casino, in which wealth is distributed largely by luck – that is, by random fluctuations in the inflation rate. In the long run, a 'casino economy' is likely to perform poorly, as its unpredictability discourages people from working and saving. (Why bother if inflation can take away your savings overnight?) Rather, a high-inflation economy encourages people to use up resources in trying to anticipate inflation and protect themselves against it.

## Interference with long-run planning

The fifth and final cost of inflation we shall examine is its tendency to interfere with the long-run planning of households and firms. Many economic decisions take place within a long time horizon. Planning for retirement, for example, may begin when workers are in their twenties or thirties. And firms develop long-run investment and business strategies that look decades into the future. Clearly, high and erratic inflation can make long-term planning difficult. Suppose, for example, that you want to enjoy a certain standard of living when you retire. How much of your income do you need to save to make your dreams a reality? That depends on what the goods and services you plan to buy will cost 30 or 40 years from now. With high and erratic inflation, even guessing what your chosen lifestyle will cost by the time you retire is extremely difficult. You may end up saving too little and having to compromise on your retirement plans; or you may save too much, sacrificing more than you need to during your working years. Either way, inflation will have proved costly.

In summary, inflation damages the economy in a variety of ways. Some of its effects are difficult to quantify and are therefore controversial. But most economists agree that a low and stable inflation rate is instrumental in maintaining a healthy economy.

## RECAP The true costs of inflation

The public sometimes confuses changes in *relative prices* (such as the price of oil) with inflation, which is a change in the *overall level of prices*. This confusion can cause problems, because the remedies for undesired changes in relative prices and for inflation are different.

There are a number of true costs of inflation, which together tend to reduce economic growth and efficiency. These include:

- *Shoe-leather costs*, or the costs of economising on cash (for example, by making more frequent trips to the bank or installing a computerised cash management system).

- *'Noise' in the price system*, which occurs when general inflation makes it difficult for market participants to interpret the information conveyed by prices.
- *Distortions of the tax system*, for example, when provisions of the tax code are not indexed.
- Unexpected *redistributions of wealth*, as when higher-than-expected inflation hurts wage earners to the benefit of employers or hurts creditors to the benefit of debtors.
- Interference with *long-term planning*, arising because people find it difficult to forecast prices over long periods.

## Hyperinflation

Although there is some disagreement about whether inflation rate of, say, 5 per cent per year imposes important costs on an economy, few economists would question the fact that an inflation rate of 500 per cent or 1,000 per cent per year disrupts economic performance. A situation in which the inflation rate is extremely high is called **hyperinflation**. Although there is no official threshold above which inflation becomes hyperinflation, inflation rates in the range of 500 to 1,000 per cent per year would surely qualify. Since the 1970s, episodes of hyperinflation have occurred in several Latin American countries (including Argentina and Brazil), in Israel and in several countries attempting to make the transition from communism to capitalism – including Russia, where inflation exceeded 2,000 per cent in 1992. In Europe the classic example of hyperinflation is the case of Germany in the early 1920s. Following its defeat in the First World War, Germany was faced with the dual problem of rebuilding its devastated economy and the burden imposed by the Treaty of Versailles which required Germany to pay war reparations (or compensation) to France and Britain. Rather than impose ever-higher taxes on its citizens, the German government resorted to printing money which, as we will see in Chapter 23, ultimately leads to accelerating inflation. For example, in the last quarter of 1923 (October–December) prices were a staggering 53,000 per cent higher than in the previous quarter (July–September).

**hyperinflation** a situation in which the inflation rate is extremely high

Hyperinflation greatly magnifies the costs of inflation. For example, shoe-leather costs – a relatively minor consideration in times of low inflation – become quite important during hyperinflation, when people may visit the bank two or three times per day to hold money for as short a time as possible. With prices changing daily, or even hourly, markets work quite poorly, slowing economic growth. Massive redistributions of wealth take place, impoverishing many. Not surprisingly, episodes of hyperinflation rarely last more than a few years; they are so disruptive that they quickly lead to a public outcry for relief.

### Economic naturalist 19.3 How costly is high inflation?

Economic theory suggests that high inflation rates, especially those associated with hyperinflation, reduce economic efficiency and growth. Most economists believe that the economic costs associated with high inflation outweigh the perceived benefits, yet we continue to see episodes of high inflation throughout the world. In reality, how costly are high inflation rates?

Economists Stanley Fischer, Ratna Sahay and Carlos A. Végh examined the economic performance of 133 market economies over the period 1960–96 and uncovered 45 episodes of high inflation (12-month inflation rates greater than 100 per cent) among 25 different countries.[2] They found that, while uncommon, episodes of

[2] Fischer, Sahay and Végh (2002).

high inflation impose significant economic costs on the countries experiencing them. During periods of high inflation, these countries saw real GDP per person fall by an average of 1.6 per cent per year, real consumption per person fall by an average of 1.3 per cent per year and real investment per person fall by an average of 3.3 per cent per year. During low-inflation years these same countries experienced positive growth in each of these variables. In addition, during periods of high inflation, these countries' trade and government budget deficits were larger than during low-inflation years.

Falling output and consumption levels caused by high inflation reduce the economic well-being of households and firms, and have a disproportionate effect on poor workers, who are least likely to have their wages indexed to the inflation rate and thus avoid a real loss in purchasing power. As pointed out in the last section, high inflation rates also distort relative prices in the marketplace, leading to a *misallocation of resources* that can have long-term economic consequences. Falling investment in new capital caused by high inflation, for example, leads not only to a slowdown in current economic activity but also to reduced growth rates of future output. Because of these adverse economic effects, policy makers have an incentive to keep inflation rates low.

## Inflation and interest rates

So far, we have focused on the *measurement* and *economic* costs of inflation. Another important aspect of inflation is its close relationship to other key macroeconomic variables. For example, economists have long realised that during periods of high inflation *interest rates* tend to be high as well. We shall close this chapter with a look at the relationship between inflation and interest rates, which will provide a useful background to the chapters to come.

### Inflation and the real interest rate

Earlier in our discussion of the ways in which inflation redistributes wealth, we saw that inflation tends to hurt creditors and help debtors by reducing the value of the money with which debts are repaid. The effect of inflation on debtors and creditors can be explained more precisely using an economic concept called the **real interest rate**. An example will illustrate.

**real interest rate** the annual percentage increase in the purchasing power of a financial asset; the real interest rate on any asset equals the nominal interest rate on that asset minus the inflation rate

Suppose that there are two neighbouring countries, Alpha and Beta. In Alpha, whose currency is called the alphan, the inflation rate is zero and is expected to remain at zero. In Beta, where the currency is the betan, the inflation rate is 10 per cent and is expected to remain at that level. Bank deposits pay 2 per cent annual interest in Alpha and 10 per cent annual interest in Beta. In which country are bank depositors getting a better deal?

You may answer Beta, since interest rates on deposits are higher in that country. But if you think about the effects of inflation, you will recognise that Alpha, not Beta, offers the better deal to depositors. To see why, think about the change over a year in the real purchasing power of deposits in the two countries. In Alpha, someone who deposits 100 alphans in the bank on 1 January will have 102 alphans on 31 December. As there is no inflation in Alpha, and goods and services will cost the same at the end of the year as at the beginning, the 102 alphans represent a 2 per cent increase in buying power.

In Beta, the depositor who deposits 100 betans on 1 January will have 110 betans by the end of the year – 10 per cent more than she started with. But the prices of goods and services in Beta, we have assumed, will also rise by 10 per cent. Thus the Beta depositor can afford to buy precisely the same amount of goods and services at the end of the year as she could at the beginning; she gets no increase in buying power. So the Alpha depositor has the better deal, after all.

Economists refer to the annual percentage increase in the *real* purchasing power of a financial asset as the real interest rate, or the *real rate of return* on that asset. In our example, the real purchasing power of deposits rises by 2 per cent per year in Alpha and by 0 per cent per year in Beta. So the real interest rate on deposits is 2 per cent in Alpha and 0 per cent in Beta. The real interest rate should be distinguished from the more familiar market interest rate, also called the **nominal interest rate**. The nominal interest rate is the annual percentage increase in the nominal, or euro, value of an asset.

**nominal interest rate** (or market interest rate) the annual percentage increase in the nominal value of a financial asset

As the example of Alpha and Beta illustrates, we can calculate the real interest rate for any financial asset, from a bank deposit to a government bond, by subtracting the rate of inflation from the market or nominal interest rate on that asset. So in Alpha, the real interest rate on deposits equals the nominal interest rate (2 per cent) minus the inflation rate (0 per cent), or 2 per cent. Likewise in Beta, the real interest rate equals the nominal interest rate (10 per cent) minus the inflation rate (10 per cent), or 0 per cent.

We can write this definition of the real interest rate in very simple mathematical terms:

$$r = i - \pi$$

where

$r$ = the real interest rate
$i$ = the nominal, or market, interest rate
$\pi$ = the inflation rate

## Example 19.12 Real interest rates in the 1970s, 1980s and 1990s

Following are interest rates on 20-year British government bonds for selected years in the 1970s, 1980s and 1990s. In which of these years did the financial investors who bought these bonds get the best deal? The worst deal?

| Year | Interest rate (%) | Inflation rate (%) |
|---|---|---|
| 1970 | 9.2 | 6.5 |
| 1975 | 14.4 | 24.0 |
| 1980 | 13.8 | 18.0 |
| 1985 | 10.6 | 6.1 |
| 1990 | 11.1 | 9.4 |
| 1995 | 8.3 | 3.3 |
| 2000 | 4.7 | 2.9 |

Financial investors and lenders do best when the *real* (not the nominal) interest rate is high, since the real interest rate measures the increase in their *purchasing power*. We can calculate the real interest rate for each year by subtracting the inflation rate from the nominal interest rate. The results are 2.7 per cent for 1970, –9.6 per cent for 1975, –4.2 per cent for 1980, 4.5 per cent for 1985, 1.7 per cent for 1990, 5 per cent for 1995 and 1.8 per cent for 2000. For purchasers of government bonds, the best of these years was 1995, when they enjoyed a real return of 5 per cent. The worst year was 1975, when their real return was actually negative. In other words, despite receiving 14.4 per cent nominal interest, financial investors ended up losing purchasing power in 1975, as the inflation rate exceeded the interest rate earned by their investments. Once again the effect of inflation is *distributive*. For example, in 1975, when the real rate of interest was close to –10 per cent, the effect of high inflation was to redistribute purchasing power from lenders (bond holders) to borrowers (government).

Figure 19.2 shows the real interest rate in Germany and the United Kingdom since 1960, as measured by the nominal interest rate minus the inflation rate. Note that in both countries, and especially in the United Kingdom, the real interest rates were negative in the 1970s, a decade of high inflation, but became strongly positive as inflation subsided in the 1980s and 1990s.

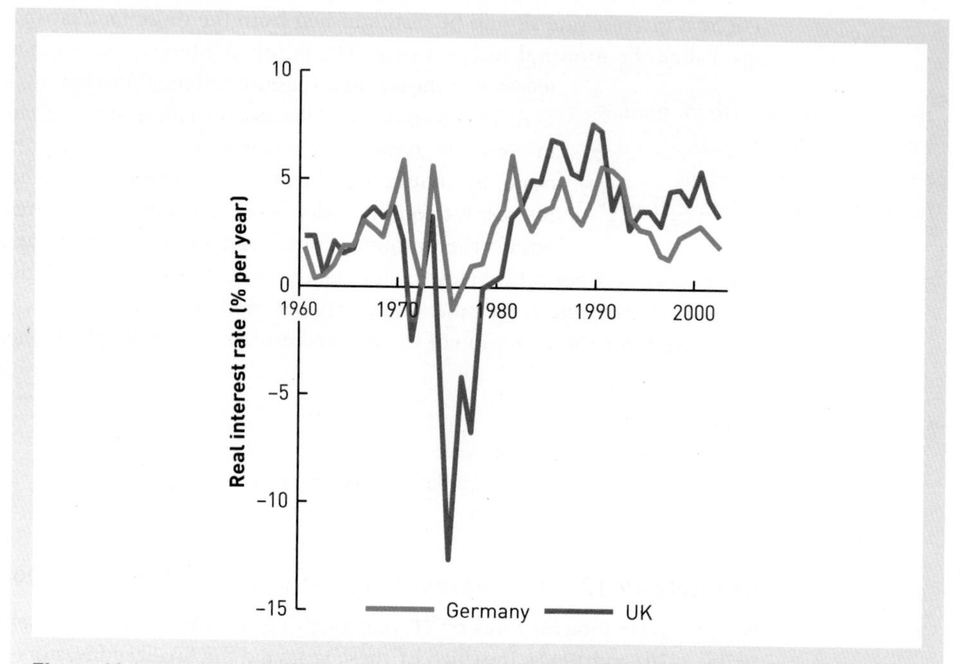


**Figure 19.2 The Real Interest in Germany and the United Kingdom, 1960–2002.** The real interest rate is the nominal interest rate – here, the short-term rate – minus the rate of inflation. In the United Kingdom the real interest rate was negative in the 1970s when inflation was exceptionally high.

The concept of the real interest rate helps to explain more precisely why an unexpected surge in inflation is bad for lenders and good for borrowers. For any given nominal interest rate that the lender charges the borrower, the higher the inflation rate, the lower the real interest rate the lender actually receives. So unexpectedly high inflation leaves the lender worse off. Borrowers, on the other hand, are better off when inflation is unexpectedly high, because their real interest rate is lower than anticipated.

Although unexpectedly high inflation hurts lenders and helps borrowers, a high rate of inflation that is expected may not redistribute wealth at all, because expected inflation can be built into the nominal interest rate. Suppose, for example, that the lender requires a real interest rate of 2 per cent on new loans. If the inflation rate is confidently expected to be zero, the lender can get a 2 per cent real interest rate by charging a nominal interest rate of 2 per cent. But if the inflation rate is expected to be 10 per cent, the lender can still ensure a real interest rate of 2 per cent by charging a nominal interest rate of 12 per cent. Thus high inflation, if it is *expected*, need not hurt lenders – as long as the lenders can adjust the nominal interest they charge to reflect the expected inflation rate.

**Exercise 19.7** What is the real rate of return to holding cash? (**Hint:** Does cash pay interest?) Does this real rate of return depend on whether the rate of inflation is correctly anticipated? How does your answer relate to the idea of shoe-leather costs?

## The Fisher effect

Earlier we mentioned the observation that interest rates tend to be high when inflation is high and low when inflation is low. This relationship can be seen in Figure 19.3, which shows the German inflation rate and a nominal interest rate from 1960 to 2002. Notice that the *spikes* and *troughs* (or high and low values) for the nominal interest rate tend to coincide with spikes and troughs in the inflation rate. Hence, nominal interest rates have tended to be high in periods of high inflation, such as the late 1970s, and relatively low in periods of low inflation, such as the early 1960s and the late 1990s.

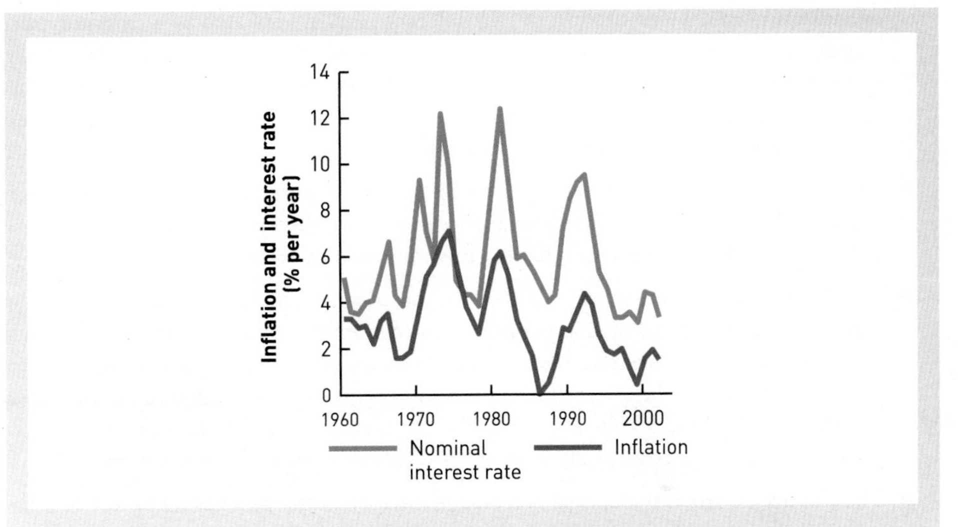


**Figure 19.3 Inflation and Interest Rates in Germany, 1960–2002.** On average, nominal interest rates tend to be high when inflation is high and low when inflation is low, a phenomenon called the 'Fisher effect'.

Why do interest rates tend to be high when inflation is high? Our discussion of real interest rates provides the answer. Suppose that inflation has recently been high, so borrowers and lenders anticipate that it will be high in the near future. We would expect lenders to raise their nominal interest rate so that their real rate of return will be unaffected. For their part, borrowers are willing to pay higher nominal interest rates when inflation is high, because they understand that the higher nominal interest rate serves only to compensate the lender for the fact that the loan will be repaid in euros of reduced real value – in real terms, their cost of borrowing is unaffected by an equal increase in the nominal interest rate and the inflation rate. Conversely, when inflation is low, lenders do not need to charge so high a nominal interest rate to ensure a given real return. Thus nominal interest rates will be high when inflation is high and low when inflation is low. This tendency for nominal interest rates to follow inflation rates is called the **Fisher effect**, after the early twentieth-century American economist Irving Fisher, who first pointed out the relationship.

**Fisher effect** the tendency for nominal interest rates to be high when inflation is high and low when inflation is low

## Summary

- The basic tool for measuring inflation is the *consumer price index*, or CPI. The CPI measures the cost of purchasing a fixed basket of goods and services in any period relative to the cost of the same basket of goods and services in a base year. The *inflation rate* is the annual percentage rate of change in the price level as measured by a *price index* such as the CPI.
- The official inflation rate, based on the CPI, may *overstate* the true inflation rate for two reasons. First, it may not adequately reflect improvements in the quality of goods and services. Second, the method of calculating the CPI ignores the fact that consumers can substitute cheaper goods and services for more expensive ones.
- A *nominal quantity* is a quantity that is measured in terms of its current money value. Dividing a nominal quantity, such as a family's income or a worker's wage in euros, by a price index, such as the CPI, expresses that quantity in terms of real purchasing power. This procedure is called *deflating* the nominal quantity. If nominal quantities from two different years are deflated by a common price index, the purchasing power of the two quantities can be compared. To ensure that a nominal payment, such as a pension, represents a constant level of real purchasing power, the nominal payment should be increased each year by a percentage equal to the inflation rate. This method of adjusting nominal payments to maintain their purchasing power is called *indexing*.
- The public sometimes confuses increases in the *relative prices* for specific goods or services with inflation, which is an increase in the *general price level*. Since the remedies for a change in relative prices are different from the remedies for inflation, this confusion can cause problems.
- Inflation imposes a number of true costs on the economy, including 'shoe-leather' costs, which are the real resources that are wasted as people try to economise on cash holdings, 'noise' in the price system, distortions of the tax system, unexpected redistributions of wealth, and interference with long-run planning. Because of these costs, most economists agree that sustained economic growth is more likely if inflation is low and stable. *Hyperinflation*, a situation in which the inflation rate is extremely high, greatly magnifies the costs of inflation and is highly disruptive to the economy.
- The *real interest rate* is the annual percentage increase in the purchasing power of a financial asset. It is equal to the *nominal*, or *market*, *interest rate* minus the inflation rate. When inflation is unexpectedly high, the real interest rate is lower than anticipated, which hurts lenders but benefits borrowers. When inflation is unexpectedly low, lenders benefit and borrowers are hurt. To obtain a given real rate of return, lenders must charge a high nominal interest rate when inflation is high and a low nominal interest rate when inflation is low. The tendency for nominal interest rates to be high when inflation is high and low when inflation is low is called the *Fisher effect*.


## Key terms

**consumer price index (CPI)** (525)
**deflating (a nominal quantity)** (529)
**deflation** (528)
**Fisher effect** (547)
**hyperinflation** (543)
**indexing** (532)
**nominal interest rate** (545)
**nominal quantity** (530)
**price index** (527)
**price level** (536)
**rate of inflation** (527)
**real interest rate** (544)
**real quantity** (530)
**real wage** (531)
**relative price** (536)

## Review questions

1. Explain why changes in the cost of living for any particular individual or family may differ from changes in the official cost-of-living index, the CPI.
2. What is the difference between the *price level* and the *rate of inflation* in an economy?
3. Why is it important to adjust for inflation when comparing nominal quantities (for example, workers' average wages) at different points in time? What is the basic method for adjusting for inflation?
4. Describe how indexation might be used to guarantee that the purchasing power of the wage agreed to in a multi-year labour contract will not be eroded by inflation.
5. Give two reasons why the official inflation rate may understate the 'true' rate of inflation. Illustrate by examples.
6. 'It's true that unexpected inflation redistributes wealth, from creditors to debtors, for example. But what one side of the bargain loses the other side gains. So from the perspective of the society as a whole, there is no real cost.' Do you agree? Discuss.
7. How does inflation affect the real return on holding cash?
8. **True or false:** If both the potential lender and the potential borrower correctly anticipate the rate of inflation, inflation will not redistribute wealth from the creditor to the debtor. Explain.

## Problems

1. A government survey determines that typical family expenditures each month in the year designated as the base year are as follows:

 20 pizzas, €10 each
 Rent, €600 per month
 Petrol and car maintenance, €100
 Phone service, €50

 In the year following the base year, the survey determines that pizzas have risen to €11 each, rent is €640, petrol and car maintenance have risen to €120 and the phone service has dropped in price to €40.

 a. Find the CPI in the subsequent year and the rate of inflation between the base year and the subsequent year.
 b. The family's nominal income rose by 5 per cent between the base year and the subsequent year. Are they worse off or better off in terms of what their income is able to buy?

2. The table below gives values for the EU HICP for each year from 1990 to 2001. For each year, beginning with 1991, calculate the rate of inflation from the previous year. What happened to inflation rates over the 1990s?

| | |
|---|---|
| 1990 | 81.7 |
| 1991 | 85.9 |
| 1992 | 89.3 |
| 1993 | 92.4 |
| 1994 | 95.0 |
| 1995 | 97.7 |
| 1996 | 100.0 |
| 1997 | 101.7 |
| 1998 | 103.0 |
| 1999 | 104.3 |
| 2000 | 106.2 |
| 2001 | 108.6 |

3. Here is a hypothetical income tax schedule, expressed in nominal terms, for 2002.

| Family income (€) | Taxes due (% of income) |
|---|---|
| <20,000 | 0 |
| 20,000–30,000 | 10 |
| 30,000–50,000 | 20 |
| >50,000 | 25 |

The government wants to ensure that families with a given real income are not pushed up into higher tax brackets by inflation. The CPI is 175 in 2002 and 192.5 in 2004. How should the income tax schedule be adjusted for 2004 to meet the government's objective?

4. The typical consumer's food basket in the base year 2000 is as follows:

30 chickens @ €3.00 each
10 hams @ €6.00 each
10 steaks @ €8.00 each

A chicken feed shortage causes the price of chickens to rise to €5.00 each in 2001. Hams rise to €7.00 each, and the price of steaks is unchanged.

a. Calculate the change in the 'cost-of-eating' index between 2000 and 2001.

b. Suppose that consumers are completely indifferent between two chickens and one ham. For this example, how large is the substitution bias in the official 'cost-of-eating' index?

5. Here are the actual UK. per-litre prices for unleaded premium petrol for selected years from 1990 to 2004 with the value of the CPI for those years. Would it be fair to say that most of the changes in petrol prices during this period were due to general inflation, or were factors specific to the oil market playing a role as well?

| Year | Price (pence/litre) | CPI (1996 = 100) |
|---|---|---|
| 1990 | 38.37 | 81.1 |
| 1995 | 53.44 | 97.6 |
| 2000 | 75.38 | 105.6 |
| 2004 | 76.20 | 111.2 |

6. Repeat Example 19.10 from the text (shoe-leather costs at Manuel's Hardware). Calculate shoe-leather costs (relative to the original situation, in which Manuel goes to the bank once a week) assuming that

a. Inflation is 5 per cent rather than 10 per cent.

b. Inflation is 5 per cent and Manuel's trips to the bank cost €2 each.

c. Inflation remains at 10 per cent and a trip to the bank costs €4, but Manuel needs €10,000 per day to transact with customers.

7. On 1 January 2000, Albert invested €1,000 at 6 per cent interest per year for three years. The CPI on 1 January 2000, stood at 100. On 1 January 2001, the CPI stood at 100. On 1 January 2002, it was 110 and on 1 January 2003, the day Albert's investment matured, the CPI was 118. Find the real rate of interest earned by Albert in each of the three years and his total real return over the three-year period. Assume that interest earnings are reinvested each year and earn interest.

8. Frank is lending €1,000 to Sarah for two years. Frank and Sarah agree that Frank should earn a 2 per cent real return per year.

a. The CPI is 100 at the time that Frank makes the loan. It is expected to be 110 in one year and 121 in two years. What nominal rate of interest should Frank charge Sarah?

b. Suppose Frank and Sarah are unsure about what the CPI will be in two years. Show how Frank and Sarah could index Sarah's annual repayments to ensure that Frank gets an annual 2 per cent real rate of return.

9. In the base year for computing the CPI expenditures of the typical consumer break down as follows:

| Item | % |
|---|---|
| Food and beverages | 17.8 |
| Housing | 42.8 |
| Clothing | 6.3 |
| Transportation | 17.2 |
| Medical care | 5.7 |
| Entertainment | 4.4 |
| Other goods, services | 5.8 |
| Total | 100.0 |

Suppose that since the base year the prices of food and beverages have increased by 10 per cent, the price of housing has increased by 5 per cent, and the price of medical care has increased by 10 per cent. Other prices are unchanged. Find the CPI for the current year.

## Answers to in-chapter exercises

19.1 The cost of the family's basket in 2000 remains at €680, as in Table 19.1. If the rent on their flat falls to €400 in 2004, the cost of reproducing the 2000 basket of goods and services in 2004 is €620 (€400 for rent + €150 for hamburgers + €70 for train tickets). The CPI for 2004 is accordingly €620/€680, or 0.912. So in this example, the cost of living fell nearly 9 per cent between 2000 and 2004.

19.2 To construct your own PPI, you would need to determine the basket of goods and services that you personally purchased in the base year. Your PPI in each period would then be defined as the cost of your personal basket in that period relative to its cost in the base year. To the extent that your mix of purchases differs from that of the typical consumer, your cost-of-living index will differ from the official CPI. For example, if in the base year you spent an above-average share of your budget on goods and services that have risen relatively rapidly in price, your personal inflation rate will be higher than the CPI inflation rate.

19.3 To find the CPI using 1972 as the base year we divide each value by the 1972 index. Multiplying by 100 this gives: 1972 = 100, 1973 = 108.5, 1974 = 127.1, 1975 = 157.8, 1976 = 184. Allowing for rounding, these values give the same inflation rates as in Example 19.2. Hence the choice of the base year does not alter our results.

19.4 Sharapova's real earnings, in 1982–84 dollars, were $1 million/1.89, or $529,100. In real terms Sharapova earned about 2.5 times (529,100/207,272) Navratilova's 1990 prize money.

19.5 For women, real wages were 170.3/1.261 = £135.05 in 1990 and 356/1.813 = £196.35 in 2003, an increase of 45 per cent. For men, real wages were 282.20/1.261 = £223.79 in 1990 and 486.8/1.813 = £268.50 in 2003, an increase of 20 per cent. Hence while both sexes experienced an increase in real wages the increase in real female wages was 2.5 times the increase in male wages.

19.6 At the end of the first year the pension should increase by the rate of inflation 2 per cent. Hence the money value will be 1.02 × 2,000 = €2,040. At the end of the second year when inflation is 3 per cent the pension will be 1.03 × 2,040 = €2,101.2. As inflation is 4 per cent in the third year the pension will increase to 1.04 × 2,101.2 = €2,185.2.

19.7 The real rate of return to cash, as with any asset, is the nominal interest rate less the inflation rate. But cash pays no interest; that is, the nominal interest rate on cash is zero. Therefore, the real rate of return on cash is minus the inflation rate. In other words, cash loses buying power at a rate equal to the rate of inflation. This rate of return depends on the actual rate of inflation and does not depend on whether the rate of inflation is correctly anticipated.

If inflation is high so that the real rate of return on cash is strongly negative, people will take actions to try to reduce their holdings of cash, such as going to the bank more often. The costs associated with trying to reduce holdings of cash are what economists call 'shoe-leather costs'.

## References

Fischer, S., R. Sahay and C. A. Végh (2002) 'Modern Hyper- and High Inflations', *Journal of Economic Literature*, 11, pp. 837–80.

Shapiro, M. and J. Wilcox (1996) 'Mismeasurement in the Consumer Price Index: An Evaluation', in B. Bernanke and J. Rotemberg (eds), *NBER Macroeconomics Annual*.

# Part 7

# The Economy in the Long Run

For millennia the great majority of the world's inhabitants eked out a spare existence by tilling the soil. Only a small proportion of the population lived above the level of subsistence, learned to read and write, or travelled more than a few kilometres from their birthplaces. Large cities grew up, serving as imperial capitals and centres of trade, but the great majority of urban populations lived in dire poverty, subject to malnutrition and disease.

Then, in the 1700s, a fundamental change occurred. Spurred by technological advances and entrepreneurial innovations, a process of economic growth began. Sustained over many years, this growth in the economy's productive capacity has transformed almost every aspect of how we live – from what we eat and wear to how we work and play. What caused this economic growth? And why have some countries enjoyed substantially greater rates of growth than others? As the Nobel Prize winner Robert E. Lucas, Jr put it in a classic article on economic development: 'The consequences for human welfare involved in questions like these are simply staggering: Once one starts to think about them, it is hard to think about anything else.' Although most people would attach less significance to these questions than Lucas did, they are undoubtedly of very great importance.

The subject of Part 7 is the behaviour of the economy in the long run, including the factors that cause the economy to grow and develop. Chapter 20 begins by tackling the causes and consequences of economic growth. A key conclusion of the chapter is that improvements in average labour productivity are the primary source of rising living standards; hence policies to improve living standards should focus on stimulating productivity. Chapter 21 studies long-term trends in the labour market, analysing the long-run effects of economic growth on real wages and employment opportunities. As the creation of new capital goods is an important factor underlying rising productivity, Chapter 22 examines the processes of saving and capital formation. Chapter 23 introduces the concept of money and examines its relationship to inflation in the long run. In addition, this chapter introduces the European Central Bank (ECB) and describes how it can promote economic stability. Chapter 24 discusses the role of banks, bond markets and stock markets in allocating saving to productive uses, as well as the role of international capital flows, which facilitate the allocation of saving across countries.

# 20

# Economic Growth, Productivity and Living Standards

A speaker at a conference on the effects of economic growth and development on society posed the following question: 'Which would you rather be? An ordinary, middle-class French or British citizen today, or the richest person in Europe at the time of Napoleon?'

A member of the audience spoke out immediately: 'I can answer that question in one word, dentistry.'

The answer may have caused laughter but it was nonetheless a good answer. Dentistry in Europe at the time of Napoleon – whether the patient was rich or poor – was a primitive affair. Most dentists simply pulled a patient's rotten teeth, with a shot of brandy for anaesthetic. Other types of medical care were not much better than dentistry. Eighteenth- and early-nineteenth-century doctors had no effective weapons against tuberculosis, typhoid fever, diphtheria, influenza, pneumonia and other communicable diseases. Such illnesses, now quite treatable, were major killers in Napoleon's time. Infants and children were particularly susceptible to deadly infectious diseases and even a well-to-do family could often lose two or three children to these illnesses.

Medical care is not the only aspect of ordinary life that has changed drastically since the late 1770s. Today we can use the Channel Tunnel to travel between London and Paris in a matter of hours; in 1800 the same journey could take several days. We can now fly from European capital cities to places such as Beijing, Tokyo and Los Angeles in less than a day; even in 1950 similar journeys could take weeks, or even months.

No doubt you can think of other enormous changes in the way average people live, even over the past few decades. Computer technologies and the Internet have changed the ways people work and study in just a few years, for example. Though these changes are due in large part to scientific advances, such discoveries by themselves usually have little effect on most people's lives. New scientific knowledge leads to widespread improvements in living standards only when it is *commercially applied*. Better understanding of the human immune system, for example, has little impact unless it leads to new therapies or drugs. And a new drug will do little to help unless it is affordable to those who need it.

A tragic illustration of this point is the AIDS epidemic in Africa. Although some new drugs will moderate the effects of the virus that causes AIDS, they are so expensive that they are of little practical value in poverty-stricken African nations grappling with the disease. But even if the drugs were affordable, they would have limited benefit without modern hospitals, trained health professionals and adequate nutrition and sanitation. In short, most improvements in a nation's living standard are the result not just of scientific and technological advances but of an *economic system* that makes the benefits of those advances available to the average person.

In this chapter we shall explore the sources of economic growth and rising living standards in the modern world. We shall begin by reviewing the remarkable economic growth in the industrialised countries, as measured by real GDP per person. Since the mid-nineteenth century (and earlier in some countries), a radical transformation in living standards has occurred. What explains this transformation? The key to rising living standards is a *continuing increase in average labour productivity*, which depends on several factors, from the skills and motivation workers bring to their jobs to the legal and social environment in which they work. We shall analyse each of these factors and discuss its implications for government policies to promote growth. We shall also discuss the costs of rapid economic growth and consider whether there may be limits to the amount of economic growth a society can achieve.

## The remarkable rise in living standards: the record

The advances in health care and transportation mentioned in the beginning of this chapter illustrate only a few of the impressive changes that have taken place in people's material well-being since 1800, particularly in industrialised countries such as France, Germany, the United Kingdom and the United States. To study the factors that affect living standards systematically, however, we must go beyond anecdotes and adopt a specific measure of economic well-being in a particular country and time.

In Chapter 18 we introduced the concept of *real GDP* as a basic measure of the level of economic activity in a country. Recall that, in essence, real GDP measures the physical volume of goods and services produced within a country's borders during a specific period, such as a quarter or a year. Consequently, real GDP *per person* provides a measure of the quantity of goods and services available to the typical resident of a country at a particular time. Although, as we saw in Chapter 18, real GDP per person is certainly not a perfect indicator of economic well-being it is positively related to a number of pertinent variables, such as life expectancy, infant health and literacy. Lacking a better alternative, economists have focused on real GDP per person as a key measure of a country's living standard and stage of economic development.

Figure 17.2 (p. 480) showed the remarkable growth in real GDP per person that occurred in Europe and the United States between 1900 and 2000. For comparison, Table 20.1 shows real GDP per person in eight major countries in selected years from 1870 to 2000 (US dollars are used to facilitate comparisons). Figure 20.1 displays the same data graphically for five of the eight countries.

| Country<br>(1) | 1870<br>(2) | 1913<br>(3) | 1950<br>(4) | 1979<br>(5) | 2000<br>(6) | Annual % change 1870–2000<br>(7) | Annual % change 1950–2000<br>(8) |
|---|---|---|---|---|---|---|---|
| Australia | 5,626 | 7,385 | 9,561 | 18,033 | 24,708 | 1.1 | 1.9 |
| Canada | 2,447 | 5,791 | 9,362 | 20,899 | 26,604 | 1.8 | 2.1 |
| France | 2,249 | 4,401 | 6,049 | 17,801 | 22,447 | 1.8 | 2.6 |
| Germany | 1,205 | 2,320 | 5,005 | 18,014 | 23,247 | 2.3 | 3.1 |
| Italy | 2,248 | 3,167 | 4,042 | 13,331 | 21,930 | 1.8 | 3.4 |
| Japan | 963 | 1,825 | 2,216 | 16,899 | 24,772 | 2.5 | 4.8 |
| United Kingdom | 3,500 | 5,374 | 7,832 | 14,889 | 21,142 | 1.4 | 2.0 |
| United States | 2,843 | 6,745 | 11,921 | 22,480 | 32,629 | 1.9 | 2.0 |

**Table 20.1** Real GDP per Person in Selected Countries, 1870–2000 (1995 US Dollars)

*Note*: Rebased to 1995 and updated to 2000 by the authors using OECD *Quarterly National Accounts*. 'Germany' refers to West Germany in 1950 and 1979.

*Sources*: Derived from Maddison (1988, Tables A2, B2–B4).

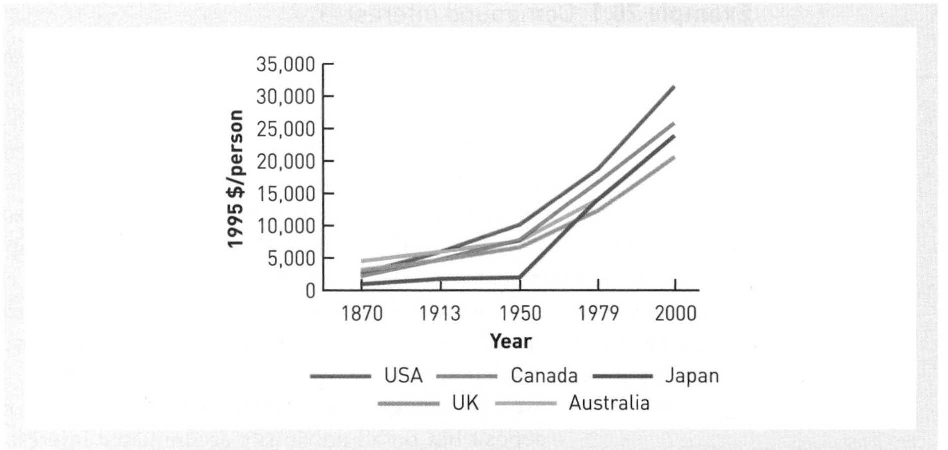


**Figure 20.1 Real GDP per Person in Five Industrialised Countries, 1870–2000.** Economic growth has been especially rapid since the 1950s, particularly in Japan.

The data in Table 20.1 and Fig. 20.1 tell a dramatic story. For example, in the United States (which was already a relatively wealthy industrialised country in 1870), real GDP per person grew more than 11-fold between 1870 and 2000. In Japan, real GDP per person grew more than 25-fold over the same period. Underlying these statistics is an amazingly rapid process of economic growth and transformation, through which in just a few generations relatively poor agrarian societies became highly industrialised economies – with average standards of living that could scarcely have been imagined in 1870. As Fig. 20.1 shows, a significant part of this growth has occurred since 1950, particularly in Japan.

A note of caution is in order. The further back in time we go, the less precise are historical estimates of real GDP. Most governments did not keep official GDP statistics until after the Second World War; production records from earlier periods are often incomplete or of questionable accuracy. Comparing economic output over a century or more is also problematic because many goods and services that are produced today were unavailable – indeed, inconceivable – in 1870. How many nineteenth-century horse-drawn wagons, for example, would be the economic equivalent of a BMW 328i car or an Airbus jet? Despite the difficulty of making precise comparisons, however, we can say with certainty that the variety, quality and quantity of available goods and services increased enormously in industrialised countries during the nineteenth and twentieth centuries, a fact reflected in the data on real GDP per capita.

## Why 'small' differences in growth rates matter

Columns (7) and (8) of Table 20.1 show the annual growth rates of real GDP per person, both for the entire 1870–2000 period and the more recent years, 1950–2000. At first glance these growth rates don't seem to differ much from country to country. For example, for the period 1870–2000, the highest growth rate is 2.5 per cent (Japan) and the lowest is 1.1 per cent (Australia). But consider the long-run effect of this seemingly 'small' difference in annual growth rates. In 1870, in terms of output per person, Australia was by far the richest of the eight countries listed in Table 20.1, with a real GDP per person nearly six times that of Japan. Yet by 2000 Japan had not only caught up with but had exceeded Australia. This remarkable change in economic fortunes is the result of the apparently small difference between a 1.1 per cent growth rate and a 2.5 per cent growth rate, maintained over 130 years.

The fact that what seem to be small differences in growth rates can have large long-run effects results from what is called the *power of compound interest*.

### Example 20.1 Compound interest: 1

In 1800 your great-great-grandfather deposited the equivalent of €10.00 in a bank account at 4 per cent interest. Interest is compounded annually (so that interest paid at the end of each year receives interest itself in later years). Great-great-grandpa's will specified that the account be turned over to his most direct descendant (you) in 2000. When you withdrew the funds in that year, how much was the account worth?

The account was worth €10.00 in 1800; €10.00 × 1.04 = €10.40 in 1801; €10.00 × 1.04 × 1.04 = €10.00 × $(1.04)^2$ = €10.82 in 1802; and so on. Since 200 years elapsed between 1800, when the deposit was made, and the year 2000, when the account was closed, the value of the account in the year 2000 was €10.00 × $(1.04)^{200}$, or €10.00 × 1.04 to the 200th power. Using a calculator, you will find that €10.00 times 1.04 to the 200th power is €25,507.50 – a good return for a €10.00 deposit!

**Compound interest** – an arrangement in which interest is paid not only on the original deposit but on all previously accumulated interest – is distinguished from *simple interest*, in which interest is paid only on the *original deposit*. If your great-great-grandfather's account had been deposited at 4 per cent simple interest, it would have accumulated only 40 cents each year (4 per cent of the original €10.00 deposit), for a total value of €10.00 + 200 × €0.40 = €90.00 after 200 years. The tremendous growth in the value of his account came from the compounding of the interest – hence the phrase 'the power of compound interest'.

**compound interest** the payment of interest not only on the original deposit but on all previously accumulated interest

### Example 20.2 Compound interest: 2

Refer to Example 20.1. What would your great-great-grandfather's €10.00 deposit have been worth after 200 years if the annual interest rate had been 2 per cent?

At 2 per cent interest the account would be worth €10.00 in 1800; €10.00 × 1.02 = €10.20 in 1801; €10.00 × $(1.02)^2$ = €10.40 in 1802; and so on. In the year 2000 the value of the account would be €10.00 × $(1.02)^{200}$, or €524.85. If the interest rate were 6 per cent, after 200 years the account would be worth €0.00 × $(1.06)^{200}$, or €1,151,259.04. Let's summarise the results of Examples 20.1 and 20.2:

| Interest rate (%) | Value of €10 after 200 years (€) |
|---|---|
| 2 | 524.85 |
| 4 | 25,507.50 |
| 6 | 1,151,259.04 |

The power of compound interest is that, even at relatively low rates of interest, a small sum, compounded over a long enough period, can greatly increase in value. A more subtle point, illustrated by Examples 20.1 and 20.2, is that small differences in interest rates matter a lot. The difference between a 2 per cent and a 4 per cent interest rate doesn't seem tremendous, but over a long period of time it implies large differences in the amount of interest accumulated on an account. Likewise, the effect of switching from a 4 per cent to a 6 per cent interest rate is enormous, as our calculations show.

Economic growth rates are similar to compound interest rates. Just as the value of a bank deposit grows each year at a rate equal to the interest rate, so the size of a nation's economy expands each year at the rate of economic growth. This analogy suggests that even a relatively modest rate of growth in output per person – say, 1 to 2 per cent per year – will produce tremendous increases in average living standards over a long period. And relatively small *differences* in growth rates, as in the case of Australia versus Japan, will ultimately produce very different living standards. Over the long run, then, the *rate of economic growth* is an extremely important variable. Hence, government policy changes or other factors that affect the long-term growth rate even by a small amount will have a major economic impact.

**Exercise 20.1**

Suppose that real GDP per capita in the United Kingdom had grown at 2.5 per cent per year, as Japan's did, instead of the actual 1.4 per cent per year, from 1870 to 2000. How much larger would real GDP per person have been in the United Kingdom in 2000?

## Why nations become rich: the crucial role of average labour productivity

What determines a nation's economic growth rate? To get some insight into this vital question, we shall find it useful to express real GDP per person as the product of two terms: *average labour productivity* and the *share of the population that is working*.

To do this, let $Y$ equal total real output (as measured by real GDP, for example), $N$ equal the number of employed workers and $POP$ equal the total population. Then real GDP per person can be written as $Y/POP$; average labour productivity, or output per employed worker, equals $Y/N$; and the share of the population that is working is $N/POP$. The relationship between these three variables is

$$\frac{Y}{POP} = \frac{Y}{N} \times \frac{N}{POP}$$

which, as you can see by cancelling out $N$ on the right-hand side of the equation, always holds exactly. In words, this basic relationship is

Real GDP per person = Average labour productivity × Share of population employed

This expression for real GDP per person tells us something very basic and intuitive: The quantity of goods and services that each person can consume depends on (1) how much each worker can produce and (2) how many people (as a fraction of the total population) are working. Furthermore, because real GDP per person equals average labour productivity times the share of the population employed, real GDP per person can *grow* only to the extent that there is *growth* in worker productivity and/or the fraction of the population that is employed.

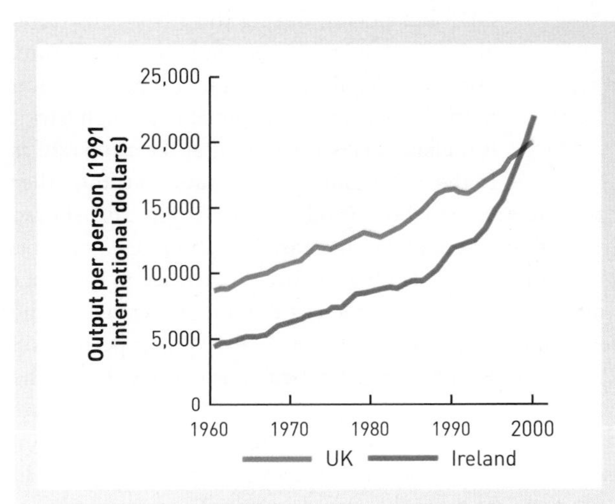


**Figure 20.2 Real GDP per Person, Ireland and the United Kingdom, 1960–2000.**

Figures 20.2, 20.3 and 20.4 use data for Ireland and the United Kingdom over 1960–2000 to illustrate the behaviour of the three key variables in the relationship above. Figure 20.2 shows real GDP per person, Fig. 20.3 shows real GDP per person employed (average labour productivity) and Fig. 20.4 shows the portion of the population (not just the working-age population) that was employed during that period. Figures 20.2 and 20.3 demonstrate the remarkable growth of the Irish economy, especially in the 1990s. Between 1960 and 2000 Irish output per person

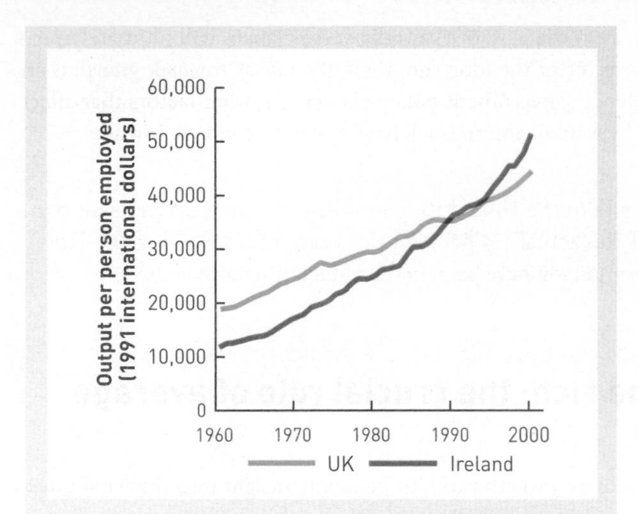


**Figure 20.3 Real GDP per Person Employed, Ireland and the United Kingdom, 1960–2000.**

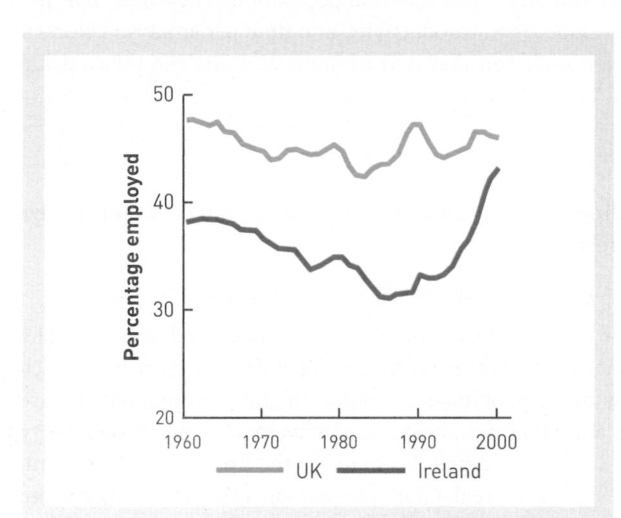


**Figure 20.4 Percentage of the Population Employed Ireland and the United Kingdom, 1960–2000.**

grew by over 400 per cent and output per person employed by 350 per cent. In contrast, UK output per person increased by 130 per cent and output per person employed by 140 per cent. This does not imply that the UK economy performed badly. Indeed, by 2000 the average British citizen enjoyed about twice as many goods and services as in 1960 which is broadly in line with the record of other European economies. However, by any standards the performance of the Irish economy has been exceptional, especially in the 1980s. For example, in 1960 the real income of the average Irish citizen was about 50 per cent of the income of the average British citizen, but by 2000 Irish income per head was 9 per cent greater than in the United Kingdom. Figures 20.3 and 20.4 show that increases in both labour productivity and the share of the population holding a job contributed to this dramatic rise in Irish living standards.

Let us look a bit more closely at these two contributing factors, beginning with the share of the population that is employed. In the case of Ireland as Fig. 20.4 shows, between 1960 and the mid-1980s the number of people employed declined from 38 to 31 per cent of the entire population but then increased rapidly to 43 per cent by 2000. The growing tendency of women to work outside the home, an increase in the share of the general population of working age and inward migration were important reasons for this rise in employment. Although the rising share of the population with jobs contributed significantly to the increase in real Irish GDP per person during the 1990s, this trend almost certainly will not continue in the future. For example, although women's participation in the labour force may remain at a high *level* it is unlikely to continue *rising* at the same rate as in the 1980s and 1990s. What about the other factor that determines output per person, average labour productivity? As Fig. 20.3 shows, between 1960 and 2000, average Irish labour productivity increased by about 350 per cent, and dominates the rise in numbers employed in explaining the overall increase in GDP per person. The UK data tell a slightly different story. Despite the fact that the percentage of the total population in employment declined between 1960 and 2000, real GDP per person still increased by about 130 per cent. This rise in British living standards was entirely due to the growth in average labour productivity, $Y/N$.

This quick look at recent data supports a more general conclusion. In the long run, increases in output per person arise primarily from *increases in average labour productivity*. In simple terms, the more people can produce, the more they can consume. To understand why economies grow, then, we must understand the reasons for increased labour productivity.

### RECAP Economic growth and productivity

Real GDP per person, a basic indicator of living standards, has grown dramatically in the industrialised countries. This growth reflects the *power of compound interest*: even a modest growth rate, if sustained over a long period of time, can lead to large increases in the size of the economy.

Output per person equals average labour productivity times the share of the population that is employed. In the long run, increases in output per person and hence living standards arise primarily from increases in average labour productivity.

## Determinants of average labour productivity

What determines the productivity of the average worker in a particular country at a particular time? Popular discussions of this issue often equate worker productivity with the willingness of workers of a given nationality to work hard. Everything else being equal, a culture that promotes hard work certainly tends to increase worker productivity. But intensity of effort alone cannot explain the huge differences in average labour productivity that we observe around the world. For example, average labour productivity in countries such as Ireland and the United Kingdom is about 100 times what it is in Bangladesh, though there is little doubt that Bangladeshis work very hard. Likewise, the differences in the growth of Irish and British labour productivity, as illustrated in Fig. 20.3, do not imply that Irish workers work three times harder than their English, Scottish or Welsh counterparts.

In this section we shall examine six factors that appear to account for the major differences in average labour productivity, both between countries and between generations. Later in the chapter we shall discuss how economic policies can influence these factors to spur productivity and growth.

### Human capital

To illustrate the factors that determine average labour productivity, we introduce two prototypical assembly line workers, Lucy and Ethel.

#### Example 20.3 Lucy and Ethel on the assembly line

Lucy and Ethel have jobs wrapping chocolate bars and placing them into boxes. Lucy, a trainee wrapper, can wrap only 100 bars per hour. Ethel, who has had on-the-job training, can wrap 300 bars per hour. Lucy and Ethel each work 40 hours per week. Find average labour productivity, in terms of bars wrapped per week and bars wrapped per hour, (a) for Lucy, (b) for Ethel and (c) for Lucy and Ethel as a team.

We have defined average labour productivity in general terms as *output per worker*. Note, though, that the measurement of average labour productivity depends on the time period that is specified. For example, the data presented in Fig. 20.3 tell us how much the average worker produces *in a year*. In this example we are concerned with how much Lucy and Ethel can produce *per hour* of work or *per week* of work. Any one of these ways of measuring labour productivity is equally valid, as long as we are clear about the time unit we are using.

Lucy and Ethel's hourly productivities are given in the example: Lucy can wrap 100 bars per hour and Ethel can wrap 300. Lucy's weekly productivity is (40 hours/week) × (100 bars wrapped/hour) = 4,000 wrapped bars per week. Ethel's weekly productivity is (40 hours/week) × (300 bars wrapped/hour) = 12,000 bars per week.

Together Lucy and Ethel can wrap 16,000 bars per week. As a team, their average weekly productivity is (16,000 bars wrapped)/(2 weeks of work), or 8,000 bars per week. Their average hourly productivity as a team is (16,000 bars wrapped)/(80 hours of work) = 200 bars per hour. Notice that, taken as a team, the two women's productivity lies midway between their individual productivities.

Ethel is more productive than Lucy because she has had on-the-job training, which has allowed her to develop her wrapping skills to a higher level than Lucy's. Because of her training, Ethel can produce more than Lucy can in a given number of hours.

**Exercise 20.2** Suppose Ethel has additional training in chocolate bar wrapping and learns how to wrap 500 bars per hour. Find the output per week and output per hour for Lucy and Ethel, both individually and as a team.

Economists would explain the difference in the two women's performance by saying that Ethel has more human capital than Lucy. *Human capital* comprises the talents, education, training and skills of workers. Workers with a large stock of human capital are more productive than workers with less training. For example, a secretary who knows how to use a word processing program will be able to type more letters than one who doesn't; a motor mechanic who is familiar with computerised diagnostic equipment will be able to fix engine problems that less well-trained mechanics cannot.

## Economic naturalist 20.1 Why did West Germany and Japan recover so successfully from the devastation of the Second World War?

Germany and Japan sustained extensive destruction of their cities and industries during the Second World War and entered the postwar period impoverished. Yet within 30 years both countries had not only been rebuilt but had become worldwide industrial and economic leaders. What accounts for these 'economic miracles'?

Many factors contributed to the economic recovery of the two countries, including the substantial aid provided by the United States to Europe under the Marshall Plan and to Japan during the US occupation. Most economists agree, however, that high levels of *human capital* played a crucial role in both countries.

At the end of the war, Germany's population was exceptionally well educated, with a large number of highly qualified scientists and engineers. The country also had (and still has today) an extensive apprentice system that provided on-the-job training to young workers. As a result, Germany had a *skilled industrial workforce*. In addition, the area that became West Germany benefited substantially from an influx of skilled workers from East Germany and the rest of Soviet-controlled Europe, including 20,000 trained engineers and technicians. Beginning as early as 1949, this concentration of human capital contributed to a major expansion of Germany's technologically sophisticated, highly productive manufacturing sector. By 1960, West Germany was a leading exporter of high-quality manufactured goods, and its citizens enjoyed one of the highest standards of living in Europe.

Japan also began the postwar period with a skilled and educated labour force. In addition, occupying American forces restructured the Japanese school system and encouraged all Japanese to obtain a good education. Even more so than the Germans, however, the Japanese emphasized on-the-job training. As part of a *lifetime employment system*, under which workers were expected to stay with the same company their entire career, Japanese firms invested extensively in worker training. The payoff to these investments in human capital was a steady increase in average labour productivity, particularly in manufacturing. By the 1980s, Japanese manufactured goods were among the most advanced in the world and Japan's workers among the most skilled.

Although high levels of human capital were instrumental in the rapid economic growth of West Germany and Japan, human capital alone cannot create a high living standard. A case in point is Soviet-dominated East Germany, which had a level of human capital similar to West Germany's after 1945 but did not enjoy the same economic growth. For reasons we shall discuss later in the chapter (see Economic naturalist 20.4, p. 570), the communist system imposed by the Soviets utilised East Germany's human capital far less effectively than the economic systems of Japan and West Germany.

Human capital is analogous to *physical capital* (such as machines and factories) in that it is acquired primarily through the investment of time, energy and money. For example, to learn how to use a word processing program, a secretary might need to attend a technical school at night. The cost of going to school includes not only the tuition paid but also the *opportunity cost* of the secretary's time spent attending class and studying. The benefit of the schooling is the increase in wages the secretary will earn when the course has been completed. We know by the *Cost–Benefit Principle* (Chapter 1) that the secretary should learn word processing only if the benefits exceed the costs, including the opportunity costs. In general, then, we would expect to see people acquire additional education and skills when the difference in the wages paid to skilled and unskilled workers is significant.

## Physical capital

Workers' productivity depends not only on their skills and effort but also on the tools they have to work with. Even the most skilled surgeon cannot perform open-heart surgery without sophisticated equipment, and an expert computer programmer is of limited value without a computer. These examples illustrate the importance of *physical capital*, such as factories and machines. More and better capital allows workers to produce more efficiently, as Example 20.4 shows.

### **Example 20.4** Lucy and Ethel get automated

Refer to Example 20.3. Lucy and Ethel's boss acquired an electric wrapping machine, which is designed to be operated by one worker. Using this machine, an untrained worker can wrap 500 bars per hour. What are Lucy and Ethel's hourly and weekly outputs now? Will the answer change if the boss gets a second machine? A third?

Suppose for the sake of simplicity that a wrapping machine must be assigned to one worker only. (This assumption rules out sharing arrangements, in which one worker uses the machine on the day shift and another on the night shift.) If the boss buys just one machine, she will assign it to Lucy. (Why? See Exercise 20.3.) Now Lucy will be able to wrap 500 bars per hour, while Ethel can wrap only 300 per hour. Lucy's weekly output will be 20,000 wrapped bars (40 hours × 500 bars wrapped per hour). Ethel's weekly output is still 12,000 wrapped bars (40 hours × 300 bars wrapped per hour). Together they can now wrap 32,000 bars per week, or 16,000 bars per week each. On an hourly basis, average labour productivity for the two women taken together is 32,000 bars wrapped per 80 hours of work, or 400 bars wrapped per hour – twice their average labour productivity before the boss bought the machine.

With two wrapping machines available, both Lucy and Ethel could use a machine. Each could wrap 500 bars per hour, for a total of 40,000 wrapped bars per week. Average labour productivity for both women taken together would be 20,000 wrapped bars per week, or 500 wrapped bars per hour.

What would happen if the boss purchased a third machine? With only two workers, a third machine would be useless: it would add nothing to either total output or average labour productivity.

**Exercise 20.3** Using the assumptions made in Examples 20.3 and 20.4, explain why the boss should give the single available wrapping machine to Lucy rather than Ethel. (**Hint:** Use the *Principle of Increasing Opportunity Cost*, Chapter 3.)

The wrapping machine is an example of a *capital good*, which was defined in Chapter 18 as a long-lived good, which is itself produced and used to produce other goods and services. Capital goods include machines and equipment (such as computers, earthmovers or assembly lines) as well as buildings (such as factories or office buildings).

Capital goods such as the wrapping machine enhance workers' productivity. Table 20.2 summarises the results from Examples 20.3 and 20.4. For each number of machines the boss might acquire (column (1)), Table 20.2 gives the total weekly output of Lucy and Ethel taken together (column (2)), the total number of hours worked by the two women (column (3)) and average output per hour (column (4)), equal to total weekly output divided by total weekly hours.

Table 20.2 demonstrates two important points about the effect of additional capital on output. First, for a given number of workers, adding more capital generally increases both total output and average labour productivity. For example, adding the first wrapping machine increases weekly output (column (2)) by 16,000 bars and average labour productivity (column (4)) by 200 bars wrapped per hour.

| Number of machines (capital) (1) | Total number of bars wrapped each week (output) (2) | Total hours worked per week (3) | Bars wrapped per hour worked (productivity) (4) |
|---|---|---|---|
| 0 | 16,000 | 80 | 200 |
| 1 | 32,000 | 80 | 400 |
| 2 | 40,000 | 80 | 500 |
| 3 | 40,000 | 80 | 500 |

**Table 20.2** Capital, Output and Productivity in the Chocolate Bar Wrapping Factory

The second point illustrated by Table 20.2 is that the more capital is already in place, the smaller the benefits of adding extra capital. Notice that the first machine adds 16,000 bars to total output, but the second machine adds only 8,000. The third machine, which cannot be used since there are only two workers, does not increase output or productivity at all. This result illustrates a general principle of economics, called **diminishing returns to capital**. According to the principle of diminishing returns to capital, if the amount of labour and other inputs employed is held constant, then the greater the amount of capital already in use the less an additional unit of capital adds to production. In the case of the wrapping factory, diminishing returns to capital implies that the first wrapping machine acquired adds more output than the second, which in turn adds more output than the third.

**diminishing returns to capital** if the amount of labour and other inputs employed is held constant, then the greater the amount of capital already in use, the less an additional unit of capital adds to production

Diminishing returns to capital are a natural consequence of firms' incentive to use each piece of capital as productively as possible. To maximise output, managers will assign the first machine that a firm acquires to the most productive use available, the next machine to the next most productive use, and so on – an illustration of the *Principle of Increasing Opportunity Cost* (Chapter 3). When many machines are available, all the highly productive ways of using them already have been exploited. Thus adding yet another machine will not raise output or productivity by very much. If Lucy and Ethel are already operating two wrapping machines, there is little point to buying a third machine, except perhaps as a replacement or spare.

The implications of Table 20.2 can be applied to the question of how to stimulate economic growth. First, increasing the amount of capital available to the workforce will tend to increase output and average labour productivity. The more adequately equipped workers are, the more productive they will be. Second, the degree to which productivity can be increased by an expanding stock of capital is limited. Because of diminishing returns to capital, an economy in which the quantity of capital available to each worker is already very high will not benefit much from further expansion of the capital stock.

Is there empirical evidence that giving workers more capital makes them more productive? Figure 20.5 shows the relationship between average labour productivity (real GDP per worker) and the amount of capital per worker in 15 major countries, including the 8 industrialised countries listed in Table 20.1. Figure 20.5 shows a strong relationship between the amounts of capital per worker and productivity, consistent with the theory. Note, though, that the relationship between capital and productivity is somewhat weaker for the richest countries. For example, Germany has more capital per worker than the United States, but German workers are less productive than American workers on average. Diminishing returns to capital may help to explain the weakening of the relationship between capital and productivity at high levels of capital. In addition, Fig. 20.5 does not account for many other differences among countries, such as differences in economic systems or government policies. Thus we should not expect to see a perfect relationship between the two variables.

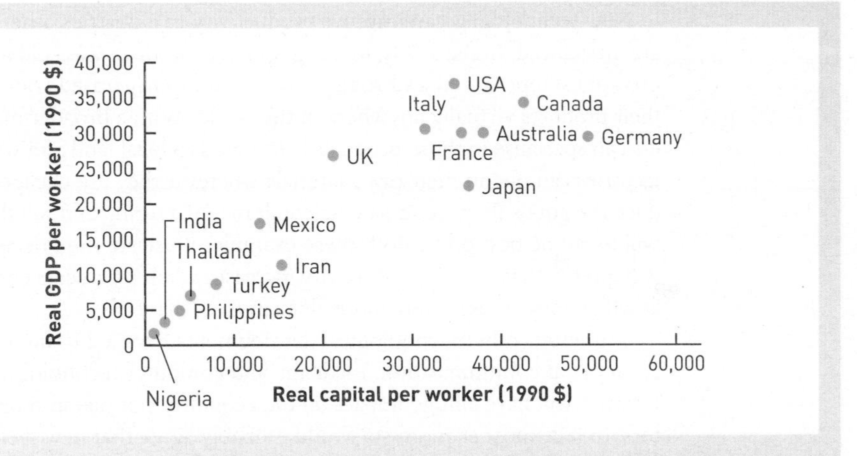


**Figure 20.5 Average Labour Productivity and Capital per Worker in 15 Countries, 1990.** Countries with large amounts of capital per worker also tend to have high average labour productivity, as measured by real GDP per worker.

*Source*: Penn World Tables, www.nber.org. Countries included are those listed in Table 20.1, plus all countries with populations of 40 million or more for which data are available.

## Land and other natural resources

Besides capital goods, other *inputs to production* help to make workers more productive, among them land, energy and raw materials. Fertile land is essential to agriculture, and modern manufacturing processes make intensive use of energy and raw materials.

In general, an abundance of natural resources increases the productivity of the workers who use them. For example, a farmer can produce a much larger crop in a land-rich country such as the United States or Australia than in a country where the soil is poor or arable land is limited in supply. With the aid of modern farm machinery and great expanses of land, American farmers are today so productive that even though they constitute less than 3 per cent of the population, they provide enough food not only to feed the country but to export to the rest of the world.

Although there are limits to a country's supply of arable land, many other natural resources, such as petroleum and metals, can be obtained through international markets. Because resources can be obtained through trade, countries need not possess large quantities of natural resources within their own borders to achieve economic growth. Indeed, a number of countries have become rich without substantial natural resources of their own, including Japan, Hong Kong, Singapore and Switzerland. Just as important as possessing natural resources is the ability to *use them productively* – for example, by means of advanced technologies.

## Technology

Besides human capital, physical capital and natural resources, a country's ability to develop and apply new, more productive technologies will help to determine its productivity. Consider just one industry, transportation. In 1800, the horse and carriage were the primary means of transportation – a slow and costly method indeed. But in the nineteenth century, technological advances to the steam engine (invented in the eighteenth century) supported the expansion of river-borne transportation and the development of national rail networks. In the twentieth century, improvements in the internal combustion engine (a late nineteenth-century invention) and the development of aviation, supported by the construction of an extensive infrastructure of roads and airports, have produced increasingly rapid, cheap and reliable transport. Technological change has clearly been a driving force in the transportation revolution.

New technologies can improve productivity in industries other than the one in which they are introduced. In the 1770s, most agricultural produce was sold locally. Today the availability of rapid shipping, rail and road networks and refrigerated transport allows farmers to sell their products virtually anywhere in the world. With a broader market in which to sell, farmers can specialise in those products best suited to local land and weather conditions. Similarly, factories can obtain their raw materials wherever they are cheapest and most abundant, produce the goods they are most efficient at manufacturing and sell their products wherever they will fetch the best price. Both these examples illustrate the *Principle of Comparative Advantage* (Chapter 2) that overall productivity increases when producers concentrate on those activities at which they are relatively more efficient (see Chapter 3).

Numerous other technological developments have led to increased productivity, including advances in communication, medicine and computer technology. All indications are that the Internet will have a huge impact on the economy, not just in retailing but in many other sectors. In fact, most economists would probably agree that new technologies are the *single most important source of productivity improvement*, and hence of economic growth in general.

However, economic growth does not automatically follow from breakthroughs in basic science. To make the best use of new knowledge, an economy needs **entrepreneurs** who can exploit scientific advances commercially, as well as a *legal and political environment* that encourages the practical application of new knowledge.

**entrepreneurs** people who create new economic enterprises

**Exercise 20.4** A new kind of wrapping paper has been invented that makes wrapping chocolate bars quicker and easier. The use of this paper *increases* the number of bars a person can wrap by hand by 200 per hour, and the number of bars a person can wrap by machine by 300 per hour. Using the data from Examples 20.3 and 20.4, construct a table like Table 20.2 that shows how this technological advance affects average labour productivity. Do diminishing returns to capital still hold?

**Exercise 20.5** A Senegalese worker who emigrates to France is likely to find that his average labour productivity is much higher in France than it was at home. The worker is, of course, the same person he was when he lived in Senegal. How can the simple act of moving to France increase the worker's productivity? What does your answer say about the incentive to emigrate?

## Entrepreneurship and management

The productivity of workers depends in part on the people who help to decide what to produce and how to produce it: entrepreneurs and managers. Entrepreneurs are people who create new economic enterprises. Because of the new products, services, technological processes and production methods they introduce, entrepreneurs are critical to a dynamic, healthy economy. Individuals such as Henry Ford (automobiles), Bill Gates (software) and Richard Branson (airlines) have played central roles in the development of their industries both nationally and internationally – and, not incidentally, amassed huge personal fortunes in the process. These people and others like them have been criticised for some of their business practices, in some cases with justification. Clearly, though, they and dozens of other prominent business leaders of the twentieth-century contributed significantly to economic growth. Henry Ford, for example, developed the idea of *mass production*, which lowered costs sufficiently to bring automobiles within reach of the average family. Ford began his business in his garage, a tradition that has been maintained by thousands of innovators ever since.

Entrepreneurship, like any form of creativity, is difficult to teach, although some of the supporting skills, such as financial analysis and marketing, can be learned in college or business school. How, then, does a society encourage entrepreneurship? History suggests that the entrepreneurial spirit will always exist; the challenge to society is to channel entrepreneurial energies in economically productive ways. For example, economic policy makers need to ensure that taxation is not so heavy, and regulation not so inflexible, that small businesses – some of which will eventually become big businesses – cannot get off the ground. Sociological factors may play a role as well. Societies in which business and commerce are considered to be beneath the dignity of refined, educated people are less likely to produce successful entrepreneurs (see Economic naturalist 20.2 below). Overall, a social and economic environment that allows entrepreneurship to flourish appears to promote economic growth and rising productivity, perhaps especially so in high-technology eras like our own.

### **Example 20.5** Lucy and Ethel become entrepreneurs

After many years working on the assembly line Lucy and Ethel decide to use their experience in the chocolate industry to start their own business. Using their savings and a loan from their friendly bank manager, Lucy and Ethel open a shop – Lucy & Ethel's Chocolate Factory – selling specialised hand-made chocolates. The shop is an instant success and Lucy and Ethel cash in by franchising their brand nationwide with outlets in all major cities. As a result, their incomes increase from thousands to millions of euro per year. This increase in income is a measure of Lucy and Ethel's contribution to GDP. How does the success of the Lucy & Ethel's Chocolate Factory affect their average labour productivity? Their average labour productivity (in per-hour terms) is their contribution to GDP divided by the number of hours they work on their franchise operation. As Lucy and Ethel's income has increased dramatically, their average labour productivity as entrepreneurs will be many times what it was when they were chocolate bar wrappers.

Example 20.5 illustrates the importance of creative entrepreneurship: had they not discovered their latent entrepreneurial skills, Lucy and Ethel would still be working on the assembly line, where their average labour productivity would be much lower.

## Economic naturalist 20.2 Why did medieval China stagnate economically?

The Sung period in China (AD 960–1270) was one of considerable technological sophistication; its inventions included paper, waterwheels, water clocks, gunpowder and possibly the compass. Yet no significant industrialisation occurred, and in subsequent centuries Europe saw more economic growth and technological innovation than China. Why did medieval China stagnate economically?

According to research by economist William Baumol,[1] the main impediment to industrialisation during the Sung period was a social system that inhibited entrepreneurship. Commerce and industry were considered low-status activities, not fit for an educated person. In addition, the emperor had the right to seize his subjects' property and to take control of their business enterprises – a right that greatly reduced his subjects' incentives to undertake business ventures. The most direct path to status and riches in medieval China was to go through a system of demanding civil service examinations given by the government every three years. The highest scorers on these national examinations were granted lifetime positions in the imperial bureaucracy, where they wielded much power and often became wealthy, in part through corruption. Not surprisingly, medieval China did not develop a dynamic entrepreneurial class, and consequently its scientific and technological advantages did not translate into sustained economic growth. China's experience shows why scientific advances alone cannot guarantee economic growth; to have economic benefits, scientific knowledge must be *commercially applied* through new products and new, more efficient means of producing goods and services.

Although entrepreneurship may be more glamorous, managers – the people who run businesses on a daily basis – also play an important role in determining average labour productivity. Managerial jobs span a wide range of positions, from the supervisor of the loading dock to the CEO (chief executive officer) at the helm a large multinational company. Managers work to satisfy customers, deal with suppliers, organise production, obtain financing, assign workers to jobs and motivate them to work hard and effectively. Such activities enhance labour productivity. For example, in the 1970s and 1980s, Japanese managers introduced new production methods that greatly increased the efficiency of Japanese manufacturing plants. Among them was the *just-in-time* (JIT) inventory system, in which suppliers deliver production components to the factory just when they are needed, eliminating the need for factories to stockpile components. Japanese managers also pioneered the idea of organising workers into semi-independent production teams, which allowed workers more flexibility and responsibility than the traditional assembly line.

## The political and legal environment

So far, we have emphasised the role of the private sector in increasing average labour productivity. But government, too, has a role to play in fostering improved productivity. One of the key contributions government can make is to provide a *political and legal environment* that encourages people to behave in economically productive ways – to work hard, save and invest wisely, acquire useful information and skills, and provide the goods and services that the public demands.

[1] Baumol (1990).

One specific function of government that appears to be crucial to economic success is the establishment of *well-defined property rights*. Property rights are well defined when the law provides clear rules for determining who owns what resources (through a system of deeds and titles, for example) and how those resources can be used. Imagine living in a society in which a dictator, backed by the military and the police, could take whatever he wanted, and regularly did so. In such a country, what incentive would you have to raise a large crop or to produce other valuable goods and services? Very little, since much of what you produced would probably be taken away from you. Unfortunately, in many countries of the world today, this situation is far from hypothetical.

Political and legal conditions affect the growth of productivity in other ways, as well. Political scientists and economists have documented the fact that *political instability* can be detrimental to economic growth. This finding is reasonable, since entrepreneurs and savers are unlikely to invest their resources in a country whose government is unstable, particularly if the struggle for power involves civil unrest, terrorism or guerrilla warfare. For example, one hoped-for benefit of the Northern Ireland peace process was a so-called, but yet to be fully realised, 'peace dividend' in terms of greater investment, higher economic growth and lower unemployment.

However, government can do much more than guaranteeing well-defined property rights and political stability. In particular, government can promote the growth of free and flexible markets which encourage the development of new technologies and products by providing incentives to entrepreneurship, innovation and higher productivity. Economic naturalist 20.3 provides a European example.

## Economic naturalist 20.3 The Lisbon Agenda

In March 2000 Europe's political leaders agreed a 10-year strategy designed to promote economic growth and employment in the European Union. Of particular concern was that, relative to the United States, Europe continued to experience a low rate of job creation, higher and more persistent unemployment and lower labour productivity. The aim of the new strategy, which has subsequently become known as the *Lisbon Agenda*, was to transform Europe into 'the most competitive and dynamic knowledge-based economy in the world', a goal to be achieved by a series of *structural reforms* in labour, product and financial markets. At the heart of the Lisbon Agenda is the realisation that to exploit the full benefits of economic integration Europe must provide greater incentives for innovation, job creation and competitiveness by promoting flexible and responsive labour markets, more efficient welfare and tax systems which encourage job-seeking and do not over-penalise successful and innovative high-income earners, and a reduction in the administrative 'red tape' which stifles innovation and entrepreneurship. For example, some estimates suggest that whereas it took just one week to establish a new business in the United States it could take up to twelve weeks, and cost four times more, in Europe. Likewise, in some European countries there are limits on the maximum working week and unions have a legal right to be involved in management decisions such as a decision to close a plant or retail outlet. More generally, high and long-lived unemployment benefits, generous redundancy payments and labour laws which make 'hiring and firing' unduly difficult and expensive are seen as disincentives to job creation, investment and innovation.

Most mid-term reviews of the Lisbon Agenda agree that it has failed to deliver. The fundamental problem is that labour market institutions and welfare systems have evolved in different ways and there is no common or one-size model to which all countries can agree. On the one side, countries such as France and Germany favour an approach which promotes social cohesion rather than individualism whereas others such as Ireland and the United Kingdom have moved toward more flexible systems which put greater emphasis on incentives and economic efficiency. If the Lisbon Agenda is to succeed, Europe must find a way to reconcile these differences.

## Economic naturalist 20.4 Why did communism fail?

For more than 70 years, from the Russian Revolution in 1917 until the collapse of the Soviet Union in 1991, communism was believed by many to pose a major challenge to market-based economic systems. Yet, by the time of the Soviet Union's break-up, the poor economic record of communism had become apparent. Indeed, low living standards in communist countries, compared with those achieved in the West, were a major reason for the popular discontent that brought down the communist system in Europe. Economically speaking, why did communism fail?

The poor growth records of the Soviet Union and other communist countries did not reflect a lack of resources or economic potential. The Soviet Union had a highly educated workforce; a large capital stock; a vast quantity of natural resources, including land and energy; and access to sophisticated technologies. Yet, at the time of its collapse, output per person in the Soviet Union was probably less than one-seventh what it was in the United States.

Most observers would agree that the *political and legal environment* that established the structure of the communist economic system was a major cause of its ultimate failure. The economic system of the Soviet Union and other communist countries had two main elements. First, the capital stock and other resources were owned by the government rather than by individuals or private corporations. Second, most decisions regarding production and distribution were made and implemented by a government planning agency rather than by individuals and firms interacting through markets. This system performed poorly, we now understand, for several reasons.

One major problem was the *absence of private property rights*. With no ability to acquire a significant amount of private property, Soviet citizens had little incentive to behave in economically productive ways. The owner of an American or Japanese firm is strongly motivated to cut costs and to produce goods that are highly valued by the public, because the owner's income is determined by the firm's profitability. In contrast, the performance of a Soviet firm manager was judged on whether the manager produced the quantities of goods specified by the government's plan – irrespective of the quality of the goods produced or whether consumers wanted them. Soviet managers had little incentive to reduce costs or produce better, more highly valued products, as any extra profits would accrue to the government and not to the manager; nor was there any scope for entrepreneurs to start new businesses. Likewise, workers had little reason to work hard or effectively under the communist system, as pay rates were determined by the government planning agency rather than by the economic value of what the workers produced.

A second major weakness of the communist system was the *absence of free markets*. In centrally planned economies (CPEs), markets are replaced by detailed government plans that specify what should be produced, and how. But, as we saw in the case of London's food supply (Chapter 3), the co-ordination of even relatively basic economic activities can be extremely complex and require a great deal of information, much of which is dispersed among many people. In a market system, changes in prices both convey information about the goods and services people want and provide suppliers with the incentives to bring these goods and services to market. Indeed, as we know from the *Equilibrium Principle* (Chapter 3), a market in equilibrium leaves individuals with no *unexploited opportunities*. Central planners in communist countries proved far less able to deal with this complexity than decentralised markets. As a result, under communism, consumers suffered constant shortages and shoddy goods.

After the collapse of communism, many formerly communist countries began the difficult transition to a market-orientated economic system. Changing an entire economic system (the most extreme example of a *structural policy*) is a slow and difficult task, and many countries saw economic conditions worsen at first rather than improve. *Political instability* and the absence of a modern *legal framework*, particularly laws applying to commercial transactions, have often hampered the progress of reforms. However, a number of formerly communist countries, including Poland, the Czech Republic and the former East Germany, have succeeded in implementing Western-style market systems and have begun to achieve significant economic growth.

**RECAP Determinants of average labour productivity**

Key factors determining average labour productivity in a country include:

- The skills and training of workers – *human capital*
- The quantity and quality of *physical capital* – machines, equipment and buildings
- The availability of land and other *natural resources*
- The sophistication of the *technologies* applied in production
- The effectiveness of *management* and *entrepreneurship*
- The broad *social and legal environment*.

## The worldwide productivity slowdown – and recovery?

During the 1950s and 1960s most of the major industrialised countries saw rapid growth in real GDP and average labour productivity. In the 1970s, however, productivity growth began to slow down around the world. Slower growth in real GDP and in average living standards followed.

The slowdown in the growth of labour productivity is documented in Table 20.3, which gives data for five major industrialised countries. Note the sharp decline in productivity growth in all five countries during 1973–79 compared with 1960–73. Japan's case was particularly striking: its productivity growth rate fell from 7.6 per cent per year in 1960–73 to 2.7 per cent in 1973–79. In the United States, annual productivity growth fell from 2.3 per cent before 1973 to just 0.6 per cent per year during 1973–79. During the period 1979–2000, productivity growth improved somewhat in the United States and the United Kingdom but, in all five countries, the rate of productivity improvement since 1979 has been much slower than it was prior to 1973.

The sudden decline in worldwide productivity growth around 1973 is puzzling to economists and policy makers alike. What might have caused it? In the 1970s and 1980s many

| | Percentage growth, annual rates | | |
|---|---|---|---|
| **Country** | **1960–73** | **1973–79** | **1979–2000** |
| France | 4.6 | 2.3 | 1.8 |
| Germany | 4.0 | 2.6 | 2.0 |
| Japan | 7.6 | 2.7 | 2.0 |
| United Kingdom | 2.8 | 1.3 | 1.7 |
| United States | 2.3 | 0.6 | 1.7 |

**Table 20.3** Average Labour Productivity Growth Rates in Selected Countries, 1960–2000

economists thought that the fourfold increase in oil prices that followed the Arab–Israeli war (1973) might have caused the slowdown. However, oil prices (relative to the prices of other goods) eventually returned to pre-1973 levels, but productivity growth did not. Thus oil prices are no longer thought to have played a critical role in the slowdown.

One view of the slowdown in productivity since 1973 is that (at least in part) it is not a real phenomenon but the result of *poor measurement of productivity growth*. According to this argument, many of the productivity improvements that occur in modern services-orientated economies are difficult to capture in economic statistics. For example, the computerisation of inventories allows supermarkets to offer customers a wider variety of products, with less chance that a particular product will be out of stock. ATMs and online banking allow people to make financial transactions 24 hours a day, not just when the bank is open. Many medical procedures can be done far more quickly, safely and painlessly today than just a few years ago (see Economic naturalist 19.2). In theory, all these improvements in the quality of services should be captured in real GDP, and hence in productivity measures. In reality, accurate measurement of improvements in quality is difficult, as we saw when discussing biases in the CPI in Chapter 19, and some improvements may be missed. If the productivity slowdown is not real but reflects only poor measurement, then economists need not worry about it.

Another explanation has been called the *technological depletion hypothesis*.[2] According to this hypothesis the high rates of productivity in the 1950s and 1960s reflected an unusual period of 'catch-up' after the Second World War (see Economic naturalist 17.1). Although scientific and technical advances continued to be made during the 1930s and 1940s (many of which arose from military research), depression and war prevented them from being adapted to civilian use. During the 1950s and 1960s, the backlog of technological breakthroughs was applied commercially, producing high rates of productivity growth at first and then a sharp decline in new technological opportunities. Once the catch-up period was over, productivity growth slowed. According to this hypothesis, then, the slowdown in productivity growth since the 1970s reflects a *dearth of technological opportunities* relative to the immediate postwar period. From this perspective, the 1950s and 1960s were the exception, and the period since the 1970s represents a return to more normal rates of productivity growth.

Although the rate of productivity growth since the 1980s has generally been low, in recent years there have been some hints of a possible recovery in productivity, particularly in the United States. Between 1991 and 2000, US productivity growth averaged nearly 2.3 per cent per year, close to the rate achieved prior to 1973. Will this increase in productivity growth be sustained? Optimists argue that the United States is currently leading a new technological revolution, sparked by advances in computers, communications, genetics and other fields, which will allow productivity to continue to grow indefinitely. Others are more cautious, arguing that the long-run commercial value of the new technologies has yet to be proven. A great deal is riding on which view turns out to be correct.

---

[2] Nordhaus (1982).

## The costs of economic growth

Both this chapter and Chapter 18 emphasised the positive effects of economic growth on the average person's living standard. But should societies always strive for the highest possible rate of economic growth? The answer is no. Even if we accept for the moment the idea that increased output per person is always desirable, attaining a higher rate of economic growth does impose costs on society.

What are the costs of increasing economic growth? The most straightforward is the cost of creating *new capital*. We know that by expanding the capital stock we can increase future productivity and output. But, to increase the capital stock, we must divert resources that could otherwise be used to increase the supply of consumer goods. For example, to add more robot-operated assembly lines, a society must employ more of its skilled technicians in building industrial robots and fewer in designing video games. To build new factories, more resources must be assigned to factory construction and less to improving the housing stock. In short, high rates of investment in new capital require people to tighten their belts, consume less and save more – a real *economic cost*.

Should a country undertake a high rate of investment in capital goods at the sacrifice of consumer goods? The answer depends on the extent that people are willing and able to sacrifice consumption today to have a bigger economic 'pie' tomorrow. In a country that is very poor, or is experiencing an economic crisis, people may prefer to keep consumption relatively high and savings and investment relatively low. The midst of a thunderstorm is not the time to be putting something aside for a rainy day! But in a society that is relatively well off, people may be more willing to make sacrifices to achieve higher economic growth in the future.

Consumption sacrificed to *capital formation* is not the only cost of achieving higher growth. In Europe and the United States in the nineteenth and early twentieth centuries, periods of rapid economic growth were often times in which many people worked extremely long hours at dangerous and unpleasant jobs. While those workers helped to build the economy that we enjoy today, the costs were great in terms of reduced leisure time and, in some cases, workers' health and safety.

Other costs of growth include the cost of the research and development (R&D) that is required to improve technology and the costs of acquiring training and skill (human capital). The fact that a higher living standard tomorrow must be purchased at the cost of current sacrifices is an example of the *Scarcity Principle* (Chapter 1), that having more of one good thing usually means having less of another. Because achieving higher economic growth imposes real economic costs, we know from the *Cost–Benefit Principle* (Chapter 1) that higher growth should be pursued only if the benefits outweigh the costs.

## Promoting economic growth

If a society decides to try to raise its rate of economic growth, what are some of the measures that policy makers might take to achieve this objective? Here is a short list of suggestions, based on our discussion of the factors that contribute to growth in average labour productivity – and, hence, output per person.

### Policies to increase human capital

Because skilled and well-educated workers are more productive than unskilled labour, governments in most countries try to increase the human capital of their citizens by supporting education and training programmes. In many European countries, governments provide free public education at all levels from primary school to university. Most countries also support active labour market programmes which provide job training for unskilled youths, disabled workers and older workers whose skills have become obsolete.

## Economic naturalist 20.5 Why do almost all countries provide free state education?

All industrial countries provide their citizens free education through to secondary school and most subsidise college and other tertiary education. Why?

Most Europeans are so used to the idea of free public education that this question may seem odd. But why should the government provide free education when it does not provide even more essential goods and services, such as food or, in some cases, medical care? Furthermore, educational services can be, and indeed commonly are, supplied and demanded on the private market, without the aid of the government.

An important argument for free, or at least subsidised, education is that the private demand curve for educational services does not include all the *social benefits* of education. (Recall the *Equilibrium Principle*, Chapter 3, which states in part that a market in equilibrium may not exploit all the gains achievable from collective action.) For example, the democratic political system relies on an educated citizenry to operate effectively – a factor that an individual demander of educational services has little reason to consider. From a narrower economic perspective, we might argue that individuals do not capture the full economic returns from their schooling. For example, people with high human capital, and thus high earnings, pay more taxes – funds that can be used to finance government services and aid the less fortunate. Because of income taxation, the private benefit to acquiring human capital is less than the social benefit, and the demand for education on the private market may be less than optimal from society's viewpoint. Similarly, educated people are more likely than others to contribute to technological development, and hence to general productivity growth, which may benefit many other people besides themselves. Finally, another argument for public support of education is that poor people who would like to invest in human capital may not be able to do so because of insufficient income.

The Nobel Laureate Milton Friedman, among many economists, suggested that these arguments may justify government grants, called educational *vouchers*, to help citizens purchase educational services in the private sector, but they do *not* justify the government providing education directly, as through the state school system. Defenders of state education, on the other hand, argue that the government should have some direct control over education in order to set standards and monitor quality. What do you think?

## Policies that promote saving and investment

Average labour productivity increases when workers can utilise a sizeable and modern capital stock. To support the creation of new capital, government can encourage high rates of saving and investment in the private sector. Many provisions in the tax code are designed expressly to stimulate households to save and firms to invest. For example, households may get tax relief when they save in specially designated schemes and firms can be given tax credits, which reduce their tax bills when they invest in new capital. Private sector saving and investment are discussed in greater detail in Chapter 22.

Government can contribute directly to capital formation through *public investment*, or the creation of government-owned capital. Public investment includes the building of roads, bridges, airports, dams and, in some countries, energy and communications networks. For example, the construction of highway systems reduces long-haul transportation costs and improves productivity throughout the economy. Today, the web of computers and communications links we call the Internet is having a similar effect. Many research studies have confirmed that government investment in the *infrastructure*, the public capital that supports private sector economic activities, can be a significant source of growth.

## Policies that support research and development

Productivity is enhanced by technological progress, which in turn requires investment in R&D. In many industries, private firms have an adequate incentive to conduct R&D activities. There is no need, for example, for the government to finance research for developing a better underarm deodorant. But some types of knowledge, particularly basic scientific knowledge, may have widespread economic benefits that cannot be captured by a single private firm. The developers of the silicon computer chip, for example, were instrumental in creating huge new industries, yet they received only a small portion of the profits flowing from their inventions. Because society in general, rather than the individual inventors, may receive much of the benefit from basic research, government may need to support basic research. Government also sponsors a great deal of applied research, particularly in military and space applications. To the extent that national security allows, the government can increase growth by sharing the fruits of such research with the private sector. For example, the Global Positioning System (GPS), which was developed originally for military purposes, is now available in private passenger vehicles, helping drivers find their way.

## The legal and political framework

Although economic growth comes primarily from activities in the private sector, the government plays an essential role in providing the framework within which the private sector can operate productively. We have discussed the importance of secure property rights and a well-functioning legal system, of an economic environment that encourages entrepreneurship and of political stability and the free and open exchange of ideas. Government policy makers should also consider the potential effects of tax and regulatory policies on activities that increase productivity, such as investment, innovation and risk taking. Policies that affect the legal and political framework are examples of *structural macroeconomic policies* (see Chapter 17).

## The poorest countries: a special case?

Radical disparities in living standards exist between the richest and poorest countries of the world (see Table 18.4 for some data). Achieving economic growth in the poorest countries is thus particularly urgent. Are the policy prescriptions of this section relevant to those countries, or are very different types of measures necessary to spur growth in the poorest nations?

To a significant extent, the same factors and policies that promote growth in richer countries apply to the poorest countries as well. Increasing human capital by supporting education and training, increasing rates of saving and investment, investing in public capital and infrastructure, supporting R&D and encouraging entrepreneurship are all measures that will enhance economic growth in poor countries.

However, to a much greater degree than in richer countries, most poor countries need to improve the legal and political environment that underpins their economies. For example, many developing countries have poorly developed or corrupt legal systems, which discourage entrepreneurship and investment by creating uncertainty about property rights. Taxation and regulation in developing countries are often heavy-handed and administered by inefficient bureaucracies, to the extent that it may take months or years to obtain the approvals needed to start a small business or expand a factory. Regulation is also used to suppress market forces in poor countries; for example, the government, rather than the market, may determine the allocation of bank credit or the prices for agricultural products. Structural policies that aim to ameliorate these problems are important preconditions for generating growth in the poorest countries. But probably most important – and most difficult, for some countries – is establishing political stability and the rule of law. Without political stability, domestic and foreign savers will be reluctant to invest in the country, and economic growth will be difficult (if not impossible) to achieve.

Can rich countries help poor countries to develop? Historically, richer nations have tried to help by providing financial aid through loans or grants from individual countries (foreign aid) or by loans made by international agencies, such as the World Bank and the International Monetary Fund (IMF). Experience has shown, however, that financial aid to countries that do not undertake structural reforms, such as reducing excessive regulation or improving the legal system, is of limited value. To make their foreign aid most effective, rich countries should help poor countries achieve *political stability* and undertake the necessary reforms to the *structure of their economies*.

## Economic naturalist 20.6 Promoting growth and cohesion in Europe

For the first twenty years of its existence the group of countries now called the European Union was a club of six relatively rich nations – Belgium, France, Germany, Italy, Luxembourg and the Netherlands. The first enlargement occurred in 1973 when the United Kingdom, Denmark and Ireland joined, to be followed by Greece in 1981 and Spain and Portugal in 1986. One significant feature of these enlargements was the inclusion of four relatively poor countries – Ireland, Greece, Portugal and Spain – with real incomes per person between 55 and 65 per cent of the European average. Up to that point regional policy, or measures to help disadvantaged areas, had been mostly left to individual countries. However, the inclusion of these four poorer countries posed a new problem for the Union. If the process of economic integration was to promote higher living standards then a way had to be found for the benefits to be enjoyed by all members. The Union responded to this challenge by redirecting policy from general growth-promoting policies to a strategy which would favour the poorer members and help them catch up with the richest countries. In the late 1980s and early 1990s the Union introduced a series of measures under the general titles of *Structural and Cohesion Funds* designed to channel resources toward its more disadvantaged members. Structural Funds could be used in disadvantaged regions in all member states but the Cohesion Funds could be allocated only to the 'poor four' – Greece, Ireland, Portugal and Spain – who became known as the Cohesion Countries. The purpose of these funds was to promote economic growth and convergence by investing in areas such as infrastructure and human capital.

Figure 20.6 shows the growth of real GDP per person, as a percentage of the EU average, in the four Cohesion Countries since 1980. Compared with Greece, Portugal and Spain, Ireland is the obvious success story, with GDP per person increasing from 64 per cent of the EU average in 1980 to 115 per cent in 2001. One theory suggests that Ireland made better use of Structural and Cohesion Funds by targeting them on key areas such as the transport infrastructure and job training programmes. However, while compared with the other Cohesion Countries, Ireland may have made better use of EU funding, the funds by themselves are only a part, and probably a relatively small part, of the Irish economic miracle, often referred to

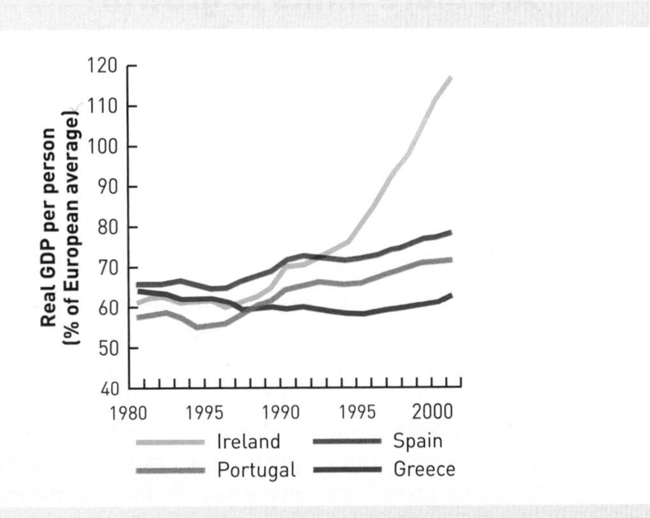


**Figure 20.6 Real GDP per Person in the Cohesion Economies, 1980–2001.** The figure shows real GDP per person, as a percentage of the EU average, in the four Cohesion Country economies – Greece, Ireland, Portugal and Spain. Only Ireland has managed to reach and even exceed the average level of GDP per person in the European Union. The others still lag well behind.

as the 'Celtic Tiger'. Economists are generally agreed that there is no single factor explaining the phenomenal performance of the Irish economy. Relatively low wages (at least in the 1980s and early 1990s), a young and educated labour force together with EU funding certainly played significant roles. However, if one factor stands out it is not EU funding but the introduction of the Single European Market (SEM) in 1993. Unifying the European market provided a direct incentive for American multinationals to invest and produce in Europe. While all EU countries have attracted foreign direct investment (FDI), Ireland had several advantages not enjoyed by the others, namely a low rate of profits tax and the fact that it was an English-speaking country. As a result Ireland attracted a disproportionate amount of FDI. Large international companies such as Dell, Intel, Microsoft and Monsanto now have major production facilities in Ireland supplying both the EU and US markets. Not only did these companies create employment but, by introducing cutting-edge technology, they improved the skills and productivity of the Irish labour force which, as we saw at the start of this chapter, is a necessary condition for sustained economic growth.

The 2004 enlargement of the European Union to include countries in central and eastern Europe with income levels less half of the EU average poses an even greater problem. In the future, EU funding will be directed toward these new accession states. However, as the experience of Greece, Ireland, Portugal and Spain shows, Structural and Cohesion Funds, although important, are unlikely to solve the problem by themselves.

## Are there limits to growth?

Earlier in this chapter we saw that even relatively low rates of economic growth, if sustained for a long period, will produce huge increases in the size of the economy. This fact raises the question of whether economic growth can continue indefinitely without depleting natural resources and causing massive damage to the global environment. Does the basic truth that we live in a finite world of finite resources imply that, ultimately, economic growth must come to an end?

The concern that economic growth may not be sustainable is not a new one. An influential book, *The Limits to Growth* (1972)[3] reported the results of computer simulations that suggested that unless population growth and economic expansion were halted, the world would soon run out of natural resources, drinkable water and breathable air. This book, and later works in the same vein, raises some fundamental questions that cannot be done full justice here. However, in some ways its conclusions are misleading.

One problem with the 'limits to growth' theory lies in its underlying concept of *economic growth*. Those who emphasise the environmental limits on growth assume implicitly that economic growth will always take the form of more of what we have now – more smoky factories, more polluting cars, more fast-food restaurants. If that were indeed the case, then surely there would be limits to the growth the planet can sustain. But growth in real GDP does not necessarily take such a form. Increases in real GDP can also arise from new or higher-quality products. For example, not too long ago tennis rackets were relatively simple items made primarily of wood. Today they are made of newly invented synthetic materials and designed for optimum performance using sophisticated computer simulations. Because these new high-tech tennis rackets are more valued by consumers than the old wooden ones, they increase the real GDP. Likewise, the introduction of new pharmaceuticals has contributed to economic growth, as have the expanded number of TV channels, digital sound and Internet-based sales. Thus, economic growth need not take the form of more and more of the same old stuff; it can mean newer, better and perhaps cleaner and more efficient goods and services.

A second problem with the 'limits to growth' conclusion is that it overlooks the fact that increased wealth and productivity expand society's capacity to take measures to safeguard the environment. In fact, the most polluted countries in the world are not the richest but those that are in a relatively early stage of industrialisation (see Economic naturalist 20.7). At this stage, countries must devote the bulk of their resources to basic needs – food, shelter, health care – and continued industrial expansion. In these countries, clean air and water may be viewed as luxuries rather than as basic needs. In more economically developed countries, where the most basic needs are more easily met, extra resources are available to keep the environment clean. Thus continuing economic growth may lead to less, not more, pollution.

A third problem with the pessimistic view of economic growth is that it ignores the power of the market and other social mechanisms to deal with scarcity. During the oil-supply disruptions of the 1970s, newspapers were filled with headlines about the energy crisis and the imminent depletion of world oil supplies. Yet in 2005 the world's known oil reserves were actually *greater* than they were in the 1970s. Today's energy situation is so much better than was expected in the 1970s because the market went to work. Reduced oil supplies led to an increase in prices that changed the behaviour of both demanders and suppliers. Consumers insulated their homes, purchased more energy-efficient cars and appliances, and switched to alternative sources of energy. Suppliers engaged in a massive hunt for new reserves, opening up major new sources in Latin America, China and the North Sea. In short, *market forces* solved the energy crisis.

---

[3] Meadows, Meadows, Randers and Behrens, III (1972).

In general, shortages in any resource will trigger price changes that induce suppliers and demanders to deal with the problem. Simply extrapolating current economic trends into the future ignores the power of the market system to recognise shortages and make the necessary corrections. Government actions spurred by political pressures, such as the allocation of public funds to preserve open space or reduce air pollution, can be expected to supplement market adjustments.

Despite the shortcomings of the 'limits to growth' perspective, most economists would agree that not all the problems created by economic growth can be dealt with effectively through the market or the political process. Probably most important, global environmental problems, such as the possibility of global warming or the ongoing destruction of rain forests, are a particular challenge for existing economic and political institutions. Environmental quality is not bought and sold in markets and thus will not automatically reach its optimal level through market processes (recall the *Equilibrium Principle*, Chapter 3). Nor can local or national governments effectively address problems that are global in scope. Unless international mechanisms are established for dealing with global environmental problems, these problems may become worse as economic growth continues.

## Economic naturalist 20.7 Why is the air quality so poor in Mexico City?

Developing countries such as Mexico, which are neither fully industrialised nor desperately poor, often have severe environmental problems. Why?

One concern about economic growth is that it will cause ever-increasing levels of environmental pollution. Empirical studies show, however, that the relationship between pollution and real GDP per person is more like an inverted U (see Fig. 20.7). In other words, as countries move from very low levels of real GDP per person to 'middle-income' levels, most measures of pollution tend to worsen, but environmental quality improves as real GDP per person rises even further. One study of the relationship between air quality and real GDP per person found that the level of real GDP per person at which air quality is the worst – indicated by point *A*

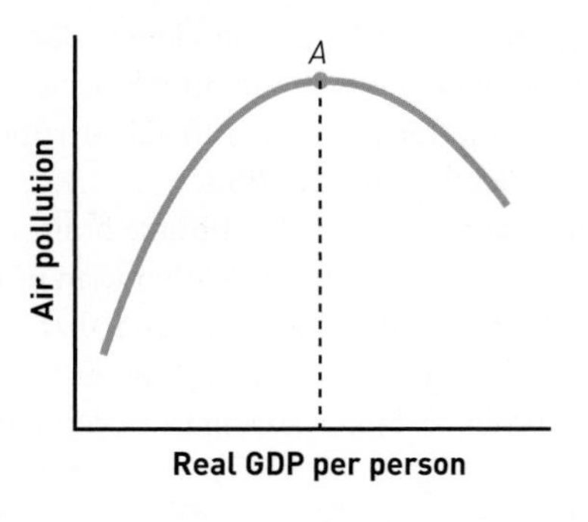


**Figure 20.7 The Relationship between Air Pollution and Real GDP per Person.** Empirically, air pollution increases with real GDP per person up to a point and then begins to decline. Maximum air pollution (point *A*) occurs at a level of real GDP per person roughly equal to that of Mexico.

in Fig. 20.7 – is roughly equal to the average income level in Mexico.[4] And indeed, the air quality in Mexico City is exceptionally poor, as any visitor to that sprawling metropolis can attest.

That pollution may worsen as a country industrialises is understandable, but why does environmental quality improve when real GDP per person climbs to very high levels? There are a variety of explanations for this phenomenon. Compared with middle-income economies, the richer economies are more concentrated in 'clean', high-value services such as finance and software production as opposed to pollution-intensive industries such as heavy manufacturing. Rich economies are also more likely to have the expertise to develop sophisticated and cost-effective anti-pollution technologies. But the main reason the richer economies tend to be cleaner is the same reason that the homes of rich people are generally cleaner and in better condition than the homes of the poor. As income rises above the level necessary to fulfil basic needs, more resources remain to dedicate to 'luxuries' like a clean environment (the *Scarcity Principle*, Chapter 1). For the rich family, the extra resources will pay for a cleaning service; for the rich country, they will pay for pollution control devices in factories and on cars. Indeed, anti-pollution laws are generally tougher and more strictly enforced in rich countries than in middle-income and poor countries.

## RECAP Economic growth: developments and issues

- Labour productivity growth slowed throughout the industrialised world in the early 1970s. One possible explanation is that *productivity growth* has become harder to measure; another is the *technological depletion hypothesis*, that technological opportunities occur less frequently today than in the immediate postwar period. Some evidence suggests a recent resurgence in productivity growth in the United States.
- Economic growth has substantial costs, notably the sacrifice of *current consumption* that is required to free resources for creating new capital and new technologies. Higher rates of growth should be pursued only if the benefits outweigh the costs.
- Policies for promoting economic growth include policies to increase *human capital* (education and training); policies that promote *saving and capital formation*; policies that support R&D; and the provision of a *legal and political framework* within which the private sector can operate productively. Deficiencies in the legal and political framework (for example, official corruption or poorly defined property rights) are a special problem for many developing countries.
- Some have argued that *finite resources* imply ultimate limits to economic growth. This view overlooks the facts that growth can take the form of better, rather than more, goods and services; that increased wealth frees resources to safeguard the environment; and that political and economic mechanisms exist to address many of the problems associated with growth. However, these mechanisms may not work well when environmental or other problems arising from economic growth are global in scope.

[4] Grossman and Krueger (1993).

## Summary


- Since 1800 the industrialised nations have seen enormous improvements in living standards, as reflected in large increases in real GDP per person. Because of the power of *compound interest*, relatively small differences in growth rates, if continued over long periods, can produce large differences in real GDP per person and average living standards. Thus, the rate of *long-term economic growth* is an economic variable of critical importance.
- Real GDP per person is the product of *average labour productivity* (real GDP per employed worker) and the share of the population that is *employed*. Growth in real GDP per person can occur only through growth in average labour productivity, in the share of the population that is working, or both. In the period since 1960, increases in the share of the US population holding a job contributed significantly to rising real GDP per person. But since the 1960s, as in most earlier periods, the main source of the increase in real GDP per person was rising average labour productivity.
- Among the factors that determine labour productivity are the talents, education, training and skills of workers, or *human capital*; the quantity and quality of the *physical capital* that workers use; the availability of land and other *natural resources;* the application of *technology* to the production and distribution of goods and services; the effectiveness of *entrepreneurs* and managers; and the broad *social and legal environment*. Because of *diminishing returns to capital*, beyond a certain point expansion of the capital stock is not the most effective way to increase average labour productivity. Economists generally agree that new technologies are the most important single source of improvements in productivity.
- Since the 1970s the industrial world has experienced a *slowdown* in productivity growth. Some economists have suggested that the 'slowdown' is more the result of an inability to measure increases in the quality of output than of any real economic change. Others have suggested that the exploitation of a backlog of technological opportunities following the Great Depression and the Second World War led to unusually high growth rates in the 1950s and 1960s, a view called the *technological depletion hypothesis*. In this view, the slower growth in US productivity since about 1970 in fact reflects a return to a more normal rate of growth. US productivity growth has picked up since about 1991, however, possibly as the result of new technologies.
- Economic growth has costs as well as benefits. Prominent among them is the need to sacrifice *current consumption* to achieve a high rate of investment in new capital goods; other costs of growing more quickly include extra work effort and the costs of R&D. Thus more economic growth is not necessarily better; whether increased economic growth is desirable depends on whether the benefits of growth outweigh the costs.
- Among the ways in which government can *stimulate economic growth* are by adopting policies that encourage the creation of human capital; that promote saving and investment, including public investment in infrastructure; that support R&D, particularly in the basic sciences; and that provide a legal and political framework that supports private sector activities. The poorest countries, with poorly developed legal, tax and regulatory systems, are often in the greatest need of an improved legal and political framework and increased political stability.
- Are there *limits to growth?* Arguments that economic growth must be constrained by environmental problems and the limits of natural resources ignore the fact that economic growth can take the form of increasing quality as well as increasing quantity. Indeed, increases in output can provide additional resources for cleaning up the environment. Finally, the market system, together with political processes, can solve many of the problems associated with economic growth. On the other hand, global environmental problems, which can be handled by neither the market nor by individual national governments, have the potential to constrain economic growth.

## Key terms

**compound interest** (558)
**diminishing returns to capital** (564)
**entrepreneurs** (566)

## Review questions

1. What has happened to real GDP per person in the industrialised countries since 1900? What implications does this have for the average person?
2. Why do economists consider growth in average labour productivity to be the key factor in determining long-run living standards?
3. What is 'human capital'? Why is it economically important? How is new human capital created?
4. You have employed five workers of varying physical strength to dig a ditch. Workers without shovels have zero productivity in ditch digging. How should you assign shovels to workers if you don't have enough shovels to go around? How should you assign any additional shovels that you obtain? Using this example, discuss (a) the relationship between the availability of physical capital and average labour productivity and (b) the concept of diminishing returns to capital.
5. Discuss how talented entrepreneurs and effective managers can enhance average labour productivity.
6. What major contributions can the government make to the goal of increasing average labour productivity?
7. What explanations have been offered for the slowdown in productivity growth observed in industrial countries since the early 1970s?
8. Discuss the following statement: 'Because the environment is fragile and natural resources are finite, ultimately economic growth must come to an end.'

## Problems

Problems marked with an asterisk (*) are more difficult.

1. Richland's real GDP per person is €10,000, and Poorland's real GDP per person is €5,000. However, Richland's real GDP per person is growing at 1 per cent per year and Poorland's is growing at 3 per cent per year. Compare real GDP per person in the two countries after 10 years and after 20 years. Approximately how many years will it take Poorland to catch up with Richland?

2. Refer to Table 20.3 for growth rates of average labour productivity over the periods 1960–73, 1973–79 and 1979–2000. Suppose that growth of average labour productivity in France had continued at its 1960–73 rate until 2000. Proportionally, how much higher would French average labour productivity in 2000 have been, compared with its actual value? (**Note:** You do not need to know the actual values of average labour productivity in any year to solve this problem.) Does your answer shed light on why economists consider the post-1973 productivity slowdown to be an important issue?

3. Data for Canada, Germany and Japan on the ratio of employment to population in 1979 and 2000 are as in the table below.

| Country | 1979 | 2000 |
|---|---|---|
| Canada | 0.45 | 0.46 |
| Germany | 0.34 | 0.33 |
| Japan | 0.47 | 0.51 |

Using data from Table 20.1, find average labour productivity for each country in 1979 and in 2000. How much of the increase in output per person in each country over the 1979–2000 period is due to increased labour productivity? To increased employment relative to population?

4. Joanne has just completed high school and is trying to determine whether to go to college for two years or go directly out to work. Her objective is to maximise the savings she will have in the bank five years from now. If she goes directly out to work she will earn €20,000 per year for each of the next five years. If she goes to college, for each of the next two years she will earn nothing – indeed, she will have to borrow €6,000 each year to cover tuition and books. This loan must be repaid in full three years after graduation. If she graduates from college, in each of the subsequent three years her wages will be €38,000 per year. Joanne's total living expenses and taxes, excluding tuition and books, equal €15,000 per year.

a. Suppose for simplicity that Joanne can borrow and lend at 0 per cent interest. On purely economic grounds, should she go to college or work?

b. Does your answer to part (a) change if she can earn €23,000 per year with only a high-school qualification?

c. Does your answer to part (a) change if Joanne's tuition and books cost €8,000 per year?

d.* Suppose that the interest rate at which Joanne can borrow and lend is 10 per cent per year, but other data are as in part (a). Savings are deposited at the end of the year they are earned and receive (compound) interest at the end of each subsequent year. Similarly, the loans are taken out at the end of the year in which they are needed, and interest does not accrue until the end of the subsequent year. Now that the interest rate has risen, should Joanne go to college or go to work?

5. The Good'n'Fresh Grocery Store has two checkout lanes and four employees. Employees are equally skilled, and all are able either to operate a cash register (checkers) or bag groceries (baggers). The store owner assigns one checker and one bagger to each lane. A lane with a checker and a bagger can check out 40 customers per hour. A lane with a checker only can check out 25 customers per hour.

a. In terms of customers checked out per hour, what is total output and average labour productivity for the Good'n'Fresh Grocery Store?

b. The owner adds a third checkout lane and register. Assuming that no employees are added, what is the best way to reallocate the workers to tasks? What is total output and average labour productivity (in terms of customers checked out per hour) now?

c. Repeat part (b) for the addition of a fourth checkout lane, and a fifth. Do you observe diminishing returns to capital in this example?

6. Harrison, Carla and Fred are housepainters. Harrison and Carla can paint 30 $m^2$ per hour using a standard paintbrush, and Fred can paint 25 $m^2$ per hour. Any of the three can paint 60 $m^2$ per hour using a roller.

a. Assume that Harrison, Carla and Fred have only paintbrushes at their disposal. What is the average labour productivity, in terms of $m^2$ per painter-hour, for the three painters taken as a team? Assume that the three painters always work the same number of hours.

b. Repeat part (a) for the cases in which the team has one, two, three or four rollers available. Are there diminishing returns to capital?

c. An improvement in paint quality increases the area that can be covered per hour (by either brushes or rollers) by 20 per cent. How does this technological improvement affect your answers to part (b)? Are there diminishing returns to capital? Does the technological improvement increase or reduce the economic value of an additional roller?

7. Hester's Hatchery raises fish. At the end of the current season she has 1,000 fish in the hatchery. She can harvest any number of fish that she wishes, selling them to restaurants for €5 apiece. Because big fish make little fish, for every fish that she leaves in the hatchery this year she will have two fish at the end of next year. The price of fish is expected to be €5 each next year as well. Hester relies entirely on income from current fish sales to support herself.

a. How many fish should Hester harvest if she wants to maximise the growth of her stock of fish from this season to next season?

b. Do you think maximising the growth of her fish stock is an economically sound strategy for Hester? Why or why not? Relate to the text discussion on the costs of economic growth.

c. How many fish should Hester harvest if she wants to maximise her current income? Do you think this is a good strategy?

d. Explain why Hester is unlikely to harvest either all or none of her fish, but instead will harvest some and leave the rest to reproduce.

8. **True or false:** For advances in basic science to translate into improvements in standards of living, they must be supported by favourable economic conditions. Discuss, using concrete examples where possible to illustrate your arguments.

## Answers to in-chapter exercises

20.1 If the United Kingdom had grown at the Japanese rate for the period 1870–2000, then, from the figures in Table 20.1, real GDP per person in 2000 would have been ($3,500) × ($1.025^{200}$) = $86,730. Actual GDP per person in the United Kingdom in 2000 was $21,142, so at the higher rate of growth, output per person would have been $86,730/$21,142 = 4.1 times higher.

20.2 As before, Lucy can wrap 4,000 bars per week, or 100 bars per hour. Ethel can wrap 500 bars per hour, and working 40 hours weekly she can wrap 20,000 bars per week. Together Lucy and Ethel can wrap 24,000 bars per week. Since they work a total of 80 hours between them, their output per hour as a team is 24,000 bars wrapped per 80 hours = 300 bars wrapped per hour, midway between their hourly productivities as individuals.

20.3 Because Ethel can wrap 300 bars per hour by hand, the benefit of giving Ethel the machine is 500 – 300 = 200 additional bars wrapped per hour. Because Lucy wraps only 100 bars per hour by hand, the benefit of giving Lucy the machine is 400 additional bars wrapped per hour. So the benefit of giving the machine to Lucy is greater than of giving it to Ethel. Equivalently, if the machine goes to Ethel, then Lucy and Ethel between them can wrap 500 + 100 = 600 bars per hour, but if Lucy uses the machine the team can wrap 300 + 500 = 800 bars per hour. So output is increased by letting Lucy use the machine.

20.4 Now, working by hand, Lucy can wrap 300 bars per hour and Ethel can wrap 500 bars per hour. With a machine, either Lucy or Ethel can wrap 800 bars per hour. As in Exercise 20.3, the benefit of giving a machine to Lucy (500 bars per hour) exceeds the benefit of giving a machine to Ethel (300 bars per hour), so if only one machine is available Lucy should use it.

The table analogous to Table 20.2 now looks like this:

Relationship of Capital, Output and Productivity in the Chocolate Bar Wrapping Factory

| Number of machines (*K*) | Bars wrapped per week (*Y*) | Total hours worked (*N*) | Average hourly labour productivity (*Y*/*N*) |
|---|---|---|---|
| 0 | 32,000 | 80 | 400 |
| 1 | 52,000 | 80 | 650 |
| 2 | 64,000 | 80 | 800 |
| 3 | 64,000 | 80 | 800 |

Comparing this table with Table 20.2, you can see that technological advance has increased labour productivity for any value of *K*, the number of machines available.

Adding one machine increases output by 20,000 bars wrapped per week, adding the second machine increases output by 12,000 bars wrapped per week, and adding the third machine does not increase output at all (because there is no worker available to use it). So diminishing returns to capital still hold after the technological improvement.

20.5 Although the individual worker is the same person as he was in Senegal, by going to France he gains the benefit of factors that enhance average labour productivity in this country relative to his homeland. These include more and better capital to work with, more natural resources per person, more advanced technologies, sophisticated entrepreneurs and managers and a political–legal environment that is more conducive to high productivity. It is not guaranteed that the value of the immigrant's human capital will rise, but normally it will. Since increased productivity leads to higher wages and living standards, on economic grounds the worker has a strong incentive to emigrate to France if he is able to do so.

## References

Baumol, W. (1990) 'Entrepreneurship: Unproductive and Destructive', *Journal of Political Economy*, October, pp. 893–921.

Grossman, G. M. and A. B. Krueger (1993) 'Environmental Impacts of a North American Free Trade Agreement', in P. Garber (ed.), *The Mexico–US Free Trade Agreement* (Cambridge, MA: MIT Press).

Maddison, A. (1988) *Phases of Capitalist Development* (Oxford: Oxford University Press).

Meadows, D., D. L. Meadows, J. Randers and W. W. Behrens III (1972) *The Limits to Growth* (New York: New American Library).

Nordhaus, W. (1982) 'Economic Policy in the Face of Declining Productivity Growth', *European Economic Review*, May–June, pp. 131–58.

# 21

# Workers, Wages and Unemployment in the Modern Economy

In Chapter 20 we examined the remarkable economic growth and increased productivity that has occurred in the industrialised world since 1800. These developments have greatly increased the quantity of goods and services that the economy can produce. But we have not yet discussed how the fruits of economic growth are distributed. Has everyone benefited equally from economic growth and increased productivity? Or is the population divided between those who have caught the 'train' of economic modernisation, enriching themselves in the process, and those who have been left at the station?

To understand how economic growth and change affect different groups, we must turn to the *labour market*. Except for retirees and others receiving government support, most people rely almost entirely on wages and salaries to pay their bills and save for the future. Hence it is in the labour market that most people will see the benefits of the economic growth and increasing productivity. This chapter describes and explains some important trends in the labour markets of industrial countries. Using a supply and demand model of the labour market, we focus first on several important trends in real wages and employment. In the second part of the chapter we turn to the problem of unemployment, especially long-term unemployment. We shall see that two key factors contributing to recent trends in wages, employment and unemployment are the *globalisation* of the economy, as reflected in the increasing importance of international trade, and ongoing *technological change*. By the end of the chapter, you will understand better the connection between these macroeconomic developments and the economic fortunes of workers and their families.

## Five important labour market trends

In recent decades, at least five trends have characterised labour markets in the industrialised world. We divide these trends into two groups: those affecting real wages and those affecting employment and unemployment.

## Trends in real wages

### 1 Over the twentieth century, all industrial countries have enjoyed substantial growth in real wages

In most European countries the average worker's yearly earnings in 2000 could command nearly twice as many goods and services as in 1960 and about four times as much as in 1929, just prior to the Great Depression. Similar trends have prevailed in other industrialised countries such as the United States and Canada.

### 2 As shown by column (1) of Table 21.1 the rate of real wage growth in both Europe and America has slowed since 1973

Though the post-Second World War period has seen impressive increases in real wages, the fastest rates of increase occurred during the 1960s and early 1970s. In the 1960s real wages per employee in the then EU rose by an impressive 5.1 per cent per year. However, growth in real wages slowed to 3 per cent in the 1970s, to 1 per cent in the 1980s and to 0.8 per cent in the 1990s.

| | Annual growth rate (%) | | | | | |
|---|---|---|---|---|---|---|
| | Real Wages (1) | | Employment (2) | | Unemployment (3) | |
| **Period** | **EU** | **USA** | **EU** | **USA** | **EU** | **USA** |
| 1961–73 | 5.0 | 2.7 | 0.3 | 2.0 | 2.0 | 4.7 |
| 1974–85 | 1.5 | 0.7 | 0.1 | 1.8 | 3.8 | 6.5 |
| 1986–95 | 1.2 | 0.6 | 0.6 | 1.7 | 8.5 | 7.1 |
| 1996–2000 | 0.6 | 2.2 | 1.2 | 2.0 | 9.4 | 5.6 |

**Table 21.1** Labour Market Trends, 1961–2000

*Note*: Real wages: average percentage change in the real wage. Employment: percentage change in numbers employed. Unemployment rate: percentage of the labour force unemployed.

*Source*: *The European Economy*, Commission of the European Communities, www.europa _eu.int/comm _finance/publications.

### 3 Recent decades have brought a pronounced increase in wage inequality, especially in the United States

A growing gap in real wages between skilled and unskilled workers has been of particular concern especially in the United States. Indeed, the real wages of the least-skilled, least-educated workers have actually *declined* since the early 1970s, by as much as 25–30 per cent according to some studies. At the same time, the best-educated, highest-skilled workers have enjoyed continuing gains in real wages. Many observers worry that the United States is developing a 'two-tier' labour market: plenty of good jobs at good wages for the well-educated and highly skilled, but less and less opportunity for those without schooling or skills.

Outside the United States, particularly in Western Europe, the trend toward wage inequality has been much less pronounced. But, as we shall see, employment trends in Europe have not been as encouraging as in the United States. Let's turn now to the trends in employment and unemployment.

## Trends in employment and unemployment

### 4 Compared with the United States, the rate of job creation in Europe remains relatively low

As column (2) of Table 21.1 shows, the increase in employment since the 1960s has been much lower in Europe than in the United States.

### 5 Western European countries have been suffering high rates of unemployment for almost two decades

In the European Union an average of 9.4 per cent of the workforce was unemployed over the period 1990–2001, compared with just 5.6 per cent in the United States. Over the same period, French unemployment averaged 10.9 per cent and German unemployment 7.9 per cent.

Given the trend toward increasing wage inequality in the United States and the persistence of high unemployment in Europe, we may conclude that a significant fraction of the industrial world's labour force has not been sharing in the recent economic growth and prosperity. Whereas in the United States the problem takes the form of low and falling real wages for unskilled workers, in Europe work is often simply unavailable for the unskilled, and sometimes even for the skilled.

What explains these trends in employment and wages? In the remainder of the chapter we shall show that a supply and demand analysis of the labour market can help to explain these important developments.

### RECAP Important labour market trends

- Over a long period, average real wages have risen substantially in both Europe and in other industrialised countries.
- Despite the long-term upward trend in real wages, real wage growth has slowed significantly in both Europe and the United States since the early 1970s.
- In the United States, wage inequality has increased dramatically since the 1960s. The real wages of most unskilled workers have actually declined, while the real wages of skilled and educated workers have continued to rise. This trend is less pronounced in Europe.
- The growth in numbers employed has been significantly lower in Europe than the United States.
- Since about 1980, European nations have experienced very high rates of unemployment compared with the United States.

## Supply and demand in the labour market

In Chapter 3 we saw how supply and demand analysis can be used to determine equilibrium prices and quantities for individual goods and services. The same approach is equally useful for studying labour market conditions. In the market for labour, the 'price' is the wage paid to workers in exchange for their services. The wage is expressed per unit of time – for example, per hour or per year. The 'quantity' is the amount of labour firms use, which in this book we shall generally measure by the number of *workers employed*. Alternatively, we could state the quantity of labour in terms of the number of *hours worked*; the choice of units is a matter of convenience.

Who are the demanders and suppliers in the labour market? Firms and other employers demand labour in order to produce goods and services. Virtually all of us supply labour during some phase of our lives. Whenever people work for pay, they are supplying labour services at a price equal to the wage they receive. In this chapter, we shall discuss both the supply of and demand for labour, with an emphasis on the demand side of the labour market. Changes in the demand for labour turn out to be key in explaining the aggregate trends in wages and employment described in the preceding section.

The labour market is studied by microeconomists as well as macroeconomists, and both use the tools of supply and demand. However, microeconomists focus on issues such as the determination of wages for specific types of jobs or workers. In this chapter we take the macroeconomic approach and examine factors that affect aggregate, or economywide, trends in employment and wages.

## Wages and the demand for labour

Let us start by thinking about what determines the number of workers employers want to hire at any given wage – that is, the demand for labour. As we shall see, the demand for labour depends both on the *productivity* of labour and the *price* that the market sets on workers' output. The more productive workers are, or the more valuable the goods and services they produce, the greater the number of workers an employer will want to hire at any given wage.

Table 21.2 shows the relationship between output and the number of workers employed at the Big Computer Company (BCC), which builds and sells computers. Column (1) of Table 21.2 shows some different possibilities for the number of technicians BCC could employ in its plant. Column (2) shows how many computers the company can produce each year, depending on the number of workers employed. The more workers, the greater the number of computers BCC can produce. For the sake of simplicity, we shall assume that the plant, equipment and materials the workers use to build computers are fixed quantities.

Column (3) of Table 21.2 shows the *marginal product* of each worker, the extra production that is gained by adding one more worker. Note that each additional worker adds less to total production than the previous worker did. The tendency for marginal product to decline as

| Number of workers (1) | Computers produced per year (2) | Marginal product (3) | Value of marginal product (at €3,000/computer) (4) |
|---|---|---|---|
| 0 | 0 | | |
| | | 25 | 75,000 |
| 1 | 25 | | |
| | | 23 | 69,000 |
| 2 | 48 | | |
| | | 21 | 63,000 |
| 3 | 69 | | |
| | | 19 | 57,000 |
| 4 | 88 | | |
| | | 17 | 51,000 |
| 5 | 105 | | |
| | | 15 | 45,000 |
| 6 | 120 | | |
| | | 13 | 39,000 |
| 7 | 133 | | |
| | | 11 | 33,000 |
| 8 | 144 | | |

**Table 21.2** Production and Marginal Product for Big Computer Company

**diminishing returns to labour** if the amount of capital and other inputs in use is held constant, then the greater the quantity of labour already employed, the less each additional worker adds to production

more and more workers are added is called **diminishing returns to labour**. The principle of diminishing returns to labour states that if the amount of capital and other inputs in use is held constant, then the greater the quantity of labour already employed, the less each additional worker adds to production.

The principle of diminishing returns to labour is analogous to the principle of diminishing returns to capital discussed in Chapter 20. The economic basis for these principles is the same – that is, the *Principle of Increasing Opportunity Cost*, also known as the *Low-Hanging-Fruit Principle* (Chapter 2). As we saw in Chapter 20, a firm's managers want to use their available inputs in the most productive way possible. So an employer who has one worker will assign that worker to the most productive job. If she hires a second worker, she will assign that worker to the second most productive job. The third worker will be given the third most productive job available, and so on. The greater the number of workers already employed, the lower the marginal product of adding another worker, as shown in Table 21.1.

If BCC computers sell for €3,000 each, then column (4) of Table 21.2 shows the *value of the marginal product* of each worker. The value of a worker's marginal product is the amount of extra revenue that the worker generates for the firm. Specifically, the value of the marginal product of each BCC worker is that worker's marginal product, stated in terms of the number of additional computers produced, multiplied by the price of output, here €3,000 per computer. We now have all the information necessary to find BCC's demand for workers.

### **Example 21.1** BCC's demand for labour

Suppose that the going wage for computer technicians is €60,000 per year. BCC managers know that this is the wage being offered by all their competitors, so they cannot hire qualified workers for less. How many technicians will BCC hire? What would the answer be if the wage were €50,000 per year?

BCC will hire an extra worker if and only if the value of that worker's marginal product (which equals the extra revenue the worker creates for the firm) exceeds the wage BCC must pay. The going wage for computer technicians, which BCC takes as given, is €60,000 per year. Table 21.2 shows that the value of the marginal product of the first, second and third workers each exceeds €60,000. Hiring these workers will be profitable for BCC because the extra revenue each generates exceeds the wage that BCC must pay. However, the fourth worker's marginal product is worth only €57,000. If BCC's managers hired a fourth worker, they would be paying €60,000 in extra wages for additional output that is worth only €57,000. Since hiring the fourth worker is a money-losing proposition, BCC will hire only three workers. Thus the quantity of labour BCC demands when the going wage is €60,000 per year is three technicians.

If the market wage for computer technicians were €50,000 per year instead of €60,000, the fourth technician would be worth hiring, since the value of his marginal product, €57,000, would be €7,000 more than his wages. The fifth technician would also be worth hiring, since the fifth worker's marginal product is worth €51,000–€1,000 more than the going wage. The value of the marginal product of a sixth technician, however, is only €45,000, so hiring a sixth worker would not be profitable. When wages are €50,000 per year then, BCC's labour demand is five technicians.

**Exercise 21.1** How many workers will BCC hire if the going wage for technicians is €35,000 per year?

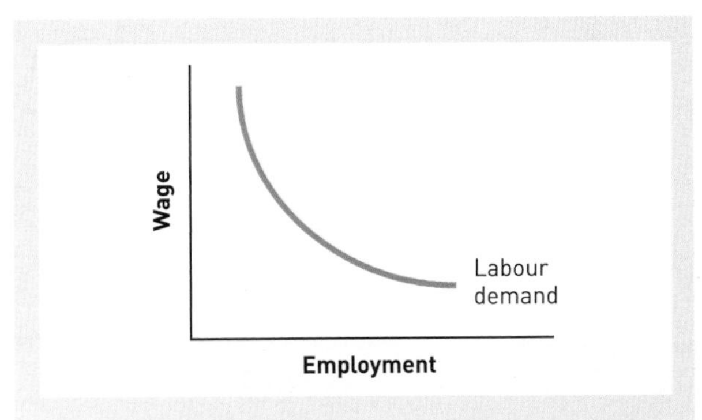


**Figure 21.1 The Demand Curve for Labour.** The demand curve for labour is downward-sloping. The higher the wage, the fewer workers employers will hire.

The lower the wage a firm must pay, the more workers it will hire. Thus the demand for labour is like the demand for other goods or services in that the quantity demanded rises as the price (in this case, the wage) falls. Figure 21.1 shows a hypothetical labour demand curve for a firm or industry, with the wage on the vertical axis and employment on the horizontal axis. All else being equal, the higher the wage, the fewer workers a firm or industry will demand.

In our example thus far we have discussed how labour demand depends on the *nominal*, or euro, wage and the *nominal* price of workers' output. Equivalently, we could have expressed the wage and the price of output in *real* terms – that is, measured relative to the average price of goods and services. The wage measured relative to the general price level is the *real wage*; as we saw in Chapter 19, the real wage expresses the wage in terms of its purchasing power. The price of a specific good or service measured relative to the general price level is called the *relative price* of that good or service. Because our main interest is in real rather than nominal wages, from this point on we shall analyse the demand for labour in terms of the real wage and the relative price of workers' output, rather than in terms of nominal variables.

## Shifts in the demand for labour

The number of workers that BCC will employ at any given real wage depends on the value of their marginal product, as shown in column (4) of Table 21.2. Changes in the economy that increase the value of workers' marginal product will increase the value of extra workers to BCC, and thus BCC's demand for labour at any given real wage. In other words, any factor that *raises the value of the marginal product of BCC's workers* will shift BCC's labour demand curve to the right.

Two main factors could increase BCC's labour demand: (1) an increase in the relative price of the company's output (computers) and (2) an increase in the productivity of BCC's workers. Example 21.2 illustrates the first of these possibilities, Example 21.3 the second.

### **Example 21.2** The relative price of computers and BCC's demand for labour

Suppose an increase in the demand for BCC's computers raises the relative price of its computers to €5,000 each. How many technicians will BCC hire now, if the real wage is €60,000 per year? If the real wage is €50,000?

The effect of the increase in computer prices is shown in Table 21.3. Columns (1)–(3) of the table are the same as in Table 21.2. The number of computers a given number of technicians can build (column (2)) has not changed; hence, the marginal product of particular technicians (column (3)) is the same. But because computers can now be sold for €5,000 each instead of €3,000, the *value* of each worker's marginal product has increased by two-thirds (compare column (4) of Table 21.3 with column (4) of Table 21.2).

How does the increase in the relative price of computers affect BCC's demand for labour? Recall from Example 21.1 that when the price of computers was €3,000 and the going wage for technicians was €60,000, BCC's demand for labour was three workers. But now, with computers selling for €5,000 each, the value of the marginal product of each of the first seven workers exceeds €60,000 (Table 21.3). So if the real wage of computer technicians is still €60,000, BCC would increase its demand from three workers to seven.

| Number of workers (1) | Computers produced per year (2) | Marginal product (3) | Value of marginal product (€5,000/computer) (4) |
|---|---|---|---|
| 0 | 0 | | |
| | | 25 | 125,000 |
| 1 | 25 | | |
| | | 23 | 115,000 |
| 2 | 48 | | |
| | | 21 | 105,000 |
| 3 | 69 | | |
| | | 19 | 95,000 |
| 4 | 88 | | |
| | | 17 | 85,000 |
| 5 | 105 | | |
| | | 15 | 75,000 |
| 6 | 120 | | |
| | | 13 | 65,000 |
| 7 | 133 | | |
| | | 11 | 55,000 |
| 8 | 144 | | |

**Table 21.3** Production and Marginal Product for Big Computer Company after an Increase in Computer Prices

Suppose instead that the going real wage for technicians is €50,000. In Example 21.1, when the price of computers was €3,000 and the wage was €50,000, BCC demanded five workers. But if computers sell for €5,000, we can see from column (4) of Table 21.3 that the value of the marginal product of even the eighth worker exceeds the wage of €50,000. So if the real wage is €50,000, the increase in computer prices raises BCC's demand for labour from five workers to eight.

**Exercise 21.2** How many workers will BCC hire if the going real wage for technicians is €100,000 per year and the relative price of computers is €5,000? Compare your answer with the demand for technicians at a wage of €100,000 when the price of computers is €3,000.

The general conclusion to be drawn from Example 21.2 is that an increase in the *relative price of workers' output increases the demand for labour*, shifting the labour demand curve to the right, as shown in Fig. 21.2. A higher relative price for workers' output makes workers more valuable, leading employers to demand more workers at any given real wage.

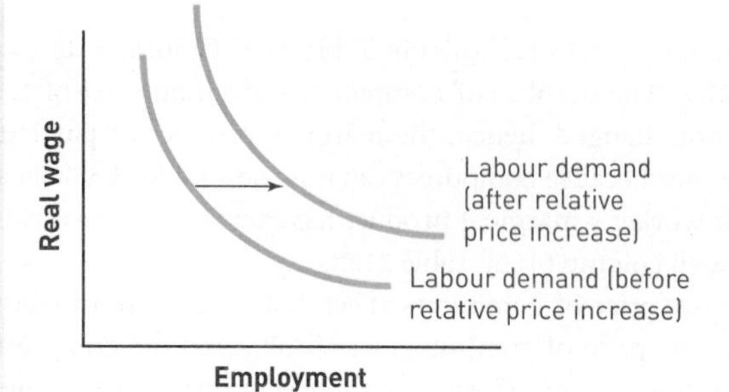


**Figure 21.2 A Higher Relative Price of Output Increases the Demand for Labour.** An increase in the relative price of workers' output increases the value of their marginal product, shifting the labour demand curve to the right.

The second factor that affects the demand for labour is worker productivity. Since an increase in productivity increases the value of a worker's marginal product, it also increases the demand for labour, as Example 21.3 shows.

### Example 21.3 Worker productivity and BCC's demand for labour

Suppose that BCC adopts a new technology that reduces the number of components to be assembled, permitting each technician to build 50 per cent more machines per year. Assume that the relative price of computers is €3,000 per machine. How many technicians will BCC hire if the real wage is €60,000 per year?

| Number of workers (1) | Computers produced per year (2) | Marginal product (3) | Value of marginal product (€3,000/computer) (4) |
|---|---|---|---|
| 0 | 0 | | |
| | | 37.5 | 112,500 |
| 1 | 37.5 | | |
| | | 34.5 | 103,500 |
| 2 | 72 | | |
| | | 31.5 | 94,500 |
| 3 | 103.5 | | |
| | | 28.5 | 85,500 |
| 4 | 132 | | |
| | | 25.5 | 76,500 |
| 5 | 157.5 | | |
| | | 22.5 | 67,500 |
| 6 | 180 | | |
| | | 19.5 | 58,500 |
| 7 | 199.5 | | |
| | | 16.5 | 49,500 |
| 8 | 216 | | |

**Table 21.4** Production and Marginal Product for BCC after an Increase in Worker Productivity

Table 21.4 shows workers' marginal products and the value of their marginal products after the 50 per cent increase in productivity, assuming that computers sell for €3,000 each.

Before the productivity increase, BCC would have demanded three workers at a wage of €60,000 (Table 21.2). After the productivity increase, however, the value of the marginal product of the first six workers exceeds €60,000 (see Table 21.4, column (4)). So at a wage of €60,000, BCC's demand for labour increases from three workers to six.

**Exercise 21.3** How many workers will BCC hire after the 50 per cent increase in productivity if the going real wage for technicians is €50,000 per year? Compare this figure with the demand for workers at a €50,000 wage before the increase in productivity.

In general, an increase in worker productivity increases the demand for labour, shifting the labour demand curve to the right, as in Fig. 21.3.

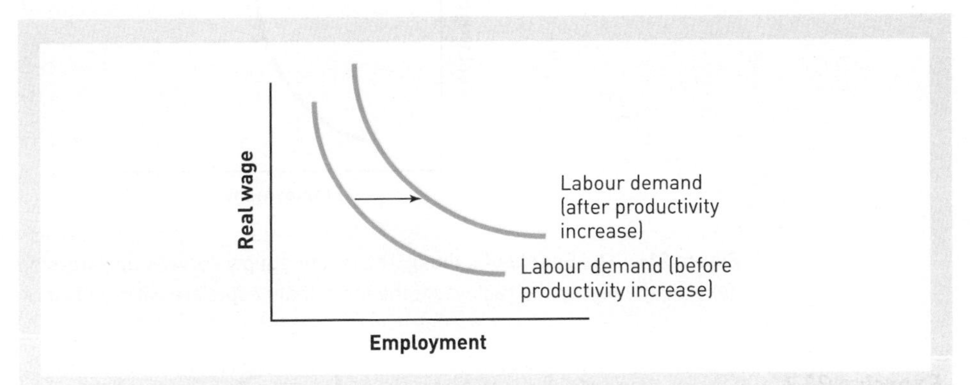


**Figure 21.3 Higher Productivity Increases the Demand for Labour.** An increase in productivity raises workers' marginal product and – assuming no change in the price of output – the value of their marginal product. Since a productivity increase raises the value of marginal product, employers will hire more workers at any given real wage, shifting the labour demand curve to the right.

## The supply of labour

We have discussed the demand for labour by employers; to complete the story we need to consider the supply of labour. The suppliers of labour are workers and potential workers. At any given real wage, potential suppliers of labour must decide if they are willing to work. The total number of people who are willing to work at each real wage is the *supply of labour*.

### Example 21.4 Will you mow your neighbour's lawn or go to the beach?

You were planning to go to the beach today, but your neighbour asks you to mow his lawn. You like the beach a lot more than cutting grass. Do you take the job?

Unless you are motivated primarily by neighbourliness, your answer to this job offer would probably be, 'It depends on how much my neighbour will pay.' You may not be willing to take the job for €5 or €10, unless you have a severe and immediate need for cash, but you might take it for €30. This minimum payment, the *reservation price* you set for your labour, is the compensation level that leaves you just indifferent between working and not working.

In economic terms, deciding whether to work at any given wage is a straightforward application of the *Cost–Benefit Principle* (Chapter 1). The cost to you of mowing the lawn is the opportunity cost of your time (or the value you put on a day at the beach) plus the cost you place on having to work in unpleasant conditions. You can measure this total cost in euros simply by asking yourself, 'What is the minimum amount of money I would take to mow the lawn instead of going to the beach?' The minimum payment that you would accept is the same as your *reservation price*. The benefit of taking the job is measured by the pay you receive, which will go toward that new DVD player you want. You should take the job only if the promised pay (the benefit of working) exceeds your reservation price (the cost of working).

In this example, your willingness to supply labour is greater the higher the wage. In general, the same is true for the population as a whole. Certainly people work for many reasons, including personal satisfaction, the opportunity to develop skills and talents, and the chance to socialise with co-workers. Still, for most people, income is one of the principal benefits of working, so the higher the real wage, the more willing they are to sacrifice other possible uses of their time. The fact that people are more willing to work when the wage they are offered is higher is captured in the upward slope of the supply curve of labour (see Fig. 21.4).

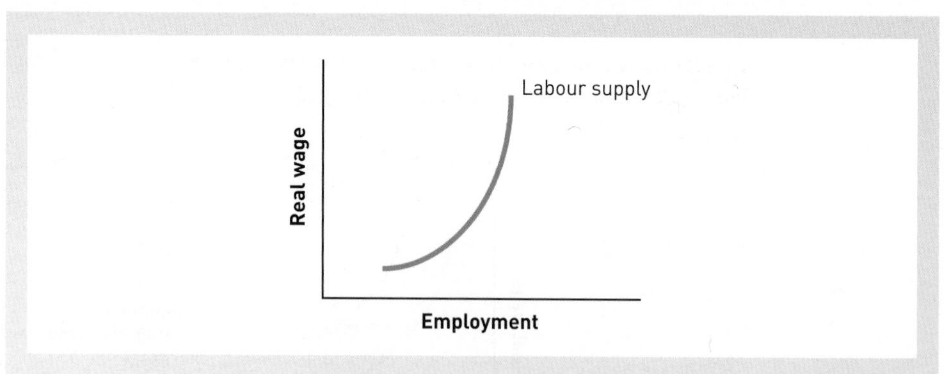


**Figure 21.4 The Supply of Labour.** The labour supply curve is upward-sloping because, in general, the higher the real wage, the more that people are willing to work.

**Exercise 21.4** You want to make a career in broadcasting. The local radio station is offering an unpaid summer job that would give you valuable experience. Your alternative to the summer job is to earn €3,000 working in a car wash. How would you decide which job to take? Would a decision to take the summer job contradict the conclusion that the labour supply curve is upward-sloping?

### Shifts in the supply of labour

Any factor that affects the quantity of labour offered at a given real wage will shift the labour supply curve. At the macroeconomic level, the most important factor affecting the supply of labour is the size of the *working-age population*, which is influenced by factors such as the domestic birth-rate, immigration and emigration rates and the ages at which people normally first enter the workforce and at which they retire. All else being equal, an increase in the working-age population raises the quantity of labour supplied at each real wage, shifting the labour supply curve to the right. Changes in the percentage of people of working age who seek employment – for example, as a result of social changes that encourage women to work outside the home – can also affect the supply of labour.

Now that we have discussed both the demand for and supply of labour, we are ready to apply supply and demand analysis to real-world labour markets. But first, try your hand at using supply and demand analysis to answer the Exercise 21.5.

**Exercise 21.5** In some countries, trade unions typically favour tough restrictions on immigration, while employers tend to favour more liberal rules. Why? (**Hint:** How is an influx of potential workers likely to affect real wages?)

## RECAP Supply and demand in the labour market

- **The demand for labour** The extra production gained by adding one more worker is the *marginal product* of that worker. The *value of the marginal product* of a worker is that worker's marginal product times the relative price of the firm's output. A firm will employ a worker only if the worker's value of marginal product, which is the same as the extra revenue the worker generates for the firm, exceeds the real wage that the firm must pay. The lower the real wage, the more workers the firm will find it profitable to employ. Thus the labour demand curve, like most demand curves, is downward-sloping.

  For a given real wage, any change that increases the value of workers' marginal products will increase the demand for labour and shift the labour demand curve to the right. Examples of factors that increase labour demand are an increase in the relative price of workers' output and an increase in productivity.
- **The supply of labour** An individual is willing to supply labour if the real wage that is offered is greater than the opportunity cost of the individual's time. Generally, the higher the real wage, the more that people are willing to work. Thus the labour supply curve, like most supply curves, is upward-sloping.
- For a given real wage, any factor that increases the number of people available and willing to work increases the supply of labour and shifts the labour supply curve to the right. Examples of facts that increase labour supply include an increase in the working-age population or an increase in the share of the working-age population seeking employment.

We are now ready to analyse the important trends in real wages, employment and unemployment discussed earlier in the chapter. We shall do so in Economic naturalists 21.1–21.4.

# Explaining the trends in real wages

## Economic naturalist 21.1 Why have real wages increased by so much in the industrialised countries?

As we discussed, real annual earnings in the industrialised countries have tripled or quadrupled since 1929. These increases have greatly improved the standard of living of workers in these countries. Why have real wages increased by so much in Europe and the United States?

The large increase in real wages results from the sustained growth in productivity experienced by the industrialised countries during the twentieth century. (Figure 17.2 on p. 480 shows the growth of output per worker in Europe and the United States from 1900 to 2000.) As illustrated by Fig. 21.5, increased productivity raises the demand for labour, increasing employment and the real wage.

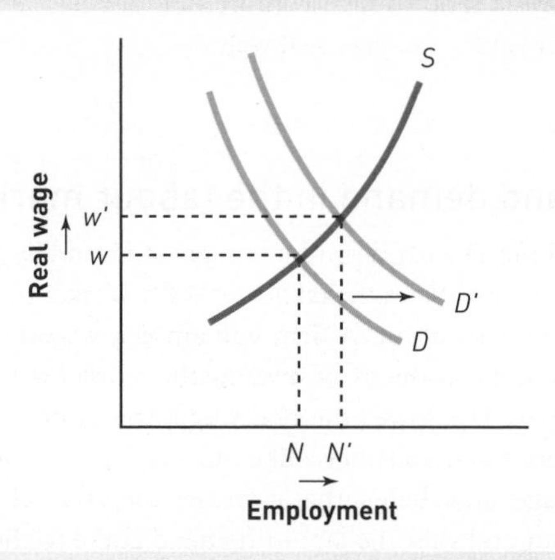


**Figure 21.5 An Increase in Productivity Raises the Real Wage.** An increase in productivity raises the demand for labour, shifting the labour demand curve from *D* to *D'*. The real wage rises from *w* to *w'*, and employment rises from *N* to *N'*.

Of the factors contributing to productivity growth in the industrialised countries, two of the most important were (1) the dramatic technological progress that occurred during the twentieth century and (2) large increases in capital stocks, which provided workers with more and better tools with which to work. Labour supply increased during the century as well, of course (not shown in Fig. 21.5). However, the increases in labour demand, driven by rapidly expanding productivity, have been so great as to overwhelm the depressing effect on real wages of increased labour supply.

**Economic naturalist 21.2 Table 21.1 shows that (a) the growth of real wages has slowed since the 1970s and, with the exception of the late 1990s, the slowdown has been more pronounced in the United States, (b) employment has expanded at a slower rate in Europe than in the United States. What accounts for these trends?**

Supply and demand analysis tells us that a slowdown in real wage growth must result from slower growth in the demand for labour, more rapid growth in the supply of labour, or both. On the demand side, recall from Chapter 20 that since the early 1970s most industrialised nations have experienced a slowdown in productivity growth. Thus, one possible explanation for the slowdown in the growth of real wages since the early 1970s is the *decline in the pace of productivity gains*.

Some evidence for a relationship between productivity and real wages is given in Table 21.5, which shows the average annual growth rates in real wages and labour productivity for the 1960s, 1970s, 1980s and 1990s. You can see that the growth in productivity corresponds closely to the growth in real earnings. Particularly striking is the rapid growth of both productivity and real wages during the 1960s and early 1970s. Since 1973, growth in both productivity and real wages has been significantly slower especially in the United States, although some improvement is apparent in US labour productivity and real wages during the late 1990s. Hence, the behaviour of labour productivity is an important factor in explaining the slowdown in real wage growth since the 1970s. Slower productivity growth means smaller shifts in the labour demand curve (Fig. 21.5) and, given labour supply, smaller increases in real wages. This has happened in both Europe and America since 1973.

| | Annual growth rate (%) | | | | | |
|---|---|---|---|---|---|---|
| | Real wages[1] | | Productivity[1] | | Labour force[1] | |
| Period | EU (1) | USA (2) | EU (3) | USA (4) | EU (5) | USA (6) |
| 1961–73 | 5.0 | 2.7 | 4.9 | 2.4 | | |
| 1974–85 | 1.5 | 0.7 | 1.9 | 1.0 | 0.6[2] | 2.1[2] |
| 1986–95 | 1.2 | 0.6 | 1.9 | 1.1 | 0.5 | 1.4 |
| 1996–2000 | 0.6 | 2.2 | 1.3 | 2.1 | 0.6 | 1.2 |

**Table 21.5** Real Wages, Productivity and Labour Supply, 1961–2000

*Notes*: 1. Real wages are average percentage change in the real wage. Productivity is real GDP divided by civilian employment. Labour force is employed plus unemployed.
2. 1977–85.

*Source*: *The European Economy*, Commission of the European Communities, www.europa_eu.int/comm_finance/publications and *OECD Employment Outlook*, www.oecd.org.

While the effects of the slowdown in productivity on the demand for labour are an important reason for declining real wage growth in both Europe and the United States, they can't be the whole story. We know this because, with labour supply held constant, slower growth in labour demand would lead to reduced rates of employment growth, as well as reduced growth in real wages. While this has been true of many European countries, we know (Table 21.1) that job growth in the United States has been rapid in recent decades. Large increases in employment in the face of slow growth of labour demand can be explained only by simultaneous increases in the *supply of labour* (see Exercise 21.6).

Columns (5) and (6) of Table 21.5 show that labour supply in the United States has grown rapidly since the 1960s – at more than twice the European rate. As we saw in Chapter 18, increased participation in the labour market by women has increased the US supply of labour since the mid-1970s. Other factors, including high rates of immigration, also help to explain the increase in the supply of labour. The combination of slower growth in *labour demand* (the result of the productivity slowdown) and accelerated growth in *labour supply* (the result of increased participation by women in the workforce, together with other factors) helps to explain why real wage growth has been sluggish for many years in the United States, even as employment has grown rapidly. Likewise, the combination of the productivity slowdown and sluggish growth in the labour supply explains why both real wage and employment growth have been low in Europe.

**Exercise 21.6** Assume that both Europe and America start with the same real wages and employment and draw a demand and supply diagram to explain how differences in the growth of the labour supply can explain (1) why real wages have increased faster in Europe and (2) why employment has grown faster in the United States. You can assume that productivity growth is the same in each economy. What could account for the rapid increase in US real wage growth since 1996?

## Increasing wage inequality

Another important labour market trend, especially in the United States, is the increasing *inequality in wages* earned by skilled and unskilled workers, We next discuss two reasons for this increasing inequality: (1) globalisation and (2) technological change.

### Economic naturalist 21.3 Why has the gap between the wages of skilled and unskilled workers widened in recent years? 1: globalisation

Many commentators have blamed the increasing divergence between the wages of skilled and unskilled workers on the phenomenon of 'globalisation'. This popular term refers to the fact that, to an increasing extent, the markets for many goods and services are becoming *international*, rather than national or local in scope. While Europeans have long been able to buy products from all over the world, the ease with which goods and services can cross borders is increasing rapidly. Within the European Union the elimination of tariffs (taxes on imports) and the creation of the Single Market have dramatically reduced barriers to trade between member states. In North America, the North American Free Trade Agreement (NAFTA), has also reduced tariffs on goods and services traded among Canada, Mexico and the United States. Also, via organisations such as the General Agreements on Tariffs and Trade (GATT) and the World Trade Organisation (WTO), trade between Europe, North America, Africa and Asia has been gradually liberalised. In addition, factors such as free capital mobility and technological advances such as the Internet have promoted globalisation.

The main economic benefit of globalisation is increased *specialisation* and the *efficiency* that it brings. Instead of each country trying to produce everything its citizens consume, each can concentrate on producing those goods and services at which it is relatively more efficient. As implied by the *Principle of Comparative Advantage* (Chapter 2), the result is that consumers of all countries enjoy a greater variety of goods and services, of better quality and at lower prices, than they would without international trade.

The effects of globalisation on the *labour* market are mixed, however, which explains why some politicians and pressure groups oppose free trade agreements. Expanded trade means that consumers stop buying certain goods and services from domestic producers and switch to foreign-made products. Consumers would not make this switch unless the foreign products were better, cheaper, or both, so expanded trade clearly makes them better off. But the workers and firm owners in the domestic industries that lose business may well suffer from the increase in foreign competition.

The effects of increasing trade on the labour market can be analysed using Fig. 21.6. Figure 21.6 contrasts the supply and demand for labour in two different industries, (a) textiles and (b) computer software. Imagine that, initially, there is little or no international trade in these two goods. Without trade, the demand for workers in each industry is indicated by the curves marked $D_{textiles}$ and $D_{software}$ respectively. Wages and employment in each industry are determined by the intersection of the demand curves and the labour supply curves in each industry. As we have drawn Fig. 21.6, initially, the real wage is the same in both industries, equal to $w$. Employment is $N_{textiles}$ in textiles and $N_{software}$ in software.

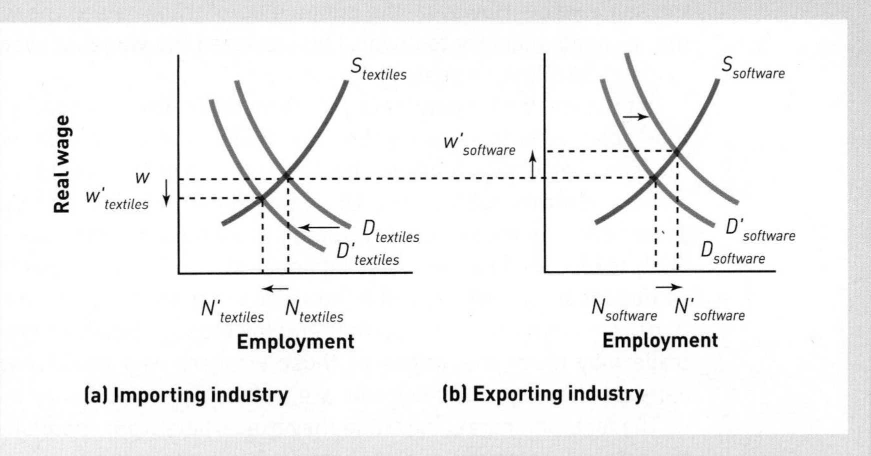


**Figure 21.6 The Effect of Globalisation on the Demand for Workers in Two Industries.** Initially, real wages in the two industries are equal at $w$. After an increase in trade, (a) demand for workers in the importing industry (textiles) declines, lowering real wages and employment, while (b) demand for workers in the exporting industry (software) increases, raising real wages and employment in that industry.

What will happen when this economy is opened up to trade? For example, the enlargement of the European Union to include countries in central and eastern Europe, or CEECs, has liberalised trade between the more prosperous countries of the old EU15 and new member states such as Poland and Hungary. Under the process of trade liberalisation, countries will begin to produce for export those goods or services at which they are relatively more efficient and to import goods or services that they are relatively less efficient at producing. Suppose the country in this example is a Western country which is relatively more efficient at producing software than at manufacturing textiles. With the opening of trade, the country gains new foreign markets for its software and begins to produce for export as well as for domestic use. Meanwhile, because the country is relatively less efficient at producing textiles, consumers begin to purchase foreign-made textiles, which are cheaper or of higher quality, instead of the domestic product. In short, software becomes an exporting industry and textiles an importing industry.

These changes in the demand for domestic products are translated into changes in the demand for labour. The opening of export markets increases the demand for domestic software, raising its relative price. The higher price for domestic software, in turn, raises the value of the marginal products of software workers, shifting the labour demand curve in the software industry to the right, from $D_{software}$ to $D'_{software}$ in Fig. 21.6(b). Wages in the software industry rise, from $w$ to $w'_{software}$, and employment in the industry rises as well. In the textile industry the opposite happens. Demand for domestic textiles falls as consumers switch to imports. The relative price of domestic textiles falls with demand, reducing the value of the marginal product of textile workers and hence the demand for their labour, to $D'_{textiles}$ in Fig. 21.6(a). Employment in the textile industry falls, and the real wage falls as well, from w to $w'_{textiles}$.

In sum, Fig. 21.6 shows how globalisation can contribute to *increasing wage inequality*. Initially, we assumed that software workers and textile workers received the same wage. However, the opening up of trade raised the wages of workers in the 'winning' industry (software) and lowered the wages of workers in the 'losing' industry (textiles), increasing inequality.

In practice, the tendency of trade to increase wage inequality may be even worse than depicted here, because the great majority of the world's workers, particularly those in developing countries, have relatively low skill levels. Thus, when industrialised countries such as the United Kingdom, France, Germany and the United States open up trade with developing countries, the domestic industries that are likely to face the toughest international competition are those that use mostly low-skilled labour. Conversely, the industries that are likely to do the best in international competition are those that employ mostly skilled workers. Thus increased trade may lower the wages of those workers who are already poorly paid and increase the wages of those who are well paid.

The fact that increasing trade may exacerbate wage inequality explains some of the political resistance to globalisation, but in general it does not justify attempts to reverse the trend. Increasing trade and specialisation is a major source of improvement in living standards, in both Europe and abroad, so trying to stop the process is counter-productive. Indeed, the economic forces behind globalisation – primarily, the desire of consumers for better and cheaper products and of producers for new markets – are so powerful that the process would be hard to stop even if government officials were determined to do so.

Rather than trying to stop globalisation, helping the labour market to adjust to the effects of globalisation is probably a better course. To a certain extent, indeed, the economy will adjust on its own. Figure 21.6 showed that, following the opening to trade, real wages and employment fall in (a) textiles and rise in (b) software. At that point, wages and job opportunities are much more attractive in the software industry than in textiles. Will this situation persist? Clearly, there is a strong incentive for workers who are able to do so to leave the textile industry and seek employment in the software industry.

The movement of workers between jobs, firms and industries is called **labour mobility**. In our example, labour mobility will tend to reduce labour supply in textiles and increase it in software, as workers move from the contracting industry to the growing one. This process will reverse some of the increase in wage inequality by raising wages in textiles and lowering them in software. It will also shift workers from a less competitive sector to a more competitive sector. To some extent, then, the labour market can adjust on its own to the effects of globalisation.

**labour mobility** the movement of workers between jobs, firms and industries

Of course, there are many barriers to a textile worker becoming a software engineer. So there may also be a need for *transition aid* to workers in the affected sectors. Ideally, such aid helps workers train for and find new jobs. Because trade and specialisation increase the total economic 'pie', the 'winners' from globalisation can afford the taxes necessary to finance retraining for the 'losers' and still enjoy a net benefit from increased trade.

A second source of increasing wage inequality is ongoing technological change that favours more highly skilled or educated workers. Economic naturalist 21.4 examines the effect of technological change on the labour market.

## Economic naturalist 21.4 Why has the gap between the wages of less-skilled and higher-skilled workers widened in recent years? 2: technological change

How has the pattern of technological change contributed to increasing inequality of wages?

As we have seen, new scientific knowledge and the technological advances associated with it are a major source of improved productivity and economic growth. Increases in worker productivity are in turn a driving force behind wage increases and higher average living standards. In the long run and on average, technological progress is undoubtedly the worker's friend.

This sweeping statement is not true at all times and in all places, however. Whether a particular technological development is good for a particular worker depends on the effect of that innovation on the worker's value of marginal product and, hence, on his or her wage. For example, at one time the ability to add numbers rapidly and accurately was a valuable skill; a clerk with that skill could expect advancement and higher wages. However, the invention and mass production of the electronic calculator has rendered human calculating skills less valuable, to the detriment of those who have that skill.

History is replete with examples of workers who opposed new technologies out of fear that their skills would become less valuable. In England in the early nineteenth century, rioting workmen destroyed newly introduced labour-saving machinery. The name of the workers' reputed leader, Ned Ludd, has been preserved in the term *Luddite*, meaning a person who is opposed to the introduction of new technologies.

How do these observations bear on wage inequality? According to some economists, many recent technological advances have taken the form of **skill-biased technological change** – that is, technological change that affects the marginal product of higher-skilled workers differently from that of lower-skilled workers. Specifically, technological developments since the 1980s appear to have favoured more-skilled and educated workers. Developments in automobile production are a case in point. The advent of mass production techniques in the 1920s provided highly paid work for several generations of relatively low-skilled car workers. But automobile production, like the automobiles themselves, has become considerably more sophisticated. The simplest production jobs have been taken over by robots and computer-controlled machinery, which require skilled operatives who know how to use and maintain the new equipment. Consumer demands for luxury features and customised options have also raised the car makers' demand for highly skilled craftspeople. Thus, in general, the skill requirements for jobs in automobile production have risen. Similarly, few office workers today can escape the need to use computer applications, such as word processing and spreadsheets. In many places, primary school teachers are expected to know how to set up a web page or use the Internet.

**skill-biased technological change** technological change that affects the marginal products of higher-skilled workers differently from those of lower-skilled workers

Figure 21.7 illustrates the effects of technological change that favours skilled workers. Figure 21.7(a) shows the market for unskilled workers; Fig. 21.7(b) shows the market for skilled workers. The demand curves labelled $D_{unskilled}$ and $D_{skilled}$ show the demand for each type of worker before a skill-biased technical change. Wages and employment for each type of worker are determined by the intersection

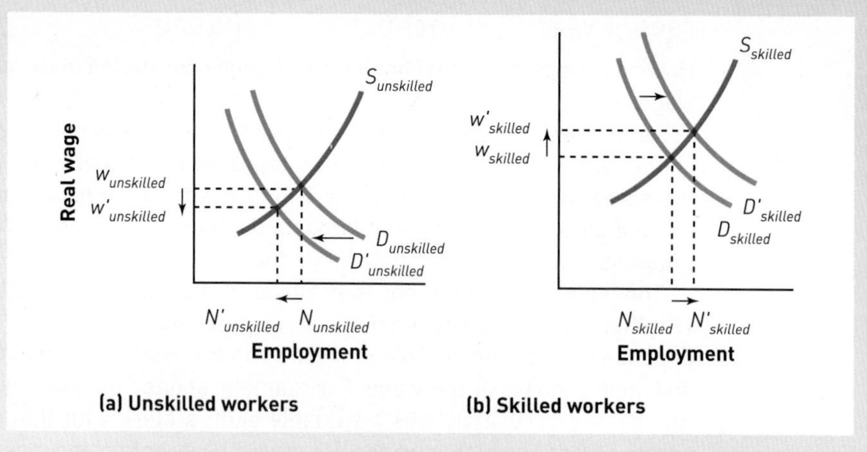


**Figure 21.7 The Effect of Skill-Biased Technological Change on Wage Inequality.** The figure shows the effects of a skill-biased technological change that increases the marginal product of skilled workers and reduces the marginal product of unskilled workers. The resulting increase in the demand for skilled workers raises their wages (b), while the decline in demand for unskilled workers reduces their wages (a). Wage inequality increases.

of the demand and supply curves in each market. Figure 21.7 shows that, even before the technological change, unskilled workers received lower real wages than skilled workers ($w_{unskilled} < w_{skilled}$), reflecting the lower marginal products of the unskilled.

Now suppose that a new technology – computer-controlled machinery, for example – is introduced. This technological change is biased toward skilled workers, which means that it raises their marginal productivity relative to unskilled workers. We will assume in this example that the new technology also lowers the marginal productivity of unskilled workers, perhaps because they are unable to use the new technology, but all that is necessary for our conclusions is that they benefit less than skilled workers. Figure 21.7 shows the effect of this change in marginal products. In panel (b) the increase in the marginal productivity of skilled workers raises the demand for those workers; the demand curve shifts rightward to $D'_{skilled}$. Accordingly, the real wages and employment of skilled workers also rise. In contrast, because they have been made less productive by the technological change, the demand for unskilled workers shifts leftward to $D'_{unskilled}$ (Fig. 21.7(a)). Lower demand for unskilled workers reduces their real wages and employment.

In summary, this analysis supports the conclusion that technological change that is biased in favour of skilled workers will tend to increase the *wage gap* between the skilled and unskilled. Empirical studies have confirmed the role of skill-biased technological change in recent increases in wage inequality.

Because new technologies that favour skilled workers increase wage inequality, should government regulators act to block them? As in the case of globalisation, most economists would argue against trying to block new technologies, since technological advances are necessary for economic growth and improved living standards. If the Luddites had somehow succeeded in preventing the introduction of labour-saving machinery in Great Britain, economic growth and development over the past few centuries might have been greatly reduced.

The remedies for the problem of wage inequalities caused by technological change are similar to those for wage inequalities caused by globalisation. First among them is *worker mobility*. As the pay differential between skilled and unskilled work increases, unskilled workers will have a stronger incentive to acquire education and skills, to everyone's benefit. A second remedy is transition aid. Government policy makers should consider programmes that will help workers to retrain if they are able, or provide income support if they are not.

## Both sides gain from free trade

In Economic naturalists 21.3 and 21.4 we saw that the processes of globalisation, free trade and technological change can lead to greater wage inequality within a *single country*. However, international trade is a *two-way process*. One country's imports are another's exports, and if one country is importing more, its partner country must be exporting more. For example, suppose that Germany is the domestic country in Economic naturalist 21.3. Opening trade with other countries leads to lower wages in the German textile industry because demand shifts from domestic to foreign production which implies a corresponding increase in the demand for textiles in countries exporting to Germany. What are the effects on wages and employment in these new partner countries? This question is considered in Economic naturalist 21.5.

## Economic naturalist 21.5 EU enlargement: the impact of trade and technological change.

In May 2004 ten new member states, mostly CEE nations (Estonia, Hungary, Latvia and Poland, etc.), joined the European Union. Unlike previous enlargements which opened EU membership to relatively wealthy countries such as Sweden and the United Kingdom, the countries joining in 2004 had living standards well below the EU average. Slovakian real GDP per person, for example, is about 40 per cent of the EU average. Also, although there are significant differences between the accession countries, a common feature is that in terms of technology, management skills and the quality of goods and services produced, they generally lag behind their Western partners (France, Germany, the United Kingdom, etc.). Hence we might expect the new members of the Union to benefit in two ways: gains from trade with the West and greater access to superior Western technology.

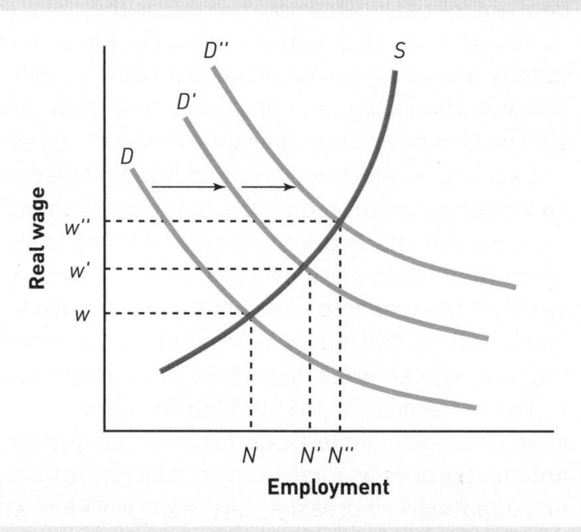


**Figure 21.8 EU Enlargement: the Effect on Wages and Employment in Accession Countries.** The figure shows that effects of opening Western markets to new member states. Full access to the EU market enables accession countries to specialise in products in which they are relatively efficient. Increased Western demand for these products raises the value of the workers' marginal product, shifting the labour demand curve to the right and leading to higher real wages and employment. Exploiting Western technology and management skills also leads to improved labour productivity with further gains in real wages and employment.

Figure 21.8 illustrates the possible effects of EU enlargement on real wages and employment in the accession countries. Following on from Economic naturalist 21.3, we shall assume that Germany is the domestic country and Poland is its new partner. We shall also assume that Poland is relatively more efficient in textile production and Germany in the production of the capital goods (machines, etc.) required to produce textiles, and that German-made capital goods are more technologically advanced than their Polish equivalents. As Poland's accession to the European Union opens free trade between Poland and Germany, we would expect

Poland to specialise in textile production and Germany in capital goods. Hence Poland will export textiles to Germany and import capital equipment. Figure 21.8 shows the effects on wages and employment in the Polish textile industry. Opening trade increases German demand for Polish textiles, raising their relative prices, which increases the value of the marginal product of Polish textile workers and shifts the labour demand curve to the right from $D$ to $D'$. As a result real wages will rise from $w$ to $w'$ and employment from $N$ to $N'$. If Polish textile manufacturers replace their capital equipment with more technologically advanced machines imported from Germany, the technological improvement will lead to an increase in the productivity and skills of textile workers, shifting the labour demand curve further to the right from $D'$ to $D''$, with wages rising to $w''$ and employment to $N''$.

Hence both sides gain from free trade. Germany gains by importing Polish textiles and switching resources from textile production to the goods such as software and capital equipment in which it is relatively more efficient. Poland gains because access to the German market enables it to specialise in industries where it is relatively efficient, and to take advantage of German technology which improves the skills and productivity of Polish textile workers. More generally, as the accession countries now have full access to the Single Market we can expect to see changes in trade patterns between 'Western' and 'Eastern' Europe, with each group specialising in the areas where they are relatively efficient. The resulting gains, together with the opportunity to import Western technology and management skills, should eventually raise living standards in the CEE countries.

## RECAP Explaining the trends in real wages

The long-term increase in real wages enjoyed by workers in industrial countries results primarily from large *productivity gains*, which have raised the demand for labour. Technological progress and an expanded and modernised capital stock are two important reasons for these long-term increases in productivity.

The slowdown in real wage growth that began in the 1970s resulted in part from the slowdown in productivity growth (and, hence, the slower growth in labour demand) that occurred at about the same time. Both globalisation and skill-biased technological change contribute to wage inequality. *Globalisation* raises the wages of workers in exporting industries by raising the demand for those workers, while reducing the wages of workers in importing industries. *Technological change* that favours more-skilled workers increases the demand for such workers, and hence their wages, relative to the wages of less-skilled workers.

Attempting to block either globalisation or technological change is not the best response to the problem of wage inequality. To some extent, *worker mobility* (movement of workers from low-wage to high-wage industries) will offset the inequality created by these forces. Where mobility is not practical, transition aid – government assistance to workers whose employment prospects have worsened – may be the best solution.

# Labour force trends: unemployment

Earlier in this chapter we saw that since the 1970s the growth of employment in Europe has been significantly lower than in the United States, while unemployment has been higher. Over the forty years between 1961 and 2000 the numbers employed in the European Union increased at an annual average rate of 0.45 per cent compared with 1.9 per cent in the United States. Over the same period the average annual rate of unemployment was approximately the same (6 per cent) in both economies, but since the mid-1990s US unemployment has declined to relatively low levels while European unemployment has remained persistently high. In 2000 the US unemployment rate reached an historic low of 4 per cent of the labour force – although it increased to 6 per cent in the 2001 recession. In the same year the French unemployment rate was 9.3 and the German rate 7.8.

As we saw in Chapter 18, a high unemployment rate has serious economic, psychological and social costs. Understanding the causes of unemployment and finding ways to reduce it are therefore major concerns for macroeconomists. Hence, prior to explaining these trends in unemployment (Economic naturalist 21.6, p. 611) we first discuss the causes and costs of three types of unemployment – frictional, structural and cyclical.

## Types of unemployment and their costs

**frictional unemployment** the short-term unemployment associated with the process of matching workers with jobs

**structural unemployment** the long-term and chronic unemployment that exists even when the economy is producing at a normal rate

**cyclical unemployment** the extra unemployment that occurs during periods of recession

Economists have found it useful to think of unemployment as being of three broad types: **frictional unemployment**, **structural unemployment** and **cyclical unemployment**. Each type of unemployment has different causes and imposes different economic and social costs.

### Frictional unemployment

The function of the labour market is to *match available jobs with available workers*. If all jobs and workers were the same, or if the set of jobs and workers were static and unchanging, this matching process would be quick and easy. But the real world is more complicated. In practice, both jobs and workers are highly *heterogeneous*. Jobs differ in their location, in the skills they require, in their working conditions and hours and in many other ways. Workers differ in their career aspirations, their skills and experience, their preferred working hours, their willingness to travel and so on.

The real labour market is also *dynamic*, or constantly changing and evolving. On the demand side of the labour market, technological advances, globalisation and changing consumer tastes spur the creation of new products, new firms and even new industries, while outmoded products, firms and industries disappear. Thus CD players have replaced record players, and word processors have replaced typewriters. As a result of this upheaval, new jobs are constantly being created, while some old jobs cease to be viable. The workforce in a modern economy is equally dynamic. People move, gain new skills, leave the labour force for a time to rear children or go back to school and even change careers.

Because the labour market is heterogeneous and dynamic, the process of matching jobs with workers often takes time. For example, a software engineer who loses or quits her job may take weeks or even months to find another software company which has a job requiring her specific skills. In her search she will probably consider alternative areas of software development or even totally new challenges. She may also want to think about different regions of the country in which software companies are located, or even different countries. During the period in which she is searching for a new job, she is counted as *unemployed*.

Short-term unemployment that is associated with the process of matching workers with jobs is called *frictional unemployment*. The *costs* of frictional unemployment are low and may even be negative; that is, frictional unemployment may be economically beneficial. First, frictional unemployment is short-term, so its psychological effects and direct economic losses are minimal. Second, to the extent that the search process leads to a better match between worker and job, a period of frictional unemployment is actually productive, in the sense that it leads to higher output over the long run. Indeed, a certain amount of frictional unemployment seems essential to the smooth functioning of a rapidly changing, dynamic economy.

## Structural unemployment

A second major type of unemployment is *structural unemployment*, or the long-term and chronic unemployment that exists even when the economy is producing at a normal rate. Several factors contribute to structural unemployment. First, *a lack of skills, language barriers*, or *discrimination* keeps some workers from finding stable, long-term jobs. Migrant farm workers and unskilled construction workers who find short-term or temporary jobs from time to time, but never stay in one job for very long, fit the definition of chronically unemployed.

Second, economic changes sometimes create a *long-term mismatch* between the skills some workers have and the available jobs. Under the forces of globalisation the European textile and coal mining industries, for example, have declined over the years, while the computer and financial services industries have grown rapidly. Ideally, textile workers and miners who lose their jobs will be able to find new jobs in computer firms and financial institutions (worker mobility), so that their unemployment will only be frictional in nature. In practice, of course, many ex-textile workers and miners lack the education, ability and training necessary to work in the computer and financial services industries. Since their skills are no longer in demand, these workers may drift into chronic or long-term unemployment.

In most countries structural unemployment is identified with long-term unemployment (Chapter 18), generally defined as unemployment with more than six months' duration. Table 21.6 gives estimates of long-term unemployment in the European Union, France, Germany, the United Kingdom and the United States for 2002. Clearly, chronic long-term unemployment is a greater problem for Europe than for the United States. Economic naturalist 21.6 (p. 611) discusses this difference in greater detail.

| Duration | % of total unemployed | | | | |
|---|---|---|---|---|---|
| | EU15 | France | Germany | UK | USA |
| 6 months and over | 59.0 | 53.4 | 64.8 | 38.8 | 18.3 |
| 12 months and over | 41.4 | 33.8 | 47.9 | 21.3 | 8.5 |

**Table 21.6** Long-Term Unemployment, 2002

*Source*: *OECD Employment Outlook*, Commission of the European Communities, www.europa_eu.int/comm_finance/publications.

Finally, structural unemployment can result from *structural features of the labour market* that act as barriers to employment. Examples of such barriers include trade unions and minimum wage laws, both of which may keep wages above their market-clearing level, creating unemployment. We shall discuss some of these structural features shortly.

The *costs* of structural unemployment are much higher than those of frictional unemployment. Because structurally unemployed workers do little productive work over long periods, their idleness causes substantial economic losses to both the unemployed workers and to society. Structurally unemployed workers also lose out on the opportunity to develop new skills on the job, and their existing skills wither from disuse. Long spells of unemployment are also much more difficult for workers to cope with psychologically than the relatively brief spells associated with frictional unemployment.

## Cyclical unemployment

The third type of unemployment occurs during periods of recession (that is, periods of unusually low production) and is called *cyclical unemployment*. The sharp peaks in unemployment shown in Fig. 18.2 (p. 515) reflect the cyclical unemployment that occurs during recessions. Cyclical unemployment occurs when the economy experiences a decline in the demand for the goods and services it produces – computers, software, textiles, cars, etc. Because fewer goods and services are being bought producers such as computer and car manufacturers start to cut back on production and lay off workers. Provided that policy makers take the appropriate actions to boost demand, such as cutting interest rates and reducing income taxes, increases in cyclical unemployment are likely to be short-lived. However, if corrective action is not taken, workers who lose their jobs because of a decline in demand may become long-term unemployed. We shall study cyclical unemployment and its remedies in later chapters dealing with recessions and macroeconomic policy.

In principle, frictional, structural and cyclical unemployment add up to the *total unemployment rate*. In practice, sharp distinctions often cannot be made between the different categories, so any breakdown of the total unemployment rate into the three types of unemployment is necessarily subjective and approximate.

**Exercise 21.7** In Fig. 21.6, free trade leads to a decline in employment in the importing country's textile industry. Would you classify unemployed textile workers as frictional, structural or cyclical unemployment? What is the appropriate policy to help unemployed textile workers?

## Impediments to full employment

In discussing structural unemployment, we mentioned that *structural features* of the labour market may contribute to long-term and chronic unemployment. Let us discuss a few of those features.

### Minimum-wage laws

Many countries have *minimum-wage laws*, which prescribe the lowest hourly wage that employers may pay to workers. Basic supply and demand analysis shows that if the minimum-wage law has any effect at all, it must raise the unemployment rate. Figure 21.9 shows why. Figure 21.9 shows the demand and supply curves for low-skilled workers, to whom the minimum wage is most relevant. The market-clearing real wage, at which the quantity of labour demanded equals the quantity of labour supplied, is *w*, and the corresponding level of employment of low-skilled workers is *N*. Now suppose there is a legal minimum wage $w_{min}$ that exceeds the market-clearing wage *w*, as shown in Fig. 21.9. At the minimum wage, the number of people who want jobs, $N_B$, exceeds the number of workers that employers are willing to hire, $N_A$. The result is unemployment in the amount $N_B - N_A$, also equal to the length of the line segment *AB* in Fig. 21.9. If there were no minimum wage, this unemployment would not exist in competitive labour markets, since the labour market would clear at wage *w*.

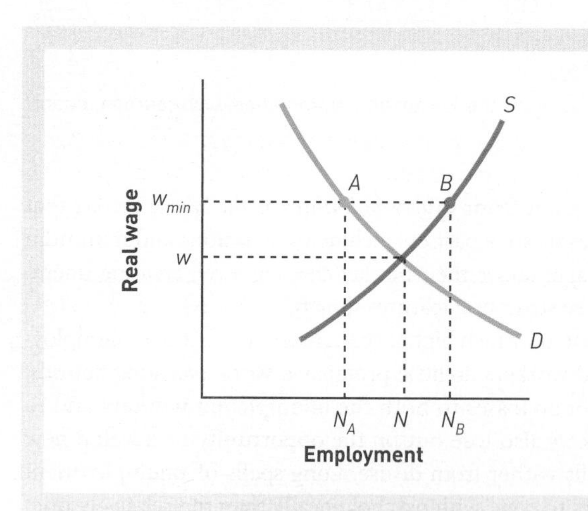


**Figure 21.9 A Legal Minimum Wage May Create Unemployment.** If the minimum wage $w_{min}$ exceeds the market-clearing wage *w* for low-skilled workers, it will create unemployment equal to the difference between the number of people who want to work at the minimum wage, $N_B$, and the number of people that employers are willing to hire, $N_A$.

If minimum wages create unemployment, why are they politically popular? A minimum wage creates two classes of workers: those who are lucky enough to find jobs at the minimum wage and those who are shut out because the minimum wage exceeds the market-clearing wage. Workers who do find jobs at the minimum wage will earn more than they would have otherwise, because the minimum wage is higher than the market-clearing wage. If the minimum wage were put to a vote, the number of workers who benefit from the legislation, and who could thus be expected to support it, might well exceed the number of workers who are hurt by it. In creating groups of 'winners' and 'losers', minimum-wage legislation resembles rent-control legislation (see Chapter 3). But, like rent controls, minimum wages create *economic inefficiency*. Other methods of attacking poverty, such as direct grants to the working poor, might prove more effective.

As Fig. 21.9 illustrates, minimum wages can lead to higher unemployment. How widespread is this effect? Minimum wages will have the greatest impact when they are set above the competitive or market-clearing wage ($w$ in Fig. 21.9) and when they apply to a high proportion of the workforce. Table 21.7 gives some indication of the coverage of minimum wages in the United Kingdom, the Netherlands and the United States. The first row gives the minimum wage as a percentage of average monthly earnings in industry and services while the second gives the percentage of full-time workers with earnings on the minimum wage. In no case does the minimum wage exceed 50 per cent of the average wage, and the proportion of workers covered is very low. Hence, on this evidence minimum wages do not appear to have significant economic effects of the type illustrated in Fig. 21.9.

| | UK | Netherlands | USA |
|---|---|---|---|
| Minimum wage as a percentage of average monthly earnings in industry and services | 34.4 | 49.3 | 34.4 |
| Percentage of full-time workers with earnings on the minimum wage | 1.8 | 2.3 | 1.5 |

**Table 21.7** Minimum wages
*Source*: Eurostat, http://eurostat.cec.eu.int.

## Trade unions

Trade or labour unions are organisations that negotiate with employers on behalf of workers. Among the issues that unions negotiate, which are embodied in the contracts they draw up with employers, are the wages workers earn, rules for hiring and firing, the duties of different types of workers, working hours and conditions, and procedures for resolving disputes between workers and employers. Unions gain negotiating power by their power to call a strike – that is, to refuse work until a contract agreement has been reached.

Through the threat of a strike, a union can usually get employers to agree to a wage that is higher than the market-clearing wage. Thus Fig. 21.9 could represent conditions in a unionised industry if $w_{min}$ is interpreted as the union wage instead of the legal minimum wage. As in the case of a minimum wage, a union wage that is higher than the market-clearing wage leads to unemployment, in the amount $N_B - N_A$ in Fig. 21.9. Furthermore, a high union wage creates a trade-off similar to the one created by a minimum wage. Those workers who are lucky enough to get jobs as union members will be paid more than they would be otherwise. Unfortunately, their gain comes at the expense of other workers who are unemployed as a result of the artificially high union wage.

Are unions good for the economy? That is a controversial, emotionally charged question. Early in the twentieth century, some employers who faced little local competition for workers exploited their advantage by forcing workers to toil long hours in dangerous conditions for low pay. Through bitter and sometimes bloody confrontations with these companies, labour organisations succeeded in eliminating many of the worst abuses. Unions also point with pride to their historic political role in supporting progressive labour legislation, such as laws that banned child labour. Finally, union leaders often claim to increase productivity and promote democracy in the workplace by giving workers some voice in the operations of the firm.

Opponents of unions, while acknowledging that these organisations may have played a positive role in the past, question their value in a modern economy. Today, more and more workers are professionals or semi-professionals, rather than production workers, so they can move relatively easily from firm to firm. Indeed, many labour markets have become national or even international, so today's workers have numerous potential employers. Thus the forces of *competition* – the fact that employers must persuade talented workers to work for them – should provide adequate protection for workers. Indeed, opponents would argue that unions are becoming increasingly self-defeating, since firms that must pay artificially high union wages and abide by inflexible work rules will not be able to compete in a global economy. The ultimate effect of such handicaps will be the failure of unionised firms and the loss of union jobs. Indeed, unions are in decline in many European countries with the highest incidence of union membership in the public sector – civil servants, school teachers and the police.

However, in some European countries low union membership does not necessarily imply that unions have become less influential. The reason is that labour laws often require that wages agreed between firms and unions apply to all workers in the industry regardless of whether they are union members. For example, in France union membership covers only about 10 per cent of the non-government workforce but because French law requires non-unionised firms to accept the wages agreed by unionised firms, union bargaining can affect up to 90 per cent of the workforce in certain industries. In contrast about 35 per cent of the UK workforce belongs to trade unions but because British law does not require that wages agreed in unionised firms should also apply to non-unionised firms, union wage bargaining affects only approximately 40 per cent of the workforce.

### Unemployment benefits

Another structural feature of the labour market that may increase the unemployment rate is the availability of *unemployment benefits*, or government transfer payments to unemployed workers. Unemployment benefits provide an important safety-net because they help the unemployed to maintain a decent standard of living while they are looking for a job. But because their availability allows the unemployed to search longer or less intensively for a job, it may lengthen the average amount of time the typical unemployed worker is without a job.

Most economists would argue that unemployment benefits should be generous enough to provide basic support to the unemployed but not so generous as to remove the incentive actively to seek work. Thus, unemployment benefits should last for only a limited time, and should be set at levels below the income a worker receives when working.

### Other government regulations

Besides minimum-wage legislation, many other government regulations bear on the labour market. They include *health and safety regulations*, which establish the safety standards employers must follow, and rules that prohibit racial or gender-based discrimination in hiring. Many of these regulations are beneficial (see Chapter 13 for further discussion). In some cases, however, the costs of complying with regulations may exceed the benefits they provide. Further, to the extent that regulations increase employer costs and reduce productivity, they depress the demand for labour, lowering real wages and contributing to unemployment. For maximum economic efficiency, legislators should use the cost–benefit criterion (Chapter 1) when deciding what regulations to impose on the labour market.

The points raised in this section can help us to understand one of the important labour market trends discussed earlier in the chapter, namely, the persistence of high unemployment in Western Europe.

## Economic naturalist 21.6 Why are unemployment rates so high in Western Europe?

Since the 1980s, unemployment has been exceptionally high in the major countries of Western Europe, as Fig. 21.10 shows. Over 1993–2000, for example, the average unemployment rate was 9.6 per cent in the European Union, 8.5 per cent in Germany and more than 11 per cent in France, compared with 5.2 per cent in the United States. However, as Fig. 21.10 shows, there are important differences between European countries. While unemployment remains high in France and Germany it has declined rapidly in Ireland and the United Kingdom. Why has unemployment been so stubbornly high in some European countries and declined in others?

One explanation for the high unemployment in major European countries is the existence of structural 'rigidities' in their labour markets. Relative to the United States, European labour markets are highly regulated. European governments set rules in matters ranging from the number of weeks of vacation workers must receive to the reasons for which a worker can be dismissed. Minimum wages tend to be relatively high in Europe, and unemployment benefits are much more generous than in the United States. European unions are also far more powerful than those in the United States; in countries such as France their wage agreements are often extended by law to all firms in the industry, whether or not they are unionised. This lack of flexibility in labour markets – which some observers refer to as *Eurosclerosis* – causes higher frictional and structural unemployment.

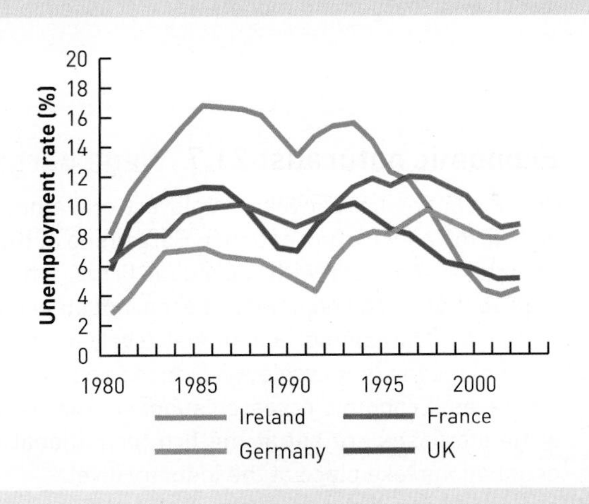


**Figure 21.10 Unemployment Rates in Western Europe, 1960–2002.** In France and Germany, unemployment rates have been high for more than a decade. In Ireland and the United Kingdom, unemployment has been declining since the early 1990s.

*Source*: *The European Economy*, Commission of the European Communities, www.europa_eu.int/comm_finance/publications.

If European labour markets are so dysfunctional, why has serious European unemployment emerged only since the 1980s? One explanation turns on the increasing pace of *globalisation and skill-biased technological change*. As we saw, these two factors decrease the demand for less-skilled labour relative to the demand for skilled labour. In the United States, falling demand has depressed the wages of the less skilled, increasing wage inequality. But in Western Europe, high minimum wages, union contracts, generous unemployment insurance and other factors may have created a *floor* for the wage that firms could pay or that workers would accept. As the marginal productivity of the less skilled dropped below that floor, firms no longer found it profitable to employ those workers, swelling the ranks of the unemployed. Thus the combination of labour market rigidity and the declining marginal productivity of low-skilled workers may be responsible for the European unemployment problem.

Evidence for the idea that inflexible labour markets have contributed to European unemployment comes from the United Kingdom, where the government of Prime Minister Margaret Thatcher instituted a series of reforms beginning in the early 1980s. Britain has since largely deregulated its labour market so that it functions much more like that in the United States. Fig. 21.10 shows that unemployment in Britain has gradually declined and is now lower than in most other Western European countries. Labour market reforms like those in Britain are examples of *structural policies*.

Ireland is another European country in which unemployment has declined rapidly since the 1980s. The decline in Irish unemployment has largely been associated with rapid productivity growth and an increasing demand for labour (Fig. 20.3). Also, like the United Kingdom, Ireland has taken steps toward labour market deregulation. However unlike the United Kingdom and many other European countries, Ireland has used a form of wage bargaining which sets wage increases at the *national* level rather than at the firm or industry level. The implications of these different wage bargaining models are discussed in Economic naturalist 21.7.

## Economic naturalist 21.7 Wage bargaining models

Wage negotiations between employers and employees can take place at three levels – firm, industry and national. Bargaining at the *firm* level means that employees or unions negotiate with individual firms, whereas bargaining at *industry* level implies that firms and unions in each industry collectively agree industrywide wage increases. Bargaining at national level, or *social partnership* as it is known in Ireland, means that employers, unions and government agree economywide wage increases. Economic research suggests that employment is best protected when wage increases are set at the firm or national level and most vulnerable when negotiations take place at the industry level.

Consider an airline industry with two firms, FlyEasy and FlyFast. When unions and employers bargain at the firm level each will pay close attention to the effect of their negotiations on their competitors. For example, if FlyFast unions push for higher wage increases than FlyEasy unions, they run the risk that their firm will lose competitiveness and that customers will shift to FlyEasy, resulting in possible job losses at FlyFast. However, if both unions jointly negotiate with the airline industry they know that each firm with retain its competitive position as both FlyEasy and FlyFast will pay the same wage increases, although the industry may suffer a competitive loss relative to other forms of transport. Hence, bargaining at firm level is more likely to exert a moderating influence on wage demands thus reducing the adverse effects on employment. Likewise, when wage increases are set at the national level, unions, employers and government (the *social partners*) are more likely to pay closer attention to national objectives and the economy's international competitiveness, resulting in more moderate wage increases. In the case of Ireland, the social partners collectively agreed to moderate wage increases in order to address the alarmingly high unemployment rates of the 1980s. As Fig. 21.10 shows, countries which use the firm-level (United Kingdom) or national-level (Ireland) models have lower unemployment rates than countries where wage bargaining is at industry level (France and Germany).

## RECAP Unemployment

Economists distinguish among three broad types of unemployment. *Frictional unemployment* is the short-term unemployment that is associated with the process of matching workers with jobs. *Structural unemployment* is the long-term or chronic unemployment that occurs even when the economy is producing at a normal rate. *Cyclical unemployment* is the extra unemployment that occurs during periods of recession. Frictional unemployment may be economically beneficial, as improved matching of workers and jobs may increase output in the long run. Structural and cyclical unemployment impose heavy economic costs on workers and society, as well as psychological costs on workers and their families.

*Structural features* of the labour market may cause structural unemployment. Examples of such features are legal minimum wages or union contracts that set wages above market-clearing levels; unemployment insurance, which allows unemployed workers to search longer or less intensively for a job; and government regulations that impose extra costs on employers. Regulation of the labour market is not necessarily undesirable, but it should be subject to the *cost–benefit* criterion. Heavy labour market regulation and high unionisation rates in Western Europe help to explain the persistence of high unemployment rates in those countries.

## Summary

- Since the 1970s the American and European labour markets have developed in different ways. Both have experienced a slowdown in the growth of *real wages* but employment and wage inequality have increased more rapidly in America. Western Europe has experienced less wage inequality but significantly higher rates of *unemployment* than the United States.
- Trends in real wages and employment can be studied using a supply and demand model of the labour market. The productivity of labour and the relative price of workers' output determine the *demand for labour*. Employers will hire workers only as long as the value of the marginal product of the last worker hired equals or exceeds the wage the firm must pay. Because of *diminishing returns to labour*, the more workers a firm employs, the less additional product will be obtained by adding yet another worker. The lower the going wage, the more workers will be hired; that is, the demand for labour curve slopes downward. Economic changes that increase the value of labour's marginal product, such as an increase in the relative price of workers' output or an increase in productivity, shift the labour demand curve to the right. Conversely, changes that reduce the value of labour's marginal product shift the labour demand curve to the left.

- The *supply curve for labour* shows the number of people willing to work at any given real wage. Since more people will work at a higher real wage, the supply curve is upward-sloping. An increase in the working-age population or a social change that promotes labour market participation (such as increased acceptance of women in the labour force) will raise labour supply and shift the labour supply curve to the right.
- Improvements in *productivity*, which raise the demand for labour, account for the bulk of increases in real wages since 1900. The slowdown in real wage growth that has occurred since the 1960s is the result of slower growth in labour demand, which was caused in turn by a slowdown in the rate of productivity improvement, and of more rapid growth in labour supply. Slower growth in labour supply has also contributed to Europe's poor employment record.
- Two reasons for the increasing wage inequality in the United States are economic globalisation and *skill-biased technological change*. Both have increased the demand for, and hence the real wages of, relatively skilled and educated workers. Attempting to block globalisation and technological change is counter-productive, however, since both factors are essential to economic growth and increased productivity. To some extent, the movement of workers from lower-paying to higher-paying jobs or industries (*worker mobility*) will counteract the trend toward wage inequality. A policy of providing transition aid and training for workers with obsolete skills is a more useful response to the problem.
- There are three broad types of unemployment: frictional, structural and cyclical. *Frictional unemployment* is the short-term unemployment associated with the process of matching workers with jobs in a dynamic, heterogeneous labour market. *Structural unemployment* is the long-term and chronic unemployment that exists even when the economy is producing at a normal rate. It arises from a variety of factors, including language barriers, discrimination, structural features of the labour market, lack of skills, or long-term mismatches between the skills workers have and the available jobs. *Cyclical unemployment* is the extra unemployment that occurs during periods of recession. The costs of frictional unemployment are low, as it tends to be brief and to create more productive matches between workers and jobs. But structural unemployment (which is often long term) and cyclical unemployment (which is associated with significant reductions in real GDP) are relatively more costly.
- *Structural features* of the labour market that may contribute to unemployment include minimum wage laws, which discourage firms from hiring low-skilled workers; labour unions, which can set wages above market-clearing levels; unemployment benefits, which reduce the incentives of the unemployed to find work quickly; and other regulations, which – although possibly conferring benefits – increase the costs of employing workers, for example, when wages negotiated in unionised firms apply to non-unionised firms in the same industry. The labour market 'rigidity' created by government regulations and union contracts is more of a problem in Europe than in the United States, which may account for Europe's high unemployment rates.
- *Wage bargaining*, which can take place at firm, industry and national level, may also have an effect on employment. The evidence suggests that employment is best protected when wages are negotiated at the firm or national level and most vulnerable when wages are set at the industry level.

## Key terms

**cyclical unemployment** (606)
**diminishing returns to labour** (590)
**frictional unemployment** (606)
**labour mobility** (601)
**skill-biased technological change** (602)
**structural unemployment** (606)

## Review questions

1. List and discuss the five important labour market trends given in the chapter. How do these trends differ between Europe and the United States? How do these trends either support or qualify the proposition that increasing labour productivity leads to higher standards of living?
2. Alice is very skilled at fixing manual typewriters. Would you expect her high productivity to result in a high real wage for her? Why or why not?
3. The Acme Corporation is considering hiring Jane Smith. Based on her other opportunities in the job market, Jane has told Acme that she will work for them for €40,000 per year. How should Acme determine whether to employ her?
4. Why did real wage growth slow down for 30 years beginning in the early 1970s?
5. What are two major factors contributing to increased inequality in wages? Briefly, why do these factors raise wage inequality? Contrast possible policy responses to increasing inequality in terms of their effects on economic efficiency.
6. List three types of unemployment and their causes. Which of these types is economically and socially the least costly? Explain.
7. Describe some of the structural features of European labour markets that have helped to keep European unemployment rates high. If these structural features create unemployment, why don't European governments just eliminate them?
8. How would you expect the 2004 enlargement of the European Union to affect wages and employment in the new member states?

## Problems

1. Production data for Bob's Bicycle Factory are in the table below:

| Number of workers | Bikes assembled/day |
|---|---|
| 1 | 10 |
| 2 | 18 |
| 3 | 24 |
| 4 | 28 |
| 5 | 30 |

Other than wages, Bob has costs of €100 (for parts and so on) for each bike assembled.

a. Bikes sell for €130 each. Find the marginal product and the value of the marginal product for each worker (don't forget about Bob's cost of parts).

b. Make a table showing Bob's demand curve for labour.

c. Repeat part (b) for the case in which bikes sell for €140 each.

d. Repeat part (b) for the case in which worker productivity increases by 50 per cent. Bikes sell for €130 each.

2. The marginal product of a worker in a light bulb factory equals 30 – $N$ bulbs per hour, where $N$ is the total number of workers employed. Light bulbs sell for €2 each, and there are no costs to producing them other than labour costs.

a. The going hourly wage for factory workers is €20 per hour. How many workers should the factory manager hire? What if the wage is €30 per hour?

b. Graph the factory's demand for labour.

c. Repeat part (b) for the case in which light bulbs sell for €3 each.

d. Suppose the supply of factory workers in the town in which the light bulb factory is located is 20 workers (in other words, the labour supply curve is vertical at 20 workers). What will be the equilibrium real wage for factory workers in the town if light bulbs sell for €2 each? If they sell for €3 each?

3. How would each of the following be likely to affect the real wage and employment of unskilled workers on an automobile plant assembly line?

a. Demand for the type of car made by the plant increases.

b. A sharp increase in the price of petrol causes many commuters to switch to public transport.

c. Because of alternative opportunities, people become less willing to do factory work.

d. The plant management introduces new assembly line methods that increase the number of cars unskilled workers can produce per hour while reducing defects.

e. Robots are introduced to do most basic assembly line tasks.

f. The workers unionise.

4. How would each of the following factors be likely to affect the economywide supply of labour?

a. European regulations increase the mandatory retirement age.

b. Increased productivity causes real wages to rise.

c. An emergency leads to many young people being drafted into the armed forces.

d. More people decide to have children (consider both short-run and long-run effects).

e. Unemployment benefits are made more generous.

5. Either skilled or unskilled workers can be used to produce a small toy. The marginal product of skilled workers, measured in terms of toys produced per day, equals $200 - N_s$, where $N_s$ is the number of skilled workers employed. Similarly, the marginal product of unskilled workers is $100 - N_u$, where $N_u$ is the number of unskilled workers employed. The toys sell for €3 each.

a. Assume that there are 100 skilled workers and 50 unskilled workers available (and the labour supply curves for each group are vertical). In euros, what will be the equilibrium wage for each type of worker? (**Hint:** What are the marginal products and the values of marginal product for each type of worker when all workers are employed?)

b. Electronic equipment is introduced that increases the marginal product of skilled workers (who can use the equipment) to $300 - N_s$. The marginal product of unskilled workers is unaffected. Now what are the equilibrium wages for the two groups?

c. Suppose that unskilled workers find it worthwhile to acquire skills when the wage differential between skilled and unskilled workers is €300 per day or greater. Following the introduction of the electronic equipment, how many unskilled workers will become skilled? (**Hint:** How many workers would have to shift from the unskilled to the skilled category to make the equilibrium difference in wages precisely equal to €300 per day?) What are equilibrium wages for skilled and unskilled workers after some unskilled workers acquire training?

6. An economy with no foreign trade produces sweaters and dresses. There are 14 workers in the sweater industry and 26 workers in the dress industry. The marginal product of workers in the sweater industry, measured in sweaters produced per day, is $20 - N_S$, where $N_S$ is the number of workers employed in the sweater industry. The marginal product of workers in the dress industry, measured in dresses produced per day, is $30 - N_D$, where $N_D$ is the number of workers employed in the dress industry.

a. Initially, sweaters sell for €40 apiece and dresses are €60 apiece. Find the equilibrium wage in each industry.

b. The economy opens up to trade. Foreign demand for domestically produced sweaters is strong, raising the price of sweaters to €50 each. But foreign competition reduces demand for domestically produced dresses so that they now sell for €50 each. Assuming that workers cannot move between industries, what are the wages in each industry now? Who has been hurt and who has been helped by the opening up to trade?

c. Now suppose that workers can move freely from one industry to the other, and will always move to the industry that pays the higher wage. In the long run, how many of the 40 workers in the economy will be in each industry? What wages will they receive? In the long run, are domestic workers hurt or helped by the opening up to foreign trade? Assume that sweaters and dresses continue to sell for €50.

7. For each of the following scenarios, state whether the unemployment is frictional, structural or cyclical. Justify your answer.

a. Ted lost his job when the steel mill closed down. He lacks the skills to work in another industry and so has been unemployed for over a year.

b. Alice was laid off from her job at the car plant because the recession reduced the demand for cars. She expects to get her job back when the economy picks up.

c. Lance is an unskilled worker who works for local removal companies during their busy seasons. The rest of the year he is unemployed.

d. Gwen had a job as an office clerk but quit when her husband was transferred to another city. She looked for a month before finding a new job that she liked.

e. Tao looked for a job for six weeks after finishing college. He turned down a couple of offers because they didn't let him use the skills he had acquired at college, but now he has a job in the area that he trained for.

f. Karen, a software engineer, lost her job when the dot.com company she was working for went bankrupt. She had interviews at five companies before accepting a new job in another firm in the same industry.

8. The demand for and supply of labour in a certain industry are given by the equations

$$N_d = 400 - 2w$$
$$N_s = 240 + 2w$$

where $N_d$ is the number of workers employers want to hire, $N_s$ is the number of people willing to work, and both labour demand and labour supply depend on the real wage $w$, which is measured in euros per day.

a. Find employment and the real wage in labour market equilibrium.

b. Suppose the minimum wage is €50 per day. Find employment and unemployment. Is anyone made better off by the minimum wage? Worse off? In answering the last part of the question, consider not only workers but employers and other people in the society, such as consumers and tax-payers.

c. Repeat part (b) except now assume that a union contract requires that workers be paid €60 per day.

d. Repeat part (b) but, instead of a minimum wage, suppose there is an unemployment benefit that pays €50 per day. Workers are indifferent between earning a wage of €50 per day and remaining unemployed and collecting the benefit.

e. Repeat part (b), assuming that the minimum wage is €50 per day. However, assume that the cost of complying with government regulations on workplace safety reduces labour demand to $N_d = 360 - 2w$.

## Answers to in-chapter exercises

**21.1** The value of the marginal product of the seventh worker is €39,000, and the value of the marginal product of the eighth worker is €33,000. So the seventh but not the eighth worker is profitable to hire at a wage of €35,000.

**21.2** With the computer price at €5,000, it is profitable to hire three workers at a wage of €100,000, since the third worker's value of marginal product (€105,000) exceeds €100,000 but the fourth worker's value of marginal product (€95,000) is less than €100,000. At a computer price of €3,000, we can refer to Table 21.2 to find that not even the first worker has a value of marginal product as high as €100,000, so at that computer price BCC will hire no workers. In short, at a wage of €100,000, the increase in the computer price raises the demand for technicians from zero to three.

**21.3** The seventh but not the eighth worker's value of marginal product exceeds €50,000 (Table 21.4), so it is profitable to hire seven workers if the going wage is €50,000. From Table 21.2, before the increase in productivity, the first five workers have values of marginal product greater than €50,000, so the demand for labour at a given wage of €50,000 is five workers. Thus the increase in productivity raises the quantity of labour demanded at a wage of €50,000 from five workers to seven workers.

**21.4** Even though you are receiving no pay, the valuable experience you gain working at the radio station is likely to raise the pay you will be able to earn in the future, so it is an investment in human capital. You also find working in the radio station more enjoyable than working in a car wash, presumably. To decide which job to take, you should ask yourself, 'Taking into account both the likely increase in my future earnings and my greater enjoyment from working in the radio station, would I be willing to pay €3,000 to work in the radio station rather than in the car wash?' If the answer is yes, then you should work in the radio station, otherwise you should go to the car wash.

A decision to work in the radio station does not contradict the idea of an upward-sloping labour supply curve, if we are willing to think of the total compensation for that job as including not just cash wages but also such factors as the value of the training that you receive. Your labour supply curve is still upward-sloping in the sense that the greater the value you place on the radio station experience, the more likely you are to accept the job.

**21.5** Immigration to a country raises labour supply – indeed, the search for work is one of the most powerful factors drawing immigrants in the first place. As shown in the figure below, an increase in labour supply will tend to lower the wages that employers have to pay (from $w$ to $w'$), while raising overall employment (from $N$ to $N'$). Because of its tendency to

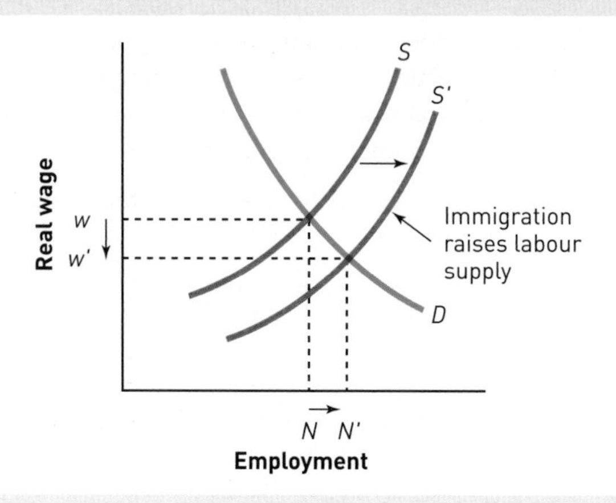

reduce real wages, labour unions generally oppose large-scale immigration, while employers support it.

Although the figure shows the overall, or *aggregate*, supply of labour in the economy, the specific effects of immigration on wages depend on the skills and occupations of the immigrants. In many European countries, immigration policy makes the reunification of families the main reason for admitting immigrants, and for the most part immigrants are not screened by their education or skills. Some countries also have a good deal of *illegal* immigration, made up largely of people looking for economic opportunity. These two factors create a tendency for new immigrants to be relatively low-skilled. Since immigration tends to increase the supply of unskilled labour by more than it does skilled labour, it depresses the wages of domestic low-skilled workers more than it does the wages of domestic high-skilled workers. Some economists, such as George Borjas of Harvard University, have argued that low-skilled immigration is another important factor reducing the wages of less-skilled workers relative to workers with greater skills and education. Borjas favours the approach used by Canada which gives preference to potential immigrants with relatively high levels of skills and education.

21.6 In the figure below both Europe and the United States start with the same initial values of the real wage ($w$) and employment ($N$) and each experiences the same increase in labour demand (from $D$ to $D'$), the result of productivity growth. In Europe, modest growth in labour supply shifts the supply curve to $S_{EU}$ establishing wage and employment levels at $w_{EU}$ and $N_{EU}$. In the United States the larger increase in labour supply (from $S$ to $S_{US}$) results in a lower wage relative to Europe ($w_{US}$) and higher employment ($N_{US}$). Since 1996, more rapid productivity growth, which raises labour demand more quickly and shifts the demand curve further to the right, accounts for faster growth in American real wages.

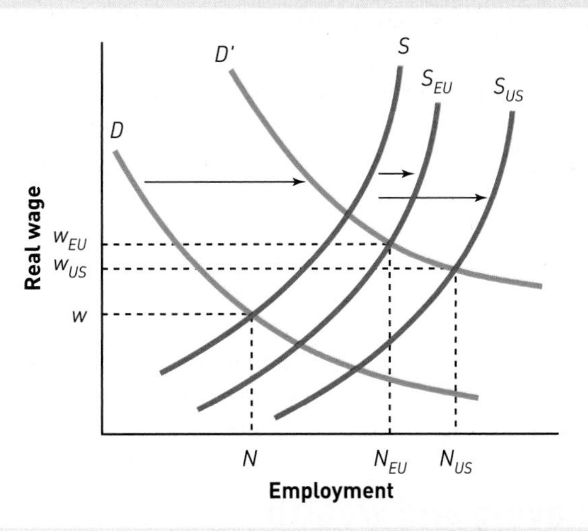


21.7 Unemployed textile workers are most likely to be classified as structural unemployed. They become unemployed because free trade leads to a reallocation of resources from the domestic textile industry to software production. The appropriate policy is to retrain unemployed textile workers to take jobs in the expanding software industry.

# 22

# Saving and Capital Formation

Saving is important, to both individuals and to nations. People need to save to provide for their retirement and for other future needs, such as their children's education or a new home. An individual's or a family's savings can also provide a crucial buffer in the event of an economic emergency, such as the loss of a job or unexpected medical bills. At the national level, the production of new capital goods – factories, equipment and housing – is an important factor promoting economic growth and higher living standards. As we shall see in this chapter, the resources necessary to produce new capital come primarily from a nation's collective saving.

In this chapter we shall look at saving and its links to the formation of new capital. We begin by defining the concepts of saving and wealth and exploring the connection between them. We shall consider why people choose to save, rather than spend all their income. We then turn to national saving – the collective saving of households, businesses and government. Because national saving determines the capacity of an economy to create new capital, it is the more important measure of saving from a macroeconomic perspective.

We next discuss capital formation. Most decisions to invest in new capital are made by firms. As we shall see, a firm's decision to invest is in many respects analogous to its decision about whether to increase employment; firms will choose to expand their capital stocks when the benefits of doing so exceed the costs. We end the chapter by showing how national saving and capital formation are related, using a supply and demand approach.

## Saving and wealth

**saving** current income minus spending on current needs

**saving rate** saving divided by income

**wealth** the value of assets minus liabilities

**assets** anything of value that one owns

In general, the **saving** of an economic unit – whether a household, a business, a university or a nation – may be defined as its *current income* minus its *spending on current needs*. For example if the Rossis family earns €1,000 per week, spends €900 weekly on living expenses such as rent, food, clothes and entertainment and deposit the remaining €100 in a bank account, its saving is €100 per week. The **saving rate** of any economic unit is its saving divided by its income. Since the Rossis save €100 from a weekly income of €1,000, their saving rate is €100/€1,000, or 10 per cent.

The saving of an economic unit is closely related to its **wealth**, or the value of its assets minus its liabilities. **Assets** are anything of value that one *owns*, either *financial* or *real*. Examples of financial assets that you or your family might own include cash, bank accounts, shares in companies and government bonds. Examples of real assets include property, jewellery, consumer durables like cars and valuable collectibles.

**liabilities** the debts one owes

**Liabilities**, on the other hand, are the debts one *owes*. Examples of liabilities are credit card balances, bank loans and mortgages.

Accountants list the assets and liabilities of a family, a firm, a university or any other economic unit on a *balance sheet*. Comparing the values of the assets and liabilities helps them to determine the economic unit's wealth, also called its *net worth*.

### Example 22.1 The Rossis construct their balance sheet

To take stock of their financial position, the Rossis list their assets and liabilities on a balance sheet. The result is shown in Table 22.1. What is the Rossis' wealth?

| Assets | | Liabilities | |
|---|---|---|---|
| Cash | €100 | Mortgage | €200,000 |
| Bank account | 1,200 | Credit card balance | 250 |
| Shares | 1,000 | | |
| Car (market value) | 3,500 | | |
| House (market value) | 250,000 | | |
| **Total** | **€255,800** | | **€200,250** |
| | | **Net worth** | **€55,550** |

**Table 22.1** The Rossis' Balance Sheet

The Rossis' financial assets are their cash holdings (notes and coin), the balance in their bank account and the current value of their shares. Together their financial assets are worth €2,300. They also list €253,500 in real assets – the sum of the market values of their car and house. The Rossis' total assets, both financial and real, come to €255,800. Their liabilities are the mortgage on their home and the balance due on their credit card, which total €200,250. The Rossis' wealth, or net worth, then, is the value of their assets (€255,800) minus the value of their liabilities (€200,250), or €55,550.

**Exercise 22.1** What would the Rossis' net worth be if their mortgage was €270,000 rather than €250,000? Construct a new balance sheet for the household.

Saving and wealth are related, because saving contributes to wealth. To understand this relationship better, we must distinguish between *stocks* and *flows*.

## Stocks and flows

**flow** a measure that is defined per unit of time

**stock** a measure that is defined at a point in time

Saving is an example of a **flow**, a measure that is defined *per unit of time*. For example, the Rossis' savings are €100 *per week*. Wealth, in contrast, is a **stock**, a measure that is defined *at a point in time*. The Rossis' wealth of €55,550, for example, is their wealth on a particular date.

To visualise the difference between stocks and flows, think of water running into a bath. The amount of water in the bath at any specific moment – for example, 100 litres at 7.15 p.m. – is a *stock*, because it is measured at a specific point in time. The rate at which the water flows into the bath – for example, 5 litres per minute – is a *flow*, because it is measured per unit of time. In many cases, a flow is the *rate of change* in a stock: if we know that there are 100 litres of water in the bath at 7.15 p.m., for example, and that water is flowing in at 5 litres per minute, we can easily determine that the stock of water will be changing at the rate of 5 litres per minute and will equal 105 litres at 7.16 p.m., 110 litres at 7.17 p.m. and so on, until the bath overflows.

The relationship between saving (a *flow*) and wealth (a *stock*) is similar to the relationship between the flow of water into a bath and the stock of water in the bath in that the *flow* of saving causes the *stock* of wealth to change at the same rate. Indeed, as Example 22.2 illustrates, every euro that a person saves adds a euro to her wealth.

### **Example 22.2** The link between saving and wealth

The Rossis save €100 per week. How does this saving affect their wealth? Does the change in their wealth depend on whether the Rossis use their saving to accumulate assets or to reduce their liabilities?

The Rossis could use the €100 they saved this week to increase their assets – for example, by adding the €100 to their bank account – or to reduce their liabilities – for example, by paying off their credit card balance. Suppose they add the €100 to their bank account, increasing their assets by €100. Since their liabilities are unchanged, their wealth also increases by €100, to €55,650 (see Table 22.1).

If the Rossis decide to use the €100 they saved this week to pay off their credit card balance, they reduces it from €250 to €150. That action would reduce liabilities by €100, leaving their assets unchanged. Since wealth equals assets minus liabilities, reducing their liabilities by €100 increases their wealth by €100, to €55,650. Thus, saving €100 per week raises the Rossis' stock of wealth by €100 a week, regardless of whether they use their saving to increase assets or reduce liabilities. In either case the *flow* of saving leads to an increase in the *stock* of wealth.

The close relationship between saving and wealth explains why saving is so important to an economy. Higher rates of saving today lead to faster accumulation of wealth, and the wealthier a nation is, the higher its standard of living. Thus a high rate of saving today contributes to an improved *standard of living* in the future.

**Exercise 22.2**

Continuing with the Rossis, assume that Table 22.1 is their family balance sheet on 1 January 2004. Assume that the following transactions take place over 2004. (a) The Rossis save €400 per month. (b) The market value of the Rossis' car falls by €1,000. (c) The market value of the Rossis' house increases by 10 per cent. (d) The Rossis' have monthly mortgage payments of €300, of which €100 is interest on the debt and €200 is repayment on the loan. Other items in their balance sheet remain unchanged. Find the Rossis' net worth on 1 January 2005.

## Capital gains and losses

Though saving increases wealth, it is not the only factor that determines wealth. Wealth can also change because of changes in the values of the real or financial *assets* one owns. Suppose the Rossis' shares rise in value, from €1,000 to €1,500. This increase in the value of the Rossis' shares raises their total assets by €500 without affecting their liabilities. As a result, the Rossis' wealth rises by €500, from €255,800 to €256,300 and their net worth from €55,550 to €56,050 (see Table 22.2).

**capital gains** increases in the value of existing assets

**capital losses** decreases in the value of existing assets

Changes in the value of existing assets are called **capital gains** when an asset's value increases and **capital losses** when an asset's value decreases. Just as capital gains increase wealth, capital losses decrease wealth. Capital gains and losses are not counted as part of saving, however. Instead, the change in a person's wealth during any period equals the saving done during the period plus capital gains or minus capital losses during that period. In terms of an equation,

Change in wealth = Saving + Capital gains – Capital losses

| Assets | | Liabilities | |
|---|---|---|---|
| Cash | €100 | Mortgage | €200,000 |
| Checking account | 1,200 | Credit card balance | 250 |
| Shares | 1,500 | | |
| Car (market value) | 3,500 | | |
| House (market value) | 250,000 | | |
| **Total** | **€256,300** | | **€200,250** |
| | | **Net worth** | **€56,050** |

**Table 22.2** The Rossis' Balance Sheet after an Increase in the Value of Their Shares

**Exercise 22.3** How would each of the following actions or events affect the Rossis' *saving* and their *wealth*?

a. The Rossis deposit €100 in the bank at the end of the week as usual. They also charge €150 to their credit card, raising the balance to €400.
b. The Rossis use €400 from their bank account to pay off their credit card bill.
c. The Rossis' old car is recognised as a classic. Its market value rises from €3,500 to €4,000.
d. A fall in property prices reduces the value of the Rossis' house by €20,000.

We have seen how saving is related to the accumulation of wealth. To understand why people choose to save, however, we need to examine their *motives for saving*.

## RECAP Saving and wealth

In general, *saving* is current income minus spending on current needs. *Wealth* is the value of assets – anything of value that one owns – minus liabilities – the debts one owes. Saving is measured per unit of time (for example, euros per week) and thus is a *flow*. Wealth is measured at a point in time and thus is a *stock*. In the same way as the flow of water through the tap increases the stock of water in a bathtub, the flow of saving increases the stock of wealth.

Wealth can also be increased by *capital gains* (increases in the value of existing assets) or reduced by *capital losses* (decreases in asset values).

## Why do people save?

Why do people save part of their income instead of spending everything they earn? Economists have identified at least three broad reasons for saving. First, people save to meet certain *long-term objectives*, such as a comfortable retirement. By saving part of their income during their most productive working years, households can support a higher standard of living during their retirement years. In fact, saving, and borrowing, are means by which households can move expenditure on goods and services, or consumption, across time. When a household saves it is refraining from consumption by spending less than its income.

However as saving increases the household's stock of wealth it will be possible to spend more on goods and services and consume above income in future years. Put another way, saving means that households are substituting *future* for *current* consumption. Conversely, if a household borrows this year it can consume above its current income. But as borrowing today has to be repaid in subsequent years the household must consume less than its income at some point in the future. Hence borrowing is a means by which households can substitute *present* for *future* consumption. Economists refer to this transfer of consumption across time as **intertemporal substitution**.

**intertemporal substitution** a means of moving consumption across time by substituting consumption in one year for consumption in another year

Figure 22.1 illustrates how intertemporal substitution can enable a household to follow different consumption and income paths over its lifetime. For many households *income from employment* starts at a relatively low level but rises as the working members acquire job skills and experience and then declines at retirement. This life-cycle profile of earned income is illustrated by the hump-shaped income curve in Fig. 22.1. If households could not save or borrow then their life-cycle consumption would follow the same path. However, by borrowing in the early years when income is relatively low and expenditure on housing, children, etc. is high, the household can support a higher level of consumption. As income rises in the more productive years of its life-cycle the household can use its greater resources to repay earlier borrowing and save, or accumulate wealth, to support consumption during its retirement years when the household is running its wealth down, or *dis-saving*. Because this type of saving and borrowing enables the household to separate its consumption path from its life-cycle income profile, economists refer to it as **life-cycle saving**.

**life-cycle saving** saving to smooth out the household's consumption path

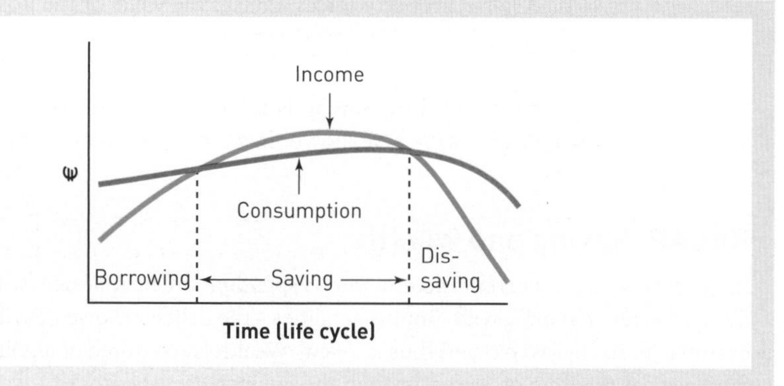


**Figure 22.1 Life-Cycle Saving.** By saving and borrowing, households can separate their life-cycle consumption path from their income profile.

A second reason to save is to protect oneself and family against *unexpected setbacks* – the loss of a job, for example, or a costly health problem. Saving for protection against potential emergencies is called **precautionary saving**.

**precautionary saving** saving for protection against unexpected setbacks, such as the loss of a job or a medical emergency

**bequest saving** saving done for the purpose of leaving an inheritance

A third reason to save is to accumulate an *estate* to leave to one's heirs, usually one's children but possibly a favourite charity or other worthy cause. Saving for the purpose of leaving an inheritance, or bequest, is called **bequest saving.**

To be sure, people usually do not mentally separate their saving into these three categories; rather, all three reasons for saving motivate most savers to varying degrees. Economic naturalist 22.1 shows how these reasons for saving can explain differences between household saving in Europe and the United States.

## Economic naturalist 22.1 Why do Europeans save more than Americans?

Household saving in the United States, which has always been comparatively low, has fallen even further since the 1990s. Figure 22.2 shows recent trends in household saving rates in France, Germany and the United States and clearly illustrates that Europeans save more than Americans. Why do US households save so little compared with their European counterparts?

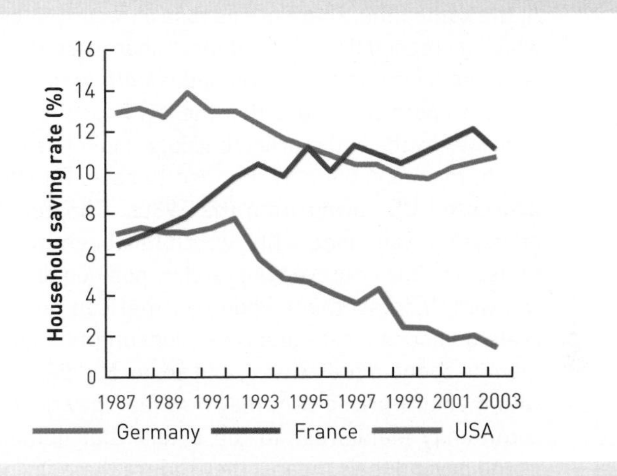


**Figure 22.2 Household Saving Rates as a Percentage of Disposable Income, 1987–2003.** European household saving rates are now significantly higher than in United States.

*Source*: OECD, www.oecd.org.

Economists do not agree on the reasons for differences between household saving rates in Europe and the United States, although many hypotheses have been suggested. It is possible that higher saving rates in Europe may have as much to do with historical and psychological factors as with economics. The United States has not known sustained economic hardship since the Great Depression of the 1930s. Most European economies, on the other hand, suffered devastation in the Second World War whereas the American economy prospered. Also, during the Cold War period (1950– 89), parts of Western Europe were very much on the 'front line', creating greater uncertainty about the future than in the United States. Although the immediate effects of world wars have faded into memory they may have implanted a much stronger inertia (old habits die hard) in European saving behaviour compared with that of the United States. Perhaps a less prosperous and more volatile history has led to stronger *precautionary* and *bequest* motives for saving in Europe than in the United States.

*Life-cycle* reasons may also explain part of the differences between European and American household saving behaviour. In Chapter 20 (Fig. 20.1) we saw that in the 1990s income per person increased more rapidly in the United States than in Europe. If this rise in the relative US standard of living is viewed as permanent then it reduces the need to save from current income to support future consumption.

Three other factors present in both America and Europe, but more prominent in the United States, may help to explain recent differences in saving rates. First, the pace of *financial innovation* has been much more rapid in the United States than in Europe, giving American households greater access to credit markets and reducing *precautionary* motives for saving. For example, unlike in some European countries, US home owners find it relatively easy to borrow against their home equity (the difference between the market value of a family's home and its mortgage liability). Second, during the 1990s an increasing number of Americans acquired stocks, either directly through purchases or indirectly through their pension and retirement funds. At the same time, share prices rose at record rates. The strongly rising 'bull market', which increased the prices of most shares, enabled many Americans to enjoy significant capital gains and increased wealth without saving much, if anything. Indeed, some economists argued that the low household saving rate of the 1990s is partially *explained* by the bull market; because capital gains increased household wealth by so much, many people saw no need to save. Finally, *demonstration effects* may have depressed US saving from the 1980s. Chapter 21 discussed the phenomenon of increasing wage inequality, which has been much more pronounced in the United States and has improved the relative position of more American skilled and educated workers. Increased spending by American households at the top of the earnings scale on houses, cars and other consumption goods may have led those just below them to spend more as well, and so on. Middle-class families that were once content with medium-priced cars may now feel they need Volvos and BMWs to keep up with community standards. To the extent that demonstration effects lead families to spend beyond their means, they reduce their saving rate.

## Saving and the real interest rate

Most people don't save by putting cash in a tin. Instead, they make *financial investments* that they hope will provide a good return on their saving. For example, a bank account may pay interest on the account balance. More sophisticated financial investments, such as government bonds or shares (see Chapter 24), also pay returns in the form of interest payments, dividends or capital gains. High returns are desirable, of course, because the higher the return, the faster one's savings will grow.

The rate of return that is most relevant to saving decisions is the *real interest rate*, denoted $r$. Recall from Chapter 19 that the real interest rate is the rate at which the real purchasing power of a financial asset increases over time. The real interest rate equals the market, or nominal, interest rate ($i$) minus the inflation rate ($\pi$).

The real interest rate is relevant to savers because it is the 'reward' for saving. Suppose you are thinking of increasing your saving by €1,000 this year, which you can do if you give up your habit of going to the cinema once a week. If the real interest rate is 5 per cent, then in a year your extra saving will give you extra purchasing power of €1,050, measured in today's money. But if the real interest rate were 10 per cent, your sacrifice of €1,000 this year would be rewarded by €1,100 in purchasing power next year. Obviously, all else being equal, you would be more willing to save today if you knew the reward next year would be greater. In either case the cost of the extra saving – giving up your weekly night out – is the same. But the *benefit* of the extra saving, in terms of increased purchasing power next year, is higher if the real interest rate is 10 per cent rather than 5 per cent.

### Example 22.3 By how much does a high savings rate enhance a family's future living standard?

The Spends and the Thrifts are similar families, except that the Spends save 5 per cent of their income each year and the Thrifts save 20 per cent. The two families began to save in 1980 and plan to continue to save until their respective breadwinners retire in the year 2015. Both families earn €40,000 a year in real terms in the labour market, and both put their savings in a fund that has yielded a real return of 8 per cent per year, a return they expect to continue into the future. Compare the amount that the two families consume in each year from 1980 to 2015, and compare the families' wealth at retirement.

In the first year, 1980, the Spends saved €2,000 (5 per cent of their €40,000 income) and consumed €38,000 (95 per cent of €40,000). The Thrifts saved €8,000 in 1980 (20 per cent of €40,000) and hence consumed only €32,000 in that year, €6,000 less than the Spends. In 1981, the Thrifts' income was €40,640, the extra €640 representing the 8 per cent return on their €8,000 savings. The Spends saw their income grow by only €160 (8 per cent of their savings of €2,000) in 1981. With an income of €40,640, the Thrifts consumed €32,512 in 1981 (80 per cent of €40,640) compared with €38,152 (95 per cent of €40,160) for the Spends. The consumption gap between the two families, which started out at €6,000, thus fell to €5,640 after one year.

Because of the more rapid increase in the Thrifts' wealth and hence interest income, each year the Thrifts' income grew faster than the Spends'; each year the Thrifts continued to save 20 per cent of their higher incomes compared with only 5 per cent for the Spends. Figure 22.3 shows the paths followed by the consumption spending of the two families. You can see that the Thrifts' consumption, though starting at a lower level, grows more quickly. By 1995 the Thrifts had overtaken the Spends, and from that point onward, the amount by which the Thrifts outspent the Spends grew with each passing year. Even though the Spends continued to consume 95 per cent of their income each year, their income grew so slowly that by 2000, they were consuming nearly €3,000 a year less than the Thrifts (€41,158 a year versus €43,957). And by the time the two families retire, in 2015, the Thrifts will be consuming more than €12,000 per year more than the Spends (€55,774 versus €43,698). Even more striking is the difference between the retirement nest eggs of the two families. Whereas the Spends will enter retirement with total accumulated savings of just over €77,000, the Thrifts will have more than €385,000, five times as much.

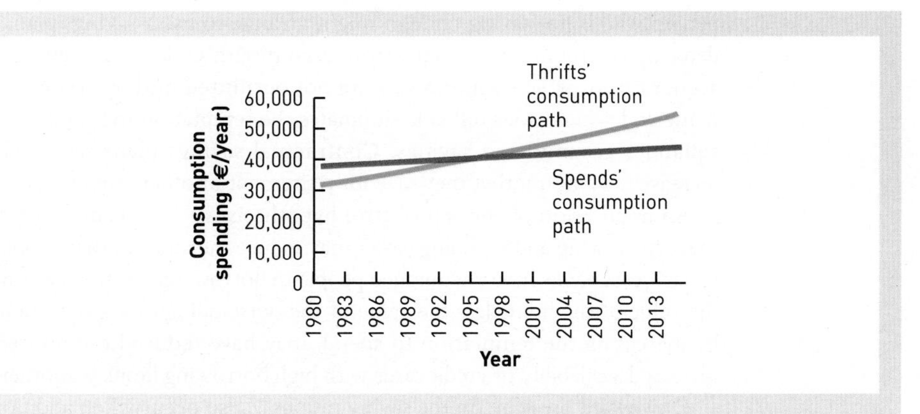


**Figure 22.3 Consumption Trajectories of the Thrifts and the Spends.** The figure shows consumption spending in each year by two families, the Thrifts and the Spends. Because the Thrifts save more than the Spends, their annual consumption spending rises relatively quickly. By the time of the retirement in the year 2015, the Thrifts are both consuming significantly more each year than the Spends and also have a retirement nest egg that is five times larger.

These dramatic differences depend in part on the assumption that the real rate of return is 8 per cent, a relatively high rate of return from a historical perspective. However, the point of the example, which remains valid under alternative assumptions about the real interest rate and saving rates, is that, because of the power of *compound interest*, a high rate of saving pays off in the long run.

While a higher real interest rate increases the reward for saving and encourages people to save, another force counteracts that extra incentive. Recall that a major reason for saving is to attain specific goals such as a comfortable retirement. If the goal is a specific amount – say, €25,000 for a down-payment on a home – then a higher rate of return means that households can save *less* and still reach their goal, because funds that are put aside will grow more quickly. For example, to accumulate €25,000 at the end of five years, at a 5 per cent interest rate a person would have to save about €4,309 per year. At a 10 per cent interest rate, reaching the €25,000 goal would require saving only about €3,723 per year. To the extent that people are *target savers* who save to reach a specific goal, higher interest rates actually decrease the amount they need to save.

In sum, a higher real interest rate has both positive and negative effects on saving – a *positive* effect because it increases the reward for saving and a *negative* effect because it reduces the amount people need to save each year to reach a given target. Empirical evidence suggests that, in practice, higher real interest rates lead to modest increases in saving.

## Saving, self-control and demonstration effects

The reasons for saving we have just discussed are based on the notion that people are *rational decision makers* who will choose their saving rates to maximise their welfare over the long run. Yet many psychologists, and some economists, have argued instead that people's saving behaviour is based as much on *psychological* as on economic factors. For example, psychologists stress that many people lack the *self-control* to do what they know is in their own best interest. People smoke or eat greasy food, despite the known long-term health risks. Similarly, they may have good intentions about saving but lack the self-control to put aside as much as they ought to each month.

One way to strengthen self-control is to remove temptations from the immediate environment. A person who is trying to quit smoking will make a point of not having cigarettes in the house, and a person with a weight problem will avoid going to a bakery. Similarly, a person who is not saving enough might arrange to use a savings plan, through which a predetermined amount is deducted from each month's salary payment and set aside in a special account from which withdrawals are not permitted until retirement. Making saving automatic and withdrawals difficult eliminates the temptation to spend all of current earnings or squander accumulated savings. Contractual savings plans have helped many people to increase the amount that they save for retirement or other purposes.

An implication of the self-control hypothesis is that consumer credit arrangements that make borrowing and spending easier may reduce the amount that people save. For example, in recent years banks have encouraged people to borrow against the *equity* in their homes – that is, the value of the home less the value of the outstanding mortgage. Such financial innovations, by increasing the temptation to spend, may have reduced the household saving rate. The increased availability of credit cards with high borrowing limits is another temptation.

Downward pressure on the saving rate may also occur when additional spending by some consumers stimulates additional spending by others. Such *demonstration effects* arise when people use the spending of others as a yardstick by which to measure the adequacy of their own living standards. For example, a family in an upper-middle-class suburb in which the average house has 1,000 $m^2$ of living space might regard a 500 $m^2$ house as being uncomfortably small – too cramped, for example, to entertain friends in the manner to which community members have become accustomed. In contrast, a similar family living in a low-income neighbourhood might find the very same house luxuriously large.

The implication of demonstration effects for saving is that families who live among others who consume more than they do may be strongly motivated to increase their own consumption spending. When satisfaction depends in part on *relative* living standards, an upward spiral may result in which household spending is higher, and saving lower, than would be best for either the individual families involved or for the economy as a whole.

### RECAP Why do people save?

Motivations for saving include saving to meet long-term objectives, such as retirement (*life-cycle saving*), saving for emergencies (*precautionary saving*) and saving to leave an inheritance or bequest (*bequest saving*). The amount that people save also depends on macroeconomic factors, such as the real interest rate. A higher real interest rate stimulates saving by increasing the reward for saving, but it can also depress saving by making it easier for savers to reach a specific savings target. On balance, a higher real interest rate appears to lead to modest increases in saving.

Psychological factors may also affect saving rates. If people have *self-control* problems, then financial arrangements (such as automatic payroll deductions) that make it more difficult to spend will increase their saving. People's saving decisions may also be influenced by *demonstration effects*, as when people feel compelled to spend at the same rate as their neighbours, even though they may not be able to afford to do so.

## National saving and its components

Thus far, we have been examining the concepts of saving and wealth from the individual's perspective. But macroeconomists are interested primarily in saving and wealth for the country as a whole. In this section we shall study *national saving*, or the *aggregate saving* of the economy. National saving includes the saving of business firms and the government as well as that of households. Later in the chapter we shall examine the close link between national saving and the rate of capital formation in an economy.

### The measurement of national saving

To define the saving rate of a country as a whole, we shall start with a basic accounting identity that was introduced in Chapter 18. According to this identity, for the economy as a whole, production (or income) must equal total expenditure. In symbols, the identity is

$$Y = C + I + G + NX$$

where $Y$ stands for either production or aggregate income (which must be equal), $C$ equals consumption expenditure, $I$ equals investment spending, $G$ equals government purchases of goods and services and $NX$ equals net exports.

For now, let's assume that net exports ($NX$) is equal to zero, which would be the case if a country did not trade at all with other countries or if its exports and imports were always balanced. With net exports set at zero, the condition that output equals expenditure becomes

$$Y = C + I + G$$

To determine how much saving is done by the nation as a whole, we can apply the general definition of saving. As for any other economic unit, a nation's saving equals its *current income* less its *spending on current needs*. The current income of the country as a whole is its GDP, or $Y$ – that is, the value of the final goods and services produced within the country's borders during the year.

Identifying the part of total expenditure that corresponds to the nation's spending on current needs is more difficult than identifying the nation's income. The component of aggregate spending that is easiest to classify is investment spending $I$. We know that investment spending – the acquisition of new factories, equipment and other capital goods, as well as residential construction – is done to expand the economy's future productive capacity or provide more housing for the future, not to satisfy current needs. So investment spending clearly is *not* part of spending on current needs.

Deciding how much of consumption spending by households, $C$, and government purchases of goods and services, $G$, should be counted as spending on current needs is less straightforward. Certainly most consumption spending by households – on food, clothing, utilities, entertainment and so on – is for current needs. But consumption spending also includes purchases of long-lived *consumer durables*, such as cars, furniture and appliances. Consumer durables are only partially used up during the current year; they may continue to provide service, in fact, for years after their purchase. So household spending on consumer durables is a combination of spending on current needs and spending on future needs.

As with consumption spending, most government purchases of goods and services are intended to provide for current needs. However, like household purchases, a portion of government purchases is devoted to the acquisition or construction of long-lived capital goods, such as roads, bridges, schools, government buildings and military hardware. And like consumer durables, these forms of *public capital* are only partially used up during the current year; most will provide useful services far into the future. So, like consumption spending, government purchases are in fact a mixture of spending on current needs and spending on future needs.

Although in reality not all spending by households and the government is for current needs, in practice determining precisely how much of such spending is for current needs and how much is for future needs is extremely difficult. For simplicity's sake, in this book we shall treat *all* of both consumption expenditures ($C$) and government purchases ($G$) as spending on current needs. But bear in mind that because consumption spending and government purchases do in fact include some spending for future rather than current needs, treating all of $C$ and $G$ as spending on current needs will understate the true amount of national saving.

**national saving** the saving of the entire economy, equal to GDP less consumption expenditures and government purchases of goods and services, or $Y - C - G$

If we treat all consumption spending and government purchases as spending on current needs, then the nation's saving is its income $Y$ less its spending on current needs, $C + G$. So we can define **national saving** $S$ as

$$S = Y - C - G \tag{22.1}$$

Figure 22.4 shows the national saving rates (national saving as a percentage of GDP) for the years 1960–2002 for France, Germany and the United Kingdom and shows that, since about 1970, European national saving rates have tended to decline. As we shall see next, the reason for this decline is partly related to the behaviour of government rather than private saving.

## Private and public components of national saving

To understand national saving better, we shall divide it into two major components: *private* saving, which is saving done by households and businesses, and *public* saving, which is saving done by the government.

To see how national saving breaks down into public and private saving, we work with the definition of national saving, $S = Y - C - G$. To distinguish private sector income from public sector income, we must expand this equation to incorporate taxes as well as payments made by the government to the private sector. Government payments to the private sector include

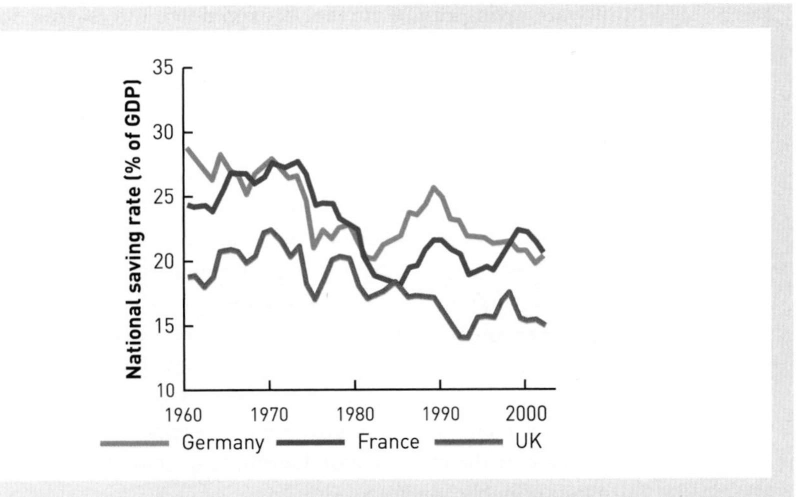


**Figure 22.4 National Savings Rates.** France, Germany and the United Kingdom, 1960–2002. European national savings rates (as a percentage of GDP) have declined since the 1970s.

*Source*: *The European Economy*, Commission of the European Communities, www.europa_eu.int/comm_finance/publications.

both *transfers* and *interest* paid to individuals and institutions holding government bonds. **Transfer payments** are payments the government makes to the public for which it receives no current goods or services in return. Unemployment benefits, welfare payments and pensions to government workers are transfer payments.

**transfer payments** payments the government makes to the public for which it receives no current goods or services in return

Let $T$ stand for taxes paid by the private sector to the government *less* transfer payments and interest payments made by the government to the private sector. Since $T$ equals private sector tax payments minus the various benefits, and interest payments the private sector receives from the government, we can think of $T$ as net taxes. If we add and then subtract $T$ from the definition of national saving, $S = Y - C - G$, we get

$$S = Y - C - G + T - T$$

Rearranging this equation and grouping terms, we obtain

$$S = (Y - T - C) + (T - G) \tag{22.2}$$

This equation splits national saving $S$ into two parts, *private saving*, or $Y - T - C$ and public saving, $T - G$.

**private saving** the saving of the private sector of the economy is equal to the after-tax income of the private sector minus consumption expenditures ($Y - T - C$); private saving can be further broken down into household saving and business saving

**Private saving**, $Y - T - C$, is the saving of the private sector of the economy. Why is $Y - T - C$ a reasonable definition of private saving? Remember that saving equals current income minus spending on current needs. The income of the private (non-governmental) sector of the economy is the economy's total income $Y$ less net taxes paid to the government, $T$. The private sector's spending on current needs is its consumption expenditures $C$. So private sector saving, equal to private sector income less spending on current needs, is $Y - T - C$. Letting $S_{private}$ stand for private saving, we can write the definition of private saving as

$$S_{private} = Y - T - C$$

Private saving can be further broken down into saving done by households and business firms. *Household saving*, also called personal saving, is saving done by families and individuals. Household saving corresponds to the familiar image of families putting aside part of their incomes each month, and it is the focus of much attention in the news media. Businesses use the revenues from their sales to pay workers' salaries and other operating costs, to pay taxes and to provide dividends to their shareholders. The funds remaining after these payments have been made are equal to *business saving*. A business firm's savings are available for the purchase of new capital equipment or the expansion of its operations. Alternatively, a business can put its savings in the bank for future use.

**public saving** the saving of the government sector is equal to net tax payments minus government purchases ($T - G$)

**Public saving**, $T - G$, is the saving of the government sector, both local and national. Net taxes $T$ are the income of the government. Government purchases $G$ represent the government's spending on current needs (remember that, for the sake of simplicity, we are ignoring the investment portion of government purchases). Thus $T - G$ fits our definition of saving, in this case by the public sector. Letting $S_{public}$ stand for public saving, we can write out the definition of public saving as

$$S_{public} = T - G$$

Using Eq. (22.2) and the definitions of private and public saving, we can rewrite national saving as

$$S = S_{private} + S_{public} \tag{22.3}$$

This equation confirms that national saving is the *sum of private saving and public saving*.

## Public saving and the government budget

Although the idea that households and businesses can save is familiar to most people, the fact that the *government can also save* is less widely understood. Public saving is closely linked to the government's decisions about spending and taxing. Governments finance the bulk of their spending by taxing the private sector. If taxes and spending in a given year are equal, the government is said to have a *balanced budget*. If in any given year the government's spending exceeds its tax collections, the difference is called the **government budget deficit**. If the government runs a deficit, it must make up the difference by borrowing from the public through issuance of government bonds. Algebraically, the government budget deficit can be written as $G - T$, or government purchases minus net tax collections.

**government budget deficit** the excess of government spending over tax collections ($G - T$)

**government budget surplus** the excess of government tax collections over government spending ($T - G$); the government budget surplus equals public saving

In some years, the government may spend less than it collects in taxes. The excess of tax collections over government spending is called the **government budget surplus**. When a government has a surplus, it uses the extra funds to pay off its outstanding debt to the public. Algebraically, the government budget surplus may be written as $T - G$, or net tax collections less government purchases.

If the algebraic expression for the government budget surplus, $T - G$, looks familiar, that is because it is also the definition of public saving, as we saw earlier. Thus, *public saving is identical to the government budget surplus*. In other words, when the government collects more in taxes than it spends, public saving will be *positive*. When the government spends more than it collects in taxes so that it runs a deficit, public saving will be *negative*.

Example 22.4 illustrates the relationships among public saving, the government budget surplus and national saving.

### Example 22.4 Government saving

Suppose that in a fictional country called Euroland, government is organised on two levels, central and local. The following are last year's data on revenues and expenditures for each level of Euroland's government, in million euro. Find (a) the central government's budget surplus or deficit, (b) the budget surplus or deficit of local governments and (c) the contribution of the total government sector to national saving.

| Item | € million |
|---|---|
| Central government: | |
| Receipts | 2,000 |
| Expenditures | 1,800 |
| Local governments: | |
| Receipts | 1,200 |
| Expenditures | 1,150 |

The central government's receipts minus its expenditures were 2,000 – 1,800 = 200, so the central government ran a budget surplus of €200 million. Local government receipts minus expenditures were 1,200 – 1,150 = 50, so local governments ran a collective budget surplus of €50 million. The budget surplus of the entire public sector – that is, the central government surplus plus the local surplus – was 200 + 50 = 250, or €250 million. So the contribution of the government sector to Euroland's national saving was €250 million.

**Exercise 22.4** Continuing Example 22.4, the table below shows the analogous data on government revenues and expenditures five years previously. Again, find (a) the central government's budget surplus or deficit, (b) the budget surplus or deficit of local governments and (c) the contribution of the government sector to national saving.

| Item | € million |
|---|---|
| Central government: | |
| Receipts | 1,420 |
| Expenditures | 1,640 |
| Local governments: | |
| Receipts | 950 |
| Expenditures | 875 |

If you did Exercise 22.4 correctly, you would have found that the government sector's contribution to national saving in 1995 was *negative*. The reason is that the central and local governments taken together ran a *budget deficit* in that year, reducing national saving by the amount of the budget deficit.

Figure 22.4 showed the French, German and UK national saving rates since 1960. Figure 22.5 shows the behaviour since 1960 of the two components of national saving: private saving and public saving each measured as a percentage of GDP. Note that private saving played a major role in national saving during these years, while the role of public saving was relatively modest. The contribution of public saving has also varied considerably over time. Until about 1970, governments typically ran a surplus, making a positive contribution to national saving. But by the mid-1990s, public saving had turned negative, reflecting budget deficits, especially in the United Kingdom.

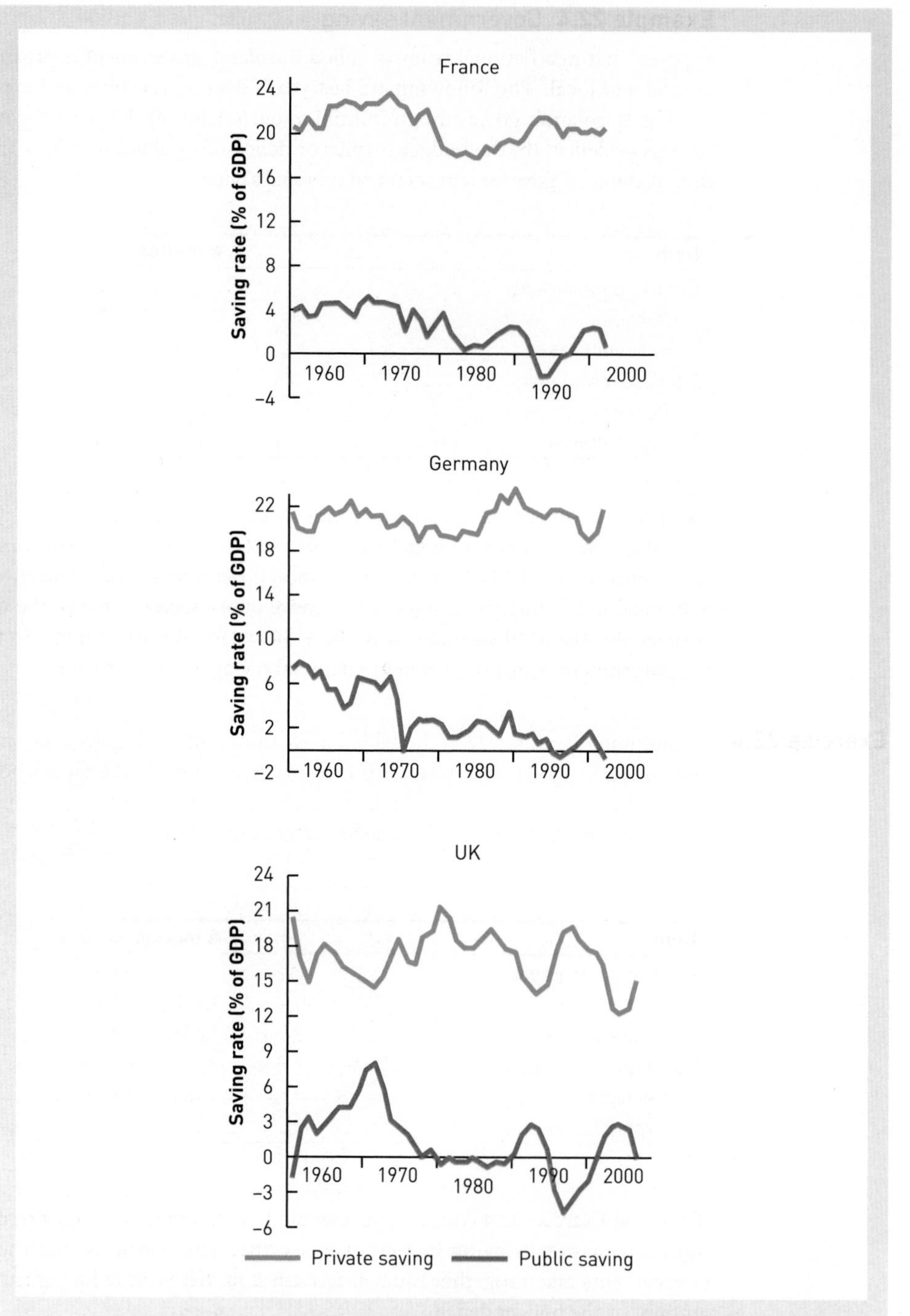


**Figure 22.5 Private and Public Saving, 1960–2002.** Of the components of national saving, private saving (business and households) is the most important.

*Source*: *The European Economy*, Commission of the European Communities, www.europa_eu.int/comm_finance/publications.

## RECAP National saving and its components

- *National saving*, the saving of the economy as a whole, is defined by $S = Y - C - G$, where $Y$ is GDP, $C$ is consumption spending and $G$ is government purchases of goods and services. National saving is the sum of public saving and private saving: $S = S_{private} + S_{public}$.
- *Private saving*, the saving of the private sector, is defined by $S_{private} = Y - T - C$, where $T$ is net tax payments. Private saving can be broken down further into household saving and business saving.
- *Public saving*, the saving of the government, is defined by $S_{public} = T - G$. Public saving equals the government budget surplus, $T - G$. When the government budget is in surplus, government saving is positive; when the government budget is in deficit, public saving is negative.

# Investment and capital formation

From the point of view of the economy as a whole, the importance of national saving is that it provides the funds needed for *investment*. Investment – the creation of new capital goods and housing – is critical to increasing average labour productivity and improving standards of living.

What factors determine whether, and how much, firms choose to invest? Firms acquire new capital goods for the same reason that they hire new workers: they expect that doing so will be profitable. We saw in Chapter 21 that the profitability of employing an extra worker depends primarily on two factors: the cost of employing the worker and the value of the worker's marginal product. In the same way, firms' willingness to acquire new factories and machines depends on the expected *cost* of using them and the expected *benefit*, equal to the value of the marginal product that they will provide.

### **Example 22.5** Should Manuel buy a motor cycle: 1?

Manuel is currently working in an office earning €15,600 after taxes but is considering buying a motor cycle and going into the courier business delivering letters and small packages around Madrid. He can buy a €4,000 motor cycle by taking out a loan at 6 per cent annual interest. With this cycle and his own labour Manuel reckons he can net €20,000 per year after deduction of costs such as petrol and maintenance. Of the €20,000 net revenues, 20 per cent must be paid to the government in taxes. Assume that the motor cycle can always be resold for its original purchase price of €4,000. Should Manuel buy the motor cycle?

To decide whether to invest in the capital good (the motor cycle), Manuel should compare the financial benefits and costs. With the motor cycle he can earn revenue of €20,000, net of petrol and maintenance costs. However, 20 per cent of that, or €4,000, must be paid in taxes, leaving Manuel with €16,000. Manuel could earn €15,600 after taxes by working at his current job, so the financial benefit to Manuel of buying the motor cycle is the difference between €16,000 and €15,600, or €400; €400 is the value of the *marginal product* of the motor cycle. Why is the motor cycle's marginal product €400? Because by using it to operate his courier service the motor cycle adds €400 to Manuel's income.

Since the motor cycle does not lose value over time and since running and maintenance costs have already been deducted, the only remaining cost Manuel should take into account is the interest on the loan for the motor cycle. Manuel must pay 6 per cent interest on €4,000, or €240 per year. Since this financial cost is less than the financial benefit of €400, the value of the motor cycle's marginal product, Manuel should buy the motor cycle.

Manuel's decision might change if the costs and benefits of his investment in the motor cycle change, as Example 22.6 shows.

### Example 22.6 Should Manuel buy a motor cycle: 2?

With all other assumptions the same as in Example 22.5, decide whether Manuel should buy the motor cycle:

**a.** If the interest rate is 12 per cent rather than 6 per cent.

**b.** If the purchase price of the motor cycle is €8,000 rather than €4,000.

**c.** If the tax rate on Manuel's net revenues is 21 per cent rather than 20 per cent.

**d.** If the motor cycle maintenance costs are higher so that Manuel's net revenues will be €19,500 rather than €20,000.

**e.** If Manuel can use his savings held in a bank deposit at 5 per cent interest to finance the purchase rather than borrowing the €4,000. What would Manuel's decision be if the deposit rate was 7 per cent?

In each case, Manuel must compare the financial costs and benefits of buying the motor cycle.

**a.** If the interest rate is 12 per cent, then the interest cost will be 12 per cent of €4,000, or €480, which exceeds the value of the motor cycle's marginal product (€400). Manuel should not buy the motor cycle.

**b.** If the cost of the motor cycle is €8,000 then Manuel must borrow €8,000 instead of €4,000. At 6 per cent interest, his interest cost will be €480 – too high to justify the purchase, since the value of the motor cycle's marginal product is €400.

**c.** If the tax rate on net revenues is 21 per cent, then Manuel must pay 21 per cent of his €20,000 net revenues, or €4,200 in taxes. After taxes, his revenues will be €15,800, which is only €200 more than he could make working at his current job. Furthermore, the €200 will not cover the €240 in interest that Manuel would have to pay. So, again, Manuel should not buy the motor cycle.

**d.** If the motor cycle is less efficient than originally expected so that Manuel can earn net revenues of only €19,500, Manuel will pay €3,900 in taxes leaving €15,600 – the same amount he could earn by staying in his office job. So in this case, the value of the motor cycle's marginal product is zero. At any interest rate greater than zero, Manuel should not buy the motor cycle.

**e.** If Manuel cashes in €4,000 of his savings to buy the motor cycle he gives up interest of 5 per cent or €200 per year. Since the financial cost is less than the value of the motor cycle's marginal product of €400, Manuel should buy the motor cycle and use his savings rather than take a loan at 6 per cent. With 7 per cent interest on deposits Manuel would give up interest of €280 per year, which is less than the value of the motor cycle's marginal product but greater than the cost of taking a loan. Manuel should by the motor cycle but finance the purchase with a loan rather than using his savings.

**Exercise 22.5** Repeat Example 22.5, but assume that, over the course of the year, wear and tear reduces the resale value of the motor cycle from €4,000 to €3,800. Should Manuel buy the motor cycle?

In Example 22.5 we saw that Manuel will invest in the motor cycle if the value of its marginal product (VMP) is greater than the financing cost of the investment. With the rate of interest at 6 per cent the financing cost of borrowing the €4,000 necessary to buy the motor cycle is €240 ($0.06 \times 4{,}000$). Hence the investment is profitable so long as the VMP is greater than

€240. More generally, if we let $P_K$ denote the purchase price of the capital and $r$ denote the real rate of interest then the financing cost is $rP_K$ and the investment will be profitable so long as

$$\text{VMP} > rP_K$$

Dividing both sides of this condition by the capital cost $P_K$ gives

$$\text{VMP}/P_K > r$$

**rate of return** on an investment equals the value of marginal product expressed as a percentage of the purchase price

The ratio of the VMP to the purchase price is the **rate of return** on the investment. In the case of Manuel's motor cycle $P_K$ = €4,000 and the VMP is €400. Hence the rate of return is 400/4,000 = 0.1 or 10 per cent. As the rate of return exceeds the real rate of interest, 6 per cent, the investment is profitable.

### Example 22.7 Should Manuel buy a motor cycle: 3?

Repeat Example 22.5, explaining Manuel's decision by comparing the rate of return on the investment with the financing cost.

**a.** As the financing cost of 12 per cent exceeds the 10 per cent rate of return Manuel should not buy the motor cycle.

**b.** As the purchase price is €8,000 the rate of return is 400/8,000 = 0.05 or 5 per cent which is less than the 6 per cent financing cost, Manuel should not buy the motor cycle.

**c.** As the value of the marginal product is only €200 the investment's rate of return is 200/4,000 = 0.05 or 5 per cent which is less than the 6 per cent financing cost, Manuel should not buy the motor cycle.

**d.** As the value of the marginal product is zero the rate of return is also zero. Manuel should not buy the motor cycle.

**e.** As the rate of return, 10 per cent, is greater than the financing costs of 5 or 7 per cent, Manuel should make the investment.

The examples involving Manuel and the motor cycle illustrate the main factors firms must consider when deciding whether to invest in new capital goods. On the cost side, two important factors are the *price of capital goods* and the *real interest rate*. Clearly, the more expensive new capital goods are, the more reluctant firms will be to invest in them. Buying the motor cycle was profitable for Manuel when its price was €4,000, but not when its price was €8,000.

Why is the real interest rate an important factor in investment decisions? The most straightforward case is when a firm has to borrow to purchase its new capital. The real interest rate then determines the real cost to the firm of paying back its debt. Since financing costs are a major part of the total cost of owning and operating a piece of capital, a higher real interest rate makes the purchase of capital goods less attractive to firms, all else being equal.

Even if a firm does not need to borrow to buy new capital – say, because it has accumulated enough profits to buy the capital outright – the real interest rate remains an important determinant of the desirability of an investment. If a firm does not use its accumulated profits to acquire new capital, most likely it will use those profits to acquire financial assets such as bonds, which will earn the firm the real rate of interest. If the firm uses its profits to buy capital rather than to purchase a bond, it forgoes the opportunity to earn the real rate of interest on its funds. Thus the real rate of interest measures the *opportunity cost* of a capital investment. Since an increase in the real interest rate raises the opportunity cost of investing in new capital, it lowers the willingness of firms to invest, even if they do not literally need to borrow to finance new machines or equipment.

On the benefit side, the key factor in determining business investment is the *value of the marginal product* of the new capital (VMP), which should be calculated net of both operating and maintenance expenses and taxes paid on the revenues the capital generates. The ratio of the value of the marginal product to the capital cost is the *rate of return* to the investment. If the rate of return exceeds the real rate of interest the investment will be profitable. The value of the marginal product and the rate of return are affected by several factors. For example, a technological advance that allows a piece of capital to produce more goods and services would increase the value of its marginal product and rate of return, as would lower taxes on the revenues produced by the new capital. An increase in the relative price of the good or service that the capital is used to produce will also increase the value of the marginal product and, hence, the desirability of the investment. For example, if the going price for courier services were to rise then, all else being equal, investing in the motor cycle would become more profitable for Manuel.

## Economic naturalist 22.2 Why has investment in computers increased so much since the 1980s?

Since about 1980, investment in new computer systems has risen sharply. While this trend is present in many countries it is especially true of the United States (see Fig. 22.6). Purchases of new computers and software by American firms now exceed 2.5 per cent of GDP and amount to about 15 per cent of all private non-residential investment. Why has investment in computers increased so much?

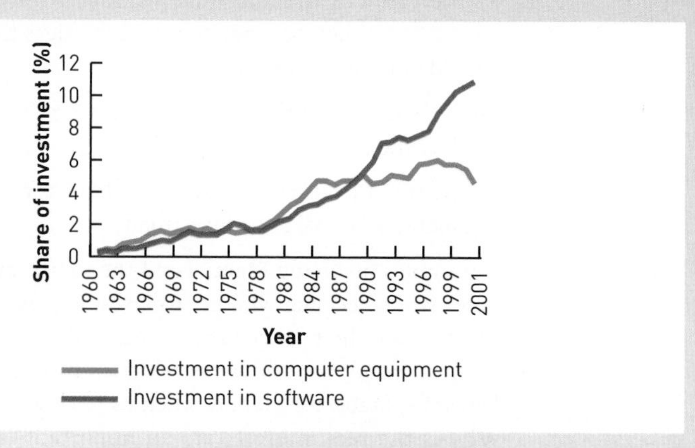


**Figure 22.6 Investment in Computers and Software, 1960–2001.** Investment in computer equipment and software since 1960 shown as a percentage of private non-residential investment. Computer-related investments by US firms have risen significantly since about 1980, but investment in computer equipment dropped sharply in 2000 and 2001.
*Source*: Bureau of Economic Analysis, http://www.bea.gov/.

Investment in computers has increased by much more than other types of investment. Hence, the factors that affect all types of investment (such as the real interest rate and the tax rate) are not likely to be responsible for the boom. The two main causes of increased investment in computers appear to be the declining price of *computing power* and the increase in the value of the *marginal product* of computers. In recent years, the price of computing power has fallen at a precipitous rate. An industry rule of thumb is that the amount of computing power that is obtainable at a given price doubles every 18 months. As the price of computing power falls, an investment in computers becomes more and more likely to pass the *cost–benefit* test.

On the benefit side, for some years after the beginning of the computer boom economists were unable to associate the technology with significant productivity gains. Defenders of investment in computer systems argued that the improvements in goods and services computers create were particularly hard to measure. How does one quantify the value to consumers of 24/7 access to cash or of the ability to make airline reservations online? Critics responded that the expected benefits of the computer revolution may have proved illusory because of problems such as user-unfriendly software and poor technical training. However, US productivity has increased noticeably since the 1990s and many people now credit the improvement to investment in computers and computer-related technologies such as the Internet. As more firms become convinced that computers do add significantly to productivity and profits, the boom in computer investment can be expected to continue.

### RECAP Factors that affect investment

Any of the following factors will increase the willingness of firms to invest in new capital:

1. A decline in the price of new capital goods
2. A decline in the real interest rate
3. Technological improvement that raises the marginal product of capital
4. Lower taxes on the revenues generated by capital
5. A higher relative price for the firm's output.

## Saving, investment and financial markets

Saving and investment are determined by different forces. Ultimately, though, in an economy without international borrowing and lending, *national saving must equal investment*. The supply of savings (by households, firms and the government) and the demand for savings (by firms that want to purchase or construct new capital) are equalised through the workings of *financial markets*. Figure 22.7 illustrates this process. Quantities of national saving and investment are measured on the horisontal axis; the real interest rate is shown on the vertical axis. As we shall see, in the market for saving, the real interest rate functions as the 'price'.

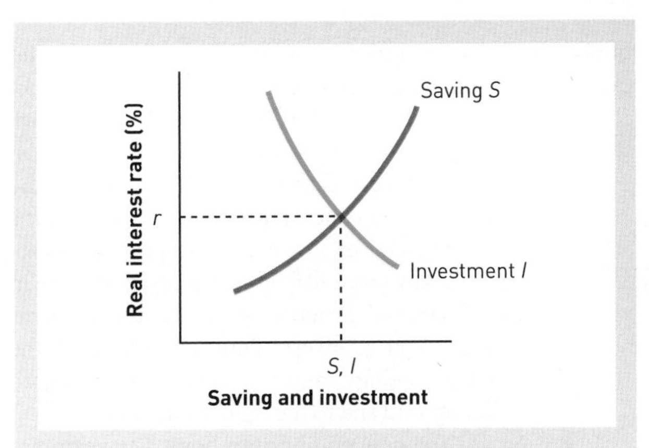


**Figure 22.7 The Supply of and Demand for Savings.** Savings are supplied by households, firms and the government and demanded by borrowers wishing to invest in new capital goods. The suppply of saving (S) increases with the real interest rate, and the demand for saving by investors (I) decreases with the real interest rate. In financial market equilibrium, the real interest rate takes the value that equates the quantity of saving supplied and demanded.

In Fig. 22.7 the supply of savings is shown by the upward-sloping curve marked *S*. This curve shows the quantity of national saving that households, firms and the government are willing to supply at each value of the real interest rate. The saving curve is upward-sloping because empirical evidence suggests that increases in the real interest rate stimulate saving. The demand for saving is given by the downward-sloping curve marked *I*. This curve shows the quantity of investment in new capital that firms would choose and hence the amount they would need to borrow in financial markets, at each value of the real interest rate. Because higher real interest rates raise the cost of borrowing and reduce firms' willingness to invest, the demand for saving curve is downward-sloping.

Putting aside the possibility of borrowing from foreigners (discussed in Chapter 24), a country can invest only those resources that its savers make available. In equilibrium, then, desired investment (the demand for savings) and desired national saving (the supply of savings) must be equal. As Fig. 22.7 suggests, desired saving is equated with desired investment through adjustments in the real interest rate, which functions as the 'price' of saving. The movements of the real interest rate clear the market for savings in much the same way as the price of apples clears the market for apples. In Fig. 22.7, the real interest rate that clears the market for saving is $r$, the real interest rate that corresponds to the intersection of the supply and demand curves.

The forces that push the real interest rate toward its equilibrium level are similar to the forces that lead to equilibrium in any other supply and demand situation. Suppose, for example, that the real interest rate exceeded $r$. At a higher real interest rate, savers would provide more funds than firms would want to invest. As lenders (savers) competed among themselves to attract borrowers (investors), the real interest rate would be bid down. The real interest rate would fall until it equalled $r$, the only interest rate at which both borrowers and lenders are satisfied, and no opportunities are left unexploited in the financial market (recall Chapter 3's *Equilibrium Principle*). What would happen if the real interest rate were *lower* than $r$?

Changes in factors *other than the real interest rate* that affect the supply of or demand for saving will shift the curves, leading to a new equilibrium in the financial market. Changes in the real interest rate cannot shift the supply or demand curves, just as a change in the price of apples cannot shift the supply or demand for apples, because the effects of the real interest rate on savings are already incorporated in the slopes of the curves. Examples 22.7 and 22.8 will illustrate the use of the supply and demand model of financial markets.

## Example 22.8 The effects of new technology

Exciting new technologies have been introduced in recent years, ranging from the Internet to new applications of genetics. A number of these technologies appear to have great commercial potential. How does the introduction of new technologies affect saving, investment and the real interest rate?

The introduction of any new technology with the potential for commercial application creates profit opportunities for those who can bring the fruits of the technology to the public. In economists' language, the *technological breakthrough* raises the marginal product and the rate of return of new capital. Figure 22.8 shows the effects of a technological breakthrough, with a resulting increase in the marginal product of capital. At any given real interest rate, an increase in the marginal product of capital makes firms more eager to invest. Thus, the advent of the new technology causes the demand for saving to shift upward and to the right, from $I$ to $I'$.

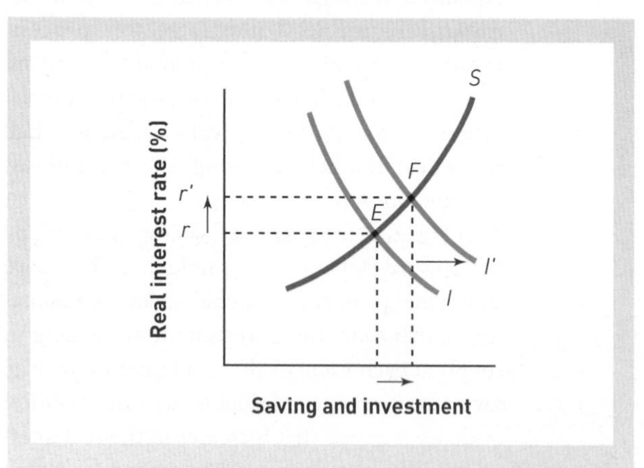


**Figure 22.8 The Effects of a New Technology on National Saving and Investment.** A technological breakthrough raises the marginal product of new capital goods, increasing desired investment and the demand for savings. The real interest rate rises, as do national saving and investment.

At the new equilibrium point $F$, investment and national saving are higher than before, as is the real interest rate, which rises from $r$ to $r'$. The rise in the real interest rate reflects the increased demand for funds by investors as they race to apply the new technologies. Because of the incentive of higher real returns, saving increases as well. Example 22.8 examines the effect of changing fiscal policies on the market for saving.

### Example 22.9 An increase in the government budget deficit

Suppose the government increases its spending without raising taxes, thereby increasing its budget deficit (or reducing its budget surplus). How will this decision affect national saving, investment and the real interest rate?

National saving includes both private saving (saving by households and businesses) and public saving, which is equivalent to the government budget surplus. An increase in the government budget deficit (or a decline in the surplus) reduces public saving. Assuming that private saving does not change, the reduction in public saving will reduce national saving as well.

Figure 22.9 shows the effect of the increased government budget deficit on the market for saving and investment. At any real interest rate, a larger deficit reduces national saving, causing the saving curve to shift to the left, from *S* to *S'*. At the new equilibrium point *F*, the real interest rate is higher at *r'*, and both national saving and investment are lower. In economic terms, the government has dipped further into the pool of private savings to borrow the funds to finance its budget deficit. The government's extra borrowing forces investors to compete for a smaller quantity of available saving, driving up the real interest rate. The higher real interest rate makes investment less attractive, assuring that investment will decrease along with national saving.

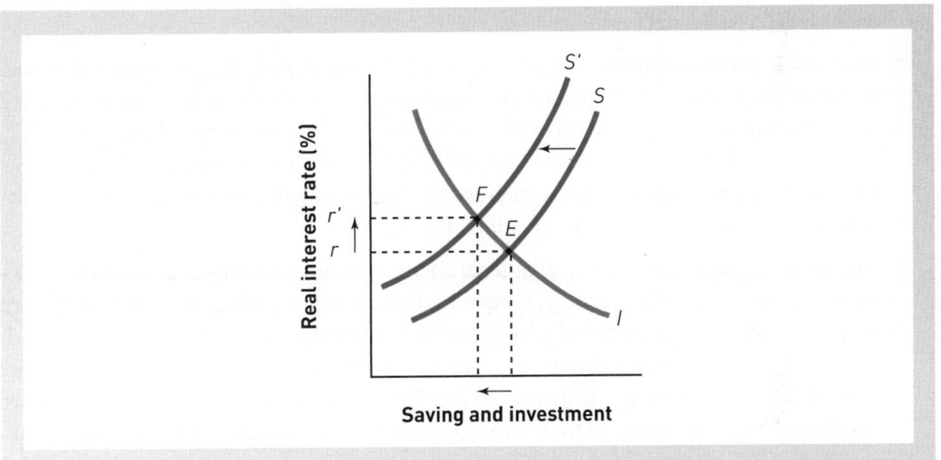


**Figure 22.9 The Effects of an Increase in the Government Budget Deficit on National Saving and Investment.** An increase in the government budget deficit reduces the supply of saving, raising the real interest rate and lowering investment. The tendency of increased goverment deficits to reduce investment in new capital is called *crowding out*.

**crowding out** the tendency of increased government deficits to reduce investment spending

The tendency of government budget deficits to reduce investment spending is called **crowding out**. Reduced investment spending implies slower capital formation, and thus lower economic growth, as we saw in Chapter 20. This adverse effect of budget deficits on economic growth is probably the most important cost of deficits, and a major reason why economists advise governments to minimise their deficits.

**Exercise 22.6** Suppose the general public become less concerned about the future and save less at each rate of interest. How will the change in public attitudes affect the rate of capital formation and economic growth?

At the national level, a high savings rate leads to greater investment in new capital goods and thus higher standards of living. At the individual or family level, a high saving rate promotes the accumulation of wealth and the achievement of economic security. In this chapter we have studied some of the factors that underlie saving and investment decisions. Chapters 23 and 24 will look more closely at how savers hold their wealth and at how the financial system allocates the pool of available savings to the most productive investment projects.

## Summary

- In general, *saving* equals current income minus spending on current needs; the *saving rate* is the percentage of income that is saved. *Wealth*, or net worth, equals the market value of assets (real or financial items of value) minus liabilities (debts). Saving is a *flow*, being measured in euros per unit of time; wealth is a *stock*, measured in euros at a point in time. As the amount of water in a bathtub changes according to the rate at which water flows in, the stock of wealth increases at the saving rate. Wealth also increases if the value of existing assets rises (*capital gains*) and decreases if the value of existing assets falls (*capital losses*).
- Individuals and households save for a variety of reasons, including *life-cycle* objectives; the need to be prepared for an emergency (*precautionary saving*); and the desire to leave an inheritance (*bequest saving*). The amount people save is also affected by the real interest rate, which is the 'reward' for saving. Evidence suggests that higher real interest rates lead to modest increases in saving. Saving can also be affected by psychological factors, such as the degree of self-control and the desire to consume at the level of one's neighbours (demonstration effects).
- The saving of an entire country is *national saving, S*. National saving is defined by $S = Y - C - G$, where $Y$ represents total output or income, $C$ equals consumption spending and $G$ equals government purchases of goods and services. National saving can be broken up into private saving (or $Y - T - C$) and public saving (or $T - G$), where $T$ stands for taxes paid to the government less transfer payments and interest paid by the government to the private sector. Private saving can be further broken down into household saving and business saving. In most countries, the bulk of national saving is done by the private sector.
- *Public saving* is equivalent to the government budget surplus, $T - G$; if the government runs a budget deficit, then public saving is negative.
- *Investment* is the purchase or construction of new capital goods, including housing. Firms will invest in new capital goods if the benefits of doing so outweigh the costs. Two factors that determine the cost of investment are the price of new capital goods and the real interest rate. The higher the real interest rate, the more expensive it is to borrow, and the less likely firms are to invest. The benefit of investment is the value of the marginal product of new capital, which depends on factors such as the productivity of new capital goods, the taxes levied on the revenues they generate and the relative price of the firm's output.
- In the absence of international borrowing or lending, the supply of and demand for national saving must be equal. The *supply* of national saving depends on the saving decisions of households and businesses and the fiscal policies of the government (which determine public saving). The *demand* for saving is the amount business firms want to invest in new capital. The real interest rate, which is the 'price' of borrowed funds, changes to equate the supply of and demand for national saving. Factors that affect the supply of or demand for saving will change saving, investment and the equilibrium real interest rate. For example, an increase in the government budget deficit will reduce national saving and investment and raise the equilibrium real interest rate. The tendency of government budget deficits to reduce investment is called *crowding out*.

## Key terms

assets (620)
bequest saving (624)
capital gains (622)
capital losses (622)
crowding out (641)
flow (621)
government budget deficit (632)
government budget surplus (632)
intertemporal substitution (624)
liabilities (621)
life-cycle saving (624)
national saving (630)
precautionary saving (624)
private saving (631)
public saving (632)
rate of return (637)
saving (620)
saving rate (620)
stock (621)
transfer payments (631)
wealth (620)

## Review questions

1. Explain the relationship between saving and wealth, using the concepts of flows and stocks. Is saving the only means by which wealth can increase? Explain.
2. Give three basic motivations for saving. Illustrate each with an example. What other factors would psychologists cite as being possibly important for saving?
3. Define *national saving*, relating your definition to the general concept of saving.
4. Why are household saving rates in Europe higher than in the United States?
5. Why do increases in real interest rates reduce the quantity of saving demanded? (**Hint:** Who are the 'demanders' of saving?)
6. Name one factor that could increase the supply of saving and one that could increase the demand for saving. Show the effects of each on saving, investment and the real interest rate.

## Problems

1. a. Corey has a mountain bike worth €300, a credit card debt of €150, €200 in cash, a Paul McCartney autograph worth €400, €1,200 in a bank account and an electricity bill due for €250. Construct Corey's balance sheet and calculate his net worth. For parts (b)–(d), explain how the event affects Corey's assets, liabilities and wealth.

   b. Corey discovers that his Paul McCartney autograph is a worthless forgery.

   c. Corey uses €150 from his wages to pay off his credit card balance. The remainder of his earnings is spent.

   d. Corey writes a €150 cheque on his bank account to pay off his credit card balance.

   Of the events in parts (b)–(d), which, if any, corresponds to saving on Corey's part?
2. State whether each of the following is a *stock* or a *flow*, and explain.

   a. The gross domestic product (GDP)

   b. National saving

   c. The value of the French housing stock on 1 January 2003

   d. The amount of British currency in circulation as of this morning

   e. The government budget deficit

   f. The quantity of outstanding government debt on 1 January 2003

**3.** Ellie and Vince are a married couple, both with university degrees and jobs. How would you expect each of the following events to affect the amount they save each month? Explain your answers in terms of the basic motivations for saving.

**a.** Ellie learns she is pregnant.

**b.** Vince reads in the paper about possible layoffs in his industry.

**c.** Vince had hoped that his parents would lend financial assistance toward the couple's planned purchase of a house, but he learns that they can't afford it.

**d.** Ellie announces that she would like to go to law school in the next few years.

**e.** A boom in the stock market greatly increases the value of the couple's retirement funds.

**f.** Vince and Ellie agree that they would like to leave a substantial amount to local charities in their wills.

**4.** Suppose that the government introduces a new special savings scheme (SSS) to encourage households to save more. An individual who deposits part of current earnings in an SSS does not have to pay income taxes on the earnings deposited, nor are any income taxes charged on the interest earned by the funds in the SSS. However, when the funds are withdrawn from the SSS, the full amount withdrawn is treated as income and is taxed at the individual's current income tax rate. In contrast, an individual depositing in a non-SSS account has to pay income taxes on the funds deposited and on interest earned in each year but does not have to pay taxes on withdrawals from the account. Another feature of SSSs which is different from a standard saving account is that funds deposited in an SSS cannot be withdrawn prior to retirement, except upon payment of a substantial penalty.

**a.** Greg, who is five years from retirement, receives a €10,000 bonus at work. He is trying to decide whether to save this extra income in an SSS account or in a regular savings account. Both accounts earn 5 per cent nominal interest, and Greg is in the 30 per cent tax bracket in every year (including his retirement year). Compare the amounts that Greg will have in five years under each of the two saving strategies, net of all taxes. Is the SSS a good deal for Greg?

**b.** Would you expect the availability of SSSs to increase the amount that households save? Discuss in light of (1) the response of saving to changes in the real interest rate and (2) psychological theories of saving.

**5.** In part (a)–(c), use the economic data given to find national saving, private saving, public saving and the national saving rate.

**a.** Household saving = 200    Business saving = 400
Government purchases of goods and services = 100
Government transfers and interest payments = 100
Tax collections = 150    GDP = 2,200

**b.** GDP = 6,000    Tax collections = 1,200
Government transfers and interest payments = 400
Consumption expenditures = 4,500
Government budget surplus = 100

**c.** Consumption expenditures = 4,000    Investment = 1,000
Government purchases = 1,000    Net exports = 0
Tax collections = 1,500
Government transfers and interest payments = 500

6. Ellie and Vince are trying to decide whether to purchase a new home. The house they want is priced at €200,000. Annual expenses such as maintenance, taxes and insurance equal 4 per cent of the house's value. If properly maintained, the house's real value is not expected to change. The real interest rate in the economy is 6 per cent, and Ellie and Vince can qualify to borrow the full amount of the purchase price (for simplicity, assume no down-payment) at that rate.

   a. Ellie and Vince would be willing to pay €1,500 monthly rent to live in a house of the same quality as the one they are thinking about purchasing. Should they buy the house?

   b. Does the answer to part (a) change if they are willing to pay €2,000 monthly rent?

   c. Does the answer to part (a) change if the real interest rate is 4 per cent instead of 6 per cent?

   d. Does the answer to part (a) change if the developer offers to sell Ellie and Vince the house for €150,000?

   e. Why do home-building companies dislike high interest rates?

7. The builder of a new cinema complex is trying to decide how many screens she wants. Below are her estimates of the number of patrons the complex will attract each year, depending on the number of screens available.

| Number of screens | Total number of patrons |
|---|---|
| 1 | 40,000 |
| 2 | 75,000 |
| 3 | 105,000 |
| 4 | 130,000 |
| 5 | 150,000 |

8. After paying the movie distributors and meeting all other non-interest expenses, the owner expects to net €2.00 per ticket sold. Construction costs are €1,000,000 per screen.

   a. Make a table showing the value of marginal product for screen 1– screen 5. What property is illustrated by the behaviour of marginal products?

   b. How many screens will be built if the real interest rate is 5.5 per cent?

   c. If the real interest rate is 7.5 per cent?

   d. If the real interest rate is 10 per cent?

   e. If the real interest rate is 5.5 per cent, how far would construction costs have to fall before the builder would be willing to build a five-screen complex?

9. For each of the following scenarios, use supply and demand analysis to predict the resulting changes in the real interest rate, national saving and investment. Show all your diagrams.

   a. The legislature passes a 10 per cent investment tax credit. Under this programme, for every €100 that a firm spends on new capital equipment, it receives an extra €10 in tax refunds from the government.

   b. A reduction in military spending moves the government's budget from deficit into surplus.

   c. A new generation of computer-controlled machines becomes available. These machines produce manufactured goods much more quickly and with fewer defects.

   d. The government raises its tax on corporate profits. Other tax changes are also made, such that the government's deficit remains unchanged.

   e. Concerns about job security raise precautionary saving.

   f. New environmental regulations increase firms' costs of operating capital.

## Answers to in-chapter exercises

**22.1** If the Rossis' mortgage was €270,000 instead of €200,000, their liabilities would be €270,250 instead of €200,250. In this case the Rossis' wealth is negative, since assets of €255,800 less liabilities of €270,250 equals –€14,450. Negative wealth or net worth means that the family owes more than it owns.

**22.2** (a) If the Rossis save €400 per month their bank account will increase by €4,800 to €6,000. (b) A €1,000 reduction in the value of their car reduces its resale price to €2,500. (c) A 10 per cent increase in the value of the Rossis' house increases its market value by €25,000 to €275,000. (d) Interest payments are a cost of servicing the mortgage debt and do not reduce the liability. However, the monthly loan repayments of €200 reduce the outstanding loan balance by €2,400 to €197,600. Hence, the Rossis' balance sheet on 1 January 2005 is:

| Assets | | Liabilities | |
|---|---|---|---|
| Cash | €100 | Mortgage | €197,600 |
| Bank account | 6,000 | Credit card balance | 250 |
| Shares | 1,000 | | |
| Car (market value) | 2,500 | | |
| House (market value) | 275,000 | | |
| **Total** | **€284,600** | | €197,850 |
| | | **Net worth** | **€86,750** |

**22.3** **a.** The Rossis set aside their usual €100, but they also incur a new liability of €150. So their net saving for the week is *minus* €50. Since their assets (their bank account account) have increased by €100 but their liabilities (their credit card balance) have increased by €150, their wealth has also declined by €50.

**b.** In paying off their credit card bill, the Rossis reduce their assets by €400 by drawing down their bank account and reduce their liabilities by the same amount by reducing their credit card balance to zero. Thus there is no change in the Rossis' wealth. There is also no change in their saving (note that the Rossis' income and spending on current needs have not changed).

**c.** The increase in the value of the Rossis' car raises their assets by €500. So their wealth also rises by €500. Changes in the value of existing assets are not treated as part of saving, however, so their saving is unchanged.

**d.** The decline in the value of the Rossis' house is a capital loss of €20,000. Their assets and wealth fall by €20,000. Their saving is unchanged.

**22.4** The central government had expenditures greater than receipts, so it ran a deficit. The central deficit equalled expenditures of 1,640 minus revenues of 1,420, or €220 million. Equivalently, the central budget surplus was *minus* €220 million. Local governments had a surplus, equal to receipts of 950 minus expenditures of 875, or €75 million. The entire public sector ran a deficit of €145 million as the central deficit of 220 outweighed the local surplus of €75. (You can also find this answer by adding central to local expenditures and comparing this number to the sum of central and local receipts.) The public sector's contribution to national saving five years ago was negative, equal to –€145 million.

**22.5** The loss of value of €200 over the year is another financial cost of owning the motor cycle, which Manuel should take into account in making his decision. His total cost is now €240 in interest costs plus €200 in anticipated loss of value of the motor cycle (known as *depreciation*), or €440. This exceeds the value of marginal product, €400, and so now Manuel should not buy the motor cycle.

**22.6** Household saving is part of national saving. A decline in household saving, and hence national saving, at any given real interest rate shifts the saving supply curve to the left. The results are as in Fig. 22.9. The real interest rate rises and the equilibrium values of national saving and investment fall. Lower investment is the same as a lower rate of capital formation, which would be expected to slow economic growth.

# 23

# Money, Prices and the European Central Bank

The Aztec people, who dominated central Mexico until the coming of the Spanish in the sixteenth century, are perhaps best remembered today for their elaborate ceremonies that culminated in human sacrifice. But the Aztec empire also had a sophisticated economic system, which included active trade not only in a wide variety of agricultural goods – such as corn, tomatoes and peanuts – but also in manufactured items, including jewellery, sandals, cloaks, baskets, alcohol and weapons. Slaves and captives – some designated for sacrifice – were also bought and sold. Trade was carried out in local markets, notably in the Aztec capital city, located where Mexico City now stands, and over long distances, as far north as present-day Arizona, for example.[1]

Despite ample supplies of gold, the Aztecs did not use metallic coins to carry out their market transactions, as most European peoples did. Instead, they often used chocolate or, more specifically, cacao 'beans' (the seeds of the cacao plant). Prices of goods or services were quoted in cacao beans, in much the same way that today we quote prices in terms of euros. Cacao beans could also be used to purchase goods, to pay for a service, or to make change – for example, to balance a transaction when a good of greater value was traded for one of lesser value. For larger items, prices were quoted in terms of bags of approximately 24,000 cacao beans, although large purchases might actually be paid for with something easier to carry than bags of cacao beans, such as woven cloaks.

In Aztec society cacao beans fulfilled what we would still regard as the fundamental role of money – an asset which is generally used to *finance transactions between individuals*. Cacao beans do not of course play this role today but when defining what money is and what money does the same principle applies. In modern economies, money is any asset which individuals, firms and governments use to finance transactions. We use money to pay for day-to-day items such as newspapers, bus fares and haircuts. We also use it to settle regular bills such as telephone accounts and credit card debts. Firms use money to purchase supplies of materials and components and to pay wages and salaries to their employees. Governments use money to pay for public services such as education, health care and policing. While the idea of money appears straightforward we must be careful to distinguish between the day-to-day use of the term *money* and the manner in which economists define money.

---

[1] See Weatherford (1997).

In everyday language, people often use the word *money* to mean 'income' or 'wealth', as in 'That job pays good money' or 'I wish I had as much money as she does'. Economists would rephrase these sayings as 'That job pays a high *income*' or 'I wish I had as much *wealth* as she does'. In distinguishing the role of money, economists give a much more specific meaning to the term. To the economist, **money** is any asset that can be used in making purchases.

**money** any asset that can be used in making purchases

Common examples of money in the modern world are *currency* and *coin*. A chequing account balance represents another asset that can be used in making payments (as when you write a cheque to pay for your weekly groceries) and so is also counted as money. In contrast, shares or equity, for example, cannot be used directly in most transactions. Shares must first be sold – that is, converted into cash or a chequing account deposit – before further transactions, such as buying your groceries, can be made.

Historically, a wide variety of objects have been used as money, including not only cacao beans but also gold and silver coins, shells, beads, feathers and, in the W. Pacific Yap islands, large, immovable boulders. Prior to the use of metallic coins, by far the most common form of money was the cowrie, a type of shell found in the South Pacific. Cowries were used as money in some parts of Africa until very recently, being officially accepted for payment of taxes in Uganda until the beginning of the twentieth century. Today money can be virtually intangible, as in the case of your chequing account balance, which exists only in the form of an entry in your bank's computer.

In this chapter we discuss the role of money in modern economies: why it is important, how it is measured, how it is created. Money plays a major role in everyday economic transactions but, as shall will see, it is also quite important at the macro level. For example, as we mentioned in Chapter 17, one of the three main types of macroeconomic policy, monetary policy, relates primarily to decisions about how much money should be allowed to circulate in the economy. In most countries monetary policy is the responsibility of the national Central Bank. Central Banks are institutions established by government to conduct monetary policy and supervise the banking system. In the United Kingdom the Central Bank is called the **Bank of England** and in the United States it is the **Federal Reserve System** (Fed). In the European Union the **European Central Bank** (or ECB) is the central bank for those countries which now use the euro as their common currency. The ECB was established by the 1993 Treaty on European Union (TEU), commonly referred to as the 'Maastricht Treaty' because it was agreed in the Dutch city bearing that name. Because the ECB determines the Eurosystem's money supply, this chapter also introduces the ECB and discusses some of the policy tools at its disposal. Finally, the chapter discusses the important relationship between the amount of money in circulation and the rate of inflation in an economy.

## Money and its uses

Why do people use money? Money has three principal uses: a *medium of exchange*, a *unit of account* and a *store of value*.

**medium of exchange** an asset used in purchasing goods and services

**barter** the direct trade of goods or services for other goods or services

Money serves as a **medium of exchange** when it is used to purchase goods and services, as when you pay cash for a newspaper or write a cheque to cover your telephone bill. This is perhaps money's most crucial function. Think about how complicated daily life would become if there were no money. Without money, all economic transactions would have to be in the form of **barter**, which is the direct trade of goods or services for other goods or services. Barter is highly inefficient because it requires that each party to a trade has something that the other party wants, a so-called *double coincidence of wants*. For example, under a barter system, a musician could get her dinner only by finding someone willing to trade food for a musical performance. Finding such a match of needs, where each party happens to want exactly what the other person has to offer, would be difficult to do on a regular basis. In a world with money, the musician's problem is considerably simpler. First, she must find someone who is willing to pay money for her musical performance. Then, with the money received, she can purchase the food and other goods and services that she needs. In a society that uses money, it is not necessary that the person who wants to hear music and the person willing to provide food to the musician be one and the same. In other words, there need not be a double coincidence of wants for trades of goods and services to take place.

By eliminating the problem of having to find a double coincidence of wants in order to trade, the use of money in a society permits individuals to specialise in producing particular goods or services, as opposed to having every family or village produce most of what it needs. *Specialisation* greatly increases economic efficiency and material standards of living, as we discussed in Chapter 2 (the *Principle of Comparative Advantage*). This usefulness of money in making transactions explains why savers hold money, even though money generally pays a low rate of return. Cash, for example, pays no interest at all, and the balances in chequing accounts usually pay a lower rate of interest than could be obtained in alternative financial investments.

**unit of account** a basic measure of economic value

Money's second function is as a *unit of account*. As a **unit of account**, money is the basic yardstick for measuring *economic value*. In the countries which use the euro as their currency virtually all prices – including the price of labour (wages) and the prices of financial assets, such as government bonds – are expressed in euros. In the United States these prices are measured in dollars and in the United Kingdom in pounds sterling. Expressing economic values in a common unit of account allows for easy comparisons. For example, milk can be measured in litres and coal in tonnes, but to judge whether 1,000 litres of milk is economically more or less valuable than a tonne of coal, we express both values in money terms. The use of money as a unit of account is closely related to its use as a medium of exchange; because money is used to buy and sell things, it makes sense to express prices of all kinds in money terms.

**store of value** an asset that serves as a means of holding wealth

As a **store of value**, its third function, money is a way of holding wealth. For example, the miser who stuffs cash into his mattress or buries gold coins under the old oak tree at midnight is holding wealth in money form. Likewise, if you regularly keep a balance in your chequing account, you are holding part of your wealth in the form of money. Although money is usually the primary medium of exchange or unit of account in an economy, it is not the only store of value. There are numerous other ways of holding wealth, such as owning bonds, shares or property.

For most people, money is not a particularly good way to hold wealth, apart from its usefulness as a medium of exchange. Unlike government bonds and other types of financial assets, most forms of money pay no interest, and there is always the risk of cash being lost or stolen. However, cash has the advantage of being anonymous and difficult to trace, making it an attractive store of value for smugglers, drug dealers and others who want their assets to stay out of the view of national tax authorities.

### Economic naturalist 23.1 Private money: Ithaca Hours and LETS

Since money is such a useful tool, why is money usually issued only by governments? Are there examples of privately issued money?

Money is usually issued by the government, not private individuals, but in part this reflects legal restrictions on private money issuance. Where the law allows, private moneys do sometimes emerge.[2] For example, privately issued currencies

[2] Good (1998).

circulate in more than 30 US communities. In Ithaca, New York, a private currency known as 'Ithaca Hours' has circulated since 1991. Instituted by town resident Paul Glover, each Ithaca Hour is equivalent to $10, the average hourly wage of workers in the county. The bills, printed with specially developed inks to prevent counterfeiting, honour local people and the environment. An estimated 1,600 individuals and businesses have earned and spent Hours. Founder Paul Glover argues that the use of Hours, which can't be spent elsewhere, induces people to do more of their shopping in the local economy.

A more high-tech form of private money is associated with computerised trading systems called LETS, for Local Electronic Trading System. These are quite popular in Australia, New Zealand and Great Britain (the United States has about 10 of them). Participants in a LETS post a list of goods and services they would like to buy or sell. When transactions are made, the appropriate number of 'computer credits' is subtracted from the buyer's account and added to the seller's account. People are allowed to have negative balances in their accounts, so participants have to trust other members not to abuse the system by buying many goods and services and then quitting. LETS credits exist in the computer only and are never in the form of paper or metal. In this respect LETS may foreshadow the electronic monetary systems of the future.

What do Ithaca Hours and LETS credits have in common? By functioning as a medium of exchange, each facilitates trade within a community.

## Measuring money

How much money, defined as financial assets usable for making purchases, is there in the economy at any given time? This question is not simple to answer because in practice it is not easy to draw a clear distinction between those assets that should be counted as money and those that should not. Euro notes are certainly a form of money, and a van Gogh painting certainly is not. However, in some countries, brokerage firms now offer accounts that allow their owners to combine financial investments in stocks and bonds with cheque-writing and credit card privileges. Should the balances in these accounts, or some part of them, be counted as money? It is difficult to tell.

Economists skirt round the problem of deciding what is and isn't money by using several alternative definitions, which vary in how broadly the concept of money is defined. In the Eurosystem the ECB uses three definitions. The first is a relatively 'narrow' definition of the amount of money in the economy called **M1**. M1 is the sum of currency outstanding and balances held in deposits on which the holder can write cheques and withdraw cash from ATMs, etc. Deposits of this type are called 'overnight' deposits. The second definition is a broader measure of money, called **M2**, and includes all the assets in M1 plus some additional deposits that are usable in making payments, but at greater cost or inconvenience than the use of currency or cheques. These deposits normally require advance notice of withdrawal and may carry a penalty if withdrawn early. The final, and broadest, definition is money called **M3**, which comprises all assets in M2 and certain marketable instruments issued by financial institutions. These instruments have high liquidity, which means they can be easily sold without significant risk of capital loss and are considered to be close substitutes for the type of the deposit included in M1 and M2. Table 23.1 lists the components of M1, M2 and M3 and also gives the amount of each type of asset outstanding

M1 sum of currency outstanding and balances held in chequing accounts

M2 all the assets in M1 plus some additional assets that are usable in making payments but at greater cost or inconvenience than the use of currency or cheques

M3 all assets in M2 plus marketable securities with a high degree of liquidity and price certainty as of January 2004. We shall see that in formulating monetary policy the ECB relies most heavily on M3. For most illustrative purposes, however, it is sufficient to think of money as the sum of currency outstanding and balances in overnight accounts, or M1.

| | | |
|---|---|---|
| **M1** | | 2,712.4 |
| Currency | 396.7 | |
| Overnight deposits | 2,315.7 | |
| **M2** | | 5,258.2 |
| M1 | 2,712.4 | |
| Deposits with up to 2 years' maturity | 1,029.1 | |
| Deposits requiring up to 3 months' notice of withdrawal | 1,516.7 | |
| **M3** | | |
| M2 | 5,258.2 | 6,158.3 |
| Marketable instruments | 900.1 | |

**Table 23.1** Components of M1, M2 and M3, January 2004 (€ billion)

*Notes*: Billion euros adjusted for seasonal variation. In M1, currency refers to cash and overnight deposits are deposits which can immediately be converted into currency. M2 includes all components of M1 plus deposits with maturity up to two years or redeemable at up to three months' notice. M3 comprises all assets in M2 plus money market instruments such as repurchase agreements, money market fund shares/units and debt securities with maturity of up to two years

*Source*: ECB, *Monthly Bulletin* (April 2004), www.ecb.int.

### RECAP Money and its uses

*Money* is any asset that can be used in making purchases, such as currency or a chequing account. Money serves as a *medium of exchange* when it is used to purchase goods and services. The use of money as a medium of exchange eliminates the need for *barter* and the difficulties of finding a 'double coincidence of wants'. Money also serves as a *unit of account* and a *store of value.*

The ECB uses three measures of money M1, M2 and M3. M1, a more narrow measure, is made up primarily of currency and balances held in chequing accounts. The broader measures, M2 and M3, include all the assets in M1 plus some additional assets usable in making payments.

## Commercial banks and the creation of money

What determines the amount of money in the economy? If the economy's supply of money consisted entirely of currency, the answer would be simple: the supply of money would just be equal to the value of the currency created and circulated by the government. However, as we have seen, in modern economies the money supply consists not only of currency but also of deposit balances held by the public in commercial (that is, private) banks. The determination of the money supply in a modern economy thus depends in part on the *behaviour of commercial banks and their depositors*.

To see how the existence of commercial banks affects the money supply, we shall use the example of a fictional country, the Republic of Euroland. Initially, we assume, Euroland has no commercial banking system. To make trading easier and eliminate the need for barter, the government directs the Central Bank of Euroland to put into circulation 1 million identical paper notes, called euros. The Central Bank prints the euros and distributes them to the populace. At this point, the Euroland money supply is 1 million euros.

However, the citizens of Euroland are unhappy with a money supply made up entirely of paper euros, since the notes may be lost or stolen. In response to the demand for safekeeping of money, some Euroland entrepreneurs set up a system of commercial banks. At first, these banks are only storage vaults where people can deposit their euros. When people need to make a payment they can either physically withdraw their euros or, more conveniently, write a cheque on their account. Cheques give the banks permission to transfer euros from the account of the person paying by cheque to the account of the person to whom the cheque is made out. With a system of payments based on cheques, the paper euros need never leave the banking system, although they flow from one bank to another as a depositor of one bank makes a payment to a depositor in another bank. Deposits do not pay interest in this economy; indeed, the banks can make a profit only by charging depositors fees in exchange for safeguarding their cash.

Let us suppose for now that people prefer bank deposits to cash and deposit all of their euros with the commercial banks. With all euros in the vaults of banks, the balance sheet of all of Euroland's commercial banks taken together is as shown in Table 23.2.

The *assets* of the commercial banking system in Euroland are the paper euros sitting in the vaults of all the individual banks. The banking system's *liabilities* are the deposits of the banks' customers, since chequing account balances represent money owed by the banks to the depositors.

| Assets | | Liabilities | |
|---|---|---|---|
| Currency | 1,000,000 euros | Deposits | 1,000,000 euros |

**Table 23.2** Consolidated Balance Sheet of Euroland Commercial Banks: Initial

**bank reserves** cash or similar assets held by commercial banks for the purpose of meeting depositor withdrawals and payments

**100 per cent reserve banking** a situation in which banks' reserves equal 100 per cent of their deposits

Cash or similar assets held by banks are called **bank reserves**. In this example, bank reserves, for all the banks taken together, equal 1,000,000 euros – the currency listed on the asset side of the consolidated balance sheet. Banks hold reserves to meet depositors' demands for cash withdrawals or to pay cheques drawn on their depositors' accounts. In this example, the bank reserves of 1,000,000 euros equal 100 per cent of banks' deposits, which are also 1,000,000 euros. A situation in which bank reserves equal 100 per cent of bank deposits is called **100 per cent reserve banking**.

Bank reserves are held by banks in their vaults, rather than circulated among the public, and thus are *not* counted as part of the money supply. However, bank deposit balances, which can be used in making transactions, *are* counted as money. So, after the introduction of 'safekeeper' banks in Euroland, the money supply, equal to the value of bank deposits, is 1,000,000 euros, which is the same as it was prior to the introduction of banks.

After a while, to continue the story, the commercial bankers of Euroland begin to realise that keeping 100 per cent reserves against deposits is not necessary. True, a few euros flow in and out of the typical bank as depositors receive payments or write cheques, but for the most part the stacks of paper euros just sit there in the vaults, untouched and unused. It occurs to the bankers that they can meet the random inflow and outflow of euros to their banks with reserves that are less than 100 per cent of their deposits. After some observation, the bankers conclude that keeping reserves equal to only 10 per cent of deposits is enough to meet the random ebb and flow of withdrawals and payments from their individual banks. The remaining 90 per cent of deposits, the bankers realise, can be lent out to borrowers to earn interest.

So the bankers decide to keep reserves equal to 100,000 euros, or 10 per cent of their deposits. The other 900,000 euros they lend out at interest to Euroland cheese producers who want to use the money to make improvements to their farms. After the loans are made, the balance sheet of all of Euroland's commercial banks taken together has changed, as shown in Table 23.3.

| Assets | | Liabilities | |
|---|---|---|---|
| Currency (= reserves) | 100,000 euros | Deposits | 1,000,000 euros |
| Loans to farmers | 900,000 euros | | |

**Table 23.3** Consolidated Balance Sheet of Euroland Commercial Banks after One Round of Loans

**reserve–deposit ratio** bank reserves divided by deposits

**fractional-reserve banking system** a banking system in which bank reserves are less than deposits so that the reserve–deposit ratio is less than 100 per cent

After the loans are made, the banks' reserves of 100,000 euros no longer equal 100 per cent of the banks' deposits of 1,000,000 euros. Instead, the **reserve–deposit ratio**, which is bank reserves divided by deposits, is now equal to 100,000/1,000,000, or 10 per cent. A banking system in which banks hold fewer reserves than deposits so that the reserve–deposit ratio is less than 100 per cent is called a **fractional-reserve banking system**.

Notice that 900,000 euros have flowed out of the banking system (as loans to farmers) and are now in the hands of the public. But farmers use these funds to pay for improvements to their farms and the 900,000 euros will be paid to contractors specialising in farm improvements. As we have assumed that private citizens prefer bank deposits to cash for making transactions these contractors will redeposit the 900,000 euros in the banking system. After these deposits are made, the consolidated balance sheet of the commercial banks is as in Table 23.4.

| Assets | | Liabilities | |
|---|---|---|---|
| Currency (= reserves) | 1,000,000 euros | Deposits | 1,900,000 euros |
| Loans to farmers | 900,000 euros | | |

**Table 23.4** Consolidated Balance Sheet of Euroland Commercial Banks after Euros Are Redeposited

Notice that bank deposits, and hence the economy's money supply, now equal 1,900,000 euros. In effect, the existence of the commercial banking system has permitted the creation of new money. These deposits, which are liabilities of the banks, are balanced by assets of 1,000,000 euros in reserves and 900,000 euros in loans owed to the banks.

The story does not end here. On examining their balance sheets, the bankers are surprised to see that they once again have 'too many' reserves. With deposits of 1,900,000 euros and a 10 per cent reserve–deposit ratio, they need only 190,000 euros in reserves. But they have 1,000,000 euros in reserves – 810,000 too many. Since lending out their excess euros is always more profitable than leaving them in the vault, the bankers proceed to make another 810,000 euros in loans. Eventually these lent-out euros are redeposited in the banking system, after which the consolidated balance sheet of the banks is as shown in Table 23.5.

| Assets | | Liabilities | |
|---|---|---|---|
| Currency (= reserves) | 1,000,000 euros | Deposits | 2,710,000 euros |
| Loans to farmers | 1,710,000 euros | | |

**Table 23.5** Consolidated Balance Sheet of Euroland Commercial Banks after Two Rounds of Loans and Redeposits

Now the money supply has increased to 2,710,000 euros, equal to the value of bank deposits. Despite the expansion of loans and deposits, however, the bankers find that their reserves of 1,000,000 euros *still* exceed the desired level of 10 per cent of deposits, which are 2,710,000 euros. And so yet another round of lending will take place.

**Exercise 23.1** Determine what the balance sheet of the banking system of Euroland will look like after a third round of lending to farmers and redeposits of euros into the commercial banking system. What is the money supply at that point?

The process of expansion of loans and deposits will end only when reserves equal 10 per cent of bank deposits, because as long as reserves exceed 10 per cent of deposits the banks will find it profitable to lend out the extra reserves. Since reserves at the end of every round equal 1,000,000 euros, for the reserve deposit ratio to equal 10 per cent, total deposits must equal 10,000,000 euros. Further, since the balance sheet must balance, with assets equal to liabilities, we know as well that at the end of the process loans to cheese producers must equal 9,000,000 euros. If loans equal 9,000,000 euros, then bank assets, the sum of loans and reserves (1,000,000 euros), will equal 10,000,000 euros, which is the same as bank liabilities (bank deposits). The final consolidated balance sheet is as shown in Table 23.6.

| Assets | | Liabilities | |
|---|---|---|---|
| Currency (= reserves) | 1,000,000 euros | Deposits | 10,000,000 euros |
| Loans to farmers | 9,000,000 euros | | |

**Table 23.6** Final Consolidated Balance Sheet of Euroland Commercial Banks

The money supply, which is equal to total deposits, is 10,000,000 euros at the end of the process. We see that the existence of a fractional-reserve banking system has multiplied the money supply by a factor of 10, relative to the economy with no banks or the economy with 100 per cent reserve banking. Put another way, with a 10 per cent reserve–deposit ratio, each guilder deposited in the banking system can 'support' 10 euros worth of deposits.

To find the money supply in this example more directly, we observe that deposits will expand through additional rounds of lending as long as the ratio of bank reserves to bank deposits exceeds the reserve–deposit ratio desired by banks. When the actual ratio of bank reserves to deposits equals the desired reserve–deposit ratio, the expansion stops. So ultimately, deposits in the banking system satisfy the following relationship:

$$\frac{\text{Bank reserves}}{\text{Bank deposits}} = \text{Desired reserve–deposit ratio}$$

This equation can be rewritten to solve for bank deposits:

$$\text{Bank deposits} = \frac{\text{Bank reserves}}{\text{Desired reserve–deposit ratio}} \tag{23.1}$$

In Euroland, since all the currency in the economy flows into the banking system, bank reserves equal 1,000,000 euros. The reserve–deposit ratio desired by banks is 0.10. Therefore, using Eq. (23.1), we find that bank deposits equal (1,000,000 euros)/0.10, or 10,000,000 euros, the same answer we found in the consolidated balance sheet of the banks, Table 23.6.

**Exercise 23.2** Find deposits and the money supply in Euroland if the banks' desired reserve–deposit ratio is 5 per cent rather than 10 per cent. What if the total amount of currency circulated by the Central Bank is 2,000,000 euros and the desired reserve–deposit ratio remains at 10 per cent?

## The money supply with both currency and deposits

In the example of Euroland we assumed that all money is held in the form of deposits in banks. In reality, of course, people keep only part of their money holdings in the form of bank accounts and hold the rest in the form of currency. Fortunately, allowing for the fact that people hold both currency and bank deposits does not greatly complicate the determination of the money supply, as Example 23.1 shows.

### Example 23.1 The money supply with both currency and deposits

Suppose that the citizens of Euroland choose to hold a total of 500,000 euros in the form of currency and to deposit the rest of their money in banks. Banks keep reserves equal to 10 per cent of deposits. What is the money supply in Euroland?

The money supply is the sum of currency in the hands of the public and bank deposits. Currency in the hands of the public is given as 500,000 euros. What is the quantity of bank deposits? Since 500,000 of the 1,000,000 euros issued by the Central Bank are being used by the public in the form of currency, only the remaining 500,000 euros are available to serve as bank reserves. We know that deposits equals bank reserves divided by the reserve–deposit ratio, so deposits are 500,000 euros/0.10 = 5,000,000 euros. The total money supply is the sum of currency in the hands of the public (500,000 euros) and bank deposits (5,000,000 euros), or 5,500,000 euros.

We can write a general relationship that captures the reasoning of Example 23.1. First, let us write out the fact that the money supply equals currency plus bank deposits:

$$\text{Money supply} = \text{Currency held by the public} + \text{Bank deposits}$$

We also know that bank deposits equal bank reserves divided by the reserve–deposit ratio that is desired by commercial banks (Eq. (23.1)). Using that relationship to substitute for bank deposits in the expression for the money supply, we get bank reserves:

$$\text{Money supply} = \text{Currency held by public} + \frac{\text{Bank reserves}}{\text{Desired reserve–deposit ratio}} \tag{23.2}$$

We can use Eq. (23.2) to confirm our answer to Example 23.1. In that example, currency held by the public is 500,000 euros, bank reserves are 500,000 euros, and the desired reserve–deposit ratio is 0.10. Plugging these values into Eq. (23.2), we get that the money supply equals 500,000 + 500,000/0.10 = 5,500,000, the same answer we found before.

### Example 23.2 The money supply at Christmas

During the Christmas season people choose to hold unusually large amounts of currency for shopping. With no action by the Central Bank, how would this change in currency holding affect the national money supply?

To illustrate with a numerical example, suppose that initially bank reserves are 500, the amount of currency held by the public is 500, and the desired reserve deposit ratio in the banking system is 0.2. Inserting these values into Eq. (23.2), we find that the money supply equals 500 + 500/0.2 = 3,000.

Now suppose that because of Christmas shopping needs, the public increases its currency holdings to 600 by withdrawing 100 from commercial banks. These withdrawals reduce bank reserves to 400. Using Eq. (23.2) we find now that the money supply is 600 + 400/0.2 = 2,600. So the public's increased holdings of currency have caused the money supply to drop, from 3,000 to 2,600. The reason for the drop is that with a reserve–deposit ratio of 20 per cent, every euro in the vaults of banks can 'support' 5 euros of deposits and hence 5 euros of money supply. However, the same euro in the hands of the public becomes 1 euro of currency, contributing only 1 euro to the total money supply. So when the public withdraws cash from the banks, the overall money supply declines. (We shall see in the next section, however, that in practice the Central Bank has means to offset the impact of the public's actions on the money supply.)

### RECAP Commercial banks and the creation of money

Part of the money supply consists of deposits in private commercial banks. Hence the behaviour of commercial banks and their depositors help to determine the money supply.

Cash or similar assets held by banks are called *bank reserves*. In modern economies, banks' reserves are less than their deposits, a situation called *fractional-reserve banking*. The ratio of bank reserves to deposits is called the *reserve–deposit ratio*; in a fractional-reserve banking system, this ratio is less than 1.

The portion of deposits not held as reserves can be lent out by the banks to earn interest. Banks will continue to make loans and accept deposits as long as the reserve–deposit ratio exceeds its desired level. This process stops only when the actual and desired reserve–deposit ratios are equal. At that point, total bank deposits equal bank reserves divided by the desired reserve–deposit ratio, and the money supply equals the currency held by the public plus bank deposits (see Eq. (23.2)).

## The European Central Bank

On 1 January 1999 eleven member states of the European Union adopted a common currency called the *euro*. These countries were Austria, Belgium, Finland, France, Germany, Ireland, Italy, Luxemburg, the Netherlands, Portugal and Spain. Greece joined in January 2001 but the United Kingdom, Sweden and Denmark decided to opt out of the euro and retain their national currencies. Together the countries using the euro as their currency form the **Eurosystem** or the euro area. In effect the participating countries agreed to eliminate their national currencies (francs, guilders, lira, etc.) and replace them with the new common currency. At the same time, control of monetary policy in each country passed from their national Central Banks to the newly established **European Central Bank (ECB)** based in Frankfurt. The ECB is at the centre of a new central banking system known as the **European System of Central Banks (ESCB)**, which consists of the ECB and the national Central Banks (NCBs) of all EU member states including those of the non-participating countries. However, while the non-participating Central Banks, such as the Bank of England, are part of the ESCB, they play no role in its decision-making process. To distinguish between those member states which use the euro as their common currency and those who have retained their national currencies, the ECB uses the term *Eurosystem* to refer to the former.

**Eurosystem** those EU member states which use the euro as their currency and for whom the ECB is their Central Bank

**European System of Central Banks (ESCB)** the ECB and the national Central Banks of all member states including those who do not use the euro as their currency

**European Central Bank (ECB)** the Central Bank of the Eurosystem which comprises all countries using the euro as their currency

## Decision-making bodies of the ECB

The ECB is responsible for the *formulation and implementation of a single monetary policy* throughout the entire euro area and for the supervision and regulation of the banking and financial system. It has two key decision-making bodies: the Executive Board and **Governing Council**. The Executive Board consists of the President and Vice-president of the ECB plus four others appointed on the recommendation of the EU's Ecofin Council (the council of finance ministers) after consultation with the European Parliament (EP) and the heads of government of the participating member states. The **Governing Council** consists of all members of the Executive Board plus the governors of the NCBs participating in the Eurosystem. The President and Vice-President are normally former governors of NCBs; the other members of the Executive Board are selected on the basis of their experience in financial matters and appointed for a non-renewable eight-year term. NCB governors must be appointed by their governments for a minimum term of five years. The Governing Council is the supreme decision-making body of the ECB. It formulates monetary policy for the entire Eurosystem and has a monopoly on decisions relating to interest rates and the supply of reserves to the banking system. The Executive Board prepares information relevant to meetings of the Governing Council and is responsible for implementing policy decisions. A full description of both bodies and their membership can be found on the ECB website www.ecb.int.

**Governing Council** the ECB's supreme decision-making body

The **General Council** of the ECB is an additional body that controls for the fact that not all EU member states have adopted the euro as their currency. It is composed of the President and Vice-President of the ECB plus Central Bank governors from all EU states, irrespective of whether they use the euro as their currency. Its principal function is to oversee and strengthen *policy co-ordination* between participating and non-participating countries. The General Council has no role in formulating monetary policy and will be dissolved when and if all EU member states adopt the euro as their currency and the ECB as their Central Bank.

## Voting rights in the Governing Council

As originally designed, Governing Council decisions were taken by a simple majority of the 18 voting members (6 members of the Executive Board plus the 12 NCB governors), with each member having a single vote. Hence the governor of Germany's national Central Bank, the Bundesbank, has the same voting weight as the governor of the Central Bank of Ireland despite the fact that Germany accounts for over 30 per cent of the Eurosystem's GDP while Ireland accounts for approximately 1 per cent. However, as we shall see, the ECB has been designed as a highly independent Central Bank free from political influence, with members of the Governing Council acting in a personal capacity rather than as representatives of national governments.

With the accession of 10 additional EU member countries in May 2004 the potential size of the Governing Council has increased from 15 to 25 NCB governors plus members of the Executive Board. To accommodate this expansion in membership the European Council has approved a new voting system under which the six members of the Executive Board will continue to have permanent votes but a rotation system will be introduced to limit the voting numbers of NCB governors once the number of euro area countries exceeds 15. This new voting system will evolve in two stages:

- **Stage 1** This stage applies when the number of participating countries exceeds 15 but is fewer than 22. When membership of the Eurosystem reaches 16 the participating countries will be divided into two groups according to the size of their economies. Group 1 will consist of the five largest economies and the other will form Group 2. Table 23.7 describes how the voting rights will vary with the size of the Eurosystem.

| | Number of participating countries | | | | | |
|---|---|---|---|---|---|---|
| | 16 | 17 | 18 | 19 | 20 | 21 |
| **Group 1** | | | | | | |
| No. of: | | | | | | |
| Countries | 5 | 5 | 5 | 5 | 5 | 5 |
| Votes | 5 | 5 | 5 | 4 | 4 | 4 |
| **Group 2** | | | | | | |
| No. of: | | | | | | |
| Countries | 11 | 12 | 13 | 14 | 15 | 16 |
| Votes | 10 | 10 | 10 | 11 | 11 | 11 |
| Total votes: | 15 | 15 | 15 | 15 | 15 | 15 |

**Table 23.7** Two-Group Voting System
*Source*: ECB, www.ecb.int.

- **Stage 2** When the number of participating countries exceeds 21 a three-group system will apply. As at Stage 1, countries will be allocated to different groups depending on the size of their economies. Group 1 will again consist of the five largest economies with the size of Groups 2 and 3 depending on the number of countries in the Eurosystem. Table 23.8 describes how voting rights will evolve in Stage 2.

| | Number of participating countries | | | | | |
|---|---|---|---|---|---|---|
| | 22 | 23 | 24 | 25 | 26 | 27 |
| **Group 1** | | | | | | |
| No. of: | | | | | | |
| Countries | 5 | 5 | 5 | 5 | 5 | 5 |
| Votes | 4 | 4 | 4 | 4 | 4 | 4 |
| **Group 2** | | | | | | |
| No. of: | | | | | | |
| Countries | 11 | 12 | 12 | 13 | 13 | 14 |
| Votes | 8 | 8 | 8 | 8 | 8 | 8 |
| **Group 3** | | | | | | |
| No. of: | | | | | | |
| Countries | 6 | 6 | 7 | 7 | 8 | 8 |
| Votes | 3 | 3 | 3 | 3 | 3 | 3 |
| Total votes: | 15 | 15 | 15 | 15 | 15 | 15 |

**Table 23.8** Three-Group Voting System
*Source*: ECB, www.ecb.int.

Note that, irrespective of the number of countries, the number of votes on the Governing Council will remain constant at 21, the 6 members of the Executive Board plus 15 Central Bank governors.

## ECB independence

The statutes governing the ESCB are contained in the Treaty on European Union (1993), which is often referred to as the Maastricht Treaty or TEU. Articles 107 and 108 of the Treaty stipulate three key provisions designed to establish the crucial principle of Central Bank independence. (1) The ECB, the NCBs and members of their decision-making bodies are prohibited from taking instructions from EU institutions and national governments. (2) EU institutions and governments are likewise prohibited from attempting to influence members of ECB decision-making bodies. (3) The ESCB is prohibited from lending to national governments and EU institutions. We should also note that the statutes of the ECB can be altered only by revising the Maastricht Treaty which requires unanimity among all member states and in some cases a national referendum. These provisions ensure that ECB decisions on monetary policy are free from political influence and that voting members of the Governing Council can act in what they perceive as the best interests of the Eurosystem rather than as political representatives of national governments.

There are two reasons why this high level of Central Bank independence was deemed necessary. First, prior to the introduction of the ECB, Germany's Central Bank, the Bundesbank, was designed on similar principles of political independence. In contrast, policy decisions taken by most other national Central Banks were, to varying degrees, influenced by political authorities. As Germany was the largest and in many respects the most successful economy in the Union, it had most to lose from transferring responsibility for monetary policy from its own Central Bank to a new Europewide institution which would make decisions based on European rather than specific German interests. Hence, Germany used its strategic position within the Union to influence the design of the ECB and to ensure political independence. Second, a considerable body of economic research suggests a negative correlation between the level of Central Bank independence and inflation performance. That is, independent Central Banks appear to deliver lower average inflation rates than Central Banks that take policy decisions from government. This research also suggests that granting independence to a Central Bank does not lead to higher average unemployment or lower growth rates.

## A mandate for price stability

Central Banks are generally concerned with two broad policy objectives: *price stability* and *stabilisation*. Price stability means the maintenance of a relatively low rate of inflation, while stabilisation implies that policy is directed toward moderating increases in cyclical unemployment as defined in Chapter 21. During inflationary periods we would normally expect Central Banks to tighten monetary policy by reducing the money supply and increasing interest rates whereas the opposite policy might be expected when unemployment is rising in recessionary periods.

With respect to the ECB it is important to note that Article 105 of the Maastricht Treaty appears to suggest some restrictions on the Bank's freedom to choose between price stability and stabilisation. This Article states that: 'the primary objective of the ESCB shall be to maintain price stability.' However, the Treaty also states that: 'without prejudice to the objective of price stability, the ESCB shall support the general economic policies in the Community … as laid down in Article 2.' These objectives explicitly include a high level of employment and sustainable non-inflationary economic growth.

Several points are worth noting. First, there is a clear *hierarchy of objectives*. Under the terms of the Treaty, which is legally binding in the European Union, the ECB has a primary mandate for the maintenance of price stability or low inflation within the euro area. Other objectives can be given significant weight in the Bank's decision making only if the policy does not undermine or prejudice the primary mandate for price stability. This, it should be noted, was also the guiding principle of Germany's Bundesbank. Second, at no point does the Treaty offer a definition of *price stability*, which appears to be at the discretion of the ECB. Indeed, one of the Bank's first actions was to pronounce that it defined price stability as an inflation rate between zero and 2 per cent per annum. More recently the Bank has attempted to clarify this definition by stating that the Governing Council aims to 'maintain inflation rates below but close to 2 per cent over the medium term.'[3] Third, the ECB does not expect to achieve its inflation target on a continuous basis. Rather it aims at achieving the target *over the 'medium term'* which, although undefined, can be reasonably assumed to be an average inflation rate over a period of one to two years. Because of random or unexpected events, such as a sudden rise in oil prices, we may observe short periods when the inflation rate exceeds the target. If the Governing Council considers such a rise in inflation to be temporary then it may not interpret it as a breach of its mandate. If, however, the rise in inflation is more persistent then the Council may consider it as a threat to its target and react accordingly. That is, the Bank does not necessarily interpret its mandate as a requirement to keep inflation below 2 per cent on a month-to-month or continuous basis. Rather, it appears to suggest that its mandate will be fulfilled if the average inflation rate over the medium term is below 2 per cent.

Finally, it is important to note that the ECB's definition of price stability relates to the *average inflation rate in the Eurosystem* and not to inflation in a particular country. It could well be the case that the average inflation rate across the euro area is consistent with the ECB's mandate but that some countries are experiencing inflation above 2 per cent. While this may be of concern to the ECB, especially if the outliers are large countries such as France and Germany, it is unlikely to lead to policy changes unless the Governing Council sees it as a threat to inflation in the Eurosystem as a whole. In other words, the ECB is primarily concerned with European averages rather than events in particular countries.

As we shall see in later chapters, monetary policy can affect many important macroeconomic variables, including interest rates, inflation, unemployment and exchange rates. Because of its ability to affect key variables, particularly financial variables such as interest rates, financial market participants pay close attention to ECB actions and announcements. As a necessary first step in understanding how ECB policies have the effects that they do, we shall focus on the basic question of how the ECB affects the supply of money and interest rates, leaving for later the explanation of how changes in these variables affect the economy.

## RECAP The European Central Bank

The European Central Bank (or ECB), is the Central Bank of the Eurosystem which consists of those countries using the *euro* as their common currency. The ECB is responsible for the formulation and implementation of monetary policy throughout the Eurosystem. Under the provisions of the Maastricht Treaty the ECB is a highly independent Central Bank and is free from political influence from EU institutions and national governments. Its key decision-making body, the Governing Council, determines monetary policy in the interests of the Eurosystem as a whole rather than in the interests of individual countries. The Bank has, however, a primary mandate for maintaining *price stability*, which it now defines as a medium-term inflation rate below but close to 2 per cent per year.

In Chapter 30 we shall discuss the economic rationale underlying the desirability of monetary union in Europe. Before that, Economic naturalist 23.2 outlines the key steps leading to the introduction of the single currency and the ECB.

[3] See ECB (2004), also available on the ECB website www.ecb.int.

## Economic naturalist 23.2 The three steps to monetary union

In June 1988 the European Council, meeting as the heads of governments of member states, established a Committee on Economic and Monetary Union, chaired by Jacques Delors, the then President of the European Commission. The purpose of this committee was to consider an appropriate strategy which would lead to a successful monetary union between the member states. The Delors Committee reported one year later and proposed a three-stage plan for the establishment of a European monetary union.

### Stage One

This began on 1 July 1990 and consisted of three key elements:

- First, restrictions on the movement of capital between member states were abolished.
- Second, the Committee of Governors of the NCBs was required to strengthen co-ordination of monetary policies between member states, with the objective of achieving greater price stability.
- Third, and most important, an Intergovernmental Conference was established to review the legal and constitutional structures necessary for proceeding to full monetary union. This Conference resulted in the *Treaty on European Union*, often referred to as the *Maastricht Treaty*, which was agreed in December 1991 and came into force in 1993.

The Maastricht Treaty and its Protocols contains the Statutes of the ESCBs and the criteria which member states were required to satisfy before being admitted into the monetary union. These criteria set targets for a range of key economic indicators such as inflation, interest rates and government budget deficits and subsequently became known as the Maastricht Convergence Criteria. The Treaty also required governments to introduce legislation designed to strengthen the independence of their national Central Banks.

### Stage Two

This commenced on 1 January 1994 and established the European Monetary Institute (EMI) which replaced the Committee of Governors of the NCBs. While the EMI can be seen as a forerunner to the ECB it had no responsibility for monetary policy, which remained the prerogative of the individual NCBs. Rather, its principal function was to make the practical preparations necessary for the establishment of the ESCBs and the introduction of the single currency. In May 1998 the European Council agreed that 11 member states (Austria, Belgium, Finland, France, Germany, Ireland, Italy, Luxemburg, the Netherlands, Portugal and Spain) satisfied the convergence criteria and could proceed to Stage Three. Greece was deemed not to satisfy the criteria, but was admitted in 2001, while Denmark, Sweden and the United Kingdom decided to opt out. The Council also appointed the President and Vice-President of the ECB, the members of the Executive Board and agreed that Stage Three should commence on 1 January 1999. The ECB was formally established in June 1998 with full responsibility for the conduct of monetary policy at the start of the final stage.

### Stage Three

This commenced on 1 January 1999 when responsibility for the conduct and implementation of monetary policy passed from the NCBs to the ECB based in Frankfurt. Participating countries continued to use their national currencies but the exchange rates between them were irrevocably fixed from the start of the final stage. In January 2002 these so-called 'legacy currencies' were withdrawn and replaced with euro notes and coins which are now the single and only currency of the entire Eurosystem.

From an administrative and practical perspective the creation of the Eurosystem and the introduction of the single currency has been an outstanding success. Although it is still possible to see shops in countries such as France and Italy that quote prices in both euro and their old national currencies the vast majority of Europeans now regard the euro as their domestic currency and the ECB has emerged as a highly credible and efficient Central Bank, second only to the United States' Federal Reserve System in international importance. However, the economic rationale underlying the euro and its ultimate success in promoting the economic well-being of Europe's citizens is another matter, to be considered in Chapter 30.

## Controlling the money supply: open-market operations

All Central Banks have a primary responsibility for formulating monetary policy, which involves decisions about the appropriate size of the money supply. As we saw in the previous section, Central Banks control the money supply by changing the supply of reserves held by commercial banks. The Central Bank has several ways of affecting the supply of bank reserves. By far the most important of these are **open-market operations (OMOs)**. We shall first give a general explanation of OMDs and then describe a specific form used by the ECB known as *main refinancing operations*.

**open-market operations (OMOs)** open-market purchases and open-market sales

Suppose that the Central Bank wants to increase bank reserves, with the ultimate goal of increasing bank deposits and the money supply. To accomplish this the Central Bank buys financial assets, usually government bonds, from the public. To simplify the actual procedure a bit, think of the Central Bank as paying for the bonds it acquires with newly printed money. Assuming that the public is already holding all the currency that it wants, they will deposit the cash they receive as payment for their bonds in commercial banks. Thus, the reserves of the commercial banking system will increase by an amount equal to the value of the bonds purchased by the Central Bank. The increase in bank reserves will lead in turn, through the process of lending and redeposit of funds described earlier, to an expansion of bank deposits and the money supply, as summarised by Eq. (23.2). The Central Bank's purchase of government bonds from the public is called an **open-market purchase**.

**open-market purchase** the purchase of government bonds from the public by the ECB for the purpose of increasing the supply of bank reserves and the money supply

To reduce bank reserves and hence the money supply, the Central Bank reverses the procedure. It sells some of the government bonds that it holds (acquired in previous open-market purchases) to the public. Assume that the public pays for the bonds by writing cheques on their accounts in commercial banks. Then, when the Central Bank presents the cheques to the commercial banks for payment, reserves equal in value to the government bonds sold by the Central Bank are transferred from the commercial banks to the Central Bank. The Central Bank retires these reserves from circulation, lowering the supply of bank reserves and, hence, the overall money supply. The sale of government bonds by the Central

**open-market sale** the sale by the ECB of government bonds to the public for the purpose of reducing bank reserves and the money supply

Bank to the public for the purpose of reducing bank reserves and hence the money supply is called an **open-market sale**. Open-market purchases and sales together are called *open-market operations*.

### Example 23.3 Increasing the money supply by OMOs

In a particular economy, currency held by the public is 1,000 euros, bank reserves are 200 euros and the desired reserve–deposit ratio is 0.2. What is the money supply? How is the money supply affected if the Central Bank prints 100 euros and uses this new currency to buy government bonds from the public? Assume that the public does not wish to change the amount of currency it holds.

As bank reserves are 200 euros and the reserve–deposit ratio is 0.2, bank deposits must equal 200 euros/0.2, or 1,000 euros. The money supply, equal to the sum of currency held by the public and bank deposits, is therefore 2,000 euros, a result you can confirm using Eq. (23.2).

The open-market purchase puts 100 more euros into the hands of the public. We assume that the public continues to want to hold 1,000 euros in currency, so they will deposit the additional 100 euros in the commercial banking system, raising bank reserves from 200 to 300 euros. As the desired reserve–deposit ratio is 0.2, multiple rounds of lending and redeposit will eventually raise the level of bank deposits to 300 euros/0.2, or 1,500 euros. The money supply, equal to 1,000 euros held by the public plus bank deposits of 1,500 euros, equals 2,500 euros. So the open-market purchase of 100 euros, by raising bank reserves by 100 euros, has increased the money supply by 500 euros. Again, you can confirm this result using Eq. (23.2).

**Exercise 23.3** Continuing Example 23.3, suppose that instead of an open-market purchase of 100 euros the Central Bank conducts an open-market sale of 50 euros worth of government bonds. What happens to bank reserves, bank deposits and the money supply?

## Main refinancing operations

OMOs are ways in which the Central Bank influences the supply of reserves to the banking system. As described above, these operations were assumed to take the form of transactions between the Central Bank and the public with the supply of reserves to the banking system affected indirectly. For example, to increase the supply of reserves the Central Bank conducts an open-market purchase by buying bonds directly from the public. Bank reserves are changed indirectly when the public deposits the proceeds with commercial banks. This is the traditional or general method of conducting OMOs. However, OMOs can take other forms. In the Eurosystem the most important type of OMO is known as a **main refinancing operation**. This is a technique by which the ECB can directly influence the supply of reserves to the banking system.

**main refinancing operations** the type of OMO used by the ECB to control the supply of reserves to the banking system

Main refinancing operations work as follows. Each week the ECB announces a tender, an amount of reserves that it is prepared to lend to commercial banks. The commercial banks may wish to borrow reserves for a variety of reasons. For example, their current holding may fall short of what is required given their deposit liabilities or they may need additional stocks of euro notes. Borrowing reserves from the ECB enables the banks to maintain and increase their lending which, as we have seen, leads to a multiple increase in deposits and the supply of money. Hence, the greater the volume of reserves which the ECB makes available the greater the capacity of the commercial banks to increase lending to the public and, using Eq. (23.2), the faster the rate of growth of the money supply. Likewise, if the ECB reduces the amount of reserves available to the commercial banks, the slower the growth in bank lending and the money supply.

This can be illustrated by a simple example. As we shall see later in this chapter there is a key relationship between the *rate at which the money supply increases* and the *rate of inflation*. Given this relationship, suppose that the ECB estimates that its inflation target can be best achieved if the maximum growth rate of the Eurosystem's money supply is 4 per cent per annum. However, ECB economists also estimate that without ECB intervention the money supply is set to increase by more than 4 per cent. To offset this excessive rate of monetary growth the ECB can reduce the amount of reserves it makes available to the banking system, leading to slower growth in bank lending, deposit creation and the supply of money. Conversely, if the ECB estimates that the rate of monetary growth is well below 4 per cent it may increase the amount of reserves that the banking system can borrow, leading to an acceleration in bank lending and the money supply. These examples can be checked using Eq. (23.2).

However, the amount of reserves that the banks may wish to borrow from the ECB does not only depend on the amount available. It also depends on the cost or interest rate that the banks must pay to borrow from the ECB. Other things being equal, the higher the cost the lower the amount the banks will want to borrow at the ECB's weekly tender. Conversely, the lower the interest rate charged by the ECB the greater the commercial banks' willingness to borrow. The interest rate that the banks pay to borrow reserves is known as the **main refinancing rate**. In practice, banks can bid for different amounts of reserves at varying interest rates. The main refinancing rate is the minimum rate at which banks can bid for reserves and is officially referred to as the *minimum rate bid*. For simplicity we will continue to use the name main refinancing rate – or, more simply, the refinancing rate.

**main refinancing rate** the interest rate which commercial banks pay to borrow reserves from the ECB

The refinancing rate is set by the ECB's Governing Council and is widely regarded as the key interest rate in the Eurosystem. Indeed, many Governing Council meetings are preceded by intense media speculation on the possibility that the Council may decide to change the main refinancing rate. An increase in the refinancing rate is most likely when the Governing Council estimates that the annualised rate of inflation is set to exceed the target. If the Governing Council decides that monetary conditions are a threat to its target it may increase the main refinancing rate. As the banks have to pay more to borrow from the ECB they will, at least in part, pass this increased cost on to their customers, leading to higher interest rates on bank loans and a slowdown in the demand for credit. Following the analyses in previous sections, lower growth in bank lending leads to slower growth in bank deposits and the money supply. Conversely, if the Governing Council decides that monetary conditions are not a threat to the inflation target it may decide to reduce the main refinancing rate, which leads to lower interest rates on bank loans and an increased demand for credit, leading to faster deposit creation and monetary growth.

Changes in the main refinancing rate lead to important changes throughout the banking sector. Other things being equal, increases in the main refinancing rate lead to higher interest rates and slower monetary growth while reductions have the opposite effects.

## Controlling the money supply: changing reserve requirements

As Eq. (23.2) shows, the economy's money supply depends on three factors: the amount of currency the public chooses to hold, the supply of bank reserves and the reserve–deposit ratio maintained by the commercial banks. For given quantities of currency held by the public and of reserves held by the banks, an increase in the reserve–deposit ratio reduces the money supply, as you can see from Eq. (23.2). A higher reserve–deposit ratio implies that banks lend out a smaller share of their deposits in each of the rounds of lending and redeposit described earlier, limiting the overall expansion of loans and deposits. In the Eurosystem the ECB requires the commercial banks to hold a reserve–deposit ratio of at least 2 per cent. These reserves are held as deposits at the NCBs and are called *required reserves*.

Changes in required reserves can be used to affect the money supply, although the ECB does not usually use them in this way. For example, suppose that the commercial banks are maintaining a 2 per cent reserve–deposit ratio, and the ECB wants to contract the money supply. By raising required reserves to, say, 3 per cent of deposits, the ECB could force commercial banks to raise their reserve–deposit ratio, at least until it reached 3 per cent. As you can see from Eq. (23.2), an increase in the reserve–deposit ratio lowers deposits and the money supply. Similarly, a reduction in required reserves by the ECB might allow at least some banks to lower their ratio of reserves to deposits. A decline in the economywide reserve–deposit ratio would in turn cause the money supply to rise.

## Economic naturalist 23.3 The Federal Reserve System

The Federal Reserve System (or the Fed), is the Central Bank of the United States. The Fed was created by the Federal Reserve Act, passed by Congress in 1913, and began operations in 1914. Like all Central Banks, the Fed is a publicly owned agency. Like the ECB, the Fed is also a highly independent Central Bank, but unlike the ECB the Fed does not have a primary mandate for price stability. While the Federal Reserve Act requires the Fed to promote public goals such as economic growth, low inflation and the smooth operation of financial markets, these objectives are not ranked.

The Federal Reserve Act also established a system of 12 regional Federal Reserve banks, each associated with a geographical area called a Federal Reserve District. Congress hoped that the establishment of Federal Reserve banks around the country would ensure that different regions were represented in the national policy-making process. In fact, the regional Feds regularly assess economic conditions in their districts and report this information to policy makers in Washington. Regional Federal Reserve banks also provide various services, such as cheque-clearing services, to the commercial banks in their district. These regional Federal Reserve Banks are the Fed's equivalent of the ESCB's NCBs.

At the national level, the leadership of the Federal Reserve System is provided by its *Board of Governors*. The Board of Governors, together with a large professional staff, is located in Washington, DC and is the Fed's equivalent of the ECB in Frankfurt. The Board consists of seven governors, who are appointed by the President of the United States to 14-year terms. The terms are staggered so that one governor comes up for reappointment every other year. The President also appoints one of these Board members to serve as chairman of the Board of Governors for a term of four years. The Fed chairman, along with the secretary of the Treasury, is probably one of the two most powerful economic policy makers in the United States government, after the President.

**Federal Open Markets Committee (FOMC)** the key decision-making body in the Federal Reserve System and the Fed's equivalent of the ECB's Governing Council

Decisions about monetary policy are made by a 12-member committee called the **Federal Open Markets Committee (FOMC)**. The FOMC consists of the seven Fed governors, the president of the Federal Reserve Bank of New York, and four of the presidents of the other regional Federal Reserve banks, who serve on a rotating basis. The FOMC meets approximately eight times a year to review the state of the economy and to determine monetary policy and is the Fed's equivalent of the ECB's Governing Council.

*In October 2005, President Bush nominated Professor Bernanke to succeed Alan Greenspan as Chair of the Federal Reserve Board of Governors*

### Economic naturalist 23.4 The Bank of England

The Bank of England is the Central Bank of the United Kingdom. It was established in 1694 and is the second oldest Central Bank in the world. The Swedish central bank, the Riksband, established in 1668 has the honour of being the oldest central bank still operating today. Following the May 1997 general election the new British Chancellor of the Exchequer, Gordon Brown, announced that the government was granting independence to the Bank of England. Prior to this, monetary policy had been decided by the UK government and implemented by the Bank. The subsequent Bank of England Act 1998 established a new decision-making body known as the **Monetary Policy Committee (MPC)**. Membership of the MPC consists of the Governor of the Bank, two Deputy Governors, the Bank's Chief Economist and four external members appointed by the government. The MPC is responsible for the conduct of monetary policy in the United Kingdom and is the Bank's equivalent of the ECB's Governing Council and the Fed's FOMC.

**Monetary Policy Committee (MPC)** the key decision-making body in the Bank of England

Like the ECB's Governing Council, the MPC has a mandate to deliver price stability and, without prejudice to that objective, to support the government's economic policy, including objectives for economic growth and employment. There are, however, several important differences. Whereas the ECB has the freedom to define what it understands by 'price stability' the UK inflation target is set by the government rather than the MPC. Given this inflation target, currently 2 per cent, the MPC has the freedom to decide on the monetary policy required to fulfil its mandate. The MPC is also required to publish a quarterly Inflation Report containing a detailed analysis of monetary and price developments in the United Kingdom and the economic justification for the Bank's policy decisions. Also, unlike meetings of the Governing Council, the minutes and voting record of the MPC are published and available, along with the its Inflation Reports, on the Bank's website, www.bankofengland.co.uk.

## Money and prices

From a macroeconomic perspective, a major reason that control of the supply of money is important is that, in the long run, *the amount of money circulating in an economy and the general level of prices are closely linked*. Indeed, it is virtually unheard of for a country to experience high, sustained inflation without a comparably rapid growth in the amount of money held by its citizens. The economist Milton Friedman summarised the inflation–money relationship by saying that 'Inflation is always and everywhere a monetary phenomenon.' We shall see in Part 8 that, over short periods, inflation can arise from sources other than an increase in the supply of money. But over a longer period, and particularly for more severe inflations, Friedman's dictum is certainly correct: the rate of inflation and the rate of growth of the money supply are closely related.

The existence of a close link between money supply and prices should make intuitive sense. Imagine a situation in which the available supply of goods and services is approximately fixed. Then the more cash (say, euros) that people hold, the more they will be able to bid up the prices of the fixed supply of goods and services. Thus a large money supply relative to the supply of goods and services (too much money chasing too few goods) tends to result in high prices. Likewise, a rapidly *growing* supply of money will lead to quickly *rising* prices – that is, inflation.

## Velocity

To explore the relationship of money growth and inflation in a bit more detail, it is useful to introduce the concept of **velocity**. In economics, *velocity* is a measure of the speed at which money circulates. For example, a given euro might pass from your hand to the grocer's when you buy a litre of milk. The same euro may then pass from the grocer to his supplier, from the supplier to the dairy farmer who produced the milk, from the farmer to the feed supply store owner and so on. The more quickly money circulates from one person to the next, the higher its velocity. More formally, velocity is defined as the value of transactions completed in a period of time divided by the stock of money required to make those transactions. The higher this ratio, the faster the 'typical' euro is circulating.

**velocity** a measure of the speed at which money circulates, or, equivalently, the value of transactions completed in a period of time divided by the stock of money required to make those transactions; numerically, $V = (P \times Y)/M$, where $V$ is velocity, $P \times Y$ is nominal GDP and $M$ is the money supply whose velocity is being measured

As a practical matter, we usually do not have precise measures of the total value of transactions taking place in an economy; so, as an approximation, economists often measure the total value of transactions in a given period by nominal GDP for that period. A numerical value of velocity can then be obtained from the following formula:

$$\text{Velocity} = \frac{\text{Value of transactions}}{\text{Money stock}}$$

$$= \frac{\text{Nominal GDP}}{\text{Money stock}}$$

Let $V$ stand for velocity and let $M$ stand for the particular money stock being considered (for example, M1 or M2). Nominal GDP (a measure of the total value of transactions) equals the price level $P$ times real GDP $Y$. Using this notation, we can write the definition of velocity as

$$V = \frac{P \times Y}{M} \tag{23.3}$$

### Example 23.4 The velocity of money in the Eurosystem economy

In 2002 M1 was €2,439.3 billion, M2 was €4,913.6 billion and nominal Eurosystem GDP was €7,073.3 billion. Find the velocity of M1 and of M2 for that year. Using Eq. (23.3), velocity for M1 is given by

$$V = \frac{7{,}073.3}{2{,}439.3} = 2.89$$

Similarly, velocity for M2 was

$$V = \frac{7{,}073.3}{4{,}913.6} = 1.44$$

You can see that the velocity of M1 is higher than that of M2. This makes sense: because the components of M1, such as cash and chequing accounts, are used more frequently for transactions, each euro of M1 'turns over' more often than the average euro of M2.

A variety of factors determines velocity. A leading example is advances in payment technologies, such as the introduction of credit cards and debit cards or the creation of networks of automatic teller machines (ATMs). These new technologies and payment methods have allowed people to carry out their daily business while holding less cash, and have thus tended to increase velocity over time.

**Exercise 23.4** In 2002 M3 was €5,768.1 billion and nominal GDP €7,073.3 billion. Find the velocity of M3 and compare it with the estimates for M1 and M2 in Example 23.4.

## Money and inflation in the long run

We can use the definition of velocity to see how money and prices are related in the long run. First, rewrite the definition of velocity, Eq. (23.3), by multiplying both sides by the money stock $M$. This yields

$$M \times V = P \times Y \tag{23.4}$$

**quantity equation** money times velocity equals nominal GDP: $M \times V = P \times Y$

Equation (23.4), a famous relationship in economics, is called for historical reasons the **quantity equation**. The quantity equation states that money times velocity equals nominal GDP. Because the quantity equation is simply a rewriting of the definition of velocity, Eq. (23.3), it always holds exactly.

The quantity equation is historically important because late nineteenth- and early twentieth-century monetary economists, such as Yale's Irving Fisher, used this relationship to theorise about the relationship between money and prices. We can do the same thing here. To keep things simple, imagine that velocity $V$ is determined by current payments' technologies and thus is approximately constant over the period we are considering. Likewise, suppose that real output $Y$ is approximately constant. If we use a bar over a variable to indicate that the variable is constant, we can rewrite the quantity equation as

$$M \times \bar{V} = P \times \bar{Y} \tag{23.5}$$

where we are treating $\bar{V}$ and $\bar{Y}$ as fixed numbers.

Now look at Eq. (23.5) and imagine that for some reason the ECB increases the money supply $M$ by 10 per cent. Because $\bar{V}$ and $\bar{Y}$ are assumed to be fixed, Eq. (23.5) can continue to hold only if the price level $P$ also rises by 10 per cent. That is, according to the quantity equation, a 10 per cent increase in the money supply $M$ should cause a 10 per cent increase in the price level $P$, that is, an inflation of 10 per cent. As explained in Economic naturalist 23.2 this relationship between money and prices plays a role in the ECB's monetary policy strategy.

The intuition behind this conclusion is the one we mentioned earlier. If the quantity of goods and services $Y$ is approximately constant (and assuming also that velocity $V$ is also constant), an increase in the supply of money will lead people to bid up the prices of the available goods and services. Thus high rates of money growth will tend to be associated with high rates of inflation. Figure 23.1 shows this relationship for 10 countries in Latin America during the period 1995–2001. You can see that countries with higher rates of money growth tend also to have higher rates of inflation. The relationship between money growth and inflation is not exact, in part because – contrary to the simplifying assumption we made earlier – velocity and output are not constant but vary over time.

If high rates of money growth lead to inflation, why do countries allow their money supplies to rise quickly? Usually, rapid rates of money growth are the result of large government budget deficits. Particularly in developing countries or countries suffering from war or political instability, governments sometimes find that they cannot raise sufficient taxes or borrow enough from the public to cover their expenditures. In this situation, the government's only recourse may be to print new money and use this money to pay its bills. If the resulting increase in the amount of money in circulation is large enough, the result will be inflation. This type of policy is often referred to as *monetary financing* which means that Central Banks lend money to governments to finance budget deficits. However, as the provisions of the Maastricht Treaty prevent the ECB from lending to national governments and EU institutions, monetary financing is effectively prohibited within the Eurosystem.

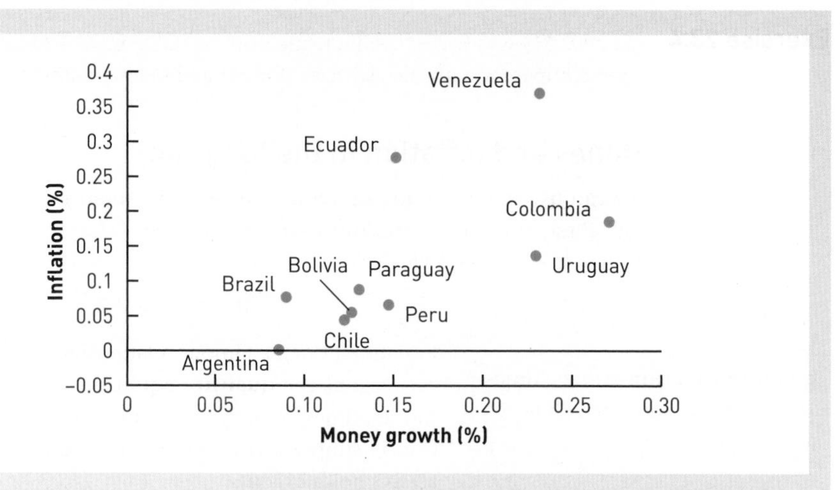


**Figure 23.1 Inflation and Money Growth in Latin America, 1995–2001.** Latin American countries with higher rates of growth in their money supplies also tended to have higher rates of inflation between 1995 and 2001. (The data for Argentina and Uruguay end in 2000 and the data for Ecuador end in 1997. In 1997 Ecuador abandoned its currency, the sucre, and began using US dollars instead.)
*Source*: International Monetary Fund, International Financial Statistics

## Economic naturalist 23.5 The ECB's reference value for monetary growth

The long-run relationship between money and prices is more than a simple theoretical relationship. It fact it appears to play a role in determining the ECB's policy strategy and the Governing Council has set a *reference value* for the growth of M3 which it believes is consistent with its target inflation rate of approximately 2 per cent per annum. To see how this reference value is determined, let the symbol $\Delta$ denote the *annual percentage* change in each variable in the quantity theory equation. Hence $\Delta M$ denotes the percentage change in the money supply and $\Delta P$ the percentage change in the price level, or the rate of inflation, etc. Using this notation, we can rewrite Eq. (23.4) in terms of percentage changes:

$$\Delta M = \Delta Y - \Delta V + \Delta P$$

According to the ECB's publication *The Monetary Policy of the ECB* (ECB 2004), the Bank estimates the medium-to-long-term trend growth rate for real GDP ($\Delta Y$) in the Eurosystem at approximately 2 per cent. Due to financial innovations the ECB also expects the velocity of M3 ($\Delta V$) to decline by 0.5 per cent per year on average. Hence the ECB expects $\Delta Y = 2$ and $\Delta V = -0.5$. Substituting these values into the above equation along with the 2 per cent inflation target ($\Delta P = 2$) gives a reference value for $\Delta M = 4.5$ per cent per year. Given its estimates for GDP growth and velocity, this is the rate of monetary growth which the ECB believes is consistent with its stated inflation target. When the ECB's Governing Council meets it will have up-to-date information on the actual and predicted future rates of monetary growth. If these figures exceed the 4.5 per cent reference value the Governing Council *may* decide to tighten policy and raise interest rates. Alternatively, if the rate of monetary growth is well below the reference value the Council *may* take the opportunity to ease policy and reduce interest rates. There is, however, no hard and fast rule. Information on monetary growth rates are just a small part of the information which the Council will have available and its decisions are also influenced by movements in a wide range of other variables such as short-run variations in economic growth, oil prices, wages, exchange rates, etc. Indeed there have been many occasions when the actual rate of monetary growth has exceeded the reference value but has not led to an increase in interest rates. However, the existence of the reference value indicates that the ECB pays attention to the *long-run relationship* between monetary growth and inflation.

## RECAP Money and prices

A high rate of money growth generally leads to inflation. The larger the amount of money in circulation, the higher the public will bid up the prices of available goods and services.

*Velocity* measures the speed at which money circulates; equivalently, it is the value of transactions completed in a period of time divided by the stock of money required to make those transactions. A numerical value for velocity can be obtained from the equation $V = (P \times Y)/M$, where $V$ is velocity, $P \times Y$ is nominal GDP (a measure of the total value of transactions) and $M$ is the money supply.

The *quantity equation* states that money times velocity equals nominal GDP, or, in symbols, $M \times V = P \times Y$. The quantity equation is a restatement of the definition of velocity and thus always holds. If velocity and output are approximately constant, the quantity equation implies that a given percentage increase in the money supply leads to the same percentage increase in the price level. In other words, the *rate of growth of the money supply equals the rate of inflation*.

## Summary

- *Money* is any asset that can be used in making purchases, such as currency and chequing account balances. Money has three main functions: it is a *medium of exchange*, which means that it can be used in transactions; it is a *unit of account*, in that economic values are typically measured in units of money (e.g. euros); and it is a store of value, a means by which people can hold wealth. In practice it is difficult to measure the money supply since many assets have some money-like features. A relatively narrow measure of money is M1, which includes currency and chequing accounts. Broader measures of money such as M2 and M3 include all the assets in M1 plus additional assets that are somewhat less convenient to use in transactions.
- Because bank deposits are part of the money supply, the behaviour of commercial banks and of bank depositors affects the amount of money in the economy. A key factor is the *reserve–deposit* ratio chosen by banks. *Bank reserves* are cash or similar assets held by commercial banks, for the purpose of meeting depositor withdrawals and payments. The reserve–deposit ratio is bank reserves divided by deposits in banks. A banking system in which all deposits are held as reserves practises *100 per cent reserve banking*. Modern banking systems have reserve–deposit ratios less than 100 per cent, and are called *fractional-reserve banking systems*.
- Commercial banks *create money* through multiple rounds of lending and accepting deposits. This process of lending and increasing deposits comes to an end when banks' reserve–deposit ratios equal

their desired levels. At that point, bank deposits equal bank reserves divided by the desired reserve deposit ratio. The money supply equals currency held by the public plus deposits in the banking system.

- The *Eurosystem* consists of those EU member states who use the euro as their currency. The original 11 countries were Austria, Belgium, Finland, France, Germany, Ireland, Italy, Luxemburg, the Netherlands, Portugal and Spain. Greece joined in January 2001 but the United Kingdom, Sweden and Denmark decided to opt out of the euro and retain their national currencies.
- The Central Bank of the Eurosystem is called the *European Central Bank* (or the ECB). The ECB is part of the *European System of Central Banks* (ESCB), which includes the ECB and the national Central Banks (NCBs) of member states of the European Union, although non-euro countries do not participate in policy decisions. The ESCB was established by the Maastricht Treaty and became fully operational on 1 January 1999. The ECB's main responsibilities are formulating monetary policy for the Eurosystem and regulating financial markets, especially banks. The *Governing Council* is the ECB's supreme decision-making body and is made up of the President and Vice-President of the ECB, other members of the *Executive Board* and the governors of the NCBs. The *Executive Board* consists of the President and Vice-President of the ECB plus four others appointed on the basis of their expertise and experience in financial matters.
- The ECB can affect the money supply indirectly through its control of the supply of *bank reserves*. The principal method which the ECB uses to control the money supply is called a *main refinancing operation* in which the ECB lends reserves to the commercial banks. The main refinancing rate is the interest rate that banks pay to borrow from the ECB. The *main refinancing rate* is regarded as the key interest rate in the Eurosystem and is set by the ECB's *Governing Council.*
- The Central Bank of the United States is called the *Federal Reserve System* (or the Fed). The Fed's two main responsibilities are making monetary policy (which means determining how much money will circulate in the economy), and overseeing and regulating financial markets, especially banks. Created in 1914, the Fed is headed by a *Board of Governors* made up of seven governors appointed by the President of the United States. One of these seven governors is appointed chairman. The *Federal Open Market Committee* (FOMC), which meets about eight times a year to determine monetary policy, is made up of the seven governors and five of the presidents of the regional Federal Reserve banks.
- The Central Bank of the United Kingdom is called the *Bank of England*. The *Monetary Policy Committee*, (or MPC), is the Bank's policy decision-making body and consists of the Governor of the Bank of England, two Deputy Governors, the Bank's Chief Economist and four members appointed by the government. The Bank of England Act 1998 gives the Bank a mandate for price stability and grants the MPC operational independence in formulating monetary policy. However, the inflation target or definition of price stability is set by the government rather than the MPC.
- In the long run, the rate of growth of the money supply and the rate of inflation are closely linked because a larger amount of money in circulation allows people to bid up the prices of existing goods and services. *Velocity* measures the speed at which money circulates; equivalently, it is the value of transactions completed in a period of time, divided by the stock of money required to make those transactions. Velocity is defined by the equation $V = (P \times Y)/M$, where $V$ is velocity, $P \times Y$ is nominal GDP (a measure of the total value of transactions) and $M$ is the money supply. The definition of velocity can be rewritten as the *quantity equation*, $M \times V = P \times Y$. The quantity equation shows that, if velocity and output are constant, a given percentage increase in the money supply will lead to the same percentage increase in the price level.
- The ECB has established a 4.5 per cent *reference value* for the growth of the broad monetary aggregate M3. This reference value is the rate of monetary growth which the ECB believes to be consistent with its medium-term inflation target of approximately 2 per cent. Deviations between the actual rate of monetary growth and the reference value *may* indicate a change in interest rates.

## Key terms

**100 per cent reserve banking** (653)
**Bank of England** (649)
**bank reserves** (653)
**barter** (649)
**European Central Bank (ECB)** (657)
**European System of Central Banks (ESCB)** (657)
**Eurosystem** (657)
**Federal Open Markets Committee** (666)
**fractional-reserve banking system** (654)
**Governing Council (of the ECB)** (658)
**M1** (651)
**M2** (651)
**M3** (651)
**main refinancing operations** (664)
**main refinancing rate** (665)
**medium of exchange** (649)
**Monetary Policy Committee (MPC)** (667)
**money** (649)
**open-market operations (OMOs)** (663)
**open-market purchase** (663)
**open-market sale** (664)
**quantity equation** (669)
**reserve–deposit ratio** (654)
**store of value** (650)
**unit of account** (650)
**velocity** (668)

## Review questions

1. What is *money*? Why do people hold money even though it pays a lower return than other financial assets?
2. Suppose that the introduction of debit cards means that the public reduces its currency holdings by 50 per cent. If the Central Bank takes no action, what will happen to the national money supply? Explain.
3. The Central Bank wants to reduce the economy's money supply. Describe the various actions it might take, and explain how each action would accomplish the bank's objective.
4. What would you expect to happen to the Eurosystem's money supply if the ECB raised its main refinancing rate?
5. What are the main policy-making bodies in the ECB, the Fed and the Bank of England?
6. What is the ECB's definition of price stability in the Eurosystem?
7. Define *velocity*. How has the introduction of new payments technologies, such as ATMs, affected velocity? Explain.
8. Use the quantity equation to explain why money growth and inflation tend to be closely linked.

## Problems

1. During the Second World War, an Allied soldier named Robert Radford spent several years in a large German prisoner-of-war (POW) camp. At times, more than 50,000 prisoners were held in the camp, with some freedom to move about within the compound. Radford later wrote an account of his experiences. He described how an economy developed in the camp, in which prisoners traded food, clothing and other items. Services, such as haircuts, were also exchanged. Lacking paper money, the prisoners began to use cigarettes (provided monthly by the Red Cross) as money. Prices were quoted, and payments made, using cigarettes.
   a. In Radford's POW camp, how did cigarettes fulfil the three functions of money?
   b. Why do you think the prisoners used cigarettes as money, as opposed to other items of value such as squares of chocolate or pairs of boots?

c. Do you think a non-smoking prisoner would have been willing to accept cigarettes in exchange for a good or service in Radford's camp? Why or why not?

2. Using the ECB website, www.ecb.int, obtain recent data on M1, M2 and M3 (see Table 23.1). By what percentage have the three monetary aggregates grown over the past year?

3. Redo the example of Euroland in the text (see Tables 23.2–23.6), assuming that (a) initially, the Euroland Central Bank puts 5,000,000 euros into circulation, and (b) the commercial banks desire to hold reserves of 20 per cent of deposits. As in the text, assume that the public holds no currency. Show the consolidated balance sheets of Euroland commercial banks after the initial deposits (compare with Table 23.2), after one round of loans (compare with Table 23.3), after the first redeposit of euros (compare with Table 23.4) and after two rounds of loans and redeposits (compare with Table 23.5). What are the final values of bank reserves, loans, deposits and the money supply?

4. a. Bank reserves are 100, the public holds 200 in currency and the desired reserve–deposit ratio is 0.25. Find deposits and the money supply.

b. The money supply is 500, and currency held by the public equals bank reserves. The desired reserve–deposit ratio is 0.25. Find the currency held by the public and bank reserves.

c. The money supply is 1,250, of which 250 is currency held by the public. Bank reserves are 100. Find the desired reserve–deposit ratio.

5. When a Central Bank increases bank reserves by €1, the money supply rises by more than €1. The amount of extra money created when the Central Bank increases bank reserves by €1 is called the *money multiplier*.

a. Explain why the money multiplier is generally greater than 1. In what special case would it equal 1?

b. The initial money supply is €1,000, of which €500 is currency held by the public. The desired reserve–deposit ratio is 0.2. Find the increase in money supply associated with increases in bank reserves of €1, €5 and €10. What is the money multiplier in this economy?

c. Find a general rule for calculating the money multiplier.

d. Suppose the ECB wanted to reduce the money multiplier, perhaps because it believes that change would give it more precise control over the money supply. What action could the ECB take to achieve its goal?

6. Real GDP is €8 billion, nominal GDP is €10 billion, M1 is €2 billion and M2 is €5 billion.

a. Find velocity for M1 and for M2.

b. Show that the quantity equation holds for both M1 and M2.

7. You are given the following data for 2004 and 2005:

| Item | 2004 | 2005 |
|---|---|---|
| Money supply | 1,000 | 1,050 |
| Velocity | 8.0 | 8.0 |
| Real GDP | 12,000 | 12,000 |

a. Find the price level for 2004 and 2005. What is the rate of inflation between the two years?

b. What is the rate of inflation between 2004 and 2005 if the money supply in 2005 is 1,100 instead of 1,050?

c. What is the rate of inflation between 2004 and 2005 if the money supply in 2005 is 1,100 and output in 2005 is 12,600?

## Answers to in-chapter exercises

23.1 Table 23.5 shows the balance sheet of banks after two rounds of lending and redeposits. At that point deposits are 2,710,000 euros and reserves are 1,000,000 euros. Since banks have a desired reserve–deposit ratio of 10 per cent, they will keep 271,000 euros (10 per cent of deposits) as reserves and lend out the remaining 729,000 euros. Loans to farmers are now 2,439,000 euros. Eventually the 729,000 euros lent to the farmers will be redeposited into the banks, giving the banks deposits of 3,439,000 euros and reserves of 1,000,000 euros. The balance sheet is as shown in the table below.

| Assets | | Liabilities | |
|---|---|---|---|
| Currency (= reserves) | 1,000,000 euros | Deposits | 3,439,000 euros |
| Loans to farmers | 2,439,000 euros | | |

Notice that assets equal liabilities. The money supply equals deposits, or 3,439,000 euros. Currency held in the banks as reserves does not count in the money supply.

23.2 Because the public holds no currency, the money supply equals bank deposits, which in turn equal bank reserves divided by the reserve–deposit ratio (Eq. (23.1)). If bank reserves are 1,000,000 and the reserve–deposit ratio is 0.05, then deposits equal 1,000,000/0.05 = 20,000,000 euros, which is also the money supply. If bank reserves are 2,000,000 euros and the reserve–deposit ratio is 0.10, then the money supply and deposits are again equal to 20,000,000 euros, or 2,000,000/0.10.

23.3 If the Central Bank sells 50 euros of government bonds in exchange for currency, the immediate effect is to reduce the amount of currency in the hands of the public by 50 euros. To restore their currency holding to the desired level of 1,000 euros, the public will withdraw 50 euros from commercial banks, reducing bank reserves from 200 euros to 150 euros. The desired reserve–deposit ratio is 0.2, so ultimately deposits must equal 150 euros in reserves divided by 0.2, or 750 euros. (Note that to contract deposits, the commercial banks will have to 'call in' loans, reducing their loans outstanding.) The money supply equals 1,000 euros in currency held by the public plus 750 euros in deposits, or 1,750 euros. Thus the open-market purchase has reduced the money supply from 2,000 to 1,750 euros.

23.4 Using Eq. (23.3), velocity for M3 is given by

$$V = \frac{7{,}073.3}{5{,}768.1} = 1.22$$

The velocity of M3 is lower than that of M1 and M2. The reason is that some components of M3 such as debt securities are used less frequently than, say, cash and chequing accounts to finance transactions. Indeed some of these assets may have to be converted into cash or chequing accounts before they can be use to facilitate transactions. Hence each euro of M3 'turns over' less frequently than the average euro of M1 or M2.

## References

ECB (2004) *The Monetary Policy of the ECB* (Frankfurt: European Central Bank).

Good, B. A. (1998) 'Private Money: Everything Old is New Again', Federal Reserve Bank of Cleveland, *Economic Commentary*, 1 April.

Weatherford, J. (1997) *The History of Money: From Sandstone to Cyberspace* (New York: Crown Publishers).

# 24

# Financial Markets and International Capital Flows

In Chapter 22 we discussed the importance of national saving. Under most circumstances, a high rate of national saving permits a high rate of capital formation, which both economic logic and experience predict will tend to increase labour productivity and living standards. However, creating new capital does not *guarantee* a richer and more productive economy. History is full of examples of 'white elephants', capital projects in which millions, and even billions, of euros were invested with little economic benefit: nuclear power plants that were never opened, massive dams whose main effect was to divert water supplies and disrupt the local agriculture, new technologies that just didn't work as planned.

A healthy economy not only saves adequately but also *invests those savings in a productive way*. In market economies, such as those in Western Europe and North America, channelling society's savings into the best possible capital investments is the role of the *financial system*: banks, stock markets, bond markets and other financial markets and institutions. For this reason, many economists have argued that the development of well-functioning financial markets is a crucial precursor to sustained economic growth. In the first part of this chapter we shall discuss some major financial markets and institutions and their role in directing saving to productive uses.

Many of the people who purchased shares in US companies during the rollercoaster years of the late 1990s and early 2000s were Europeans, looking to the United States for profitable investment opportunities. More broadly, in the modern world, saving often flows across national boundaries, as savers purchase financial assets in countries other than their own and borrowers look abroad for sources of financing. Flows of funds between lenders and borrowers located in different countries are referred to as **international capital flows**. We shall discuss the international dimension of saving and capital formation in the second part of the chapter. As we shall see, for many countries *foreign savings* provide an important supplement to domestic savings as a means of financing the formation of new capital.

**international capital flows** flows of funds between lenders and borrowers located in different countries

## The financial system and the allocation of saving to productive uses

We have emphasised the importance of high rates of saving and capital formation for economic growth and increased productivity. High rates of saving and investment by themselves are not sufficient, however. A case in point is the former Soviet Union (FSU), which had very high rates of saving and investment but often used its resources very inefficiently – for example, by constructing massive but poorly designed factories that produced inferior goods at high cost. A successful economy not only saves but also uses its savings wisely by applying these limited funds to the investment projects that seem likely to be the most productive.

In the Soviet Union, a centralised bureaucracy made decisions about the allocation of saving to alternative uses. Because the bureaucrats in Moscow had relatively poor information and because they allowed themselves to be influenced by non-economic considerations such as political favouritism, they often made poor decisions. In market economies such as the United Kingdom, Germany and the United States, in contrast, savings are allocated by means of a decentralised, market-orientated financial system. In these countries the financial system consists both of financial *institutions*, such as banks, and financial *markets*, such as bond markets and stock markets.

In market economies the financial system improves the allocation of savings in at least two distinct ways. First, the financial system provides *information* to savers about which of the many possible uses of their funds is likely to prove most productive and hence pay the highest return. By evaluating the potential productivity of alternative capital investments, the financial system helps to direct savings to its best uses. Second, financial markets help savers to *share the risks* of individual investment projects. Sharing of risks protects individual savers from bearing excessive risk, while at the same time making it possible to direct savings to projects, such as the development of new technologies, which are risky but potentially very productive as well.

In the following two sections we shall briefly discuss three key components of the financial system: the banking system, the bond market and the stock market. In doing so we can elaborate on the role of the financial system as a whole in providing information about investment projects and in helping savers to share the risks of lending.

## The banking system

The banking system consists of commercial banks, of which there are thousands in Europe. Commercial banks are privately owned firms that accept deposits from individuals and businesses and use those deposits to make loans. Banks are the most important example of a class of institutions called **financial intermediaries**, firms that extend credit to borrowers using funds raised from savers. Other examples of financial intermediaries are building societies and credit unions.

**financial intermediaries** firms that extend credit to borrowers using funds raised from savers

Why are financial intermediaries such as banks, which 'stand between' savers and investors, necessary? Why don't individual savers just lend directly to borrowers who want to invest in new capital projects? The main reason is that, through specialisation, banks and other intermediaries develop a *comparative advantage* in evaluating the quality of borrowers – the information-gathering function that we referred to a moment ago. Most savers, particularly small savers, do not have the time or the knowledge to determine for themselves which borrowers are likely to use the funds they receive most productively. In contrast, banks and other intermediaries have gained expertise in performing the information-gathering activities necessary for profitable lending, including checking out the borrower's background, determining whether the borrower's business plans make sense and monitoring the borrower's activities during the life of the loan. Because banks specialise in evaluating potential borrowers, they can perform this function at a much lower cost, and with better results, than individual savers can on their own. Banks also reduce the costs of gathering information about potential borrowers by *pooling the savings* of many individuals to make large loans. Each large loan needs to be evaluated only once, by the bank, rather than separately by each of the hundreds of individuals whose savings may be pooled to make the loan.

Banks help savers by eliminating their need to gather information about potential borrowers and by directing their savings toward higher-return, more productive investments. Banks help borrowers as well, by providing access to credit that might otherwise not be available. Unlike a large corporation, which typically has many ways to raise funds, a small business that wants to buy a new computer or remodel its offices will have few options other than going to a bank. Because the bank's lending officer has developed expertise in evaluating small business loans, and may even have an ongoing business relationship with the small-business owner, the bank will be able to gather the information it needs to make the loan at a reasonable cost. Likewise, household who want to borrow for projects such as home improvement will find few alternatives to a bank. In sum, banks' expertise at gathering information about alternative lending opportunities allows them to bring together small savers, looking for good uses for their funds, and small borrowers with worthwhile investment projects.

In addition to being able to earn a return on their savings, a second reason that people hold bank deposits is to make it easier to make payments. Most bank deposits allow the holder to write a cheque against them or draw on them using a debit card or ATM card. For many transactions, paying by cheque or debit card is more convenient than using cash. For example, it is safer to send a cheque through the post than to send cash, and paying by cheque gives you a record of the transaction, whereas a cash payment does not. We discussed the role of banks in the creation of money in Chapter 23.

## Economic naturalist 24.1 How has the banking crisis in Japan affected the Japanese economy?

During the 1980s, real estate and share prices soared in Japan. Japanese banks made many loans to real estate developers and the banks themselves acquired shares in corporations. However, in the early 1990s land prices plummeted in Japan, leading many bank borrowers to default on their loans. Share prices also came down sharply, reducing the value of banks' shareholdings. The net result was that most Japanese banks fell into severe financial trouble, with many large banks near to bankruptcy. What has been the effect of this crisis, which has lasted more than a decade, on the Japanese economy?

Relative to countries such as the United Kingdom and the United States, which have more developed share and bond markets, Japan has traditionally relied very heavily on banks to allocate its savings. Thus, when the severe financial problems of the banks prevented them from operating normally, many borrowers found it unusually difficult to obtain credit – a situation known as a 'credit crunch'. Smaller borrowers, such as small and medium-sized businesses, had been particularly dependent on banks for credit, and thus suffered disproportionately.

The Japanese economy, after many years of robust growth, suffered a severe recession throughout the 1990s. Many factors contributed to this sharp slowdown. However, the virtual breakdown of the banking system certainly did not help the situation, as credit shortages interfered with smaller firms' ability to make capital investments and, in some cases, to purchase raw materials and pay workers. The

Japanese government recognised the problem but has responded very slowly, in large part out of reluctance to bear the high costs of returning the banks to a healthy financial condition. Meanwhile, the Japanese economy has continued to perform poorly.

## Bonds and shares

Large and well-established companies that wish to obtain funds for investment will sometimes go to banks. Unlike the typical small borrower, however, a larger firm usually has alternative ways of raising funds, notably through the corporate bond market and the stock market. We first discuss some of the mechanics of bonds and shares, and then return to the role of bond and stock markets in allocating saving.

### Bonds

**bond** a legal promise to repay a debt, usually including both the principal amount and regular interest payments

**principal amount** the amount originally lent

**coupon rate** the interest rate promised when a bond is issued

**coupon payments** regular interest payments made to the bondholder

A **bond** is a legal promise to repay a debt, usually including both the **principal amount**, which is the amount originally lent, and regular interest payments. The promised interest rate when a bond is issued is called the **coupon rate** and the regular interest payments made to the bondholder are called coupon payments. The **coupon payment** of a bond that pays interest annually equals the coupon rate times the principal amount of the bond. For example, if the principal amount of a bond is €1,000,000 and its coupon rate is 5 per cent, then the annual coupon payment made to the holder of the bond is 0.05 times €1,000,000, or €50,000.

Corporations and governments frequently raise funds by issuing bonds and selling them to savers. The coupon rate that a newly issued bond has to promise in order to be attractive to savers depends on a number of factors, including the bond's term, its credit risk and its tax treatment. The *term* of a bond is the length of time before the debt it represents is fully repaid, a period that can range from 30 days to 30 years or more. Generally lenders will demand a higher interest rate to lend for a longer term. *Credit risk* is the risk that the borrower will go bankrupt and thus not repay the loan. A borrower that is viewed as 'risky' will have to pay a higher interest rate to compensate lenders for taking the chance of losing all or part of their financial investment. For example, so-called 'high-yield bonds', less formally known as 'junk bonds', are bonds issued by firms judged to be risky by credit-rating agencies; these bonds pay higher interest rates than bonds issued by companies thought to be less risky.

Bonds also differ in their *tax treatment*. For example, in some countries interest paid on bonds issued by local governments may be exempt from taxes, or taxed at a low rate. Because of this tax advantage, lenders are willing to accept a lower interest rate on these bonds.

Bondholders are not required to hold bonds until *maturity*, the time at which they are supposed to be repaid by the issuer, but are always free to sell their bonds in the *bond market*, an organised market run by professional bond traders. The market value of a particular bond at any given point in time is called the *price* of the bond. As it turns out, there is a close relationship between the price of a bond at a given point of time and the *interest rate* prevailing in financial markets at that time, as illustrated by Example 24.1.

#### **Example 24.1** Bond prices and interest rates

On 1 January 2004, Tanya purchases a newly issued, two-year government bond with a principal amount of €1,000. The coupon rate on the bond is 5 per cent, paid annually. Hence Tanya, or whoever owns the bond at the time, will receive a coupon payment of €50 (5 per cent of €1,000) on 1 January, 2005, and €1,050 (a €50 coupon payment plus repayment of the original €1,000 lent) on 1 January, 2006.

On 1 January 2005, after receiving her first year's coupon payment, Tanya decides to sell her bond to raise the funds to take a vacation. She offers her bond for sale in the bond market. How much can she expect to get for her 'used' bond if the prevailing interest rate in the bond market is 6 per cent? If the prevailing interest rate is 4 per cent?

As we mentioned, the price of a 'used' bond at any point in time depends on the prevailing interest rate. Suppose first that, on 1 January 2005, when Tanya takes her bond to the bond market, the prevailing interest rate on newly issued one-year bonds is 6 per cent. Would another saver be willing to pay Tanya the full €1,000 principal amount of her bond? No, because the purchaser of Tanya's bond will receive €1,050 in one year, when the bond matures; whereas if he uses his €1,000 to buy a new one-year bond paying 6 per cent interest, he will receive €1,060 (€1,000 principal repayment plus €60 interest) in one year. So Tanya's bond is not worth €1,000 to another saver.

How much would another saver be willing to pay for Tanya's bond? Since newly issued one-year bonds pay a 6 per cent return, he will buy Tanya's bond only at a price that allows him to earn at least that return. As the holder of Tanya's bond will receive €1,050 (€1,000 principal plus €50 interest) in one year, the price for her bond that allows the purchaser to earn a 6 per cent return must satisfy the equation

$$\text{Bond price} \times 1.06 = €1{,}050$$

Solving the equation for the bond price, we find that Tanya's bond will sell for €1,050/1.06, or just under €991. To check this result, note that in one year the purchaser of the bond will receive €1,050 or €59 more than he paid. His rate of return is €59/€991, or 6 per cent, as expected.

What if the prevailing interest rate had been 4 per cent rather than 6 per cent? Then the price of Tanya's bond would satisfy the relationship bond price × 1.04 = €1,050, implying that the price of her bond would be €1,050/1.04, or almost €1,010. What happens if the interest rate when Tanya wants to sell is 5 per cent, the same as it was when she originally bought the bond? You should show that in this case the bond would sell at its face value of €1,000.

This example illustrates a general principle, that *bond prices and interest rates are inversely related*. When the interest rate being paid on newly issued bonds rises, the price that financial investors are willing to pay for existing bonds falls, and vice versa.

**Exercise 24.1**

Three-year government bonds are issued at a face value (principal amount) of 100 and a coupon rate of 7 per cent, interest payable at the end of each year. One year prior to the maturation of these bonds, a newspaper headline reads, 'Bad Economic News Causes Prices of Bonds to Plunge', and the story reveals that these three-year bonds have fallen in price to 96. What has happened to interest rates? What is the one-year interest rate at the time of the newspaper story?

Issuing bonds is one means by which a company or a government can obtain funds from savers. Another important way of raising funds, but one restricted to corporations, is by issuing shares to the public.

## Shares

**share (or equity)** a claim to partial ownership of a firm

**dividend** a regular payment received by shareholders for each share that they own

A **share (or equity)** is a claim to partial ownership of a firm. For example, if a company has 1 million shares outstanding, ownership of one share is equivalent to ownership of one-millionth of the company. Shareholders receive returns on their shares in two forms. First, shareholders receive a regular payment called a **dividend** for each share they own. Dividends are determined by the firm's management and usually depend on the firm's recent profits. Second, shareholders receive returns in the form of *capital gains* when the price of their share increases (we discussed capital gains and losses in Chapter 22).

Prices of shares are determined through trading on a stock exchange, such as the London or Frankfurt stock exchanges. A share's price rises and falls as the demand for the share changes. Demand for shares in turn depends on factors such as news about the prospects of the company. For example, the share price of a pharmaceutical company that announces the discovery of an important new drug is likely to rise on the announcement because financial investors expect the company to become more profitable in the future. Example 24.2 illustrates numerically some key factors that affect share prices.

### **Example 24.2** How much should you pay for a share of EuroFly.com?

You have the opportunity to buy shares in a new low-cost airline called EuroFly.com, which plans to sell cheap flights over the Internet. Your stockbroker estimates that the company will pay €1.00 per share in dividends a year from now, and that in a year the market price of the company will be €80.00 per share. Assuming that you accept your broker's estimates as accurate, what is the most that you should be willing to pay today per share of EuroFly.com? How does your answer change if you expect a €5.00 dividend? If you expect a €1.00 dividend but an €84.00 share price in one year?

Based on your broker's estimates, you conclude that in one year each share of EuroFly.com you own will be worth €81.00 in your pocket – the €1.00 dividend plus the €80.00 you could get by reselling the shares. Finding the maximum price you would pay for the share today therefore boils down to asking how much would you invest today to have €81.00 a year from today. Answering this question in turn requires one more piece of information, which is the expected rate of return that you require in order to be willing to buy shares in this company.

How would you determine your required rate of return to hold shares in EuroFly.com? For the moment, let's imagine that you are not too worried about the potential riskiness of the share, either because you think that it is a 'sure thing' or because you are a devil-may-care type who is not bothered by risk. In that case, your required rate of return to hold EuroFly.com should be about the same as you can get on other financial investments, such as government bonds. The available return on other financial investments gives the *opportunity cost* of your funds. So, for example, if the interest rate currently being offered by government bonds is 6 per cent, you should be willing to accept a 6 per cent return to hold EuroFly.com as well. In that case, the maximum price you would pay today for a share of EuroFly.com satisfies the equation

$$\text{Share price} \times 1.06 = €81.00$$

This equation defines the share price you should be willing to pay if you are willing to accept a 6 per cent return over the next year. Solving this equation yields share price = €81.00/1.06 = €76.42. If you buy EuroFly.com for €76.42, then your return over the year will be (€81.00 – €76.42)/€76.42 = €4.58/€71.42 = 6 per cent, which is the rate of return you required to buy the shares.

If instead the dividend is expected to be €5.00, then the total benefit of holding EuroFly.com shares in one year, equal to the expected dividend plus the expected price, is €5.00 + €80.00, or €85.00. Assuming again that you are willing to accept a 6 per cent return to hold EuroFly.com, the price you are willing to pay today satisfies the relationship share price × 1.06 = €85.00. Solving this equation for the share price yields €85.00/1.06 = €80.19. Comparing with the previous case we see that a higher expected dividend in the future increases the value of EuroFly.com shares today. That's why good news about the future prospects of a company – such as the announcement by a pharmaceutical company that it has discovered a useful new drug – affects its share price immediately.

If the expected future price of the share is €84.00, with the dividend at €1.00, then the value of holding the share in one year is once again €85.00, and the calculation is the same as the previous one. Again, the price you should be willing to pay for the share is €80.19.

These examples show that an increase in the future dividend or in the future expected share price raises the share price today, whereas an increase in the return a saver requires to hold the share lowers today's share price. Since we expect required returns in the stock market to be closely tied to market interest rates, this last result implies that increases in interest rates tend to depress share prices as well as bond prices.

Our examples also took the future share price as given. But what determines the future share price? Just as today's share price depends on the dividend that shareholders expect to receive this year and the share price a year from now, the share price a year from now depends on the dividend expected for next year and the share price two years from now, and so on. Ultimately, then, today's share price is affected not only by the dividend expected this year but by future dividends as well. A company's ability to pay dividends depends on its earnings. Thus, as we noted in the example of the pharmaceutical company that announces the discovery of a new drug, news about future earnings – even earnings quite far in the future – is likely to affect a company's share price immediately.

**Exercise 24.2**

As in Example 24.2, you expect a share of EuroFly.com to be worth €80.00 per share in one year, and also to pay a dividend of €1.00 in one year. What should you be willing to pay for the share today if the prevailing interest rate, equal to your required rate of return, is 4 per cent? What if the interest rate is 8 per cent? In general, how would you expect share prices to react if economic news arrives that implies that interest rates will rise in the very near future?

In Example 24.2 we assumed that you were willing to accept a return of 6 per cent to hold EuroFly.com, the same return that you could get on a government bond. However, financial investments in the stock market are quite risky in that returns to holding shares can be highly variable and unpredictable. For example, although you expect a share of EuroFly.com to be worth €80.00 in one year, you also realise that there is a chance it might sell as low as €50.00 or as high as €110.00 per share. Most financial investors dislike risk and unpredictability and thus have a higher required rate of return for holding risky assets like shares than for holding relatively safe assets such as government bonds. The difference between the required rate of return to hold risky assets and the rate of return on safe assets, like government bonds, is called the **risk premium**. Example 24.3 illustrates the effect of financial investors' dislike of risk on share prices.

**risk premium** the rate of return that financial investors require to hold risky assets minus the rate of return on safe assets

### Example 24.3 Riskiness and share prices

Continuing Example 24.2, suppose that EuroFly.com is expected to pay a €1.00 dividend and have a market price of €80.00 per share in one year. The interest rate on government bonds is 6 per cent per year. However, to be willing to hold a risky asset like a share of EuroFly.com, you require an expected return four percentage points higher than the rate paid by safe assets such as government bonds (a risk premium of 4 per cent). Hence you require a 10 per cent expected return to hold EuroFly.com. What is the most you would be willing to pay for the share now? What do you conclude about the relationship between perceived riskiness and share prices?

As a share of EuroFly.com is expected to pay €81.00 in one year and the required return is 10 per cent, we have share price × 1.10 = €81.00. Solving for the share price, we find the price to be €81.00/1.10 = €73.64, less than the price of €76.42 we found when there was no risk premium and the required rate of return was 6 per cent (Example 24.2). We conclude that financial investors' dislike of risk, and the resulting risk premium lowers the prices of risky assets like shares.

**RECAP Factors affecting share prices**

- An increase in expected *future dividends* or in the expected *future market price* of a share raises the current price of the share.
- An increase in *interest rates*, implying an increase in the required rate of return to hold shares, lowers the current price of shares.
- An increase in *perceived riskiness*, as reflected in an increase in the risk premium, lowers the current price of shares.

## Bond markets, stock markets and the allocation of saving

Like banks, bond markets and stock markets provide a means of channelling funds from savers to borrowers with productive investment opportunities. For example, a company that is planning a capital investment but does not want to borrow from a bank has two other options: it can issue new bonds, to be sold to savers in the bond market, or it can issue new shares in itself, which are then sold in the stock market. The proceeds from the sales of new bonds or shares are then available to the firm to finance its capital investment.

How do share and bond markets help to ensure that available savings are devoted to the most productive uses? As we mentioned earlier, two important functions served by these markets are gathering information about prospective borrowers and helping savers to share the risks of lending.

### The informational role of bond and stock markets

Savers and their financial advisers know that to get the highest possible returns on their financial investments, they must find the potential borrowers with the most profitable opportunities. This knowledge provides a powerful incentive to scrutinise potential borrowers carefully.

For example, companies considering a new issue of shares or bonds know that their recent performance and plans for the future will be carefully studied by financial investors and professional analysts working for specialised firms in cities such as London and New York which are noted for their expertise. If the analysts and other potential purchasers have doubts about the future profitability of the firm, they will offer a relatively low price for the newly issued shares or they will demand a high interest rate on newly issued bonds. Knowing this, a company will be reluctant to go to the bond or stock market for financing unless its management is confident that it can convince financial investors that the firm's planned use of the funds will be profitable. Thus the ongoing search by savers and their financial advisers for high returns leads the bond and stock markets to direct funds to the uses that appear most likely to be productive.

### Risk-sharing and diversification

Many highly promising investment projects are also quite risky. The successful development of a new drug to lower cholesterol could create billions of euros in profits for a drug company; but if the drug turns out to be less effective than some others on the market, none of the development costs will be recouped. An individual who lends her life savings to help finance the development of the anti-cholesterol drug may enjoy a handsome return but also takes the chance of losing everything. Savers are generally reluctant to take large risks, so without some means of reducing the risk faced by each saver it might be very hard for the company to find the funds to develop the new drug.

**diversification** the practice of spreading one's wealth over a variety of different financial investments to reduce overall risk

Bond and stock markets help reduce risk by giving savers a means to *diversify* their financial investments. **Diversification** is the practice of spreading one's wealth over a variety of different financial investments to reduce overall risk. The idea of diversification follows from the adage that 'you shouldn't put all your eggs in one basket'. Rather than putting all of her savings in one very risky project, a financial investor will find it much safer to allocate a small amount of savings to each of a large number of shares and bonds. That way, if some financial assets fall in value, there is a good chance that others will rise in value, with gains offsetting losses. Example 24.4 illustrates the benefits of diversification.

### Example 24.4 The benefits of diversification

Hugh has €1,000 to invest and is considering two shares, the Smith Umbrella Company and the Jones Suntan Lotion Company. Suppose the price of each share depends on how good the summer is. If the summer turns out to be cold and wet the price of Smith Umbrella shares will rise by 10 per cent but will remain unchanged if the summer is hot and sunny. Likewise, the price of Jones Suntan shares is expected to rise by 10 per cent if the summer is good but will remain unchanged if it is bad. The chance of a good summer is 50 per cent, and the chance of bad summer is also 50 per cent. How should Hugh invest his €1,000?

If Hugh were to invest all his €1,000 in Smith Umbrella, he has a 50 per cent chance of earning a 10 per cent return, in the event of a bad summer, and a 50 per cent chance of earning zero, if the summer is good.

His average, or expected, return is 50 per cent times 10 per cent plus 50 per cent times zero, or 5 per cent. Similarly, an investment in Jones Suntan yields 10 per cent return half of the time, when it's sunny, and 0 per cent return the other half of the time, when it rains, for an average return of 5 per cent.

Although Hugh can earn an *average* return of 5 per cent in either share, investing in only one share or the other is quite risky, since the actual return he receives varies widely depending on whether there is rain or shine. Can Hugh *guarantee* himself a 5 per cent return, avoiding the uncertainty and risk? Yes, all he has to do is put €500 into each of the two shares. If it rains, he will earn €50 on his Smith Umbrella share and nothing on his Jones Suntan. If it's sunny, he will earn nothing on Smith Umbrella but €50 on Jones Suntan. Rain or shine, he is guaranteed to earn €50 – a 5 per cent return – without risk.

The existence of bond markets and stock markets make it easy for savers to diversify by putting a small amount of their savings into each of a wide variety of different financial assets, each of which represents a share of a particular company or investment project. From society's point of view, diversification makes it possible for risky but worthwhile projects to obtain funding, without individual savers having to bear too much risk.

**mutual fund** a financial intermediary that sells shares in itself to the public, then uses the funds raised to buy a wide variety of financial assets

For the typical person, a particularly convenient way to diversify is to buy bonds and shares indirectly through **mutual funds**. A mutual fund is a financial intermediary that sells shares in itself to the public, then uses the funds raised to buy a wide variety of financial assets. Holding shares in a mutual fund thus amounts to owning a little bit of many different financial assets, which helps to achieve diversification. The advantage of mutual funds is that it is usually less costly and time-consuming to buy shares in one or two mutual funds than to buy many different shares and bonds directly. Mutual funds have become increasingly popular in the United States since the 1990s.

### Economic naturalist 24.2 Why did the US stock market rise sharply in the 1990s, then fall in the new millennium?

Share prices soared during the 1990s in the United States. The Standard & Poor's 500 index, which summarises the share price performance of 500 major companies, rose 60 per cent between 1990 and 1995, then more than doubled between 1995 and 2000. However, in the first two years of the new millennium this index lost nearly half its value. Why did the US stock market boom in the 1990s and go bust in the early 2000s?

The prices of shares depend on their purchasers' expectations about future dividends and share prices and on the rate of return required by potential shareholders. The required rate of return in turn equals the interest rate on safe assets plus the risk premium. In principle, a rise in share prices could be the result of increased optimism about future dividends, a fall in the required return, or some combination of these. Probably both factors contributed to the boom in share prices in the 1990s. Dividends grew rapidly, reflecting the strong overall performance of the US economy. Encouraged by the promise of new technologies, many financial investors expected future dividends to be even higher.

There is also evidence that the risk premium that people required to hold shares fell during the 1990s, thereby lowering the total required return and raising share prices. One possible explanation for a decline in the risk premium in the 1990s is increased diversification. The number and variety of mutual funds available increased markedly. Millions of Americans invested in these funds, including many who had never owned shares before or had owned shares in only a few companies. This increase in diversification for the typical stock market investor may have lowered the *perceived risk* of holding shares, which in turn reduced the risk premium and raised share prices.

After 2000 both of these favourable factors reversed. The growth in dividends was disappointing to shareholders, in large part because many high-tech firms did not prove as profitable as had been hoped. An additional blow was a series of corporate accounting scandals in 2002, in which it became known that some large firms had taken illegal or unethical actions to make their profits seem larger than they in fact were. A number of factors – including a recession, a major terrorist attack and the accounting scandals – also increased shareholders' concerns about the riskiness of shares, so that the risk premium they required to hold shares rose from its 1990s low. The combination of lower expected dividends and a higher premium for risk sent share prices sharply downward.

## International capital flows

Our discussion thus far has focused on financial markets operating within a given country, such as the United Kingdom. However, economic opportunities are not necessarily restricted by national boundaries. The most productive use of a British citizen's savings might be located outside the United Kingdom, such as purchasing shares in an American company or a partnership agreement with a Polish enterprise. Likewise, the best way for a French saver to diversify her assets and reduce her risks could be to hold bonds and shares from a number of different countries. Over time, extensive financial markets have developed to permit *cross-border* borrowing and lending. Financial markets in which borrowers and lenders are residents of different countries are called *international* financial markets.

International financial markets differ from domestic financial markets in at least one important respect: unlike a domestic financial transaction, an international financial transaction is subject to the laws and regulations of at least two countries, the country that is home to the *lender* and the country that is home to the *borrower*. The size and vitality of international financial markets thus depend on the degree of political and economic co-operation among countries. For example, during the relatively peaceful decades of the late nineteenth and early twentieth centuries, international financial markets were remarkably highly developed. Great Britain, at the time the world's dominant economic power, was a major international lender, despatching its savings for use around the globe. However, during the turbulent years 1914–45, two world wars and the Great Depression substantially reduced both international finance and international trade in goods and services. The extent of international finance and trade returned to the levels achieved in the late nineteenth century only in the 1980s.

In thinking about international financial markets, it is useful to understand that lending is economically equivalent to acquiring a real or financial asset, and borrowing is economically equivalent to selling a real or financial asset. For example, savers lend to companies by purchasing shares or bonds, which are financial assets for the lender and financial liabilities for the borrowing firms. Similarly, lending to a government is accomplished in practice by acquiring a government bond – a financial asset for the lender and a financial liability for the borrower, in this case the government. Savers can also provide funds by acquiring real assets such as land; if I purchase a parcel of land from you, though I am not making a loan in the usual sense, I am providing you with funds that you can use for consuming or investing. In lieu of interest or dividends from a bond or a share, I receive the rental value of the land that I purchased.

Purchases or sales of real and financial assets across international borders (which are economically equivalent to lending and borrowing across international borders) are known as *international capital flows*. From the perspective of a particular country, say the United Kingdom, purchases of domestic (UK) assets by foreigners are called **capital inflows**; purchases of foreign assets by domestic (UK) households and firms are called **capital outflows**. To remember these terms, it may help to keep in mind that capital inflows represent funds 'flowing in' to the country (foreign savers buying domestic assets), while capital outflows are funds 'flowing out' of the country (domestic savers buying foreign assets). The difference between the two flows is expressed as *net capital inflows* – capital inflows minus capital outflows – or *net capital outflows* – capital outflows minus capital inflows. Note that capital inflows and outflows are *not* counted as exports or imports, because they refer to the purchase of existing real and financial assets rather than currently produced goods and services.

**capital inflows** purchases of domestic assets by foreign households and firms

**capital outflows** purchases of foreign assets by domestic households and firms

From a macroeconomic perspective, international capital flows play two important roles. First, they allow countries whose productive investment opportunities are greater than domestic savings to fill in the gap by borrowing from abroad. Second, they allow countries to run *trade imbalances* – situations in which the country's exports of goods and services do not equal its imports of goods and services. The rest of this chapter discusses these key roles. We begin by analysing the important link between international capital flows and trade imbalances.

## Capital flows and the balance of trade

**trade balance (or net exports)** the value of a country's exports less the value of its imports in a particular period (quarter or year)

In Chapter 18 we introduced the term *net exports (NX)*, the value of a country's exports less the value of its imports. An equivalent term for the value of a country's exports less the value of its imports is the **trade balance**. Because exports need not equal imports in each quarter or

**trade surplus** when exports exceed imports, the difference between the value of a country's exports and the value of its imports in a given period

**trade deficit** when imports exceed exports, the difference between the value of a country's imports and the value of its exports in a given period

year, the trade balance (or net exports) need not always equal zero. If the trade balance is positive in a particular period so that the value of exports exceeds the value of imports, a country is said to have a **trade surplus** for that period equal to the value of its exports minus the value of its imports. If the trade balance is negative, with imports greater than exports, the country is said to have a **trade deficit** equal to the value of its imports minus the value of its exports.

Figure 24.1 shows the components of the trade balance for four European countries over 1970 to 2003. Figure 24.1 shows the trade balance for two large economies, the United Kingdom and France, and two smaller economies, Belgium and Ireland. In each case the blue line represents exports as a percentage of GDP and the red line represents imports as a percentage of GDP. When exports exceed imports, the vertical distance between the two lines gives the trade surplus as a percentage of GDP. When imports exceed exports, the vertical distance between the two lines represents the trade deficit. Several points are worth noting. First, with the exception of the United Kingdom, international trade has become increasingly important since the 1970s. For example, in 1970, 34.2 per cent of Irish GDP was exported and imports equalled 42.4 per cent of GDP. However, by 2000, exports accounted for 98 per cent of GDP and imports 84.4 per cent. In Belgium, exports increased from 51.9 per cent of GDP to 85.5 per cent and imports from 49.7 per cent to 81.8 per cent over the same 30-year period. Second, international trade is relatively more important for the smaller economies. In 2000, exports accounted for only 28.5 per cent of French GDP and 27.9 per cent British GDP, compared with 98 per cent for Ireland and 85.5 per cent for Belgium. Third, Fig. 24.1 shows that Belgium and Ireland consistently ran trade surpluses from the mid-1980s and France from the early 1990s. By contrast, the United Kingdom has been running a trade deficit since the early 1980s. Why has the UK trade balance been in deficit for so long? We shall answer that question later in this section.

The trade balance represents the difference between the value of goods and services exported by a country and the value of goods and services imported by the country. We have previously referred to the trade balance as net exports or *NX*. Net capital inflows represent the difference between purchases of domestic assets by foreigners and purchases of foreign assets by domestic residents. We shall use *KI* to denote net capital inflows. Hence:

$NX = \text{Exports} - \text{Imports}$
$KI = \text{Capital inflows} - \text{Capital outflows}$

There is a precise and very important link between these two imbalances, which is that in any given period, *the trade balance and net capital inflows sum to zero*. For future reference, let us write this relationship as an equation:

$$NX + KI = 0 \tag{24.1}$$

The relationship given by Eq. (24.1) is an *identity*, meaning that it is true by definition. To see why Eq. (24.1) holds, consider what happens when (for example) a British resident purchases an imported good, say a Japanese-manufactured car priced at £20,000. Suppose the British buyer pays by cheque so that the Japanese car manufacturer now holds £20,000 in an account with a British bank. What will the Japanese manufacturer do with this £20,000? Basically, there are two possibilities.

First, the Japanese company may use the £20,000 to buy British-produced goods and services, such as British-manufactured car parts or vacations in London for its executives. In this case, the United Kingdom has £20,000 in exports to balance the £20,000 car import. Because exports equal imports, the British trade balance is unaffected by these transactions (for these transactions, $NX = 0$). And because no assets are bought or sold, there are no capital inflows

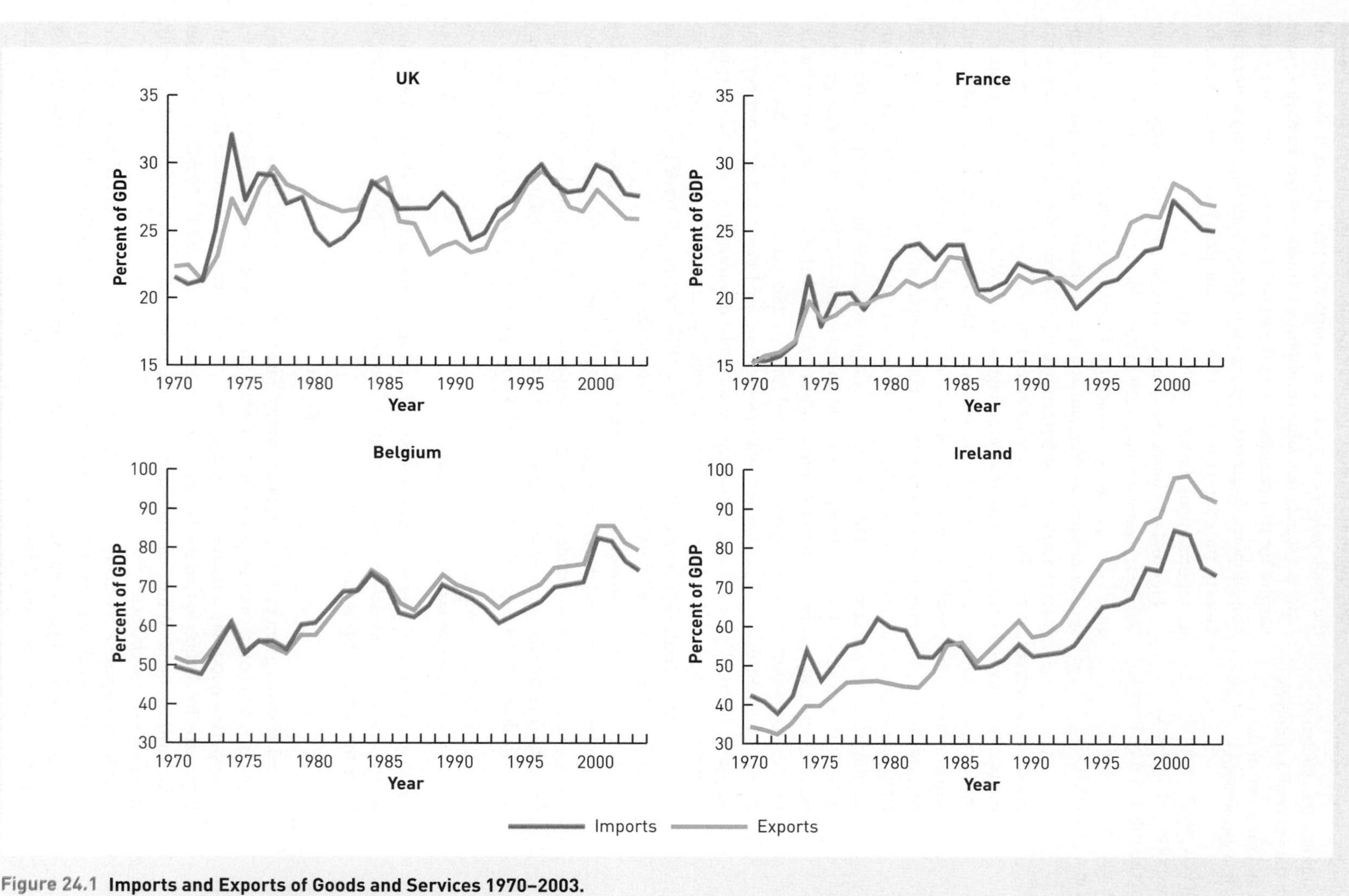


**Figure 24.1 Imports and Exports of Goods and Services 1970–2003.**

*Source: The European Economy*, Commission of the European Communities, www.europa_eu.int/comm_finance/publications.

or outflows ($KI = 0$). So, under this scenario, the condition that the trade balance plus net capital inflows equals zero, as stated in Eq. (24.1), is satisfied.

Alternatively, the Japanese car producer might use the £20,000 to acquire British assets, such as a UK government bond or some land adjacent to its plant in Sunderland. In this case, the United Kingdom compiles a trade deficit of £20,000, because the £20,000 car import is not offset by an export ($NX = -£20,000$). But there is a corresponding capital inflow of £20,000, reflecting the purchase of a British asset by the Japanese ($KI = £20,000$). So once again the trade balance and net capital inflows sum to zero, and Eq. (24.1) is satisfied.[1]

In fact, there is a third possibility, which is that the Japanese car company might swap its pounds with some other party outside the United Kingdom. For example, the company might sell its pounds to another Japanese firm or individual in exchange for Japanese yen. Alternatively, the Japanese exporter might lodge the pounds in a Tokyo bank in exchange for a deposit denominated in yen. However, the acquirer of the pounds would then have the same two options as the car company – to buy British goods and services or acquire British assets – so that the equality of net capital inflows and the trade deficit would continue to hold.

**Exercise 24.3** A German bank purchases a €20,000 Japanese government bond. Explain why Eq. (24.1) is satisfied no matter what the Japanese government does with the €20,000 it receives for its bond.

## Determinants of international capital flows

Capital inflows, recall, are purchases of domestic assets by foreigners, while capital outflows are purchases of foreign assets by domestic residents. For example, capital inflows into the United Kingdom include foreign purchases of items such as shares and bonds issued by UK companies, UK government bonds and real assets such as land or buildings owned by UK residents. Why would foreigners want to acquire UK assets – and, conversely, why would UK citizens and firms want to acquire assets abroad?

The basic factors that determine the attractiveness of any asset, either domestic or foreign, are *return* and *risk*. Financial investors seek high real returns; thus, with other factors (such as the degree of risk and the returns available abroad) held constant, a higher real interest rate in the home country promotes capital inflows by making domestic assets more attractive to foreigners. By the same token, a higher real interest rate in the home country reduces capital outflows by inducing domestic residents to invest their savings at home. Thus, all else being equal, a higher real interest rate at home leads to net capital inflows. Conversely, a low real interest rate at home tends to create net capital outflows, as financial investors look abroad for better opportunities. Figure 24.2 shows the relationship between a country's net capital inflows and the real rate of interest pre-

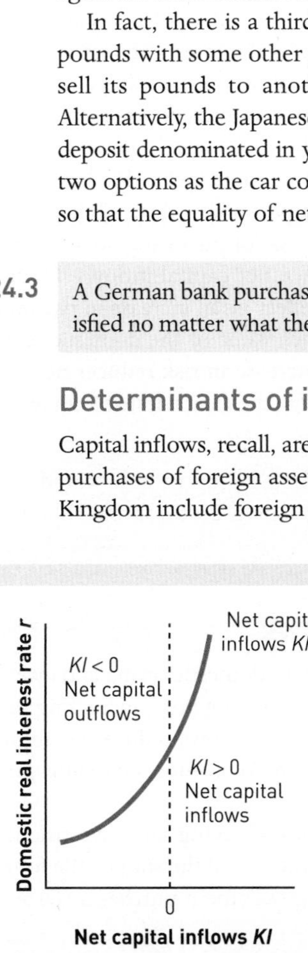

**Figure 24.2 Net Capital Inflows and the Real Interest Rate.** Holding constant the degree of risk and the real returns available abroad, a high real interest rate in the home country will induce foreigners to buy domestic assets, increasing capital inflows. A high real rate in the home country also reduces the incentive for domestic savers to buy foreign assets, reducing capital outflows. Thus, all else being equal, the higher the domestic real interest rate $r$, the higher will be net capital inflows $KI$.

[1] If the Japanese company simply left the €20,000 in the British bank, it would still count as a capital inflow, since the deposit would still be a UK asset acquired by foreigners.

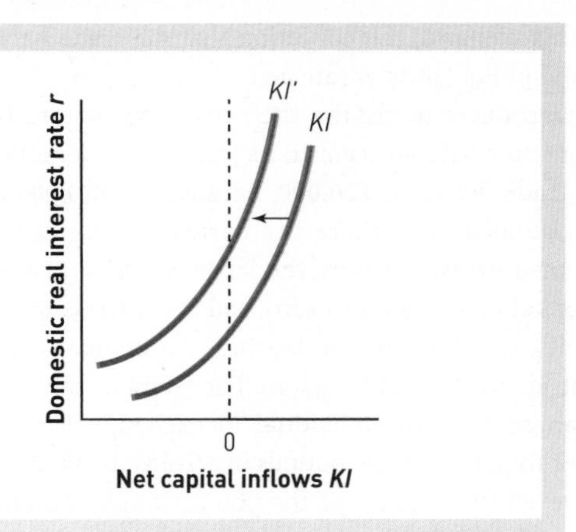


**Figure 24.3 An Increase in Risk Reduces Net Capital Inflows.** An increase in the riskiness of domestic assets, arising, for example, from an increase in political instability, reduce the willingness of foreign and domestic savers to hold domestic assets. The supply of capital inflows declines at each value of the domestic real interest rate, shifting the *KI* curve to the left.

vailing in that country. When the domestic real interest rate is high, net capital inflows are positive (foreign purchases of domestic assets exceed domestic purchases of foreign assets). But when the real interest rate is low, net capital inflows are negative (that is, the country experiences net capital outflows).

The effect of risk on capital flows is the opposite of the effect of the real interest rate. For a given real interest rate, an increase in the riskiness of domestic assets reduces net capital inflows, as foreigners become less willing to buy the home country's assets and domestic savers become more inclined to buy foreign assets. For example, political instability, which increases the risk of investing in a country, tends to reduce net capital inflows. Figure 24.3 shows the effect of an increase in risk on capital flows: at each value of the domestic real interest rate, an increase in risk reduces net capital inflows, shifting the capital inflows curve to the left.

**Exercise 24.4** For a given real interest rate and riskiness in the home country, how would you expect net capital inflows to be affected by an increase in real interest rates abroad? Show your answer graphically.

## Saving, investment and capital inflows

International capital flows have a close relationship to domestic saving and investment. As we shall see next, capital inflows augment the domestic saving pool, increasing the funds available for investment in physical capital, while capital outflows reduce the amount of saving available for investment. Thus capital inflows can help to promote economic growth within a country, and capital outflows to restrain it.

To derive the relationship among capital inflows, saving and investment, recall from Chapter 18 that total output or income $Y$ must always equal the sum of the four components of expenditure: consumption ($C$), investment ($I$), government purchases ($G$) and net exports ($NX$). Writing out this identity, we have

$$Y = C + I + G + NX$$

Next, we subtract $C + G + NX$ from both sides of the identity to obtain

$$Y - C - G - NX = I$$

In Chapter 22 we saw that national saving $S$ is equal to $Y - C - G$. Furthermore, Eq. (24.1) states that the trade balance plus capital inflows equals zero, or $NX + KI = 0$, which implies that $KI = -NX$. If we substitute $S$ for $Y - C - G$ and $KI$ for $-NX$ in the above equation, we find that

$$S + KI = I \tag{24.2}$$

Equation (24.2), a key result, says that the sum of national saving $S$ and capital inflows from abroad $KI$ must equal domestic investment in new capital goods, $I$. In other words, in an open economy, the pool of saving available for domestic investment includes not only *national saving* (the saving of the domestic private and public sectors) but funds from *savers abroad* as well.

Chapter 22 introduced the saving–investment diagram, which shows that in a closed economy, the supply of saving must equal the demand for saving. A similar diagram applies to an open economy, except that the supply of saving in an open economy includes net capital inflows as well as domestic saving. Figure 24.4 shows the open-economy version of the saving–investment diagram. The domestic real interest rate is shown on the vertical axis and saving and investment flows on the horizontal axis. As in a closed economy, the downward-sloping curve $I$ shows the demand for funds by firms that want to make capital investments. The solid upward-sloping curve, marked $S + KI$, shows the total supply of saving, including *both* domestic saving $S$ and net capital inflows from abroad $KI$. Also shown, for comparison, is the supply of domestic saving, marked $S$. You can see that for higher values of the domestic real interest rate, net capital inflows are positive, so the $S + KI$ curve falls to the right of the curve $S$ showing domestic saving only. But at low enough values of the real interest rate $r$, the economy sustains net capital outflows, as savers look abroad for higher returns on their financial investments. Thus, at low values of the domestic real interest rate, the net supply of savings is lower than it would be in a closed economy, and the $S + KI$ curve falls to the left of the domestic supply of saving curve $S$. As Fig. 24.4 shows, the equilibrium real interest rate in an open economy, $r^*$, is the level that sets the total amount of saving supplied (including capital inflows from abroad) equal to the amount of saving demanded for purposes of domestic capital investment.

Figure 24.4 also indicates how net capital inflows can benefit an economy. A country that attracts significant amounts of foreign capital flows will have a larger pool of total saving and hence both a lower real interest rate and a higher rate of investment in new capital than it otherwise would. The United States and Canada both benefited from large inflows of capital in the early stages of their economic development, as do many developing countries today. Because capital inflows tend to react very sensitively to risk, an implication is that countries that are politically stable and safeguard the rights of foreign investors will attract more foreign capital and thus grow more quickly than countries without those characteristics.

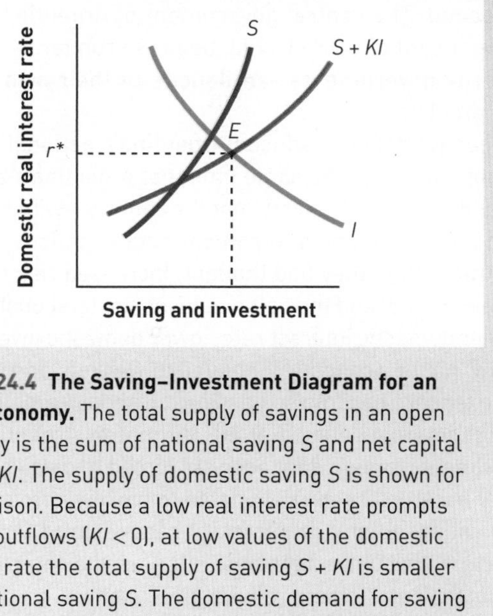

**Figure 24.4 The Saving–Investment Diagram for an Open Economy.** The total supply of savings in an open economy is the sum of national saving $S$ and net capital inflows $KI$. The supply of domestic saving $S$ is shown for comparison. Because a low real interest rate prompts capital outflows ($KI < 0$), at low values of the domestic interest rate the total supply of saving $S + KI$ is smaller than national saving $S$. The domestic demand for saving for purposes of capital investment is shown by the curve labelled $I$. The equilibrium real interest rate $r^*$ sets the total supply of saving, including capital inflows, equal to the domestic demand for saving.

Although capital inflows are generally beneficial to the countries that receive them, they are not costless. Countries that finance domestic capital formation primarily by capital inflows face the prospect of paying interest and dividends to the foreign financial investors from whom they have borrowed. A number of developing countries have experienced *debt crises*, arising because the domestic investments they made with foreign funds turned out poorly, leaving them insufficient income to pay what they owed their foreign creditors. An advantage to financing domestic capital formation primarily with domestic saving is that the returns from the country's capital investments accrue to domestic savers rather than flow abroad.

### Economic naturalist 24.3 Why did the Argentine economy collapse in 2001–02?

Argentina, with a wealth of natural resources and an educated population, has long been among the most prosperous economies of Latin America. However, in 2001–02 the country faced a severe economic crisis. Political dissatisfaction reached so high a level that Argentines rioted in the streets of Buenos Aires, and the country had five different presidents within a span of a few months. Why did the Argentine economy collapse?

Because Argentina is a developing economy with extensive human and natural resources, investments in new capital goods in that country could potentially be very profitable. However, Argentina's national saving rate is among the lowest in Latin America. To make up the difference between the demand for investment (new capital goods) and the domestic supply of saving, Argentina borrowed extensively from abroad – that is, *capital inflows* to Argentina were large. These capital inflows helped Argentina to invest more and grow more quickly than it otherwise might have (see Fig. 24.4, which shows how capital inflows *KI* augment the available pool of domestic saving *S*). However, the rapid capital inflows also implied that, over time, Argentina was building up a large debt to foreigners. Foreigners remained willing to lend to Argentina so long as they expected to earn good returns on their loans.

Unfortunately, in the late 1990s the situation in Argentina took a turn for the worse. In 1998, following a three-year growth boom, the Argentine economy slowed considerably. Moreover, partly as a result of the slowing economy, which reduced tax receipts and raised the public's demands for government services, the government budgetary situation worsened. The central government of Argentina, which had a budget surplus of over 2 per cent of GDP in 1993, began to run large deficits. Free-spending provincial and city governments ran deficits of their own, which exacerbated the nation's fiscal problem.

The increased government budget deficits reduced Argentina's national saving, increasing the need to borrow abroad. But at the same time that Argentina's borrowing needs were rising, foreign lenders began to worry that the country – with its slowing economy, high debt burden and worsening government budget deficits – was a much riskier location for investment than they had thought. Increased risk reduces the supply of capital inflows (see Fig. 24.3) and thus also reduces the total pool of saving available; the result is a higher domestic interest rate, lower domestic investment and hence a weakening economy. As the economy continued to weaken, and government budgets worsened, foreign lenders became so pessimistic about Argentina that they would lend only at very high interest rates, if at all. Ultimately Argentina was unable to repay even the interest on its foreign debt and was forced to *default* (refuse to pay). At that point the country became essentially unable to borrow abroad at any price. Investment in Argentina collapsed and real interest rates soared. As of this writing, Argentina is negotiating with public agencies, such as the International Monetary Fund (IMF), to try to obtain loans to help rebuild its economy.

## The saving rate and the trade deficit

We have seen that a country's exports and imports do not necessarily balance in each period. Indeed, as illustrated by Fig. 24.2 the United Kingdom has run a trade deficit, with its imports exceeding exports, for many years. What causes trade deficits? Stories in the media sometimes claim that trade deficits occur because a country produces inferior goods that no one wants to buy or because other countries impose unfair trade restrictions on imports. Despite the popularity of these explanations, however, there is little support for them in either economic theory or evidence. For example, the United States has a large trade deficit with China, but no one would claim that US goods are generally inferior to Chinese goods. And many developing countries have significant trade deficits even though they, rather than their trading partners, tend to impose the more stringent restrictions on trade.

Economists argue that, rather than the quality of a country's exports or the existence of unfair trade restrictions, a low rate of national saving is the primary cause of trade deficits.

To see the link between national saving and the trade deficit, recall the identity $Y = C + I + G + NX$. Subtracting $C + I + G$ from both sides of this equation and rearranging, we get $Y - C - G - I = NX$. Finally, recognising that national saving $S$ equals $Y - C - G$, we can rewrite the relationship as

$$S - I = NX \qquad (24.3)$$

Equation (24.3) can also be derived directly from Eqs (24.1) and (24.2). According to Eq. (24.3), if we hold domestic investment ($I$) constant, a high rate of national saving $S$ implies a high level of net exports $NX$, while a low level of national saving implies a low level of net exports. Furthermore, if a country's national saving is less than its investment, or $S < I$, then Eq. (24.3) implies that net exports $NX$ will be negative. That is, the country will have a trade deficit. The conclusion from Eq. (24.3) is that, holding domestic investment constant, low national saving tends to be associated with a trade deficit ($NX < 0$), and high national saving to be associated with a trade surplus ($NX > 0$).

Why does a low rate of national saving tend to be associated with a trade deficit? A country with a low national saving rate is one in which households and the government have high spending rates, relative to domestic income and production. Since part of the spending of households and the government is devoted to imported goods, we would expect a low-saving, high-spending economy to have a high volume of imports. Furthermore, a low-saving economy consumes a large proportion of its domestic production, reducing the quantity of goods and services available for export. With high imports and low exports, a low-saving economy will experience a trade deficit.

A country with a trade deficit must also be receiving capital inflows, as we have seen. (Equation (24.1) tells us that if a trade deficit exists so that $NX < 0$, then it must be true that $KI > 0$ – net capital inflows are positive.) Is a low national saving rate also consistent with the existence of net capital inflows? The answer is yes. A country with a low national saving rate will not have sufficient savings of its own to finance domestic investment. Thus there will probably be many good investment opportunities in the country available to foreign savers, leading to capital inflows. Equivalently, a shortage of domestic saving will tend to drive up the domestic real interest rate, which attracts capital flows from abroad.

We conclude that a low rate of national saving tends to create a trade deficit, as well as to promote the capital inflows that must accompany a trade deficit. Economic naturalist 24.4 illustrates this effect for the case of the United Kingdom.

## Economic naturalist 24.4 Saving, investment and the UK trade deficit

As shown by Fig. 24.1, the United Kingdom experienced a trade deficit during the 1990s and into the early years of the twenty-first century. Figure 24.5 shows national saving, investment and the trade balance for the United Kingdom from 1990 to 2003 (all measured relative to GDP). Note that national saving and investment were roughly in balance in 1997 and the trade balance was close to zero in that year. In all other years, investment exceeded national saving which, according to Eq. (24.3), implies a trade deficit. Hence Fig. 24.5 illustrates that an excess of investment over national saving implies a trade deficit.

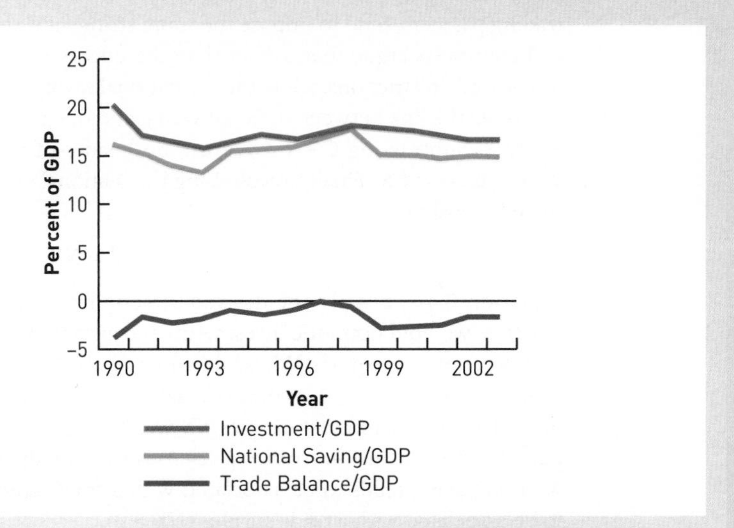


**Figure 24.5 National Saving, Investment and the Trade Balance in the United Kingdom 1990–2003.** Since 1990, national saving has been less than domestic investment, implying a trade deficit.

*Source*: *The European Economy*, Commission of the European Communities, www.europa_eu.int/comm_finance/publications.

Is the UK trade deficit a problem? Recall from Eq. (24.2) that when national saving is less than investment the shortfall must be financed by *positive net capital inflows*, or $KI = I - S$. Hence, the trade deficit implies that the United Kingdom is relying heavily on foreign savings to finance its domestic capital formation (net capital inflows). These foreign loans must ultimately be repaid, with interest. If the foreign savings are invested well and the UK economy grows, repayment will not pose a problem. However, if economic growth in the United Kingdom slackens, repaying the foreign lenders will impose an economic burden in the future.

## RECAP International capital flows and the balance of trade

- Purchases or sales of assets across borders are called *international capital flows*. If a person, firm or government in (say) the United Kingdom borrows from abroad, we say that there is a capital inflow into the United Kingdom. In this case, foreign savers are acquiring UK assets. If a person, firm, or government in the United Kingdom lends to someone abroad, thereby acquiring a foreign asset, we say that there has been a capital outflow from the United Kingdom to the foreign country. Net capital inflows to a given country equal capital inflows minus outflows.
- If a country imports more goods and services than it exports, it must borrow abroad to cover the difference. Likewise, a country that exports more than it imports will lend the difference to foreigners. Thus, as a matter of accounting, the trade balance *NX* and net capital inflows *KI* must *sum to zero* in every period.

- The funds available for *domestic investment* in new capital goods equal the sum of domestic saving and net capital inflows from abroad. The higher the return and the lower the risk of investing in the domestic country, the greater will be the capital inflows from abroad. Capital inflows benefit an economy by providing more funds for capital investment, but they can become a burden if the returns from investing in new capital goods are insufficient to pay back the foreign lenders.
- An important cause of a trade deficit is a *low national saving rate*. A country that saves little and spends a lot will tend to import a greater quantity of goods and services than it is able to export. At the same time, the country's low saving rate implies a need for more foreign borrowing to finance domestic investment spending.

To this point in the book we have discussed a variety of issues relating to the long-run performance of the economy, including economic growth, the sources of increasing productivity and improved living standards, the determination of real wages and the determinants of saving and capital formation. Beginning with Chapter 25, we shall take a more short-run perspective, examining first the causes of recessions and booms in the economy and then turning to policy measures that can be used to affect these fluctuations.

## Summary

- Besides balancing saving and investment in the aggregate, financial markets and institutions play the important role of allocating saving to the *most productive investment projects*. The financial system improves the allocation of saving in two ways. First, it provides information to savers about which of the many possible uses of their funds are likely to prove must productive, and hence pay the highest return. For example, *financial intermediaries* such as banks develop expertise in evaluating prospective borrowers, making it unnecessary for small savers to do that on their own. Similarly, share and bond analysts evaluate the business prospects of a company issuing shares of share or bonds, which determines the price the share will sell for or the interest rate the company will have to offer on its bond. Second, financial markets help savers share the risks of lending by permitting them to *diversify* their financial investments. Individual savers often hold shares through *mutual funds*, a type of financial intermediary that reduces risk by holding many different financial assets. By reducing the risk faced by any one saver, financial markets allow risky but potentially very productive projects to be funded.
- Corporations that do not wish to borrow from banks can obtain finance by issuing bonds or shares. A *bond* is a legal promise to repay a debt, including both the *principal amount* and regular interest payments. The prices of existing bonds decline when interest rates rise. A *share* is a claim to partial ownership of a firm. The price of a share depends positively on the *dividend* the share is expected to pay and on the expected future price of the share and negatively on the rate of return required by financial investors to hold the share. The required rate of return in turn is the sum of the return on safe assets and the additional return required to compensate financial investors for the riskiness of shares, called the *risk premium*.
- The *trade balance*, or net exports, is the value of a country's exports less the value of its imports in a particular period. Exports need not equal imports in each period. If exports exceed imports, the difference is called a *trade surplus*, and if imports exceed exports, the difference is called a *trade deficit*. Trade takes place in assets as well as goods and services. Purchases of domestic assets (real or financial) by foreigners are called *capital inflows*, and purchases of foreign assets by domestic savers are called *capital outflows*. Because imports that are not financed by sales of exports must be financed by sales of assets, the trade balance and net capital inflows sum to zero.

- The higher the real interest rate in a country, and the lower the risk of investing there, the higher its capital inflows. The *availability of capital inflows* expands a country's pool of saving, allowing for more domestic investment and increased growth. A drawback to using capital inflows to finance domestic capital formation is that the returns to capital (interest and dividends) accrue to foreign financial investors rather than to domestic residents.
- A low rate of national saving is the primary cause of *trade deficits*. A low-saving, high-spending country is likely to import more than a high-saving country. It also consumes more of its domestic production, leaving less for export. Finally, a low-saving country is likely to have a high real interest rate, which attracts net capital inflows. Because the sum of the trade balance and capital inflows is zero, a high level of net capital inflows is consistent with a large trade deficit.

## Key terms

bond (679)
capital inflows (686)
capital outflows (686)
coupon payments (679)
coupon rate (679)
diversification (684)
dividend (680)
financial intermediaries (677)
international capital flows (676)
mutual fund (684)
principal amount (679)
risk premium (682)
share (or equity) (680)
trade balance (or net exports) (686)
trade deficit (687)
trade surplus (687)

## Review questions

1. Give two ways that the financial system can help to improve the allocation of savings. Illustrate with examples.
2. Judy plans to sell a bond that matures in one year and has a principal value of €1,000. Can she expect to receive €1,000 in the bond market for the bond? Explain.
3. Suppose you are much less concerned about risk than is the typical person. Are shares a good financial investment for you? Why or why not?
4. Share prices surge but the prices of government bonds remain stable. What can you infer from the behaviour of bond prices about the possible causes of the increase in share values?
5. From the point of view of a given country – say, Spain – give an example of a capital inflow and a capital outflow.
6. How are capital inflows or outflows related to domestic investment in new capital goods?
7. Explain with examples why, in any period, a country's net capital inflows equal its trade deficit.
8. How would increased political instability in a country probably affect capital inflows, the domestic real interest rate and investment in new capital goods? Show this graphically.

## Problems

1. Simon purchases a bond, newly issued by the Amalgamated Corporation, for €1,000. The bond pays €60 to its holder at the end of the first and second years and pays €1,060 upon its maturity at the end of the third year.

a. What are the principal amount, the term, the coupon rate and the coupon payment for Simon's bond?

b. After receiving the second coupon payment (at the end of the second year), Simon decides to sell his bond in the bond market. What price can he expect for his bond if the one-year interest rate at that time is 3 per cent? 8 per cent? 10 per cent?

c. Can you think of a reason that the price of Simon's bond after two years might fall below €1,000, even though the market interest rate equals the coupon rate?

2. Shares in Brothers Grimm Plc, manufacturers of gingerbread houses, are expected to pay a dividend of €5.00 in one year and to sell for €100 per share at that time. How much should you be willing to pay today per share of Grimm:

a. If the safe rate of interest is 5 per cent and you believe that investing in Grimm carries no risk?

b. If the safe rate of interest is 10 per cent and you believe that investing in Grimm carries no risk?

c. If the safe rate of interest is 5 per cent but your risk premium is 3 per cent?

d. Repeat parts (a)–(c), assuming that Grimm is not expected to pay a dividend but that the expected price is unchanged.

3. Your financial investments consist of UK government bonds maturing in 10 years and shares in a start-up company doing research in pharmaceuticals. How would you expect each of the following news items to affect the value of your assets? Explain.

a. Interest rates on newly issued government bonds rise.

b. Inflation is forecast to be much lower than previously expected (**Hint:** Recall the Fisher effect from Chapter 19.) Assume for simplicity that this information does *not* affect your forecast of the sterling value of the pharmaceutical company's future dividends and share price.

In parts (c)–(f), interest rates on newly issued government bonds are assumed to remain unchanged.

c. Large swings in the stock market increase financial investors' concerns about market risk.

d. The start-up company whose share you own announces the development of a valuable new drug. However, the drug will not come to market for at least five years.

e. The pharmaceutical company announces that it will not pay a dividend next year.

f. The UK government announces a system of price controls on prescription drugs.

4. You have €1,000 to invest and are considering buying some combination of the shares of two UK companies, Oldspin Plc and Newspin Plc. Shares of Oldspin will pay a 10 per cent return if the Conservative Party is elected, an event you believe to have a 40 per cent probability; otherwise the shares pay a zero return. Shares of Newspin will pay 8 per cent if the Labour Party is elected (a 60 per cent probability), zero otherwise. Assume that either the Conservatives or Labour will be elected.

a. If your only concern is maximising your average expected return, with no regard for risk, how should you invest your €1,000?

b. What is your expected return if you invest €500 in each share? (**Hint:** Consider what your return will be if Labour wins and if the Conservatives win, then weight each outcome by the probability that that event occurs.)

c. The strategy of investing €500 in each share does *not* give the highest possible average expected return. Why might you choose it anyway?

d. Devise an investment strategy that guarantees at least a 4.4 per cent return, no matter which party wins.

e. Devise an investment strategy that is riskless – that is, one in which the return on your €1,000 does not depend at all on which party wins.

5. How do each of the following transactions affect (1) the trade surplus or deficit and (2) capital inflows or outflows for the United Kingdom? Show that in each case the identity that the trade balance plus net capital inflows equals zero applies.

a. A UK exporter sells software to Israel. She uses the Israeli shekels received to buy shares in an Israeli company.

b. A Mexican firm uses proceeds from its sale of oil to the United Kingdom to buy UK government debt.

c. A Mexican firm uses proceeds from its sale of oil to the United Kingdom to buy oil-drilling equipment from a UK firm.

d. A Mexican firm receives British pounds from selling oil to the United Kingdom. A French firm accepts the pounds as payment for drilling equipment. The French firm uses the pounds to buy UK government debt.

6. Use a diagram such as Fig. 24.4 to show the effects of each of the following on the real interest rate and capital investment of a country that is a net borrower from abroad.

a. Investment opportunities in the country improve owing to the development of new technologies.

b. The government budget deficit rises.

c. Domestic citizens decide to save more.

d. Foreign investors believe that the riskiness of lending to the country has increased.

7. A country's domestic supply of saving, domestic demand for saving for purposes of capital formation and supply of net capital inflows are given by the following equations:

$$S = 1{,}500 + 2{,}000r$$
$$I = 2{,}000 - 4{,}000r$$
$$KI = -100 + 6{,}000r$$

a. Assuming that the market for saving and investment is in equilibrium, find national saving, capital inflows, domestic investment and the real interest rate.

b. Repeat part (a), assuming that desired national saving declines by 120 at each value of the real interest rate. What effect does a reduction in domestic saving have on capital inflows?

c. Concern about the economy's macroeconomic policies causes capital inflows to fall sharply so that now $KI = -700 + 6{,}000r$. Repeat part (a). What does a reduction in capital inflows do to domestic investment and the real interest rate?

## Answers to in-chapter exercises

24.1 Since bond prices fell, interest rates must have risen. To find the interest rate, note that bond investors are willing to pay only 96 today for a bond that will pay back 107 (a coupon payment of 7 plus the principal amount of 100) in one year. To find the one-year return, divide 107 by 96 to get 1.115. Thus the interest rate must have risen to 11.5 per cent.

**24.2** A Eurofly.com share will be worth €81.00 in one year – the sum of its expected future price and the expected dividend. At an interest rate of 4 per cent, its value today is €81.00/1.04 = €77.88. At an interest rate of 8 per cent, the share's current value is €81.00/1.08 = €75.00. Recall from Example 24.2 that when the interest rate is 6 per cent, the value of a share of EuroFly.com is €76.42. Since higher interest rates imply lower share values, news that interest rates are about to rise should cause the stock market to fall.

**24.3** The purchase of the Japanese bond is a capital outflow for Germany, or $KI$ = – €20,000. The Japanese government now holds €20,000. What will it do with these funds? There are basically three possibilities. First, it might use the funds to purchase German goods and services. In that case the German trade balance equals +€20,000, and the sum of the trade balance and capital inflows is zero. Second, the Japanese government might acquire German assets – for example, euro-denominated deposits in a German bank. In that case a capital inflow to Germany of €20,000 offsets the original capital outflow. Both the trade balance and net capital outflows individually are zero, and so their sum is zero.

Finally, the Japanese government might use the €20,000 to purchase goods, services or assets from outside Germany – oil from Saudi Arabia, for example. But then the recipient of the €20,000 is holding the funds, and it has the same options that the Japanese government did. Eventually, the funds will be used to purchase German goods, services or assets, satisfying Eq. (24.1). Indeed, even if the recipient holds on to the funds (in cash, or as a German bank deposit), they would still count as a capital inflow to Germany, as euros or accounts in a German bank are German assets acquired by foreigners.

**24.4** An increase in the real interest rate abroad increases the relative attractiveness of foreign financial investments to both foreign and domestic savers. Net capital inflows to the home country will fall at each level of the domestic real interest rate. The supply curve of net capital inflows shifts left, as in Fig. 24.3.

# Part 8

# The Economy in the Short Run

In previous chapters we have seen that over long periods of time the economy's average rate of growth is the crucial determinant of living standards. But short-term fluctuations in the economy's growth rate also affect economic welfare. In particular, periods of slow or negative economic growth, known as *recessions*, may create significant economic hardship and dissatisfaction. Recessions are periods of below-average economic growth, and for many people, especially those who lose their jobs, they are periods in which living standards may actually fall. In Part 8 we shall explore the causes of short-term fluctuations in key economic variables, including output, unemployment and inflation, and we shall discuss the options available to government policy makers for stabilising the economy.

Chapter 25 provides some background for our study of recessions and shows how fluctuations in spending, or *aggregate demand*, may lead to short-run fluctuations in output and employment. In Chapters 26–28 we develop a framework for the analysis of short-term fluctuations and the alternative policy responses. Chapter 26 explains how changes in fiscal policy – policies relating to government spending and taxation – can be used to stabilise spending and output. Chapter 27 focuses on monetary policy, a second tool for stabilising output and employment. Finally, Chapter 28 incorporates inflation into the analysis, discussing both the sources of inflation and the policies that can be used to control it.

# 25 Short-Term Economic Fluctuations

In Part 7 we discussed the factors that determine long-run economic growth. Over the broad sweep of history, those factors determine the economic success of a society. Indeed, over a span of 30, 50, or 100 years, relatively small differences in the rate of economic growth can have an enormous effect on the average person's standard of living. But even though the economic 'climate' (long-run economic conditions) is the ultimate determinant of living standards, changes in the economic 'weather' (short-run fluctuations in economic conditions) are also important. A good long-run growth record is not much consolation to a worker who has lost her job due to a recession. Recessions and periods of sustained inflation are also bad news for governments as their management of the economy is often a key factor in deciding how people vote at elections.

In this part of the book we study short-term fluctuations in economic activity, commonly known as *recessions* and *expansions*. Our main focus will be on the *causes* of short-term fluctuations, as well as the available *policy responses*. Because the analysis of short-term economic fluctuations can become complex and even controversial, we shall proceed in a step-by-step fashion. We shall start, in this chapter, with some background on the history and characteristics of short-term economic fluctuations and then introduce a basic – and oversimplified – model of booms and recessions, which we shall refer to as the *basic Keynesian model* in honour of its principal originator, the British economist John Maynard Keynes. The basic Keynesian model focuses on the components of aggregate spending, such as consumption spending by households and investment spending by firms, and the effects of changes in spending on total real GDP. Because the basic Keynesian model does not take into account the 'self-correcting' tendencies of the economy, it tends to overstate the need for government intervention to offset fluctuations. In Chapters 26–28 we shall add new features to the model to make it more realistic. By the end of Part 8, we shall have discussed the major causes of short-term economic fluctuations, as well as the options that policy makers have in responding to them.

## Recessions and expansions

As background to the study of short-term economic fluctuations, let us review the historical record of the fluctuations in the British economy. Figure 25.1 shows the path of real GDP in the United Kingdom since 1920 (Fig. 17.1 provides an even longer data series). As you can see,

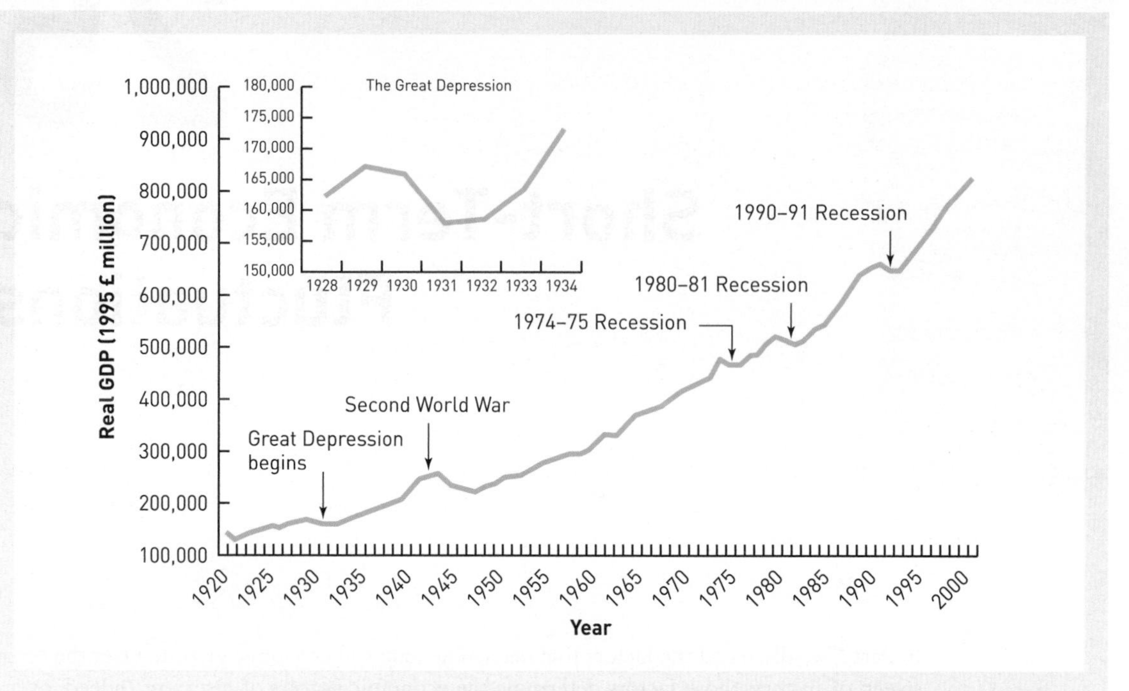


**Figure 25.1 Fluctuations in Real UK GDP, 1920–2000.** Real GDP does not grow smoothly but goes through phases of expansion and recession. The inset highlights the Great Depression of 1930–32.

the growth path of real GDP is not always smooth; the bumps and wiggles correspond to short periods of faster or slower growth.

A period in which the economy is growing at a rate significantly *below* normal is called a **recession** or a *contraction*. An extremely severe or protracted recession is called a **depression**. From Fig. 25.1 you should be able to pick out the Great Depression, which had a devastating impact on all industrial economies between 1929 and 1933. You can also see that the UK economy was volatile in the mid-1970s, the early 1980s and 1990s, with serious recessions in 1974–75, 1980–81 and 1990–91. Most European countries, together with the United States and Japan, experienced recessions around the same times as the United Kingdom. Each of these recessions was preceded by significant increases in oil prices. In the 1970s and early 1980s this was the result of action taken by the Organisation of Petroleum Exporting Countries (OPEC) which cut production and raised oil prices in 1973 and again in 1979. In 1990–91 the rise in oil prices was related to Iraq's invasion of Kuwait and the resulting Gulf War.

**recession (or contraction)** a period in which the economy is growing at a rate significantly below normal

**depression** a particularly severe or protracted recession

The opposite of a recession is an **expansion** – a period in which the economy is growing at a rate that is significantly *above* normal. A particularly strong and protracted expansion is called a **boom**. In the United Kingdom, strong expansions are evident for most of the 1950s, the mid-1960s, the late 1980s and toward the end of the twentieth century (see Fig. 25.1). In fact the expansion of the 1950s prompted the Prime Minister Harold Macmillan, to fight, and win, the 1959 general election under the slogan 'You have never had it so good'. As can also be seen from Fig. 25.1, on average, expansions have endured much longer than recessions.

**expansion** a period in which the economy is growing at a rate significantly above normal

**boom** a particularly strong and protracted expansion

Although Fig. 25.1 shows only twentieth-century data, periods of expansion and recession have been a feature of industrial economies since at least the late eighteenth century. Karl Marx and Friedrich Engels referred to these fluctuations, which they called 'commercial crises', in their *Communist Manifesto* (1848). In the United States, economists have been studying short-term fluctuations for at least a century. The traditional term for these fluctuations is *business cycles*, and they are still often referred to as *cyclical fluctuations*. Neither term is accurate, though; as Fig. 25.1 shows, economic fluctuations are not 'cyclical' at all in the sense that they recur at predictable intervals, but instead are *irregular in their length and severity*. This irregularity makes the dates of turning points, known as *peaks* and *troughs*, extremely hard to predict, despite the fact that professional forecasters have devoted a great deal of effort and brainpower to the task.

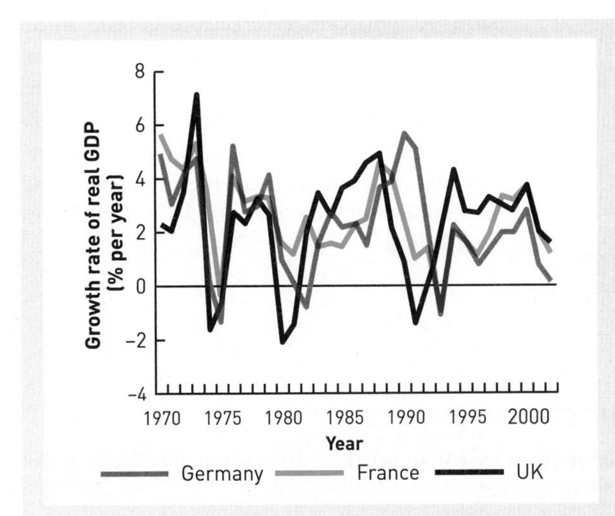


**Figure 25.2 Real GDP Growth in Three European Countries, 1970–2002.** Annual growth rates for Germany, France and the United Kingdom.

*Source: The European Economy*, Commission for the European Communities, www.europa_eu.int/ comm_finance/publications

Expansions and recessions are not usually limited to a few industries or regions but are *felt throughout the economy*. Indeed, the largest fluctuations may have a *global impact*. For instance, the Great Depression of the 1930s affected most of the world's economies; Canada, Japan and the United States, as well as most countries in Western Europe, experienced the recessions of 1974–75, 1980–81 and 1990–91. Figure 25.2 shows growth rates of real GDP over the period 1970–2002 for France, Germany and the United Kingdom. You can see that all three countries experienced peaks and troughs at approximately the same time and especially in the case of the 1974–75 recession.

*Unemployment* is a key indicator of short-term economic fluctuations. The unemployment rate typically rises sharply during recessions and recovers (although more slowly) during expansions. Figure 25.3 shows the UK unemployment rate since 1970 and illustrates that unemployment starts to rise steeply once a recession starts. Recall from Chapter 21 that the part of unemployment that is associated with recessions is called *cyclical unemployment*. Beyond this increase in unemployment, labour market conditions generally worsen during recessions. For example, during recessions real wages grow more slowly, workers are less likely to receive promotions or bonuses, and new entrants to the labour force (such as college graduates) have a much tougher time finding attractive jobs.

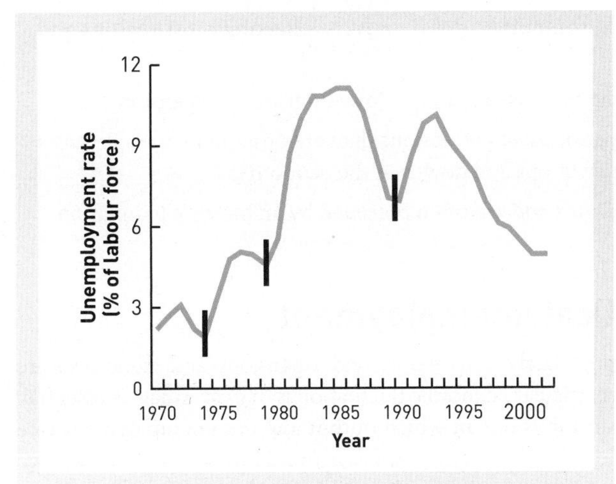


**Figure 25.3 UK Unemployment, 1970–2002.** UK unemployment since 1970. The start of a recession is indicated by a vertical bar. Note that unemployment increases rapidly after the start of each recession.

Generally, industries that produce *durable goods* – such as cars, houses and capital equipment – are more affected than others by recessions and booms. In contrast, industries that provide *services* and *non-durable goods* such as food are much less sensitive to short-term

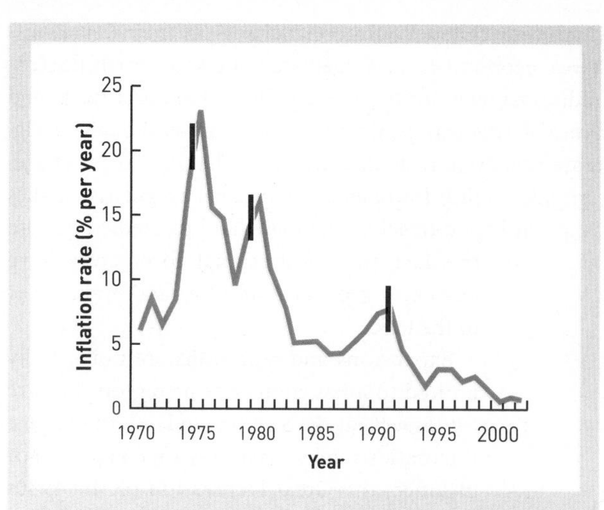


**Figure 25.4 UK Inflation, 1970–2002.** UK inflation since 1970. Recessions are indicated by the vertical bars. Note that inflation declines after each recession.

fluctuations. Thus an automobile worker or a construction worker is far more likely to lose his job in a recession than is a barber or a baker. Like unemployment, *inflation* follows a typical pattern in recessions and expansions, though it is not so sharply defined. Figure 25.4 shows the UK inflation rate since 1970; in Fig. 25.4, vertical bars indicate periods of recession. As you can see, recessions tend to be followed by a decline in the rate of inflation. Furthermore, many – though not all – post-war recessions have been preceded by increases in inflation, as Fig. 25.4 shows. The behaviour of inflation during expansions and recessions will be discussed more fully in Chapter 28.

## RECAP Recessions, booms and their characteristics

- A *recession* is a period in which output is growing more slowly than normal. An *expansion*, or *boom*, is a period in which output is growing more quickly than normal.
- The beginning of a recession is called the *peak*, and its end (which corresponds to the beginning of the subsequent expansion) is called the *trough*.
- The sharpest recession in the history of most industrial countries was the initial phase of the *Great Depression* in 1929–33. Severe recessions also occurred in the early 1970s, 1980s and 1990s. Each of these recessions followed large increases in world oil prices.
- *Short-term economic fluctuations* (recessions and expansions) are irregular in length and severity, and thus are difficult to predict.
- Expansions and recessions have *widespread* (and sometimes *global*) *impacts*, affecting most regions and industries.
- *Unemployment* rises sharply during a recession and falls, usually more slowly, during an expansion.
- *Durable goods* industries are more affected by expansions and recessions than are other industries. Services and non-durable goods industries are less sensitive to ups and downs in the economy.
- Recessions tend to be followed by a *decline in inflation* and are often preceded by an increase in inflation.

## Output gaps and cyclical unemployment

If policy makers are to respond appropriately to recessions and expansions, and economists are to study them, knowing whether a particular economic fluctuation is 'big' or 'small' is essential. Intuitively, a 'big' recession or expansion is one in which output and the unemployment rate deviate significantly from their normal or trend levels. In this section we shall attempt to be more precise about this idea by introducing the concept of the **output gap**, which measures how far output is from its normal level at a particular time. We shall also revisit the idea of *cyclical unemployment*, or the deviation of unemployment from its normal level. Finally, we shall examine how these two concepts are related.

**output gap** the difference between the economy's potential output and its actual output at a point in time ($Y^* - Y$)

## Potential output and the output gap

The concept of potential output is a useful starting point for thinking about the measurement of expansions and recessions. **Potential output**, also called *potential GDP* or *full-employment output*, is the amount of output (real GDP) that an economy can produce when using its resources, such as capital and labour, at normal rates. Potential output is not a fixed number but *grows over time*, reflecting increases in both the amounts of available capital and labour and their productivity. We discussed the sources of growth in potential output (the economy's productive capacity) in Chapter 20. We shall use the symbol $Y^*$ to signify the economy's potential output at a given point in time.

**potential output (or potential GDP or full-employment output)** the amount of output (real GDP) that an economy can produce when using its resources, such as capital and labour, at normal rates

Why does a nation's output sometimes grow quickly and sometimes slowly, as shown for the United Kingdom in Fig. 25.1? Logically, there are two possibilities. First, changes in the rate of output growth may reflect changes in the rate at which the country's potential output is increasing. For example, unfavourable weather conditions, such as a severe drought, would reduce the rate of potential output growth in an agricultural economy, and a decline in the rate of technological innovation might reduce the rate of potential output growth in an industrial economy. Under the assumption that the country is using its resources at normal rates, so that actual output equals potential output, a significant slowdown in potential output growth would tend to result in recession. Similarly, new technologies, increased capital investment, or a surge in immigration that swells the labour force could produce unusually brisk growth in potential output, and hence an economic boom.

Undoubtedly, changes in the rate of growth of potential output are part of the explanation for expansions and recessions. In the United States, for example, the economic boom of the second half of the 1990s was propelled in part by new information technologies, such as the Internet. And the severe slowdown in Japan during the decade of the 1990s reflected in part a reduction in the growth of potential output, arising from factors such as slower growth in the Japanese labour force and capital stock. When changes in the rate of GDP growth reflect changes in the growth rate of potential output, the appropriate policy responses are those discussed in Chapter 20. In particular, when a recession results from slowing growth in potential output, the government's best response is to try to promote saving, investment, technological innovation, human capital formation and other activities that support growth.

A second possible explanation for short-term economic fluctuations is that *actual output does not always equal potential output*. For example, potential output may be growing normally, but for some reason the economy's capital and labour resources may not be fully utilised, so that actual output is significantly below the level of potential output. This low level of output, resulting from underutilisation of economic resources, would generally be interpreted as a recession. Alternatively, capital and labour may be working much harder than normal – firms may put workers on overtime, for example – so that actual output expands beyond potential output, creating a boom.

At any point in time, the difference between potential output and actual output is called the *output gap*. Recalling that $Y^*$ is the symbol for potential output and that $Y$ stands for actual output (real GDP), we can express the output gap as $Y^* - Y$. A positive output gap – when actual output is below potential, and resources are not being fully utilised – is called a **recessionary gap**. A negative output gap – when actual output is above potential, and resources are being utilised at above-normal rates – is referred to as an **expansionary gap**.

**recessionary gap** a positive output gap, which occurs when potential output exceeds actual output ($Y^* > Y$)

**expansionary gap** a negative output gap, which occurs when actual output is higher than potential output ($Y > Y^*$)

Policy makers generally view both recessionary gaps and expansionary gaps as problems. It is not difficult to see why a recessionary gap is bad news for the economy: when there is a recessionary gap, capital and labour resources are not being fully utilised, and output and employment are below normal levels. This is the sort of situation that poses problems for politicians' re-election prospects. An expansionary gap is considered a problem by policy makers for a more subtle reason: what's wrong, after all, with having higher output and employment than normal? A prolonged expansionary gap is problematic because, when faced with a demand for their products that significantly exceeds their normal capacity, firms tend to raise prices. Thus an expansionary gap typically results in increased inflation, which reduces the efficiency of the economy in the longer run. (We discuss the genesis of inflation in more detail in Chapter 28.) Figure 25.5 shows estimated output gaps for EU countries in 2003. Note that the gap is measured as the percentage deviation of actual output $Y$ from potential output $Y^*$, or $(Y^* - Y)/Y^*$. Hence a positive value indicates a recessionary gap. Figure 25.5 shows that only Greece and Ireland were experiencing expansionary gaps and that the two largest economies, France and Germany, were experiencing significant recessionary gaps.

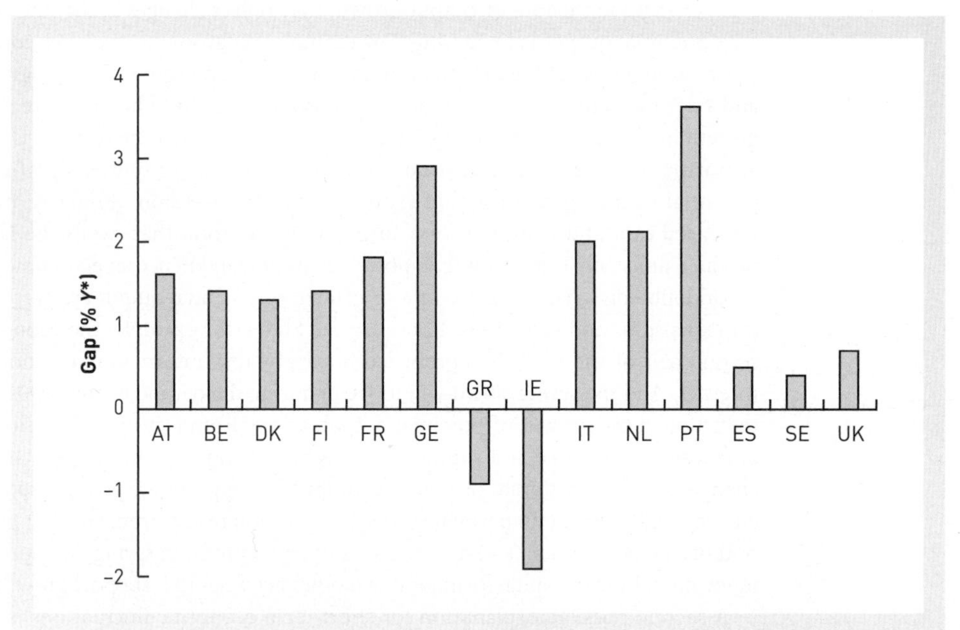


**Figure 25.5 Output Gaps for EU Member States, 2003.** The gap is measured as the percentage deviation of $Y$ from $Y^*$. A positive value indicates a recessionary gap.
*Source*: OECD, *Economic Outlook*, No. 75, www.oecd.org.

Whenever an output gap exists, whether it is recessionary or expansionary, policy makers have an incentive to try to eliminate the gap by returning actual output to potential. In Chapters 26–28 we shall discuss both how output gaps arise and the tools that policy makers have for *stabilising* the economy – that is, bringing actual output into line with potential output.

## The natural rate of unemployment and cyclical unemployment

Whether recessions arise because of slower growth in potential output or because actual output falls below potential, they bring bad times. In either case output falls (or at least grows more slowly), implying reduced living standards. Recessionary output gaps are particularly frustrating for policy makers, however, because they imply that the economy has the *capacity* to produce more, but for some reason available resources are not being fully utilised. Recessionary gaps are *inefficient* in that they unnecessarily reduce the total economic 'pie', making the typical person worse off.

An important indicator of the low utilisation of resources during recessions is the *unemployment rate*. In general, a *high* unemployment rate means that labour resources are not being fully utilised, so that output has fallen below potential (a recessionary gap). By the same logic, an unusually *low* unemployment rate suggests that labour is being utilised at a rate greater than normal, so that actual output exceeds potential output (an expansionary gap).

To understand the relationship between the output gap and unemployment better, recall from Chapter 21 the three broad types of unemployment: frictional unemployment, structural unemployment and cyclical unemployment. *Frictional unemployment* is the short-term unemployment that is associated with the matching of workers and jobs. Some amount of frictional unemployment is necessary for the labour market to function efficiently in a dynamic, changing economy. *Structural unemployment* is the long-term and chronic unemployment that occurs even when the economy is producing at its normal rate. Structural unemployment often results when workers' skills are outmoded and do not meet the needs of employers – so, for example, steelworkers may become structurally unemployed as the steel industry goes into a long-term decline, unless those workers can retrain to find jobs in growing industries. Finally, *cyclical unemployment* is the extra unemployment that occurs during periods of recession. Unlike cyclical unemployment, which is present only during recessions, frictional unemployment and structural unemployment are always present in the labour market, even when the economy is operating normally. Economists call the part of the total unemployment rate that is attributable to frictional and structural unemployment the **natural rate of unemployment**. Put another way, the natural rate of unemployment is the unemployment rate that prevails when cyclical unemployment is zero, so that the economy has neither a recessionary nor an expansionary output gap. We will denote the natural rate of unemployment as $u^*$.

**natural rate of unemployment** the part of the total unemployment rate that is attributable to frictional and structural unemployment; equivalently, the unemployment rate that prevails when cyclical unemployment is zero, so that the economy has neither a recessionary nor an expansionary output gap

Cyclical unemployment, which is the difference between the total unemployment rate and the natural rate, can be expressed as $u - u^*$, where $u$ is the actual unemployment rate and $u^*$ denotes the natural rate of unemployment. In a recession, the actual unemployment rate $u$ exceeds the natural unemployment rate $u^*$, so cyclical unemployment, $u - u^*$, is positive. When the economy experiences an expansionary gap, in contrast, the actual unemployment rate is lower than the natural rate, so that cyclical unemployment is negative. Negative cyclical unemployment corresponds to a situation in which labour is being used more intensively than normal, so that actual unemployment has dipped below its usual frictional and structural levels.

## RECAP Output gaps and cyclical unemployment

Potential output is the amount of output (real GDP) that an economy can produce when using its resources, such as capital and labour, at normal rates. The output gap, $Y^* - Y$, is the difference between potential output $Y^*$ and actual output $Y$. When actual output is below potential, the resulting output gap is called a *recessionary gap*. When actual output is above potential, the difference is called an *expansionary gap*. A recessionary gap reflects a waste of resources, while an expansionary gap threatens to ignite inflation; hence policy makers have an incentive to try to eliminate both types.

The *natural rate of unemployment*, $u^*$, is the sum of the frictional and structural unemployment rates. It is the rate of unemployment that is observed when the economy is operating at a normal level, with no output gap.

*Cyclical unemployment*, $u - u^*$, is the difference between the actual unemployment rate $u$ and the natural rate of unemployment $u^*$. Cyclical unemployment is positive when there is a recessionary gap, negative when there is an expansionary gap and zero when there is no output gap.

## Why do short-term fluctuations occur? A preview and a parable

What causes periods of recession and expansion? In the preceding section we discussed two possible reasons for slowdowns and speed-ups in real GDP growth. First, growth in *potential output* itself may slow down or speed up, reflecting changes in the growth rates of available capital and labour and in the pace of technological progress. Second, even if potential output is growing normally, *actual output* may be higher or lower than potential output – that is, expansionary or recessionary output gaps may develop. Earlier in this book we discussed some of the reasons why growth in potential output can vary, and the options that policy makers have for stimulating growth in potential output. But we have not yet addressed the question of how output gaps can arise, or what policy makers should do in response. The causes and cures of output gaps will be a major topic of Chapters 26–28. Here is a brief preview of the main conclusions of those chapters:

1. In a world in which prices adjusted immediately to balance the quantities supplied and demanded for all goods and services, output gaps would not exist. However, for many goods and services, the assumption that prices will adjust immediately is not realistic. Instead, many firms adjust the prices of their output only periodically. In particular, rather than changing prices with every variation in demand, firms tend to adjust to changes in demand in the short run by varying the quantity of *output* they produce and sell. This type of behaviour is known as 'meeting the demand' at a pre-set price.
2. Because in the short run firms tend to meet the demand for their output at preset prices, changes in the amount that customers decide to spend will affect output. When total spending is low for some reason, output may fall below potential output; conversely, when spending is high, output may rise above potential output. In other words, *changes in economywide spending* are the primary cause of output gaps. Thus government policies can help to eliminate output gaps by influencing total spending. For example, the government can affect total spending directly simply by changing its own level of purchases.
3. Although firms tend to meet demand in the short run, they will not be willing to do so indefinitely. If customer demand continues to differ from potential output, firms will eventually adjust their prices to eliminate output gaps. If demand exceeds potential output (an *expansionary* gap), firms will raise their prices aggressively, spurring inflation. If demand falls below potential output (a *recessionary* gap), firms will raise their prices less aggressively or even cut prices, reducing inflation.
4. Over the longer run, price changes by firms eliminate any output gap and bring production back into line with the economy's potential output. Thus the economy is 'self-correcting' in the sense that it operates to eliminate output gaps over time. Because of this self-correcting tendency, in the long run actual output equals potential output, so that output is determined by the *economy's productive capacity* rather than by the rate of spending. In the long run, total spending influences only the rate of inflation.

These ideas will become clearer as we proceed through Chapters 26–28. Before plunging into the details of the analysis, though, let us consider an example that illustrates the links between spending and output in the short and long run.

Bill produces gourmet ice cream on his premises on London's Oxford Street and sells it directly to the public. What determines the amount of ice cream that Bill produces on a daily basis? The productive capacity, or potential output, of the shop is one important factor. Specifically, Bill's potential output of ice cream depends on the amount of capital (number of ice cream makers) and labour (number of workers) that he employs, and on the productivity of that capital and labour. Although Bill's potential output usually changes rather slowly, on occasion it can fluctuate significantly – for example, if an ice cream maker breaks down or Bill contracts the flu.

The main source of day-to-day variations in Bill's ice cream production, however, is not changes in potential output but fluctuations in the *demand* for ice cream by the public. Some of these fluctuations in spending occur predictably over the course of the day (more demand in the afternoon than in the morning, for example), the week (more demand on weekends), or the year (more demand in the summer and during the tourist season). Other changes in demand are less regular – more demand on a hot summer day than a cool one. Some changes in demand are hard for Bill to interpret: for example, a surge in demand for rocky road strawberry ice cream on one particular Tuesday could reflect a permanent change in consumer tastes, or it might just be a random, one-time event.

How should Bill react to these ebbs and flows in the demand for ice cream? The basic supply and demand model that we introduced in Chapter 3, if applied to the market for ice cream, would predict that the price of ice cream should change with every change in the demand for ice cream. For example, prices should rise on hot sunny days, and they should fall on cold rainy days, when most people would prefer a hot drink to an ice cream cone. Indeed, taken literally, the supply and demand model of Chapter 3 predicts that ice cream prices should change almost most moment to moment. Imagine Bill standing in front of his shop like an auctioneer, calling out prices in an effort to determine how many people are willing to buy at each price!

Of course, we do not expect to see this behaviour by an ice cream parlour owner. Price-setting by auction does in fact occur in some markets, such as the market for grain or the stock market, but it is not the normal procedure in most retail markets, such as the market for ice cream. Why this difference? The basic reason is that sometimes the economic benefits of hiring an auctioneer and setting up an auction exceed the costs of doing so, and sometimes they do not. In the market for grain, for example, many buyers and sellers gather together in the same place at the same time to trade large volumes of standardised goods (tonnes of grain). In that kind of situation, an auction is an efficient way to determine prices and balance the quantities supplied and demanded. In an ice cream parlour, by contrast, customers come in by twos and threes at random times throughout the day. Some want shakes, some cones and some sodas. With small numbers of customers and a low sales volume at any given time, the costs involved in selling ice cream by auction are much greater than the benefits of allowing prices to vary with demand.

So how does Bill, the ice cream parlour manager, deal with changes in the demand for ice cream? Observation suggests that he begins by setting prices based on the best information he has about the demand for his product and the costs of production. Perhaps he prints up a menu or makes a sign announcing the prices. Then, over a period of time, he will keep his prices fixed and serve as many customers as want to buy (up to the point where he runs out of ice cream or room in the parlour at these prices). This behaviour is what we call 'meeting the demand' at pre-set prices, and it implies that *in the short run*, the amount of ice cream Bill produces and sells is determined by the demand for his products.

However, *in the long run* the situation is quite different. Suppose, for example, that Bill's ice cream earns a citywide reputation for its freshness and flavour. Day after day Bill observes long queues in his ice cream parlour. His ice cream maker is overworked, as are his employees and his table space. There can no longer be any doubt that, at current prices, the quantity of ice cream the public wants to consume exceeds what Bill is able and willing to supply on a normal basis (his potential output). Expanding the ice cream parlour is an attractive possibility, but not one (we assume) that is immediately feasible. What will Bill do?

Certainly one thing Bill can do is raise his prices. At higher prices, Bill will earn higher profits. Moreover, raising ice cream prices will bring the quantity of ice cream demanded closer to Bill's normal production capacity – his potential output. Indeed, when the price of

Bill's ice cream finally rises to its equilibrium level, the parlour's actual output will equal its potential output. Thus, over the long run, ice cream prices adjust to their equilibrium level, and the amount that is sold is determined by potential output.

This example illustrates in a simple way the links between spending and output – except, of course, that we must think of this story as applying to the whole economy, not to a single business. The key point is that there is an important difference between the short run and the long run. In the short run, producers often choose not to change their prices, but rather to meet the demand at pre-set prices. Because output is determined by demand, in the short run total spending plays a central role in determining the level of economic activity. Thus Bill's ice cream parlour enjoys a boom on an unusually hot day, when the demand for ice cream is strong, while an unseasonably cold day brings an ice cream recession. But in the long run, prices adjust to their *market-clearing levels*, and output equals potential output. Thus the quantities of inputs and the productivity with which they are used are the primary determinants of economic activity in the long run, as we saw in Chapter 20. Although total spending affects output in the short run, in the long run its main effects are on prices.

## Economic naturalist 25.1 Why did the Coca-Cola Company test a vending machine that 'knows' when the weather is hot?

According to the *New York Times* (28 October 1999, p. C1), the Coca-Cola Company has quietly tested a soda vending machine that includes a temperature sensor. Why would Coca-Cola want a vending machine that 'knows' when the weather is hot?

When the weather is hot, the demand for refreshing soft drinks rises, increasing their market-clearing price. To take advantage of this variation in consumer demand, the vending machines that Coca-Cola tested were equipped with a computer chip that gave them the capability to raise prices automatically when the temperature climbs. The company's chairman and chief executive, M. Douglas Ivester, described in an interview how the desire for a cold drink increases during a sports championship final held in the summer heat. 'So it is fair that it should be more expensive,' Mr Ivester was quoted as saying. 'The machine will simply make this process automatic.' Company officials suggested numerous other ways in which vending machine prices could be made dependent on demand. For example, machines could be programmed to reduce prices during off-peak hours or at low-traffic machines.

In traditional vending machines, cold drinks are priced in a way analogous to the way Bill prices his ice cream: a price is set, and demand is met at the pre-set price, until the machine runs out of soda. The weather-sensitive vending machine illustrates how technology may change pricing practices in the future. Indeed, increased computing power and access to the Internet have already allowed some firms, such as airline companies, to change prices almost continuously in response to variations in demand. Conceivably, the practice of meeting demand at a pre-set price may some day be obsolete.

On the other hand, Coca-Cola's experiments with 'smart' vending machines also illustrate the barriers to fully flexible pricing in practice. First, the new vending machines are more costly than the standard model. In deciding whether to use them, the company must decide whether the extra profits from variable pricing justify the extra cost of the machines. Second, in early tests many consumers reacted negatively to the new machines, complaining that they take unfair advantage of thirsty customers. In practice, customer complaints and concerns about 'fairness' make companies less willing to vary prices sensitively with changing demand.?

### Spending and output in the short run

The story of Bill's ice cream parlour suggested that when prices are slow to change, spending might be an important factor influencing fluctuations in short-run output. We shall now focus on this link at the aggregate or macro level. To fix our ideas we first consider a parable about two countries called Big-Land and Small-Land. Big-Land is a large economy producing a wide range of goods and services. Small-Land is a much smaller economy and its industry is highly specialised in one good which, for the sake of illustration, we shall assume to be shoes. We shall also assume that most of Small-Land's shoe production is exported and sold to households in Big-Land. Of course Small-Land will have firms other than shoe manufacturers. The majority of Small-Land's workforce may be employed in shoe factories but they spend their incomes on the many goods and services produced or sold domestically. These would include food sold by supermarkets, clothes, restaurant meals, petrol, haircuts, etc. Even though many of these goods may be produced in Big-Land their distribution and sale creates jobs in Small-Land. Workers who supply these goods earn income, which, of course, is part of Small-Land's GDP. We shall assume that Small-Land's GDP is currently equal to potential GDP, or $Y^*$.

Now suppose that households in Big-Land become uncertain about the future of Big-Land's economy and decide to increase their regular savings by reducing consumption expenditures. This could be due to political instability or external events such as war in a region important to Big-Land's economy. Whatever the cause, lower spending by consumers in Big-Land means that they will purchase fewer shoes produced in Small-Land. The immediate effect will be that shoe producers in Small-Land will find that sales are less than expected and they will start to accumulate stocks of unsold shoes. Initially they may add this unsold production to their inventories, but if low sales persist they will eventually cut back on production and make some of their workers redundant. As profits and incomes fall, Small-Land's GDP will start to decline and Small-Land will experience a recessionary gap, $Y^* > Y$.

Unfortunately this is not the end of the story. Small-Land's government may pay benefits to unemployed shoe workers, but these are likely to be well below what these workers were earning in wages and salaries. With lower incomes, unemployed shoe-workers will spend less on food, clothes, restaurant meals, petrol and haircuts, etc. As sales of these goods decline the firms supplying them will scale down their businesses and lay off some of their workers, creating a vicious circle with further declines in spending and more redundancies. In this scenario, the problem is not a lack of productive capacity – Small-Land's factories, shops and restaurants have not lost their ability to produce – but rather *insufficient spending* to support the normal level of production.

## John Maynard Keynes and the Keynesian revolution

The idea that a decline in *aggregate spending* may cause output to fall below its potential level was one of the key insights of *John Maynard Keynes*, a highly influential British economist of the first half of the twentieth century. The goal of this chapter is to present a theory, or model, of how recessions and expansions may arise from fluctuations in aggregate spending, along the lines first suggested by Keynes. This model, which we call the *basic Keynesian model*, is also known as the *Keynesian cross*, after the diagram that is used to illustrate the theory. In the body of the chapter we will emphasise a numerical and graphical approach to the basic Keynesian model.

### John Maynard Keynes

John Maynard Keynes (1883–1946), perhaps the most influential economist of the twentieth century, was a remarkable individual who combined a brilliant career as an economic theorist with an active life in diplomacy, finance, journalism and the arts. Keynes (pronounced 'canes') first came to prominence at the end of the First World War when he attended the Versailles peace conference as a representative of the British Treasury. He was appalled by the short-sightedness of the diplomats at the conference, particularly their insistence that the defeated Germans make huge compensatory payments (called *reparations*) to the victorious nations. In his widely read book written in 1919, *The Economic Consequences of the Peace,* Keynes argued that the reparations imposed on Germany were impossibly large, and that attempts to extract the payments would prevent Germany's economic recovery and perhaps lead to another war. Unfortunately for the world, he turned out to be right.

In the period between the two world wars, Keynes held a professorship at Cambridge, where his father had taught economics. Keynes' early writings had been on mathematics and logic, but after his experience in Versailles he began to work primarily on economics, producing several well-regarded books. He developed an imposing intellectual reputation, editing Great Britain's leading scholarly journal in economics, writing articles for newspapers and magazines, advising the government and playing a major role in the political and economic debates of the day. On the side, Keynes made fortunes both for himself and for King's College (a part of Cambridge University) by speculating in international currencies and commodities. He was also an active member of the Bloomsbury Group, a circle of leading artists, performers and writers that included E. M. Forster and Virginia Woolf. In 1925 Keynes married the glamorous Russian ballerina Lydia Lopokova and Keynes devoted significant energies to managing his wife's career and promoting the arts in Britain.

## The Keynesian revolution

Like other economists of the time, Keynes struggled to understand the Great Depression that gripped the world in the 1930s. His work on the problem led to the publication in 1936 of *The General Theory of Employment, Interest and Money*. In the *General Theory*, Keynes tried to explain how economies can remain at low levels of output and employment for protracted periods. He stressed a number of factors, most notably that *aggregate spending* may be too low to permit full employment during such periods. Keynes recommended increases in government spending as the most effective way to increase aggregate spending and restore full employment.

The *General Theory* is a difficult book, reflecting Keynes' own struggle to understand the complex causes of the Depression. In retrospect, some of the *General Theory's* arguments seem unclear or even inconsistent. Yet the book is full of fertile ideas, many of which had a worldwide impact and eventually led to what has been called the *Keynesian revolution*. Over the years, many economists have added to or modified Keynes' conception, to the point that Keynes himself, were he alive today, probably would not recognise much of what is now called 'Keynesian economics'. But the ideas that insufficient aggregate spending can lead to recession and that government policies can help to restore full employment are still critical to Keynesian theory.

In 1937 a heart attack curtailed Keynes' activities, but he remained an important figure on the world scene. In 1944 he led the British delegation to the international conference in Bretton Woods, New Hampshire, which established the key elements of the postwar international monetary and financial system, including the International Monetary Fund (IMF) and the World Bank. Keynes died in 1946.

We shall begin with a brief discussion of the key assumptions of the basic Keynesian model. We shall then turn to the important concept of total, or aggregate, *planned spending* in the economy. We shall show how, in the short run, the rate of aggregate spending helps to determine the level of output, which can be greater than or less than potential output. In other words, depending on the level of spending, the economy may develop an output gap. 'Too little' spending leads to a recessionary output gap, while 'too much' creates an expansionary output gap.

An implication of the basic Keynesian model is that government policies that affect the level of spending can be used to reduce or eliminate output gaps. Policies used in this way are called *stabilisation policies*. Keynes himself argued for the active use of fiscal policy – policy relating to government spending and taxes – to eliminate output gaps and stabilise the economy. In the latter part of this chapter we shall show why Keynes thought fiscal policy could help to stabilise the economy, and we shall discuss the usefulness of fiscal policy as a stabilisation tool.

The basic Keynesian model is not a complete or entirely realistic model of the economy, since it applies only to the relatively short period during which firms do not adjust their prices but instead meet the demand forthcoming at pre-set prices. Furthermore, by treating prices as fixed, the basic Keynesian model presented in this chapter does not address the determination of *inflation*. Nevertheless, this model is an essential building block of leading current theories of short-run economic fluctuations and stabilisation policies. In Chapters 26–28 we shall extend the basic Keynesian model to incorporate inflation and other important features of the economy.

## The Keynesian model's crucial assumption: firms meet demand at pre-set prices

The basic Keynesian model is built on a key assumption. This is that firms do not continuously change their prices as supply and demand conditions change; rather, over short periods, firms tend to keep their prices fixed and *meet the demand* that is forthcoming at those prices. As we will see, the assumption that firms vary their production in order to meet demand at pre-set prices implies that fluctuations in spending will have powerful effects on the nation's real GDP.

> **Key assumption of the basic Keynesian model:** In the short run, firms meet the demand for their products at pre-set prices.

Firms do not respond to every change in the demand for their products by changing their prices. Instead, they typically set a price for some period, then *meet the demand* at that price. By 'meeting the demand', we mean that firms produce *just enough to satisfy their customers* at the prices that have been set.

The assumption that, over short periods of time, firms meet the demand for their products at pre-set prices is generally realistic. Think of the stores where you shop. The price of a pair of jeans does not fluctuate from moment to moment according to the number of customers who enter the store or the latest news about the price of denim. Instead, the store posts a price and sells jeans to any customer who wants to buy at that price, at least until the store runs out of stock. Similarly, the corner pizza restaurant may leave the price of its large pizza unchanged for months or longer, allowing its pizza production to be determined by the number of customers who want to buy at the pre-set price.

Firms do not normally change their prices frequently because doing so would be costly. Economists refer to the costs of changing prices as **menu costs**. In the case of the pizza restaurant, the menu cost is literally just that – the cost of printing up a new menu when prices change. Similarly, the clothing store faces the cost of remarking all its merchandise if the manager changes the prices. But menu costs may also include other kinds of costs – for example, the cost of doing a market survey to determine what price to charge and the cost of informing customers about price changes. Economic naturalist 25.2 discusses how technology may affect menu costs in the future.

**menu costs** the costs of changing prices

Menu costs will not prevent firms from changing their prices indefinitely. As we saw in the case of Bill's ice cream parlour, too great an imbalance between demand and supply, as reflected by a difference between sales and potential output, will eventually lead firms to change their prices. If no one is buying jeans, for example, at some point the clothing store will mark down its prices. Or if the pizza restaurant becomes the local hot spot, with a queue of customers stretching out the door, eventually the manager will raise the price of a large pizza. Like many other economic decisions, the decision to change prices reflects a *cost–benefit* comparison: prices should be changed if the benefit of doing so – the fact that sales will be brought more nearly in line with the firm's normal production capacity – outweighs the menu costs associated with making the change. As we have stressed, the basic Keynesian model developed in this chapter ignores the fact that prices will eventually adjust, and should therefore be interpreted as applying to the short run.

## Economic naturalist 25.2 Will new technologies eliminate menu costs?

Thanks to new technologies, changing prices and informing customers about price changes is becoming increasingly less costly. Will technology eliminate menu costs as a factor in price-setting? Keynesian theory is based on the assumption that the costs of changing prices, which economists refer to as *menu costs*, are sufficiently large to prevent firms from adjusting prices immediately in response to changing market conditions. However, in many industries, new technologies have eliminated or greatly reduced the direct costs of changing prices. For example, the use of bar codes to identify individual products, together with scanner technologies, allows a grocery store manager to change prices with just a few keystrokes, without having to change the price label on each can of soup or loaf of bread. Airlines use sophisticated computer software to implement complex pricing strategies, under which two travellers on the same flight to London may pay very different fares, depending on whether they are business or vacation travellers and on how far in advance their flights were booked. Online retailers, such as booksellers, have the ability to vary their prices by type of customer and even by individual customer, while other Internet-based companies, such as eBay and Priceline, allow for negotiation over the price of each individual purchase. As described in Economic naturalist 25.1, the Coca-Cola Company experimented with a vending machine that automatically varied the price of a soft drink according to the outdoor temperature, charging more when the weather is hot.

Will these reductions in the direct costs of changing prices make the Keynesian theory, which assumes that firms meet demand at pre-set prices, less relevant to the real world? This is certainly a possibility that macroeconomists must take into account. However, it is unlikely that new technologies will completely eliminate the costs of changing prices any time soon. Gathering the information about market conditions needed to set the profit-maximising price – including the prices charged by competitors, the costs of producing the good or service and the likely demand for the product – will remain costly for firms. Another cost of changing prices is the use of the valuable managerial time and attention needed to make informed pricing decisions. A more subtle cost of changing prices – particularly raising prices – is that doing so may lead regular customers to rethink their choice of suppliers and decide to search for a better deal elsewhere.

## Planned aggregate expenditure

In the Keynesian theory discussed in this chapter, output at each point in time is determined by the amount that people throughout the economy want to spend – what we shall refer to as **planned aggregate expenditure** (PAE). Specifically, planned aggregate expenditure is *total planned spending on final goods and services*.

**planned aggregate expenditure** (PAE) total planned spending on final goods and services

The four components of spending on final goods and services were introduced in Chapter 18:

1. *Consumer expenditure*, or simply *consumption* ($C$), is spending by households on final goods and services. Examples of consumer expenditure are spending on food, clothes and entertainment and on consumer durable goods such as cars, DVD players and furniture.
2. *Investment* ($I$) is spending by firms on new capital goods, such as office buildings, factories and equipment. Spending on new houses and apartment buildings (residential investment) and increases in inventories (inventory investment) are also included in investment.
3. *Government purchases* ($G$) is spending by governments (national and local) on goods and services. Examples of government purchases include spending on new roads, schools and hospitals, military hardware, the services of government employees, such as soldiers, police and government office workers and the salaries paid to politicians. Recall from Chapter 18 that *transfer payments* – such as social security benefits and unemployment insurance – and interest on the government debt are *not* included in government purchases. Transfer payments and interest contribute to aggregate expenditure only at the point when they are spent by their recipients (for example, when a recipient of unemployment benefits uses the funds to buy food, clothing or other consumption goods).
4. *Net exports* ($NX$) equals exports minus imports. Exports are sales of domestically produced goods and services to foreigners; imports are purchases by domestic residents of goods and services produced abroad. Net exports represents the *net demand for domestic goods by foreigners*.

Together these four types of spending – by households, firms, the government and the rest of the world – sum to total, or aggregate, spending.

### Planned spending versus actual spending

In the Keynesian model, output is determined by planned aggregate expenditure, or 'planned spending', for short. Could *planned* spending ever differ from *actual* spending? The answer is yes. The most important case is that of a firm that sells either less or more of its product than expected. As was noted in Chapter 18, additions to the stocks of goods sitting in a firm's warehouse are treated in official government statistics as *inventory investment* by the firm. In effect, government statisticians assume that the firm buys its unsold output from itself; they then count those purchases as part of the firm's investment spending.[1]

Suppose, then, that a firm's actual sales are *less* than expected, so that part of what it had planned to sell remains in the warehouse. In this case, the firm's actual investment, including the unexpected increases in its inventory, is greater than its planned investment, which did not include the added inventory. Suppose we agree to let $I^P$ equal the firm's planned investment, including planned inventory investment. A firm that sells less of its output than planned, and therefore adds more to its inventory than planned, will find that its actual investment (including unplanned inventory investment) exceeds its planned investment, so that $I > I^P$.

[1] For the purpose of measuring GDP, treating unsold output as being purchased by its producer has the advantage of ensuring that actual production and actual expenditure are equal.

What about a firm that sells *more* of its output than expected? In that case, the firm will add less to its inventory than it planned, so actual investment will be less than planned investment, or $I < I^P$. Example 25.1 gives a numerical illustration.

### Example 25.1 Actual and planned investment

The Fly-by-Night Kite Company produces €5,000,000 worth of kites during the year. It expects sales of €4,800,000 for the year, leaving €200,000 worth of kites to be stored in the warehouse for future sale. During the year, Fly-by-Night adds €1,000,000 in new production equipment as part of an expansion plan. Find Fly-by-Night's actual investment $I$ and its planned investment $I^P$ if actual kite sales turn out to be €4,600,000. What if they are €4,800,000? What if they are €5,000,000?

Fly-by-Night's planned investment $I^P$ equals its purchases of new production equipment (€1,000,000) plus its planned additions to inventory (€200,000), for a total of €1,200,000 in planned investment. The company's planned investment does not depend on how much it actually sells.

If Fly-by-Night sells only €4,600,000 worth of kites, it will add €400,000 in kites to its inventory instead of the €200,000 worth originally planned. In this case, actual investment equals the €1,000,000 in new equipment plus the €400,000 in inventory investment, so $I = €1,400,000$. We see that when the firm sells less output than planned, actual investment exceeds planned investment ($I > I^P$).

If Fly-by-Night has €4,800,000 in sales, then it will add €200,000 in kites to inventory, just as planned. In this case, actual and planned investment are the same:

$$I = I^P = €1,200,000$$

Finally, if Fly-by-Night sells €5,000,000 worth of kites, it will have no output to add to inventory. Its inventory investment will be zero, and its total actual investment (including the new equipment) will equal €1,000,000, which is less than its planned investment of €1,200,000 ($I < I^P$).

Because firms that are meeting the demand for their product or service at pre-set prices cannot control how much they sell, their actual investment (including inventory investment) may well differ from their planned investment. However, for households, the government and foreign purchasers, we may reasonably assume that actual spending and planned spending are the same. Thus, from now on we will assume that, for consumption, government purchases and net exports, *actual spending equals planned spending*.

With these assumptions, we can define planned aggregate expenditure by the following equation:

$$PAE = C + I^P + G + NX \qquad (25.1)$$

Equation (25.1) says that planned aggregate expenditure is the sum of planned spending by households, firms, governments and foreigners. We use a superscript $p$ to distinguish planned investment spending by firms, $I^P$, from actual investment spending, $I$. However, because planned spending equals actual spending for households, the government, and foreigners, we do not need to use superscripts for consumption, government purchases or net exports.

## Consumer spending and the economy

The largest component of planned aggregate expenditure – nearly two-thirds of total spending – is consumption spending, denoted $C$. As already mentioned, consumer spending includes household purchases of goods, such as groceries and clothing; services, such as health care, concerts and legal fees; and consumer durables, such as cars, furniture and home computers. Thus consumers' willingness to spend affects sales and profitability in a wide range of industries. (Households' purchases of new homes are usually classified as investment, rather than consumption; but home purchases represent another channel through which household decisions affect total spending.)

What determines how much people plan to spend on consumer goods and services in a given period? While many factors are relevant, a particularly important determinant of the amount people plan to consume is their after-tax, or *disposable*, income. All else being equal, households and individuals with higher disposable incomes will consume more than those with lower disposable incomes. Keynes himself stressed the importance of disposable income in determining household consumption decisions, claiming a 'psychological law' that people would tie their spending closely to their incomes.

Recall from Chapter 22 that the disposable income of the private sector is the total production of the economy, $Y$, less net taxes (taxes minus transfers), or $T$. So we can assume that consumption spending ($C$) increases as disposable income ($Y - T$) increases. As already mentioned, other factors may also affect consumption, such as the real interest rate, also discussed in Chapter 22. For now we shall ignore those other factors, returning to some of them later.

A general equation that captures the link between consumption and the private sector's disposable income is

$$C = \bar{C} + c(Y - T) \qquad (25.2)$$

**consumption function** the relationship between consumption spending and its determinants, in particular disposable (after-tax) income

This equation, which we shall dissect in a moment, is known as the **consumption function**. It relates consumption spending to its determinants, in particular to disposable (after-tax) income.

Let us look at the consumption function, Eq. (25.2), more carefully. The right-hand side of Eq. (25.2) contains two terms, $\bar{C}$ and $c(Y - T)$. The first term, $\bar{C}$, is a constant term in the equation that is intended to capture factors *other than disposable income* that affect consumption. For example, suppose consumers were to become more optimistic about the future, so that they desire to consume more and save less at any given level of their current disposable incomes. An increase in desired consumption at any given level of disposable income would be represented in the consumption function as an increase in the term $\bar{C}$.

We can imagine other factors that may affect the term $\bar{C}$ in the consumption function. Suppose, for example, that there is a boom in the stock market or a sharp increase in home prices, making consumers feel wealthier and hence more inclined to spend, for a given level of current disposable income. This effect could be captured by assuming that $\bar{C}$ increases. Likewise, a fall in home prices or share prices that made consumers feel poorer and less inclined to spend would be represented by a decrease in $\bar{C}$. Economists refer to the effect of changes in asset prices on households' wealth and hence their consumption spending as the **wealth effect** of changes in asset prices.

**wealth effect** the tendency of changes in asset prices to affect households' wealth and thus their spending on consumption goods

**marginal propensity to consume** (MPC), or, $c$, the amount by which consumption rises when disposable income rises by one euro. We assume that $0 < c < 1$

The second term on the right-hand side of Eq. (25.2), $c(Y - T)$, reflects the effect of disposable income, $Y - T$, on consumption. The parameter $c$, a fixed number, is called the *marginal propensity to consume*. The **marginal propensity to consume** (MPC) is the amount by which consumption rises when current disposable income rises by one euro. Presumably, if people receive an extra euro of income, they will consume part of the euro and save the rest. In other words, their consumption will increase, but by less than the full euro of extra income. Thus it is realistic to assume that the marginal propensity to consume is greater than 0 (an increase in income leads to an increase in consumption) but less than 1 (the increase in consumption will be less than the full increase in income). Mathematically, we can summarise these assumptions as $0 < c < 1$.

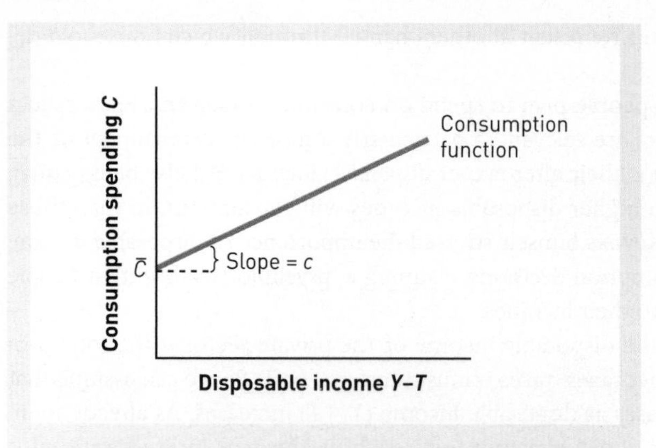


Figure 25.6 **A Consumption Function.** The consumption function relates households' consumption spending, *C*, to disposable income, *Y* – *T*. The vertical intercept of this consumption function is the exogenous component of consumption, $\bar{C}$, and the slope of the line equals the marginal propensity to consume, *c*.

Figure 25.6 shows a hypothetical consumption function, with consumption spending (*C*) on the vertical axis and disposable income (*Y* – *T*) on the horizontal axis. The intercept of the consumption function on the vertical axis equals exogenous consumption $\bar{C}$, and the slope of the consumption function equals the marginal propensity to consume, *c*.

To see how this consumption function fits reality, compare Fig. 25.6 to Fig. 25.7, which shows the relationship between aggregate real consumption expenditures and real disposable income in the United Kingdom for the period 1960–2003. Figure 25.7, a type of diagram called a *scatter plot*, shows aggregate real consumption on the vertical axis and aggregate real disposable income on the horizontal axis. Each point on the graph corresponds to a year between 1960 and 2003. The position of each point is determined by the combination of consumption and disposable income associated with that year. As you can see, there is indeed a close relationship between aggregate consumption and disposable income: higher disposable income implies higher consumption.

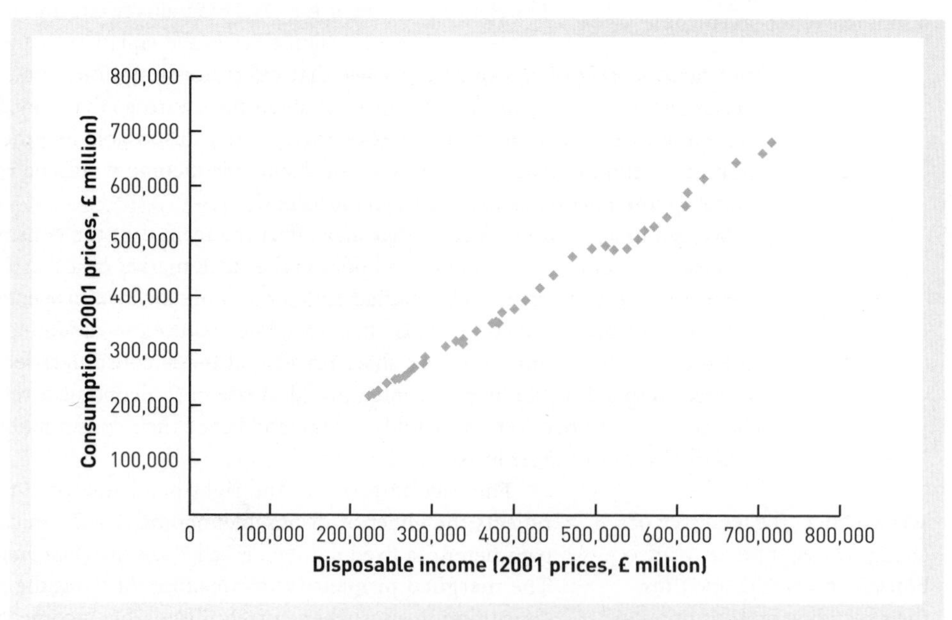


Figure 25.7 **The UK Consumption Function, 1960–2003.** Each point represents a combination of real consumption and real disposable income for a specific year between 1960 and 2003. Note the strong positive correlation between income and consumption.

## Planned aggregate expenditure and output

Thinking back to Small-Land, recall that an important element of the story involved the links among production, income and spending. As Small-Land's shoe factories reduced production, the incomes of factory workers fell. Reduced incomes, in turn, forced workers to curtail their spending – which led to still lower production and further reductions in income. This vicious circle led the economy further and further into recession.

The logic of the Small-Land story has two key elements: (1) declines in production (which imply declines in the income received by producers) lead to reduced spending; and (2) reductions in spending lead to declines in production and income. In this section we look at the first part of the story, the effects of production and income on *spending*. We return later in this chapter to the effects of spending on production and income.

Why do changes in production and income affect planned aggregate spending? The consumption function, which relates consumption to disposable income, is the basic source of this relationship. Because consumption spending $C$ is a large part of planned aggregate spending, and because consumption depends on output $Y$, aggregate spending as a whole depends on output. Example 25.2 illustrates this relationship numerically.

### **Example 25.2** Linking planned aggregate expenditure to output

In a particular economy, the consumption function is

$$C = 620 + 0.8(Y - T)$$

so that the intercept term in the consumption function, $\bar{C}$, equals 620, and the marginal propensity to consume, $c$, equals = 0.8. Also, suppose we are given planned investment spending $I^P = 220$, government purchases $G = 300$, net exports $NX = 20$ and taxes $T = 250$.

Write a numerical equation linking planned aggregate expenditure ($PAE$) to output $Y$. How does planned spending change when output and hence income change?

Recall the definition of planned aggregate expenditure, Eq. (25.1):

$$PAE = C + I^P + G + NX$$

To find a numerical equation for planned aggregate expenditure, we need to find numerical expressions for each of its four components. The first component of spending, consumption, is defined by the consumption function, $C = 620 + 0.8(Y - T)$. Since taxes $T = 250$, we can substitute for $T$ to write the consumption function as $C = 620 + 0.8(Y - 250)$. Now plug this expression for $C$ into the definition of planned aggregate expenditure above to get

$$PAE = [620 + 0.8(Y - 250)] + I^P + G + NX$$

where we have just replaced $C$ by its value as determined by the consumption function. Similarly, we can substitute the given numerical values of planned investment $I^P$, government purchases G and net exports $NX$ into the definition of planned aggregate expenditure to get

$$PAE = [620 + 0.8(Y - 250)] + 220 + 300 + 20$$

To simplify this equation, first note that $0.8(Y - 250) = 0.8Y - 200$, then add all the terms that don't depend on output $Y$. The result is:

$$\begin{aligned} PAE &= (620 - 200 + 220 + 300 + 20) + 0.8Y \\ &= 960 + 0.8Y \end{aligned}$$

The final expression shows the relationship between planned aggregate expenditure and output in this numerical example. Note that, according to this equation, a €1 increase in $Y$ leads to an increase in $PAE$ of (0.8)(€1), or 80 cents. The reason for this is that the marginal propensity to consume, $c$, in this example is 0.8. Hence a €1 increase in income raises consumption spending by 80 cents. Since consumption is a component of total planned spending, total spending rises by 80 cents as well.

**autonomous expenditure** the portion of planned aggregate expenditure that is independent of output

The solution to Example 25.2 illustrates a general point: PAE can be divided into two parts, a part that *depends* on output ($Y$) and a part that is *independent* of output. The portion of PAE that is independent of output is called **autonomous expenditure**. In Example 25.2, autonomous expen-

**induced expenditure** the portion of planned aggregate expenditure that depends on output $Y$

diture is the constant term in the equation for PAE, or 960. This portion of planned spending, being a fixed number, does not vary when output varies. By contrast, the portion of PAE that depends on output ($Y$) is called **induced expenditure**. In Example 25.2, induced expenditure equals $0.8Y$, the second term in the expression for PAE. Note that the numerical value of induced expenditure depends, by definition, on the numerical value taken by output. Autonomous expenditure and induced expenditure together equal PAE.

## RECAP Planned aggregate expenditure

Planned aggregate expenditure (*PAE*) is total planned spending on final goods and services. The four components of planned spending are consumer expenditure ($C$), planned investment ($I^P$), government purchases ($G$) and net exports ($NX$). Planned investment differs from actual investment when firms' sales are different from what they expected, so that additions to inventory (a component of investment) are different from what firms anticipated.

The largest component of aggregate expenditure is *consumer expenditure*, or simply consumption. Consumption depends on disposable, or after-tax, income, according to a relationship known as the *consumption function*, stated algebraically as $C = \bar{C} + c(Y - T)$.

The constant term in the consumption function, $\bar{C}$, captures factors *other than disposable income* that affect consumer spending. For example, an increase in housing or stock prices that makes households wealthier and thus more willing to spend – an effect called the *wealth effect* – could be captured by an increase in $\bar{C}$. The slope of the consumption function equals the *marginal propensity to consume*, c, where $0 < c < 1$. This is the amount by which consumption rises when disposable income rises by one euro.

Increases in output $Y$, which imply equal increases in income, cause consumption to rise. As consumption is part of PAE, planned spending depends on output as well. The portion of PAE that depends on output is called *induced expenditure*. The portion of PAE that is independent of output is called *autonomous expenditure*.

# Short-run equilibrium output

Now that we have defined PAE and seen how it is related to output, the next task is to see how *output* itself is determined. Recall the assumption of the basic Keynesian model: in the short run, producers leave prices at pre-set levels and simply meet the demand that is forthcoming at those prices. In other words, during the short-run period in which prices are pre-set, firms produce an amount that is equal to PAE. Accordingly, we define **short-run equilibrium output** as the level of output at which output $Y$ equals *PAE*:

**short-run equilibrium output** the level of output at which output $Y$ equals planned aggregate expenditure *PAE*; short-run equilibrium output is the level of output that prevails during the period in which prices are predetermined

$$Y = PAE \tag{25.3}$$

We can now find the short-run equilibrium output for the economy described in Example 25.2. In that economy *PAE* is given by:

$$PAE = 960 + 0.8Y$$

Using Eq. (25.3) to equate $Y$ and *PAE* gives

$$Y = 960 + 0.8Y$$

or

$$Y(1 - 0.8) = 960$$

Dividing both sides by 0.2 (1 – 0.8) gives the value for short-run equilibrium output:

$$Y = 960/0.2 = 4{,}800$$

Hence, in the economy described by Example 25.2, short-run equilibrium output is 4,800.

Because the determination of short-run equilibrium output is important to the subject matter of this chapter and Chapters 26–28, we shall develop two general methods which can be used to solve for the equilibrium value of $Y$. Example 25.3 presents an algebraic approach while Example 25.4 presents a more intuitive tabular, or numeric, method.

### Example 25.3 Solving short-run equilibrium output (the algebraic approach)

We have seen that the economy reaches its short-run equilibrium output when *actual* output $Y$ equals *planned* aggregate expenditure $PAE$:

$$Y = PAE$$

Equation (25.1) says that planned aggregate expenditure is the sum of four components – consumption ($C$), planned investment ($I^P$), government purchases ($G$) and net exports ($NX$):

$$PAE = C + I^P + G + NX$$

The components of $PAE$ can be sub-divided into two types, *induced* (depends on output) and *autonomous* (independent of output). Consumption spending is determined by the consumption function, Eq. (25.2), and consists of both induced and autonomous components:

$$C = \bar{C} + c(Y - T)$$

The first term $\bar{C}$ captures factors other than income that affect consumption and is autonomous. Substituting the consumption function into the definition of $PAE$ gives

$$\begin{aligned} PAE &= [\bar{C} + c(Y - T)] + I^P + G + NX \\ &= [\bar{C} - cT + I^P + G + NX] + cY \end{aligned}$$

We have assumed that tax revenues ($T$), planned investment ($I^P$), government purchases ($G$) and net exports ($NX$) are all autonomous (do not depend on $Y$). Using a over-bar to denote a given value of an autonomous variable we can define *total autonomous expenditures*, denoted by $\bar{A}$, as

$$\bar{A} = \bar{C} - c\bar{T} + \bar{I} + \bar{G} + \overline{NX}$$

Which is the first term in the equation for $PAE$. Hence:

$$PAE = \bar{A} + cY$$

This equation simply divides $PAE$ into an autonomous component, $\bar{A}$, and an induced component, $cY$. As equilibrium output is the level of output at which $Y = PAE$ the economy will reach its short-run equilibrium when

$$Y = \bar{A} + cY$$

or

$$Y(1 - c) = \bar{A}$$

Dividing both sides by $(1 - c)$ gives

$$Y = \left(\frac{1}{1 - c}\right)\bar{A} \tag{25.4}$$

Equation (25.4) gives short-run equilibrium output in terms of total autonomous expenditures $\bar{A}$ and the marginal propensity to consume, $c$. For given values of total autonomous expenditures and the marginal propensity to consume, Eq. (25.4) can be used to determine the short-run equilibrium value of the economy's output. In Example 25.2, $\bar{C} = 620$, $\bar{I} = 220$, $\bar{G} = 300$, $\overline{NX} = 20$, $\bar{T} = 250$ and $c = 0.8$ Hence:

$$\bar{A} = [620 - 200 + 220 + 300 + 20] = 960$$

and

$$Y = \left(\frac{1}{1-0.8}\right) 960 = 4{,}800$$

Which is the same answer as before.

**Exercise 25.1** Suppose the economy can be described as follows: consumption function is $C = 860 + 0.6(Y - T)$, $I^P = 900$, $G = 800$, $NX = 200$ and $T = 600$. Using the method described in Example 25.3, find short-run equilibrium output in this economy.

For those who may find algebra difficult, Example 25.4 illustrates an alternative and perhaps more intuitive method to solve for short-run equilibrium output.

### Example 25.4 Solving short-run equilibrium output (the numeric approach)

We can find the short-run equilibrium for the economy described in Example 25.2 using Table 25.1. Column (1) of Table 25.1 gives some possible values for short-run equilibrium output. To find the correct value, we must compare each to the value of *PAE* at that output level. Column (2) shows the value of *PAE* corresponding to the values of short-run equilibrium output in column (1). Recall that in Example 25.2, planned spending is determined by the equation $PAE = 960 + 0.8Y$.

| Output *Y* (1) | Planned aggregate expenditure *PAE* = 960 + 0.8*Y* (2) | *Y* – *PAE* (3) | *Y* = *PAE*? (4) |
|---|---|---|---|
| 4,000 | 4,160 | –160 | No |
| 4,200 | 4,320 | –120 | No |
| 4,400 | 4,480 | –80 | No |
| 4,600 | 4,640 | –40 | No |
| 4,800 | 4,800 | 0 | Yes |
| 5,000 | 4,960 | 40 | No |
| 5,200 | 5,120 | 80 | No |

**Table 25.1** Numerical Determination of Short-Run Equilibrium Output

Because consumption rises with output, total planned spending (which includes consumption) rises also. But if you compare columns (1) and (2), you will see that when output rises by 200, planned spending rises by only 160. That is because the *marginal propensity to consume* (MPC) in this economy is 0.8, so that each euro in added income raises consumption and planned spending by 80 cents.

Again, short-run equilibrium output is the level of output at which $Y = PAE$ – or, equivalently, $Y - PAE$, = 0. Looking at Table 25.1, we can see there is only one level of output that satisfies that condition, $Y = 4{,}800$. At that level, output and *PAE* are precisely equal, so that producers are just meeting the demand for their goods and services.

In this economy, what would happen if output differed from its equilibrium value of 4,800? Suppose, for example, that output were 4,000. Looking at the column (2) of Table 25.1, you can see that when output is 4,000, PAE equals 960 + 0.8(4,000), or 4,160. Thus if output is 4,000, firms are not producing enough to meet the demand. They will find that as sales exceed the amounts they are producing, their inventories of finished goods are being depleted by 160 per year, and that actual investment (including inventory investment) is less than planned investment. Under the assumption that firms are committed to meeting their customers' demand, firms will respond by expanding their production.

Would expanding production to 4,160, the level of planned spending firms faced when output was 4,000, be enough? The answer is no, because of *induced expenditure*. That is, as firms expand their output, aggregate income (wages and profits) rises with it, which in turn leads to higher levels of consumption. Indeed, if output expands to 4,160, planned spending will increase as well, to 960 + 0.8(4,160), or 4,288. So an output level of 4,160 will still be insufficient to meet demand. As Table 25.1 shows, output will not be sufficient to meet planned aggregate expenditure until it expands to its short-run equilibrium value of 4,800.

What if output were initially greater than its equilibrium value – say, 5,000? From Table 25.1 we can see that when output equals 5,000, planned spending equals only 4,960 – less than what firms are producing. So at an output level of 5,000, firms will not sell all they produce, and they will find that their merchandise is piling up on store shelves and in warehouses (actual investment, including inventory investment, is greater than planned investment). In response, firms will cut their production runs. As Table 25.1 shows, they will have to reduce production to its equilibrium value of 4,800 before output just matches planned spending.

**Exercise 25.2** Construct a table like Table 25.1 for the economy described in Exercise 25.1 What is short-run equilibrium output in this economy? (**Hint:** Try using values for output above 5,000.)

We have used two approaches to solve for short-run equilibrium output – the algebraic model in Example 25.3 and the numeric model in Example 25.4. Both give the same answer for the economy described in Example 25.2, $Y = 4{,}800$. Figure 25.8 illustrates this solution graphically. Output $Y$ is plotted on the horizontal axis and planned aggregate expenditure $PAE$ on the vertical axis. The figure contains two lines, one of which is a 45° line extending from the origin. In general, a 45° line from the origin includes the points at which the variable on the vertical axis equals the variable on the horizontal axis. Hence, in this case, the 45° line represents the equation $Y = PAE$. Since short-run equilibrium output must satisfy the equation $Y = PAE$, the combination of output and spending that satisfies this condition must lie somewhere on the 45° line in Fig. 25.8.

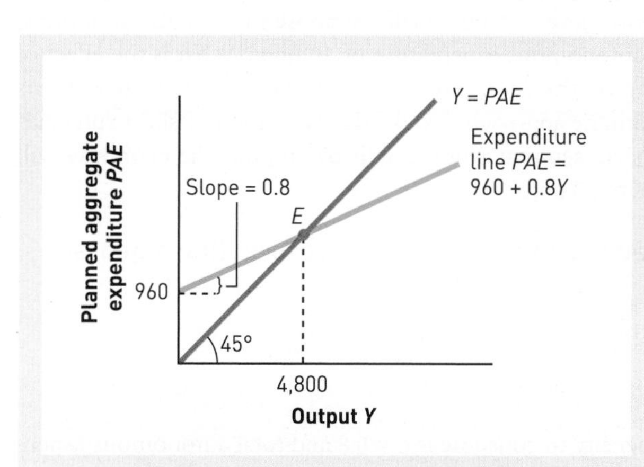


**Figure 25.8 Determination of Short-Run Equilibrium Output (Keynesian Cross).** The 45° line represents the short-run equilibrium condition $Y = PAE$. The line $PAE = 960 + 0.8Y$, referred to as the 'expenditure line', shows the relationship of $PAE$ to output. Short-run equilibrium output (4,800) is determined at the intersection of the two lines, point $E$. This type of diagram is known as a 'Keynesian cross'.

The second line in Fig. 25.8, less steep than the 45° line, shows the relationship between planned aggregate expenditure $PAE$ and output $Y$. Because it summarises how planned spending depends on output, we shall call this line the *expenditure line*. In this example, we know that the relationship between $PAE$ and output (the equation for the expenditure line) is

$$PAE = 960 + 0.8Y$$

According to this equation, when $Y = 0$, the value of $PAE$ is 960. Thus 960 is the intercept of the expenditure line, as shown in Fig. 25.8. Notice that *the intercept of the expenditure line equals autonomous expenditure*, a result that will always hold. The slope of the line relating aggregate demand to output is 0.8, the value of the coefficient of output in the equation $PAE = 960 + 0.8Y$. Where does the number 0.8 come from? (**Hint:** What determines by how much aggregate spending increases when output rises by a euro?)

Only one point in Figure 25.8 is consistent with *both* the definition of short-run equilibrium output, $Y = PAE$, and the given relationship between planned spending and output, $PAE = 960 + 0.8Y$. That point is the intersection of the two lines, point *E*. At point *E*, short-run equilibrium output equals 4,800, which is the same value that we obtained in Examples 25.3 and 25.4. At points to the right of *E*, output exceeds planned aggregate expenditure. Hence, to the right of point *E*, firms will be producing more than they can sell, which will lead them to reduce their rate of production. By contrast, to the left of point *E*, planned aggregate spending exceeds output. In that region, firms will not be producing enough to meet demand, and they will tend to increase their production. Only at point *E*, where output equals 4,800, will firms be producing enough to just satisfy planned spending on goods and services.

The diagram in Fig. 25.8 is often called the *Keynesian cross*, after its characteristic shape. The Keynesian cross shows graphically how short-run equilibrium output is determined in a world in which producers meet demand at predetermined prices.

## Planned spending and the output gap

We are now ready to use the basic Keynesian model to show how insufficient spending can lead to a recession. To illustrate the effects of spending changes on output, we shall continue to work with the economy introduced in Example 25.2. We have shown that in this economy, short-run equilibrium output equals 4,800. Let us now make the additional assumption that potential output in this economy also equals 4,800, or $Y^* = 4{,}800$, so that initially there is no output gap. Starting from this position of full employment, suppose that consumers become more pessimistic about the future, so that they begin to spend less at every level of current disposable income. We can capture this change by assuming that $\bar{C}$, the constant term in the consumption function, falls to a lower level. To be specific, suppose that $\bar{C}$ falls by 10 units, which in turn implies a decline in autonomous expenditure of 10 units. What is the effect of this reduction in planned spending on the economy? Examples 25.5 and 25.6 answer this question using the algebraic and numeric approaches to the determination of short-run equilibrium output. In each case, we shall see that when $\bar{C}$ falls by 10 units the economy will experience a recessionary gap equal to 50 units.

### **Example 25.5** A fall in planned spending leads to a recession (the algebraic approach)

From Eq. (25.4) we know that short-run equilibrium output is given by:

$$Y = \left(\frac{1}{1-c}\right)\bar{A}$$

In Example 25.2 the marginal propensity to consume is $c = 0.8$ and total autonomous expenditures are

$$\begin{aligned}\bar{A} &= \bar{C} - c\bar{T} + \bar{I} + \bar{G} + \overline{NX}\\ &= 620 - 200 + 220 + 300 + 20\\ &= 960\end{aligned}$$

which gives an equilibrium value for *Y* equal to 4,800 ($960/0.2 = 4{,}800$). If the autonomous component of consumption $\bar{C}$ falls by 10 units then the new value for total autonomous expenditure will be

$$\begin{aligned}\bar{A} &= \bar{C} - c\bar{T} + \bar{I} + \bar{G} + \overline{NX}\\ &= 610 - 200 + 220 + 300 + 20\\ &= 950\end{aligned}$$

and the new value for short-run equilibrium output is

$$Y = \left(\frac{1}{1-0.8}\right)950 = 4{,}750$$

Hence, a 10 unit fall in autonomous expenditure results in a 50 unit unit fall in equilibrium output (4,800 – 4,750). The recessionary gap, $Y^* - Y$, is 50-units.

### Example 25.6 A fall in planned spending leads to a recession (the numeric approach)

Table 25.2 illustrates the numeric approach which is in the same form as Table 25.1. The key difference is that in Table 25.2 planned aggregate expenditure is given by $PAE = 950 + 0.8Y$, rather than by $PAE = 960 + 0.8Y$, as in Table 25.1.

| Output *Y* (1) | Planned aggregate expenditure $PAE = 950 + 0.8Y$ (2) | *Y* – *PAE* (3) | *Y* = *PAE*? (4) |
|---|---|---|---|
| 4,600 | 4,630 | −30 | No |
| 4,650 | 4,670 | −20 | No |
| 4,700 | 4,710 | −10 | No |
| 4,750 | 4,750 | 0 | Yes |
| 4,800 | 4,790 | 10 | No |
| 4,850 | 4,830 | 20 | No |
| 4,900 | 4,870 | 30 | No |
| 4,950 | 4,910 | 40 | No |
| 5,000 | 4,950 | 50 | No |

**Table 25.2** Determination of Short-Run Equilibrium Output after a Fall in Spending

As in Table 25.1, column (1) shows alternative possible values of output *Y*, and column (2) shows the levels of planned aggregate expenditure *PAE* implied by each value of output in column (1). Notice that 4,800, the value of short-run equilibrium output found in Table 25.1, is no longer an equilibrium; when output is 4,800, planned spending is 4,790, so output and planned spending are not equal. As Table 25.2 shows, following the decline in planned aggregate expenditure, short-run equilibrium output is 4,750, the only value of output for which $Y = PAE$. Thus a drop of 10 units in autonomous expenditure has led to a 50 unit decline in short-run equilibrium output. If full-employment output is 4,800, then the recessionary gap shown in Fig. 25.9 is 4,800 – 4,750 = 50 units.

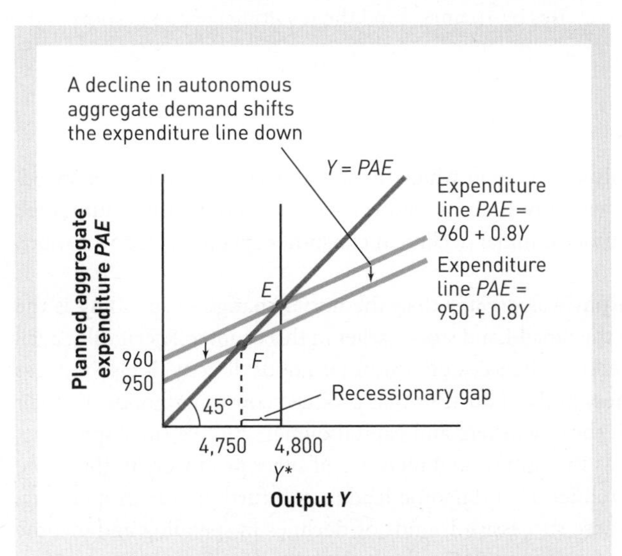


**Figure 25.9 A Decline in Planned Spending Leads to a Recession.** A decline in consumers' willingness to spend at any current level of disposable income reduces planned automous expediture and shifts the expenditure line down. The short-run equilibrium point drops from *E* to *F*, reducing output and opening up a recessionary gap.

We can also illustrate the effects of the decline in consumer spending on the economy using the Keynesian cross diagram. Figure 25.9 shows the original short-run equilibrium point of the model (*E*), at the intersection of the 45° line, along which $Y = PAE$, and the original expenditure line, representing the equation $PAE = 960 + 0.8Y$. As before, the initial value of short-run equilibrium output is 4,800, which we have now assumed also corresponds to potential output $Y^*$. But what happens if $\bar{C}$ declines by 10, reducing autonomous expenditure by 10 as well?

Originally, autonomous expenditure in this economy was 960, so a decline of 10 units causes it to fall to 950. Instead of the economy's planned spending being described by the equation $PAE = 960 + 0.8Y$, as initially, it is now given by $PAE = 950 + 0.8Y$. What does this change imply for the graph in Fig. 25.9? Since the intercept of the expenditure line (equal to autonomous expenditure) has decreased from 960 to 950, the effect of the decline in consumer spending will be to shift the expenditure line down in parallel fashion, by 10 units. Figure 25.9 indicates this downward shift in the expenditure line. The new short-run equilibrium point is at point *F*, where the new, lower expenditure line intersects the 45° line.

Point *F* is to the left of the original equilibrium point *E*, so we can see that output and spending have fallen from their initial levels. Since output at point *F* is lower than potential output, 4,800, we see that the fall in consumer spending has resulted in a recessionary gap in the economy. More generally, starting from a situation of full employment (where output equals potential output), any decline in autonomous expenditure leads to a recession. Examples 25.5 and 25.6 show that a decline in autonomous expenditure, arising from a decreased willingness of consumers to spend, causes short-run equilibrium output to fall and opens up a recessionary gap. The same conclusion applies to declines in autonomous expenditure arising from other sources. Suppose, for example, that firms become disillusioned with new technologies and cut back their planned investment in new equipment. In terms of the model, this reluctance of firms to invest can be interpreted as a decline in planned investment spending $I^P$. Under our assumption that planned investment spending is autonomous and does not depend on output, planned investment is part of autonomous expenditure. So a decline in planned investment spending depresses autonomous expenditure and output, in precisely the same way that a decline in the autonomous part of consumption spending does. Similar conclusions apply to declines in other components of autonomous expenditure, such as government purchases and net exports, as we shall see in later applications.

**Exercise 25.3** Using the economy described in Exercise 25.1, assume that consumers become *more* confident about the future. As a result, $\bar{C}$ rises by 10 units. Find the resulting change in short-run equilibrium output.

## The multiplier

In Examples 25.5 and 25.6 we analysed a case in which the initial decline in consumer spending (as measured by the fall in $\bar{C}$) was only 10 units, and yet short-run equilibrium output fell by 50 units. Why did a relatively modest initial decline in consumer spending lead to a much larger fall in output?

The reason the impact on output was greater than the initial change in spending is the 'vicious circle' effect suggested by the Small-Land story earlier in this chapter. Specifically, a fall in consumer spending not only reduces the sales of consumer goods directly; it also reduces the incomes of workers and owners in the industries that produce consumer goods. As their incomes fall, these workers and capital owners reduce their spending, which reduces the output and incomes of *other* producers in the economy. These reductions in income lead to still further cuts in spending. Ultimately, these successive rounds of declines in spending and income may lead to a decrease in *PAE* and output that is significantly greater than the change in spending that started the process.

**income–expenditure multiplier** the effect of a 1 unit change in autonomous expenditure on short-run equilibrium output; for example, a multiplier of 5 means that a 10 unit decrease in autonomous expenditure reduces short-run equilibrium output by 50 units

The effect on short-run equilibrium output of a 1 unit change in autonomous expenditure is called the **income–expenditure multiplier**, or the *multiplier* for short. To find the value of the multiplier recall that Eq. (25.4) determines short-run equilibrium output as

$$Y = \left(\frac{1}{1-c}\right)\bar{A}$$

If the marginal propensity to consume $c = 0.8$ then $1/(1-c)$ equals $1/0.2$ or 5 and each unit change in total autonomous expenditures $\bar{A}$ results in a 5-unit change in $Y$. For example, if $\bar{A} = 1{,}000$ then equilibrium $Y = 5{,}000$. However, if $\bar{A}$ falls by 100 to 900 then equilibrium $Y$ declines by 500 to 4,500. Hence, for each unit change in $\bar{A}$, $Y$ changes by 5 units (500/100). More generally, as a 1 unit change in $\bar{A}$ leads to a change in $Y$ equal to $1/(1-c)$ it follows that the term $1/(1-c)$ is the *multiplier*. The idea that a change in spending may lead to a significantly larger change in short-run equilibrium output is a key feature of the basic Keynesian model. The Appendix to this chapter provides a more rigorous derivation of the multiplier.

As we shall see in Chapter 26, the size of the multiplier is important in determining the effectiveness of *fiscal policy* as a means to stabilise the economy. Hence, it is important to ask what determines the value of the multiplier? Clearly, the marginal propensity to consume (MPC) out of disposable income $c$ is crucial. If the MPC is large, then, as disposable income falls, people will reduce their spending sharply, and the multiplier effect will be large. Conversely, if the MPC is small, households will not reduce their expenditure by as much when income falls, and the multiplier will be smaller. For example, if $c = 0.8$ the multiplier is 5. However if $c = 0.6$ the multiplier is $1/0.4 = 2.5$. As shown in Example 25.7, the openness of the economy to international trade can also affect the value of the multiplier.

### **Example 25.7** The multiplier and imports

So far, we have assumed that expenditures on imports are autonomous (do not depend on $Y$). However, imports are part of *domestic expenditures* and may change as $Y$ changes. As incomes increase we would expect households to spend more on goods and services, including those produced in other economies. For example, in 2003 approximately 33 per cent of total GDP in the European Union was spent on imports, and in small countries such as Belgium and Ireland the percentage was much higher, at 75 per cent or more. Likewise, part of investment expenditures by firms and government purchases will be spent on imported goods. Note that this is why we have included *net* exports (exports minus imports) in our definition of total planned aggregate expenditures:

$$PAE = C + I^P + G + NX$$

For example, if a Belgian household buys a camera manufactured in Japan, the camera is part of Japan's GDP not Belgium's. However, as the expenditure is included in domestic consumption, $C$, and net exports, $NX$, it cancels out in our definition of $PAE$. If the camera costs €500 its purchase increases $C$ by €500 and reduces $NX$ by €500, leaving total expenditure on *domestically* produced goods unaffected. As expenditures on consumption, investment and government purchases all include imports, it seems unrealistic to assume that imports are totally autonomous. Suppose we were to relax this assumption and assume that imports vary with $Y$. We shall see that for a given value of the marginal propensity to consume, this reduces the value of the multiplier.

The last term in the equation for $PAE$ denotes net exports, or exports less imports. Denoting exports as $EX$ and imports as $IM$ we can define net exports as

$$NX = EX - IM$$

and $PAE$ as

$$PAE = C + I^P + G + EX - IM$$

The consumption function

$$C = \bar{C} + c(Y - T)$$

implies that consumption, which includes expenditure on imports, is an induced expenditure. To treat imports as an induced expenditure we introduce an additional equation, which we shall call the **import function**:

**import function** the relationship between imports and income

**marginal propensity to import** the proportion of a change in income which is spent on imports

$$IM = mY$$

The parameter $m$ is a constant greater than zero but less than one ($0 < m < 1$) and is known as the **marginal propensity to import**. For example, if $m = 0.4$ a €100 increase in $Y$ leads to (or induces) a €40 increase in expenditure on imports. Likewise, if $Y$ falls by €100, expenditure on imports will fall by €40.

Using the consumption and import functions to substitute for $C$ and $IM$ in the equation for $PAE$ gives

$$\begin{aligned} PAE &= [\bar{C} + c(Y - T)] + I^P + G + EX - mY \\ &= [\bar{C} - cT + I^P + G + EX] + (c - m)Y \end{aligned}$$

Treating the first term on the right-hand side as total autonomous expenditures, $\bar{A}$, we get

$$PAE = \bar{A} + (c - m)Y$$

As equilibrium output is the level at which $Y = PAE$ the economy will reach its short-run equilibrium when

$$Y = \bar{A} + (c - m)Y$$

or

$$Y(1 - c + m) = \bar{A}$$

Dividing both sides by $(1 - c + m)$ gives equilibrium $Y$ as

$$Y = \left(\frac{1}{1 - c + m}\right)\bar{A} \qquad (25.5)$$

The multiplier is the term $1/(1 - c + m)$ which is smaller than the previous value $1/(1 - c)$. For example if $c = 0.8$ and $m = 0.2$, the multiplier is $1/0.4 = 2.5$ as compared with 5 when imports are autonomous ($m = 0$). To explain why treating imports as an induced expenditure reduces the value of the multiplier, suppose that autonomous expenditures fall by 10 units leading to an 8 unit fall in consumption. We have seen that this creates a 'vicious circle' leading to further declines in consumption and, if $m = 0$ and the multiplier is 5, an eventual fall in $Y$ of 50 units. In this case the entire fall in consumption falls on domestic production. However, if $m = 0.2$ the initial decline in consumption can be broken down into 6 units on domestic production and 2 units on imports, and as imports are not part of $Y$ the effect on domestic production is smaller and each round of the 'vicious circle' leads to a smaller decline in economic activity.

It follows that the greater the marginal propensity to import the lower the value of the multiplier. For example, we have seen that when $c = 0.8$ and $m = 0.2$ the multiplier is 2.5. However, if $c = 0.8$ and $m = 0.3$ the value of the multiplier falls to $1/(1 - 0.8 + 0.3) = 2$. In short, the more important are imports in domestic expenditure the lower the multiplier is likely to be. This, as we have seen, this is characteristic of several European economies and especially the smaller ones in which imports account for a high proportion of total expenditure.

**Exercise 25.4** Repeat Exercise 25.3 but this time assume that next exports are $NX = 2{,}600 - 0.4Y$ (imports are an induced expenditure and the marginal propensity to import $m = 0.4$). Explain why your answer differs from that in Exercise 25.3.

## RECAP Finding short-run equilibrium output

Short-run equilibrium output is the level of output at which output equals planned aggregate expenditure – or, in symbols, $Y = PAE$. For a specific sample economy, short-run equilibrium output can be solved for algebraically, numerically or graphically.

The graphical solution is based on a diagram called the *Keynesian cross*. The Keynesian cross diagram includes two lines: a 45° line that represents the condition $Y = PAE$, and the expenditure line, which shows the relationship of *PAE* to output. Short-run equilibrium output is determined at the intersection of the two lines. If short-run equilibrium output differs from potential output, an *output gap* exists.

Increases in autonomous expenditure shift the expenditure line upward, increasing short-run equilibrium output; decreases in autonomous expenditure shift the expenditure line downward, leading to declines in short-run equilibrium output. Decreases in autonomous expenditure that drive actual output below potential output are a source of *recessions*.

Generally, a one unit change in autonomous expenditure leads to a larger change in short-run equilibrium output, reflecting the working of the *income–expenditure multiplier*. The multiplier arises because a given initial increase in spending raises the incomes of producers, which leads them to spend more, raising the incomes and spending of other producers and so on.

As imports are expenditures on foreign output the value of the multiplier will be lower when the economy is open to international trade.

## Summary

- Real GDP does not grow smoothly. Periods in which the economy is growing at a rate significantly below normal are called *recessions*; periods in which the economy is growing at a rate significantly above normal are called *expansions*. A severe or protracted recession, like the long decline that occurred between 1929 and 1933, is called a *depression*, while a particularly strong expansion is called a *boom*. Most European economies experienced recession in the early 1970s, 1980s and 1990s. Each of these recessions was preceded by a rise in oil prices.
- Short-term economic fluctuations are irregular in length and severity, and are thus hard to forecast. Expansions and recessions are typically felt throughout the economy and may even be *global* in scope. *Unemployment* rises sharply during recessions, while *inflation* tends to fall during or shortly after a recession. Durable goods industries tend to be particularly sensitive to recessions and booms, whereas services and non-durable goods industries are less sensitive.
- *Potential output*, also called potential GDP or full employment output, is the amount of output (real GDP) that an economy can produce when it is using its resources, such as capital and labour, at normal rates. The difference between potential output and actual output is the *output gap*. When output is below potential, the gap is called a *recessionary gap*; when output is above potential, the difference is called an *expansionary gap*. Recessions can occur either because potential output is growing unusually slowly or because actual output is below potential. Because recessionary gaps represent wasted resources and expansionary gaps threaten to create inflation, policy makers have an incentive to try to eliminate both types.
- The *natural rate of unemployment* is the part of the total unemployment rate that is attributable to *frictional* and *structural* unemployment. Equivalently, the natural rate of unemployment is the rate of unemployment that exists when the output gap is zero. *Cyclical* unemployment, the part of unemployment that is associated with recessions and expansions, equals the total unemployment rate less the natural unemployment rate.

- The basic Keynesian model shows how fluctuations in planned *aggregate expenditure*, or total *planned spending*, can cause actual output to differ from potential output. Too little spending leads to a *recessionary* output gap; too much spending creates an *expansionary* output gap. This model relies on the crucial assumption that firms do not respond to every change in demand by changing prices. Instead, they typically set a price for some period, then meet the demand forthcoming at that price. Firms do not change prices continually because changing prices entails costs, called *menu costs*.
- *Planned aggregate expenditure* (*PAE*) is total planned spending on final goods and services. The four components of total spending are consumption, investment, government purchases and net exports. Planned and actual consumption, government purchases and net exports are generally assumed to be the same. *Actual* investment may differ from planned investment, because firms may sell a greater or lesser amount of their production than they expected. If firms sell less than they expected, for example, they are forced to add more goods to inventory than anticipated. And because additions to inventory are counted as part of investment, in this case actual investment (including inventory investment) is greater than planned investment.
- Consumption is related to disposable, or after-tax, income by a relationship called the *consumption function*. The amount by which desired consumption rises when disposable income rises by one euro is called the *marginal propensity to consume* (*MPC*, or *c*). The MPC is always greater than 0 but less than 1 (that is, $0 < c < 1$).
- An increase in real output raises planned aggregate expenditure, since higher output (and, equivalently, higher income) encourages households to consume more. PAE can be broken down into two components, autonomous expenditure and induced expenditure. *Autonomous expenditure* is the portion of planned spending that is independent of output; *induced expenditure* is the portion of spending that depends on output.
- In the period in which prices are fixed, the *short-run equilibrium output* is the level of output that just equals planned aggregate expenditure. Short-run equilibrium can be determined algebraically or numerically by a table which compares alternative values of output and the planned spending implied by each level of output. Short-run equilibrium output can also be determined graphically in a Keynesian cross diagram, drawn with planned aggregate expenditure on the vertical axis and output on the horizontal axis. The Keynesian cross contains two lines: an expenditure line, which relates planned aggregate expenditure to output, and a 45° line, which represents the condition that short-run equilibrium output equals planned aggregate expenditure. Short-run equilibrium output is determined at the point at which these two lines intersect.
- Changes in *autonomous expenditure* will lead to changes in short-run equilibrium output. In particular, if the economy is initially at full employment, a fall in autonomous expenditure will create a recessionary gap and a rise in autonomous expenditure will create an expansionary gap. The amount by which a one unit increase in autonomous expenditure raises short-run equilibrium output is called the *multiplier*. An increase in autonomous expenditure not only raises spending directly; it also raises the incomes of producers, who in turn increase their spending and so on. Hence the multiplier is greater than 1; that is, a 1 euro increase in autonomous expenditure tends to raise short-run equilibrium output by more than 1 euro. Because imports may vary with income, the value of the multiplier will be lower when the economy is open to international trade. This is an important feature of the smaller European economies.
- In Chapters 26–28 our study of recessions and expansions will focus on government policies that influence aggregate spending may help to eliminate output gaps. In the long run, however, firms' price changes will eliminate output gaps – that is, the economy will 'self-correct' – and total spending will influence only the rate of inflation.

## Key terms

autonomous expenditure (721)
boom (704)
consumption function (719)
depression (704)
expansion (704)
expansionary gap (707)
income–expenditure multiplier (728)
import function (730)
induced expenditure (722)
marginal propensity to consume (MPC) (719)
marginal propensity to import (730)
menu costs (715)
natural rate of unemployment (709)
output gap (706)
planned aggregate expenditure (PAE) (717)
potential output (707)
recession (or contraction) (704)
recessionary gap (707)
short-run equilibrium output (722)
wealth effect (719)

## Review questions

1. Define *recession* and *expansion*. What are the beginning and ending points of a recession called? Which have been longer on average, recessions or expansions?
2. How is each of the following likely to be affected by a recession: the natural unemployment rate, the cyclical unemployment rate and the inflation rate?
3. Define *potential output*. Is it possible for an economy to produce an amount greater than potential output? Explain.
4. **True or false:** When output equals potential output, the unemployment rate is zero. Explain.
5. What is the key assumption of the basic Keynesian model? Explain why this assumption is needed if one is to accept the view that aggregate spending is a driving force behind short-term economic fluctuations.
6. Give an example of a good or service whose price changes very frequently and one whose price changes relatively infrequently. What accounts for the difference?
7. Define *planned aggregate expenditure* (*PAE*) and list its components. Why does planned spending change when output changes?
8. Explain how planned spending and actual spending can differ. Illustrate with an example.
9. Sketch a graph of the consumption function, labelling the axes of the graph. Discuss the economic meaning of (a) a movement from left to right along the graph of the consumption function; and (b) a parallel upward shift of the consumption function. Give an example of a factor that could lead to a parallel upward shift of the consumption function.
10. Sketch the Keynesian cross diagram. Explain in words the economic significance of the two lines graphed in the diagram. Given only this diagram, how could you determine autonomous expenditure, induced expenditure, the marginal propensity to consume and short-run equilibrium output?
11. Define the *multiplier*. In economic terms, why is the multiplier greater than 1?

## Problems

1. Acme Manufacturing is producing €4,000,000 worth of goods this year and expects to sell its entire production. It is also planning to purchase €1,500,000 in new equipment during the year. At the beginning of the year the company has €500,000 in inventory in its warehouse. Find actual investment and planned investment if

   a. Acme actually sells €3,850,000 worth of goods.

   b. Acme actually sells €4,000,000 worth of goods.

   c. Acme actually sells €4,200,00 worth of goods.

Assuming that Acme's situation is similar to that of other firms, in which of these three cases is output equal to short-run equilibrium output?

2. Data on before-tax income, taxes paid and consumption spending for the Simpson family in various years is given below.

| Before-tax income (€) | Taxes paid (€) | Consumption spending (€) |
|---|---|---|
| 25,000 | 3,000 | 20,000 |
| 27,000 | 3,500 | 21,350 |
| 28,000 | 3,700 | 22,070 |
| 30,000 | 4,000 | 23,600 |

   a. Graph the Simpsons' consumption function and find their household's marginal propensity to consume.

   b. How much would you expect the Simpsons to consume if their income was €32,000 and they paid taxes of €5,000?

   c. Homer Simpson wins a lottery prize. As a result, the Simpson family increases its consumption by €1,000 at each level of after-tax income. ('Income' does not include the prize money.) How does this change affect the graph of their consumption function? How does it affect their marginal propensity to consume?

3. An economy is described by the following equations:

$$C = 1{,}800 + 0.6(Y - T)$$
$$I^P = 900$$
$$G = 1{,}500$$
$$NX = 100$$
$$T = 1{,}500$$
$$Y^* = 9{,}000$$

   a. Using the algebraic method, find the short-run equilibrium value for output in this economy.

   b. What is the value of the multiplier in this economy?

   c. Find autonomous expenditure and induced expenditure in this economy.

   d. Is the economy experiencing an output gap? If so, what is its value?

   e. Find the effect on short-run equilibrium output of a decrease in planned investment from 900 to 800.

   f. Find the effect on short-run equilibrium output of an increase in autonomous consumption from 1,800 to 1,900.

4. For the economy described in Problem 3:

   a. Construct a table like Table 25.1 to find short-run equilibrium output. Consider possible values for short-run equilibrium output ranging from 8,200 to 9,000.

   b. Show the determination of short-run equilibrium output for this economy using the Keynesian cross diagram.

5. For the economy described in Problem 3, suppose that net exports are given by $NX = 950 - mY$. If the marginal propensity to import is $m = 0.1$:

a. Find the value for short-run equilibrium output.

b. Find the value for the multiplier. Why does it differ from the answer in Problem 3?

c. Repeat parts (e) and (f) in Problem 3. Why do your answers differ?

## Answers to in-chapter exercises

25.1 The equation for equilibrium output is

$$Y = \left(\frac{1}{1-c}\right)\bar{A}$$

As the consumption function is $C = 860 + 0.6(Y - T)$, the marginal propensity to consume $c = 0.6$ and $1 - c = 0.4$. Total autonomous expenditures are

$$\begin{aligned}\bar{A} &= \bar{C} - c\bar{T} + \bar{I} + \bar{G} + \overline{NX}\\ &= 860 - 360 + 900 + 800 + 200\\ &= 2{,}400\end{aligned}$$

Hence equilibrium $Y$ is

$$Y = \left(\frac{1}{1-0.6}\right)2{,}400 = 6{,}000$$

25.2 First we need to find an equation that relates planned aggregate expenditure $PAE$ to output $Y$:

$$PAE = \bar{A} + cY$$

The marginal propensity to consume is $c = 0.6$ and total autonomous expenditure is

$$\begin{aligned}\bar{A} &= \bar{C} - c\bar{T} + \bar{I} + \bar{G} + \overline{NX}\\ &= 860 - 360 + 900 + 800 + 200\\ &= 2{,}400\end{aligned}$$

Hence:

$$PAE = 2{,}400 + 0.6Y$$

Using this relationship we construct a table analogous to Table 25.1. Some trial and error is necessary to find an appropriate range of guesses for output (column (1)).

Determination of short-run equilibrium output

| Output *Y* (1) | Planned aggregate expenditure *PAE* = 2,400 + 0.6*Y* (2) | *Y* – *PAE* (3) | *Y* = *PAE*? (4) |
|---|---|---|---|
| 5,000 | 5,400 | –400 | No |
| 5,200 | 5,520 | –320 | No |
| 5,400 | 5,640 | –240 | No |
| 5,600 | 5,760 | –160 | No |
| 5,800 | 5,880 | –80 | No |
| 6,000 | 6,000 | 0 | Yes |
| 6,200 | 6,120 | 80 | No |
| 6,400 | 6,240 | 160 | No |
| 6,600 | 6,360 | 240 | No |

Short-run equilibrium output equals 6,000, as that is the only level of output that satisfies the condition $Y = PAE$.

25.3 The equation for equilibrium output is

$$Y = \left(\frac{1}{1-c}\right)\bar{A}$$

With a 10 unit increase in $\bar{C}$, the consumption function is $C = 870 + 0.6(Y - T)$, the marginal propensity to consume $c = 0.6$ and $1 - c = 0.4$. Total autonomous expenditures are

$$\begin{aligned}\bar{A} &= \bar{C} - c\bar{T} + \bar{I} + \bar{G} + \overline{NX} \\ &= 870 - 360 + 900 + 800 + 200 \\ &= 2{,}410\end{aligned}$$

Hence equilibrium $Y$ is

$$Y = \left(\frac{1}{1-0.6}\right)2{,}410 = 6{,}025$$

Hence equilibrium output increases by 25 units, which equals the increase in autonomous consumption (10) times the multiplier (2.5).

25.4 The equation for equilibrium output is

$$Y = \left(\frac{1}{1-c+m}\right)\bar{A}$$

The marginal propensity to consume is $c = 0.6$ and the marginal propensity to import is $m = 0.6$. Hence $1 - c + m = 0.8$ and the multiplier is $1/0.8 = 1.25$. Total autonomous expenditures are

$$\begin{aligned}\bar{A} &= \bar{C} - c\bar{T} + \bar{I} + \bar{G} + \overline{NX} \\ &= 860 - 360 + 900 + 800 + 2{,}600 \\ &= 4{,}800\end{aligned}$$

Hence equilibrium $Y$ is

$$Y = \left(\frac{1}{1-0.6+0.4}\right)4{,}800 = 6{,}000$$

A 10 unit increase in $\bar{C}$ increases autonomous expenditures to 4,810 and the new equilibrium value for $Y$ is

$$Y = \left(\frac{1}{1-0.6+0.4}\right)4{,}810 = 6{,}012.5$$

Hence equilibrium output increases by 12.5 units, which equals the increase in autonomous consumption (10) times the multiplier (1.25). The increase in equilibrium $Y$ is smaller than in Exercise 25.3 because part of the increase in $\bar{C}$ is spent on imported goods, which are not part of domestic output.

## Appendix The multiplier in the basic Keynesian model

This Appendix gives a more complete explanation of the *income–expenditure multiplier* in the basic Keynesian model. In Example 25.5, we saw that a drop in autonomous expenditure of 10 units caused a decline in short-run equilibrium output of 50 units, five times as great as the initial change in spending. Hence the multiplier in this example is 5.

To see why this multiplier effect occurs, note that the initial decrease of 10 in consumer spending (more precisely, in the constant term of the consumption function, $\bar{C}$) in Example 25.5 has two effects. First, the fall in consumer spending directly reduces planned aggregate expenditure by 10 units. Second, the fall in spending also reduces by 10 units the incomes of producers (workers and firm owners) of consumer goods. Under the assumption of Example 25.5 that the marginal propensity to consume is 0.8, the producers of consumer goods will therefore reduce *their* consumption spending by 8, or 0.8 times their income loss of 10. This reduction in spending cuts the income of *other* producers by 8 units, leading them to reduce their spending by 6.4, or 0.8 times their income loss of 8. These income reductions of 6.4 lead still other producers to cut their spending by 5.12, or 0.8 times 6.4, and so on. In principle this process continues indefinitely, although after many rounds of spending and income reductions the effects become quite small.

When all these 'rounds' of income and spending reductions are added, the *total* effect on planned spending of the initial reduction of 10 in consumer spending is

$$10 + 8 + 6.4 + 5.12 + \ldots$$

The three dots indicate that the series of reductions continues indefinitely. The total effect of the initial decrease in consumption can also be written as

$$10[1 + 0.8 + (0.8)^2 + (0.8)^3 + \ldots]$$

This expression highlights the fact that the spending that takes place in each round is 0.8 times the spending in the previous round (0.8), because that is the marginal propensity to consume out of the income generated by the previous round of spending.

A useful algebraic relationship, which applies to any number $x$ greater than 0 but less than 1, is

$$1 + x + x^2 + x^3 + \ldots = \frac{1}{1-x}$$

If we set $x = 0.8$, this formula implies that the total effect of the decline in consumption spending on aggregate demand and output is

$$10\left(\frac{1}{1-08}\right) = 10\left(\frac{1}{0.2}\right) = 10 \times 5 = 50$$

This answer is consistent with our earlier calculation, which showed that short-run equilibrium output fell by 50 units, from 4,800 to 4,750.

By a similar analysis we can also find a general algebraic expression for the multiplier in the basic Keynesian model. Recalling that $c$ is the marginal propensity to consume out of disposable income, we know that a 1 unit increase in autonomous expenditure raises spending and income by 1 unit in the first round; by $c \times 1 = c$ units in the second round; by $c \times c = c^2$ units in the second round; by $c \times c^2 = c^3$ units in the third round; and so on. Thus the total effect on short-run equilibrium output of a 1 unit increase in autonomous expenditure is given by

$$1 + c + c^2 + c^3 + \ldots$$

Applying the algebraic formula given above, and recalling that $0 < c < 1$, we can rewrite this expression as $1/(1 - c)$. Thus, in a basic Keynesian model with a marginal propensity to consume of $c$, the multiplier equals $1/(1 - c)$. Note that if $c = 0.8$, then $1/(1 - c) = 1/(1 - 0.8) = 5$, which is the same value of the multiplier we found numerically above.

# 26

# Stabilising the Economy: the Role of Fiscal Policy

According to the basic Keynesian model, inadequate spending is an important cause of recessions. To fight recessions – at least those caused by insufficient demand rather than slow growth of potential output – policy makers must find ways to stimulate planned spending. Policies that are used to affect planned aggregate expenditure (PAE), with the objective of eliminating output gaps, are called **stabilisation policies**. Policy actions intended to increase planned spending and output are called **expansionary policies**; expansionary policy actions are normally taken when the economy is in recession. It is also possible, as we have seen, for the economy to be 'overheated', with output greater than potential output (an expansionary gap). The risk of an expansionary gap, as we shall see in more detail later, is that it may lead to an increase in inflation. To offset an expansionary gap, policy makers will try to reduce spending and output. **Contractionary policies** are policy actions intended to reduce planned spending and output.

**stabilisation policies** government policies that are used to affect planned aggregate expenditure, with the objective of eliminating output gaps

**expansionary policies** government policy actions intended to increase planned spending and output

**contractionary policies** government policy actions designed to reduce planned spending and output

The two major tools of stabilisation policy are *monetary policy* and *fiscal policy*. Recall that monetary policy refers to decisions about the size of the money supply, whereas fiscal policy refers to decisions about the government's budget – how much the government spends and how much tax revenue it collects. In this chapter we focus on how fiscal policy can be used to influence spending in the basic Keynesian model, as well as on some practical issues that arise in the use of fiscal policy in the real world. Monetary policy will be discussed in Chapters 27 and 28.

Fiscal policy is especially important in a European context. Recall from Chapter 23 that countries in the Eurosystem have transferred responsibility for monetary policy from their national Central Banks to the European Central Bank (ECB) based in Frankfurt. This sacrifice of policy independence means that individual countries can no longer use monetary policy to stabilise their domestic economies. Hence when countries such as France and Italy are faced with recession they cannot increase their domestic money supplies and reduce interest rates to offset a decline in aggregate spending. Likewise, when faced with inflationary pressures they cannot cool the economy by reducing the money supply and increasing interest rates.

Rather, they must accept the monetary policy set by the ECB. While this policy may be appropriate for the Eurosystem as a whole there can be no guarantee that it will be appropriate for individual countries such as France, Italy and other members of the Eurosystem.

Given that monetary policy is no longer an option, *fiscal policy* would appear to become much more important as it is now the only macroeconomic stabilisation policy available to national governments. However, although fiscal policy remains the responsibility of national governments we shall see that countries within the Eurosystem have placed limits on their fiscal independence through an agreement known as the *Stability and Growth Pact* (SGP). Later in this chapter we shall take a close look at the SGP and ask why it is considered necessary, and how successful it has been. There is, however, one important point that we should note at this stage. As stated above, fiscal policy refers to the government's budget, which we have defined as the difference between government purchases, G, and net taxes, *T*. Changes in the budget deficit ($G - T$), can be taken as a key indicator of the strength and direction of fiscal policy. For example, a decision to increase the budget deficit by increasing G and/or reducing *T* would normally be seen as an indicator of an *expansionary* policy. Conversely, a decision to reduce the deficit by cutting G and/or increasing *T* can be interpreted as a *contractionary* policy.

These are *discretionary* policy changes. That is, the government takes decisions to spend more or less on specific projects (build new roads, increase the wages of public sector workers, cancel plans to purchase new military equipment, etc.) or to cut or increase taxation. However, it is important to note that the deficit can change even if the government does not alter its spending and tax plans. Most government tax revenue comes from income taxes and taxes on expenditure, and as the economy moves into recession we would expect these revenues to fall as incomes and expenditures decline with output. Likewise, we would expect transfer payments such as unemployment benefits to increase as the *number claiming* these benefits grows during recession (remember that net taxes *T* are tax revenues less transfer payments). Conversely we would expect tax revenues to increase and transfer payments to fall during an expansion as incomes rise and the *number claiming* unemployment benefits declines. That is, we would expect to observe *automatic* changes in the government's deficit as the economy moves from recession to expansion – increasing in recession, declining in an expansion. So long as tax revenues vary with the level of economic activity and transfer payments vary with the number claiming benefit, the deficit will automatically change over the course of the business cycle. When analysing the role and effectiveness of fiscal policy it will be important to distinguish between *discretionary* and *automatic* changes in the government's deficit. The next two sections discuss *discretionary* fiscal policy, or government decisions to change its purchases and taxation. The following section discusses *automatic* changes in the government deficit and highlights their role in helping to stabilise the economy. Once we have dealt with the discretionary and automatic aspects of fiscal policy we can then analyse the SGP which, as we shall see, limits government budget deficits to 3 per cent of a country's GDP.

## Discretionary fiscal policy: changes in government purchases

Decisions about government spending represent one of the two main components of discretionary fiscal policy, the other being decisions about taxes and transfer payments. As was mentioned in Chapter 25, Keynes himself felt that changes in *government purchases* were probably the most effective tool for reducing or eliminating output gaps. His basic argument was straightforward: government purchases of goods and services, being a component of planned aggregate expenditure, directly affect total spending. If output gaps are caused by too much or too little total spending, then the government can help to guide the economy toward full employment by changing its own level of spending. Keynes' views seemed to be vindicated by the events of the 1930s, notably the fact that the Depression did not finally end until governments greatly increased their military spending in the latter part of the decade.

Example 26.1 shows how increased government purchases of goods and services can help to eliminate a recessionary gap. (The effects of government spending on transfer programmes, such as unemployment benefits, are a bit different. We shall return to that case shortly.)

### Example 26.1 An increase in the government's purchases eliminates a recessionary gap

Recall the economy described by Example 25.5. In that economy the consumption function was $C = 620 + 0.8(Y - T)$, $\bar{I} = 220$, $\bar{G} = 300$, $\overline{NX} = 20$ and $\bar{T} = 250$. We found that PAE was given by the equation $PAE = 960 + 0.8Y$, so that autonomous expenditure equalled 960 and short-run equilibrium output was 4,800. We also found that the multiplier equalled 5 and a 10 unit fall in autonomous consumption spending $\bar{C}$ created a 50 unit recessionary gap. How can the government eliminate the output gap and restore full employment by changing its purchases of goods and services $G$?

To offset the effects of the consumption decline, the government would have to restore autonomous expenditure to its original value, 960. Under our assumption that government purchases are simply given and do not depend on output, government purchases are part of autonomous expenditure, and changes in government purchases change autonomous expenditure one-for-one. Thus, to increase autonomous expenditure from 950 to 960, the government should simply increase its purchases by 10 units (for example, by increasing spending on road construction). According to the basic Keynesian model, this increase in government purchases should return autonomous expenditure and hence output to their original levels.

We can illustrate this by using the model for short-run equilibrium output described in Chapter 25. In that model short-run equilibrium output is determined by the equation

$$Y = \left(\frac{1}{1-c}\right)\bar{A}$$

where $1/(1-c)$ is the multiplier and $\bar{A}$ is total autonomous expenditures, defined as

$$\bar{A} = \bar{C} - c\bar{T} + \bar{I} + \bar{G} + \overline{NX}$$

As in other parts of this book we shall use the Greek letter delta, or $\Delta$, as shorthand for the phrase 'change in'. Hence

$$\Delta Y = \left(\frac{1}{1-c}\right)\Delta\bar{A} \tag{26.1}$$

which simply says that the change in output equals the multiplier times the change in total autonomous expenditures. For example, if $c = 0.8$ the multiplier will be 5 and a 1 unit fall in $\bar{A}$ leads to a 5 unit fall in output. In Example 25.5, $\Delta\bar{A} = \Delta\bar{C} = -10$ and $\Delta Y = -50$. To offset the effects of this decline in autonomous consumption expenditures the government would have to increase its purchases by a similar amount. With the other components of autonomous expenditure constant, the resulting change in $Y$ would be

$$\Delta Y = \left(\frac{1}{1-c}\right)[\Delta\bar{C} + \Delta\bar{G}] \tag{26.2}$$

Hence, to stabilise $Y$ at its equilibrium level, the government would have to set $\Delta\bar{G} = -\Delta\bar{C}$. In Example 25.5, $\Delta\bar{C} = -10$ and government would have to increase $\bar{G}$ by 10 units, or $\Delta\bar{G} = +10$ to prevent output from falling.

The effect of the increase in government purchases is shown graphically in Fig. 26.1. After the 10 unit decline in the autonomous component of consumption spending $\bar{C}$, the economy is at point $F$, with a 50 unit recessionary gap. A 10 unit increase in government purchases raises autonomous expenditure by 10 units, raising the intercept of the expenditure line by 10 units and causing the expenditure line to shift upward in parallel fashion. The economy returns to point $E$, where short-run equilibrium output equals potential output ($Y = Y^* = 4{,}800$) and the output gap has been eliminated.

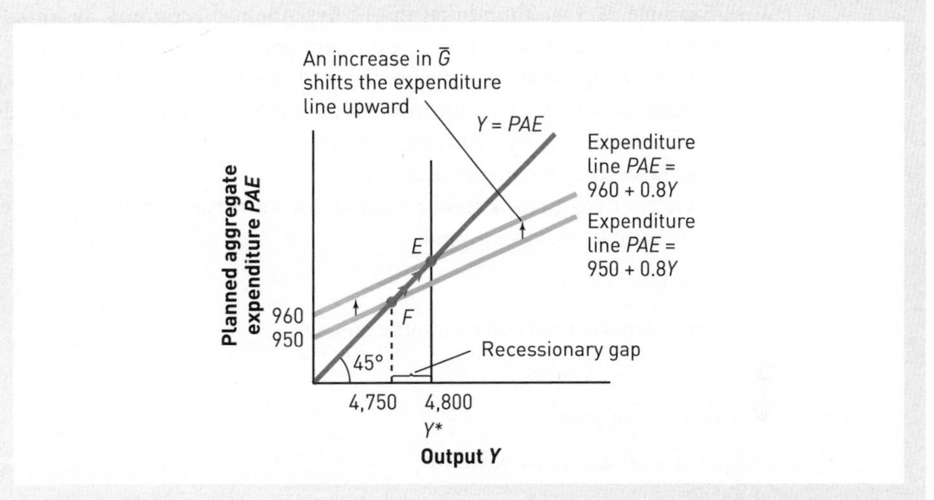


Figure 26.1 **An Increase in Government Purchases Eliminates a Recessionary Gap.** After a 10 unit decline in the autonomous part of consumer spending $C$, the economy is at point $F$, with a recessionary gap of 50 (see Fig. 25.9). A 10 unit increase in government purchases raises autonomous expenditure by 10 units, shifting the expenditure line back to its original position and raising the equilibrium point from $F$ to $E$. At point $E$, where output equals potential output ($Y - Y^* = 4{,}800$), the output gap has been eliminated.

**Exercise 26.1** Using the economy described in Example 26.1 assume that consumers become more rather than less confident and increase consumption by 10 units at each level of disposable income, leading to an expansionary output gap. Discuss how a change in government purchases could be used to eliminate this output gap.

## Discretionary fiscal policy: changes in taxes and transfers

Besides making decisions about government purchases of goods and services, fiscal policy makers also determine the level and types of *taxes* to be collected and *transfer payments* to be made. (Transfer payments, recall, are payments made by the government to the public, for which no current goods or services are received. Examples of transfer payments are unemployment benefits, welfare benefits and income support payments to farmers. Once again, transfer payments are *not* included in government purchases of goods and services.) The basic Keynesian model implies that, like changes in government purchases, changes in the level of taxes or transfers can be used to affect PAE and thus eliminate output gaps.

Unlike changes in government purchases, however, changes in taxes or transfers do not affect planned spending directly. Instead they work indirectly, by changing *disposable income* in the private sector. For example, either a tax cut or an increase in government transfer payments increases disposable income, equal to $Y - T$. According to the consumption function, when disposable income rises, households should spend more. Thus a tax cut or increase in transfers should increase PAE. Likewise, an increase in taxes or a cut in transfers, by lowering households' disposable income, will tend to lower planned spending. Example 26.2 illustrates the effects of a tax cut on spending and output.

## Example 26.2 Using a tax cut to close a recessionary gap

In Example 25.5 we found that in our hypothetical economy, an initial drop in consumer spending of 10 units creates a recessionary gap of 50 units. Example 26.1 showed that this recessionary gap could be eliminated by a 10 unit increase in government purchases. Suppose that, instead of increasing government purchases, fiscal policy makers decided to stimulate consumer spending by changing the level of tax collections. By how much should they change taxes to eliminate the output gap?

To answer we go back to our solution for short-run equilibrium output in Example 25.3. In that example, *PAE* was given by

$$PAE = \bar{A} + cY$$

where $\bar{A}$ denotes total autonomous expenditure:

$$\bar{A} = \bar{C} - c\bar{T} + \bar{I} + \bar{G} + \overline{NX}$$

which we can write as

$$\bar{A} = [\bar{C} + \bar{I} + \bar{G} + \overline{NX}] - c\bar{T}$$

or

$$\bar{A} = \bar{A}' - c\bar{T}$$

where $\bar{A}' = [\bar{C} + \bar{I} + \bar{G} + \overline{NX}]$. Hence we can express *PAE* as

$$PAE = \bar{A}' + cY - cT$$

As equilibrium output is the level of output at which $Y = PAE$, the economy will reach its short-run equilibrium when

$$Y = \bar{A}' + cY - c\bar{T}$$

or

$$Y(1 - c) = \bar{A}' - c\bar{T}$$

Dividing both sides by $(1 - c)$ gives

$$Y = \left(\frac{1}{1-c}\right)\bar{A}' - \left(\frac{c}{1-c}\right)\bar{T}$$

Hence, with autonomous expenditures constant, a 1 unit change in taxation causes a change in equilibrium output equal to $c/(1 - c)$ units, or

$$\Delta Y = -\left(\frac{c}{1-c}\right)\Delta\bar{T} \tag{26.3}$$

**tax multiplier** the effect of a 1 unit change in autonomous taxes on short-run equilibrium output. Because the marginal propensity to consume is less than one, the tax multiplier will be smaller than the income-expenditure multiplier

For example, if $c = 0.8$ then $c/(1 - c) = 0.8/0.2 = 4$ and a 1 unit cut in taxes increases $Y$ by 4 units. Hence, to close a recessionary gap of 50 units government must cut taxes by 12.5 units. As the term $c/(1 - c)$ gives the change in short-run equilibrium output that results from a 1 unit change in taxes it is called the **tax multiplier**. Note that because the marginal propensity to consume is less than one $(0 < c < 1)$, the tax multiplier will be smaller than the income–expenditure multiplier, $1/(1 - c)$. When, for example, $c = 0.8$ the tax multiplier is 4 but the income–expenditure multiplier is 5.

We can illustrate the difference between the tax and income–expenditure multipliers by referring to the economy described in Example 26.1. In that economy the source of the recessionary gap is the reduction in household consumption spending of 10 units at each level of output $Y$ – that is, the constant term $\bar{C}$ in the consumption function is assumed to have fallen by 10 units. To eliminate this recessionary gap, the change in taxes must induce households to increase their consumption spending by 10 units at each output level. However, although a 10 unit tax cut will increase disposable income by an equal amount it will lead to a smaller increase in consumption. The reason is that the marginal propensity to consume out of disposable income in our example is 0.8, so that consumption spending increases by only 0.8 times the amount of the tax cut. (The rest of the tax cut is saved.) An increase in autonomous expenditure of 8 units is not enough to return output to its full-employment level, in this example.

To raise consumption spending by 10 units, fiscal policy makers must instead cut taxes by 12.5 units. A tax cut of 12.5 increases disposable income by an equal amount and induces households to increase their consumption by 10 units at each level of output, which offsets the 10 unit decrease in $\bar{C}$ and restores the economy to full employment.

Note that since $T$ refers to *net taxes*, or taxes less transfers, the same result could be obtained by increasing transfer payments by 12.5 units. Because households spend 0.8 times any increase in transfer payments they receive, this policy would also raise consumption spending by 10 units at any level of output.

Graphically, the effect of the tax cut is identical to the effect of the increase in government purchases, shown in Fig. 26.1. Because it leads to a 10 unit increase in consumption at any level of output, the tax cut shifts the expenditure line up by 10 units. Equilibrium is attained at point $E$ in Fig. 26.1, where output again equals potential output.

**Exercise 26.2**

In a particular economy, a 20 unit increase in planned investment moved the economy from an initial situation with no output gap to a situation with an expansionary gap. Describe two ways in which fiscal policy could be used to offset this expansionary gap. Assume that the marginal propensity to consume equals 0.5.

### Example 26.3 The balanced-budget multiplier

Example 26.1 illustrated a case in which fiscal policy can be used to stabilise the economy by increasing government purchases while Example 26.2 illustrated how the same objective can be achieved by a tax cut. Note that in each case the government's budget deficit ($G - T$) will increase. In the first case, the deficit increases because the government is spending more on roads, schools, etc. and in the second because tax revenue is reduced. Suppose that the budget deficit is already running at a high level and the government does not want to increase it further. Does this mean that fiscal policy cannot be used to stabilise the economy? The answer is no. To see why, assume that the government decides to finance an increase in its expenditures by imposing higher taxes. If, for example, G is increased by 10 units then taxes will also be increased by 10, leaving the deficit unchanged.

In Example 26.2 we saw that short-run equilibrium output can be expressed as

$$Y = \left(\frac{1}{1-c}\right)\bar{A}' - \left(\frac{c}{1-c}\right)\bar{T}$$

where $\bar{A}' = [\bar{C} + \bar{I} + \bar{G} + \overline{NX}]$. Now suppose that government increases G and finances the additional expenditure by imposing higher taxes. Again using $\Delta$ as shorthand for 'the change in', the resulting change in $Y$ is (with other components of autonomous expenditure constant):

$$\Delta Y = \left(\frac{1}{1-c}\right)\Delta\bar{G} - \left(\frac{c}{1-c}\right)\Delta\bar{T}$$

However, as this policy implies that $\Delta\bar{G} = \Delta\bar{T}$, then

$$\begin{aligned}\Delta Y &= \left(\frac{1}{1-c}\right)\Delta\bar{G} - \left(\frac{c}{1-c}\right)\Delta\bar{G} \\ &= \left(\frac{1-c}{1-c}\right)\Delta\bar{G} \\ &= \Delta\bar{G}\end{aligned} \tag{26.4}$$

Hence, an increase in government purchases financed by an equal increase in taxation leads to an equal increase in output. If, for example, $\bar{G}$ and $\bar{T}$ are both increased by 10 units, short-run equilibrium output will also increase by 10 units. This effect is known as the **balanced-budget multiplier**, which is the effect on output of a change in government purchases financed by an equal change in taxation. As equilibrium output changes by the same amount, the balanced budget multiplier equals one.

**balanced-budget multiplier** the effect on short-run equilibrium output of an increase in government purchases financed by an equal increase in taxation. As the change in output equals the change in government purchases, the balanced budget multiplier equals one

In Examples 26.1 and 26.2 we saw that a 10 unit fall in autonomous consumption expenditures reduced output by 50 units and that government can offset this by either increasing purchases by 10 units (income–expenditure multiplier = 5) or cutting taxes by 12.5 units (tax multiplier = 4). In each case the fiscal expansion results in a *higher budget deficit*. If the government wishes to avoid a larger deficit it must finance higher purchases by increasing taxes. Hence, as the balanced-budget multiplier is one, the government must increase both expenditure and tax revenues by 50 units to offset the effect of the 10 unit fall in autonomous consumption.

**Exercise 26.3** In a particular economy, a 20 unit increase in planned investment moved the economy from an initial situation with no output gap to a situation with an expansionary gap. Suppose that the government wants to use fiscal policy offset this expansionary gap but does not want to change its deficit. What action should the government take? Assume that the marginal propensity to consume equals 0.5.

## RECAP Fiscal policy and planned spending

Fiscal policy includes two general tools for affecting total spending and eliminating output gaps: (1) changes in *government purchases* and (2) changes in *taxes or transfer payments*. An increase in government purchases increases autonomous expenditure by an equal amount. A reduction in taxes or an increase in transfer payments increases autonomous expenditure by an amount equal to the marginal propensity to consume times the reduction in taxes or increase in transfers. The ultimate effect of a fiscal policy change on short-run equilibrium output equals the change in autonomous expenditure times the multiplier. Accordingly, if the economy is in recession, an increase in government purchases, a cut in taxes or an increase in transfers can be used to stimulate spending and eliminate the recessionary gap. As the income–expenditure multiplier is greater than the tax and balanced-budget multipliers, changes in government purchases financed by borrowing are the most effective way to stabilise the economy.

## Automatic stabilisers

So far, our discussion on fiscal policy has assumed that government takes *discretionary* decisions to increase or decrease the level of government purchases, transfer payments and taxation in order to stabilise the economy. For example, in Example 26.1 the government *decides* to increase its purchases by 10 units in order to close the recessionary gap. Likewise, in Example 26.2 government *decides* to reduce taxation by 12.5 units. Because they result from explicit policy decisions these changes in G and *T* are referred to as **discretionary fiscal policy**. However, as mentioned in the introduction to this chapter, under slightly more realistic assumptions the economy will have a built-in stabilisation mechanism which operates independently of discretionary policy changes. This mechanism works through changes in the *government budget deficit* which dampen fluctuations in economic activity by automatically increasing in a recession and decreasing during an expansion. It is referred to as an **automatic stabiliser** effect.

**discretionary fiscal policy** decisions by government to increase or decrease the levels of government purchases, transfer payments and taxation

**automatic stabilisers** automatic changes in the government budget deficit which help to dampen fluctuations in economic activity

In Chapter 22, we defined the government budget deficit as government purchases G minus *net taxes T*:

$$\text{Government deficit} = G - T$$

Recall that *net taxes* were defined as tax revenues minus transfer payments (unemployment benefits, social welfare payments, etc.). We also assumed that both G and *T* were *autonomous*. That is, government sets G and *T* and their levels do not vary as output *Y* changes. While this is a useful simplifying assumption it is unrealistic in most modern economies. For example, think what actually happens to tax revenues and transfer payments as the economy moves into recession. Most tax revenue comes from taxes on household incomes (income tax) and expenditures (value added tax) and from profits earned by firms (corporate taxes). During a recession some households will experience declining incomes and, given the consumption function, this will induce an automatic decline in consumption expenditures. Hence, we would expect revenue from income and expenditure taxes to fall during a recession. Company profits will also decline, resulting in reduced revenue from taxes on profits. Conversely, as the economy expands, revenues from income, expenditure and profits taxes will automatically rise. Transfer payments, on the other hand, will move in the opposite direction. If unemployment rises in recession, more households will be claiming unemployment benefit and total transfer payments will automatically increase. Conversely, as the economy recovers and unemployment falls, fewer households will claim unemployment benefits, leading to a decline in government expenditure on transfer payments. We can express this idea as

$$T = tY$$

where *t* can be thought of as the average rate of tax. If, for example, $t = 0.25$ then each time *Y* falls by €1 tax revenues will fall by €0.25, or 25 cents. Likewise if *Y* increases by €1 tax revenues will increase by €0.25. Note that these changes are completely automatic. They do not require any action by government such as a change in the rate of taxation, *t*. It also follows that at a constant level of government purchases G, the government deficit will automatically rise during recession and automatically fall during an expansion. Example 26.4 shows that this makes an important difference to our analysis of how changes in autonomous expenditures affect short-run equilibrium output.

### Example 26.4 Automatic stabilisers

To explain what automatic stabilisers are and how they work we shall compare two economies called *A* and *B*. We will assume that tax revenues are completely autonomous in *A* but vary with output in *B*. The following models describe each economy.

| | **Economy *A*** | **Economy *B*** |
|---|---|---|
| Planned consumption | $C = 620 + 0.8(Y - T)$ | $C = 480 + 0.8(Y - T)$ |
| Autonomous expenditures | $I^p = 220G = 500NX = 20$ | $I^p = 220G = 1{,}200NX = 20$ |
| Tax revenues | $T = 500$ | $T = 0.25Y$ |

In economy *A*, *PAE* is the sum of planned consumption, planned investment, government purchases and net exports, or

$$PAE = [620 + 0.8(Y - 500)] + 220 + 500 + 20$$

As $0.8(Y - 500) = 0.8Y - 400$ we can add all terms which don't depend on *Y* to get

$$\begin{aligned} PAE &= 620 - 400 + 220 + 500 + 20 + 0.8Y \\ &= 960 + 0.8Y \end{aligned}$$

We know that in short-run equilibrium $PAE = Y$, hence

$$Y = 960 + 0.8Y$$

or

$$Y - 0.8Y = (1 - 0.8)Y = 960$$

As $1 - 0.8 = 0.2$ we get

$$Y = 960/0.2 = 4{,}800$$

Hence in economy *A* equilibrium output is 4,800. Note also that the government deficit $(G - T)$ is zero as both *G* and *T* are set at 500. Now suppose that net exports were to fall by 10 units, reducing autonomous expenditures from 960 to 950. *PAE* would then be

$$PAE = 950 + 0.8Y$$

To find the new equilibrium level of output we equate *PAE* and *Y*:

$$Y = 950 + 0.8Y$$

which gives

$$Y = 950/0.2 = 4{,}750$$

which is a fall of 50 units (4,800 – 4,750). Hence in economy *A*, a 10 unit fall in autonomous expenditures opens a 50 unit recessionary gap. Note that as *T* does not change with *Y* the government deficit $(G - T)$ is still zero.

We shall now perform the same exercise for economy *B*. In *B*, *PAE* is

$$PAE = [480 + 0.8(Y - 0.25Y] + 220 + 1{,}200 + 20$$

As $0.8(Y - 0.25Y) = 0.8Y - 0.2Y = 0.6Y$ we can again add up all terms which do not depend on *Y*:

$$\begin{aligned} PAE &= 480 + 220 + 1{,}200 + 20 + 0.6Y \\ &= 1{,}920 + 0.6Y \end{aligned}$$

We know that in short-run equilibrium $PAE = Y$, hence

$$Y = 1{,}920 + 0.6Y$$

or

$$Y = 1{,}920/0.4 = 4{,}800$$

Hence in economy *B* the initial equilibrium output is also 4,800. To find the government deficit we need to find tax revenues $T = 0.25Y$. As $Y = 4{,}800$ we get $T = 0.25 \times 4{,}800 = 1{,}200$. As the government purchases are 1,200 economy *B* also has a zero deficit. Now suppose that, as in economy $A$, net exports were to fall by 10 units, reducing autonomous expenditures from 1,920 to 1,910. $PAE$ would then be:

$$PAE = 1{,}910 + 0.6Y$$

To find the new equilibrium level of output we equate $PAE$ and $Y$:

$$Y = 1{,}910 + 0.6Y$$

which gives

$$Y = 1{,}910/0.4 = 4{,}775$$

which is a 25 unit fall in $Y$ (4,800 – 4,775). Hence in economy $B$ a 10 unit fall in autonomous expenditure opens a 25 unit recessionary gap. Tax revenues are $T = 0.25Y = 1{,}193.75$ and the government's budget deficit $(G - T)$ is $1{,}200 - 1193.75 = 6.25$.

Hence each economy starts with the same equilibrium output and each experiences the same decline in autonomous expenditure. However the fall in $A$'s output is twice the fall in $B$'s output. Why is the fall in output lower in economy $B$? The answer is that because less tax is paid to the government as income falls, disposable or after-tax income $(Y - T)$ falls by a smaller amount in $B$. As a result, consumption expenditure falls by less in $B$. For example, suppose a typical household earns €1,000 per week before tax and lives in economy $A$. If the household is taxed at €250 per week its disposable income is €750. Suppose before-tax income falls to €900. As the household still has to pay €250 tax its disposable income will also fall by €100 to €650. However, if the household lives in $B$ and is taxed at 25 per cent ($t = 0.25$) its tax liability will fall from €250 to €225 (25 per cent of 900) and disposable income will fall by less, from €750 to €675. Hence, planned consumption, which depends on disposable income, will fall by less in economy $B$, leading to a smaller fall in output.

This effect helps to *stabilise* the economy in the sense that the recessionary gap is smaller when tax revenues vary with income. It is also *automatic* because it does not require any discretionary action by the government such as a change in government purchases $G$ or the rate of taxation $t$. Hence, it is referred to as an *automatic stabiliser*. Another way to think of the automatic stabiliser effect is that the government deficit automatically increases as $Y$ falls and partially offsets the contractionary impact of a fall in autonomous expenditure.

Automatic stabilisers also work in the opposite direction. For example, if the economy experiences an increase in autonomous expenditures, tax revenues will increase as $Y$ increases thus reducing the increase in disposable income and planned consumption.

Without automatic stabilisers both expansionary and recessionary gaps would be larger and more prolonged. Hence, automatic stabilisers help to dampen the size and duration of cyclical fluctuations in economic activity. We shall see that one reason why countries in the Eurosystem have agreed to put limits on national government deficits is to ensure that automatic stabilisers can work effectively.

**Exercise 26.4** Repeat Example 26.4 but this time assume a 10 unit increase in net exports. Find the changes in $Y$ and $(G - T)$ for economies $A$ and $B$.

### Example 26 .5 Automatic stabilisers and the income-expenditure multiplier

In Example 26.4 we saw that the same fall in net exports had a greater effect on output in economy $A$ than in economy $B$. As net exports are part of total autonomous expenditures this implies that the income-expenditure multiplier must be smaller in economy $B$. Remember that the income-expenditure multiplier is the effect of a 1 unit change in autonomous expenditure on short-run equilibrium output and equals $1/(1 - c)$. In economy $A$ the marginal propensity to consume $c = 0.8$ and the income-expenditure multiplier is

$1/(1-0.8)=5$. Hence, a 10 unit fall in net exports opens a recessionary gap of 50 units. However, in economy *B* the marginal propensity to consume is also 0.8 but the same fall in net exports results in a 25 unit fall in output, which implies that the multiplier is 2.5. To see why, we will go back to our definition of planned aggregate expenditure:

$$PAE = C + I^p + G + NX$$

In both *A* and *B* the consumption function is

$$C = \bar{C} + c\,(Y - T)$$

In *A*, taxes are autonomous, $T = \bar{T}$, but vary with income in *B*, $T = tY$. Hence *B*'s consumption function is

$$C = \bar{C} + c\,(Y - tY)$$
$$= \bar{C} + c\,(1 - t)Y$$

and *PAE* in *B* is

$$PAE = [\bar{C} + c\,(1 - t)Y] + I^p + G + NX$$

Assuming planned investment, government purchases and net exports to be autonomous:

$$PAE = [\bar{C} + \bar{I} + \bar{G} + \overline{NX}] + c\,(1 - t)Y$$
$$= \bar{A}' + c\,(1 - t)Y$$

where

$$\bar{A}' = [\bar{C} + \bar{I} + \bar{G} + \overline{NX}]$$

As short-run equilibrium output is the level of output at which *Y* equals *PAE*:

$$Y = \bar{A}' + c\,(1 - t)Y$$

or

$$Y[1 - c\,(1 - t)] = \bar{A}'$$

Dividing both sides by $[1 - c\,(1 - t)]$ gives

$$Y = \left(\frac{1}{1 - c\,(1 - t)}\right)\bar{A}' \tag{26.5}$$

Hence, in economy *B* a 1 unit fall in autonomous expenditure reduces *Y* by $1/[1 - c(1 - t)]$ units which is the value of the income–expenditure multiplier. In *B*, $c = 0.8$ and $t = 0.25$ and the multiplier is 2.5 as compared with 5 in *A*. Note that in *A* a €100 increase in autonomous expenditure increases disposable income by the same amount, leading to a €80 rise in consumption. However, in *B* a €100 rise in autonomous expenditure increases disposable income by €75 (the other €25 goes to the government in taxes) leading to a €60 rise in consumption. Hence, letting taxes vary with income reduces the value of the income–expenditure multiplier and dampens the impact of a change in autonomous expenditures on output.

**Exercise 26.5** In a particular economy, the consumption function is $C = 600 - 0.75(Y - T)$ and $T = tY$. The other components of autonomous expenditures are $\bar{I} = \bar{G} = \overline{NX} = 100$. If $t = 1/3$ (one-third) find the changes in *Y* and the government deficit if net exports were to fall by 37.5 units.

## The problem of deficits

In this chapter we have seen that the government's budget deficit is a key indicator of the strength and direction of fiscal policy. Other things being equal, an increase in the deficit indicates an expansionary fiscal policy while a decrease indicates a contractionary policy. We have also seen that changes in the deficit are partly the result of discretionary decisions taken by government to change taxes or purchases and partly the result of automatic changes in net taxes as the economy moves from recession to expansion. While discretionary and automatic changes in the deficit are important stabilisation instruments, sustained government deficits can be harmful to the economy. As we saw in Chapter 22, higher government deficits reduce national saving, which in turn reduces investment in new capital goods – an important source of long-run economic growth. Also, deficits have to be financed by *borrowing* and if they persist over long periods the government's debt will increase continuously. Recall from Chapter 22 that the government deficit or surplus is a *flow* or the amount that the government borrows or saves in each year, but the government's outstanding debt is a *stock* resulting from the accumulation of previous deficits. For example, if government borrows €1 million in two consecutive years its stock of outstanding debt will be €2 million higher by the end of the second year. Hence a continuous flow of borrowing adds to the stock of *outstanding debt*.

Persistent government deficits and increasing debt can create problems when economies are closely integrated and especially when they use a common currency. In particular, expansionary fiscal policy by one or a group of countries can lead to *negative externalities* which impose costs on partner countries whose fiscal policies may be more conservative. Recall from Chapter 11 that we defined a negative externality as *a cost of an activity that falls on people other than those who pursue the activity*. We shall see that differences in fiscal policies within a monetary union may give rise to three possible negative externalities. The first is the effect on *interest rates*, the second is the impact on *exchange rates* and the third relates to *debt sustainability*.

## Interest rates

To focus our ideas we shall assume that there are two countries in a monetary union, *A* and *B*. Suppose that *A*'s government has a zero deficit while *B*'s government continuously increases its deficit by increasing its purchases and cutting taxes. Other things being equal, increased government borrowing by *B*, which is necessary to finance its deficit, leads to higher real interest and, as we saw in Example 22.8, lower national saving and investment in economy *B*. However, in a monetary union, partner countries share common interest rates, which implies that higher real interest rates in *B* may spill over to *A* resulting in lower investment and a slowdown in *A*'s economy leading to an increase in *A*'s government deficit. Hence country *A* experiences a negative externality because it bears the cost of an activity (increased deficits) pursued by its partner. In the terminology of Chapter 22, higher real interest rates in *B* will lead to capital outflows from *A* to *B* and the resulting excess demand for capital in *A* will force a corresponding rise in *A*'s interest rates. There is, however, one important qualification to this argument. If financial markets in *A* and *B* are small relative to world markets then they may be considered as *price takers*, with the implication that they can borrow outside the monetary union with little or no effect on domestic interest rates. That is, they face a perfectly elastic supply curve for capital at the current 'world' interest rate. In this sense they are analogous to the perfectly competitive firm, discussed in Chapter 6, which faces a perfectly elastic demand curve at the market price. Just as the output of the competitive firm does not affect the market price, borrowing by a single country may not affect the market, or world, rate of interest. For example, if a member country of the Eurosystem finances its deficit by borrowing in US dollars then its activities will have little effect on euro interest rates.

## Exchange rates

An exchange rate is the price of *one currency in terms of the other*. For example, if 1 euro buys 1.2 US dollars, or €1 = $1.2, then the dollar–euro exchange rate is 1.2. As we shall see in Chapter 29, like other prices the exchange rate is determined by demand and supply on the *foreign exchange market* – the market in which currencies are traded for each other. If, for example, market participants decide to sell (or supply) dollars to buy (or demand) euros then the dollar price of 1 euro will increase, which we refer to as an *appreciation* of the euro. Conversely, if market participants decide to sell (or supply) euros to buy (or demand) dollars then the dollar price of 1 euro will decrease, which we refer to as a *depreciation* of the euro. Now suppose that a Eurosystem country such as France starts to run large government deficits financed by borrowing in US dollars. As the French government borrows these dollars to pay for projects such as road building and new schools it must sell the dollars and buy euros, leading to a possible appreciation of the euro. As the euro appreciates in value, foreign goods become less expensive to Europeans and European goods more expensive to foreigners. Other things being equal, an increase in the euro exchange rate will lead to a decline in net exports and, as we have seen, a short-run fall in equilibrium output. However, because Belgium, Germany, Ireland, Italy, etc. also use the euro as their currency the impact of the euro's appreciation will be spread across the *entire system*. Hence increased deficits in one country can affect economic activity in its monetary union partners.

## Debt sustainability

Panel (a) in Fig. 26.2 shows the behaviour of government deficits in Belgium and Italy over the period 1980–2000 while panel (b) shows the outstanding debt of these countries. Both deficits and debts are expressed as percentages of each country's GDP.

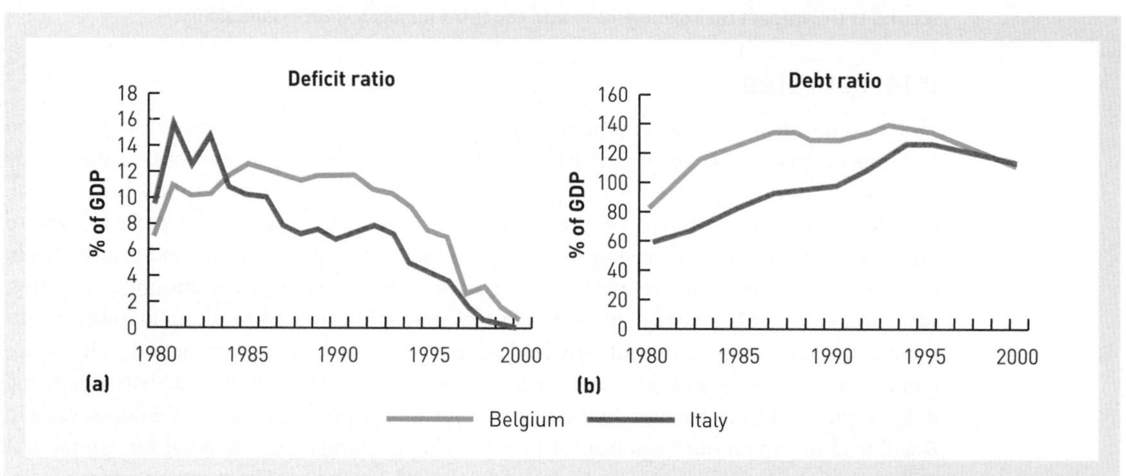


**Figure 26.2 Deficit and Debt Ratios, Belgium and Italy, 1980–2000, percentage of actual GDP.**
*Source: OECD Economic Outlook*, www.oecd.org.

Figure 26.2 illustrates that continuous borrowing to finance large government deficits leads to an ever-increasing stock of outstanding debt. By the early 1990s, government debt in both countries was well in excess of 100 per cent of GDP. Much the same was true of other countries such as Greece and Ireland whose debt ratios reached 100 per cent of GDP in the late 1980s, although the Irish debt ratio declined significantly over the 1990s. One way in which such countries can deal with an increasing debt ratio is to finance deficits by borrowing from their national Central Banks. Effectively, this means that rather than borrowing from the private sector the government prints the money necessary to finance its deficit, a policy known as *monetary financing*. As we saw in Chapter 23, monetary financing leads to an increase in the money supply and rising inflation which reduces the real value, and hence the burden, of the government's debt. However, Article 103 of the Maastricht Treaty explicitly prohibits the

**no-bailout clause** a provision in the Maastricht Treaty which prohibits the ESCB from lending to national governments

ESCB from lending to national governments. This Article is known as the **no-bailout clause**, and it means that responsibility for financing deficits and paying off debt remains at the *national* level.

The no-bailout clause implies that to stop their debt from rising, governments must reduce their deficits by cutting expenditures and/or increasing taxes. Unfortunately such measures are politically unpopular and governments with time horizons focused on the next election are often unwilling to countenance such harsh fiscal measures. However, if deficits remain high and the debt continues to grow then international financial markets may question the government's willingness to take the necessary corrective action and demand an interest rate premium to continue lending – or, in extreme cases, refuse to finance deficits by purchasing additional government debt. Such an outcome not only would force hard contractionary fiscal policies on the delinquent country but could also spill over into partner monetary union countries. One reason for this spillover is that in the Eurosystem all government debt is denominated in euros, which means that international investors may not distinguish between debt issues by different governments. German, French, Italian and Irish government bonds, etc. may simply be seen as *euro-denominated assets* rather than debt issued by different countries, with the consequence that a loss of confidence in bonds issued by one government may spill over into debt issued by the others. Once again, the actions of one country can affect its partners – the *externality effect*.

The authors of the Maastricht Treaty were very aware of the risks associated with large government deficits. Article 104 of the Treaty decrees that 'Member States shall avoid excess government deficits' and stipulates reference or target values for both government deficits and debt ratios. Specifically, to qualify for membership of the Eurosystem a country's deficit could not exceed 3 per cent of GDP and its debt ratio could not exceed 60 per cent. These conditions were part of the Maastricht Convergence Criteria and became known as the *Excessive Deficit Procedure*. The condition for the debt ratio was, however, qualified. Countries with debt ratios above 60 per cent of GDP could be deemed to satisfy the criteria provided that the ratio was 'diminishing sufficiently and approaching the reference value at a satisfactory pace'. As shown in Fig. 26.2, neither Belgium nor Italy could have satisfied the debt criterion without this qualification.

While the Excessive Deficit Procedure proved to be successful in bringing deficits under control it would have been inconsistent with Article 104 of the Treaty if these restraints were removed once the monetary union actually started. As we have seen above, it is important that member countries avoid large deficits once they adopt the single currency. To prevent this from happening the countries joining the Eurosystem agreed to control their deficits by negotiating the *Stability and Growth Pact* (SGP), discussed in Economic naturalist 26.1.

## Economic naturalist 26.1 The Stability and Growth Pact

The SGP, more commonly known as the Stability Pact, was negotiated at the December 1996 European summit in Dublin and finally agreed six months later at the Amsterdam summit. As in the Excessive Deficit Procedure the SGP establishes a 3 per cent reference value for government deficits. The European Commission monitors the fiscal positions of each country and reports to the Council of Economic and Finance Ministers, or Ecofin. If Ecofin rules that a country has breached the 3 per cent reference value it can issue recommendations and a deadline for corrective action. Countries that fail to comply with these recommendations can be subject to sanctions or fines. For example, if a country runs a deficit between 3 and 4 per cent of its GDP the fine is 0.2 per cent of GDP. If the deficit is between 4 and 5 per cent of GDP the fine is increased to 0.3 per cent of GDP and so on. The maximum fine is 0.5 per cent and applies to countries whose deficit exceeds 6 per cent of GDP.

The SGP recognises that countries may breach the 3 per cent reference value because of exceptional economic conditions such as a severe recession. Hence, if real GDP declines by more than 2 per cent in a given year the SGP grants an exemption for countries whose deficit is in excess of the reference value. When the decline in real GDP is between 0.75 and 2 per cent the country concerned can apply for an exemption from fines which may be granted if Ecofin agrees that the country is experiencing exceptional economic conditions. However, when the fall in real GDP is less than 0.75 per cent, exemptions are not permitted. Table 26.1 summarises the major provisions of the SGP.

| | | **Fines** | | |
|---|---|---|---|---|
| Deficit (% of GDP) | 3–4 | 4–5 | 5–6 | 6 and above |
| Fine (% of GDP) | 0.2 | 0.3 | 0.4 | 0.5 |
| | | **Exemptions** | | |
| Decline in GDP | | | | |
| 2% or more | | Automatic | | |
| 0.75–2% | | Can be granted in exceptional circumstances | | |
| Less than 0.75% | | No exemption | | |

**Table 26.1** The Stability and Growth Pact

## The SGP and automatic stabilisers

In addition to compliance with the 3 per cent reference value the SGP also requires the European Commission and individual governments in the Eurosystem to agree *Stability Programmes* for their deficit and debt ratios. The purpose of these Stability Programmes is to ensure that each government's budgetary position is 'close to balance or in surplus' over the 'medium term'. In practice, this means that governments should aim for *balanced budgets*, or *zero deficits*, over the course of the business cycle. To illustrate, remember that we have defined expansionary and recessionary gaps as the deviation of actual output $Y$ from potential or full-employment output $Y^*$. In proportionate or percentage terms the expansionary or recessionary gap is

$$\text{Gap} = \left(\frac{Y^* - Y}{Y^*}\right)$$

Hence if the gap is +0.01, or +1 per cent, the economy is operating at 1 per cent below its potential output, $Y^*$, a recessionary gap. Conversely, if the gap is –0.01, or –1 per cent, the economy is operating at 1 per cent above $Y^*$, an expansionary gap. Now consider an economy which records gaps of –1 per cent, 0 and +1 per cent over three successive years (the medium term). That is, the economy moves from an expansionary gap in year one to a recessionary gap in year three. In this economy the SGP and the Stability Programmes require that the average value for the government deficit should be close to zero over these three years and should be close to zero or in surplus in year two when $Y = Y^*$. For example, the terms of the SGP would be satisfied if the deficit was –2 per cent of GDP in year one, zero in year two and +2 per cent in year three. (Remember that the deficit is defined as government purchases $G$ minus net taxes $T$ so that a negative value implies a surplus or $T > G$.)

One important reason for setting these *medium-term targets* is that they allow automatic stabilisers to operate at their maximum effectiveness and give governments greater flexibility in using discretionary policy. In Example 26.4 we saw that when a recessionary gap appears the automatic stabiliser effect means that net taxes decline with output, leading to smaller declines in disposable incomes and consumption expenditures. If this did not happen then the fall in total expenditures would be greater leading to a larger recessionary gap. Table 26.2 illustrates how adherence to the SGP and Stability Programmes enhances the effectiveness of automatic stabilisers and gives greater scope for discretionary fiscal policy. Table 26.2 illustrates two hypothetical examples, labelled *A* and *B*, of how the deficit might behave as the economy moves from an expansion recession.

| Output gap (% of $Y^*$) | Deficit (% of GDP) Policy *A* | Policy *B* |
|---|---|---|
| -6 | -3.0 | -1.0 |
| -5 | -2.5 | -0.5 |
| -4 | -2.0 | 0.0 |
| -3 | -1.5 | 0.5 |
| -2 | -1.0 | 1.0 |
| -1 | -0.5 | 1.5 |
| 0 | 0.0 | 2.0 |
| 1 | 0.5 | 2.5 |
| 2 | 1.0 | 3.0 |
| 3 | 1.5 | 3.5 |
| 4 | 2.0 | 4.0 |
| 5 | 2.5 | 4.5 |
| 6 | 3.0 | 5.0 |
| Average | 0.0 | 1.96 |

**Table 26.2 The Stability Pact and Automatic Stabilisers**. Each 1 per cent increase in the recessionary gap leads to an automatic 0.5 per cent increase in the deficit.

In each case, we assume that there are no discretionary policy changes and that a 1 per cent recessionary gap automatically increases the deficit by 0.5 per cent of GDP. For example, when the recessionary gap increases from zero to 1 per cent we assume the deficit automatically increases by 0.5 per cent of GDP. Likewise, when the recessionary gap increases from 1 to 2 per cent the deficit automatically increases by an additional 0.5 per cent of GDP, and so on. If policy *A* is followed the deficit is zero when $Y = Y^*$ and averages to zero as the economy moves from expansion to recession. However, in policy *B* the deficit is 2 per cent of GDP when $Y = Y^*$ and averages to 1.96 per cent. Hence the government complies with the medium-term targets of the SGP in policy *A* but does not in policy *B*. Now suppose that actual output equals potential output and the government is following policy *A* by setting its deficit at zero. If the economy moves into recession the government has the flexibility to let the deficit increase and would breach the 3 per cent reference value only when the recessionary gap reaches 6 per cent, which in most cases would correspond to a severe recession. Also, because the government is complying with the SGP it has the opportunity to introduce discretionary increases in its purchases and/or lower tax rates to reinforce the automatic stabiliser effect and stop the economy moving further into recession. For example, at a recessionary gap of 1 per cent the government has the option to increase the deficit by up to 2.5 per cent by discretionary policy changes. By contrast, if the government followed policy *B* its deficit would be 2 per cent at the onset of recession and the 3 per cent reference value would be breached at a recessionary gap of 2 per cent. To comply with the terms of the SGP the government would have to prevent a further rise in the deficit by cutting its expenditures and/or increasing taxes. That is, the government would have to disable the automatic effect by introducing a contractionary fiscal policy which, of course, would deepen the recession. In short, by adhering to the terms of the SGP, governments can let automatic stabilisers work effectively and have greater scope for discretionary fiscal policy.

## Problems with the SGP

While it is generally agreed that fiscal discipline is necessary for a successful monetary union the SGP is not without its critics. In fact the last President of the European Commission, Romano Prodi, was reported as calling the SGP 'stupid' and *The Economist* magazine labelled it 'the stupidity pact'. Much of this criticism comes from the fact that rigid adherence to the SGP may require governments to take *contractionary measures* when the economy is in recession. Using the example in Table 26.2, suppose the government is following policy *B* and is faced with a 2 per cent recessionary gap. Given that its deficit will be 3 per cent of GDP the required corrective action might be a switch to policy *A* which, if successful, would reduce the deficit to 1 per cent. This, however, would require the government to reduce expenditure and/or increase taxation, which, as illustrated by Examples 26.1 and 26.2, leads to a fall in output and widens the recessionary gap. Hence, while it is important that governments avoid excessive deficits it is also important that even errant governments should not be forced to take measures which may lead to lower growth and higher unemployment when the economy is faced with a recessionary gap and rising unemployment.

A high-profile example is the situation faced by France and Germany in 2002 and 2003. In 2002 the French deficit was 3.3 per cent of GDP and the German deficit 3.5 per cent. The European Commission and Ecofin ruled that both countries were in breach of the SGP and recommended corrective action to be taken, with fines to be imposed in 2004 if the deficits did not fall below 3 per cent. However, by 2003 the French deficit had increased to 4.1 per cent of GDP and the German deficit to 3.9 per cent. While the failure of France and Germany to comply with the SGP led to a prolonged dispute between their governments and Ecofin, the important question is why the French and German deficits increased over 2002–03. In both cases, the main cause was growing recessionary gaps which, via automatic stabilisers, led to higher deficits. In France the recessionary gap increased from 0.1 per cent in 2002 to 1.8 per cent in 2003 and in Germany it increased from 1.3 per cent to 2.9 per cent at the same time. Given that both countries were stuck in recession there would have been little economic logic in forcing their governments to use contractionary fiscal policies designed to bring the deficits closer to the 3 per cent reference value but at the cost of further aggravating the underlying economic problem.

The examples of France and Germany illustrate an inconsistency in the SGP. There is a strong case for putting limits on government deficits but there is an equally strong argument for permitting discretion and flexibility when governments are faced with slow economic growth and high unemployment. One possible way out of this dilemma is to set deficit targets in terms of the **cyclically adjusted budget deficit** rather than the actual deficit. This idea is explained in Example 26.6.

**cyclically adjusted budget deficit** eliminates automatic changes by evaluating the government's budget deficit at a constant level of output

### Example 26.6 The cyclically adjusted budget deficit

We have seen that increases in the French and German deficits over 2002–03 resulted in the threat of fines if the governments failed to comply with Ecofin's recommendations for corrective action. However, corrective action in the form of contractionary fiscal measures would have been inappropriate at a time when both economies were experiencing recession and could have weakened or even disabled the automatic stabilisers. An alternative approach that avoids penalising governments whose deficits are increasing because of automatic stabiliser effects is to judge their performance on discretionary actions only. This, however, requires that we can decompose changes in the actual deficit into components due to *automatic* changes and *discretionary* policy. This is what the *cyclically adjusted budget deficit* attempts to do.

The *cyclically adjusted budget deficit* separates automatic from discretionary changes by evaluating each year's deficit at a *constant level of output*. Evaluating the deficit at a constant level of output means that automatic changes, which depend on output changes, are eliminated in the calculation, so that the measured change in the deficit reflects discretionary policy only. As automatic changes are the result of cyclical changes or year-to-year variations in output the resulting measure is known as the *cyclically adjusted budget deficit*. Although the cyclically adjusted budget deficit can be calculated at any constant level of output it is common to use the economy's full-employment or potential output $Y^*$.

To illustrate, consider an economy in which autonomous expenditures $\bar{A}' = 2{,}240$, potential output $Y^* = 5{,}600$, government purchases $G = 1{,}500$ and net taxes are $T = 0.25Y$. Suppose that planned investment falls by 100 and government attempts to stabilise the economy with a 20 unit increase in G. If the income-expenditure multiplier is 2.5 find the change in the government's deficit. How much of the change in the deficit is due to discretionary fiscal policy and how much is due to automatic stabiliser effects?

As autonomous expenditures are 2,240 and the multiplier is 2.5 then, using Eq. (26.5), equilibrium output is 5,600 which equals $Y^*$. Net taxes are 25 per cent of $Y$ or 1,400. As $G =$ 1,500 the government deficit is 100. If investment falls by 100 units and the government increases G by 20 units the net fall in autonomous expenditure will be 80 units. As the multiplier is 2.5 output will fall by 200 units, to 5,400. Net taxes will fall to 1,350 (25 per cent of 5,400) and as G now equals 1,520 the deficit will increase by 70 to 170. The cyclically adjusted deficit is $(G - tY^*)$ or $1{,}520 - 1{,}400 = 120$. Hence, of the 70 unit increase in the actual deficit, 20 are due to discretionary policy changes and 50 to the automatic stabiliser effect.

This approach is analogous to the calculation of the consumer price index discussed in Chapter 19. In that case we measured the cost of a fixed basket of goods at the prices prevailing in each year. As the quantities of goods are held constant, any change in their cost must be due to changes in prices. Likewise, evaluating the deficit at a constant level of output means that automatic changes, which only happen when output changes, are eliminated and the resulting change reflects changes in discretionary policy only.

Figure 26.3 shows the actual and adjusted deficits for France and Germany over 1999–03. The adjusted deficit measures the contribution of discretionary fiscal policy and the automatic component, which is the difference between the actual and cyclically adjusted deficits, measures the contribution of automatic stabilisers. Note that the automatic component is positive when the actual deficit is greater than the adjusted deficit. In 2003, the actual German deficit was 3.9 per cent of GDP, which can be broken down into a cyclical component equal to 2.3 per cent of GDP and an automatic component equal to 1.6 per cent. Without the automatic component, which was due to the widening recessionary gap, the German deficit would have been within the 3 per cent reference value as required by the SGP. By basing the reference value on the cyclically adjusted rather than the actual deficit there would have been no reason to recommend corrective action at a time when the German

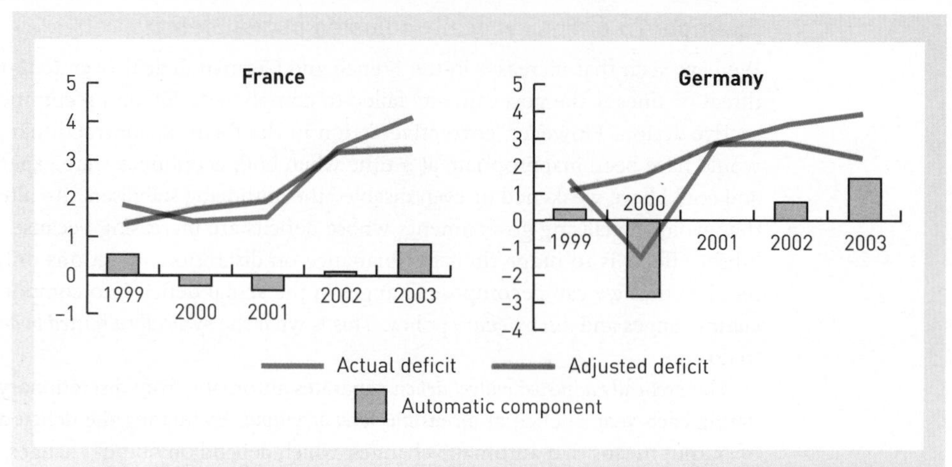


**Figure 26.3 Actual and Adjusted Deficits, France and Germany, 1999–2003, percentage of actual/potential GDP.**

*Source*: *OECD Economic Outlook*, No. 75, www.oecd.org.

economy was moving further into recession. Hence, there is an obvious case for focusing on the adjusted rather than the actual budget deficit. France, on the other hand, was in a different position. The actual deficit was 4.1 per cent of GDP and the adjusted deficit was 3.3, leaving an automatic component of 0.8 per cent. The relatively large adjusted deficit was mostly the result of President Chirac fulfilling his election pledge to cut taxes, a discretionary change. Hence, based on the cyclically adjusted deficit there was still a case for recommending corrective action by reversing the tax changes or cutting government expenditures. However, the correction needed to bring the adjusted deficit into line with the reference value would have been less severe than that required to reduce the actual deficit to below 3 per cent.

Basing the 3 per cent reference value on the cyclically adjusted rather than the actual deficit has the advantage of reducing the need to take corrective action in the form of tax hikes and expenditure cuts at a time when the economy is in recession. Should the SGP be reformed in this way? To date, the European Commission and most economists seem to favour a move in this direction. There is, however, one important caveat. Like many other concepts in applied economics, calculating the cyclically adjusted deficit is far from a precise science and there is a danger that governments, the Commission and Ecofin could become embroiled in arguments about estimation methods. Unless there is a binding agreement on how cyclically adjusted deficits are to be estimated it would be difficult to classify deficits as excessive and requiring corrective action. What, for example, would have happened in 2003 if France had argued that using an alternative, and perhaps equally valid, estimator its adjusted deficit was actually 2.3 rather than 3.3 per cent of GDP?

In March 2005 the Eurosystem governments did agree to reform the SGP, but not in the manner discussed above. Rather, they simply agreed to widen the concept of 'exceptional' circumstances under which the excessive deficit procedure could be breached. In effect there are no hard and fast rules and the Commission must judge each case on its merits. Hence, when considering the need for corrective action the Commission must take account of claimed 'special' circumstances underlying a rise in government deficits. These circumstances might include 'necessary' additional spending on infrastructural projects, education, health services, war, aid to developing countries and, in the case of Germany, the costs of unification. Although unlikely but by no means impossible, the cost of staging major events such as the Olympic Games could conceivably be counted as an exceptional circumstance. The extent to which these changes will weaken the SGP remains to be seen and may depend on the resolve shown by the Commission in dealing with errant governments whose claims for special circumstances may simply reflect fiscal indiscipline or thinly designed attempts to maintain political popularity.

## Fiscal policy as a stabilisation tool: two qualifications

The basic Keynesian model might lead you to think that precise use of fiscal policy can eliminate output gaps. But, as is often the case, the real world is more complicated than economic models suggest. We close the chapter with two qualifications about the use of fiscal policy as a stabilisation tool.

### Fiscal policy and the supply side

We have focused so far on the use of fiscal policy to affect planned aggregate expenditure. However, most economists would agree that *fiscal policy may affect potential output as well as planned aggregate expenditure* (PAE). On the spending side, for example, investments in public capital – such as roads, airports and schools – can play a major role in the growth of potential output, as we discussed in Chapter 20. On the other side of the ledger, tax and transfer programmes may well affect the incentives, and thus the economic behaviour, of households and firms. For example, a high tax rate on interest income may reduce the willingness of people to save for the future, while a tax break on new investment may encourage firms to increase their rate of capital formation. Such changes in saving or investment will in turn affect potential output. Many other examples could be given of how taxes and transfers affect economic behaviour, and thus possibly affect potential output as well.

Some critics of the Keynesian theory have gone so far as to argue that the *only* effects of fiscal policy that matter are effects on potential output. This was essentially the view of the so-called *supply-siders*, a group of American economists and journalists whose influence reached a high point during President Reagan's first term of office (1981–85). Supply-siders focused on the need for tax cuts, arguing that lower tax rates would lead people to work harder (because they would be allowed to keep a larger share of their earnings), to save more and to be more willing to innovate and take risks. Through their arguments that lower taxes would substantially increase potential output, with no significant effect on planned spending, the supply-siders provided crucial support for the large tax cuts that took place under the Reagan administration. Supply-sider ideas also were used to support the long-term income tax cut passed under President George W. Bush in 2001.

A more balanced view is that fiscal policy affects *both* planned spending *and* potential output. Thus, in making fiscal policy, government officials should take into account not only the need to stabilise planned aggregate expenditure but also the likely effects of government spending, taxes and transfers on the economy's *productive capacity*.

### The relative inflexibility of fiscal policy

The second qualification about the use of fiscal policy is that *fiscal policy is not always flexible enough to be useful for stabilisation*. Our examples have implicitly assumed that the government can change spending or taxes relatively quickly in order to eliminate output gaps. In reality, changes in government spending or taxes must usually go through a lengthy legislative process, which reduces the ability of fiscal policy to respond in a timely way to economic conditions. Another factor that limits the flexibility of fiscal policy is that fiscal policy makers have many other objectives besides stabilising aggregate spending – from ensuring an adequate national defence to providing income support to the poor. What happens if, say, the need to strengthen the national defence requires an increase in government spending, but the need to contain planned aggregate expenditure requires a decrease in government spending? Such conflicts can be difficult to resolve through the political process.

This lack of flexibility means that fiscal policy is less useful for stabilising spending than the basic Keynesian model suggests. Nevertheless, most economists view fiscal policy as an important stabilising force, for two reasons. The first is the presence of automatic stabilisers. These automatic changes in government spending and tax collections help to stabilise the economy by increasing planned spending during recessions and reduce it during expansions, *without the delays inherent in the legislative process*. The second reason that fiscal policy is an important stabilising force is that although fiscal policy may be difficult to change quickly, it may still be useful for dealing with prolonged episodes of recession: the Great Depression of the 1930s and the Japanese slump of the 1990s are two cases in point. However, because of the relative lack of flexibility of fiscal policy, in modern economies aggregate spending is more usually stabilised through *monetary policy*. The stabilising role of monetary policy is the subject of Chapter 27.

## Summary

- To eliminate output gaps and restore full employment, the government employs *stabilisation policies*. The two major types of stabilisation policy are monetary policy and fiscal policy. Stabilisation policies work by changing planned aggregate expenditure (PAE) and hence short-run equilibrium output. For example, an increase in government purchases raises autonomous expenditure directly, so it can be used to reduce or eliminate a recessionary gap. Similarly, a cut in taxes or an increase in transfer payments increases the public's disposable income, raising consumption spending at each level of output by an amount equal to the marginal propensity to consume times the cut in taxes or increase in transfers. Higher consumer spending, in turn, raises short-run equilibrium output.
- *Fiscal policy* can be expansionary or contractionary. An *expansionary* policy is one which increases planned spending and output while a *contractionary* policy has the opposite effect. The government budget deficit is the key indicator of the strength and direction of fiscal policy. An increase in the deficit indicates an expansionary policy while a fall indicated a contractionary policy. As the income-expenditure multiplier is greater than the tax and balanced-budget multipliers, changes in government purchases financed by borrowing are the most effective way to stabilise the economy.
- Decisions to change government purchases and tax rates are types of *discretionary* fiscal policy. However, as net taxes vary with economic activity the budget deficit will automatically rise during recessions and fall during expansions. This is the *automatic stabiliser effect* which helps to dampen cyclical fluctuations in economic activity. In the absence of automatic stabilisers recessions would be deeper and more prolonged.
- Persistent government deficits are harmful to the economy because they can reduce national saving and investment. In a monetary union such as the Eurosystem, high deficits in one or a group of countries can result in negative externality effects, which can be lead to a loss of confidence and offset the benefits of a common currency. Hence countries in the Eurosystem have agreed a *Stability and Growth Pact* (SGP), which limits government deficits to 3 per cent of GDP.
- Two qualifications must be made to the use of fiscal policy as a stabilisation tool. First, fiscal policy may affect *potential output* as well as *aggregate spending*. Second, because changes in fiscal policy must go through a lengthy legislative process, fiscal policy is not always flexible enough to be useful for *short-run stabilisation*. However, *automatic stabilisers* can overcome the problem of legislative delays and contribute to economic stability.

## Key terms

automatic stabilisers (745)
balanced-budget multiplier (744)
contractionary policies (738)
cyclically adjusted budget deficit (754)
discretionary fiscal policy (745)
expansionary policies (738)
no-bailout clause (751)
stabilisation policies (738)
tax multiplier (742)

## Review questions

1. Define *stabilisation policies*. Distinguish between expansionary and contractionary stabilisation policies.
2. The government wishes to stimulate planned aggregate expenditure and is considering two alternative policies: a €50 million increases in government purchases and a €50 million tax cut. Which policy will have the greatest impact on planned aggregate expenditure? Why?
3. Define the *balanced-budget multiplier*. In economic terms, why is the balanced-budget multiplier equal to one?
4. Explain the concept of an *automatic stabiliser* and distinguish between automatic and discretionary changes in the government budget deficit.
5. Explain why high government deficits can lead to *negative externalities* between closely integrated national economies.
6. What are the principal features of the *Stability and Growth Pact* (SGP).
7. Define the concept of the *cyclically adjusted budget deficit*. How does the adjusted deficit differ from the actual deficit?
8. Is there a case for recasting the Stability Pact's 3 per cent reference value for government deficits in terms of the adjusted rather than the actual government deficit?
9. Explain how fiscal policy can affect potential output as well as aggregate spending.
10. Explain why fiscal policy may not be sufficiently flexible to deal with or short-run stablisation problems.

## Problems

Problems marked with an asterisk (*) are more difficult.

1. For the following economy, find autonomous expenditure, the multiplier, short-run equilibrium output and the output gap. By how much would government purchases have to change to eliminate the output gap?

$$C = 3{,}000 + 0.5(Y - T)$$
$$I^p = 1{,}500$$
$$G = 2{,}500$$
$$NX = 200$$
$$T = 2{,}000$$
$$Y^* = 12{,}000$$

2. An economy is described by the following equations:

$$C = 1{,}800 + 0.6(Y - T)$$
$$I^p = 900$$

$$G = 1{,}500$$
$$NX = 100$$
$$T = 1{,}500$$
$$Y^* = 9{,}000$$

Find the effect on short-run equilibrium output of:

**a.** An increase in government purchases from 1,500 to 1,600.

**b.** A decrease in tax collections from 1,500 to 1,400 (leaving government purchases at their original value).

**c.** An increase in government purchases from 1,500 to 1,600 financed by an equal increase in taxation.

**3.** An economy is initially at full employment, but a 20 unit decrease in planned investment spending (a component of autonomous expenditure) pushes the economy into recession. Assume that the MPC of this economy is 0.75 and that the multiplier is 4.

**a.** How large is the recessionary gap after the fall in planned investment?

**b.** By how much would the government have to change its purchases to restore the economy to full employment?

**c.** Alternatively, by how much would the government have to change taxes?

**d.*** Suppose that the government's budget is initially in balance, with government spending equal to taxes collected. A balanced-budget law forbids the government from running a deficit. Is there anything that fiscal policy makers could do to restore full employment in this economy, assuming that they do not want to violate the balanced-budget law?

**4.** An economy is described by the following equations:

$$C = 40 = 0.8\,(Y - T)$$
$$I^P = 70$$
$$G = 120$$
$$NX = 10$$
$$T = 150$$
$$Y^* = 580$$

**a.** Find the value of short-run equilibrium output. (**Hint:** The economy is fairly close to full employment.)

**b.** By how much would government purchases have to change in order to eliminate any output gap? By how much would taxes have to change? Show the effects of these fiscal policy changes in a Keynesian cross diagram.

**c.** Repeat part (b) assuming that $Y^* = 630$.

**5.*** This problem illustrates the workings of automatic stabilisers. Suppose that the components of planned spending in an economy are: $C = \bar{C} + c\,(Y - T)$, $I^P = \bar{I}$, $G = \bar{G}$ and $NX = \overline{NX}$. However, suppose that, realistically, taxes are not fixed but depend on income. Specifically, we assume

$$T = tY$$

where $t$ is the fraction of income paid in taxes (the tax rate). As we shall see in this problem, a tax system of this sort serves as an automatic stabiliser, because taxes collected automatically fall when incomes fall.

**a.** Find an algebraic expression for short-run equilibrium output in this economy.

**b.** Find an algebraic expression for the multiplier – that is, the amount that output changes when autonomous expenditure changes by 1 unit. Compare the expression you found to the formula for the multiplier when taxes are fixed. Show that making taxes proportional to income reduces the multiplier.

**c.** Explain how reducing the size of the multiplier helps to stabilise the economy, holding constant the typical size of fluctuations in the components of autonomous expenditure.

**d.** Suppose $\overline{C} = 500$, $\overline{I} = 1{,}500$, $\overline{G} = 2{,}000$, $\overline{NX} = 0$, $c = 0.8$ and $t = 0.25$. Calculate numerical values for short-run equilibrium output and the multiplier.

## Answers to in-chapter exercises

**26.1** This exercise is just the reverse of Example 26.1. An increase in $\overline{C}$ of 10 units raises autonomous expenditure by 10 units. Using Eq. (26.1) a 10 unit increase in $\overline{A}$ increases $Y$ by 50 units, to 4,850. Note that as the marginal propensity to consume is 0.8 the multiplier is 5 so that a 10 unit rise in autonomous expenditure leads to a 50 unit increase in $Y$. To offset this increase in output and eliminate the output gap, government must *reduce* G by 10 units which leads to a 50 unit fall in output and stabilises $Y$ at 4,800 (Eq. (26.2)).

**26.2** The 20 unit increase in planned investment is a 20 unit increase in autonomous expenditure, which will lead to a greater increase in short-run equilibrium output. To offset the 20 unit increase in autonomous expenditure by means of fiscal policy, the government can reduce its purchases by 20 units. Alternatively, it could raise taxes (or cut transfers) to reduce consumption spending. Since $MPC = 0.5$, to reduce consumption spending by 20 units at each level of output, the government will need to increase taxes (or reduce transfers) by 40 units. At each level of output, a 40 unit tax increase will reduce disposable income by 40 units and cause consumers to reduce their spending by $0.5 \times 40 = 20$ units, as needed to eliminate the expansionary output gap.

**26.3** To offset an expansionary output gap the government would normally reduce its purchases and/or increase taxation. If it wishes to keep the deficit ($G - T$) constant then it must set $\Delta\overline{G} = -\Delta\overline{T}$ (Eq. (26.4)). As the balanced-budget multiplier is 1 the change in G and $T$ must equal the output gap. If marginal propensity to consume is 0.5 the income-expenditure multiplier will be 5 and a 20 unit increase in planned investment will increase $Y$ by 100 units. Hence government must set $\Delta\overline{G} = -100$ and $\Delta\overline{T} = +100$.

**26.4** This exercise is just the reverse of Example 26.4. In that Example a 10 unit fall in net exports reduced output by 50 units in economy $A$ and 25 units in economy $B$. As net exports are part of autonomous expenditures it follows that the income–expenditure multiplier is 5 ($10 \times 5 = 50$) in $A$ and 2.5 ($10 \times 2.5 = 25$) in $B$. Hence, a 10 unit increase in net exports will increase output by 50 units in $A$ and 25 units in $B$. In $A$ net taxes do not change with $Y$ and the deficit will be unaffected. In $B$, $T = tY$ and the tax rate $t = 0.25$. As the increase in net exports increases $B$'s output by 25 units to 4,825 tax revenues will rise from 1,200 to 1,206.25. With government purchases fixed at 1,200 the government will now have a surplus (or negative deficit) of 6.25. Because tax revenues increase with $Y$ the increase in disposable income and consumption expenditures will be lower in $B$, leading to a smaller expansionary output gap.

**26.5** Using Eq. (26.5), the multiplier is $1/(1 - 0.75(1 - 1/3)) = 2$ and autonomous expenditures are $\overline{A}' = 900$. Hence equilibrium $Y$ is 1,800. Tax revenues are $tY = 600$. As government purchases are 100 the deficit $G - T = -500$. A 37.5 unit fall in next exports reduces autonomous expenditure by 37.5 to 862.5 and, given that the multiplier is 2, $Y$ falls by 75 units to 1,725. Tax revenues $tY = 575$ and the deficit is $-475$. Hence the government deficit increases by 25 units which helps to stabilise the economy by dampening the fall in $Y$.

# 27

# Stabilising the Economy: the Role of Monetary Policy

Individuals charged with responsibility for monetary policy, such as the ECB's Governing Council, are often subjected to close public scrutiny aimed at ascertaining their views on the state of the economy and how they might react to current and future developments. The reason for the intense public interest in ECB decisions about monetary policy – and especially the level of interest rates – is that those decisions have important implications both for financial markets and for the Eurosystem economy in general. Decisions taken by the ECB's Governing Council can affect returns to small savers, the financial plans of large corporations and whether you change you car this year or next. Regardless of whether an individual is the chief executive of a large Dutch electronics company or owns a small restaurant in the west of Ireland, the deliberations of the Governing Council can have important implications for business success and financial well-being. Hence, it is not surprising that every speech and interview from a member of the Governing Council is closely analysed for clues about the future course of policy

In this chapter we examine the workings of monetary policy, one of the two major types of *stabilisation policy*. (The other type, fiscal policy, was discussed in Chapter 26.) As we saw in Chapter 26, stabilisation policies are government policies that are meant to influence *planned aggregate expenditure (PAE)*, with the goal of eliminating *output gaps*. Both types of stabilisation policy – monetary and fiscal – are important and have been useful at various times. However, monetary policy, which can be changed quickly by a decision of the ECB's Governing Council, is more flexible and responsive than fiscal policy. Also, within the Eurosystem there is, as yet, no central fiscal authority equivalent to the ECB. As we saw in Chapter 26, national governments have, subject to the provisions of the Stability and Growth Pact (SGP), freedom to change tax and expenditure levels depending on the conditions in their own economies. Under normal circumstances, therefore, monetary policy is used more actively than fiscal policy to help stabilise the Eurosystem's economy.

We shall begin this chapter by discussing how the ECB uses its ability to control the money supply to influence the level of interest rates. We then turn to the economic effects of changes in interest rates. Building on our analysis of the basic Keynesian model in Chapter 25, we shall see that, in the short run, monetary policy works by affecting planned spending and thus short-run equilibrium output. We shall defer discussion of the other major effect of monetary policy actions, changes in the rate of inflation, to Chapter 28.

## The ECB and interest rates

When we introduced the ECB in Chapter 23, we focused on the Bank's tools for controlling the Eurosystem's *money supply*. Unlike the United States or the United Kingdom, the Eurosystem is not a single country with a national government. While each country in the Eurosystem retains its own national Central Bank (NCB) these banks are now part of the European System of Central Banks (ESCB), headed by the Frankfurt-based ECB. As the policy set by the ECB's Governing Council prevails in all participating countries we can, from a monetary policy perspective, think of the Eurosystem as a single country. In short, because the Eurosystem is a full monetary union with a single currency and a unified Central Bank we can think of the Eurosystem's money supply in the same way as we think of the US or the UK money supply. Likewise, because it has a single monetary policy, interest rates are equal in all Eurosystem economies, from Finland to Greece, just as the same interest rates are common to all American states, from North Dakota to Texas. In this sense, and perhaps only in this sense, we can think of the Eurosystem, but not the European Union, as a single political and monetary entity. Hence, for the purpose of analysing monetary policy we shall treat the Eurosystem as a single country.

Determining the *money supply* is the primary task of monetary policy makers. But if you follow the economic news regularly, you may find the idea that the ECB's job is to control the money supply a bit foreign, because the news media nearly always focus on the Bank's decisions about *interest rates*. Indeed, the announcement the ECB makes after each meeting of the Governing Council nearly always concerns its decisions on the *refinancing rate* which, as we saw in Chapter 23, is the key interest rate in the Eurosystem.

Actually, there is no contradiction between the two ways of looking at monetary policy – as control of the money supply or as the setting of interest rates. As we shall see in this section, controlling the money supply and controlling the nominal interest rate are two sides of the same coin: any value of the money supply chosen by the ECB implies a specific setting for the nominal interest rate, and vice versa. The reason for this close connection is that the nominal interest rate is effectively the 'price' of money (or, more accurately, its *opportunity cost*). So, by controlling the quantity of money supplied to the economy, the ECB, or any Central Bank, also controls the 'price' of money (the *nominal interest rate*).

To understand better how the ECB determines interest rates, we shall look first at the market for money, beginning with the demand side of that market. We shall see that, given the demand for money by the public, the ECB can control interest rates by changing the amount of money it supplies. Later we shall show how the ECB uses the control of interest rates to influence planned spending and the state of the Eurosystem's economy.

### The demand for money

Recall from Chapter 23 that *money* refers to the set of assets, such as cash and chequing accounts, that are usable in transactions. Money is also a store of value, like stocks, bonds or real estate – in other words, a type of financial asset. As a financial asset, money is a way of *holding wealth*.

Anyone who has some wealth must determine the *form* in which they wish to hold that wealth. For example, if Louis has wealth of €10,000, he could, if he wished, hold all €10,000 in cash. Or he could hold €5,000 of his wealth in the form of cash and €5,000 in government bonds. Or he could hold €1,000 in cash, €2,000 in a chequing account, €2,000 in government bonds and €5,000 in rare stamps. Indeed, there are thousands of different real and financial assets to choose from, all of which can be held in different amounts and combinations, so Louis' choices are virtually infinite. The decision about the forms in which to hold one's wealth is called the **portfolio allocation decision**.

**portfolio allocation decision** the decision about the forms in which to hold one's wealth

What determines the particular *mix of assets* that Louis or another wealth holder will choose? All else being equal, people generally prefer to hold assets that they expect to pay a high *return* and do not carry too much *risk*. They may also try to reduce the overall risk they face through *diversification* – that is, by owning a variety of different assets.[1] Many people own some real assets, such as a car or a home, because they provide services (transportation or shelter) and often a financial return (an increase in value, as when the price of a home rises in a strong housing market).

Here we do not need to analyse the entire portfolio allocation decision, but only one part of it – namely, the decision about how much of one's wealth to hold in the form of *money* (cash and chequing accounts). The amount of wealth an individual chooses to hold in the form of money is that individual's **demand for money**. So if Louis decided to hold his entire €10,000 in the form of cash, his demand for money would be €10,000. But if he were to hold €1,000 in cash, €2,000 in a chequing account, €2,000 in government bonds and €5,000 in rare stamps, his demand for money would be only €3,000 – that is, €1,000 in cash plus the €2,000 in his chequing account.

**demand for money** the amount of wealth an individual chooses to hold in the form of money

### Example 27.1 The Rossis' demand for money

Example 22.1 presented the balance sheet of a household called the Rossis (see Table 22.1). What is their demand for money? If the Rossis wanted to increase their money holdings by €100, how could they do so? What if they wanted to reduce their money holdings by €100?

Looking back at Table 22.1, we see that the Rossis' balance sheet shows five different asset types: cash, a bank account, shares of stock, a car and furniture. Of these assets, the first two (the cash and the bank account) are forms of money. As shown in Table 22.1, the Rossis' money holdings consist of €100 in cash and €1,200 in their bank account. Thus the Rossis' *demand for money* – the amount of wealth they choose to hold in the form of money – is €1,300.

There are many different ways in which the Rossis could increase their money holdings, or demand for money, by €100. They could sell €100 worth of shares in companies and deposit the proceeds in the bank. That action would leave the total value of their assets and wealth unchanged (because the decrease in their shareholdings would be offset by the increase in their bank account) but would increase their money holdings by €100. Another possibility would be to take a €100 cash advance on their credit card. That action would increase both their money holdings and their assets by €100 but would also increase their liabilities – specifically, their credit card balance – by €100. Once again, the Rossis' total wealth would not change, though their money holdings would increase.

To reduce their money holdings, the Rossis need only use some of their cash or bank account balance to acquire a non-money asset or pay down a liability. For example, if they were to buy an additional €100 of shares by writing a cheque against their bank account, their money holdings would decline by €100. Similarly, writing a cheque to reduce their credit card balance by €100 would reduce their money holdings by €100. You can confirm that although the Rossis' money holdings decline, in neither case does their total wealth change.

How much money should an individual (or household) choose to hold? Application of the *Cost–Benefit Principle* (Chapter 1) tells us that an individual should increase her money holdings only so long as the benefit of doing so exceeds the cost. As we saw in Chapter 23, the principal *benefit* of holding money is its usefulness in carrying out transactions. The Rossis' shares, their car and their house are all valuable assets, but they cannot use them to buy groceries or pay telephone bills. They can make routine payments using cash or their bank account, however. Because of its usefulness in daily transactions, the Rossis will almost

[1] Chapter 24 discusses risk, return and diversification in more detail.

certainly want to hold some of their wealth in the form of money. Furthermore, if the Rossis are a high-income family, they will probably choose to hold more money than a family with a lower income would, because they are likely to spend more and carry out more transactions than the low-income household.

The Rossis' benefit from holding money is also affected by the technological and financial sophistication of the society they live in. For example, in most European countries, developments such as credit cards, debit cards and ATMs have generally reduced the amount of money people need in order to carry out routine transactions, decreasing the public's demand for money at given levels of income. Although money is an extremely useful asset, there is also a cost to holding money – more precisely, an *opportunity cost* – which arises from the fact that most forms of money pay little or no interest. Cash pays zero interest, and many bank accounts pay either no interest or very low rates. For the sake of simplicity, we will just assume that *the nominal interest rate on money is zero*. In contrast, most alternative assets, such as bonds or shares, pay a positive nominal return. A bond, for example, pays a fixed amount of interest each period to the holder, while stocks pay dividends and may also increase in value (capital gains).

The cost of holding money arises because, in order to hold an extra euro of wealth in the form of money, a person must reduce by 1 euro the amount of wealth held in the form of higher-yielding assets, such as bonds or shares. The *opportunity cost* of holding money is measured by the interest rate that could have been earned if the person had chosen to hold interest-bearing assets instead of money. All else being equal, the higher the nominal interest rate, the higher the opportunity cost of holding money and hence the less money people will choose to hold.

We have been talking about the demand for money by individuals, but businesses also hold money to carry out transactions with customers and to pay workers and suppliers. The same general factors that determine individuals' money demand also affect the demand for money by businesses. That is, in choosing how much money to hold, a business, like an individual, will compare the benefits of holding money for use in transactions with the opportunity cost of holding a non-interest-bearing asset. Although we shall not differentiate between the money held by individuals and the money held by businesses in discussing money demand, you should be aware that, in modern economies, businesses hold a significant portion – more than half – of the total money stock. Example 27.2 illustrates the determination of money demand by a business owner.

### **Example 27.2** How much money should Kim's restaurants hold?

Kim owns several successful restaurants. Her accountant informs her that on the typical day her restaurants are holding a total of €50,000 in cash on the premises. The accountant points out that if Kim's restaurants reduced their cash holdings, Kim could use the extra cash to purchase interest-bearing government bonds.

The accountant proposes two methods of reducing the amount of cash Kim's restaurants hold. First, she could increase the frequency of cash pickups by her armoured car service. The extra service would cost €500 annually but would allow Kim's restaurants to reduce their average cash holding to €40,000. Second, in addition to the extra pickups, Kim could employ a computerised cash management service to help her keep closer tabs on the inflows and outflows of cash at her restaurants. The service costs €700 a year, but the accountant estimates that, together with more frequent pickups, the more efficient cash management provided by the service could help Kim reduce average cash holdings at her restaurants to €30,000.

The interest rate on government bonds is 6 per cent. How much money should Kim's restaurants hold? What if the interest rate on government bonds is 8 per cent?

Kim's restaurants need to hold cash to carry out their normal business, but holding cash also has an opportunity cost, which is the interest those funds could be earning if they were held in the form of government bonds instead of zero-interest cash. As the interest rate on government bonds is 6 per cent, each €10,000 by which Kim can reduce her restaurants' money holdings yields an annual benefit of €600 (6 per cent of €10,000).

If Kim increases the frequency of pickups by her armoured car service, reducing the restaurants' average money holdings from €50,000 to €40,000, the benefit will be the additional €600 in interest income that Kim will earn. The cost is the €500 charged by the armoured car company. Since the benefit exceeds the cost, Kim should purchase the extra service and reduce the average cash holdings at her restaurants to €40,000.

Should Kim go a step further and employ the cash management service as well? Doing so would reduce average cash holdings at the restaurants from €40,000 to €30,000, which has a benefit in terms of extra interest income of €600 per year. However, this benefit is less than the cost of the cash management service, which is €700 per year. So Kim should *not* employ the cash management service and instead should maintain average cash holdings in her restaurants of €40,000.

If the interest rate on government bonds rises to 8 per cent, then the benefit of each €10,000 reduction in average money holdings is €800 per year (8 per cent of €10,000) in extra interest income. In this case, the benefit of employing the cash management service, €800, exceeds the cost of doing so, which is €700. So Kim should employ the service, reducing the average cash holdings of her business to €30,000. Example 27.2 shows that a higher nominal interest rate on alternative assets reduces the quantity of money demanded.

**Exercise 27.1**

The interest rate on government bonds falls from 6 per cent to 4 per cent. How much cash should Kim's restaurants hold now?

## The Rossis, Kim and the ECB

Suppose the Rossis live in a small town in the south of Italy and Kim lives in Finland. Like many citizens of the European Union they may know little about the ECB, what it does and how decisions taken by the Governing Council in Frankfurt affect them and their neighbours. However, these decisions have important implications for the Rossis and Kim. Suppose the ECB decides to increase interest rates. Because the ECB's policy is common to all countries, interest rates will start to rise in right across the Eurosystem from southern Italy to Finland. As interest rates rise, the Rossis will find that the opportunity cost of holding money has increased, providing them with an incentive to economise on their money holdings. The same is true for Kim. Higher interest rates are an incentive for Kim to reduce the average cash holdings at her restaurants. In short, decisions taken in Frankfurt will affect the demand for money by individuals and firms in all countries using the euro as their currency.

# Macroeconomic factors that affect the demand for money

In any household or business the demand for money will depend on a variety of individual circumstances. For example, a high-volume retail business that serves thousands of customers each day will probably choose to have more money on hand than a legal firm that bills clients and pays employees monthly. But while individuals and businesses vary considerably in the amount of money they choose to hold, three macroeconomic factors affect the demand for money quite broadly: the nominal interest rate, real output and the price level. As we shall see next, the nominal interest rate affects the cost of holding money throughout the economy, while real output and the price level affect the benefits of money.

- *The nominal interest rate (i)* We have seen that the interest rate paid on alternatives to money, such as government bonds, determines the opportunity cost of holding money. The higher the prevailing nominal interest rate, the greater the opportunity cost of holding money, and hence the less money individuals and businesses will demand.

  What do we mean by *the* nominal interest rate? As we have seen, there are thousands of different assets, each with its own interest rate (rate of return). So can we really talk about *the* nominal interest rate? The answer is that, while there are many different assets, each with its own corresponding interest rate, the rates on those assets tend to *rise and fall together*. This is to be expected, because if the interest rates on some assets were to rise sharply while the rates on other assets declined, financial investors would flock to the assets paying high rates and refuse to buy the assets paying low rates. So, although there are many different interest rates in practice, speaking of the general level of interest rates usually does make sense. In this book, when we talk about *the* nominal interest rate, what we have in mind is some average measure of interest rates. This simplification is one more application of the macroeconomic concept of *aggregation*, introduced in Chapter 17.

  The nominal interest rate is a macroeconomic factor that affects the cost of holding money. A macroeconomic factor that affects the *benefit* of holding money is real income or output.

- *Real income or output (Y)* An increase in aggregate real income or output – as measured, for example, by real GDP – raises the quantity of goods and services that people and businesses want to buy and sell. When the economy enters a boom, for example, people do more shopping and stores have more customers. To accommodate the increase in transactions, both individuals and businesses need to hold more money. Thus higher real output raises the demand for money.

  A second macroeconomic factor affecting the benefit of holding money is the price level.

- *The price level (P)* The higher the prices of goods and services, the more euros are needed to make a given set of transactions. Thus a higher price level is associated with a higher demand for money.

  Today, when a couple of teenagers go out for a movie and snacks on Saturday night, they need probably five times as much cash as their parents did 25 years ago. Because the prices of movie tickets and popcorn have risen steeply over 25 years, more money (that is, more euros) is needed to pay for a Saturday night date than in the past. By the way, the fact that prices are higher today does *not* imply that people are worse off today than in the past, because nominal wages and salaries have also risen substantially. In general, however, higher prices do imply that people need to keep a greater number of euros available, in cash or in a chequing account.

## The money demand curve

**money demand curve** shows the relationship between the aggregate quantity of money demanded *M* and the nominal interest rate *i*; because an increase in the nominal interest rate increases the opportunity cost of holding money, which reduces the quantity of money demanded, the money demand curve slopes down

For the purposes of monetary policy making, economists are most interested in the aggregate, or economywide, demand for money. The interaction of the aggregate demand for money, determined by the public, and the supply of money, which is set by the ECB, determines the *nominal interest rate* that prevails in the economy.

The economywide demand for money can be represented graphically by the **money demand curve** (see Fig. 27.1). The money demand curve relates the aggregate quantity of money demanded *M* to the nominal interest rate *i*. The quantity of money demanded *M* is a nominal quantity, measured in euros. Because an increase in the nominal interest rate increases the opportunity cost of holding money, which reduces the quantity of money demanded, the money demand curve slopes down.

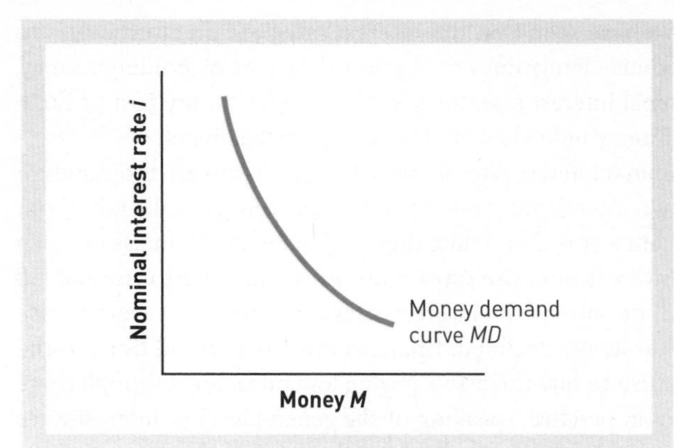


**Figure 27.1 The Money Demand Curve.** The money demand curve relates the economywide demand for money to the nominal interest rate. Because an increase in the nominal interest rate raises the opportunity cost of holding money, the money demand curve slopes down.

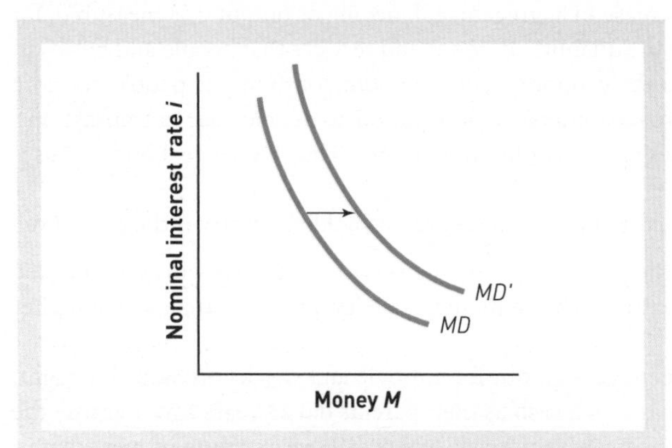


**Figure 27.2 A Shift in the Money Demand Curve.** At a given nominal interest rate, any change that makes people want to hold more money – such as an increase in the general price level or in real GDP – will shift the money demand curve to the right.

If we think of the nominal interest rate as the 'price' (more precisely, the opportunity cost) of money and the amount of money people want to hold as the 'quantity', the money demand curve is analogous to the demand curve for a good or service. As with a standard demand curve, the fact that a higher price of money leads people to demand less of it is captured in the downward slope of the demand curve. Furthermore, as in a standard demand curve, changes in factors other than the price of money (the nominal interest rate) can cause the demand curve for money to shift. For a given nominal interest rate, any change that makes people want to hold more money will shift the money demand curve to the right, and any change that makes people want to hold less money will shift the money demand curve to the left. We have already identified two macroeconomic factors other than the nominal interest rate that affect the economy wide demand for money: *real output* and the *price level*. Because an increase in either of these variables increases the demand for money, it shifts the money demand curve rightward, as shown in Fig. 27.2. Similarly, a fall in real output or the general price level reduces money demand, shifting the money demand curve leftward.

The money demand curve may also shift in response to other changes that affect the cost or benefit of holding money, such as the technological and financial advances we mentioned earlier. For example, the introduction of ATMs reduced the amount of money that people chose to hold and thus shifted the economywide money demand curve to the left.

## RECAP Money demand

For the economy as a whole, the demand for money is the amount of wealth that individuals, households, and businesses choose to hold in the form of *money*. The opportunity cost of holding money is measured by the *nominal interest rate* i, which is the return that could be earned on alternative assets such as bonds. The benefit of holding money is its usefulness in transactions.

Increases in real GDP (*Y*) or the price level (*P*) raise the nominal volume of transactions and thus the economywide demand for money. The demand for money is also affected by technological and financial innovations, such as the introduction of ATMs, that affect the costs or benefits of holding money.

The money demand curve relates the economywide demand for money to the nominal interest rate. Because an increase in the nominal interest rate raises the opportunity cost of holding money, the money demand curve slopes downward.

Changes in factors other than the nominal interest rate that affect the demand for money can shift the money demand curve. For example, increases in real GDP or the price level raise the demand for money, shifting the money demand curve to the right, whereas decreases shift the money demand curve to the left.

## The supply of money and money market equilibrium

Where there is demand, can supply be far behind? As we have seen, the *supply* of money is controlled by the Central Bank – in the Eurosystem, the ECB. For any Central Bank, the primary tool for controlling the money supply is *open-market operations* (OMOs). As described in Chapter 23 the ECB uses a type of OMO called *main refinancing operations* by which the Bank directly controls the supply of reserves available to the commercial banks. We shall assume that this enables the ECB to set the Eurosystem's money supply at whatever level it wishes. More precisely, this means that, unlike the demand for money, the supply of money does not vary with the rate of interest.

Figure 27.3 shows the demand for and the supply of money in a single diagram. The nominal interest rate is on the vertical axis, and the nominal quantity of money (in euros) is on the horizontal axis. As we have seen, because a higher nominal interest rate increases the opportunity cost of holding money, the money demand curve slopes downward. Because we are assuming that the ECB fixes the supply of money, we have drawn the *money supply curve* as a vertical line that intercepts the horizontal axis at the quantity of money chosen by the ECB, denoted $M$. Note that unlike the demand for money, the money supply is fixed at $M$ at all rates of interest.

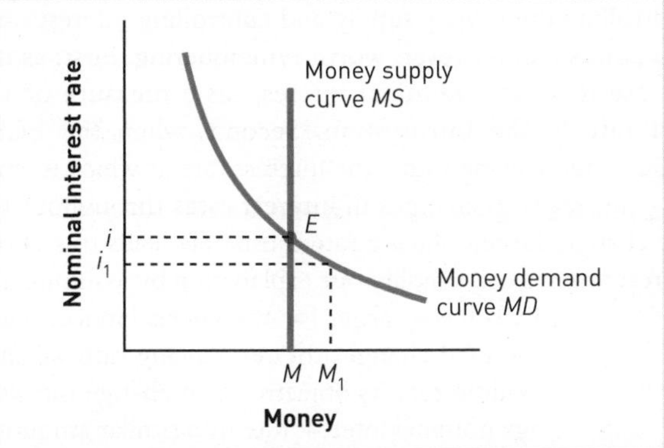

Nominal interest rate
Money supply curve *MS*
*E*
$i$
$i_1$
Money demand curve *MD*
$M$ $M_1$
Money

**Figure 27.3 Equilibrium in the Market for Money.** Equilibrium in the market for money occurs at point $E$, where the demand for money by the public equals the amount of money supplied by the ECB. The equilibrium nominal interest rate, which equates the supply of and demand for money, is $i$.

As in standard supply and demand analysis, equilibrium in the market for money occurs at the intersection of the supply and demand curves, shown as point $E$ in Fig. 27.3. The equilibrium amount of money in circulation, $M$, is simply the amount of money the ECB chooses to supply. The equilibrium nominal interest rate $i$ is the interest rate at which the quantity of money demanded by the public, as determined by the money demand curve, equals the fixed supply of money made available by the ECB.

To understand how the market for money reaches equilibrium, it may be helpful to recall the relationship between interest rates and the market price of bonds that was introduced in Chapter 24 (see Example 24.1). As we saw there, the prices of existing bonds are *inversely related* to the current interest rate. Higher interest rates imply lower bond prices, and lower interest rates imply higher bond prices. With this relationship between interest rates and bond prices in mind, let us ask what happens if, say, the nominal interest rate is initially below the equilibrium level in the market for money – for example, at a value such as $i_1$ in Fig. 27.3. At that interest rate the public's demand for money is $M_1$, which is greater than the actual amount of money in circulation, equal to $M$. How will the public – households and firms – react if the amount of money they hold is less than they would like? To increase their holdings of money, people will try to sell some of the interest-bearing assets they hold, such as bonds. But if everyone is trying to sell bonds and there are no willing buyers, then all that the attempt to reduce bond holdings will achieve is to drive down the price of bonds, in the same way that a glut of apples will drive down the price of apples.

A fall in the price of bonds, however, is equivalent to an increase in *interest rates*. Thus the public's collective attempt to increase its money holdings by selling bonds and other interest-bearing assets, which has the effect of lowering bond prices, also implies higher market interest rates. As interest rates rise, the quantity of money demanded by the public will decline (represented by a right-to-left movement along the money demand curve), as will the desire to sell bonds. Only when the interest rate reaches its equilibrium value, *i* in Fig. 27.3, will people be content to hold the quantities of money and other assets that are actually available in the economy.

**Exercise 27.2** Describe the adjustment process in the market for money if the nominal interest rate is initially above rather than below its equilibrium value. What happens to the price of bonds as the money market adjusts toward equilibrium?

## How the ECB controls the nominal interest rate

We began this section by noting that the public and the press usually talk about ECB policy in terms of decisions about the nominal interest rate rather than the money supply. Indeed, policy makers themselves usually describe policy in terms of setting a value for the interest rate rather than fixing the money supply at a particular level. We now have the necessary background to understand why controlling the money supply and controlling interest rates are essentially the same thing. Two points are, however, worth remembering. First, as discussed earlier in this chapter, we use the term 'nominal interest' as a measure of the economywide or average interest rate in the Eurosystem. Second, when the ECB's Governing Council decides to change its refinancing rate – the interest rate at which it lends reserves to the commercial banks – this leads to changes in interest rates throughout the Eurosystem. As an ECB decision to change the refinancing rate ultimately leads to a corresponding change in the average interest rate we can simplify our explanation by assuming the ECB has a target for the latter. Hence, when the ECB changes the refinancing rate we shall assume that its objective is to change the average nominal interest rate by a similar amount.

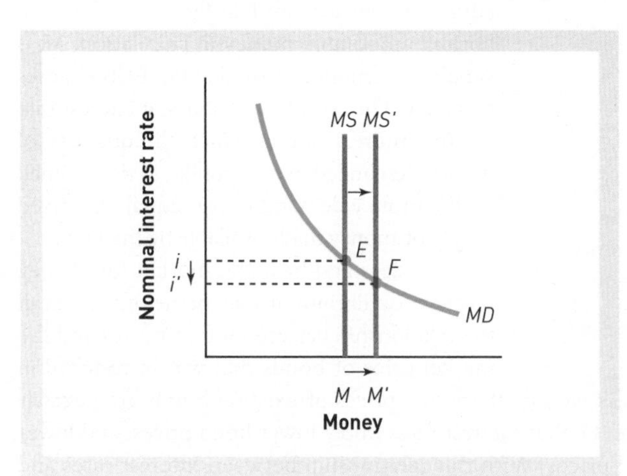


**Figure 27.4 The ECB Lowers the Nominal Interest Rate.** The ECB can lower the equilibrium nominal interest rate by increasing the supply of money. For the given money demand curve, an increase in the money supply from *M* to *M'* shifts the equilibrium point in the money market from *E* to *F*, lowering the equilibrium nominal interest rate from *i* to *i'*.

Figure 27.3 showed that the nominal interest rate is determined by equilibrium in the market for money. Let us suppose that for some reason the ECB decides to lower the interest rate. As we shall see, to lower the interest rate the ECB must increase the supply of money, which can be accomplished by increasing the amount of reserves it makes available to the banking system. Following the analysis of Chapter 23, increasing the supply of reserves leads to higher bank lending, deposit creation and an increased money supply.

Figure 27.4 shows the effects of such an increase in the money supply. If the initial money supply is *M*, then equilibrium in the money market occurs at point *E* and the equilibrium nominal interest rate is *i*. Now suppose the ECB increases the money supply to *M'*. This increase in the money supply shifts the vertical money supply curve to the right, which shifts the equilibrium in the money market from point $E$ to point $F$ (see Fig. 27.4). Note that at point $F$ the equilibrium nominal interest rate has declined, from $i$ to $i'$. The nominal interest rate must decline if the public is to be persuaded to hold the extra money that has been injected into the economy. The key point is that if the ECB wishes to fix the money supply at the higher level $M'$ then it must permit the nominal rate of interest to fall to $i'$ in order to retain equality between the demand for and supply of money.

Now consider the same sequence from a different perspective. In Fig. 27.4 the initial interest rate is $i$ and the money supply is $M$ as given by the vertical line $MS$ with equilibrium at $E$. Suppose that the ECB announces a cut in its refinancing rate with the intention of reducing the average nominal interest rate to $i'$. A lower interest rate leads to an increased demand for money which can be satisfied only if the ECB simultaneously permits the money supply to increase from $M$ to $M'$. That is, the money supply curve must shift to $MS'$ if a new money market equilibrium is to be established at $F$ with $i$ equal to $i'$.

Now compare these two examples. In the first case the ECB increases the money supply from $M$ to $M'$. For the public to willingly hold these higher money balances the interest rate must fall from $i$ to $i'$. In the second case the ECB reduces the interest rate from $i$ to $i'$. To satisfy the increased demand for money, the money supply must increase from $M$ to $M'$. Hence, saying that the ECB sets the money supply at $M'$ is exactly the same as saying that it sets the average interest rate at $i'$. It follows that there is no contradiction between these two ways of describing monetary policy – controlling the *money supply* or setting interest rates. Any value of the money supply implies a specific level for *nominal interest rates*, and vice versa.

A similar scenario unfolds if the ECB decides to raise interest rates. To raise interest rates, the ECB must *reduce* the money supply. A reduction of the money supply is accomplished by reducing the amount of reserves it makes available to commercial banks. With fewer reserves available the banks must contract lending, leading to a fall in deposits and, using Eq. (23.2), a lower money supply. For the money market to restore equilibrium the rate of interest must rise to reduce the demand for money in line with supply. Alternatively, if the ECB announces an increase in interest rates the demand for money will fall (we move up the demand for money curve) requiring a corresponding fall in the money supply to restore equilibrium. Again, control of the money supply and control of interest rates is really the same thing. A target level for one implies a given level for the other.

As Figs 27.3 and 27.4 illustrate, control of the interest rate is not separate from control of the money supply. If ECB officials choose to set the nominal interest rate at a particular level, they can do so only by setting the money supply at a level consistent with the *target interest rate*. The ECB *cannot* set the interest rate and the money supply independently, since for any given money demand curve, a particular interest rate implies a particular size of the money supply, and vice versa.

Since monetary policy actions can be expressed in terms of either the interest rate or the money supply, why does the ECB (and almost every other Central Bank) choose to communicate its policy decisions to the public in terms of an interest rate change rather than a money supply change? One reason, as we shall see shortly, is that the main effects of monetary policy on both the economy and financial markets are exerted through interest rates. Consequently, the interest rate is often the best summary of the overall impact of ECB actions. Another reason for focusing on interest rates is that they are more familiar to the public than the money supply. Finally, interest rates can be monitored continuously in the financial markets, which make the effects of ECB policies on interest rates easy to observe. By contrast, measuring the amount of money in the economy requires collecting data on bank deposits, with the consequence that several weeks may pass before policy makers and the public know precisely how ECB actions have affected the money supply.

## Economic naturalist 27.1 What's so important about the refinancing rate?

Although thousands of interest rates and other financial data are easily available, the interest rate that is perhaps most closely watched by the public, politicians, the media and the financial markets is the *refinancing rate*. What is the refinancing rate, and why is it so important?

As we have seen, the **refinancing rate** is the interest rate at which the ECB lends reserves to the commercial banks. For example, a bank that has insufficient reserves to meet its legal reserve requirements (see Chapter 23) might borrow from the ECB to make good the shortfall. The media and financial analysts always pay close attention to the refinancing rate because it is the key indicator of *monetary policy* in the Eurosystem. Indeed, at the close of every meeting of the ECB's Governing Council, it is announced whether the refinancing rate will be increased, decreased or left unchanged. The ECB may also indicate the likely direction of future changes in the refinancing rate. Thus more than any other financial variable, changes in the refinancing rate indicate the ECB's plans for monetary policy.

Figure 27.5 shows the behaviour of the refinancing rate since the ECB started operations in January 1999. As you can see, the ECB has allowed this interest rate to vary considerably in response to economic conditions. Later in the chapter we shall consider two specific episodes in which the ECB changed the refinancing rate in response to conditions in the Eurosystem's economy.

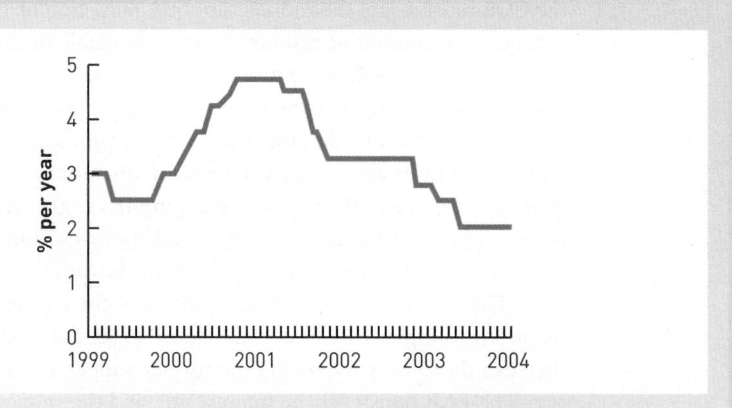


**Figure 27.5 The ECB's Main Refinancing Rate, 1999–2004.** The refinancing rate is the interest rate which commercial banks pay to borrow reserves from the ECB. It is set by the ECB's Governing Council and is the key interest rate in the Eurosystem.

## Can the ECB control the real interest rate?

Through its control of the money supply the ECB can control the economy's *nominal* interest rate. But many important economic decisions, such as the decisions to save and invest, depend on the *real* interest rate. To affect those decisions, the ECB must exert some control over the real interest rate.

Most economists believe that the ECB can control the real interest rate, at least for some period. To see why, recall the definition of the real interest rate from Chapter 19:

$$r = i - \pi$$

The real interest rate *r* equals the nominal interest rate *i* minus the rate of inflation $\pi$. We have seen that the ECB can control the nominal interest rate quite precisely. Furthermore, for reasons that we shall discuss in Chapter 28, inflation appears to change relatively slowly in response to changes in policy or economic conditions. Because inflation tends to adjust slowly, actions by the ECB to change the nominal interest rate generally lead the real interest rate to change by about the same amount.

The idea that the ECB can set the real interest rate appears to contradict the analysis in Chapter 22, which concluded that the real interest rate is determined by the condition that national saving must equal investment in new capital goods. This apparent contradiction is rooted in a difference in the time frame being considered. Because inflation does not adjust quickly, the ECB can control the real interest rate over the short run. In the long run, however – that is, over periods of several years or more – the inflation rate and other economic variables will adjust, and the balance of saving and investment will determine the real interest rate. Thus the ECB's ability to influence consumption and investment spending through its control of the real interest rate is strongest in the short run.

In discussing the ECB's control over interest rates, we should also return to a point mentioned earlier in this chapter: in reality, not just one but many thousands of interest rates are seen in the economy. Because interest rates tend to move together (allowing us to speak of *the* interest rate), an action by the ECB to change the refinancing rate generally causes other interest rates to change in the same direction. However, the tendency of other interest rates (such as the long-term government bond rate or the rate on bonds issued by corporations) to move in the same direction as the refinancing rate is only a tendency, not an exact relationship. In practice, then, the ECB's control of other interest rates may be somewhat less precise than its control of the refinancing rate – a fact that complicates the ECB's policy making.

### RECAP The ECB and interest rates

In the market for money, the money demand curve slopes downward, reflecting the fact that a higher nominal interest rate increases the opportunity cost of holding money and thus reduces the amount of money people want to hold. The money supply curve is *vertical* at the quantity of money that the ECB chooses to supply. The *equilibrium nominal interest rate i* is the interest rate at which the quantity of money demanded by the public equals the fixed supply of money made available by the ECB.

The ECB controls the nominal interest rate by changing the *supply of money*. We have seen that controlling the money supply and controlling the interest rates are essentially the same thing. The ECB typically expresses its policy intentions in terms of a target for a specific nominal interest rate – the *refinancing rate* – which is the rate at which the Bank lends reserves to the commercial banks. Reducing the refinancing rate increases the money supply and lowers the equilibrium nominal interest rate. Conversely, increasing the refinancing rate reduces the money supply and increases the nominal interest rate. The ECB can prevent changes in the demand for money from affecting the nominal interest rate by adjusting the quantity of money supplied. Because inflation is slow to adjust, in the short run the ECB can control the real interest rate (equal to the nominal interest rate minus the inflation rate) as well as the nominal interest rate. In the long run, however, the real interest rate is determined by the balance of saving and investment.

## The effects of ECB actions on the economy

Now that we have seen how the ECB can influence interest rates (both nominal and real), we can consider how monetary policy can be used to eliminate output gaps and stabilise the economy. The basic idea is relatively straightforward. As we shall see in this section, planned aggregate expenditure (PAE) is affected by the level of *real interest rates* prevailing in the economy. Specifically, a lower real interest rate encourages higher planned spending by households and firms, while a higher real interest rate reduces spending. By adjusting the real interest rate, the ECB can move planned spending in the desired direction. Under the assumption of the basic Keynesian model that firms produce just enough goods and services to meet the demand for their output, the ECB's stabilisation of planned spending leads to stabilisation of aggregate output and employment as well. In this section we shall first explain how planned aggregate expenditure is related to the real interest rate. Then we shall show how the ECB can use changes in the real interest rate to fight a recession or inflation.

## Planned aggregate expenditure and the real interest rate

In Chapter 25 we saw how planned spending is affected by changes in real output $Y$. Changes in output affect the private sector's disposable income $(Y - T)$, which in turn influences consumption spending – a relationship captured by the *consumption function*.

A second variable that has potentially important effects on aggregate expenditure is the real interest rate $r$. In Chapter 24, in our discussion of saving and investment, we saw that the real interest rate influences the behaviour of both households and firms.

For households, the effect of a higher real interest rate is to increase the reward for saving, which leads households to save more.[2] At a given level of income, households can *save more* only if they *consume less*. Thus, saying that a higher real interest rate *increases* saving is the same as saying that a higher real interest rate *reduces* consumption spending at each level of income. The idea that higher real interest rates reduce household spending makes intuitive sense. Think, for example, about people's willingness to buy consumer durables, such as cars or furniture. Purchases of consumer durables, which are part of consumption spending, are often financed by borrowing from a bank, credit union or finance company. When the real interest rate rises, the monthly finance charges associated with the purchase of a car or a piano are higher, and people become less willing or able to make the purchase. Thus a higher real interest rate reduces people's willingness to spend on consumer goods, holding constant disposable income and other factors that affect consumption.

Besides reducing consumption spending, a higher real interest rate also discourages firms from making capital investments. As in the case of a consumer thinking of buying a car or a piano, when a rise in the real interest rate increases financing costs firms may reconsider their plans to invest. For example, upgrading a computer system may be profitable for a manufacturing firm when the cost of the system can be financed by borrowing at a real interest rate of 3 per cent. However, if the real interest rate rises to 6 per cent, doubling the cost of funds to the firm, the same upgrade may not be profitable and the firm may choose not to invest. We should also remember that residential investment – the building of houses and flats – is also part of investment spending. Higher interest rates, in the form of higher mortgage rates, certainly discourage this kind of investment spending as well.

The conclusion is that, at any given level of output, *both consumption spending and planned investment spending decline when the real interest rate increases*. Conversely, a fall in the real interest rate tends to stimulate consumption and investment spending by reducing financing costs. Example 27.3 is a numerical illustration of how PAE can be related to the real interest rate and output.

---

[2] Because a higher real rate of interest also reduces the amount households must save to reach a given target, the net effect of a higher real interest rate is ambiguous. However, empirical evidence suggests that higher real interest rates do lead to an increase in household saving.

### Example 27.3 PAE and the real interest rate

In a certain economy, the components of planned spending are given by

$$C = 640 + 0.8(Y - T) - 400r$$
$$I^P = 250 - 600r$$
$$G = 300$$
$$NX = 20$$
$$T = 250$$

Find the relationship of planned aggregate expenditure to the real interest rate $r$ and output $Y$ in this economy. Find autonomous expenditure and induced expenditure.

This example is similar to Example 25.2, except that now the real interest rate $r$ is allowed to affect both consumption and planned investment. For example, the final term in the equation describing consumption, $-400r$, implies that a 1 per cent (0.01) increase in the real interest rate reduces consumption spending by $400(0.01) = 4$ units. Similarly, the final term in the equation for planned investment tells us that, in this example, a 1 per cent increase in the real interest rate lowers planned investment by $600(0.01) = 6$ units. Thus the overall effect of a 1 per cent increase in the real interest rate is to lower planned aggregate expenditure by 10 units, the sum of the effects on consumption and investment. As in the earlier examples, disposable income $(Y - T)$ is assumed to affect consumption spending through a marginal propensity to consume of 0.8 (see the first equation), and government purchases $G$, net exports $NX$ and taxes $T$ are assumed to be fixed numbers.

To find an equation that describes the relationship of PAE to output, we can begin as in Chapter 25 with the general definition of planned aggregate expenditure:

$$PAE = C + I^P + G + NX$$

Substituting for the four components of expenditure, using the equations describing each type of spending, we get

$$PAE = [640 + 0.8(Y - 250) - 400r] + [250 - 600r] + 300 + 20$$

The first term in brackets on the right-hand side of this equation is the expression for consumption, using the fact that taxes $T = 250$; the second bracketed term is planned investment; and the last two terms correspond to the given numerical values of government purchases and net exports. If we simplify this equation and group together the terms that do not depend on output $Y$ and the terms that do depend on output, we get

$$PAE = [(640 - 0.8 \times 250 - 400r) + (250 - 600r) + 300 + 20] + 0.8Y$$

or, simplifying further,

$$PAE = [1{,}010 - 1{,}000r] + 0.8Y \qquad (27.1)$$

In Eq. (27.1), the term in brackets is *autonomous expenditure*, the portion of PAE that does not depend on output. Notice that in this example *autonomous expenditure depends on the real interest rate r*. Induced expenditure, the portion of PAE that does depend on output, equals $0.8Y$ in this example.

### Example 27.4 The real interest rate and short-run equilibrium output

In the economy described in Example 27.3, the real interest rate $r$ is set by the Central Bank to equal 0.05 (5 per cent). Find short-run equilibrium output.

We found in Example 27.3 that, in this economy, PAE is given by Eq. (27.1). We are given that the Central Bank sets the real interest rate at 5 per cent. Setting $r = 0.05$ in Eq. (27.1) gives

$$PAE = [1{,}010 - 1{,}000 \times (0.05)] + 0.8Y$$

Simplifying, we get

$$PAE = 960 + 0.8Y$$

So, when the real interest rate is 5 per cent, autonomous expenditure is 960 and induced expenditure is $0.8Y$. Short-run equilibrium output is the level of output that equals planned aggregate spending. To find short-run equilibrium output, we could now apply the methods used in Chapter 25. Short-run equilibrium output would be determined as the value of output such that output just equals PAE, or

$$Y = PAE$$

Substituting for *PAE* gives

$$Y = 960 + 0.8Y$$

Hence short-run equilibrium output is

$$Y = 960/0.2 = 4{,}800$$

Short-run equilibrium output can also be found using the numeric method (Table 25.1) or graphically, using the Keynesian cross diagram from Chapter 25. Note that since the equation for planned aggregate output is the same as in Example 25.2, Figure 25.3 applies equally well here.

**Exercise 27.3** For the economy described in Example 27.4, suppose the Central Bank sets the real interest rate at 3 per cent rather than at 5 per cent. Find short-run equilibrium output using the algebraic and numeric methods described in Chapter 25. (**Hint:** Consider values between 4,500 and 5,500.)

## The ECB fights a recession

We have seen that the ECB can control the real interest rate, and that the real interest rate in turn affects planned spending and short-run equilibrium output. Putting these two results together, we can see how ECB actions may help to stabilise the economy.

Suppose the economy faces a *recessionary gap* – a situation in which real output is below potential output, and planned spending is 'too low'. To fight a recessionary gap, the ECB should reduce the real interest rate, stimulating consumption and investment spending. According to the theory we have developed, this increase in planned spending will cause output to rise, restoring the economy to full employment. Example 27.5 illustrates this point by extending Example 27.4.

### Example 27.5 The ECB fights a recession

For the economy described in Example 27.4, suppose that potential output $Y^*$ equals 5,000. As before, the ECB has set the real interest rate equal to 5 per cent. At that real interest rate, what is the output gap? What should the ECB do to eliminate the output gap and restore full employment? You are given that the multiplier in this economy is 5.

In Example 27.4 we showed that with the real interest rate at 5 per cent, short-run equilibrium output for this economy is 4,800. Potential output is 5,000, so the output gap ($Y - Y^*$) equals 5,000 – 4,800 = 200. Because actual output is below potential, this economy faces a recessionary gap.

To fight the recession, the ECB should lower the real interest rate, raising aggregate expenditure until output reaches 5,000, the full-employment level. That is, the ECB's objective is to increase output by 200. Because the multiplier equals 5, to increase output by 200 the ECB must increase autonomous expenditure by 200/5 = 40 units. By how much should the ECB reduce the real interest rate to increase autonomous expenditure by 40 units? Autonomous expenditure in this economy is [1,010 – 1,000$r$], as you can see from Eq. (27.1), so that each percentage point reduction in $r$ increases autonomous expenditure by 1,000 × (0.01) = 10 units. To increase autonomous expenditure by 40, then, the ECB should lower the real interest rate by 4 percentage points, from 5 per cent to 1 per cent.

The ECB's recession-fighting policy is shown graphically in Fig. 27.6. The reduction in the real interest rate raises planned spending at each level of output, shifting the expenditure line upward. When the real interest rate equals 1 per cent, the expenditure line intersects the $Y = PAE$ line at $Y$ = 5,000, so that output and potential output are equal. A reduction in interest rates by the ECB, made with the intention of reducing a recessionary gap in this way, is an example of an *expansionary* monetary policy.

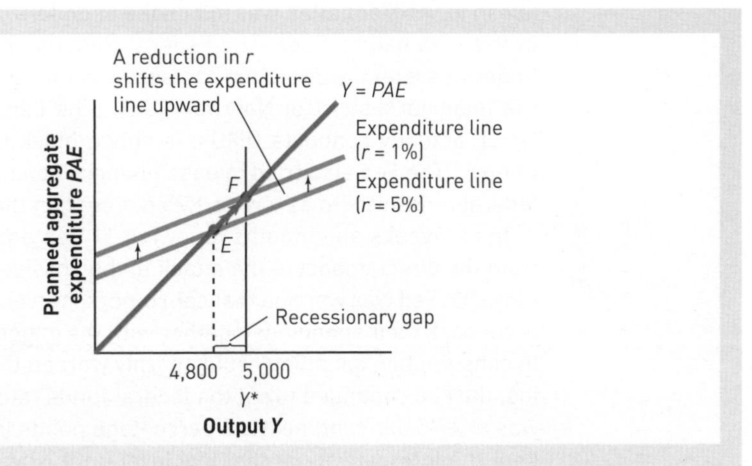


**Figure 27.6 The ECB Fights a Recession.** When the real interest rate is 5 per cent, the expenditure line intersects the $Y = PAE$ line at point $E$. At that point output is 4,800, below the economy's potential output of 5,000 (a recessionary gap of 200). If the ECB reduces the real interest rate to 1 per cent, stimulating consumption and investment spending, the expenditure line will shift upward. At the new point of intersection $F$, output will equal potential ouput at 5,000.

**Exercise 27.4** Continuing Example 27.5, suppose that potential output is 4,850 rather than 5,000. By how much should the ECB cut the real interest rate to restore full employment? You may take as given that the multiplier is 5.

## Economic naturalist 27.2 How did the Central Banks respond to recession and the terror attacks in 2001?

Late 2000 and early 2001 was a period of marked slowdown in the global economy. The US economy began slowing in the last quarter of 2000, with investment in high-tech equipment falling particularly sharply. In the euro area the annualised growth of real GDP declined from 4.2 per cent in the second quarter of 2000 to 1.6 per cent in the same quarter in 2001. To make matters worse, on 11 September 2001, terrorist attacks on New York City and Washington shocked the world and led to serious problems in the travel and financial industries, among others. How did the ECB, and other Central Banks react to these events?

The ECB first began to respond to growing evidence of an economic slowdown during the first part of 2001 when it reduced the refinancing rate from 4.75 to 4.50 per cent (a cut of 25 basis points) in May and by a similar amount in August. Over this period the Federal Reserve was even more aggressive, cutting the federal funds rate (the approximate US equivalent to the refinancing rate) by more than 2 per cent in successive steps. By summer's end, however, there was still considerable uncertainty in both Europe and the United States about the likely severity and persistence of the economic slowdown.

The picture changed suddenly on 11 September 2001, when the terror attacks on the World Trade Centre and the Pentagon killed more than 3,000 people. The terrorist attacks imposed great economic as well as human costs. The physical damage in lower Manhattan was in billions of dollars, and many offices and businesses in the area had to close. The Federal Reserve in its role as supervisor of the US financial system, worked hard to assist in the restoration of normal operations in the financial district of New York City. (The Federal Reserve Bank of New York, which actually conducts OMOs, is only a block from the site of the World Trade Centre.) The Fed also tried to ease financial conditions by temporarily lowering the federal funds rate to as low as 1.25 per cent, in the week following the attack.

In the weeks and months following 11 September, the Fed turned its attention from the direct impact of the attack to the possible indirect effects on the US economy. The Fed was worried that consumers, nervous about the future, would severely cut back their spending; together with the ongoing weakness in investment, a fall in consumption spending could sharply worsen the recession. To stimulate spending, the Fed continued to cut the federal funds rate. By January 2002, the funds rate was at 1.75 per cent, nearly 5 percentage points lower than a year earlier. The Fed kept the interest rate at that low level until November 2002, when it lowered the federal funds rate another 0.5 percentage points, to 1.25 per cent.

The Fed's actions were paralleled by the ECB. In the wake of the terrorist attacks the Governing Council cut interest rates by 50 basis points on 18 September and by a similar amount in early November. The decision on the first of these cuts was deemed so urgent that it was taken by an extraordinary meeting of the Governing Council held by teleconference on 17 September 2001. Most economists agree that expansionary actions by major Central Banks such as the Fed and the ECB played a constructive role in reducing the economic impact of the 11 September attacks. However, the recession which had started in both the United States and Europe prior to the attacks still persisted. Within the Eurosystem the growth of real GDP was less than 1 per cent per annum by mid-2002. As a result, the ECB engaged in more interest rate cuts, reducing the refinancing rate from 2.75 to 2 per cent between December 2002 and June 2003. By late 2003/early 2004 there were definite signs of recovery in the United States. However, despite the actions taken by the ECB the performance of the Eurosystem's economy remained disappointing with a meagre 0.6 per cent annualised growth rate in the last quarter of 2003 compared with 3.4 per cent in the United States.

## The ECB fights inflation

To this point we have focused on the problem of stabilising *output*, without considering inflation. In Chapter 28 we shall see how ongoing inflation can be incorporated into our analysis. For now, we shall simply note that one important cause of inflation is an *expansionary output gap* – a situation in which planned spending, and hence actual output, exceeds potential output. When an expansionary gap exists, firms find that the demand for their output exceeds their normal rate of production. Although firms may be content to meet this excess demand at previously determined prices for some time, if the high demand persists they will ultimately raise their prices, spurring inflation.

Because an expansionary gap tends to lead to inflation, the ECB moves to eliminate expansionary gaps as well as recessionary gaps. The procedure for getting rid of an expansionary gap – a situation in which output is 'too high' relative to potential output – is the reverse of that for fighting a recessionary gap, a situation in which output is 'too low'. As we have seen, the cure for a recessionary gap is to *reduce* the real interest rate, an action that stimulates planned spending and increases output. The cure for an expansionary gap is to *raise* the real interest rate, which reduces consumption and planned investment by raising the cost of borrowing. The resulting fall in planned spending leads in turn to a decline in output and to a reduction in inflationary pressures.

### **Example 27.6** The ECB fights inflation

For the economy studied in Examples 27.4 and 27.5, assume that potential output is 4,600 rather than 5,000. At the initial real interest rate of 5 per cent, short-run equilibrium output is 4,800, so this economy has an expansionary gap of 200. How should the ECB change the real interest rate to eliminate this gap?

In Example 27.5 we were told that the multiplier in this economy is 5. Hence, to reduce total output by 200, the ECB needs to reduce autonomous expenditure by $200/5 = 40$ units. From Eq. (27.1), we know that autonomous expenditure in this economy is $[1{,}010 - 1{,}000r]$, so that each percentage point (0.01) increase in the real interest rate lowers autonomous expenditure by 10 units ($1{,}000 \times 0.01$). We conclude that to eliminate the inflationary gap, the ECB should raise the real interest rate by 4 percentage points (0.04), from 5 per cent to 9 per cent. The higher real interest rate will reduce planned aggregate expenditure and output to the level of potential output, 4,600, eliminating inflationary pressures.

The effects of the ECB's inflation-fighting policy are shown in Fig. 27.7. With the real interest rate at 5 per cent, the expenditure line intersects the $Y = PAE$ line at point $E$, where output

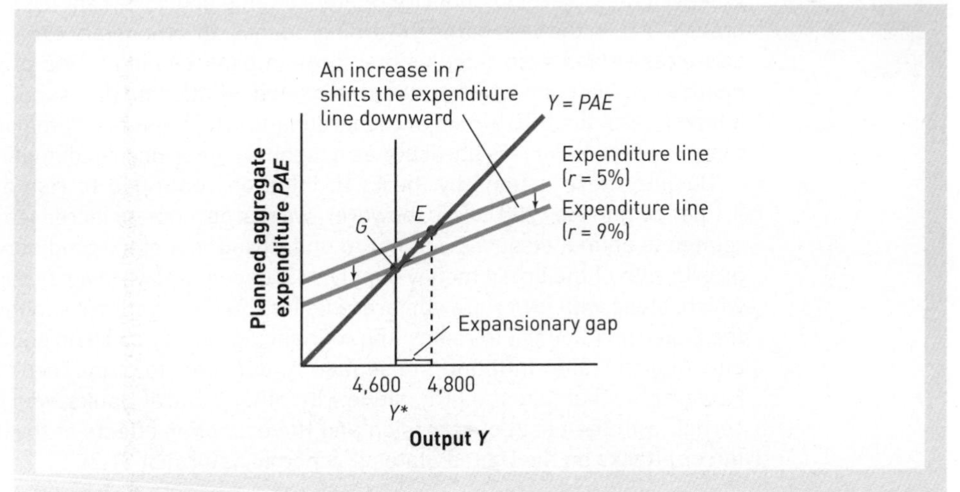


**Figure 27.7 The ECB Fights Inflation.** When the real interest rate is 5 per cent, the expenditure line intersects the $Y = PAE$, or 45°, line at point $E$, where short-run equilibrium output equals 4,800. If potential output is 4,600, an expansionary output gap of 200 exists. If the ECB raises the real interest rate to 9 per cent, reducing $PAE$, the expenditure line shifts downward. At the new intersection point $G$, actual output equals potential output at 4,600, and the expansionary gap is eliminated.

equals 4,800. To reduce planned spending and output, the ECB raises the real interest rate to 9 per cent. The higher real interest rate slows consumption and investment spending, moving the expenditure line downward. At the new equilibrium point G, actual output equals potential output at 4,600. The ECB's raising of the real interest rate – a contractionary policy action – has thus eliminated the expansionary output gap and, with it, the threat of inflation.

## Economic naturalist 27.3 Why did the ECB increase the refinancing rate seven times between April 1999 and October 2000?

When the ECB commenced operations in January 1999 the Eurosystem's inflation rate was just under 1 per cent per annum. By the end of 1999 inflation was running at 1.7 per cent and exceeded 2 per cent by mid-2000. This surge in inflation was due to a series of factors, the most important of which were rising oil prices and a significant depreciation of the euro's value against currencies such as sterling and the dollar. In January 1999 1 euro was worth $1.16. By the end of 1999 its value had fallen to $1.01 and by mid-2000 reached $0.90. This steady depreciation of the new currency increased inflationary pressure by directly impacting on import prices and by increasing the *competitiveness*, and hence the *demand for*, European goods and services on world markets. The ECB reacted to these developments by increasing the refinancing rate on seven occasions between April 1999 and October 2002. The cumulative effect was to increase the refinancing rate from 2.5 to 4.75 per cent. There were two reasons why the ECB reacted in this way. First, as explained in Chapter 23, the Maastricht Treaty had given the Bank a mandate for price stability which the ECB subsequently defined as an inflation rate between zero and 2 per cent. Hence, as the Eurosystem's inflation rate approached the upper end of the target range the ECB honoured its mandate and increased interest rates in an attempt to moderate the inflationary surge. Second, by late 1999 the Bank had become increasingly concerned about the growth of the money supply which was above 6 per cent in early 2000 and exceeded the Governing Council's reference value of 4.5 per cent (see Economic naturalist 23.2). In the view of the Governing Council, this monetary expansion was seen as excessive and associated with a surge in bank lending to the private sector to finance consumption which further intensified inflationary pressures. By increasing interest rates the ECB aimed at moderating these pressures by making bank loans more expensive and less attractive as a means of financing consumption.

Despite these actions by the ECB, inflation continued to rise and peaked at 3.1 per cent in May 2001. This, however, was largely due to increases in food prices related to animal diseases and not to underlying monetary conditions. Indeed, the growth rate of the broad money supply, M3, declined toward 4 per cent in late 2000 which, along with lower growth forecasts for the Eurosystem's economy, convinced the Governing Council to reduce the refinancing rate by 25 basis points in both May and August 2001. Inflation subsequently declined to 2 per cent by end 2001. However, by that date the ECB, along with other Central Banks, was primarily concerned with the onset of recession and the economic effects of the 11 September terror attacks on the United States (Economic naturalist 27.2).

ECB interest rate policies affect the economy as a whole, but they have a particularly important effect on financial markets. The introduction to this chapter noted the lengths that financial market participants will go to in an attempt to anticipate ECB policy changes. Economic naturalist 27.4 illustrates the type of information financial investors look for, and why it is so important to them.

### Economic naturalist 27.4 Why does news of inflation hurt the stock market?

Financial market participants watch data on inflation extremely closely. A report that inflation is increasing or is higher than expected often causes share prices to fall sharply. Why does bad news about inflation hurt the stock market?

Investors in the financial markets worry about inflation because of its likely impact on ECB policy. Financial investors understand that the ECB, or any Central Bank, when faced with signs of an inflationary surge, is likely to raise interest rates in an attempt to reduce planned spending and 'cool down' the economy. This type of contractionary policy action hurts share prices in two ways. First, it slows down *economic activity*, reducing the expected sales and profits of companies whose shares are traded in the stock market. Lower profits, in turn, reduce the dividends those firms are likely to pay their shareholders.

Second, higher real interest rates reduce the *value of shares* by increasing the required return for holding shares. We saw in Chapter 24 that an increase in the return financial investors require in order to hold shares lowers current stock prices. Intuitively, if interest rates rise, interest-bearing alternatives to shares such as newly issued government bonds will become more attractive to investors, reducing the demand for, and hence the price of, shares.

## The ECB'S policy reaction function

The ECB attempts to stabilise the economy by manipulating the real interest rate. When the economy faces a recessionary gap, the ECB may reduce the real interest rate in order to stimulate spending. When an expansionary gap exists, so that inflation threatens to become a problem, the ECB can restrain spending by raising the real interest rate. Economists sometimes find it convenient to describe the behaviour of Central Banks in terms of a **policy reaction function**. In general, a policy reaction function describes how the action a policy maker takes depends on the state of the economy. Here, the policy maker's action is the bank's choice of the real interest rate, and the state of the economy is given by factors such as the output gap or the inflation rate. Economic naturalist 27.5 describes one attempt to quantify a Central Bank policy reaction function.

**policy reaction function** describes how the action a policy maker takes depends on the state of the economy

### Economic naturalist 27.5 What is the Taylor rule?

In 1993 economist John Taylor proposed a 'rule,' now known as the Taylor rule, to describe Central Bank behaviour.[3] Although the Taylor rule was originally proposed to describe the Federal Reserve's behaviour it has general application and can be used to explain the policy reactions of most Central Banks, including the ECB. What is the Taylor rule? Do the ECB and other Central Banks always follow it?

The rule Taylor proposed is not a 'rule' in any legal sense but is instead an attempt to describe the Central Bank's behaviour in terms of a *quantitative policy reaction function*. Taylor's 'rule' can be written as

$$r = a - b\frac{(Y^* - Y)}{Y^*} + c\,(\pi - \pi^*)$$

[3] Taylor (1993).

where $r$ is the *real interest rate* set by the Central Bank, expressed as a decimal (for example, 5 per cent = 0.05); $Y^* - Y$ is the current *output gap* (the difference between potential and actual output); $(Y^* - Y)/Y^*$ is the output gap relative to *potential output*, $\pi$ is the actual *inflation rate* and $\pi^*$ is the Central Bank's *target inflation rate*. Both $\pi$ and $\pi^*$ are expressed as decimals (for example, a 2 per cent inflation rate is expressed as 0.02). According to the Taylor rule, the Central Bank responds to both output gaps and deviations in the rate of inflation from its target level. The coefficients $b$ and $c$ describe the strength of these responses. For example, if $b$ and $c$ both equal 0.5 then the formula implies that if a recessionary gap equal to a fraction 0.01 of potential output develops, the Central Bank will reduce the real interest rate by 0.5 percentage points (that is, 0.5 times 0.01 or 0.005). Similarly, if inflation rises by 1 percentage point (0.01) relative to the target, according to the Taylor rule the Central Bank will increase the real interest rate by 0.5 percentage points (0.005). The coefficient $a$ estimates the real rate of interest set by the Central Bank when $Y = Y^*$ and inflation is on target. Taylor has shown that the values $a = 0.01$, $b = 0.5$ and $c = 0.5$ describe the normal behavior of the Fed reasonably accurately. Thus the Taylor rule is a real-world example of a policy reaction function. The ECB, established in 1999, is still a relatively young Central Bank and we have insufficient data to derive precise estimates for the coefficients $a$, $b$ and $c$. However, Economic naturalists 27.2 and 27.3 suggest that the ECB does react to the both output gaps and excessive inflation.

Although the Taylor rule has worked well as a description of the Fed's behaviour, we reiterate that it is not a 'rule' in any legal sense. All Central Banks are perfectly free to deviate from it and do so when circumstances warrant. Still, the Taylor rule provides a useful benchmark for assessing, and predicting, Central Bank actions.

**Exercise 27.5** This exercise asks you to apply the Taylor rule. Suppose that the Central Bank's target inflation rate is 2 per cent but actual inflation is 5 per cent and the output gap is zero. If the Taylor rule parameters have the values $a = 0.01$, $b = 0.5$ and $c = 0.5$, at what value should the Central Bank set the real interest rate? The nominal interest rate? Suppose that the Central Bank were to receive new information showing that there is a 1 per cent recessionary gap (inflation is still 5 per cent). According to the Taylor rule, how should the Central Bank change the real interest rate, if at all?

Notice that, according to the Taylor rule, the ECB responds to two variables – the output gap and inflation. In principle, any number of economic variables, from stock market prices to the value of the euro in terms of the dollar, could affect ECB policy and thus appear in the policy reaction function. For the sake of simplicity, in applying the policy reaction function idea in Chapter 28, we shall assume that the ECB's choice of the real interest rate depends on only one variable – the *rate of inflation*. This simplification will not change our main results in any significant way. Furthermore, as we shall see, having the ECB react only to inflation captures the most important aspect of its behaviour – namely, its tendency to raise the real interest rate when the economy is 'overheating' (experiencing an expansionary gap) and to reduce it when the economy is sluggish (experiencing a recessionary gap). It is also consistent with the ECB's primary mandate for price stability, as discussed in Chapter 23.

Table 27.1 describes an example of a policy reaction function according to which the ECB reacts only to inflation. We assume that the target rate of inflation $\pi^*$ is zero. According to the policy reaction function given in Table 27.1, the higher the rate of inflation, the higher the real interest rate set by the ECB. This relationship is consistent with the idea that the Central Bank responds to inflationary pressures by raising the real interest rate. Figure 27.8 is a graph of this policy reaction function. The vertical axis of the graph shows the real interest rate chosen by the ECB; the horizontal axis shows the rate of inflation. The upward slope of the policy reaction function captures the idea that the ECB reacts to increases in inflation by raising the real interest rate.

| Actual rate of inflation ($\pi$) | Real interest rate set by ECB ($r$) |
|---|---|
| 0.00 (= 0%) | 0.02 (= 2%) |
| 0.01 | 0.03 |
| 0.02 | 0.04 |
| 0.03 | 0.05 |
| 0.04 | 0.06 |

**Table 27.1** A Policy Reaction Function for the ECB

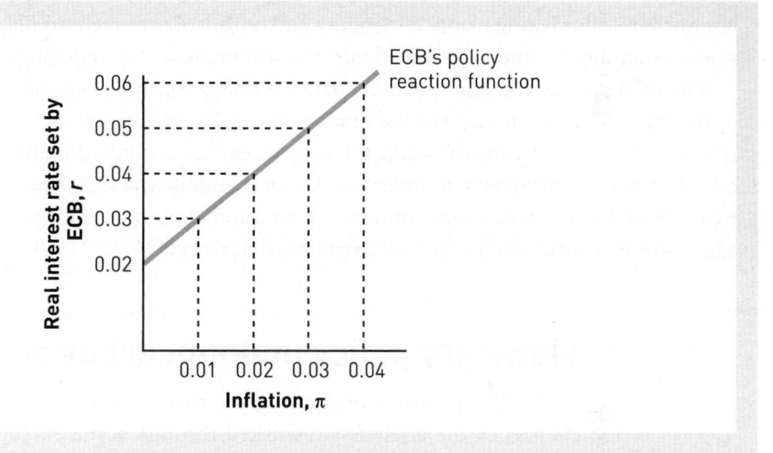


**Figure 27.8 An Example of an ECB Policy Reaction Function.** This hypothetical example of a policy reaction function for the ECB shows the real interest rate the ECB sets in response to any given value of the inflation rate. The upward slope captures the idea that the ECB raises the real interest rate when inflation rises. The numerical values in the figure are from Table 27.1.

How does the ECB determine its policy reaction function? In practice, the process is a complex one, involving a combination of statistical analysis of the economy and human judgement. However, two useful insights into the process can be drawn even from the simplified policy reaction function shown in Table 27.1 and Fig. 27.8. First, as we mentioned earlier in the chapter, though the ECB controls the real interest rate in the short run, in the long run the real interest rate is determined by the *balance of saving and investment*. To illustrate the implication of this fact for the ECB's choice of policy reaction function, suppose that the ECB estimates the long-run value of the real interest rate (as determined by the supply and demand for saving) to be 4 per cent, or 0.04. By examining Table 27.1, we can see that the ECB's policy reaction function implies a long-run value of the real interest rate of 4 per cent only if the inflation rate in the long run is 2 per cent. Thus the ECB's choice of this policy reaction function makes sense only if the ECB's long-run target rate of inflation is 2 per cent. We conclude that one important determinant of the ECB's policy reaction function is the policy makers' objective for inflation.

Second, the ECB's policy reaction function contains information not only about the Bank's long-run inflation target but also about how aggressively it plans to *pursue that target*. To illustrate, suppose the ECB's policy reaction function was very flat, implying that the ECB changes the real interest rate rather modestly in response to increases or decreases in inflation. In this case, we would conclude that the ECB does not intend to be very aggressive in its attempts to offset movements in inflation away from the target level. In contrast, if the reaction function slopes steeply upward, so that a given change in inflation elicits a large adjustment of the real interest rate by the ECB, we would say that the ECB plans to be quite aggressive in responding to changes in inflation. Given its mandate for price stability we might reasonably assume that the ECB would be fairly aggressive in combating sustained inflationary pressures.

### RECAP Monetary policy and the economy

An increase in the real interest rate reduces both *consumption spending* and *planned investment spending*. Through its control of the real interest rate, the ECB is thus able to influence planned spending and short-run equilibrium output. To fight a *recession* (a recessionary output gap), the ECB should *lower* the real interest rate, stimulating planned spending and output. Conversely, to fight the threat of *inflation* (an expansionary output gap), the ECB should *raise* the real interest rate, reducing planned spending and output.

The ECB's policy reaction function relates its policy action (specifically, its setting of the real interest rate) to the state of the economy. For the sake of simplicity, we consider a policy reaction function in which the real interest rate set by the ECB depends only on the rate of inflation. Because the ECB raises the real interest rate when inflation rises, in order to restrain spending, the ECB's policy reaction is upward-sloping. The ECB's policy reaction function contains information about the Bank's long-run target for inflation and the aggressiveness with which it intends to pursue that target.

## Monetary policy making: art or science?

In this chapter we have analysed the basic economics underlying real-world monetary policy. As part of the analysis we worked through some examples showing the calculation of the real interest rate that is needed to restore output to its full-employment level. While those examples are useful in understanding how monetary policy works – as with our analysis of fiscal policy in Chapter 26 – they overstate the precision of monetary policy making. The real-world economy is highly complex, and our knowledge of its workings is imperfect. For example, though we assumed in our analysis that the ECB knows the exact value of potential output, in reality potential output can be estimated only approximately. As a result, at any given time the ECB has only a rough idea of the size of the output gap. Similarly, ECB policy makers have only an approximate idea of the effect of a given change in the real interest rate on planned spending, or the length of time before that effect will occur. Because of these uncertainties, the ECB tends to proceed cautiously. ECB policy makers avoid large changes in interest rates and rarely raise or lower the refinancing rate more than one-half of a percentage point (from 3.50 per cent to 3.00 per cent, for example) at any one time. Indeed, the typical change in the interest rate is one-quarter of a percentage point.

Is monetary policy making, then, an art or a science? In practice, it appears to be both. Scientific analyses, such as the development of detailed statistical models of the economy, have proved useful in making monetary policy. But human judgement based on long experience – what has been called the 'art' of monetary policy – plays a crucial role in successful policy making, and is likely to continue to do so.

## Summary

- *Monetary policy* is one of two types of stabilisation policy, the other being fiscal policy. In the Eurosystem there is no central fiscal authority which has the ability to conduct fiscal policy for all participating economies. Hence, monetary policy as determined by the ECB is the principal stabilisation instrument. Although the ECB operates by controlling the money supply, the media's attention nearly always focuses on the ECB's decisions about interest rates, not the money supply. There is no contradiction between these two ways of looking at monetary policy, however, as the ECB's ability to control the money supply is the source of its ability to control interest rates.
- The *nominal interest rate* is determined in the market for money, which has both a demand side and a supply side. For the economy as a whole, the *demand for money* is the amount of wealth households and businesses choose to hold in the form of money (such as cash or chequing accounts). The demand for money is determined by a comparison of cost and benefits. The opportunity cost of holding money, which pays either zero interest or very low interest, is the interest that could have been earned by holding interest-bearing assets instead of money. Because the nominal interest rate measures the opportunity cost of holding a euro in the form of money, an increase in the nominal interest rate reduces the quantity of money demanded. The benefit of money is its usefulness in carrying out transactions. All else being equal, an increase in the volume of transactions increases the demand for money. At the macroeconomic level, an increase in the price level or in real GDP increases the euro volume of transactions, and thus the demand for money.
- The *money demand curve* relates the aggregate quantity of money demanded to the nominal interest rate. Because an increase in the nominal interest rate increases the opportunity cost of holding money, which reduces the quantity of money demanded, the money demand curve slopes down. Factors other than the nominal interest rate that affect the demand for money will shift the demand curve to the right or left. For example, an increase in the price level or real GDP increases the demand for money, shifting the money demand curve to the right.
- The European Central Bank (ECB) determines the supply of money through the use of *open-market operations* (OMOs). The supply curve for money is vertical at the value of the money supply set by the ECB. Money market equilibrium occurs at the nominal interest rate at which the money demand equals the money supply. The ECB can reduce the nominal interest rate by increasing the money supply (shifting the money supply curve to the right) or increase the nominal interest rate by reducing the money supply (shifting the money supply curve to the left). The nominal interest rate that the ECB controls is the *refinancing rate*, which is the rate at which commercial banks borrow reserves from the ECB.
- In the short run, the ECB can control the *real interest rate* as well as the nominal interest rate. Recall that the real interest rate equals the nominal interest rate minus the inflation rate. Because the inflation rate adjusts relatively slowly, the ECB can change the real interest rate by changing the nominal interest rate. In the long run, the real interest rate is determined by the *balance of saving and investment* (Chapter 22).
- The ECB's actions affect the Eurosystem economy because changes in the real interest rate affect *planned spending*. For example, an increase in the real interest rate raises the cost of borrowing, reducing consumption and planned investment. Thus, by increasing the real interest rate, the ECB can reduce planned spending and short-run equilibrium output. Conversely, by reducing the real interest rate, the ECB can stimulate planned aggregate expenditure and thereby raise short-run equilibrium output.
- A *policy reaction function* describes how the action a policy maker takes depends on the state of the economy. For example, a policy reaction function for the ECB could specify the real interest rate set by the ECB for each value of inflation.
- In practice, the ECB's information about the level of potential output and the size and speed of the effects of its actions is imprecise. Monetary policy making is thus as much an art as a science.

## Key terms

demand for money (764)
money demand curve (767)
policy reaction function (781)
portfolio allocation decision (763)

## Review questions

1. What is the *demand for money*? How does the demand for money depend on the nominal interest rate? On the price level? On income? Explain in terms of the costs and benefits of holding money.
2. Show graphically how the ECB controls the nominal interest rate. Can the ECB control the real interest rate?
3. What effect does an open-market purchase of bonds by the ECB have on nominal interest rates? Discuss in terms of (a) the effect of the purchase on bond prices and (b) the effect of the purchase on the supply of money.
4. You hear a news report that employment growth is lower than expected. How do you expect that report to affect market interest rates? Explain. (**Hint:** Assume that ECB policy makers have access to the same data as you do.)
5. Why does the real interest rate affect planned aggregate expenditure? Give examples.
6. The ECB faces a recessionary gap. How would you expect it to respond? Explain step by step how its policy change is likely to affect the economy.
7. The ECB decides to take a *contractionary* policy action. What would you expect to happen to the nominal interest rate, the real interest rate and the money supply? Under what circumstances is this type of policy action most likely to be appropriate?
8. Define the *policy reaction function*. Sketch a policy reaction function relating the ECB's setting of the real interest rate to inflation.
9. Discuss why the analysis of this chapter overstates the precision with which monetary policy can be used to eliminate output gaps.

## Problems

Problems marked with an asterisk (*) are more difficult.

1. During the heavy Christmas shopping season, sales by retail stores, online sales firms and other merchants rise significantly.
   a. What would you expect to happen to the money demand curve during the Christmas season? Show graphically.
   b. If the ECB took no action, what would happen to nominal interest rates around Christmas?
   c. In fact, nominal interest rates do not change significantly in the fourth quarter of the year, due to deliberate ECB policy. Explain and show graphically how the ECB can ensure that nominal interest rates remain stable around Christmas.

2. The following table shows Uma's estimated annual benefits of holding different amounts of money:

| Average money holdings (€) | Total benefit (€) |
|---|---|
| 500 | 35 |
| 600 | 47 |
| 700 | 57 |
| 800 | 65 |
| 900 | 71 |
| 1,000 | 75 |
| 1,100 | 77 |
| 1,200 | 77 |

a. How much money will Uma hold on average if the nominal interest rate is 9 per cent? 5 per cent? 3 per cent? Assume that she wants her money holding to be a multiple of €100. (**Hint:** Make a table comparing the extra benefit of each additional €100 in money holdings with the opportunity cost, in terms of forgone interest, of additional money holdings.)

b. Graph Uma's money demand curve for interest rates between 1 per cent and 12 per cent.

3. How would you expect each of the following to affect the economywide demand for money? Explain.

a. Competition among brokers forces down the commission charge for selling holdings of bonds or stocks.

b. Grocery stores begin to accept credit cards in payment.

c. Financial investors become concerned about increasing riskiness of stocks.

d. Online banking allows customers to check balances and transfer funds between chequing and mutual fund investments 24 hours a day.

e. The economy enters a boom period.

f. Political instability increases in developing nations.

4. Suppose the economywide demand for money is given by $P(0.2Y - 25{,}000i)$. The price level $P$ equals 3.0 and real output $Y$ equals 10,000. At what value should the ECB set the nominal money supply if

a. It wants to set the nominal interest rate at 4 per cent?

b. It wants to set the nominal interest rate at 6 per cent?

5. An economy is described by the following equations:

$$C = 2{,}600 + 0.8(Y - T) - 10{,}000r$$
$$I^P = 2{,}000 - 10{,}000r$$
$$G = 1{,}800$$
$$NX = 0$$
$$T = 3{,}000$$

The real interest rate, expressed as a decimal, is 0.10 (that is, 10 per cent). Find a numerical equation relating planned aggregate expenditure to output. Using a table or other method, solve for short-run equilibrium output. Show your result graphically using the Keynesian cross diagram.

**6.** For the economy described in Problem 5:

**a.** Potential output $Y^*$ equals 12,000. What real interest rate should the ECB set to bring the economy to full employment? You may take as given that the multiplier for this economy is 5.

**b.** Repeat part (a) for the case in which potential output $Y^* = 9{,}000$.

**c.*** Show that the real interest rate you found in part (a) sets national saving at potential output, defined as $Y^* - C - G$, equal to planned investment, $I^P$. This result shows that the real interest rate must be consistent with equilibrium in the market for saving when the economy is at full employment.

**7.*** Here is another set of equations describing an economy:

$$C = 14{,}400 + 0.5(Y - T) - 40{,}000r$$
$$I^P = 8{,}000 - 2{,}000r$$
$$G = 7{,}000$$
$$NX = -1{,}800$$
$$T = 3{,}000$$
$$Y^* = 40{,}000$$

**a.** Find a numerical equation relating planned aggregate expenditure to output and to the real interest rate.

**b.** At what value should the ECB set the real interest rate to eliminate any output gap? (**Hint:** Set output $Y$ equal to the value of potential output given above in the equation you found in part (a). Then solve for the real interest rate that also sets planned aggregate expenditure equal to potential output.)

**8.** Supposing that the ECB follows the Taylor rule (Economic naturalist 27.5), find the real interest rate and the nominal interest rate that the ECB will set in each of the following situations:

**a.** Inflation of 4 per cent and an expansionary gap equal to 1 per cent of potential output.

**b.** Inflation of 2 per cent and a recessionary gap equal to 2 per cent of potential output.

**c.** Inflation of 6 per cent and no output gap.

**d.** Inflation of 2 per cent and a recessionary gap of 5 per cent. (Can the ECB set a negative real interest rate? If so, how?)

## Answers to in-chapter exercises

**27.1** At 4 per cent interest, the benefit of each €10,000 reduction in cash holdings is €400 per year (4 per cent × €10,000). In this case the cost of the extra armoured car service, €500 a year, exceeds the benefit of reducing cash holdings by €10,000. Kim's restaurants should therefore continue to hold €50,000 in cash. Comparing this result with Example 27.2, you can see that the demand for money by Kim's restaurants is lower the higher the nominal interest rate.

**27.2** If the nominal interest rate is above its equilibrium value, then people are holding more money than they would like. To bring their money holdings down, they will use some of their money to buy interest-bearing assets such as bonds.

If everyone is trying to buy bonds, however, the price of bonds will be bid up. An increase in bond prices is equivalent to a fall in market interest rates. As interest rates fall, people will be willing to hold more money. Eventually interest rates will fall enough that people are content to hold the amount of money supplied by the ECB, and the money market will be in equilibrium.

**27.3** If $r = 0.03$, then consumption is $C = 640 + 0.8(Y - 250) - 400(0.03) = 428 + 0.8Y$, and planned investment is $I^p = 250 - 600(0.03) = 232$. Using the algebraic method, planned aggregate expenditure is given by

$$\begin{aligned} PAE &= C + I^p + G + NX \\ &= (428 + 0.8Y) + 232 + 300 + 20 \\ &= 980 + 0.8Y \end{aligned}$$

To find short-run equilibrium output we set $Y = PAE$ which gives $Y = 980 + 0.8Y$. Hence:

$$Y = 980/0.2 = 4{,}900$$

Using the numeric method we can construct a table analogous to Table 25.1. As usual, some trial and error is necessary to find an appropriate range of guesses for output (column (1)).

**Determination of Short-Run Equilibrium Output**

| Output *Y* (1) | Planned aggregate expenditure *PAE* = 980 + 0.8*Y* (2) | *Y* - *PAE* (3) | *Y* = *PAE*? (4) |
|---|---|---|---|
| 4,500 | 4,580 | - 80 | No |
| 4,600 | 4,660 | - 60 | No |
| 4,700 | 4,740 | - 40 | No |
| 4,800 | 4,820 | - 20 | No |
| 4,900 | 4,900 | 0 | Yes |
| 5,000 | 4,980 | 20 | No |
| 5,100 | 5,060 | 40 | No |
| 5,200 | 5,140 | 60 | No |
| 5,300 | 5,220 | 80 | No |
| 5,400 | 5,300 | 100 | No |
| 5,500 | 5,380 | 120 | No |

Short-run equilibrium output equals 4,900, as that is the only level of output that satisfies the condition $Y = PAE$.

Hence, lowering the real interest rate from 5 per cent to 3 per cent increases short-run equilibrium output from 4,800 to 4,900.

**27.4** When the real interest rate is 5 per cent, output is 4,800. Each percentage point reduction in the real interest rate increases autonomous expenditure by 10 units. Since the multiplier in this model is 5, to raise output by 50 units the real interest rate should be cut by 1 percentage point, from 5 per cent to 4 per cent. Increasing output by 50 units, to 4,850, eliminates the output gap.

**27.5** If $\pi = 0.05$, $\pi^* = 0.02$ and the output gap is zero, we can plug these values into the Taylor rule to obtain

$$r = 0.01 - 0.5(0) + 0.5(0.03) = 0.025 = 2.5 \text{ per cent}$$

So the real interest rate implied by the Taylor rule when inflation is 5 per cent and the output gap is zero is 2.5 per cent. The nominal interest rate equals the real rate plus the inflation rate, or 2.5 per cent + 5 per cent = 7.5 per cent.

If there is a recessionary gap of 1 per cent of potential output, the Taylor rule formula becomes

$$r = 0.01 - 0.5(0.01) + 0.5(0.03) = 0.02 = 2 \text{ per cent}$$

The nominal interest rate implied by the Taylor rule in this case is the 2 per cent real rate plus the 5 per cent inflation rate, or 7 per cent. So the Taylor rule has the ECB lowering the interest rate when the economy goes into recession, which is both sensible and realistic.

## Appendix Monetary policy in the basic Keynesian model

This Appendix extends the algebraic analysis of the basic Keynesian model that was presented in Chapter 25 to include the role of monetary policy. The main difference from Chapter 25 is that in this analysis the real interest rate is allowed to affect planned spending. We shall not describe the supply and demand for money algebraically but will simply assume that the ECB can set the real interest rate $r$ at any level it chooses.

The real interest rate affects consumption and planned investment. To capture these effects, we shall modify the equations for those two components of spending as follows:

$$C = \bar{C} + c(Y - T) - ar$$
$$I^P = \bar{I} - br$$

The first equation is the consumption function with an additional term, equal to $-ar$. Think of $a$ as a fixed number, greater than zero, that measures the strength of the interest rate effect on consumption. Thus the term $-ar$ captures the idea that when the real interest rate $r$ rises, consumption declines by $a$ times the increase in the interest rate. Likewise, the second equation adds the term $-br$ to the equation for planned investment spending. The parameter $b$ is a fixed positive number that measures how strongly changes in the real interest rate affect planned investment; for example, if the real interest rate $r$ rises, planned investment is assumed to decline by $b$ times the increase in the real interest rate. We continue to assume that government purchases, taxes and net exports are exogenous variables, so that $G = \bar{G}$, $T = \bar{T}$ and $NX = \overline{NX}$.

To solve for short-run equilibrium output, we start as usual by finding the relationship of planned aggregate expenditure (*PAE*) to output. The definition of planned aggregate expenditure is

$$PAE = C + I^P + G + NX$$

Substituting the modified equations for consumption and planned investment into this definition, along with the exogenous values of government spending, net exports, and taxes, we get

$$PAE = [\bar{C} + c(Y - \bar{T}) - ar] + [\bar{I} - br] + \bar{G} + \overline{NX}$$

The first term in brackets on the right-hand side describes the behaviour of consumption, and the second bracketed term describes planned investment. Rearranging this equation in order to group together terms that depend on the real interest rate and terms that depend on output, we find

$$PAE = [\bar{C} - c\bar{T} + \bar{I} + \bar{G} + \overline{NX}] - (a + b)r + cY$$

This equation is similar to the equation for *PAE* in Chapter 25 (p. 723), except that it has an extra term, $-(a + b)r$, on the right-hand side. This extra term captures the idea that an increase in the real interest rate reduces consumption and planned investment, lowering planned spending. Notice that the term $-(a + b)r$ is part of autonomous expenditure, since it does not depend on output. Since autonomous expenditure determines the intercept of the expenditure line in the Keynesian cross diagram, changes in the real interest rate will shift the expenditure line up (if the real interest rate decreases) or down (if the real interest rate increases).

To find short-run equilibrium output, we uses the definition of short-run equilibrium output to set $Y = PAE$ and solve for $Y$:

$$\begin{aligned} Y &= PAE \\ &= [\bar{C} - c\bar{T} + \bar{I} + \bar{G} + \overline{NX}] - (a + b)r + cY \\ Y(1 - c) &= [\bar{C} - c\bar{T} + \bar{I} + \bar{G} + \overline{NX}] - (a - b)r \\ Y &= \left(\frac{1}{1 - c}\right)[(\bar{C} - c\bar{T} + \bar{I} + \bar{G} + \overline{NX}) - (a + b)r] \end{aligned} \quad (27A.1)$$

Equation (27A.1) shows that short-run equilibrium output once again equals the multiplier, $1/(1-c)$, times autonomous expenditure, $\bar{C} - c\bar{T} + \bar{I} + \bar{G} + \overline{NX} - (a+b)r$. Autonomous expenditure in turn depends on the real interest rate $r$. Equation (27A.1) also shows that the impact of a change in the real interest rate on short-run equilibrium output depends on two factors: (1) the effect of a change in the real interest rate on consumption and planned investment, which depends on the magnitude of $(a+b)$; and (2) the size of the multiplier, $1/(1-c)$, which relates changes in autonomous expenditure to changes in short-run equilibrium output. The larger the effect of the real interest rate on planned spending, and the larger the multiplier, the more powerful will be the effect of a given change in the real interest rate on short-run equilibrium output.

To check Eq. (27A.1), we can use it to resolve Example 27.4 (see p. 775). In that example, we are given $\bar{C} = 640$, $\bar{I} = 250$, $\bar{G} = 300$, $\overline{NX} = 20$, $\bar{T} = 250$, $c = 0.8$, $a = 400$ and $b = 600$. The real interest rate set by the Central Bank is 5 per cent, or 0.05. Substituting these values into Eq. (27A.1) and solving, we obtain

$$Y = \left(\frac{1}{1.08}\right)[640 - 0.08 \times 250 + 250 + 300 + 20 - (400 + 600) \times 0.05]$$
$$= 5 \times 960 = 4{,}800$$

This is the same result as we found in Example 27.4.

**For those that require expanding coverage of this topic, there is an appendix on the IS-LM model provided at the end of the book.**

## References

Taylor, J. (1993) 'Discretion versus Policy Rules in Practice', *Carnegie–Rochester Conference Series on Public Policy*, pp. 195–227.

# 28

# Inflation and Aggregate Supply

In Chapter 23, we saw that under the terms of the Treaty on European Union (TEU, 1993), commonly known as the Maastricht Treaty, the European Central Bank (ECB) has a primary mandate for the maintenance of price stability in the Eurosystem. Although the Treaty does not offer a precise definition of price stability it is generally understood to mean the maintenance of low inflation which the ECB has defined as a medium-term inflation rate below but close to 2 per cent. Hence the ECB's primary objective is to achieve an inflation rate of approximately 2 per cent over the medium term. This chapter we will discuss the policies that the ECB can use to achieve this target and how it might react to sudden surges in the Eurosystem's inflation rate. In order to fully understand these policies we must first introduce the basic framework for understanding *inflation*, and why it changes over time.

In Chapters 25–27 we made the assumption that firms are willing to meet the demand for their products at pre-set prices. When firms simply produce what is demanded, the level of planned aggregate expenditure determines the economy's real GDP. If the resulting level of short-run equilibrium output is lower than potential output, a *recessionary* output gap develops, and if the resulting level of output exceeds potential output, the economy experiences an *expansionary* gap. As we saw in Chapters 26 and 27, policy makers can attempt to eliminate output gaps by taking actions that affect the level of autonomous expenditure, such as changing the level of government spending or taxes (fiscal policy) or using the Central Bank's control of the money supply to change the real interest rate (monetary policy).

The basic Keynesian model is useful for understanding the role of spending in the short-run determination of output, but it is too simplified to provide a fully realistic description of the economy. The main shortcoming of the basic Keynesian model is that it does not explain the behaviour of *inflation*. Although firms may meet demand at pre-set prices for a time, as assumed in the basic Keynesian model, prices do *not* remain fixed indefinitely. Indeed, sometimes they may rise quite rapidly – the phenomenon of high inflation – imposing significant costs on the economy in the process. In this chapter we shall extend the basic Keynesian model to allow for ongoing inflation. As we shall show, the extended model can be conveniently represented by a new diagram, called the *aggregate demand–aggregate supply diagram*. Using this extended analysis, we shall be able to show how macroeconomic policies affect inflation as well as output, illustrating in the process the difficult trade-offs that policy makers sometimes face. We shall emphasise numerical and graphical analysis of output and inflation in the body of the chapter. The Appendix at the end of the chapter presents an algebraic treatment. As in previous chapters, we shall continue to treat the Eurosystem as a single economy with a common currency and a unified Central Bank.

## Inflation, spending and output: the aggregate demand curve

**aggregate demand (*AD*) curve** shows the relationship between short-run equilibrium output $Y$ and the rate of inflation $\pi$; the name of the curve reflects the fact that short-run equilibrium output is determined by, and equals, total planned spending in the economy: increases in inflation reduce planned spending and short-run equilibrium output, so the aggregate demand curve is downward-sloping

To begin incorporating inflation into the model, our first step is to introduce a new relationship, called the **aggregate demand curve**, which is shown graphically in Fig. 28.1. The aggregate demand (*AD*) curve shows the relationship between short-run equilibrium output $Y$ and the *rate of inflation*, denoted $\pi$. The name of the curve reflects the fact that, as we have seen, short-run equilibrium output is determined by total planned spending, or demand, in the economy. Indeed, by definition, short-run equilibrium output *equals* planned aggregate expenditure, so that we could just as well say that the *AD* curve shows the relationship between inflation and spending.[1]

We shall see shortly that, all else being equal, an increase in the rate of inflation tends to *reduce short-run equilibrium output*. Therefore, in a diagram showing inflation $\pi$ on the vertical axis and output $Y$ on the horizontal axis (Fig. 28.1), the aggregate demand curve is downward-sloping.[2] Note that we refer to the *AD* 'curve', even though the relationship is drawn as a straight line in Fig. 28.1. In general, the *AD* curve can be either straight or curving.

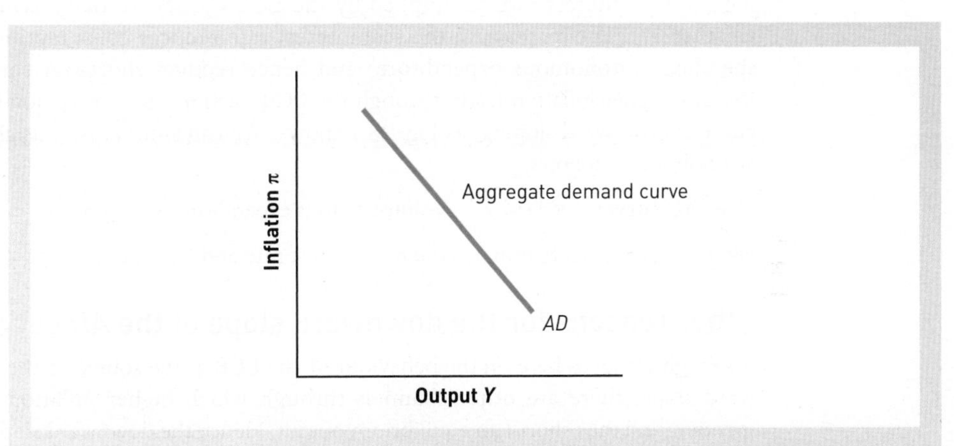


**Figure 28.1 The Aggregate Demand Curve.** The aggregate demand curve *AD* shows the relationship between short-run equilibrium output $Y$ and the rate of inflation $\pi$. Because short-run equilibrium output equals planned spending, the *AD* curve also shows the relationship between inflation and planned spending. The downward slope of the *AD* curve implies that an increase in inflation reduces short-run equilibrium output.

[1] It is important to distinguish the *AD* curve from the expenditure line, introduced as part of the Keynesian cross diagram (Fig. 25.8). The upward-sloping expenditure line shows the relationship between planned aggregate expenditure and output. Again, the *AD* curve shows the relationship between short-run equilibrium output (which equals planned spending) and inflation.

[2] Economists sometimes define the *AD* curve as the relationship between aggregate demand and the *price level*, rather than inflation, which is the *rate of change* of the price level. The definition used here both simplifies the analysis and yields results more consistent with real-world data. For a comparison of the two approaches, see Romer (2000). The graphical analysis used in this chapter follows closely the approach Romer recommends.

Why does higher inflation lead to a lower level of planned spending and short-run equilibrium output? As we shall see next, one important reason is the ECB's response to *increases in inflation*.

## Inflation, the ECB and the *AD* curve

One of the primary responsibilities of the ECB, or any Central Bank, is to maintain a low and stable rate of inflation. For example, following its mandate for price stability the ECB has tried to keep inflation in the Eurosystem below but close to 2 per cent. By keeping inflation low, the Bank tries to avoid the costs that high inflation impose on the economy.

What can the ECB do to keep inflation low and stable? As we have already mentioned, one situation that is likely to lead to increased inflation is an *expansionary output gap*, in which short-run equilibrium output exceeds potential output. When output is above potential output, firms must produce at above-normal capacity to meet the demands of their customers. Like Bill's ice cream parlour, described in Chapter 25, firms may be willing to do this for a time. But eventually they will adjust to the high level of demand by raising prices, contributing to inflation. To control inflation, then, the ECB needs to dampen planned spending and output when they threaten to exceed potential output.

How can the ECB avoid a situation of economic 'overheating', in which spending and output exceed potential output? As we saw in Chapter 27, the ECB can act to reduce autonomous expenditure, and hence short-run equilibrium output, by raising the *real interest rate*. This behaviour by the ECB is a key factor that underlies the link between inflation and output that is summarised by the *AD* curve. When inflation is high, the ECB responds by raising the real interest rate (as implied by the ECB's *policy reaction function*, introduced in Chapter 27). The increase in the real interest rate reduces consumption and investment spending (autonomous expenditure) and hence reduces short-run equilibrium output. Because higher inflation leads, through the ECB's actions, to a reduction in output, the *AD* curve is downward-sloping, as Fig. 28.1 shows. We can summarise this chain of reasoning symbolically as follows:

***AD* curve:** $\pi \uparrow \Rightarrow r \uparrow \Rightarrow$ autonomous expenditure $\downarrow \Rightarrow Y \downarrow$

where, recall, $\pi$ is inflation, $r$ is the real interest rate and $Y$ is output.

## Other reasons for the downward slope of the *AD* curve

Although we focus here on the behaviour of the ECB as the source of the *AD* curve's downward slope, there are other channels through which higher inflation reduces planned spending and thus short-run equilibrium output. Hence the downward slope of the *AD* curve does not depend on the ECB behaving in the particular way just described.

One additional reason for the downward slope of the *AD* curve is the effect of inflation on the *real value of money* held by households and businesses. At high levels of inflation, the purchasing power of money held by the public declines rapidly. This reduction in the public's real wealth may cause households to restrain consumption spending, reducing short-run equilibrium output.

A second channel by which inflation may affect planned spending is through *distributional effects*. Studies have found that people who are less well off are often hurt more by inflation than wealthier people are. For example, retirees on fixed incomes and workers receiving the minimum wage (which is set in euro terms) lose buying power when prices are rising rapidly. Less affluent people are also likely to be relatively unsophisticated in making financial investments and hence less able than wealthier citizens to protect their savings against inflation.

People at the lower end of the income distribution tend to spend a greater percentage of their disposable income than do wealthier individuals. Thus, if a burst of inflation redistributes resources from relatively high-spending, less-affluent households toward relatively high-saving, more-affluent households, overall spending may decline.

A third connection between inflation and aggregate demand arises because higher rates of inflation generate *uncertainty* for households and businesses. When inflation is high, people become less certain about what things will cost in the future, and uncertainty makes planning more difficult. In an uncertain economic environment, both households and firms may become more cautious, reducing their spending as a result.

A final link between inflation and total spending operates through the *prices of domestic goods and services sold abroad*. As we shall see in Chapter 29, the foreign price of domestic goods depends in part on the rate at which the domestic currency, such as the euro, exchanges for foreign currencies, such as the dollar or sterling. However, for constant rates of exchange between currencies, a rise in domestic inflation causes the prices of domestic goods in foreign markets to rise more quickly. As domestic goods become relatively more expensive to prospective foreign purchasers, export sales decline. Net exports are part of aggregate expenditure, and so once more we find that increased inflation is likely to reduce spending. All these factors contribute to the downward slope of the *AD* curve, together with the behaviour of the ECB.

## Shifts of the *AD* curve

The downward slope of the *AD*, curve shown in Fig. 28.1 reflects the fact that *all other factors held constant*, a higher level of inflation will lead to lower planned spending and thus lower short-run equilibrium output. Again, a principal reason higher inflation reduces planned spending and output is that the ECB tends to react to increases in inflation by raising the real interest rate, which in turn reduces consumption and planned investment, two important components of planned aggregate expenditure.

However, even if inflation is held constant, various factors can affect planned spending and short-run equilibrium output. Graphically, as we shall see in this section, these factors will cause the *AD* curve to shift. Specifically, for a given level of inflation, if there is a change in the economy that *increases* short-run equilibrium output, the *AD* curve will shift to the *right*. If, on the other hand, the change *reduces* short-run equilibrium output at each level of inflation, the *AD* curve will shift to the *left*. We shall focus on two sorts of changes in the economy that shift the aggregate demand curve: (1) changes in spending caused by factors other than output or interest rates, which we shall refer to as *exogenous* changes in spending; and (2) changes in the ECB's monetary policy, as reflected in a shift in the ECB's policy reaction function.

### Changes in spending

We have seen that planned aggregate expenditure depends both on output (through the consumption function) and on the real interest rate (which affects both consumption and planned investment). However, many factors other than output or the real interest rate can affect planned spending. For example, at given levels of output and the real interest rate, fiscal policy affects the level of government purchases, and changes in consumer confidence can affect consumption spending. Likewise, new technological opportunities may lead firms to increase their planned investment, and an increased willingness of foreigners to purchase domestic goods will raise net exports. We shall refer to changes in planned spending unrelated to changes in output or the real interest rate as *exogenous* changes in spending.

For a given inflation rate (and thus for a given real interest rate set by the ECB), an exogenous increase in spending raises short-run equilibrium output, for the reasons we have discussed in Chapters 26 and 27. Because it increases output at each level of inflation, *an exogenous increase in spending shifts the AD curve to the right*. This result is illustrated graphically in Fig. 28.2. Imagine, for example, that a rise in the stock market or house prices makes consumers more willing to spend (the wealth effect). Then, for each level of inflation, aggregate spending and short-run equilibrium output will be higher, a change which is shown as a shift of the *AD* curve to the right, from *AD* to *AD*'.

Similarly, at a given inflation rate, an exogenous decline in spending – for example, a fall in government purchases resulting from a more restrictive fiscal policy – causes short-run equilibrium output to fall. We conclude that *an exogenous decrease in spending shifts the AD curve to the left.*

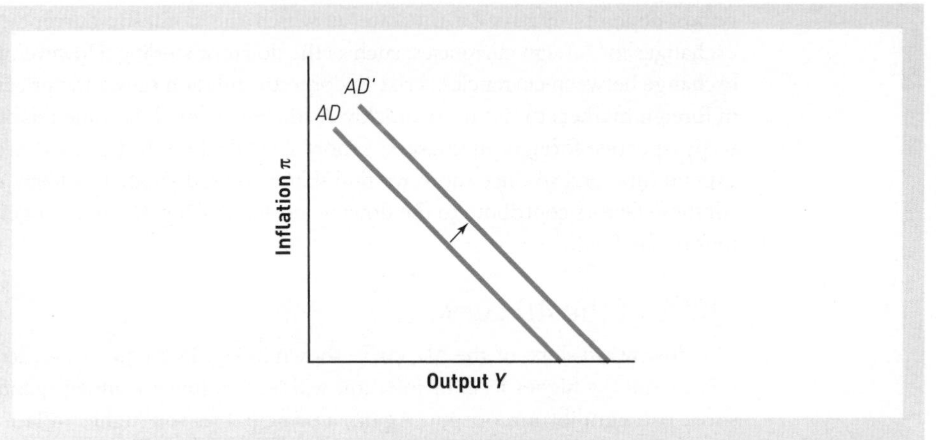


**Figure 28.2 Effect of an Increase in Exogenous Spending.** The *AD* curve is seen both before (*AD*) and after (*AD*') an increase in exogeneous spending – specifically, an increase in consumption spending resulting from a rise in the stock market. If the inflation rate and the real interest rate set by the ECB are held constant, an increase in exogenous spending raises short-run equilibrium output. As a result, the *AD* curve will shift to the right, from *AD* to *AD*'.

**Exercise 28.1** Determine how the following events will affect the *AD* curve:

a. Due to widespread concerns about future weakness in the economy, businesses reduce their spending on new capital.
b. A reduction in income taxes by governments in the Eurosystem.

## Changes in the ECB's policy reaction function

Recall that the ECB's policy reaction function describes how the ECB sets the real interest rate at each level of inflation. This relationship is built into the *AD* curve – indeed, it accounts in part for the curve's downward slope. As long as the ECB sets the real interest rate according to an unchanged reaction function, its adjustments in the real rate will not cause the *AD* curve to shift. Under normal circumstances the ECB generally follows a stable policy reaction function.

However, on occasion the ECB may choose to be significantly 'tighter' or 'easier' than normal for a given rate of inflation. For example, if inflation is high and has stubbornly refused to decrease, the ECB might choose a tighter monetary policy, setting the real interest rate higher than normal at each given rate of inflation. This change of policy can be interpreted as an upward shift in the ECB's policy reaction function, as shown in Fig. 28.3(a). A decision by the ECB to become more 'hawkish' about inflation – that is, to set the real interest rate at a higher level for each given rate of inflation – reduces planned expenditure and thus short-run equilibrium output at each inflation rate. Thus an upward shift of the ECB's policy reaction function leads the *AD* curve to shift to the left (Fig. 28.3(b)).

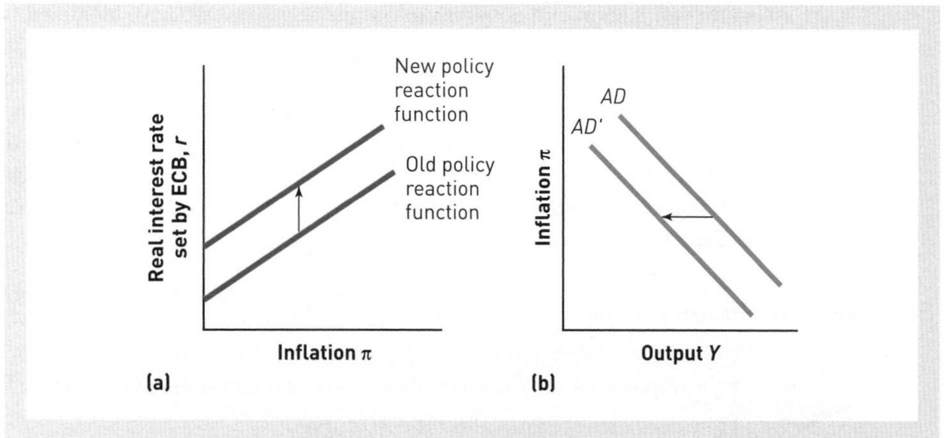


**Figure 28.3 A Shift in the ECB's Policy Reaction Function.** If inflation has remained too high for an extended period, the ECB may choose a 'tighter' monetary policy, by setting the real interest rate at a higher level than usual for each given rate of inflation. Graphically, this change corresponds to an upward movement in the ECB's policy reaction function (a). This change to a tighter monetary policy shifts the *AD* curve to the left (b). If a protracted recession led the ECB to decide to set a lower real interest rate at each level of inflation, the ECB's policy reaction function would shift downward and the *AD* curve would shift to the right.

Similarly, if the Eurosystem's economy is experiencing an unusually severe and protracted recession, the ECB may choose to change its policies and set the real interest rate lower than normal, given the rate of inflation. This change in policy can be interpreted as a downward shift of the ECB's policy reaction function. Given the rate of inflation, a lower-than-normal setting of the real interest rate will lead to higher levels of expenditure and short-run equilibrium output. Therefore, a downward shift of the ECB's policy reaction function causes the *AD* curve to shift to the right.

**Exercise 28.2** Explain why a shift in monetary policy like that shown in Fig. 28.3 can be interpreted as a decline in the ECB's long-run 'target' for the inflation rate. (**Hint:** In the long run, the real interest rate set by the ECB must be consistent with the real interest rate determined in the market for saving and investment.)

## Shifts of the *AD* curve versus movements along the *AD* curve

Let us end this section by reviewing and summarising the important distinction between *movements along* the *AD* curve and *shifts* of the *AD* curve.

The downward slope of the *AD* curve captures the *inverse relationship* between inflation, on the one hand, and short-run equilibrium output, on the other. As we have seen, a rise in the inflation rate leads the ECB to raise the real interest rate, according to its policy reaction function. The higher real interest rate, in turn, depresses planned spending and hence lowers short-run equilibrium output. The downward slope of the *AD* curve embodies this relationship among inflation, spending and output. Hence changes in the inflation rate, and the resulting changes in the real interest rate and short-run equilibrium output, are represented by *movements along* the *AD* curve. In particular, as long as the ECB sets the real interest rate in accordance with a fixed policy reaction function, changes in the real interest rate will *not* shift the *AD* curve.

However, any factor that changes the short-run equilibrium level of output *at a given level of inflation* will *shift* the *AD* curve – to the right if short-run equilibrium output increases, or to the left if short-run equilibrium output decreases. We have identified two factors that can shift the *AD* curve: exogenous changes in spending (that is, changes in spending unrelated to output or the real interest rate) and changes in the ECB's policy reaction function. An exogenous increase in spending or a downward shift of the ECB's policy reaction function increases short-run equilibrium output at every level of inflation, hence shifting the *AD* curve to the right. An exogenous decline in spending or an upward shift in the ECB's policy reaction function decreases short-run equilibrium output at every level of inflation, shifting the *AD* curve to the left.

**Exercise 28.3** What is the difference, if any, between the following?

a. An upward shift in the ECB's policy reaction function

b. A response by the ECB to higher inflation, for a given policy reaction function.

How does each scenario affect the *AD* curve?

## RECAP The aggregate demand (*AD*) curve

- The *AD* curve shows the relationship between *short-run equilibrium output* and *inflation*. Higher inflation leads the ECB to raise the real interest rate, which reduces autonomous expenditure and thus short-run equilibrium output. Therefore, the *AD* curve slopes downward.
- The *AD curve may also slope downward* because (1) higher inflation reduces the real value of money held by the public, reducing wealth and spending; (2) inflation redistributes resources from less affluent people, who spend a high percentage of their disposable income, to more affluent people, who spend a smaller percentage of disposable income; (3) higher inflation creates greater uncertainty in planning for households and firms, reducing their spending; and (4) for a constant rate of exchange between the euro and other currencies, rising prices of domestic goods and services reduce foreign sales and hence net exports (a component of aggregate spending).
- An exogenous *increase* in spending raises short-run equilibrium output at each value of inflation, and so shifts the *AD* curve to the right. Conversely, an exogenous *decrease* in spending shifts the *AD* curve to the left.
- A change to an *easier* monetary policy, as reflected by a downward shift in the ECB's policy reaction function, shifts the *AD* curve to the right. A change to a *tighter*, more anti-inflationary monetary policy, as reflected by an upward shift in the ECB's policy reaction function, shifts the *AD* curve to the left.
- Assuming no change in the ECB's reaction function, changes in inflation correspond to movements *along* the *AD* curve; they do not *shift* the *AD* curve.

# Inflation and aggregate supply

Thus far in this chapter we have focused on how changes in inflation affect spending and short-run equilibrium output, a relationship captured by the *AD* curve. But we have not yet discussed how inflation itself is determined. In the rest of the chapter we shall examine the main factors that determine the inflation rate in modern industrial economies, as well as the options that policy makers have to control inflation. In doing so, we shall introduce a useful diagram for analysing the behaviour of output and inflation, called the *aggregate demand–aggregate supply diagram*.

Physicists have noted that a body will tend to keep moving at a constant speed and direction unless it is acted upon by some outside force – a tendency they refer to as *inertia*. Applying this concept to economics, many observers have noted that inflation seems to be inertial, in the sense that it tends to remain roughly constant as long as the economy is at full employment and there are no external shocks to the price level. In the first part of this section we shall discuss why inflation behaves in this way.

However, just as a physical object will change speed if it is acted on by outside forces, so various economic forces can change the rate of inflation. Later in this section we shall discuss three factors that can cause the inflation rate to change. The first is the presence of an *output gap*: inflation tends to rise when there is an expansionary output gap and to fall when there is a recessionary output gap. The second factor that can affect the inflation rate is a shock that directly affects prices, which we will refer to as an *inflation shock*. A large increase in the price of imported oil, for example, raises the price of petrol, heating oil and other fuels, as well as of goods made with oil or services using oil. Finally, the third factor that directly affects the inflation rate is a *shock to potential output*, or a sharp change in the level of potential output – a natural disaster that destroys a significant portion of a country's factories and businesses is one extreme example. Together, inflationary shocks and shocks to potential output are known as *aggregate supply shocks*.

## Inflation inertia

In low-inflation industrial economies like that of the Eurosystem today, inflation tends to change relatively slowly from year to year, a phenomenon that is sometimes referred to as *inflation inertia*. If the rate of inflation in one year is 2 per cent, it may be 3 per cent or even 4 per cent in the next year. But unless the nation experiences very unusual economic conditions, inflation is unlikely to rise to 6 per cent or 8 per cent or fall to –2 per cent in the following year. This relatively sluggish behaviour contrasts sharply with the behaviour of economic variables such as stock market or commodity prices, which can change rapidly from day to day. For example, oil prices might well rise by 20 per cent over the course of a year and then fall 20 per cent over the next year. Yet since the early 1990s, the inflation rate in most advanced economies has generally remained in the range of 2–3 per cent per year.

Why does inflation tend to adjust relatively slowly in modern industrial economies? To answer this question, we must consider two closely related factors that play an important role in determining the inflation rate: the behaviour of the public's *inflation expectations* and the existence of *long-term wage and price contracts*.

First, consider the public's expectations about inflation. In negotiating future wages and prices, both buyers and sellers take into account the rate of inflation they expect to prevail in the next few years. As a result, today's *expectations* of future inflation may help to determine the future inflation rate. Suppose, for example, that an office worker called Fred and his boss Colleen agree that performance this past year justifies an increase of 2 per cent in his real wage for next year. What *nominal*, or euro, wage increase should they agree on? If Fred believes that inflation is likely to be 3 per cent over the next year, he will ask for a 5 per cent increase in his nominal wage to obtain a 2 per cent increase in his real wage. If Colleen also expects that inflation will be 3 per cent, she should be willing to go along with a 5 per cent nominal increase, knowing that it implies only a 2 per cent increase in Fred's real wage. Thus the rate at which Fred and Colleen *expect* prices to rise affects the rate at which at least one price – Fred's nominal wage – *actually* rises.

A similar dynamic affects the contracts for production inputs other than labour. For example, if Colleen is negotiating with her office supply company, the prices she will agree to pay for next year's deliveries of copy paper and staples will depend on what she expects the inflation rate to be. If Colleen anticipates that the price of office supplies will not change relative to the prices of other goods and services, and that the general inflation rate will be 3 per cent, then she should be willing to agree to a 3 per cent increase in the price of office supplies. On the other hand, if she expects the general inflation rate to be 6 per cent, then she will agree to pay 6 per cent more for copy paper and staples next year, knowing that a nominal increase of 6 per cent implies no change in the price of office supplies relative to other goods and services.

Economywide, then, the higher the expected rate of inflation, the more nominal wages and the cost of other inputs will tend to rise. But if wages and other costs of production grow rapidly in response to expected inflation, firms will have to raise their prices rapidly as well in order to cover their costs. Thus a high rate of expected inflation tends to lead to a high rate of actual inflation. Similarly, if expected inflation is low, leading wages and other costs to rise relatively slowly, actual inflation should be low as well.

**Exercise 28.4**

Assume that employers and workers agree that real wages should rise by 2 per cent next year.

a. If inflation is expected to be 2 per cent next year, what will happen to nominal wages next year?
b. If inflation is expected to be 4 per cent next year, rather than 2 per cent, what will happen to nominal wages next year?
c. Use your answers from parts (a) and (b) to explain how an increase in expected inflation will tend to affect the following year's actual rate of inflation.

The conclusion that actual inflation is partially determined by expected inflation raises the question of what determines *inflation expectations*. To a great extent, people's expectations are influenced by their recent experience. If inflation has been low and stable for some time, people are likely to expect it to continue to be low. But if inflation has recently been high, people will expect it to continue to be high. If inflation has been unpredictable, alternating between low and high levels, the public's expectations will likewise tend to be volatile, rising or falling with news or rumours about economic conditions or economic policy.

Figure 28.4 illustrates schematically how low and stable inflation may tend to be *self-perpetuating*. As Fig. 28.4 shows, if inflation has been low for some time, people will continue to expect low inflation. Increases in nominal wages and other production costs will thus tend to be small. If firms raise prices only by enough to cover costs, then actual inflation will be low, as expected. This low actual rate will in turn promote low expected inflation, perpetuating the 'virtuous circle'. The same logic applies in reverse in an economy with high inflation: a persistently high inflation rate leads the public to expect high inflation, resulting in higher increases in nominal wages and other production costs. This in turn contributes to a high rate of actual inflation, and so on in a vicious circle. This role of inflation expectations in the determination of wage and price increases helps to explain why inflation often seems to adjust slowly.

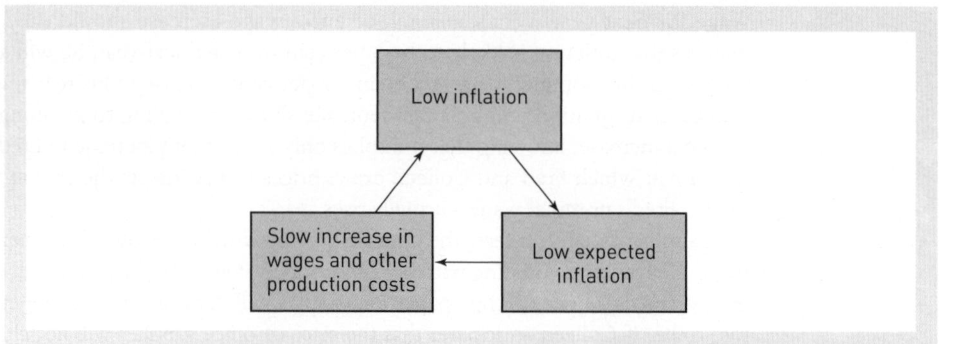


**Figure 28.4 A Virtuous Circle of Low Inflation and Low Expected Inflation.** Low inflation leads people to expect low inflation in the future. As a result, they agree to accept small increases in wages and in the prices of the goods and services they supply, which keeps inflation – and expected inflation – low. In a similar way, high inflation leads people to expect high inflation, which in turn tends to produce high inflation.

The role of inflation expectations in the slow adjustment of inflation is strengthened by a second key element, the existence of *long-term wage and price contracts*. Union wage contracts, for example, can extend for two to three years into the future. Likewise, contracts that set the prices manufacturing firms pay for parts and raw materials often cover several years. Long-term contracts serve to 'build in' wage and price increases that depend on inflation expectations at the time the contracts were signed. For example, a union negotiating in a high-inflation environment is much more likely to demand a rapid increase in nominal wages over the life of the contract than would a union in an economy in which prices are stable.

To summarise, in the absence of external shocks, inflation tends to remain relatively stable over time – at least in low-inflation industrial economies such as those of the Eurosystem. In other words, inflation is *inertial* (or as some people put it, 'sticky'). Inflation tends to be inertial for two main reasons. The first is the behaviour of people's expectations of inflation. A low inflation rate leads people to expect low inflation in the future, which results in reduced pressure for wage and price increases. Similarly, a high inflation rate leads people to expect high inflation in the future, resulting in more rapid increases in wages and prices. Second, the effects of expectations are reinforced by the existence of long-term wage and price contracts, which is the second reason inflation tends to be stable over time. Long-term contracts tend to build in the effects of people's inflation expectations.

Although the rate of inflation tends to be inertial, it does of course change over time. We next discuss a key factor causing the inflation rate to change.

**Exercise 28.5** Based on Fig. 28.4, discuss why Central Banks have a strong incentive to maintain a low inflation rate in the economy.

## The output gap and inflation

An important factor influencing the rate of inflation is the *output gap*, or the difference between potential output and actual output ($Y^* - Y$). We have seen that, in the short run, firms will meet the demand for their output at previously determined prices. For example, Bill's ice cream parlour will serve ice cream to any customer who comes into the shop at the prices posted behind the counter. The level of output that is determined by the demand at pre-set prices is called *short-run equilibrium output*.

At a particular time the level of short-run equilibrium output may happen to equal the economy's long-run productive capacity, or potential output. But that is not necessarily the case. Output may exceed potential output, giving rise to an *expansionary* gap, or it may fall short of potential output, producing a *recessionary* gap. Let us consider what happens to inflation in each of these three possible cases: no output gap, an expansionary gap and a recessionary gap.

If actual output equals potential output, then by definition there is no output gap. When the output gap is zero, firms are satisfied, in the sense that their sales equal their normal production rates. As a result, firms have no incentive either to reduce or increase their prices *relative* to the prices of other goods and services. However, the fact that firms are satisfied with their sales does *not* imply that inflation – the rate of change in the overall price level – is zero.

To see why, let us go back to the idea of inflation inertia. Suppose that inflation has recently been steady at 2 per cent per year, so that the public has come to expect an inflation rate of 2 per cent per year. If the public's inflation expectations are reflected in the wage and price increases agreed to in long-term contracts, then firms will find their labour and materials costs are rising at 2 per cent per year. To cover their costs, firms will need to raise their prices by 2 per cent per year. Note that if all firms are raising their prices by 2 per cent per year, the *relative* prices of various goods and services in the economy – say, the price of ice cream relative to the price of a taxi ride – will not change. Nevertheless, the economywide rate of inflation equals 2 per cent, the same as in previous years. We conclude that, if the *output gap is zero, the rate of inflation will tend to remain the same.*

Suppose instead that an *expansionary* gap exists, so that most firms' sales exceed their normal production rates. As we might expect in situations in which the quantity demanded exceeds the quantity firms desire to supply, firms will ultimately respond by trying to increase their relative prices. To do so, they will increase their prices by more than the increase in their costs. If all firms behave this way, then the general price level will begin to rise more rapidly than before. Thus, when an *expansionary gap exists, the rate of inflation will tend to increase.*

Finally, if a *recessionary* gap exists, firms will be selling an amount less than their capacity to produce, and they will have an incentive to cut their relative prices so they can sell more. In this case, firms will raise their prices less than needed to cover fully their increases in costs, as determined by the existing inflation rate. As a result, when a *recessionary gap exists, the rate of inflation will tend to decrease.* These important results are summarised in Table 28.1.

| Relationship of output to potential output | | Behaviour of inflation |
|---|---|---|
| 1. No output gap<br>$Y = Y^*$ | → | Inflation remains unchanged |
| 2. Expansionary gap<br>$Y > Y^*$ | → | Inflation rises<br>$\pi \uparrow$ |
| 3. Recessionary gap<br>$Y < Y^*$ | → | Inflation falls<br>$\pi \downarrow$ |

**Table 28.1** The Output Gap and Inflation

### Example 28.1 Spending changes and inflation

In Chapters 26 and 27 we saw that changes in spending can create expansionary or recessionary gaps. Therefore, based on the discussion above, we can conclude that changes in spending also lead to changes in the rate of inflation. If the economy is currently operating at potential output, what effect will a fall in consumer confidence that makes consumers less willing to spend at each level of disposable income have on the rate of inflation in the economy?

A decrease in exogenous consumption spending, $C$, for a given level of inflation, output and real interest rates, reduces aggregate expenditures and short-run equilibrium output. If the economy was originally operating at potential output, the reduction in consumption will cause a recessionary gap, since actual output, $Y$, will now be less than potential output, $Y^*$. As indicated above, when $Y < Y^*$, the rate of inflation will tend to fall because firms' sales fall short of normal production rates, leading them to slow down the rate at which they increase their prices.

**Exercise 28.6** Suppose that firms become optimistic about the future and decide to increase their investment in new capital. What effect will this have on the rate of inflation, assuming that the economy is currently operating at potential output?

## The aggregate demand–aggregate supply diagram

The adjustment of inflation in response to an output gap can be shown conveniently in a diagram. Figure 28.5, drawn with inflation $\pi$ on the vertical axis and real output $Y$ on the horizontal axis, is an example of an *aggregate demand–aggregate supply diagram* (or *AD–AS diagram*, for short). Figure 28.5 has three elements, one of which is the downward-sloping *AD* curve, introduced earlier in the chapter. Recall that the *AD* curve shows how planned aggregate spending (PAE), and hence short-run equilibrium output, depend on the inflation rate. The second element is a vertical line marking the economy's potential output $Y^*$. Because potential output represents the economy's long-run productive capacity, we will refer to this vertical line as the **long-run aggregate supply line**, or *LRAS* line. The third element in Fig. 28.5, and a new one, is the *short-run aggregate supply line*, labelled *SRAS* in Fig. 28.5. **The short-run aggregate supply (*SRAS*) line** is a horizontal line that shows the current rate of inflation in the economy, which in the figure is labelled $\pi$. We can think of the current rate of inflation as having been determined by *past expectations of inflation* and *past pricing decisions*. The short-run aggregate supply line is horizontal because, in the short run, producers supply whatever output is demanded at pre-set prices.

**long-run aggregate supply (*LRAS*) line** a vertical line showing the economy's potential output $Y^*$

**short-run aggregate supply (*SRAS*) line** a horizontal line showing the current rate of inflation, as determined by past expectations and pricing decisions

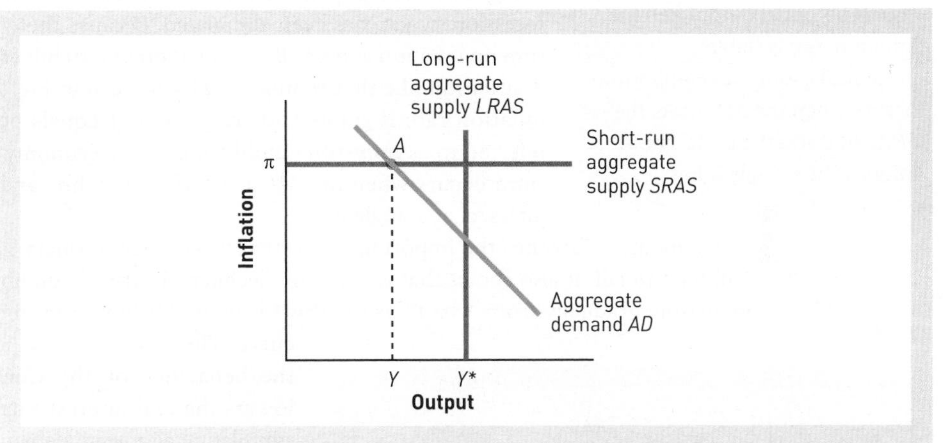


**Figure 28.5 The Aggregate Demand–Aggregate Supply (*AD–AS*) Diagram.** This diagram has three elements: the *AD* curve, which shows how short-run equilibrium output depends on inflation; the long-run aggregate supply (*LRAS*) line, which marks the economy's potential output $Y^*$, and the short-run aggregate supply (*SRAS*) line, which shows the current value of inflation $\pi$. Short-run equilibrium output, which is equal to $Y$ here, is determined by the intersection of the *AD* curve and the *SRAS* line (point *A*). Because actual output $Y$ is less than potential output $Y^*$, this economy has a recessionary gap.

The *AD–AS* diagram can be used to determine the level of output prevailing at any particular time. As we have seen, the inflation rate at any moment is given directly by the position of the *SRAS* line – for example, current inflation equals $\pi$ in Fig. 28.5. To find the current level of output, recall that the *AD* curve shows the level of short-run equilibrium output at any given rate of inflation. Since the inflation rate in this economy is $\pi$, we can infer from Fig. 28.5 that short-run equilibrium output must equal $Y$, which corresponds to the intersection of the *AD* curve and the *SRAS* line (point *A* in Fig. 28.5). Notice that in Fig. 28.5, short-run equilibrium output $Y$ is smaller than potential output $Y^*$, so there is a *recessionary gap* in this economy.

**short-run equilibrium** a situation in which inflation equals the value determined by past expectations and pricing decisions and output equals the level of short-run equilibrium output that is consistent with that inflation rate; graphically, short-run equilibrium occurs at the intersection of the *AD* curve and the *SRAS* line

The intersection of the *AD* curve and the *SRAS* line (point *A* in Fig. 28.5) is referred to as the point of **short-run equilibrium** in this economy. When the economy is in short-run equilibrium, inflation equals the value determined by past expectations and past pricing decisions, and output equals the level of short-run equilibrium output that is consistent with that inflation rate.

Although the economy may be in short-run equilibrium at point *A* in Fig. 28.5, it will not remain there. The reason is that, at point *A*, the economy is experiencing a recessionary gap (output is less than potential output, as indicated by the *LRAS* line). As we have just seen, when a recessionary gap exists, firms are not selling as much as they would like to and so they slow down the rate at which they increase their prices. Eventually, the low level of aggregate demand that is associated with a recessionary gap causes the inflation rate to fall.

The adjustment of inflation in response to a recessionary gap is shown graphically in Fig. 28.6. As inflation declines, the *SRAS* line moves downward, from *SRAS* to *SRAS*'. Because of inflation inertia (caused by the slow adjustment of the public's inflation expectations and the existence of long-term contracts), inflation adjusts downward only gradually. However, as long as a recessionary gap exists, inflation will continue to fall, and the *SRAS* line will move downward until it intersects the *AD* curve at point *B* in Fig. 28.6. At that point, actual output equals potential output and the recessionary gap has been eliminated. Because there is no further pressure on inflation at point *B*, the inflation rate stabilises at the lower level. A situation like that represented by point *B* in Fig. 28.6, in which the inflation rate is stable and actual output equals potential output, is referred to as **long-run equilibrium** of the economy. Long-run equilibrium occurs when the *AD* curve, the *SRAS* line and the *LRAS* line all intersect at a single point.

**long-run equilibrium** a situation in which actual output equals potential output and the inflation rate is stable; graphically, long-run equilibrium occurs when the *AD* curve, the *SRAS* line and the *LRAS* line all intersect at a single point

Figure 28.6 illustrates the important point that when a recessionary gap exists, inflation will tend to fall. It also shows that as inflation declines, short-run equilibrium output rises, increasing gradually from *Y* to *Y** as the short-run equilibrium point moves down the *AD* curve. The source of this increase in output is the behaviour of the Central Bank, which lowers the real interest rate as inflation falls, stimulating aggregate demand. Falling inflation stimulates spending and output in other ways, such as by reducing uncertainty.[3] As output rises, cyclical unemployment also declines. This process of falling inflation, falling real interest rates, rising output and falling unemployment continues until the economy reaches full employment at point *B* in Fig. 28.6, the economy's long-run equilibrium point.

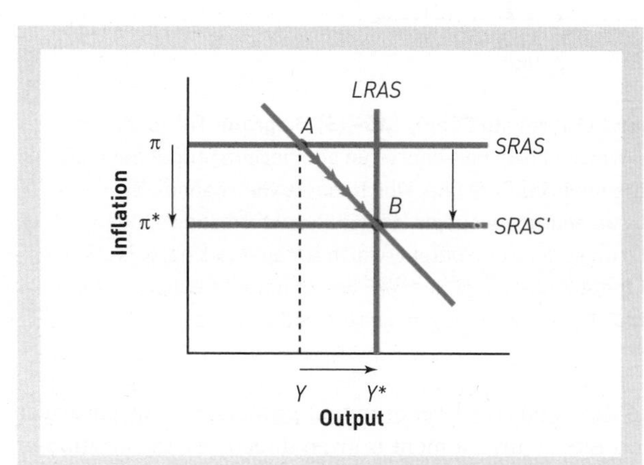


**Figure 28.6 The Adjustment of Inflation when a Recessionary Gap Exists.** At the initial short-run equilibrium point *A*, a recessionary gap exists, which puts downward pressure on inflation. As inflation gradually falls, the *SRAS* line moves downward until it reaches *SRAS*', and actual output equals potential output (point *B*). Once the recessionary gap has been eliminated, inflation stabilises at $\pi^*$, and the economy settles into long-run equilibrium at the intersection of *AD*, *LRAS* and *SRAS*' (point *B*).

What happens if instead of a recessionary gap, the economy has an expansionary gap, with output greater than potential output? An expansionary gap would cause the rate of inflation to *rise*, as firms respond to high demand by raising their prices more rapidly than their costs are rising. In graphical terms, an expansionary gap would cause the *SRAS* line to move upward over time. Inflation and the *SRAS* line would continue to rise until the economy reached long-run equilibrium, with actual output equal to potential output. This process is illustrated in Fig. 28.7. Initially, the economy

[3] Our explanation for the downward slope of the *AD* curve, earlier in the chapter, described some of these other factors.

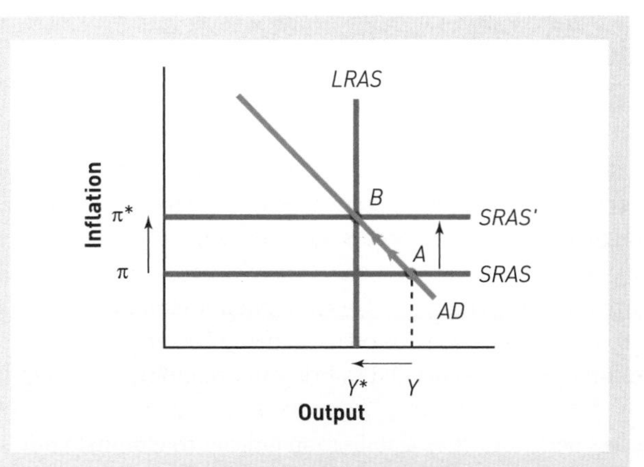


**Figure 28.7 The Adjustment of Inflation when an Expansionary Gap Exists.** At the initial short-run equilibrium point *A*, an expansionary gap exists. Inflation rises gradually (the *SRAS* line moves upward) and output falls. The process continues until the economy reaches long-run equilibrium at point *B*, where inflation stabilises and the output gap is eliminated.

is in short-run equilibrium at point *A*, where $Y > Y^*$ (an expansionary gap). The expansionary gap causes inflation to rise over time; graphically, the short-run aggregate supply line moves upward, from *SRAS* to *SRAS'*. As the *SRAS* line rises, short-run equilibrium output falls – the result of the Central Bank's tendency to increase the real interest rate when inflation rises. Eventually the *SRAS* line intersects the *AD* curve *LRAS* and line at point *B*, where the economy reaches long-run equilibrium, with no output gap and stable inflation.

## The self-correcting economy

Our analysis of Figs 28.6 and 28.7 makes an important general point: the economy tends to be *self-correcting* in the long run. In other words, given enough time, output gaps tend to disappear without changes in monetary or fiscal policy (other than the change in the real interest rate embodied in the Central Bank's policy reaction function). Expansionary output gaps are eliminated by rising inflation, while recessionary output gaps are eliminated by falling inflation. This result contrasts sharply with the basic Keynesian model, which does not include a self-correcting mechanism. The difference in results is explained by the fact that the basic Keynesian model concentrates on the short-run period, during which prices do not adjust, and does not take into account the changes in prices and inflation that occur over a longer period.

Does the economy's tendency to self-correct imply that aggressive monetary and fiscal policies are not needed to stabilise output? The answer to this question depends crucially on the *speed* with which the self-correction process takes place. If self-correction takes place very slowly, so that actual output differs from potential for protracted periods, then active use of monetary and fiscal policy can help to stabilise output. But if self-correction is rapid, then active stabilisation policies are probably not justified in most cases, given the *lags* and *uncertainties* that are involved in policy making in practice. Indeed, if the economy returns to full employment quickly, then attempts by policy makers to stabilise spending and output may end up doing more harm than good, for example, by causing actual output to 'overshoot' potential output.

The speed with which a particular economy corrects itself depends on a variety of factors, including the prevalence of long-term contracts and the efficiency and flexibility of product and labour markets. (For a case study, see the comparison of US and European labour markets in Chapter 21.) However, a reasonable conclusion is that the greater the initial output gap, the longer the economy's process of self-correction will take. This observation suggests that stabilisation policies should not be used actively to try to eliminate relatively small output gaps, but that they may be quite useful in remedying large gaps – for example, when the unemployment rate is exceptionally high.

## RECAP *AD–AS* and the self-correcting economy

The economy is in short-run equilibrium when inflation equals the value determined by past expectations and pricing decisions, and output equals the level of short-run equilibrium output that is consistent with that inflation rate. Graphically, short-run equilibrium occurs at the intersection of the *AD* curve and the *SRAS* line.

The economy is in long-run equilibrium when actual output equals potential output (there is no output gap) and the inflation rate is stable. Graphically, long-run equilibrium occurs when the *AD* curve, the *SRAS* line and the *LRAS* line intersect at a common point.

Inflation adjusts gradually to bring the economy into long-run equilibrium (a phenomenon called the economy's *self-correcting* tendency). Inflation rises to eliminate an expansionary gap and falls to eliminate a recessionary gap. Graphically, the *SRAS* line moves up or down as needed to bring the economy into long-run equilibrium.

The more rapid the self-correction process, the less need for active stabilisation policies to eliminate output gaps. In practice, policy makers' attempts to eliminate output gaps are more likely to be helpful when the output gap is large than when it is small.

# Sources of inflation

We have seen that inflation can rise or fall in response to an output gap. But what creates the output gaps that give rise to changes in inflation? And are there factors besides output gaps that can affect the inflation rate? In this section we use the *AD–AS* diagram to explore the *ultimate sources of inflation*. We first discuss how excessive growth in aggregate spending can spur inflation, then turn to factors operating through the supply side of the economy.

## Excessive aggregate spending

One important source of inflation in practice is excessive aggregate spending – or, in more colloquial terms, 'too much spending chasing too few goods'. Example 28.2 illustrates this.

### **Example 28.2** Government deficits and inflation

Excessive government budget deficits are sometimes associated with increased inflation. Explain why, using the *AD–AS* diagram (Fig. 28.5). Can the ECB do anything to prevent the increase in inflation caused by budget deficits?

A government's budget deficit is the *excess of government spending over tax revenues*. In Fig. 28.2 we saw that higher government expenditures (G) shift the *AD* curve to the *right*. The same is true for reductions in tax revenues (*T*) which increase disposable incomes, leading to higher consumption expenditures. As consumption is a key component of total expenditure in the economy, aggregate demand will increase at any given level of inflation: that is, the *AD* curve will shift to the *right*. Hence higher government deficits are potentially inflationary because increased spending and lower taxation raises total demand relative to the economy's productive capacity. In the face of rising sales, firms increase their prices more quickly, raising the inflation rate.

Figure 28.8 illustrates this process. We will assume that the aggregate demand and aggregate supply curves in Fig. 28.8 illustrate the Eurosystem as a whole. Suppose that the Eurosystem's economy is initially in long-run equilibrium at point *A*, where the aggregate demand curve *AD* intersects both the short-run and long-run aggregate supply lines, *SRAS* and *LRAS*, respectively. Point *A* is a long-run equilibrium point, with output equal to potential output and stable inflation. Now suppose that governments across the Eurosystem decide to start increasing their budget deficits. We saw earlier that, for a given level of inflation, an exogenous increase in spending raises short-run equilibrium output, shifting the *AD* curve to the right. Figure 28.8 shows the aggregate demand curve shifting rightward, from *AD* to *AD*', as the result of increased deficits. The economy moves to a new, short-run equilibrium at point *B*, where *AD′* intersects *SRAS*. Note that at point *B* actual output has risen above potential, creating an expansionary gap. Because inflation is inertial and does not change in the short run, the immediate effect of the increase in government deficits is only to increase output, just as we saw in the Keynesian cross analysis of Chapter 25.

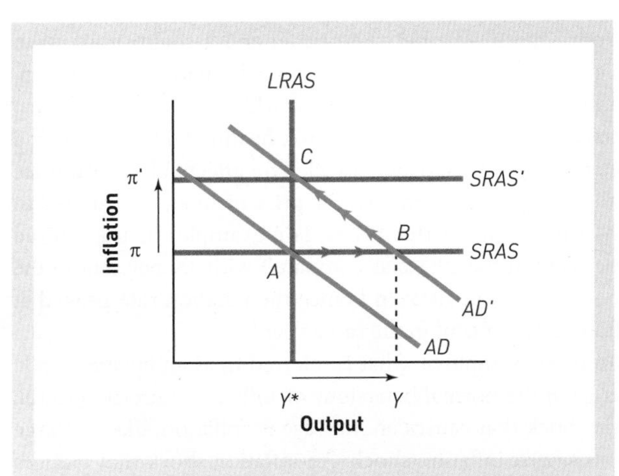


**Figure 28.8 Budget Deficits and Inflation.** An increase in government budget deficits shifts the *AD* curve to the right, from *AD* to *AD'*. At the new short-run equilibrium point *B*, actual output has risen above potential output *Y**, creating and expansionary gap. This gap leads to a rise in inflation, shown as an upward movement of the *SRAS* line from *SRAS* to *SRAS'*. At the new long-run equilibrium point *C*, actual output has fallen back to the level of potential output, but inflation is higher at $\pi'$.

The process doesn't stop there, however, because inflation will not remain the same indefinitely. At point *B* an expansionary gap exists, so inflation will gradually begin to increase. Figure 28.8 shows this increase in inflation as a shift of the *SRAS* line from its initial position to a higher level, *SRAS′*. When inflation has risen to $\pi'$, enough to eliminate the output gap (point *C*), the economy is back in long-run equilibrium. Hence, the increase in output created by higher government deficits temporary, in the long run, actual output returns to the level of potential output, but at a higher rate of inflation.

Does the ECB have the power to prevent the increased inflation induced by a rise in government deficits? The answer is yes. We saw earlier that a decision by the ECB to set a higher real interest rate at any given level of inflation – an upward shift in the policy reaction function – will shift the *AD* curve to the left. So if the ECB aggressively tightens monetary policy (shifts its reaction function) as government deficits increase, it can reverse the rightward shift of the *AD* curve caused by increased government spending. Offsetting the rightward shift of the *AD* curve in turn avoids the development of an expansionary gap, with its inflationary consequences. The ECB's policy works because the higher real interest rate it sets at each level of inflation acts to reduce consumption and investment spending. The reduction in private spending offsets the increase in demand by governments, eliminating – or at least moderating – the inflationary impact of the higher deficits.

We should not conclude, by the way, that avoiding the inflationary consequences of higher deficits is *costless* to society. As we have just noted, inflation can be avoided only if consumption and investment are reduced by a policy of higher real interest rates. Effectively, the private sector must give up some resources so that more output can be devoted to public purposes. This reduction in resources reduces both current living standards (by reducing consumption) and future living standards (by reducing investment). Also, one reason behind the Eurosystem's Stability and Growth Pact (SGP), as discussed in Chapter 26, is to prevent national governments from running excessive deficits which would require the ECB to undertake the type of contractionary monetary policy discussed above.

**Exercise 28.7** In Example 28.1 we found that a decline in consumer spending tends to reduce the rate of inflation. Using the *AD–AS* diagram (Fig. 28.5), illustrate the short-run and long-run effects of a fall in consumer spending on inflation. How does the decline in spending affect output in the short run and in the long run?

**inflation shock** a sudden change in the normal behaviour of inflation, unrelated to the nation's output gap

Whereas output gaps cause gradual changes in inflation, on occasion an economic shock can cause a relatively rapid increase or decrease in inflation. Such jolts to prices, which we call **inflation shocks**, are the subject of the next section.

## Inflation shocks

In late 1973, at the time of the Yom Kippur War between Israel and a coalition of Arab nations, the Organisation of Petroleum Exporting Countries (OPEC) dramatically cut its supplies of crude oil to the industrialised nations, quadrupling world oil prices. The sharp increase in oil prices was quickly transferred to the price of petrol, heating oil and goods and services that were heavily dependent on oil, such as air travel. The effects of the oil price increase, together with agricultural shortages that increased the price of food, contributed to a significant rise in European inflation rates in the 1970s. For example, in the United Kingdom inflation averaged 10.6 per cent in the 1970s, as compared with 3.9 per cent in the 1960s, and reached a peak of over 20 per cent in 1975. In France the inflation rate peaked at almost 15 per cent in 1974 and in Italy at 21 per cent in the same year.[4]

The increase in inflation in 1970s is an example of what is referred to as an *inflation shock*. An inflation shock is a sudden change in the normal behaviour of inflation, unrelated to the economy's output gap. An inflation shock that causes an increase in inflation, like the large rise in oil prices in 1973, is called an *adverse* inflation shock. An inflation shock that reduces inflation, such as the sharp decline in oil prices that occurred in 1986, is called a *favourable* inflation shock. Economic naturalist 28.2 gives more details on the economic effects of inflation shocks.

### Economic naturalist 28.1 Why did inflation escalate in the 1970s?

During the 1970s, inflation in Western Europe averaged around 11 per cent per annum as compared with just under 4 per cent for the 1960s. For most countries the peak came around 1974–75 just after the quadrupling in world oil prices. Why did inflation increase so much in the 1970s?

We have already described the quadrupling of oil prices in late 1973 and the sharp increases in agricultural prices at about the same time, which together constituted an *adverse inflation shock*. A second inflation shock occurred in 1979, when the turmoil of the Iranian Revolution restricted the flow of oil from the Middle East and doubled oil prices yet again.

Figure 28.9 shows the effects of an adverse inflation shock on a hypothetical economy. Before the inflation shock occurs, the economy is in long-run equilibrium at point *A*, at the intersection of *AD*, *LRAS* and *SRAS*. At point *A* actual output is equal to potential output *Y**, and the inflation rate is stable at $\pi$. However, an adverse inflation shock directly increases inflation, so that the *SRAS* line shifts rapidly upward to *SRAS'*. A new short-run equilibrium is established at point *B*, where *SRAS'* intersects the aggregate demand curve *AD*. In the wake of the inflation shock, inflation rises to $\pi'$ and output falls, from *Y** to *Y'*. Thus an inflation shock

[4] In Chapter 19 we distinguished between relative price changes (changes in the prices of individual goods) and inflation (changes in the overall price level). In the 1973–74 episode, changes in the prices of individual categories of goods, such as energy and food, were sufficiently large and pervasive that the overall price level was significantly affected. Thus these relative price changes carried an inflationary impact as well.

creates the worst possible scenario: higher inflation coupled with a recessionary gap. The combination of inflation and recession has been referred to as *stagflation*, or stagnation plus inflation. Most European countries experienced a stagflation in 1973–75, after the first oil shock, and again in 1980, after the second oil shock.

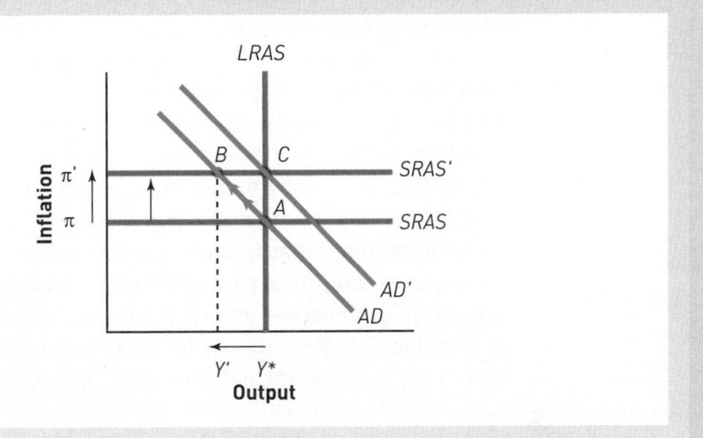


**Figure 28.9 The Effects of an Adverse Inflation Shock.** Starting from long-run equilibrium at point *A*, an adverse inflation shock directly raises current inflation, causing the *SRAS* line to shift upward to *SRAS'*. At the new short-run equilibrium, point *B*, inflation has risen to $\pi'$ and output has fallen to *Y'*, creating a recessionary gap. If the Central Bank does nothing, eventually the economy will return to point *A*, restoring the original inflation rate but suffering a long recession in the process. The Central Bank could ease monetary policy by reducing the real rate of interest at each rate of inflation, shifting the *AD* curve to *AD'* and restoring full employment more quickly at point *C*. The cost of this strategy is that inflation remains at its higher level.

An adverse inflation shock poses a difficult problem for macroeconomic policy makers. To see why, suppose that monetary and fiscal policies were left unchanged following an inflationary shock. In that case, inflation would eventually abate and return to its original level. Graphically, the economy would reach its short-run equilibrium at point *B* in Fig. 28.9 soon after the inflation shock. However, because of the recessionary gap that exists at point *B*, eventually inflation would begin to drift downward, until finally the recessionary gap was eliminated. Graphically, this decline in inflation would be represented by a downward movement of the *SRAS* line, from *SRAS'* back to *SRAS*. Inflation would stop declining only when long-run equilibrium is restored, at point *A* in Fig. 28.9, where inflation is at its original level of $\pi$ and output equals potential output.

However, although a 'do-nothing' policy approach would ultimately eliminate both the output gap and the surge in inflation, it would also put the economy through a deep and protracted recession, as actual output remains below potential output until the inflation adjustment process is completed. To avoid such an economically and politically costly outcome, policy makers might opt to eliminate the recessionary gap more quickly. By setting a lower real interest rate at any given level of inflation – a downward shift in the policy reaction function – the Central Bank could shift the *AD* curve to the right, from *AD* to *AD'*, taking the economy to a new long-run equilibrium, point *C* in Fig. 28.9. This expansionary policy would help to restore output to the full-employment level more quickly, but as Fig. 28.9 shows, it would also allow inflation to stabilise at the new, higher level.

In sum, inflation shocks pose a problem for policy makers. If they leave their policies unchanged – a 'steady-as-she-goes' approach – inflation will eventually subside, but the economy may experience a lengthy and severe recession. If instead they act aggressively to expand aggregate spending, the recession will end more quickly, but inflation will stabilise at a higher level. In Chapter 23 we discussed the long-run relationship between inflation and money growth. The example of an inflation shock shows that inflation does not always originate from excessive money growth; it can arise from a variety of factors. However, our analysis also shows that, in the absence of monetary policy's easing, inflation that arises from factors such as inflation shocks will eventually die away. By contrast, *sustained* inflation requires that monetary policy remain easy – that is, policy makers allow the money supply to rise rapidly. In this respect, our analysis of this chapter is consistent with the earlier long-run analysis, which concluded that sustained inflation is possible only if monetary policy is sufficiently expansionary. This is discussed more fully in Economic naturalist 28.2 below.

**Exercise 28.8** Inflation shocks can also be beneficial for the economy, such as when oil prices declined in the late 1990s. What effect would a decrease in oil prices have on output and inflation?

## Shocks to potential output

In analysing the effects of increased oil prices in the 1970s, we assumed that potential output was unchanged in the wake of the shock. However, the sharp rise in oil prices during that period probably affected the economy's potential output as well. Oil is an input into many production processes, it is also a major source of generating energy, which is crucial to nearly all production. Energy in some form drives machinery, powers computers and lights offices and factories. Hence energy prices are an important cost of production and a rise in oil prices can be seen as an increase in input prices to suppliers of goods and services. Higher energy prices therefore lead to higher costs and reduced output levels which in the long run may cause firms to cut back on investment plans, leading to a smaller capital stock and a lower potential output.

If the increases in oil prices did reduce potential output, their inflationary impact would have been compounded. Figure 28.10 illustrates the effects on the economy of a sudden decline in potential output. For the sake of simplicity, the figure includes only the effects of the reduction in potential output, and not the direct effect of the inflation shock. (Problem 7 at the end of the chapter asks you to combine the two effects.)

Suppose once again that the economy is in long-run equilibrium at point *A*. Then potential output falls unexpectedly, from $Y^*$ to $Y^{*\prime}$, shifting the long-run aggregate supply line leftward from *LRAS* to *LRAS*'. After this decline in potential output, is the economy still in long-run equilibrium at point *A*? The answer is no, because output now exceeds potential output at that point. In other words, an *expansionary gap* has developed. This gap reflects the fact that although planned spending has not changed, the capacity of firms to supply goods and services has been reduced.

As we have seen, an expansionary gap leads to rising inflation. In Fig. 28.10, increasing inflation is represented by an upward movement of the *SRAS* line. Eventually the short-run aggregate supply line reaches *SRAS*', and the economy reaches a new long-run equilibrium at

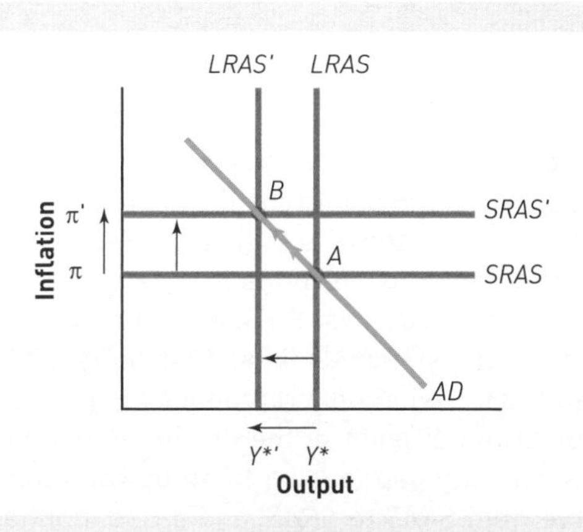


**Figure 28.10 The Effects of a Shock to Potential Output.** The economy is in long-run equilibrium at point *A* when a decline in potential output, from *Y** to *Y**', creates an expansionary gap. Inflation rises, and the short-run aggregate supply line shifts upward from *SRAS* to *SRAS*'. A new long-run equilibrium is reached at point *B*, where actual output equals the new, lower level of potential output, *Y**', and inflation has risen to π'. Because it is the result of a fall in potential output, the decline in output is permanent.

point *B*. (Why is point *B* a long-run, and not just a short-run, equilibrium?) At that point, output has fallen to the new, lower level of potential output, *Y**' and inflation has risen to π'.

**aggregate supply shock** either an inflation shock or a shock to potential output; adverse aggregate supply shocks of both types reduce output and increase inflation

Sharp changes in potential output and inflation shocks are both referred to as **aggregate supply shocks**. As we have seen, an adverse aggregate supply shock of either type leads to lower output and higher inflation, and therefore poses a difficult challenge for policy makers. Economic naturalist 28.2 explains the dilemma which aggregate supply shocks can cause.

## Economic naturalist 28.2 The policy maker's dilemma

Sharp changes in potential output and inflation shocks are both referred to as *aggregate supply shocks*. As we have seen, an adverse aggregate supply shock of either type leads to lower output and higher inflation, and therefore poses a difficult challenge for policy makers. A difference between the two types of aggregate supply shocks is that the output losses associated with an adverse inflation shock are temporary (because the economy self-corrects and will ultimately return to its initial level of potential output), but those associated with a fall in potential output are permanent (output remains lower even after the economy has reached a new long-run equilibrium).

The distinction between adverse inflation shocks and a decline in permanent output can create a dilemma for the policy maker. If the shock is temporary then, as we have seen, the Central Bank may respond by easing monetary policy and shifting the *AD* line to the right in order to stabilise output at its potential level (point *C* in Fig. 28.9) If the shock is permanent then, as we shall see, the appropriate response may be to adopt a 'do-nothing' approach and let the economy stabilise at the lower level of permanent output (point *B* in Fig. 28.10) However, those responsible for policy may simply observe a fall in actual output followed by a rise in inflation. As both are consistent with each type of shock it may not be clear whether they are the result of a shock to permanent output or an adverse inflation shock. Hence, the policy maker's dilemma is to decide if the observed fall in output and rise in inflation are the result of an adverse inflation shock or a decline in permanent output, a decision that will determine the appropriate policy reaction.

Suppose the shock is actually the result of a decline in permanent output but the Central Bank misinterprets it as temporary. In order to offset what it thinks is a recession, the Central Bank may attempt to stabilise output by lowering the real rate of interest. Panels (a) and (b) of Fig. 28.11 illustrate the effects of this action. Figure 28.11(a) simply reproduces Fig. 28.10. Starting from the initial long-run equilibrium at point *A*, the decline in potential output from $Y^*$ to $Y^{*\prime}$ creates an expansionary gap leading to an upward shift in the short-run aggregate supply curve from *SRAS* to *SRAS*' and a rise in inflation from $\pi$ to $\pi'$. The new long-run equilibrium is point *B* with output at $Y^{*\prime}$ and inflation at $\pi'$.

Figure 28.11(b) illustrates what happens if the Central Bank misinterprets the fall in output as temporary and eases monetary policy. By cutting the real rate of interest at the inflation rate $\pi'$, the Central Bank will shift the *AD* line to the right, from *AD* to *AD*', taking the economy to a new equilibrium at *C*. However, because actual output $Y^*$ is now greater than the new potential output $Y^{*\prime}$ the point *C* is a short-run rather than a long-run equilibrium position. The resulting expansionary gap ($Y^* - Y^{*\prime}$) leads to a rise in inflation and, as we have seen, an upward shift in the short-run aggregate supply line from *SRAS*' to *SRAS*'' establishing a new long-run equilibrium at point *D*. At *D* output has fallen to the new lower permanent level of $Y^{*\prime}$ but inflation has risen again to $\pi''$. Hence, by misinterpreting the data the policy maker runs the risk of failing to reverse the decline in output and pays a price in terms of higher equilibrium inflation.

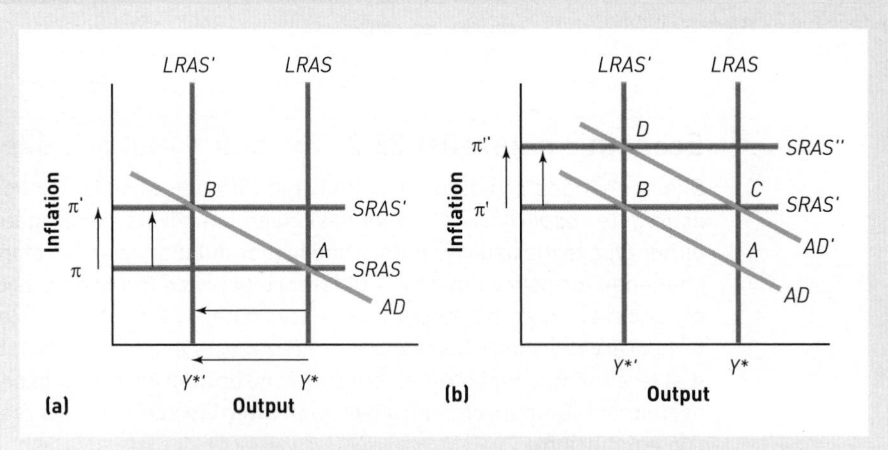


**Figure 28.11 The Policy Maker's Dilemma.** Starting from the long-run equilibrium point at *A* the supply shock leads to a permanent decline in potential output and a rise in inflation, moving the economy to point *B*. If the Central Bank misinterprets the shock as temporary it may reduce the real rate of interest, shifting the *AD* line to *AD*' and establishing a new short-run equilibrium at point *C* (panel (b)). As actual output $Y^*$ now exceeds potential output $Y^{*\prime}$ the resulting expansionary gap shifts the *SRAS* line to *SRAS*'', establishing a new long-run equilibrium at point *D* with a higher inflation rate of $\pi''$ but no gain in terms of permanently higher output.

This example also illustrates the point made in Chapter 27, that policy making is both an art and a science. Although we have classified aggregate supply shocks as either temporary or permanent, most shocks such as the oil price increases of the 1970s probably contain elements of both. Unfortunately shocks do not come labelled 'permanent' or 'temporary' and the policy maker's task is to decide which component is the most important. While statistical models and economic analysis (science) may be of considerable help, the complexity and uncertainty surrounding the real-world economy will always require judgement on the part of the policy maker (art).

## Economic naturalist 28.3 The advantage of an independent Central Bank

Figure 28.11 also illustrates the advantage of an independent Central Bank. As explained in Chapter 23, research suggests that independent Central Banks appear to deliver lower average inflation rates as compared with Central Banks that take policy decisions from government. To see way this might happen we will reverse the situation in Economic naturalist 28.2 and assume that the Central Bank solves the dilemma correctly and is convinced that the shock is permanent. We will also assume that, following Economic naturalist 28.2, the Central Bank knows that in the face of an adverse shock to permanent output, easing monetary policy will result only in higher inflation without any long-run gains in terms of higher output. If the Central Bank is independent it will most likely take a 'do-nothing' approach and let the economy stabilise at point *B* in Fig. 28.11(a) with the equilibrium inflation rate equal to $\pi'$. Now suppose that the Central Bank is not independent but takes policy decisions from government. Governments are elected by voters who become concerned when economic activity slows down and unemployment starts to rise. As government may be more concerned with its short-term popularity and the need to get re-elected than with the long-run equilibrium inflation rate, it may instruct the Central Bank to relax monetary policy. In the short term, this will move the economy toward point *C* in Fig. 28.11(b). The decline in output will be delayed, which may satisfy voters and protect the government's short-term political position. However, as we have seen, in the long run the economy will stabilise at point *D* with a lower level of permanent output and a higher inflation rate equal to $\pi''$. By contrast, the decision-making bodies in independent Central Banks, such as the ECB's Governing Council or the Bank of England's Monetary Policy Committee (MPC), do not have to worry about short-term popularity or the need to get re-elected. In short, the costs of higher equilibrium inflation without any compensation in terms of higher potential output are more likely to be avoided with a Central Bank free from political influence.

## RECAP Sources of inflation

Inflation may result from *excessive spending*, which creates an expansionary output gap and puts upward pressure on inflation. An example is an increase in government deficits, which shift the *AD* curve to the right and intensify inflationary pressures. Monetary policy can be used to offset excessive deficits, preventing higher inflation from emerging.

Inflation may also arise from an *aggregate supply shock*, either an inflation shock or a shock to potential output. An inflation shock is a sudden change in the normal behaviour of inflation, unrelated to the output gap. An example of an inflation shock is a rise in energy and food prices large enough to raise the overall price level. An inflation shock creates *stagflation*, a combination of recession and higher inflation.

Stagflation poses a difficult dilemma for policy makers. If they take no action, eventually inflation will subside and output will recover, but in the interim the economy may suffer a protracted period of recession. If they use monetary or fiscal policy to increase aggregate demand, they will shorten the recession but will also lock in the higher level of inflation.

A shock to potential output is a sharp change in potential output. Like an adverse inflation shock, an adverse shock to potential output results in both higher inflation and lower output. Because lower potential output implies that productive capacity has fallen, however, output does not recover following a shock to potential output, as it eventually does following an inflation shock.

## Controlling inflation

High or even moderate rates of inflation can impose significant costs to the economy. Indeed, since the 1960s a consensus has developed among economists and policy makers that *low and stable inflation* is important and perhaps necessary for sustained economic growth. What, then, should policy makers do if the inflation rate is too high? As Example 28.3 will show, inflation can be slowed by policies that shift the aggregate demand curve leftward. Unfortunately, although they produce long-term gains in productivity and economic growth, such policies are likely to impose significant *short-run costs* in the form of lost output and increased unemployment.

### Example 28.3 The effects of anti-inflationary monetary policy

Suppose that, although the economy is at full employment, the inflation rate is 10 per cent – too high to be consistent with economic efficiency and long-term economic growth. The Central Bank decides to tighten monetary policy to reduce the inflation rate to 3 per cent. What will happen to output, unemployment and inflation in the short run? In the long run?

The economic effects of a monetary tightening are very different in the short and long run. Figure 28.12(a) shows the short-run effect. Initially, the economy is in long-run equilibrium at point *A*, where actual output equals potential output. But at point *A* the inflation rate, 10 per cent, is high, as indicated by the aggregate supply line, *SRAS*.

To bring inflation down to 3 per cent, what can policy makers do? To get 'tough' on inflation, the Central Bank must set the real interest rate at a level higher than normal, given the rate of inflation. In other words, the Central Bank must shift its policy reaction function upward, as in Fig. 28.3(a). At a constant rate of inflation, an increase in the real interest rate set by the Central Bank will reduce consumption and investment spending, lowering aggregate demand at every inflation rate. As we saw earlier in the chapter, this monetary tightening by the Central Bank causes the *AD* curve to shift leftward, from *AD* to *AD'* in Fig. 28.12(a).

After the Central Bank's action, the *AD'* curve and the *SRAS* line intersect at point *B* in Fig. 28.12(a), the new short-run equilibrium point. At point *B* actual output has fallen to *Y*, which is less than potential output *Y**. In other words, the Central Bank's action has allowed a *recessionary gap* to develop, one result of which will be that unemployment will exceed the natural rate. At point *B*, however, the inflation rate has not changed, remaining at 10 per cent. We conclude that, in the short run, a monetary tightening pushes the economy into recession but has little or no effect on the inflation rate, because of *inflation inertia*.

The short-run effects of the anti-inflationary shift in monetary policy – lower output, higher unemployment and little or no reduction of inflation – are, to say the least, not very encouraging, and they explain why such policy shifts are often highly unpopular in their early

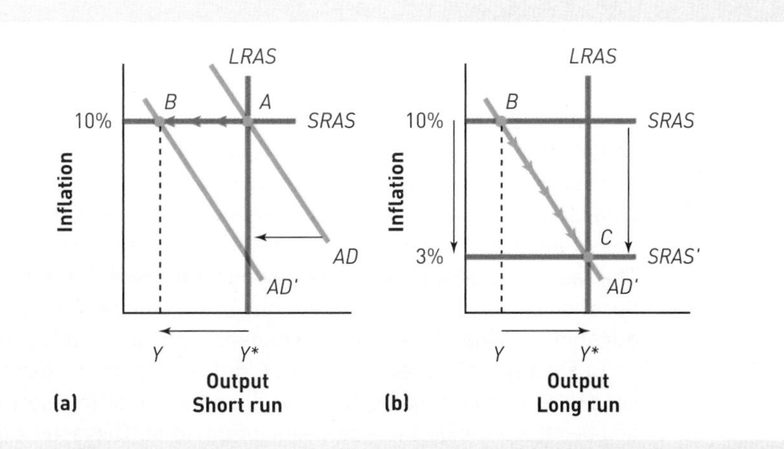


**Figure 28.12 Short-Run and Long-Run Effects of an Anti-Inflationary Monetary Policy.** (a) Initially the economy is in long-run equilibrium at point *A*, with actual output equal to potential and the inflation rate at 10 per cent. If an anti-inflationary policy shift by the Central Bank shifts the *AD* curve to the left, from *AD* to *AD'*, the economy will reach a new short-run equilibrium at point *B*, at the intersection of *AD'* and *SRAS*. As short-run equilibrium output falls to *Y*, a recessionary gap opens up. The inflation rate does not change in the short run. (b) Following the tightening of monetary policy, a recessionary gap exists at point *B*, which eventually causes inflation to decline. The short-run aggregate supply line moves downward, from *SRAS* to *SRAS'*. Long-equilibrium is restored at point *C*. In the long run, real output returns to potential and inflation stabilises at a lower level (3 per cent in this figure).

stages. Fortunately, however, we have not reached the end of the story, because the economy will not remain at point *B* indefinitely. The reason is that the existence of a recessionary gap at that point eventually causes inflation to decline, as firms become more reluctant to raise their prices in the face of weak demand.

Graphically, the eventual decline in inflation that results from a recessionary gap is represented by the downward movement of the short-run aggregate supply line, from *SRAS* to *SRAS'* in Fig. 28.12(b). Inflation will continue to fall until the economy returns to long-run equilibrium at point *C*. At that point, actual output has returned to potential, and the inflation rate has stabilised at 3 per cent. So we see that a tight monetary policy inflicts *short-term pain* (a decline in output, high unemployment, and a high real interest rate) to achieve a *long-term gain* (a permanent reduction in inflation). Incidentally, the result that an upward shift in the monetary policy reaction function leads to a permanently lower rate of inflation suggests a useful alternative way to think about such shifts: an upward shift in the Central Bank's reaction function is equivalent to a decline in its long-term target for inflation (see Exercise 28.2). Similarly, a downward shift in Central Bank's reaction function could be interpreted as an increase in its long-term inflation target.

One important implication of Example 28.3 is that a *temporary slowdown in economic activity* is the price that has to be paid for a lower equilibrium inflation rate. Key questions, discussed in Economic naturalist 28.4, are: How high is this price, and how long does it take for the economy to adjust to its new lower inflation equilibrium?

**Exercise 28.9** Show the typical time paths of output, inflation and the real interest rate when the Central Bank employs an anti-inflationary monetary policy. Draw a separate graph for each variable, showing time on the horizontal axis. Be sure to distinguish the short run from the long run. Specific numerical values are not necessary.

## Economic naturalist 28.4 Inflation adjustment and Central Bank credibility

Example 28.3 illustrates that anti-inflationary monetary policies may succeed in achieving a lower equilibrium inflation rate but only at the cost of a short-term increases in unemployment and lower output. Looking at Fig. 28.12, it should be clear that the extent and persistence of this recessionary gap will depend on the speed at which the equilibrium inflation rate falls to its lower equilibrium value. The faster the *SRAS* line shifts down toward *SRAS'* in Fig. 28.12(b) the shorter the duration of the recession and the faster the adjustment of *Y* back to *Y**. Hence, a key question is: What determines the *speed* with which actual inflation adjusts?

To answer that, recall that earlier in this chapter our discussion on inflation inertia concluded that *inflation expectations* are a key factor in determining the speed at which actual inflation adjusts to a new equilibrium level. The faster expectations of future inflation adjust to a lower level, the faster actual inflation will decline. While many factors may influence inflationary expectations, the *credibility* which the public attaches to the Central Bank and its policies is among the most important. By 'credibility' we simply mean the confidence which the public has in the Central Bank's ability and willingness to see its policy through to fulfilment. If the public are confident that the Central Bank will, despite a short-term rise in unemployment, maintain its anti-inflationary policy then we can expect inflationary expectations to be revised rapidly. Alternatively, if – say, on the basis of its past record – the public expect that the Central Bank may weaken or reverse its policy once a recessionary gap emerges then inflationary expectations may be revised slowly, if at all. In terms of Fig. 28.12(a), maintaining the policy means that the Central Bank will keep the real interest high enough to hold the *AD* line at *AD'*, despite the fall in output. Weakening the policy means that, as output starts to decline, the Central Bank will ease policy and let the *AD* line drift back to its initial position at *AD*. In the first case, it is reasonable to assume that the public will become convinced that the equilibrium inflation rate will fall in the near future leading to a more rapid downward revision of inflationary expectations and a faster adjustment to the new equilibrium at *C* in Fig. 28.12(b). In the second case, the public may be much less convinced that the new policy will be maintained, with the consequence that inflationary expectations may not be revised downward and the inflation rate will remain at its initial high level.

The credibility that the public attaches to Central Bank policy is therefore critical to the revision of expectations and the speed at which the economy adjusts to the lower equilibrium inflation rate. In other words, inflation inertia is likely to be weaker and less persistent when the public is confident that the Central Bank will deliver on its inflation target. What characteristics should Central Banks have to ensure that the public has confidence in their ability and willingness to maintain a tight anti-inflationary policy even when output is falling and unemployment rising? We give two answers, both relevant in a European context – Central Bank independence and pre-commitments to other objectives.

As we saw in Economic naturalist 28.3, monetary policy is more likely to respond to short-run variations in economic activity when Central Banks take instructions from politicians. Governments are elected by voters who become concerned when economic activity slows down and unemployment starts to rise. As a government may be more concerned with its short-term popularity and the need to get re-elected than with the long-run equilibrium inflation rate, it may instruct the Central Bank to relax monetary policy when a temporary recessionary gap emerges. Conversely, policy makers in politically independent Central Banks normally have fixed terms of office and do not need to get re-elected or be concerned with their short-term popularity. Hence it is possible that the public may, other things being equal, place greater confidence in the anti-inflationary policies of independent Central Banks. Given the ECB's mandate for price stability and its high level of independence, this is perhaps one reason why the Maastricht Treaty required governments of EU member states to introduce legislation designed to increase the political independence of their national Central Banks prior to the start of full monetary union in 1999.

Central Bank credibility may also be enhanced if the bank has a pre-commitment to other targets which require a lower equilibrium inflation rate. The Maastricht Convergence Criteria provide one possible example. As we saw in Chapter 23, to be admitted to the new monetary union, member states were required to satisfy a number of criteria which became known as the Maastricht Convergence Criteria. One of these criteria was convergence to a low and stable inflation rate. Specifically, a country would be deemed eligible if its annual inflation rate was not more than 1.5 per cent higher than the average of the three lowest inflation rates in the European Union. This posed a problem for several countries, such as Italy, whose inflation rate was approximately twice the European average for most of the 1980s and into the early 1990s. Hence, to satisfy the Maastricht criteria, Italy and several other countries had to introduce tough anti-inflationary policies of the type illustrated by Fig. 28.12. Italy's problem was that because of its high inflation history the public was unlikely to place much credibility in a new policy which, following many that had failed in the past, promised to deliver a lower equilibrium inflation rate. Other things being equal, this low credibility implied that Italy might have to pay a high price in terms of slower economic growth and higher unemployment in order to reduce its equilibrium inflation rate. However, the Italian government and its Central Bank now had an overriding objective which was to be admitted to the new monetary union. Success in achieving this objective meant that the benefits from a tight monetary policy would be much greater than those associated with lower inflation. They would also include the political advantages of being at the forefront of a major European initiative with a seat 'at the table' and full voting rights on the Governing Council of the new ECB. The firm commitment of the Italian government and the majority of its electorate to monetary union may have enhanced the credibility of monetary policy in the 1990s because the primary commitment was not low inflation *per se*, but qualification for the new monetary regime, which required a strong anti-inflationary policy.

The stance of Italian monetary policy over this period may be gauged from the annual rate of growth of the money supply which fell from 9 per cent in 1991 to under 1 per cent in 1998 and was actually negative in 1995. Over the same period unemployment increased from 8 to 12 per cent but the inflation rate declined from 7 to under 3 per cent, which enabled Italy to satisfy the Maastricht criteria. In short, without its firm commitment to monetary union and its effects on policy credibility, Italian inflation, judged on previous performance, might have declined more slowly and, if the policy had been pursued, resulted in even higher unemployment.

## RECAP Controlling inflation

Inflation can be controlled by policies that shift the aggregate demand curve leftward, such as a move to a 'tighter' monetary policy (an upward shift in the monetary policy reaction function). In the short run, the effects of an anti-inflationary monetary policy are felt largely on *output*, so that a disinflation (a substantial reduction in inflation) may create a significant recessionary gap. According to the theory, in the long run, output should return to potential and inflation should decline. The extent and persistence of the recessionary gap may depend on *inflationary expectations* and the *credibility* which the public attaches to the Central Bank's policy.

## Summary

- This chapter has extended the basic Keynesian model to include *inflation*. First, we showed how planned spending and short-run equilibrium output are related to inflation, a relationship that is summarised by the *aggregate demand* (*AD*) *curve*. Second, we discussed how inflation itself is determined. In the short run, inflation is determined by past expectations and pricing decisions, but in the longer run, inflation adjusts as needed to eliminate output gaps.
- The *aggregate demand (AD) curve* shows the relationship between short-run equilibrium output and inflation. Because short-run equilibrium output is equal to planned spending, the aggregate demand curve also relates spending to inflation. Increases in inflation reduce planned spending and short-run equilibrium output, so the aggregate demand curve is downward-sloping.
- The *inverse relationship* of inflation and short-run equilibrium output is the result, in large part, of the behaviour of the Central Bank. To keep inflation low and stable, the Central Bank reacts to rising inflation by increasing the real interest rate. A higher real interest rate reduces consumption and planned investment, lowering planned aggregate expenditure and hence short-run equilibrium output. Other reasons that the *AD* curve slopes downward include the effects of inflation on the real value of money, distributional effects (inflation redistributes wealth from the poor, who save relatively little, to the more affluent, who save more), uncertainty created by inflation and the impact of inflation on foreign sales of domestic goods.
- For any given value of inflation, an *exogenous increase in spending* (that is, an increase in spending at given levels of output and the real interest rate) raises short-run equilibrium output, shifting the *AD* curve to the right. Likewise, an *exogenous decline in spending* shifts the *AD* curve to the left. The *AD* curve can also be shifted by a change in the Central Bank's policy reaction function. If the Central Bank gets 'tougher', shifting up its reaction function and thus choosing a higher real interest rate at each level of inflation, the *AD* curve will shift to the left. If the Central Bank gets 'easier,' shifting down its reaction function and thus setting a lower real interest rate at each level of inflation, the *AD* curve will shift to the right.
- In low-inflation industrial economies such as most of those in Western Europe today, inflation tends to be *inertial*, or slow to adjust to changes in the economy. This inertial behaviour reflects the fact that inflation depends in part on people's expectations of future inflation, which in turn depend on their recent experience with inflation. Long-term wage and price contracts tend to 'build in' the effects of people's expectations for multi-year periods. In the aggregate demand–aggregate supply (*AD–AS*) diagram, the *short-run aggregate supply (SRAS) line* is a horizontal line that shows the current rate of inflation, as determined by past expectations and pricing decisions.
- Although inflation is inertial, it does change over time in response to *output gaps*. An expansionary gap tends to raise the inflation rate, because firms raise their prices more quickly when they are facing demand that exceeds their normal productive capacity. A recessionary gap tends to reduce the inflation rate, as firms become more reluctant to raise their prices.
- The economy is in *short-run equilibrium* when the inflation rate equals the value determined by past expectations and pricing decisions, and output equals the level of short-run equilibrium output that is consistent with that inflation rate. Graphically, short-run equilibrium occurs at the intersection of the *AD* curve and the *SRAS* line. If an output gap exists, however, the inflation rate will adjust to eliminate the gap. Graphically, the *SRAS* line moves upward or downward as needed to restore output to its full-employment level. When the inflation rate is stable and actual output equals potential output, the economy is in *long-run equilibrium*. Graphically, long-run equilibrium corresponds to the common intersection point of the *AD* curve, the *SRAS* line and the long-run aggregate supply (*LRAS*) line, a vertical line that marks the economy's *potential output*.

- Because the economy tends to move toward long-run equilibrium on its own through the adjustment of the inflation rate, it is said to be *self-correcting*. The more rapid the self-correction process, the smaller the need for active stabilisation policies to eliminate output gaps. In practice, the larger the output gap, the more useful such policies are.
- One source of inflation is *excessive spending*, which leads to expansionary output gaps. Aggregate supply shocks are another source of inflation. *Aggregate supply shocks* include both *inflation shocks* – sudden changes in the normal behaviour of inflation, created, for example, by a rise in the price of imported oil – and shocks to potential output. Adverse supply shocks both lower output and increase inflation, creating a difficult dilemma for policy makers.
- To *reduce inflation*, policy makers must shift the aggregate demand curve to the left, usually through a shift in monetary policy toward greater 'tightness'. In the short run, the main effects of an anti-inflationary policy may be reduced output and higher unemployment, as the economy experiences a recessionary gap. These short-run costs of *disinflation* must be balanced against the long-run benefits of a lower rate of inflation. Over time, output and employment will return to normal levels and inflation declines. Both the extent and persistence of these short-run costs may be determined by *inflationary expectations* and the *credibility* which the public attaches to Central Bank policy.

## Key terms

**aggregate demand (*AD*) curve** (793)
**aggregate supply shock** (811)
**inflation shock** (808)
**long-run aggregate supply (*LRAS*) line** (803)
**long-run equilibrium** (804)
**short-run aggregate supply (*SRAS*) line** (803)
**short-run equilibrium** (803)

## Review questions

1. What two variables are related by the aggregate demand (*AD*) curve? Explain how the behaviour of the ECB helps to determine the slope of this curve. List and discuss two other factors that lead the curve to have the slope that it does.
2. State how each of the following affects the *AD* curve, and explain:
   a. An increase in government purchases.
   b. A cut in taxes.
   c. A decline in planned investment spending by firms.
   d. A decision by the Central Bank to lower the real interest rate at each level of inflation.
3. Why does the overall rate of inflation tend to adjust more slowly than prices of commodities, such as oil or grain?
4. Discuss the relationship between output gaps and inflation. How is this relationship captured in the aggregate demand–aggregate supply (*AD–AS*) diagram?
5. Sketch an aggregate demand–aggregate supply (*AD–AS*) diagram depicting an economy away from long-run equilibrium. Indicate the economy's short-run equilibrium point. Discuss how the economy reaches long-run equilibrium over a period of time. Illustrate the process in your diagram.
6. **True or false:** The economy's self-correcting tendency makes active use of stabilisation policy unnecessary. Explain.

7. Why does an adverse inflation shock pose a particularly difficult dilemma for policy makers?

8. Most Central Banks place great value on keeping inflation low and stable. Why do they view this objective as so important?

## Problems

Problems marked with an asterisk (*) are more difficult.

1. We saw in Chapter 27 that short-run equilibrium output falls when the Central Bank raises the real interest rate. Suppose the relationship between short-run equilibrium output $Y$ and the real interest rate $r$ set by the Central Bank is given by

$$Y = 1{,}000 - 1{,}000r$$

Suppose also that the Central Bank's reaction function is the one shown in Table 27.1 and reproduced in the Appendix to this chapter (Table 28A.1). For whole-number inflation rates between 0 and 4 per cent, find the real interest rate set by the Central Bank and the resulting short-run equilibrium output. Graph the *AD* curve numerically.

2. For the economy in Problem 1, suppose that potential output $Y^* = 960$. From the policy reaction function in Table 28A.1, what can you infer about the Central Bank's objective for the inflation rate in the long term?

3. An economy's aggregate demand curve (the relationship between short-run equilibrium output and inflation) is described by the equation

$$Y = 13{,}000 - 20{,}000\pi$$

Initially, the inflation rate is 4 per cent, or $\pi = 0.04$. Potential output $Y^*$ equals 12,000.

a. Find inflation and output in short-run equilibrium.

b. Find inflation and output in long-run equilibrium.

Show your work.

4. This problem asks you to trace out the adjustment of inflation when the economy starts with an output gap. Suppose that the economy's aggregate demand curve is

$$Y = 1{,}000 - 1{,}000\pi$$

where $Y$ is short-run equilibrium output and $\pi$ is the inflation rate, measured as a decimal. Potential output $Y^*$ equals 950, and the initial inflation rate is 10 per cent ($\pi = 0.10$).

a. Find output and inflation for this economy in short-run equilibrium and in long-run equilibrium.

b. Suppose that, each quarter, inflation adjusts according to the following rule:

This quarter's inflation = Last quarter's inflation – $0.0004(Y^* - Y)$

Starting from the initial value of 10 per cent for inflation, find the value of inflation for each of the next five quarters. Does inflation come close to its long-run value?

5. For each of the following, use an *AD–AS* diagram to show the short-run and long-run effects on output and inflation. Assume the economy starts in long-run equilibrium.

a. An increase in consumer confidence that leads to higher consumption spending.

b. A reduction in taxes.

c. An easing of monetary policy by the Central Bank (a downward shift in the policy reaction function).

d. A sharp drop in oil prices.

e. A war that raises government purchases.

6. Suppose that the government cuts taxes in response to a recessionary gap, but because of legislative delays the tax cut is not put in place for 18 months. Using an *AD–AS* diagram and assuming that the government's objective is to stabilise output and inflation, show how this policy action might actually prove to be counter-productive.

7. Suppose that a permanent increase in oil prices both creates an inflationary shock and reduces potential output. Use an *AD–AS* diagram to show the effects of the oil price increase on output and inflation in the short run and the long run, assuming that there is no policy response. What happens if the Central Bank responds to the oil price increase by tightening monetary policy?

8. An economy is initially in recession. Using the *AD–AS* diagram, show the process of adjustment

a. If the Central Bank responds by easing monetary policy (moving its reaction function down).

b. If the Central Bank takes no action.

What are the costs and benefits of each approach, in terms of output loss and inflation?

9.* Planned aggregate expenditure in Lotusland depends on real GDP and the real interest rate according to the following equation:

$$PAE = 3{,}000 + 0.8Y - 2{,}000r$$

The Bank of Lotusland, the Central Bank, has announced that it will set the real interest rate according to the following policy reaction function:

| **Actual rate of inflation ($\pi$)** | **Real interest rate ($r$)** |
|---|---|
| 0.00 | 0.02 |
| 0.01 | 0.03 |
| 0.02 | 0.04 |
| 0.03 | 0.05 |
| 0.04 | 0.06 |

For the rates of inflation given, find autonomous expenditure and short-run equilibrium output in Lotusland. Graph the *AD* curve.

10.* An economy is described by the following equations:

$$C = 1{,}600 + 0.6(Y - T) - 2{,}000r$$

$$I^p = 2{,}500 - 1{,}000r$$

$$G = \bar{G} = 2{,}000$$

$$NX = \overline{NX} = 50$$

$$T = T = 2{,}000$$

Suppose also that the Central Bank's policy reaction function is the same as in Problem 9.

a. Find an equation relating planned spending to output and the real interest rate.

b. Construct a table showing the relationship between short-run equilibrium output and inflation, for inflation rates between 0 and 4 per cent. Using this table, graph the *AD* curve for the economy.

c. Repeat parts (a) and (b), assuming that government purchases have increased to 2,100. How does an increase in government purchases affect the *AD* curve?

11.* For the economy described in Problem 10, suppose that the Central Bank's policy reaction function is as follows:

| Actual rate of inflation ($\pi$) | Real interest rate ($r$) |
|---|---|
| 0.00 | 0.040 |
| 0.01 | 0.045 |
| 0.02 | 0.050 |
| 0.03 | 0.055 |
| 0.04 | 0.060 |

a. Construct a table showing the relationship between short-run equilibrium output and the inflation rate for values of inflation between zero and 4 per cent. Graph the aggregate demand curve of the economy.

b. Suppose that the Central Bank decides to lower the real interest rate by 0.5 percentage point at each value of inflation. Repeat part (a). How does this change in monetary policy affect the aggregate demand curve?

## Answers to in-chapter exercises

**28.1** a. At the current level of inflation, output and real interest rate, an exogenous reduction in business spending on new capital will reduce planned investment, causing a decline in overall aggregate expenditures (*AE*), and a reduction in short-run equilibrium output. Because output has fallen for a given level of inflation, the decrease in business spending leads to a leftward shift in the *AD* curve.

b. At the current level of inflation, output and real interest rate, a reduction in income taxes increases consumers' disposable income ($Y - T$), which leads to an exogenous increase in consumption at all income levels, as illustrated in Chapter 26. The upward shift in the consumption function increases overall aggregate expenditures (*AE*) and leads to an increase in short-run equilibrium output. Because output has increased for a given level of inflation, the reduction in income taxes leads to a rightward shift in the *AD* curve.

**28.2** In the long run, the real interest rate set by the ECB must be consistent with the real interest rate determined in the market for saving and investment. To find the ECB's long-run inflation target, take as given the real interest rate determined in the long run by the market for saving and investment and read off the corresponding inflation rate from the ECB's policy reaction function. As the figure below illustrates, a tightening of ECB policy (an upward shift of the policy reaction function) implies that, for any given long-run real interest rate, the ECB's inflation target must be lower.

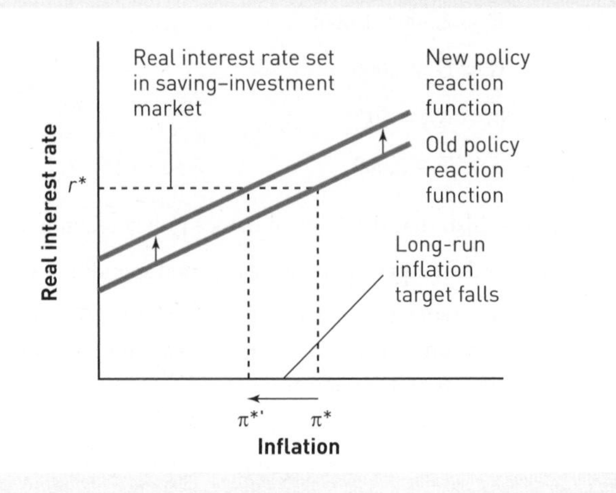

28.3 a. An upward shift in the ECB's policy reaction function means that the ECB is raising the real interest rate associated with a given level of inflation. An increase in the real interest rate causes both consumption and planned investment spending to fall, reducing overall aggregate expenditures and short-run equilibrium output. Thus, a shift in the ECB's policy reaction function causes the output level to fall for a given level of inflation, resulting in a leftward shift in the *AD* curve.

b. The ECB's policy reaction function illustrates that the ECB responds to rising inflation rates by raising the real interest rate (a move *along* the policy reaction function), which causes a reduction in overall aggregate expenditures and short-run equilibrium output. However, in this case the ECB's response to higher inflation causes a move *along* a given *AD* curve.

Note that while the two actions appear to be similar, there is a key difference. In the first case, the ECB is changing its policy rule for a *given inflation rate* while, in the second case, the ECB is responding to a *changing inflation rate*. Changes in aggregate spending for a given inflation rate shift the *AD* curve, while changes in aggregate spending resulting from ECB policy responses to a rise or fall in inflation lead to moves along a given *AD* curve.

28.4 a. If inflation is expected to be 2 per cent next year and workers are expecting a 2 per cent increase in their real wages, then they will expect, and ask for, a 4 per cent increase in their nominal wages.

b. If inflation is expected to be 4 per cent next year, rather than 2 per cent, workers will expect, and ask for, a 6 per cent increase in their nominal wages.

c. If wage costs rise, firms will need to increase the prices of their goods and services to cover their increased costs, leading to an increase in inflation. In part (b), when expected inflation was 4 per cent, firms will be faced with larger increases in nominal wages than in part (a), when expected inflation was only 2 per cent. Thus, we can expect firms to raise prices by more when expected inflation is 4 per cent than when expected inflation is 2 per cent. From this example, we can conclude that increased inflationary expectations lead to higher inflation.

28.5 If the inflation rate is high, the economy will tend to stay in this high-inflation state due to expectations of high inflation and the existence of long-term wage and price contracts, while if the inflation rate is low, the economy will likewise tend to stay in this low-inflation state, for similar reasons. However, since high inflation rates impose economic costs on society, as pointed out in Chapter 19, Central Banks have an incentive to avoid the high-inflation state by keeping inflation low, which helps to maintain people's expectations of low inflation and leads to lower future inflation rates – perpetuating the 'virtuous circle' illustrated in Fig. 28.4.

28.6 An increase in spending on new capital by firms for a given level of inflation, output and real interest rate increases aggregate expenditures and short-run equilibrium output. Since the economy was originally operating at potential output, the increase in investment spending will lead to an expansionary gap; actual output, $Y$, will now be greater than potential output, $Y^*$. When $Y > Y^*$, the rate of inflation will tend to rise.

28.7 The effects will be the opposite of those illustrated in Fig. 28.8. Beginning in a long-run equilibrium with output equal to potential output and stable inflation (that is, where the aggregate demand (*AD*) curve intersects both the short-run and long-run aggregate supply lines (*SRAS* and *LRAS*, respectively)), the fall in consumption spending will initially lead to a leftward shift in the *AD* curve and the economy moves to a new, lower, short-run equilibrium output level at the same inflation rate. The shift in *AD* creates a recessionary gap, since $Y$ is now less than $Y^*$. The immediate effect of the decrease in consumption spending is only to reduce output. However, over time, inflation will fall because of the recessionary gap. As inflation falls the *SRAS* line will shift downward. The Central Bank responds to the fall in inflation by reducing real interest rates, leading to an increase in aggregate expenditure and output, a move down along the new *AD* curve. When inflation has fallen enough (and real interest rates have fallen enough) to eliminate the output gap the economy will be back in long-run equilibrium where output equals potential output but the inflation rate will be lower than before the fall in consumption spending.

**28.8** A decrease in oil prices is an example of a 'beneficial' inflation shock and the economic effects of such a shock are the reverse of those illustrated in Fig. 28.9. In this case, starting from a long-run equilibrium where output equals potential output, a beneficial inflation shock reduces current inflation, causing the *SRAS* line to shift downward. The downward shift in the *SRAS* curve leads to a short-run equilibrium with lower inflation and higher output, creating an expansionary gap. If the Central Bank does nothing, eventually the *SRAS* will begin to shift upward and the economy will return to its original inflation and output levels. However, the Central Bank may instead choose to tighten its monetary policy by shifting up its policy reaction function, raising the current real interest rate, shifting the *AD* curve to the left and restoring equilibrium at potential GDP, but at the new, lower inflation rate.

**28.9**

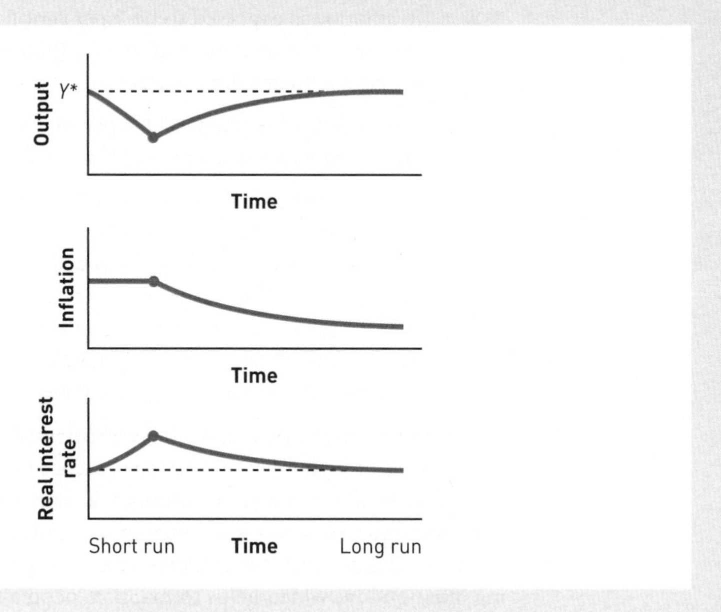

# Appendix The algebra of aggregate demand and aggregate supply

In this Appendix we shall derive the aggregate demand (*AD*) curve algebraically. Then we shall show how together aggregate demand and aggregate supply determine the short-run and long-run equilibrium points of the economy.

## The aggregate demand curve

In the Appendix to Chapter 27, Eq. (27A.1) showed that short-run equilibrium output depends on both exogenous components of expenditure and the real interest rate:

$$Y\left(\frac{1}{1-c}\right)[\bar{C} - c\bar{T} + \bar{I} + \bar{G} + \overline{NX} - (a+b)r] \tag{27A.1}$$

where $1/(1-c)$ is the multiplier, $\bar{C} - c\bar{T} + \bar{I} + \bar{G} + \overline{NX}$ is the exogenous component of planned spending, the term in brackets is autonomous expenditure and $a$ and $b$ are positive numbers that measure the effect of changes in the real interest rate on consumption and planned investment, respectively.

The aggregate demand (*AD*) curve incorporates the behaviour of the Central Bank, as described by its policy reaction function. According to its policy reaction function, when inflation rises, the Central Bank raises the real interest rate. Thus the Central Bank's policy reaction function can be written as an equation relating the real interest rate $r$ to inflation $\pi$:

$$r = \bar{r} + g\pi \tag{28A.1}$$

where $\bar{r}$ and $g$ are positive constants chosen by Central Bank officials. This equation states that when inflation $\pi$ rises by 1 percentage point – say, from 2 to 3 per cent per year – the Central Bank responds by raising the real interest rate by $g$ percentage points. So, for example, if $g = 0.5$, an increase in inflation from 2 to 3 per cent would lead the Central Bank to raise the real interest rate by 0.5 per cent. The intercept term $\bar{r}$ tells us at what level the Central Bank would set the real interest rate if inflation happened to be zero (so that the term $g\pi$ dropped out of the equation).

Equations (27A.1) and (28A.1) together allow us to derive the *AD* curve. We can think of the curve as being derived in two steps: first, for any given value of inflation $\pi$, use the policy reaction function, Eq. (28A.1), to find the real interest rate set by the Central Bank. Second, for that real interest rate, use Eq. (27A.1) to find short-run equilibrium output $Y$. The relationship between inflation and short-run equilibrium output derived in these two steps is the *AD* curve.

Alternatively, we can combine the equation for short-run equilibrium output with the equation for the policy reaction function by substituting the right-hand side of Eq. (28A.1) for the real interest rate $r$ in Eq. (27A.1):

$$Y\left(\frac{1}{1-c}\right)[\bar{C} - c\bar{T} + \bar{I} + \bar{G} + \overline{NX} - (a+b)(\bar{r} + g\pi)] \tag{28A.2}$$

This equation, which is the general algebraic expression for the *AD* curve, summarises the link between inflation and short-run equilibrium output, as shown graphically in Fig. 28.1. Note that Eq. (28A.2) implies that an increase in inflation $\pi$ reduces short-run equilibrium output $Y$, so that the *AD* curve is downward-sloping.

For a numerical illustration, we can use the parameter values from Example 27.3. For the economy studied in Example 27.3, we assumed that $\bar{C} = 640$, $\bar{T} = 250$, $\bar{I} = 250$, $\bar{G} = 300$, $\overline{NX} = 20$, $c = 0.8$, $a = 400$ and $b = 600$. To derive the *AD* curve, we also need values for the Central Bank's policy reaction function; for illustration, we use the policy reaction function shown in Table 27.1, reproduced here for convenience as Table 28A.1.

| Actual rate of inflation ($\pi$) | Real interest rate set by Central Bank ($r$) |
|---|---|
| 0.00 (= 0%) | 0.02 (= 2%) |
| 0.01 | 0.03 |
| 0.02 | 0.04 |
| 0.03 | 0.05 |
| 0.04 | 0.06 |

**Table 28A.1** A Policy Reaction Function for the Central Bank

Table 28A.1 relates the Central Bank's choice of the real interest rate to the inflation rate. To derive the *AD* curve, it will be useful to express the policy reaction function in the form of an equation like Eq. (28A.1). To do this, note that when inflation $\pi$ equals zero, the real interest rate $r$ equals 2 per cent. Therefore, the constant term in the Central Bank's policy reaction function $\bar{r}$ equals 2 per cent, or 0.02. Second, Table 28A.1 shows that the real interest rate rises one point for each point that inflation rises; therefore the slope $g$ of the reaction function equals 1.0. So the Central Bank's policy reaction function can be expressed as

$$r = 0.02 + \pi$$

which is Eq. (28A.1) with $\bar{r} = 0.02$ and $g = 1$.

Substituting these numerical values into Eq. (28A.2) and simplifying, we get the following numerical equation for the *AD* curve:

$$Y = 5[640 - 0.8(250) + 250 + 300 + 20 - (400 + 600)(0.02 + \pi)] \tag{28A.3}$$

$$Y = 4{,}950 - 5{,}000\pi \tag{28A.4}$$

Note that in this equation, higher values of inflation imply lower values of short-run equilibrium output, so the *AD* curve is downward-sloping. To check this equation, suppose that inflation is 3 per cent, so that the Central Bank sets the real interest rate at 5 per cent (see Table 28A.1). Setting $\pi = 0.03$ in Eq. (28A.4) yields $Y = 4{,}800$. This is consistent with the answer we found in Example 27.4, where we showed for the same economy that when $r = 0.05$ (the value of the real interest rate set by the Central Bank when $\pi = 0.03$), then short-run equilibrium output $Y = 4{,}800$.

## Shifts of the *AD* curve

Recall that exogenous changes in spending or in the Central Bank's policy reaction function will shift the *AD* curve (see pp. 795–7). These results follow from Eq. (28A.2). First, the equation shows that for a given rate of inflation $\pi$, an increase in exogenous spending, $\bar{C} - c\bar{T} + \bar{I} + \bar{G} + \overline{NX}$, will raise short-run equilibrium output $Y$. Thus an increase in exogenous spending shifts the *AD* curve to the right; conversely, a decrease in exogenous spending shifts the *AD* curve to the left.

A shift in the Central Bank's policy reaction can be captured by a change in the intercept term $\bar{r}$ in Eq. (28A.1). For example, suppose the Central Bank tightens monetary policy by setting the real interest rate 1 per cent higher than before at every level of inflation. Such a change is equivalent to raising the intercept term $\bar{r}$ in the policy reaction function by 0.01. If you look at Eq. (28A.2), you will see that with the level of inflation held constant, an increase in $\bar{r}$ reduces short-run equilibrium output. Thus a tightening of monetary policy (an upward movement in the monetary policy reaction function) shifts the *AD* curve to the left. Conversely, an easing of monetary policy (represented by a decline in $\bar{r}$ or a downward shift in the policy reaction function) shifts the *AD* curve to the right.

**Exercise 28A.1**

a. For the economy described above, find an algebraic equation for the *AD* curve after an exogenous increase in spending (say, in planned investment) of 10 units.
b. For the economy described above, find an algebraic equation for the *AD* curve after a tightening of monetary policy which involves setting the real interest rate 1 per cent higher at each level of inflation.

## Short-run equilibrium

Recall that in short-run equilibrium, inflation is equal to its previously determined value, and the *SRAS* line is horizontal at that value. At that level of inflation, the level of output in short-run equilibrium is given by the *AD* curve, Eq. (28A.2). For instance, in the economy described, suppose the current value of inflation is 5 per cent. The value of short-run equilibrium output is therefore

$$Y = 4{,}950 - 5{,}000\pi = 4{,}950 - 5{,}000(0.05)$$
$$= 4{,}700$$

## Long-run equilibrium

In long-run equilibrium, actual output $Y$ equals potential output $Y^*$. Thus, in long-run equilibrium, the inflation rate can be obtained from the equation for the *AD* curve by substituting $Y^*$ for $Y$. To illustrate, let us write the equation for the *AD* curve in this sample economy, Eq. (28A.4), once again:

$$Y = 4{,}950 - 5{,}000\pi$$

Suppose, in addition, that potential output $Y^* = 4{,}900$. Substituting this value for $Y$ in the aggregate demand equation yields

$$4{,}900 = 4{,}950 - 5{,}000\pi$$

Solving for the inflation rate $\pi$ we get

$$\pi = 0.01 = 1 \text{ per cent}$$

When this economy is in long-run equilibrium, then, the inflation rate will be 1 per cent. If we start from the value of inflation in short-run equilibrium, 5 per cent, we can see that the short-run aggregate supply line must shift downward until inflation reaches 1 per cent before long-run equilibrium can be achieved.

# Answers to in-appendix exercises

28A.1 The algebraic solutions for the *AD* curves in each case, obtained by substituting the numerical values into the formula, are given below.

a. $Y = 5{,}000 - 5{,}000\pi$

b. $Y = 4{,}900 - 5{,}000\pi$

# References

Romer, D. (2000) 'Keynesian Macroeconomics without the LM Curve', *Journal of Economic Perspectives*, Spring, pp. 149–70.

# Part 9 The International Economy

One of the defining recent economic trends is the 'globalisation' of national economies. Since the mid-1980s, the value of international trade has increased at nearly twice the rate of world GDP, and the volume of international financial transactions has expanded at many times that rate. From a long-run perspective, the rapidly increasing integration of national economies we see today is not unprecedented: before the First World War, Great Britain was the centre of an international economic system that was in many ways nearly as 'globalised' as our own, with extensive international trade and lending. But even the most far-seeing nineteenth-century merchant or banker would be astonished by the sense of *immediacy* that recent revolutionary changes in communications and transportation have imparted to international economic relations. For example, teleconferencing and the Internet now permit people on opposite sides of the globe to conduct 'face-to-face' business negotiations and transactions.

We have introduced international dimensions of the economy at several points in this book already (for example, in our discussion of comparative advantage and trade in Chapter 2 and our analysis of the labour market effects of globalisation in Chapter 21). Chapter 16 continued our analysis of international trade, considering both the broad benefits of trade and the reasons why we sometimes see attempts to block or reduce trade. In Chapter 17 we drew attention to the increasing economic interdependence among nations and stressed the importance of this trend for the European Union which now consists of twenty-five countries. Working together these countries have progressively dismantled barriers to trade and formed a unified trading block called the European Single Market. As explained in Chapter 23, twelve of these countries have also eliminated their national currencies and adopted the euro as their common currency with responsibility for monetary policy transferred from national Central Banks (NCBs) to the European Central Bank (ECB). Hence, while globalisation has increased interdependence between Europe and other regions such as North America and Asia, the process of economic integration has also increased interdependence among European economies.

In Part 9 we shall look at the monetary aspects of this integration process. Chapter 29 focuses on a particularly important variable, the *exchange rate* or the price of one currency in terms of another. The exchange rate plays a key role in determining *patterns of trade* and has important implications for the effectiveness of its macroeconomic policies. Understanding what the exchange rate is, how it is determined and how it can – or, in some cases, cannot – be controlled will help us to understand why some European countries have decided to adopt a single currency that completely eliminates exchange rates between them. It will also help us understand why other European countries decided to opt out of the euro and retain policy independence. Chapter 30 discusses the economic rationale for monetary union. By focusing on the costs and benefits of a common currency we shall try to access the criteria for a successful monetary union and ask if European countries can expect to be net beneficiaries from joining the euro.

# 29

# Exchange Rates and the Open Economy

Dealing with exchange rates and different currencies can be confusing. A New York couple approaching retirement decides to buy a dream home in Europe. After extensive research on the Internet they whittle the options down to two houses, one in the west of Ireland and one in the Scottish highlands. After visiting both properties they cannot decide which they prefer. 'Its easy,' said the wife, 'let's choose the cheapest.' Her husband agrees and checks the prices. The Irish property is on offer at 300,000 euros and the Scottish at 250,000 pounds. Finding the comparison difficult the husband says, 'Which is the cheapest in real money?' (by which he means the American dollar). 'I haven't a clue,' replies the wife 'but I have just read that since our trip the dollar has appreciated against the euro and the pound has depreciated against the dollar, what does that mean?' To which her husband replies, 'It means we are moving to Florida!'

Regardless of whether they are interested in a foreign property, negotiating a business deal or simply chilling out in another country, dealing with unfamiliar currencies is a problem every international traveller faces. These problems can be further complicated by the fact that *exchange rates* may change unpredictably. Thus the number of Russian rubles, Japanese yen, Australian dollars or US dollars that one euro can buy may vary over time, sometimes quite a lot.

The economic consequences of variable exchange rates are much broader than their impact on travel and tourism, however. For example, the competitiveness of European exports depends in part on the prices of European goods in terms of foreign currencies, which in turn depend on the *exchange rate* between the euro and those currencies. Likewise, the prices Europeans pay for imported goods depend in part on the value of their currency relative to the currencies of the countries that produce those goods. Exchange rates also affect the value of financial investments made across national borders. For countries that are heavily dependent on trade and international capital flows – the majority of the world's nations and certainly most European countries – fluctuations in the exchange rate may have a significant economic impact.

This chapter discusses exchange rates and the role they play in open economies. We will start by distinguishing between the *nominal exchange rate* – the rate at which one national currency trades for another – and the *real exchange rate* – the rate at which one country's goods trade for another's. We shall show how exchange rates affect the prices of exports and imports, and thus the pattern of trade.

Next we shall turn to the question of how exchange rates are determined. Exchange rates may be divided into two broad categories, flexible and fixed. The value of a *flexible* exchange rate is determined freely in the market for national currencies, known as the *foreign exchange market*. Flexible exchange rates vary continually with changes in the supply of and demand for national currencies. In contrast, the value of a *fixed* exchange rate is set by the government at a constant level. Because most large industrial countries have a flexible exchange rate, we shall focus on that case first. We shall see that a country's monetary policy plays a particularly important role in determining the exchange rate. Furthermore, in an open economy with a flexible exchange rate, the exchange rate becomes a tool of monetary policy, in much the same way as the real interest rate.

Although most large industrial countries have a flexible exchange rate, many small and developing economies fix their exchange rates, so we shall consider the case of fixed exchange rates as well. We shall explain first how a country's government (usually, its Central Bank) goes about maintaining a fixed exchange rate at the officially determined level. Though fixing the exchange rate generally reduces day-to-day fluctuations in the value of a nation's currency, we shall see that, at times, a fixed exchange rate can become severely unstable, with potentially serious economic consequences. We shall close the chapter by discussing the relative merits of fixed and flexible exchange rates.

## Exchange rates

The economic benefits of trade between nations in goods, services and assets are similar to the benefits of trade within a nation. In both cases, trade in goods and services permits greater specialisation and efficiency, whereas trade in assets allows financial investors to earn higher returns while providing funds for worthwhile capital projects. However, there is a difference between the two cases, which is that trade in goods, services and assets *within* a country normally involves a single currency – euros, sterling, dollars, yen, or whatever the country's official form of money happens to be – whereas trade *between* nations usually involves dealing in different currencies. So, for example, if a Dutch resident wants to purchase an automobile manufactured in South Korea, she (or more likely, the automobile dealer) must first trade euros for the Korean currency, called the won. The Korean car manufacturer is then paid in won. Similarly, a British pension fund wishing to purchase shares in a US company (a US financial asset) must first trade sterling for dollars and then use the dollars to purchase the shares.

### Economic naturalist 29.1 Exchange rates and openness

The more an economy engages international trade the more important exchange rates are likely to be. For example, the euro value of French wine exports to the United States will in part depend on the exchange rate between the euro and the dollar. Likewise, the amount which British households spend on beef imports from Argentina will vary with the exchange rate between the Argentine peso and the British pound. Hence, the more a country exports and imports the greater the importance of exchange rates. When countries are heavily engaged in international trade we refer to them as relatively *open economies*. Conversely, when international trade accounts for a small percentage of total economic activity we refer to the country as a relatively *closed economy*. Openness matters, and the more open the economy is the greater the importance of international trade and exchange rates.

Table 29.1 presents some measures of openness for European economies. Columns (1) and (2) give each country's total exports and imports as a percentage of its GDP. The greater are these ratios the more open the economy and the greater

| | Total exports | Total imports | Intra-EU exports | Intra-EU imports |
|---|---|---|---|---|
| | As % of GDP | | As % of total | |
| | (1) | (2) | (3) | (4) |
| Austria | 52.8 | 50.6 | 38.3 | 44.1 |
| Belgium | 83.9 | 80.2 | 68.7 | 65.5 |
| Denmark | 44.3 | 38.7 | 44.0 | 52.7 |
| Finland | 38.7 | 30.3 | 46.8 | 46.5 |
| France | 27.1 | 25.0 | 47.6 | 50.0 |
| Germany | 35.9 | 31.6 | 45.7 | 38.6 |
| Greece | 20.9 | 27.7 | 16.7 | 44.4 |
| Ireland | 93.7 | 75.0 | 49.2 | 33.5 |
| Italy | 27.0 | 26.0 | 42.2 | 45.4 |
| Netherlands | 62.6 | 57.5 | 52.4 | 36.3 |
| Portugal | 30.3 | 37.6 | 57.4 | 67.8 |
| Spain | 28.4 | 29.9 | 47.2 | 53.5 |
| Sweden | 44.0 | 37.5 | 41.4 | 49.3 |
| United Kingdom | 26.2 | 29.2 | 39.3 | 39.0 |
| European Union | 35.1 | 33.4 | 46.4 | 44.9 |

**Table 29.1** European Economies: Measures of Openness, 2002

the importance of exchange rates. As we might expect, small economies such as Belgium and Ireland have a greater dependence on international trade than larger economies such as France and Germany. In 2002, Belgium exports accounted for 83.9 per cent of the country's GDP and imports accounted for 80.2 per cent of total domestic spending. The corresponding figures for France are 27.1 and 25 per cent, suggesting that France is much less dependent on international trade than is Belgium. In short, small economies appear to be more open than large economies.

Columns (3) and (4) of Table 29.1 illustrate the importance of each country's trade with its EU partners, or intra-EU trade (trade within the Union). Column (3) gives each country's exports to its EU partners as a percentage of its total world exports while column (4) gives imports from EU countries as a percentage of total imports from all countries. For the majority of countries, intra-EU trade either exceeds or is very close to 50 per cent of total trade, which is an important reason why European countries have always been anxious to limit the extent of exchange rate fluctuations between their currencies and, ultimately, opted for monetary union and the complete elimination of intra-Union exchange rates.

## Nominal exchange rates

Because international transactions generally require that one currency be traded for another, the relative values of different currencies are an important factor in international economic relations. The rate at which two currencies can be traded for each other is called the **nominal exchange rate**, or more simply the *exchange rate*, between the two currencies. For example, if 1 euro can be exchanged for 1.20 US dollars, the nominal exchange rate between the European and US currencies is 1.20 dollars per euro. Each country has many

**nominal exchange rate** the rate, or price, at which two currencies can be traded for each other

nominal exchange rates, one corresponding to each currency against which its own currency is traded. Thus the euro's value can be quoted in terms of British pounds, Swedish krona, Israeli shekels, Russian rubles, or dozens of other currencies. Table 29.2 gives exchange rates between the euro and six other currencies, as published by the ECB on 24 August 2004.

| Country | Foreign currency/euro (1) | Euro/foreign currency (2) |
|---|---|---|
| United States (dollar) | 1.2139 | 0.8238 |
| United Kingdom (pound) | 0.6725 | 1.487 |
| Japan (yen) | 133.02 | 0.0075 |
| Denmark (krone) | 7.4378 | 0.1344 |
| Sweden (krona) | 9.1613 | 0.1092 |
| Switzerland (Swiss franc) | 1.541 | 0.6489 |

**Table 29.2** Nominal Exchange Rates for the Euro
*Source*: ECB, www.ecb.int, 24 August 2004.

As Table 29.2 shows, exchange rates can be expressed either as the amount of foreign currency needed to purchase one euro (column (1)) or as the number of euros needed to purchase one unit of the foreign currency (column (2)). These two ways of expressing the exchange rate are equivalent: each is the *reciprocal* of the other. For example, on 24 August, the exchange rate between the euro and the dollar could have been expressed either as 1.2139 dollars per euro or as 0.8238 euros per dollar, where $0.8238 = 1/1.2139$.

### Example 29.1 Nominal exchange rates

Based on Table 29.2, find the exchange rate between the British and American currencies. Express the exchange rate in both dollars per pound and pounds per dollar.

From Table 29.2, we see that 0.6725 pounds will buy one euro, and that 1.2139 dollars will buy also buy one euro. Therefore 0.6725 pounds and 1.2139 dollars are equal in value:

$$0.6725 \text{ pounds} = 1.2139 \text{ dollars}$$

Dividing both sides of this equation by 1.2139 we get

$$0.5540 \text{ pounds} = 1 \text{ dollar}$$

In other words, the British–American exchange rate can be expressed as 0.5540 pounds per dollar. Alternatively, the exchange rate can be expressed as $1/0.5540 = 1.8051$ dollars per pound.

**Exercise 29.1** From the business section of the newspaper or an online source (try the ECB at www.ecb.int or Pacific Exchange Rate Service at www.fx.sauder.ubc.ca) find recent quotations of the value of the euro against the US dollar, the British pound and the Japanese yen. Based on these data find the exchange rate (a) between the pound and the dollar and (b) between the dollar and the yen. Express the exchange rates you derive in two ways (e.g. both as pounds per dollar and as dollars per pound).

Figure 29.1 shows the nominal exchange rate for the euro against the US dollar from the euro's launch in 1999 to the end of 2004. The exchange rate is measured as the number of dollars per euro. You can see from Fig. 29.1 that the euro's value fluctuated over these four years. Starting from a value of approximately 1.16 dollars per euro in January 1999 the exchange rate fell consistently, reaching a low of just over 0.80 dollars per euro in early 2002.

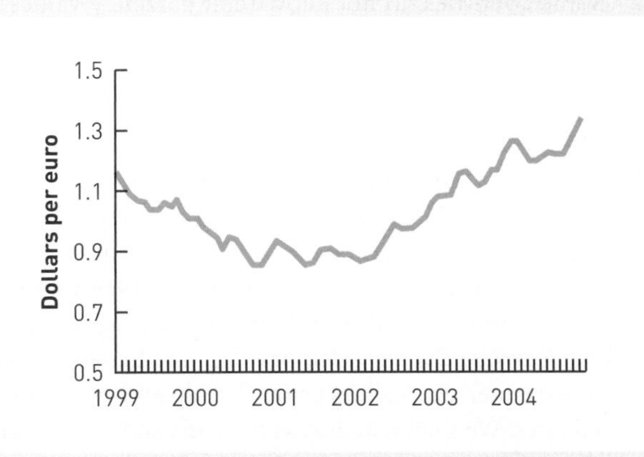


**Figure 29.1 The Dollar–Euro Nominal Exchange Rate, 1999–2004.** This figure shows the value of the euro in terms of US dollars from its launch in January 1999 to the end of 2004. *Source*: Pacific Exchange Rate Service, www.fx.sauder.ubc.ca.

However, since then the exchange rate has steadily increased to over 1.30 dollars per euro at the close of 2004. (If you are interested in more recent changes, use an online source such as ECB at www.ecb.int or Pacific Exchange Rate Service at www.fx.sauder.ubc.ca to check movements in the dollar–euro exchange rate since 2004.)

**appreciation** an increase in the value of a currency relative to other currencies

**depreciation** a decrease in the value of a currency relative to other currencies

An increase in the value of a currency relative to other currencies is known as an **appreciation**; a decline in the value of a currency relative to other currencies is called a **depreciation**. So we can say that the euro depreciated in 1999 and 2001 and appreciated in 2002 and 2003. We shall discuss the reasons a currency may appreciate or depreciate later in this chapter.

In this chapter we shall use the symbol *e* to stand for a country's nominal exchange rate. Although the exchange rate can be expressed either as foreign currency units per unit of domestic currency, or vice versa, as we saw in Table 29.2, let us agree to define *e* as the number of units of the foreign currency that the domestic currency will buy. For example, if we treat the Eurosystem as the 'home' or 'domestic' country and the United States as the 'foreign' country, *e* will be defined as the number of US dollars that one euro will buy. Defining the nominal exchange rate this way implies that an *increase* in *e* corresponds to an *appreciation*, or a strengthening, of the home currency, while a *decrease* in *e* implies a *depreciation*, or weakening, of the home currency.

## Flexible versus fixed exchange rates

**flexible (floating) exchange rate** an exchange rate whose value is not officially fixed but varies according to the supply of and demand for the currency in the foreign exchange market

**foreign exchange market** the market on which currencies of various nations are traded for one another

As we saw in Fig. 29.1, the exchange rate between the euro and the US dollar is not constant but varies continually. Indeed, changes in the exchange rates between currencies occur daily, hourly, even minute by minute. Such fluctuations in the value of a currency are normal for countries such as the United Kingdom, the United States and the Eurosystem which have a **flexible** or **floating exchange rate**. The value of a flexible exchange rate is not officially fixed but varies according to the supply of and demand for the currency in the **foreign exchange market** – the market on which currencies of various nations are traded for one another. We shall discuss the factors that determine the supply of and demand for currencies shortly.

Some countries do not allow their currency values to vary with market conditions but instead maintain a **fixed exchange rate**. The value of a fixed exchange rate is set by official government policy. A government that establishes a fixed exchange rate typically determines the exchange rate's value independently, but sometimes exchange rates are set according to an agreement among a number of governments. Between the end of the Second World War and the early 1970s most of the world's currencies operated within the *Bretton Woods* exchange rate system which required a fixed value against the US dollar, (see Economic naturalist 29.3, p. 853). From 1979 to 1999 countries in the European Union attempted to fix the value of their currencies against a composite or 'basket' currency known as the *European Currency Unit* or ECU, (see Economic naturalist 29.4, p. 855). In the next part of the chapter we shall focus on flexible exchange rates, but shall return later to the case of fixed rates. We shall also discuss the costs and benefits of each type of exchange rate.

**fixed exchange rate** an exchange rate whose value is set by official government policy

## The real exchange rate

**real exchange rate** the price of the average domestic good or service *relative* to the price of the average foreign good or service, when prices are expressed in terms of a common currency

The nominal exchange rate tells us the price of the domestic currency in terms of a foreign currency. As we shall see in this section, the **real exchange rate** tells us the price of the average *domestic good or service* in terms of the average *foreign good or service*. We shall also see that a country's real exchange rate has important implications for its ability to sell its exports abroad.

To provide a background for discussing the real exchange rate, imagine that you are in charge of purchasing for a French corporation that is planning to acquire a large number of new computers. The company's computer specialist has identified two models, one British-made and one French-made, that meet the necessary specifications. Since the two models are essentially equivalent, the company will buy the one with the lower price. However, since the computers are priced in the currencies of the countries of manufacture, the price comparison is not so straightforward. In this case the British computer is priced in pounds sterling and the French computer in euros. Your mission – should you decide to accept it – is to determine which of the two models is cheaper.

To complete your assignment you will need two pieces of information: the nominal exchange rate between the euro and sterling and the prices of the two models in terms of the currencies of their countries of manufacture. Example 29.2 shows how you can use this information to determine which model is cheaper.

### Example 29.2 Comparing prices expressed in different currencies

A French-made computer costs €2,250, and a similar British-made computer costs £2,100. If the nominal exchange rate is £0.70 per euro, which computer is the better buy?

To make this price comparison, we must measure the prices of both computers in the *same currency*. To make the comparison in euros, we first convert the British computer's price into euros. The price in terms of sterling is £2,100, and we are told that £0.70 = €1. To find the euro price of the British computer we observe that for any good or service,

$$\text{Price in sterling} = \text{Price in euros} \times \text{Value of euro in terms of sterling}$$

Note that the value of a euro in terms of sterling is just the sterling–euro exchange rate. Making this substitution and solving, we get

$$\text{Price in euros} = \frac{\text{Price in sterling}}{\text{Sterling–euro exchange rate}}$$

$$= \frac{£2{,}100}{£0.70} = 3{,}000$$

Notice that the pound symbol (£) appears in both the numerator and the denominator of the ratio, so it cancels out. Our conclusion is that the French computer is cheaper than the British computer at €2,250, or €750 less than the price of the British computer, €3,000. The French computer is the better deal.

**Exercise 29.2** Continuing Example 29.2, compare the prices of the French and British computers by expressing both prices in terms of sterling.

In Example 29.2, the fact that the French computer was cheaper implied that your firm would choose it over the British-made computer. In general, a country's ability to compete in international markets depends in part on the prices of its goods and services *relative* to the prices of foreign goods and services, when the prices are measured in a common currency. In the hypothetical example of the French and British computers, the price of the domestic (French) good relative to the price of the foreign (British) good is €2,250/€3,000, or 0.75. So the French computer is 25 per cent less expensive than the British computer, putting the French product at a competitive advantage.

More generally, economists ask whether *on average* the goods and services produced by a particular country are expensive relative to the goods and services produced by other countries. This question can be answered by the country's *real exchange rate*. Specifically, a country's real exchange rate is the price of the average domestic good or service *relative* to the price of the average foreign good or service, when prices are expressed in terms of a common currency.

To obtain a formula for the real exchange rate, recall that $e$ equals the nominal exchange rate (the number of units of foreign currency per unit of domestic currency) and that $P$ equals the domestic price level – as measured, for example, by the consumer price index (CPI). In what follows we shall treat the euro as the domestic currency and use $P$ as a measure of the price of the 'average' domestic good or service measured in euros. Similarly, let $P^f$ equal the foreign price level. We will use $P^f$ as the measure of the price of the 'average' foreign good or service measured in foreign currency (sterling, dollars, yen, etc.).

The real exchange rate equals the price of the average domestic good or service relative to the price of the average foreign good or service. It would not be correct, however, to define the real exchange rate as the ratio $P/P^f$, because the two price levels are expressed in *different currencies*. As we saw in Example 29.2, to convert foreign prices into domestic, we must divide the foreign price by the exchange rate. By this rule, the price in domestic currency of the average foreign good or service equals $P^f/e$. Treating the *euro as the domestic currency*, we can now write the real exchange rate as

$$\text{Real exchange rate} = \frac{\text{Price of domestic good}}{\text{Price of foreign good, in euros}} = \frac{P}{P^f/e}$$

To simplify this expression, multiply the numerator and denominator by $e$ to get

$$\text{Real exchange rate (for computers)} = \frac{eP}{P^f} \qquad (29.1)$$

which is the formula for the real exchange rate.

To check this formula, let us use it to re-solve our computer example, Example 29.2. (For this exercise, we imagine that computers are the only good produced in France and Britain, so the real exchange rate becomes just the price of French computers relative to British computers.) In that example, the nominal exchange rate $e$ was £0.70/€1, the domestic, or French, price $P$ (of a computer) was €2,250, and the foreign price $P^f$ was £2,100. Applying Eq. (29.1), we get

$$\text{Real exchange rate (for computers)} = \frac{(\pounds 0.71/€1) \times €2.250}{\pounds 2{,}100}$$
$$= \frac{\pounds 1{,}575}{\pounds 2{,}100}$$
$$= 0.75$$

which is the same answer as we got earlier.

The real exchange rate, an overall measure of the cost of domestic goods relative to foreign goods, is an important economic variable. In Example 29.2, the real exchange rate for computers indicates that the price of domestic (French) production is less than the price of foreign (British) computers when measured in the same currency. Other things being equal, British firms and households have an incentive to buy French-made computers, thus increasing French exports to the United Kingdom. Likewise, French firms and households will find imported British computers expensive relative to French-made computers, thus reducing French imports from the United Kingdom. Hence, a low real exchange rate implies that domestic producers will find it easier exporting to other countries because domestic goods are competitive relative to foreign goods (foreign goods will be 'overpriced'), while domestic goods will sell well in the home country (because imported goods are expensive relative to goods produced at home). Since a low real exchange rate tends to increase exports and reduce imports, we conclude that net exports will tend to be higher when the *real exchange rate is low*. Conversely, if the real exchange rate is high, then the home country will find it more difficult to export (because its goods are expensive relative to foreign goods), while domestic residents will buy more imports (because imports are cheaper relative to domestic goods). Thus net exports will tend to be low when the *real exchange rate is high*.

Equation (29.1) also shows that the real exchange rate tends to move in the same direction as the nominal exchange rate $e$ (since an increase in $e$ reduces the price of foreign goods measured in domestic currency). To the extent that real and nominal exchange rates move in the same direction, we can conclude that net exports will be hurt by a high nominal exchange rate and helped by a low nominal exchange rate.

A decrease in the real exchange rate is known as a *real depreciation of the domestic currency*. As a lower real exchange rate makes domestic goods more competitive relative to foreign goods a real depreciation will, other things being equal, lead to an increase in net exports. Conversely, an increase in the real exchange rate is known as a *real appreciation of the domestic currency*. As a higher real exchange rate makes domestic goods less competitive relative to foreign goods a real appreciation will, other things being equal, lead to a decline in net exports.

## Economic naturalist 29.2 Does a strong currency imply a strong economy?

Politicians and the public sometimes take pride in the fact that their national currency is 'strong', meaning that its value in terms of other currencies is high or rising. Likewise, policy makers sometimes view a depreciating ('weak') currency as a sign of economic failure. Does a strong currency necessarily imply a strong economy?

Contrary to popular impression, there is no simple connection between the strength of a country's currency and the strength of its economy. For example, Fig. 29.1 shows that the value of the euro relative to the US dollar rose steadily throughout most of 2002 and 2003. However, in both years US economic growth exceeded growth in the Eurosystem. In 2003, for example, real US GDP increased by 3.1 per cent compared with only 0.4 per cent in the Eurosystem. The following sections will analyse how exchange rates are determined, and why they change over time.

## RECAP Exchange rates

- The *nominal exchange rate* between two currencies is the rate at which the currencies can be traded for each other. More precisely, the nominal exchange rate *e* for any given country is the number of units of foreign currency that can be bought for one unit of the domestic currency.
- An *appreciation* is an increase in the value of a currency relative to other currencies (a rise in *e*); a *depreciation* is a decline in a currency's value (a fall in *e*).
- An exchange rate can be either *flexible* – meaning that it varies freely according to supply of and demand for the currency in the foreign exchange market – or *fixed*, meaning that its value is established by official government policy.
- The *real exchange rate* is the price of the average domestic good or service relative to the price of the average foreign good or service, when prices are expressed in terms of a common currency. A useful formula for the real exchange rate is $eP/P^f$, where *e* is the nominal exchange rate, *P* is the domestic price level, and $P^f$ is the foreign price level.
- An *increase* in the real exchange rate implies that domestic goods are becoming more expensive relative to foreign goods, which tends to reduce exports and stimulate imports. Conversely, a *decline* in the real exchange rate tends to increase net exports.

# Determination of the exchange rate

Countries that have flexible exchange rates, such as the United Kingdom, the United States and those which use the euro as their common currency, see the international values of their currencies change continually. What determines the value of the nominal exchange rate at any point in time? In this section, we shall try to answer this basic economic question. Again, our focus for the moment is on flexible exchange rates, whose values are determined by the foreign exchange market. Later in the chapter, we shall discuss the case of fixed exchange rates.

## A simple theory of exchange rates: purchasing power parity

**purchasing power parity (PPP)** the theory that nominal exchange rates are determined as necessary for the law of one price to hold

**law of one price** if transportation costs are relatively small, the price of an internationally traded commodity must be the same in all locations

The most basic theory of how nominal exchange rates are determined is called **purchasing power parity** (or **PPP**). To understand this theory, we must first discuss a fundamental economic concept, called the **law of one price**. The law of one price states that if transportation costs are relatively small, the price of an internationally traded commodity must be the same in all locations. For example, if transportation costs are not too large, the price of 1 kg of wheat ought to be the same in Bombay, India and Sydney, Australia. Suppose that were not the case – that the price of wheat in Sydney were only half the price in Bombay. In that case, grain merchants would have a strong incentive to buy wheat in Sydney and ship it to Bombay, where it could be sold at double the price of purchase. As wheat left Sydney, reducing the local supply, the price of wheat in Sydney would rise, while the inflow of wheat into Bombay would reduce the price in Bombay. According to the *Equilibrium Principle* (Chapter 3), the international market for wheat would return to equilibrium only when unexploited opportunities to profit had been eliminated – specifically, only when the prices of wheat in Sydney and in Bombay became equal or nearly equal (with the difference being less than the cost of transporting wheat from Australia to India).

If the law of one price were to hold for all goods and services (which is not a realistic assumption, as we shall see shortly), then the value of the nominal exchange rate would be determined as in Example 29.3.

### **Example 29.3** How many Indian rupees equal one Australian dollar: 1?

Suppose that 1 kg of grain costs 5 Australian dollars in Sydney and 150 rupees in Bombay. If the law of one price holds for grain, what is the nominal exchange rate between Australia and India?

Because the market value of 1 kg of grain must be the same in both locations, we know that the Australian price of wheat must equal the Indian price of wheat, so that

5 Australian dollars = 150 Indian rupees

Dividing by 5, we get

1 Australian dollar = 30 Indian rupees

Thus the nominal exchange rate between Australia and India should be 30 rupees per Australian dollar.

**Exercise 29.3** The price of gold is $300 per ounce in New York and 2,500 kronor per ounce in Stockholm, Sweden. If the law of one price holds for gold, what is the nominal exchange rate between the US dollar and the Swedish krona?

Example 29.3 and Exercise 29.3 illustrate the application of the *purchasing power parity* (*PPP*) theory. According to the PPP theory, nominal exchange rates are determined as necessary for the law of one price to hold.

A particularly useful prediction of the PPP theory is that in the long run, the currencies of countries that experience *significant inflation will tend to depreciate*. To see why, we shall extend the analysis in Example 29.3.

### **Example 29.4** How many Indian rupees equal one Australian dollar: 2?

Suppose that India experiences significant inflation so that the price of 1 kg of grain in Bombay rises from 150 to 300 rupees. Australia has no inflation, so the price of grain in Sydney remains unchanged at 5 Australian dollars. If the law of one price holds for grain, what will happen to the nominal exchange rate between Australia and India?

As in Example 29.3, we know that the market value of 1 kg of grain must be the same in both locations. Therefore,

5 Australian dollars = 300 rupees

Equivalently,

1 Australian dollar = 60 rupees

The nominal exchange rate is now 60 rupees per Australian dollar. Before India's inflation, the nominal exchange rate was 30 rupees per Australian dollar (Example 29.3). So in this example, inflation has caused the rupee to *depreciate* against the Australian dollar. Conversely, Australia, with no inflation, has seen its currency *appreciate* against the rupee. Note that in this example the difference between the Australian and Indian inflation rates exactly matches the appreciation of the Australian dollar. Australian inflation is zero and Indian inflation is 100 per cent (150 to 300 rupees). If PPP is correct and the value of the Australian dollar rises from 30 to 60 rupees then the currency appreciates by 100 per cent against the rupee. From Eq. (29.1) we know that the real exchange rate can be expressed as $eP/P^f$. In this case $e$ is the rupee–Australian dollar nominal exchange rate, $P$ is the Australian price and $P^f$ is the Indian price. Hence, the 100 per cent increase in $P^f$ (Indian inflation) is exactly matched by a 100 per cent increase in $e$ (appreciation of the Australian dollar) leaving the real exchange rate unaffected. Hence, if PPP holds exactly, the real exchange rate should be constant. If this is correct then we can write Eq. (29.1) as $eP = P^f$ which is simply the *law of one price* – that prices should be equal when measured in a common currency. Using a dot above a variable to denote its percentage change, or rate of inflation, we can express this relationship as

$$\dot{e} = \dot{P}^f - \dot{P} \tag{29.2}$$

**relative purchasing power parity** the theory that the nominal rate of appreciation or depreciation equals the difference in inflation rates between the two countries

which implies that the appreciation or depreciation of the domestic currency equals the difference between the foreign and domestic inflation rates. In Example 29.4 $\dot{P}^f$ (Indian inflation) = 100 per cent, $\dot{P} = 0$ (Australian inflation) and $\dot{e} = 100$ per cent (appreciation of the Australian dollar). Hence the appreciation of the Australian dollar equals the difference between the two inflation rates. When expressed as in Eq. (29.2), PPP is known as the theory of **relative purchasing power parity**.

While we may not expect PPP or relative PPP to hold at all times and for all goods, the link between inflation and depreciation or appreciation of the nominal exchange rate makes economic sense. Inflation implies that a nation's currency is losing purchasing power in the domestic market. Analogously, exchange rate depreciation implies that the nation's currency is losing purchasing power in international markets. Figure 29.2 shows annual rates of inflation and nominal exchange rate depreciation for 10 European countries over 1973–80, the years following the 1973 oil price shock. Inflation is measured as the excess of each country's inflation rate over the German inflation rate, called the *inflation differential*, and depreciation is measured relative to the German Deutsche Mark. As you can see, inflation varied greatly among European countries during the period. Figure 29.2 shows that, as the PPP theories imply, countries with higher inflation during the 1970s tended to experience the most rapid depreciation of their currencies.

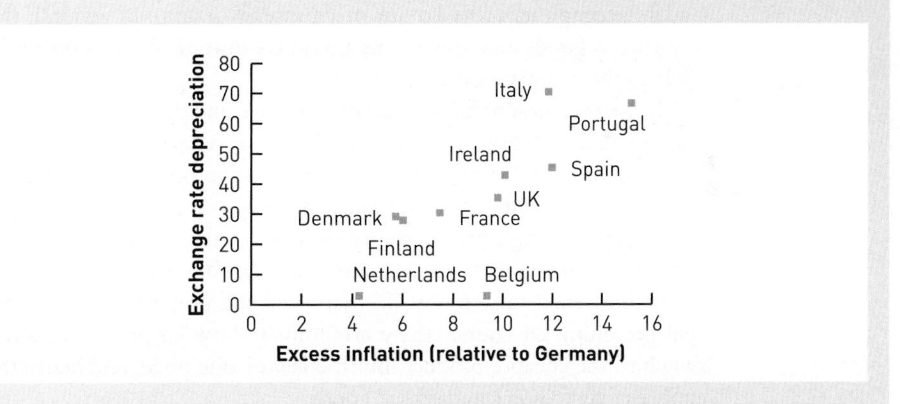


**Figure 29.2 Inflation and Currency Depreciation in Europe, 1973–80.** The figure plots the difference between each country's average rate of inflation and the German inflation rate, against the rate of currency depreciation against the DM over 1973–80. High inflation relative to Germany was associated with rapid depreciation of the nominal exchange rate.

## Shortcomings of the PPP theory

Empirical studies have found that the PPP theory is useful for predicting changes in nominal exchange rates over the relatively long run. In particular, this theory helps to explain the tendency of countries with high inflation to experience depreciation of their exchange rates, as shown in Fig. 29.2. However, the theory is less successful in predicting *short-run* movements in exchange rates.

A particularly dramatic failure of the PPP theory occurred in the years following the euro's launch on 1 January 1999. As Fig. 29.1 indicates, between 1999 and 2001 the value of the euro fell by nearly 30 per cent relative to the dollar. This strong depreciation was followed by an even more rapid appreciation during 2002 and 2003. PPP theory could explain this rollercoaster behaviour only if inflation were far higher in Europe than in United States from 1999 to 2001, and far lower in 2002 and 2003. In fact, European inflation was similar to inflation in the United States throughout both periods.

Why does the PPP theory work less well in the short run than in the long run? Recall that this theory relies on the *law of one price*, which says that the price of an internationally traded commodity must be the same in all locations. The law of one price works well for goods such as grain or gold, which are standardised commodities that are traded widely. However, not all goods and services are *traded internationally*, and not all goods are *standardised commodities*.

Many goods and services are not traded internationally, because the assumption underlying the law of one price – that transportation costs are relatively small – does not hold for them. For example, for Indians to export haircuts to Australia, they would need to transport an Indian barber to Australia every time a Sydney resident desired a trim. Because transportation costs prevent haircuts from being traded internationally, the law of one price does not apply to them. Thus, even if the price of haircuts in Australia were double the price of haircuts in India, market forces would not necessarily force prices toward equality in the short run. (Over the long run, some Indian barbers might emigrate to Australia.) Other examples of *non-traded goods and services* are agricultural land, buildings, heavy construction materials (whose value is low relative to their transportation costs) and highly perishable foods. In addition, some products use non-traded goods and services as inputs: a McDonald's hamburger served in Moscow has both a tradable component (frozen hamburger patties) and a non-tradable component (the labour of counter workers). In general, the greater the share of non-traded goods and services in a nation's output, the less precisely the PPP theory will apply to the country's exchange rate.[1]

The second reason that the law of one price and the PPP theory sometimes fail to apply is that not all internationally traded goods and services are perfectly standardised commodities, like grain or gold. For example, German-made automobiles and Japanese-made automobiles are not identical; they differ in styling, horsepower, reliability and other features. As a result, some people strongly prefer one nation's cars to the other's. Thus if Japanese cars cost 10 per cent less than German cars, Japanese automobile exports will not necessarily flood the German market, since many Germans will still prefer German-made cars even at a 10 per cent premium. Of course, there are limits to how far prices can diverge before people will switch to the cheaper product. But the law of one price, and hence the PPP theory, will not apply exactly to non-standardised goods.

To summarise, the PPP theory works reasonably well as an explanation of exchange rate behaviour over the long run, but not in the short run. Because transportation costs limit international trade in many goods and services, and because not all goods that are traded are standardised commodities, the law of one price (on which the PPP theory is based) works only imperfectly in the short run. To understand the short-run movements of exchange rates we need to incorporate some additional factors. In the next section we shall study a supply and demand framework for the determination of exchange rates.

[1] Trade barriers, such as tariffs and quotas, also increase the costs associated with shipping goods from one country to another. Thus trade barriers reduce the applicability of the law of one price in much the same way as physical transportation costs do.

## Determination of the exchange rate: a supply and demand analysis

Although the PPP theory helps to explain the long-run behaviour of the exchange rate, supply and demand analysis is more useful for studying its short-run behaviour. In this section, we shall analyse the short-run behaviour of exchange rates by using a simple demand and supply model similar that in Chapter 3. However, in this case the market is the *foreign exchange market* which, as we have seen, is a market on which different currencies (euros, dollars, sterling, yen, etc.) are traded for one another and the price is the nominal exchange rate or the value of one currency in terms of another currency. To focus our attention on Europe we shall concentrate on the market for euros. For convenience we shall use the terms 'Eurosystem' and 'Europe' as meaning the same thing, even though many European countries do not use the euro as their currency. This is a simplifying assumption which enables us to focus on the fundamentals of the foreign exchange market. As we shall see, euros are demanded in the foreign exchange market by foreigners who seek to purchase European goods and assets and are supplied by European residents who need foreign currencies to buy foreign goods and assets. The *equilibrium exchange rate* is the value of the euro that equates the number of euros supplied and demanded in the foreign exchange market. Our aim is to analyse the supply of and demand for euros, and thus the euro exchange rate.

One note before we proceed: in Chapter 27 we described how the supply of money by the ECB and the demand for money by the public help to determine the nominal interest rate. However, the supply of and demand for money in the domestic economy, as presented in Chapter 27, are *not* equivalent to the supply of and demand for euros in the foreign exchange market. As mentioned, the foreign exchange market is the market in which the currencies of various nations are traded for one another. The supply of euros to the foreign exchange market is *not* the same as the money supply set by the ECB; rather, it is the number of euros households and firms in the Eurosystem offer to trade for other currencies. Likewise, the demand for euros in the foreign exchange market is *not* the same as the domestic demand for money, but the number of euros holders of foreign currencies seek to buy. To understand the distinction, it may help to keep in mind that while the ECB determines the total supply of euros in the Eurosystem economy, a euro does not 'count' as having been supplied to the foreign exchange market until some holder of euros, such as a household or firm, tries to trade it for a foreign currency.

### The supply of euros

Anyone who holds euros – from an international bank to a Russian citizen whose euros are buried in the back garden – is a potential *supplier of euros* to the foreign exchange market. In practice, however, the principal suppliers of euros to the foreign exchange market are European households and firms. Why would a European household or firm want to supply euros in exchange for foreign currency? There are two major reasons. First, a European household or firm may need foreign currency to *purchase foreign goods or services*. For example, a Dutch automobile importer may need yen to purchase Japanese cars, or an Italian tourist may need dollars to make purchases in New York. In each case the European household or firm must supply euros to buy the foreign currency. Second, a European household or firm may need foreign currency to *purchase foreign assets*. For example, an Irish pension fund may wish to acquire shares issued by American companies. Because American assets are normally priced in dollars, the pension fund will need to trade euros for dollars to acquire these assets.

The supply of euros to the foreign exchange market is illustrated in Fig. 29.3. We shall focus on the market in which euros are traded for US dollars, but bear in mind that similar markets exist for every other pair of traded currencies. The vertical axis of Fig. 29.3 shows the dollar–euro exchange rate as measured by the number of dollars that can be purchased with each euro. The horizontal axis shows the number of euros being traded in the market.

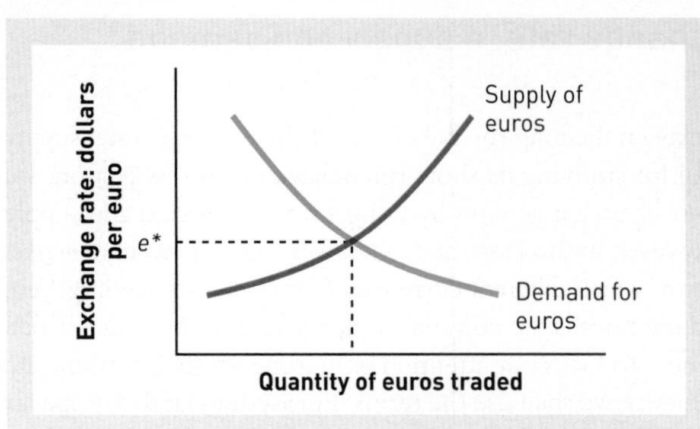


Figure 29.3 **The Supply and Demand for Euros in the Dollar–Euro Market.** The supply of euros is upward-sloping because an increase in the number of dollars offered for each euro makes US goods, services and assets more attractive to European buyers. Similarly, the demand for euros is downward-sloping because holders of dollars will be less willing to buy euros the more expensive they are in terms of dollars. The equilibrium rate $e^*$, also called the *fundamental value of the exchange rate*, equates the quantities of euros supplied and demanded.

Note that the supply curve for euros is *upward-sloping*. In other words, the more dollars each euro can buy, the more euros people are willing to supply to the foreign exchange market. Why? At given prices for American goods, services and assets, the more dollars a euro can buy, the cheaper those goods, services and assets will be in euro terms. For example, if a video game costs $55 in the United States, and a euro can buy $1.00, the euro price of the video game will be €55. However, if a euro can buy $1.10, then the euro price of the same video game will be €50 (or $55/$1.10). Assuming that lower euro prices will induce Europeans to increase their expenditures on American goods, services and assets, a higher dollar–euro exchange rate will increase the supply of euros to the foreign exchange market. Thus the supply curve for euros is upward-sloping.

### The demand for euros

In the dollar–euro foreign exchange market, demanders of euros are those who wish to acquire euros in exchange for dollars. Most demanders of euros in the dollar–euro market are American households and firms, although anyone who happens to hold dollars is free to trade them for euros. Why demand euros? The reasons for acquiring euros are analogous to those for acquiring dollars. First, households and firms that hold dollars will demand euros so that they can *purchase European goods and services*. For example, an American importer who wants to purchase French wine needs euros to pay the French exporter, and an American student studying in a European university must pay tuition fees in euros. The importer or the student can acquire the necessary euros only by offering dollars in exchange. Second, households and firms demand euros in order to *purchase European assets*. The purchase of Irish real estate by an American company or the acquisition of German bonds by an American mutual fund are two examples.

The demand for euros is represented by the *downward-sloping* curve in Fig. 29.3. The curve slopes downward because the more dollars an American citizen must pay to acquire a euro, the less attractive European goods, services and assets will be. Hence the demand for euros will be low when euros are expensive in terms of dollars and high when euros are cheap in terms of dollars.

### The equilibrium value of the euro

**fundamental value of the exchange rate (or equilibrium exchange rate)** the exchange rate that equates the quantities of the currency supplied and demanded in the foreign exchange market

As mentioned earlier, the Eurosystem maintains a flexible, or floating, exchange rate, which means that the value of the dollar–euro exchange rate is determined by the forces of supply and demand in the foreign exchange market. In Fig. 29.3 the equilibrium value of the euro is $e^*$, the dollar–euro exchange rate at which the quantity of euros supplied equals the quantity of euros demanded. The equilibrium value of the exchange rate is also called the **fundamental value of the exchange rate**. In general, the equilibrium value of the euro is not constant but changes with shifts in the supply of and demand for euros in the foreign exchange market.

### Changes in the supply of euros

Recall that people supply euros to the dollar–euro foreign exchange market in order to purchase American goods, services and assets. Factors that affect the desire of European households and firms to acquire American goods, services, and assets will therefore affect the supply of euros to the foreign exchange market. Some factors that will *increase* the supply of euros, shifting the supply curve for euros to the right, include:

- An *increased preference for American goods*. For example, suppose that Californian wine becomes more popular in Europe. To acquire the dollars needed to buy more Californian wine, European wine importers will increase their supply of euros to the foreign exchange market.
- An *increase in European real GDP*. An increase in European real GDP will raise the incomes of Europeans, allowing them to consume more goods and services (recall the *consumption function*, introduced in Chapter 26). Some part of this increase in consumption will take the form of goods imported from the United States. To buy more American goods, Europeans will supply more euros to acquire the necessary dollars.
- An *increase in the real interest rate on American assets*. Recall that European households and firms acquire dollars in order to purchase American assets as well as goods and services. Other factors, such as risk, held constant, the higher the real interest rate paid by American assets, the more American assets Europeans will choose to hold. To purchase additional American assets, European households and firms will supply more euros to the foreign exchange market.

Conversely, reduced demand for American goods, a lower European GDP, or a lower real interest rate on American assets will *reduce* the number of dollars Europeans need, in turn reducing their supply of euros to the foreign exchange market and shifting the supply curve for euros to the left. Of course, any shift in the supply curve for euros will affect the equilibrium exchange rate, as Example 29.5 shows.

### **Example 29.5** Video games, the euro and the dollar

Suppose American firms come to dominate the video game market, with games that are more exciting and realistic than those produced in Europe. All else being equal, how will this change affect the relative value of the euro and the dollar?

The increased quality of American video games will increase the demand for the games in Europe. To acquire the dollars necessary to buy more American video games, European importers will supply more euros to the foreign exchange market. As Fig. 29.4 shows, the increased supply of euros will reduce the value of the euro: in other words, a euro will buy fewer dollars than it did before. At the same time, the dollar will increase in value: a given number of dollars will buy more euros than it did before.

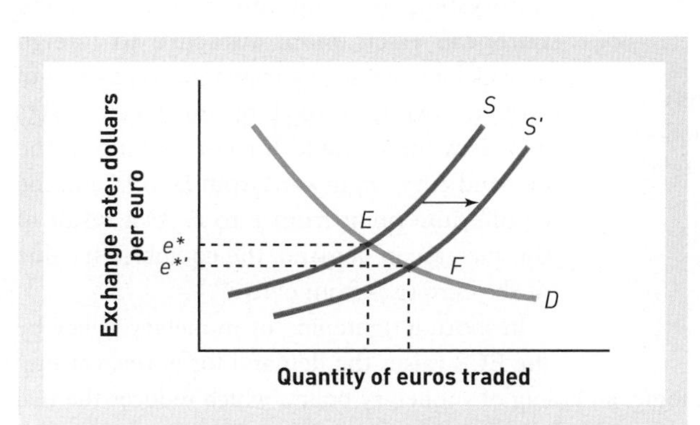


Figure 29.4 **An Increase in the Supply of Euros Lowers the Value of the Euro.** To buy more American video games Europeans must supply more euros to the foreign exchange market to acquire the dollars they need to buy the games. The supply curve for euros shifts from *S* to *S'*, lowering the equilibrium value of the euro from *e** to *e*'*.

**Exercise 29.4** The United States goes into a recession, and real GDP falls. All else being equal, how is this economic weakness likely to affect the value of the euro?

### Changes in the demand for euros

The factors that can cause a change in the demand for euros in the foreign exchange market, and thus a shift of the euro demand curve, are analogous to the factors that affect the supply of euros. Factors that will *increase* the demand for euros include:

- An *increased preference for European goods*. For example, airlines in the United States might find that planes built by the French company Airbus are superior to others such as the US-built Boeing, and decide to expand the number of Airbus planes in their fleets. To buy the European planes, US airlines would demand more euros on the foreign exchange market.
- An *increase in real GDP abroad*, which implies higher incomes abroad, and thus more demand for imports from Europe.
- An *increase in the real interest rate on European assets*, which would make those assets more attractive to foreign savers. To acquire additional European assets, foreign savers would demand more euros.

## Monetary policy and the exchange rate

Of the many factors that could influence a country's exchange rate, among the most important is the *monetary policy of the country's Central Bank*. As we shall see, monetary policy affects the exchange rate primarily through its effect on the real interest rate.

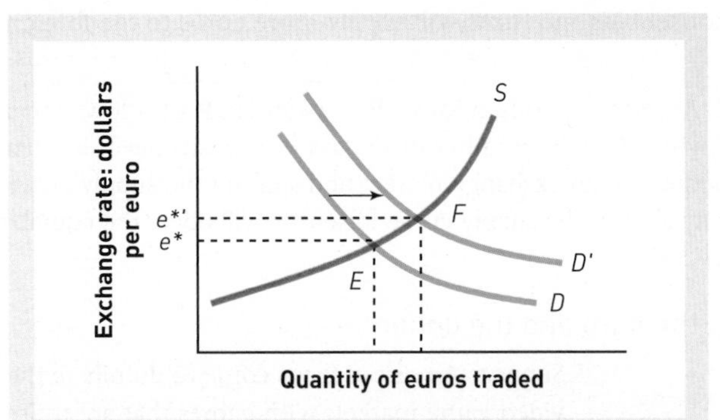


**Figure 29.5 A Tighter Monetary Policy Strengthens the Euro.** Tighter monetary policy in Europe raises euro real interest rates, increasing the demand for euro assets by foreign savers. An increased demand for European assets increases the demand for euros. The demand curve for euros shifts from *D* to *D*', increasing the equilibrium value of the euro from e* to *e**'.

Suppose that the ECB is concerned about inflation and tightens monetary policy in response. The effects of this policy change on the value of the euro are shown in Fig. 29.5. Before the policy change, the equilibrium value of the exchange rate is $e^*$, at the intersection of supply curve *S* and the demand curve *D*. The tightening of monetary policy raises the Eurosystem real interest rate *r*, making European assets more attractive to foreign financial investors. The increased willingness of foreign investors to buy European assets increases the demand for euros, shifting the demand curve rightward from *D* to *D*' and the equilibrium point from *E* to *F*. As a result of this increase in demand, the equilibrium value of the euro rises from $e^*$ to $e^{*\prime}$.

In short, a tightening of monetary policy by the ECB raises the demand for euros, causing the euro to *appreciate*. By similar logic, an easing of monetary policy, which reduces the real interest rate, would weaken the demand for the euro, causing it to *depreciate*.

### The exchange rate as a tool of monetary policy

In a closed economy, monetary policy affects aggregate demand solely through the *real interest rate*. For example, by raising the real interest rate, a tight monetary policy reduces consumption and investment spending. We shall see next that in an open economy with a flexible exchange rate, the exchange rate serves as another channel for monetary policy, one that reinforces the effects of the real interest rate.

To illustrate, suppose that policy makers are concerned about inflation and decide to restrain aggregate demand. To do so, they increase the real interest rate, reducing consumption and investment spending. But, as Fig. 29.5 shows, the higher real interest rate also increases the demand for euros, causing the euro to appreciate. The stronger euro, in turn, further reduces aggregate demand. Why? As we saw in discussing the real exchange rate, a stronger euro reduces the cost of imported goods, *increasing imports*. It also makes European exports more costly to foreign buyers, which tends to *reduce exports*. Recall that net exports – or exports minus imports – is one of the four components of aggregate demand. Thus, by reducing exports and increasing imports, a stronger euro (more precisely, a higher real exchange rate) reduces aggregate demand.

In sum, when the exchange rate is flexible, a tighter monetary policy reduces net exports (through a stronger euro) as well as consumption and investment spending (through a higher real interest rate). Conversely, an easier monetary policy weakens the euro and stimulates net exports, reinforcing the effect of the lower real interest rate on consumption and investment spending. Thus, relative to the case of a closed economy we studied earlier, monetary policy is more effective in an *open economy with a flexible exchange rate*.

## RECAP Determining the exchange rate

- The most basic theory of nominal exchange rate determination, *purchasing power parity* (PPP), is based on the *law of one price*. The law of one price states that if transportation costs are relatively small, the price of an internationally traded commodity must be the same in all locations. According to the PPP theory, the nominal exchange rate between two currencies can be found by setting the price of a traded commodity in one currency equal to the price of the same commodity expressed in the second currency.
- A useful prediction of the PPP theory is that the currencies of countries that experience significant inflation will tend to *depreciate* over the long run. However, the PPP theory does not work well in the short run. The fact that many goods and services are *non-traded*, and that not all traded goods are *standardised*, reduces the applicability of the law of one price, and hence of the PPP theory.
- Supply and demand analysis is a useful tool for studying the short-run determination of the exchange rate. European households and firms supply euros to the foreign exchange market to acquire foreign currencies, which they need to purchase foreign goods, services and assets. Foreigners demand euros in the foreign exchange market to purchase European goods, services and assets. The *equilibrium exchange rate*, also called the fundamental value of the exchange rate, equates the quantities of euros supplied and demanded in the foreign exchange market.
- An increased preference for foreign goods, an increase in European real GDP, or an increase in the real interest rate on foreign assets will increase the supply of euros on the foreign exchange market, *lowering* the value of the euro. An increased preference for European goods by foreigners, an increase in real GDP abroad, or an increase in the real interest rate on European assets will increase the demand for euros, *raising* the value of the euro.
- A tight monetary policy raises the real interest rate, increasing the demand for euros and *strengthening* the euro. A stronger euro reinforces the effects of tight monetary policy on aggregate spending by reducing net exports, a component of aggregate demand. Conversely, an easy monetary policy lowers the real interest rate, *weakening* the euro.

# Fixed exchange rates

So far, we have focused on the case of flexible exchange rates, the relevant case for most large industrial countries such as the United Kingdom, the United States and the Eurosystem. However, the alternative approach, *fixing the exchange rate*, has been quite important historically. Prior to the introduction of the euro in 1999 most European countries had a strong preference for fixed exchange rates between their currencies. One reason is that exchange rate flexibility and volatility is often seen as a threat to trade between European countries and the continuing process of economic integration. In this section we shall see how our conclusions change when the nominal exchange rate is fixed rather than flexible. One important difference is that when a country maintains a fixed exchange rate, its ability to use monetary policy as a *stabilisation tool* is greatly reduced.

## How to fix an exchange rate

In contrast to a flexible exchange rate, whose value is determined solely by supply and demand in the foreign exchange market, the value of a fixed exchange rate is determined by the government (in practice, usually the finance ministry with the co-operation of the Central Bank). Today, the value of a fixed exchange rate is usually set in terms of a major currency (for instance, several countries in Central and Eastern Europe (CEE) link their currency to the euro and China pegs its currency to the US dollar), or relative to a 'basket' of currencies, typically those of the country's trading partners. Historically, currency values were often fixed in terms of gold or other precious metals, but in recent years precious metals have rarely if ever been used for that purpose.

Once an exchange rate has been fixed, the government usually attempts to keep it unchanged for some time.[2] However, sometimes economic circumstances force the government to change the value of the exchange rate. A reduction in the official value of a currency is called a **devaluation**; an increase in the official value is called a **revaluation**. The devaluation of a fixed exchange rate is analogous to the *depreciation* of a flexible exchange rate; both involve a reduction in the currency's value. Conversely, a revaluation is analogous to an *appreciation*.

**devaluation** a reduction in the official value of a currency (in a fixed exchange rate system)

**revaluation** an increase in the official value of a currency (in a fixed exchange rate system)

**overvalued exchange rate** an exchange rate that has an officially fixed value greater than its fundamental value

**undervalued exchange rate** an exchange rate that has an officially fixed value less than its fundamental value

Example 29.6 uses the demand and supply model to illustrate how exchange rates are fixed and the problems associated with maintaining an official exchange rate at a level different from the its fundamental value. When the officially fixed value of an exchange rate is *greater* than its fundamental value, the exchange rate is said to be **overvalued**. The official value of an exchange rate can also be *lower* than its fundamental value, in which case the exchange rate is said to be **undervalued**.

### Example 29.6 Fixing the euro–sterling exchange rate

Let us consider an illustrative case in which the United Kingdom fixes the value of sterling against the euro, perhaps in preparation for eventual membership of the Eurosystem. We will assume that the demand for and supply of *sterling* in the foreign exchange market are

$$\text{Demand} = 25{,}000 - 3{,}000e$$

$$\text{Supply} = 17{,}000 + 2{,}000e$$

where $e$ is the nominal exchange rate measured in euros per pound sterling. Note that in this example sterling is the *domestic currency* and the euro is the *foreign currency*. Hence the nominal exchange rate is the value of £1 in terms of euros, or the amount of the foreign currency required to buy one unit of the domestic currency. This is the same definition as in Example

[2] There are exceptions to this statement. Some countries employ a *crawling peg system*, under which the exchange rate is fixed at a value that changes in a pre-announced way over time. For example, the government may announce that the value of the fixed exchange rate will fall 2 per cent each year. Other countries use a *target zone* system, in which the exchange rate is allowed to deviate by a small amount from its fixed value. To focus on the key issues, we shall assume that the exchange rate is fixed at a single value for a protracted period.

29.2, except that in that example the euro is the domestic currency and sterling the foreign currency. In both cases the nominal exchange rates is defined as the amount of the foreign currency required to buy one unit of the domestic currency.

To find the fundamental value of sterling, equate the demand and supply for sterling:

$$25{,}000 - 3{,}000e = 17{,}000 + 2{,}000e$$

Solving for $e$, we get

$$8{,}000 = 5{,}000e$$

$$e = 1.60$$

So the fundamental value of the exchange rate is €1.60 per pound sterling, or £1 = €1.60. We will assume that the UK authorities decide to fix the euro value of sterling at €1.60. One possible reason for doing this is that the United Kingdom has decided to adopt the euro as its currency and wishes to fix the exchange rate at its fundamental value to facilitate a smooth transition toward full membership of the Eurosystem. We shall refer to this fixed rate as the *official* exchange rate. As the official rate equals the fundamental or equilibrium rate this illustration of a fixed exchange rate is clearly identical to a flexible exchange rate. Why? Because the official rate is just sufficient to equate the demand for and supply of sterling and clear the foreign exchange market. Now suppose that this situation is disturbed by a fall in the demand for sterling. For example, low economic growth in countries such as France and Germany may lead to a decline in the demand for British goods and services in these countries. As foreign firms and households are purchasing fewer British exports their demand for sterling will decline. Suppose that with supply unchanged, the new demand for sterling is given by

$$\text{Demand} = 24{,}500 - 3{,}000e$$

(note that for any value of $e$ the demand for sterling is reduced by 500). To find the new fundamental value of sterling we equate this new demand to supply.

$$24{,}500 - 3{,}000e = 17{,}000 + 2{,}000e$$

Solving for $e$, we get

$$7{,}500 = 5{,}000e$$

$$e = 1.50$$

Hence the fundamental value of sterling has fallen from £1 = €1.60 to £1 = €1.50. Figure 29.6 provides an illustration of these changes. The curves *D* and *S* represent the initial demand and supply curves. Equilibrium is established at point *A* and the fundamental exchange rate is 1.60. The decline in the demand for sterling is illustrated by a leftward shift in the demand curve to *D'* and a new equilibrium at point *B* determining the lower equilibrium exchange rate at 1.50. The UK authorities could, of course, react to this situation by devaluing the official exchange rate to bring it into line with the new fundamental rate of £1 = €1.50. However, we shall assume that despite the change in the fundamental exchange rate the authorities decide against devaluation and opt to hold the official exchange rate at £1 = €1.60. Why might they decide against devaluation? One reason is that, other things being equal, a devalued currency results in higher import prices which may lead to inflationary pressures in the domestic economy. More generally, once governments start to follow a fixed exchange rate policy they are often reluctant to devalue their currency because the media and opposition politicians may interpret it as a policy failure leading to a loss of government credibility. Finance ministers do not like appearing on TV to explain why they have devalued the national currency. In either case, we shall assume that the official rate is held above the fundamental rate. That is, the euro–sterling exchange rate is *overvalued*.

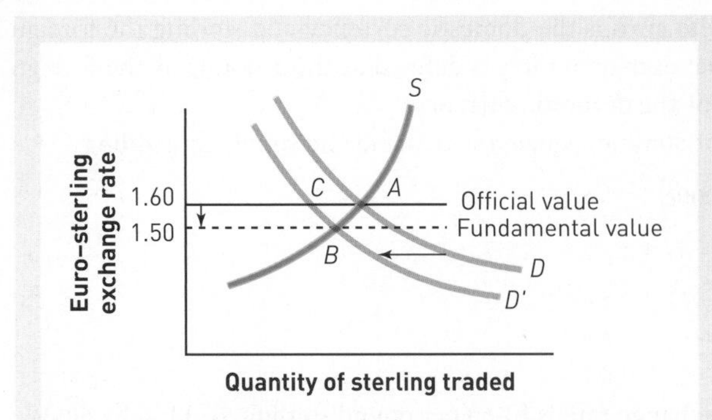


**Figure 29.6 An Overvalued Exchange Rate.** The initial demand for and supply of sterling are given by the curves *D* and *S*. Market equilibrium is at *A* and the initial value of the fundamental exchange rate is £1 = €1.60, which coincides with the official value. Due to a fall in British exports foreigners demand less sterling, shifting the demand curve to *D'*, establishing a new equilibrium at *B* and a lower fundamental exchange rate of £1 = €1.50. To avoid a devaluation the authorities maintain the official rate at £1 = €1.60. As the official rate is now greater than the fundamental rate, sterling is overvalued. To maintain the exchange rate, above its fundamental value the Central Bank must purchase sterling in the quantity *CA* each period.

What problems does an overvalued exchange rate pose for the UK authorities? Figure 29.6 shows that at the official exchange rate of £1 = €1.60, the private sector supply of sterling (point *A*) exceeds the private sector demand (point *C* on *D'*). Hence there is an excess supply of sterling in the foreign exchange market equal to the length of the line segment *CA*. We can calculate the value of this excess supply by substituting $e = 1.60$ into our demand and supply equations for *D'* and *S*.

$$\text{Demand} = 24{,}500 - 3{,}000 \times 1.60 = 19{,}700$$

$$\text{Supply} = 17{,}000 + 2{,}000 \times 1.60 = 20{,}200$$

$$\text{Excess supply} = 20{,}200 - 19{,}700 = 500$$

If demand and supply are measured in millions of pounds, the excess supply of sterling is £500 million per period.With a flexible exchange rate excess supply would result in the market price falling toward its equilibrium level. In this case the excess supply of sterling would force the exchange rate down to its fundamental level of £1 = €1.50 and establish an equilibrium at point *B* in Fig. 29.6. How can the authorities prevent this from happening? One possibility is that the United Kingdom could try to maintain its overvalued exchange rate by restricting international transactions. Imposing quotas on imports and prohibiting domestic households and firms from acquiring foreign assets would effectively reduce the supply of sterling to the foreign exchange market, raising the fundamental value of the currency. However, restrictions of this type are illegal within the European Union. Also, restrictions on trade and capital flows are extremely costly to the economy, because they reduce the gains from specialisation and trade and deny domestic households and firms access to foreign capital markets. Thus, a policy of restricting international transactions, even if permitted, to maintain a fixed exchange rate is likely to do more harm than good.

More realistically, to keep sterling from falling below its official value of 1.60, the UK authorities must purchase an amount of sterling equal to the excess supply of £500 million in each period. If the government followed this strategy, then at the official exchange rate of £1 = €1.60, the total demand for sterling would consist of private demand at point *C* in Fig. 29.6, or 19,700 plus official demand *CA*, or 500, and equal the private supply (point *A*, 20,200). So long as the authorities continue to purchase 500 per period the exchange rate will be held constant at its official rate 1.60. This situation is analogous to government attempts to keep the price of a commodity, such as grain or milk, above its market level. To maintain an official price of grain that is above the market-clearing price, the government must stand ready to purchase the excess supply of grain forthcoming at the official price. In the same way, to keep the 'price' of its currency above the market-clearing level, the government must buy the excess supply at the official price.

**international reserves** foreign currency assets held by a Central Bank for the purpose of purchasing the domestic currency in the foreign exchange market

To be able to purchase its own currency and maintain an overvalued exchange rate, the government (usually the Central Bank) must hold foreign currency assets, called **international reserves**, or simply *reserves*.

**balance-of-payments deficit** the net decline in a country's stock of international reserves over a year

**balance-of-payments surplus** the net increase in a country's stock of international reserves over a year

For example, the Bank of England may hold euro deposits in German banks or German government debt, which it can sell for euros to buy sterling in the foreign exchange market as needed. Because a country with an overvalued exchange rate must use part of its reserves to support the value of its currency in each period, over time its available reserves will decline. The net decline in a country's stock of international reserves over a year is called its **balance-of-payments deficit**. Conversely, if a country experiences a net increase in its international reserves over the year, the increase is called its **balance-of-payments surplus**.

In Example 29.6, maintaining the official euro–sterling exchange rate at a level above the fundamental value means that the United Kingdom will experience a balance-of-payments deficit equal to £500 million per period. As this deficit is financed by using reserves to buy sterling it is also the amount by which the Bank of England's stock of foreign exchange reserves will fall in each period. Although the Bank can maintain an overvalued exchange rate for a time by offering to buy back its own currency at the official price, there is a limit to this strategy, since no country's stock of international reserves is infinite. Eventually the Central Bank will run out of reserves. When this happens the Central Bank can no longer buy the excess supply of its currency and the fixed exchange rate will collapse. As we shall see next, the collapse of a fixed exchange rate can be quite sudden and dramatic.

**Exercise 29.5**

Repeat Example 29.6 but this time assume that after the fall in net exports the new demand for sterling is 24,000 – 3,000*e*. If the official exchange rate is fixed at £1.60 what do you conclude about the relationship between the degree of currency overvaluation and the resulting balance-of-payments deficit?

**Exercise 29.6**

Repeat Example 29.6 but this time assume an *increase* in British net exports and a higher demand for sterling given by 25,500 – 3,000*e*. What action must the Bank of England take to maintain the official exchange rate £1 = €1.60?

## Speculative attacks

**speculative attack** a massive selling of domestic currency assets by financial investors

A government's attempt to maintain an overvalued exchange rate can be ended quickly and unexpectedly by the onset of a **speculative attack**. A speculative attack involves massive selling of domestic currency assets by both domestic and foreign financial investors. For example, in a speculative attack on sterling, financial investors would attempt to get rid of any *financial assets* – stocks, bonds and deposits in banks – *denominated in sterling*. A speculative attack is most likely to occur when financial investors fear that an overvalued currency will soon be devalued, since in a devaluation, financial assets denominated in the domestic currency suddenly become worth much less in terms of other currencies. Ironically, speculative attacks, which are usually prompted by *fear* of devaluation, may turn out to be the cause of devaluation. Thus a speculative attack may actually be a *self-fulfilling prophecy*.

The effects of a speculative attack are shown in Fig. 29.7 which continues the story told in Fig. 29.6. The supply and demand for sterling are indicated by the curves marked $S$ and $D'$, implying a fundamental value of sterling of 1.50 euros per pound. As before, the official value of the sterling is £1 = £1.60 – greater than the fundamental value – so sterling is *overvalued*. To maintain the official rate at 1.60, the Bank of England must use its international reserves to *continually* buy back sterling, in the amount corresponding to the line segment *CA* in Fig. 29.7.

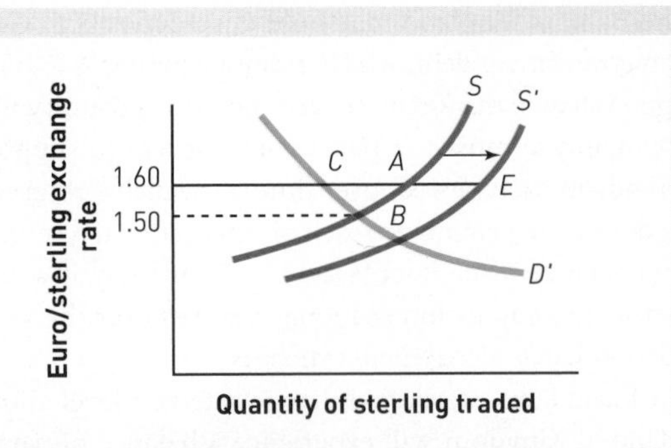


**Figure 29.7 A Speculative Attack on Sterling.** Initially, sterling is overvalued at €1.60 per £1. To maintain this official exchange rate the Central Bank must buy sterling in the amount *CA* per period. Fearing devaluation, financial investors launch a speculative attack selling sterling-denominated assets and supply additional sterling to the foreign exchange market. As a result, the supply curve for sterling shifts from *S* to *S'*, lowering the fundamental value further and forcing the Central Bank to buy sterling in the amount *CE* to maintain the official exchange rate at 1.60. This more rapid loss of reserves may lead the Central Bank to devalue sterling.

Suppose, though, that financial investors fear that the United Kingdom may soon devalue its currency, perhaps because the international reserves are getting dangerously low. If sterling were to be devalued from its official value of £1 = €1.60 to its fundamental value of £1 = €1.50, then a 1 million sterling investment, worth €1.6 million at the official exchange rate, would suddenly be worth only €1.5 million. To try to avoid these losses, financial investors will sell their sterling-denominated assets and offer the sterling proceeds on the foreign exchange market to buy assets denominated in other currencies. The resulting flood of sterling into the market will shift the supply curve of sterling to the right, from *S* to *S'* in Fig. 29.7. Effectively, speculators are being offered a one-way bet. If sterling is devalued they gain by repurchasing sterling assets at the lower exchange rate. If sterling is not devalued, the value of assets in their portfolios will not change. For example, if a speculator sells assets worth £1 million, or €1.60 million, at the official exchange rate they can repurchase these assets for €1.50 million if the exchange rate is devalued to £1 = €1.50. Alternatively, if the devaluation does not happen the value of the speculators' investment remains constant at €1.60 or £1 million.

This speculative attack creates a serious problem for the British authorities. Prior to the attack, maintaining the value of the sterling required the Central Bank to spend each period an amount of international reserves corresponding to the line segment *CA*. Now suddenly the Central Bank must spend a larger quantity of reserves, equal to the distance *CE* in Fig. 29.7, to maintain the fixed exchange rate. These extra reserves are needed to purchase the sterling being sold by panicky financial investors. In practice, such speculative attacks often force a devaluation by reducing the Central Bank's reserves to the point where further defence of the fixed exchange rate is considered hopeless. Thus a speculative attack ignited by fears of devaluation may actually end up producing the very devaluation that was feared.

## Exchange rate systems

Historically, relatively small countries have independently fixed the values of their currencies against the currency of a major trading partner. Argentina and Hong Kong have pegged against the US dollar while CEE transition economies have attempted to maintain stable currency values against the German Mark and now the euro. Likewise, between the foundation of the State in 1922 and 1979 the Irish authorities maintained a fixed one-to-one exchange rate between the Irish pound and sterling. In these cases the responsibility for maintaining the fixed exchange rate normally rests with the smaller country and the fixed exchange rate policy is rarely the result of a co-operative agreement between the two countries concerned. To protect international trade and promote economic integration, countries in Western Europe have also favoured fixed exchange rates between their currencies. However, rather than follow independent exchange rate policies European countries attempted to maintain stable currency values by collectively agreeing to operate a *fixed-exchange system*.

Economic naturalists 29.3 and 29.4 describe two important exchange rate systems – the Bretton Woods System, which included most of the world's major currencies, and the European Monetary System (EMS) which lasted from 1979 to the introduction of the euro in 1999.

## Economic naturalist 29.3 The Bretton Woods exchange rate system

### The US dollar as a key reserve currency

In July 1944 representatives from forty-four countries met in the town of Bretton Woods, New Hampshire, with the aim of restoring order to the postwar international monetary system. Following prolonged debate, they finally agreed that the best way forward was to adopt a fixed-exchange rate system proposed by the United States. The new regime was named the **Bretton Woods system** and was to be administered by a new international institution called the International Monetary Fund or IMF (the IMF is discussed, later in the chapter).

**Bretton Woods system** an exchange rate system centred on the US dollar

The Bretton Woods exchange rate system was centred on the US dollar. All participating countries were assigned a *central* or *parity value* against the dollar and agreed to maintain the actual exchange rate within ±1 per cent of this central parity. Hence if the British pound's central value was £1 = $5 the Bank of England would be expected to maintain the actual dollar–sterling exchange rate within the range $5 ± 1 per cent or $4.95–$5.05. Note that this permitted the exchange rate between currencies other than the dollar to deviate by up to ±2 per cent. If, for example, the British pound were to appreciate by 1 per cent against the dollar while the French franc simultaneously depreciated by 1 per cent, then the pound would have appreciated by 2 per cent against the franc. Once currencies approached the outer limits of the permitted fluctuation range their Central Banks were required to use international reserves to buy or sell their currency in order to keep the actual exchange rate within the permitted fluctuation band. To work smoothly, this required an adequate supply of liquidity in the form of *international reserves*. Most international reserves were held in dollars or gold but only the dollar was convertible against gold at a fixed price of $35 per ounce. To obtain gold, other Central Banks had first to acquire dollars and purchase gold at the fixed price. This made the dollar equivalent to gold and greatly increased the liquidity or the supply of reserves available to the international financial system. The Bretton Woods system also recognised that currencies may become undervalued or overvalued relative to their parity values and permitted realignments or changes in the parity exchange rates. One of the most dramatic devaluations was that of the British pound in November 1967 when the Prime Minister Harold Wilson famously told his electorate 'the pound in your pocket has not been devalued!'

The Bretton Woods system was anchored on the US dollar and its success depended on the dollar's stability. As the key reserve currency it was essential that the dollar should be in adequate supply to provide the liquidity necessary for Central Banks to maintain their currencies within the agreed bands of fluctuation. This was generally the case between the end of the Second World War and the mid-

1960s. Over this period America and most continental European countries achieved steady growth and growing economic prosperity. However, for the system to work smoothly it was essential that the dollar should not be undersupplied or oversupplied. A dollar shortage would reduce liquidity, putting downward pressure on the dollar–gold price, leading to a possible revaluation of the dollar, or a cut in the official gold price of $35 per ounce. Conversely, a dollar surplus put would put upward pressure on the dollar–gold price, leading to a possible devaluation of the dollar, or a rise in the official gold price. In the event it was the latter that led to the collapse of the Bretton Woods exchange rate system in the early 1970s.

Following more than a decade of relative stability American macroeconomic policy changed dramatically in the mid-1960s when government expenditures started to rise at an alarming rate. There were two reasons for this. First intensification of the Vietnam War led to large increases in government military purchases. Second, President Johnson's 'Great Society' programmes greatly increased government expenditures on public education, urban renewal and welfare services. The result of this fiscal expansion was a rise in US inflation and, at fixed nominal exchange rates a real appreciation of the dollar and a loss of competitiveness leading to a decline in US net exports. By the early 1970s the United States was experiencing a significant balance-of-payments deficit, leading to an excess supply of dollars on the world's foreign exchange markets. As with any other commodity an excess supply of dollars will eventually lead to a fall in its market price. In the case of the dollar, this meant an increase in the dollar–gold price and devaluation against *all currencies* in the Bretton Woods system. Private speculators started to sell dollars and buy gold in anticipation that the official dollar–gold price would be increased. This expectation was fulfilled in December 1971 when, at the Smithsonian Institution in Washington, DC, the member countries agreed to increase the gold price to $38 per ounce and devalue the dollar by 8 per cent against the other currencies. Unfortunately the Smithsonian Agreement failed to restore confidence in the system. The US balance of payments deficit continued and speculation mounted against the dollar, resulting in an additional 10 per cent devaluation in February 1973. Despite this, speculative attacks continued and the Bretton Woods system survived only because Central Banks in Europe and Asia were soaking up the excess supply by continuously buying dollars to prevent its value from falling further. This proved unsustainable and in March 1973 the Bretton Woods parities were abandoned. Since then, the world's major currencies such as sterling, the yen – and, since 1999, the euro – have been floating against the dollar.

### The International Monetary Fund

The International Monetary Fund (IMF) was established after the Second World War. An international agency, the IMF is controlled by a 24-member Executive Board. Eight Executive Board members represent individual countries (China, France, Germany, Japan, Russia, Saudi Arabia, the United Kingdom and the United States); the other 16 members each represent a group of countries. A managing director oversees the IMF's operations and its approximately 2,600 employees.

The original purpose of the IMF was to help manage the Bretton Woods system. Under Bretton Woods, the IMF's principal role was to *lend international reserves* to member countries who needed them so that those countries could maintain their exchange rates at the official parity values. However, by 1973 the United States, the United Kingdom, Germany and most other industrial nations had abandoned fixed exchange rates for flexible rates, leaving the IMF to find a new mission. Since 1973 the IMF has been involved primarily in lending to developing countries. It lent heavily to Mexico when that country experienced speculative attacks in 1994, and it made loans to East Asian countries during the 1997–98 crisis. Other countries that have received large IMF loans include Russia and Brazil.

The IMF's performance in recent crises has been controversial. Many observers credit the IMF with helping Mexico, the East Asian nations and others to recover quickly from the effects of speculative attacks and contend that the IMF plays a vital role in maintaining international economic stability. However, some critics have charged that the IMF has required recipients of its loans to follow economic policies – such as tight monetary policies and fiscal cutbacks – that have turned out to be ill-advised. Others have claimed that the IMF's loans help foreign financial investors and the richest people in the countries receiving loans, rather than the average person. (The IMF has been severely embarrassed by reports that much of the nearly $5 billion it lent to Russia in 1998 disappeared into the bank accounts of unscrupulous citizens, including gangsters.)

The IMF has also come into conflict with the *World Bank*, a separate international institution that was set up at about the same time as the IMF. The World Bank (or IBRD), whose mission is to provide long-term loans to help poor nations develop their economies, has complained that IMF interventions in poor countries interfered with World Bank programmes and objectives. In 2000, a report commissioned by the US Congress recommended reducing the IMF's powers (as well as, incidentally, those of the World Bank). The debate over the IMF's proper role will no doubt continue.

## Economic naturalist 29.4 The European Monetary System

Following the collapse of the Bretton Woods system European governments attempted to maintain some degree of exchange rate stability by keeping their dollar exchange rates within ±2.25 per cent of the old Bretton Woods parity rates, a system known as 'The Snake'. Effectively this permitted the exchange rate between any two European currencies to deviate by up to 9 per cent. If currency *A* moves from the bottom to the top of its band against the dollar, an appreciation of 4.5 per cent, while currency *B* simultaneously moves in the opposite direction, a 4.5 per cent depreciation, the cumulative result is that *A* has appreciated by 9 per cent against *B*. Some countries considered a potential ±9 per cent fluctuation margin to be excessive and the system was modified to limit the potential fluctuation range between any two currencies to 4.5 per cent – 'The Snake in the Tunnel'. However, failure to co-ordinate policies and different responses to the 1973 oil price shock meant that these systems were doomed to failure. As can be seen from Fig. 29.2, over the six years following the oil price shock the French franc depreciated by approximately 30 per cent against the German Mark and the Italian lira by more than 50 per cent. Fearing that this exchange rate instability could damage international trade and threaten the process of European integration, France and Germany proposed a new exchange rate system designed to restore order and stability to the foreign exchange markets and establish a *zone of monetary stability* in Europe. In 1978 the nine member states of the then EC reached agreement and the new **European Monetary System (EMS)** was launched in March 1979. The key features of the EMS were the **European Currency Unit (ECU)**, the **Exchange Rate Mechanism (ERM)** and *realignments*.

**European Monetary System (EMS)** the system by which EU countries attempted to fix exchange rates, 1979–98

**European Currency Unit (ECU)** composite or 'basket' currency including specific amounts of EMS currencies

**Exchange Rate Mechanism (ERM)** countries in the ERM maintained their bilateral exchange rates within an agreed band of fluctuation around the central rate

- *The European Currency Unit* The ECU was a composite or 'basket' currency that included specific amounts of all EMS currencies (German Mark, French franc, Irish pound, etc.). The contribution of each currency reflected the economic importance of the different countries. Hence, the German Mark accounted for over 30 per cent of the ECU while the Irish pound contributed just over 1 per cent. Each currency was assigned a central value against the ECU which was used to fix *bilateral central values* between pairs of currencies. For example, suppose the ECU central rates for the Deutsche Mark (DM) and the French franc (FF) are

  1 ECU = 2.5 DM and 1 ECU = 6.0 FF

  Then 2.5 DM has the same value as 6 FF:

  2.5 DM = 6.0 FF

  Dividing both sides by 2.5 gives the bilateral central rate for the DM in terms of the FF:

  1 DM = 2.4 FF

  Alternatively dividing both sides by 2.4 gives the bilateral central rate for the FF in terms of the DM:

  0.4167 DM = 1 FF

  Once the central rates against the ECU are determined we can calculate the bilateral central rates between any pair of currencies. This matrix of EMS bilateral central rates was known as *The Parity Grid*.

- *The Exchange Rate Mechanism* Participation in the ERM required countries to maintain their bilateral exchange rates within an agreed band of fluctuation around the central rate. For most countries this band was set at ± 2.25 per cent around the central rate. Hence, if the FF–DM central rate is 1 DM = 2.4 FF, then Germany would be required to maintain the actual exchange with the range 2.4 + 2.25 per cent (2.2414) and 2.4 – 2.25 per cent (2.34). Belgium, Denmark, France, Germany, Ireland, the Netherlands and Luxemburg adopted the ±2.25 per cent fluctuation band while Italy operated in a wider ±6 per cent band. The United Kingdom, while a member of the EMS and a contributor to the ECU basket, opted out of the ERM and maintained a flexible exchange rate throughout the 1980s.

- *Realignments* Realignments were the method by which countries could change their central rates against the ECU and therefore against other currencies in the ERM. In effect realignment usually meant a *devaluation* or *revaluation* of the currency or currencies concerned.

Figure 29.8 illustrates a typical realignment. For purposes of illustration we assume that the exchange rate in question is that between the Italian lira and the German DM. For simplicity we assume that the lira's central rate in terms of DMs is initially set at its fundamental value or $e^*$ in Fig. 29.8. The solid lines directly above and below $e^*$ determine the width of the lira's permitted fluctuation band against the DM. This fluctuation band is labelled *B* in the Fig. 29.8. So long as Italy maintains the actual exchange rate within this band it is fulfilling its ERM commitments. Now suppose that, as was often the case, Italian inflation increases relative to German inflation. Eventually this excess inflation will make Italian goods less competitive, leading to a fall in net exports and a lower demand for the lira in the foreign

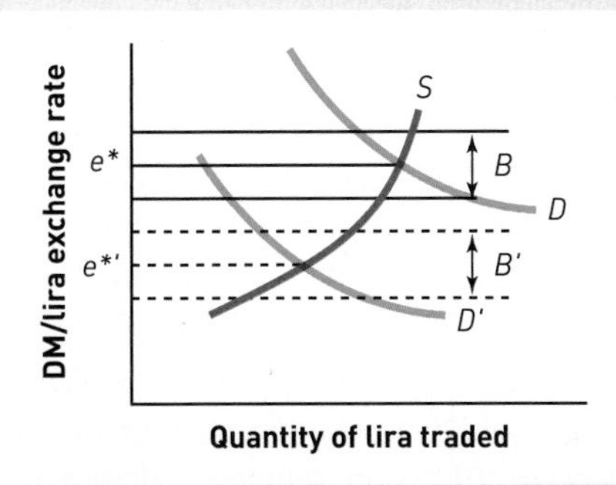


**Figure 29.8 EMS Realignment.** The lira's central rate in terms of DM is initially set at its fundamental value or $e^*$ and its permitted fluctuation band is $B$. If the Italian inflation rises relative to German inflation Italian goods become less competitive leading to a decline in net exports and a shift in the demand curve for lira from $D$ to $D'$ establishing a new fundamental value at $e^{*\prime}$. As the actual exchange rate must remain within $B$ the lira is overvalued and open to speculative attack. The realignment reduces the central rate to $e^{*\prime}$. As the actual exchange rate must be within the new fluctuation band $B'$, the lira is effectively devalued.

exchange market. This is illustrated by a leftward shift in the demand curve from $D$ to $D'$ and a decline in the lira's fundamental value from $e^*$ to $e^{*\prime}$. Note that the new equilibrium value lies outside the lira's permitted range of fluctuation against the DM. So long as the lira remains within its ERM band $B$ it will be overvalued because the actual rate will exceed its fundamental value. We have seen that overvalued currencies can be open to speculative attack, leading to uncertainty and turmoil in the foreign exchange markets. In Figure 29.8 the fall in the demand for the lira will push the actual exchange rate towards the bottom of its permitted fluctuation band and encourage speculators to start selling lira in anticipation that it will not be able to stay within the band. To accommodate these differences in inflation rates and forestall speculation, the EMS permitted a realignment of the currency's central rate. In Fig. 29.8 a realignment might reduce the lira's central rate to the new equilibrium value $e^{*\prime}$ with a new fluctuation band $B'$ which has the same width as $B$ but is located around the lower central rate. After the realignment takes place the actual DM–lira exchange rate will have to drop into $B'$ implying a devaluation of the lira. The intention was that so long as realignments could be agreed quickly the incidence and strength of speculative attacks might be minimised.

The history of the EMS can be divided into three distinct periods which we shall label 'soft', 'hard' and 'flexible'.

- *The soft EMS: 1979–86* The early years of the EMS were characterised by a lack of policy co-ordination among the participating countries. Germany, committed to price stability, favoured tight monetary policies while other countries such as France and Italy were more concerned with unemployment and followed more expansionary monetary policies. This lack of co-ordination resulted in large inflation differentials. Between 1979 and 1985 German inflation averaged 4 per cent per annum compared with 10 per cent for France and 15 per cent for Italy. As a result the high-inflation countries experienced continuous balance of payments difficulties, requiring frequent realignments to correct for the competitive losses resulting from excess inflation. Between September 1979 and August 1986 the Italian lira was devalued five times and the French franc four times. The low-inflation DM, on the other hand, was revalued on six occasions. The cumulative effect was that the lira lost almost 50 per cent of its value against the DM and the franc 30 per cent. Also, the financial markets were quick to learn that persistent inflation differentials would lead to realignments and launched frequent attacks against the high-inflation currencies. Over these years, the EMS was far from being the zone of monetary stability intended by its designers.

- *The hard EMS: 1987–92* By 1986 there was common agreement that the EMS could deliver stability only if the participating countries could agree on a high level of policy co-ordination. A major problem in finding a co-operative solution was that Germany was unlikely to moderate its strong anti-inflationary policies to accommodate more inflation-prone countries such as France and Italy. Germany may have wanted a more stable EMS but not at the price of weakening its commitment to price stability. The solution, although not publicly announced, was to grant Germany leadership of the EMS. Germany was free to determine its own monetary policy and the other countries followed. Effectively the other Central Banks acted as 'Bundesbank clones'. The move to German leadership resulted in a much greater convergence of inflation rates within the EMS. Over 1987–91 the average German inflation rate was just over 2 per cent per annum but the average French rate fell to 3 per cent and the Italian rate to 5.6 per cent. Realignments and speculative attacks became very infrequent and even the British joined the ERM in 1991. Anchored on German monetary policy the ERM appeared to be fulfilling its potential as a zone of monetary stability. However, things were not what they seemed and in mid-September 1992 speculators launched a series of massive attacks against several EMS currencies, and especially against sterling and the lira. The reasons behind these attacks will be discussed more fully in Economic naturalist 29.6. In essence, they resulted from a growing policy conflict between Germany and the other large countries. The fall of the Berlin Wall and German reunification was accompanied by a dramatic increase in government spending and an inflationary surge. Committed to price stability the Bundesbank increased German interest rates to offset the rise in inflation. As Germany had effective leadership of the EMS, higher DM interest rates were transmitted across the other participating countries. This, however, coincided with recession in the United Kingdom and Italy. These countries required lower interest rates to combat recession and increasing unemployment, but their commitment to maintain a stable exchange rate with Germany meant that they had to accept higher rather than lower interest rates. International financial markets became convinced that the United Kingdom and Italy would have to choose between using monetary policy to stabilise their economies and their commitment to maintaining a stable exchange rate. They bet heavily on the first and massive speculation forced sterling and the lira to leave the ERM and depreciate against the DM. At least two important lessons can be learned from this period:
  - First, a fixed exchange rate system can work properly only if all countries *face the same problems and require the same policies*. Once these problems differ, with some countries requiring high interest rates to fight inflation and the others needing lower interest rates to offset recession, the resulting policy

conflict will eventually lead to one of the groups breaking free and following the monetary policy best suited to their own economies.
- Second, if the goal is to achieve full monetary integration and an end to exchange rate instability the obvious path is to *full monetary union*, which completely eliminates national currencies and, by definition, exchange rates.

- *The flexible ERM: 1993–99* The speculative attacks that started in mid-1992 continued periodically throughout the first half of 1993. In order to reduce the incidence of these attacks the EMS countries agreed to replace the narrow ±2.25 per cent fluctuation band with a much wider ±15 per cent band in August 1993. The introduction of these wider bands greatly reduced incentives for speculative attacks. For speculators to gain, the currency must be devalued, which in the ERM meant that the actual exchange rate would jump from its initial fluctuation band into a lower band. For example, in Fig. 29.8 so long as the Italian authorities attempt to keep the lira within the initial fluctuation band $B$ it will remain overvalued relative to its fundamental value $e^{*\prime}$, providing speculators with an incentive to continue selling the currency in the expectation that the central rate will be realigned to $e^{*\prime}$. Once this happens the actual exchange rate must jump into the new band $B'$ and the currency will be devalued. However, the wider the band the greater the probability that the new equilibrium value will be within the initial fluctuation band. When this is the case the Central Bank does not have to defend the currency. It can simply let the exchange rate depreciate toward the lower fundamental value and speculators are not presented with an incentive to sell the currency in the expectation that it will have to be realigned.

**Exercise 29.7** Redraw Fig. 29.8 but this time make the initial fluctuation band $B$ wide enough so that it includes the lower fundamental value $e^{*\prime}$. Why might this reduce the probability of a speculative attack against the lira?

The EMS came to an end on 31 December 1998 when the euro replaced the ECU. Some months prior to this the eleven countries committed to membership of the Eurosystem had agreed to irrevocably fix the exchange rates between their currencies. Although euro notes and coin did not appear for another two years the system of irrevocably fixed exchange rates meant that national currencies were effectively eliminated on 1 January 1999. At the same time the ECB assumed full responsibility for monetary policy within the entire Eurosystem. Introduction of the single monetary policy meant that policy co-ordination between Central Banks would no longer be an issue. The policy decided by the ECB would apply to all countries in the Eurosystem irrespective of the needs of individual economies. In Chapter 30 we shall see that full monetary union does not necessarily eliminate the problem of different countries', requiring different policies and that the single or 'one-size-fits-all' monetary policy may not be optimum for all countries.

## Monetary policy and the fixed exchange rate

We have seen that there is no really satisfactory way of maintaining a fixed exchange rate above its fundamental value for an extended period. A Central Bank can maintain an overvalued exchange rate for a time by using international reserves to buy up the excess supply of its currency in the foreign exchange market. But a country's international reserves are limited and may eventually be exhausted by the attempt to keep the exchange rate artificially high. Moreover, speculative attacks often hasten the collapse of an overvalued exchange rate.

An alternative to trying to maintain an overvalued exchange rate is to take actions that increase the exchange rate's fundamental value. If the exchange rate's fundamental value can be raised enough to equal its official value, then the overvaluation problem will be eliminated. The most effective way to change the exchange rate's fundamental value is through *monetary policy*. As we saw earlier in the chapter, a tight monetary policy that raises the real interest rate will increase the demand for the domestic currency, as domestic assets become more attractive to foreign financial investors. Increased demand for the currency will, in turn, raise its fundamental value.

The use of monetary policy to support a fixed exchange rate can be illustrated by referring to Fig. 29.6. With the decline in the demand for sterling, demand and supply are given by the curves *D*' and *S*, so the fundamental value of sterling equals €1.50 – less than the official value of €1.60 – and sterling is overvalued. This time, however, the Central Bank uses monetary policy to eliminate the overvaluation problem. To do so, the Central Bank increases the domestic real interest rate, making sterling denominated assets more attractive to foreign financial investors and raising the demand curve for sterling from *D*' back to its initial position. After this increase in the demand for sterling, the fundamental value of sterling equals the officially fixed value, as can be seen in Fig. 29.6. Because sterling is no longer overvalued, it can be maintained at its fixed value without loss of international reserves or fear of speculative attack. However, as will be illustrated by Economic naturalist 29.6, this policy may not succeed if international investors are totally convinced that the currency may be devalued. Conversely, an easing of monetary policy (a lower real interest rate) could be used to remedy an undervaluation, in which the official exchange rate is below the fundamental value.

Although monetary policy can be used to keep the fundamental value of the exchange rate equal to the official value, using monetary policy in this way has one very important implication: if monetary policy is used to set the fundamental value of the exchange rate equal to the official value, it is *no longer available for stabilising the domestic economy*. Suppose, for example, that the domestic economy were suffering a recession due to insufficient aggregate demand and at the same time its exchange rate is overvalued. The combination of recession and an overvalued exchange rate poses a policy dilemma. To combat recession the Central Bank should lower the real interest rate to increase spending and output, but to protect the exchange rate it must *raise* the real interest rate to increase the demand for its currency and eliminate overvaluation. *Clearly, it cannot do both*. This was the dilemma faced by the UK authorities in September 1992. Maintaining a fixed exchange rate with Germany required higher interest rates while fighting recession required the opposite. Speculators bet on the second – and, as we shall see in Economic naturalist 29.6 – won decisively.

Conversely, suppose that the domestic economy were suffering an expansionary gap and at the same time its exchange rate is undervalued. To combat the inflationary pressures associated with an expansionary gap the Central Bank should *increase* the real interest rate to reduce spending, but to protect the exchange rate it must *lower* the real interest rate to reduce the demand for its currency and eliminate undervaluation.

Hence, if officials decide to maintain the fixed exchange rate, they must give up any hope of fighting recessions or inflation by using monetary policy. The fact that a fixed exchange rate limits or eliminates the use of monetary policy for the purpose of stabilising aggregate demand is one of the most important features of a fixed exchange rate system. This relationship between stabilisation policy and exchange rate policy is discussed further in Economic naturalist 29.5.

## Economic naturalist 29.5 The impossible trinity

The principle of the 'impossible trinity' means that a country can choose only two of the following three types of policy: policy independence, a fixed exchange rate and capital mobility. It cannot have all three at the same time. *Policy independence* means that monetary policy can be used to stabilise the domestic economy. For example, when the economy is experiencing a recessionary gap the Central Bank can stimulate aggregate demand by reducing real interest rates. *Fixed exchange rate* means that the Central Bank can maintain a fixed or relatively stable value of the domestic currency against other currencies. *Capital mobility* means that financial investors are free to buy and sell different currencies in any quantity and at any time. In the years following the Second World War, many countries imposed restrictions on capital movement, which prevented domestic investors from selling assets to obtain the foreign currency necessary to purchase assets denominated in another currency. If effective, these restrictions can limit the ability of speculators to force devaluations by selling assets denominated in the currency under attack. For example, in Fig. 29.7 restrictions on capital movement would prohibit investors from selling sterling-denominated assets and prevent the supply curve for sterling shifting from *S* to *S*', thus making it easier for the Central Bank to maintain an overvalued exchange rate. However, we have already noted that restrictions on the free movement of capital can reduce the gains from specialisation and trade and are generally agreed to be harmful to the economy. Also, as part of the Single Market Programme and in preparation for the euro, the European Union prohibited these restrictions from the early 1990s. Recall from Economic naturalist 23.2 that Stage One of EMU required that restrictions on the movement of capital between member states should be abolished. Hence, capital mobility can be taken as a given.

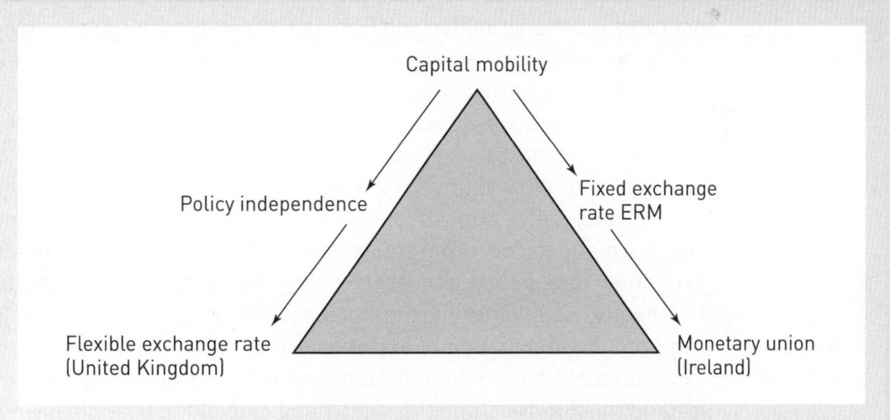


**Figure 29.9 The Impossible Trinity.** Given free movement of capital, countries must choose between policy independence and fixed exchange rates.

Figure 29.9 illustrates the 'impossible trinity'. Free capital mobility is located at the apex or top of the triangle. The bottom corners of the triangle locate the two extremes of completely flexible exchange rates and monetary union. Given capital mobility, the impossible trinity implies that countries must ultimately choose between these two points. To illustrate, consider the exchange rate policies of the United Kingdom and Ireland in the years before the euro was launched. The United Kingdom had removed controls on capital movement in the early 1980s and Ireland in the 1990s. Hence both start at the top of the triangle and must decide which side they wish to move along.

Suppose, as is the case to date, the United Kingdom decides that the Bank of England should retain policy independence – that is, the ability to respond to recessionary or expansionary gaps by reducing or increasing real interest rates. If the Bank were to reduce real interest rates to combat a recession this would also reduce the demand for sterling-denominated assets, leading to a fall in sterling's fundamental exchange rate. Conversely, if the Bank were to fight inflation by raising real interest rates it would also make sterling-denominated assets more attractive, leading to an increased demand for sterling and a rise in the fundamental exchange rate. Hence, given capital mobility, policy independence implies that the United Kingdom must accept a flexible exchange rate. In Fig. 29.9, the United Kingdom has moved along the left-hand side of the triangle giving a combination of capital mobility and a flexible exchange rate. This, to date, has been the UK choice.

Suppose Ireland has different preferences and opts for exchange rate stability by fixing the value of its currency against a leading currency such as the DM. This is what Ireland attempted to do from 1979 to 1999 when it participated in the ERM. To maintain a fixed exchange rate against the DM, the Irish authorities cannot permit Irish interest rates to deviate from German interest rates. If Irish interest rates were to fall below German interest rates, investors would sell Irish assets, which increases the supply of the Irish currency, leading to depreciation. Conversely, if Irish interest rates were to rise above German interest rates, investors would purchase Irish assets, which increases the demand for Irish currency, leading to an appreciation. Hence, to maintain a fixed exchange rate against the DM, Irish interest rates must stay in line with German interest rates, which implies the sacrifice of policy independence. However, we have seen that when economic conditions differ and partner countries require different policies, fixed exchange rate systems are open to speculative attack and difficult to defend when combined with capital mobility. So long as Ireland retained its own currency it had an exchange rate against Germany and any significant deviation from German monetary policy could lead to speculative attacks forcing a change in the official exchange rate. However, when Ireland faced different problems from Germany it needed to modify its exchange rate policy and exert policy independence to stabilise the economy. Ultimately, rigid adherence to an absolutely fixed value for the domestic currency required the elimination of exchange rates by adopting a common currency. In Fig. 29.9 complete elimination of exchange rate instability with Germany required that Ireland must move along the right-hand side of the triangle giving a combination of capital mobility and monetary union.

Economic naturalists 29.6 and 29.7 illustrate what can happen when countries attempt to ignore the constraints imposed by the impossible trinity.

## Economic naturalist 29.6 Breaking the Bank of England: sterling and the 1992 ERM crisis

When the EMS commenced operation in early 1979 the United Kingdom was the only member state to opt out of the ERM which, as we have seen, was a system designed to limit fluctuations between participating currencies. However, in October 1990 the British Prime Minister Margaret Thatcher gave in to pressure from her more pro-European cabinet colleagues and agreed that sterling should participate in the ERM. In terms of Fig. 29.9 the United Kingdom was, for a short time at least, moving down the right-hand side of the triangle. Sterling entered the ERM at a central rate of 2.95 DM per pound sterling (which was probably overvalued) and operated in the wide band, which permitted the exchange rate to fluctuate by ±6 per cent around the central rate. Less than two years later, on Wednesday, 16 September 2002, a series of massive speculative attacks forced sterling and the Italian lira not just to be devalued but to leave the ERM completely. What caused the 1992 ERM crisis and prompted such speculation against these currencies?

Somewhat ironically, the background to the crisis lay in the United States, which had started to experience a severe recession in the late 1980s. The recession spread to several European countries and especially the United Kingdom, where unemployment increased from 7.3 per cent to over 10 per cent between 1989 and 1992. The Federal Reserve (Fed) reacted to the US recession by aggressively cutting interest rates, which resulted in a decline in the three-month money market rate from 8.4 per cent in 1989 to 3.5 per cent in 1991. However, because the British authorities had sacrificed policy independence by joining the ERM they were unable to respond to recession in a similar manner. This situation was further complicated by German reunification, which dramatically increased government spending and created an inflationary surge in the German economy. To moderate the rise in inflation, Germany's Central Bank, the Bundesbank, followed an opposite path to the Fed and sharply increased short-term interest rates. As the other EMS currencies were linked to the DM via the ERM this rise in interest rates spread across the system. The widening differential between European and American interest rates increased the attractiveness of European assets, leading to a higher demand for European currencies and a steady appreciation against the dollar. As the United States accounted for approximately 12 per cent of UK exports, this loss of competitiveness against the dollar was a further blow to the British economy.

By mid-1992 the United Kingdom could be described as a country facing recession and rising unemployment combined with high interest rates and an overvalued currency. Germany, on the other hand, was experiencing an expansionary gap and rising inflation. Maintaining high interest rates and a strong currency may have been the appropriate policy for Germany but not for the United Kingdom, which required lower interest rates and a more competitive exchange rate. However, so long as the United Kingdom maintained its currency link with Germany it could not deviate far from German monetary policy. Britain was now caught on the horns of the impossibility trinity. Given capital mobility, it had to choose between maintaining a fixed exchange rate and using monetary policy to stabilise the domestic economy. As the recession deepened, financial markets became convinced that the British authorities would opt for the latter and launched a massive speculative attack against sterling. At first the Bank of England attempted to defend the exchange rate by buying sterling in the foreign exchange market and on Wednesday, 16 September increased its key lending rate, called the *base interest rate*, from

10 to 12 per cent and threatened a further 3 per cent increase as an incentive for speculators to stop selling sterling. The markets were not convinced and continued to sell large amounts of the British currency in anticipation of devaluation. With reserves falling rapidly the United Kingdom had little choice but to abandon its fixed exchange rate policy and at 7 p.m. that evening the government announced that Britain would leave the ERM and float against the other European currencies. The announced increases in interest rates were reversed and by the end of 1992 sterling had depreciated by 16 per cent against the dollar and by 11 per cent against the DM.

Having driven sterling out of the ERM, the speculators turned their attention to other European economies such as Belgium, France, Italy and Spain which, like the United Kingdom, were experiencing low growth and required lower interest and more competitive exchange rates. The Italian lira was also forced out of the ERM and the Spanish peseta was devalued twice. Speculative attacks continued throughout the first half of 1993 and in August the narrow ±2.25 ERM fluctuation band was abandoned and replaced with a much wider ±15 per cent band. Given this wide range of permitted fluctuation, the ERM was now a closer approximation to a flexible exchange rate system than to a fixed exchange rate system.

The attempt to circumvent the impossible trinity by defending the exchange rate is estimated to have cost the Bank of England £4 billion in reserves. One of the most prominent speculators, George Soros, is thought to have earned up to £0.5 billion from the crisis and became known as 'the man who broke the Bank of England'. Wednesday, 16 September 1992 is sometimes referred to as 'Black Wednesday'. However, for the remaining years of the decade and into the new century the UK economy generally outperformed countries such as France and Germany, leading proponents of flexible exchange rates to call that day 'Golden Wednesday'.

## Economic naturalist 29.7 Ireland's struggle for (economic) independence

When the British pound left the ERM on 16 September 1992 it depreciated strongly against other European currencies and especially the DM. Put another way, the European currencies appreciated against sterling. This caused special problems for Ireland. The United Kingdom was Ireland's most important trading partner, accounting for approximately 30 per cent of Irish exports and 40 per cent of imports. As the Irish pound, initially unaffected by the crisis, still operated in the narrow ±2.25 per cent ERM fluctuation band it followed the DM's appreciation against sterling. On 16 September one Irish pound (IR£) bought 0.973 pounds sterling. By early October the exchange rate had increased to IR£1 = £1.10 and remained well above the one-for-one parity value for the rest of the year, leading to a decline in Ireland's competitiveness *vis-à-vis* its most important trading partner. Irish goods rapidly became more expensive in the United Kingdom with British goods becoming cheaper in Ireland. (You should check this using our definition of the real exchange rate.) This threatened jobs not only in Irish firms exporting to the United Kingdom but also in those competing with British imports on the Irish market. In many cases, these firms operated in relatively labour-intensive sectors such as textiles and food processing. Hence the appreciation of the Irish pound presented a direct threat to Irish jobs and net exports.

The obvious solution was to restore competitiveness by devaluing the Irish pound. Realigning against the DM would have enabled the Irish pound to follow sterling's depreciation and prevent a serious competitive loss against the United Kingdom. This was the unambiguous view taken by foreign exchange markets and, anticipating devaluation, speculators launched an attack on the Irish currency. Capital flowed out of the country, interest rates rose to record levels and the Central Bank of Ireland was forced to use its reserves to purchase ever-increasing quantities of Irish pounds in order to defend its overvalued currency. However, the Irish government, supported by institutions ranging from the Catholic Church to the Congress of Trade Unions, took the opposite view and steadfastly refused to countenance devaluation. The government's stance was politically motivated and reflected a strong ambition that Ireland should be seen as a country fully committed to the European ideal rather than as part of a greater 'sterling zone'. The previous devaluations of the Irish pound, in 1983 and 1986, had followed sustained periods of sterling weakness and the government was determined that the experience would not be repeated. In short, Ireland was, once again, attempting to demonstrate its independence from Britain. Unfortunately political independence does not guarantee economic independence and on 30 January 1993 with the Central Bank's reserves close to exhaustion the Irish pound was devalued by 10 per cent, the largest single devaluation in the history of the ERM. Following the devaluation capital flowed back into the Irish pound and interest rates fell dramatically. When the ERM fluctuation bands were increased to ±15 per cent in August 1993 the Irish authorities used the greater flexibility to their advantage. In periods when sterling was weak against the DM the Irish pound was permitted to follow the British currency by depreciating within the wide band and thereby maintaining competitiveness against the United Kingdom. Clearly a 10 per cent depreciation has very different political connotations from a 10 per cent devaluation!

One important lesson from the Irish experience is that PPP does not hold in the short run. Recall our definition of the real exchange rate as $eP/P^f$. In this case $e$ is the sterling–Irish pound nominal exchange rate, $P$ is the domestic or Irish price level and $P^f$ is the foreign or British price level. If PPP held continuously we would expect to observe a fall in the Irish price level to compensate for the rise in the nominal exchange rate and keep competitiveness constant. However, this did not happen. As the nominal exchange rate appreciated the domestic price level did not decline, leading to a real appreciation of the Irish pound and a severe loss in competitiveness.

## Economic naturalist 29.8 What were the causes and consequences of the East Asian crisis of 1997–98?

From the 1970s the countries of East Asia enjoyed impressive economic growth and stability. But the 'East Asian miracle' seemed to end in 1997, when a wave of speculative attacks hit the region's currencies. Thailand, which had kept a constant value for its currency in terms of the US dollar for more than a decade, was the first to come under attack, but the crisis spread to other countries, including South

Korea, Indonesia and Malaysia. Each of these countries was ultimately forced to devalue its currency. What caused this crisis, and what were its consequences?

Because of the impressive economic record of the East Asian countries, the speculative attacks on their currencies were unforeseen by most policy makers, economists and financial investors. With the benefit of hindsight, however, we can identify some problems in the East Asian economies that contributed to the crisis. Perhaps the most serious problems concerned their *banking systems*. In the decade prior to the crisis, East Asian banks received large inflows of capital from foreign financial investors hoping to profit from the 'East Asian miracle'. Those inflows would have been a boon if they had been well invested but unfortunately many bankers used the funds to make loans to family members, friends or the politically well-connected – a phenomenon that became known as *crony capitalism*. The results were poor returns on investment and defaults by many borrowers. Ultimately, foreign investors realised that the returns to investing in East Asia would be much lower than expected. When they began to sell off their assets, the process snowballed into a fully fledged speculative attack on the East Asian currencies.

Despite assistance by international lenders such as the IMF (see p. 854), the effects of the speculative attacks on the East Asian economies were severe. The prices of assets such as stocks and land plummeted, and there were banking panics in several nations. In an attempt to raise the fundamental values of their exchange rates and stave off additional devaluation, several of the countries increased their real interest rates sharply. However, the rise in real interest rates depressed aggregate demand, contributing to sharp declines in output and rising unemployment.

Fortunately, by 1999 most of the East Asian economies had begun to recover. Still, the crisis impressed the potential dangers of fixed exchange rates quite sharply on the minds of policy makers in developing countries. Another lesson from the crisis is that banking regulations need to be structured so as to promote economically sound lending rather than crony capitalism.

## RECAP Fixed exchange rates

- The value of a *fixed exchange rate* is set by the government. The official value of a fixed exchange rate may differ from its fundamental value, as determined by supply and demand in the foreign exchange market. An exchange rate whose officially fixed value exceeds its fundamental value is *overvalued*; an exchange rate whose officially fixed value is below its fundamental value is *undervalued*.
- For an *overvalued* exchange rate, the quantity of the currency supplied to the foreign exchange market at the official exchange rate exceeds the quantity demanded. The government can maintain an overvalued exchange rate for a time by using its international reserves (foreign currency assets) to purchase the excess supply of its currency. The net decline in a country's stock of international reserves during the year is its balance-of-payments deficit.
- Because a country's international reserves are limited, it cannot maintain an *overvalued* exchange rate indefinitely. Moreover, if financial investors fear an impending devaluation of the exchange rate, they may launch a speculative attack, selling domestic currency assets and supplying large amounts of the country's currency to the foreign exchange market – an action that exhausts the country's reserves even more quickly. Because rapid loss of reserves may force a devaluation, financial investors' fear of devaluation may prove to be a self-fulfilling prophecy.

- A *tight monetary policy*, which increases the real interest rate, raises the demand for the currency and hence its fundamental value. By raising a currency's fundamental value to its official value, tight monetary policies can eliminate the problem of overvaluation and stabilise the exchange rate. However, if monetary policy is used to set the fundamental value of the exchange rate, it is no longer available for stabilising the domestic economy.

## Should exchange rates be fixed or flexible?

Should countries adopt fixed or flexible exchange rates? In briefly comparing the two systems, we shall focus on two major issues: (1) the effects of the exchange rate system on monetary policy and (2) the effects of the exchange rate system on trade and economic integration.

On the issue of monetary policy, we have seen that the type of exchange rate a country has strongly affects the Central Bank's ability to use monetary policy to stabilise the economy. A flexible exchange rate actually strengthens the impact of monetary policy on aggregate demand. But a fixed exchange rate prevents policy makers from using monetary policy to stabilise the economy, because they must instead use it to keep the exchange rate's fundamental value at its official value (or else risk speculative attack).

In large economies such as those of the United States and the Eurosystem, giving up the power to stabilise the domestic economy via monetary policy makes little sense. Thus large economies should nearly always employ a flexible exchange rate. However, in small economies, giving up this power may have some benefits. An interesting case is that of Argentina, which for the period 1991–2001 maintained a one-to-one exchange rate between its peso and the US dollar. Although prior to 1991 Argentina had suffered periods of hyperinflation, while the peso was pegged to the dollar Argentina's inflation rate essentially equalled that of the United States. By tying its currency to the dollar and giving up the freedom to set its monetary policy, Argentina attempted to commit itself to avoiding the inflationary policies of the past, and instead placed itself under the 'umbrella' of the Federal Reserve. Unfortunately, early in 2002 investors' fears that Argentina would not be able to repay its international debts led to a speculative attack on the Argentine peso. The fixed exchange rate collapsed, the peso depreciated and Argentina experienced an economic crisis. The lesson is that a fixed exchange rate alone cannot stop inflation in a small economy, if other policies are not sound as well. Large fiscal deficits, which were financed by foreign borrowing, ultimately pushed Argentina into crisis. Although not as dramatic, much the same happened in the EMS between 1979 and 1986. As we saw in Economic naturalist 29.4, the EMS was far from a 'zone of monetary stability' over these years and the fundamental cause was a failure to co-ordinate macroeconomic policies. Germany followed tight anti-inflationary monetary policies while other countries, such as France and Italy, were more concerned with unemployment and attempted to follow more expansionary policies. This resulted in large inflation differentials requiring frequent realignments to correct for competitive losses. In summary, macroeconomic policies must be consistent with the maintenance of a fixed exchange rate. If they are not, the fixed exchange rate is likely to collapse under the pressure of speculative attacks.

The second important issue is the effect of the exchange rate on trade and economic integration. Proponents of fixed exchange rates argue that fixed rates promote international trade and cross-border economic co-operation by reducing uncertainty about future exchange rates. For example, a firm that is considering building up its export business knows that its potential profits will depend on the future value of its own country's currency relative to the currencies of the countries to which it exports. Under a flexible exchange rate regime, the value of the home currency fluctuates with changes in supply and demand and is therefore difficult to predict far in advance. Such uncertainty may make the firm reluctant to expand its export business. Supporters of fixed exchange rates argue that if the exchange rate is officially fixed, uncertainty about the future exchange rate is reduced or eliminated.

One problem with this argument, which has been underscored by episodes such as the East Asian crisis, the Argentine crisis and the problems faced by the EMS in the early 1990s is that fixed exchange rates are not guaranteed to remain fixed for ever. Although they do not fluctuate from day to day as flexible rates do, a speculative attack on a fixed exchange rate may lead suddenly and unpredictably to a large devaluation. Thus a firm that is trying to forecast the exchange rate 10 years into the future may face as much uncertainty if the exchange rate is fixed as if it is flexible.

The potential instability of fixed exchange rates and their detrimental effects on international trade was an important reason why countries in Western Europe agreed to abandon their national currencies and adopt a common currency, the euro, in 1999. It turns out that the question of whether a common currency actually promotes trade between partner countries is important in assessing the gains from monetary union. We shall return to this issue in Chapter 30.

## Summary

- The *nominal exchange rate* between two currencies is the rate at which the currencies can be traded for each other. A rise in the value of a currency relative to other currencies is called an *appreciation*; a decline in the value of a currency is called a *depreciation*.
- Exchange rates can be flexible or fixed. The value of a *flexible exchange rate* is determined by the supply and demand for the currency in the *foreign exchange market*, the market on which currencies of various nations are traded for one another. The government sets the value of a *fixed exchange rate*.
- The *real exchange rate* is the price of the average domestic good or service *relative* to the price of the average foreign good or service, when prices are expressed in terms of a common currency. An increase in the real exchange rate implies that domestic goods and services are becoming more expensive relative to foreign goods and services, which tends to reduce exports and increase imports. Conversely, a decline in the real exchange rate tends to increase net exports.
- A basic theory of nominal exchange rate determination, the *purchasing power parity* (*PPP*) theory, is based on the *law of one price*. This states that if transportation costs are relatively small, the price of an internationally traded commodity must be the same in all locations. According to the PPP theory, we can find the nominal exchange rate between two currencies by setting the price of a commodity in one currency equal to the price of the commodity in the second currency. The PPP theory correctly predicts that the currencies of countries that experience significant inflation will tend to depreciate in the long run. However, the fact that many goods and services are not traded internationally, and that not all traded goods are standardised, makes the PPP theory less useful for explaining short-run changes in exchange rates.
- Supply and demand analysis is a useful tool for studying the determination of exchange rates in the short run. The equilibrium exchange rate, also called the *fundamental value of the exchange rate*, equates the quantities of the currency supplied and demanded in the foreign exchange market. A currency is supplied by domestic residents who wish to acquire foreign currencies to purchase foreign goods, services and assets. An increased preference for foreign goods, an increase in the domestic GDP, or an increase in the real interest rate on foreign assets will all increase the supply of a currency on the foreign exchange market and thus lower its value. A currency is demanded by foreigners who wish to purchase domestic goods, services and assets. An increased preference for domestic goods by foreigners,

an increase in real GDP abroad, or an increase in the domestic real interest rate will all increase the demand for the currency on the foreign exchange market and thus increase its value.

- If the exchange rate is flexible, a *tight* monetary policy (by raising the real interest rate) increases the demand for the currency and causes it to appreciate. The stronger currency reinforces the effects of the tight monetary policy on aggregate demand by reducing net exports. Conversely an *easy* monetary policy lowers the real interest rate and weakens the currency, which in turn stimulates net exports.
- The value of a *fixed exchange rate* is officially established by the government. A fixed exchange rate whose official value exceeds its fundamental value in the foreign exchange market is said to be *overvalued*. An exchange rate whose official value is below its fundamental value is *undervalued*. A reduction in the official value of a fixed exchange rate is called a *devaluation*; an increase in its official value is called a *revaluation*.
- For an overvalued exchange rate, the quantity of the currency supplied at the official exchange rate exceeds the quantity demanded. To maintain the official rate, the country's Central Bank must use its *international reserves* (foreign currency assets) to purchase the excess supply of its currency in the foreign exchange market. Because a country's international reserves are limited, it cannot maintain an overvalued exchange rate indefinitely. Moreover, if financial investors fear an impending devaluation of the exchange rate, they may launch a *speculative attack*, selling their domestic currency assets and supplying large quantities of the currency to the foreign exchange market. Because speculative attacks cause a country's Central Bank to spend its international reserves even more quickly, they often force a devaluation.
- A tight monetary policy, by raising the fundamental value of the exchange rate, can eliminate the problem of overvaluation. However, if monetary policy is used to set the fundamental value of the exchange rate equal to the official value, it is no longer available for stabilising the domestic economy. Thus under fixed exchange rates, monetary policy has little or no power to affect *domestic output and employment*.
- The 'impossible trinity' teaches us that in a world characterised by free capital mobility countries must choose between *domestic stabilisation* and *fixed exchange rates*. If they opt for the latter they cannot use macroeconomic policies to stabilise their domestic economies.
- Because a fixed exchange rate implies that monetary policy can no longer be used for domestic stabilisation, most large countries employ a *flexible exchange rate*. A fixed exchange rate may benefit a small country by forcing its Central Bank to follow the monetary policies of the country to which it has tied its rate. Advocates of fixed exchange rates argue that they increase trade and economic integration by making the exchange rate more predictable. However, the threat of speculative attacks greatly reduces the long-term predictability of a fixed exchange rate. Ultimately, countries may require *monetary union* if their economies are to be fully insulated from the detrimental effects of exchange rate instability.

## Key terms

**appreciation** (835)
**balance-of-payments deficit** (851)
**balance-of-payments surplus** (851)
**Bretton Woods system** (853)
**depreciation** (835)
**devaluation** (848)
**European Currency Unit (ECU)** (855)
**European Monetary System (EMS)** (855)
**Exchange Rate Mechanism (ERM)** (855)
**fixed exchange rate** (836)
**flexible (floating) exchange rate** (835)
**foreign exchange market** (835)
**fundamental value of the exchange rate** (844)
**international reserves** (850)
**law of one price** (839)
**nominal exchange rate** (833)
**overvalued exchange rate** (848)
**purchasing power parity (PPP)** (839)
**real exchange rate** (836)
**relative purchasing power parity** (841)
**revaluation** (848)
**speculative attack** (841)
**undervalued exchange rate** (848)

## Review questions

1. Japanese yen trade at 110 yen per dollar and Mexican pesos trade at 10 pesos per dollar. What is the nominal exchange rate between the yen and the peso? Express it in two ways.
2. Define the *nominal exchange rate* and the *real exchange rate*. How are the two concepts related? Which type of exchange rate most directly affects a country's ability to export its goods and services?
3. Would you expect the law of one price to apply to crude oil? To fresh milk? To taxi rides? To compact discs produced in different countries by local recording artists? Explain your answer in each case.
4. Why do German households and firms supply euros to the foreign exchange market? Why do Americans demand euros in the foreign exchange market?
5. Under a flexible exchange rate, how does an easing of monetary policy (a lower real interest rate) affect the value of the exchange rate? Does this change in the exchange rate tend to weaken or strengthen the effect of the monetary ease on output and employment? Explain.
6. Define an *overvalued exchange rate*. Discuss four ways in which government policy makers can respond to an overvaluation. What are the drawbacks of each approach?
7. Use a supply and demand diagram to illustrate the effects of a speculative attack on an overvalued exchange rate. Why do speculative attacks often result in a devaluation?
8. Contrast fixed and flexible exchange rates in terms of how they affect (a) the ability of monetary policy to stabilise domestic output and (b) the predictability of future exchange rates.

## Problems

1. Using the data in Table 29.2, find the nominal exchange rate between the Swiss franc and the Japanese yen. Express it in two ways. How do your answers change if the franc appreciates by 10 per cent against the euro while the value of the yen against the euro remains unchanged?
2. A British-made automobile is priced at £20,000. A comparable US-made car costs $26,000. One pound trades for $1.50 in the foreign exchange market. Find the real exchange rate for automobiles from the perspective of the United States and from the perspective of Great Britain. Which country's cars are more competitively priced?
3. Between last year and this year, the CPI in Blueland rose from 100 to 110 and the CPI in Redland rose from 100 to 105. Blueland's currency unit, the blue, was worth €1 last year and is worth 90 cents this year. Redland's currency unit, the red, was worth 50 cents last year and is worth 45 cents this year.

   Find the percentage change from last year to this year in Blueland's *nominal* exchange rate with Redland and in Blueland's *real* exchange rate with Redland. (Treat Blueland as the home country.) Relative to Redland, do you expect Blueland's exports to be helped or hurt by these changes in exchange rates?
4. The demand for German-made cars in Japan is given by

   Japanese demand = 10,000 – 0.001(Price of German cars in yen)

   Similarly, the demand for Japanese-made cars in the Germany is

   German demand = 30,000 – 0.2(Price of Japanese cars in euros)

The domestic price of a German-made car is €20,000, and the domestic price of a Japanese-made car is ¥2,500,000. From the perspective of Germany, find the real exchange rate in terms of cars and net exports of cars to Japan, if:

a. The nominal exchange rate is 100 yen per euro.

b. The nominal exchange rate is 125 yen per euro.

How does an appreciation of the euro affect German net exports of automobiles (considering only the Japanese market)?

5. a. Gold is $350 per ounce in the United States and 2,800 pesos per ounce in Mexico. What nominal exchange rate between US dollars and Mexican pesos is implied by the PPP theory?

b. Mexico experiences inflation so that the price of gold rises to 4,200 pesos per ounce. Gold remains $350 per ounce in the United States. According to the PPP theory, what happens to the exchange rate? What general principle does this example illustrate?

c. Gold is $350 per ounce in the United States and 4,200 pesos per ounce in Mexico. Crude oil (excluding taxes and transportation costs) is $30 per barrel in the United States. According to the PPP theory, what should a barrel of crude oil cost in Mexico?

d. Gold is $350 per ounce in the United States. The exchange rate between the United States and Canada is 0.70 US dollars per Canadian dollar. How much does an ounce of gold cost in Canada?

6. How would each of the following be likely to affect the value of the euro, all else being equal? Explain.

a. Shares in European companies are perceived as having become much riskier financial investments.

b. American households decide to purchase less French, Spanish and Italian wine and more Australian, Chilean and South African Wine.

c. As East Asian economies recover from recession, international financial investors become aware of many new, high-return investment opportunities in the region.

d. The US government imposes higher tariffs on imported European goods.

e. Faced with rising inflation, the ECB decides to increase real interest rates.

f. European consumers increase their spending on imported goods.

7. The demand for and supply of Polish zlotys in the foreign exchange market are

$$Demand = 30{,}000 - 8{,}000e$$

$$Supply = 25{,}000 + 12{,}000e$$

where the nominal exchange rate is expressed as euros per zloty.

a. What is the fundamental value of the zloty?

b. The zloty is fixed at 0.30 euros. Is the zloty overvalued, undervalued, or neither? Find the balance-of-payments deficit or surplus in both zlotys and euros. What happens to the country's international reserves over time?

c. Repeat part (b) for the case in which the zloty is fixed at 0.20 euros.

8. The annual demand for and supply of zlotys in the foreign exchange market is as given in Problem 7. The zloty is fixed at 0.30 euros per zloty. The country's international reserves are €600. Foreign financial investors hold chequing accounts in the country in the amount of 5,000 zlotys.

a. Suppose that foreign financial investors do not fear a devaluation of the zloty, and thus do not convert their zloty chequing accounts into euros. Can the zloty be maintained at its fixed value of 0.30 euros for the next year?

b. Now suppose that foreign financial investors come to expect a possible devaluation of the zloty to 0.25 euros. Why should this possibility worry them?

c. In response to their concern about devaluation, foreign financial investors withdraw all funds from their chequing accounts and attempt to convert those zlotys into euros. What happens?

d. Discuss why the foreign investors' forecast of devaluation can be considered a 'self-fulfilling prophecy'.

9. Eastland's currency is called the eastmark, and Westland's currency is called the westmark. In the market in which eastmarks and westmarks are traded for each other, the supply of and demand for eastmarks are given by

$$Demand = 25{,}000 - 5{,}000e - 50{,}000(r_E - r_W)$$

$$Supply = 18{,}500 + 8{,}000e - 50{,}000(r_E - r_W)$$

The nominal exchange rate $e$ is measured as westmarks per eastmark, and $r_E$ and $r_W$ are the real interest rates prevailing in Eastland and Westland, respectively.

a. Explain why it makes economic sense for the two real interest rates to appear in the demand and supply equations in the way they do.

b. Initially, $r_E = r_W = 0.10$, or 10 per cent. Find the fundamental value of the eastmark.

c. The Westlandian Central Bank grows concerned about inflation and raises Westland's real interest rate to 12 per cent. What happens to the fundamental value of the eastmark?

d. Assume that the exchange rate is flexible and that Eastland does not change its real interest rate following the increase in Westland's real interest rate. Is the action of the Westlandian Central Bank likely to increase or reduce aggregate demand in Eastland? Discuss.

e. Now suppose that the exchange rate is fixed at the value you found in part (b). After the action by the Westlandian Central Bank, what will the Eastlandian Central Bank have to do to keep its exchange rate from being overvalued? What effect will this action have on the Eastlandian economy?

f. In the context of this example, discuss the effect of fixed exchange rates on the ability of a country to run an independent monetary policy.

## Answers to in-chapter exercises

29.1 Answers will vary, depending on when the data are obtained.

29.2 The euro price of the French computer is €2,250 and the exchange rate is £0.70 = €1. As each euro is worth £0.70, the sterling price of the French computer is £0.70 × 2,250 = £1,575 which is £525 less than the price of the British computer. Note that at the exchange rate £0.70 = €1, the price difference is 525/0.70 = €750 which is the same as in Example 29.2. Thus the conclusion that the French model is cheaper does not depend on the currency in which the comparison is made.

29.3 Since the law of one price holds for gold, its price per ounce must be the same in New York and Stockholm:

$300 = 2,500 kronor

Dividing both sides by 300, we get

$1 = 8.33 kronor

So the exchange rate is 8.33 kronor per dollar.

**29.4** A decline in US GDP reduces consumer incomes and hence imports. As Americans are purchasing fewer imports, they demand fewer euros on the foreign exchange market, so the demand curve for euros shifts to the left. Reduced demand lowers the equilibrium value of the euro.

**29.5** Equating demand and supply gives: $24{,}000 - 3{,}000e = 17{,}000 + 2{,}000e$. Solving for the equilibrium exchange rate gives $e = 1.4$ or £1 = 1.40. Hence the decline in sterling's fundamental value is greater than in Example 29.6. If the Bank of Engand continues to maintain the official rate at £1 = €1.6 then demand equals $24{,}000 - 3{,}000 \times 1.6 = 19{,}200$ and supply equals $17{,}000 + 2{,}000 \times 1.6 = 20{,}200$. The quantity supplied at the official rate exceeds the quantity demanded by 1,000. The Bank of England will have to purchase £1,000 each period, so its balance-of-payments deficit will equal £1,000, or $1000 \times 1.6 = 1{,}600$ euros. This balance-of-payments deficit is larger than we found in Example 29.6. We conclude that the greater the degree of overvaluation, the larger the country's balance-of-payments deficit is likely to be.

**29.6** Equating demand and supply gives: $25{,}500 - 3{,}000e = 17{,}000 + 2{,}000e$. Solving for the equilibrium exchange gives $e = 1.7$ or £1 = 1.70. As the official rate 1.6 is less than the fundamental value sterling is *undervalued*. If the Bank of England continues to maintain the official rate at £1 = €1.6 then demand equals $25{,}5000 - 3{,}000 \times 1.6 = 20{,}700$ and supply equals $17{,}000 + 2{,}000 \times 1.6 = 20{,}200$. The quantity demanded at the official rate now exceeds the quantity supplied by 500. To meet the excess demand for sterling the Bank of England will have to sell 500 each period, so its balance-of-payments *surplus* will equal £500, or $500 \times 1.6 = 800$ euros. In contrast to the case of an overvalued exchange rate, here the Central Bank is providing its own currency to the foreign exchange market and receiving foreign currencies in return.

**29.7** The figure below illustrates the case in which the initial fluctuation band is wide enough to include the new fundamental value for the lira.

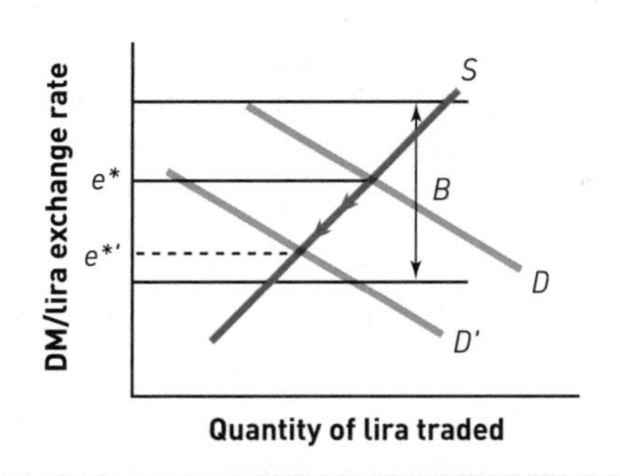


The fall in the demand for the lira shifts the demand curve to *D*', establishing a new fundamental value at $e^{*\prime}$. However, in this case $e^{*\prime}$ is within *B* and the actual exchange rate can fall toward its fundamental value without reaching the lower limit and sparking fears of a realignment and devaluation of the lira.

# 30 Monetary Union: the Theory of Optimum Currency Areas

Twelve member states of the European Union – Austria, Belgium, Finland, France, Germany, Greece, Ireland, Italy, Luxemburg, the Netherlands, Portugal and Spain – now use a common currency called the euro. Although the United Kingdom, Sweden and Denmark have, to date, decided to opt out of the euro and retain their national currencies, at least some of the new accession countries such as Poland, Hungary and the Czech Republic may join in the near future.

In this chapter we ask why these countries have taken what appears to be the irreversible step of replacing their national currencies with a common currency and transferring authority for monetary policy from national Central Banks (NCBs) and elected governments to the ECB. In short, is the use of the euro justified on economic criteria? We should, of course, note that for many politicians and euro enthusiasts the introduction of the European common currency was seen as a *political* initiative designed to deepen the process of integration among member states and enhance the EU's influence on the world stage. While these political aspects cannot be discounted, it must also be recognised that the euro has important *economic* implications. This chapter deals with these economic implications by focusing on the costs and benefits of a common currency. To help us think about costs and benefits in a systematic way we use a framework called the *Theory of Optimum Currency Areas*. This approach is similar to the *Cost–Benefit Principle* discussed in Chapter 1. To recap, an individual, firm or society should take an action if, and only if, the extra benefits from the action are at least as great as the extra costs. Hence, according to the Theory of Optimum Currency Areas a country should join a monetary union if, and only if, the benefits outweigh the costs. If, based on the *Cost–Benefit Principle*, a country estimates that joining a monetary union with other countries will result in a net gain then it forms an **optimum currency area** with those countries. For example, if two countries such as France and Germany conclude that each will gain by replacing their national currency with a common currency then they form an optimum currency area. However, if for a third country such as the United Kingdom the costs exceed the benefits then it does not form an optimum currency area with France and Germany.

**optimum currency area** a group of countries for which the benefits of replacing national currencies with a common currency exceed the costs

In this chapter, we shall see that the loss of policy independence is the principal cost of joining a monetary union. Benefits, on the other hand, include savings from the elimination of currency transactions costs and exchange rate uncertainty. We shall also ask what characteristics economies must have to ensure that the benefits are greater than the costs. That is, what types of economies are most likely to form an optimum currency area? As we shall see, economies are best suited to monetary union when economic activity is *closely synchronised* and they *trade extensively with each other*.

## Costs and benefits of a common currency

The most important cost of participating in a monetary union is the *sacrifice of policy independence*, especially the loss of monetary and exchange rate policy as a means of stabilising the domestic economy. The principal benefit, on the other hand, is the reduction in *transactions costs* and *exchange rate uncertainty* that occurs when international trade is financed by a single currency rather than by different national currencies. From an economics perspective, whether or not an individual country should join a monetary union will depend on whether the benefits outweigh the costs. One point should, however, be borne in mind. The relative importance of the costs and benefits may change once a country joins a monetary union. We shall see that in some cases the use of a common currency may actually lead to an increase in the benefits and a reduction in the costs. For example, as will be explained in this chapter, the costs may outweigh the benefits when the amount of international trade between partner countries is low. However, if the use of a common currency promotes trade between members of a monetary union, then forming the union may lead to a net gain by increasing the benefits and reducing the costs.

### Costs: the loss of policy independence

In Chapters 27 and 28, we saw that monetary policy is an important method by which Central Banks can offset *recessionary* and *expansionary gaps*. For example, when a country faces a recessionary gap its Central Bank can stimulate consumption and investment by cutting the real rate of interest. Conversely, when a country faces an expansionary gap the Central Bank can slow the economy down with higher real interest rates which increase saving and reduce aggregate demand. Further, in Chapter 29 we saw that the effectiveness of monetary policy is enhanced when the country operates a *flexible exchange rate*. If, for example, the Central Bank eases monetary policy to offset a recession, lower domestic interest rates will lead to capital outflows and a depreciation of the domestic currency, providing a stimulus to net exports and a further boost to aggregate demand. Alternatively, if the Central Bank tightens policy in the face of an expansionary gap, higher interest rates will lead to capital inflows and an appreciation of the domestic currency which slows the growth in aggregate demand by reducing net exports. In short, monetary policy will be most effective when the country operates a flexible exchange rate.

When a country joins a monetary union such as the Eurosystem it automatically sacrifices its ability to use independent monetary and exchange rate policy to stabilise its domestic economy. Rather it must accept the single monetary policy as determined by the monetary union's Central Bank. How important is this loss of policy independence? According to the Theory of Optimum Currency Areas the cost of sacrificing policy independence by participating in a monetary union will depend on whether partner countries experience similar or different problems at the same time. In terms of the optimum currency area literature, problems are likely to be similar when partner countries experience **symmetric shocks**: for example, partner countries face recessionary or expansionary gaps at the same time. Conversely, countries will face different problems when shocks are **asymmetric**: for example, one country faces a recessionary gap while its partners face an expansionary gap.

**symmetric shocks** affect different economies in the same way and at the same time

**asymmetric shocks** affect different economies in different ways at the same time

To explain the importance of symmetric and asymmetric shocks recall from Chapter 28 that the aggregate demand curve (*AD*) shows the relationship between the economy's short-run equilibrium output *Y* and the rate of inflation, $\pi$. Aggregate demand is, of course, another name for *planned expenditure*, which we previously defined as the sum of consumption *C*, investment *I*, government purchases *G* and net exports *NX*. Hence we can define a **demand shock** as a sudden or unexpected change in planned aggregate expenditure (*PAE*). As we saw in Fig. 28.2, an increase in autonomous expenditure will increase aggregate demand at any level of *Y* and shift the *AD* curve to the *right*. Conversely, a decrease in autonomous expenditure will reduce aggregate demand at each level of *Y* and shift the *AD* curve to the *left*. We shall refer to an increase in autonomous expenditure as a **positive demand shock** and a decrease in autonomous expenditure as a **negative demand shock**. For example, if firms decide to spend more on investment, aggregate demand will increase at any given level of output, shifting the *AD* curve to the *right* – a positive demand shock. Likewise if, at any given level of disposable income, households decide to spend less on consumption the *AD* curve will shift to the *left* – a negative demand shock.

**demand shock** sudden or unexpected change in planned aggregate expenditure (PAE)

**positive demand shock** an increase in autonomous expenditure which shifts the aggregate demand curve to the right

**negative demand shock** a decrease in autonomous expenditure which shifts the aggregate demand curve to the left

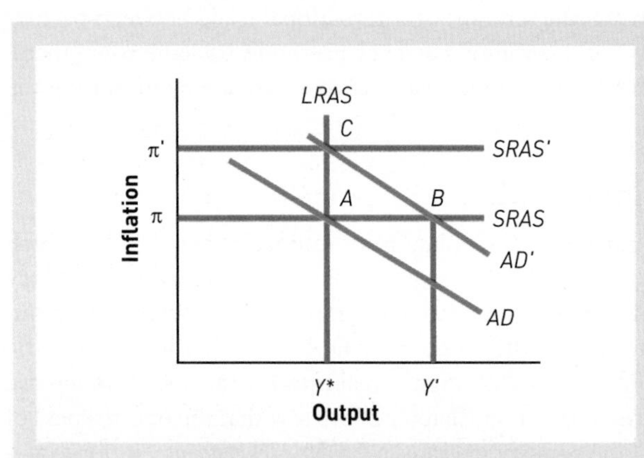


**Figure 30.1 A Positive Demand Shock.** Starting from the long-run equilibrium at point *A* a positive demand shock shifts *AD* to *AD'*. At the new short-run equilibrium *B*, output is *Y'* and the expansionary gap is *Y*Y'*. To stabilise the economy, the Central Bank should tighten monetary policy by increasing the real interest rate, which reduces consumption and investment and shifts the aggregate demand curve back to *AD* restoring long-run equilibrium at point *A*. In an open economy with a flexible exchange rate, the rise in the domestic interest rate will also lead to an appreciation of the domestic currency, which reduces net exports and reinforces the effect of the higher real interest rate on consumption and investment spending. However, if the country participated in a monetary union the domestic Central Bank could not use monetary policy to stabilise the economy. Eventually the expansionary gap would force a rise in inflation, shifting *SRAS* up toward *SRAS'*. Long-run equilibrium would eventually be restored at point *C*, but at the cost of a higher inflation rate at $\pi'$.

Figure 30.1 illustrates a positive demand shock and Fig. 30.2 a negative demand shock. (Note that these figures are similar to those we used to analyse the relationship between inflation and aggregate supply in Chapter 28.) In each case, we start at the same long-run equilibrium point *A* with output equal to its potential level $Y^*$. In Fig. 30.1 we assume an increase in autonomous expenditure which shifts the aggregate demand curve from *AD* to *AD'* establishing a new short-run equilibrium at point *B*, opening an expansionary gap equal to $Y^*Y'$. Conversely in Fig. 30.2 we assume a decrease in autonomous expenditure which shifts the aggregate demand curve to the left and opens a recessionary gap equal to $Y'Y^*$. Note that, as in Chapter 28, we assume *inflation inertia*, which means that inflation adjusts slowly to a shock.

Consider two economies which, for the sake of illustration, we shall assume to be the United Kingdom and Germany. If the United Kingdom and Germany both experience a similar increase or decrease in autonomous expenditure we can say that the shock is *symmetric* in the sense that each economy faces the same problem at the same time. If, for example, both experience a negative shock then both will face a recessionary gap. Alternatively if the United Kingdom were to experience a negative demand shock while Germany is either unaffected or experiences a positive shock, then the shock is *asymmetric* in the

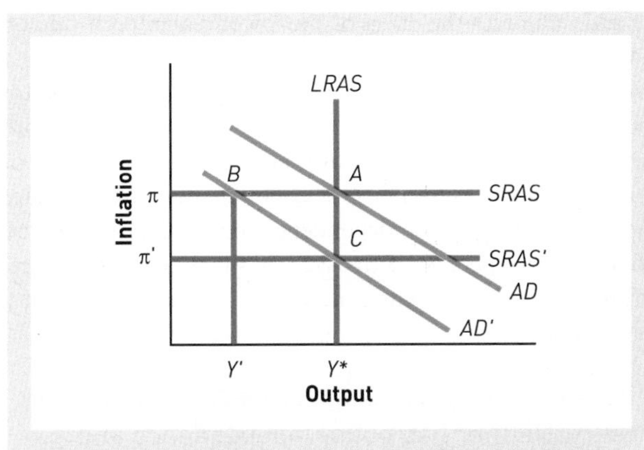


**Figure 30.2 A Negative Demand Shock.** Starting from the long-run equilibrium at point *A* a negative demand shock shifts *AD* to *AD'*. At the new short-run equilibrium, point *B*, output is *Y'* and the recessionary gap is *Y'Y**. To stabilise the economy, the Central Bank should ease monetary policy by reducing the real interest rate, which increases consumption and investment and shifts the aggregate demand curve back to *AD*, restoring long-run equilibrium at point *A*. In an open economy with a flexible exchange rate, the fall in the domestic interest rate will also lead to a depreciation of the domestic currency, which stimulates net exports and reinforces the effect of the lower real interest rate on consumption and investment spending. However, if the country participated in a monetary union the domestic Central Bank could not use monetary policy to stabilise the economy. Eventually the recessionary gap would force a fall in inflation, shifting *SRAS* down toward *SRAS'*. Long-run equilibrium would eventually be restored at point *C* at a lower inflation rate $\pi'$, but at the cost of a prolonged recession.

sense that they face different problems at the same time. How can each economy adjust to positive or negative shocks? We shall see that the answer will depend on whether Germany and the United Kingdom are members of a monetary union and whether the shocks are symmetric or asymmetric. To explain, we shall consider the two policy scenarios. In Scenario One both countries retain their own currencies while Scenario Two assumes that they are members of a monetary union and use a common currency.

## Scenario One: neither economy is a member of a monetary union and both have retained policy independence

### *Symmetric shocks*

Suppose that Germany and the United Kingdom both experience a symmetric demand shock as illustrated by either Fig. 30.1 or Fig. 30.2. If the shock is positive both countries will experience an expansionary output gap equal to *Y*Y'* in Fig. 30.1. As each country has retained policy independence both Central Banks can react by tightening monetary policy and increasing the real rate of interest which, as we have seen, reduces consumption and investment and shifts the aggregate demand curve to the left, restoring long-run equilibrium at point *A* in Fig. 30.1. Conversely, if both countries experience a negative demand shock both will face a recessionary gap equal to *Y'Y** in Fig. 30.2. In this case, both Central Banks can react by easing monetary policy and cutting the real rate of interest, which stimulates consumption and investment and shifts the aggregate demand curve to the right, restoring long-run equilibrium at point *A* in Fig. 30.2. In short, so long as the shock is symmetric we can expect both Central Banks to respond in a similar fashion.

### *Asymmetric shocks*

Suppose that Germany experiences a positive demand shock and the United Kingdom a negative shock. As Germany faces an expansionary gap, we would expect its Central Bank to react to the shock by increasing the real interest rate, which leads to a fall in consumption and investment and closes the expansionary gap by shifting the *AD* curve to the left. Further, as we saw in Chapter 29, a rise in the domestic real rate of interest will lead to an appreciation of the German currency and a fall in net exports, which reinforces the impact on aggregate demand. Conversely, the British Central Bank can react to the recessionary gap by easing monetary policy and reducing the real rate of interest which, as we have seen, increases consumption and investment and shifts the aggregate demand curve back to *AD*, restoring long-run equilibrium at point *A* in Fig. 30.2. Also, in an open economy with a flexible exchange rate, a cut in the domestic interest rate will lead to a depreciation of the British currency, which stimulates net exports and reinforces the effect of the lower real interest rate on consumption and investment spending.

Note that so long as each economy retains policy independence it does not matter whether shocks are symmetric or asymmetric. In the case of a symmetric shock, both Central Banks are free to either increase or decrease interest rates in response to a positive or negative shock. Alternatively, when the shock is asymmetric one can increase interest rates while the other can cut interest rates. In short, policy independence means that the Central Banks are free to stabilise their economies irrespective of the type of shock they experience. As we shall see in Scenario Two, this is not the case when the countries are members of a monetary union and use a common currency.

### Scenario Two: Germany and the United Kingdom are members of a monetary union and use a common currency. Neither has policy independence and monetary policy is decided by an independent Central Bank that reacts to unionwide shocks to output and inflation rather than to the problems of a single member country

#### *Symmetric shocks*

Suppose both economies experience a positive demand shock, as illustrated by Fig. 30.1. As the resulting expansionary gap is common to all members of the monetary union we can reasonably expect the Central Bank to offset the resulting inflationary pressures by tightening monetary policy and raising interest rates which, as we have seen, eliminates the expansionary gap in both economies by shifting their *AD* curves to the left. Alternatively if each country experiences a similar negative demand shock, as illustrated by Fig. 30.2, we can expect the Central Bank to offset the decline in output by easing monetary policy and cutting interest rates which, as we have seen, eliminates the recessionary gap in both economies by shifting their *AD* curves to the right. Note that the adjustment to symmetric shocks is similar to that in Scenario One. The only difference is that the appropriate stabilisation policy is undertaken by the Central Bank of the monetary union rather than by the British and German Central Banks following independent but similar policies.

#### *Asymmetric shocks*

As in Scenario One, we shall assume that Germany experiences a positive demand shock and the United Kingdom a negative shock. However, in contrast to Scenario One neither country has policy independence, with the consequence that Germany's Central Bank will be unable to respond to the expansionary gap and Britain's Central Bank to the recessionary gap. Is it probable that the Central Bank of the monetary union will react by changing interest rates? For two reasons, the answer is most likely no. First, as the adjustment problem is different between Germany and the United Kingdom the Central Bank cannot help one country without harming the other. For example, an increase in interest rates would ease inflationary pressure in Germany but make the UK recession deeper. Conversely, if the Central Bank were to cut interest rates the policy would close the UK's recessionary gap but widen the German expansionary gap. Second, the Central Bank is responsible for stabilising the monetary union's aggregate output rather than the output of individual countries. Hence, if the decline in Britain's GDP is approximately offset by the increase in Germany's GDP the monetary union's aggregate output may remain relatively constant, requiring no action by the Central Bank.

In the absence of Central Bank intervention both economies will have to rely on the *self-correcting adjustment mechanism* described in Chapter 28. In Germany, the expansionary gap would eventually force a rise in inflation shifting *SRAS* up toward *SRAS*' in Fig. 30.1, restoring equilibrium at point *C* but at the cost of a higher inflation rate at $\pi'$. In the United Kingdom the recessionary gap would force a fall in inflation shifting *SRAS* down toward *SRAS'* in Fig. 30.2, restoring equilibrium at point *C* with a lower inflation rate $\pi'$, but at the cost of a prolonged recession. Note that this is not the end of the story. As German inflation now exceeds British inflation German exports to the United Kingdom will become less competitive and British imports more attractive to German households and firms. Conversely, British exports will become more competitive on the German market and imports from Germany less attractive to British households and firms. Hence, German net exports will decline, shifting the German *AD* curve back to the left in Fig. 30.1. On the other hand, UK net exports will increase, shifting the *AD* curve to the right in Fig. 30.2. This process will continue until the *inflation differential* is eliminated and both economies return to their initial long-run equilibrium positions, point *A* in both figures. However, in the absence of a proactive stabilisation policy by Central Banks the adjustment back to long-run equilibrium is likely to be long and painful.

Scenarios One and Two illustrate an important principle underlying the Theory of Optimum Currency Areas. In a monetary union there is a single or 'one-size' monetary policy which is common to all members. When shocks are symmetric and member countries face similar problems at the same time the single policy will be appropriate across the union and the one-size monetary policy fits all. Hence, the cost of sacrificing policy independence is likely to be relatively low when member countries experience symmetric shocks. Other things being equal, such countries are more likely to form an optimum currency area. However, if shocks are asymmetric and the countries face different problems at the same time the single or one-size monetary policy will not fit all members and, as described in Scenario Two, the loss of policy independence can lead to prolonged adjustment. Other things being equal, such countries are less likely to form an optimum currency area.

## Costs: the importance of flexible markets and inflation inertia

We have seen that the loss of policy independence is most likely to be significant when countries experience asymmetric shocks. Does this necessarily mean that these countries should never consider forming a monetary union? For two reasons, the answer is no. First, as will be explained later in this chapter, a monetary union also yields benefits which may outweigh the costs even if the latter are high. Second, if a country's commodity and labour markets are flexible in the sense that prices and wages respond rapidly to excess demand or supply then the cost of sacrificing policy independence may be significantly reduced even if shocks tend to be asymmetric. To explain, we shall return to the example in which the United Kingdom and Germany form a monetary union and assume a negative demand shock which affects the United Kingdom only. Hence the shock is asymmetric in that the United Kingdom experiences a recessionary gap while Germany is unaffected and continues to produce its potential or full-employment output $Y^*$. In terms of Fig. 30.2 the United Kingdom moves from point *A* to point *B* while Germany remains at the initial equilibrium point *A*.

If the United Kingdom is part of a monetary union it does not have policy independence and its Central Bank cannot offset the recession by easing monetary policy and reducing interest rates. Also, as the United Kingdom does not have an independent currency it cannot stimulate net exports by letting its exchange rate depreciate. Rather the United Kingdom will have to rely on the self-correcting adjustment process described in Chapter 28. Remember that when the United Kingdom experiences a recessionary gap British firms will not be selling as much as they had planned and will eventually slow down the rate at which they increase prices. This will lead to a decline in inflation and the *SRAS* curve will move downward to *SRAS'* establishing a new equilibrium at point *C* in Fig. 30.2 with $Y$ again equal to $Y^*$. What is important is the *speed* at which inflation declines – or, in the terminology of Chapter 28, the strength of *inflation inertia* in the UK economy. Recall from Chapter 28 that inflation inertia is a phenomenon which occurs when inflation changes slowly from year to year with the consequence that a relatively constant inflation rate leads households and firms to expect that the current inflation rate will persist into the future. Crucially this expectation of a stable inflation rate is built into long-term wage and price contracts. For example, suppose that in Fig. 30.2 the initial inflation rate $\pi$ is 3 per cent. If this inflation rate is expected to persist into the future then both employers and employees will agree an annual increase of 3 per cent in money wages and, if the expectation is realised, the average real wage will remain constant. Suppose that this is the situation when the United Kingdom experiences a negative demand shock. How will firms react? As firms have unsold output they may respond by slowing down the rate at which they increase prices, leading to a fall in the inflation rate. As inflation declines the *SRAS* curve shifts downward along *AD'*stimulating demand and establishing a new long-run equilibrium at point *C* in Fig. 30.2 with output restored to its potential level $Y^*$. However, this is possible only if inflationary expectations are revised downward and reflected in *money wage contracts*. For example, if the new equilibrium inflation rate $\pi'$ is 1 per cent then in order reduce the rate of price increase firms will require that money wage contracts are renegotiated to reflect lower inflation. If this does not happen and money wage contracts remain fixed at 3 per cent, firms will be unwilling to reduce the rate of price increase to 1 per cent as this would result in a 2 per cent, rise in real wages, making increased production unprofitable. Hence, so long as wage and other price contracts remain fixed at 3 per cent, firms will not reduce the rate at which they increase prices. Rather they will respond by cutting output and laying off workers, leading to a recessionary gap and a short-run equilibrium at point *B* in Fig. 30.2.

It follows that the recession will persist until money wage and price contracts are revised to reflect a lower rate of inflation. If this takes a long time then the recession will be prolonged and painful. Alternatively if inflationary expectations and wage contracts are revised quickly the recession will be shorter and adjustment to full employment quicker. Put another way, if inflation inertia is strong and the inflation rates declines slowly the recession will be prolonged and the cost of sacrificing policy independence high. Alternatively, if inflation inertia is weak and the inflation rate falls rapidly then the recession will be short-lived and the cost of sacrificing policy independence will be lower. Figure 30.3 illustrates these two possible adjustment paths for output. Note that time is measured on the horizontal axis. When inflation inertia is weak and contracts revised quickly the recession will be short-lived and relatively mild, as illustrated by the solid curve. However, when inflation inertia is strong, contracts will be revised more slowly and, as shown by the dashed line, the recession will be deeper and more prolonged.

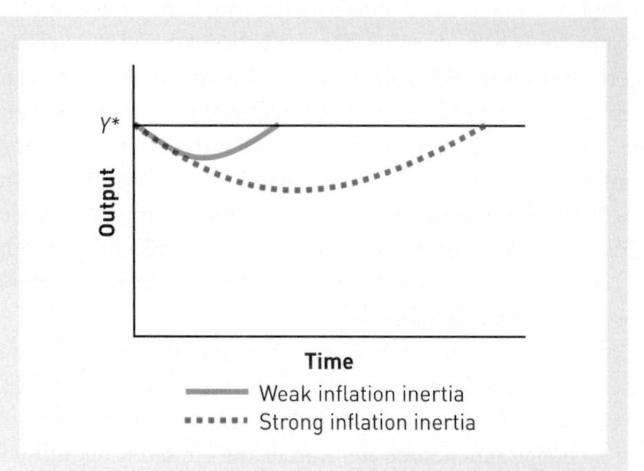


**Figure 30.3 Output Adjustment.** The figure illustrates alternative time paths for output adjustment following a negative demand shock. When inflation inertia is weak, inflationary expectations and wage contracts are rapidly revised and the recession is relatively short. However, when inflation inertia is strong, it takes much longer to revise expectations and wage contracts, leading to a prolonged recession, as illustrated by the dashed line.

## Costs: the importance of labour mobility

*Labour mobility* is often seen as a key criterion for a successful monetary union, especially when inflation inertia is strong and partner countries experience asymmetric shocks. To illustrate, suppose that following a negative demand shock newly unemployed British workers migrate to partner countries with greater employment opportunities. If this is the case then unemployment rate would not increase and there would be no need for a decline in the rate of inflation. As unemployed workers leave the country in search of job opportunities elsewhere there will be no pressure to reduce either the rate of price or wage inflation and firms would simply produce a lower equilibrium output with a smaller labour force. Unfortunately labour mobility between partner countries is not a panacea for asymmetric shocks and strong inflation inertia. Indeed labour mobility may have adverse effects on the domestic economy. If newly unemployed workers migrate and settle permanently in other countries then the labour force will decline, leading to a fall in potential output. For example, in Fig. 30.2 a smaller labour force would reduce the United Kingdom's potential output from $Y^*$ to $Y'$. The United Kingdom might avoid a short-run adjustment problem but only at the cost of a lower level of long-run GDP.

## Benefits: eliminating transaction costs

Using different currencies also imposes *costs* on individuals and firms. For individuals, the most obvious cost is the commission that must be paid to banks for exchanging currencies. If, for example, a British family wants to acquire euros before going on an Italian holiday it will normally have to pay a commission or fee to its bank for the privilege of converting sterling to euros. This commission is the *cost of the exchange transaction*. If, on the other hand, the United Kingdom were to adopt the euro as its currency the family could finance the holiday in its own domestic currency (the euro) and the transaction cost of converting sterling to euros would be eliminated. Hence, using a common currency implies obvious benefits to individuals who engage in foreign travel. A related benefit is that using a common currency leads to greater *price transparency* and simplifies *price comparisons*. Suppose a female member of the family is attracted to a dress in a Milan fashion house. Knowing that a similar dress is also available in London's Knightsbridge she has to compare two prices, one in euros and the other in sterling. This requires knowledge of the appropriate euro–sterling exchange rate required to make the conversion, which might be the exchange rate used by her credit card company rather than that published in the financial pages of newspapers. Also, as the exchange rate may change between the date of purchase and that of receiving a credit card bill, which may also include a transactions fee, the price actually paid can be greater or less than that assumed at the time the dress was bought in Milan. Although more indirect than the cost of exchanging currencies in banks these difficulties in making correct price comparisons are an obvious inconvenience to the traveller and a cost arising from the use of different currencies. However, as with currency exchange costs these inconveniences are eliminated by the use of a common currency and present another gain to the international traveller.

Similar gains also accrue to firms engaged in international trade. To illustrate, consider a British importer who signs a contract to purchase French-made automobile parts. As the British importer works in pounds sterling while the French exporter works in euros the completion of the contract requires that one currency must be exchanged for the other. If, for example, the price is agreed in euros then the importer must sell sterling to purchase euros in order to complete the purchase. If the contract price is €1 million and the current exchange rate between the euro and sterling is €1 = £0.7 then to purchase €1 million the importer must supply £700,000 to the foreign exchange market. However, the importer will normally buy the euros from a bank, which charges commission on the transaction. If the bank's commission is 1 per cent, the total cost to the importer is £707,000 (£700,000 plus 1 per cent or £7,000 commission) and the transactions cost is £7,000. Alternatively, if the price is agreed in pounds sterling the French exporter will receive £700,000 which it then sells to a French bank in return for a deposit denominated in euros. At an exchange rate of €1 = £0.70, or £1 = €1/0.7, the £700,000 will be worth €1 million. However, if the French bank also charges 1 per cent commission the net value of the sterling payment will be £693,000 (£700,000 less 1 per cent or £7,000 commission) or €990,000. Hence, the commission or transaction cost is also £7,000 or €10,000.

**transaction costs** costs involved in exchanging one currency for another

The **transactions costs** involved in exchanging one currency for another are like a tax which the purchaser pays but receives nothing in return, and result in a *deadweight loss* equivalent to the loss resulting from indirect taxation discussed in Chapter 7. Eliminating this deadweight loss by using a common currency means that banks will lose commission on foreign exchange transactions. This, however, is a transitional problem requiring banks to reallocate staff and resources to other profitable lines of business such as loan assessment and improved customer relations. Hence, the elimination of transaction costs in financing international trade is a potentially important gain from using a common currency. In its study 'One Market, One Money' (1990), the European Commission estimated that the gains from the elimination of transaction costs could be as much as €20 billion or approximately half of 1 per cent of the then EU GDP.

## Benefits: eliminating exchange rate uncertainty

When countries use different currencies, uncertainty over future exchange rate movements can impose additional costs on firms by complicating international investment decisions. To illustrate, consider a French automobile manufacturer, who currently supplies the British market by producing in France and exporting to the United Kingdom. Suppose the manufacturer is considering a switch to supplying the UK market locally by investing in a new plant located in England. If the decision is taken today it may be next year or longer before the plant is working at full production and automobiles are being sold on the UK market. These sales and the manufacturer's profits will be in pounds sterling but the French firm may wish to convert its profits into euros in order to pay dividends to its French shareholders or make further investments within the Eurosystem. However, as the sterling–euro exchange is subject to uncertainty the firm cannot be sure of the euro value of its future sterling profits. If, for example, sterling were to depreciate over the first year of the investment then the euro value of the firm's profits would be lower than expected. Conversely, if sterling appreciates then the euro value of the firm's profits would be higher than expected. This uncertainty surrounding future exchange rate movements is an unnecessary complication in the firm's decision, which should be based on criteria such as efficiency and maximising the return to its shareholders. However, exchange rate fluctuations mean that future returns to an investment can change dramatically if the sterling–euro exchange rate moves in an unexpected manner. As a common currency eliminates exchange rates between partner countries it also eliminates *exchange rate uncertainty* and removes unnecessary and perhaps misleading complications surrounding decisions on which country is the more efficient and profitable as a location for production. This is another important gain from the use of a common currency.

## RECAP Costs and benefits of a common currency

- *Sacrificing policy independence* is the most important cost of joining a monetary union. Rather than being able to use monetary and exchange rate policy to stabilise their domestic economies, member countries must rely on the policy followed by the monetary union's Central Bank.
- The *cost of sacrificing policy independence* is likely to be highest when countries experience asymmetric shocks and face different problems at the same time. Conversely, it will be relatively low when shocks are symmetric and countries face similar problems at the same time.
- A *low level of inflation inertia* and flexible labour markets can compensate for the loss of policy independence and speed up adjustment to shocks.
- *Labour mobility* between partner countries can also compensate for the loss of policy independence. However, it can also lead to a lower level of potential output.
- *Eliminating currency transactions costs* and *exchange rate uncertainty* are major benefits of a common currency.

## Comparing costs and benefits: the *CC* and *BB* schedules

To compare the costs and benefits of a monetary union we shall consider the United Kingdom's decision on whether it should join the Eurosystem and use the euro as its domestic currency. From an economics perspective the decision should depend on whether the benefits outweigh the costs. Hence it is appropriate to ask what characteristics the UK economy should have if the benefits are to be large and the costs low. We have seen that the costs may be low when the United Kingdom experiences symmetric shocks relative to the Eurosystem economies. More generally, the cost of sacrificing policy independence will be reduced when the British business cycle is synchronised with business cycles in the Eurosystem economies such as France, Germany and Italy. When this is the case the United Kingdom will experience recessions and expansions at the same time as the other countries and will require the same type of stabilisation policy. In short, **synchronised business cycles** imply that partner countries face similar problems at the same time and that the 'one-size' monetary policy fits all members.

**synchronised business cycles** mean that countries experience recession or expansion at the same time and require similar rather than different stabilisation policies

When are business cycles likely to be synchronised and shocks symmetric? One possible answer is that synchronisation is more likely when partner economies produce and trade a similar range of goods and services. To illustrate, suppose that the United Kingdom and Germany are major producers of two types of good called manufactured goods and financial services. Now consider an adverse shock which reduces the world demand for financial services. As both Britain and Germany are major suppliers of financial services then both will be affected and the shock is more likely to be symmetric. Alternatively, consider a situation in which the United Kingdom is highly specialised in financial services with a small manufacturing sector whereas Germany specialises in manufacturing and supplies few financial services. In this case a shock to the financial sector will have a greater impact on the British economy and is more likely to be asymmetric. There is, however, one important qualification to this conclusion. Suppose the United Kingdom is a significant importer of German manufactured goods while Germany imports financial services from the United Kingdom. In this case, an adverse shock to the financial sector will affect both economies. It will affect the United Kingdom directly via the demand for financial services, and Germany indirectly because, as UK economic growth slows, British demand for German manufactured goods will also decline, leading to a corresponding slowdown in the German economy. Hence we can conclude that when countries produce similar types of goods and services, shocks are more likely to be symmetric and business cycles synchronised. Conversely, when countries are highly specialised in different goods, shocks are more likely to be asymmetric and business cycles unsynchronised. However, when specialised economies trade extensively with each other, shocks to one can lead to similar problems in the other, increasing the degree of synchronisation and reducing the cost of sacrificing policy independence.

Turning to the benefits, we have seen that eliminating currency transaction costs and exchange rate uncertainty are major gains from using a common currency. How significant are these gains to an economy such as the United Kingdom? As with costs, the answer depends on the extent of trade and integration between the United Kingdom and its partner economies. The closer the interdependence and the greater the volume of trade between the United Kingdom and the Eurosystem the greater the gains from eliminating currency transaction costs and exchange rate uncertainty are likely to be. Hence, the higher the degree of economic integration and the larger the amount of trade with its potential euro partners the more the United Kingdom will benefit from joining the Eurosystem.

We can sum up this argument as follows. Similar industrial structures and the interdependence produced by international trade leads to greater *synchronisation* among partner economies. Other things being equal, these characteristics are more likely if the economies are highly integrated, by which we mean that they produce a similar range of goods and services and/or trade extensively with each other. Also, the higher the degree of economic integration the lower the cost and the greater the benefit from joining a monetary union. Figure 30.4 illustrates this conclusion. The

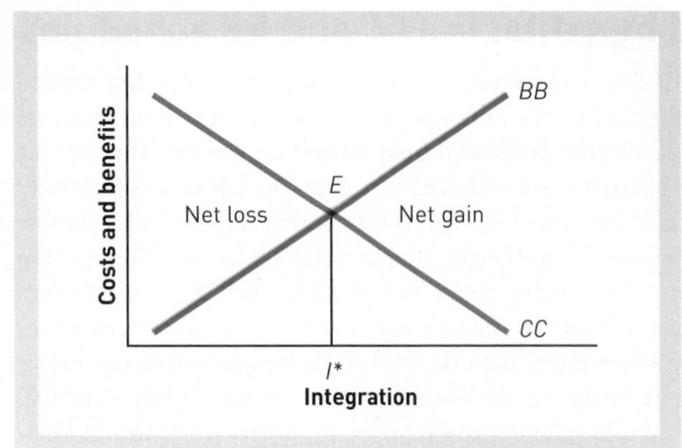


**Figure 30.4 Cost and Benefits Compared.** The *CC curve* illustrates the idea that the cost of a common currency declines with the degree of integration between partner countries, while the upward-sloping *BB* curve illustrates the corresponding idea that the gains increase with the degree of integration. $I^*$ indicates the degree of integration at which the costs of joining the monetary union just equal the benefits. If economic integration between the United Kingdom and its potential partners is lower than $I^*$, costs will exceed benefits and the United Kingdom will experience a net loss. Conversely, if integration is greater than $I^*$, the benefits will be greater than the costs, and the United Kingdom will experience a net gain.

horizontal axis measures the degree of economic integration between the United Kingdom and the Eurosystem while costs and benefits are measured on the vertical axis. The downward-sloping *Cost* or *CC curve* illustrates the idea that costs decline with the degree of integration between the United Kingdom and its potential partners while the upward-sloping *Benefit* or *BB curve* illustrates the corresponding idea that the gains to the United Kingdom increase with the degree of integration.

In Fig. 30.4, costs and benefits are equal at the intersection point *E* which also defines the level of integration $I^*$ required for the United Kingdom to break even by participating in the Eurosystem. At any level of integration below $I^*$ costs exceed benefits and joining the euro would result in a net loss to the United Kingdom. Conversely, at any level of integration greater than $I^*$ benefits exceed costs and the United Kingdom would experience a net gain. Hence, provided that we can accurately measure the degree of integration and the associated costs and benefits it is relatively simply to decide whether or not the United Kingdom should join the Eurosystem. If the degree of integration between the United Kingdom and the Eurosystem is greater than $I^*$ in Fig. 30.4 then the gains outweigh the losses and the economic case for joining is proven. What happens if the degree of integration between the United Kingdom and the Eurosystem economies is less than $I^*$? Does this necessarily mean that the United Kingdom should retain its own currency and stay out of the euro? Economic naturalists 30.1 and 30.2 explain why it may be justified to join even if the initial level of integration is less than $I^*$.

## Economic naturalist 30.1 Mr Brown's five economic tests for joining the euro

Shortly after his appointment as Chancellor of the Exchequer (or Finance Minister), in May 1997, Gordon Brown announced five economic tests or criteria to be used in assessing the costs and benefits of British entry to the Eurosystem. These tests are:

- *The convergence test* Are business cycles and economic structures compatible so that the United Kingdom could live with euro interest rates?
- *The flexibility test* If problems emerge, is there sufficient flexibility to deal with them?
- *The investment test* Would joining the euro create better conditions for firms making long-term decisions to invest in the United Kingdom?
- *The financial services test* What impact would joining the euro have on the financial services industry?
- *The growth and employment test* Will the euro promote higher economic growth and a permanent increase in employment?

Note that the convergence test requires that the British economy should be synchronised with that of the Eurosystem so that the common or 'one-size' monetary policy is appropriate to the problems faced by the British economy while the flexibility test requires that labour markets be sufficiently flexible to ensure a rapid response to possible asymmetric shocks.

After four years of intensive research by the Treasury, Mr Brown subsequently announced that the United Kingdom passed the investment and financial services tests but that the conditions relating to convergence and flexibility were not satisfied. As the first two tests were also deemed to be preconditions for meeting the growth and employment test the Chancellor decided that Britain was not ready for participation in the euro. Mr. Brown's decision is therefore consistent with the approach taken in this chapter. In terms of Fig. 30.4 the United Kingdom was placed to the left of the critical integration level $I^*$, implying a net loss from joining the euro. However, some economists have argued that although membership of the Eurosystem could result in a net loss this would be a temporary phenomenon that would decline in the longer run. This argument is explained in Economic naturalist 30.2.

## Economic naturalist 30.2 Does a common currency promote convergence?

Britain's decision not to participate in the euro is partly based on the argument that its economy is not convergent with that of the Eurosystem and that its markets lack the flexibility to deal with asymmetric shocks. Proponents of the common currency, on the other hand, have argued that the fastest way to meet the convergence and flexibility tests is to join the monetary union today. There are two aspects to this argument. The first suggests that using a common currency will reduce the costs and increase the benefits by promoting *trade and integration*. The second suggests that membership of a monetary union will lead to greater *labour market flexibility* and reduce the costs associated with any given level of integration.

### Convergence

In a series of research papers Andrew Rose of the University of California, Berkeley, tested the hypothesis that a common currency promotes trade between partner currencies. Using data on almost 200 countries Rose (2000) found that trade between countries using the same currency can be as much as three times greater than trade between countries using different currencies. Rose also found that a reduction in exchange rate volatility, a proxy for uncertainty, could have a significant positive effect on international trade. Figure 30.5 illustrates the implications of these findings for the UK decision on euro membership. Suppose that, based on Mr Brown's tests, the degree of integration or convergence between the United Kingdom and the Eurosystem is $I'$ in Fig. 30.5. As $I'$ is below the break-even level $I^*$ the United Kingdom would suffer a net loss equal to the distance *AB*. We can think of the difference between $I^*$ and $I'$ as the United Kingdom's *convergence gap*, or the extent to which integration falls short of the level required for costs to be offset by benefits. However, Rose is correct in stating that joining the euro will promote trade between the United Kingdom and the Eurosystem and, as increased trade leads to greater interdependence among economies, it will also lead to greater convergence and integration. It follows that joining the euro today may imply a short-run loss but it will also speed up the convergence process, as indicated by the arrows in Fig. 30.5. As trade increases and the United Kingdom becomes more and more integrated with the Eurosystem it moves downward along its *CC* schedule from point *A* and upward along its *BB* schedule from point *B* toward, and perhaps beyond, the break-even point *E*. That is, trade increases interdependence between the United Kingdom and the Eurosystem and closes the convergence gap.

This conclusion depends on the validity of the Rose hypothesis that a common currency actually promotes trade among partner countries. One problem with Rose's data is that they include very few examples of monetary unions being formed, and where they exist they involve very small countries with little in common with large industrial countries such as the United Kingdom and other European economies. The data, however, include more examples in which existing monetary unions were dissolved. Hence to some extent the validity of Rose's findings depends upon a symmetric effect in that ending a monetary union has an equal but opposite effect on trade. That is, if forming a monetary union leads to an increase in trade then dissolving a union should lead to a decline in trade between the countries concerned. Unfortunately many of the monetary unions considered by Rose were dissolved for reasons such as war and international sanctions which would have led to a decline in trade irrespective of whether the countries concerned used a common currency. One exception is the 50-year monetary union between Ireland and the United Kingdom which, as we saw in Chapter 29, ended in 1979 when the United Kingdom decided not to participate in the ERM. This event has been studied by two Irish economists Rodney Thom and Brendan Walsh of University College Dublin (2002), who concluded that ending the monetary union had no significant effect on Anglo-Irish trade. Hence, while Rose's hypothesis may be compelling to euro advocates it is by no means fully supported by the evidence and cannot be unquestionably accepted as a means of closing the convergence gap.

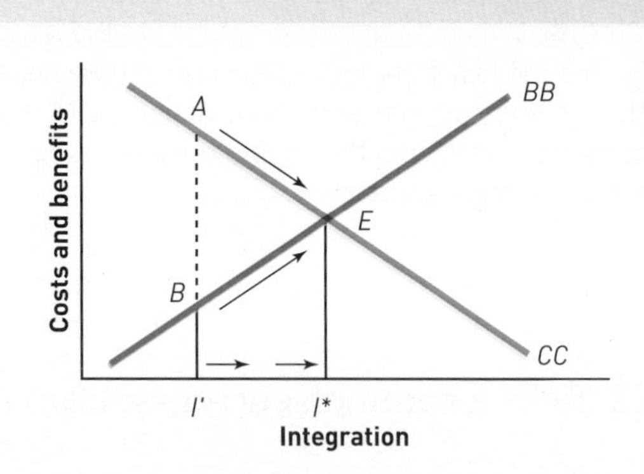


**Figure 30.5 Trade and Economic Convergence.** Prior to joining the euro the degree of economic integration between the United Kingdom and its potential partners is *I'*. If the United Kingdom joins it will experience a net loss equal to the distance *AB*. However, if the use of a common currency promotes trade between partner countries it will also increase the degree of economic integration, moving the United Kingdom closer to the break-even level *I**.

## Flexibility

Earlier in this chapter we saw that the costs of sacrificing policy independence may be relatively high when inflation inertia is strong and labour markets respond slowly to adverse shocks. Specifically, if, following a negative demand shock, money wage contracts are not renegotiated to reflect lower expected inflation then the adjustment back to long-run equilibrium can be prolonged and painful. Can this situation be changed by participation in a monetary union? One possible reason for the slow adjustment of wage and price contracts is that both sides know that their domestic Central Bank may intervene by reducing real interest rates and let the currency depreciate in order to stimulate aggregate demand. Why, for example, should trade unions accept lower wage increases if they can be confident that their

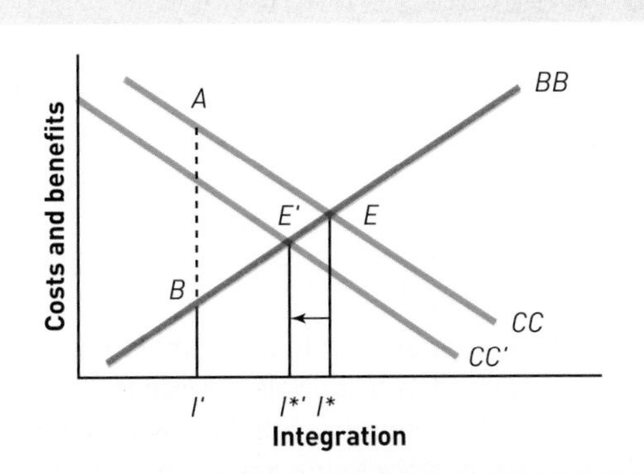


**Figure 30.6 Economic Convergence and Flexibility.** Prior to joining the euro the degree of economic integration between the United Kingdom and its potential partners is *I'*. If the United Kingdom joins it will experience a net loss equal to the distance *AB*. However, if employers and employees realise that they can no longer rely on their own Central Bank to stabilise the economy, inflation inertia may decline, shifting the *CC* curve to the left to *CC'*, reducing the break-even level of integration to *I*'*.

national Central Bank will protect employment by easing monetary policy? Likewise, if the country experiences a positive demand shock, employers are less likely to agree to higher wage increases if they know that the Central Bank will offset inflationary pressures by increasing interest rates and tightening monetary policy. In short, independent stabilisation policy may be regarded as a substitute for market flexibility and a reason for strong inflation inertia. Hence, so long as the domestic Central Bank retains policy independence it is more likely that inflationary expectations will be revised slowly and inflation inertia will be relatively strong. This situation changes dramatically once the country joins a monetary union. The domestic Central Bank loses its independence and neither employers nor employees can be confident that the union's Central Bank will intervene in the face of asymmetric shocks. Hence, it is possible that labour market participants will respond more quickly to shocks, leading to a decline in inflation inertia and a corresponding fall in the cost of sacrificing policy independence. Figure 30.6 illustrates this effect. As before, the degree of integration or convergence between the United Kingdom and the Eurosystem is *I'* and if the United Kingdom decides to join the Eurosystem it experiences a net loss equal to the distance *AB*. However, if inflation inertia declines, the cost will fall at any given level of integration as illustrated by the leftward shift in the United Kingdom's *CC* curve to *CC'*. As a result, the critical break-even level of integration falls to *I*'* narrowing the convergence gap between the United Kingdom and its partner countries.

Although this argument holds, it cannot be regarded as a panacea for Europe's labour market rigidities, which are more a consequence of strong labour laws and sophisticated social welfare systems than of Central Bank policies. In particular, Europe's relatively high levels of redundancy payment and generous welfare benefits reduce the hardships associated with unemployment and make it less likely that workers will accept the rate of wage increase necessary to maintain their jobs in the wake of an adverse shock.

### Is the European Union an optimum currency area?

We have seen that countries form an optimum currency area if the benefits of using a common currency outweigh the costs and that this is more likely if countries experience symmetric shocks and trade extensively with each other. Given that twelve European countries now use a common currency, it is important to ask if they satisfy these key criteria. Economic naturalists 30.3, 30.4 and 30.5 provide some evidence on this issue.

## Economic naturalist 30.3 Are shocks symmetric?

Figure 30.7 uses evidence on demand and supply shocks reported by Jarko Fidrmuc and Iikka Korhonen in a Bank of Finland Discussion Paper (2001). The difference between demand and supply shocks is that the former are assumed to have a *temporary* impact on output while the latter have a *permanent* effect. Demand shocks thus include those illustrated by Figs 30.1 and 30.2 as well as the type of inflation shock discussed in Chapter 28 (see, for example, Fig. 28.9). Supply shocks, on the other hand, can be thought of as shocks to *potential output* (as illustrated in Fig. 28.10). Using data on inflation and output, Fidrmuc and Korhonen were able to estimate the degree to which shocks to specific countries are correlated with equivalent average shocks to the Eurosystem as a whole. A high degree of correlation means that the two events tend to occur together. Hence the closer the correlations are to the maximum value of one the greater the symmetry between each country and the Eurosystem. These results enable us to identify three distinct groups of countries. The first group comprises what might be called the 'European Core': France, Germany, Belgium, Italy, the Netherlands and perhaps Portugal and Austria. These countries all exhibit relatively high *supply-side correlations* suggesting symmetry with the Eurosystem average. Although the correlations for demand shocks are much lower it must be remembered that the estimates are based on pre-euro data and the low demand-side correlations may simply reflect the fact that these countries had their own currencies and to some extent followed independent policies. For example, suppose that, following a negative demand shock, some countries take immediate action by cutting interest rates while others take a 'do-nothing' approach and let their economies adjust gradually. As we would expect much faster adjustment in the former it would not be surprising if the economies diverged significantly. This type of asymmetry should, however, disappear in a monetary union with all countries subject to a common monetary policy. Hence, there is some evidence

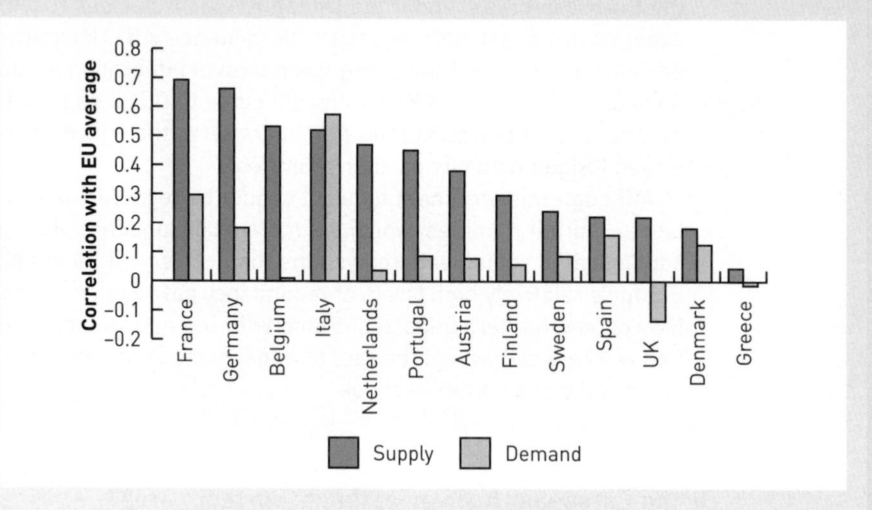


**Figure 30.7 Demand and Supply Shocks.** The figure shows the correlation of demand and supply shocks in individual countries with average shocks in the European Union. A high value indicates that shocks are strongly correlated with the European average and therefore symmetric.

*Source*: Fidrmuc and Korhonen (2001).

to suggest that shocks to these economies are or may become symmetric and that they may be close to the idea of an optimum currency area.

The second group consists of Denmark, Sweden and the United Kingdom, or the three countries that initially opted out of the euro. Given the *relatively low values for supply-side shocks* and, in the case of the United Kingdom *negative correlation of demand-side shocks*, it is unlikely that these countries are symmetric with the Eurosystem average. Hence on this evidence they do not form an optimum currency area with the core economies.

The third group consists of Finland, Greece, Ireland and Spain. These countries are all members of the Eurosystem but the *low correlations with the average demand and supply shocks* suggest that they are not part of a European optimum currency area.

## Economic naturalist 30.4 How important is intra-EU trade?

Figure 30.8 shows the percentage of each economy's GDP exported to other EU countries in 1993, 1998 and 2003. This period is of particular interest because it covers the start of the Single European Market (SEM) in 1993 and the introduction of the euro in 1999, both of which might be expected to stimulate trade between partner countries. Although most economies have experienced an increase in intra-EU trade since 1993 the majority still export less than 20 per cent of their GDP to other EU economies – and for some of the larger countries, such as France and Italy, the figure is closer to 10 per cent, suggesting that trade within the Union still falls short of what might be

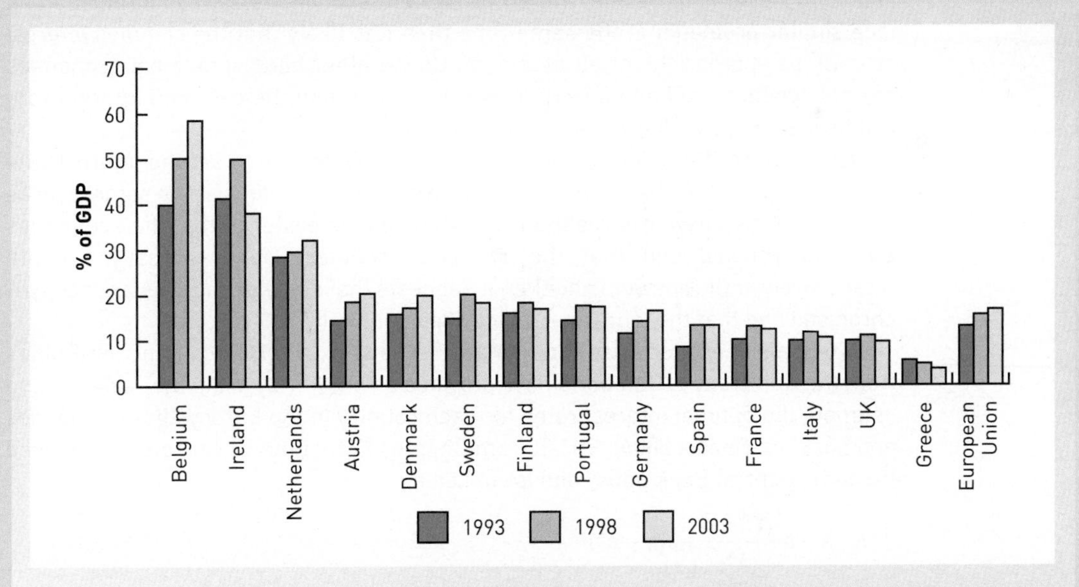


**Figure 30.8 Intra-EU Exports as a Percentage of GDP, 1993, 1998 and 2003.** Intra-EU exports are shown as a percentage of each country's GDP. Trade within the Union is more important to smaller countries. Although most countries show an increase in intra-EU trade since 1993 the majority still export less than 20 per cent of total output to other EU economies.

*Source*: *The European Economy* (Spring 2004). Commission of the European Communities, www.europa_eu.int/comm_finance/publications.

considered necessary for the majority of countries to form an optimum currency area. There do, however, appear to be three country groupings, which are close to but not identical with those identified in Fig. 30.7. First, some of the countries using the euro have seen an increase in their intra-EU trade since 1998. This is especially true of 'European Core' economies such as Austria, Belgium, Germany and the Netherlands. However, other euro countries such as France and Italy have seen a slight fall in their intra-EU exports since 1998. Second, the United Kingdom and Sweden, two of the countries which opted out of the euro, have seen a decline in intra-EU exports since 1998 while the third country, Denmark, has experienced the reverse with its intra-EU trade increasing. Finally, Finland, Greece, Ireland and Spain, the group of euro countries which Fig. 30.7 places outside a possible optimum currency area, have all have experienced either no growth or a decline in intra-EU exports since 1998. As with the evidence on demand and supply shocks this suggests that if an optimum currency area exists it is, at present, limited to a group of 'European Core' economies such as Austria, Belgium, Germany, France, Italy and the Netherlands. Economic naturalist 30.5 provides some additional evidence.

## Economic naturalist 30.5 Does the 'one-size' monetary policy fit all?

In the Eurosystem a single or 'one-size' monetary policy applies to all participating countries. Interest rates set by the ECB in Frankfurt apply from Galway to Vienna and from Helsinki to Seville. If the Eurosystem economies are synchronised and face similar problems at the same time then it is likely that the *common interest rate* will be appropriate for all members. On the other hand, if national economies are not synchronised and face different problems then the common interest rate will be inappropriate for at least some members.

Now consider the following question: If NCBs were free to set the interest rate most appropriate for their own economies would they set rates at the same level as the ECB? If the answer is yes then we can take it as evidence that the economies are synchronised and that the one-size monetary policy actually fits all. Alternatively, if the answer is no then it suggests that some economies are not synchronised and that the 'one-size' policy does not fit all.

Two Spanish economists, Adolfo Maza Fernández, and Blanca Sánchez-Robles from the University of Cantabria have provided an answer by using the Taylor rule to estimate the optimal interest rates for each country in the Eurosystem (Fernández and Sánchez-Robles 2004). Recall from Chapter 27 that the Taylor rule can be used to model Central Bank policy and is written as

$$r = a - b\frac{(Y^* - Y)}{Y^*} + c(\pi - \pi^*)$$

As in Chapter 27, $r$ is the interest rate set by the Central Bank, expressed as a decimal (for example, 5 per cent = 0.05); $Y^* - Y$ is the current output gap (the difference between potential and actual output); $(Y^* - Y)/Y^*$ is the output gap relative to potential output, $\pi$ is actual the inflation rate and $\pi^*$ is the Central Bank's target inflation rate. Both $\pi$ and $\pi^*$ are expressed as decimals (for example, a 2 per cent inflation rate is expressed as 0.02). According to the Taylor rule, the Central Bank responds

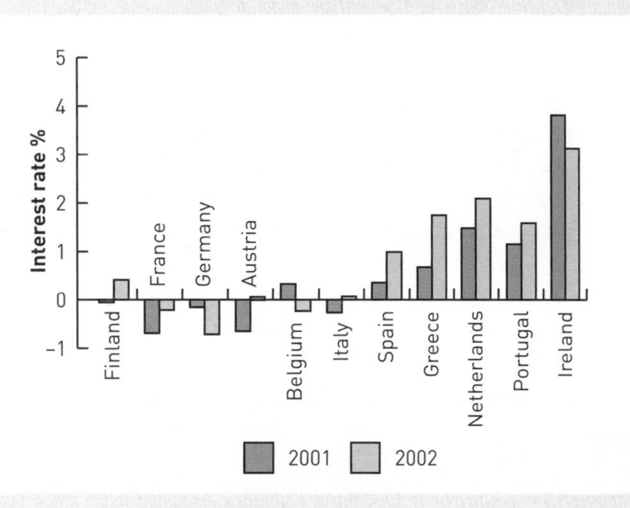


**Figure 30.9 Optimal Interest Rates, 2001 and 2002.** The figure shows the difference between the optimal interest rate for each euro country and the average rate set by the ECB in 2001 and 2002. A positive value indicates that the ECB interest rate was below that which would be predicted by the Taylor rule.

*Source*: Fernández and Sánchez-Robles (2004).

to both output gaps and deviations in the rate of inflation from its target level. The coefficients $b$ and $c$ describe the strength of these responses. For example, if $b$ and $c$ both equal 0.5 then the formula implies that if a recessionary gap equal to a fraction 0.01 of potential output develops, the Central Bank will reduce the real interest rate by 0.5 percentage points (that is, 0.5 times 0.01, or 0.005). Similarly, if inflation rises by 1 percentage point (0.01) relative to the target, according to the Taylor rule the Central Bank will increase the real interest rate by 0.5 percentage points (0.005). The coefficient $a$ estimates the rate of interest set by the Central Bank when $Y = Y^*$ and inflation is on target.

Based on their estimates of the parameters $a$, $b$ and $c$ and actual data for inflation and output gaps Fernández and Sánchez-Robles (2004) report the interest rates which would have been optimal for each economy over the period January 1999–January 2003. By comparing these interest rates with those set by the ECB we can compute an indicator of how appropriate the single monetary policy is for each country. Figure 30.9 summarises the results for 2001 and 2002. Each column measures the difference between the optimal country interest rate and the average rate set by the ECB in that year, 4.27 per cent in 2001 and 3.21 per cent in 2002. (Fernández and Sánchez-Robles 2004 use nominal rather than real interest rates.) A positive value indicates that the rate set by the ECB is below that which the NCB would have set if it could determine policy independently, while a negative value indicates the reverse. The greater the absolute value, the greater the difference between the optimal country rates and the ECB rate.

The results are broadly consistent with those in Economic naturalists 30.3 and 30.4. For so-called 'European Core' economies, such as Austria, Belgium, Germany, France and Italy, the differences between the predicted optimal rate for each economy and the actual ECB rate is less than 1 per cent, suggesting that they are well served by ECB policy. That is, the 'one-size' monetary policy appears to fit these economies. At the other end of the scale countries such as Greece, Ireland, the Netherlands and Portugal appear to have required interest rates much higher than those set by the ECB. This difference is largely because these countries experienced output gaps and inflation rates significantly different from the Eurosystem average. For example, in 2002 the Irish output gap $(Y^* - Y)/Y^*$ was −2.3 per cent as compared with 0.1 per cent for the entire euro area. Likewise, Irish inflation was 6 per cent, or approximately 4 per cent higher than the euro average for 2002. Hence, the 'one-size' monetary policy may fit some but by no means all members of the Eurosystem.

## Summary

- This chapter used the *Theory of Optimum Currency Areas* to assess the suitability of economies for monetary union. This approach uses the *Cost–Benefit Principle* discussed in Chapter 1. The *Cost–Benefit Principle* states that an individual, firm or society should take an action if, and only if, the extra benefits from the action are at least as great as the extra costs. Hence, a country should join a monetary union if, and only if, the benefits outweigh the costs. Benefits include gains from the elimination of currency transactions costs and exchange rate uncertainty, as well as greater price transparency. Sacrificing policy independence is the most important cost of joining a monetary union.
- Once in a monetary union individual countries cannot use monetary and exchange rate policies to stabilise their economies. Rather, they must rely on the single or 'one-size' policy as determined by the union's Central Bank, and the cost of sacrificing policy independence will depend on whether shocks are *symmetric* or *asymmetric*. A symmetric shock implies that countries face similar problems (recessionary or expansionary gaps) at the same time. Conversely, asymmetric shocks mean that countries experience different problems at the same time. For example, one may face a recessionary gap while the other may face an expansionary gap. When shocks are symmetric and countries face similar problems at the same time the single policy will be appropriate across the union and the 'one-size' monetary policy fits all. Hence, the cost of sacrificing policy independence is likely to be relatively low when member countries experience symmetric shocks. Other things being equal, such countries are more likely to form an optimum currency area. Conversely, when shocks are asymmetric countries will require different policies and the 'one-size' policy is unlikely to fit all, implying that some countries may experience difficult adjustment problems. However, a low level of inflation inertia and flexible labour markets can compensate for the loss of policy independence.
- The cost of sacrificing policy independence will be relatively low if shocks are symmetric and economic activity is synchronised. Likewise, benefits are likely to be highest when countries trade extensively with each other and have convergent or integrated economies. The *CC* and *BB* curves illustrate how costs decline and benefits increase with the degree of integration between economies. The point at which these curves intersect defines the break-even level of integration or $I^*$ for a country considering membership of a monetary union. Countries with lower levels of integration will experience a net loss by participating in a monetary union and are not part of an optimum currency area.
- Based on the results of Gordon Brown's five economic tests for joining the euro it appears that the degree of integration between the United Kingdom and the Eurosystem is below the break-even level $I^*$, implying that the British economy would experience a net loss if it replaced sterling with the euro. This, however, does not necessarily mean that the United Kingdom should continue to opt out of the euro. On the hypothesis that a common currency promotes trade between partner countries, joining

the euro today may lead to greater *interdependence* and *integration* between the United Kingdom and the euro economies: that is, using the euro may lead to faster convergence pushing the United Kingdom closer to and even beyond the break-even integration point. However, while this hypothesis has significant support it is by no means fully justified on the available evidence.

- Economic research on issues such as the symmetry of shocks and the impact of the single monetary policy on individual countries suggests that the twelve members of the Eurosystem do not form an optimum currency area. The data do, however, identify a 'European Core' grouping for which economic activity is synchronised and the single policy is appropriate. Although the evidence is mixed, this group probably includes Austria, Belgium, France, Germany, Italy and the Netherlands.

## Key terms

**asymmetric shocks** (875)
**demand shock** (876)
**negative demand shock** (876)
**optimum currency areas** (874)
**positive demand shock** (876)
**sychronised business cycles** (883)
**symmetric shocks** (875)
**transactions costs** (882)

## Review questions

1. What are the principal costs and benefits of a monetary union? How are these costs and benefits related to the degree of economic integration between partner countries?
2. You are asked to advise the Scottish Parliament on the economic case for Scotland using the euro rather than sterling as its currency. List the main points in your report.
3. Give some plausible examples of symmetric and asymmetric shocks.
4. Approximately 70 per cent of Irish imports and 30 per cent of exports are with countries outside the euro area. Using a diagram such as Fig. 30.1 or 30.2, illustrate how a significant appreciation of the euro against other currencies might affect the Irish economy.
5. Why is the ECB unlikely to react to asymmetric shocks within the Eurosystem?
6. Suppose a country in the Eurosystem experiences an asymmetric negative demand shock. If the ECB does not respond by changing euro interest rates, how might this economy adjust to the shock?
7. Explain how low inflation inertia and labour market flexibility may compensate for the loss of policy independence when a country joins a monetary union.
8. Do you agree with the UK position that it cannot join the euro until the British economy is fully integrated with that of the Eurosystem?
9. Suppose the parameters of the Taylor rule are estimated as, $a = 0.03$, $b = 0.4$ and $c = 0.6$. For a particular Eurosystem country, potential output $Y^* = 100$, actual output $Y = 105$, inflation $\pi = 4$ per cent and the target inflation rate is $\pi^* = 2$ per cent. Using the Taylor rule, what is the optimal interest rate for this country? If the ECB sets its interest rate at 3 per cent, what problems might this country face?

## References

European Commission (1990) 'One Market, One Money', *The European Economy* (Brussels: Commission of the European Communities).

Fernández, A. M. and B. Sánchez-Robles (2004) 'An Attempt to Model the ECB's Monetary Policy', University of Cantabria, Working Paper.

Fidrmuc, J. and I. Korhonen (2001) 'Similarity of Supply and Demand Shocks between the Euro Area and the CEECs', Bank of Finland Discussion Paper, 14.

Rose, A. K. (2000) 'One Money, One Market: The Effect of Common Currencies on Trade', *Economic Policy*, April, pp. 8–45.

Thom, R. and B. M. Walsh ( 2002) 'The Effect of Currency Unions on Trade: Lessons from the Irish Experience', *European Economic Review*, June, pp. 1111–23.

# Appendix: The IS-LM Model

Chapter 25 introduced the Keynesian model and defined short-run equilibrium as a position in which the level of output $Y$ equals planned aggregate expenditure *PAE*. Chapter 27 takes the analysis a step further by introducing the money market and allowing planned expenditures to vary with the rate of interest. Chapter 27 also established that for a given level of output the equilibrium rate of interest is determined by equality between the demand for and supply of money. Hence, in this expanded model the economy consists of two markets, the market for goods and services and the market for money.

These markets are inter-linked. For a given rate of interest, as determined in the money market, we can use the model describing the market for goods and services to determine the equilibrium level of output. Conversely, for a given level of output, as determined in the market for goods and services, we can use the model describing the market for money to determine the equilibrium value of the rate of interest. Furthermore, a change in the equilibrium in one market will lead to a change in the equilibrium in the other market. For example, as we saw in Chapter 26, an increase in autonomous expenditure leads, via the income–expenditure multiplier, to an increase in the level of output. However, as explained in Chapter 27, an increase in aggregate income increases the demand for money and, given the supply of money, leads to a higher equilibrium interest rate. Likewise, an increase in the money supply reduces the equilibrium rate of interest which stimulates consumption and investment and, via the multiplier, increases the equilibrium level of output.

In short, we cannot determine equilibrium in one market independently from equilibrium in the other. Rather, we must determine the equilibrium values of income and the interest rate simultaneously. This task is achieved by the IS-LM model, which uses the equilibrium conditions in each market to simultaneously determine the equilibrium values for the level of output and the rate of interest.

## The IS curve

The IS curve plots combinations of the rate of interest and the level of output for which the market for goods and services is in equilibrium. Recall that in the appendix to Chapter 27 we saw that the short-run equilibrium in the market for goods and services can be described by the equation:

$$Y = \left(\frac{1}{1-c}\right)\left[\bar{A} - (a+b)r\right] \tag{1}$$

Where $\bar{A} = \bar{C} - c\bar{T} + \bar{I} + \bar{G} + \overline{NX}$ and the term $-(a + b)r$ captures the idea that when the real rate of *interest* $r$ rises or falls planned expenditures fall or rise by $(a + b)$ times the change in $r$. We have also seen, in Chapter 19, that the real rate of interest equals the difference between the nominal rate of interest ($i$) and the rate of inflation ($\pi$). That is, $r = i - \pi$. However in Chapter 27 we assumed that because inflation changes slowly the central bank can control the real rate of interest over the short-run. To simplify we shall assume that inflation is constant and equal to zero so that $r = i$ in the short-run. For convenience we shall also assume that the economy is closed to international trade and capital flows ($NX = KI = 0$) and that the term $(a + b)$ equals a value denote by $f$. Given these assumptions we can write Equation 1 as:

$$Y = \left(\frac{1}{1-c}\right)\left[\bar{A} - fi\right] \tag{2}$$

Equation (2) defines $(Y, i)$ combinations which give equilibrium in the market for goods and services and is known as the IS equation. Figure 1 presents a graphical illustration of this equation. The top part of Figure 1 illustrates the determination of equilibrium $Y$ and is similar to the Keynesian Cross diagram, Fig. 27.6 in the text. With a rate of interest equal to $i_1$ the expenditure line is $PAE_1$ and equilibrium output is determined at the point A on the 45 degree line ($Y = PAE$) with $Y = Y_1$. The bottom part of Figure 1 has the interest rate on the vertical axis and output on the horizontal. The point C defines the interest rate, output combination $(i_1, Y_1)$ which gives equilibrium in the market for goods and services. If the interest rate were to fall to a lower level $i_2$ then, as illustrated in Chapter 27, the expenditure line shifts up to $PAE_2$ and equilibrium output is determined at the point B on the 45 degree line ($Y = PAE$) with $Y = Y_2$. In the bottom part of Figure 1 the point D defines a second interest rate, output combination $(i_2, Y_2)$, which also gives equilibrium in the market for goods and services. The points C and D are $(i, Y)$ combinations which determine equilibrium in the market for goods and services. The line joining these points is known as the *IS curve*.[1]

### **Example 1**: The IS curve

In a certain economy, $c = 0.8$, $f = 1{,}000$ and $\bar{A} = 1{,}010$. Derive the IS curve when $i = 0.05$, or 5 per cent and when $i = 0.01$, or 1% .

Using Equation (2) for:

$$i = 0.05\text{: } Y = \left(\frac{1}{0.2}\right)\left[1{,}010 - 1{,}000(0.05)\right] = 4{,}800$$

$$i = 0.01\text{: } Y = \left(\frac{1}{0.2}\right)\left[1{,}010 - 1{,}000(0.01)\right] = 5{,}000$$

Hence in Figure 1 the point C corresponds to an $(i, Y)$ combination (0.05, 4,800) and the point D to a combination (0.01, 5,000). As both combinations give equilibrium in the market for goods and services both lie on the IS curve.

#### *The slope of the IS curve*

The IS curve has a negative slope because a reduction in the interest rate stimulates planned aggregate expenditure and via the multiplier leads to a higher equilibrium level of output. That is, to maintain equilibrium in the market for goods and services $i$ and $Y$ must change in opposite directions. To derive the slope of the IS curve we can rewrite Equation (2) as:

$$i = \left(\frac{1}{f}\right)\bar{A} - \left(\frac{1-c}{f}\right)Y \tag{3}$$

Letting the Greek letter delta or $\Delta$ denote the phrase 'change in', then for a constant level of autonomous expenditure $\bar{A}$:

$$\Delta i = -\left(\frac{1-c}{f}\right)\Delta Y$$

And the slope of the IS curve is:

$$\left(\frac{\Delta i}{\Delta Y}\right)_{IS} = -\left(\frac{1-c}{f}\right)$$

[1] The IS, or Investment-Saving, curve gets its name from the fact that in a closed economy without international trade and capital flows, the equilibrium level of $Y$ also corresponds to equality between domestic saving and investment. See Chapter 24.

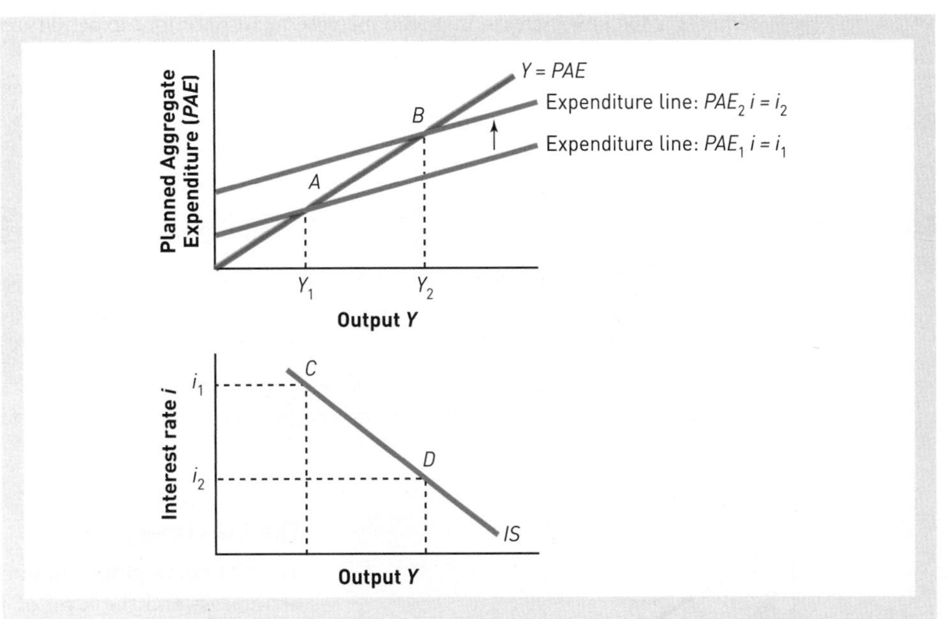


**Figure 1 The IS Curve.** The IS curve traces interest rate and output combinations which give equilibrium in the market for goods and services.

Hence given the value of the marginal propensity to consume $c$, the slope of the IS curve depends on the parameter $f$ which measures the response of consumption and investment to the rate of interest. Other things equal, the greater is $f$, or the greater the responsiveness of consumption and investment to interest rate changes, the smaller the slope and the flatter the IS curve.

*The position of the IS curve*

At a given rate of interest the position of the IS curve will shift when autonomous expenditures change. Recall that the IS equation (2) is:

$$Y = \left(\frac{1}{1-c}\right)[\bar{A} - fi]$$

At any given rate of interest an increase in autonomous expenditure $\bar{A}$ will, via the multiplier, lead to a higher level of output. For example suppose that $\bar{A} = 1{,}010$, $c = 0.8$, $f = 1{,}000$. Then for:

$$i = 0.01\text{: } Y = \left(\frac{1}{0.2}\right)\left[1{,}010 - 1{,}000(0.05)\right] = 5{,}000$$

$$i = 0.05\text{: } Y = \left(\frac{1}{0.2}\right)\left[1{,}010 - 1{,}000(0.05)\right] = 4{,}800$$

If $\bar{A}$ increases by 100 then for:

$$i = 0.01\text{: } Y = \left(\frac{1}{0.2}\right)\left[1{,}110 - 1{,}000(0.01)\right] = 5{,}500$$

$$i = 0.05\text{: } Y = \left(\frac{1}{0.2}\right)\left[1{,}110 - 1{,}000(0.05)\right] = 5{,}300$$

Hence at each rate of interest a 100 unit increase in autonomous expenditure requires a 500 unit increase in $Y$ to maintain equilibrium in the market for goods and services. This effect is illustrated by Figure 2. Starting from the point A with $i = 0.05$, a 100 unit increase in $\bar{A}$

requires a 500 unit increase in $Y$ (the increase in autonomous expenditures times the multiplier) to maintain equilibrium in the market for goods and services. As this result will hold at any given level of the interest rate it follows that an increase in autonomous expenditures shifts the IS curve to the right. Conversely, a reduction in autonomous expenditures shifts the IS curve to the left.

**Exercise 1**

In Euroland the components of planned aggregate expenditure are given by

$$C = \bar{C} + c(Y - T) - ai$$
$$I^P = \bar{I} - bi$$
$$\bar{G} = 200 \quad T = 320 \quad NX = 0$$

Where $\bar{C} = 1{,}245$, $\bar{I} = 310$, $a = 1{,}000$, $b = 500$ and $c = 0.75$. Derive the equation for Euroland's IS curve and find the equilibrium values of $Y$ when $i = 0.01$ and when $i = 0.03$.

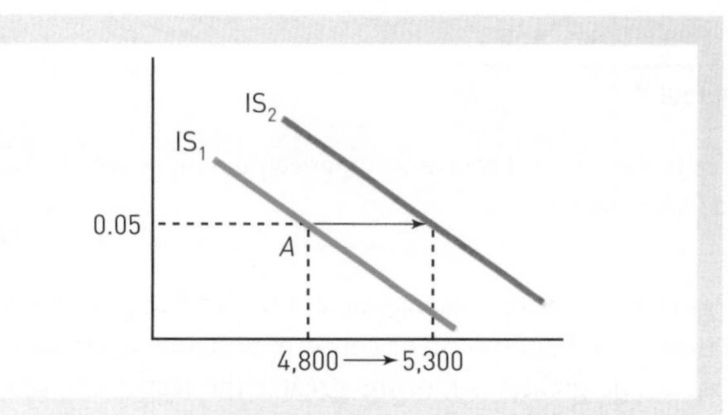


**Figure 2 The Position of the IS Curve.** At each rate of interest an increase in autonomous expenditure increases $Y$ and shifts the IS curve to the right from $IS_1$ to $IS_2$. Conversely, a fall in autonomous expenditure reduces $Y$ and shifts the IS curve to the left.

## The LM curve

The LM curve plots combinations of the rate of interest and the level of output for which the money market is in equilibrium. In that Chapter 27 we saw that the demand for money depends on a number of variables including the nominal rate of interest $i$ and the level of real output $Y$ and that the money supply is determined exogenously by the central bank. To illustrate the derivation of the LM curve, suppose that the market for money can be described as:

| | |
|---|---|
| *Demand* | $M^D = kY - hi$ |
| *Supply* | $M^S = \bar{M}$ |
| *Equilibrium* | $M^D = M^S$ |

The first equation specifies the demand for money as a function of the level of real output $Y$ and the nominal rate of interest $i$. The parameter $k$ models the transaction demand for money. For example, if $k = 0.2$ then a €1,000 increase in income increases the demand for money by €200. Likewise the parameter $h$ models the idea that the interest rate is the opportunity cost of money. Hence, if $k = 1{,}000$ then a 1 per cent increases in the interest rate, or a rise equal to 0.01, reduces the demand for money by €10. The second equation assumes that the money supply is autonomous and set by the central bank and the third equation defines equilibrium in the money market. Substituting the first two equations into the equilibrium condition gives:

$$kY - hi = \bar{M}$$

Re-arranging gives:

$$i = \frac{1}{h}\left[kY - \bar{M}\right] \tag{4}$$

Equation (4) defines $(Y, i)$ combinations which give equilibrium in the market for money and is known as the LM equation. Figure 3 presents a graphical illustration of this equation. The left-hand panel of Figure 3 illustrates the market for money. The money supply is fixed by the central bank at MM and the demand for money is negatively related to the interest rate. At a given level of income $Y = Y_1$ the demand for money curve is $L_1$ and the money market equilibrium is at the point A. The right-hand panel of Figure 3 has the interest rate on the vertical axis and output on the horizontal and the point C defines an interest rate, output combination $(i_1, Y_1)$ which gives equilibrium in the money market. If income were to rise to a higher level $Y_2$ then the demand for money curve shifts up to $L_2$ and equilibrium in the money market is determined at the point B with $i = i_2$. In the right-hand panel the point D defines a second interest rate, output combination $(i_2, Y_2)$ which also gives equilibrium in the money market. Hence points such as C and D are $(i, Y)$ combinations which determine equilibrium in the market for money. The line joining these points is known as the *LM curve*.[2]

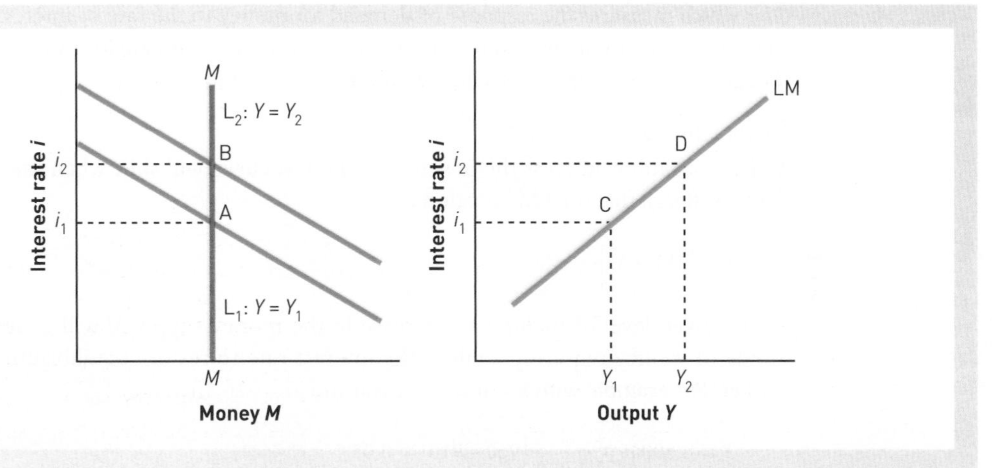


**Figure 3 The LM Curve.** The LM curve traces interest rate and output combinations which give equilibrium in the money market.

## Example 2: The LM curve

In a certain economy, $k = 0.2$, $h = 1{,}000$ and $\bar{M} = 910$. Derive the LM curve when $Y = 4{,}800$ and when $Y = 5{,}000$.

Using Equation (4) for:

$$Y = 4{,}800: i = \frac{1}{1{,}000}\left[960 - 910\right] = 0.05$$

$$Y = 5.000: i = \frac{1}{1{,}000}\left[1{,}000 - 910\right] = 0.09$$

Hence in Figure 3 the point C corresponds to an $(i, Y)$ combination (0.05, 4,800) and the point D to a combination (0.09, 5,000). As both combinations give equilibrium in the market for goods and services both lie on the LM curve.

### *The slope of the LM curve*

The LM curve has a positive slope because, as explained in Chapter 27, an increase in $Y$ increases the demand for money, which given the money supply shifts the demand for money curve to the right resulting in a higher interest rate. That is, to maintain equilibrium in the money market $i$ and $Y$ must change in the same direction. We can use Equation (3) to derive

[2] The LM curve gets it name from the money market equilibrium condition in which the demand for money, or in Keynesian terminology Liquidity Preference (L), equals the money supply (M).

the slope of the LM curve. Letting the Greek letter delta or Δ denote the phrase 'change in', then for a constant money supply $\bar{M}$:

$$\Delta i = \frac{k}{h}\Delta Y$$

And the slope of the LM curve is:

$$\left(\frac{\Delta i}{\Delta Y}\right)_{LM} = \frac{k}{h}$$

Hence given the value of the parameter $k$ the slope of the LM curve depends on the parameter $h$ which measures the response of demand for money to the rate of interest. Other things equal, the greater is $h$, or the greater the responsiveness of demand for money to interest rate changes, the smaller the slope and the flatter the LM curve.

### *The position of the LM curve*

At a given rate of interest the position of the LM curve will shift when the money supply changes. Recall that the LM equation is:

$$i = \frac{1}{h}\left[kY - \bar{M}\right]$$

At any given level of income an increase in the money supply $\bar{M}$ will generate an excess supply of money requiring a fall in the interest rate to restore equilibrium in the money market. For example with $k = 0.2$, $h = 1{,}000$ and $\bar{M} = 910$, then for:

$$Y = 4{,}800: i = \frac{1}{1{,}000}\left[960 - 910\right] = 0.05$$

$$Y = 5.000: i = \frac{1}{1{,}000}\left[1{,}000 - 910\right] = 0.09$$

If $\bar{M}$ increases by 10 to 910, then for:

$$Y = 4{,}800: i = \frac{1}{1{,}000}\left[960 - 920\right] = 0.04$$

$$Y = 5.000: i = \frac{1}{1{,}000}\left[1{,}000 - 920\right] = 0.08$$

Hence at each level of $Y$ a 20 unit increase in the money supply requires a 1 per cent, or 0.01, fall in $i$ to maintain equilibrium in the money market. This effect is illustrated by Figure 4. Starting from the point A with $Y = 4{,}800$, a 10 unit increase in $\bar{M}$ requires a 0.01 fall in $i$ to maintain equilibrium in the money market. As this result will hold at any given level of income it follows that an increase in the money supply shifts the LM curve down to the right. Conversely, a reduction in the money supply shifts the LM curve to the left.

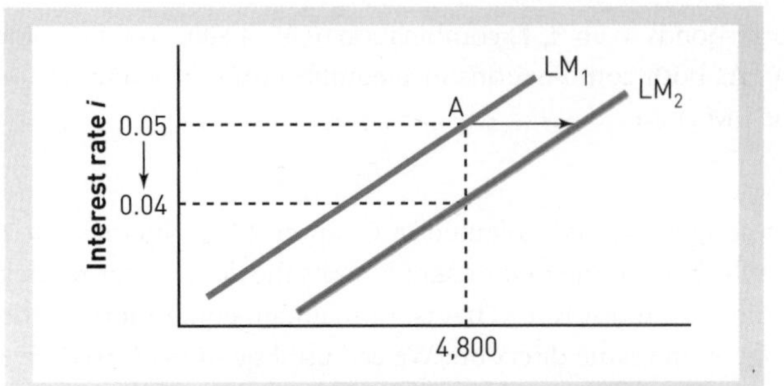


**Figure 4 The Position of the LM Curve.** At each level of $Y$ an increase in the money supply reduces $i$ and shifts the LM curve to the right from $LM_1$ to $LM_2$. Conversely, a reduction in the money supply shifts the LM curve to the left.

**Exercise 2**

Suppose the money market in Euroland can be described by:

| | |
|---|---|
| *Demand* | $M^D = kY - hi$ |
| *Supply* | $M^S = \bar{M}$ |
| *Equilibrium* | $M^D = M^S$ |

Where $k = 0.2$, $h = 2{,}800$ and $\bar{M} = 972$

Derive the equation for Euroland's LM curve and find the equilibrium values of $i$ when $Y = 5{,}140$ and when $Y = 5{,}420$.

## General equilibrium

The IS and LM curves describe equilibrium in two inter-linked markets. The IS curve traces $(i, Y)$ combinations at which $Y = PAE$, the equilibrium condition in the market for goods and services; while the LM curve traces $(i, Y)$ combinations at which $M^D = M^S$, the equilibrium condition in the money market. Hence together they determine the *general equilibrium* condition for the economy. That is, the $(i, Y)$ combination which gives simultaneous equilibrium in all markets. Figure 5 illustrates this overall or general equilibrium position. The intersection of the IS and LM curves at point E defines the $(i, Y)$ combination, which gives simultaneous equilibrium in the market for goods and services $(Y = PAE)$ and in the money market $(M^D = M^S)$.

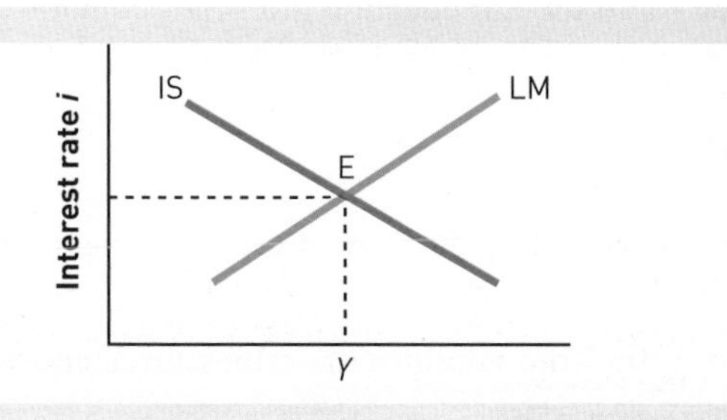


**Figure 5 General Equilibrium.** The intersection of the IS and LM curves at point E defines the $(i, Y)$ combination which gives simultaneous equilibrium in the market for goods and services $(Y = PAE)$ and in the money market $(M^D = M^S)$.

### Example 3: General equilibrium

Suppose that in a given economy $\bar{A} = 1{,}010$, $\bar{M} = 910$, $c = 0.8$, $f = 1{,}000$, $h = 1{,}000$ and $k = 0.2$. Use the IS-LM model to find the equilibrium values for $Y$ and $i$.

Recall that we can write the IS and LM equations as:

$$\text{IS: } i = \left(\frac{1}{f}\right)\bar{A} - \left(\frac{1-c}{f}\right)Y$$

$$\text{LM: } i = \frac{1}{h}\left[kY - \bar{M}\right]$$

Equating the right-hand side of each equation gives:

$$\left(\frac{1}{f}\right)\bar{A} - \left(\frac{1-c}{f}\right)Y = \left(\frac{k}{h}\right)Y - \left(\frac{1}{h}\right)\bar{M}$$

Collecting the terms in $Y$ gives:

$$\left[\frac{k}{h} + \frac{1-c}{f}\right]Y = \left(\frac{1}{f}\right)\bar{A} + \left(\frac{1}{h}\right)\bar{M}$$

Or:

$$\left[\frac{fk + h(1-c)}{hf}\right]Y = \left(\frac{1}{f}\right)\bar{A} + \left(\frac{1}{h}\right)\bar{M}$$

Hence equilibrium Y is given by:

$$Y = \frac{hf}{fk + h(1-c)}\left[\left(\frac{1}{f}\right)\bar{A} + \left(\frac{1}{h}\right)\bar{M}\right]$$

$$= \frac{hf}{fk + h(1-c)}\left[\frac{1}{hf}(h\bar{A} + f\bar{M})\right]$$

$$= \frac{1}{fk + h(1-c)}[h\bar{A} + f\bar{M}] \tag{5}$$

Using the assumed values $\bar{A} = 1{,}010$, $\bar{M} = 910$, $c = 0.8$, $f = 1{,}000$, $h = 1{,}000$ and $k = 0.2$ gives the equilibrium value for $Y$:

$$Y = \frac{1}{400}[(1{,}000)1{,}010 + (1{,}000)910] = 4{,}800$$

Substituting the equilibrium value for $Y$ into the LM equation gives the equilibrium rate of interest:

$$i = \frac{1}{1{,}000}[0.2(4{,}800) - 910] = 0.05$$

Hence in this economy equilibrium $Y = 4{,}800$ and equilibrium $i = 0.05$ or 5.0 per cent.

**Exercise 3**

Using the data in Exercises 1 and 2, find the equilibrium values for $Y$ and $i$ in the Euroland economy.

We will now use the IS-LM model to illustrate the effects of stabilisation policies on the equilibrium values of $Y$ and $i$.

### Stabilisation policy: Closing a recessionary gap

Suppose that, as in Example 3, $\bar{A} = 1{,}010$, $\bar{M} = 910$, $c = 0.8$, $f = 1{,}000$, $h = 1{,}000$ and $k = 0.2$. We have seen that in this economy equilibrium $Y = 4{,}800$ and equilibrium $i = 0.05$ or 5 per cent. Now suppose that the full employment or natural level of output $Y^*$ is 5,000, implying a recessionary gap equal to 200. We shall now illustrate how fiscal and monetary policies can be used to close the recessionary gap.

### **Example 4.** Using fiscal policy to close a recessionary gap

At any given rate of interest an increase in government expenditure $\bar{G}$ will lead to an increase in autonomous expenditure $\bar{A}$ and, as we have seen, shifts the IS curve to the right closing the recessionary gap. By how much does government have to increase $\bar{G}$? Letting the Greek $\Delta$ denote 'change in' and using Equation (5), the change in output is:

$$\Delta Y = \frac{h}{fk + h(1-c)}\Delta\bar{G}$$

$$= \frac{1{,}000}{400}\Delta\bar{G} \tag{6}$$

Hence at a given money supply, $\Delta\bar{M} = 0$, $\Delta Y$ will equal 2.5, or 1,000/400, times the change in autonomous expenditure and for $Y$ to increase by 200 $\bar{G}$ must be increased by 80. That is:

$$\Delta Y = 2.5[80] = 200$$

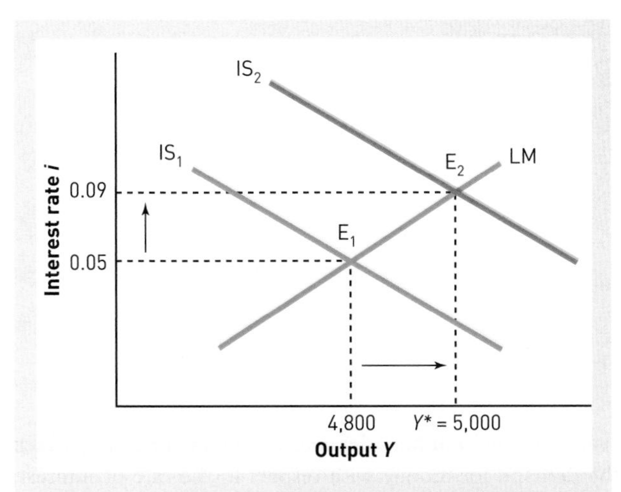


**Figure 6 Closing a Recessionary Gap: Fiscal Policy.** Starting from a recessionary gap equal to 200, an 80 unit increase in government expenditure shifts the IS curve from $IS_1$ to $IS_2$ and closes the recessionary gap. Income increases by 200 but the higher level of $Y$ leads to an excess demand for money and a higher equilibrium rate of interest.

However, following the analysis of Chapter 27, an increase in $Y$ will increase the demand for money and, at a fixed money supply, lead to a higher rate of interest. From Equation (4) the change in the interest rate needed to maintain equilibrium in the money market is:

$$\Delta i = \frac{k}{h}[\Delta Y]$$

$$= \frac{0.2}{1{,}000}[200] = 0.04$$

Hence the equilibrium interest rate will increase from 0.05 to 0.09, or 9 per cent. This effect is illustrated by Figure 6. Starting from the point $E_1$ with $i = 0.05$ and $Y = 4{,}800$, an increase in $\bar{G}$ closes the recessionary gap by shifting the IS curve to the right and establishing a new equilibrium at the point $E_2$ with $Y = 5{,}000$ and $i = 0.09$.

**Exercise 4**

Using the data in Exercise 3, suppose the natural level of income in Euroland is $Y^* = 5{,}840$. (a) By how much would Euroland's government have to change government expenditure for equilibrium $Y$ to equal $Y^*$? (b) What is the resulting change in the equilibrium rate of interest?

### *Crowding out*

Figure 22.9 illustrated the crowding out effect defined as the tendency of increased government deficits to increase interest rates and reduce investment spending. The IS-LM model can be used to analyse the crowding out effect in greater detail. First, note that the IS-LM analysis of fiscal policy differs from that in Chapter 26. In Chapter 26 the impact of an increase in government expenditure on $Y$ is given by:

$$\Delta Y = \frac{1}{1-c}\Delta\bar{G}$$

Hence with the marginal propensity to consume $c = 0.8$, the multiplier $1/(1 - c)$ is equal to 5 and an 80 unit increase in $\bar{G}$ leads to a 400 unit increase in $Y$ as compared to a 200 increase in the IS-LM model. The key difference is that in Chapter 26 we used a 'partial equilibrium' Keynesian model which assumes that the rate of interest is constant at all levels of $Y$. In contrast, the IS-LM general equilibrium model permits the market for goods and services to interact with the money market. Hence as $Y$ increases, the demand for money increases forcing a rise in the rate of interest which in turn lowers consumption and investment spending and partially offsets the effect of the fiscal stimulus. This offsetting effect is equivalent to the *crowding out* effect discussed in Chapter 22. Using arrows to denote the direction of change this sequence can be illustrated as:

$$\underbrace{\uparrow \bar{G} \rightarrow \uparrow Y}_{Multiplier} \rightarrow \underbrace{\uparrow M^D \rightarrow \uparrow i}_{Money\ Market} \rightarrow \underbrace{\downarrow C, I \rightarrow \downarrow Y}_{Crowding\ Out}$$

To assess the strength of this crowding out effect, recall that in the IS-LM model equilibrium $Y$ is given by Equation (5):

$$Y = \frac{1}{fk + h(1-c)}\left[h\bar{A} + f\bar{M}\right]$$

And the income–expenditure multiplier is:

$$\frac{\Delta Y}{\Delta \bar{G}} = \frac{h}{fk + h(1-c)} = \frac{1}{\frac{fk}{h} + (1-c)}$$

For given values of $c$, $k$ and $f$ the value of the multiplier depends on the parameter $h$, which measures the responsiveness of the demand for money with respect to the rate of interest. The higher is the parameter $h$, the smaller is $fk/h$ and the greater the value of the multiplier. For example, with $c = 0.8$, $f = 1{,}000$, $k = 0.2$ and $h = 1{,}000$ the multiplier is 2.5. But with $h = 4{,}000$ the multiplier increases to 4. Hence the greater the responsiveness of the demand for money with respect to the rate of interest, the weaker the crowding out effect and the greater the effectiveness of fiscal policy.

To explain the reasoning behind this result, recall from Equation (4) that for a given change in $Y$ the change in $i$ required to maintain equilibrium in the market for money is given by:

$$\Delta i = \frac{k}{h}\Delta Y$$

Hence the greater is $h$, the smaller is the change in $i$ required to restore equilibrium in the market for money and the smaller the rise in $i$, the lower the crowding out impact on consumption and investment.

### **Example 5**. Crowding out

Suppose that $\bar{A} = 1{,}010$, $\bar{M} = 910$, $c = 0.8$, $f = 1{,}000$, $k = 0.2$, equilibrium $Y = 4{,}800$ and equilibrium $i = 0.05$. If government expenditure is increased by 80, find the change in the equilibrium values of $Y$ and $i$ when $h = 1{,}000$ and when $h = 4{,}000$.

In Example 4 we saw that when $h = 1{,}000$ the multiplier is 2.5 and an 80 unit increase in $\bar{G}$ leads to a 200 unit increase in $Y$ and a 4 per cent increase in $i$. With $h = 4{,}000$:

$$\Delta Y = \frac{h}{fk + h(1-c)}\Delta \bar{G}$$

$$= \frac{4{,}000}{1{,}000}(80) = 320 \qquad (7)$$

In this case the multiplier equals 4 and an 80 unit increase in government expenditure will increase $Y$ by 320. The change in $i$ required to maintain equilibrium in the market for money is given by:

$$\Delta i = \frac{k}{h}\Delta Y = \frac{0.2}{4{,}000}(320) = 0.016$$

And the new equilibrium interest rate is 0.066, or 6.6 per cent. Hence the greater is $h$, the greater the multiplier and the smaller the increase in the interest rate required to restore equilibrium in the money market. Other things equal, the smaller the increase in $i$, the smaller the decline in consumption and investment and the weaker the crowding out effect. This result is illustrated by Figure 7, which shows that the flatter the LM curve, the smaller the impact on $i$ and the greater the impact on $Y$.

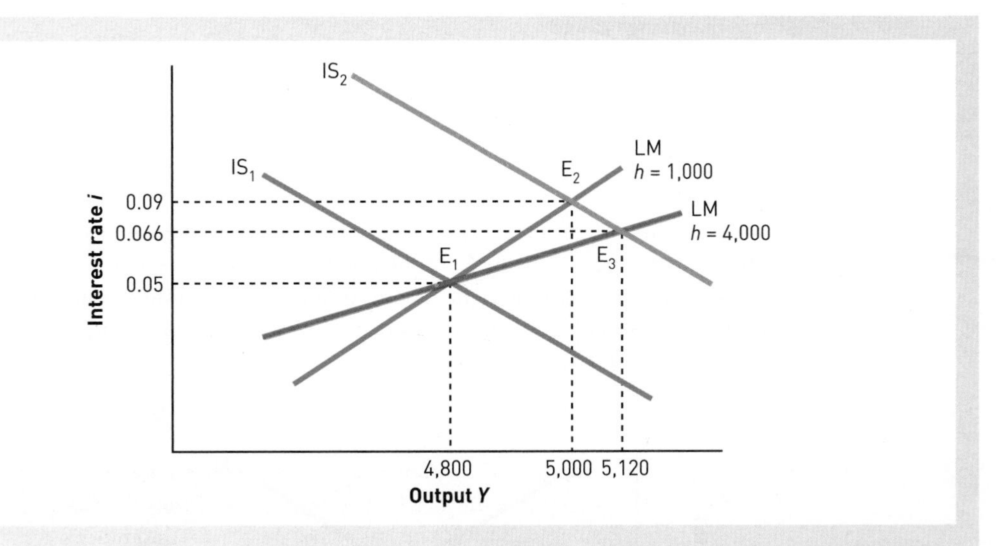


**Figure 7 Crowding Out.** When $h$ = 1,000 an 80 unit increase in government expenditure increases $Y$ from 4,800 to 5,000 and $i$ from 0.05 to 0.09. With $h$ = 4,000 the LM curve is flatter and the same increase in government expenditure increases $Y$ by 320 to 5,120 and $i$ by 0.016 to 0.066.

**Exercise 5**

Using the data in Exercise 3 recall what is the value of Euroland's income–expenditure multiplier? What is the value of Euroland's multiplier if the parameter $h = 3{,}600$ rather than 2,800? What does this imply for the effectiveness of fiscal policy in Euroland?

### Example 6. Using monetary policy to close a recessionary gap

Recall that we are assuming that $\bar{A} = 1{,}010$, $\bar{M} = 910$, $c = 0.8$, $f = 1{,}000$, $h = 1{,}000$, $k = 0.2$, $Y = 4{,}800$, $i = 0.05$ and that the economy faces a recessionary gap equal to 200. At any given level of $Y$ an increase in the money supply $\bar{M}$ will lead to a fall in the interest rate and, as we have seen, shifts the LM curve to the right closing the recessionary gap. By how much does the central bank have to increase $\bar{M}$? Letting the Greek $\Delta$ denote 'change in' and using Equation (5), the change in output is:

$$\Delta Y = \frac{f}{fk + h(1-c)} \Delta\bar{M}$$

$$= \frac{1{,}000}{400} \Delta\bar{M} \qquad (8)$$

Hence with $\Delta\bar{A} = 0$, $\Delta Y$ will equal 2.5, or 1,000/400, times the change in the money supply and for $Y$ to increase by 200 $\bar{M}$ must be increased by 80. That is:

$$\Delta Y = 2.5[80] = 200$$

To find the change in the rate of interest we can use the LM equation:

$$i = \frac{1}{h}\left[kY - \bar{M}\right]$$

Hence the change in $i$ is:

$$\Delta i = \frac{k}{h}\Delta Y - \frac{1}{h}\Delta \bar{M}$$

$$= \frac{0.2}{1,000}(200) - \frac{1}{1,000}(80) = -0.04$$

Hence the equilibrium interest rate will fall from 0.05 to 0.01, or 1 per cent. This effect is illustrated by Figure 8. Starting from the point $E_1$ with $i = 0.05$ and $Y = 4,800$, an increase in $\bar{M}$ shifts the LM curve to the right. The resulting fall in the rate of interest closes the recessionary gap by stimulating consumption and investment, establishing a new equilibrium at the point $E_2$ with $Y = 5,000$ and $i = 0.01$.

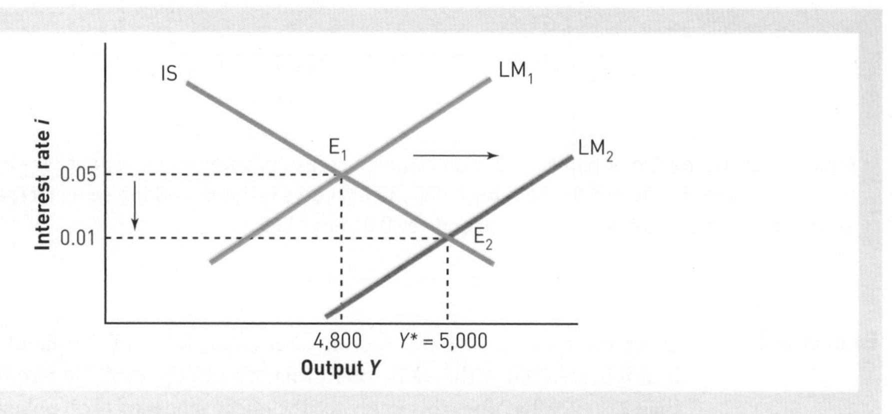


**Figure 8 Closing a Recessionary Gap: Monetary Policy.** The increase in $\bar{M}$ shifts the LM curve from $LM_1$ to $LM_2$ resulting in a lower rate of interest and closes the recessionary gap by simulating consumption and investment leading to an increase in $Y$.

To assess the effectiveness of monetary policy we use Equation (8):

$$\Delta Y = \frac{f}{fk + h(1-c)}\Delta \bar{M}$$

The term:

$$\frac{f}{fk + h(1-c)} = \frac{1}{k + h(1-c)/f}$$

measures the change in equilibrium $Y$ resulting from each unit change in $\bar{M}$ and can be thought of as the *'money multiplier'* or the effect of a 1 unit change in the nominal money supply on short-run equilibrium output. For given values of $c$, $k$ and $h$ the value of the money multiplier depends on the parameter $f$, which measures the responsiveness of consumption and investment to changes in the rate of interest. The higher is the parameter $f$, the smaller is $h(1-c)/f$ and the greater the value of the money multiplier. For example, with $c = 0.8$, $h = 1,000$, $k = 0.2$ and $f = 1,000$ the money multiplier is 2.5. But with $f = 4,000$ value of the money multiplier increases to 4. Hence the greater the responsiveness of consumption and investment to changes in the rate of interest, the greater the effectiveness of monetary policy. However if $f = 4,000$ the money multiplier will be $1/0.25 = 4$ and an 80 unit increase in the money supply will increase equilibrium $Y$ by 320. The corresponding change in the interest rate is given by:

$$\Delta i = \frac{k}{h}\Delta Y - \frac{1}{h}\Delta\bar{M}$$

$$= \frac{0.2}{1{,}000}(320) - \frac{1}{1{,}000}(80) = -0.016$$

Hence the equilibrium interest rate will fall from 0.05 to 0.034. We can explain the reasoning behind this result as follows. Using arrows to denote the direction of change the process by which monetary policy leads to a change in *Y* can be illustrated as:

$$\uparrow M \rightarrow \downarrow i \rightarrow \uparrow PAE \rightarrow Y$$

That is, an increase in the money supply leads to a fall in the rate of interest, which stimulates planned aggregate expenditure (consumption and investment) and leads to a higher level of output. The second link in this chain depends on the parameter *f*, which measures the responsiveness of consumption and investment to changes in the rate of interest. Hence the greater is *f*, the greater the impact on *PAE* and the greater the increase in *Y*. This relationship between the strength of monetary policy and the slope of the IS curve is illustrated by Figure 9, which shows that the flatter the IS curve, or the greater is *f*, the smaller the impact on *i* and the greater the impact on *Y*.

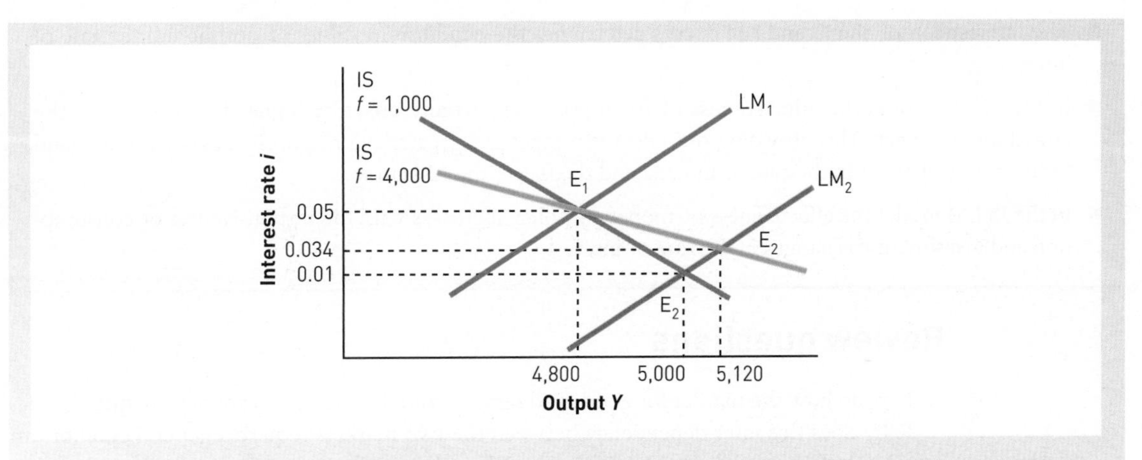


**Figure 9. The Strength of Monetary Policy.** When $f = 1{,}000$ an 80 unit increase in $\bar{M}$ increases *Y* from 4,800 to 5,000 and reduces *i* from 0.05 to 0.01. With $f = 4{,}000$ the IS curve is flatter and the same increase in $\bar{M}$ increases *Y* by 320 to 5,120 and *i* by 0.016 to 0.034.

**Exercise 6** Using the data in Exercise 3 suppose the natural level of income in Euroland is $Y^* = 5{,}625$. (a) By how much would Euroland's central bank have to change the money supply for equilibrium *Y* to equal $Y^*$? (b) What is the resulting change in the equilibrium rate of interest?

## Summary

- The IS-LM model is a general equilibrium model which simultaneously determines the equilibrium values of income and the rate of interest.
- The IS curve plots income and interest rate combinations which give equilibrium in the market for goods and services, while the LM curve plots similar combinations for the money market.
- The slope of the IS curve depends on the responsiveness of consumption and investment to changes in the rate of interest. The more responsive are consumption and investment, the lower the slope and the flatter the IS curve.
- An increase in autonomous expenditure shifts the IS curve to the right and a decrease shifts the curve to the left.
- The slope of the LM curve depends on the responsiveness of the demand for money to changes in the rate of interest. The more responsive is the demand for money, the lower the slope and the flatter the LM curve.
- An increase in the money supply shifts the LM curve to the right and a decrease shifts the curve to the left.
- The intersection of the IS and LM curves determines the equilibrium values of output and the rate of interest.
- In the IS-LM model the effectiveness of fiscal policy is partially offset by higher interest rates – the crowding out effect. This crowding out effect is weaker the greater the responsiveness of the demand for money to changes in the rate of interest and the flatter the LM curve.
- In the IS-LM model the effectiveness of monetary policy increases with the responsiveness of consumption and investment to changes in the rate of interest.

## Review questions

1. Explain how the market for goods and services and the market for money are inter-linked. Why does this inter-dependency between the two markets require a general equilibrium model of income determination rather than the simple Keynesian model introduced in Chapter 25?
2. Explain why the slope of the IS curve depends on the responsiveness of consumption and investment to changes in the rate of interest. If consumption and investment become more responsive to changes in the rate of interest does this make the IS curve flatter or steeper?
3. Explain why the slope of the LM curve depends on the responsiveness of the demand for money to changes in the rate of interest. If the demand for money becomes less responsive to changes in the rate of interest does this make the LM curve flatter or steeper?
4. Explain how an increase in government expenditure shifts the position of the IS curve.
5. Explain how a reduction in the money supply shifts the position of the LM curve.
6. Using the IS-LM model, explain how (a) an increase in government expenditure and (b) a reduction in the money supply affect the equilibrium values for the level of income and the rate of interest.
7. Explain the concept of crowding out. Why does the strength of fiscal policy depend on the responsiveness of the demand for money to changes in the rate of interest?
8. Would the effectiveness of monetary policy be strengthened or weakened if consumption and investment became more responsive to changes in the rate of interest?

## Answers to appendix exercises

1. Along the IS curve the market for goods and services is in equilibrium and $PAE = Y$. $PAE$ is given by: $PAE = C + I^P + G + NX$. Substituting for the components of $PAE$ gives:

$$PAE = [\bar{C} + c(Y - T) - ai] + [\bar{I} - bi] + \bar{G}$$
$$= [\bar{C} + \bar{I} + \bar{G} - cT] - fi + cY$$
$$= \bar{A} - fi + cY$$

Where $\bar{A} = \bar{C} + \bar{I} + \bar{G} - cT$ and $f = (a + b)$. Equating $PAE$ to $Y$ gives equilibrium output as

$$Y = \bar{A} - fi + cY$$
$$= \left(\frac{1}{1-c}\right)[\bar{A} - fi]$$

Which is the equation for Euroland's IS curve. Given the assumed values $\bar{A} = 1{,}515$ and $f = 1{,}500$, equilibrium $Y$ is given by:

$$Y = \left(\frac{1}{0.25}\right)[1{,}515 - 1{,}500i]$$

Hence:

$$\text{For } i = 0.01 \quad Y = \left(\frac{1}{0.25}\right)[1{,}515 - 1{,}500(0.01)] = 6{,}000$$

$$\text{For } i = 0.03 \quad Y = \left(\frac{1}{0.25}\right)[1{,}515 - 1{,}500(0.03)] = 5{,}880$$

As the $(i, Y)$ combinations (0.01, 6,000) and (0.03, 5,880) give equilibrium in the market for goods and services they are points on Euroland's IS curve.

2. Along the LM curve the market for money is in equilibrium and $M^D = M^S$. Hence in equilibrium

$$kY - hi = \bar{M}$$

or:

$$i = \left(\frac{1}{h}\right)[kY - \bar{M}]$$

Which is the equation for Euroland's LM curve. At each value of $Y$, the equilibrium interest rate is given by:

$$i = \left(\frac{1}{2{,}800}\right)[0.2Y - 972]$$

Hence:

$$\text{For } Y = 5{,}140 \quad i = \left(\frac{1}{2{,}800}\right)[0.2x5{,}140 - 972] = 0.02$$

$$\text{For } Y = 5{,}420 \quad i = \left(\frac{1}{2{,}800}\right)[0.2x5{,}420 - 972] = 0.04$$

As the $(i, Y)$ combinations (0.02, 5,140) and (0.04, 5,420) give equilibrium in the market for money they are points on Euroland's LM curve.

3. In Exercise 1 we saw that the equation for Euroland's IS curve is:

$$Y = \left(\frac{1}{1-c}\right)[\bar{A} - fi]$$

Re-arranging gives:

$$i = \left(\frac{1}{f}\right)\bar{A} - \left(\frac{1-c}{f}\right)Y$$

Likewise in Exercise 2 we saw that the equation for Euroland's LM curve is:

$$i = \left(\frac{1}{h}\right)[kY - \bar{M}]$$

Equating these two expressions gives:

$$\left(\frac{1}{f}\right)\bar{A} - \left(\frac{1-c}{f}\right)Y = \left(\frac{1}{h}\right)[kY - \bar{M}]$$

Re-arranging gives the equilibrium value for $Y$:

$$Y = \left(\frac{1}{fk + h(1-c)}\right)[h\bar{A} + f\bar{M}]$$

$$= \left(\frac{1}{1{,}000}\right)[2{,}800x1{,}515 + 1{,}500x972] = 5{,}700$$

Substituting $Y = 5{,}700$ into the LM equation gives the equilibrium interest rate:

$$i = \left(\frac{1}{2{,}800}\right)[0.2x5{,}700 - 972] = 0.06$$

Hence in Euroland equilibrium $Y = 5{,}700$ and equilibrium $i = 0.06$ or 6 per cent.

4. As equilibrium $Y = 5{,}700$ and $Y^* = 5{,}840$ Euroland faces a recessionary gap equal to 140.

   a. In Exercise 3 we saw that equilibrium $Y$ is given by:

$$Y = \left(\frac{1}{1{,}000}\right)[2{,}800\bar{A} + 1{,}500\bar{M}]$$

Where $\bar{A} = 1{,}515$ and $\bar{M} = 972$. As autonomous government expenditure $\bar{G}$ is a component of $\bar{A}$, the change in $Y$ resulting from a change in $\bar{G}$ is:

$$\Delta Y = 2.8\Delta\bar{G}$$

For $\Delta Y = 140$

$$\Delta\bar{G} = 140/2.8 = 50$$

Hence the multiplier is 2.8 and to close a recessionary gap equal to 140 the government must increase autonomous expenditure by 50.

   b. In Exercise 2 we saw that the equation for Euroland's LM curve is:

$$i = \left(\frac{1}{h}\right)[kY - \bar{M}]$$

At a constant money supply the change in the rate of interest is:

$$\Delta i = \left(\frac{1}{h}\right)[k\Delta Y]$$

$$= \left(\frac{0.2}{2{,}800}\right)140 = 0.01$$

Hence the equilibrium interest rate increases by 0.01 or 1 per cent.

**5.** In Exercise 3 we saw that equilibrium $Y$ is given by:

$$Y = \left(\frac{1}{fk + h(1-c)}\right)[h\bar{A} + f\bar{M}]$$

The income expenditure multiplier is:

$$\frac{\Delta Y}{\Delta \bar{A}} = \frac{h}{fk + h(1-c)}$$

With $f = 1{,}500$, $k = 0.2$, $c = 0.75$ and $h = 2{,}800$ the multiplier is:

$$\frac{\Delta Y}{\Delta \bar{A}} = \frac{2{,}800}{300 + 700} = 2.8$$

Hence increasing government expenditure by €1 million results in a €2.8 million increase in $Y$. However, if $h = 3{,}600$ the multiplier is:

$$\frac{\Delta Y}{\Delta \bar{A}} = \frac{3{,}600}{300 + 900} = 3.0$$

And increasing government expenditure by €1 million results in a €3 million increase in $Y$. It follows that other things equal the greater the value of the parameter $h$, the greater the multiplier and the greater the impact of fiscal policy on income.

**6.** As equilibrium $Y = 5{,}700$ and $Y^* = 5{,}625$ Euroland faces an expansionary gap equal to 75.

**a.** In Exercise 3 we saw that equilibrium $Y$ is given by:

$$Y = \left(\frac{1}{fk + h(1-c)}\right)[h\bar{A} + f\bar{M}]$$

$$= \left(\frac{1}{1{,}000}\right)[2{,}800\bar{A} + 1{,}500\bar{M}]$$

Where $\bar{A} = 1{,}515$ and $\bar{M} = 972$. At a given level of autonomous expenditure $\bar{A}$, the change in $Y$ resulting from a change in $\bar{M}$ is:

$$\Delta Y = 1.5\Delta\bar{M}$$

For $\Delta Y = -75$

$$\Delta\bar{M} = -75/1.5 = -50$$

Hence to close an expansionary gap equal to 75 the central bank must reduce the money supply by 50.

**b.** In Exercise 2 we saw that the equation for Euroland's LM curve is:

$$i = \left(\frac{1}{h}\right)[kY - \bar{M}]$$

For $k = 0.2$, $\Delta Y = -75$ and $\Delta\bar{M} = 50$. The resulting change in the rate of interest is:

$$\Delta i = \left(\frac{1}{h}\right)[k\Delta Y - \Delta\bar{M}]$$

$$= \left(\frac{1}{2{,}800}\right)[-15 + 50] = 0.0125$$

Hence the equilibrium interest rate increases by 0.0125 or 1.25 per cent.

# Glossary

**100 per cent reserve banking** a situation in which banks' reserves equal 100 per cent of their deposits
**absolute advantage** one person has an absolute advantage over another if an hour spent in performing a task earns more than the other person can earn in an hour at the task
**accounting profit** the difference between a firm's total revenue and its explicit cost
**adverse selection** the pattern in which insurance tends to be purchased disproportionately by those who are most costly for companies to insure
**aggregate demand (*AD*) curve** shows the relationship between short-run equilibrium output *Y* and the rate of inflation $\pi$; the name of the curve reflects the fact that short-run equilibrium output is determined by, and equals, total planned spending in the economy: increases in inflation reduce planned spending and short-run equilibrium output, so the aggregate demand curve is downward-sloping
**aggregate supply shock** either an inflation shock or a shock to potential output; adverse aggregate supply shocks of both types reduce output and increase inflation
**aggregation** the adding up of individual economic variables to obtain economywide totals
**allocative function of price** to direct resources away from overcrowded markets and toward markets that are underserved
**appreciation** an increase in the value of a currency relative to other currencies
**assets** anything of value that one owns
**asymmetric information** where buyers and sellers are not equally informed about the characteristics of products or services
**asymmetric shocks** affect different economies in different ways at the same time
**attainable point** any combination of goods that can be produced using currently available resources
**autarky** a situation in which a country is economically self-sufficient
**automatic stabilisers** automatic changes in the government budget deficit which help to dampen fluctuations in economic activity
**autonomous expenditure** the portion of planned aggregate expenditure that is independent of output
**average benefit** the total benefit of undertaking *n* units of an activity divided by *n*
**average cost** the total cost of undertaking *n* units of an activity divided by *n*
**average labour productivity** output per person employed
**average total cost (ATC)** total cost divided by total output
**average variable cost (AVC)** variable cost divided by total output
**balanced-budget multiplier** the effect on short-run equilibrium output of an increase in government purchases financed by an equal increase in taxation. As the change in output equals the change in government purchases, the balanced budget multiplier equals one
**balance-of-payments deficit** the net decline in a country's stock of international reserves over a year
**balance-of-payments surplus** the net increase in a country's stock of international reserves over a year
**Bank of England** the central bank of the United Kingdom
**bank reserves** cash or similar assets held by commercial banks for the purpose of meeting depositor withdrawals and payments
**barrier to entry** any force that prevents firms from entering a new market
**barter** the direct trade of goods or services for other goods or services
**basic elements of a game** the players, the strategies available to each player and the payoffs each player receives for each possible combination of strategies
**bequest saving** saving done for the purpose of leaving an inheritance
**Bertrand competition** firms choose a price and accept that quantity sold depends on demand at that price
**better-than-fair gamble** a gamble whose expected value is positive
**bond** a legal promise to repay a debt, usually including both the principal amount and regular interest payments

**boom** a particularly strong and protracted expansion
**Bretton Woods system** an exchange rate system centred on the US dollar
**buyer's reservation price** the largest euro amount the buyer would be willing to pay for a good
**buyer's surplus** the difference between the buyer's reservation price and the price he or she actually pays
**capital gains** increases in the value of existing assets
**capital good** a long-lived good, which is itself produced and used to produce other goods and services
**capital inflows** purchases of domestic assets by foreign households and firms
**capital losses** decreases in the value of existing assets
**capital outflows** purchases of foreign assets by domestic households and firms
**cartel** a coalition of firms that agrees to restrict output for the purpose of earning an economic profit
**'cash on the table'** economic metaphor for unexploited gains from exchange
**central planning** the allocation of economic resources is determined by a political and administrative mechanism that gathers information as to technology, resource availability and end demands for goods and services
**change in demand** a shift of the entire demand curve
**change in supply** a shift of the entire supply curve
**change in the quantity demanded** a movement along the demand curve that occurs in response to a change in price
**change in the quantity supplied** a movement along the supply curve that occurs in response to a change in price
**closed economy** an economy that does not trade with the rest of the world
**Coase theorem** if at no cost people can negotiate the purchase and sale of the right to perform activities that cause externalities, they can always arrive at efficient solutions to the problems caused by externalities
**collective good** a good or service that, to at least some degree, is non-rival but excludable
**comparative advantage** one person has a comparative advantage over another in a task if his or her opportunity cost of performing a task is lower than the other person's opportunity cost
**compensating wage differential** a difference in the wage rate – negative or positive – that reflects the attractiveness of a job's working conditions
**commitment device** a way of changing incentives so as to make otherwise empty threats or promises credible
**commitment problem** a situation in which people cannot achieve their goals because of an inability to make credible threats or promises
**common market** the member states agree to free up trade in services and to permit liberalised (in the limiting case, free) movement of labour and capital
**complements** two goods are complements in consumption if an increase in the price of one causes a leftward shift in the demand curve for the other (or if a decrease causes a rightward shift)
**compound interest** the payment of interest not only on the original deposit but on all previously accumulated interest
**constant (or parameter)** a quantity that is fixed in value
**constant returns to scale** a production process is said to have constant returns to scale if, when all inputs are changed by a given proportion, output changes by the same proportion
**consumer price index (CPI)** for any period, measures the cost in that period of a standard basket of goods and services relative to the cost of the same basket of goods and services in a fixed year, called the *base year*
**consumer surplus** the difference between a buyer's reservation price for a product and the price actually paid
**consumption expenditure (or consumption)** spending by households on goods and services, such as food, clothing and entertainment
**consumption function** the relationship between consumption spending and its determinants, in particular disposable (after-tax) income
**consumption possibilities** the combinations of goods and services that a country's citizens might feasibly consume
**contractionary policies** government policy actions designed to reduce planned spending and output
**costly-to-fake principle** to communicate information credibly to a potential rival, a signal must be costly or difficult to fake

**cost-plus regulation** a method of regulation under which the regulated firm is permitted to charge a price equal to its explicit costs of production plus a mark-up to cover the opportunity cost of resources provided by the firm's owners
**coupon payments** regular interest payments made to the bondholder
**coupon rate** the interest rate promised when a bond is issued
**Cournot competition** firms choose an output and accept the market price
**credible promise** a promise that is in the interests of the promissor to keep when the time comes to act.
**credible threat** a threat to take an action that is in the threatener's interest to carry out
**cross-price elasticity of demand** the percentage by which the quantity demanded of the first good changes in response to a 1 per cent change in the price of the second
**crowding out** the tendency of increased government deficits to reduce investment spending
**customer discrimination** the willingness of consumers to pay more for a product produced by members of a favoured group, even if the quality of the product is unaffected
**customs union** the members, in addition to permitting free trade between them, agree to a single and common set of trade restrictions (or 'commercial policy') with respect to non-members
**cyclical unemployment** the extra unemployment that occurs during periods of recession
**cyclically adjusted budget deficit** eliminates automatic changes by evaluating the government's budget deficit at a constant level of output
**deadweight loss** the reduction in total economic surplus that results from the adoption of a policy
**decision tree (or game tree)** a diagram that describes the possible moves in a game in sequence and lists the payoffs that correspond to each possible combination of moves
**deflating (a nominal quantity)** the process of dividing a nominal quantity by a price index (such as the CPI) to express the quantity in real terms
**deflation** a situation in which the prices of most goods and services are falling over time so that inflation is negative
**demand curve** a schedule or graph showing the quantity of a good that buyers wish to buy at each price
**demand for money** the amount of wealth an individual chooses to hold in the form of money
**demand shock** sudden or unexpected change in planned aggregate expenditure (PAE)
**dependent variable** a variable in an equation whose value is determined by the value taken by another variable in the equation
**depreciation** a decrease in the value of a currency relative to other currencies
**depression** a particularly severe or protracted recession
**devaluation** a reduction in the official value of a currency (in a fixed exchange rate system)
**differentiation** finding the slope or rate of change of a function using algebra rather than geometry
**diminishing returns to capital** if the amount of labour and other inputs employed is held constant, then the greater the amount of capital already in use, the less an additional unit of capital adds to production
**diminishing returns to labour** if the amount of capital and other inputs in use is held constant, then the greater the quantity of labour already employed, the less each additional worker adds to production
**disappearing political discourse** the theory that people who support a position may remain silent, because speaking out would create a risk of being misunderstood
**discouraged workers** people who say they would like to have a job but have not made an effort to find one in the recent past
**discretionary fiscal policy** decisions by government to increase or decrease the levels of government purchases, transfer payments and taxation
**diversification** the practice of spreading one's wealth over a variety of different financial investments to reduce overall risk
**dividend** a regular payment received by shareholders for each share that they own
**dominant strategy** one that yields a higher payoff no matter what the other players in a game choose
**dominated strategy** any other strategy available to a player who has a dominant strategy
**duration** the length of an unemployment spell

**economic efficiency** (also called **efficiency**) occurs when all goods and services are produced and consumed at their respective socially optimal levels

**economic loss** an economic profit that is less than zero

**economic profit (or supernormal profit or excess profit)** the difference between a firm's total revenue and the sum of its explicit and implicit costs

**economic rent** that part of the payment for a factor of production that exceeds the owner's reservation price

**economics** the study of how people make choices under conditions of scarcity and of the results of those choices for society

**economic surplus** the economic surplus from taking any action is the benefit of taking that action minus its cost

**economic union** there is centralised effective decision making on economic policies affecting the countries of the union

**economic of scale** *see* increasing returns to scale

**efficient (or Pareto efficient)** a situation is efficient if no change is possible that will help some people without harming others

**efficient markets hypothesis** the theory that the current price of stock in a company reflects all the relevant information about its current and future earnings prospects

**efficient point** any combination of goods for which currently available resources do not allow an increase in the production of one good without a reduction in the production of the other

**elastic** demand is elastic with respect to price if the price elasticity of demand is greater than 1

**emissions trading** a system whereby firms can trade emission reductions, with the result that any given level of emissions reduction is undertaken by those with the lowest costs of achieving reductions

**employer discrimination** an arbitrary preference by an employer for one group of workers over another

**entrepreneurs** people who create new economic enterprises

**equation** a mathematical expression that describes the relationship between two or more variables

**equilibrium** a system is in equilibrium when there is no tendency for it to change

**equilibrium exchange rate** *see* fundamental value of the exchange rate

**equilibrium price** and **equilibrium quantity** the values of price and quantity for which quantity supplied and quantity demanded are equal

**equity** *see* share

**European Central Bank (ECB)** the Central Bank of the Eurosystem which comprises all countries using the euro as their currency

**European Currency Unit (ECU)** composite or 'basket' currency including specific amounts of EMS currencies

**European Monetary System (EMS)** the system by which EU countries attempted to fix exchange rates, 1979–98

**European System of Central Banks (ESCB)** the ECB and the national Central Banks of all member states including those who do not use the euro as their currency

**Eurosystem** those EU member states which use the euro as their currency and for whom the ECB is their Central Bank

**excess demand** the amount by which quantity demanded exceeds quantity supplied when the price of a good lies below the equilibrium price

**excess profit** *see* economic profit

**excess supply** the amount by which quantity supplied exceeds quantity demanded when the price of a good exceeds the equilibrium price

**Exchange Rate Mechanism (ERM)** countries in the ERM maintained their bilateral exchange rates within an agreed band of fluctuation around the central rate

**expansion** a period in which the economy is growing at a rate significantly above normal

**expansionary gap** a negative output gap, which occurs when actual output is higher than potential output ($Y > Y^*$)

**expansionary policies** government policy actions intended to increase planned spending and output

**expected value of a gamble** the sum of the possible outcomes of the gamble multiplied by their respective probabilities

**explicit costs** the actual payments a firm makes to its factors of production and other suppliers
**external benefit (or positive externality)** a benefit of an activity received by people other than those who pursue the activity
**external cost (or negative externality)** a cost of an activity that falls on people other than those who pursue the activity
**externality** an external cost or benefit of an activity
**factor of production** an input used in the production of a good or service
**fair gamble** a gamble whose expected value is zero
**Federal Open Markets Committee (FOMC)** the key decision-making body in the Federal Reserve System and the Fed's equivalent of the ECB's Governing Council
**final goods or services** goods or services consumed by the ultimate user; because they are the end products of the production process, they are counted as part of GDP
**financial intermediaries** firms that extend credit to borrowers using funds raised from savers
**fiscal policy** decisions that determine the government's budget, including the amount and composition of government expenditures and government revenues
**Fisher effect** the tendency for nominal interest rates to be high when inflation is high and low when inflation is low
**fixed cost** the sum of all payments made to the firm's fixed factors of production
**fixed exchange rate** an exchange rate whose value is set by official government policy
**fixed factor of production** an input whose quantity cannot be altered in the short run
**flexible (floating) exchange rate** an exchange rate whose value is not officially fixed but varies according to the supply of and demand for the currency in the foreign exchange market
**flow** a measure that is defined per unit of time
**foreign exchange market** the market on which currencies of various nations are traded for one another
**fractional-reserve banking system** a banking system in which bank reserves are less than deposits so that the reserve–deposit ratio is less than 100 per cent
**free-rider problem** an incentive problem in which too little of a good or service is produced because non-payers cannot be excluded from using it
**free-trade area** group of countries that has agreed to permit goods produced in one of them to be imported into any other member country free of tariff or quota restrictions
**frictional unemployment** the short-term unemployment associated with the process of matching workers with jobs
**full-employment output** *see* potential output
**fundamental value of the exchange rate (or equilibrium exchange rate)** the exchange rate that equates the quantities of the currency supplied and demanded in the foreign exchange market
**Gini coefficient** a measure of equality of distribution that compares the actual distribution with a benchmark of absolute equality
**Governing Council** the ECB's supreme decision-making body
**government budget deficit** the excess of government spending over tax collections ($G - T$)
**government budget surplus** the excess of government tax collections over government spending ($T - G$); the government budget surplus equals public saving
**government purchases** purchases by central and local governments of final goods and services; government purchases do *not* include *transfer payments*, which are payments made by the government in return for which no current goods or services are received, nor do they include interest paid on the government debt
**gross domestic product (GDP)** the market value of the final goods and services produced in a country during a given period
**human capital** an amalgam of factors such as education, training, experience, intelligence, energy, work habits, trustworthiness and initiative that affect the value of a worker's marginal product
**human capital theory** a theory of pay detemination that says a worker's wage will be proportional to his or her stock of human capital

**hurdle method of price discrimination** the practice by which a seller offers a discount to all buyers who overcome some obstacle

**hyperinflation** a situation in which the inflation rate is extremely high

**imperfectly competitive firm** a firm that has at least some control over the market price of its product

**implicit costs** the opportunity costs of the resources supplied by the firm's owners

**import function** the relationship between imports and income

**income effect** the change in the quantity demanded of a good that results because of a change in real income of purchasers arising from the price change

**income elasticity of demand** the percentage by which quantity demanded changes in response to a 1 per cent change in income

**income–expenditure multiplier** the effect of a 1 unit change in autonomous expenditure on short-run equilibrium output; for example, a multiplier of 5 means that a 10 unit decrease in autonomous expenditure reduces short-run equilibrium output by 50 units

**increasing returns to scale** a production process is said to have increasing returns to scale if, when all inputs are changed by a given proportion, output changes by more than that proportion; also called **economies of scale**

**independent variable** a variable in an equation whose value determines the value taken by another variable in the equation

**indexing** the practice of increasing a nominal quantity each period by an amount equal to the percentage increase in a specified price index; indexing prevents the purchasing power of the nominal quantity from being eroded by inflation

**indifference curve** a smoothly convex curve; its slope is the consumer's marginal rate of substitution (MRS) between two goods

**induced expenditure** the portion of planned aggregate expenditure that depends on output $Y$

**inefficient point** any combination of goods for which currently available resources enable an increase in the production of one good without a reduction in the production of the other

**inelastic** demand is inelastic with respect to price if the price elasticity of demand is less than 1

**inferior good** one whose demand curve shifts leftward when the incomes of buyers increase and rightward when the incomes of buyers decrease

**inflation shock** a sudden change in the normal behaviour of inflation, unrelated to the nation's output gap

**in-kind transfer** a payment made not in the form of cash, but in the form of a good or service

**intermediate goods or services** goods or services used up in the production of final goods and services and therefore not counted as part of GDP

**international capital flows** flows of funds between lenders and borrowers located in different countries

**international reserves** foreign currency assets held by a Central Bank for the purpose of purchasing the domestic currency in the foreign exchange market

**intertemporal substitution** a means of moving consumption across time by substituting consumption in one year for consumption in another year

**investment** spending by firms on final goods and services, primarily capital goods and housing

**'invisible hand' theory** Adam Smith's theory that the actions of independent, self-interested buyers and sellers will often result in the most efficient allocation of resources

**involuntary part-time workers** people who say they would like to work full-time but are able to find only part-time work

**IS curve** a graph showing combinations of income and the rate of interest which give equilibrium in the market for goods and services

**IS-LM model** a general equilibrium model of the economy which simultaneously determines the equilibrium values of aggregate income and the rate of interest

**labour force** the total number of employed and unemployed people in the economy

**labour mobility** the movement of workers between jobs, firms and industries

**labour union** a group of workers who bargain collectively with employers for better wages and working conditions

**law of diminishing marginal utility** the tendency for the additional utility gained from consuming an additional unit of a good to diminish as consumption increases beyond some point

**law of diminishing returns** a property of the relationship between the amount of a good or service produced and the amount of a variable factor required to produce it; it says that when some factors of production are fixed, increased production of the good eventually requires ever-larger increases in the variable factor
**law of one price** if transportation costs are relatively small, the price of an internationally traded commodity must be the same in all locations
**'lemons' model** George Akerlof's explanation of how asymmetric information tends to reduce the average quality of goods offered for sale
**liabilities** the debts one owes
**life-cycle saving** saving to smooth out the household's consumption path
**LM curve** a graph showing combinations of output and the rate of interest which give equilibrium in the money market
**long run** a period of time of sufficient length that all the firm's factors of production are variable
**long-run aggregate supply (*LRAS*) line** a vertical line showing the economy's potential output $Y^*$
**long-run equilibrium** a situation in which actual output equals potential output and the inflation rate is stable; graphically, long-run equilibrium occurs when the *AD* curve, the *SRAS* line and the *LRAS* line all intersect at a single point
**Lorenz curve** the graph of the cumulative distribution of income or wealth by percentages of households or individuals from poorest to richest
**M1** sum of currency outstanding and balances held in chequing accounts
**M2** all the assets in M1 plus some additional assets that are usable in making payments but at greater cost or inconvenience than the use of currency or cheques
**M3** all assets in M2 plus marketable securities with a high degree of liquidity and price certainty
**macroeconomic policies** government actions designed to affect the performance of the economy as a whole
**macroeconomics** the study of the performance of national economies and the policies that governments use to try to improve that performance
**main refinancing operations** the type of OMO used by the ECB to control the supply of reserves to the banking system
**main refinancing rate** the interest rate which commercial banks pay to borrow reserves from the ECB
**marginal benefit** the increase in total benefit that results from carrying out one additional unit of an activity
**marginal cost** the increase in total cost that results from carrying out one additional unit of an activity
**marginal cost** as output changes from one level to another, the change in total cost divided by the corresponding change in output
**marginal product of labour (MP)** the additional output a firm gets by employing one additional unit of labour
**marginal propensity to consume (MPC)**, or, $c$, the amount by which consumption rises when disposable income rises by one euro. We assume that $0 < c < 1$
**marginal propensity to import** the proportion of a change in income which is spent on imports
**marginal revenue** the change in a firm's total revenue that results from a one-unit change in output
**marginal utility** the additional utility gained from consuming an additional unit of a good
**market** the market for any good consists of all buyers or sellers of that good
**market equilibrium** occurs in a market when all buyers and sellers are satisfied with their respective quantities at the market price
**market power** a firm's ability to raise the price of a good without losing all its sales
**means-tested** a benefit programme whose benefit level declines as the recipient earns additional income
**medium of exchange** an asset used in purchasing goods and services
**menu costs** the costs of changing prices
**merit goods** goods produced under non-market conditions by the state for political reasons
**microeconomics** the study of individual choice under scarcity and its implications for the behaviour of prices and quantities in individual markets
**Monetary Policy Committee (MPC)** the key decision-making body in the Bank of England
**monetary policy** determination of the nation's money supply

**monetary union** the member states have a single currency

**money** any asset that can be used in making purchases

**money demand curve** shows the relationship between the aggregate quantity of money demanded $M$ and the nominal interest rate $i$; because an increase in the nominal interest rate increases the opportunity cost of holding money, which reduces the quantity of money demanded, the money demand curve slopes down

**money multiplier** the effect of a 1 unit change in the nominal money supply on short-run equilibrium output; for example, a multiplier equal to 2 implies that a €100 million increase in the money supply increases short-run equilibrium output by €200 million

**monopolistically competitive firm** one of a large number of firms that produce slightly differentiated products that are reasonably close substitutes for one another

**moral hazard** the tendency of people to expend less effort protecting those goods that are insured against theft or damage

**mutual fund** a financial intermediary that sells shares in itself to the public, then uses the funds raised to buy a wide variety of financial assets

**Nash equilibrium** any combination of strategies in which each player's strategy is his or her best choice, given the other players' strategies

**national saving** the saving of the entire economy, equal to GDP less consumption expenditures and government purchases of goods and services, or $Y - C - G$

**natural monopoly** a monopoly that results from economies of scale

**natural rate of unemployment** the part of the total unemployment rate that is attributable to frictional and structural unemployment; equivalently, the unemployment rate that prevails when cyclical unemployment is zero, so that the economy has neither a recessionary nor an expansionary output gap

**negative demand shock** a decrease in autonomous expenditure which shifts the aggregate demand curve to the left

**negative externality** *see* **external cost**

**negative income tax (NIT)** a system under which the government would grant every citizen a cash payment each year, financed by an additional tax on earned income

**net exports** exports minus imports

**no-bailout clause** a provision in the Maastricht Treaty which prohibits the ESCB from lending to national governments

**nominal exchange rate** the rate, or price, at which two currencies can be traded for each other

**nominal GDP** a measure of GDP in which the quantities produced are valued at current-year prices; nominal GDP measures the *current money value* of production

**nominal interest rate** (or market interest rate) the annual percentage increase in the nominal value of a financial asset

**nominal price** the absolute price of a good in euro terms

**nominal quantity** a quantity that is measured in terms of its current euro value

**non-excludable good** a good that is difficult, or costly, to exclude non-payers from consuming

**non-rival good** a good whose consumption by one person does not diminish its availability for others

**normal good** one whose demand curve shifts rightward when the incomes of buyers increase and leftward when the incomes of buyers decrease

**normal profit** the opportunity cost of the resources supplied by a firm's owners, equal to accounting profit minus economic profit

**normative analysis** addresses the question of whether a policy *should* be used; normative analysis inevitably involves the values of the person doing the analysis

**oligopolist** a firm that produces a product for which only a few rival firms produce close substitutes

**open economy** an economy that trades with other countries

**open-market operations (OMOs)** open-market purchases and open-market sales

**open-market purchase** the purchase of government bonds from the public by the ECB for the purpose of increasing the supply of bank reserves and the money supply

**price elasticity of demand** percentage change in quantity demanded that results from a 1 per cent change in price

**price elasticity of supply** the percentage change in quantity supplied that occurs in response to a 1 per cent change in price

**price index** a measure of the average price of a given class of goods or services relative to the price of the same goods and services in a base year

**price level** a measure of the overall level of prices at a particular point in time as measured by a price index such as the CPI

**price setter** a firm with at least some latitude to set its own price

**price taker** a firm that has no influence over the price at which it sells its product

**principal amount** the amount originally lent

**prisoner's dilemma** a game in which each player has a dominant strategy, and when each plays it, the resulting payoffs are smaller than if each had played a dominated strategy

**private saving** the saving of the private sector of the economy is equal to the after-tax income of the private sector minus consumption expenditures ($Y - T - C$); private saving can be further broken down into household saving and business saving

**producer surplus** the amount by which price exceeds the seller's reservation price

**production possibilities curve** a graph that describes the maximum amount of one good that can be produced for every possible level of production of the other good

**profit** the total revenue a firm receives from the sale of its product minus all costs – explicit and implicit – incurred in producing it

**profitable firm** a firm whose total revenue exceeds its total cost

**profit-maximising firm** a firm whose primary goal is to maximise the difference between its total revenues and total costs

**progressive tax** one in which the proportion of income paid in taxes rises as income rises

**proportional income tax** one under which all tax-payers pay the same proportion of their incomes in taxes

**protectionism** the view that free trade is injurious and should be restricted

**public good** a good or service that, to at least some degree, is both non-rival and non-excludable

**public saving** the saving of the government sector is equal to net tax payments minus government purchases ($T - G$)

**purchasing power parity (PPP)** the theory that nominal exchange rates are determined as necessary for the law of one price to hold

**pure commons good** one for which non-payers cannot easily be excluded and for which each unit consumed by one person means one less unit available for others

**pure monopoly** the only supplier of a unique product with no close substitutes

**pure private good** one for which non-payers can easily be excluded and for which each unit consumed by one person means one less unit available for others

**pure public good** a good or service that, to a high degree, is both non-rival and non-excludable

**quantity equation** money times velocity equals nominal GDP: $M \times V = P \times Y$

**quota** a legal limit on the quantity of a good that may be imported

**rate of inflation** the annual percentage rate of change in the price level, as measured, for example, by the CPI

**rate of return** on an investment equals the value of marginal product expressed as a percentage of the purchase price

**rational person** someone with well-defined goals who tries to fulfil those goals as best she can

**rationing function of price** to distribute scarce goods to those consumers who value them most highly

**reaction function** shows the preferred response of a firm in terms of a decision variable as a response to a value of that variable chosen by the other firm(s)

**real exchange rate** the price of the average domestic good or service *relative* to the price of the average foreign good or service, when prices are expressed in terms of a common currency

**real GDP** a measure of GDP in which the quantities produced are valued at the prices in a base year rather than at current prices; real GDP measures the actual *physical volume* of production

**open-market sale** the sale by the ECB of government bonds to the public for the purpose of reducing bank reserves and the money supply

**opportunity cost** the opportunity cost of an activity is the value of the next-best alternative that must be forgone in order to undertake the activity

**optimal combination of goods** the affordable combination that yields the highest total utility

**optimum currency area** a group of countries for which the benefits of replacing national currencies with a common currency exceed the costs

**output gap** the difference between the economy's potential output and its actual output at a point in time ($Y^* - Y$)

**overvalued exchange rate** an exchange rate that has an officially fixed value greater than its fundamental value

**Pareto efficient** *see* efficient

**participation rate** the percentage of the working-age population in the labour force (that is, the percentage that is either employed or looking for work)

**payoff matrix** a table that describes the payoffs in a game for each possible combination of strategies

**perfect hurdle** a threshold that completely segregates buyers whose reservation prices lie above it from others whose reservation prices lie below it, imposing no cost on those who jump the hurdle

**perfectly competitive market** a market in which no individual supplier has significant influence on the market price of the product

**perfectly discriminating monopolist** a firm that charges each buyer exactly his or her reservation price

**perfectly elastic demand** demand is perfectly elastic with respect to price if price elasticity of demand is infinite

**perfectly elastic supply** supply is perfectly elastic with respect to price if elasticity of supply is infinite

**perfectly inelastic demand** demand is perfectly inelastic with respect to price if price elasticity of demand is zero

**perfectly inelastic supply** supply is perfectly inelastic with respect to price if elasticity is zero

**planned aggregate expenditure (PAE)** total planned spending on final goods and services

**policy reaction function** describes how the action a policy maker takes depends on the state of the economy

**poll tax** a tax that collects the same amount from every tax-payer

**portfolio allocation decision** the decision about the forms in which to hold one's wealth

**positional arms control agreement** an agreement in which contestants attempt to limit mutually offsetting investments in performance enhancement

**positional arms race** a series of mutually offsetting investments in performance enhancement that is stimulated by a positional externality

**positional externality** occurs when an increase in one person's performance reduces the expected reward of another in situations in which reward depends on relative performance

**positive analysis** addresses the economic consequences of a particular event or policy, not whether those consequences are desirable

**positive demand shock** an increase in autonomous expenditure which shifts the aggregate demand curve to the right

**positive externality** *see* **external benefit**

**potential output (or potential GDP or full-employment output)** the amount of output (real GDP) that an economy can produce when using its resources, such as capital and labour, at normal rates

**poverty threshold** the level of income below which a family is 'poor'

**precautionary saving** saving for protection against unexpected setbacks, such as the loss of a job or a medical emergency

**present value** for an annual interest rate $r$, the present value ($PV$) of a payment ($M$) to be received $T$ years from now is the amount that would have to be deposited today at interest rate $r$ to generate a balance of $M$

**price ceiling** a maximum allowable price, specified by law

**price discrimination** the practice of charging different buyers different prices for essentially the same good or service

**real interest rate** the annual percentage increase in the purchasing power of a financial asset; the real interest rate on any asset equals the nominal interest rate on that asset minus the inflation rate
**real price** the euro price of a good relative to the average euro price of all other goods
**real quantity** a quantity that is measured in physical terms – for example, in terms of quantities of goods and services
**real wage** the wage paid to workers measured in terms of real purchasing power; the real wage for any given period is calculated by dividing the nominal (euro) wage by the CPI for that period
**recessionary gap** a positive output gap, which occurs when potential output exceeds actual output ($Y^* > Y$)
**recession (or contraction)** a period in which the economy is growing at a rate significantly below normal
**regressive tax** a tax under which the proportion of income paid in taxes declines as income rises
**regulation** legal intervention in markets to alter the way in which firms or consumers behave
**relative price** the price of a specific good or service in comparison to the prices of other goods and services
**relative purchasing power parity** the theory that the nominal rate of appreciation or depreciation equals the difference in inflation rates between the two countries
**repeated prisoner's dilemma** a standard prisoner's dilemma that confronts the same players repeatedly
**reserve–deposit ratio** bank reserves divided by deposits
**residual demand curve** shows the price and output combinations available to a firm given other firms' decisions
**revaluation** an increase in the official value of a currency (in a fixed exchange rate system)
**risk averse person** someone who would refuse any fair gamble
**risk neutral person** someone who would accept any gamble that is fair or better
**risk premium** the rate of return that financial investors require to hold risky assets minus the rate of return on safe assets
**saving** current income minus spending on current needs
**saving rate** saving divided by income
**seller's reservation price** the smallest money amount for which a seller would be willing to sell an additional unit, generally equal to marginal cost
**seller's surplus** the difference between the price received by the seller and his or her reservation price
**share (or equity)** a claim to partial ownership of a firm
**short run** a period of time sufficiently short that at least some of the firm's factors of production are fixed
**short-run aggregate supply (*SRAS*) line** a horizontal line showing the current rate of inflation, as determined by past expectations and pricing decisions
**short-run equilibrium** a situation in which inflation equals the value determined by past expectations and pricing decisions, and output equals the level of short-run equilibrium output that is consistent with that inflation rate; graphically, short-run equilibrium occurs at the intersection of the *AD* curve and the *SRAS* line
**short-run equilibrium output** the level of output at which output $Y$ equals planned aggregate expenditure *PAE*; short-run equilibrium output is the level of output that prevails during the period in which prices are predetermined
**skill-biased technological change** technological change that affects the marginal products of higher-skilled workers differently from those of lower-skilled workers
**slope** in a straight line, the ratio of the vertical distance the straight line travels between any two points (**rise**) to the corresponding horizontal distance (**run**)
**socially optimal quantity** the quantity of a good that results in the maximum possible economic surplus from producing and consuming the good
**speculative attack** a massive selling of domestic currency assets by financial investors
**stabilisation policies** government policies that are used to affect planned aggregate expenditure, with the objective of eliminating output gaps
**statistical discrimination** the practice of making judgements about the quality of people, goods or services based on the characteristics of the groups to which they belong
**stock** a measure that is defined at a point in time
**store of value** an asset that serves as a means of holding wealth

**structural policy** government policies aimed at changing the underlying structure, or institutions, of the nation's economy

**structural unemployment** the long-term and chronic unemployment that exists even when the economy is producing at a normal rate

**substitutes** two goods are substitutes in consumption if an increase in the price of one causes a rightward shift in the demand curve for the other (or if a decrease causes a leftward shift)

**substitution effect** the change in the quantity demanded of a good that results because buyers switch to substitutes when the price of the good changes

**sunk cost** a cost that is beyond recovery at the moment a decision must be made

**supernormal profit** *see* economic profit

**supply curve** a curve or schedule showing the quantity of a good that sellers wish to sell at each price

**symmetric shocks** affect different economies in the same way and at the same time

**synchronised business cycles** mean that countries experience recession or expansion at the same time and require similar rather than different stabilisation policies

**tacit collusion** firms behaving in a manner that resembles what might emerge from a collusive agreement because they recognise their interdependence

**tariff** a tax imposed on an imported good

**tax multiplier** the effect of a 1 unit change in autonomous taxes on short-run equilibrium output. Because the marginal propensity to consume is less than one, the tax multiplier will be smaller than the income–expenditure multiplier

**The Federal Reserve System** the central bank of the United States consisting of the Board of Governors in Washington DC and twelve Regional Federal Reserve Banks

**time value of money** the fact that a given euro amount today is equivalent to a larger euro amount in the future, because the money can be invested in an interest-bearing account in the meantime. After $T$ years: $PV - M/(1 - r)T$

**tit-for-tat** a strategy for the repeated prisoner's dilemma in which players co-operate on the first move, then mimic their partner's last move on each successive move

**total cost** the sum of all payments made to the firm's fixed and variable factors of production

**total surplus** the difference between the buyer's reservation price and the seller's reservation price

**trade balance (or net exports)** the value of a country's exports less the value of its imports in a particular period (quarter or year)

**trade creation** replacing more costly domestic production by less costly imported goods

**trade deficit** when imports exceed exports, the difference between the value of a country's imports and the value of its exports in a given period

**trade diversion** replacing lower-cost imports by higher-cost imports

**trade surplus** when exports exceed imports, the difference between the value of a country's exports and the value of its imports in a given period

**trade symmetry** freeing trade has symmetrical effects as between sectors and countries

**tragedy of the commons** the tendency for a resource that has no price to be used until its marginal benefit falls to zero

**transaction costs** costs involved in exchanging one currency for another

**transfer payments** payments the government makes to the public for which it receives no current goods or services in return

**ultimatum bargaining game** one in which the first player has the power to confront the second player with a take-it-or-leave-it offer

**unattainable point** any combination of goods that cannot be produced using currently available resources

**undervalued exchange rate** an exchange rate that has an officially fixed value less than its fundamental value

**unemployment rate** the number of unemployed people divided by the labour force

**unemployment spell** a period during which an individual is continuously unemployed

**unit elastic** demand is unit elastic with respect to price if the price elasticity of demand equals 1

**unit of account** a basic measure of economic value

**value added** for any firm, the market value of its product or service minus the cost of inputs purchased from other firms

**value of marginal product of labour (VMP)** the money value of the additional output a firm gets by employing one additional unit of labour

**variable** a quantity that is free to take a range of different values

**variable cost** the sum of all payments made to the firm's variable factors of production

**variable factor of production** an input whose quantity can be altered in the short run

**velocity** a measure of the speed at which money circulates, or, equivalently, the value of transactions completed in a period of time divided by the stock of money required to make those transactions; numerically, $V = (P \times Y)/M$, where $V$ is velocity, $P \times Y$ is nominal GDP and $M$ is the money supply whose velocity is being measured

**vertical intercept** in a straight line, the value taken by the dependent variable when the independent variable equals zero

**wealth** the value of assets minus liabilities

**wealth effect** the tendency of changes in asset prices to affect households' wealth and thus their spending on consumption goods

**winner-take-all labour market** one in which small differences in human capital translate into large differences in pay

**world price** the price at which a commodity is traded internationally

**X-inefficiency** where market power results in inefficient production rather than higher profits

# Index


100 per cent reserve banking 653–4

ability signal, conspicuous consumption as 353–4
absolute advantage 37–8
  defining 37
accelerated depreciation 541
accounting profit 209–12
  defining 209
*AD–AS* diagram *see* aggregate demand–aggregate supply diagram
AD curve *see* aggregate demand curve
adding value, middlemen 342–3
adverse selection, information 355–6
advertising cigarettes 282–3
aggregate demand (*AD*) curve 793–8
  algebra 825–7
  ECB 794–8
aggregate demand–aggregate supply diagram (*AD–AS* diagram) 802–5
aggregate supply
  algebra 825–7
  inflation 792–827
  inflation inertia 799–801
  output gap and inflation 801–2
aggregate supply shocks 811–14
  defining 811
aggregation
  defining 489
  macroeconomics 489–90
allocative function of price 212–13
analysis
  reaction function 297–300
  residual demand curve 296
  tools 296–7
anti-poverty programmes, 'invisible hand' 226–7
anti-trust laws, enforcing 266–7
appreciation 834–5
  defining 835
approach, this text's 14–15
arbitration agreements 333
Argentina, economy collapse 692
assets 620–1
  defining 620
asymmetric information 348–57
asymmetric shocks 875–9
  defining 875
ATC *see* average total cost
attainable point, defining 44
autarky 435
  defining 435
automated price-setting 712, 716
automatic stabilisers
  defining 745
  fiscal policy 745–8
  income-expenditure multiplier 747–8
  SGB 752–7
autonomous expenditure 721–2
  defining 721
availability, goods/services, GDP 512
AVC *see* average variable cost
average benefits 10–13
  defining 11
average costs 10–13
  defining 11
average labour productivity 480–2
  *see also* economic growth
  China 568
  communism 570–1
  defining 480
  determinants 561–71
  human capital 561–3
  land 565–6
  legal environment 568–71
  Lisbon Agenda 569–70
  natural resources 565–6
  physical capital 563–5
  political environment 568–71
  role 559–61
  technology 566–7, 572
  worldwide slowdown/recovery 571–2
average total cost (ATC) 163–7
  defining 163
average variable cost (AVC) 163–7
  defining 163
average–marginal distinction, Cost–Benefit Principle 10–13

balance-of-payments deficit 851
  defining 851
balance-of-payments surplus 851
  defining 851
balance of trade *see* trade balance
balanced-budget multiplier 743–4
  defining 744
Bank of England 649
  crisis (1992) 863–4
  defining 649
  MPC 667
bank reserves 653–6
  defining 653
banks/banking
  100 per cent reserve banking 653–4
  Bank of England 649, 667, 863–4
  banking system 677–83
  commercial banks 652–7
  crises 678–9, 863–4
  ECB *see* European Central Bank
  fractional-reserve banking system 654
  price stability 660–1
  reserve–deposit ratio 654
  World Bank (IBRD) 855
barriers to entry 219–20
  defining 219
barter 649–50
  defining 649
basic elements of a game 274–6
  defining 274
behaviour, oligopolistic markets 295–304
beliefs, oligopolistic markets 295–304
bequest saving 624–6
Bertrand competition 298–300
  defining 298
better-than-fair gamble 346
  defining 346
blunders, regulatory 398–9
bond markets 683–5
  diversification 683–5
  informational role 683
  risk-sharing 683–5
bonds 679–80
  defining 679
booms 704
  defining 704
Boskin Commission, inflation 534–5
Bretton Woods system
  defining 853
  exchange rates 853–4
budget deficits, inflation 806–7
budget share, price elasticity of demand 96
buyers and sellers, markets 61–5
buyer's reservation price 63
  defining 63
buyer's surplus 83
  defining 83
by-products, sale of 419

calculus 28–34
campaign spending limits 333
capital
  creating 573
  human *see* human capital
  physical *see* physical capital
capital flows, international 685–95
capital formation, investment 635–9
capital gains 622–3
  defining 622
capital good 500–1, 563–4
  defining 500
capital income, GDP 505–14

capital inflows
defining 686
investment 690–4
real interest rates 689
risk 689–90
saving 690–4
capital losses 621–2
defining 622
capital mobility, 'impossible trinity' 861–2
capital outflows, defining 686
capitalist economies 61
cardinal utility 137
cartels 279–83, 301
*see also* collusion
defining 279
case studies, regulation 400–9
cash on the table 83–4
defining 84
Central Banks *see* European Central Bank; European System of Central Banks
central planning
defining 60
vs market 60–1
central planning change in demand, defining 73
change in demand 73
defining 73
change in supply 73
defining 73
change in the quantity demanded 73
defining 73
change in the quantity supplied 73
defining 73
China
average labour productivity 568
entrepreneurship 568
cigarette advertising 282–3
cigarette pricing 303
cigarette taxes 87–8
closed economy 431–41
defining 431
Coase theorem
defining 317
externalities 316–19, 320
collective goods 412–13
defining 412
collusion 301
*see also* cartels
tacit 300–4
commercial banks, money 652–7
commitment device 291–2
defining 291
commitment problems
defining 291
games 291–2
preferences 294–5
rational search 347–8
common currency
*see also* monetary union
benefits 875–93
costs 875–93
exchange rates uncertainty 882
flexible markets 879–80
inflation inertia 879–80
labour mobility 880–1
policy independence 875–9
transaction costs 881–2
common market 465–8
defining 465
communism, average labour productivity 570–1
comparative advantage 36–57, 566–7
defining 38
international trade 52–3, 430–9
opportunity costs 37–41
principle 38–41
production possibilities 43–9
sources 41–3
compensating wage differentials 376–7
defining 377
competition
Bertrand 298–300
Cournot 298–300
perfect 179–81
profit maximisation 179–81
competition authorities, regulation 399–400
complements 74
defining 74
compound interest
defining 558
living standards 557–9
conspicuous consumption
as ability signal 353–4
information 353–4
constant returns to scale 245
defining 245
constants (or parameters), defining 21
consumer price index (CPI)
defining 525
measuring inflation 533–6
price level measurement 525–7
consumer rationality 141–3
defining 142
consumer spending, PAE 718–19
consumer surplus
defining 145
demand 145–8
consumption expenditure (consumption)
defining 503
GDP 503–5
PAE 717
consumption function 719–20
defining 719
United Kingdom 720
consumption possibilities
defining 434
international trade 434–9
contractionary policies 738–9
defining 738
contractions *see* recessions
convergence, monetary union 884–6, 887
copyrights, market power 244
cost concepts 160–1
cost-plus regulation 264–5
defining 264
cost-saving innovations, 'invisible hand' 222–3
cost side, markets 153–81
Cost–Benefit Principle 4–7
average–marginal distinction 10–13
decision pitfalls 8–14
opportunity costs 9, 113
proportions 8, 113
sunk costs 10, 113
cost–benefit test, information 344
costly-to-fake principle
defining 350
information 350–1
coupon payments 679
defining 679
coupon rate 679
defining 679
Cournot competition 298–300
defining 298
CPI *see* consumer price index
credibility problem
information 350–1
trading 350–1
credible promises 288–90
defining 289
credible threats 288–90
defining 288
crises
banks/banking 678–9, 863–4
East Asian (1997–8) 865–6
ERM (1992) 863–4
Japan (1990s) 678–9
cross-price elasticity of demand 107–8
defining 107
crowding out
defining 641
investment 641
customer discrimination 378–9
defining 378
customs union 465–8
defining 465
cyclical unemployment 607–8
defining 606
natural rate of unemployment 708–9
output gap 706–9
cyclically adjusted budget deficit, SGB 755–7

deadweight loss 199–202
defining 199
debt sustainability, fiscal policy 750–2
decision pitfalls, Cost–Benefit Principle 8–14

decision tree (or game tree) 286–8
deflating (a nominal quantity) 529–32
  defining 529
deflation 528
delegated regulation 399–400
demand 121–52
  consumer surplus 145–8
  euros 844
  fixed income allocation 127–30
  income differences 135–6
  income effect 131–3
  law of demand 122–4
  origins 123
  substitution effect 131–3
  translating wants into 125–33
demand and supply *see* supply and demand
demand curve 62–3
  defining 62
  indifference curve analysis 136–8
  individual 143–8
  market 143–8
  perfectly competitive firms 158–9
  public goods 416–18
  rules 80–2
demand for labour
  shifts 591–3
  wages 589–91
demand for money 763–9
  defining 764
  macroeconomic factors 766–9
demand shocks 875–9
  defining 876
demonstration effects, saving 628–9
dependent variables, defining 21
depreciation 834–5
  accelerated 541
  defining 835
depressions
  defining 704
  Great Depression 477–8, 484, 704
devaluation 848–52, 855–9
  defining 848
differentiation
  calculus 31–4
  defining 32
diminishing marginal rate of substitution (DMRS) 140
diminishing marginal utility (DMU) 127–30, 136–43
  defining 127
  DMU model 138–43
diminishing returns to capital 564–5
  defining 564
diminishing returns to labour 589–90
  defining 590
disappearing political discourse 357–9
  defining 358
discounts, monopolies 257–60, 263
discouraged workers
  defining 518
  unemployment 518
discretionary fiscal policy 739–45
  defining 745
discrimination
  *see also* price discrimination
  customer 378–9
  by employers 377–8
  labour market 377
  by others 378–9
  parental 379
  statistical 354–5
distribution, measuring, income/wealth 383–4
diversification
  benefits 684
  bond markets/stock markets 683–5
  defining 684
dividends 680–3
  defining 680
DMRS *see* diminishing marginal rate of substitution
DMU *see* diminishing marginal utility
dominant strategy 275–6
  defining 275
dominated strategy 275–6
  defining 276
donation, funding by 418
duration
  defining 517
  unemployment 517–18
dynamic gains, Single Market Programme 470–2

Earned Income Tax Credit (EITC) 389–91
earnings, differences in 371–81
East Asian crisis (1997–8) 865–6
ECB *see* European Central Bank
economic efficiency 84–5
  defining 84
economic gains
  free trade 469, 603
  Single Market Programme 470–2
economic growth 49–52, 555–85
  *see also* average labour productivity
  costs 573
  EU 576–7
  human capital 573–4
  investment/saving policy 574–5
  legal framework 575
  limits 578–80
  macroeconomics 478–80
  policies 573–7
  political framework 575
  poor countries 575–6
  PPC 49–52
  promoting 573–7
  research and development 575
  saving/investment policy 574–5
  trends, EU 472
economic inequality, GDP 511
economic loss 211–12
  defining 211
economic models, role 7
economic naturalism 15–17
economic profit 209–12
  defining 209
  vs economic rent 220–2
economic rent
  defining 220
  vs economic profit 220–2
economic surplus 6, 1145–8
  defining 6
  maximisation 327
  minimum wages 390–1
  taxes 198–200
economic tests, monetary union 884–5
economic union 465–8
  defining 465
economic value of work 366–8
economic well-being, GDP 509, 511–14
economics, defining 4
economies of scale
  *see also* natural monopoly
  defining 245
  fixed costs 246–9
  market power 245
ECU *see* European Currency Unit
education and health, GDP 512–13
education provision 574
efficiency 84–5
  defining 84
  equilibrium 182–6
  and exchange 182–207
  first-come, first-served policies 191–5
  goals 185–6
  marginal cost pricing 195–6
  market equilibrium 182–6
  price adjustment prevention 186–95
  price ceilings 186–9
  protectionism 449
  public services 195–6
  taxes 196–202
Efficiency Principle 84–5
efficient markets hypothesis
  defining 229
  'invisible hand' 229–32
efficient (Pareto efficient), defining 183
efficient point, defining 45
EITC *see* Earned Income Tax Credit
elastic demand, defining 95
elasticity 93–120
  price elasticity of demand 94–108
  price elasticity of supply 108–15
  taxes 200–1
emissions trading 402–4
  defining 403
employer discrimination 377–8
employment
  *see also* unemployment
  impediments to full 608–13
  levels 369–81

regulations, government 610
trade unions 609–10
trends 587
EMS *see* European Monetary System
entrepreneurs 566–8
defining 566
entrepreneurship 566–8
China 568
and management 567–8
environment
emissions trading 402–4
environmental quality, GDP 510–11
environmental regulation 400–4
protection 400–4
equations
defining 21
working with 21–8
equilibrium
*see also* market equilibrium
defining 65
efficiency 182–6
labour market 369–70
market 65–72, 1182–6
money market 769–70
vs social optimum 232–3
equilibrium exchange rate 844
equilibrium price 65–6
defining 65
equilibrium quantity 65–6
defining 65
equilibrium value, euros 844
equilibrium wage 369–81
ERM *see* Exchange Rate Mechanism
ESCB *see* European System of Central Banks
EU *see* European Union
euro(s)
demand 844, 846
equilibrium value 844
introduction 853, 859
joining tests 884–5
supply 843–6
Europe
GDP 705
saving 625–6
Europe, Western, unemployment rate 611–12
European Central Bank (ECB) 657–63, 762–6
*AD* curve 794–8
advantages 813
credibility 816–17
decision-making bodies 658–9
defining 657
effects, economy 773–84
Governing Council 658–9
independence 659–60
inflation 778–81, 794–8, 816–17
interest rates 763–7, 770–3
monetary growth 670–1
nominal interest rates 770–3
policy reaction function 781–4, 796–7
price stability 660–1
recessions 776–8
refinancing rate 767, 780
terror attacks 777–8
European Currency Unit (ECU) 855–6
defining 855
European Monetary System (EMS) 855–9
European System of Central Banks (ESCB) 657–63
defining 657
European Union (EU) 455–74
birth 456–7
economic gains 469
economic growth 576–7
enlargement 604–5
freeing trade, economics of 457–64
GDP 576–7
growth 456–7
integration, international 465–8
intra-EU trade 889–90
optimum currency area 887–92
output gaps 708
Single Market Programme 470–2
technological change impact 604–5
trade creation 468–9
trade diversion 468–9
trade impact 604–5
excess demand 67–9
defining 67
excess profit 209–12
defining 209
excess supply 66–9
defining 66
excessive aggregate spending, inflation 806–8
exchange
and efficiency 182–207
opportunity costs 37–8, 43
Exchange Rate Mechanism (ERM) 855–9
crisis (1992) 863–4
defining 855
exchange rates 831–73
Bretton Woods system 853–4
common currency 882
determination 839–46
equilibrium 844
fiscal policy 749–50
fixed 835–6, 847–52, 859–68
fixing 848–51
flexible 867–8
flexible vs fixed 835–6
fundamental value of the exchange rate (equilibrium exchange rate) 844
monetary policy 846–7
nominal 833–5
open economy 831–73
openness 832–3
overvalued 848, 849–50
PPP 839–42
prices, comparing 836–8
real 836–9
strong currencies/economies 836–8
supply and demand 843–4
systems 852–4
uncertainty 882
undervalued 848
exclusive contracting, natural monopoly 265–6
expansionary gaps 707
defining 707
expansionary policies 738–9
defining 738
expansions 703–6
defining 704
macroeconomics 483
expectations, supply determinant 169
expected value of a gamble 346
defining 346
expenditure method, GDP measurement 502–5
explicit costs 209–12
defining 209
export subsidies 463–4, 468
export taxes 463–4
exports
*see also* international capital flows
goods/services 688
external benefits 312–13
defining 312
external costs 312–13
defining 312
taxes 201
externalities 312–40
Coase theorem 316–19, 320
defining 312
graphical portrayal 314–16
legal remedies 320–2
negative 322–3
optimal amount 322–3
positional 329–35
resource allocation 313–22

factor of production 159–60
defining 159
fair gamble 346
defining 346
Federal Open Markets Committee (FOMC) 666
defining 666
Federal Reserve System (Fed) 666
female labour market, GDP 498–9
final goods or services 499–501
defining 499
financial intermediaries 677–8
defining 677
financial markets 676–99
investment 639–42
saving 639–42
first-come, first-served policies, efficiency 191–5

fiscal policy 487–9, 738–61
automatic stabilisers 745–8
balanced-budget multiplier 743–4
debt sustainability 750–2
deficits 748–52
defining 487
discretionary 739–45
exchange rates 749–50
government purchases 739–41
inflexibility 757–8
interest rates 749
planned spending 738–44
role 738–61
stabilisers, automatic 745–8
stabilising the economy 738–61
supply side 757
taxes 741–4
transfer payments 741–4
Fisher effect
inflation 547
nominal interest rates 547
fixed costs 160–1
defining 160
economies of scale 246–9
fixed exchange rates 847–52
defining 836
vs flexible exchange rates 835–6, 867–8
'impossible trinity' 861–2
monetary policy 859–67
fixed factor of production 159–60
defining 159
fixed income allocation, demand 127–30
(in)flexibility, fiscal policy 757–8
flexibility, monetary union 884, 886–7
flexibility of inputs, price elasticity of supply 111–12
flexible exchange rates
defining 835
vs fixed exchange rates 835–6, 867–8
flexible markets, common currency 879–80
flow 621
*see also* international capital flows
defining 621
FOMC *see* Federal Open Markets Committee
foreign exchange market 835–6
defining 835
fractional-reserve banking system 654
defining 654
free-market economies 61
free-rider problem 414
defining 345
information 344–5
non-payers, excluding 418
free trade
agreements 52–3
economic gains 469, 603
free-trade agreements 52–3
NAFTA 52–3
free-trade areas (FTAs) 465–8
defining 465
freeing trade, economics of 457–64
frictional unemployment 606
defining 606
FTAs *see* free-trade areas
fuel prices 113–15
full-employment output *see* potential output
fundamental value of the exchange rate (equilibrium exchange rate) 844
defining 844

gainers and losers 460–1
defining 460
gains, economic
dynamic gains 471–2
free trade 469
integrating factor markets 470–1
Single Market Programme 470–2
static gains 470–1
gamble inherent in search 346–7
game theory 274–7
basic elements of a game 274–6
defining 275
dominant strategy 275–6
Nash equilibrium 276–7
payoff matrix 275–6
game tree (or decision tree) 286–8
games
commitment problems 291–2
credible threats/promises 288–90
oligopolistic markets 295–304
repeated 300–4
timing 286–92
ultimatum bargaining game 286–8
GDP *see* gross domestic product
Gini coefficient 383–4
defining 383
glossary 895–907
goals, efficiency 185–6
Governing Council
defining 658–9
ECB 658–9
government 397–425
public health/security 409–25
regulation 397–409, 610
government budget deficit
defining 632
national saving 632–5, 641
government budget surplus
defining 632
national saving 632–5
government deficits, inflation 806–7
government licences/franchises, market power 244
government purchases 504
defining 504
fiscal policy 739–41
PAE 717
recessionary gaps 739–41
graphical approach, profit maximisation 163–7
graphical interpretation, price elasticity of demand 99–101
graphical portrayal, externalities 314–16
graphs, working with 21–8
Great Depression 477–8, 484, 704
gross domestic product (GDP) 495–514
availability, goods/services 512
capital income 505–14
consumption expenditure (consumption) 503–5
defining 496
economic inequality 511
economic well-being 509, 511–14
education and health 512–13
environmental quality 510–11
EU 576–7
Europe 705
expansions/recessions 703–5
expenditure method 502–5
female labour market 498–9
fluctuations 703–5
health and education 512–13
incomes of capital and labour 505–14
labour income 505–14
labour market 498–9
leisure time 509
living standards 556–61
market value 496–9
measuring economy's output 496–502
nominal 506–9
non-market economic activities 510
pollution 579–80
poverty 511
quality of life 511
real 506–9
recessions/expansions 703–5
resource depletion 510–11
growth, economic *see* economic growth

Harmonised Index of Consumer Prices (HICP), inflation 528–9
health and education, GDP 512–13
health and safety, regulation 406–9
health care sector, inflation 535–6
HICP *see* Harmonised Index of Consumer Prices
horizontal addition, individual demand curve 144–5
Hours, Ithaca 650–1
house sizes 134
human capital 371–2
average labour productivity 561–3
defining 371
economic growth 573–4
human capital theory 371–2
defining 371
hurdle method of price discrimination 260–3

defining 260
hyperinflation 543–4
defining 543

IBRD *see* World Bank
IMF *see* International Monetary Fund
imperfect competition 241–72
forms 242–3
market power 241–72
imperfectly competitive firms 158–9, 242–3
defining 159, 242
vs perfectly competitive firms 243
prisoner's dilemma 279–83
implicit costs 209–12
defining 209
import function 729–30
defining 730
import quotas *see* quotas
import taxes 463–4
imports
*see also* international capital flows
goods / services 688
income–expenditure multiplier 728–30
multiplier 729–30
'impossible trinity' 861–2
in-kind transfers
defining 386
redistribution 386
incentives
defective 406–9
regulation 406–9
income
distribution, measuring 383–4
redistribution 385–91
income effect 63
defining 63
demand 131–3
income elasticity of demand
defining 108
price elasticity of demand 107–8
income–expenditure multiplier, automatic stabilisers 747–8
income tax
EITC 389–91
NIT 386–7
progressive tax 416
proportional income tax 414–16
redistribution 387–8
income–expenditure multiplier 728–30
defining 728
imports 729–30
Keynesian model 737
incomes of capital and labour, GDP 505–14
increasing returns to scale 245
defining 245
independent variables, defining 21
indexing
defining 531
to maintain buying power 531–2
indifference curve 140–3
analysis 136–8
defining 140
demand curve 136–8
individual demand curve 143–8
horizontal addition 144–5
individual productivity, PPC 45–6
induced expenditure 721–2
defining 722
industrial pollution
environmental regulation 400–4
GDP 579–80
inefficient point, defining 44
inelastic demand, defining 95
inequality
income / wealth 382–5
moral problem 384–5
trends 382–4, 598–603
wages 598–603
inferior goods 76
defining 76
inflation
*AD* curve 793–8
adjusting for 529–33
aggregate supply 792–827
Boskin Commission 534–5
budget deficits 806–7
controlling 814–17
costs 536–43
CPI 533–6
deflation 528
ECB 778–81, 794–8, 816–17
excessive aggregate spending 806–8
Fisher effect 547
government deficits 806–7
health care sector 535–6
HICP 528–9
hyperinflation 543–4
inertia 799–801, 879–80
interest rates 544–7
long run 669–71
long-run planning 542
macroeconomics 484–5
measuring 524–52
monetary policy 814–15
money 669–71
'noise', price system 539–40
output gap 801–2
planning, long-run 542
price level 536–7
rate of 527–9
recessionary gaps 804–5
redistribution, wealth 541–2
relative prices 536–7
'shoe-leather' costs 538–9
sources 806–14
stock markets 781
'true' 533–6
United Kingdom 706
wealth redistribution 541–2
inflation shocks 808–14
defining 808
inflexibility, fiscal policy 757–8
information
adverse selection 355–6
asymmetric 348–57
conspicuous consumption 353–4
cost–benefit test 344
costly-to-fake principle 350–1
credibility problem 350–1
economics of 341–62
free-rider problem 344–5
'lemons' model 349–55
middlemen 341–3
moral hazard 356
optimal amount 344–5
political discourse 357–9
rational search 345–8
statistical discrimination 354–5
informational role, bond markets / stock markets 683
input prices, supply determinant 168
inputs control, market power 244
integrating factor markets, static gains 470–1
integration, international
EU 465–8
impact, economic growth trend 472
interdependence
incentives 406–9
international 485–6
prisoner's dilemma 278–86
interest rates
ECB 763–7, 770–3
fiscal policy 749
inflation 544–7
nominal 545–7, 767, 770–3
real 544–7, 626–8
intermediate goods or services 499–501
defining 499
international capital flows 685–95
defining 676
determinants 689–90
international interdependence 485–6
International Monetary Fund (IMF) 854–67
international reserves 850–1
defining 850
international trade 429–54
*see also* European Union
comparative advantage 52–3, 430–9
consumption possibilities 434–9
policy 429–54
production possibilities 431–4
protectionism 443–9
quotas 445–9
supply and demand 439–42
tariffs 443–5
winners / losers 441–2
intertemporal substitution
defining 624
saving 624

investment
  actual/planned 718
  capital formation 635–9
  capital inflows 690–4
  crowding out 641
  defining 503–4
  economic growth 574–5
  financial markets 639–42
  GDP 503–4
  PAE 717
  planned/actual 718
  saving 639–42
  technology 640
'invisible hand' 208–9
  in action 222–32
  anti-poverty programmes 226–7
  cost-saving innovations 222–3
  defining 212
  efficient markets hypothesis 229–32
  free entry/exit 219–20
  markets 224–8
  monopoly case 254–6
  price functions 212–13
  queuing 222
  regulated markets 224–6
  responses to profits/losses 213–19
  stock market 227–8
  theory 212–20
involuntary part-time workers
  defining 518
  unemployment 518
Ireland, economic independence 864–5
IS curve 895–898
IS-LM 895
Ithaca Hours 650–1

Japan, banking crisis (1990s) 678–9

Keynes, John Maynard 713–14
Keynesian cross 725–6
Keynesian model
  assumption 715–16
  monetary policy 790–1
  multiplier 737
Keynesian revolution 714–15

labour
  demand 369
  supply curve 369–70
labour force 514–16
  defining 515
  trends 605–13
labour income, GDP 505–14
labour market
  demand for labour 589–93
  discrimination 377
  equilibrium 369–70
  female 498–9
  GDP 498–9
  supply and demand 588–93
  supply of labour 594–5
  trends 586–8
  winner-take-all 380–1
labour mobility 601
  common currency 880–1
  defining 601
labour productivity *see* average labour productivity
labour union, defining 372
land, average labour productivity 565–6
law of demand 122–4
law of diminishing marginal utility 127–30
defining 127
law of diminishing returns 159–60
  defining 159
law of supply 167–8
legal environment, average labour productivity 568–71
legal framework, economic growth 575
legal remedies, externalities 320–2
leisure time, GDP 509
'lemons' model
  defining 349
  information 349–55
LETS *see* Local Electronic Trading System
liabilities 621
  defining 621
life-cycle saving 624–6
limits, economic growth 578–80
Lisbon Agenda, average labour productivity 569–70
living standards 555–85
  compound interest 557–9
  GDP 556–61
  macroeconomics 478–80
  rise 556–61
  saving 627–8
LM curve 898–901
Local Electronic Trading System (LETS) 651
long run 159–60
  defining 159
  inflation 669–71
long-run aggregate supply (*LRAS*) line 803
  anti-inflationary monetary policy 814–15
  defining 803
long-run equilibrium 804
  defining 804
long-run planning, inflation 542
Lorenz curve 383
  defining 383
losses, responses to profits/losses 213–19
The Low-Hanging-Fruit Principle 49
*LRAS* line *see* long-run aggregate supply line

M1, M2, M3, money 651–2
Maastricht Treaty, no-bailout clause 750–1
macroeconomic factors, demand for money 766–9
macroeconomic policies, defining 478, 488–9
macroeconomics 477–94
  aggregation 489–90
  defining 14
  economic growth 478–80
  expansions 483
  inflation 484–5
  interdependence, international 485–6
  living standards 478–80
  major issues 478–86
  policy 478, 487–9
  productivity 480–2
  recessions 483
  studying 491
  unemployment 483–5
main refinancing operations 664–5
  defining 664
main refinancing rate 665
  defining 665
management, entrepreneurship and 567–8
many-person economy, PPC 48–9
marginal benefits 10–13
  defining 11
marginal cost pricing
  efficiency 195–6
  public services 195–6
marginal costs 10–13, 160–1, 179
  defining 11, 160
marginal product of labour (MP) 367–8
  defining 367
marginal propensity to consume (MPC) 719–20
  defining 719
marginal propensity to import 730
  defining 730
marginal revenue 249
  defining 249
  monopolists 250–1
marginal utility 125–30
  defining 126
market demand curve 143–8
market equilibrium 65–72
  defining 66
  efficiency 182–6
market exchange, regulation 399
market power
  consequences 241–72
  copyrights 244
  defining 244
  economies of scale 245
  exploitation, counteracting 405–6
  government licences/franchises 244
  government regulation 405–6
  imperfect competition 241–72
  inputs control 244
  network economies 245–6
  patents 244

regulation 405–6
sources 244–6
market shifts 370
market value, GDP 496–9
market, vs central planning 60–1
markets
buyers and sellers 61–5
cost side 153–81
defining 62
efficient markets hypothesis 229–32
flexible 879–80
'invisible hand' 224–8
perfectly competitive 157–63
regulated 224–6
social welfare 83–5
stock markets 227–8, 683–5
winner-take-all 380–1
maximum-profit condition 165–7
means testing
defining 387
redistribution 387
medium of exchange 649–50
defining 649
menu costs 715–16
defining 715
technology 712, 716
merit goods 411
defining 411
microeconomics, defining 14
middlemen
adding value 342–3
information 341–3
minimum-wage laws 608–9
minimum wages 388–91
mobility of inputs, price elasticity of supply 112
models, economic *see* economic models
monetary policy 487–9, 762–91
anti-inflationary 814–15
art or science? 781
defining 487
exchange rates 846–7
fixed exchange rates 859–67
Keynesian model 790–1
role 762–91
stabilising the economy 762–91
Monetary Policy Committee (MPC) 667
defining 667
monetary union 465–8
*see also* common currency
defining 465
economic tests 884–5
optimum currency areas 874–94
steps 662–3
money 648–75
commercial banks 652–7
creating 652–7
defining 649
demand 763–9
inflation 669–71
Ithaca Hours 650–1
LETS 651
M1, M2, M3 651–2
measuring 651–2
and prices 667–71
private 650–1
supply 656–7, 663–7, 769–70
uses 649–52
velocity 668–70
money demand curve 767–9
defining 767
money market equilibrium 769–70
money multiplier 906
money supply 656–7, 663–7, 763
OMOs 663–5
reserve requirements 665–7
monopolies
discounts 257–60, 263
economies of scale 245
'invisible hand' 254–6
natural monopoly 245, 263–7
profit maximisation 181
state regulation 264–5
monopolistically competitive firms 242–3
defining 242
monopolists
marginal revenue 250–1
profit maximisation 249, 254
profit-maximising decision rule 251–4
moral hazard
defining 356
information 356
moral problem, income inequality 384–5
MP *see* marginal product of labour
MPC *see* marginal propensity to consume; Monetary Policy Committee
multiplier 728–30
defining 728
imports 729–30
Keynesian model 737
mutual funds 684
defining 684

NAFTA *see* North American Free Trade Agreement
Nash equilibrium
defining 276
game theory 276–7
prices 299
national saving 629–35
*see also* saving
components 630–5
defining 630
government budget deficit 632–5, 641
government budget surplus 632–5
measuring 629–30
private components 630–5
private saving 630–5
public components 630–5
public saving 630–5
transfer payments 630–1
natural monopoly 245
*see also* economies of scale
defining 245
exclusive contracting 265–6
public policy 263–7
state ownership/management 263–4
natural rate of unemployment 708–9
cyclical unemployment 708–9
defining 709
natural resources, average labour productivity 565–6
needs, vs wants 123–4
negative demand shocks 875–9
defining 876
negative externalities 322–3
*see also* external costs
negative income tax (NIT) 386–7
defining 386
negotiations costs 400–2
net exports (NX) 504
*see also* trade balance
defining 504
PAE 717
network economies, market power 245–6
NIT *see* negative income tax
no-bailout clause, Maastricht Treaty 750–1
'No-Cash-on-the-Table' Principle 84–5
No-Free-Lunch Principle *see* Scarcity Principle
'noise', price system, inflation 539–40
nominal exchange rates 833–5
defining 833
nominal GDP
defining 507
vs real GDP 506–9
nominal interest rates 545–7
defining 545
demand for money 767
ECB 770–3
Fisher effect 547
nominal price 135
defining 135
nominal quantity
defining 530
deflating 529–32
non-excludable goods 411–13
defining 411
non-market economic activities, GDP 510
non-payers, excluding 418
non-rival goods 411–13
defining 411
normal goods 76
defining 76
normal profit 210–12
defining 210
normative analysis 488–9
defining 488
North American Free Trade Agreement (NAFTA) 52–3

NX *see* net exports
oligopolist, defining 242
oligopolistic markets 295–304
OMOs *see* open-market operations
open economy 431–5, 831–73
  defining 431
  exchange rates 831–73
open-market operations (OMOs)
  defining 663
  money supply 663–5
open-market purchase 663–4
  defining 663
open-market sale 663–4
  defining 664
openness
  exchange rates 832–3
  measuring 832–3
opportunity costs 6–7
  comparative advantage 37–41
  Cost–Benefit Principle 9, 113
  defining 6
  exchange 37–8, 43
  ignoring 9, 113
  importance 154–7
  supply 154–7
optimal combination of goods 130
  defining 130
optimum currency areas 874–94
  defining 874
  EU 887–92
  monetary union 874–94
ordinal utility 137
output
  *AD* curve 793–8
  PAE 720–2
  potential 707–8
  profit maximisation 161–2
output gap
  cyclical unemployment 706–9
  defining 706
  EU 708
  inflation 801–2
  planned spending 726–8
output/spending, short run 713
overbooking 191–5
overvalued exchange rate 848, 849–50
  defining 848

PAE *see* planned aggregate expenditure
parental discrimination 379
Pareto efficient, defining 183
participation rate 514–16
  defining 515
patents, market power 244
payoffs, relative performance 330–1
peer influence 123
perfect competition, profit maximisation 179–81
perfect hurdle 261
perfectly competitive firms
  demand curve 158–9
  vs imperfectly competitive firms 243
  supply curve 153–68
perfectly competitive markets
  defining 157
  profit-maximising firms 157–63
perfectly competitive supply 153–81
perfectly discriminating monopolist 260
  defining 260
perfectly elastic demand 102
  defining 102
perfectly elastic supply 110–11
  defining 111
perfectly inelastic demand 102–3
  defining 103
perfectly inelastic supply 109–10
  defining 110
physical capital, average labour productivity 563–5
pitfalls, decision 8–14
pizza price controls 72
planned aggregate expenditure (PAE) 717–31
  components 717
  consumer spending 718–19
  contractionary policies 738–9
  expansionary policies 738–9
  output 720–2
  real interest rates 774–6
  spending, planned vs actual 717–18
  stabilisation policies 738–9
planned spending
  fiscal policy 738–44
  output gap 726–8
  recessions 726–8
planning, long-run, inflation 542
policy
  economic growth 573–7
  fiscal 487–9, 738–61
  international trade 429–54
  macroeconomics 478, 487–9
  monetary 487–9
  natural monopoly 263–7
  structural 487–9
policy independence
  common currency 875–9
  'impossible trinity' 861–2
policy reaction function
  defining 781
  ECB 781–4, 796–7
political discourse
  disappearing 357–9
  information 357–9
political environment, average labour productivity 568–71
political framework, economic growth 575
poll tax 414–15
  defining 415
pollution
  environmental regulation 400–4
  GDP 579–80
poor countries, economic growth 575–6
portfolio allocation decision 763–4
  defining 763
positional arms control agreements 332–5
  defining 332
  social norms 333–5
positional arms races 331–2
  defining 332
positional externalities 329–35
positional externality 331–2
positive analysis 488–9
  defining 488
positive demand shocks 875–9
  defining 876
positive externality
  *see also* external benefit
potential GDP *see* potential output
potential output 707–8
  defining 707
poverty
  GDP 511
  'invisible hand'/anti-poverty programmes 226–7
poverty threshold, defining 388
'poverty trap' 387
power, market *see* market power
PPC *see* production possibilities curve
PPP *see* purchasing power parity; relative purchasing power parity
precautionary saving 624–6
preferences
  commitment problems 294–5
  strategic role 292–5
present value 228
  defining 228
price adjustment prevention, efficiency 186–95
price ceilings
  defining 72
  efficiency 186–9
price discrimination 258–63
  defining 258
  examples 261–3
  hurdle method 260–3
price elasticity of demand 94–108
  budget share 96
  calculating 104
  changes 101–3
  cross-price elasticity of demand 107–8
  defining 94
  determinants 95–6
  graphical interpretation 99–101
  income elasticity of demand 107–8
  midpoint formula 103–4
  representative estimates 96–7
  substitution possibilities 95–6
  time 96
  total expenditure 104–7
  using 97–9
price elasticity of supply 108–15
  defining 108
  determinants 111–15

flexibility of inputs 111–12
mobility of inputs 112
substitute inputs 112
supply bottlenecks 115
time 112–15
unique and essential inputs 115
price incentives, environmental regulation 400–4
price index, defining 527
price level
defining 536
demand for money 767
inflation 536–7
measuring 524–52
price mechanisms 403–4
price setter 241
defining 241
price-setting, technology 712, 716
price stability, banks/banking 660–1
price subsidies 189–91
price taker, defining 157
price wars 303–4
prices
allocative function 212–13
cigarettes 303
comparing, exchange rates 836–8
flexible 712
fuel 113–15
functions 212–13
money and 667–71
Nash equilibrium 299
rationing function 212–13
relative 458–9
seasonal price movements 82
supply determinant 168, 1169
world price 440–1
principal amount 679
defining 679
Principle of Increasing Opportunity Cost 49
prisoner's dilemma 278–86, 461
defining 278
everyday life 283–5
imperfectly competitive firms 279–83
repeated 285–6
tit-for-tat 285–6
private contracting 418–19
private money 650–1
private ownership, property rights 326–9
private provision, public goods 418–20
private saving
defining 631
national saving 630–5
producer surplus 172–3
defining 172
production possibilities
comparative advantage 43–9
international trade 431–4
production possibilities curve (PPC) 43–52, 431–4
defining 43
individual productivity 45–6
many-person economy 48–9
shift factors 49–52
specialisation 46–7, 49–52
productivity
*see also* average labour productivity
individual 45–6
macroeconomics 480–2
profit
*see also* economic profit
defining 157
responses to profits/losses 213–19
role 209–12
types 209–12
profit maximisation
analysis 256–7
competition 179–81
graphical approach 163–7
maximum-profit condition 165–7
monopolists 249, 254
monopoly case 181
output 161–2
perfect competition 179–81
simple mathematics 179–81
profit-maximising decision rule, monopolists 251–4
profit-maximising firms
defining 157
perfectly competitive markets 157–63
profitable firm 163
defining 163
progressive tax 416
defining 416
property rights 323–40
private ownership 326–9
tragedy of the commons 323–9
unpriced resources 324–6
proportional income tax 414–16
defining 415
proportions, Cost–Benefit Principle 8, 13
protectionism
defining 443
efficiency 449
international trade 443–9
public goods 411–20
defining 411
demand curve 416–18
paying for 413–16
private provision 418–20
public health/security 409–25
public policy, natural monopoly 263–7
public saving
defining 632
national saving 630–5
public services
efficiency 195–6
marginal cost pricing 195–6
purchasing power parity (PPP)
defining 839
exchange rates 839–42
shortcomings 841–2
pure commons goods 412–13
defining 412
pure monopoly 242–3
defining 242
pure private goods 412–13
defining 412
pure public goods 412–13
defining 412

quality of life, GDP 511
quantity equation
defining 669
money 669
queuing, 'invisible hand' 222
quotas
defining 443
effects 446–9
international trade 445–9

rate of inflation 527–9
defining 527
rate of return 637–9
defining 637
rational choice, indifference curve analysis 136–43
rational person 5–6
defining 5
rational search
commitment problems 347–8
gamble inherent in 346–7
information 345–8
rational spending rule 131
application 133–6
defining 131
rationing function of price 212–13
reaction function
analysis 297–300
defining 297
real exchange rates 836–9
defining 836
real GDP
defining 507
vs nominal GDP 506–9
real income or output, demand for money 767
real interest rates 544–7
capital inflows 689
defining 544
PAE 774–6
saving 626–8
short-run equilibrium output 775–6
real price 135
defining 135
real quantity 530
defining 530
real wages 531–2
defining 531
realignments, EMS 855–9
recessionary gaps 707
defining 707
government purchases 739–41
inflation 804–5
taxes 742–3

recessions 703–6
defining 704
ECB 776–8
macroeconomics 483
planned spending 726–8
redistribution
in-kind transfers 386
income 385–91
income tax 387–8
inflation 541–2
means testing 387
universality 387
wealth 541–2
welfare payments 386
refinancing rate, ECB 767, 780
regressive tax 414–15
defining 415
regulated markets, 'invisible hand' 224–6
regulation
blunders 398–9
case studies 400–9
competition authorities 399–400
defining 397
delegated 399–400
environmental 400–4
framework 399–400
government 397–409, 610
health and safety 406–9
incentives, defective 406–9
market exchange 399
market power exploitation 405–6
pollution 400–4
security 398–9
supply 398–9
relative performance, payoffs 330–1
relative prices 458–9
defining 458, 536
inflation 536–7
relative purchasing power parity (PPP) 840–1
rent controls 61, 69–71
repeated games 300–4
repeated prisoner's dilemma 285–6
defining 285
research and development, economic growth 575
reserve requirements, money supply 665–7
reserve–deposit ratio
banks/banking 654
defining 654
reserves 850–1
defining 850
residual demand curve
analysis 296
defining 296
resource depletion, GDP 510–11
resources
allocation, externalities 313–22
unpriced 324–6
revaluation 848, 855–9
defining 848
risk averse person 346
defining 346
risk, capital inflows 689–90
risk neutral 346
defining 346
risk premium 682
defining 682
risk-sharing, bond markets/stock markets 683–5

safety, health and *see* health and safety
saving 620–47
*see also* national saving
allocation 683–5
bequest 624–6
capital inflows 690–4
defining 620
demonstration effects 628–9
Europe 625–6
financial markets 639–42
financial system 677
intertemporal substitution 624
investment 639–42
life-cycle 624–6
living standards 627–8
national saving 629–35
precautionary 624–6
productive uses 677
real interest rates 626–8
reasons 623–9
self-control 628–9
supply and demand 639–40
technology 640
United States 625–6
wealth 622–3
saving/investment policy, economic growth 574–5
saving rate
defining 620
trade deficit 692–4
Scarcity Principle 4–5
school starting dates 333
search, rational
commitment problems 347–8
gamble inherent in 346–7
information 345–8
seasonal price movements 82
security of supply, regulation 398–9
security, public health/security 409–25
self-control, saving 628–9
self-correcting economy 804–6
selfishness 293–4
sellers and buyers, markets 61–5
seller's reservation price 64–5
defining 64
seller's surplus 83
defining 83
SGB *see* Stability and Growth Pact
share prices, stock markets 685
shares 680–3
factors affecting 680–3
shift factors, PPC 49–52
shifts, supply curve 77–82
shocks
common currency 875–9
demand and supply 888–9
inflation 808–14
to potential output 808–14
symmetry 888–9
'shoe-leather' costs, inflation 538–9
short run 159–60
defining 159
spending/output 713
short-run aggregate supply (*SRAS*) line 803
anti-inflationary monetary policy 814–15
defining 803
short-run equilibrium 803–4
defining 803
short-run equilibrium output 722–6, 731
algebraic approach 723–4
defining 722
numeric approach 724–6
real interest rates 775–6
tax-multiplier 742–3
short-term economic fluctuations 703–37
reasons 710–12
shutdown condition 162–3
Single Market Programme, EU 470–2
skill-biased technological change 602–3
Smith, Adam 208–9
smoking, taxes 87–8
social norms, positional arms control agreements 333–5
social optimum, vs equilibrium 232–3
social welfare, markets 83–5
socially optimal quantity 84–5
defining 84
specialisation
gains from 46–7
PPC 46–7, 49–52
quantity 52
speed 51–2
speculative attacks 851–2, 855–9, 863–4
defining 851
spending, *AD* curve 793–8
spending/output, short run 713
*SRAS* line *see* short-run aggregate supply line
stabilisation policies 738–9
defining 738
stabilisers, automatic, fiscal policy 745–8
stabilising the economy
fiscal policy 738–61
monetary policy 762–91
Stability and Growth Pact (SGB) 751–7
automatic stabilisers 752–7
cyclically adjusted budget deficit 755–7
problems 754–7

standards of living *see* living standards
state ownership/management, natural monopoly 263–4
state regulation, private monopolies 264–5
static gains, integrating factor markets 470–1
statistical discrimination
  defining 355
  information 354–5
stock markets 683–5
  diversification 683–5
  inflation 781
  informational role 683
  'invisible hand' 227–8
  risk-sharing 683–5
  share prices 685
  United States 685
stocks 621–2
  defining 621
store of value 650
  defining 650
strategic role, preferences 292–5
strategic thinking 273–311
structural policy 487–9
  defining 487
structural unemployment 607
  defining 606
subsidies
  export 463–4, 468
  international trade 463–4, 468
  price 189–91
substitute inputs, price elasticity of supply 112
substitutes 74
  defining 74
substitution effect 63
  defining 63
  demand 131–3
substitution possibilities, price elasticity of demand 95–6
substitution, role 134–5
sunk costs
  Cost–Benefit Principle 10, 113
  defining 10
supernormal profit 209–12
  defining 209
suppliers, supply determinant 168–9
supply
  application of theory 169–73
  determinants 168–9
  euros 843–6
  law of 167–8
  money 656–7, 663–7, 769–70
  opportunity costs 154–7
  perfectly competitive 153–81
  regulation 398–9
  security 398–9
supply and demand 58–90
  central planning vs market 60–1
  exchange rates 843–4
  international trade 439–42
  labour market 588–93
  saving 639–40
  shocks 888–9
supply bottlenecks, price elasticity of supply 115
supply curve 64–5
  defining 64
  labour 369–70
  perfectly competitive firm 153–68
  rules 80–2
  shifts 77–82
supply of labour 594–5
  shifts 595
supply side, fiscal policy 757
surplus
  *see also* economic surplus
  buyer's 83
  consumer 145–8
  producer 172–3
  total 83
symmetric shocks 875–9
  defining 875
synchronised business cycles 883–4
  defining 883

tables, working with 21–8
tacit collusion 300–4
  defining 301
tariffs
  defining 443
  implications 462–3
  imposing 462–3
  international trade 443–5
  removing 462–3
tax multiplier 742–3
  defining 742
  short-run equilibrium output 742–3
tax system, distortions 540–1
taxes
  *see also* tariffs
  distortions 540–1
  economic surplus 198–200
  efficiency 196–202
  EITC 389–91
  elasticity 200–1
  export 463–4
  external costs 201
  fiscal policy 741–4
  import 463–4
  income tax 540–1
  income tax and redistribution 387–8
  NIT 386–7
  poll tax 414–15
  progressive tax 416
  proportional income tax 414–16
  public goods 414–15
  recessionary gaps 742–3
  regressive tax 414–15
  smoking 87–8
  yachts 98–9
Taylor rule 781–2
technological change impact, EU 604–5
technology
  average labour productivity 566–7, 572
  investment 640
  menu costs 712, 716
  price-setting 712, 716
  saving 640
  skill-biased technological change 602–3
  supply determinant 168
terror attacks, ECB 777–8
tests, monetary union 884–5
time
  price elasticity of demand 96
  price elasticity of supply 112–15
time value of money 228
  defining 228
timing
  games 286–92
  oligopolistic markets 295–304
tit-for-tat, prisoner's dilemma 285–6
total cost 160–1
  defining 160
total surplus 83
  defining 83
trade balance (net exports) 686–9
  capital flows 686–9
  defining 686
trade creation
  defining 468
  EU 468–9
trade deficit 687
  defining 687
  saving rate 692–4
  United Kingdom 693–4
trade diversion
  defining 463
  EU 468–9
  international trade 463
trade impact, EU 604–5
trade, international *see* international trade
trade-offs 3
trade restrictions
  *see also* quotas; tariffs
  consequences 461–4
trade surplus 687
  defining 687
trade symmetry 459–60
  defining 459
trade unions 372–6
  employment 609–10
  labour union 372
trading
  *see also* international trade
  credibility problem 350–1
  emissions 403
  freeing trade, economics of 457–64
  gains from 457–61

tragedy of the commons
defining 323
property rights 323–9
transaction costs
common currency 881–2
defining 882
eliminating 881–2
transfer payments
defining 630
fiscal policy 741–4
national saving 630–1
Treaty on European Union (TEU) *see* Maastricht Treaty
trends
economic growth, EU 472
employment 587
inequality 382–4, 598–603
labour force 605–13
labour market 586–8
unemployment 587, 605–13
wages 587, 596–605

ultimatum bargaining game 286–8
defining 288
unattainable point, defining 44
undervalued exchange rate 848
defining 848
unemployment 514–18
*see also* employment
costs 516–17
cyclical 606, 607–8, 706–9
discouraged workers 518
duration 517–18
frictional 606
involuntary part-time workers 518
macroeconomics 483–5
measuring 514–16
natural rate of 708–9
structural 607
trends 587, 605–13
types 606–8
United Kingdom 705
unemployment benefits 610
unemployment rate 514–18
defining 514
vs 'true' unemployment 518
Western Europe 611–12
unemployment spell 517–18
defining 517
union, monetary *see* monetary union
unions, trade *see* trade unions
unique and essential inputs, price elasticity of supply 115
unit elastic demand, defining 95
unit of account 650
defining 650
United Kingdom
consumption function 720
inflation 706
trade deficit 693–4
unemployment 705
United States
saving 625–6
stock markets 685
universality, redistribution 387
utility
cardinal 137
DMU 127–30, 1136
ordinal 137
wants 125–7
utility function assumption 137–8
defining 137

value added 500–1
defining 500
value, adding, middlemen 342–3
value of marginal product of labour (VMP) 367–8
defining 367
value of work, economic 366–8
variable cost 160–1
defining 160
variable factor of production 159–60
defining 159
variables, defining 21
velocity
defining 668
money 668–70
VMP *see* value of marginal product of labour

wage differentials
compensating 376–7
sources 379–80
wages
demand for labour 589–91
inequality 598–603
minimum 388–91
minimum-wage laws 608–9
trends 587, 596–605
wage bargaining models 612–13
wants
measuring 125–7
vs needs 123–4
origins 123
translating to demand 125–33
utility 125–7
water shortages 124
wealth 620–3
defining 620
distribution, measuring 383–4
saving 622–3
wealth effect 719–20
defining 719
*The Wealth of Nations* 208–9
wealth redistribution, inflation 541–2
welfare payments, redistribution 386
Western Europe, unemployment rate 611–12
winner-take-all markets 380–1
women's labour market, GDP 498–9
work, economic value of 366–8
workplace health and safety 406–9
World Bank (IBRD) 855
world price 440–1
defining 440

X-inefficiency 264
defining 264

yachts, taxing 98–9